ECONOMICS

THIRD EDITION

MICHAEL PARKIN
MELANIE POWELL
KENT MATTHEWS

ADDISON-WESLEY
Harlow, England ◆ Reading, Massachusetts ◆ Menlo Park, California ◆ New York ◆ Don Mills, Ontario ◆ Amsterdam
◆ Bonn ◆ Sydney ◆ Singapore ◆ Tokyo ◆ Madrid ◆ San Juan ◆ Milan ◆ Mexico City ◆ Seoul ◆ Taipei

©Addison Wesley Longman Limited 1997

Addison Wesley Longman Limited
Edinburgh Gate,
Harlow, Essex
CM20 2JE,
England

and Associated Companies throughout the world.

Many of the designations used by manufacturers and sellers to distinguish their products are claimed as trademarks. Addison Wesley Longman has made every attempt to supply information about manufacturers and their products mentioned in this book.

First printed 1997.

ISBN 0-201-40373-0

British Library Cataloguing-in-Publication Data

A catalogue record for this book is available from the British Library.

Commissioning Editor:	**Paula Harris**
Senior Production Editor:	**Susan Harrison**
Editor:	**Lee Hodder**
Editorial Assistant:	**Anna Herbert**
Production Control Manager:	**Jim Allman**
Production Assistant:	**Alison Martin**
Copy-Editor:	**Penelope Williams**
Proofreader:	**Cynthia Roberts**
Indexer:	**Indexing Specialists, Hove**
Design Manager:	**Kevin Ancient**
Cover Design Artist:	**Mark Sturridge**
Marketing Executive:	**Lucy Everest**
Page Design, Layout and Reproduction:	**Express Graphics Ltd.**
Features Typesetter:	**Meridian Colour Repro Ltd.**
Technical Illustrator:	**Richard Parkin, RWP Graphics**
Printer:	**R.R. Donnelly & Sons Co.**

Many thanks to everyone at Addison Wesley Longman, past and present, who have contributed to this text.

ABOUT THE AUTHORS

Michael Parkin received his training at the Universities of Leicester and Essex in England. Currently in the Department of Economics at the University of Western Ontario, Canada, Professor Parkin has held faculty appointments at Brown University, the University of Manchester, the University of Essex and Bond University. He has served on the editorial boards of the *American Economic Review* and the *Journal of Monetary Economics* and as managing editor of the *Canadian Journal of Economics*. Professor Parkin's research on macroeconomics, monetary economics and international economics has resulted in over 160 publications in journals and edited volumes, including the *American Economic Review*, the *Journal of Political Economy*, the *Review of Economic Studies*, the *Journal of Monetary Economics* and the *Journal of Money, Credit and Banking*. It became most visible to the public with his work on inflation that discredited the use of wage and price controls. Michael Parkin also spearheaded the movement toward European monetary union. Professor Parkin is an experienced and dedicated teacher of introductory economics.

Melanie Powell took her first degree at Kingston University and her MSc in economics at Birkbeck College, London University. She spent three years as a research fellow in health economics at York University before moving on to become a principal lecturer heading the economics division of the business school at Leeds Metropolitan University. Melanie Powell then moved to Leeds University where she is the director of economic studies at the Leeds University Business School. Her main interest as a micro economist is in applied welfare economics and health policy. Her publications include papers on economic aspects of alcohol and tobacco consumption, health policy and European tax policy, as well as a book on the Economics of Social Policy. Her current research into economic decision making under uncertainty uses experimental techniques.

Kent Matthews received his training as an economist at the London School of Economics, Birkbeck College University of London and the University of Liverpool. He is currently the Sir Julian Hodge Professor of Banking and Finance at the University of Wales, Cardiff. He has held research appointments at the London School of Economics, the National Institute of Economic and Social Research, the Bank of England, and Lombard Street Research Ltd and faculty positions at the Universities of Liverpool, Western Ontario, Leuven, and Liverpool John Moores. He is the author (co-author) of 4 books and over 30 articles in scholarly journals and edited volumes.

BRIEF CONTENTS

Part 1 Introduction   1

CHAPTER 1
What is Economics?   5

CHAPTER 2
Making and Using Graphs   25

CHAPTER 3
Production, Growth and Trade   44

CHAPTER 4
Demand and Supply   68

CHAPTER 5
Elasticity   97

CHAPTER 6
Markets in Action   122

Part 2 Markets for Goods and Services   147

CHAPTER 7
Utility and Demand   151

CHAPTER 8
Possibilities, Preferences and Choices   171

CHAPTER 9
Organizing Production   201

CHAPTER 10
Output and Costs   225

CHAPTER 11
Competition   258

CHAPTER 12
Monopoly   284

CHAPTER 13
Monopolistic Competition and Oligopoly   310

Part 3 Markets for Factors of Production   340

CHAPTER 14
Pricing and Allocating Factors of Production   344

CHAPTER 15
Labour Markets   370

CHAPTER 16
Capital and Natural Resource Markets   393

CHAPTER 17
Uncertainty and Information   416

Part 4 Markets and Governments   438

CHAPTER 18
Market Failure and Public Choice   441

CHAPTER 19
Regulation and Privatization   465

CHAPTER 20
Externalities, the Environment and Knowledge   493

CHAPTER 21
Inequality, Redistribution and Welfare   517

Part 5 Preliminaries and Long-term Fundamentals   543

CHAPTER 22
A First Look at Macroeconomics   547

CHAPTER 23
Measuring GDP, Inflation and Economic Growth   574

CHAPTER 24
Employment, Unemployment and Wages   600

CHAPTER 25
Investment, Capital and Interest   625

CHAPTER 26
Long-term Economic Growth   653

Part 6 Macroeconomic Fluctuations and Policies   681

CHAPTER 27
Aggregate Supply and Aggregate Demand   684

CHAPTER 28
Expenditure Multipliers   710

CHAPTER 29
The Government Budget and Fiscal Policy   741

CHAPTER 30
Money   767

CHAPTER 31
The Central Bank and Monetary Policy   799

CHAPTER 32
Inflation   831

CHAPTER 33
The Business Cycle   860

CHAPTER 34
Macroeconomic Policy Challenges   890

Part 7 The Global Economy   916

CHAPTER 35
Trading with the World   919

CHAPTER 36
The Balance of Payments and the Exchange Rate   950

CHAPTER 37
Emerging Economies   980

CONTENTS

Part 1
Introduction 1
TALKING WITH SHEILA DOW

CHAPTER 1
WHAT IS ECONOMICS? 5

Some Economic Questions 6

How Economists Think 8

Scarcity 8
Choice and Opportunity Cost 8
Marginal Analysis 9
Substitution and Incentives 9
Competition and Second Round Effects 10

What Economists Do 11

Microeconomics and Macroeconomics 11
Economic Analysis 11
Economic Policy 14
Agreement and Disagreement 15

The Economy: An Overview 16

Decision Makers and Choices 17
Markets 17
Coordinating Decisions 19
International Linkages 21

Summary, Key Elements, Review Questions and Problems appear at the end of each chapter.

CHAPTER 2
MAKING AND USING GRAPHS 25

Three Kinds of Lies 26

Graphing Data 27

Two-variable Graphs 27
Scatter Diagrams 28
Time-series Graphs 30

Cross-section Graphs 31
Misleading Graphs 32

Graphs Used in Economic Models 32

Things That Go Up and Down Together 32
Things That Move in Opposite Directions 33
Things That are Unrelated 33
Things That Have a Maximum and a Minimum 34

The Slope of a Relationship 36

The Slope of a Straight Line 36
The Slope of a Curved Line 37

Graphing Relationships Among More Than Two Variables 38

CHAPTER 3
PRODUCTION, GROWTH AND TRADE 44

Making the Most of It 45

The Production Possibility Frontier 46

A Firm's Production Possibility Frontier 46
Efficiency 47
A Firm's Opportunity Cost of Production 48
Opportunity Costs are Inescapable 48

Increasing Opportunity Cost 49

Books versus Video Games 49
The Shape of the Frontier 50
Measuring Opportunity Cost 50
Opportunity Cost is a Ratio 50
Increasing Opportunity Costs are Everywhere 51

Economic Growth 52

The Cost of Shifting the Frontier 52
Technological Change and Capital Accumulation 53
The Economic Growth of Households 53
The Economic Growth of Nations 54

Gains from Trade 55

Comparative Advantage 55

Achieving the Gains from Trade **56**
Absolute Advantage **56**
Dynamic Comparative Advantage **58**

The Evolution of Trading Arrangements **59**

Transactions Costs **59**
Markets **59**
Property Rights **59**
Money **60**

READING BETWEEN THE LINES
OPPORTUNITY COST: THE BLACK ECONOMY **62**

ECONOMICS IN HISTORY
UNDERSTANDING THE SOURCES
OF ECONOMIC WEALTH **66**

CHAPTER 4
DEMAND AND SUPPLY **68**

Slide, Rocket and Roller-coaster **69**

Opportunity Cost and Price **70**

Demand **71**

What Determines Buying Plans? **71**
The Law of Demand **71**
Demand Schedule and Demand Curve **72**
A Change in Demand **73**
Movement Along Versus a Shift of the
Demand Curve **74**

Supply **76**

What Determines Selling Plans? **76**
The Law of Supply **76**
Supply Schedule and Supply Curve **76**
A Change in Supply **76**
Movement Along Versus a Shift of the
Supply Curve **78**

Price Determination **80**

Price as a Regulator **80**
Equilibrium **81**

Predicting Changes in Price and Quantity **82**

A Change in Demand **82**
A Change in Supply **83**

READING BETWEEN THE LINES
DEMAND AND SUPPLY: WHEAT PRICES
AND WORLD SHORTAGES **88**

ECONOMICS IN HISTORY
DISCOVERING THE LAWS OF
DEMAND AND SUPPLY **90**

CHAPTER 5
ELASTICITY **97**

OPEC's Dilemma **98**

Elasticity of Demand **99**

The Responsiveness of the
Quantity Demanded to Price **99**
Slope Depends on Units of Measurement **100**
Elasticity: A Units-free Measure **100**
Calculating Elasticity **100**
Inelastic and Elastic Demand **101**
Elasticity along a Straight-line Demand Curve **102**
The Factors that Influence the
Elasticity of Demand **103**
Elasticity, Total Revenue and Expenditure **106**

More Elasticities of Demand **107**

Cross Elasticity of Demand **107**
Income Elasticity of Demand **107**
Real-world Income Elasticities of Demand **109**

Elasticity of Supply **110**

Factor Substitution Possibilities **111**
Elasticity of Supply and the
Time-frame for Supply Decisions **111**

READING BETWEEN THE LINES
ELASTICITY: MANAGEMENT PRICING STRATEGIES **114**

CHAPTER 6
MARKETS IN ACTION **122**

Turbulent Times **123**

Housing Markets and Rent Ceilings **124**

The Market Response to a
Decrease in Supply **124**

Long-run Adjustments **124**
A Regulated Housing Market **124**
Search Activity **126**
Black Markets **126**
Rent Ceilings in Practice **126**

The Labour Market and Minimum Wages **127**

The Minimum Wage **128**
The Minimum Wage in Reality **129**

Taxes **130**

Who Pays a Sales Tax? **130**
Tax Division and Elasticity of Demand **131**
Tax Division and Elasticity of Supply **133**
Indirect Taxes in Practice **134**

Markets for Prohibited Goods **134**

A Free Market for Drugs **135**
Prohibiting a Drug **135**
Legalizing and Taxing Drugs **136**

Stabilizing Farm Revenue **137**

An Unregulated Agricultural Market **137**
Speculative Markets in Stocks **138**
Agricultural Price Support Policy **139**

READING BETWEEN THE LINES
A TAXING PROBLEM **140**

Part 2

Markets for
Goods and Services **147**
TALKING WITH ALFRED STEINHERR

CHAPTER 7
UTILITY AND DEMAND **151**

Water, Water, Everywhere **152**

Individual Demand and Market Demand **153**

Individual Consumption Choices **154**

Budget Line **154**

Preferences and Utility **154**
Total Utility **155**
Marginal Utility **155**

Maximizing Utility **157**

The Utility-maximizing Choice **157**
Equalizing Marginal Utility per Pound Spent **157**

Predictions of Marginal Utility Theory **159**

A Fall in the Price of Cinema Tickets **159**
A Rise in the Price of Cola **160**
A Rise in Income **161**
Marginal Utility and the Real World **162**

Criticisms of Marginal Utility Theory **163**

Utility Can't be Observed or Measured **163**
'People aren't that Smart' **163**

Implications of Marginal Utility Theory **164**

Consumer Surplus and the Gains from Trade **164**
Calculating Consumer Surplus **164**
The Paradox of Value **165**

READING BETWEEN THE LINES
UTILITY THEORY: PREFERRING PEA PROTEIN **166**

CHAPTER 8
POSSIBILITIES, PREFERENCES AND CHOICES **171**

Subterranean Movements **172**

Consumption Possibilities **173**

The Budget Equation **174**

Preferences and Indifference Curves **176**

Marginal Rate of Substitution **177**
Degree of Substitutability **179**

The Household's Consumption Choice **180**

Properties of the Best Affordable Point **181**

Predicting Consumer Behaviour **181**

A Change in Price **181**
The Demand Curve **182**
A Change in Income **183**

Back to the Facts **188**

Other Household Choices **188**

Labour Supply **188**
Saving **190**
Marginal Utility and Indifference Curves **191**
Differences between Theories of Choice **192**

READING BETWEEN THE LINES
INDIFFERENCE CURVES: BSE AND BEEF **186**

ECONOMICS IN HISTORY
UNDERSTANDING HUMAN BEHAVIOUR **194**

CHAPTER 9
ORGANIZING PRODUCTION **201**

An Apple a Day **202**

The Firm and its Economic Problem **203**

The Main Types of Firms **203**
The Relative Importance of
Different Sizes of Firms **205**
Uncertainty About the Future **205**
Incomplete Information **206**
The Principal–Agent Problem **207**
Coping with the Principal–Agent Problem **207**
The Pros and Cons of the Different
Types of Firms **208**

Business Finance **209**

How Firms Raise Funds **209**
Selling Shares **210**
Selling Bonds **210**
Discounting and Present Value **211**
Present Value and Marginal Analysis **212**

Opportunity Cost and Economic Profit **212**

Cost of Capital **213**
Cost of Stocks **214**
Cost of Owner's Resources **214**
Economic Profit **215**
An Example **215**

Economic Efficiency **216**

Firms and Markets **217**

Why Firms? **218**

READING BETWEEN THE LINES
CUTTING COSTS WITH OLD TECHNOLOGY **220**

CHAPTER 10
OUTPUT AND COSTS **225**

Survival of the Fittest **226**

The Firm's Objective and Constraints **227**

The Objective: Profit Maximization **227**
Market Constraints **227**
Technology Constraints **227**
The Short Run and the Long Run **227**

Short-run Technology Constraint **228**

Total Product **228**
Marginal Product **228**
Average Product **230**
Marginal Marks and Average Marks **230**
The Shapes of the Product Curves **231**

Short-run Cost **232**

Total Cost **232**
Marginal Cost **233**
Average Cost **233**
Short-run Cost Curves **234**
Why the Average Total Cost Curve
is U-Shaped **235**
Cost Curves and Product Curves **235**
Shifts in the Cost Curves **236**

Plant Size and Cost **237**

The Production Function **237**
Diminishing Returns **238**
Returns to Scale **238**
Short-run Cost and Long-run Cost **239**
The Long-run Average Cost Curve **240**
Economies and Diseconomies of Scale **241**
Returns to Scale and Economies of Scale **241**

READING BETWEEN THE LINES
OUTPUTS AND COSTS: OIL REFINING **242**

ECONOMICS IN HISTORY
UNDERSTANDING FIRMS AND COSTS **256**

Appendix to Chapter 10
Producing at Least Cost **248**

CHAPTER 11
COMPETITION 258

Rivalry in Personal Computers 259

Perfect Competition 260

Profit and Revenue 260
The Firm's Decisions in Perfect Competition 262
Profit-maximizing Output 262
Marginal Analysis 264
Economic Profit in the Short Run 264
The Firm's Short-run Supply Curve 266

Output, Price and Profit in the Short Run 267

Short-run Industry Supply Curve 267
Short-run Equilibrium 268

Output, Price and Profit in the Long Run 269

Economic Profit and
Economic Loss as Signals 269
The Effects of Entry 269
The Effects of Exit 270
Long-run Equilibrium 270
Changes in Plant Size 270

**Changing Tastes and
Advancing Technology** 272

A Permanent Change in Demand 272
External Economies and Diseconomies 273
Technological Change 275

Competition and Efficiency 276

Allocative Efficiency 276
Market Failure 276
Efficiency of Perfect Competition 280

READING BETWEEN THE LINES
COMPETITION: THE MARKET FOR
CONTAINER LINES 278

CHAPTER 12
MONOPOLY 284

The Profits of Generosity 285

How Monopoly Arises 286

No Close Substitutes 286
Barriers to Entry 286

Single-price Monopoly 287

Demand and Revenue 287
Revenue and Elasticity 289
Price and Output Decision 289

Price Discrimination 293

Price Discrimination and Total Revenue 293
Price Discrimination and Consumer Surplus 294
Discriminating among Units of a Good 294
Discriminating among Individuals 294
Discriminating between Groups 294
Profiting by Price Discrimination 296
More Perfect Price Discrimination 297
Price Discrimination in Practice 297
Limits to Price Discrimination 297

Comparing Monopoly and Competition 298

Price and Output 298
Allocative Efficiency 299
Redistribution 300
Rent Seeking 301
Gains from Monopoly 302
Incentives to Innovate 303

READING BETWEEN THE LINES
MONOPOLY IN ACTION: INVESTIGATING
A HEATING PIPE CARTEL 304

CHAPTER 13
MONOPOLISTIC COMPETITION AND OLIGOPOLY 310

Fliers and War Games 311

Varieties of Market Structure 312

Measures of Concentration 312
Limitations of Concentration Measures 313
Concentration in the UK Economy 314
Market Structures in the United Kingdom 314

Monopolistic Competition 315

Price and Output in Monopolistic Competition 316

Efficiency of Monopolistic Competition **318**
Product Innovation **318**
Selling Costs **318**
Contestable Markets **318**

Oligopoly **319**

The Kinked Demand Curve Model **319**
Dominant Firm Oligopoly **320**

Game Theory **322**

Familiar Games: What They Have in Common **322**
The Prisoners' Dilemma **322**

Oligopoly Game **324**

Cost and Demand Conditions **324**
Colluding to Maximize Profits **325**
Cheating on a Collusive Agreement **326**
The Payoff Matrix and Equilibrium **328**
Repeated Games **329**
Games and Price Wars **331**
Other Strategic Variables **331**
An R&D Game **331**
Contestable Markets **332**

READING BETWEEN THE LINES
OLIGOPOLY IN ACTION: SUPERMARKET
LOYALTY CARDS **334**

Part 3

Markets for Factors of Production **340**
TALKING WITH JOHN HEY

CHAPTER 14
PRICING AND ALLOCATING FACTORS
OF PRODUCTION **344**

Many Happy Returns **345**

Factor Prices and Incomes **346**

Factor Prices and Opportunity Costs **346**
An Overview of a Competitive Factor Market **346**

Demand for Factors **349**

Profit Maximization **349**

The Firm's Demand for Labour **350**
The Labour Demand Curve **351**
Two Conditions for Profit Maximization **352**
Changes in the Demand for Labour **353**
Market Demand **354**
Elasticity of Demand for Labour **354**

Supply of Factors **355**

Supply of Labour **355**
Supply of Capital **358**
The Supply Curve of Capital **358**
Supply of Land **359**

Incomes, Economic Rent and Transfer Earnings **362**

Large and Small Incomes **362**
Economic Rent and Transfer Earnings **362**

READING BETWEEN THE LINES
FACTOR INCOME IN FOOTBALL **360**

ECONOMICS IN HISTORY
RUNNING OUT OF RESOURCES? **368**

CHAPTER 15
LABOUR MARKETS **370**

The Sweat of Our Brows **371**

Skill Differentials **372**

The Demand for Skilled and Unskilled Labour **372**
The Supply of Skilled and Unskilled Labour **372**
Wage Rates of Skilled and Unskilled Labour **372**
Do Education and Training Pay? **374**

Union–Non-union Wage Differentials **375**

Unions' Objectives and Constraints **376**
Unions in a Competitive Labour Market **378**
Monopsony **378**
Monopsony and the Minimum Wage **380**
The Scale of Union–Non-union
Wage Differentials **380**

Wage Differentials Between the Sexes **381**

Job Types **381**
Discrimination **382**
Human Capital Differences **386**
Degrees of Specialization **386**

Equal Pay and Equal Worth Laws 387

READING BETWEEN THE LINES
PAY DIFFERENTIALS BETWEEN MEN
AND WOMEN 384

CHAPTER 16
CAPITAL AND NATURAL RESOURCE MARKETS 393

Boom and Bust 394

The Structure of Capital Markets 395

Stock Markets 395
Bond Markets 395
Loan Markets 395
The Flows of Funds 396

The Demand for Capital 396

Capital, Investment and Depreciation 396
Investment Decisions 396
The Net Present Value of a Computer 397
Demand Curve for Capital 399
The Market Demand for Capital 399

The Supply of Capital 400

The Saving Decision 400
Supply Curve of Capital 401

Interest Rates and Share Prices 402

Two Sides of the Same Coin 402
Equilibrium Interest Rate 403
Stock Market Value of a Firm 403
Price–Earnings Ratio 404
Stock Market Volume and Prices 404
Takeovers and Mergers 404

Natural Resource Markets 405

Supply and Demand in a
Natural Resource Market 405
Current Price of a Natural Resource 406
Equilibrium Stock and Flow 407
Expected Prices and Actual Prices 408
Conservation and Doomsday 409

READING BETWEEN THE LINES
LIMITED WORLD WOOD SUPPLY 410

CHAPTER 17
UNCERTAINTY AND INFORMATION 416

Lotteries and Lemons 417

Uncertainty and Risk 418

Measuring the Opportunity Cost of Risk 418
Risk Aversion and Risk Neutrality 420

Insurance 421

Insurance Industry in the United Kingdom 421

Information 423

Searching for Price Information 423
Advertising 424

Private Information 425

The Market for Used Cars 426
The Market for Loans 427
The Market for Insurance 428

Managing Risk in Financial Markets 428

Diversification to Lower Risk 428
Forward and Futures Markets 429
Rational Expectations 430

READING BETWEEN THE LINES
MARKET SIGNALS: A-LEVEL GRADE INFLATION 432

Part 4
Markets and Governments 438
TALKING WITH JOHN KAY

CHAPTER 18
MARKET FAILURE AND PUBLIC CHOICE 441

Government: Solution or Problem? 442

The Government Sector 443

The UK Government Sector 443

The Economic Theory of Government 444

Public Goods 445

Monopoly **446**
Externalities **446**
Incomplete Information and Uncertainty **446**

**Public Choice and the
Political Marketplace** **447**

Voters **447**
Politicians **447**
Bureaucrats **447**
Political Equilibrium **448**

Public Goods **448**

The Free-rider Problem **448**
Benefits and Costs of Satellites **448**
Private Provision **450**
Public Provision **451**
The Role of Bureaucrats **452**
Why Government is Large and Grows **453**
Voters Strike Back **453**

Taxes **454**

Taxes and Income **454**
Excise Taxes **455**
Why Excise Tax Rates Vary **456**
Compliance and Administration Costs **460**

READING BETWEEN THE LINES
MONITORING COSTS IN PUBLIC HEALTH CARE **458**

CHAPTER 19
REGULATION AND PRIVATIZATION **465**

Public Interest or Special Interest? **466**

Market Intervention **467**

Regulation **467**
Monopoly Control **467**
Surpluses and Their Distribution **468**

Economic Theory of Regulation **469**

Demand for Regulation **469**
Supply of Regulation **470**
Political Equilibrium **470**

Regulation and Deregulation **471**

The Scope of Regulation **471**
The Regulatory Process **472**

Natural Monopoly **473**
Public Interest or Capture? **476**
Cartel Regulation **477**
Making Predictions **478**

Monopoly and Competition Policy **479**

UK Monopoly Investigations **481**
UK Merger Investigations **481**
EU Monopolies and Mergers Investigations **482**
UK Restrictive Practices Investigations **483**
EU Restrictive Practices Investigations **483**
Public or Special Interest? **484**

Public Ownership and Privatization **484**

Public Ownership **484**
Reasons for Public Ownership **484**
Reasons for Privatization **486**

READING BETWEEN THE LINES
REGULATION AND COMPETITION IN
GAS SUPPLY **488**

CHAPTER 20
EXTERNALITIES, THE ENVIRONMENT AND KNOWLEDGE **493**

Greener and Smarter **494**

Externalities **495**

External Costs **495**
External Benefits **495**
Market Failure and Public Choice **496**

Economics of the Environment **496**

The Demand for Environmental Quality **496**
The Sources of Environment Problems **497**
Property Rights and
Environmental Externalities **498**
The Coase Theorem **500**
Emission Charges **501**
Emission Standards **501**
Marketable Permits **502**
Taxes and External Costs **503**
A Global Warming Dilemma **504**
Treaties and International Agreements **505**

Economics of Knowledge **506**

Subsidies **506**

Below-cost Provision **507**
Patents **508**

READING BETWEEN THE LINES
EXTERNALITIES AND AIR POLLUTION **510**

ECONOMICS IN HISTORY
UNDERSTANDING EXTERNALITIES **512**

CHAPTER 21
INEQUALITY, REDISTRIBUTION AND WELFARE **517**

Riches and Rags **518**

**Economic Inequality in the
United Kingdom** **519**

Lorenz Curves **519**
Inequality Over Time **520**
Who are Rich and Who are Poor? **520**
Poverty **521**

Factor Prices, Endowments and Choices **522**

Labour Market and Wages **522**
Distribution of Endowments **523**
Choices **524**

Income Redistribution **525**

Income Taxes **525**
Transfer Payments **525**
Benefits in Kind **526**
Take-up and Targeting Benefits **526**
The Impact on Income Redistribution **527**
The Leaky Bucket **527**
Reform Proposals **528**

Health-care Provision **530**

Health-care Systems **530**
Health-care Costs **530**
Private Health Care and Insurance **532**
Private Health Care and
Government Insurance **532**
National Health Services **533**
Reforming Private Systems **533**
Reforming Mixed Systems and the NHS **534**
The Impact of Reforms **534**

Ideas about Fairness **536**

End-state Theories **536**

The Big Trade-off **536**
The Process View of Justice **537**

READING BETWEEN THE LINES
HEALTH-CARE SPENDING **538**

Part 5
Preliminaries and Long-term Fundamentals **543**
TALKING WITH NICK CRAFTS

CHAPTER 22
A FIRST LOOK AT MACROECONOMICS **547**

Overheating? **548**

Origins and Issues of Macroeconomics **549**

Short-term versus Long-term Goals **549**
The Road Ahead **549**

Economic Growth **550**

Economic Growth in the United Kingdom **550**
Economic Growth Around the World **553**
Benefits and Costs of Economic Growth **555**

Jobs and Unemployment **556**

Jobs **556**
Unemployment **557**
Unemployment in the United Kingdom **557**
Unemployment Around the World **558**
Why Unemployment is a Problem **558**

Inflation **559**

Inflation in the United Kingdom **559**
Inflation Around the World **560**
Inflation and Interest Rates **560**
Inflation and the Foreign Exchange Rate **562**
Why is Inflation a Problem? **562**

International Payments **563**

The Current Account **563**
The Current Account in the United Kingdom **563**
The Capital Account **563**

Macroeconomic Policy Challenges and Tools   **564**

Policy Challenges   **564**
Policy Tools   **565**

READING BETWEEN THE LINES
THE DEVELOPED ECONOMIES IN 1995   **566**

ECONOMICS IN HISTORY
THE KEYNSIAN REVOLUTION   **572**

**CHAPTER 23
MEASURING GDP, INFLATION
AND ECONOMIC GROWTH**   **574**

Economic Barometers   **575**

Gross Domestic Product   **576**

Stocks and Flows   **576**
The Equality of Income, Expenditure
and the Value of Production   **577**
How Investment is Financed   **580**

Measuring UK GDP   **581**

The Expenditure Approach   **581**
The Factor Incomes Approach   **582**
The Output Approach   **584**

The Price Level and Inflation   **586**

Retail Prices Index   **586**
GDP Deflator   **587**
What the Inflation Numbers Mean   **588**

What Real GDP Means   **590**

International Comparisons of GDP   **590**
Economic Welfare   **591**
Phase of the Business Cycle   **593**

READING BETWEEN THE LINES
DIAGNOSING THE ECONOMY   **594**

**CHAPTER 24
EMPLOYMENT, UNEMPLOYMENT AND WAGES**   **600**

Vital Signs   **601**

Employment and Wages   **602**

Population Survey   **602**
Three Labour Market Indicators   **602**
Aggregate Hours   **604**
Wage Rates   **606**

Unemployment and Full Employment   **607**

The Anatomy of Unemployment   **607**
Types of Unemployment   **610**
Full Employment   **612**

Explaining Employment and Wage Rates   **612**

Demand and Supply in the Labour Market   **612**
The Trends in Employment and Wage Rates   **614**

Explaining Unemployment   **615**

Job Search   **618**
Job Rationing   **619**
Sticky Wages   **619**

READING BETWEEN THE LINES
UNEMPLOYMENT AND MINIMUM WAGES   **616**

**CHAPTER 25
INVESTMENT, CAPITAL AND INTEREST**   **625**

Building the Global Village   **626**

Capital and Interest   **627**

Investment Around the World   **628**
Interest Rates   **628**

Investment Decisions   **630**

The Expected Profit Rate   **630**
The Real Interest Rate   **630**
Investment Demand   **630**
Private Investment Demand
in the United Kingdom   **632**

Saving and Consumption Decisions   **633**

Real Interest Rate   **633**
Disposable Income   **633**
Purchasing Power of Net Assets   **633**
Expected Future Income   **634**
Consumption Demand and Saving Supply   **634**
Disposable Income,
Consumption Expenditure and Saving   **635**

Other Influences on
Consumption Expenditure and Saving **637**
Consumption Demand and Saving Supply
in the United Kingdom **638**

**Long-run Equilibrium in the
Global Economy** **640**

Determining the Real Interest Rate: $S = I$ **640**
Explaining Changes in the Real Interest Rate **641**
The Demand for Real GDP **642**
Determining the
Real Interest Rate: $C + I + G = Y_{POT}$ **644**

**Net Exports and Equilibrium in
the National Economy** **645**

Net Exports and the Exchange Rate **646**

READING BETWEEN THE LINES
REAL INTEREST RATES AND
CONSUMER SPENDING **648**

CHAPTER 26
LONG-TERM ECONOMIC GROWTH **653**

Economic Miracles **654**

Long-term Growth Trends **655**

Growth in the UK Economy **655**
Real GDP Growth in the World Economy **656**

The Sources of Economic Growth **657**

Preconditions for Economic Growth **657**
Saving and Investment in New Capital **658**
Growth in Human Capital **658**
Discovery of New Technologies **659**

Growth Accounting **659**

The Productivity Function **659**
Accounting for the Productivity Growth
Slowdown and Speedup **661**
Accounting for
the Productivity Slowdown: A Summary **663**
Technological Change
During the Productivity Growth Slowdown **663**

Growth Theory **664**

Classical Growth Theory **665**
Neoclassical Growth Theory **667**

New Growth Theory **669**

Achieving Faster Growth **671**

The Miracle Economies **671**
Policies for Faster Growth **671**

READING BETWEEN THE LINES
SAVING AND GROWTH **674**

ECONOMICS IN HISTORY
ECONOMIC GROWTH **676**

Part 6

Macroeconomic Fluctuations and Policies **681**

TALKING WITH PATRICK MINFORD

CHAPTER 27
AGGREGATE SUPPLY AND AGGREGATE DEMAND **684**

Catching the Wave **685**

Aggregate Supply **686**

Long-run Aggregate Supply **686**
Short-run Aggregate Supply **687**
Movements Along *LAS* and *SAS* **690**
Changes in Aggregate Supply **688**

Aggregate Demand **690**

Why the Aggregate Demand Curve
Slopes Downward **691**
Changes in the
Quantity of Real GDP Demanded **692**
Changes in Aggregate Demand **692**
Expectations **693**
International Factors **694**
Fiscal Policy **694**
Monetary Policy **695**
Shifts of the Aggregate Demand Curve **695**

Macroeconomic Equilibrium **696**

Determination of Real GDP
and the Price Level **696**
Short-run Macroeconomic Equilibrium
and Full Employment **697**
Long-term Growth and Inflation **698**

Fluctuations in Aggregate Demand **699**
Fluctuations in Aggregate Supply **700**

**Long-term Growth, Inflation
and Cycles in the UK Economy** **701**

The Evolving Economy: 1960–1994 **702**

**READING BETWEEN THE LINES
AGGREGATE SUPPLY AND
AGGREGATE DEMAND IN ACTION** **704**

**CHAPTER 28
EXPENDITURE MULTIPLIERS** **710**

Economic Amplifier or Shock Absorber? **711**

Sticky Prices and Expenditure Plans **712**

The Aggregate Implications of Sticky Prices **712**
Expenditure Plans **712**
Consumption Function and Saving Function **712**
Marginal Propensities to Consume and Save **714**
Other Influences on
Consumption Expenditure and Saving **716**
The Consumption Function **716**
Consumption as a Function of Real GDP **717**
Import Function **718**

Real GDP with a Sticky Price Level **720**

Aggregate Expenditure Schedule **720**
Aggregate Expenditure Curve **721**
Actual Expenditure,
Planned Expenditure and Real GDP **721**
Equilibrium Expenditure **722**
Convergence to Equilibrium **722**

The Multiplier **724**

The Basic Idea of the Multiplier **724**
The Multiplier Effect **725**
Why is the Multiplier Greater than 1? **725**
The Size of the Multiplier **725**
The Multiplier and the
Marginal Propensities to Consume and Save **726**
Imports and Income Taxes **727**
Business Cycle Turning Points **727**

**The Multiplier, Real GDP
and the Price Level** **729**

Aggregate Expenditure and
Aggregate Demand **729**

Aggregate Expenditure and the Price Level **729**
Equilibrium GDP and the Price Level **731**

**READING BETWEEN THE LINES
THE FRENCH MULTIPLIER IN ACTION** **734**

**Appendix to Chapter 28
Imports, Taxes and the Multiplier** **739**

**CHAPTER 29
THE GOVERNMENT BUDGET AND
FISCAL POLICY** **741**

Balancing Acts at Westminster **742**

The Government Budget **743**

Highlights of the 1995 Budget **743**
The Budget in Historical Perspective **745**
The Budget Deficit and Debt Levels
in a European Perspective **747**

Fiscal Policy Multipliers **748**

The Government Purchases Multiplier **749**
The Lump-sum Tax Multiplier **751**
The Balanced Budget Multiplier **752**
Induced Taxes and Welfare Spending **752**
International Trade and Fiscal
Policy Multipliers **753**
Automatic Stabilizers **753**

**Fiscal Policy in the Short Run
and the Long Run** **755**

Fiscal Policy and Aggregate Demand **755**
Fiscal Expansion at Potential GDP **758**
Fiscal Policy and Aggregate Supply **758**
A Burden on Future Generations? **758**
Crowding out **760**
Ricardian Equivalence **760**

**READING BETWEEN THE LINES
FISCAL POLICY IN GERMANY** **762**

**CHAPTER 30
MONEY** **767**

Money Makes the World Go Around **768**

What Is Money? **769**

Medium of Exchange **769**
Unit of Account **769**
Store of Value **770**
Commodity Money **770**
Convertible Paper Money **771**
Fiat Money **771**
Deposit Money **772**
Money in the United Kingdom Today **772**

Financial Intermediaries **775**

Banks **775**
Building Societies **776**
The Economic Functions of
Financial Intermediaries **778**

**Financial Regulation,
Deregulation and Innovation** **779**

Financial Regulation **779**
Deregulation in the 1980s **780**
Financial Innovation **780**
Deregulation, Innovation and Money **781**

How Banks Create Money **781**

Reserves: Actual and Required **781**
Creating Deposits by Making Loans in a
One-bank Economy **782**
The Deposit Multiplier **783**
Creating Deposits by Making Loans
with Many Banks **783**
The Deposit Multiplier
in the United Kingdom **785**

Money, Real GDP and the Price Level **785**

The Short-run Effects of a Change in
the Quantity of Money **785**
The Long-run Effects of a Change in
the Quantity of Money **786**
The Quantity Theory of Money **787**
The Quantity Theory and the *AS–AD* Model **788**
Historical Evidence on the
Quantity Theory of Money **790**
International Evidence on the
Quantity Theory of Money **790**
Correlation, Causation and Other Influences **791**

READING BETWEEN THE LINES
UNSTABLE MONEY **792**

ECONOMICS IN HISTORY
MONEY AND INFLATION **794**

**CHAPTER 31
THE CENTRAL BANK AND MONETARY POLICY** **799**

Inside the Old Lady **800**

The Bank of England **801**

The Origins and Functions
of the Bank of England **801**
The Bank's Financial Structure **803**
The Bank's Policy Tools **804**
Accountability and Control
of the Central Bank **805**
Dependence Versus Independence
for the Central Bank **805**

Controlling the Money Supply **806**

How an Open Market Operation Works **806**
Monetary Base and Bank Reserves **809**
The Multiplier Effect of an
Open Market Operation **809**

United Kingdom Money Supply **812**

The Demand for Money **814**

The Influences on Money Holding **814**
The Demand for Money Curve **816**
Shifts in the Demand Curve for Real Money **816**
The Demand for Money in
the United Kingdom **817**

Interest Rate Determination **818**

Interest Rates and Asset Prices **818**
Money Market Equilibrium **819**
Changing the Interest Rate **819**
The Bank of England and
Control of the Money Supply **820**

Monetary Policy **821**

The Bank of England in Action **821**
Profiting by Predicting the
Bank of England **823**
The Ripple Effects of Monetary Policy **824**
Interest Rates and the Business Cycle **824**

READING BETWEEN THE LINES
MONETARY POLICY IN THE UNITED KINGDOM **828**

CHAPTER 32
INFLATION   831

From Rome to Russia   832

Inflation and the Price Level   833

Demand-pull Inflation   834
Inflation Effect of an Increase in
Aggregate Demand   834
Wage Response   835
A Demand-pull Inflation Process   835

Cost-push Inflation   836

Initial Effect of a Decrease in
Aggregate Supply   836
Aggregate Demand Response   837
A Cost-push Inflation Process   837

Anticipating Inflation   838

Unanticipated Inflation in the Labour Market   839
How People Forecast Inflation   839
Predicting People's Forecasts   840
Rational Expectation of the Price Level   840
Anticipated Inflation   842
Unanticipated Inflation   842
The Costs of Anticipated Inflation   843

Inflation and Unemployment:
The Phillips Curve   845

The Short-run Phillips Curve   845
The Long-run Phillips Curve   846
Changes in the Natural Unemployment Rate   847
The Phillips Curve in the United Kingdom   848

Interest Rates and Inflation   849

The Effects of Inflation on
Borrowers and Lenders   849
Interest Rates and Unanticipated Inflation   850
Interest Rates and Anticipated Inflation   850
Inflation and Interest Rates in
the United Kingdom   850

The Politics of Inflation   852

Inflation Tax   852
Credibility and Reputation   853

READING BETWEEN THE LINES
INFLATION: KEEPING THE ENEMY AT BAY   854

CHAPTER 33
THE BUSINESS CYCLE   860

Must What Goes Up Always Come Down?   861

Patterns, Impulses and
Propagation Mechanisms   862

Impulses and Propagation Mechanisms   863
The Crucial Role of Investment and Capital   863
The *AS–AD* Model   863

Aggregate Demand Theories
of the Business Cycle   864

Keynesian Theory of the Cycle   864
Monetarist Theory   866
Rational Expectations Theories   866
Rational Expectations Cycle Mechanisms   868
AD–AS General Theory   869

Real Business Cycle Theory   870

The RBC Impulse   870
The RBC Mechanism   871
Criticisms of RBC Theory   874
Defence of RBC Theory   874

The 1990–1992 Recession   875

The Origins of the 1990–1992 Recession   875
Aggregate Demand and Aggregate Supply
in the 1990–1992 Recession   876
The Labour Market in the 1990s   877

The Great Depression   878

Why the Great Depression Happened   879
Can It Happen Again?   881

READING BETWEEN THE LINES
THE RECESSION WATCH IS ON   882

ECONOMICS IN HISTORY
BUSINESS CYCLES   888

CHAPTER 34
MACROECONOMIC POLICY CHALLENGES   890

What Can Policy Do?   891

Policy Goals   **892**

Long-term Real GDP Growth   **892**
The Business Cycle   **892**
Unemployment   **892**
Inflation   **892**
The Two Core Policy Indicators:
Unemployment and Inflation   **893**

Policy Tools and Performance   **894**

Recent Fiscal Policy in the European Union   **894**
Recent Monetary Policy in the
United Kingdom and the European Union   **895**

Long-term Growth Policy   **897**

National Saving Policies   **898**
Human Capital Policies   **899**
Investment in New Technologies   **899**

**Business Cycle and
Unemployment Policies**   **900**

Fixed-rule Policies   **900**
Feedback-rule Policies   **900**
Discretionary Policies   **900**
Stabilizing Aggregate Demand Shocks   **900**
Stabilizing Aggregate Supply Shocks   **904**

Inflation Policy   **906**

Avoiding Cost-push Inflation   **906**
Slowing Inflation   **908**
Inflation Reduction in Practice   **908**

READING BETWEEN THE LINES
STABILIZATION POLICY DILEMMA   **910**

Part 7

The Global Economy   916

TALKING WITH PAUL DE GRAUWE

CHAPTER 35
TRADING WITH THE WORLD   919

Silk Routes and Containers   **920**

**Patterns and Trends in
International Trade**   **921**

UK International Trade   **921**
Geographical Patterns   **922**
Trends in Trade   **923**
Balance of Trade and International Borrowing   **923**

**Opportunity Cost and
Comparative Advantage**   **924**

Opportunity Cost in Farmland   **924**
Opportunity Cost in Mobilia   **925**
Comparative Advantage   **925**

Gains from Trade   **925**

Reaping the Gains from Trade   **926**
Balanced Trade   **926**
Changes in Production and Consumption   **926**
Gains for All   **928**
Absolute Advantage   **929**

Gains from Trade in Reality   **929**

Comparative Advantage in
the Global Economy   **929**
Trade in Similar Goods   **930**

Trade Restrictions   **931**

The History of Tariffs   **931**
How Tariffs Work   **932**
Learning the Hard Way   **935**
Non-tariff Barriers   **935**
How Quotas and VERs Work   **935**
'Invisible' Non-tariff Barriers   **936**

The Case Against Protection   **937**

National Security   **937**
New Industries   **937**
Restraining Monopoly   **938**
Protection Saves Jobs   **938**
Because Foreign Labour is Cheap,
We Need a Tariff to Compete   **938**
Protection Brings Diversity and Stability   **939**
Protection Penalizes
Lax Environmental Standards   **939**
Protection Prevents Rich Countries
From Exploiting Developing Countries   **939**
Why is International Trade Restricted?   **940**
Compensating Losers   **940**
Political Outcome   **940**

READING BETWEEN THE LINES
PROTECTION VERSUS FREE TRADE 942

ECONOMICS IN HISTORY
UNDERSTANDING THE GAINS
FROM INTERNATIONAL TRADE 948

CHAPTER 36
THE BALANCE OF PAYMENTS AND
THE EXCHANGE RATE 950

A Mounting Debt and a Sinking Pound 951

Financing International Trade 952

Balance of Payments Accounts 952
Borrowers and Lenders, Debtors and Creditors 954
Current Account Balance 955
The Ricardian Case 957
The Twin Deficits Case 957
Is the UK Borrowing for
Consumption or Investment? 957

Sterling in the Global Market 958

Foreign Exchange Systems 959
Recent Exchange Rate History 960

Exchange Rate Determination 963

The Quantity of Pounds 963
The Demand for Sterling Assets 963
Changes in the Demand for Sterling Assets 964
The Supply of Sterling Assets 965
Changes in the Supply of Sterling Assets 966
The Market for Sterling 967

The European Monetary System 971

European Currency Unit 971
Exchange Rate Mechanism 971
European Monetary Union 972

READING BETWEEN THE LINES
FOREIGN EXCHANGE MARKETS IN ACTION 976

CHAPTER 37
EMERGING ECONOMIES 980

Dramatic Economic Change 981

A Snapshot of the World Economy 982

Classification of Countries 982
Incomes Per Person 982
Income Distribution 982
Economic Growth and Decline 984

Alternative Economic Systems 985

Property Rights 986
Incentives 986
Types of Economic Systems 986
Alternative Systems Compared 987
How Capitalism Copes with Scarcity 988
How Socialism Copes with Scarcity 989

Economic Transition in Russia and
Central Europe 990

History of the Soviet Union 990
Soviet-style Central Planning 991
Living Standards in the 1980s 992
Market Economy Reforms 992
Transition Problems 993
Economic Transition in Central Europe 993
East Germany 994
Czech Republic and Slovak Republic 994
Hungary 994
Poland 995

China's Emerging Market Economy 995

The Great Leap Forward 995
Deng Xiaoping's Reforms 996
China's Success 997

Other Economic Miracles in East Asia 999

READING BETWEEN THE LINES
RUSSIA'S MACROECONOMIC PERFORMANCE 1000

Glossary G–1
Index I–1

CREDITS

The publisher would like to thank the following for permission to use material in this book.

CHAPTER 1: Pin factory, **Culver Pictures**. Woman with silicon wafer, **Tony Stone Images**. Adam Smith, **The Bettmann Archive**. Cartoon, © **Chris Riddell, The Independent**. Cartoon, Minsk/Croydon, © **John Appleton, The News Chronicle**.

CHAPTER 4: Rail construction crew, Green River, **Corbis-Bettmann**. Concorde and other aircraft, **The Royal Aeronautical Society**. Antoine-Augustin Cournot and Alfred Marshall, **Stock Montage**.

CHAPTER 8: Biscuit factory, **Hulton Deutch Collection**. Woman executive, **Davina Arkell, Addison Wesley Longman**. William Stanley Jevon, **MacMillan Press**. Jeremy Bentham, **Mary Evans Picture Library**.

CHAPTER 10: Ford assembly line, **Brown Brothers**. Michael Dell, **Dell Computers**. Ronald Coase, **David Joel Photography**. Jacob Viner, **Archives of the University Department of Rare Books and Special Collections, Princeton University Library**.

CHAPTER 11: Cartoon, **M. Twohy**, © **1988 The New Yorker Magazine, Inc.**

CHAPTER 14: Traffic congestion in Manchester 1914, **Local Studies Unit, Manchester Central Library**. Stacked Cars, **Robert Hunt**. Harold Hotelling, **Wooten-Moulio**. Thomas Robert Malthus, **Mary Evans Picture Library**.

CHAPTER 15: Cartoon, © **J. Banks, The Financial Times**.

CHAPTER 17: Cartoon, © **Roger Beale, The Financial Times**.

CHAPTER 19: Cartoon, © **Nick Baker, The Financial Times**.

CHAPTER 21: River pollution, **Charles and Josett Lenars-Corbis**. Fishing on the River Thames, **Angling Times**. Arthur Cecil Pigou © **Peter Lofts**. James Buchanan, **George Mason University**.

CHAPTER 22: Spinning Jenny, **Hulton Getty Picture Collection**. BT Control Centre, **Liaison International/ Robert Harding Picture Library**. Jean-Baptiste Say,

Mary Evans Picture Library. John Maynard Keynes, **Corbis-Bettmann UPI**.

CHAPTER 26: McCormick Reaper, **Hulton Getty Picture Collection**. Fibre Optics, **Liaison International/Robert Harding Picture Library**. Joseph Schumpeter, **Corbis-Bettmann**. Robert Solow, © **L. Barry Hetherington**.

CHAPTER 27: Cartoon, © **Brian Tyrer 1996**.

CHAPTER 29: Cartoon, © **Peter Brooks / The Times, 26th July 1996**.

CHAPTER 30: Woman burning Marks and David Hume, **Bettmann Archive**. Brazilians stocking up food before price increase, © **Carlos Humberto (Contact Colorific)**. Milton Friedman, **Marshall Heinrichs, Addison Wesley Longman**.

CHAPTER 33: The Stock Exchange, **Bettmann Archive**. Boarded up shop, **Davina Arkell, Addison Wesley Longman**. Robert Lucas, **Marshall Heinrichs, Addison Wesley Longman**. Cartoon, © **David Austin, The Guardian**.

CHAPTER 34: Cartoon, © **J. Banks, The Independent Magazine**.

CHAPTER 35: Clipper Ship, **Bettmann Archive**. Container ship, **Sealand Services Inc**. David Ricardo, **Mary Evans Picture Library**.

CHAPTER 37: *Reading Between the Lines* reprinted by permission of **The Wall Street Journal** © **1994 Dow Jones & Company, Inc**. All Rights Reserved World Wide.

The publisher would like to acknowledge: **The Times Newspapers Limited** for permission to reproduce articles in *Reading Between the Lines* in Chapters 1, 9, 19, 24, 25, 27 and 36; **The Economist, London** for permission to reproduce articles in *Reading Between the Lines* in Chapters 26 and 31; and **The Office for National Statistics** (formerly the Central Statistical Office) for data used in figures and tables in this book.

The publisher has made every attempt to obtain permission to reproduce material in this book from the appropriate source. If there are any errors or ommisions please contact the publisher who will make suitable acknowledgement in the reprint.

REVIEWERS

Addison Wesley Longman would like to express appreciation for the invaluable advice and encouragement they have received from many educators in the United Kingdom and elsewhere in Europe for this edition.

Dr Angela Black, University of St Andrews

Dr S. Bradley, Lancaster University

Dr A. Carruth, University of Kent, Canterbury

Mr Martin Emmett, Chichester College

Dr P. Guldager, Aarhus Business School, Denmark

Dr Jerker Holm, Lund University, Sweden

Dr Hilary Ingham, UMIST

Dr Ian Jackson, Staffordshire University

Dr M. Keane, University College, Galway

Professor Kevin Lawler, University of Sunderland

Dr Wyn Morgan, The University of Nottingham

Dr Mats Nilsson, University of Lulea, Sweden

Professor John Struthers, University of Paisley

Professor P.C. Stubbs, University of Manchester

Table of Contents Reviewers

Martin Duffy, UMIST

John Ellis, Dorset Business School, University of Bournemouth

Dr G. Fletcher, University of Liverpool

Simon Hays, University of Newcastle

Dr Naylor, University of Warwick

Dr S. Price, City University

Dr B. Sheeham, Leeds Metropolitan University

Dr Winnett, University of Bath

Mike Woods, South Bank University

Professor Wren, University of Exeter

Addison Wesley Longman would like to give special thanks to Robert Ackrill for his contribution to the *Reading Between the Lines* in Chapter 9 and to Wyn Morgan for his input into the *Economics in History* section.

PREFACE

To change the way students see the world: this is our purpose in teaching economics and it has remained our goal in preparing the third edition of this text. There is no greater satisfaction for a teacher than to share the joy of students who have begun to understand the powerful lessons of the economic approach. But these lessons are hard to learn. Every day in the classroom we relive the challenges of gaining the insights that are called the economist's way of thinking and recall our own early struggles to master this discipline. In preparing this edition, we have been privileged to draw on our experiences not only of our students but also of the many teachers who have used the previous two editions.

The principles of economics course is constantly evolving, and the past few years have seen some major shifts of emphasis, especially in macroeconomics. Today's principles course springs from today's issues: the slowdown in productivity growth; the information revolution; the emerging market economies of Central Europe and Asia; the expansion of global trade and investment. More and more, we recognize the value of teaching long-run fundamentals as a basis for understanding these issues and as a springboard to understanding short-run economic fluctuations. This book allows students to place an early emphasis on long-run fundamentals and, for the first time, to reach the theory of long-run economic growth, including 'new' growth theory, using the familiar tools of supply and demand.

The Third Edition Approach

This edition has been crafted to meet three overriding goals:

◆ Focus on the core principles

◆ Use the core principles to explain the issues and problems of the 1990s

◆ Create a flexible teaching and learning tool

Focus on the Core Principles

The core principles of choice and opportunity cost, marginal analysis substitution and incentives, and the power of the competitive process are the focus of the micro chapters. The core tools of demand and supply are thoroughly explained and repeatedly used throughout both the micro and the macro chapters. New ideas – such as dynamic comparative advantage, game theory and its applications, the modern theory of the firm, information, public choice, new growth theory and real business cycle theory – also appear in this book. But they are described and explained by using the core principles; that is, new ideas are explained by using familiar ideas and tools.

Explain the Issues and Problems of the 1990s

The core principles and tools are also used to help students understand the issues that confront them in today's world. Among the issues that are explored, some at length, are the environment, health care, widening income gaps, the productivity growth slowdown, restraining inflation, watching for the next recession, avoiding protectionism and the consequences of the emerging markets of Central Europe and Asia. These issues are studied repeatedly by using the same core principles within economic models.

Flexible Teaching and Learning Tool

One of the most exciting facts about economics is that its teachers hold strong views about what to teach and how to teach, yet they do not hold the same view. This poses a special challenge to a text-book author, especially in the macro part of our subject. To be useful in a wide range of situations and to a diversity of teachers, a book must be flexible.

This book can be used to teach a range of microeconomic courses, including business and management economics and microeconomic policy. It can be used to teach all traditional macro courses, which emphasize short-term fluctuations in output, prices and unemployment, with either a Keynesian or monetarist emphasis. This book can also be used to teach a macroeconomics course that places an early emphasis on long-term growth. To signal this last possibility, the long-term growth chapter appears early in the book.

However, the order in which the chapters appear is only one of several orders in which they can be used. The tables on pp. I-14 to I-16 show some of the alternative possibilities for both the micro and the macro courses.

Level and Viewpoint

The emphasis in this book on using economic models creates a high degree of rigour which does not require a high level or mathematical bias. We believe economics is a serious, lively and evolving science – a science that seeks to develop a body of theory powerful enough to explain the economic world around us and that pursues its tasks by building, testing and rejecting economic models. In some areas the science has succeeded in its tasks but in others controversy persists. Where matters are settled, we present what we know; where controversy persists, we present the alternative viewpoints. This positive approach to economics is, we believe, especially valuable for students as they prepare to function in a world in which simple ideologies have become irrelevant and familiar patterns in the economic landscape have shifted and blurred.

Always recalling our own early struggles with economics, we place the student at centre stage and write for the student foremost. We are conscious that many students find economics hard. As a result, our goal has been to make the material as accessible as possible. We use a style that makes for an easy read and that doesn't intimidate. Each chapter opens with a clear list of learning objectives, a vignette that connects with the student's world and seeks to grab attention, and a statement of where we are heading. Once in the chapter, we don't reduce economics to a set of recipes to be memorized. Instead, we encourage students to try to understand each concept. To accomplish this goal, the book illustrates every principle with examples that have been selected both to hold the student's interest and to bring the subject to life. To encourage a sense of enthusiasm and confidence, when the book has explained a new principle, it puts it to work and uses it to illuminate a current real-world problem or issue.

Changes in the Third Edition

Changes in the Microeconomics Section The structure of microeconomics remains consistent with the first two editions but it reflects the central goals of the revision: to focus on the use of economic models and core concepts; to explain current issues; and to be leaner and simpler. Chapter 1 is substantially new and sets the tone for the revision. It is organized around the themes of how economists think and what economists do. Chapter 3 uses lively new examples to illustrate the core concepts of scarcity, choice and opportunity cost and gives a neat, accessible explanation of comparative advantage (and dynamic comparative advantage) and the gains from trade.

Chapter 4, the core demand and supply chapter, has a new opening section on money price, relative price and opportunity cost, and a new section that explains real-world price changes. Chapter 5 has a new illustration of the connection between elasticity and revenue and new international elasticity comparisons.

The revision of Chapter 8, an optional chapter on indifference curves, now has a section on labour–leisure and consumption–saving choices. Chapter 9 explains how agency relationships arise from incomplete information and how they lead to different types of business organizations. Chapter 10 has a simplified explanation of the connection between short-run and long-run cost of the relationship between returns to scale and the shapes of the cost curves. Chapter 11 gets to the point of the competitive model more quickly and has a new explanation of competition and efficiency, and introduces the notion of market failure. Chapter 12 introduces monopoly as an example of market failure and has a new expanded explanation and illustration of price discrimination between two groups with demand elasticities. Chapter 13 has a more streamlined coverage of the game theory approach to oligopoly and a new section on contestable markets. Chapter 15 has a new case study of trade union decline.

The chapters on markets and government have been substantially reorganized and extend the comparable chapters of the second edition. Chapter 18 previews the whole range of government expenditure, tax and public choice issues. Chapter 19 (Chapter 20 in the second edition) includes new cases and examples, such as European airlines and cable television, and has an expanded section on privatization. A new Chapter 20 explains externalities and illustrates these concepts with extensive discussion of the economics of the environment and the economics of knowledge – of education and research and development. Chapter 21 (Chapter 18 in the second edition) discusses inequality and redistribution and includes a new section on the interplay between health care and inequality and health-care reform.

Changes in the Macroeconomics Section The structure of the macroeconomics chapters has been thoroughly rethought and reworked. Chapter 22 shows the entire macro landscape including its origins and rebirth in the Great Depression; the issues it explores of long-term growth, business cycles, unemployment, inflation, and international debts and deficits; the facts it seeks to explain, both current and historical, in the United Kingdom and around the world; and the policy challenges it faces.

Chapter 23 has a streamlined treatment of the circular flow, and new material on capital and investment, wealth and saving, and national saving and international borrowing. It also has an expanded evaluation of the meaning of real GDP. A new Chapter 24 describes the measurement of employment, unemployment and the real wage rate and explains labour market trends. Chapter 25 is also new. It explains investment, saving and consumption decisions and the determination of the real interest rate. Chapters 24 and 25 are a foundation for studying both long-term growth and short-term fluctuations. Chapter 26 is a new chapter that makes growth theory accessible and relevant to the principles student. It describes growth in the UK and world economies, explains growth accounting and describes the sources of the growth slowdown of the 1970s. The chapter also describes the growth of the Asian economies and reviews policies for faster growth.

Chapter 27 draws on the best of the second edition's Chapter 24, but it now begins with long-run and short-run aggregate supply. In so doing, it sharpens the distinction between flexible and sticky price situations and paves the way for several chapters on short-run fluctuations. Chapter 28 presents the Keynesian aggregate expenditure model and multiplier. The treatment of the multiplier has been carefully revised and simplified.

Chapter 29 is completely new. It describes the components of the UK budget and its recent history and studies the effects of fiscal policy and proposals for deficit reduction. Chapters 30 and 31 cover money, the banking system and monetary policy. The coverage is similar to the second edition, but it has been streamlined and is more accessible, and includes a new section on the determination of the money supply.

Chapter 32 has a simpler and clearer explanation of the modern theory of inflation and unemployment and inflation and interest rates. Chapter 33 is substantially new. It includes an explanation of Keynesian, monetarist, rational expectations and real business cycle theories. Chapter 34 is another big picture chapter, similar in intent to the second edition's Chapter 33 but clearer and more accessible. It shows how fiscal and monetary policy have been used to achieve both short-term and long-term objectives.

The book ends with chapters that focus on the global economy. Chapter 35 has an expanded description of UK trade, a description of the GATT and a new section that uses core principles to evaluate and debunk the arguments for protection. Chapter 36 provides one of the clearest treatments of exchange rate determination currently available and includes a section on the Exchange Rate Mechanism of the European Monetary System and European Monetary Union. Lastly, Chapter 37 combines discussions of growth and development and economic systems in transition into one chapter. The coverage of current problems in Eastern and Central Europe and Asia focuses on the core principles of incentives and efficiency.

Features that Enhance the Learning Process

This third edition, like its predecessors, is packed with special features designed to enhance the learning process.

The Art Programme: Showing the Economic Action

The first and second editions of this book set new standards with their highly successful and innovative art programmes. Our goal has always been to show clearly 'where the economic action is'. The figures and diagrams in this book continue to generate enormously positive feedback, confirming our view that graphical analysis is the most important tool for teaching and learning economics. But it is a tool that gives many students much difficulty. Because many students find graphs hard to work with, the art has been designed both to be visually attractive and engaging and to communicate economic principles unambiguously and clearly. In the third edition the clear style of the data-based art that reveals the data and trends has been retained. In addition, diagrams that illustrate economic processes now consistently distinguish among key economic players (firms, households, governments and markets).

We observe a consistent protocol in style, notation and use of colour, which includes:

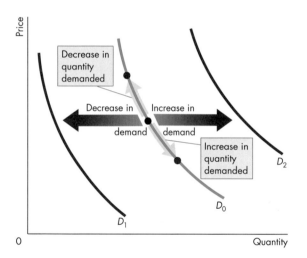

- Highlighting shifted curves, points of equilibrium and the most important features in red.
- Using arrows in conjunction with colour to lend directional movement to what are usually static presentations.
- Pairing graphs with data tables from which the curves have been plotted.
- Using colour consistently to underscore the content, and referring to such use of colour in the text and captions.
- Labelling key pieces of information in graphs with boxed notes.
- Rendering each piece electronically, so that precision is achieved.

The art programme has been developed with the study and review needs of students in mind. It has retained the following features:

- Marking the most important figures and tables with a red icon ◆ and listing them at the end of the chapter as Key Figures and Tables.
- Using complete, informative captions that encapsulate the major points in the graph, so that students can preview or review the chapter by skimming through the art.

Interviews: Leading Economists Lend a Hand

Substantive interviews with famous economists were another popular feature in the first and second editions. We are continuing the tradition and have included all new interviews – seven in total – each with an economist who has contributed significantly to advancing the thinking and practice in our discipline. Two of the interviews are with economists from continental Europe. The interviews encourage students to participate in the conversations as the economists discuss their areas of specialization, their unique contributions to economics and their general insights which are relevant to beginning students.

An interview opens each part of the book's seven parts, and each interview has been carefully edited to be self-contained. Because each interview discusses topics that are introduced formally in the subsequent chapters, students can use it as a preview to some of the terminology and theory they are about to encounter. A more careful reading afterwards will give the students a fuller appreciation of the discussion. Lastly, the whole series of interviews can be approached as an informal symposium on the subject matter of economics as it is practised today.

Reading Between the Lines: News Articles for Critical Thinking

Another feature of the previous edition that was well received is *Reading Between the Lines*. A major goal of the principles course that *Reading Between the Lines* is designed to pursue is to help students build critical thinking skills and use economic principles to interpret daily news events (and their coverage in the media). We have updated the news articles in this edition and have deliberately selected topics that appeal to students, such as Newcastle United's £15 million fee for Alan Shearer, A-level results in the United Kingdom, restrictions on alcohol in Finland and macroeconomists' performance in

Russia. Each *Reading Between the Lines* spread contains three passes at a story. It begins with a facsimile (usually abbreviated) of an actual newspaper or magazine article. These news stories come from major newspapers and magazines, including *The Economist, The Financial Times, The Sunday Times, The Guardian* and *The Independent*. The second pass presents a digest of the article's essential points. The third pass provides an economic analysis of the article. In order not to disrupt the flow of the material, these features are placed at the end of each chapter, before the chapter summary.

Economics in History: Path-breaking Ideas

The *Economics in History* feature helps students trace the evolution of path-breaking economic ideas and recognize the universality of their application, not only to the past but also to the present. For example, Adam Smith's powerful ideas about the division of labour apply to the creation of the computer chip as well as to the pin factory of the eighteenth century. In order not to disrupt the flow of the material, these features are located towards the end of chapters.

Mathematics Boxes

The mathematics boxes of the second edition have been revised and extended. Their purpose remains the same. Mathematics boxes are included to help students use a mathematical approach to explore their knowledge of economic principles if they are keen to do so. The level of mathematics is not particularly sophisticated, but the aim is to encourage students to see mathematics as just another analytical tool for resolving the economic problems and principles already encountered in the text. Students who do not find mathematics helpful or interesting can ignore these boxes. They do not contain any economic concepts or ideas that are not fully explained in a non-mathematical way in the text and figures.

Learning Aids: Pedagogy that Leads to Active Learning

The careful pedagogical plan has been refined to ensure that this book complements and reinforces classroom learning. Each chapter contains the following pedagogical elements.

Objectives   Each chapter opens with a list of objectives that enable students to set their goals as they begin the chapter.

Chapter Openers   Intriguing puzzles, paradoxes or metaphors frame the important questions that are unravelled as the chapter progresses.

Highlighted In-text Reviews   Succinct summaries for review are interspersed through the chapter. In this edition, these in-text reviews have a list format that is designed to give students a more easily digested statement of the key points.

Key Terms   Highlighted within the text, these concepts form the first part of a three-tiered review of economic vocabulary. These terms are repeated with page references at the end of the chapter and they are compiled in the end-of-book glossary.

Key Figures and Tables   The most important figures and tables are identified with a red icon ◆ and are listed at the end of each chapter.

End-of-chapter Study Material   In the third edition we have worked hard to create truly effective end-of-chapter review questions and problems and have added many new ones. As a new feature, we have included a substantial number of diagram problems. In addition, each chapter containing a *Reading Between the Lines* feature has a multipart question about this feature included in the problem section, and some chapters also have problems based on the *Economics in History* feature. Each chapter ends with a summary organized around its major headings, a list of key terms with page references, a list of key figures and tables with page references, review questions and problems.

Flexibility: Navigating the Principles Course

Pressures on the time available to teach principles courses is a powerful example of the fundamental economic problem: our wants exceed our resources and we must make choices. To facilitate these choices, a text must be flexible and contain much optional matter. The tables on pp. I-14 and I-15 explains which chapters form the core, which are extensions or applications, and the prerequisites for each chapter. The additional tables on pp. I-14 and

I-16 illustrate how the chapters can be organized to support several different micro and macro courses.

The Teaching and Learning Package

Addison Wesley's editors, the supplements authors and ourselves have worked closely together to ensure that our integrated text and supplements package provides students and instructors with a seamless learning and teaching experience. The authors of these components are outstanding educators and scholars who have used their own human capital (and that of their students) to ensure that the supplements are of the highest quality and value. The package contains three broad components:

◆ Tools to enhance learning

◆ Tools to enhance teaching

◆ Tools for the electronic classroom

Tools to Enhance Learning

Study Guide　The new third edition study guide was prepared by Brian Atkinson, formerly of the University of Central Lancashire. Carefully coordinated with the main text, each chapter of the Study Guide contains:

◆ Chapter in perspective

◆ Helpful hints

◆ An explanation of key figures and tables

◆ Self-test questions

◆ Answers to self-test questions

The Self-test section includes:

◆ Concept review questions

◆ True/false questions that ask students to explain their answers

◆ Multiple-choice questions

◆ Short-answer questions

◆ Problems

◆ Discussion questions

◆ Data questions

In each chapter of the Study Guide, students can test their cumulative understanding of the subject in a number of ways. A data question exercise asks them to apply what they've learned by analysing a news article and answering short-answer questions. Each multiple-choice test presents a selection of questions to test the students' knowledge. The self-test exercises allow students to practise exam-style questions.

Several elements of the Study Guide are geared to building critical thinking, such as the true/false questions, multiple-choice answers that include explanations of why the answer is correct, *Reading Between the Lines* exercises, problems, and discussion and data questions. Other elements are geared to making the study of economics a bit easier. The chapter in perspective provides a brief summary of key definitions, concepts and material in the textbook chapter; the helpful hints focus on ways to better understand the principles of economics and to help students understand the most important graphs, equations and techniques for problem solving; and an explanation of selected key figures and tables reviews students' understanding, and helps with exam revision.

Economics in Action Interactive Software
The second edition supplements package included truly interactive software to support student mastery of economic principles. Students around the world have used this path-breaking and widely acclaimed computer learning tool to increase their success in the principles course. With the third edition they will have fun working the tutorials and testing themselves ahead of their exams. They will also find the real-world data both illuminating and useful for projects. New releases of the software have the following features:

◆ Step-by-step, graph-based tutorials that actively engage students in exploring economic concepts.

◆ A graphing tool that allows students to graph real-world economic data.

◆ A self-testing facility that simulates a multiple-choice-test setting and gathers results

◆ A problem-solving tool that allows students to solve homework problems from the text.

Economics in the News　This supplement was prepared by Brian Atkinson. Using topical articles from *The Economist*, this book takes an event in the news and follows it with questions for student analysis, student model answers, articles to explain the essence of the story and statistical data. The book is designed to develop students' ability to think about economic issues by showing how economic models can be used to interpret the news.

Updates in Economics   This is a yearly supplement edited by Brian Atkinson. It contains topical articles linking important news items with the theory in the textbook. It is copyright free to allow instructors to copy and circulate the articles to students for private study or seminar use. It is available to qualified adopters of the textbook by contacting Addison Wesley Longman.

Tools to Enhance Teaching

Lecturer's Handbook   This has been prepared by Brian Atkinson. The Lecturer's Handbook is designed to integrate the teaching and learning package. Each chapter includes an outline of the corresponding chapter in the textbook, teaching suggestions, a list of overheads, answers to all the review questions and problems in the textbook.

Artwork on Disks   Key figures from the text are rendered in full colour on the disks. The figures are enlarged and simplified to be more legible in large classrooms. The figures on the disk can be printed out and copied on to acetates. They can also be modified to suit the needs of your course. The disks are available to qualified adopters of the textbook (contact your Addison Wesley Longman sales representative).

Tools for the Electronic Classroom

Economics in Action Software   Instructors can use *Economics in Action* interactive software in the classroom. Its full-screen display makes it possible to use as 'electronic transparencies' to do live graph manipulation. Instructors can also have students use the real-world data in *Economics in Action* to complete various course projects. Additionally, *Economics in Action* is a helpful review tool for instructors to use with their students or assign to their students to help reinforce economic principles before tests or exams.

The Parkin Internet Exchange   A new element of the Parkin package is on-line support. Whether you are a teacher or a student, you can reach the Addison Wesley Longman Internet service and more at http://www.aw.com/he on the World Wide Web. The Parkin home page includes access to mailing lists, gopher and ftp sites; a demonstration of *Economics in Action* interactive software; and links to economic resources and other discussion groups on the Internet and Web. If you have questions, comments, or suggestions for improvement, you can submit them via e-mail to us at b&e.feedback@awl.co.uk. We would love to hear from you!

Acknowledgements

One of the problems with writing an introductory text, particularly in a new edition, is that there are so many people who provide help and encouragement, either directly or indirectly, that it becomes impossible to name them all. We would like to extend our gratitude and thanks to the many people who have made a contribution to this new edition, and to all those who made such important contributions to the previous editions on which this edition is based.

In particular, the authors would like to thank their colleagues, past and present, who have helped to shape their understanding of economics and provided information and assistance in the creation of this new edition. We would also like to thank our families for their input and patience.

Melanie Powell and Kent Matthews would like to thank colleagues at the Leeds University Business School and Leeds Metropolitan University, particularly Brendan Sheehan and Dorron Otter for comments on earlier editions, colleagues at the Cardiff Business School, John Riley, Bob Macnabb and Keith Whitfield, and colleagues at Lombard Street Research Ltd, Tim Congdon, Stewart Robinson, Gabriel Stein, Rob Miller and Brendan Baker, for invaluable information. We would also like to thank Paul De Grauwe of Katholieke Universiteit Leuven, Nick Crafts of the London School of Economics and Patrick Minford of Liverpool University for their patience and instruction. In addition, thanks are extended to cartoonist Brian Tyrer for stepping in at the last minute.

Michael Parkin has acknowledged many people in the Preface to the US edition of *Economics*, including friends and colleagues and the particular input of Robin Bade, to whom the US edition is dedicated, and Richard Parkin for graphics work. The authors of this edition would extend similar tributes to these individuals for their work.

We would like to acknowledge our debt to students past and present who have used previous editions and given us invaluable feedback in the form of comments, criticisms and praise. It would not be possible to write a textbook primarily in the interests of such students without their help and input.

Last, we would like to thank the editorial and production team at Addison Wesley Longman UK. This edition was created under an incredibly tight schedule, and as a result everyone has had to work at triple speed to meet the deadlines. The consistent good humour, vigilance and patience of the team was outstanding. Without underestimating the input of other members of the team, we extend special thanks to Paula Harris and Susan Harrison, whose patience was most tested because they had the most personal contact with the authors.

As always, the proof of the pudding is in the eating! The impact and value of this book will be decided by its users and we would like to encourage all instructors and students who use this new edition to feel free to send us comments and suggestions for future developments.

Michael Parkin
Department of Economics
University of Western Ontario
London, Ontario N6A 5C2, Canada

Melanie Powell
School of Business and Economic Studies
University of Leeds, LS2 9JT, United Kingdom

Kent Matthews
Cardiff Business School
University of Wales
Cardiff, CF1 3EU, United Kingdom

ECONOMICS

THIRD EDITION

MICHAEL PARKIN
UNIVERSITY OF WESTERN ONTARIO

MELANIE POWELL
UNIVERSITY OF LEEDS

KENT MATTHEWS
UNIVERSITY OF WALES, CARDIFF

To our families and students

Part 1
INTRODUCTION

TALKING WITH SHEILA DOW

S heila Dow holds a Personal Chair in Economics at the University of Stirling, where she has taught since 1979. She previously worked as an economist for the Bank of England and for the Government of Manitoba, Canada, and has had visiting posts with the Universities of Cambridge and Toronto. Her research interests lie in money and banking theory, methodology, history of thought, regional finance and post-Keynesian economics.

Why did you specialize in economics?

Mainly because I found economics interesting. It appealed to me to try to understand how economic systems work, at different times in history and in different types of economies. And it is interesting to try to understand why particular theories emerge and others disappear. It will reveal how long ago I started to learn economics when I say that I found it a nice contrast to my other subject, pure mathematics.

I then worked for several years as a non-academic economist in the public sector. It became obvious that there are many important policy areas to which economists can make important contributions, like the design of the international financial system, or innovations in taxation. Regardless of how economists approach issues, they can contribute important insights which make policy-making more effective. It is amazing how much mileage can be made with basic concepts.

One such concept is opportunity cost. This concept is most useful in the context of fixed resources – such as a budget constraint, as in expenditure by a government department – and given needs. Economists can contribute significantly to discussions about health care provision, for example, by highlighting the trade-offs involved in opting for provision of a treatment like dialysis rather than alternative treatments. This also serves to highlight where the concept of trade-off is not relevant, for example, where preventative medicine reduces overall demands on the given budget. Another important basic concept is that of the margin. The potential for confusion among non-economists over the distinction between marginal, as opposed to average, tax rates should be enough to illustrate the point.

What are the main differences among economists in their views about markets and how they work?

Most economists would describe the workings of a real market situation in fairly similar terms. But there are different views as to whether or not markets are seen as, generally, producing socially desirable outcomes, and therefore whether and in what way governments should intervene. But the most important differences are in how economists

construct theories for analysing markets.

What are the main principles which distinguish different perspectives on the role of markets and how they work?

In mainstream economics, markets are the centrepiece of economic analysis. They are the vehicle through which individual preferences are satisfied, given factor endowments and technology. In the process they allocate resources and determine the distribution of income.
The participants in markets are isolated, rational individuals. The benchmark of analysis is the position of equilibrium in which markets clear. The norm is to assume perfect competition, but there is an expanding area of work in which the implications of imperfect competition are explored.

Other (neo-Austrian) economists share the focus on market activity, but analyse markets as a process, where flux rather than equilibrium is the norm. Others, such as post-Keynesian and Institutionalist economists, prefer to put the emphasis more on production conditions than exchange, and to see markets in terms of social

interaction rather than isolated individuals, with imperfectly competitive markets the norm. One consequence is that supply

> *'Regardless of how economists approach issues, they can contribute important insights which make policy-making more effective.'*

and demand are seen as interdependent, with production conditions influencing marketing effort and thereby demand, for example. The emphasis then is put more on how supply and demand conditions evolve over time, as a process, rather than on equilibrium outcomes of market clearing.

Within each of these approaches there are different views as to how far markets are socially beneficial, and therefore whether government intervention is required. But as a generalization, it is probably more common for mainstream and neo-Austrian economists to support *laissez-faire* policies, and for post-Keynesian and Institutionalist economists to support intervention.

Are there any basic principles on which most economists agree?

This is a hard question. Whenever I think of a possible shared principle I immediately picture some particular economist raising objections. What precludes shared principles is the absence of a shared theoretical framework.

This is not something to regret; it is inevitable when abstracting from a complex reality that some will choose one form of abstraction and some another. I don't mean just that different economists make different assumptions, but that different groups of economists use terms and concepts quite differently, so that a principle expressed by one economist might convey something quite different to another economist. 'Equilibrium', for example, means something quite different in a model where

'I found economics interesting. It appealed to me to try to understand how economic systems work, at different times in history and in different types of economies.'

everything happens at once, compared with a model analysing a process which occurs over time, and which cannot be reversed.

Is there a role for radical Marxian economics in understanding modern economies?

This is where the strength of Marxian economics lies. Marx was prescient about how capitalist economies worked and would evolve. He had a good explanation of the process of the business cycle, and the importance of power exercised by particular groups; the struggle between labour and capital, and between business capitalists and finance capitalists, for example, or the effect on labour power of a secular

rise in unemployment. It was his predictions of the process that would bring an end to capitalism, and the attempts to implement central planning, which have caused most difficulty.

What is the link between microeconomics and macroeconomics? Do economists with different perspectives have different views of this link?

The link is an obvious one, that the macroeconomy is made up of individual markets, firms and households. There has been an increasing tendency to make sure that theory encapsulates that link by requiring that macroeconomics be built on explicit micro foundations. But economic systems are extraordinarily complex. There is therefore a trade-off between choosing to separate macroeconomics and microeconomics, and accepting the limitations of a theory which extends from assumptions about individuals to the economy as a whole. The main problem to grapple with is that, traditionally, microeconomics dealt with market clearing whereas macroeconomics dealt with markets (particularly the labour market) not clearing. The link is much easier for those whose microeconomics does not require market clearing.

Can economists explain the shift towards mixed market economies and away from centralized planning in Eastern Europe?

For those who see markets as producing better outcomes than government, the explanation lies in a realization among the populace that this is the case, and the democratic demand for a better economic system. For others, the explanation lies in the shortcomings of the particular planning mechanisms employed, and in the persuasive force of the idea that markets always produce socially beneficial outcomes.

Are there any lessons from the history and development of Western European economies from which Eastern Europe can learn?

The main lesson is that, whether or not market processes are preferable to state planning, institutions and conventions are the glue which holds market

'...it is probably more common for mainstream and neo-Austrian economists to support laissez-faire *policies, and for post-Keynesian and Institutionalist economists to support intervention.'*

economies together in an uncertain world. These are not easy to generate quickly. Nor are there universal truths about which institutions and which conventions will work; so much depends on the economy's prior history.

What do you think are the most important economic problems facing the world today?

The most important problems are undoubtedly distributional, from the problems of the impoverished, unemployed underclass in Western economies to the plight of persistent low-income countries.

'It is inevitable when abstracting from a complex reality that some will choose one form of abstraction and some another.'

CHAPTER

1

WHAT IS ECONOMICS?

After studying this chapter you will be able to:

- Identify the kinds of questions that economics seeks to answer
- Explain why all economic questions arise from scarcity
- Explain the consequences of scarcity
- Explain how economists think and describe what they do
- Describe the functions and the components of the economy

WHY SHOULD YOU STUDY ECONOMICS? BECAUSE IT WILL HELP YOU TO ANSWER SOME of the most important questions about the way we live and work and the way our lives are changing. Let's look at some examples. ◆ It's hard to believe that only 20 years ago almost no one watched a film at home. But now it is an everyday event enjoyed by millions. Why? Because advances in video and communications technologies have slashed the cost of watching films at home. The technologies that are transforming our homes are also revolutionizing our farms, mines, factories, offices and shops. As a result, millions of traditional jobs have gone and millions of new jobs have been created. These facts raise the first set of important questions that economics can answer:

How does technological change affect what we consume? How does technological change affect the jobs we do and the way we work?

Film stars, pop singers, outstanding sports men and women, lawyers, doctors and the directors of big companies can earn huge incomes, while petrol pump and supermarket cashiers, day-care workers and cleaners earn just a few pounds an hour. On average, men earn more than women and white workers earn more than workers from ethnic minorities. In many rich European countries, up to 20 per cent of people are living in poverty. These facts raise a second set of important questions that economics can answer:

Some Economic Questions

What determines incomes? What factors affect poverty? Why are women and ethnic minorities persistently paid less than men even when they do similar jobs?

Over the years, the scope of West European governments has expanded from the basic provision of law and order and defence. Governments provide not only roads and railways, but also social services such as pensions, income support, education and health care. The government sector in European countries is three times as large as it was at the beginning of this century. Many European countries are struggling to contain the growth in government expenditure through cuts in welfare and privatization, while the countries of the former Soviet Union and Eastern Europe are developing market systems to replace government central planning. Most European countries have many layers of government which create laws regulating the activities of individuals and firms. For example, the European Union and national and regional governments are trying to reduce the potentially disastrous effects of the environmental damage of the 'greenhouse effect' through policies which affect the production process. These facts raise a third set of questions that economics can answer:

Is the government sector too large? Can governments produce goods and services as efficiently as private firms? Can government policy protect our environment and improve our education and health?

During the Great Depression – the early 1930s – unemployment afflicted almost one-fifth of the work-force in the industrial world. The Great Depression was a period of extreme hardship. But high unemployment is not unusual. Unemployment has been between 17 and 20 per cent in Ireland and Spain in recent years. In the European Union, more than half of unemployed people have been without work for more than one year. When the overall UK unemployment rate was 8 per cent, the unemployment rate among young people (16–19 years old) was 20 per cent. These facts raise a fourth set of questions that economics can answer:

What causes unemployment? Why are some countries and groups more severely affected than others? Why are some people more likely to be unemployed for long periods?

In 1993, the cost of living in Brazil rose by 2,500 per cent. This meant that on the Copacabana beach, a pineapple costing 15 cruzeiros on January 1 cost 400 cruzeiros by the end of the year. In the same year, prices in Russia rose by almost 1,000 per cent. In contrast, prices in the United Kingdom increased by only 3 per cent. But in the late 1970s, prices in the United Kingdom were rising by more than 20 per cent a year. These facts raise a fifth set of questions that economics can answer:

Why do prices rise? Why do prices rocket in some countries but remain stable in others? Can governments control price rises?

In the 1950s, almost all the cars and vans in the United Kingdom were made in the United Kingdom. By 1993, more than 59 per cent of cars were imported. Cars are not exceptional. We now import most of our television sets, clothing and computers. Governments impose taxes (called tariffs) on imports and also restrict the quantities of some goods that may be imported. They also enter into agreements with other governments such as non-member states joining the trading

area of the European Union. These facts raise a sixth set of questions that economics can answer:

What determines the amount of trade between nations? How do taxes on imports affect trade? How do international trade agreements affect jobs and prosperity in Europe?

Since the late 1970s, China has been undergoing a dramatic economic transformation. Incomes in that country have grown at more than 10 per cent a year, doubling every seven years. In cities such as Shanghai, incomes have grown by more than 20 per cent in some years. China is not alone. Rapid income growth has occurred in Hong Kong, India, Indonesia, Malaysia, Singapore, South Korea, Taiwan and Thailand. Incomes continue to grow in the rich countries of the world, in Western Europe, North America, Japan, Australia and New Zealand, but the pace of expansion in these countries has slowed compared with the 1960s. In stark contrast to the growth miracles, Russian incomes shrank by an alarming 12 per cent in 1993. Incomes also shrank in the Czech Republic and Hungary. These facts raise a final set of questions that economics can answer:

Why do incomes grow quickly in some countries? Why do they grow slowly or even fall in other countries? Can government policy change the rate of growth of income?

◆ ◆ ◆ ◆ These seven questions give you an idea of what economics is about. But they don't tell you what economics is. How can you tell the difference between an economic question and a non-economic question? To answer this, you need to know how economists think about economic questions, how economists identify economic questions and how they think about economic issues.

How Economists Think

Economists, as individuals, are like everyone else. They have their own private objectives and agendas and have opinions about all sorts of economic and non-economic issues. You may have already thought that the seven economic questions are largely political. They are. They have an enormous influence on the quality of human life and they generate fierce argument and debate.

Economists, as professionals, try to approach their work with the detachment, rigour and objectivity of a scientist. The first step in this process is to identify the fundamental problem from which all economic questions stem. That fundamental problem – the **economic problem** – is the fact that we have limited resources but unlimited wants.

Scarcity

When wants exceed the resources available to satisfy them, there is **scarcity**. Scarcity is everywhere. People want good health and long life, material comfort, security, physical and mental recreation, and knowledge. None of these wants is completely satisfied for everyone; and everyone has some unsatisfied wants. While some people lack even the basic needs of food and shelter, many people have all the material comfort they want, but still don't feel entirely satisfied with their state of health or life expectancy. No one feels entirely secure, even in this post-Cold War era, and no one has enough time for sport, travel, vacations and other entertainment and leisure pursuits.

Scarcity is not *poverty*. The poor and the rich face scarcity. If a child wants a 40 pence can of soft drink and a 35 pence chocolate bar but has only 50 pence in his pocket, he experiences scarcity. If a wealthy student wants to go to a party on Saturday night but also wants to spend that same night catching up on late assignments, she experiences scarcity.

Choice and Opportunity Cost

Faced with scarcity, people must make choices. When we cannot have everything we want, we choose among the available alternatives. The concepts of scarcity and choice give a definition of economics. **Economics** is the study of how people make *choices* to cope with *scarcity*.

Choosing more of one thing means having less of something else. Expressed another way, in

'Well dear, if the extra cost of food is offset by the income tax relief and what we save in petrol by not having a car pays the extra on the house, what's become of the money we were going to save by not smoking?'

Drawing by Arthur Horner, 1952 *News Chronicle*.

making choices, we must face costs. Whatever we choose to do, we could have chosen to do something else instead. There is no such thing as a free lunch. This popular phrase is not just a clever throwaway line, as the couple in the cartoon are finding out. It expresses vividly the central idea of economics: that every choice involves a cost.

Economists use the term 'opportunity cost' to emphasize that making choices in the face of scarcity implies a cost. The **opportunity cost** of any action is the best alternative forgone. The best action that you choose not to do – the forgone alternative – is the cost of the action that you choose to do.

Opportunity cost is not all the possible alternatives forgone, but the best alternative forgone. An example will make this clear. Your economics lecture is at 8:30 on a Monday morning. You contemplate two alternatives to attending the lecture: staying in bed for an hour or going jogging for an hour. You can't stay in bed and go jogging for that same hour. The opportunity cost of attending the lecture is not the pleasure of an hour in bed and the benefit of jogging for an hour. If these are the only alternatives you contemplate, then you have to decide which one you would do if you did not go to the lecture. The opportunity cost of attending a lecture for a jogger is a forgone hour of exercise; the opportunity cost of attending a lecture for a late sleeper is a forgone hour in bed.

Money Cost Versus Real Cost   We often express cost in terms of money. But this is just a convenient unit and is not a precise measure of opportunity cost. For example, the £20 spent on a book is not available for spending on two £10 CDs or on one £20 concert ticket. To calculate the opportunity cost of the book, we need to know the best alternative forgone. If CDs are the best alternative, the opportunity cost of the book is two CDs. If concert tickets are the best alternative, the opportunity cost of the book is one concert ticket.

It is especially vital to look behind the money costs when the amount that money will buy has changed. For example, a book that costs £20 today might have cost £10 in 1985. You can't conclude from this fact that the opportunity cost of a book has increased since 1985. To calculate the change in the opportunity cost of a book, you need to know the money cost of the best alternative forgone in 1985 and today. If CDs are the best alternative, and if in 1985 a CD cost £20, the opportunity cost of a book has indeed increased from one CD in 1985 to two CDs today. Why? Because book prices have increased and CD prices have decreased. But if concert tickets are the best alternative to books, and if in 1985 a concert ticket cost £5, the opportunity cost of a book has fallen from four tickets in 1985 to one ticket today. Why? Because concert ticket prices have increased faster than book prices.

The key points are that it is fine to express opportunity cost in money units as long as you remember that this is just a convenient measure. You can't compare opportunity costs between different times when the value of money has changed.

The opportunity cost of a good or service also includes the value of the time spent obtaining it. If you take an hour off work to visit your hairdresser, the opportunity cost of that visit (expressed in units of money) is the amount that you paid the hairdresser plus the wages that you lost by not being at work. So in this case, we can convert time into a money cost by using a person's hourly wage rate. Again, it's important to keep reminding yourself that the opportunity cost is not the money itself but the value of the goods and services that you would have bought with the money.

Marginal Analysis

Marginal analysis is a fundamental idea that permeates economics. The core of the idea is that people act as if they make incremental choices – choices *at the margin*. They decide whether to do a little bit more or a little bit less of an activity. In doing so, they compare the cost of a little bit more of the activity against the benefit they will get from it. For example, to decide when to stop reading this book, you compare the cost of sticking with it for another five minutes with the benefit you expect (hope) it will bring. When you get to the point at which the cost of another five minutes, reading, exceeds the benefit of another five minutes, you stop.

The cost of a small increase in an activity is called **marginal cost**[1]. For example, suppose your CD collection consists of 105 CDs and you are thinking of buying the latest Oasis release. The marginal cost of increasing your collection is the cost of the *additional* Oasis CD you are thinking about buying.

The benefit that arises from a small increase in an activity is called **marginal benefit**. For example, marginal benefit is the benefit you will get from listening to your new Oasis CD, not the benefit you'll get from all your 106 CDs after you have bought it. The reason is that you already have the benefit from your existing collection of 105 CDs, so you can't count the benefit of these as part of the benefit of the decision you are now making.

To make your decision about the Oasis CD, you compare the marginal cost of the CD with its marginal benefit. If the marginal benefit exceeds the marginal cost, you buy the new CD. If the marginal cost exceeds the marginal benefit, you don't expand your collection.

By evaluating marginal costs and marginal benefits, people are able to use their scarce resources in the way that makes them as well off as possible. This is sometimes called *optimizing* behaviour.

Substitution and Incentives

When opportunity costs change, people change their actions. Another central principle of economics, called the **principle of substitution,** is that when the opportunity cost of an activity increases, people substitute other activities in its place. Every activity has a *substitute*. Skiing is a substitute for skating; wind-surfing is a substitute for skin diving; drinking Coke is a substitute for drinking Pepsi; staying in to study economics is a substitute for going out with friends. A substitute might be

---

[1] The term 'marginal cost' has a more specific meaning which is developed in Chapter 10.

similar to the original like Pepsi and Coke, or quite different like staying in to study or going out with friends.

If the opportunity cost of Coke increases, some people will substitute Pepsi for Coke; if the opportunity cost of studying economics increases (when the exams are looming), some people will substitute going out for staying in to study. The closer the substitutes, the greater is the degree of switching that takes place when the opportunity cost changes.

Why do people substitute away from more costly activities towards less costly ones? Because they are responding to incentives. An **incentive** is an inducement to take a particular action. The inducement may be a reward (a carrot) or a penalty (a stick). Changes in marginal costs and marginal benefits – opportunity costs – are the incentives which people respond to, leading to changes in actions.

Whenever some unusual event disrupts the normal state of affairs, the economist always asks: how will opportunity costs change and what substitutions will arise from the changed incentives? For example, a frost kills Spain's Seville orange crop and sends the price of marmalade oranges through the roof. This increase in price, with all other prices remaining unchanged, increases the opportunity cost of marmalade and gives people an incentive to eat less marmalade and substitute other jams in its place. Or suppose a bumper broccoli crop sends the price of broccoli tumbling. This decrease in price, with all other prices remaining unchanged, decreases the opportunity cost of broccoli and gives people an incentive to eat more broccoli as a substitute for cauliflower and other vegetables.

Competition and Second Round Effects

Scarcity in a market environment leads to a contest for command over scarce resources, which economists call **competition.** Each individual tries to obtain as many goods and services as possible by competing with other individuals. This competition takes many forms. For example, producers compete with each other for market share and seek the highest profit available. People compete with each other for jobs and seek the highest wages available (for a given amount of work effort). Shoppers compete with each other for bargains and seek the lowest prices available.

Because of competition, the ultimate effects of an economic disturbance (the second round effects) are different from the initial effects (the first round effects). The second round effects are usually the dominant ones. For example, the first round effect of a Spanish frost is an increase in the price of Seville oranges and a substitution of other fruit (say, apricots) for jam making. The second round effects are the consequences of the increased competition for scarce Seville oranges. Marmalade makers compete with apricot eaters and other manufacturers using apricots for the available apricots and the price of apricots increases. People now search for yet other substitutes, grapefruits perhaps. As these second round effects play out, a long chain of substitutions and price changes take place, all triggered by a simple frost in Spain.

Economists try to predict second round effects by considering all the main substitutions that are likely as people compete with each other for the available resources. Trying to predict the number of vacant parking spaces in a crowded city centre is a good example of the importance of the effects of competition and of the distinction between first round and second round effects. The first round effect of a shopper going home is a vacant parking space. But the first round effect is short-lived. Competition for parking spaces results in vacant spaces being filled almost immediately. So, taking account of competition and second round effects, you predict that there are rarely any vacant spaces!

REVIEW

The economic way of thinking is based on five core ideas:

◆ All economic problems arise from scarcity and scarcity forces people to make choices and evaluate opportunity cost.

◆ Opportunity cost is the best alternative forgone, not the money cost, and includes time cost.

◆ Decisions are made by comparing marginal benefit and marginal cost.

◆ When the opportunity cost of an activity increases, the incentive to substitute an alternative activity increases.

◆ Competition creates ripples along the chain of substitution – second round effects – that dominate the first round effects.

You've now seen something of the way economists think and you have learned the five core ideas that guide this thinking. Next let's look at what economists do.

What Economists Do

Economists work on a wide array of problems, some important examples of which are covered by the questions at the start of this chapter. Economic questions can be divided into two big groups: microeconomics and macroeconomics.

Microeconomics and Macroeconomics

Microeconomics is the study of the decisions of people and businesses and the interaction of these decisions in markets. The goal of microeconomics is to explain the prices and quantities of individual goods and services. Microeconomics also studies the effects of government regulation and taxes on the prices and quantities of individual goods and services. For example, microeconomics studies the forces that determine the prices of cars and the quantities of cars produced and sold. It also studies the effects of regulations and taxes on the prices and quantities of cars.

Macroeconomics is the study of the national economy and the global economy and the way that economic aggregates fluctuate. The goal of macroeconomics is to explain *average* prices and the *total* employment, income and production. Macroeconomics also studies the effects of government actions – taxes, spending and the deficit – on total jobs and incomes. For example, macroeconomics studies the forces that determine the average cost of living in European countries, the total value of each country's production and the effects of government budget policy on these variables.

Although microeconomics and macroeconomics have their own separate focus, they use a common set of tools and ideas. Some problems have both a microeconomic and a macroeconomic dimension. An example is the invention of video games and the growth of the market in multimedia products. Microeconomics seeks to explain the prices and quantities of games, while macroeconomics

explains the effects on the total amount of spending and jobs in the economy as a whole.

Economists not only work on a wide range of questions; they also approach their work in a variety of ways. The different approaches can be described as:

◆ Economic analysis
◆ Economic policy

Economic analysis is the attempt to understand the economic world, and economic policy is the attempt to improve it. Another way of putting the distinctions is this: analysis makes *predictions* while policy offers *prescriptions*. Policy and analysis overlap in many ways, and policy cannot get far without analysis. It is not possible to make something work better without first understanding it. Let's take a closer look at these two approaches that economists take to their work.

Economic Analysis

Economics is a social science (along with political science, psychology and sociology) and a major task of economists is to discover how the economic world works. In the pursuit of this goal, economists (like all other scientists) distinguish between two types of statements:

◆ What *is*
◆ What *ought* to be

Statements about what *is* are called *positive* statements. They say what is currently believed about the way the world operates. Positive statements might be right or wrong. They can be tested by checking them against the facts. Statements about what *ought* to be are called *normative* statements. These statements depend on values and cannot be tested.

To see the distinction between positive and normative statements, consider the controversy over global warming. Some scientists believe that centuries of the burning of coal and oil are increasing the carbon dioxide content of the earth's atmosphere and leading to higher temperatures that eventually will have devastating consequences for life on this planet. 'Our planet is warming because of an increased carbon dioxide build-up in the atmosphere' is a positive statement. It can (in principle and with sufficient data) be tested. 'We ought to cut back on our use of carbon-based fuels such as coal and oil' is a normative statement. You may agree with or disagree with this statement, but you can't test it. It is based on values. Health care provides an economic example of the distinction. 'A national health service will cut the amount of work-time lost to illness' is a positive statement. 'Every citizen should have equal access to health care' is a normative statement.

It is the task of economic analysis to discover and catalogue positive statements that are consistent with what we observe in the world and that enable us to understand how the economic world works. This task is a large one and it can be broken into three steps:

◆ Observing and measuring

◆ Building models

◆ Testing theories

Observing and Measuring   By observing and measuring economic activity, economists generate large amounts of data that describe the economic reality they seek to understand. For example, they keep track of the amounts and locations of natural and human resources, wages and work hours, prices and quantities of different goods and services produced, interest rates and amounts borrowed and lent, taxes and government spending, and quantities of goods bought from and sold to other countries. Although this list is just a tiny fraction of the range of data that economists collect, it gives you the flavour of the types of data they use.

Building Models   Simple description does not tell us what has caused a change in our economy. The second step towards understanding the economic world, therefore, is to build an economic model. An **economic model** is a simplified version of some aspect of the economic world that includes only those features of the world that are needed to explain the issue at hand. All models show less detail than their counterparts in reality but are capable of generating predictions. An economic model of the market for cars will predict the likely change in the number of cars purchased if the price of cars increases by 1 per cent. What a model includes and what it leaves out result from *assumptions* about what is essential and what is inessential detail.

You can see how ignoring detail in a model is useful, even essential, to our understanding by

thinking about a model that you use every time you need a book from your library. The model in this case is the library catalogue and floor plan, which guide you to the locations of the books. The catalogue doesn't tell you whether the book you want is red or blue, and the floor plan doesn't tell you where the telephone cables run or where the electricity power points are. These details are omitted because they don't affect your search for a book.

Economic models come in many different forms. They may be a simple verbal description of an idea, they may be diagrammatic, graphical or mathematical. The ones that you will meet in this book will be in the form of ideas, diagrams and graphs. Modern economists use complex mathematical models of the economy to help predict the outcome of changes in government policy and to forecast future trends in important economic variables such as unemployment and growth.

Testing Theories   An **economic theory** is a reliable generalization that helps us to understand and predict economic choices. Economists develop economic theories by building and testing economic models. An economic model might work well or it might not work well at all. To find out, we test a theory developed from the model by seeing if the predictions of the model correspond to the facts. An economic theory is the bridge between a model and reality.

A theory is created by a process of building and testing models. For example, you may have used your library floor plan and catalogue (a model) successfully many times . You then develop the theory that if you follow the library model you will find the book you want. When you follow the floor plan and catalogue, you are testing your theory. Suppose the floor plan doesn't show that the books can only be reached by taking the north stairs because the south stairs lead to a closed fire door. You have always taken the north stairs by habit. You ask a friend to use the library model to get you a book to test your theory. Your friend takes the south stairs and finds the dead end. This particular theory must now be rejected. But you can develop a new theory, based on a new floor plan model that includes the essential assumption about a fire door between the south stairs and the bookshelves.

The process of developing theories by building and testing models is illustrated in Fig. 1.1. We begin by building a model. The model's implications are used to generate predictions about the world. Generating and testing these predictions form the basis of a theory. When predictions are in conflict with the facts, either a theory is discarded in favour of a superior alternative or we return to the model-building stage, modify our assumptions and create a new model.

While Fig. 1.1 shows the logical structure of the search for new knowledge, it does not describe the actual processes followed. In practice, scientific discovery is a human activity marked by stabs in the dark, blind alleys, flashes of insight and, occasionally, revolutionary new views. Also, some models and theories are discarded even when they fit the facts, and others are clung to even when they fail. Albert Einstein, the great physicist, put it well when he said:

'Creating a new theory is not like destroying an old barn and erecting a skyscraper in its place. It is rather like climbing a mountain, gaining new and wider views, discovering new connections between our starting point and its rich environment. But the point from which we started still exists and can be seen, although it appears smaller and forms a tiny part of our broad view gained by the mastery of the obstacles on our adventurous way up.'[2]

Economics is a young science and a long way from having achieved its goal of explaining and understanding economic activity. Its birth can be dated fairly precisely in 1776 with the publication of Adam Smith's *The Wealth of Nations* (see *Economics in History,* pp. 66–67). In the closing years of the twentieth century, economics has managed to discover a sizeable number of useful generalizations. In many areas, however, we are still going around the circle changing assumptions, performing new logical deductions, generating new predictions and getting wrong answers yet again.

The gradual accumulation of correct answers gives most practitioners some faith that their methods will, eventually, provide usable answers to the big economic questions.

[2] These words are attributed to Einstein in a letter by Oliver Sacks to *The Listener,* (November 30, 1972), 88, No. 2279, 756.

FIGURE 1.1

How Economic Theories are Developed

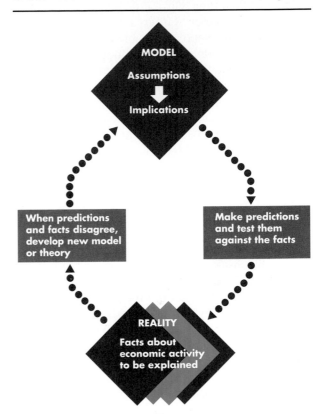

Economists develop economic theories by building and testing economic models. An economic model is based on *assumptions* about what is essential and what can be ignored and the *implications* of these assumptions. The implications of a model form the basis of *predictions* about the world. Economists test those predictions by checking them against the facts. If the predictions are in conflict with the facts, the model-building process begins again with new assumptions. Only when the predictions agree with the facts has a useful theory been developed

---

But progress in economics comes slowly and economists must be careful how they proceed. Let's look at some of the obstacles to progress in economics.

Unscrambling Cause and Effect   It is difficult in economics to isolate forces and identify what is a cause and what is the effect. The logical tool that is used by all scientists for identifying cause and effect is *ceteris paribus*. **Ceteris paribus** is a Latin term that means 'other things being equal' or 'if all other relevant things remain the same'. All successful attempts to understand the world use this device. By changing one factor at a time and holding all the other relevant factors constant, we can isolate the factor of interest to help investigate its effects in the clearest possible way.

Economic models (like the models in other sciences) enable the influence of one factor at a time to be isolated in the imaginary world of the model. Indeed, one of the strengths of model building is that it enables us to imagine what would happen if only one factor changed. But *ceteris paribus* can be a problem in economics when we try to test a model.

In the laboratory sciences, such as chemistry and physics, experiments are performed that actually hold all the relevant factors constant except for the one under investigation. In the non-experimental sciences such as economics (and astronomy), we usually observe the outcomes of the *simultaneous* operation of several, perhaps many, factors. As a result, it is hard to sort out the effects of each individual factor and to compare the effects with what a model predicts. To cope with this problem, economists take three complementary approaches.

First, they look for pairs of events in which other things were equal (or similar). An example might be to study the effects of training on the unemployment rate by comparing two European countries on the presumption that the people in the two countries are sufficiently similar. Second, economists have developed a statistical tool, called *econometrics,* which unscrambles the separate factors that simultaneously influence economic behaviour. Third, economists are beginning to design experiments which are undertaken in economic laboratories. This relatively new and exciting approach puts real subjects (often students) in a decision-making situation and varies their incentives in some way to discover how they respond to one factor at a time.

Economists work hard to avoid errors of reasoning that lead to a wrong conclusion. There are two common errors of reasoning – or fallacies – and you need to be on your guard to avoid them. They are the

◆ Fallacy of composition
◆ *Post hoc* fallacy

Fallacy of Composition The fallacy of composition is the (false) statement that what is true of the parts is true of the whole, or what is true of the whole is true of the parts. For one fishing boat (a part), using bigger nets enables more fish to be caught. But if all the fishing boats (the whole) use bigger nets, eventually over-fishing will result and everyone will catch fewer fish.

The fallacy of composition arises mainly in macroeconomics and it stems from the fact that the parts interact with each other to produce an outcome for the whole that might differ from the intended outcome of the parts. A firm lays off some workers to cut costs and improve its profits. If all firms take similar actions, incomes fall and so does spending. The firm sells less and its profits don't improve.

Post hoc Fallacy The Latin phrase *post hoc ergo propter hoc*, means 'after this, therefore because of this'. The *post hoc* fallacy is the error of reasoning about cause and effect that results from the timing of events. You see a flash of lightning and some seconds later hear a clap of thunder. But the lightning did not cause the thunder. The flash and the clap were simultaneously caused by a third factor, an electrical disturbance in the atmosphere.

Unravelling cause and effect is extremely difficult in economics. Just looking at the timing of events often doesn't help. For example, the stock market booms and some months later the economy expands, and jobs and incomes grow. Did the stock market boom cause the economy to expand? Possibly, but perhaps businesses started to plan the expansion of production because of new technology that lowered costs. As knowledge of these plans spread, the stock market reacted to anticipate the economic expansion. To disentangle cause and effect, economists use economic models and data and, to the extent that they can, perform experiments.

We've looked at the way in which economists try to understand the world – economic analysis. Let's now see how they try to contribute to improving economic performance and study economic policy.

Economic Policy

Economic policy is the attempt to devise government actions and to design institutions that might improve economic performance. Economists play two distinct roles in the formulation of economic policy.

First, they try to predict the consequence of alternative policies. For example, health economists try to predict the cost and benefits and effectiveness of alternative treatments, and alternative ways of financing and organizing health care. Economists who work on environmental issues attempt to predict changes in the cost and quality of urban air resulting from changes in vehicle emission standards. Macroeconomists, on the other hand, try to predict the effects of interest rate changes on the stock market and employment.

Second, economists evaluate alternative policies on the scale of better to worse. To do this, they must state the policy *objectives*. Provided there is clarity and openness about the policy objectives, this type of policy evaluation can be as objective and scientific as the development of economic theories. Over the years, by responding to the societies of which they are a part and interpreting sentiments expressed in the political arena, economists have developed criteria for judging policy outcomes on the better to worse scale. Four objectives of policy have emerged:

◆ Efficiency
◆ Equity
◆ Growth
◆ Stability

Efficiency When **economic efficiency** has been achieved, production costs are as low as possible and consumers want the combination of goods and services that is being produced. Three distinct conditions produce economic efficiency. They are efficient production, efficient consumption and efficient exchange.

Efficient production is achieved when each firm produces its output at the least possible cost. Cost includes costs borne by the firm and costs borne by others. Efficient consumption is achieved when everyone buys the goods and services that make them as well off as possible, by their own evaluations. Efficient exchange is achieved when everyone specializes to earn a living by doing the job that gives them the maximum possible economic benefit. Economic efficiency is desirable because when it is achieved, it is not possible to make one person better off without at the same time making someone else worse off.

Equity **Equity** is economic justice or fairness. An efficient economy is not necessarily an equitable or just one. Economic efficiency could bring very large incomes to a few people and very low incomes to the vast majority. Such a situation would be regarded as inequitable by the majority but possibly not by everyone. While economists agree that policies which improve equity are desirable, there is little consensus on the definition of equity or economic justice. There is some consensus on what constitutes extreme inequity – but equity remains a matter on which reasonable people disagree.

Growth **Economic growth** is the increase in incomes and production per person. It results from the ongoing advance of technology, the accumulation of ever larger quantities of productive equipment and ever rising standards of education. Poor societies are transformed into rich ones by economic growth. But economic growth has a cost. It uses up exhaustible natural resources, and sometimes destroys natural vegetation and damages the environment. But these are not inevitable drawbacks of economic growth and the richest countries are the ones that devote the greatest efforts to enriching and protecting the environment.

Economic growth can be encouraged or discouraged by the policies that governments adopt. For example, tax incentives for research and development might stimulate growth while tax penalties that encourage resource conservation might retard it. In reaching policy conclusions, economists must take a view about the desirable growth rate and the effects of the policies being considered on growth.

Stability **Economic stability** is the absence of wide fluctuations in the economic growth rate, the level of employment and average prices. Economic stability is desirable because it provides the best environment in which individuals and firms can make efficient decisions. Almost the whole of macroeconomics has developed to understand the problems of instability, and many macroeconomists specialize in designing policies to tame an unstable economy.

Agreement and Disagreement

Economists have a reputation for being a divided lot. Perhaps you've heard the joke: 'If you laid all the economists in the world end to end, they still wouldn't reach agreement.' There is a hint of truth in the joke, but only a hint. The fact is that there is a remarkable consensus among economists on a wide range of issues. Here is a sample of the degree of consensus on a range of issues.[3]

More than 70 per cent of economists agree that:

◆ Rent ceilings cut the availability of housing.

◆ Import restrictions have larger costs than benefits.

◆ Wage and price controls do not help to slow inflation.

◆ Wage contracts are not a primary cause of unemployment.

More than 60 per cent of economists agree that:

◆ Monopoly power of big oil companies was not the cause of a rise in the price of petrol during the Kuwait crisis.

◆ Curtailing the power of environmental agencies would not make the economy more efficient.

◆ If the budget is to be balanced, it should be balanced over a business cycle, not every year.

But on many issues, economists are divided. Among them are whether:

◆ Anti-monopoly laws should be enforced more vigorously to curtail monopoly power.

◆ Effluent taxes are better than pollution limits.

◆ The government should try to make the distribution of income more equal.

◆ Russia would be better off with rapid, 'cold-turkey' reform than gradual reform.

Some disagreements are about what is possible – *positive* matters – and some are about what is desirable – *normative* matters. Disagreements on positive issues arise when the available evidence is insufficient for a clear conclusion to be reached. Disagreements on normative issues arise from differences in values or priorities. It is hardly surprising that economists have such disagreements since they are just a reflection of similar disagreements in the larger society of which they are members.

You now know the types of questions that economists try to answer and that all economic questions and economic activity arise from scarcity. You know something about the way economists think and about the work they do. In the chapters that follow, you are going to study economic activity and discover how the European economies and the global economy work. But before we do this, let's stand back and take an overview of our economy.

The Economy: An Overview

The **economy** is a mechanism that allocates scarce resources among alternative uses. This mechanism achieves five things:

◆ What

◆ How

◆ When

◆ Where

◆ Who

1. *What* goods and services will be produced and in *what* quantities? Will more cable companies offer pay-per-view service or will more multiplex cinemas be built? Will young professionals take more exotic holidays or live in larger houses? Will more high-performance sports cars or more trucks and vans be made?

2. *How* will various goods and services be produced? Will small supermarkets operate with three check-outs and cashiers using laser scanners, or with six check-outs and cashiers keying in prices by hand? Will car factory workers weld by hand or will robots do the job? Will credit card companies use computers or clerks to read payment slips?

3. *When* will the various goods and services be produced? Will a supermarket operate 24 hours a day for 7 days a week, or just 10 hours a day for 6 days a week? Will a car factory close for the summer and lay off workers? Will there be a surge of house building in the spring, bringing higher wages and longer hours for construction workers?

4. *Where* will the various goods and services be produced? Will Barclaycard process its charge slips and accounts in the United Kingdom, or will it hire less costly labour in India and transfer its records by satellite? Will Belgium's airline

---

[3] The views of economists are taken from Richard M. Alston, J.R. Kearl and Michael B. Vaughan 'Is There a Consensus Among Economists', *American Economic Review*, (May 1992), 82, 203–209.

keep its headquarters in Belgium or move to Luxembourg where employment costs are lower? Will lower UK wage costs attract more companies or will they move to other European countries to gain higher productivity?

5. *Who* will consume the various goods and services? The distribution of economic benefits depends on the distribution of income. People with high incomes are able to consume more goods and services than people with low incomes. Who gets to consume what depends on income. Will the ski instructor consume more than the lawyer's secretary? Will the people of Europe consume more than the people of Ethiopia?

To understand how an economy works, we must identify its components and see how they interact with each other. Figure 1.2 shows a picture of an economy. This picture is of a *closed economy* – an economy that has no links to other economies. We can gain a lot of insight by studying a closed economy model. In reality, the only closed economy is the economy of the entire world – the global economy. During the 1980s, the global economy became a highly integrated mechanism for allocating scarce resources and deciding what, how, when, where and for whom the various goods and services will be produced and consumed.

These decisions by households, firms and governments are coordinated in markets – the goods markets and factor markets – which are regulated by rules that governments establish and enforce. In these markets, prices constantly adjust to keep buying and selling plans consistent.

The economy shown in Fig. 1.2 contains two types of components:

◆ Decision makers
◆ Markets

Decision Makers and Choices

Decision makers are the economic actors. They make the choices. Figure 1.2 identifies three types of decision makers:

1. Households
2. Firms
3. Governments

A *household* is any group of people living together as a decision-making unit. Every individual in the economy belongs to a household. Some households consist of a single person, while others consist either of families or of groups of unrelated individuals, such as two or three students sharing an apartment. Each household has unlimited wants and limited resources.

A *firm* is an organization that uses resources to produce goods and services. All producers are called firms, no matter how big they are or what they produce. Car makers, farmers, banks and insurance companies are all firms.

A *government* is a many-layered organization that sets laws and rules, operates a law-enforcement mechanism (courts and police forces), taxes households and firms, and provides public services such as national defence, public health, transportation and education. Governments try to influence the choices that households and firms make by changing laws and rules, taxes and spending.

Markets

In ordinary speech, the word market means a place where people buy and sell goods such as fish, meat, fruits and vegetables. In economics, market has a more general meaning. A **market** is any set-up that enables buyers and sellers to get information and to do business with each other. An example is the market in which oil is bought and sold: the world oil market. The world oil market is not a place. It is the network of oil producers, oil users, wholesalers and brokers who buy and sell. In the world oil market, decision makers do not meet physically. They make deals throughout the world by telephone, fax and direct computer link.

Figure 1.2 identifies two types of markets: goods markets and factor markets. *Goods markets* are those in which goods and services are bought and sold. *Factor markets* are those in which factors of production are bought and sold.

Factors of production are the economy's productive resources. They are classified under four headings:

1. Labour
2. Land
3. Capital
4. Entrepreneurial ability

Labour is the time and effort that people devote to producing goods and services. It is rewarded with wages. **Land** is all the natural

FIGURE 1.2

A Picture of an Economy

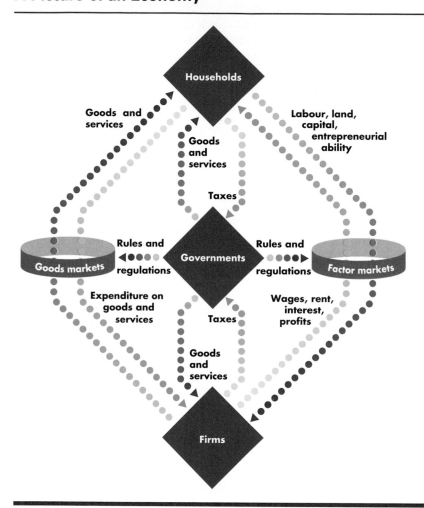

Households, firms and governments make economic decisions. Households decide how much of their labour, land, capital and entrepreneurial ability to sell or rent (the red flows) in exchange for wages, rent, interest and profits (the green flows). They also decide how much of their income to spend on the various types of goods and services available. Firms decide how much labour, land and capital to hire and how much of the various types of goods and services to produce. Governments decide which goods and services they will provide and the taxes that households and firms will pay.

resources used to produce goods and services. The return to land is rent. **Capital** is all the equipment, buildings, tools and other manufactured goods used to produce other goods and services. The return to capital is interest. **Entrepreneurial ability** is a special type of human resource that organizes the other three factors of production, makes business decisions, innovates and bears business risk. Entrepreneurship is rewarded with profit.

Households and firms make decisions that result in the transactions in the goods markets and factor markets shown in Fig. 1.2. Households decide how much of their labour, land and capital

to sell or rent on factor markets. They receive incomes in the form of wages, rent, interest and profit. Households also decide how to spend their incomes on goods and services produced by firms.

Firms decide the quantities of factors of production to hire, how to use them to produce goods and services, what goods and services to produce, and in what quantities. They sell their output in goods markets.

The flows resulting from these decisions by households and firms are shown in Fig. 1.2. The red flows are the factors of production that go from households to firms and the goods and services that go from firms to households. The green flows in the opposite direction are the payments made in exchange for these items.

A public choice process determines the rules and regulations imposed by governments, the taxes governments raise and the services they provide. These are also shown in Fig. 1.2. Of course, governments can also trade directly in both goods and services markets and factor markets, but this is not shown in Fig. 1.2.

Coordinating Decisions

Perhaps the most striking thing about the choices made by households, firms and governments is that they surely must come into conflict with each other. For example, households choose how much work to do and what type of work to specialize in, but firms choose the type and quantity of labour to employ in the production of various goods and services. In other words, households choose the types and quantities of labour to sell, and firms choose the types and quantities of labour to buy. Similarly, in markets for goods and services, households choose the types and quantities of goods and services to buy, while firms choose the types and quantities to sell.

How is it possible for the millions of individual decisions made by households, firms and governments to be consistent with each other? What makes households want to sell the same types and quantities of labour that firms want to buy? What happens if the number of households wanting to work as airline pilots exceeds the number that airlines want to hire? How do firms know what to produce so that households will buy their output? What happens if firms want to sell more hamburgers than households want to buy?

Markets Coordinate Decisions Markets coordinate individual decisions through price adjustments. To see how, think about the market for hamburgers at a major football match. Suppose that at the current price, the quantity of hamburgers being offered for sale is less than the quantity that people would like to buy. Some people who want to buy hamburgers are not able to do so. To make the choices of buyers and sellers compatible, buyers must scale down their appetites and/or more hamburgers must be offered for sale. An increase in the price of hamburgers produces this outcome. Because there is a shortage of hamburgers,

their price rises. The higher price encourages producers to offer more hamburgers for sale, perhaps by telephoning relatives to come and bring more supplies. It also curbs the appetite for hamburgers and changes some lunch plans. Fewer people buy hamburgers and more buy, say, sandwiches.

Now imagine the opposite situation. At the current price, more hamburgers are available than people want to buy. In this case, to make the choices of buyers and sellers compatible, more hamburgers must be bought and fewer must be offered for sale. A fall in the price of hamburgers achieves this outcome. Because there is a surplus of hamburgers, the price falls. The lower price discourages the production of hamburgers and encourages consumption. Decisions to produce and sell and to buy and consume are continuously adjusted and kept in balance with each other by price adjustments.

Sometimes prices get stuck or fixed. For example, the government might impose a rent ceiling or a minimum wage that prevents the price changes that would make the plans of buyers and sellers consistent. Other mechanisms then begin to operate. One possibility is that customers queue and get served on a first-come-first-served basis. Another is that stock – or stores of goods – operate as a temporary safety valve. If the price is fixed too low, firms sell more than they would like and their stocks shrink. If the price is fixed too high, firms sell less than they would like and their stocks pile up. Queues and stock changes are only a temporary solution to inconsistent buying and selling plans. Eventually, a price adjustment is needed.

We've seen how decisions coordinated in markets determine *what* gets produced – in the example, how many hamburgers are produced. Decisions coordinated in markets also determine *how* goods and services are produced. For example, hamburger producers can use gas, electric power or charcoal to cook their hamburgers. Which fuel is used depends in part on the flavour that the producer wants to achieve. It also depends on the cost and availability of the different fuels. If a fuel becomes expensive, as did oil in the 1970s, less of it is used and more of other fuels are used. By substituting one fuel for another as the costs of the different fuels change, the market solves the question of how to produce.

Drawings by Chris Riddell, 1993, *The Independent*.

Market-coordinated decisions also determine *when* goods and services are produced. If consumer spending on fast food falls temporarily and prices drop below the level that covers the wage bill and other expenses, hamburger and sandwich producers close down and lay off their workers. If consumer spending rises and fast food prices rise, firms respond by producing more hamburgers and sandwiches. Market-coordinated decisions also determine *where* goods and services are produced. If the cost of making toys rises in the United Kingdom and falls in Taiwan, toy firms switch their production to the low-cost source.

Finally, market-coordinated decisions determine *who* gets the goods and services produced. People with skills, talents and resources that are rare but highly valued command a high price, and their owners receive a large share of the economy's output. Those with skills, talents and resources that are common and less highly valued command a low price, and their owners receive a small share of output.

Alternative Coordinating Mechanisms The market is one of two alternative coordinating mechanisms. The other is a command mechanism. A *command mechanism* is a method of determining what, how, when, where and for whom goods and services are produced, using a hierarchical organization structure in which people carry out the instructions given to them. The best example of a hierarchical organization structure is the military. Commanders make decisions requiring actions that are passed down a chain of command. Soldiers and marines on the front line take the actions they are ordered to take.

An economy that relies on a command mechanism is called a *command economy*. Examples of command economies in today's world are becoming rare and only North Korea falls squarely into this category. Before they embarked on programmes of reform in the late 1980s, the Soviet Union and other countries of Eastern Europe also had command economies. You can see from the cartoon comparing towns in Russia and the United Kingdom that the allocation mechanisms in old command-based economies are quite different from coordinated market economies.

An economy that uses a market coordinating mechanism is called a *market economy*. But most real world economies use both markets and commands to coordinate economic activity. An economy that relies on both markets and command mechanisms is called a *mixed economy*.

The European mixed economies rely largely on the market as a mechanism for coordinating the decisions of individual households and firms, but they also use command mechanisms. The economy of an armed force is a command economy. Command mechanisms are also employed in other government organizations and within large firms.

FIGURE 1.3

The Global Economy

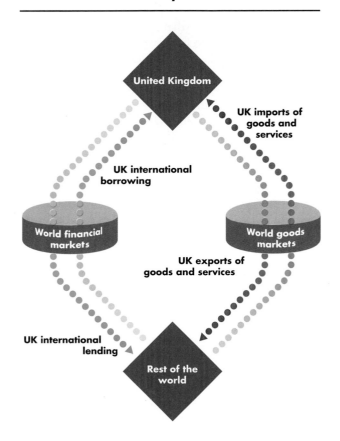

The UK economy buys and sells goods and services in world goods markets. What it buys are UK imports, and what it sells are UK exports. The UK economy also borrows from and lends to the rest of the world. UK firms set up business in other countries and foreign firms set up business in the United Kingdom. These transactions take place through the world's financial markets.

There is a command element in our legal system. By enacting laws and establishing regulations and agencies to monitor the market economy, governments influence the economic decisions of households and firms and change our economic course.

International Linkages

We've just looked at a closed economy – one that has no links with any other economy – and noted that the only closed economy is the entire world.

A national economy like the UK economy is an *open economy*. It has economic links with other economies. The economic links between the UK economy and the rest of the world are illustrated in Fig. 1.3. Firms in the open UK economy sell some of their production to the rest of the world. These sales are UK exports of goods and services. Also, firms, households and governments in the United Kingdom buy goods and services from firms in other countries. These purchases are UK imports of goods and services. These export and import transactions take place on world goods markets and are illustrated in the figure.

The total values of exports and imports are not necessarily equal to each other. When exports exceed imports, there is a surplus. When imports exceed exports, there is a deficit. A country with a surplus lends to the rest of the world and a country with a deficit borrows from the rest of the world. These international lending and borrowing transactions take place on the world financial markets and are illustrated in Fig. 1.3.

The United Kingdom has maintained a large deficit in recent years. As a consequence, it has borrowed from the rest of the world. Other countries like Germany and Japan have had surpluses. These countries have used their surpluses to lend to the rest of the world.

R E V I E W

◆ An economy is a mechanism that determines what is produced, how, when and where it is produced, and for whom it is produced.

◆ Choices made by households, firms and governments are coordinated through markets for goods and services and factors of production.

◆ Choices are sometimes coordinated by command mechanisms.

◆ ◆ ◆ ◆ In the next chapter, we will study some of the tools that economists use to describe economic performance and to build economic models. Then, in Chapter 3, we will build an economic model and use that model to sharpen our understanding of opportunity cost and to study the way in which people make choices about what to produce.

S U M M A R Y

How Economists Think

Economists see all economic questions as arising from scarcity – from the fact that wants exceed resources. Economists study the ways people cope with scarcity. Scarcity forces people to make choices and face opportunity costs. The opportunity cost of any action is the best alternative action that could have been undertaken in its place.

Two fundamental ideas permeate economics: *the margin* and *substitution*. People make decisions at the margin. They evaluate actions in incremental steps. All actions have substitutes. The higher the opportunity cost of an action, the greater is the incentive for people to seek a substitute – an alternative – action. Scarcity forces people to compete with each other for scarce resources. (pp. 8–11)

What Economists Do

Economists work on microeconomics – the study of the decisions of individual households and firms – and macroeconomics – the study of the economy as a whole and the way it fluctuates and expands over time. They attempt to *understand* the economic world using economic analysis and they attempt to *improve* economic performance by designing and evaluating economic policy.

In their attempt to understand the economic world, economists distinguish between *positive* statements – statements about what is – and *normative* statements – statements about what ought to be. Like other scientists, they try to develop theories that enable them to make sense of the world. They pursue this task by building and testing economic models – abstract, logical constructions that contain assumptions about what is essential and what can be ignored and the implications of these assumptions. The main obstacles to progress in economics are the fact that we observe the outcomes of the *simultaneous* operation of several, perhaps many, factors and that it is difficult to disentangle cause and effect. To cope with these problems, economists use the *ceteris paribus* – other things remaining the same – assumption and they develop statistical and experimental methods for isolating the factors of interest. Economists are careful to avoid the fallacy of composition (the false statement 'what is true of the parts

is true of the whole or what is true of the whole is true of the parts') and the *post hoc* fallacy (the false statement 'after this, therefore because of this').

In evaluating economic policy, economists often try to grade alternative policies on a scale of better to worse. To do this, they must choose policy *objectives* as criteria. Four objectives often used to evaluate policy are efficiency, equity, growth and stability. Of these, equity (or economic justice) is the most elusive and difficult to define.

Economists have disagreements, but they agree on a surprisingly wide range of questions. (pp. 11–16)

The Economy: An Overview

People have unlimited wants but limited resources or factors of production of labour, land and capital. The economy is a mechanism that allocates scarce resources among competing uses, determining *what*, *how*, *when*, and *where*, the various goods and services will be produced and *who* will consume them.

The economy's two key components are decision makers and markets. Economic decision makers are households, firms and governments. Households decide how much of their labour, land and capital to sell or rent and how much of the various goods and services to buy. Firms decide what factors of production to hire and which goods and services to produce. Governments decide what goods and services to provide to households and firms and how much to raise in taxes.

The decisions of households, firms and governments are coordinated through markets in which prices adjust to keep buying plans and selling plans consistent. Alternatively, coordination can be achieved by a command mechanism. European economies rely mainly on markets, but there is a command element in the actions taken by governments and large firms. The combination of market and command elements in European countries makes them mixed economies.

National economies are interlinked in the global economy. Countries exchange large quantities of goods and services – exports and imports – and undertake international borrowing and lending. (pp. 16–21)

K E Y   E L E M E N T S

Key Terms

Capital, 18
Ceteris paribus, 13
Competition, 10
Economic efficiency, 15
Economic growth, 15
Economic model, 12
Economic problem, 8
Economic stability, 15
Economic theory, 12
Economics, 8
Economy, 16
Enterpreneurial ability, 18
Equity, 15
Factors of production, 17

Incentive, 10
Labour, 17
Land, 17
Macroeconomics, 11
Marginal benefit, 9
Marginal cost, 9
Market, 17
Microeconomics, 11
Opportunity cost, 8
Principle of substitution, 9
Scarcity, 8

 Key Figure

Figure 1.2   A Picture of an Economy, 18

R E V I E W   Q U E S T I O N S

1   What is economics?

2   Give some examples, different from those in the chapter, of the questions that economics tries to answer.

3   What is scarcity and how is it different from poverty?

4   Why does scarcity force people to make choices?

5   Why does scarcity force people to face costs?

6   What is opportunity cost?

7   Why does the money we spend on something not tell us its opportunity cost?

8   Why is the time taken to do something part of its opportunity cost?

9   What is marginal cost?

10   Why is marginal cost the relevant cost for making a decision?

11   What is the principle of substitution?

12   What is an incentive and how do people respond to incentives?

13   Why does scarcity imply competition?

14   Why does competition lead to second round effects that determine the consequences of an economic disturbance?

15   Distinguish between microeconomics and macroeconomics.

16   Distinguish between positive and normative statements and list three examples of each type of statement.

17   What is an economic model?

18   What does *ceteris paribus* mean?

19   What is the fallacy of composition? Give an example.

20   What is the *post hoc* fallacy? Give an example.

21   Explain the difference between economic theory and economic policy.

22   What are the four main goals of economic policy?

23   Name the main economic decision makers.

24   List the economic decisions made by households, firms and governments.

25   What is a market?

26   What is a command mechanism?

27   How does the market determine what, how, when, where and for whom things will be produced?

PROBLEMS

1 You plan to travel round mainland Europe this summer. If you do you won't be able to take your usual job that pays £1,500 for the summer and you won't be able to live at home for free. The cost of your trip will be £2,000. What is the opportunity cost of your trip?

2 On Valentine's Day Stephen and Trudy exchanged gifts: Stephen sent Trudy red roses and Trudy bought Stephen a box of chocolates. They each spent £10. They also spent £30 on dinner and split the cost evenly. Did either Stephen or Trudy incur any opportunity costs? If so, what were they? Explain your answer.

3 Helen asks Vicky to be her bridesmaid at her wedding. Vicky accepts. Which of the following are part of her opportunity cost of being Helen's bridesmaid? Explain why they are or are not.

  a The £150 she spent on a new outfit for the occasion

  b The £50 she spent on a party for Helen's friends

  c The money she spent on a haircut a week before the wedding

  d The weekend visit she missed for her grandmother's 75th birthday, the same weekend as the wedding

  e The £10 she spent on lunch on the way to the wedding

4 The local shopping centre has free parking, but the shopping centre is always busy and it usually takes 30 minutes to find a parking space. Today when you found a vacant spot, your friend Donald also wanted it. Is parking really free at this shopping centre? If not, what did it cost you to park today? When you parked your car today did you impose any costs on Donald? Explain your answers.

5 Which of the following statements are positive and which are normative?

  a A cut in wages will reduce the number of people willing to work.

  b High interest rates prohibit many young people from buying their first home.

  c No family ought to pay more than 25 per cent of its income in taxes.

  d The government should reduce its expenditure on roads and increase its expenditure on railways.

  e Privatizing the public health services will make health provision more efficient.

  f The government ought to behave in such a way as to ensure that resources are used efficiently.

6 You have been hired by Soundtrend, a company that makes and markets tapes, records and compact discs (CDs). Your employer is going to start selling these products in a new region that has a population of 100 million people. A survey has indicated that 40 per cent of people in this region buy only popular music, 5 per cent buy only classical music and no one buys both types of music. Another survey suggests that the average income of a pop music fan in the region is £10,000 a year and that of a classical music fan is £20,000 a year. Based on a third survey, it appears that, on the average, people with low incomes spend one-quarter of 1 per cent of their income on tapes, records and CDs, while people with high incomes spend 2 per cent of their income on these products.

Build a model to enable Soundtrend to predict how much will be spent on pop music and classical music in this new region in one year. In doing so:

  a List your assumptions.

  b Work out the implications of your assumptions.

  c Highlight the potential sources of errors in your predictions.

CHAPTER

2

MAKING AND USING GRAPHS

After studying this chapter you will be able to:

◆ Make and interpret a scatter diagram, a time-series graph and a cross-section graph

◆ Distinguish between linear and non-linear relationships and between relationships that have a maximum and a minimum

◆ Define and calculate the slope of a line

◆ Graph relationships among more than two variables

BENJAMIN DISRAELI, A BRITISH PRIME MINISTER IN THE LATE NINETEENTH century, is reputed to have said that there are three kinds of lies: lies, damned lies and statistics. One of the most powerful ways of conveying statistical information is in the form of a graph. Like statistics, graphs can lie. But the right graph does not lie. It reveals a relationship that would otherwise be obscure. ◆ Graphs are a modern invention. They first appeared in the late eighteenth century, long after the discovery of logarithms and calculus. But today, in the age of the personal computer and video display, graphs have become as important as words and numbers. How do economists use graphs? What types of graphs do they use? What do graphs reveal and what can they hide? ◆ It is often said that in economics, every-thing depends on everything else. Changes in the quantity of cola consumed are caused by changes in the price of ingredients, the temperature and many other factors. How can we make and inter-pret graphs of relationships among several variables?

Three Kinds of Lies

◆ ◆ ◆ ◆ In this chapter, you are going to look at the kinds of graphs that are used in economics. You are going to learn how to make them and read them. You are also going to learn how to calculate the strength of the effect of one variable on another. If you are already familiar with graphs, you may want to skip (or skim) this chapter. Whether you study it or give it a quick pass, you can use this chapter as a handy reference.

Graphing Data

Graphs represent a quantity as a distance on a line. Figure 2.1 gives two examples. Part (a) shows temperature, measured in degrees Centigrade, as the distance on a scale. Movements from left to right show increases in temperature. Movements from right to left show decreases in temperature. The point marked 0 represents 0 degrees or freezing point. To the right of zero, the temperatures are positive. To the left of zero, the temperatures are negative (as indicated by the minus sign in front of the numbers).

Figure 2.1(b) provides another example. This time altitude, or height, is measured in thousands of metres from sea level. The point marked 0 represents sea level. Points to the right of zero represent height above sea level. Points to the left of zero (indicated by a minus sign) represent depth below sea level. There are no rigid rules about the scale for a graph. The scale is determined by the range of the variable being graphed and the space available for the graph.

Each graph in Fig. 2.1 shows just a single variable. Marking a point on either of the two scales indicates a particular temperature or a particular height. So point a represents –273 °C, the theoretical temperature of absolute zero. Point b represents 8,848 metres, the height of the world's highest mountain.

Graphing a single variable does not usually reveal much. Graphs become powerful when they show how two variables are related to each other.

Two-variable Graphs

To construct a two-variable graph, we set two scales perpendicular to each other. Figure 2.2 shows how this looks for temperature and height. Temperature is shown as it was before but height is now shown by movements up and down a vertical scale.

The two scale lines in Fig. 2.2 are called *axes*. The vertical line is called the y-axis and the horizontal line is called the x-axis. The letters x and y

---

FIGURE 2.2

Graphing Two Variables

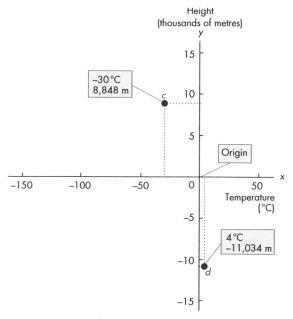

The relationship between two variables is graphed by drawing two axes perpendicular to each other. Height is measured here on the *y*-axis. Point *c* represents the top of Mount Everest, 8,848 metres above sea level (measured on the *y*-axis) with a temperature of –30 °C (measured on the *x*-axis). Point *d* represents the depth of the Mariana Trench in the Pacific Ocean, 11,034 metres below sea level with a temperature of 4 °C.

FIGURE 2.1

Graphing a Single Variable

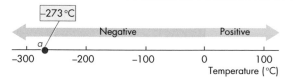

(a) Temperature

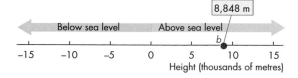

(b) Height

All graphs have a scale that measures a quantity as a distance. The two scales here measure temperature and height. Numbers to the right of zero are positive. Numbers to the left of zero are negative.

appear as labels on the axes of Fig. 2.2. Each axis has a zero point shared by the two axes. The zero point, common to both axes, is called the *origin*.

To show something in a two-variable graph, we need two pieces of information. For example, Mount Everest, the world's highest mountain, is 8,848 metres high and, on a particular day, the temperature at its peak is −30 °C. We show this information in Fig. 2.2 by marking the height of the mountain on the *y*-axis at 8,848 metres and the temperature on the *x*-axis at −30 °C. The values of the two variables that appear on the axes are marked by point *c*. The values which represent the depth and temperature of the world's deepest oceanic trench are marked by point *d*.

Two lines, called *coordinates*, can be drawn from points *c* and *d*. The line running from *c* to the horizontal axis is the *y*-coordinate, because its length is the same as the value marked off on the *y*-axis. Similarly, the line running from *d* to the vertical axis is the *x*-coordinate, because its length is the same as the value marked off on the *x*-axis.

Economists use graphs similar to the one in Fig. 2.2 to reveal and describe the relationships among economic variables. The main types of graphs used in economics are:

◆ Scatter diagrams

◆ Time-series graphs

◆ Cross-section graphs

Let's look at each of these types of graphs.

Scatter Diagrams

A **scatter diagram** plots the value of one economic variable against the value of another variable. Such a graph is used to reveal whether a relationship exists between two economic variables. It is also used to describe a relationship.

The Relationship Between Expenditure and Income   Figure 2.3 shows a scatter diagram of the relationship between consumer expenditure and income. The *x*-axis measures household income and the *y*-axis measures household expenditure. Each point shows average household expenditure and income in the United Kingdom in a given year between 1960 and 1995. The points for all seven years are 'scattered' within the graph. Each point is labelled with a two-digit number that shows us its

FIGURE 2.3

A Scatter Diagram

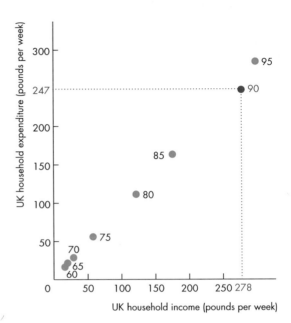

A scatter diagram shows the relationship between two variables. This scatter diagram shows the relationship between average weekly household expenditure and average weekly household income during the years 1960 to 1995. Each point shows the values of the two variables in a specific year; the year is identified by the two-digit number. For example, in 1990 average household expenditure was £247 per week and average income was £278 per week. The pattern formed by the points shows that as UK household income increases, so does household expenditure.

year. For example, the point marked 90 shows us that in 1990, each household spent £247 a week on average and had an income of £278 a week.

This graph shows us that a relationship exists between household income and expenditure. The dots form a pattern which shows us that when income increases, expenditure also increases on average.

Other Relationships   Figure 2.4 shows two other scatter diagrams. Part (a) shows the relationship between the price of cigarettes and the percentage of the population over 15 years old who smoke. The

FIGURE 2.4

More Scatter Diagrams

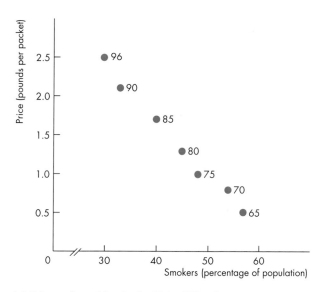

(a) Price and smoking in the United Kingdom

(b) EU unemployment and inflation

Part (a) is a scatter diagram that plots the price of a packet of cigarettes against the percentage of the population who are smokers for years between 1965 and 1995. This graph shows that as the price of cigarettes has risen, the percentage of people who smoke has decreased. Part (b) is a scatter diagram that plots the inflation rate against the unemployment rate for the European Union as a whole. This graph shows that inflation and unemployment are not closely related.

pattern formed by the points shows us that as the price of cigarettes has risen, the proportion of the population who smoke has fallen.

Part (b) looks at inflation and unemployment in the European Union. The pattern formed by the points in this graph does not reveal a clear relationship between the two variables. The graph shows us, by its lack of a distinct pattern, that there is no clear relationship between inflation and unemployment.

Correlation and Causation A scatter diagram that shows a clear relationship between two variables, such as Fig. 2.3 or Fig. 2.4(a), tells us that the two variables are highly correlated. When a high correlation is present, we can predict the value of one variable from the value of the other. But correlation does not imply causation. Of course, it is likely that high income causes high spending, and rising cigarette prices cause a reduction in the percentage

of people who smoke, but sometimes a high correlation arises by coincidence.

Breaks in the Axes Three of the axes in Fig. 2.4 have breaks in them, as shown by the small gaps. The breaks indicate that there are jumps from the origin, 0, to the first values recorded. For example, the break is used on the x axis in part (a) because in the period covered by the graph, the proportion who smoke never falls below 30 per cent. With no break in the axes of this graph, there would be a lot of empty space, all the points would be crowded into the right hand side, and we would not be able to see clearly whether a relationship existed between these two variables. By breaking the axes we are able to bring the relationship into view. In effect, we use a zoom lens to bring the relationship into the centre of the graph and magnify it so that it fills the graph.

The range of the variables plotted on the axes of a graph are an important feature of a graph, and it is a good idea to get into the habit of always looking closely at the values and the labels on the axes before you start to interpret a graph.

A scatter diagram enables us to see the relationship between two economic variables. But it does not give us a clear picture of how these variables evolve over time. To see the evolution of economic variables, we use a time-series graph.

Time-series Graphs

A **time-series graph** measures time (for example, months or years) on the x-axis and the variable or variables in which we are interested on the y-axis. Figure 2.5 shows a time-series graph. Time is measured in years on the x-axis. The variable that we are interested in – the UK inflation rate (the percentage change in retail prices) – is measured

on the y-axis. This time-series graph conveys an enormous amount of information quickly and easily:

1. It shows us the level of the inflation rate. When the line is a long way from the x-axis, the inflation rate is high. When the line is close to the x-axis, the inflation rate is low.

2. It shows us how the inflation rate changes, whether it rises or falls. When the line slopes upward, as in the early 1970s, the inflation rate is rising. When the line slopes downward, as in the early 1980s, the inflation rate is falling.

3. It shows us the speed with which the inflation rate is changing, whether it is rising or falling quickly or slowly. If the line rises or falls steeply, then the inflation rate is changing quickly. If the line is shallow, the inflation rate is rising or falling slowly. For example, inflation increased quickly from 1971 to 1974. Inflation increased again in 1978 at a similar rate, and again in the late 1980s but more slowly. Similarly, inflation was generally decreasing rapidly between 1975 and 1978, and again between 1980 and 1982, and fell more slowly after 1990.

A time-series graph also reveals trends. A **trend** is a general tendency for a variable to rise or fall. You can see that inflation had a general tendency to increase from 1967 to 1975, and then a general tendency to fall towards 1995. There is also a regular tendency for smaller fluctuations within the trend periods.

A time-series graph also lets us compare different periods quickly. Figure 2.5 shows that the 1950s and 1960s were different from later periods because the trend in inflation was constant, neither rising nor falling.

Comparing Two Time-series   Sometimes we want to use a time-series graph to compare two different variables. For example, suppose you wanted to know how the unemployment rate fluctuates with the balance of the government's budget in the United Kingdom. You can examine the unemployment and budget balance by drawing a graph of each of them on the same time scale. We can measure the government's budget balance either as a deficit or as a surplus. Figure 2.6(a) plots the unemployment rate as the orange line and the budget balance as a surplus – the blue line. The unemployment scale is on the left side of the figure and the surplus scale is on the right side

---

FIGURE 2.5

A Time-series Graph

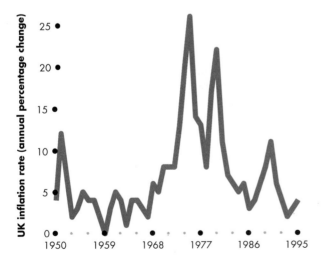

A time-series graph plots the level of a variable on the y-axis against time (day, week, month or year) on the x-axis. This graph shows the UK inflation rate each year from 1950 to 1995.

FIGURE 2.6

Seeing Relationships in Time-series Graphs

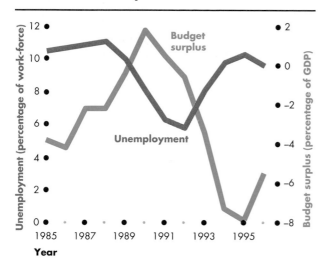

(a) Unemployment and budget surplus

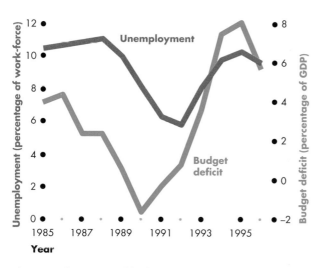

(b) Unemployment and budget deficit

These two graphs show UK unemployment and the UK government's budget balance between 1985 and 1995. The unemployment line is identical in the two parts. Part (a) shows unemployment on the left hand scale and the budget balance as a surplus – measured on the right hand scale. It is hard to see a relationship between inflation and unemployment. Part (b) shows unemployment again, but the government budget is measured as a deficit on the right hand side–the scale has been inverted. The graph now reveals a tendency for unemployment and the budget deficit to move together.

of the figure. It is not easy to see the relationship between inflation and the budget balance in Figure 2.6(a). In these situations it is often revealing to flip the scale of one of the variables over and graph it upside down. In Fig. 2.6(b) the budget balance has been inverted and plotted as a deficit. You can now see the tendency for unemployment and the budget deficit to move together.

Cross-section Graphs

A **cross-section graph** shows the values of an economic variable for different groups in a population at a point in time. Figure 2.7 is an example of a cross-section graph. It shows the percentage of 18 year olds in education and training across different developed countries in 1994. This graph uses bars rather than dots and lines, and the length of each bar indicates the percentage. Figure 2.7 enables you to compare the level of education and training for 18 year olds in these 11 countries much more quickly and clearly than by looking at a table of numbers.

FIGURE 2.7

A Cross-section Graph

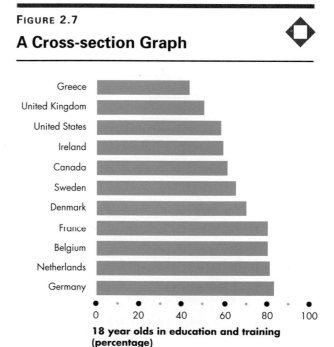

18 year olds in education and training (percentage)

A cross-section graph shows the level of a variable across the members of a population. This graph shows the percentage of 18 year olds in education and training in different developed countries.

Misleading Graphs

All types of graph – time-series graphs, scatter diagrams and cross-section graphs – can mislead. A cross-section graph gives a good example. Figure 2.8 dramatizes a point of view rather than revealing the facts. A quick glance at this graph gives the impression that the level of education and training for 18 year olds is extremely low in Greece and the United Kingdom compared with France, Belgium, Netherlands and Germany. But a closer look reveals that the scale on the axis has been stretched and percentages between zero and 40 have been chopped off the graph. You should make it a habit to look first at the numbers on the axes to avoid being misled, even if the intention of the graph is not to mislead you.

Now that we have seen how we can use graphs in economics to show economic data and relationships between variables, let us examine how economists use graphs in a more abstract way in economic models.

FIGURE 2.8

A Misleading Graph

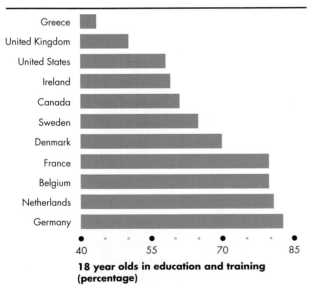

18 year olds in education and training (percentage)

A graph can mislead when it distorts the scale on one of its axes. Here, the scale measuring the percentage of 18 year olds in education and training has been stretched by chopping off values below 40 per cent. The result is that the comparison of percentages across the different countries is distorted. The percentage of 18 year olds who are in education and training looks much lower in Greece and the United Kingdom when compared with countries with the highest rate.

Graphs Used in Economic Models

The graphs used in economics are not always designed to show data. Another use of graphs is to show the relationships among the variables in an economic model. Although you will encounter many different kinds of graphs in economics, there are many similarities in their pattern. Once you have learned to recognize these patterns, they will instantly convey to you the meaning of a graph. Typical patterns show the following:

◆ Things that go up and down together

◆ Things that move in opposite directions

◆ Things that are unrelated

◆ Things that have a maximum or a minimum

Let's look at these four cases.

Things That Go Up and Down Together

Figure 2.9 shows graphs of the relationships between two variables that move up and down together. A relationship between two variables that move in the same direction is called a **positive relationship** or a **direct relationship**. Such a relationship is shown by a line that slopes upward. In the figure, there are three types of positive relationships, one shown by a straight line and two by curved lines. A relationship shown by a straight line is called a **linear relationship**. But all the lines in these three graphs are called curves. Any line on a graph – no matter whether it is straight or curved – is called a curve.

Figure 2.9(a) shows a linear relationship between the number of kilometres travelled in 5 hours and speed. A linear relationship has a constant slope. For example, point a shows us that we will travel 200 kilometres in 5 hours if our speed is 40 kilometres an hour. If we double our speed to 80 kilometres an hour, we will travel 400 kilometres in 5 hours.

Part (b) shows the relationship between distance sprinted and recovery time (recovery time being measured as the time it takes the heart rate to return to normal). This relationship is upward-sloping but the slope changes. The curved line starts out with a gentle slope but then becomes steeper as we move along the curve away from the origin.

Part (c) shows the relationship between the number of problems worked by a student and the

FIGURE 2.9

Positive (Direct) Relationships

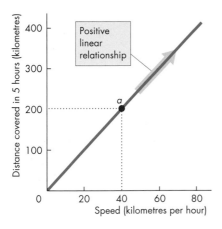

(a) Positive linear relationship

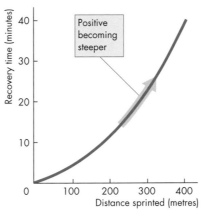

(b) Positive becoming steeper

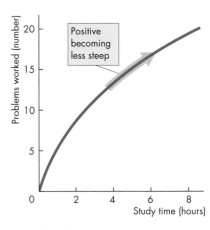

(c) Positive becoming less steep

Each part of this figure shows a positive relationship between two variables. That is, as the value of the variable measured on the *x*-axis increases, so does the value of the variable measured on the *y*-axis. Part (a) shows a linear relationship–a relationship whose slope is constant as we move along the curve. Part (b) shows a positive relation-ship whose slope becomes steeper as we move along the curve away from the origin. It is a positive relationship with an increasing slope. Part (c) shows a positive relation-ship whose slope becomes flatter as we move away from the origin. It is a positive relationship with a decreasing slope.

amount of study time. This relationship is also upward-sloping and the slope changes. This time the curved line starts out with a steep slope but then becomes more gentle as we move away from the origin.

Things That Move in Opposite Directions

Figure 2.10 shows relationships between things that move in opposite directions. A relationship between variables that move in opposite directions is called a **negative relationship** or an **inverse relationship**.

Part (a) shows the relationship between the number of hours available for playing squash and the number of hours for playing tennis. One extra hour spent playing tennis means one hour less play-ing squash and vice versa. This relationship is negative and linear.

Part (b) shows the relationship between the cost per kilometre travelled and the length of a journey. The longer the journey, the lower is the cost per kilometre. But as the journey length increases, the cost per kilometre decreases and the fall in the cost is smaller, the longer the journey. This feature of the relationship is shown by the fact that the curve slopes downward, starting out steep at a short journey length and then becoming flatter as the journey length increases.

Part (c) shows the relationship between the amount of leisure time and the number of problems worked by a student. Increasing leisure time produces an increasingly large reduction in the number of problems worked. This relationship is a negative one that starts out with a gentle slope at a small number of leisure hours and becomes steeper as the number of leisure hours increases.

Things That are Unrelated

There are many situations in which one variable is unrelated to another. No matter what happens to the value of one variable, the other variable remains constant. Sometimes we want to show the

FIGURE 2.10

Negative (Inverse) Relationships

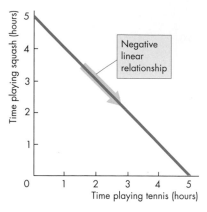

(a) Negative linear relationship

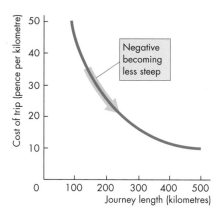

(b) Negative becoming less steep

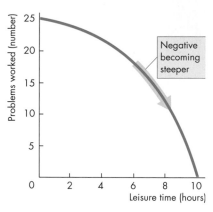

(c) Negative becoming steeper

Each part of this figure shows a negative relationship between two variables. Part (a) shows a linear relationship–a relationship whose slope is constant as we travel along the curve. Part (b) shows a negative relationship with a slope that becomes flatter as the journey length increases. Part (c) shows a negative relationship with a slope that becomes steeper as the leisure time increases.

independence between two variables in a graph. Figure 2.11 shows two ways of achieving this. In Fig. 2.11(a), your grade in economics is shown on the y-axis against the price of bananas on the x-axis. Your grade (75 per cent in this example) is unrelated to the price of bananas. The relationship between these two variables is shown by a horizontal straight line. This line slopes neither upward nor downward. In part (b), the output of French wine is shown on the x-axis and the number of rainy days a month in Ireland is shown on the y-axis. Again, the output of French wine (3 billion litres a year in this example) is unrelated to the number of rainy days in Ireland. The relationship between these two variables is shown by a vertical straight line.

Things That Have a Maximum and a Minimum

Many relationships in economic models have a maximum or a minimum. For example, firms try to make the maximum possible profit and to produce at the lowest possible cost. Figure 2.12 shows relationships that have a maximum or a minimum.

Part (a) shows the relationship between rainfall and wheat yield. When there is no rainfall, wheat will not grow, so the yield is zero. As the rainfall increases up to 10 days a month, the wheat yield also increases. With 10 rainy days each month, the wheat yield reaches its maximum at 40 tonnes a hectare (point a). Rain in excess of 10 days a month starts to lower the yield of wheat. If every day is rainy, the wheat suffers from a lack of sunshine and the yield falls back almost to zero. This relationship is one that starts out with a positive slope, reaches a maximum at which its slope is zero, and then moves into a range in which its slope is negative.

Part (b) shows the reverse case – a relationship that begins with a negative slope, falls to a minimum, and then becomes positive. An example of such a relationship is the petrol cost per kilometre as the speed of travel varies. At low speeds, the car is creeping along in a traffic jam. The number of kilometres per litre is low so the petrol cost per kilometre is high. At high speeds the car is travelling faster than its most efficient speed and, again, the number of kilometres per litre is

FIGURE 2.11

Variables that are Unrelated

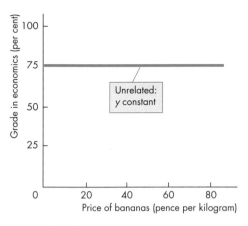

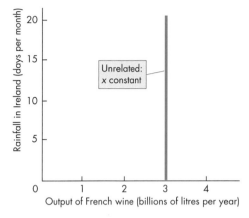

This figure shows how we can graph two variables that are unrelated to each other. In part (a), a student's grade in economics is plotted at 75 per cent regardless of the price of bananas on the x-axis. The curve is horizontal. In part (b), the output of the vineyards of France does not vary with the rainfall in Ireland. The curve is vertical.

(a) Unrelated: y constant   **(b) Unrelated: x constant**

low and the petrol cost per kilometre is high. At a speed of 55 kilometres per hour, the petrol cost per kilometre travelled is at its minimum (point b). This relationship is one that starts out with a negative slope, reaches a minimum at which its slope is zero, and then moves into a range in which its slope is positive.

Figures 2.9 through to 2.12 show 10 different shapes of graphs that we will encounter in economic models. In describing these graphs, we have talked about the slopes of curves The concept of slope is an intuitive one. But it is also a precise technical concept. Let's look more closely at the concept of slope.

FIGURE 2.12

Maximum and Minimum Points

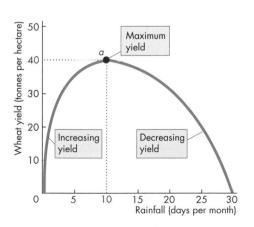

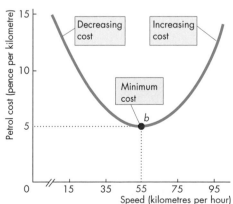

Part (a) shows a relationship that has a maximum point, a. The curve has a positive slope as it rises to its maximum point, is flat at its maximum, and then has a negative slope. Part (b) shows a relationship with a minimum point, b. The curve has a negative slope as it falls to its minimum, is flat at its minimum, and then has a positive slope.

(a) Relationship with a maximum   **(b) Relationship with a minimum**

The Slope of a Relationship

The **slope** of a relationship is the change in the value of the variable measured on the y-axis divided by the change in the value of the variable measured on the x-axis. We use the Greek letter Δ to represent 'change in'. Thus Δy means the change in the value of the variable measured on the y-axis, and Δx means the change in the value of the variable measured on the x-axis. Therefore, the slope of the relationship is

$$\frac{\Delta y}{\Delta x}$$

If a large change in the variable measured on the y-axis (Δy) is associated with a small change in the variable measured on the x-axis (Δx), the slope is large and the curve is steep. If a small change in the variable measured on the y-axis (Δy) is associated with a large change in the variable measured on the x-axis (Δx), the slope is small and the curve is flat.

We can make the idea of slope sharper by doing some calculations.

The Slope of a Straight Line

The slope of a straight line is the same regardless of where on the line you calculate it. Thus the slope of a straight line is constant. Let's calculate the slopes of the lines in Fig. 2.13. In part (a), when x increases from 2 to 6, y increases from 3 to 6. The change in x is plus 4, that is, Δx is 4. The change in y is plus 3, that is, Δy is 3. The slope of that line is

---

FIGURE 2.13

The Slope of a Straight Line

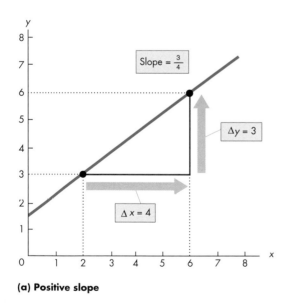

(a) Positive slope

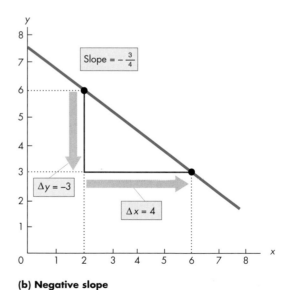

(b) Negative slope

To calculate the slope of a straight line, we divide the change in the value of the variable measured on the y-axis (Δy) by the change in the value of the variable measured on the x-axis (Δx). Part (a) shows the calculation of a positive slope. When x increases from 2 to 6, Δx equals 4. That change in x brings about an increase in y from 3 to 6, so Δy equals 3. The slope ($\Delta y/\Delta x$) equals 3/4. Part (b) shows the calculation of a negative slope. When x increases from 2 to 6, Δx equals 4. That increase in x brings about a decrease in y from 6 to 3, so Δy equals –3. The slope ($\Delta y/\Delta x$) equals –3/4.

$$\frac{\Delta y}{\Delta x} = \frac{3}{4}$$

In part (b), when x increases from 2 to 6, y decreases from 6 to 3. The change in y is minus 3, that is, Δy is –3. The change in x is plus 4, that is, Δx is 4. The slope of the curve is

$$\frac{\Delta y}{\Delta x} = \frac{-3}{4}$$

Notice that the two slopes have the same magnitude (3/4), but the slope of the line in part (a) is

positive (+3/+4) = 3/4), while that in part (b) is negative (−3/+4 = −3/4). The slope of a positive relationship is positive; the slope of a negative relationship is negative.

The Slope of a Curved Line

The slope of a curved line is not constant. It depends on where on the line we calculate it. There are two ways to calculate the slope of a curved line: at a point on the curve or across an arc of the curve. Let's look at them.

FIGURE 2.14

The Slope of a Curve

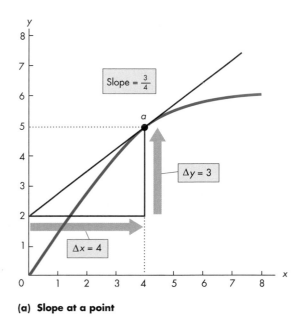

(a) Slope at a point

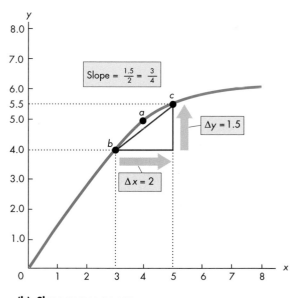

(b) Slope across an arc

To calculate the slope of the curve at point *a*, draw the red line that just touches the curve at *a* – the tangent. The slope of this straight line is calculated by dividing the change in *y* by the change in *x* along the line. When *x* increases from 0 to 4, Δx equals 4. That change in *x* is associated with an increase in *y* from 2 to 5, so Δy equals 3. The slope of the red line is 3/4. So the slope of the curve at point *a* is 3/4.

To calculate the average slope of the curve along the arc *bc*, draw a straight line from *b* to *c* in part (b). The slope of the line *bc* is calculated by dividing the change in *y* by the change in *x*. In moving from *b* to *c*, Δx equals 2, and Δy equals 1.5. The slope of the line *bc* is 1.5 divided by 2, or 3/4. So the slope of the curve across the arc *bc* is 3/4.

Slope at a Point   To calculate the slope at a point on a curve, you need to construct a straight line that has the same slope as the curve at the point in question. Figure 2.14 shows how this is done. Suppose you want to calculate the slope of the curve at point a. Place a ruler on the graph so that it touches point a and no other point on the curve, then draw a straight line along the edge of the ruler. The straight red line in part (a) is this line and it is the tangent to the curve at point a. If the ruler touches the curve only at point a, then the slope of the curve at point a must be the same as the slope of the edge of the ruler. If the curve and the ruler do not have the same slope, the line along the edge of the ruler will cut the curve instead of just touching it.

Having found a straight line with the same slope as the curve at point a, you can calculate the slope of the curve at point a by calculating the slope of the straight line. Along the straight line, as x increases from 0 to 4 ($\Delta x = 4$) y increases from 2 to 5 ($\Delta y = 3$). Therefore, the slope of the line is

$$\frac{\Delta y}{\Delta x} = \frac{3}{4}$$

Thus the slope of the curve at point a is 3/4.

Slope Across an Arc   Calculating a slope across an arc is similar to calculating an average slope. An arc of a curve is a piece of a curve. In Fig. 2.14(b), we are looking at the same curve as in part (a), but instead of calculating the slope at point a, we calculate the slope across the arc from b to c. Moving along the arc from b to c, x increases from 3 to 5 and y increases from 4 to 5.5. The change in x is 2 ($\Delta x = 2$) and the change in y is 1.5 ($\Delta y = 1.5$). Therefore, the slope of the line is

$$\frac{\Delta y}{\Delta x} = \frac{1.5}{2} = \frac{3}{4}$$

Thus the slope of the curve across the arc bc is 3/4.

In this particular example, the slope of the arc bc is identical to the slope of the curve at point a in part (a). But the calculation of the slope of a curve does not always work out so neatly. You might have some fun constructing counter-examples. Box 2.1 shows you how calculus is used to measure the slope of an arc in an algebraic example.

Graphing Relationships Among More Than Two Variables

We have seen that we can graph a single variable as a point on a straight line and we can graph the relationship between two variables as a point formed by the x and y coordinates in a two-dimensional graph. You may be thinking that although a two-dimensional graph is informative, most of the things in which you are likely to be interested involve relationships among many variables, not just two.

For example, the amount of cola consumed depends on the price of a can of cola and the temperature. If a can of cola is expensive and the temperature is low, people drink much less cola than when a can of cola is inexpensive and the temperature is high. For any given price of a can of cola, the quantity consumed varies with the temperature, and for any given temperature, the quantity of cola consumed varies with its price.

Figure 2.15 shows the relationship among three variables. The table shows the number of cans of cola consumed each day at various temperatures and cans of cola prices. How can we graph these numbers?

To graph a relationship that involves more than two variables, we consider what happens if all but two of the variables are held constant. When we hold other things constant, we are using the *ceteris paribus* assumption that is described in Chapter 1, p.15. An example is shown in Fig. 2.15(a). There, you can see what happens to the quantity of cola consumed when the price of a can varies while the temperature is held constant. The line labelled 20 °C shows the relationship between cola consumption and the price of a can of cola when the temperature stays at 20 °C. The numbers used to plot this line are those in the third column of the table in Fig. 2.15. For example, when the temperature is 20 °C, 10 cans are consumed when the price is 60 pence and 18 cans are consumed when the price is 30 pence. The curve labelled 25 °C shows the consumption of cola when the price varies and the temperature is 25 °C.

We can also show the relationship between cola consumption and temperature while holding the price of cola constant, as shown in Fig. 2.15(b).

FIGURE 2.15

Graphing a Relationship Among Three Variables

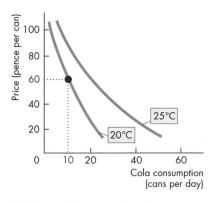

(a) Price and consumption at a given temperature

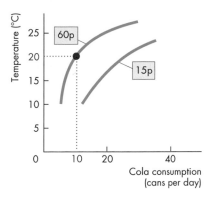

(b) Temperature and consumption at a given price

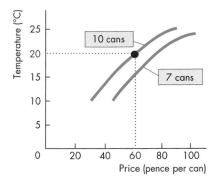

(c) Temperature and price at a given consumption

Price (pence per can)	Cola consumption (cans per day)			
	10 °C	15 °C	20 °C	25 °C
15	12	18	25	50
30	10	12	18	37
45	7	10	13	27
60	5	7	10	20
75	3	5	7	14
90	2	3	5	10
105	1	2	3	6

The quantity of cola consumed depends on its price and the temperature. The table gives some hypothetical numbers that tell us how many cans of cola are consumed each day at different prices and different temperatures. For example, if the price is 30 pence per can and the temperature is 10 °C, 10 cans of cola are consumed. In order to graph a relationship among three variables, the value of one variable is held constant. Part (a) shows the relationship between price and consumption, holding temperature constant. One curve holds temperature at 25 °C and the other at 20 °C. Part (b) shows the relationship between temperature and consumption, holding price constant. One curve holds the price at 60 pence and the other at 15 pence. Part (c) shows the relationship between temperature and price, holding consumption constant. One curve holds consumption at 10 cans and the other at 7 cans.

The curve labelled 60 pence shows how the consumption of cola varies with the temperature when cola costs 60 pence, and a second curve shows the relationship when cola costs 15 pence. For example, at 60 pence a can, 10 cans are consumed when the temperature is 20 °C and 20 cans when the temperature is 25 °C.

Figure 2.15(c) shows the combinations of temperature and price that result in a constant consumption of cola. One curve shows the combination that results in 10 cans a day being consumed, and the other shows the combination that results in

7 cans a day being consumed. A high price and a high temperature lead to the same consumption as a lower price and a lower temperature. For example, 10 cans are consumed at 20 °C and 60 pence per can and at 25 °C and 90 pence per can.

◆ ◆ ◆ ◆ With what you have learned about graphs, you can move forward with your study of economics. There are no graphs in this book that are more complicated than those that have been explained here.

SUMMARY

Graphing Data

Three types of graphs used to show economic data are scatter diagrams, time-series graphs and cross-section graphs. A scatter diagram plots the value of one economic variable against the value of another and reveals whether or not there is a relationship between the two variables. If there is a relationship, the graph reveals its nature. A time-series graph plots the value of one (or more) economic variables against time and shows the level, direction of change and speed of change of each variable. It also reveals trends. A cross-section graph shows how a variable changes across the members of a population. A graph can mislead if its scale is stretched (or squeezed) to exaggerate (or understate) a variation. (pp. 27–32)

Graphs Used in Economic Models

Graphs are used to show relationships among variables in economic models. There are five types of relationships: positive (an upward-sloping curve), negative (a downward-sloping curve), unrelated (a horizontal or vertical curve), positive and then negative (a maximum), and negative and then positive (a minimum). (pp. 32–35)

The Slope of a Relationship

The slope of a relationship is calculated as the change in the value of the variable measured on the y-axis divided by the change in the value of the variable measured on the x-axis–$\Delta y/\Delta x$. A straight line has a constant slope, but a curved line has a varying slope. To calculate the slope of a curved line, we calculate the slope at a point or across an arc. (pp. 36–38)

Graphing Relationships Among More Than Two Variables

To graph a relationship among more than two variables, we hold constant the values of all the variables except two. We then plot the value of one of the variables against the value of another. (pp. 38–39)

KEY ELEMENTS

Key Terms

Cross-section graph, 31
Direct relationship, 32
Inverse relationship, 33
Linear relationship, 32
Negative relationship, 33
Positive relationship, 32
Scatter diagram, 28
Slope, 36
Time-series graph, 30
Trend, 30

◆ Key Figures

Figure 2.3   A Scatter Diagram, 28
Figure 2.5   A Time-series Graph, 30
Figure 2.7   A Cross-section Graph, 31
Figure 2.9   Positive (Direct) Relationships, 33
Figure 2.10 Negative (Inverse) Relationships, 34
Figure 2.11 Variables That are Unrelated, 35
Figure 2.12 Maximum and Minimum Points, 35
Figure 2.13 The Slope of a Straight Line, 36
Figure 2.14 The Slope of a Curve, 37

REVIEW QUESTIONS

1 What are the three types of graphs used to show economic data?

2 Give an example of a scatter diagram.

3 Give an example of a time-series graph.

4 Give an example of a cross-section graph.

5 List three things that a time-series graph shows quickly and easily.

6 What do we mean by trend?

7 How can a graph mislead?

8 Draw some graphs to show the relationships between two variables:

  a That move in the same direction
  b That move in opposite directions
  c That have a maximum
  d That have a minimum

9 Which of the relationships in Question 8 is a positive relationship and which is a negative relationship?

10 What is the definition of the slope of a curve?

11 What are the two ways of calculating the slope of a curved line?

12 How do we graph relationships among more than two variables?

PROBLEMS

1 The unemployment rate in the United Kingdom between 1984 and 1994 was as follows:

Year	Unemployment rate (per cent per year)
1984	10.7
1985	10.9
1986	11.1
1987	10.0
1988	8.1
1989	6.3
1990	5.8
1991	8.1
1992	9.8
1993	10.3
1994	9.2

Draw a time-series graph of these data and use your graph to answer the following questions:

  a In which year was unemployment highest?
  b In which year was unemployment lowest?
  c In which years did unemployment increase?
  d In which years did unemployment decrease?
  e In which year did unemployment increase most?
  f In which year did unemployment decrease most?
  g What have been the main trends in unemployment?

2 The UK government's budget deficit as a percentage of GDP between 1984 and 1994 was as follows:

Year	Government deficit (percentage of GDP)
1984	4.2
1985	2.2
1986	2.2
1987	0.4
1988	-1.8
1989	-0.5
1990	0.6
1991	3.4
1992	7.3
1993	7.9
1994	5.5

Use these data together with those in Problem 1 to draw a scatter diagram showing the relationship between unemployment and the deficit. Then use your graph to determine whether a relationship exists between unemployment and the deficit and whether it is positive or negative.

3 Use the following information to draw a graph showing the relationship between two variables x and y.

x	0	1	2	3	4	5	6	7	8
y	0	1	4	9	16	25	36	49	64

a   Is the relationship between x and y positive or negative?

b   Does the slope of the relationship rise or fall as the value of x rises?

4   Using the data in Problem 3:

a   Calculate the slope of the relationship between x and y when x equals 4.

b   Calculate the slope of the arc when x rises from 3 to 4.

c   Calculate the slope of the arc when x rises from 4 to 5.

d   Calculate the slope of the arc when x rises from 3 to 5.

e   What do you notice that is interesting about your answers to (b), (c) and (d), compared with your answer to (a)?

5   Calculate the slopes of the following two relationships between two variables x and y

a
x	0	2	4	6	8	10
y	20	16	12	8	4	0

b
x	0	2	4	6	8	10
y	0	8	16	24	32	40

6   Draw a graph showing the following relationship between two variables x and y:

x	0	1	2	3	4	5	6	7	8	9
y	0	2	4	6	8	10	8	6	4	2

a   Is the slope positive or negative when x is less than 5?

b   Is the slope positive or negative when x is greater than 5?

c   What is the slope of this relationship when x equals 5?

d   Is y at a maximum or at a minimum when x equals 5?

7   Draw a graph showing the following relationship between two variables x and y:

x	0	1	2	3	4	5	6	7	8	9
y	10	8	6	4	2	0	2	4	6	8

a   Is the slope positive or negative when x is less than 5?

b   Is the slope positive or negative when x is greater than 5?

c   What is the slope of this relationship when x equals 5?

d   Is y at a maximum or at a minimum when x equals 5?

BOX 2.1 THE MATHEMATICS OF SLOPES

1. Linear Relationships

A straight line can be represented by the following mathematical equation:

$$y = a + bx \qquad (1)$$

y represents the value of the variable on the y-axis and x represents the value of the variable on the x-axis. Both a and b are constants, with a fixed value. Looking at Fig. B2.1, you can see three different straight line equations. In each equation, the value of a is the point at which the line crosses the y-axis – the intercept. If a increases from 2 to 3 (decreases from 3 to 2) and b does not change, the line shifts upward (downward), but the slope does not change.

Looking again at the three equations in Fig. B2.1, you can see that the value of b in each equation is the slope of the line. The slope of a straight line is given by $\Delta y/\Delta x$. So $b = \Delta y/\Delta x$. To see why, consider what would happen to y if x

increased by an amount which we will call Δx. This increase in x will lead to an increase in y by an amount which we will call Δy. We can write the result of this increase in x mathematically as:

$$y + \Delta y = a + b(x + \Delta x) \qquad (2)$$

If we subtract Equation 1 from Equation 2, we will find the difference or the value of the change which is:

$$\Delta y = b\Delta x$$

Rearranging this equation by dividing through by Δx shows you the value of the slope for a straight line, or the change in y resulting from a change in x.

$$\Delta y/\Delta x = b \qquad (3)$$

If b is positive, the line will slope upward, and if b is negative as in Fig. B2.1, the line will slope downward. The line will not change position if

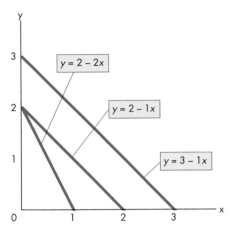

Figure B2.1

both a and b do not change. If b changes but a does not change, the line will tilt from point a as the slope changes. The figure shows that a change in the slope from −1 to −2 makes the line steeper.

2. Non-linear Relationships

In the general case, we can represent any equation as:

$$y = f(x)$$

This is a simple way of saying y is a function of x. Unlike the straight line case, the slope of a curve varies depending on the value of x. So we need a mathematical method of finding the slope of a non-linear relationship, $y = f(x)$ at any particular value of x. A graphical method would be to measure the slope of a tangent to the line at any given value of x. Another method would be to calculate the value of $\Delta y/\Delta x$ between two points on the line which are close to each other; this would approximate the value of the tangent. This is, in effect, what we do when we use calculus to find the slope of a line. The slope is then called the derivative of y with respect to x and is given by:

$$\delta y/\delta x = f'(x) \qquad \textbf{(4)}$$

where δy is a very small change in y, δx is a very small change in x, and $\delta y/\delta x$ is the rate of change of y with respect to a very small change in x – or the slope at any chosen point on the line.

Let's look at a simple example of a non-linear equation. A quadratic equation involves the square of a variable. An example is:

$$y = 5 + 3x^2 \qquad \textbf{(5)}$$

The rule for finding the derivative of y with respect to x is to ignore the constant (5), because it does not vary with x, and to multiply the coefficient of x (3), by the power of x (2), and then decrease the power of x by 1. So that gives us:

$$\delta y/\delta x = 6x \qquad \textbf{(6)}$$

This shows us that the rate of change of y with respect to a change in x, increases as x increases. If we want to find the slope of y when x takes a specific value, say 2, we substitute 2 for x in Equation 6. The slope of the line $y = 5 + 3x^2$ is equal to 12 when $x = 2$.

The general rule to find the derivative of y with respect to x.

A quadratic is just one example of the general types of non-linear functions called polynomials. A polynomial can be written in a general form as:

$$y = a + bx^n \qquad \textbf{(7)}$$

This means that y equals a constant amount a, plus a variable amount x, raised to the power n, and multiplied by the constant amount b. The rule for finding the derivative of a polynomial is to ignore the value of a as it does not vary with x, to multiply the coefficient b by the power n, and to decrease the power of x by 1. This gives us:

$$\delta y/\delta x = nbx^{n-1} \qquad \textbf{(8)}$$

From Equation 5, n is equal to 2, b is equal to 3 and $n - 1$ is equal to 1. Recall that any number raised to the power of 1 (x^1) is just the number itself (x), and any number raised to the power of 0 (x^0) is equal to 1. Try to find the derivative of the straight line

$$y = a + bx$$

to check that the slope is equal to b for any value of x.

CHAPTER 3

PRODUCTION, GROWTH AND TRADE

After studying this chapter you will be able to:

- ◆ Define the production possibility frontier
- ◆ Define efficiency
- ◆ Calculate opportunity cost
- ◆ Explain how economic growth expands production possibilities but does not provide free gifts
- ◆ Explain comparative advantage
- ◆ Explain why people specialize and how they gain from exchange

WE LIVE IN A STYLE THAT SURPRISES OUR GRANDPARENTS AND WOULD have astonished our great grandparents. We live in bigger homes, eat more, grow taller and are even born larger than they were. Video games, cellular phones, genetic engineering, personal computers and microwave ovens did not exist 20 years ago. But today it is hard to imagine life without them. Economic growth has made us richer than our grandparents. But it has not liberated us from scarcity. Why not? Why, despite our immense wealth, must we still make choices and face costs? Why are there no 'free lunches'? ◆ We see an incredible amount of specialization and exchange in the world. Each one of us specializes in a particular job – as a lawyer, a car maker, a home maker. We have become so specialized that one farm worker can feed 100 people. Only one in four of the UK work-force is employed in manu-

Making the Most of It

facturing. More than half of the work-force is employed in wholesale and retail trade, banking and finance, government and other services. Why do we specialize? How do we benefit from specialization and exchange? ◆ Over many centuries, institutions and social arrangements have evolved that we take for granted. One of them is markets. Another is property rights and a political and legal system that protects them. Yet another is money. Why have these arrangements evolved? How do they extend our ability to specialize and increase production?

◆ ◆ ◆ ◆ These are the questions that we tackle in this chapter. We begin by studying the limits to production and the concept of efficiency. We next learn how to measure opportunity cost. We also discover how we can increase production by specializing and trading with each other.

The Production Possibility Frontier

*P*roduction is the conversion of *labour, land* and *capital* into goods and services. We defined the factors of production in Chapter 1 but let's briefly recall what they are.

Labour is the time and effort that people devote to producing goods and services. It includes the physical and mental activities of the many thousands of people who make cars and cola, biscuits and glue, wallpaper and watering cans. It also includes the activities of people called *entrepreneurs* who *organize* production. *Land* is the gifts of nature that are used to produce goods and services. It includes the air, the water and the land surface, as well as the minerals that lie beneath the surface of the earth. *Capital* is the goods that have been produced and can now themselves be used in the production of other goods and services. Examples include the motorway system, the fine buildings of great cities, dams and power projects, airports and jumbo jets, car and shirt factories, and shopping centres.

A special kind of capital is called human capital. **Human capital** is the skill and knowledge of people, which arise from their education and on-the-job training. You are creating human capital right now as you work on your economics course and other subjects. Your human capital will continue to grow when you get a full-time job and become better at it. Human capital improves the *quality* of labour. Some economists have also identified another form of capital called environmental capital. **Environmental capital** includes elements of land which are lost forever when used in the production process as well as the degree of biodiversity among species and the ability of the environment to absorb waste from production.

Goods and services are all the valuable things that people produce. Goods are tangible – cars, spoons, VCRs and bread. Services are intangible – haircuts, amusement park rides and telephone calls. There are two types of goods: capital goods and consumption goods. *Capital goods* are goods that are used to produce other goods. Examples of capital goods are buildings, computers, cars and telephones. *Consumption goods* are goods that are bought by households. Some are *durable* consumption goods such as shoes and shirts, and some are non-durable such as pickled onions and toothpaste. *Consumption* is the process of using goods and services.

The quantities of goods and services that can be produced are limited by the available resources and by technology. This limit is described by our first economic model, the production possibility frontier. The **production possibility frontier** *(PPF)* marks the boundary between those combinations of goods and services that can be produced and those that cannot.

To study the production possibility frontier, we will consider just two goods at a time. They could be any two goods. In focusing on two goods, we hold the quantities produced of all the other goods constant – we use the *ceteris paribus* assumption. By this device, we look at a model in which everything remains the same except the production of the two goods that we are (currently) interested in.

Let's begin by looking at the production possibility frontier for a single firm – one that produces denim jeans.

A Firm's Production Possibility Frontier

Best Jeans Company employs 50 workers (labour). It has a small site (land), and it has a factory building that contains cutting and sewing machines (capital). The owner (entrepreneur) uses these given amounts of labour, land and capital to produce two types of jeans, comfort fit and straight leg. To find the company's production possibility frontier we need to know the maximum quantities of jeans it can produce with these fixed resources.

Figure 3.1 shows the company's production possibilities. With the fixed quantities of labour, land and capital, the maximum quantity of jeans produced is 5,000 a week. If all the available resources are used to produce comfort fit jeans, no straight legs are produced. This combination of jeans, 5,000 comfort fit and no straight legs, is just one of the company's *production possibilities* – shown in the table as possibility *a*. A second possibility is *b*. In this case, one-fifth of the resources are used to produce straight legs and the rest to produce comfort fits. The factory produces 4,000 comfort fits and 1,000 straight legs a week – still a total of 5,000 jeans a week. The pattern continues to possibility *f*, where all the available resources are devoted to producing straight legs. In this case, the factory produces 5,000 straight legs and no comfort fits.

FIGURE 3.1

The Production Possibility Frontier for Jeans

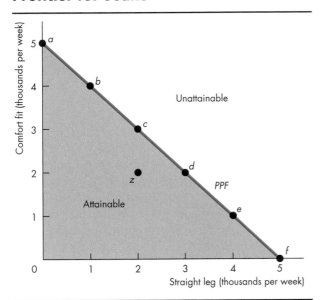

Possibility	Straight legs (thousands per week)		Comfort fits (thousands per week)
a	0	and	5
b	1	and	4
c	2	and	3
d	3	and	2
e	4	and	1
f	5	and	0

The table lists six points on Best Jeans' possibility frontier for straight legs and comfort fits. Row *a* tells us that if no straight legs are produced, the maximum quantity of comfort fits produced is 5,000 a week. The rows of the table are graphed as points *a, b, c, d, e* and *f* in the figure. The line passing through these points is Best Jeans' production possibility frontier (*PPF*). It separates what the company can attain from what it cannot attain. It can produce at any point inside the orange area or on the frontier. Points outside the frontier are unattainable. Points inside the frontier such as point *z* are inefficient because resources are being wasted or misallocated. At such points, it is possible for the owner to use the resources to produce more of either or both kinds of jeans.

The numbers in the table are plotted in the graph shown in Fig. 3.1. Thousands of straight legs are measured on the horizontal axis and thousands of comfort fits on the vertical axis. Points *a, b, c, d, e*

and *f* represent the numbers in the corresponding row of the table.

Of course, the factory does not have to produce jeans in batches of 1,000, as in the table. It could produce 1 straight leg and 4,999 comfort fits a week or any other combination that totals 5,000. All the other feasible allocations of the resources enable the factory to produce the combinations of comfort fits and straight legs described by the line that joins points *a, b, c, d, e* and *f*. This line shows Best Jeans' production possibility frontier for comfort fits and straight legs, given the fixed resources. The owner can decide to produce at any point on the frontier or at any point inside it, within the orange area. These are the attainable points. Points outside the frontier are unattainable. To produce at points beyond the frontier, the owner would need more resources. But more resources are not available, so points outside the frontier can't be reached.

Efficiency

Efficiency is achieved when it not possible to produce more of one good without producing less of some other good. Efficiency occurs only at points on the production possibility frontier. Possible production points inside the frontier, such as point *z*, are *inefficient*. They are points at which resources are being either wasted or misallocated. Resources are wasted when they are idle but could be working. For example, workers might be taking extra long coffee breaks. Resources are misallocated when they are assigned to inappropriate tasks. For example, a skilled cutter might be assigned to sewing and a skilled sewer assigned to cutting. This would be like assigning a striker to goal keeping and a goal keeper to striking in a football match. They would each work hard, but the team would not perform as well as it could. The allocation would be inefficient.

If the owner of Best Jeans has chosen an inefficient point such as *z*, the resources could be more efficiently used to produce more jeans of either or both types. The owner will strive to be efficient by avoiding waste and producing at a point on the production possibility frontier.

A Trade-off In trying to be efficient, the owner of Best Jeans must choose between the many efficient points along the *PPF*. There is a trade-off in the choice between efficient points. A **trade-off** is a constraint that entails giving up one thing to get something else. The production possibility frontier is an example of a trade-off. Your own budget is another example. With your fixed weekly resources, you must trade off seeing a film against buying magazines.

The idea of trading off one thing for another is just another way of saying that every action has an opportunity cost. Along the production possibility frontier, the owner of Best Jeans faces opportunity costs. Let's explore these trade-offs and opportunity costs more closely.

A Firm's Opportunity Cost of Production

The *opportunity cost* of an action is the best alternative forgone. Of all the things you choose not to do – the alternatives forgone – the best one is the opportunity cost of the action you choose. The concept of opportunity cost can be made precise by using the production possibility frontier. Along the frontier the Best Jeans factory is producing only two goods so it is easy to work out the best alternative forgone. Given the current resources and technology, it can produce more straight legs only if it produces fewer comfort fits. Thus the opportunity cost of producing an additional straight leg is the quantity of comfort fits forgone. Similarly, the opportunity cost of producing additional comfort fits is the quantity of straight legs forgone. At point *c*, for example, Best Jeans produces fewer straight legs and more comfort fits than at point *d*. If the owner had chosen point *d* over point *c*, the additional 1,000 straight legs would have *cost* 1,000 comfort fits. One straight cut costs one comfort fit, and one comfort fit costs one straight leg.

In this example, the opportunity costs of producing more of either type of jeans are the same. They are also constant, regardless of how many of each type is produced. That is, at any point on the *PPF* one straight leg costs one comfort fit. These opportunity costs are constant because the resources used to produce jeans are equally productive regardless of the type produced.

Opportunity Costs are Inescapable

We've just looked at opportunity costs in a denim jeans factory. But the lesson we've learned from this example is a fundamental one that applies to

every imaginable real-world situation. At any given point in time, the world has a fixed amount of labour, land and capital. By using the available technologies, these resources can be employed to produce goods and services. But there is a limit to what they can produce that defines a boundary between what is attainable and what is not attainable. This boundary is the real-world economy's production possibility frontier. On the frontier, producing more of any one good or service requires producing less of some other goods or services.

For example, a prime minister who promises better welfare and better education must at the same time, to be credible, promise either cuts in budget spending or tax increases. Higher taxes mean less money left over for holidays and other consumption goods and services. The opportunity cost of better welfare and educational services is less of other goods and services. On a smaller scale but equally important, each time you decide to rent a video you decide not to use your limited income to buy cola, or pizzas, or some other good. The opportunity cost of renting one more video is having less of something else.

R E V I E W

- ◆ The production possibility frontier (*PPF*) is the boundary between attainable and unattainable levels of production.

- ◆ Points on the *PPF* and inside it are attainable, and points outside the *PPF* are unattainable.

- ◆ Points *on* the *PPF* are efficient, and points inside it are inefficient.

- ◆ Choosing among efficient points on the *PPF* involves a trade-off and an opportunity cost.

- ◆ The opportunity cost of producing an additional unit of one good is the decrease in the number of units of another good that can be produced.

Along the production possibility curve for Best Jeans, the opportunity costs are constant. But constant opportunity costs are unusual. Generally, the opportunity cost of producing a good increases as the quantity of that good produced increases. Let's look at this more general case.

Increasing Opportunity Cost

Almost all the available labour, land and capital is relatively more productive in some activities than in others. Some people are creative and good at making entertaining movies while others are well-coordinated and good at performing challenging physical tasks. Some land is fertile and good for farming while other land is rocky and good for building shopping centres. Most capital (tools, machines and buildings) are custom-designed to do a small range of jobs – cutting and sewing machines, car assembly lines, or schools.

When each worker, each plot of land and each piece of capital is allocated to the task in which it is relatively most productive, the economy is at a point on its production possibility frontier. But there are many points on the frontier. As the economy moves along its *PPF* and produces more of one good or service and less of some others, factors of production must be assigned to tasks for which they are an increasingly poor match. Let's consider another model of a trade-off between two goods: books and video games. We will use the *ceteris paribus* assumption so that production of all other goods remains the same.

Books versus Video Games

The economy's production possibility curve for books and video games shows the limits to the production of these two goods, given the total resources available to produce them. Figure 3.2 shows this production possibility curve.

Suppose that in a year, 4,000 new games and 2,000 new books are produced – point *e* in Fig. 3.2 and possibility *e* in the table. The figure shows other production possibilities. For example, if we want a better educated population we might stop producing games and put all the creative people who devise them and all the programmers, production and marketing staff, computers, buildings and other resources used to produce games into the publishing industry to produce books. This case is shown as point *a* in the figure and possibility *a* in the table. The quantity of books produced increases to 4,000 a year and games production dries up. Alternatively, if children had their way, we might close down the publishing industry and switch the resources into producing games. This case is shown as possibility *g*.

FIGURE 3.2

The Production Possibility Frontier for Books and Video Games

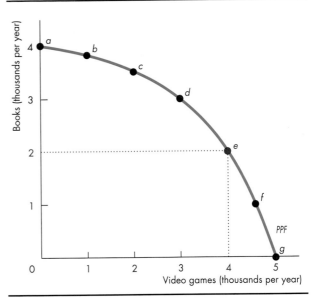

Possibility	Games (thousands of games)		Books (thousands of books)
a	0.0	and	4.0
b	1.0	and	3.8
c	2.0	and	3.5
d	3.0	and	3.0
e	4.0	and	2.0
f	4.6	and	1.0
g	5.0	and	0.0

The figure shows the production possibility frontier for books and video games, holding constant the production of all other goods and services. The *PPF* is bowed outward because resources are not equally productive in all activities. Production is at point *e* – 2,000 books and 4,000 games a year. If more resources are used to produce games, a small increase in the quantity of games produced is achieved at the cost of a large decrease in the quantity of books produced. Similarly, if more resources are allocated to books, a relatively small increase in the quantity of books is achieved at the cost of a large decrease in the quantity of games produced.

The quantity of books produced decreases to zero, and the quantity of games produced increases to 5,000 a year.

The Shape of the Frontier

Notice the shape of the production possibility frontier in Fig. 3.2. When a large quantity of books and a small quantity of games are produced – between points *a* and *d* – the frontier has a gentle slope. When a large quantity of games and a small quantity of books are produced – between points *e* and *f* – the frontier is steep. The whole frontier bows outward.

These features of the production possibility frontier are a reflection of the fact that not all resources are equally productive in all activities. Game inventors and programmers can work on books, so if they switch from making games to producing books – moving along the frontier from *e* to *a* – the production of books increases. But these people are not as good at producing books as the original publishing industry workers. So for a small increase in the quantity of books produced, the production of games falls a lot.

Similarly, publishing industry workers can produce games, but they are not as good at this activity as the people currently making games. So when publishing industry workers switch to producing games, the quantity of games produced increases by only a small amount and the quantity of books produced falls a lot.

Measuring Opportunity Cost

We can measure the opportunity cost of books and of games by using the production possibility frontier in Fig. 3.2. To do so, we calculate how many books must be given up to get more games and how many games must be given up to get more books. Figure 3.3 and its tables illustrates the calculation.

If all the available resources are used to produce books, 4,000 books and no games are produced. If we decide to produce 1,000 games, how many books do we have to give up? You can work out the answer in Fig. 3.2. To produce 1,000 games, we move from *a* to *b* and the quantity of books decreases by 200 to 3,800 a year. So the opportunity cost of the first 1,000 games is 200 books. If we decide to produce an additional 1,000 games, how many books must we give up? This time, we move from *b* to *c* and the quantity of books decreases by 300.

Figure 3.3(a) illustrates these opportunity costs. The first two rows of the table set out the opportunity costs that we have just calculated. The table also lists the opportunity costs of producing

an additional 1,000 games by moving along the production possibility frontier of Fig. 3.2 from *c* to *d*, from *d* to *e*, and from *e* to *g*. You might want to work out another example on your own to be sure that you understand this calculation. Calculate the opportunity cost of moving from *e* to *g*.

We've just worked out the opportunity cost of books. We can use the same idea to calculate the opportunity cost of games. If all the resources are used to produce games, we produce 5,000 a year and have no books. If we decide to produce 1,000 books, how many games must we give up? Again, you can work out the answer by using the information in Fig. 3.2. To produce 1,000 books, we move from *g* to *f* and the quantity of games decreases by 400 to 4,600 a year. So the opportunity cost of the first 1,000 books is 400 games. If we decide to produce an additional 1,000 books a year, how many games must we give up? This time, we move from *f* to *e* and the quantity of games decreases by 600.

Figure 3.3(b) shows these opportunity costs. The first two rows of table (b) show the opportunity costs that we have just calculated. The table also lists the opportunity costs of producing an additional 1,000 books by moving along the production possibility frontier of from *e* to *d* and from *d* to *a*. You might want to work out another example on your own to be sure that you understand what is going on. Calculate the opportunity cost of moving from *d* to *a*.

Opportunity Cost is a Ratio

The opportunity cost of producing one additional unit of a good is a ratio. It is the decrease in the quantity produced of one good divided by the increase in the quantity produced of another good as we move along the production possibility frontier. For example, in Fig. 3.3, the opportunity cost of one of the first 1,000 books is the decrease in the quantity of games, 400, divided by the increase in the quantity of books, 1,000. That is, the opportunity cost of 1 book is 0.4 games.

Because opportunity cost is a ratio, the opportunity cost of producing good *X* (the quantity of units of good *Y* forgone) is always equal to the inverse of the opportunity cost of producing good *Y* (the number of units of good *X* forgone). Let's check this proposition by returning once more to Fig. 3.3. To increase the production of games from 4,600 to 5,000, an increase of 400, the quantity of

FIGURE 3.3

Increasing Opportunity Cost

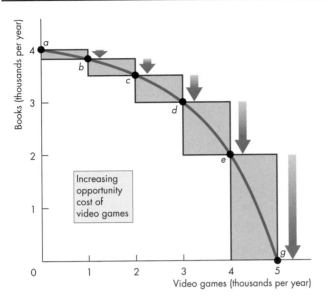

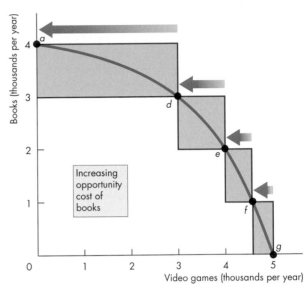

(a) Opportunity cost of video games

a) As the production of games increases:

First 1,000 games cost 200 books

Second 1,000 games cost 300 books

Third 1,000 games cost 500 books

Fourth 1,000 games cost 1,000 books

Fifth 1,000 games cost 2,000 books

(b) Opportunity cost of books

b) As the production of books increases:

First 1,000 books cost 400 games

Second 1,000 books cost 600 games

Third 1,000 books cost 1,000 games

Fourth 1,000 books cost 3,000 games

The tables record the opportunity costs of games and books, and the graphs illustrate the opportunity costs by the bars and arrows. In part (a), the opportunity cost of games increases from 200 books for the first 1,000 games to 2,000 books for the fifth 1,000 games. In part (b), the opportunity cost of books increases from 400 games for the first 1,000 books to 3,000 games for the fourth 1,000 books.

---

books must decrease from 1,000 to zero. The opportunity cost of the extra 400 games is 1,000 books, or 2.5 books per game. So, the opportunity cost of 1 book is 0.4 games and the opportunity cost of 1 game is 2.5 books (1/0.4 = 2.5).

Increasing Opportunity Costs are Everywhere

Increasing opportunity cost and the bowed-out production possibility frontier are two different ways of expressing the same idea: resources are not equally productive in all activities. Just about every

activity that you can think of is one with *increasing* opportunity cost. Two examples are producing food and producing health care. We allocate the most skilful farmers and the most fertile land to producing food. We allocate the best doctors and less fertile land to producing health care. If we shift fertile land and tractors away from farming and ask farmers to become hospital workers, the production of food drops drastically and the increase in the production of health-care services is small. The opportunity cost of a unit of health-care services rises. Similarly, if we shift our resources away from health care towards farming, we must use more doctors and nurses as farmers and more hospitals as hydroponic tomato factories. The decrease in the production of health-care services is large, but the increase in food production is small. The opportunity cost of producing a unit of food rises.

This example is extreme and unlikely, but the same considerations apply to any pair of goods or services that you can imagine: housing and diamonds, wheelchairs and golf carts, private sector or government health care. Given our limited resources, producing more of one thing always means producing less of something else, and because resources are not equally productive in all activities, the more of anything that we produce, the higher is its opportunity cost. *Reading Between the Lines* on pp 62–63 explores the opportunity cost of government services.

R E V I E W

◆ The *PPF* is bowed outward, and the opportunity cost of producing a good increases as more of it is produced.

◆ The shape of the frontier and increasing opportunity cost arise from the fact that resources are not equally productive in all activities and the resources most suitable for any given activity are the first to be used.

We've seen how the production possibility frontier shows the limits to production and measures opportunity cost; now we'll study what forces make production possibilities grow.

Economic Growth

The production possibility frontier that defines the boundary between what is attainable and what is unattainable is not static. It is constantly changing. Sometimes the production possibility frontier shifts *inward*, reducing our production possibilities. For example, when an earthquake hit Japan in 1995, the road system was damaged and so could not handle as many cars as before the earthquake. Resources were destroyed,

and the production possibility frontier shifted inward. At other times, the frontier shifts outward. For example, as the quake-damaged roads in Japan were restored, production possibilities expanded and the frontier shifted outward.

Over the years, our production possibilities have undergone enormous expansion. The expansion of our production possibilities is called **economic growth**. As a consequence of economic growth, we can now produce much more than we could 100 years ago and quite a bit more than even 10 years ago. By 2010, if the same pace of growth continues, our production possibilities will be even greater. By pushing out the frontier, can we avoid the constraints imposed on us by our limited resources? Can we avoid opportunity costs? Is the economists' quip about there being no free lunches wrong?

The Cost of Shifting the Frontier

We are going to discover that although we can and do shift the production possibility frontier outward over time, we cannot have economic growth without incurring costs. The faster the pace of economic growth, the more we have in the future but the less we can consume at the present time. Let's investigate the costs of growth by examining why economies grow and how the choice between the future and the present is made.

The two key factors that influence economic growth are technological progress and capital accumulation. **Technological progress** is the development of new and better ways of producing goods and services and the development of new goods. **Capital accumulation** is the growth of capital resources. As a consequence of technological progress and capital accumulation, we have an enormous quantity of cars and aircraft that enable us to transport more than when we had only horses and carriages; we have satellites that make transcontinental communications possible on a scale much larger than that produced by the earlier cable technology. But to develop new technologies and accumulate capital we must bear an opportunity cost. That opportunity cost is a decrease in the quantity of consumption goods and services because resources are used in research and development as well as to make new machines and other forms of capital. To understand these opportunity costs, let's return to the Best Jeans factory.

Technological Change and Capital Accumulation

Given its resources, the Best Jeans factory can produce 5,000 jeans a week. But Best Jeans' workers do not have to produce jeans. They can do other activities instead. For example, they can spend some of their time installing cutting and sewing machines.

Suppose that the owner of Best Jeans spends part of his working time keeping abreast of the latest developments in jeans-making technology. One day, he discovers a recent *technological change* that he can use in his factory. To implement his idea, he must get some of his workers to stop making jeans and to work on installing new computer-controlled cutting and sewing machines that use the new technology – *capital accumulation*.

Best Jeans production possibilities for jeans and machines are shown in Fig. 3.4. Its production possibility frontier initially is the blue curve *abc*. If Best Jeans Company devotes no resources to installing machines, it produces at point *a*. If it devotes one-fifth of its capacity to installing machines, it produces 4,000 jeans and installs 1 machine at point *b*. If it produces no jeans, it installs 2 machines at point *c*.

If Best Jeans produces at point *a* in Fig. 3.4, it remains stuck on the blue production possibility frontier. But if it moves to point *b* in Fig. 3.4 and installs 1 machine, Best Jeans increases its future production possibilities. An increase in the number of machines enables Best Jeans to produce more jeans. As a consequence, its production possibility frontier rotates outward as shown by the arrow. Best Jeans experiences economic growth.

The amount by which Best Jeans' production possibilities expand depends on how much of its resources it devotes to technological change and capital accumulation. If it devotes no resources to this activity, the frontier remains at *abc* – the original blue curve. If it cuts the current production of jeans and installs 1 machine (point *b*), then its frontier moves out in the future to the position shown by the red curve in Fig. 3.4. The fewer resources it devotes to current production of jeans and the more resources it devotes to installing machines, the greater is the expansion of its production possibilities.

But economic growth is not free for Best Jeans. To make it happen, it devotes more resources to installing new machines and less to producing jeans. Economic growth is no magic formula for

FIGURE 3.4

Economic Growth in a Jeans Factory

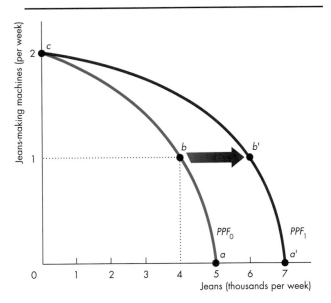

If Best Jeans devotes all its resources to producing jeans, it installs no new machines and it produces 5,000 jeans a week (point *a*). If it devotes sufficient resources to installing 1 new machine, its jeans' production falls to 4,000 a week (point *b*). But when the new machine is in place, Best Jeans can increase its production to a point on the red *PPF*. For example, if it returns to using all its resources to produce jeans, it can produce at point *a'* (7,000 a week). If it continues to devote resources to installing 1 additional machine, it can produce at point *b'* (6,000 jeans a week). So by installing machines, Best Jeans can shift its *PPF* outward. But it cannot avoid opportunity cost. To shift the frontier outward and increase its future production possibilities, Best Jeans must decrease its current production of jeans.

abolishing scarcity. Also, on the new production possibility frontier, Best Jeans continues to face opportunity costs.

The ideas about economic growth that we have explored in the setting of a denim jeans factory also apply to individual households and to nations. Let's see why.

The Economic Growth of Households

To expand its production possibilities, a family must forgo current consumption and devote resources to accumulating capital. It can accumulate claims to the income from real capital or it can accumulate human capital. For example, by forgoing current consumption and undertaking full-time schooling, members of a household can increase their earning potential and increase their future consumption.

The Economic Growth of Nations

If as a nation we devote all our resources to producing food, clothing, housing, vacations and other consumer goods and none to research, development and the accumulation of capital, we will have no more capital and no better technologies in the future than we have at present. Our production possibilities in the future will be the same as today. To expand our production possibilities in the future, we must produce fewer consumption goods today. The resources that we free up today enable us to accumulate capital and to develop better technologies for producing consumption goods in

the future. The decrease in the output of consumption goods today is the opportunity cost of economic growth and the attainment of more consumption goods in the future.

The experiences of the European Union and some East Asian economies, such as Hong Kong, provide a striking example of the effects of our choices on the rate of economic growth. In 1960, the production possibilities per person in the European Union (then the European Economic Community) were much larger than those in Hong Kong (see Fig. 3.5). The European Union devoted one-fifth of its resources to accumulating capital and the other four-fifths to consumption, as illustrated by point *a* in Fig. 3.5(a). But Hong Kong devoted more than one-third of its resources to accumulating capital and less than two-thirds to consumption, as illustrated by point *a* in Fig. 3.5(b). Both areas experienced economic growth, but growth in Hong Kong since 1960 has been much more rapid than in the European Union because

---

FIGURE 3.5

Economic Growth in the European Union and Hong Kong

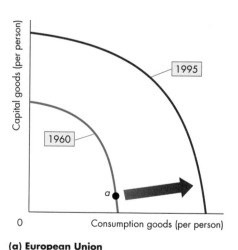

(a) European Union

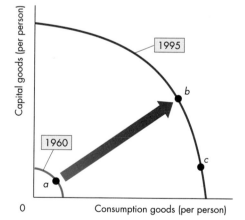

(b) Hong Kong

In 1960, the production possibilities per person in the European Union, the blue line in part (a), were much larger than those in Hong Kong, the blue line in part (b). But Hong Kong devoted a larger share of its resources to accumulating capital, than the European Union – point *a* in each part

of the figure. By 1995, the two production possibilities per person had become similar. If Hong Kong can continue to produce at point *b* on its 1995 frontier, it might overtake the European Union.

Hong Kong devotes a bigger fraction of its resources to accumulating capital.

If Hong Kong continues to devote such a large proportion of its resources to accumulating capital (point *b* on its 1995 production possibility frontier), its economy will probably continue to grow more rapidly than the economies of the European Union. Its production possibility frontier will move out beyond that of the European Union. If Hong Kong increases its consumption and decreases its capital accumulation (moving to point *c* on its 1995 production possibility frontier), then its rate of economic expansion will slow down to a rate similar to that in Europe.

Hong Kong has been the fastest-growing East Asian economy, but others, such as Singapore, Taiwan, South Korea and recently China, have performed similarly to Hong Kong and they too are closing the gap on the European Union.

REVIEW

♦ Economic growth results from technological change and capital accumulation.

♦ The opportunity cost of faster economic growth is a decrease in current consumption.

♦ By decreasing current consumption, we can devote more resources to developing new technologies and accumulating capital and can speed up the rate of economic growth.

Gains from Trade

People can produce for themselves all the goods that they consume or they can concentrate on producing one good (or perhaps a few goods) and then trade with others – exchange some of their own products for the products of others. Concentrating on the production of only one good or a few goods is called *specialization*. We are going to discover how people gain by specializing in the production of the good in which they have a *comparative advantage* and trading with each other.

Comparative Advantage

A person has a **comparative advantage** in an activity if that person can perform the activity at a lower opportunity cost than anyone else. Differences in opportunity costs arise from differences in individual abilities and from differences in the characteristics of other resources.

No one excels at everything. One person is an outstanding sales person but a poor investor; another person is a brilliant lawyer but a poor teacher. In almost all human endeavours, what one person does easily, someone else finds difficult. The same applies to land and capital. One plot of land is fertile but has no mineral deposits; another plot of land has outstanding views but is infertile. One machine has great precision but is difficult to operate; another machine is fast but often breaks down.

Although no one excels at everything, some people excel and can outperform others in many activities. But such a person does not have a comparative advantage in every activity. For example, a UK author, John Mortimer, is a better lawyer than most people. But he is an even better writer of humorous books and television scripts. His comparative advantage is writing.

Differences in individual abilities and differences in the quality of other resources mean that there are differences in individual opportunity costs of producing various goods. Such differences give rise to comparative advantage. Let's use the production possibility frontier model of the jeans factory to look at the idea of comparative advantage.

We've seen that the owner can allocate employees' time between producing jeans or installing machines. However, another choice would be to modify existing machines to produce other goods. Suppose that one of these goods is denim skirts. Also, suppose that the factory's production possibility frontier for jeans and skirts is shown in Fig. 3.6(a). As we already know from Fig. 3.1, if all the resources are used to make jeans, output will be 5,000 jeans a week. The blue *PPF* curve in Fig. 3.6(a) tells us that if all the resources are used to make skirts, the factory makes 10,000 skirts a week. But to produce skirts, production of jeans must decrease. For each 1,000 skirts produced, production of jeans must fall by 500. The opportunity cost of producing 1 skirt at Best Jeans is 0.5 jeans.

Similarly, if the owner of Best Jeans wants to increase production of jeans, production of skirts must fall. For each 1,000 jeans produced, production of skirts must fall by 2,000. So the opportunity cost of producing 1 pair of jeans at Best Jeans is 2 skirts.

Suppose there is a similar competing factory called Euro Denim Company, which also produces skirts and jeans. Euro Denim's factory has machines that are custom-made for skirt production, so they are more suitable for producing skirts than jeans. Also, Euro Denim's work-force is more accustomed to making skirts.

This difference between the two factories means that Euro Denim's production possibility frontier – shown by the blue curve in Fig. 3.6(b) – is different from Best Jeans'. If Euro Denim uses all its resources to make skirts, the factory produces 25,000 skirts a week. If all the resources are used to make jeans, the factory produces 2,000 jeans a week. To produce jeans, of course, Euro Denim must decrease production of skirts. For each 1,000 additional jeans produced, Euro Denim must reduce production of skirts by 12,500. Euro Denim's opportunity cost of producing 1 pair of jeans is 12.5 skirts.

Similarly, if the owner of Euro Denim wants to increase production of skirts, production of jeans must fall. For each 1,000 additional skirts produced, production of jeans falls by 80. So Euro Denim's opportunity cost of producing 1 skirt is 0.08 jeans.

Suppose that the owners of both factories decide to diversify by producing both jeans and skirts. Best Jeans and Euro Denim each produce the same quantities of skirts and jeans. That is, they each produce at point *a* on their respective production possibility frontiers. At this point each produces 1,400 jeans and 7,100 skirts. Their total production is 2,800 jeans and 14,200 skirts.

In which of the two goods does Euro Denim have a comparative advantage? Recall that comparative advantage is a situation in which one person's opportunity cost of producing a good is less than another person's opportunity cost of producing the same good. You can see the comparative advantage by looking at the production possibility frontiers for Euro Denim and Best Jeans in Fig. 3.6. Euro Denim's production possibility frontier is steeper than Best Jeans'. To produce one more skirt, Euro Denim gives up fewer jeans than Best Jeans. Hence Euro Denim's opportunity cost of a skirt is less than Best Jeans'. This means that Euro Denim has a comparative advantage in producing skirts.

Notice the production possibility frontier for Best Jeans is flatter than Euro Denim's. This means that Best Jeans gives up fewer skirts to produce one more pair of jeans than Euro Denim does. Best Jeans' opportunity cost of producing jeans is less than Euro Denim's, so Best Jeans has a comparative advantage in jeans production.

Achieving the Gains from Trade

If the owner of Best Jeans, who has a comparative advantage in jeans production, puts all available resources into jeans production, the factory can produce 5,000 jeans a week – point *b* on his *PPF*. If the owner of Euro Denim, who has a comparative advantage in skirt production, puts all available resources into skirt production, the factory can produce 25,000 skirts a week – point *b* on her *PPF*. By specializing, Best Jeans and Euro Denim together can produce a total of 5,000 jeans and 25,000 skirts a week.

To achieve the gains from specialization, Best Jeans and Euro Denim must trade with each other. Suppose they agree to the following deal. Each week, Euro Denim produces 25,000 skirts and Best Jeans produces 5,000 jeans. Euro Denim supplies Best Jeans with 12,500 skirts in exchange for 2,500 jeans. With this deal in place, Best Jeans and Euro Denim move along the red 'Trade line' to point *c*. At this point, each has 12,500 skirts and 2,500 jeans – an additional 1,100 jeans and an additional 5,400 skirts. These are the gains from specialization and trade, and both the parties to the trade share the gains.

Euro Denim, which produces jeans at an opportunity cost of 12.5 skirts a pair, can buy jeans from Best Jeans for a price of 5 skirts a pair. Best Jeans, which produces skirts at an opportunity cost of 0.5 jeans a skirt, can buy skirts from Euro Denim at a price of 0.2 jeans a skirt. Euro Denim buys jeans more cheaply than its opportunity cost of producing them and Best Jeans buys skirts more cheaply than its opportunity cost of producing them. By specialization and exchange, both factories get quantities of skirts and jeans that are *outside* their individual production possibility frontiers.

Absolute Advantage

We've seen that Best Jeans has a comparative advantage in producing jeans and Euro Denim has a

FIGURE 3.6

The Gains from Specialization and Trade

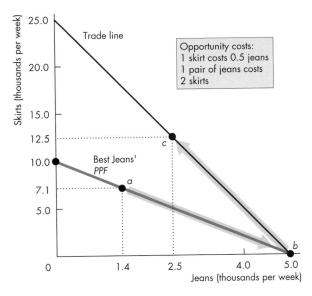

(a) Best Jeans' factory

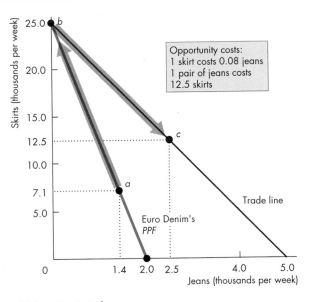

(b) Euro Denim's factory

Best Jeans (part a) and Euro Denim (part b) each produce at point *a* on their respective *PPF*. For Best Jeans, the opportunity cost of 1 pair of jeans is 2 skirts and the opportunity cost of 1 skirt is 0.5 jeans. For Euro Denim the opportunity cost of 1 pair of jeans is 12.5 skirts – higher than Best Jeans' and the opportunity cost of 1 skirt is 0.08 jeans – lower than Best Jeans'. Euro Denim has a comparative advantage in skirts and Best Jeans has a comparative advantage in jeans.

If Euro Denim specializes in skirts and Best Jeans specializes in jeans, they each produce at point *b* on their respective *PPF*. They then exchange skirts for jeans along the red 'Trade line'. Euro Denim buys jeans from Best Jeans for less than its opportunity cost of producing them, and Best Jeans buys skirts from Euro Denim for less than its opportunity cost of producing them. They each go to point *c* – a point outside their *PPF* – where a total of 2,500 jeans and 12,500 skirts are produced per week.

comparative advantage in producing skirts. We've also seen that Best Jeans can produce a larger quantity of jeans than Euro Denim, and Euro Denim can produce a larger quantity of skirts than Best Jeans. Neither factory can produce more of both goods than the other.

If one person can produce more of both goods than another person that person is said to have an **absolute advantage** in the production of both goods. In our example, neither factory has an absolute advantage.

It is tempting to suppose that when a person (factory or country) has an absolute advantage, it is not possible to benefit from specialization and exchange. But this line of reasoning is wrong. To see why, let's look again at the model of the two

factories. Suppose that the owner of Euro Denim invents and patents a production process that makes the factory four times as productive as before. With the new technology, Euro Denim can produce 100,000 skirts a week (4 times the original 25,000) if all available resources go into that activity. Alternatively, the factory can produce 8,000 jeans (4 times the original 2,000) if all the resources go into that activity. Notice that Euro Denim now has an absolute advantage in producing both goods.

We have already worked out that the gains from specialization arise when each person specializes in producing the good in which he or she has a *comparative* advantage. Recall that a person has a comparative advantage in producing a particular good if that person can produce the good at a *lower opportunity cost* than anyone else. Best Jeans' opportunity costs remain exactly the same as they were before. What has happened to Euro Denim's opportunity costs now that the factory has become four times as productive?

You can work out Euro Denim's opportunity costs by doing exactly the same calculation as before. You can see that the opportunity costs have not changed. Euro Denim can produce four times as much of both goods as before. But to increase the production of jeans by 1,000 along the new production possibility frontier, production of skirts must fall by 12,500, so the opportunity cost of 1 pair of jeans is still 12.5 skirts. To increase the production of skirts by 1,000, production of jeans must fall by 80, so the opportunity cost of 1 skirt is 0.08 jeans.

When Euro Denim becomes four times as productive as before, each unit of resources produces more output, but the opportunity costs remain the same. To produce one more pair of jeans costs the same in terms of the quantity of skirts forgone as it did previously. Since neither factory's opportunity costs have changed, Euro Denim continues to have a comparative advantage in producing skirts and Best Jeans continues to have a comparative advantage in producing jeans. So both factories continue to gain by specialization and trade.

The key point to recognize is that it is not possible for anyone, even someone who has an absolute advantage, to have a comparative advantage in everything. So gains from specialization and trade are always available.

Dynamic Comparative Advantage

Comparative advantage is not a static concept. At any given point in time, the resources available and the technologies in use determine the comparative advantages that individuals and countries have. But as technological change and capital accumulation shift the production possibility frontiers outward, so comparative advantages change. Also, people get better at doing what they do repeatedly. Just by repeatedly producing a particular good or service, people can become more productive in that activity, a phenomenon called **learning-by-doing**. Learning-by-doing is the basis of dynamic comparative advantage. **Dynamic comparative advantage** is a comparative advantage that an individual (factory or country) possesses as a result of having specialized

in a particular activity and through learning-by-doing, gained the lowest opportunity cost.

Dynamic comparative advantage applies to individuals, firms and countries. Some people have a steep 'learning curve' – they initially do not seem to be much different from anyone else but through practice and hard work they become outstanding in some activity. Boeing, the world's largest maker of wide-bodied jet aircraft, has pursued dynamic comparative advantage. As Boeing's work-force and management have gained experience in building wide-bodied aircraft, they have successively lowered costs and strengthened their comparative advantage. Singapore, South Korea, Hong Kong and Taiwan are examples of countries that have pursued dynamic comparative advantage vigorously. They have developed industries in which initially they might not have had a comparative advantage and, through learning-by-doing, have become low opportunity cost producers of high-technology products. A recent example is the decision of Singapore to develop a genetic engineering industry. It is not clear that Singapore has a comparative advantage in this activity at present, but it might acquire one as its scientists and production workers become more skilled in this area.

R E V I E W

- Production increases if people specialize in the activity in which they have a comparative advantage.
- A person has a comparative advantage in producing a good if that person's opportunity cost of producing the good is lower than everyone else's.
- Differences in opportunity cost are the source of gains from specialization and trade.
- If a person can produce more of all goods than someone else, then that person has an absolute advantage but does not have a comparative advantage in producing all goods.
- Even persons with an absolute advantage gain by specializing in the activities in which they have a comparative advantage and trading.
- Dynamic comparative advantage can result from specialization and learning-by-doing.

The Evolution of Trading Arrangements

Transactions Costs

Individuals and countries can gain by specializing in the production of those goods and services in which they have a comparative advantage. But to reap the gains from trade from billions of people specializing in millions of different activities, trade must be organized. Buyers and sellers need information and they face opportunity costs for the time taken in the trading activity. The costs of trading and negotiating are called **transactions costs**. If transactions costs are high, markets will not work smoothly. Organizing trade through social arrangements is the main way of reducing transactions costs. The most important of these social arrangements are:

◆ Markets
◆ Property rights
◆ Money

Markets

We defined a *market* in Chapter 1 as any set-up that enables buyers and sellers to get information and to do business with each other. Markets might be physical locations, such as a wholesale meat or fish market. Or they might be electronic links, such as the world oil market.

But all markets share a common feature. They link the producers and the consumers of goods and services together. Sometimes these links are direct – as in the market for haircuts – and sometimes they are indirect and involve many layers of producers of services and traders – as in the market for milk.

Markets reduce transactions costs by pooling an enormous amount of information about the plans of buyers and sellers and summarizing this information in just one number, a *price*. The price moves in response to the sum of the decisions of the buyers and sellers. It rises when there is a shortage and it falls when there is a relative abundance.

The price sends a signal to buyers and sellers. All potential buyers or sellers know their own opportunity cost of producing a good or service. By comparing this opportunity cost with the market price, each person can decide whether to become a buyer or a seller. Someone who can produce a good (or service) at an opportunity cost that is less than the market price can gain from producing and selling that good (or service). Someone who can produce a good at an opportunity cost that is greater than the market price can gain by buying the good rather than producing it.

Markets are one of the social arrangements that enable people to specialize and gain from the increased production that results from specialization.

Property Rights

Property rights are social arrangements that govern the ownership, use and disposal of factors of production and goods and services. *Real property* includes land and buildings – the things we call property in ordinary speech – and durable goods such as plant and equipment. *Financial property* includes stocks and bonds and money in the bank. *Intellectual property* is the intangible product of creative effort. This type of property includes books, music, computer programs and inventions of all kinds, and it is protected by copyrights and patents. Property rights – ownership rights – are defined and enforced through the legal system and police forces.

With no property rights, or with weakly enforced property rights, the incentive to specialize and produce the goods in which each person has a comparative advantage is weakened and some of the potential gains from specialization and trade are lost. If people can take possession of whatever they want – steal – then a good deal of society's time, energy and resources must be devoted to protection rather than production. This is inefficient. Transactions costs to trading will be higher than they would be if property rights were well established.

Establishing property rights is one of the greatest challenges facing Russia and other East European countries as they seek to develop market economies. In countries where property rights are well established, such as in West European countries, upholding intellectual property rights is still proving a challenge. Modern technologies make it relatively easy to violate property rights in audio and video material, computer programs and books. The Internet allows access to an ever-increasing source of public information.

Money

Markets and property rights enable people to specialize and trade their output. But how do people trade? There are two possible ways:

1. Barter
2. Monetary exchange

Barter   **Barter** is the direct exchange of one good or service for another. This method of trading severely limits the amount of exchange that takes place. Imagine that you have oranges but you want to get apples. You look for someone with apples who wants oranges. Economists call this a *double coincidence of wants* – when person A wants to sell exactly what person B wants to buy, and person B wants to sell exactly what person A wants to buy. Because this situation does not arise frequently, the transactions costs to trade are high in a barter system. Another way of trading by barter is to undertake a sequence of exchanges. Failing to find someone with apples who wants oranges, you might trade oranges for plums, plums for pomegranates, pomegranates for pineapples and then eventually pineapples for apples.

Although it is a cumbersome way of doing business, quite a large amount of barter still takes place. For example, before the recent changes in Eastern Europe, hairdressers in Warsaw, Poland, obtained their hairdressing equipment from England in exchange for hair clippings that they supplied to London wigmakers. Today, Australian meat processors swap cans of meat for Russian salmon, crab-meat and scallops; Australian wool growers swap wool for Russian electrical motors.

Barter has high transactions costs and is inefficient, so a better alternative has evolved.

Monetary Exchange   *Monetary exchange* is a system of trading in which a commodity, or token, that we call *money* serves as the means of payment and the medium of exchange. Money reduces transactions costs and makes millions of transactions possible that otherwise would not be worth undertaking. Imagine the chain of barter transactions you'd have to go through every day to get your coffee, Coke, textbooks, lecturer's time, lunch and all the other goods and services you consume. In a monetary exchange system, you exchange your time and effort for money and use that money to buy the goods and services you consume, cutting out the incredible hassle you'd face each day in a world of barter.

Metals such as gold, silver and copper have long served as money. Most commonly, they serve as money by being stamped as coins. Primitive societies have traditionally used commodities such as seashells as money. During the American Civil War, and for several years thereafter, people used postage stamps as money. Prisoners of war in German camps in World War II used cigarettes as money. Using cigarettes as a medium of exchange should not be confused with barter. When cigarettes play the role of money, smokers and non-smokers buy and sell goods by using cigarettes as a means of payment. Any commodity can be used as money if it is durable, easily divisible and accepted as a form of payment.

In modern societies, governments provide paper money. The banking system also provides money in the form of current accounts. Current accounts can be used for settling debts simply by writing an instruction – writing a cheque – to the bank requesting that funds be transferred to another current account. Electronic links between bank accounts, which are now becoming more widespread, enable direct transfers between different accounts without any cheques being written.

◆ ◆ ◆ ◆ You have now begun to see how economists go about the job of trying to answer economic questions. The fact of scarcity and the associated concept of opportunity cost allow us to understand why people specialize, why they trade with each other and why they have developed social arrangements such as markets, property rights, and money. One simple fact, scarcity, and its direct implications, choice and opportunity cost, explain so much!

SUMMARY

The Production Possibility Frontier

Production, which is the conversion of factors of production into goods and services, is limited by the resources available and by technology. The production possibility frontier is the boundary between production levels that are attainable and those that are not attainable when all the available resources are being used to their limit. Production can take place at any point on or inside the production possibility frontier, but it is not possible to produce outside the frontier. Points on the production possibility frontier are efficient and points inside the frontier are inefficient. Along the production possibility frontier, the opportunity cost of producing more of one good is the amount of the other good that must be given up. Opportunity cost is inescapable and confronts people with trade-offs.(pp. 46–48)

Increasing Opportunity Cost

Opportunity cost is measured as the increase in the quantity of one good divided by the decrease in the quantity of the other good as we move along the production possibility frontier. As the quantity produced of a good increases, so does the opportunity cost of producing it. This means the shape of the production possibility frontier is bowed outward. The production possibility frontier is bowed outward and opportunity cost increases because resources are not equally productive in all activities and the most suitable resources for a given activity are used first in that activity. That is, factors of production are allocated efficiently by being assigned to the tasks for which they are the best available match. As the economy moves along its production possibility frontier, producing more of one good and less of another, factors of production are assigned to tasks for which they are an increasingly poor match. (pp. 49–52)

Economic Growth

The production possibility frontier changes over time, partly because of natural forces, for example earthquakes, and partly because of the choices that we make about what to produce and consume, how much research and development to undertake and how much capital to accumulate. If we use some of today's resources for research and development and to produce capital goods, we can produce more goods and services in the future – the economy grows. But growth cannot take place without incurring costs. The opportunity cost of economic growth (of more goods and services in the future) is consuming fewer goods and services in the present. (pp. 52–55)

Gains from Trade

A person has a comparative advantage in producing a good if that person can produce the good at a lower opportunity cost than everyone else. Production can be increased if people specialize in the activity at which they have a comparative advantage. People produce the good or service for which their opportunity cost is less than everyone else's and goods produced at the lowest possible opportunity cost are exchanged – traded.

When a person is more productive than another person – is able to produce more output from fewer inputs – that person has an absolute advantage. But having an absolute advantage does not mean there are no gains from specialization and trade. Even if someone is more productive than other people in all activities, as long as the other person has a lower opportunity cost of some good, then gains from specialization and trade are available.

Comparative advantage changes over time and dynamic comparative advantage arises from learning-by-doing. (pp.55–58)

The Evolution of Trading Arrangements

Exchange in the real world involves the specialization of billions of people in millions of different activities. To make it worthwhile for each individual to specialize and to enable societies to reap the gains from trade, social arrangements have evolved. The most important of these are markets, property rights and money. These arrangements enable people to specialize, exchanging factors of production and goods and services for money, and money for factors of production and goods and services. They reduce the transactions costs associated with trading and encourage the gains from specialization and trade. (pp. 59–60)

Opportunity Cost: The Black Economy

The Essence of the Story

THE SUNDAY TIMES, 31 MARCH 1996

Moonlighters cheat taxman out of £85 billion

David Smith, Economics Editor

Britain's black economy, the amount of 'moonlighting' that escapes the attention of the taxman, is worth between £70 billion and £85 billion a year, significantly more than previously thought, according to new estimates.

The black economy covers a wide range of activities from tradesmen who insist on being paid in cash to car boot sales. It also takes in smuggling of low-duty tobacco and alcohol on the 'Calais run', prostitution and sophisticated tax evasion and, of course, the huge demand for domestic cleaners....

The new estimates show that the black economy is worth between 10% and 12% of Britain's national income or gross domestic product (GDP). Official estimates by the Inland Revenue had suggested that it ranged between 6% and 8% of GDP.

Tax cuts were supposed to put an end to the black economy by reducing the incentive to stay outside the tax system. Instead, the evidence is that the government, and those who do pay tax, are losing out through a reduced take and because many who moonlight are also receiving social security benefits....

One theory is that rises in VAT under the Tories, from 8% to 15% in 1979, and from 15% to 17.5% five years ago, may have tipped the balance in favour of black economy activity, by providing a bigger incentive not to pay the tax.

A growing black economy also explains the puzzle in Britain's unemployment figures. The jobless total has fallen by 750,000 over the past three years but recorded unemployment has risen by fewer than 500,000....

Britain has some way to go before catching up with Italy where as much as a third of economic activity is hidden. When the authorities included some of this black economy in the official data in a gambit known as Il Sorpasso (The Overtaking), the size of the official economy was boosted by 16%.

Britain's black economy is:

❏ As big as Portugal's economy and twice the size of those of Ireland and New Zealand.

❏ At least as big as the Treasury's annual receipts from income tax (£70 billion).

❏ Equivalent to the combined amount the government spends on education and health.

❏ Enough to pay out a weekly national jackpot of £10m for the next 150 years.

■ The black economy – or moonlighting – is worth between £70 billion and £85 billion in the United Kingdom.

■ New estimates suggest the black economy is equivalent to between 10 and 12 per cent of national output.

■ The black economy may have grown because increased VAT rates raise tax payments for low-paid workers.

■ When Italy included the value of the black economy in its official figures, the value of national output shot up, and Italy leaped ahead of the United Kingdom in the international economic rankings.

Economic Analysis

■ The total value of the United Kingdom's output is measured in official government statistics as gross domestic product, GDP, which is a combination of private sector output and government sector output.

■ Most government output – the welfare state, road building and other goods and services – is paid for through taxation. The opportunity cost of government output is private sector output forgone through tax payment.

■ The payoff from government output is the value of goods and services which the private sector would not supply and the extra output possible in a more fair and stable economic environment. Figure 1 shows this opportunity cost and payoff.

■ By selecting point *a* on the blue *PPF*, the UK electorate chose

to decrease private sector output from £700 billion to £440 billion and pay £260 billion in tax. The red *PPF* shows the expanded possibilities with government output in the following year.

■ If taxes are too high, some people operate in the black economy. Official figures do not count this output and an estimated £40 billion of tax revenue is lost.

■ Figure 2 shows the current official position at point *a* on the blue *PPF*. The real value of private sector output is 10 per cent higher at £770 billion pounds on the red *PPF* when the black economy is included.

■ With lower VAT rates, the electorate could choose point *b* on the red *PPF*, generating £40 billion of tax revenue and a higher value of national output.

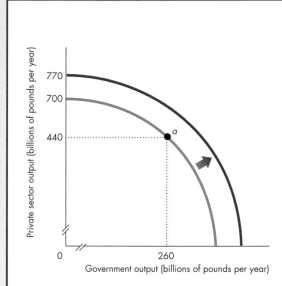

Figure 1

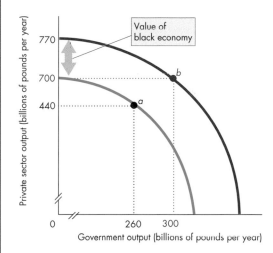

Figure 2

KEY ELEMENTS

Key Terms

Absolute advantage, 57
Barter, 60
Capital accumulation, 52
Comparative advantage, 55
Dynamic comparative advantage, 58
Economic growth, 52
Efficiency, 47
Environmental capital, 46
Human capital, 46
Learning-by-doing, 58
Production possibility frontier, 46
Property rights, 59
Technological progress, 52
Trade-off, 47
Transactions costs, 59

◆ Key Figures

Figure 3.1   The Production Possibility Frontier for Jeans, 47
Figure 3.2   The Production Possibility Frontier for Books and Video Games, 49
Figure 3.3   Increasing Opportunity Cost, 51
Figure 3.4   Economic Growth in a Jeans Factory, 53
Figure 3.5   Economic Growth in the European Union and Hong Kong, 54
Figure 3.6   The Gains from Specialization and Trade, 57

REVIEW QUESTIONS

1   How does the production possibility frontier illustrate scarcity?

2   How does the production possibility frontier illustrate efficiency?

3   How does the production possibility frontier illustrate opportunity cost?

4   Why does the production possibility frontier bow outward for most goods?

5   Why does opportunity cost generally increase as the quantity produced of a good increases?

6   What shifts the production possibility frontier outward and what shifts it inward?

7   Explain how our choices influence the pace of economic growth.

8   What is the opportunity cost of economic growth?

9   Why does it pay people to specialize and trade with each other?

10 What are the gains from specialization and trade? How do they arise?

11 Why do social arrangements such as markets, property rights and money become necessary?

12 What is money? Give some examples of money. In the late 1980s, people in Romania used Kent cigarettes to buy almost everything. Was this monetary exchange or barter? Explain your answer.

13 What are the advantages of monetary exchange over barter?

PROBLEMS

1   Suppose that Leisureland produces only two goods – food and sunscreen. The table lists its production possibilities:

a   Draw a graph of Leisureland's production possibility frontier.

b   What are the opportunity costs of producing food and sunscreen in Leisureland? List them at each output given in the table.

c   Why are the opportunity costs the same at each output level?

Food (kilograms per month)		Sunscreen (litres per month)
300	and	0
200	and	50
100	and	100
0	and	150

2 Busyland also produces only food and sunscreen, and its production possibilities are:

Food (kilograms per month)		Sunscreen (litres per month)
150	and	0
100	and	100
50	and	200
0	and	300

a Draw a graph of Busyland's production possibility frontier.

b What are the opportunity costs of producing food and sunscreen in Busyland? List them at each output given in the table.

c Why are the opportunity costs the same at each output level?

3 Suppose that in Problems 2 and 3, Leisureland and Busyland do not specialize and trade with each other. Leisureland produces and consumes 50 kilograms of food and 125 litres of sunscreen a month. Busyland produces and consumes 150 pounds of food a month and no sunscreen. Then the countries begin to trade with each other.

a What good does Leisureland export, and what good does it import?

b What good does Busyland export, and what good does it import?

c What is the maximum quantity of food and sunscreen that the two countries can produce if each country specializes in the activity at which it has the lower opportunity cost?

4 Suppose that Busyland becomes three times as productive as in Problem 3.

a Show, on a graph, the effect of the increased productivity on Busyland's production possibility frontier.

b Does Busyland now have an absolute advantage in producing both goods?

c Can Busyland gain from specialization and trade with Leisureland now that it is three times as productive? If so, what will it produce?

d What are the total gains from trade? What do these gains depend on?

5 Peter enjoys playing tennis but the more time he spends on tennis, the lower is his grade in economics. The figure shows the trade-off he faces.

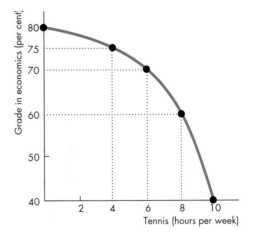

Calculate the opportunity cost of two hours of tennis if Peter increases the time he plays tennis from:

a 4 to 6 hours a week.

b 6 to 8 hours a week.

6 By using the figure in Problem 5, describe the relationship between the time Peter spends on playing tennis and the opportunity cost of an hour of tennis.

7 Study the story about the black economy in *Reading Between the Lines* on pp. 62–63.

a Describe the UK black economy.

b Explain the relationship between tax revenue and the black economy.

c What is the opportunity cost of the balck economy to government?

d What could the government do if it had the extra revenue?

8 Turn to p. 66 and read the *Economics in History* material about Adam Smith. Then:

a Explain how the division of labour creates economic wealth

b Describe the effect of automation and robotics on the division of labour in modern car manufacture. What is the link between this effect and the growth of global car markets?

'It is not from the benevolence of the butcher, the brewer, or the baker, that we expect our dinner, but from their regard to their own interest.'

Adam Smith, THE WEALTH OF NATIONS

Understanding the Sources of Economic Wealth

THE ISSUES AND IDEAS

Why do some nations become wealthy and others remain poor? Adam Smith was one of the first to try to answer this question. At the time that Smith was pondering this question, between 1760 and 1830, an 'industrial revolution' was taking place. During these years, new technologies were invented and applied to the manufacture of cotton and wool, iron, transport and agriculture.

Smith wanted to understand the sources of economic wealth, and he brought his acute powers of observation and abstraction to bear on this question. His answer was:

◆ The division of labour
◆ Free domestic and international markets

Smith identified the division of labour as the source of 'the greatest improvement in the productive powers of labour'. The division of labour became even more productive when it was applied to creating new technologies. Scientists and engineers, trained in extremely narrow fields, became specialists at inventing. Their powerful skills accelerated the advance of technology, so that by the 1820s, machines could make consumer goods faster and more accurately than any craftsman could. And by the 1850s, machines could make other machines that labour alone could never have made.

But, said Smith, the fruits of the division of labour are limited by the extent of the market. To make the market as large as possible, there must be no impediments to free trade both within a country and among countries. Smith argued that when each person makes the best possible economic choice, that choice leads as if by an 'invisible hand' to the best outcome for society as a whole.

THEN ...

Adam Smith speculated that one person, working hard, using the hand tools available in the 1770s, might possibly make 20 pins a day. Yet, he observed, by using those same hand tools but breaking the process into a number of individually small operations in which people specialize – by the division of labour – ten people could make a staggering 48,000 pins a day. One draws out the wire, another straightens it, a third cuts it, a fourth points it, a fifth grinds it. Three specialists make the head and a fourth attaches it. Finally, the pin is polished and packaged. But a large market is needed to support the division of labour: one factory employing ten workers would need to sell more than 15 million pins a year.

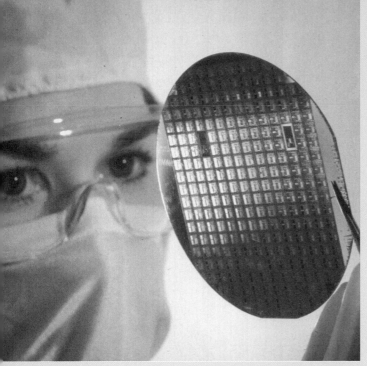

... AND NOW

Memory chips give your computer its instant-recall ability, logic chips provide its number-crunching power, and custom chips make your camera idiot-proof. The computer chip is an extraordinary example of the productivity of the division of labour. Designers lay out a chip's intricate circuits. Printers and cameras transfer an image of the design to glass plates that work like stencils. Workers prepare silicon wafers on which the circuits are printed. Some slice the wafers, others polish them, others bake them, and yet others coat them with a light-sensitive chemical. Machines transfer a copy of the circuit onto the wafer. Chemicals then etch the design onto the wafer. A further series of processes deposit atoms that act as transistors and aluminium that connects the transistors. Finally, a diamond saw or laser separates the hundreds of chips on the wafer. Every stage in the process of creating a computer chip, from its conception to its final separation from the wafer, uses other computer chips. And like the pin of the 1770s, the computer chip of the 1990s needs a large market – a global market – to support the huge quantities in which chips are produced.

THE ECONOMIST: ADAM SMITH

Adam Smith

Adam Smith was a giant of a scholar who made extraordinary contributions in ethics and jurisprudence as well as economics. Born in 1723 in Kirkcaldy, a small fishing town near Edinburgh, Scotland, he was the only child of the town's customs officer (who died before Adam was born).

His first academic appointment, at age 28, was as Professor of Logic at the University of Glasgow. He subsequently became tutor to a wealthy Scottish duke whom he accompanied on a two-year grand European tour, following which he received a pension of £300 a year – 10 times the average income at that time.

With the financial security of his pension, Smith devoted 10 years to writing *An Inquiry into the Nature and Causes of The Wealth of Nations*. This book, published in 1776, established economics as a science. Many people had written on economic issues before Adam Smith, but it was he who made economics a science. Smith's account was so broad and authoritative that no subsequent writer on economics could advance ideas without tracing their connections with Smith's ideas.

CHAPTER
4

DEMAND
AND
SUPPLY

After studying this chapter you will be able to:

◆ Distinguish between a money price and a real price

◆ Explain the main influences on demand

◆ Explain the main influences on supply

◆ Explain how prices are determined by demand and supply

◆ Explain how quantities bought and sold are determined

◆ Explain why some prices fall, some rise and some fluctuate

◆ Make predictions about price changes using the demand and supply model

S LIDE, ROCKET AND ROLLER-COASTER – ARE THESE EURODISNEY RIDES? NO. They're commonly used descriptions of the behaviour of prices. CD players have taken a price slide. In 1983, when they first became available, their price tag was around £1,000. Now you can buy one for less than £100, and during the time that CD players have been with us, the quantity bought has increased steadily. Why has there been a slide in the price of CD players? Why hasn't the increase in the quantity bought kept their price high? ◆ The prices of houses and theatre tickets were rocketing in the 1980s. Why? And why, despite their rocketing prices, did more and more people continue to buy these increasingly expensive goods? ◆ The prices of apples, corn, coffee, wheat and other agricultural commodities are examples of roller-coasters. Why does the price of apples roller-coaster even when people's taste for them hardly changes at all? ◆ Although prices may slide,

Slide, Rocket and Roller-coaster

rocket and roll, many of the things we buy have remarkably steady prices. The price of the cassette tapes that we play in a Walkman is an example. But despite their steady price, the number of tapes bought has increased each year. Why do firms sell more tapes even though they're unable to get higher prices for them, and why do people buy more tapes even though their price is no lower than it was a decade ago?

◆ ◆ ◆ ◆ We will discover the answers to these and similar questions by studying the theory of demand and supply. The central aim of this theory is to explain prices and quantities. But first, we're going to take a closer look at the concept of price. Just what do we mean by price?

Opportunity Cost and Price

Economic actions arise from *scarcity* – wants exceed the resources available to satisfy them. Faced with scarcity, people must make choices. In making choices, they are confronted with *opportunity costs*. Choices are influenced by opportunity costs. If the opportunity cost of a good or service increases, people look for less costly substitutes – the *principle of substitution* – and decrease their purchases of the more costly item.

We are going to build on these fundamental ideas and principles and construct models to help us study both the way people respond to *prices* and the forces that determine prices. But before we do that, we need to understand the relationship between opportunity cost and price.

The opportunity cost of an action is the best alternative forgone. When you buy a cup of coffee, you forgo something. If the best thing forgone is some biscuits, then the opportunity cost of buying a cup of coffee is a quantity of biscuits forgone. To calculate this quantity, we need to know the prices of the two goods.

The price of an object is the amount of money that must be given up in exchange for it. Economists refer to this everyday idea of price as the *money price*. If the money price of coffee is 50 pence a cup and the money price of biscuits is 25 pence a packet, then the opportunity cost of one cup of coffee is two packets of biscuits. To calculate this opportunity cost, we divide the price of a cup of coffee by the price of a packet of biscuits and find the *ratio* of one price to the other. The ratio of one price to another is called a **relative price** and a relative price is an opportunity cost. It is the price of good X divided by the price of good Y and it tells us how many units of good Y must be given up to get one more unit of good X.

There are trillions of relative prices – coffee to biscuits, coffee to cola, coffee to everything else, biscuits to cola, biscuits to everything else, cola to everything else – and we need a convenient way of expressing relative prices. The normal way of expressing a relative price is in terms of a 'basket' of representative goods and services rather than in terms of one particular good or service. That is, we divide the money price of a good by the price of a basket of all goods (called a *price index*). The resulting relative price is called a *real price*. A real price tells us the opportunity cost of an item in terms of how much of the basket of all goods must be given

up to buy it. A real price is expressed in units of money but based on the average prices prevailing in a given year.

Figure 4.1 gives an example of the distinction between a money price and a real price. The green line shows the money price of wheat and tells us that the money price has been rising. But this line does not tell us what has happened to the real price of wheat and hence does not tell us about its opportunity cost. The red line shows the real price of wheat measured in 1994 pounds. This line tells us what the price would have been each year if prices *on the average* had been the same as they were in 1994. The real price of wheat peaked in 1974 and it has tended to fall since that year.

The theory of demand and supply that we are about to study determines real prices, and the word

---

FIGURE 4.1

The Money Price and the Real Price of Wheat

The money price of wheat in the United Kingdom – the number of pounds that must be given up for a tonne of wheat – has fluctuated between £59.80 pounds a tonne and £124.70 a tonne. But the real price or opportunity cost of wheat, expressed in 1994 pounds, has fluctuated between £106.40 and £218.58. The money price of wheat has tended to fall, but the real price of wheat has tended to rise, a fact obscured by the behaviour of its money price.

Source: Central Statistical Office, *Annual Abstract of Statistics*, London, HMSO.

'price' means real (relative) price. When we predict that a price will fall, we do not mean that its money price will fall – although it might. We mean that its real price will fall. That is, its price will fall *relative* to the average price of other goods and services.

Let's now begin our study of demand and supply by building a model of demand.

Demand

The **quantity demanded** of a good or service is the amount that consumers plan to buy during a given time period at a particular price. Demands are different from wants. *Wants* are the unlimited desires or wishes that people have for goods and services. How many times have you thought that you would like something 'if only you could afford it' or 'if it weren't so expensive'? Scarcity guarantees that many – perhaps most – of our wants will never be satisfied. Demand reflects a decision about which wants to satisfy. If you demand something, then you've made a plan to buy it.

The quantity demanded is not necessarily the same amount as the quantity actually bought. Sometimes the quantity demanded is greater than the amount of goods available, so the quantity bought is less than the quantity demanded.

The quantity demanded is measured as an amount per unit of time. For example, suppose a person consumes one cup of coffee a day. The quantity of coffee demanded by that person can be expressed as 1 cup per day or 7 cups per week or 365 cups per year. Without a time dimension, we cannot tell whether a particular quantity demanded is large or small.

What Determines Buying Plans?

The amount of any particular good or service that consumers plan to buy depends on many factors. The main ones are:

◆ The price of the good

◆ The prices of related goods

◆ Income

◆ Expected future prices

◆ Population

◆ Preferences

Let's start our model by looking at the relationship between the quantity demanded and the price of a good. To study this relationship, we hold constant all other influences on consumers' planned purchases. We can then ask: how does the quantity demanded of the good vary as its price varies?

The Law of Demand

The law of demand states:

Other things remaining the same, the higher the price of a good, the smaller is the quantity demanded.

This law gives us a clear prediction. It is based on a theory about why a higher price reduces the quantity demanded. This theory gives two reasons[1]:

1. Substitution effect
2. Income effect

Substitution Effect   When the price of a good rises, other things remaining the same, its price rises relative to the prices of all other goods. Equivalently, its opportunity cost increases. Although each good is unique, it has substitutes – other goods that serve almost as well. As the opportunity cost of a good increases, relative to the opportunity costs of its substitutes, people buy less of that good and more of its substitutes.

Income Effect   When the price of a good rises, other things remaining the same, the price rises relative to people's incomes. Faced with a higher price and an unchanged income, the quantities demanded of at least some goods and services must decrease. Normally the good whose price has increased will be one of the goods bought in a smaller quantity.

To see the substitution effect and the income effect at work, think about blank cassette tapes, which we'll refer to as tapes. Many different goods provide a similar service to a tape; for example, a compact disc (CD), a prerecorded tape, a radio or television broadcast and a live concert. Tapes sell

---

[1] We can also derive this law from a *marginal analysis* of consumers' choices. One way to study these choices is based on the idea of *diminishing marginal utility* (the more of a good you consume, the less benefit you derive from one extra unit), which is explained in Chaper 7. Another way is based on a model of the substitution effect and income effect, which is explained in Chapter 8.

for about 90 pence each. If the price of a tape doubles to £1.80 while the prices of all the other goods remain constant, the quantity of tapes demanded decreases. People substitute compact discs and prerecorded tapes for blank tapes and, faced with a tighter budget, buy fewer tapes as well as less of other goods and services. If the price of a tape falls to 60 pence while the prices of all the other goods remain constant, the quantity of tapes demanded increases. People now substitute blank tapes for CDs and prerecorded tapes and, with a budget that has some slack from the lower price of tapes, buy more tapes as well as more of other goods and services.

Demand Schedule and Demand Curve

The table in Fig. 4.2 sets out our model of the demand schedule for tapes. A *demand schedule* lists the quantities demanded at each different price, when all the other influences on consumers' planned purchases – such as the prices of related goods, income, expected future prices, population and preferences – are held constant. For example, if the price of a tape is 30 pence, the quantity demanded is 9 million tapes a week. If the price of a tape is £1.50, the quantity demanded is 2 million tapes a week. The other rows of the table show us the quantities demanded at prices between 60 pence and £1.20.

Figure 4.2 shows the demand curve for tapes. A **demand curve** shows the relationship between the quantity demanded of a good and its price, all other influences on consumers' planned purchases remaining the same. It is a graph of a demand schedule. By convention, the quantity demanded is measured on the horizontal axis and the price is measured on the vertical axis. The points on the demand curve labelled *a* to *e* represent the rows of the demand schedule. For example, point *a* on the graph represents a quantity demanded of 9 million tapes a week at a price of 30 pence a tape.

Willingness and Ability to Pay Another way of looking at the demand curve is as a willingness-and-ability-to-pay curve. It tells us the highest price that someone is willing and able to pay for the last unit bought. If a large quantity is bought, that price is low; if a small quantity is bought, that price is high. In Fig. 4.2, if 9 million tapes are bought each week, the highest price that someone is willing to pay for the 9 millionth tape is 30 pence. But if only 2 million

FIGURE 4.2

The Demand Curve

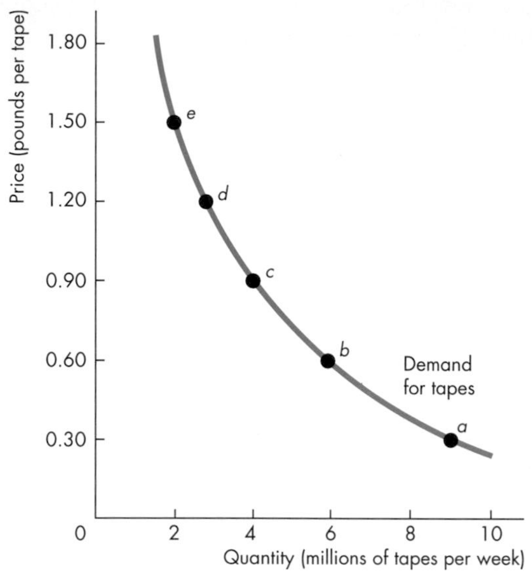

	Price (pounds per tape)	Quantity (millions of tapes per week)
a	0.30	9
b	0.60	6
c	0.90	4
d	1.20	3
e	1.50	2

The table shows a demand schedule listing the quantity of tapes demanded at each price if all other influences on buyers' plans remain the same. At a price of 30 pence a tape, 9 million tapes a week are demanded; at a price of 90 pence a tape, 4 million tapes a week are demanded. The demand curve shows the relationship between quantity demanded and price, everything else remaining the same. The demand curve slopes downward: as price decreases, the quantity demanded increases. The demand curve can be read in two ways. For a given price it tells us the quantity that people plan to buy. For example, at a price of 90 pence a tape, the quantity demanded is 4 million tapes a week. For a given quantity, the demand curve tells us the maximum price that consumers are willing to pay for the last tape bought. For example, the maximum price that consumers will pay for the 6 millionth tape is 60 pence.

tapes are bought each week, someone is willing to pay £1.50 for the last tape bought.

A Change in Demand

The term **demand** refers to the entire relationship between the quantity demanded and the price of a good, other things remaining the same. The demand for tapes is described by both the demand schedule and the demand curve in Fig. 4.2. To construct a demand schedule and demand curve, we hold constant all the other influences on consumers' buying plans. This part of the model allowed us to see how demand changes with price alone.

But we already know that demand changes with other factors like the price of related goods, people's incomes and preferences. So let's expand the model to look at how these other factors influence demand.

1. Prices of Related Goods   The quantity of any goods and services that consumers plan to buy depends in part on the price of related goods and services. There are two types: substitutes and complements.

A **substitute** is a good that can be used in place of another good. For example, a bus ride substitutes for a train ride; a hamburger substitutes for a hot dog; a pear substitutes for an apple. As we have noted, tapes have many substitutes – prerecorded tapes, CDs, radio and television broadcasts and live concerts. If the price of one of these substitutes increases, people economize on its use and buy more tapes. For example, if the price of a CD rises, more tapes are bought and there is more taping of other people's CDs – the demand for tapes increases.

A **complement** is a good used in conjunction with another good. Some examples of complements are hamburgers and chips, party snacks and drinks, cars and petrol, PCs and software. Tapes also have complements: Walkmans, tape recorders and stereo tape decks. If the price of one of these complements increases, people buy fewer tapes. For example, if the price of a Walkman rises, fewer Walkmans are bought and, as a consequence, fewer tapes are bought – the demand for tapes decreases.

2. Income   Another influence on demand is consumer income. Other things remaining the same, when income increases, consumers buy more of

most goods, and when income decreases, they buy less of most goods. Although an increase in income leads to an increase in the demand for most goods, it does not lead to an increase in the demand for all goods. Goods for which demand increases as income increases are called **normal goods**. Goods for which demand decreases when income increases are called **inferior goods**. Examples of inferior goods are cheap cuts of meat and tinned foods. These two goods are a major part of the diet of people with low incomes. As incomes increase, the demand for these goods usually declines as more expensive meat and fresh products are substituted for them.

3. Expected Future Prices   If the price of a good is expected to rise in the future, and if the good can be stored, the opportunity cost of obtaining the good for future use is lower now than it will be when the price has increased. So people substitute over time. They buy more of the good before the expected price rise and the demand for the good increases. Similarly, if the price of a good is expected to fall in the future, the opportunity cost of the good in the present is high relative to what is expected. So again, people substitute over time. They buy less of the good before its price is expected to fall, so the demand for the good now decreases.

4. Population   Demand also depends on the size and the age structure of the population. Other things remaining the same, the larger the population, the greater is the demand for all goods and services, and the smaller the population, the smaller is the demand for all goods and services. Also, other things remaining the same, the larger the proportion of the population in a given age group, the greater is the demand for the types of goods and services used by that age group.

5. Preferences   Finally, demand depends on consumer preferences. *Preferences* are an individual's attitudes towards and tastes for goods and services. For example, a rock music fanatic has a much greater taste for tapes than has a tone-deaf workaholic. As a consequence, even if they have the same incomes, their demands for tapes will be different. Preferences are shaped by past experience, genetic factors, advertising information, religious beliefs, and other cultural and social factors.

Table 4.1 summarizes the influences on demand and the direction of these influences.

Movement Along Versus a Shift of the Demand Curve

Changes in the factors that influence buyers' plans cause either a movement along the demand curve or a shift of the demand curve.

Movement Along the Demand Curve   If the price of a good changes but everything else remains the same, there is a movement along the demand curve. For example, if the price of a tape changes from 90 pence to £1.50, the result is a movement along the demand curve, from point *c* to point *e* in Fig. 4.2. The negative slope of the demand curve reveals that a decrease in the price of a good or service increases the quantity demanded – the law of demand.

A Shift of the Demand Curve   If the price of a good remains constant but some other influence on buyers' plans changes, there is a change in

---

TABLE 4.1

The Demand for Tapes

THE LAW OF DEMAND

The quantity of tapes demanded

Decreases if: | *Increases if:*

◆ The price of a tape rises | ◆ The price of a tape falls

CHANGES IN DEMAND

The demand for tapes

Decreases if: | *Increases if:*

◆ The price of a substitute falls | ◆ The price of a substitute rises
◆ The price of a complement rises | ◆ The price of a complement falls
◆ Income falls* | ◆ Income rises*
◆ The price of a tape is expected to fall in the future | ◆ The price of a tape is expected to rise in the future
◆ The population decreases | ◆ The population increases

*A tape is a normal good.

---

demand for that good. We illustrate a change in demand as a shift of the demand curve. For example, a fall in the price of a Walkman – a complement of tapes – increases the demand for tapes. We illustrate this increase in demand for tapes with a new demand schedule and a new demand curve. Whether the price of tapes is high or low, if the price of a Walkman falls, consumers buy more tapes. This is what a shift of the demand curve shows. It shows that more tapes are bought at each and every price.

Figure 4.3 illustrates such a shift. The table sets out the original demand schedule when the price of a Walkman is £125 and the new demand schedule when the price of a Walkman is £30. These numbers record the change in demand. The graph in Fig. 4.3 illustrates the corresponding shift of the demand curve. When the price of the Walkman falls, the demand curve for tapes shifts rightward.

A Change in Demand Versus a Change in Quantity Demanded   A point on the demand curve shows the quantity demanded at a given price. A movement along the demand curve shows a **change in the quantity demanded**. The entire demand curve shows demand. A shift of the demand curve shows a **change in demand**.

Figure 4.4 illustrates and summarizes these distinctions. If the price of a good falls but nothing else changes, then there is an increase in the quantity demanded of that good (a movement down the demand curve D_0). If the price rises, but nothing else changes, then there is a decrease in the quantity demanded (a movement up the demand curve D_0). When any other influence on buyers' planned purchases changes, the demand curve shifts and there is a *change* (an increase or a decrease) *in demand*. A rise in income (for a normal good), in population, in the price of a substitute or in the expected future price of the good, or a fall in the price of a complement, shifts the demand curve rightward (to the red demand curve D_2). This represents an *increase in demand*. A fall in income (for a normal good), in population, in the price of a substitute or in the expected future price of the good, or a rise in the price of a complement, shifts the demand curve leftward (to the red demand curve D_1). This represents a *decrease in demand*. (For an inferior good, the effects of changes in income are in the opposite direction to those described above.)

FIGURE 4.3

An Increase in Demand

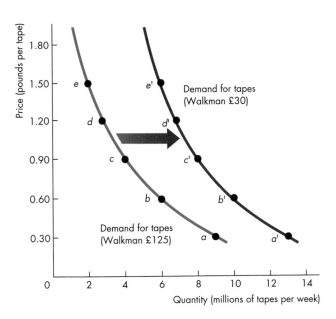

	Original demand schedule (Walkman £125)			New demand schedule (Walkman £30)	
	Price (pounds per tape)	Quantity (millions of tapes per week)		Price (pounds per tape)	Quantity (millions of tapes per week)
a	0.30	9	a'	0.30	13
b	0.60	6	b'	0.60	10
c	0.90	4	c'	0.90	8
d	1.20	3	d'	1.20	7
e	1.50	2	e'	1.50	6

A change in any influence on buyers other than the price of the good itself results in a new demand schedule and a shift of the demand curve. A change in the price of a Walkman changes the demand for tapes. At a price of 90 pence a tape (row *c* of the table), 4 million tapes a week are demanded when a Walkman costs £125 and 8 million tapes a week are demanded when a Walkman costs only £30. A fall in the price of a Walkman increases the demand for tapes because it is a complement of tapes. When demand *increases*, the demand curve shifts rightward, as shown by the shift arrow and the resulting red curve.

FIGURE 4.4

A Change in Demand Versus a Change in the Quantity Demanded

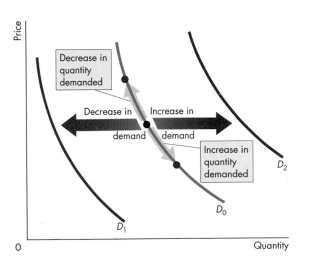

The blue arrow shows a *change in the quantity demanded* when the demand curve is D_0. A rise (fall) in the price of the good leads to a decrease (increase) in the quantity demanded and a movement along the demand curve as shown by the arrow. A change in any factor other than the price of the good, leads to a *change in demand* by shifting the demand curve – to D_2, an increase in demand and D_1, a *decrease in demand*.

R E V I E W

◆ The quantity demanded is the amount of a good that consumers plan to buy during a given period of time.

◆ Our model of demand shows the relationship between quantity demanded and price, other things remaining the same.

◆ When the price of the good changes, other things remaining the same, we can predict a change in the quantity demanded and a movement along the demand curve.

◆ When any other influences on buying plans change, we can predict a change in demand and a shift of the demand curve.

Supply

The **quantity supplied** of a good is the amount that producers plan to sell during a given time period. The quantity supplied is not the amount producers would like to sell but the amount they definitely plan to sell. But the quantity supplied is not necessarily the same as the quantity actually sold. If consumers do not want to buy the quantity producers plan to sell, the sales plans will be frustrated. Like quantity demanded, the quantity supplied is expressed as an amount per unit of time.

What Determines Selling Plans?

The amount that producers plan to sell of any particular good or service depends on many factors. The main ones are:

◆ The price of the good

◆ The prices of factors of production

◆ The prices of related goods

◆ Expected future prices

◆ The number of suppliers

◆ Technology

Let's start to build a model of supply by looking at the relationship between the price of a good and the quantity supplied. In order to study this relationship, we hold constant all the other influences on the quantity supplied. We want to know how the quantity supplied of a good varies as its price varies.

The Law of Supply

The law of supply states:

Other things remaining the same, the higher the price of a good, the greater is the quantity supplied.

This law gives us another clear prediction. The law is based on a theory about increasing opportunity cost. Increasing opportunity cost explains why a higher price leads to greater quantities supplied. The opportunity cost of supplying an additional unit of the good increases as the quantity produced increases. So the higher the price of a good, the more willing are the producers to incur a higher opportunity cost of an increase in production.

Supply Schedule and Supply Curve

The table in Fig. 4.5 sets out the supply schedule for tapes. A *supply schedule* lists the quantities supplied at each different price, when all other influences on the amount producers plan to sell remain the same. For example, if the price of a tape is 30 pence, no tapes are supplied. If the price of a tape is £1.20, 5 million tapes are supplied each week.

Figure 4.5 illustrates the supply curve for tapes. A **supply curve** shows the relationship between the quantity supplied and the price of a good, everything else remaining the same. It is a graph of a supply schedule. The points on the supply curve labelled *a* to *e* represent the rows of the supply schedule. For example, point *d* represents a quantity supplied of 5 million tapes a week at a price of £1.20 a tape.

Minimum Supply Price Just as the demand curve has two interpretations, so too does the supply curve. It shows the quantity that producers plan to sell at each possible price. It also shows the minimum price at which the last unit will be supplied. For producers to be willing to supply the 3 millionth tape each week, the price must be at least 60 pence a tape. For producers to be willing to supply the 5 millionth tape each week, they must get at least £1.20 a tape.

A Change in Supply

The term **supply** refers to the relationship between the quantity supplied of a good and its price, other things remaining the same. The supply of tapes is described by both the supply schedule and the supply curve in Fig. 4.5. To construct a supply schedule and supply curve, we hold constant all the other influences on suppliers' plans. This part of the model allowed us to see how supply changes with price alone.

But we already know that supply changes with other factors like the price of factors of production and related goods, expected future prices and technology. So let's expand the model to look at how these other factors influence supply.

1. Prices of Factors of Production The prices of the factors of production used to produce a good influence its supply. For example, an increase in the prices of the labour and the capital equipment used

FIGURE 4.5

The Supply Curve

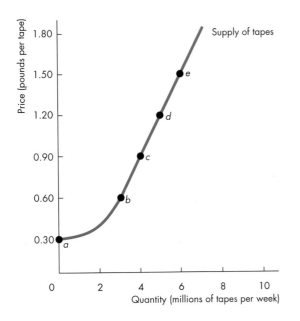

Supply of tapes

	Price (pounds per tape)	Quantity (millions of tapes per week)
a	0.30	0
b	0.60	3
c	0.90	4
d	1.20	5
e	1.50	6

The table shows the supply schedule of tapes. For example, at 60 pence a tape, 3 million tapes a week are supplied; at £1.50 a tape, 6 million tapes a week are supplied. The supply curve shows the relationship between the quantity supplied and the price, everything else remaining the same. The supply curve usually slopes upward: as the price of a good increases, so does the quantity supplied. A supply curve can be read in two ways. For a given price, it tells us the quantity that producers plan to sell. For example, at a price of 90 pence a tape, producers plan to sell 4 million tapes a week. The supply curve also tells us the minimum acceptable price at which a given quantity will be offered for sale. For example, the minimum acceptable price that will bring forth a supply of 5 million tapes a week is £1.20 a tape.

to produce tapes increases the cost of producing tapes. So for a given market price, the supplier is willing to supply fewer tapes.

2. Prices of Related Goods   The supply of a good can be influenced by the prices of related goods. For example, if a car assembly line can produce either sports cars or saloons, the quantity of saloons produced will depend on the price of sports cars and the quantity of sports cars produced will depend on the price of saloons. These two goods are *substitutes in production.* An increase in the price of a substitute in production lowers the supply of the good. Goods can also be complements in production. *Complements in production* arise when two things are, of necessity, produced together. For example, extracting chemicals from coal produces coke, coal tar and nylon. An increase in the price of any one of these by-products of coal increases the supply of the other by-products.

Blank tapes have no obvious complements in production, but they do have substitutes in production: prerecorded tapes. Suppliers of tapes can produce blank tapes and prerecorded tapes. An increase in the price of prerecorded tapes encourages producers to use their equipment to produce more prerecorded tapes and so the supply of blank tapes decreases.

3. Expected Future Prices   If the price of a good is expected to rise in the future, and if the good can be stored, the return from selling the good in the future is higher than it is in the present. So producers substitute over time. They offer a smaller quantity for sale before the expected price rise and the supply of the good decreases. Similarly, if the price of a good is expected to fall in the future, the return from selling it in the present is high relative to what is expected. So again, producers substitute over time. They offer to sell more of the good before its price is expected to fall, so the supply of the good increases.

4. The Number of Suppliers   When new firms enter a market and no firms leave a market, the quantity of the good supplied will increase. Other things remaining the same, the larger the number of firms supplying a good, the larger is the supply of the good.

5. Technology   New technologies that enable producers to use less of each factor of production or cheaper factors of production lower the cost of production and increase supply. For example, the development of a new technology for tape production by BASF, Sony and Minnesota Mining and Manufacturing (3M) has lowered the cost of producing tapes and increased their supply. Over the long term, changes in technology are the most important influence on supply.

Table 4.2 summarizes the influences on supply and the directions of those influences.

Movement Along Versus a Shift of the Supply Curve

Changes in the factors that influence producers' planned sales cause either a movement along the supply curve or a shift of the supply curve.

Movement Along the Supply Curve   If the price of a good changes but everything else influencing suppliers' planned sales remains constant, there is a movement along the supply curve. For example, if the price of tapes increases from 90 pence to £1.50 a tape, there will be a movement along the supply curve from point c (4 million tapes a week) to point e (6 million tapes a week) in Fig. 4.5. The positive slope of the supply curve reveals that an increase in the price of a good or service increases the quantity supplied – the law of supply

A Shift of the Supply Curve   If the price of a good remains the same but another influence on suppliers' planned sales changes, then there is a change in supply and a shift of the supply curve. For example, as we have already noted, technological advances lower the cost of producing tapes and increase their supply. As a result, the supply schedule changes. The table in Fig. 4.6 provides some hypothetical numbers that illustrate such a change. The table contains two supply schedules: the original, based on 'old' technology, and one based on 'new' technology. With the new technology, more tapes are supplied at each price. The graph in Fig. 4.6 illustrates the resulting shift of the supply curve. When tape-producing technology improves, the supply curve of tapes shifts rightward, as shown by the shift arrow and the red supply curve.

A Change in Supply Versus a Change in Quantity Supplied   A point on the supply curve shows the quantity supplied at a given price. A

TABLE 4.2

The Supply of Tapes

THE LAW OF SUPPLY

The quantity of tapes supplied

Decreases if:	*Increases if:*
◆ The price of a tape falls	◆ The price of a tape rises

CHANGES IN SUPPLY

The supply of tapes

Decreases if:	*Increases if:*
◆ The price of a factor of production used to produce tapes increases	◆ The price of a factor of production used to produce tapes decreases
◆ The price of a substitute in production rises	◆ The price of a substitute in production falls
◆ The price of a complement in production falls	◆ The price of a complement in production rises
◆ The price of a tape is expected to rise in the future	◆ The price of a tape is expected to fall in the future
◆ The number of firms supplying tapes decreases	◆ The number of firms supplying tapes increases
	◆ More efficient technologies for producing tapes are discovered

---

movement along the supply curve shows a **change in the quantity supplied**. The entire supply curve shows supply. A shift of the supply curve shows a **change in supply.**

Figure 4.7 illustrates and summarizes these distinctions. If the price of a good falls but nothing else changes, then there is a decrease in the quantity supplied of that good (a movement down the supply curve S_0). If the price of a good rises but nothing else changes, there is an increase in the quantity supplied (a movement up the supply curve S_0). When any other influence on sellers changes, the supply curve shifts and there is a *change in supply*. If the supply curve is S_0 and there is, say, a technological change that reduces the amounts of the factors of production needed to produce the good, then supply increases and the supply curve shifts to the red supply curve S_2. If production costs rise, supply decreases and the supply curve shifts to the red supply curve S_1.

FIGURE 4.6

An Increase in Supply

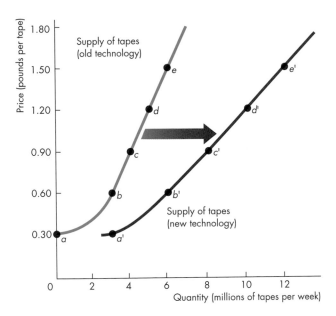

Original supply schedule (original technology)			New supply shedule (new technology)		
	Price (pounds per tape)	Quantity (millions of tapes per week)		Price (pounds per tape)	Quantity (millions of tapes per week)
a	0.30	0	a'	0.30	3
b	0.60	3	b'	0.60	6
c	0.90	4	c'	0.90	8
d	1.20	5	d'	1.20	10
e	1.50	6	e'	1.50	12

A change in any influence on sellers other than the price of the good itself results in a new supply schedule and a shift of the supply curve. For example, if BASF, Sony and 3M invent a new, cost-saving technology for producing tapes, the supply of tapes changes. At a price of 60 pence a tape (row *b* of the table), 3 million tapes a week are supplied when the producers use the old technology, and 6 million tapes a week are supplied with the new technology. An advance in technology increases the supply of tapes and the supply curve shifts rightward, as shown by the shift arrow and the resulting red curve.

FIGURE 4.7

A Change in Supply Versus a Change in the Quantity Supplied

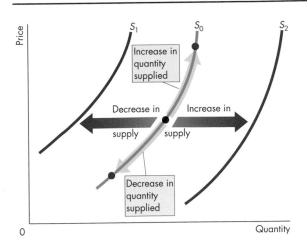

The blue arrow shows a *change in the quantity supplied* when the supply curve is S_0. A rise (fall) in the price of the good leads to a decrease (increase) in the quantity supplied and a movement along the supply curve as shown by the arrow. A change in any factor other than the price of the good, leads to a *change in supply* by shifting the supply curve – to S_2, an *increase in supply* and S_1, a *decrease in supply*.

R E V I E W

◆ The quantity supplied is the amount of a good that producers plan to sell during a given period of time.

◆ Our model of supply shows the relationship between quantity supplied and price, other things remaining the same.

◆ When the price of the good changes, other things remaining the same, we can predict a change in the quantity supplied and a movement along the supply curve.

◆ When any other influences on selling plans change, we can predict a change in supply and a shift of the supply curve.

Let's now bring the two concepts of demand and supply together to create a model which will show how prices and quantities are determined.

Price Determination

We have seen that when the price of a good rises, the quantity demanded decreases and the quantity supplied increases. We are now going to see how adjustments in price coordinate the choices of buyers and sellers.

Price as a Regulator

The price of a good regulates the quantities demanded and supplied. If the price is too high, the quantity supplied exceeds the quantity demanded. If the price is too low, the quantity demanded exceeds the quantity supplied. There is one price, and only one price, at which the quantity demanded equals the quantity supplied. Let's work out what that price is.

The table in Fig. 4.8 shows the demand schedule (from Fig. 4.2) and the supply schedule (from Fig. 4.5). If the price of a tape is 30 pence, the quantity demanded is 9 million tapes a week, but no tapes are supplied. The quantity demanded exceeds the quantity supplied by 9 million tapes a week. In other words, at a price of 30 pence a tape, there is a shortage of 9 million tapes a week. This shortage is shown in the final column of the table. At a price of 60 pence a tape, there is still a shortage but only of 3 million tapes a week. If the price of a tape is £1.20, the quantity supplied exceeds the quantity demanded. The quantity supplied is 5 million tapes a week, but the quantity demanded is only 3 million. There is a surplus of 2 million tapes a week. There is one price and only one price at which there is neither a shortage nor a surplus. That price is 90 pence a tape. At that price the quantity demanded is equal to the quantity supplied – 4 million tapes a week.

Figure 4.8 shows the market for tapes. The demand curve (of Fig. 4.2) and the supply curve (of Fig. 4.5) intersect when the price is 90 pence a tape. At that price, the quantity demanded and supplied is 4 million tapes a week. At each price *above* 90 pence a tape, the quantity supplied exceeds the quantity demanded. There is a surplus of tapes. For example, at £1.20 a tape the surplus is 2 million tapes a week, as shown by the blue arrow in the figure. At each price *below* 90 pence a tape, the quantity demanded exceeds the quantity

FIGURE 4.8

Equilibrium

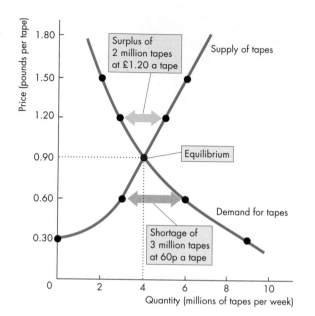

The table lists the quantities demanded and quantities supplied as well as the shortage or surplus of tapes at each price. If the price of a tape is 60 pence, 6 million tapes a week are demanded and 3 million are supplied. There is a shortage of 3 million tapes a week, and the price rises. If the price of a tape is £1.20, 3 million tapes a week are demanded but 5 million are supplied. There is a surplus of 2 million tapes a week, and the price falls. If the price of a tape is 90 pence, 4 million tapes a week are demanded and 4 million are supplied. There is neither a shortage nor a surplus. Neither buyers nor sellers have any incentive to change the price. The price at which the quantity demanded equals the quantity supplied is the equilibrium price.

Price (pounds per tape)	Quantity demanded	Quantity supplied	Shortage (-) or surplus (+)
	(millions of tapes per week)		
0.30	9	0	-9
0.60	6	3	-3
0.90	4	4	0
1.20	3	5	+2
1.50	2	6	+4

supplied. There is a shortage of tapes. For example, at 60 pence a tape, the shortage is 3 million tapes a week, as shown by the red arrow in the figure.

Equilibrium

An *equilibrium* is a situation in which opposing forces balance each other. It is a situation in which there is no tendency for change. Equilibrium in a market occurs when the price is such that the opposing forces of the plans of buyers and sellers balance each other. The **equilibrium price** is the price at which the quantity demanded equals the quantity supplied. The **equilibrium quantity** is the quantity bought and sold at the equilibrium price. The concept of equilibrium is an important element of our model. In the next section, we use it to compare the situation in a market before and after changes in demand and supply.

Let's take a closer look at the concept of an equilibrium. To see why equilibrium occurs where the quantity demanded equals the quantity supplied, we need see how buyers and sellers behave if there is a shortage or a surplus.

A Shortage Forces the Price Up   Suppose the price of a tape is 60 pence. Consumers plan to buy 6 million tapes a week and producers plan to sell 3 million tapes a week. Consumers can't force producers to sell, so the quantity actually offered for sale is 3 million tapes a week. In this situation, powerful forces operate to increase the price and move it towards the equilibrium price. Some people, unable to find the tapes they planned to buy, offer to pay more. Some producers, noticing lines of unsatisfied consumers, move their prices up. As buyers try to outbid one another, and as producers push their prices up, the price rises towards its equilibrium. The rising price reduces the shortage because it decreases the quantity demanded and increases the quantity supplied. When the price has increased to the point at which there is no longer a shortage, the forces moving the price stop operating and the price comes to rest at its equilibrium.

A Surplus Forces the Price Down   Suppose the price of a tape is £1.20. Producers plan to sell 5 million tapes a week and consumers plan to buy 3 million tapes a week. Producers cannot force consumers to buy, so the quantity actually bought is 3

million tapes a week. In this situation, powerful forces operate to lower the price and move it towards the equilibrium price. Some producers, unable to sell the quantities of tapes they planned to sell, cut their prices. Some buyers, noticing shelves of unsold tapes, offer to buy for a lower price. As producers try to undercut one another, and as buyers make lower price offers, the price falls towards its equilibrium. The falling price reduces the surplus because it increases the quantity demanded and decreases the quantity supplied. When the price has decreased to the point at which there is no longer a surplus, the forces moving the price stop operating and the price comes to rest at its equilibrium.

The Best Deal Available for Buyers and Sellers
Both situations we have just examined result in price changes. Prices were forced up or down until they hit 90 pence a tape. At that price, the quantity demanded and the quantity supplied are equal and neither buyers nor sellers can do business at a better price. Consumers pay the highest price they are willing to pay for the last unit bought, and producers receive the lowest price at which they are willing to supply the last unit sold.

When people freely make bids and offers and when buyers seek the lowest price and sellers seek the highest price, the price at which trade takes place is the equilibrium price – the quantity demanded equals the quantity supplied. You'll find a mathematical presentation of equilibrium prices and quantities in Box 4.1.

R E V I E W

◆ The equilibrium price is the price at which buyers' and sellers' plans match each other – the price at which the quantity demanded equals the quantity supplied.

◆ At prices below the equilibrium, there is a shortage and the price rises.

◆ At prices above the equilibrium, there is a surplus and the price falls.

◆ Only at the equilibrium price are there no forces acting on the price to make it change.

The theory of demand and supply that you have just studied is now a central part of economics. But this was not always the case. Only 100 years ago, the best economists of the day were quite confused about matters that today even students in introductory courses can get right (see *Economics in History* on pp. 90–91).

You'll discover in the rest of this chapter that the theory of demand and supply helps us to understand and make predictions about changes in prices – including the price slides, rockets and roller-coasters described in the chapter opener.

Predicting Changes in Price and Quantity

The theory we have just studied provides us with a powerful way of analysing influences on prices and the quantities bought and sold. According to the theory, a change in price stems from either a change in demand or a change in supply or a change in both. First, let's look at our model to discover the effects of a change in demand.

A Change in Demand

What happens to the price and quantity of tapes if demand for tapes increases? We can answer this question with a specific example. If the price of a Walkman falls from £125 to £30, the demand for tapes increases as is shown in the table in Fig. 4.9. (Recall that tapes and Walkmans are complements and that when the price of a complement falls the demand for the good increases.) The original demand schedule and the new one are set out in the first three columns of the table. The table also shows the supply schedule for tapes.

The original equilibrium price is 90 pence a tape. At that price, 4 million tapes a week are demanded and supplied. When demand increases, the price that makes the quantity demanded equal the quantity supplied is £1.50 a tape. At this price, 6 million tapes are bought and sold each week. When demand increases, both the price and the quantity increase.

Figure 4.9 shows these changes. The figure shows the original demand for and supply of tapes. The original equilibrium price is 90 pence a tape and the quantity is 4 million tapes a week. When

FIGURE 4.9

The Effects of a Change in Demand

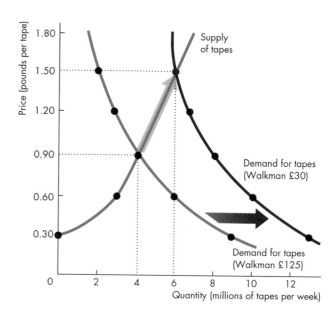

Price (pounds per tape)	Quantity demanded (millions of tapes per week)		Quantity supplied (millions of tapes per week)
	Walkman £125	Walkman £30	
0.30	9	13	0
0.60	6	10	3
0.90	4	8	4
1.20	3	7	5
1.50	2	6	6

With the price of a Walkman at £125, the demand for tapes is the blue curve. The equilibrium price is 90 pence a tape and the equilibrium quantity is 4 million tapes a week. When the price of a Walkman falls from £125 to £30, there is an increase in the demand for tapes and the demand curve shifts right – the red curve. At 90 pence a tape, there is now a shortage of 4 million tapes a week. The quantities of tapes demanded and supplied are equal at a price of £1.50 a tape. The price rises to this level and the quantity supplied increases. But there is no change in supply. The supply curve does not shift. The increase in demand increases the equilibrium price to £1.50 and increases the equilibrium quantity to 6 million tapes a week.

demand increases, the demand curve shifts rightward. The equilibrium price rises to £1.50 a tape and the quantity supplied increases to 6 million tapes a week, as is highlighted in the figure. There is an increase in the quantity supplied but *no change in supply*. That is, the supply curve does not shift.

The exercise that we've just conducted can easily be reversed. If we start at a price of £1.50 a tape, trading 6 million tapes a week, we can work out what happens if demand decreases to its original level. You can see that the decrease in demand lowers the equilibrium price to 90 pence a tape and decreases the equilibrium quantity to 4 million tapes a week. Such a decrease in demand might arise from a decrease in the price of CDs or of CD players. (CDs and CD players are substitutes for tapes.)

We can now make our two clear market predictions. Holding everything else constant:

◆ When demand increases, both the price and the quantity traded in the market increase.

◆ When demand decreases, both the price and the quantity traded in the market decrease.

A Change in Supply

Suppose that BASF, Sony and 3M introduce a new cost-saving technology in their tape-production plants. The new technology changes the supply. The new supply schedule (the one that was shown in Fig.4.6) is presented in the table in Fig. 4.10. What is the new equilibrium price and quantity? The answer is highlighted in the table: the price falls to 60 pence a tape and the quantity increases to 6 million a week. You can see why by looking at the quantities demanded and supplied at the old price of a tape. The quantity supplied at that price is 8 million tapes a week and there is a surplus of tapes. The price falls. Only when the price is 60 pence a tape does the quantity supplied equal the quantity demanded.

Figure 4.10 illustrates the effect of an increase in supply. It shows the demand curve for tapes and the original and new supply curves. The initial equilibrium price is 90 pence a tape and the original quantity is 4 million tapes a week. When the supply increases, the supply curve shifts rightward. The equilibrium price falls to 60 pence a tape and the quantity demanded increases to 6 million tapes a week, highlighted in the figure. There is an increase in the quantity demanded but *no change in demand*. That is, the demand curve does not shift.

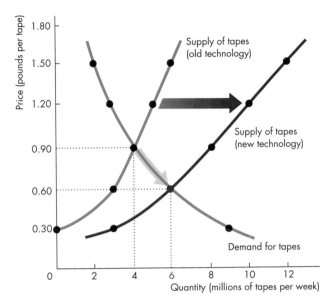

FIGURE 4.10

The Effects of a Change in Supply ◆

Price (pounds per tape)	Quantity demanded (millions of tapes per week)	Quantity supplied (millions of tapes per week)	
		Original technology	New technology
0.30	9	0	3
0.60	6	3	6
0.90	4	4	8
1.20	3	5	10
1.50	2	6	12

With the original technology, the supply of tapes is shown by the blue curve. The equilibrium price is 90 pence a tape and the equilibrium quantity is 4 million tapes a week. When the new technology is adopted, there is an increase in the supply of tapes. The supply curve shifts right – the red curve. At 90 pence a tape there is now a surplus of 4 million tapes a week. The quantities of tapes demanded and supplied are equal at a price of 60 pence a tape. The price falls to this level and the quantity demanded increases – there is a movement along the demand curve. But there is no change in demand. The demand curve does not shift. The increase in supply lowers the price of tapes to 60p and increases the quantity to 6 million tapes a week.

The exercise that we've just conducted can be reversed. If we start at a price of 60 pence a tape with 6 million tapes a week being bought and sold, we can work out what happens if supply decreases to its original level. You can see that the decrease in supply increases the equilibrium price to 90 pence a tape and decreases the equilibrium quantity to 4 million tapes a week. Such a decrease in supply might arise from an increase in the cost of labour or raw materials.

We can now make two more predictions. Holding everything else constant:

◆ When supply increases, the quantity traded increases and the price falls.

◆ When supply decreases, the quantity traded decreases and the price rises.

Reading Between the Lines on pp 88–89 explores the effect of world shortages in wheat on the demand and supply in the wheat market.

A Change in Both Supply and Demand In the above exercises, either demand or supply changed but only one at a time. In each of these cases, we can predict the direction of change of the price and the quantity. But if demand and supply change together, we cannot always say what will happen to both the price and the quantity. We'll look at two cases in which both demand and supply change. First, we'll see what happens when they both change in the same direction - both demand and supply increase (or decrease) together. Then we'll look at the case in which they move in opposite directions - demand decreases and supply increases or demand increases and supply decreases.

Demand and Supply Change in the Same Direction We've seen that an increase in the demand for tapes increases the price of tapes and increases the quantity bought and sold. We've also seen that an increase in the supply of tapes lowers the price of tapes and increases the quantity bought and sold. Let's now examine what happens in our model when both of these changes happen to occur together.

The table in Fig. 4.11 brings together the numbers that describe the original quantities demanded and supplied and the new quantities demanded and supplied after the fall in the price of a Walkman and the improved tape production technology. These same numbers are illustrated in the graph. The original (blue) demand and supply

FIGURE 4.11

The Effects of an Increase in Both Demand and Supply

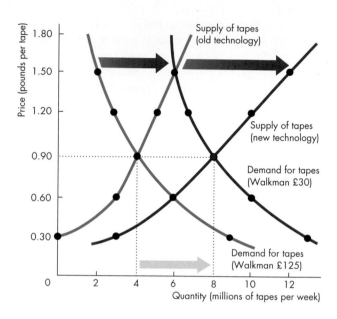

Price (pounds per tape)	Original quantities (millions of tapes per week)		New quantities (millions of tapes per week)	
	Quantity demanded (Walkman £125)	Quantity supplied (original technology)	Quantity demanded (Walkman £30)	Quantity supplied (new technology)
0.30	9	0	13	3
0.60	6	3	10	6
0.90	4	4	**8**	**8**
1.20	3	5	7	10
1.50	2	6	6	12

When a Walkman costs £125, and the old technology is used to produce tapes, the price of a tape is 90 pence and the quantity is 4 million tapes a week. A fall in the price of a Walkman increases the demand for tapes, and improved technology increases the supply of tapes. The new technology supply curve intersects the higher demand curve at 90 pence, the same price as before, but the quantity increases to 8 million tapes a week. These increases in demand and supply increase the quantity but leave the price unchanged.

curves intersect at a price of 90 pence a tape and a quantity of 4 million tapes a week. The new (red) supply and demand curves also intersect at a price of 90 pence a tape but at a quantity of 8 million tapes a week.

An increase in either demand or supply increases the quantity. Therefore when both demand and supply increase, so does quantity. But an increase in demand increases the price and an increase in supply lowers the price, so we can't say for sure which way the price will change when demand and supply increase together. In this example, the increases in demand and supply are such that the rise in price brought about by an increase in demand is offset by the fall in price brought about by an increase in supply – so the price does not change. But notice that if demand had increased slightly more than shown in the figure, the price would have risen. If supply had increased by slightly more than shown in the figure, the price would have fallen.

We can now make two more market predictions:

◆ When *both* demand and supply increase, the market quantity increases and the price increases, decreases, or remains constant.

◆ When *both* demand and supply decrease, the market quantity decreases and the price increases, decreases, or remains constant.

Demand and Supply Change in Opposite Directions   Let's now see what happens when demand and supply change together but move in *opposite* directions. We'll look yet again at the market for tapes, but this time supply increases and demand decreases. An improved production technology increases the supply of tapes as before. But now the price of CD players falls. A CD player is a *substitute* for tapes. With less costly CD players, more people buy them and switch from buying tapes to buying CDs and the demand for tapes decreases.

The table in Fig. 4.12 describes the original and new demand and supply schedules and these schedules are shown as the original (blue) and new (red) demand and supply curves in the graph. The original demand and supply curves intersect at a price of £1.50 a tape and a quantity of 6 million tapes a week. The new supply and demand curves intersect at a price of 60 pence a tape and at the original quantity of 6 million tapes a week. In this example, the decrease in demand and the increase in supply are such that the decrease in the quantity brought about by a decrease in demand is offset by the increase in

FIGURE 4.12

The Effects of a Decrease in Demand and an Increase in Supply

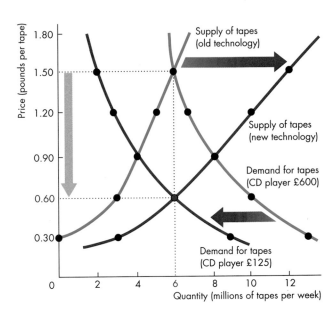

Price (pounds per tape)	Original quantities (millions of tapes per week)		New quantities (millions of tapes per week)	
	Quantity demanded (CD player £600)	Quantity supplied (original technology)	Quantity demanded (CD player £125)	Quantity supplied (new technology)
0.30	13	0	9	3
0.60	10	3	6	6
0.90	8	4	4	8
1.20	7	5	3	10
1.50	6	6	2	123

When CD players cost £600 and the old technology is used to produce tapes, the price of a tape is £1.50 and the quantity is 6 million tapes a week. A fall in the price of CD players decreases the demand for tapes, and improved technology increases the supply of tapes. The new technology supply curve intersects the lower demand curve at 60 pence, a lower price, but in this case the quantity remains constant at 6 million tapes a week. The decrease in demand and increase in supply lower the price but leave the quantity unchanged.

quantity brought about by an increase in supply – so the quantity does not change.

A decrease in demand or an increase in supply lower the price. Therefore when both a decrease in demand and an increase in supply occur together, the price falls.

A decrease in demand decreases the quantity and an increase in supply increases the quantity, so we can't say for sure which way the quantity will change when demand decreases and at the same time, supply increases. In this example, the decrease in demand and the increase in supply are such that the increase in quantity brought about by an increase in supply is offset by the decrease in quantity brought about by a decrease in demand - so the quantity does not change. But notice that if demand had decreased slightly more than shown in the figure, the quantity would have decreased. And if supply had increased by slightly more than shown in the figure, the quantity would have increased.

We can now make two more predictions:

◆ When demand decreases and supply increases, the price falls and the quantity increases, decreases, or remains constant.

◆ When demand increases and supply decreases, the price rises and the quantity increases, decreases, or remains constant.

CD Players, Houses and Apples   At the beginning of this chapter, we looked at some facts about prices and quantities of CD players, house prices and apples. Let's use the theory of demand and supply that we have just studied to explain the movements in the prices and the quantities of these goods.

A Price Slide: CD Players   Figure 4.13 (a) shows the market for CD players. In 1983, when CD players were first manufactured, few firms made them and the supply was small. The supply curve was S_0. In 1983, the demand curve was D_0. The quantities supplied and demanded in 1983 were equal at Q_0, and the real price was £1,000 (1994 pounds). As the technology for making portable CD players improved and as more and more factories began to produce CD players, the supply increased by a large amount and the supply curve shifted rightward from S_0 to S_1. At the same time, increases in incomes and a decrease in the price of CDs increased the demand for CD players. But the increase in demand was much smaller than the increase in supply. The demand curve shifted to the right from D_0 to D_1. With the new demand curve D_1

and supply curve S_1, the equilibrium price fell to £107 and the quantity increased to Q_1. The large increase in supply combined with a smaller increase in demand resulted in an increase in the quantity of CD players sold and a dramatic fall in the real price. Figure 4.13(a) shows the CD player price slide.

A Price Rocket: Houses   Figure 4.13(b) shows the market for owner occupied houses. In 1982, the supply curve for housing in the United Kingdom was S_0. The supply of housing increased between 1982 and 1989 to S_1 through new house building and more people wanting to sell existing houses to S_1. However, the increase in demand was much higher. Demand increased rapidly because of rising incomes, expectations of rising house prices, expectations of capital gains and more people wanting to set up new households - the growth in demand outstripped the growth in supply. The demand curve shifted from D_0 to D_1 between 1982 and 1989. The combined effect of a large increase in demand and a smaller increase in supply was a rapid rise in average real house prices in that period. Part (b) shows the price rocket. The quantity increased from Q_0 to Q_1. After 1990, the pressure of demand reduced and house prices fell on average.

A Price Roller-Coaster: Apples   Figure 4.13(c) shows the market for apples. The demand for apples does not change much over the years. It is described by curve D. But the supply of apples depends mainly on the weather and changes a great deal. The supply of apples fluctuates between S_0 and S_1. With good growing conditions, the supply curve is S_1. With bad growing conditions, supply decreases and the supply curve is S_0. As a consequence of fluctuations in supply, the real price of apples fluctuates between £408 per tonne (1994 prices), the maximum price, and £260 per tonne, the minimum price. The quantity fluctuates between Q_0 and Q_1. Figure 4.13(c) shows the apples price roller-coaster.

◆ ◆ ◆ ◆ By using the theory of demand and supply, you can explain past fluctuations in prices and quantities and also make predictions about future fluctuations. But you will want to do more than predict whether prices are going to rise or fall. In Chapter 5, you will examine a method of predicting *by how much* they will change. In your study of macroeconomics you will learn to explain fluctuations in the economy as a whole. In fact, the theory of demand and supply can help answer almost every economic question.

FIGURE 4.13

Price Slide, Rocket and Roller-coaster

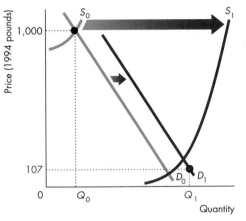

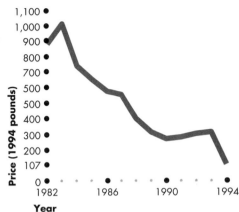

A large increase in the supply of CD players, from S_0 to S_1, between 1983 and 1994, combined with a small increase in demand, from D_0 to D_1, over the same period, resulted in a fall in the average (real) price of CD players from £1,000 in 1983 to £107 in 1994. The quantity of CDs bought and sold increases from Q_0 to Q_1 (part a). Part (b) shows this price slide.

Source: Author's calculations from retail data.

(a) Price slide: CD players

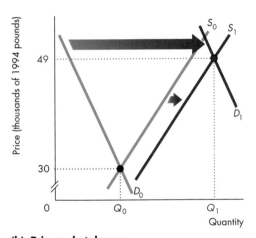

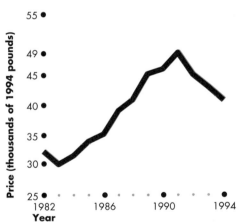

A large increase in demand for housing, from D_0 to D_1, combined with a smaller increase in the supply, resulted in a rise in the (real) average price of a house from £30,246 in 1982 to £48,695 in 1991 and an increase in the quantity, from Q_0 to Q_1 (part a). Part (b) shows this price rocket.

Source: Department of Environment, *House Price Series*, 1994, London, HMSO.

(b) Price rocket: houses

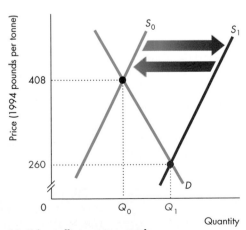

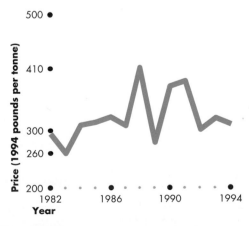

The demand for apples remains constant at D. But supply fluctuates between S_0 and S_1. As a result, the (real) price of apples has fluctuated between £260 per tonne and £408 per tonne – a roller-coaster. Part (c) shows this price roller-coaster.

Source: Central Statistical Office, *Annual Abstract of Statistics*, London, HMSO.

(c) Price roller coaster: apples

Demand and Supply: Wheat Prices and World Shortages

The Essence of the Story

THE FINANCIAL TIMES, 27 OCTOBER 1995

Rewards reaped in grain market

Alison Maitland

The strong rise in grain prices this year has taken the OECD by surprise.

...   This month the forecasting body published its first report....The study predicted world wheat prices would rise to the end of the century....

In fact, 20 years of EU export subsidies came to a halt in July, when poor grain harvests around the world and a sharp fall in stocks pushed global prices into line with the normally inflated EU market....

In the US wheat is being exported at nearly $200 a tonne – almost 70 per cent above the trade price in mid-April when the market began to move up.

Grain has become the hottest property on food commodity markets, with wheat futures in Chicago reaching 15-year highs.

The Economist Intelligence Unit says US wheat prices could break all-time records in the next six months and predicts a supply crisis if harvests in Argentina and Australia follow the same disappointing patterns of northern hemisphere producers....

Together, the US, Canada, EU, Argentina and Australia account for nearly 90 per cent of world trade. This year's US wheat crop is expected to be the smallest for four years because of the unfavourable weather....In the EU, Spanish cereals were devastated by summer drought. Argentina, which still has its harvests to come, has been suffering its most severe drought for 40 years and Australia has been affected by dry conditions.

Demand, meanwhile, is increasing. Russia faces its worst harvest for 30 years and may turn to the world market for imports. China's needs, worsened by a shortage of water, are expected to exceed the 10m tonnes of wheat it imported last year.

World grain stocks...will fall to 92m tonnes – their lowest level for 20 years – by the end of the crop year next spring. In the EU alone, a grain mountain of 33m tonnes two years ago has been knocked down to just 3m tonnes.

The position has been made worse because most cereals have been affected by crop failures and higher prices, so wheat users have been unable to switch easily to cheaper alternatives for animal feed....

Consumers in the developed world may face increases in poultry and bread prices in coming months. Bernard Matthews, the biggest turkey producer in Europe, says its prices could rise in the new year. Feed accounts for 65 per cent of the cost of raising an ovenready bird, with wheat accounting for over half the feed mix....

However, the main victims of high grain prices are developing countries, which...may be unable to finance the additional cereal imports they need,...about $3bn – or 25 per cent more than they paid last year....

The Food and Agriculture Organisation says next year's harvest 'will be crucial for world food security'. Cereal output must rise by 5 per cent to meet expected demand. Replenishing stocks to 'minimum safe levels' would need an 8–9 per cent increase in production....

It is hard to forecast next year's world output, although crops are expected to be bigger in the US and the cut in set-aside will boost EU production. But...demand for cereals from fast growing Asian countries could offset crop increases and keep stocks tight....China is expanding its livestock industry and coming to the world market for ever bigger supplies of animal feed.

- World grain prices rose sharply in 1995 and are forecast to continue rising into the twenty-first century.

- Droughts in the main producing countries cut harvests by more than 25 per cent and the world consumed more food than it produced for the third year running.

- World grain stocks are at their lowest levels for 20 years and output must rise by 5 per cent just to meet demand, and by 8–9 per cent to replenish stocks.

- World demand is rising in the short run as countries which normally grow their own wheat are forced to import grain as their crops fail.

- World demand is rising in the long run as the world's population increases. Since 1990, food production has not increased, but the world's population has increased by 440 million.

Economic Analysis

■ Figure 1 shows the world market for wheat in 1995. The demand curve for wheat, D_0, is steep as there are few substitutes in drought years. A large increase in price brings a proportionately small decrease in quantity.

■ Before the drought, the supply curve is S_0. The world price of wheat is $118 per tonne and the quantity traded is Q_0. Drought decreases the supply of wheat and the supply curve shifts leftward to S_1.

■ At $118 per tonne, the quantity of wheat traded falls to Q_1, creating a shortage. The price of wheat rises in response. As the price rises, demand decreases (a movement up the demand curve) and supply increases (a movement up the supply curve). The increase in supply reduces stocks of wheat. Quantity rises to Q_2 and price rises by 70 per cent to $200 per tonne.

■ Figure 2 shows the world market for wheat the following year. The demand curve for wheat has not changed at D_0, and the supply curve remains at S_1 if harvests are poor and some stocks remain.

■ A 6 per cent increase in the harvest shifts the supply curve rightward to S_2 in Fig. 2. Price falls to $150 per tonne and quantity increases to Q_2. An 8 per cent increase fully replenishes stocks. If China's expanding livestock industry raises world demand for wheat, the demand schedule shifts rightward to D_1. Quantity rises to Q_3, draining stocks, and price rises again to $180 per tonne.

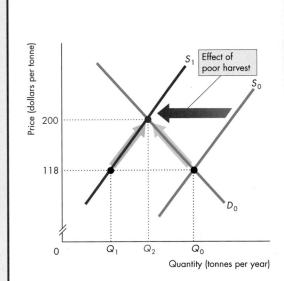

Figure 1

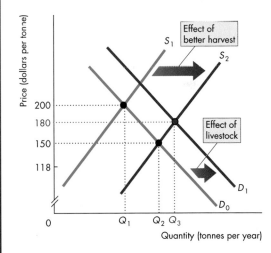

Figure 2

'...if any accident should move the scale of production from its equilibrium position, there will be instantly brought into play forces tending to push it back to that position; just as, if a stone hanging by a string is displaced from its equilibrium position, the force of gravity will at once tend to bring it back...'

Alfred Marshall, PRINCIPLES OF ECONOMICS

Discovering the Laws of Demand and Supply

THE ISSUES AND IDEAS

How are prices determined? Antoine-Augustin Cournot was the first to answer this question by using demand and supply, in the 1830s. But it was the development and expansion of the railways during the 1850s that gave the newly emerging theory its first practical applications. Railways in the 1850s were as close to the cutting edge of technology as airlines are today. And just as in the airline industry today, competition among the railways was fierce.

In England, Dionysius Lardner used demand and supply to show railway companies how they could increase their profits by cutting rates on long-distance business in which competition was fiercest, and by raising them on short-haul business in which they had less to fear from other transport suppliers.

The principles that were first worked out by Lardner in the 1850s are used by economists today to calculate the freight rates and passenger fares that will give airlines the largest possible profit. The rates that result have a lot in common with the railway rates of the nineteenth century. The airlines have local routes that feed like the spokes of a wheel into a hub on which there is little competition and on which they charge high fares (per kilometre), and they have long-distance routes between hubs on which they compete fiercely with other airlines and on which fares per kilometre are lowest.

In France, Jules Dupuit worked out how to use demand theory to calculate the value of railway bridges. His work was the forerunner of what is today called *cost-benefit analysis*. Working with the same principles invented by Dupuit, economists today calculate the costs and benefits of motorways and airports, of dams and power stations.

THEN ...

Dupuit used the law of demand to determine whether a bridge or canal would be valued enough by its users to justify the cost of building it. Lardner first worked out the relationship between the cost of production and supply and used demand and supply theory to explain the costs, prices and profits of railway operations. He also used the theory to discover ways of increasing revenue by raising rates on short-haul business and lowering them on long-distance freight.

... AND NOW

Today, using the same principles devised by Dupuit, economists calculate whether the benefits of expanding airports and air traffic control facilities are sufficient to cover their costs, and airline companies use the principles developed by Lardner to set their prices and to decide when to offer 'seat sales'. Like the railways before them, the airlines charge a high price per kilometre on short flights, for which they face little competition, and a low price per kilometre on long flights, for which competition is fierce.

THE ECONOMISTS: ANTOINE-AUGUSTIN COURNOT AND ALFRED MARSHALL

Antoine-Augustin Cournot

Antoine-Augustin Cournot (1801–1877), professor of mathematics at the University of Lyon, France, drew the first demand curve in the 1830s. The first practical application of demand theory, by Jules Dupuit (1804–1866), a French engineer/economist, was the calculation of the benefits from building a bridge – and, given that a bridge had been built, of the correct toll to charge for its use.

The laws of demand and supply and the connection between the costs of production and supply were first worked out by Dionysius Lardner (1793–1859), an Irish professor of philosophy at the University of London. Known satirically among scientists of the day as 'Dionysius Diddler', Lardner worked on an amazing range of problems from astronomy to railway engineering to economics. A colourful character, he would have been a regular guest of Clive Anderson if his talk show had been around in the 1850s. Lardner visited the Ecole des Ponts et Chaussées (the School of Bridges and Roads) in Paris and must have learned a great deal from Dupuit, who was doing his major work on economics at the time.

Many others had a hand in refining the theory of demand and supply, but the first thorough and complete statement of the theory as we know it today was that of Alfred Marshall (1842–1924) professor of political economy at the University of Cambridge, who, in 1890, published a monumental treatise – *Principles of Economics* – a work that became *the* textbook on economics for almost half a century. Marshall was an outstanding mathematician, but he kept mathematics and even diagrams in the background. His own supply and demand diagram (reproduced here at its original size) appears only in a footnote.

Alfred Marshall

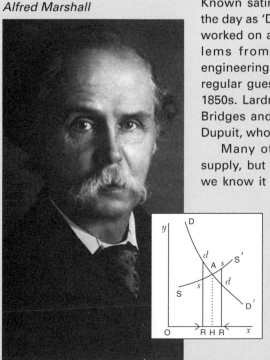

Opportunity Cost and Price

Opportunity cost is measured by a relative price – the money price of one good or service divided by the money price of another good or service. A convenient way to express opportunity cost and relative price is in terms of a 'basket' of all other goods and services – the price of one good divided by the price (index) of a basket of all goods. This relative price is called a real price. The theory of demand and supply explains how real (relative) prices are determined. (pp. 70–71)

Demand

The quantity demanded of a good or service is the amount that consumers plan to buy during a given time period at a particular price. The quantity that consumers plan to buy of any good depends on:

◆ The price of the good
◆ The prices of related goods – substitutes and complements
◆ Income
◆ Expected future prices
◆ Population
◆ Preferences

Other things remaining the same, the higher the price of a good, the smaller is the quantity demanded of that good. The relationship between the quantity demanded and price, all other influences on consumers' planned purchases remaining the same, is illustrated by the demand schedule or demand curve. A change in the price of a good produces movement along the demand curve for that good. Such a movement is called a change in the quantity demanded.

Changes in all other influences on buying plans are said to change demand. When demand changes, there is a new demand schedule and the demand curve shifts. When there is an increase in demand, the demand curve shifts rightward; when there is a decrease in demand, the demand curve shifts leftward. (pp. 71–75)

Supply

The quantity supplied of a good or service is the amount that producers plan to sell during a given time period. The quantity that producers plan to sell of any good or service depends on:

◆ The price of the good
◆ The prices of factors of production
◆ The prices of related goods
◆ Expected future prices
◆ The number of suppliers
◆ Technology

Other things remaining the same, the higher the price of a good, the larger is the quantity supplied of that good. The relationship between the quantity supplied and price, all other influences on firms' planned sales remaining the same, is illustrated by the supply schedule or supply curve. A change in the price of a good produces movement along the supply curve for that good. Such a movement is called a change in the quantity supplied.

Changes in all other influences on selling plans are said to change supply. When supply changes, there is a new supply schedule and the supply curve shifts. When there is an increase in supply, the supply curve shifts rightward; when there is a decrease in supply, the supply curve shifts leftward. (pp. 76–79)

Price Determination

Price regulates the quantities supplied and demanded. The higher the price, the greater is the quantity supplied and the smaller is the quantity demanded. At high prices, there is a surplus – an excess of the quantity supplied over the quantity demanded – and the price falls. At low prices, there is a shortage – an excess of the quantity demanded over the quantity supplied – and the price rises. There is one price and only one price at which the quantity demanded equals the quantity supplied. That price is the equilibrium price. At that price, there are no forces changing the price. (pp. 80–82)

Predicting Changes in Price and Quantity

Changes in demand and supply lead to changes in price and in the quantity bought and sold. An increase in demand leads to a rise in price and to an increase in the quantity traded. A decrease in demand leads to a fall in price and to a decrease in the quantity traded. An increase in supply leads to an increase in the quantity traded and a fall in price. A decrease in supply leads to a decrease in the quantity traded and a rise in price.

Simultaneous increases in demand and supply increase the quantity bought and sold, but the price can rise, fall, or remain constant. If the increase in demand is larger than the increase in supply, the price rises. If the increase in demand is smaller than the increase in supply, the price falls. If demand and supply increase by the same amounts, the price does not change. Simultaneous opposing changes in demand and supply such as an increase in supply and a decrease in demand decrease the price, but the quantity can increase, decrease, or remain constant. If the decrease in demand is larger than the increase in supply, the quantity traded decreases. If the decrease in demand is smaller than the increase in supply, the quantity traded increases. If the decrease in demand equals the increase in supply, the quantity traded does not change. (pp. 82–87)

K E Y   E L E M E N T S

Key Terms

Change in demand, 74
Change in supply, 78
Change in the quantity demanded, 74
Change in the quantity supplied, 78
Complement, 73
Demand, 73
Demand curve, 72
Equilibrium price, 81
Equilibrium quantity, 81
Inferior good, 73
Normal good, 73
Quantity demanded, 71
Quantity supplied, 76
Relative price, 70
Substitute, 73
Supply, 76
Supply curve, 76

◆ Key Figures and Tables

Figure 4.2	The Demand Curve, 72
Figure 4.4	A Change in Demand Versus a Change in the Quantity Demanded, 75
Figure 4.5	The Supply Curve, 77
Figure 4.7	A Change in Supply Versus a Change in the Quantity Supplied, 79
Figure 4.8	Equilibrium, 80
Figure 4.9	The Effects of a Change in Demand, 82
Figure 4.10	The Effects of a Change in Supply, 83
Table 4.1	The Demand for Tapes, 74
Table 4.2	The Supply of Tapes, 78

R E V I E W   Q U E S T I O N S

1 Distinguish between a money price and a real or relative price. Which is an opportunity cost and why?

2 Define the quantity demanded of a good or service.

3 Define the quantity supplied of a good or service.

4 List the main factors that influence the amount that consumers plan to buy and say whether an increase in the factor increases or decreases consumers' planned purchases.

5 List the main factors that influence the quantity that producers plan to sell and say whether an increase in that factor increases or decreases firms' planned sales.

6 State the law of demand and the law of supply.

7 If a fixed amount of a good is available, what does the demand curve tell us about the price that consumers are willing to pay for that fixed quantity?

8 If consumers are only willing to buy a certain fixed quantity, what does the supply curve tell us about the price at which firms will supply that quantity?

9 Distinguish between:
  a A change in demand and a change in the quantity demanded.
  b A change in supply and a change in the quantity supplied.

10 Why is the price at which the quantity demanded equals the quantity supplied the equilibrium price?

11 What is the effect on the price of a tape and the quantity of tapes sold if:
  a The price of CDs increases?
  b The price of a Walkman increases?
  c The supply of CD players increases?
  d Consumers' incomes increase and firms producing tapes switch to new cost-saving technology?
  e The prices of the factors of production used to make tapes increase?

PROBLEMS

1 Suppose that one of the following events occurs:
  a The price of petrol rises.
  b The price of petrol falls.
  c All speed limits on motorways are abolished.
  d A new fuel-effective engine that runs on cheap alcohol is invented.
  e The population doubles.
  f Robotic production plants lower the cost of producing cars.
  g A law banning all car imports from outside the European Union is passed.
  h The rates for car insurance double.
  i The minimum age for drivers is increased to 25 years.
  j A massive and high-grade oil supply is discovered in Norway.
  k The environmental lobby succeeds in closing down all nuclear power stations.
  l The price of cars rises.
  m The price of cars falls.
  n The summer temperature is 10 degrees lower than normal.

State which of the above events will produce:
  1 A movement along the demand curve for petrol.
  2 A shift of the demand curve for petrol rightward.
  3 A shift of the demand curve for petrol leftward.
  4 A movement along the supply curve of petrol.

  5 A shift of the supply curve of petrol rightward.
  6 A shift of the supply curve of petrol leftward.
  7 A movement along the demand curve for cars.
  8 A movement along the supply curve of cars.
  9 A shift of the demand curve for cars rightward.
  10 A shift of the demand curve for cars leftward.
  11 A shift of the supply curve of cars rightward.
  12 A shift of the supply curve of cars leftward.
  13 An increase in the price of petrol.
  14 A decrease in the equilibrium quantity of oil.

2 The demand and supply schedules for bags of crisps are as follows:

Price	Quantity supplied	Quantity demanded
(pence per week)	(millions of bags a week)	
10	200	0
20	180	30
30	160	60
40	140	90
50	120	120
60	100	140
70	80	160
80	60	180
90	40	200

  a What is the equilibrium price of a bag of crisps?
  b What is the equilibrium quantity of bags of crisps?

Suppose that a huge fire destroys one-half of the crisp-producing factories. Supply decreases to one-half of the amount shown in the above supply schedule.

c What is the new equilibrium price of crisps?
d What is the new equilibrium quantity of crisps?
e Has there been a shift in or a movement along the supply curve of crisps?
f Has there been a shift in or a movement along the demand curve for crisps?
g As the crisp factories destroyed by fire are rebuilt and gradually resume crisp production what will happen to:
1 The price of crisps?
2 The quantity of crisps bought?
3 The demand curve for crisps?
4 The supply curve of crisps?

3 Suppose the demand and supply schedules for crisps are those in Problem 2. An increase in the teenage population increases the demand for crisps by 40 million bags a week.

a Write out the new demand schedule for crisps.
b What is the new equilibrium quantity of crisps?
c What is the new equilibrium price of crisps?
d Has there been a shift in or a movement along the demand curve for crisps?
e Has there been a shift in or a movement

along the supply curve of crisps?

4 Suppose the demand and supply schedules for crisps are those in Problem 2. An increase in the teenage population increases the demand for crisps by 40 million bags a week, and simultaneously the fire described in Problem 2 occurs, wiping out one-half of the crisp-producing factories.

a Draw a graph of the original and new demand and supply curves.
b What is the new equilibrium quantity of crisps?
c What is the new equilibrium price of crisps?

5 Read the *Reading Between the Lines* article on pp. 88–89 again and then:

a Identify the factors which cause a change in the world supply of wheat.
b Use a diagram to show why world wheat prices have risen so much.
c What will be the impact on price of rising world demand for wheat?

6 Turn to p. 90 and read the Economics in History material. Then:

a Explain why there was so much interest in trying to understand the principles of demand and supply during the period of the industrial revolution?
b Explain why Alfred Marshall is considered to be the 'father' of modern economics?

BOX 4.1: THE MATHEMATICS OF DEMAND AND SUPPLY

1. Demand and Supply Equations

If we assume the demand curve is a straight line, it can be represented by a simple straight line equation:

$$Q^d = a - bP \qquad (1)$$

The equation says that the quantity demanded, Q^d, is equal to a constant amount, a, plus an amount that varies with price, P. Each unit increase in price, P, brings b units *decrease* in quantity demanded because the sign in front of b is negative. Figure B4.1 shows that $\Delta Q^d/\Delta P = -b$, the slope of the demand line. A change in price, P, (other things remaining the same) leads to a

movement along the demand line, Q^d. The line, Q^d, will shift if a increases or decreases. Notice that the line is drawn with quantity on the vertical axis and price on the horizontal axis from Equation 1 – the opposite way round from figures in this book. This makes no difference to the mathematics.

We can also represent the supply curve as a simple straight line equation:

$$Q^s = f + gP \qquad (2)$$

This equation says that quantity supplied, Q^s, is equal to a constant amount, f, plus an amount that varies with price, P. Each unit increase in

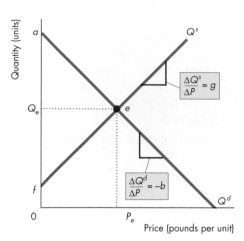

Figure B4.1 Demand and Supply

price, P, brings g units increase in quantity supplied because the sign in front of g is positive. Figure B4.1 shows that $\Delta Q^s / P = g$, the slope of the supply line. A change in price, P, (other things remaining the same) leads to a movement along the supply line, Q^s. The line, Q^s, will shift if f increases or decreases.

In equilibrium, the quantity supplied equals the quantity demanded (point e in the figure) where:

$$Q^s = Q^d \tag{3}$$

2. Equilibrium Price

You can work out the equilibrium price, P_e, without drawing a diagram by substituting Equations 1 and 2 into Equation 3. So:

$$f + gP = a - bP$$

Move all the P terms to the left and the constant, f, to the right to give:

$$(b + g)P = a - f$$

Now divide both sides by $(b + g)$ to find the equilibrium price:

$$P_e = \frac{(a - f)}{(b + g)} \tag{4}$$

You can now see the how the main predictions about price work in the equation. If a increases, demand increases and so the price must increase. If f increases, supply increases but the price must fall. If both a and f increase, both demand and supply increase, and the effect on price is ambiguous. Try these changes on a diagram to prove them to yourself.

3. Equilibrium Quantity

You can find the equilibrium quantity, Q_e, in a similar way. Substitute the equilibrium price you have just found into either the original demand or supply equations. Substituting Equation 4 into Equation 1 gives:

$$Q_e = a - \frac{b(a - f)}{(b + g)} \tag{5}$$

You can simplify this further by using $(b + g)$ as the common denominator, giving:

$$Q_e = \frac{a(b + g) - b(a - f)}{(b + g)} \tag{6}$$

If you now multiply out the brackets, the ab's cancel out to give:

$$Q_e = \frac{(ag + bf)}{(b + g)} \tag{7}$$

You can see how the main predictions about quantity work in the equilibrium quantity equation – Equation 7. If a increases, demand increases and so does quantity. If f increases, supply increases and so does quantity. If a increases and f decreases, demand increases and supply decreases, but the effect on quantity is ambiguous.

CHAPTER

5

ELASTICITY

After studying this chapter you will be able to:

◆ Define and calculate the price elasticity of demand

◆ Explain what determines the elasticity of demand

◆ Use elasticity to determine whether a price change will increase or decrease total revenue

◆ Define and calculate other elasticities of demand

◆ Define and calculate the elasticity of supply

Y OU ARE THE CHIEF ECONOMIC STRATEGIST FOR THE ORGANIZATION OF Petroleum Exporting Countries (OPEC) and you want to increase OPEC's revenue. But you have a dilemma. You know that to increase the price of oil, you must restrict its supply. You also know that to sell more oil, you must lower its price. What will you recommend: restrict supply or lower the price? Which action will increase OPEC's revenue? ◆ As OPEC's economic strategist, you need to know a lot about the demand for oil. For example, as the world economy grows, how will that growth translate into an increase in demand for oil? What about substitutes for oil? Will we discover inexpensive methods to convert coal and tar sands into usable fuel? Will nuclear energy become safe and cheap enough to compete with oil? ◆ OPEC is not the only organization with a dilemma. A bumper grape crop is good news for wine consumers. It lowers the price of wine. But is it good news for grape grow-

OPEC's Dilemma

ers? Do they get more revenue? Or does the lower price more than wipe out their gains from larger quantities sold? ◆ The government also faces a dilemma. Looking for greater tax revenue to balance its budget, it decides to increase the tax rates on tobacco and alcohol. Do the higher tax rates bring in more tax revenue? Or do people switch to substitutes for tobacco and alcohol on such a large scale that the higher tax rate brings in less tax revenue?

◆ ◆ ◆ ◆ In this chapter you will learn how to tackle questions such as the ones just posed. You will learn how we can measure in a precise way the responsiveness of the quantities bought and sold to changes in prices and other influences on buyers or sellers.

Elasticity of Demand

Let's begin by looking a bit more closely at your task as OPEC's economic strategist. You are trying to decide whether to advise a cut in production that decreases supply and shifts the supply curve leftward. To make this decision, you need to know how the quantity of oil demanded responds to a change in price. You also need some way to measure that response.

The Responsiveness of the Quantity Demanded to Price

To understand the importance of the responsiveness of the quantity of oil demanded to a change in its price, let's compare two possible scenarios in the oil industry, shown in Fig. 5.1. International oil prices are always quoted in dollars. In the two parts of the figure, the supply curves are identical, but the demand curves differ.

The supply curve S_0 in each part of the figure shows the initial supply. It intersects the demand curve, in both cases, at a price of \$10 a barrel and a quantity of 40 million barrels a day. Suppose that you contemplate a decrease in supply that shifts the supply curve from S_0 to S_1. In part (a), the new supply curve S_1 intersects the demand curve D_a at a price of \$30 a barrel and a quantity of 23 million barrels a day. In part (b), with demand curve D_b, the same supply curve shift increases the price to \$15 a barrel and decreases the quantity to 15 million barrels a day. You can see that in part (a) the price increases by more and the quantity decreases by less than it does in part (b). What happens to the total revenue of the oil producers in these two cases?

The **total revenue** from the sale of a good equals the price of the good multiplied by the quantity sold. An increase in price has two opposing effects on total revenue. It increases the revenue on each unit sold (blue area). But it also leads to a decrease in the quantity sold, which decreases revenue (red area). Either of these two opposing effects could be the larger. In case (a) the first effect is larger (blue area exceeds red area), so total revenue increases. In case (b) the second effect is larger (red area exceeds blue area), so total revenue decreases.

FIGURE 5.1

Demand, Supply and Total Revenue

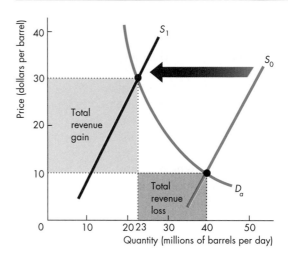

(a) More total revenue

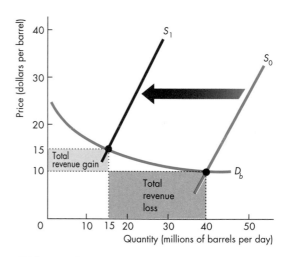

(b) Less total revenue

If supply is cut from S_0 to S_1, the price rises and the quantity decreases. In part (a), total revenue – the quantity multiplied by the price – increases from \$400 million to \$690 million a day. The increase in total revenue from a higher price (blue area) exceeds the decrease in total revenue from lower sales (red area). In part (b), total revenue decreases from \$400 million to \$225 million a day. The increase in total revenue from a higher price (blue area) is less than the decrease in total revenue from lower sales (red area). These two different responses of total revenue arise from different responses of the quantity demanded to a change in price.

Slope Depends on Units of Measurement

The difference between these two cases is the responsiveness of the quantity demanded to a change in price. Demand curve D_a is steeper than demand curve D_b. But we can't compare two demand curves simply by their slopes, because the slope of a demand curve depends on the units in which we measure the price and quantity. Also, we often need to compare the demand curves for different goods and services. For example, when deciding by how much to change tax rates, the government needs to compare the demand for oil and the demand for tobacco. Which is more responsive to price? Which can be taxed at an even higher rate without decreasing the tax revenue? Comparing the slope of the demand curve for oil with the slope of the demand curve for tobacco has no meaning since oil is measured in litres and tobacco in grams – completely unrelated units.

To overcome these problems, we need a measure of responsiveness that is independent of the units of measurement of prices and quantities. Elasticity is such a measure.

Elasticity: A Units-free Measure

The **price elasticity of demand** is a units-free measure of the responsiveness of the quantity demanded of a good to a change in its price, other things remaining the same. It is calculated by using the formula

$$\text{Price elasticity of demand} = \frac{\text{Percentage change in quantity demanded}}{\text{Percentage change in price}}$$

Elasticity is a units-free measure because the percentage change in a variable is independent of the units in which the variable is measured. For example, if we measure a price in pounds, an increase from £1.00 to £1.50 is a 50 pence increase. If we measure a price in pence, an increase from 100 pence to 150 pence is also a 50 pence increase. The first increase is 0.5 of a unit and the second increase is 50 units, but they are both 50 per cent increases.

Minus Sign and Elasticity When the price of a good *increases* along a demand curve, the quantity demanded *decreases*. Because a *positive* price change results in a *negative* change in the quantity demanded, the price elasticity of demand

is a negative number. But it is the magnitude, or *absolute value*, of the price elasticity of demand that tells us how responsive – how elastic – demand is. To compare elasticities, we use the magnitude of the price elasticity of demand and ignore the minus sign.

Calculating Elasticity

To calculate the elasticity of demand, we need to know the quantities demanded at different prices, all the other influences on consumers' buying plans remaining the same. Let's assume that we have the relevant data on prices and quantities demanded of oil and calculate the elasticity of demand for oil.

Figure 5.2 enlarges one section on the demand curve for oil and shows how the quantity demanded responds to a small change in price. Initially the price is $9.50 a barrel and 41 million barrels a day are sold – the original point in the figure. Then the price increases to $10.50 a barrel and the quantity demanded decreases to 39 million barrels a day – the new point in the figure. When the price increases by $1 a barrel, the quantity demanded decreases by 2 million barrels a day.

This calculation measures the elasticity at an average price of $10 a barrel and an average quantity of 40 million barrels.

To calculate the elasticity of demand, we express the changes in price and quantity demanded as percentages of the *average price* and the *average quantity*. By using the average price and average quantity, we calculate the elasticity at a point on the demand curve midway between the original point and the new point. The original price is $9.50 and the new price is $10.50, so the average price is $10. The $1 price increase is 10 per cent of the average price. The original quantity demanded is 41 million barrels and the new quantity demanded is 39 million barrels, so the average quantity demanded is 40 million barrels. The 2 million barrel decrease in the quantity demanded is 5 per cent of the average quantity. So the price elasticity of demand, which is the percentage change in the quantity demanded (5 per cent) divided by the percentage change in price (10 per cent), is 0.5. That is:

$$\text{Price elasticity of demand} = \frac{\%\Delta Q}{\%\Delta P}$$
$$= \frac{5\%}{10\%} = 0.5$$

FIGURE 5.2

Calculating the Elasticity of Demand

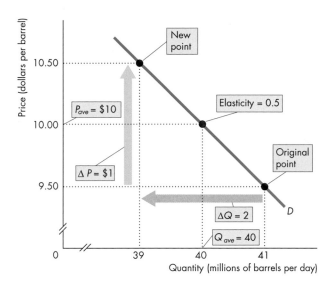

The elasticity of demand is calculated by using the formula[1] :

$$\text{Price elasticity of demand} = \frac{\text{Percentage change in quantity demanded}}{\text{Percentage change in price}}$$

$$= \frac{\%\Delta Q/Q_{ave}}{\%\Delta P/P_{ave}}$$

$$= \frac{2/40}{1/10}$$

$$= 0.5$$

[1] In the formula the Greek letter delta (Δ) stands for 'change in' and % Δ stands for 'percentage change in'.

Average Price, Average Quantity and Arc Elasticity

We use the average price and average quantity to avoid having two values for the elasticity of demand, depending on whether the price increases or decreases. A price increase of $1 is 10.5 per cent of $9.50, and 2 million barrels is 4.9 per cent of 41 million barrels. If we use these numbers to calculate the elasticity, we get 0.47. A price decrease of $1 is 9.5 per cent of $10.50, and 2 million barrels is

5.1 per cent of 39 million barrels. Using these numbers to calculate the elasticity, we get 0.54. Using the average price and average quantity demanded, the elasticity is 0.5 regardless of whether the price increases or decreases. The average price method gives an estimate of the price elasticity of demand between two points on the demand curve – between the prices $9.50 and $10.50 in this case. This is called the **arc elasticity of demand**. An example of how to find the price elasticity value at one specific point – point elasticity – is given in Box 5.1 at the end of this chapter. Examples using differential calculus are also given in the box.

Percentages and Proportions   Elasticity is the ratio of the percentage change in the quantity demanded to the percentage change in the price. It is also, equivalently, the proportionate change in the quantity demanded divided by the proportionate change in the price. The proportionate change in price is $\Delta P/P_{ave}$ and the proportionate change in quantity demanded is $\Delta Q/Q_{ave}$. The percentage changes are the proportionate changes multiplied by 100. So when we divide one percentage change by another, the 100s cancel and the result is the same as we get by using the proportionate changes.

Inelastic and Elastic Demand

Figure 5.3 shows three demand curves that cover the entire range of possible elasticities of demand. In Fig. 5.3(a), the quantity demanded is constant regardless of the price. If the quantity demanded remains constant when the price changes, then the elasticity of demand is zero and demand is said to be **perfectly inelastic**. One good that has a low elasticity of demand is insulin. Insulin is of such importance to some diabetics that they will buy the quantity that keeps them healthy at almost any price. Even at low prices, they have no reason to buy a larger quantity.

If the percentage change in the quantity demanded is less than the percentage change in price, then the magnitude of the elasticity of demand is between zero and 1 and demand is said to be **inelastic**. The demand curve in Fig. 5.2 is an example of inelastic demand. If the percentage change in the quantity demanded exceeds the percentage change in price, then the magnitude of the elasticity is greater than 1 and demand is said to be **elastic**. The dividing line between inelastic

FIGURE 5.3

Inelastic and Elastic Demand

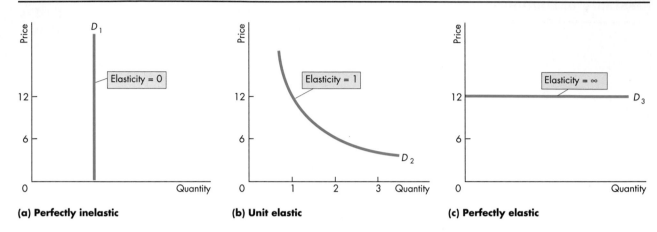

(a) Perfectly inelastic   **(b) Unit elastic**   **(c) Perfectly elastic**

Elasticity usually varies along the demand curve, but each demand curve illustrated here has a constant elasticity. The demand curve in part (a) is for a good that has a zero price elasticity of demand. The demand curve in part (b) is for a good with a unit elasticity of demand. The demand curve in part (c) is for a good with an infinite elasticity of demand.

and elastic demand is the case in which the percentage change in the quantity demanded equals the percentage change in price. In this case, the elasticity of demand is 1 and demand is said to be **unit elastic**. The demand curve in Fig. 5.3(b) is an example of unit elastic demand.

If the quantity demanded is infinitely responsive to a price change, then the magnitude of the elasticity of demand is infinity and demand is said to be **perfectly elastic**. The demand curve in Fig. 5.3(c) is an example of perfectly elastic demand. An example of a good that has a high elasticity of demand (almost infinite) is ballpoint pens from the university bookshop and from the newsagent's shop close by. If the two shops offer pens for the same price, some people buy from one and some from the other. But if the bookshop increases the price of pens, even by a small amount, while the shop close by maintains the lower price, the quantity of pens demanded from the bookshop will fall to zero. Ballpoint pens from the two shops are perfect substitutes for each other.

Elasticity along a Straight-line Demand Curve

Elasticity is not the same as slope, but the two are related. To understand how they are related, let's

look at elasticity along a straight-line demand curve – a demand curve that has a constant slope.

Figure 5.4 illustrates the calculation of elasticity along a straight-line demand curve for oil. Let's calculate the elasticity of demand for oil at an average price of $40 a barrel and an average quantity of 4 million barrels a day. To do so, imagine that the price rises from $30 a barrel to $50 a barrel. The change in the price is $20 and the average price is $40 (average of $30 and $50), which means that the proportionate change in price is

$$\frac{\Delta P}{P_{ave}} = \frac{20}{40}$$

At a price of $30 a barrel, the quantity demanded is 8 million barrels a day. At a price of $50 a barrel, the quantity demanded is zero. So the change in the quantity demanded is 8 million barrels a day and the average quantity is 4 million barrels a day (the average of 8 million and zero), so the proportionate change in the quantity demanded is

$$\frac{\Delta Q}{Q_{ave}} = \frac{8}{4}$$

Dividing the proportionate change in the quantity demanded by the proportionate change in the price gives

FIGURE 5.4

Elasticity Along a Straight-line Demand Curve

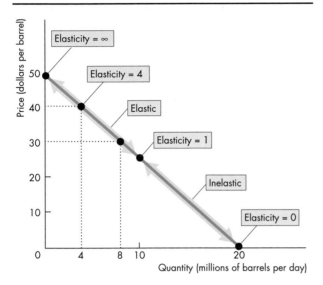

On a straight-line demand curve, elasticity decreases as the price falls and the quantity demanded increases. Demand is unit elastic at the midpoint of the demand curve (elasticity is 1). Above the midpoint demand is elastic, and below the midpoint demand is inelastic. Demand is perfectly elastic (elasticity = infinity) where quantity demanded is zero, and demand is perfectly inelastic (elasticity = zero) where the price is zero.

$$\frac{\Delta Q / Q_{ave}}{\Delta P / P_{ave}} = \frac{8/4}{20/40} = 4$$

By using this same method, we can calculate the elasticity of demand at any price and quantity along the demand curve. Because the demand curve for oil in this example is a straight line, a $20 price change brings an 8 million barrel quantity change at every average price. So in the elasticity formula, $\Delta Q = 8$ and $\Delta P = 20$ regardless of average quantity and average price. But the lower the average price, the greater is the average quantity demanded. So the lower the average price, the less elastic is demand.

Check this proposition by calculating the elasticity of demand for oil at the midpoint of the demand curve, where the price is $25 a barrel and the quantity demanded is 10 million barrels a day. The

proportionate change in price is $20 / $25 = 0.8, and the proportionate change in the quantity demanded is 8/10 = 0.8, so the elasticity of demand is 1. On a straight-line demand curve, the price elasticity is always 1 at the midpoint. Above the midpoint demand is elastic, and below the midpoint demand is inelastic. Demand is perfectly elastic (infinity) where the quantity demanded is zero and perfectly inelastic (zero) where the price is zero.

The Factors that Influence the Elasticity of Demand

Actual values of elasticities of demand have been estimated and some examples for the United Kingdom are set out in Table 5.1. You can see that these real-world elasticities of demand range from 1.4 for fresh meat, the most elastic in the table, to zero for bread, the least elastic in the table. What makes the demand for some goods elastic and the demand for others inelastic? Elasticity depends on three main factors:

◆ The closeness of substitutes

◆ The proportion of income spent on the good

◆ The time elapsed since a price change

Closeness of Substitutes   The closer the substitutes for a good or service, the more elastic is the demand for it. For example, housing has few real substitutes (sleeping on a friend's floor, in a hostel, or on the street). As a result, the demand for housing is inelastic. In contrast, metals have good substitutes such as plastics and car travel has substitutes in public transport, so the demand for these goods is elastic.

In everyday language we call some goods, such as food and housing, *necessities* and other goods, such as exotic vacations, *luxuries*. Necessities are goods that have poor substitutes and that are crucial for our well-being, so generally they have inelastic demands. Luxuries are goods that usually have many substitutes and so have elastic demands.

The degree of substitutability between two goods also depends on how narrowly (or broadly) we define them. For example, even though oil does not have a close substitute, different types of oil are close substitutes for each other. Saudi Arabian Light, a particular type of oil, is a close substitute for Alaskan North Slope, another particular type of oil. If you happen to be the economic adviser to

---

TABLE 5.1

Some Real-world Price Elasticities for the UK

Good or Service	Elasticity
ELASTIC DEMAND	
Fresh meat	1.4
Spirits	1.3
Wine	1.2
UNIT ELASTICITY	
Services	1.0
Cereals	1.0
INELASTIC DEMAND	
Durable goods	0.9
Fruit juice	0.8
Green vegetables	0.6
Tobacco	0.5
Beer	0.5
Bread	0.0

Sources: Ministry of Agriculture, Food and Fisheries *Household Food Consumption and Expenditure*, 1992, London, HMSO. C. Godfrey. Modelling Demand. In *Preventing Alcohol and Tobacco Problems*, Vol 1, (A. Maynard and P. Tether, eds), Avebury, 1990. J. Muellbauer, 'Testing the Barten Model of Household Composition Effects and the Cost of Children', *Economic Journal*, (September 1977).

Saudi Arabia (as well as the OPEC economic strategist!), you will not contemplate a unilateral price increase. Even though Saudi Arabian Light has some unique characteristics, other oils can easily substitute for it, and most buyers will be sensitive to its price relative to the prices of other types of oil. So the demand for Saudi Arabian Light is highly elastic.

This example, which distinguishes between oil in general and different types of oil, applies to many other goods and services. The elasticity of demand for meat in general is low but the elasticity of demand for beef, lamb, or chicken is high. The elasticity of demand for personal computers is low, but the elasticity of demand for an Elonex, Dell, or IBM is high.

The closeness of the substitutes for a good also depends on some other factors discussed below.

Proportion of Income Spent on the Good

Other things remaining the same, the higher the proportion of income spent on a good, the more elastic is the demand for it. If only a small fraction of income is spent on a good, then a change in its price has little impact on the consumer's overall budget. In contrast, even a small rise in the price of a good that commands a large part of a consumer's budget induces the consumer to make a radical reappraisal of expenditures.

To appreciate the importance of the proportion of income spent on a good, consider your own elasticity of demand for textbooks and crisps. If the price of textbooks doubles (increases 100 per cent), there will be a big decrease in the quantity of textbooks bought. There will be an increase in sharing and in illegal photocopying. If the price of a packet of crisps doubles, also a 100 per cent increase, there will be almost no change in the quantity of crisps demanded. Why the difference? Textbooks take a large proportion of your budget while crisps take only a tiny portion. You don't like either price increase, but you hardly notice the effects of the increased price of crisps, while the increased price of textbooks puts your budget under severe strain.

Figure 5.5 shows the proportion of income spent on food and the price elasticity of demand for food in 20 countries. This figure confirms the general tendency we have just described. The larger the proportion of income spent on food, the more price elastic is the demand for food. The general pattern is strong but there are a few exceptions in the figure. For example, Tanzania, a poor African country where average incomes are just a few per cent of incomes in the United Kingdom, and where 62 per cent of income is spent on food, the price elasticity of demand for food is 0.77. In contrast, in the United Kingdom where 15 per cent of income is spent on food, the elasticity of demand for food is 0.3. These numbers make sense. In a country that spends a large proportion of income on food, an increase in the price of food forces people to make a bigger adjustment to the quantity of food bought than in a country in which a small proportion of income is spent on food.

Time Elapsed Since Price Change   The greater the time lapse since a price change, the more elastic is demand. When a price changes, consumers often continue to buy similar quantities of a good for a while. But given enough time, they find acceptable and less costly substitutes. As this process of substitution occurs, the quantity purchased of an item that has become more expensive gradually declines. That is, given more time, it is possible to find more effective substitutes for a good or service whose price has

FIGURE 5.5

The Price Elasticity of Demand in 20 Countries

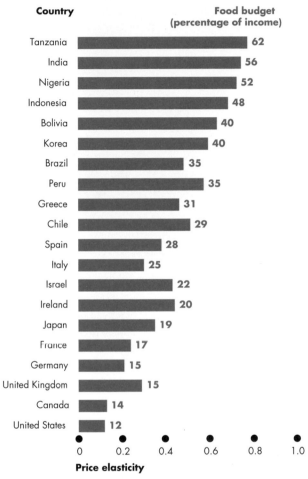

As income increases and the proportion of income spent on food decreases, the demand for food becomes less elastic.

Source: Henri Theil, Ching-Fan Chung and James L. Seale Jr., *Advances in Econometrics, Supplement 1*, 1989, *International Evidence on Consumption Patterns*. Greenwich, Connecticut JAI Press Inc.

substitutions to be made. Long-run demand describes the response of buyers to a change in price *after* sufficient time has elapsed for all the possible substitutions to be made.

An example of a long-lasting price increase was the fourfold rise in the price of oil that occurred during 1973 and 1974. The higher price of oil led to sharp increases in the costs of home heating and petrol. Initially, consumers maintained consumption at more or less their original levels. Then, gradually, buyers responded to higher oil and petrol prices by using their existing capital – boilers and gas guzzlers – in a way that economized on the more expensive fuel. But there were severe limits in the extent to which people felt it worthwhile to cut back on their consumption of the now much more costly fuel. Thermostats could be turned down but that imposed costs – costs of discomfort. Drivers could lower their average speed and economize on petrol. But that also imposed costs – costs of increases in travel time. So the short-run buyer response in the face of this sharp price increase was inelastic. With a longer time to respond, people bought more energy-efficient capital. Boilers and electric power generators became more fuel-efficient. Cars became smaller, on the average, and car and aircraft engines became more fuel-efficient.

The short-run and long-run demand curves for oil in 1974 looked like those in Fig. 5.1. Look back at that figure and refresh your memory about the demand curves in parts (a) and (b). The short-run demand curve is D_a and the long-run demand curve is D_b. The price of oil in 1974 was $10 a barrel and 40 million barrels a day were bought and sold. At that price and quantity, long-run demand, D_b, is much more elastic than short-run demand, D_a.

REVIEW

increased. It is also possible to find more uses for a good whose price has decreased.

To describe the effect of time on demand, we distinguish between two time-frames:

1. Short-run demand
2. Long-run demand

Short-run demand describes the response of buyers to a change in the price of a good *before* sufficient time has elapsed for all the possible

♦ Elasticity of demand measures the responsiveness of the quantity demanded of a good or service to a change in its price.

♦ The elasticity of demand is the percentage change in the quantity demanded of a good divided by the percentage change in its price.

♦ The elasticity of demand for a good is determined by the closeness of substitutes for it, the proportion of income spent on it, and the time lapse since its price changed.

Elasticity, Total Revenue and Expenditure

This chapter began with a dilemma. How can a producer of oil (or anything else) increase total revenue: by decreasing production to increase price, or by lowering price to sell a larger quantity? We can now answer this question by using the concept of the price elasticity of demand.

The change in a producer's total revenue (and in the total expenditure of the buyers) depends on the extent to which the quantity sold changes as the price changes. But the responsiveness of the quantity sold to a price change depends on the elasticity of demand. If demand is elastic, a 1 per cent price cut increases the quantity sold by more than 1 per cent and total revenue increases. If demand is unit elastic, a 1 per cent price cut increases the quantity sold by 1 per cent and the price decrease and the quantity increase offset each other so total revenue does not change. If demand is inelastic, a 1 per cent price cut increases the quantity sold by less than 1 per cent and total revenue decreases. The relevance of this relationship for setting prices in business is explored in *Reading Between the Lines* on pp. 114–115.

Total Revenue Test   We can use this relationship between elasticity and total revenue to estimate elasticity using a total revenue test. The total-revenue test is a method of estimating the price elasticity of demand by observing the change in total revenue that results from a price change (with all other influences on the quantity sold remaining unchanged). If a price cut increases total revenue, demand is elastic; if a price cut decreases total revenue, demand is inelastic; and if a price cut leaves total revenue unchanged, demand is unit elastic.

Figure 5.6 shows the connection between the elasticity of demand and total revenue for oil. Part (a) shows the same demand curve that you studied in Fig. 5.4. Over the price range from $50 to $25, demand is elastic. Over the price range from $25 to zero, demand is inelastic. At a price of $25, demand is unit elastic.

Figure 5.6(b) shows total revenue. At a price of $50, the quantity sold is zero so total revenue is also zero. At a price of zero, the quantity demanded is 20 million barrels a day, but at a zero price, total revenue is again zero. A price cut in the elastic range brings an increase in total revenue – the percentage increase in the quantity demanded is greater than

FIGURE 5.6
Elasticity and Total Revenue

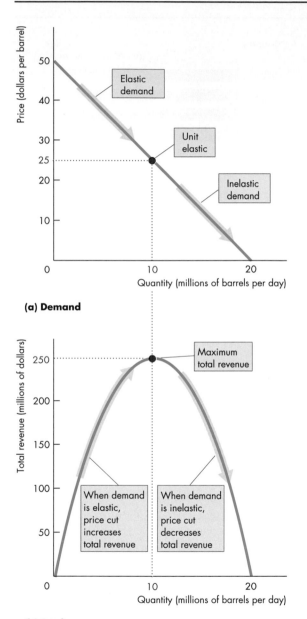

(a) Demand

(b) Total revenue

When demand for oil is elastic, in the price range from $50 to $25, a decrease in price (in part a) brings an increase in total revenue (in part b). When demand for oil is inelastic, in the price range from $25 to zero, a decrease in price (in part a) brings a decrease in total revenue (in part b). When demand is unit elastic, at a price of $25 (in part a), total revenue is at a maximum (in part b).

the percentage decrease in price. A price cut in the inelastic range brings a decrease in total revenue – the percentage increase in the quantity demanded is less than the percentage decrease in price. At the point of unit elasticity, total revenue is at a maximum. A small price change either side of $25 keeps total revenue constant. The loss in total revenue from a lower price is offset by a gain in total revenue from a greater quantity sold.

We have seen that long-run demand is more elastic than short-run demand. It is possible, therefore, that a price cut will decrease total revenue in the short run but increase total revenue in the long run. This outcome occurs if short-run demand is inelastic but long-run demand is elastic.

So far, we've studied the most widely used elasticity – the *price* elasticity of demand. But there are some other useful elasticity of demand concepts. Let's look at them.

More Elasticities of Demand

Buying plans are influenced by many factors other than price. Among these other factors are incomes and the prices of other goods. We can calculate an elasticity of demand for each of these other factors as well as for price. Let's examine some of these additional elasticities.

Cross Elasticity of Demand

The quantity of any good that consumers plan to buy depends on the prices of its substitutes and complements. We measure these influences by using the concept of the cross elasticity of demand. The **cross elasticity of demand** is a measure of the responsiveness of the demand for a good to a change in the price of a substitute or complement, other things remaining the same. It is calculated by using the formula:

$$\text{Cross elasticity of demand} = \frac{\text{Percentage change in quantity demanded}}{\text{Percentage change in the price of a substitute or complement}}$$

The cross elasticity of demand is positive for a substitute and negative for a complement. Figure 5.7 makes it clear why. When the price of coal – a substitute for oil – rises, the demand for oil increases and

the demand curve for oil shifts rightward from D_0 to D_1. Because an increase in the price of coal brings an increase in the demand for oil, the cross elasticity of demand for oil with respect to the price of coal is positive. When the price of a car – a complement of oil – rises, the demand for oil decreases and the demand curve for oil shifts leftward from D_0 to D_2. Because an increase in the price of a car brings a decrease in the demand for oil, the cross elasticity of demand for oil with respect to the price of a car is negative. So positive values identify substitutes and negative values identify complements.

Income Elasticity of Demand

As income grows, how does the demand for a particular good change? The answer depends on the income elasticity of demand for the good. The **income elasticity of demand** is a measure of the responsiveness of demand to a change in income,

FIGURE 5.7
Cross Elasticity of Demand

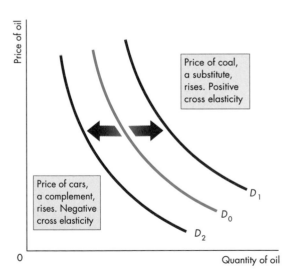

When the price of coal increases, the demand for oil, a *substitute* for coal, increases and the demand curve for oil shifts rightward from D_0 to D_1. The cross elasticity of the demand for oil with respect to the price of coal is *positive*. When the price of a car increases, the demand for oil, a *complement of cars*, decreases and the demand curve for oil shifts leftward from D_0 to D_2. The cross elasticity of the demand for oil with respect to the price of a car is *negative*.

other things remaining the same. It is calculated by using the formula:

$$\text{Income elasticity of demand} = \frac{\text{Percentage change in quantity demanded}}{\text{Percentage change in income}}$$

Income elasticities of demand can be positive or negative and fall into three interesting ranges:

1. Greater than 1 (normal good, income elastic)
2. Between zero and 1 (normal good, income inelastic)
3. Less than zero (inferior good)

Figure 5.8 illustrates these three cases. Part (a) shows an income elasticity of demand that is greater than 1. As income increases, the quantity demanded increases, but the quantity demanded increases faster than income. Some examples of income elastic goods are extreme luxuries such as ocean cruises, international travel, jewellery and works of art. But many other non-necessity goods are income elastic, such as the services of hairdressers and accountants.

Part (b) shows an income elasticity of demand that is between zero and 1. In this case, the quantity demanded increases as income increases, but income increases faster than the quantity demanded. Examples of goods in this category are food, clothing, furniture, newspapers, and magazines.

Part (c) shows an income elasticity of demand that eventually becomes negative. In this case, the quantity demanded increases as income increases until it reaches a maximum at income m. Beyond that point, as income continues to increase, the quantity demanded declines. The elasticity of demand is positive but less than 1 up to income m. Beyond income m, the income elasticity of demand is negative. Examples of goods in this category are small motorcycles, potatoes, rice and bread. Low income consumers buy most of these goods. At low income levels, the demand for such goods increases as income increases. But as income increases above point m, consumers replace these goods with superior alternatives. For example, a small car replaces the motorcycle; fruit, vegetables and meat begin to appear in a diet that was heavy in bread, rice or potatoes.

FIGURE 5.8

Income Elasticity of Demand

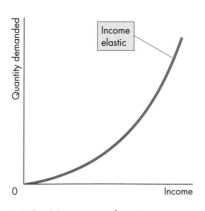

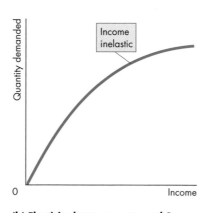

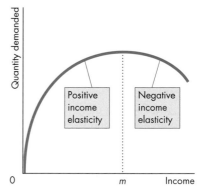

(a) Elasticity greater than 1

(b) Elasticity between zero and 1

(c) Elasticity less than 1 and becomes negative

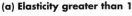

Income elasticity of demand has three ranges of values. In part (a), income elasticity of demand is greater than 1. In this case, as income increases, the quantity demanded increases but by a bigger percentage than the increase in income. In part (b), income elasticity of demand is between zero and 1. In this case, as income increases, the quantity demanded increases but by a smaller percentage than the increase in income. In part (c), the income elasticity of demand is positive at low incomes but becomes negative as income increases above level m. Maximum consumption of this good occurs at the income m.

Real-world Income Elasticities of Demand

Table 5.2 shows estimates of some income elasticities of demand in the United Kingdom. The income elasticities in the table range from 2.6 for wine to -0.3 for bread. Most basic necessities such as food and clothing are income inelastic, while luxury goods such as wines and spirits, services and durable goods – cars, electrical goods and furniture – are income elastic. Some goods such as tobacco and bread are inferior goods but their income elasticity values are close to zero.

What is a necessity and what is a luxury depend on the level of income. For people with a low income, food and clothing can be luxuries. So the *level* of income has a big effect on income elasticities of demand. Figure 5.9 shows this effect on the income elasticity of demand for food in 20 countries. In countries with low incomes, such as

Tanzania and India, the income elasticity of demand for food is – around 0.75 – while in countries with high incomes, such as the United Kingdom, France, Germany, Canada and the United States, the income elasticity of demand for food is low. These

TABLE 5.2
Some Real-world Income Elasticities of Demand for the UK

Good or Service	Elasticity
NORMAL ELASTIC DEMAND	
Wine	2.6
Services	1.8
Spirits	1.7
Durable goods	1.5
NORMAL INELASTIC DEMAND	
Fruit juice	0.9
Beer	0.6
Green vegetables	0.1
Fresh Meat	0.0
Cereals	0.0
INFERIOR	
Tobacco	−0.1
Bread	−0.3

Sources: Ministry of Agriculture, Food and Fisheries *Household Food Consumption and Expenditure*, 1992, London, HMSO. C. Godfrey. Modelling Demand. In *Preventing Alcohol and Tobacco Problems*, Vol 1, (A. Maynard and P. Tether, eds), Avebury, 1990. J. Muellbauer 'Testing the Barten Model of Household Composition Effects and the Cost of Children', *Economic Journal*, (September 1977).

FIGURE 5.9
Income Elasticities in 20 Countries

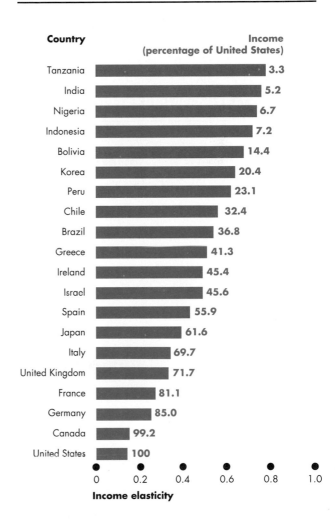

As income increases, the income elasticity of demand for food decreases. For low-income consumers, a larger percentage of any increase in income is spent on food than for high-income consumers.

Source: Henri Theil, Ching-Fan Chung and James L. Seale Jr. *Advances in Econometrics, Supplement 1*, 1989, *International Evidence on Consumption Patterns* 1989, Greenwich, Connecticut JAI Press Inc.

numbers tell us that a 10 per cent increase in income leads to an increase in the demand for food of 7.5 per cent in India and less than 4 per cent in North America and Northern Europe. These numbers make sense and confirm the idea that necessities have a lower income elasticity of demand than luxuries. What for a high-income European is a basic necessity remains beyond the reach of a low-income Indian.

Table 5.3 gives a compact summary of all the different kinds of demand elasticities you've just studied.

Elasticity of Supply

If Germany's machine tool industry expands, it will increase its demand for steel. There will be a *change in demand* for steel. Both Germany's machine tool producers and European steel producers will want to know the likely changes in the price of steel that this increase in demand could bring. A change in demand shifts the demand curve and leads to a *movement along the supply curve*.

TABLE 5.3
A Compact Glossary of Elasticities of Demand

PRICE ELASTICITIES

A relationship is described as	When the elasticity value is	Which means that
Perfectly elastic or infinitely elastic	Infinity	The smallest possible increase (decrease) in price causes an infinitely large decrease (increase) in the quantity demanded
Elastic	Less than infinity but greater than 1	The percentage decrease (increase) in the quantity demanded exceeds the percentage increase (decrease) in price
Unit elastic	1	The percentage decrease (increase) in the quantity demanded equals the percentage increase (decrease) in price
Inelastic	Greater than zero but less than 1	The percentage decrease (increase) in the quantity demanded is less than the percentage increase (decrease) in price
Perfectly inelastic or completely inelastic	Zero	The quantity demanded is the same at all prices

CROSS ELASTICITIES

A relationship is described as	When the elasticity value is	Which means that
Perfect substitutes	Infinity	The smallest possible increase (decrease) in the price of one good causes an infinitely large increase (decrease) in the quantity demanded of the other good
Substitutes	Positive, less than infinity	If the price of one good increases (decreases) the quantity demanded of the other good also increases (decreases)
Independent	Zero	The quantity demanded of one good remains constant regardless of the price of the other good
Complements	Less than zero	The quantity demanded of one good decreases (increases) when the price of the other good increases (decreases)

INCOME ELASTICITIES

A relationship is described as	When the elasticity value is	Which means that
Income elastic (normal good)	Greater than 1	The percentage increase (decrease) in the quantity demanded is greater than the percentage increase (decrease) in income
Income inelastic (normal good)	Less than 1 but greater than zero	The percentage increase (decrease) in the quantity demanded is less than the percentage increase (decrease) in income
Negative income elastic (inferior good)	Less than zero	When income increases (decreases), quantity demanded decreases (increases)

To predict the changes in price and quantity, we need to know how responsive the quantity supplied is to the price of a good. That is, we need to know the elasticity of supply.

The **elasticity of supply** measures the responsiveness of the quantity supplied of a good to a change in its price. It is calculated by using the formula:

$$\text{Elasticity of supply} = \frac{\text{Percentage change in quantity supplied}}{\text{Percentage change in price}}$$

There are two interesting cases of the elasticity of supply. If the quantity supplied is fixed regardless of the price, the supply curve is vertical. In this case, the elasticity of supply is zero. An increase in price leads to no change in the quantity supplied. Supply is perfectly inelastic. If there is a price below which nothing will be supplied and at which suppliers are willing to sell any quantity demanded, the supply curve is horizontal. In this case, the elasticity of supply is infinite. The small fall in price reduces the quantity supplied from an indefinitely large amount to zero. Supply is perfectly elastic.

The magnitude of the elasticity of supply depends on:

◆ Factor substitution possibilities
◆ The time-frame for the supply decision

Factor Substitution Possibilities

Some goods and services are produced by using unique or rare factors of production. These items have a low, and perhaps zero, elasticity of supply. Other goods and services are produced by using factors of production that are more common and that can be allocated to a wide variety of alternative tasks. Such items have a high elasticity of supply.

A Van Gogh painting has been produced by a unique type of labour – Van Gogh's. No other factor of production can be substituted for this labour. There is just one of each painting, so its supply curve is vertical and its elasticity of supply is zero. At the other extreme, wheat can be grown on land that is almost equally good for growing barley. So it is just as easy to grow wheat or barley, and the opportunity cost of wheat in terms of forgone barley is almost constant. As a result, the supply curve of wheat is almost horizontal and its elasticity of supply is large. Similarly, when a good is produced in many different

countries (for example, sugar and beef), the supply of the good is a highly elastic supply.

The supply of most goods and services lies between the two extremes. The quantity produced can be increased but only by incurring higher cost. If a higher price is offered, the quantity supplied increases. Such goods and services have an elasticity of supply between zero and infinity.

Elasticity of Supply and the Time-frame for Supply Decisions

To study the influence of the length of time elapsed since a price change, we distinguish three time-frames of supply:

◆ Momentary supply
◆ Short-run supply
◆ Long-run supply

Momentary Supply   When the price of a good rises or falls, the *momentary supply curve* describes the initial change in the quantity supplied. The momentary supply curve shows the response of the quantity supplied immediately following a price change.

Some goods, such as fruits and vegetables, have a perfectly inelastic momentary supply – a vertical supply curve. The quantities supplied depend on crop planting decisions made earlier. In the case of grapes, for example, planting decisions have to be made many years in advance of the crop being available.

Other goods, such as long-distance phone calls, have an elastic momentary supply. When many people simultaneously make a call, there is a big surge in the demand for cable, computer switching and satellite time and the quantity bought increases (up to the physical limits of the telephone system) but the price remains constant. Long-distance carriers monitor fluctuations in demand and re-route calls to ensure that the quantity supplied equals the quantity demanded without raising the price.

Long-run Supply   The *long-run supply* curve shows the response of the quantity supplied to a change in price after all the technologically possible ways of adjusting supply have been exploited. In the case of wine, the long run is the time it takes a new vineyard to grow to full maturity – about 15 years. In some cases, the long-run adjustment occurs only after a completely new production plant has been built and workers have been trained to operate it – typically a process that might take several years.

Short-run Supply   The *short-run supply curve* shows how the quantity supplied responds to a price change when only some of the technologically possible adjustments to production have been made. The first adjustment usually made is in the amount of labour employed. To increase output in the short run, firms make their employees work overtime and perhaps hire additional workers. To decrease their output in the short run, firms lay off workers or reduce their hours of work. With the passage of time, firms can make additional adjustments, perhaps training additional workers or buying additional tools and other equipment. The short-run response to a price change, unlike the momentary and long-run responses, is not a unique response but a sequence of adjustments.

Three Supply Curves   Figure 5.10 shows three supply curves that correspond to the three time-frames. They are the supply curves in the world market for grapes on a given day in which the price is £2 a kilogram and the quantity of grapes grown is 3 million kilograms. Each supply curve passes through that point. Momentary supply is perfectly inelastic, as shown by the blue curve *MS*. As time passes, the quantity supplied becomes more responsive to price and is shown by the short-run supply curve, *SS*. As yet more time passes, the supply curve becomes the red long-run curve *LS*, the most elastic of the three supplies.

The momentary supply curve, *MS*, shows how quantity supplied responds to a price change the moment that it occurs. The blue momentary supply curve shown here is perfectly inelastic. The purple short-run supply curve, *SS*, shows how the quantity supplied responds to a price change after some adjustments to production have been made. The red long-run supply curve, *LS*, shows how the quantity supplied responds to a price change when all the technologically possible adjustments to the production process have been made.

The momentary supply curve is vertical because, on a given day, no matter what the price of grapes, producers cannot change their output. They have picked, packed and shipped their crop to market and the quantity available for that day is fixed. The short-run supply curve slopes upward because producers can take actions quite quickly to change

FIGURE 5.10

Supply: Momentary, Short-run and Long-run

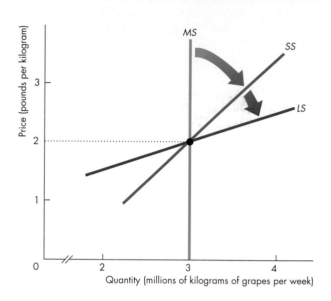

The momentary supply curve, *MS*, is perfectly inelastic The short-run supply curve, *SS*, is more elastic as quantity supplied responds to a price change after some adjustments to production have been made. The long-run supply curve, *LS*, is even more elastic as quantity supplied responds to a price change when all the technologically possible adjustments to the production process have been made.

the quantity supplied in response to a price change. They can, for example, stop picking and leave grapes to rot on the vine if the price falls by a large amount. Or they can use more fertilizers and improved irrigation and increase the yields of their existing vines if the price rises. In the long run, they can plant more vines and increase the quantity supplied even more in response to a given price rise.

◆ ◆ ◆ ◆ You have now studied the theory of demand and supply, and you have learned how to measure the responsiveness of the quantity demanded to changes in prices and income. You have also learned how to measure the responsiveness of the quantity supplied to a change in the price. In the next chapter, we are going to use what we have learned to study some real world markets – markets in action.

S U M M A R Y

Elasticity of Demand

Elasticity of demand is a measure of the responsiveness of the quantity demanded of a good to a change in its price. It enables us to calculate the effect of a change in supply on price, quantity bought, and total revenue. Elasticity of demand is calculated as the percentage change in the quantity demanded divided by the percentage change in price.

The larger the magnitude of the elasticity of demand, the greater is the responsiveness of the quantity demanded to a given change in price. When the percentage change in the quantity demanded is smaller than the percentage change in price, demand is inelastic. When the percentage change in the quantity demanded equals the percentage change in price, demand is unit elastic. When the percentage change in the quantity demanded is larger than the percentage change in price, demand is elastic. Along a straight-line demand curve, demand is elastic at prices above the midpoint price, unit elastic at the midpoint price and inelastic at prices below the midpoint price.

Elasticity depends on how easily one good serves as a substitute for another, the proportion of income spent on the good and the length of time that has elapsed since the price change. We use two time-frames to analyse demand: short run and long run. Short-run demand describes the initial response of buyers to a price change. Long-run demand describes the response of buyers to a price change after all possible adjustments have been made. Short-run demand is usually less elastic than long-run demand.

If demand is elastic, a decrease in price leads to an increase in total revenue. If demand is unit elastic, a decrease in price leaves total revenue unchanged. If demand is inelastic, a decrease in price leads to a decrease in total revenue. (pp. 99–107)

More Demand Elasticities

Cross elasticity of demand measures the responsiveness of demand for one good to a change in the price of another good (a substitute or a complement). Cross elasticity of demand is calculated as the percentage change in the quantity demanded of one good divided by the percentage change in the price of another good. The cross elasticity of demand with respect to the price of a substitute is positive. The cross elasticity of demand with respect to the price of a complement is negative.

Income elasticity of demand measures the responsiveness of demand to a change in income. Income elasticity of demand is calculated as the percentage change in the quantity demanded divided by the percentage change in income. The larger the income elasticity of demand, the greater is the responsiveness of demand to a given change in income. When income elasticity is between zero and 1, demand is income inelastic. In this case, as income increases demand increases but the percentage of income spent on the good decreases. When income elasticity is greater than 1, demand is income elastic. In this case, as income increases demand increases and the percentage of income spent on the good also increases. When income elasticity is less than zero, demand is negative income elastic. In this case, as income increases demand decreases. For normal goods, the income elasticity of demand is positive. For inferior goods, the income elasticity of demand is negative. Inferior goods are consumed only at low incomes. (pp. 107–110)

Elasticity of Supply

The elasticity of supply measures the responsiveness of the quantity supplied of a good to a change in its price. Elasticity of supply is calculated as the percentage change in the quantity supplied of a good divided by the percentage change in its price. Supply elasticities are usually positive and range between zero (vertical supply curve) and infinity (horizontal supply curve).

Supply decisions have three time-frames: momentary, long run, and short run. Momentary supply refers to the response of suppliers to a price change at the instant that the price changes. Long-run supply refers to the response of suppliers to a price change when all the technologically feasible adjustments in production have been made. Short-run supply refers to the response of suppliers to a price change after some adjustments in production have been made. For many goods, momentary supply is perfectly inelastic. Supply becomes more elastic as suppliers have more time to respond to price changes. (pp. 110–112)

Elasticity: Management Pricing Strategies

The Essence of the Story

THE FINANCIAL TIMES, 24 APRIL 1996

Knowing when the price is right

Vanessa Houlder

'Pricing is managers' biggest marketing headache,' noted Robert ... Dolan of the Harvard Business School in last September's *Harvard Business Review*. 'It's where they feel the most pressure to perform and the least certain that they are doing a good job.'

Yet managers are only too aware of the rewards of a better pricing strategy. It offers...a possibly substantial increase in profits, without heavy upfront costs....

Pricing issues are now at, or near, the top of the corporate agenda. A recent survey of 50 large UK and US companies... found that a majority agreed that insufficient attention was given to revenue opportunities, especially in pricing....

Even in traditionally cut-throat markets...companies could gain...the order of 5 to 10 per cent of return on sales....

The problem is not usually a lack of familiarity with pricing options...but the under-exploitation of these options as a result of roadblocks within the organisation...and insufficient use of available data....

The finance division is usually keen to set prices so that they cover costs and achieve their profit objectives, [but] the marketing and sales staff want prices set low enough to achieve their sales objectives....Many businesses fail to explore the concept of price elasticity, or how a price change will effect the quantity sold....

Companies could do more with existing sales data....Analysis of electronic point of sales data...can yield valuable, detailed information, such as the variation of the price elasticities with the size of the store, its geographical location and its distance from the nearest competitor. That information is an important weapon because it means that stores with relatively price-insensitive customers can charge higher prices....

At present, highly price-sensitive consumers are relatively few in number. A survey by the Henley Centre found that the percentage of European consumers who always looked for the cheapest products when shopping ranged from a maximum of 45 per cent (of German consumers) to a minimum of 20 per cent (of British consumers). In many markets, consumers show a particularly resilient respect for price as an indicator of quality....

A similar point is made by the London-based Centre for Economics and Business Research....Currently, consumers are largely unaware of the price of staple food and so are insensitive to moderate price changes, it says....

- Getting prices right is one of the most important decisions marketing managers have to make.

- The majority of managers agree that more attention should be paid to the extra revenue — up to 10 per cent more — which could be gained by more accurate pricing.

- Managers are wary of raising prices because quantity sold will fall and they rarely analyse data to calculate the price elasticity of demand for their products.

- An examination of existing electronic point-of-sale data in supermarkets, for example, could reveal the relationship between price elasticities and factors such as region, store size, local competition and customer attitude to quality.

- Managers could use this information to target price changes to raise profits.

Economic Analysis

■ Figure 1 shows the demand curve, D_L, for fresh fish in a local supermarket, where the price is £2 per kilogram and 100 kilograms are sold each day.

■ The marketing manager believes that demand for fresh fish is inelastic as there are no other supermarkets or fish shops within an hour's drive.

■ With the information in Fig. 2, the marketing manager could calculate the value of price elasticity of demand for fresh fish for the supermarket at the current price as follows:

$$\frac{\Delta Q/Q_{ave}}{\Delta P/P_{ave}} = \frac{10/100}{100/200} = 0.2$$

■ This shows that demand is inelastic, and a rise in price from £2 to £2.50 a kilogram will raise revenue and profit, if costs remain the same.

■ The rise in revenue of £47.50 (95 × £0.50) exceeds the fall in revenue of £10.00 (5 × £2), resulting in a total revenue increase of £37.50 per day.

■ Suppose that there was a competing fresh fish seller within a five minute drive. The demand curve for fresh fish might look more like D_H in Fig. 2.

■ In this case the price elasticity of demand is elastic as shown in the following calculation:

$$\frac{\Delta Q/Q_{ave}}{\Delta P/P_{ave}} = \frac{80/100}{100/200} = 1.6$$

■ The manager can now see that the proposed price rise would lead to a fall in revenue of £50 a day. The rise in revenue of £30 (60 × £0.50) is less than the fall in revenue of £80 (40 × £2).

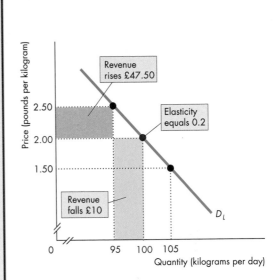

Figure 1

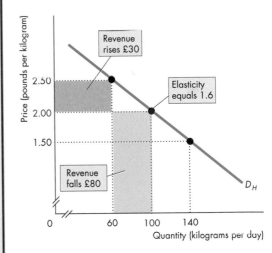

Figure 2

KEY ELEMENTS

Key Terms

Arc elasticity of demand, 101
Cross elasticity of demand, 107
Elastic, 101
Elasticity of supply, 111
Income elasticity of demand, 107
Inelastic, 101
Perfectly elastic, 102
Perfectly inelastic, 101
Price elasticity of demand, 100
Total revenue, 99
Unit elastic, 102

◆ Key Figures and Table

Figure 5.2   Calculating the Elasticity of Demand,
101
Figure 5.3   Inelastic and Elastic Demand, 102
Figure 5.4   Elasticity Along a Straight-Line
Demand Curve, 103
Figure 5.6   Elasticity and Total Revenue, 106
Figure 5.7   Cross Elasticity of Demand, 107
Figure 5.9   Income Elasticity of Demand, 108
Table 5.3   A Compact Glossary of Elasticities of
Demand, 110

REVIEW QUESTIONS

1   Define the price elasticity of demand.

2   Why is elasticity a more useful measure of responsiveness than slope?

3   Draw a graph, or describe the shape of a demand curve that represents a good that has an elasticity of demand equal to:

   a   Infinity
   b   Zero
   c   Unity

4   What three factors determine the size of the elasticity of demand?

5   What do we mean by short-run demand and long-run demand?

6   Explain why the short-run demand curve is usually less elastic than the long-run demand curve.

7   What is the connection between elasticity and total revenue? If the elasticity of demand for books is 1, by how much does a 10 per cent increase in the price of books change total revenue?

8   Define the income elasticity of demand.

9   Give an example of a good whose income elasticity of demand is:

   a   Greater than 1
   b   Positive but less than 1
   c   Less than zero

10   Define the cross elasticity of demand. Is the cross elasticity of demand positive or negative?

11   Define the elasticity of supply. Is the elasticity of supply positive or negative?

12   Give an example of a good whose elasticity of supply is:

   a   Zero
   b   Greater than zero but less than infinity
   c   Infinity

13   What do we mean by momentary, short-run, and long-run supply?

14   Why is momentary supply perfectly inelastic for many goods?

15   Why is long-run supply more elastic than short-run supply?

PROBLEMS

1 The demand schedule for video camera rental per day is

Price (pounds)	Quantity demanded (number per day)
0	150
1	125
2	100
3	75
4	50
5	25
6	0

a At what price is the elasticity of demand equal to:
1 1?
2 Infinity?
3 Zero?
b At what price is total revenue maximized?
c Calculate the elasticity of demand for a rise in the rental price from £4 to £5.

2 Assume that the demand for video camera rentals in Problem 1 increases by 10 per cent at each price.

a Draw the old and new demand curves.
b Calculate the elasticity of demand for a rise in the rental price from £4 to £5.

Compare your answer with that to Problem 1(c).

3 Which item in each of the following pairs has the larger elasticity of demand:

a *The Economist* newspaper or newspapers in general?
b Vacations or vacations in Africa?
c Broccoli or vegetables?

4 You have been hired as an economic consultant by OPEC and given the following schedule showing the world demand for oil:

Price (dollars per barrel)	Quantity demanded (millions of barrels per day)
10	60,000
20	50,000
30	40,000
40	30,000
50	20,000

Your advice is needed on the following questions:
a If the supply of oil is decreased so that the price rises from $20 to $30 a barrel, will the total revenue from oil sales increase or decrease?
b What will happen to total revenue if the supply of oil is decreased further and the price rises to $40 a barrel?
c What is the price that will achieve the highest total revenue?
d What quantity of oil will be sold at the price that answers Problem 4(c)?
e What are the values of the price elasticity of demand for price changes of $10 a barrel at average prices of $15, $25, $35 and $45 a barrel?
f What is the elasticity of demand at the price that maximizes total revenue?
g Over what price range is the demand for oil inelastic?

5 State the sign (positive or negative) and, where possible, the range (less than 1, 1, greater than 1) of the following elasticities:

a The price elasticity of demand for ice cream at the point of maximum total revenue.
b The cross elasticity of demand for ice cream with respect to the price of frozen yoghurt.
c The income elasticity of demand for Caribbean cruises.
d The income elasticity of demand for toothpaste.
e The elasticity of supply of Irish salmon.
f The cross elasticity of demand for corn ready to be popped with respect to the price of popcorn machines.

6 The following table gives some data on the demand for long-distance telephone calls:

Price (pence per minute)	Quantity demanded (millions of minutes per day)	
	Short-run	Long-run
10	700	1,000
20	500	500
30	300	0

At a price of 20 pence a minute:

a Calculate the elasticity of short-run demand.
b Calculate the elasticity of long-run demand.
c Is the demand for calls more elastic in the short run or the long run?

7 In Problem 6, does total expenditure on calls increase or decrease as the price of a call decreases from 20 pence a minute to 10 pence a minute?

8 The following table gives some data on the supply of long-distance phone calls:

Price (pence per minute)	Quantity supplied (thousands per day)	
	Short-run	Long-run
10	300	0
20	500	500
30	700	10,000

At a price of 20 pence a minute, calculate the elasticity of:

a Short-run supply.
b Long-run supply.

9 In Problem 8, which supply is more elastic and why? Compare the elasticities of supply when the price of a call is 15 pence a minute and when it is 25 pence a minute.

10 Read the article in *Reading Between the Lines* on pp. 114–115 and answer the following questions.

a Why might it be in the interests of a supermarket to raise prices for price-insensitive customers?
b What is the effect on the demand for a supermarket's goods of an increase in local competition?

BOX 5.1 CALCULATING POINT ELASTICITIES OF DEMAND

The formula for calculating price elasticity of demand gives us an estimate of the elasticity along a section of the demand curve as shown in Fig. B5.1. Although it is called arc elasticity it

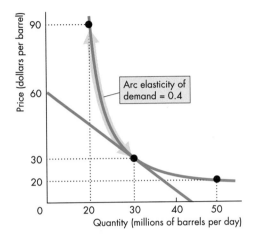

Figure B5.1

could be a section from a curved or straight-line demand curve. The formula from Fig. 5.2 is:

$$\text{Arc price elasticity of demand} = \frac{\Delta Q / \Delta Q_{ave}}{\Delta P / P_{ave}} \quad \textbf{(1)}$$

You can rearrange the formula as:

$$\text{Arc price elasticity of demand} = \frac{\Delta Q / \Delta P}{Q_{ave} / P_{ave}} \quad \textbf{(2)}$$

In Equation 2, the numerator is the ratio of the change in quantity demanded to the change in the price along a portion of the demand curve – the inverse of the slope. The denominator is the ratio of the average quantity demanded to the average price along that portion.

If we want to find the price elasticity of demand at a given point on the demand curve – the point elasticity – we can use the arc elasticity formula but make the arc infinitely small. The

average price and quantity demanded on this infinitely small arc would then be the price and quantity demanded at the point we are interested in. To do this, substitute P for P_{ave} and Q for Q_{ave} in Equation 2, to give:

$$\text{Point price elasticity of demand} = \frac{\Delta Q / \Delta P}{Q / P} \quad \textbf{(3)}$$

Remember a positive price change results in a negative change in the quantity demanded. Both arc and point price elasticity of demand are therefore negative. However, it is often common practice to drop the minus sign so that elasticities are reported as the absolute value.

The Straight-line Demand Curve Case

Figure 5.4 showed that the point elasticity of demand is infinity when the price is $50 a barrel. Let's use the point elasticity formula to check this value.

First, we need to know the slope of the demand curve at the point of interest. Because this is a straight-line demand curve, the slope is constant. An easy way to calculate the slope is to consider what happens if the price falls from $50 to $0, while the quantity demanded increases from 0 to 20 million barrels a day. The slope is:

$$\frac{\Delta P}{\Delta Q} = \frac{-50}{20,000,000} = \frac{-5}{2,000,000} \quad \textbf{(4)}$$

The formula for point price elasticity of demand in Equation 3 uses $\Delta Q / \Delta P$ (the inverse of the slope) which is:

$$\frac{\Delta Q}{\Delta P} = \frac{2,000,000}{-5} = -400,000 \quad \textbf{(5)}$$

To calculate the point price elasticity of demand, we also need the values of P and Q. At the point of interest, $P = \$50$ and $Q = 0$. Now substitute these values of P and Q, together with the value of $\Delta Q/\Delta P$ from Equation 5, into Equation 3 to give:

$$\text{Point price elasticity} \atop \text{of demand} = \frac{-400,000}{0/50}$$

$$= -400,000/1 \times 50/0$$

$$= -20,000,000/0$$

$$= -\infty$$

The elasticity of demand at this point is the absolute value of the point elasticity of demand which is infinity. Try calculating the point elasticity of demand when the price is 0 and the quantity demanded is 20 million barrels a day.

2. The General Demand Curve Case

Figure B5.1 shows a curved demand curve for oil. In this figure the arc elasticity of demand between $30 and $90 a barrel is 0.4. Let's use the arc elasticity formula above to check this. The change in price is $60 and the change in quantity is 10,000,000. The average price and quantity are:

$$P_{ave} = \frac{\$90 + \$30}{2} = \$60$$

$$Q_{ave} = \frac{20,000,000 + 30,000,000}{2} = 25,000,000$$

Putting these values into the arc price elasticity formula from Equation 1 gives:

$$\text{Arc price elasticity} \atop \text{of demand} = \frac{10,000,000}{25,000,000} \times \frac{60}{60} = \frac{10}{25} = 0.4$$

Now let's use Equation 3 to calculate the point price elasticity of demand when the price is $30 a barrel from Fig. B5.1. To calculate the point elasticity of demand we need the inverse of the slope of the demand curve at the point where the price is $30 a barrel. One way to calculate the slope $(\Delta P/\Delta Q)$ of a curve is to measure the slope of a tangent to the curve at the point of interest. If you draw a tangent to the demand curve in Fig. B5.1 at the price of $30 a barrel, you will find that it cuts the y-axis at $59 a barrel ($\Delta P$) and cuts the x-axis at 45 million barrels (ΔQ). Substituting these values into Equation 5 gives:

$$\frac{\Delta Q}{\Delta P} = \frac{-45,000,000}{59} = -76,000,000$$

When $P = \$30$, $Q = 30,000,000$. Substituting these values into Equation 3 gives:

$$\text{Point price elasticity} \atop \text{of demand} = \frac{-76,000,000}{(30,000,000/30)} = -0.76$$

The point elasticity of demand when the price is $30 a barrel is the absolute value of the point price elasticity of demand which is equal to 0.76.

3. Using Calculus to Calculate Point Elasticity

The formula for point elasticity of demand using calculus is:

$$\text{Point price elasticity} = \frac{\delta Q/\delta P}{Q/P} \qquad \text{(6)}$$

Suppose that a demand curve is described by:

$$Q = 100 - P^2 \qquad \text{(7)}$$

Let's calculate the point price elasticity of demand when the price is 5. Substituting $P = 5$ into Equation 7 gives:

$$Q = 100 - 5^2$$
$$Q = 75$$

To find how the quantity demanded responds to a small change in price, differentiate Equation 7 with respect to P (see Box 2.1) to give:

$$\delta Q/\delta P = -2P \qquad \text{(8)}$$

Substitute $P = 5$ into Equation 8 to give:

$$\delta Q/\delta P = -10$$

So we know $P = 5$, $Q = 75$, and $\delta Q/\delta P = -10$. Substituting these values into Equation 6, we get:

$$\text{Point price elasticity} \atop \text{of demand} = \frac{-10}{(75/5)} = \frac{-10}{15} = -0.67$$

The point elasticity of demand when the price is $5 is the absolute value of the point price elasticity of demand which is equal to 0.67.

4. Constant Elasticity

You saw some examples of demand curves with constant elasticity in Fig. 5.3. We can use a mathematical representation of a demand curve with constant elasticity to explore its properties. Look at the demand curve whose equation is given by:

$$Q = kP^{-a} \qquad (9)$$

The values of k and a are constants. The equation has a point price elasticity of demand of $-a$.
To show why, we will use the calculus formula for point price elasticity of demand. The first step is to differentiate Q with respect to P:

$$\delta Q/\delta P = -akP^{-(a+1)} \qquad (10)$$

Substituting Equation 10 into Equation 6 gives:

$$\text{Point price elasticity of demand} = \frac{\delta Q/\delta P}{Q/P} = \frac{-akP^{-(a+1)}}{Q/P}$$

But notice the equation of the demand curve is

$$Q = kP^{-a} \text{ or } Q = k/P^a$$

So,

$$Q/P = k/(P \times P^a)$$
$$= k/P^{(a+1)}$$
$$= kP^{-(a+1)}$$

Substituting this value of Q/P into Equation 6 gives:

$$\text{Point price elasticity of demand} = \frac{-akP^{-(a+1)}}{kP^{-(a+1)}} = -a$$

So price elasticity of demand is the absolute value of the point price elasticity of demand at any point which is equal to a. Using this approach, see if you can work out the value of the price elasticity of demand for the following demand curve:

$$Q = \frac{12}{P} = 12P^{-1}$$

CHAPTER

6

MARKETS
IN
ACTION

After studying this chapter you will be able to:

◆ Explain the short-run and long-run effects of a change in supply on price and the quantity bought and sold

◆ Explain the short-run and long-run effects of a change in demand on price and the quantity bought and sold

◆ Explain the effects of price controls

◆ Explain how excise taxes affect prices

◆ Explain how making a good illegal affects its price and the quantity consumed

◆ Explain why farm prices and revenues fluctuate

◆ Explain how stores and farm policies limit price and revenue fluctuations

I N JANUARY 1995, THE NETHERLANDS SUFFERED A DEVASTATING FLOOD THAT destroyed many homes but killed few people. How did the housing market cope with this enormous shock? What happened to rents and to the quantity of housing services available in the flooded regions? Would rent controls have helped to keep housing affordable? ◆ Almost every day, new machines are invented that save labour and increase productivity. How do labour markets cope with consequences of technological change? Does a falling demand for labour drive wages lower and lower? Is it necessary to have minimum wage laws to prevent wages from falling? ◆ Almost everything we buy is taxed. How do taxes affect the prices and quantities of the things we buy? Do prices increase by the full amount of the tax so that we, the buyers, pay? Or does the seller bear part of the tax? ◆ Trading in items such as auto-

Turbulent Times

matic firearms, certain drugs and enriched uranium is illegal. Does prohibiting trade in these goods actually restrict the amount of these goods consumed? And how does it affect the prices paid by those who trade illegally? ◆ In 1988, grain yields were extremely low as crops were devastated by drought. Yields recovered in 1991 but stocks of grain were low worldwide. How do farm prices and revenues react to such output fluctuations? How do the actions of speculators and agricul-tural policy influence farm revenues?

◆ ◆ ◆ ◆ In this chapter, we use the theory of demand and supply (of Chapter 4) and the concept of elasticity (of Chapter 5) to answer questions such as those just posed. We're going to begin by studying how a market responds to a severe supply shock.

Housing Markets and Rent Ceilings

To see how unregulated markets cope with supply shocks, let's consider the consequences of the flood in the Gelderland province of the Netherlands in January 1995. How did the region cope with such a vast reduction in the supply of housing? Almost overnight, 70,000 people left the area and their devastated homes behind them. The floods wrecked homes and businesses causing more than £700 million worth of damage.

The Market Response to a Decrease in Supply

The market for housing in the worst affected area in the Gelderland province is shown in Fig. 6.1. The demand curve for housing before the flood is D in part (a). There are two supply curves: the short-run supply curve, labelled SS, and the long-run supply curve, labelled LS. The short-run supply curve shows how the quantity of housing supplied varies as the price (rent) varies, while the number of houses and blocks of flats remains constant. Supply varies with the intensity with which existing buildings are used. The quantity of housing supplied increases if families decide to rent out rooms that they previously used themselves, and decreases if families decide to use rooms they previously rented out to others.

The long-run supply curve shows how the quantity supplied varies over the period of renovation and rebuilding. We will assume that the long-run supply curve is perfectly elastic, as shown. This is reasonable as the cost of building is much the same regardless of whether there are 5,000 or 15,000 flats and houses in existence.

The equilibrium price (rent) and quantity are determined at the point of intersection of the *short-run* supply curve and the demand curve. Before the flood, the equilibrium rent is 400 guilders a month and the quantity is 10,000 units of housing. In addition (for simplicity), the housing market is assumed to be on its long-run supply curve, LS. Let's now look at the situation immediately after the flood.

Figure 6.1(a) shows the new situation. The damage to buildings decreases the supply of housing and shifts the short-run supply curve SS leftward to SS_A. If people use the remaining housing units with the same intensity as before the flood and if the rent remains at 400 guilders a month, only 4,400 units of housing are available. But rents do not remain at 400 guilders a month. With only 4,400 units of housing available, the maximum rent that someone is willing to pay for the last available apartment is 600 guilders a month. So to get a flat, a higher rent than 400 guilders is offered. Rents rise as people try to outbid each other for the available housing. In Figure 6.1(a), they rise to 500 guilders a month. At this rent, the quantity of housing supplied is 7,400 units. People economize on their use of space and make spare rooms, attics and basements available to others.

The response we've just seen takes place in the short run. What happens in the long run?

Long-run Adjustments

With sufficient time for renovation and building, supply will increase. The long-run supply curve tells us that in the long run, housing will be supplied at a rent of 400 guilders a month. Because the current rent of 500 guilders a month is higher than the long-run supply price of housing, there will be a rush to supply new housing. As time passes, more housing is renovated or rebuilt, and the short-run supply curve gradually shifts rightward.

Figure 6.1(b) illustrates the long-run adjustment. As more housing is available, the short-run supply curve shifts rightward and intersects the demand curve at lower rents and higher quantities. The market equilibrium follows the arrows down the demand curve. The process ends when there is no further profit in renovating or building housing units. Such a situation occurs at the original rent of 400 guilders a month and the original quantity of 10,000 units of housing.

The analysis of the short-run and long-run response of a housing market that we've just studied applies to a wide range of other markets. It applies regardless of whether the initial shock is to supply (as it is here) or demand.

A Regulated Housing Market

We've just seen how a housing market responds to a decrease in supply. We've also seen that a key part of the adjustment process is a rise in rents. Suppose the government passes a law to stop rents from rising – it imposes a price ceiling. A **price ceiling** is a regulation making it illegal to charge a price

FIGURE 6.1

The Gelderland Housing Market in 1995

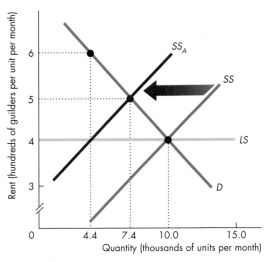

(a) After flood

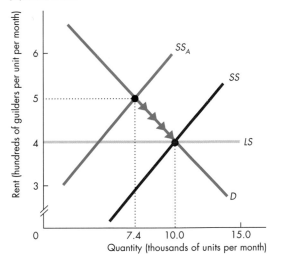

(b) Long-run adjustment

Before the flood, the local housing market in the worst affected area is in equilibrium with 10,000 housing units being rented each month at 400 guilders a month (part a). After the flood, the short-run supply curve shifts from *SS* to *SS*ₐ. The rent rises to 500 guilders a month, and the quantity of housing falls to 7,400 units.

With rents at 500 guilders a month, it is profitable to renovate or rebuild flats and houses quickly. As the renovation and rebuilding programme proceeds, the short-run supply curve shifts rightward (part b). Rents gradually fall to 400 guilders a month and the quantity of housing gradually increases to 10,000 units.

higher than a specified level. When a price ceiling is applied to rents in housing markets it is called a **rent ceiling**. How does a rent ceiling affect the way the housing market works?

The effect of a price (rent) ceiling depends on whether it is imposed at a level that is above or below the equilibrium price (rent). A price ceiling set above the equilibrium price has no effect. The reason is that the market forces are not constrained by the price ceiling. The force of the law and the market forces are not in conflict. But a price ceiling below the equilibrium price has powerful effects on a market. The reason is that it prevents the price from acting as the regulator of the quantities demanded and supplied. The force of the law and the market forces are in conflict, and one (or both) of these forces must yield to some degree. Let's study the effects of a price ceiling set below the equilibrium price by returning to the flood region.

What would have happened after the flood if a rent ceiling of 400 guilders a month – the rent before the flood – had been imposed by the government? This question and some answers are illustrated in Fig. 6.2. If a rent ceiling holds the rent at 400 guilders a month, then the quantity of housing supplied is 4,400 units and the quantity demanded is 10,000 units. So there is a shortage of 5,600 units of housing – the quantity demanded exceeds the quantity supplied by 5,600 units.

When the quantity demanded exceeds the quantity supplied, the smaller quantity – the quantity supplied – determines the actual quantity bought and sold. The reason is that suppliers cannot be forced to offer housing for rent, and at a monthly rent of 400 guilders, they are willing to offer only 4,400 units.

So the immediate effect of a rent ceiling of 400 guilders a month is that only 4,400 units of housing are available and a demand for a further 5,600 units is unsatisfied. But the story does not end here. Somehow the 4,400 units of available housing must be allocated among the people demanding 10,000 units. How is this allocation achieved?

In an unregulated market, the shortage would drive the rent up (as shown in Fig. 6.1(a)) and the price mechanism would regulate the quantities demanded and supplied and allocate the scarce housing resources. As long as one person was willing to pay a higher price than another person's minimum supply price, the price would rise and the quantity of housing available would increase. When a rent ceiling blocks the market mechanism by

FIGURE 6.2

A Rent Ceiling

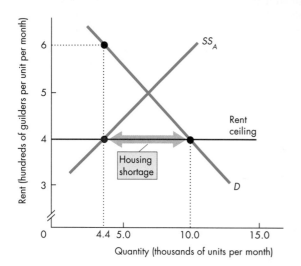

If there had been a rent ceiling of 400 guilders a month after the flood, the quantity of housing supplied would have been stuck at 4,400 units. People would willingly have paid 600 guilders a month for the 4.4 thousandth unit. Because the last unit of housing available is worth more than the regulated rent, frustrated buyers will spend time searching for housing and frustrated buyers and sellers will make deals in a black market.

making rent increases illegal, two developments occur. They are:

♦ Search activity
♦ Black markets

Search Activity

When the quantity demanded exceeds the quantity supplied, many suppliers have nothing to sell and many demanders have nothing to buy. So unsatisfied demanders devote time and other resources to searching for a supplier. The time spent looking for someone with whom to do business is called **search activity**. Of course, without full information, some search activity occurs in markets even if prices adjust freely, but search activity increases when markets are regulated.

Search activity is costly. It uses time and other resources – telephones, cars, petrol – that could be used in other productive ways. People look for any kind of information about newly available housing to try to avoid the queues. The *total cost* of housing is equal to the rent – the regulated price – plus the cost of search activity – an unregulated price. So rent ceilings might control the rent portion of the cost of housing, but they do not control the total cost. The total cost may well be *higher* than the unregulated market price.

Black Markets

A **black market** is an illegal trading arrangement in which buyers and sellers do business at a price higher or lower than the legally imposed price. There are many markets that are regulated or taxed and in which economic forces result in black market trading. In countries like Italy and the United Kingdom, the black market is estimated to be worth more than 10 per cent of national output.

In regulated housing markets, a black market usually takes the form of a buyer and a seller colluding to avoid the rent ceiling. They have a written agreement that uses the regulated rent, but agree informally to raise the actual rent. The level of the black market rent depends mainly on how tightly the government polices its rent ceiling regulations, the chances of being caught violating them and the scale of the penalties imposed for violations.

At one extreme, the chance of being caught violating a rent ceiling is small. In this case, the black market will function similarly to an unregulated market, and the black market rent and quantity traded will be close to the unregulated equilibrium. At the other extreme, where policing is highly effective and where large penalties are imposed on violators, the rent ceiling will restrict the quantity traded. In the flood example, strict enforcement of the rent ceiling would restrict the quantity of housing available to 4,400 units. A small number of people would offer housing for sale at 600 guilders a month – the highest price that a buyer is willing to pay – and the government would detect and punish some of the black market traders.

Rent Ceilings in Practice

Rent controls have been widely used throughout Europe and North America. They were introduced in the United Kingdom after World War I and eventually covered most of the rented market. Remember that the private rented sector comprised more than 50 per cent of the total housing market at that time. When rent ceilings are in force, frustrated renters and landlords constantly seek ways of increasing rents that do not violate the letter of the law but defeat its purpose. One common way of increasing the effective rent is for a new tenant to pay the landlord a high price for worthless fittings – £1,000 for threadbare curtains or several thousand pounds for a superficial repainting job. Another is for the tenant to pay a high price for new locks and keys – a device called 'key money'.

But to the extent that the law does prevent the rent from adjusting to bring the quantity demanded into equality with the quantity supplied, factors other than rent must allocate the scarce housing. One of these factors is discrimination, on the basis of race, ethnicity, or sex.

The effects of rent ceilings in cities such as London, Paris and New York have led Assar Lindbeck, chairman of the economic science Nobel Prize committee and a professor at the University of Stockholm, to suggest that rent ceilings are the most effective means yet invented for destroying cities, even more effective than the hydrogen bomb. By the time the UK government decided to remove rent controls in 1989, the size of the private rented sector had dwindled to less than 10 per cent of the housing market.

REVIEW

◆ A decrease in the supply of housing increases equilibrium rents.

◆ In the short run, higher rents result in a decrease in the quantity of housing demanded and an increase in the quantity supplied as existing houses and blocks of flats are used more intensively.

◆ In the long run, higher rents stimulate building. The supply of housing increases and rents fall.

◆ Rent ceilings limit the ability of the housing market to respond to change and can result in a permanent housing shortage.

We've studied the effects of a change in supply in the housing market. Let's now look at the effects of a change in demand in the labour market.

The Labour Market and Minimum Wages

For most of us, the labour market is the most important market in which we participate. It is the interaction of demand and supply in the labour market that influences the jobs we get and the wages we earn. Firms make decisions about the quantity of labour to demand and households make decisions about the quantity of labour to supply. The wage rate balances the quantities demanded and the quantities supplied and determines the level of employment. But the labour market is constantly being bombarded by shocks, particularly from technological advances. This means that wages and employment prospects are constantly changing.

Labour-saving technology is constantly being invented. As a result, the demand for certain types of labour, usually the least skilled types, is constantly decreasing. How does the labour market cope with this continuous decrease in the demand for unskilled labour? Does it mean that the wages of unskilled workers are constantly falling? Let's find out.

Figure 6.3 shows the market for unskilled labour. Labour is demanded by firms and, other things remaining the same, the lower the wage rate, the greater is the quantity of labour demanded. The demand curve for labour, D in part (a), shows this relationship between the wage rate and the quantity of labour demanded. Labour is supplied by households and, other things remaining the same, the higher the wage rate, the greater is the quantity of labour supplied. But the longer the period of adjustment, the greater is the elasticity of supply of labour. Thus there are two supply curves, a short-run supply curve SS and a long-run supply curve LS.

The short-run supply curve shows how the hours of labour supplied by a given number of workers changes as the wage rate changes. To get employees to work longer hours, firms must offer higher wages, so the short-run supply curve is upward sloping.

The long-run supply curve shows the relationship between the quantity of labour supplied and the wage rate after enough time has passed for people to acquire new skills and move to new locations and new types of jobs. The number of people in the unskilled labour market depends on the opportunity cost – the unskilled wage rate

FIGURE 6.3

A Market for Unskilled Labour

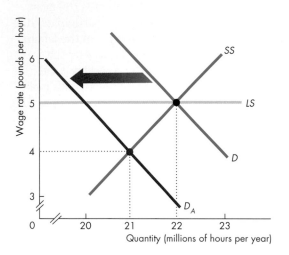

(a) After invention

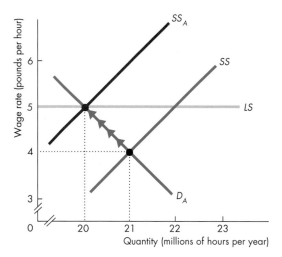

(b) Long-run adjustment

A market for unskilled labour is in equilibrium (part a) at a wage rate of £5 an hour with 22 million hours of labour a year being employed. A labour-saving invention shifts the demand curve from D to D_A. The wage rate falls to £4 an hour and employment decreases to 21 million hours a year. With the lower wage, some workers leave this market and the short-run supply curve starts to shifts to SS_A (part b). The wage rate gradually increases, and the employment level decreases. Ultimately, wages return to £5 an hour and employment falls to 20 million hours a year.

compared with skilled wages and the value of leisure time. If the wage rate is high enough, people will enter this market. When it is too low, people leave the labour market – to seek training to enter the skilled labour market, to retire, or to work at home.

Because people are free to enter and leave the unskilled labour market, the long-run supply curve is highly elastic. In Fig. 6.3, for simplicity, the long-run supply curve is assumed to be perfectly elastic (horizontal). The unskilled labour market is in equilibrium at a wage rate of £5 an hour and 22 million hours of labour are employed.

What happens if a labour-saving technology decreases the demand for unskilled labour? Figure 6.3(a) shows the short-run effects of such a change. The demand curve before the new technology is introduced is D. After the introduction of the new technology, the demand curve shifts leftward, to D_A. The wage rate falls to £4 an hour, and the quantity of labour employed decreases to 21 million hours. But this is not the end of the story.

People who are now earning only £4 an hour look around for other opportunities. They see that there are many other jobs for workers with more skills that pay wages above £4 an hour. One by one, workers decide to quit the market for unskilled labour. Some may retire, but many go to college to get new qualifications, or take jobs that pay less initially but offer on-the-job training. As a result, the short-run supply curve begins to shift leftward.

Figure 6.3(b) shows the long-run adjustment. As the short-run supply curve shifts leftward, it intersects the demand curve D_A at higher wage rates and lower levels of employment. In the long run, the short-run supply curve must shift all the way to SS_A. At this point, the wage has returned to £5 an hour, and employment has decreased to 20 million hours a year.

If the adjustment process we've just described is long and drawn out, wages remain low for a long period. In such a situation, the government is tempted to intervene in the labour market by legislating a minimum wage to protect the lowest-paid workers.

The Minimum Wage

A **minimum wage law** is a regulation that makes hiring labour below a specified wage illegal. If the minimum wage is set *below* the equilibrium wage, it has no effect. The law and the market forces are not in conflict. But if a minimum wage is set *above* the equilibrium wage, the minimum wage is in conflict with the market forces and does have some effects on the labour market. Let's study these effects by returning to the market for unskilled labour.

Suppose that when the wage rate falls to £4 an hour (in Fig. 6.3(a)) the government imposes a minimum wage of £5 an hour. What are the effects of this law? The answer can be found by studying Fig. 6.4. The minimum wage is shown as the horizontal red line labelled 'Minimum wage'. At the minimum wage, only 20 million hours of labour are demanded (point *a*) but 22 million hours of labour are supplied (point *b*). Because the number of hours demanded is less than the number of hours supplied, 2 million hours of available labour are unemployed.

What are the workers doing with their unemployed hours? They are searching for work. With only 20 million hours of labour employed, there are many people willing to supply their labour for wage rates much lower than the minimum wage. In fact, the 20 millionth hour of labour will be supplied for as little as £3. How do we know that there are people willing to work for as little as £3 an hour?

Look again at Fig. 6.4. When only 20 million hours of work are available, you can read off from the supply curve that the lowest wage at which workers are willing to supply that 20 millionth hour is £3. Someone who manages to find a job will earn £5 an hour – £2 an hour more than the lowest wage rate at which someone is willing to work. Therefore it pays the unemployed workers to engage in search activity. Even though only 20 million hours of labour actually get employed, each person spends time and effort searching for one of the scarce jobs.

The Minimum Wage in Reality

Minimum wage laws are used by most governments in Europe and North America. The United Kingdom and Ireland are the only members of the European Union that do not have minimum wage laws. The UK Labour Party has proposed introducing a minimum wage. Many European countries have a statutory national minimum wage across all industries, adjusted at regular intervals for changes in

FIGURE 6.4

Minimum Wages and Unemployment

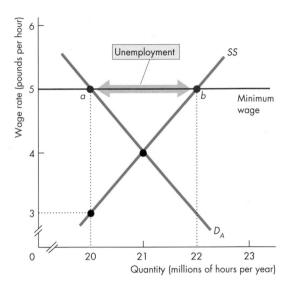

The demand curve for labour is D_A and the supply curve is *SS*. In an unregulated market, the wage rate is £4 an hour and 21 million hours of labour a year are employed. If a minimum wage of £5 an hour is imposed, only 20 million hours are hired but 22 million hours are available. This results in unemployment – *ab* – of 2 million hours a year. With only 20 million hours being demanded, some workers will willingly supply that 20 millionth hour for £3. These frustrated unemployed workers will spend time and other resources looking for a job.

the price level or average earnings. In Belgium and Greece, the national minimum wage is set by a process of collective bargaining with trade unions, and a similar process determines industry minimum wages in Denmark, Germany and Italy.

There is now a hot debate about whether to introduce a Europe-wide minimum wage as part of the European Union's new labour market strategy. Some economists believe that bringing down the barriers to trade in the new single European market will increase competition and create an increasingly low-wage work-force – a process called *social dumping*. Firms will be attracted to low-wage countries and governments will start to compete for this investment by cutting back welfare provision, training and employer costs. Growth will be limited to the low-skill, low-wage sector. Minimum wages are needed to halt the downward pressure on wages.

Other economists believe that minimum wages will fuel inflation as higher paid workers try to raise their wages to keep the same differentials with the lowest paid workers. Minimum wages also stop the market reaching equilibrium and low paid workers only gain higher wages at the opportunity cost of fewer jobs. As low wages are more common among young people, existing minimum wage laws may explain why the highest rates of unemployment in Europe are among such people.

In Chapter 15 we will look at some examples of when minimum wages do not lead to unemployment.

R E V I E W

◆ A decrease in the demand for unskilled labour lowers the equilibrium wage.

◆ In the short run, lower wages result in a decrease in the quantity of unskilled labour supplied and an increase in the quantity demanded.

◆ In the long run, lower wages encourage some people to leave the work-force and others to train and obtain skills. The supply of unskilled labour decreases and wages rise.

◆ Minimum wage regulations limit the ability of the labour market to respond to change and can result in high rates of unemployment among the low paid workers.

Let's look at the effects of another set of government actions on markets – taxes.

Taxes

In 1994, the UK government raised more than £6.4 billion – an average of £1,150 per person – from indirect tax, that is taxes on the goods and services we buy. These taxes include value added tax (VAT), sales taxes on goods and services like insurance and housing, and excise taxes on petrol, alcoholic beverages and tobacco. VAT is an *ad valorem* tax – a tax set as a percentage of the selling price on all transactions. All countries in the European Union levy this tax, but different countries impose different rates. Excise taxes are usually specific taxes – a specific amount of tax per unit, say 5 pence per cigarette levied on the manufacturer. Sales taxes may be *ad valorem* or specific taxes but are levied at the final point of sale.

If a good or service is taxed, you pay the retail price *plus* an additional amount, the *tax*. What are the effects of taxes on the prices and quantities of goods bought and sold? Do the prices of the goods and services you buy increase by the full amount of the tax? Isn't it always you – the consumer – who pays the entire tax? It can be, but usually it isn't. It is even possible that you actually pay none of the tax, forcing the seller to pay it for you. Let's see how we can make sense of these apparently absurd statements.

Who Pays a Sales Tax?

To study the effect of a tax, we start by looking at a market in which there is no tax. We'll then introduce a tax – a specific sales tax – and see what changes arise. The results for other forms of tax are not examined here but they are similar.

Figure 6.5 shows the market for CD players. The demand curve is D and the supply curve is S. The equilibrium price of a CD player is £100, and the quantity traded is 5,000 players a week.

Suppose the government puts a £10 sales tax on CD players. What are the effects of this tax on the price and quantity in the market for CD players? To answer this question, we need to work out what happens to demand and supply in this market.

When a good is taxed it has two prices – a price that excludes the tax and a price that includes it. Consumers respond only to the price that includes the tax. Producers respond only to the price they receive – the price that excludes the tax. The tax is like a wedge between these two prices.

Let's think of the price on the vertical axis of Fig. 6.5 as the price paid by the consumer that includes the tax. When a tax is imposed, there is no shift in demand. The demand curve shows quantities demanded at different levels of the total price, with or without a tax.

But the supply curve *does* shift. When a sales tax is imposed on a good, it is offered for sale at a higher

FIGURE 6.5

The Sales Tax

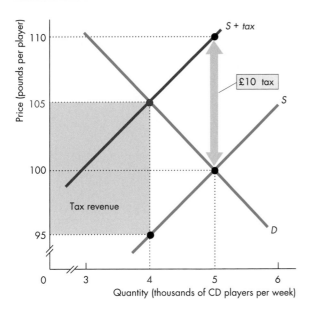

The demand curve for CD players is *D* and the supply curve is *S*. With no tax, the price is £100 a player and 5,000 players a week are bought and sold. Then a sales tax of £10 a player is imposed. The price on the vertical axis is the price *including* the tax. The demand curve does not change, but supply decreases and the supply curve shifts leftward. The curve *S* + *tax* shows the terms on which sellers will make CD players available. The vertical distance between the supply curve *S* and the new supply curve *S* + *tax* equals the tax – £10 a player.

    The new equilibrium is at a price of £105 with 4,000 CD players a week bought and sold. The tax increases the price by less than the tax, decreases the price received by the supplier, and decreases the quantity bought and sold. It brings in revenue to the government equal to the blue shaded area.

price than in a no-tax situation. The supply curve shifts leftward to *S* + *tax*. The new supply curve is found by adding the tax to the minimum price that suppliers are willing to accept for each quantity sold. For example, with no tax, suppliers are willing to sell 4,000 players a week for £95 a player. So with a £10 tax, they will supply 4,000 players a week for £105 – a price that includes the tax. The new supply curve *S* + *tax* lies to the left of the original curve – supply has decreased – and the vertical distance between the original supply curve *S* and

the new supply curve *S* + *tax* equals the tax. The curve *S* + *tax* describes the price at which the good is available to buyers.

    A new equilibrium is determined where the new supply curve intersects the demand curve – at a price of £105 and a quantity of 4,000 CD players a week. The £10 sales tax has increased the price paid by the consumer by only £5 (£105 versus £100), which is less than the £10 tax. And it has decreased the price received by the supplier by £5 (£95 versus £100). The £10 tax paid is made up of the higher price to the buyer and the lower price to the seller.

    The tax brings in tax revenue to the government equal to the tax per item multiplied by the items sold. It is illustrated by the blue area in Fig. 6.5. The £10 tax on CD players brings in a tax revenue of £40,000 a week.

    In this example, the buyer and the seller split the tax equally; the buyer pays £5 a player and so does the seller. The proportion of the tax paid by the buyer and the seller is determined by the elasticity of demand and supply. In extreme cases, the buyer or the seller might have to pay the entire tax. Let's look at these cases.

Tax Division and Elasticity of Demand

The division of the total tax between buyers and sellers also depends on the elasticity of demand. Again, there are two extreme cases:

◆ Perfectly inelastic demand – buyer pays.
◆ Perfectly elastic demand – seller pays.

Perfectly Inelastic Demand   Figure 6.6(a) shows the market for insulin, a life-saving daily medication for diabetics. The quantity demanded is 100,000 bottles a day, regardless of the price. Each one of the 100,000 diabetics in the population would sacrifice all other goods and services for their daily insulin dose. In the absence of a national health service, demand for insulin would reflect this fact and would be perfectly inelastic. It is shown by the vertical curve *D*. The supply curve of insulin is *S*. With no tax, the price is £2 a bottle, and the quantity is 100,000 bottles a day.

    If insulin is taxed at 20 pence a bottle, we must add the tax to the minimum price at which the drug companies are willing to sell insulin to determine the post-tax supply to consumers. The result is a new supply curve *S* + *tax*. The price rises to

FIGURE 6.6

Sales Tax and the Elasticity of Demand

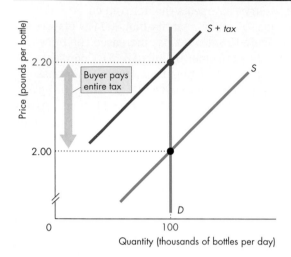

(a) Inelastic demand

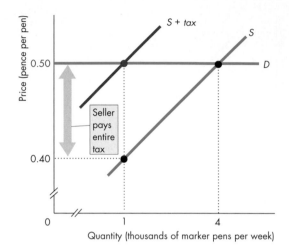

(b) Elastic demand

Part (a) shows the market for insulin. The demand for insulin is perfectly inelastic, as shown by the curve *D*. The supply curve of insulin is *S*. With no tax the price is £2 a bottle and 100,000 bottles a day are bought. A sales tax of 20 pence a bottle increases the price at which sellers are willing to make insulin available, and shifts the supply curve to *S + tax*. The price rises to £2.20 a bottle, but the quantity bought does not change and buyers pay the entire tax.

Part (b) shows the market for pink marker pens. The demand for pink marker pens is perfectly elastic at the price of other coloured marker pens – 50 pence a pen. The demand curve is *D*, the supply curve is *S*, and with no tax the price of a pink marker pen is 50 pence and 4,000 a week are bought. A sales tax of 10 pence a pink pen decreases the supply of pink marker pens, shifting the supply curve to *S + tax*. The price remains at 50 pence a pen, and the quantity of pink markers sold decreases to 1,000 a week. Suppliers pay the entire tax.

£2.20 a bottle, but the quantity does not change. The buyer pays the entire sales tax of 20 pence a bottle.

Perfectly Elastic Demand   Figure 6.6(b) shows the market for pink marker pens. Apart from a few pink freaks, no one cares whether they use a pink, blue, yellow, or green marker pen. If pink markers are less expensive than the others, everyone will use pink. If pink markers are more expensive than the others, no one will use them. The demand for pink marker pens is perfectly elastic at the price of other coloured marker pens – 50 pence a pen in Fig. 6.6(b). The demand curve for pink markers is the horizontal curve *D*. The supply curve is *S*. With no tax, the price of a pink marker is 50 pence and 4,000 a week are bought at that price.

If the sales tax of 10 pence a pen is levied on

pink, and only pink, marker pens, we must add the tax to the minimum price at which suppliers are willing to sell them to determine the post-tax supply to consumers. The new supply curve is *S + tax*. The price remains at 50 pence a pen, and the quantity of pink markers decreases to 1,000 a week. The 10 pence tax has left the price paid by the consumer unchanged, but decreased the amount received by the supplier by the full amount of the tax – 10 pence a pen. As a result, sellers decrease the quantity offered for sale.

In most markets, demand is neither perfectly inelastic nor perfectly elastic, so the tax is split between the buyer and the seller. But the division depends on the elasticity of demand and will rarely be equal. The more inelastic the demand and the more elastic the supply, the larger is the portion of the tax paid by the buyer.

FIGURE 6.7

Sales Tax and the Elasticity of Supply

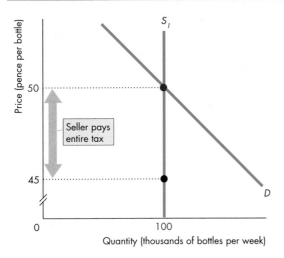

(a) Inelastic supply

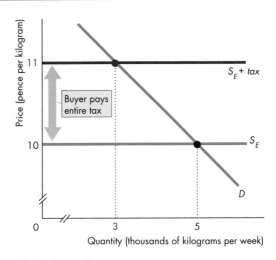

(b) Elastic supply

Part (a) shows the market for water from a mineral spring. Supply is perfectly inelastic and the supply curve is S_I. The demand curve is D, and with no tax the price is 50 pence a bottle. A sales tax of 5 pence decreases the price received by sellers, but the price remains at 50 pence a bottle and the number of bottles bought remains the same. Suppliers pay the entire tax.

Part (b) shows the market for sand from which silicon is extracted. Supply is perfectly elastic at a price of 10

pence a kilogram. The supply curve is S_E, the demand curve is D, and with no tax the price is 10 pence a kilogram and 5,000 kilograms a week are bought. A sales tax of 1 penny a kilogram increases the minimum price at which sellers are willing to supply to 11 pence a kilogram. The supply curve shifts to $S_E + tax$. The price increases to 11 pence a kilogram, the quantity bought decreases to 3,000 kilograms a week, and buyers pay the entire tax.

Tax Division and Elasticity of Supply

The division of the total tax between buyers and sellers depends, in part, on the elasticity of supply. There are two extreme cases:

◆ Perfectly inelastic supply – seller pays.
◆ Perfectly elastic supply – buyer pays.

Perfectly Inelastic Supply Figure 6.7(a) shows the market for water from a mineral spring which flows at a constant rate that can't be controlled. The quantity supplied is 100,000 bottles a week, regardless of the price. The supply is perfectly inelastic and the supply curve is S_I. The demand curve for the water from this spring is D. With no tax, the price is 50 pence a bottle and the 100,000 bottles that flow from the spring are bought at that price.

If the spring water is taxed at 5 pence a bottle, we must add the tax to the minimum price at which the spring owners are willing to sell the water to determine the terms on which this water will be available to consumers. But the spring owners are able to supply only one quantity – 100,000 bottles a week – at any price (greater than zero). Consumers, on the other hand, are willing to buy the 100,000 bottles available each week only if the price is 50 pence a bottle. So the price remains at 50 pence a bottle, and the suppliers pay the entire tax. The tax of 5 pence a bottle reduces the price received by suppliers to 45 pence a bottle.

Perfectly Elastic Supply Figure 6.7(b) shows the market for sand from which computer-chip makers extract silicon. There is a virtually unlimited quantity of sand available, and its owners are willing to supply any quantity at a price of 10 pence a kilogram. So supply is perfectly elastic – the supply curve S_E. The demand curve for sand is D. With no tax, the price is 10 pence a kilogram, and 5,000 kilograms a week are bought at that price.

If sand is taxed at 1 penny a kilogram, we must add the tax to the minimum price at which the suppliers are willing to sell the sand to determine the supply to computer-chip makers. Suppliers of sand are willing to supply any quantity at 10 pence a kilogram, without a tax. With the 1 penny tax, they are willing to supply any quantity at 11 pence a kilogram along the curve $S_E + tax$. A new equilibrium is determined where the new supply curve intersects the demand curve – at a price of 11 pence a kilogram and a quantity of 3,000 kilograms a week. The sales tax has increased the price paid by consumers by the full amount of the tax – 1 penny a kilogram – and has decreased the quantity sold.

We've seen that when supply is perfectly inelastic, the seller pays the entire tax and when supply is perfectly elastic, the buyer pays it. In the usual case, where supply is neither perfectly inelastic nor perfectly elastic, the tax is split between the seller and the buyer. But the division depends on the elasticity of supply. The more elastic the supply, the larger is the portion of the tax paid by the buyer.

Indirect Taxes in Practice

We've looked at the range of possible effects of a sales tax by studying extreme cases. In practice, supply and demand are rarely perfectly elastic or inelastic. So does our model of tax help us to understand government tax policy? Let's see. We know that governments tend to choose goods such as alcohol, tobacco and petrol for excise taxes. Why? Because they have a low elasticity of demand. Although the tax raises the price and the quantity bought falls, it does not fall by much. Tax revenue will rise even if the tax is increased. Of course, governments must raise the specific tax on goods every year to keep the real value of the tax constant. Otherwise revenue will start to fall, other things remaining the same. Alternative reasons for taxing these goods are examined in Chapter 20 and in the next section.

◆ The effect of the sales tax depends on the elasticities of supply and demand.

◆ For a given demand curve, the more elastic the supply, the larger is the price increase, the larger is the quantity decrease, and the larger is the portion of the tax paid by the buyer.

◆ For a given supply curve, the less elastic the demand, the larger is the price increase, the smaller is the quantity decrease, and the larger is the portion of the tax paid by the buyer.

Taxes are just one method of changing prices and quatities. Let's look at another: prohibiting trade in a good.

Markets for Prohibited Goods

The markets for many goods and services are regulated, and buying and selling some goods is prohibited – the goods and services are illegal. The best known examples are drugs. Alcohol and tobacco are currently legally available drugs, but their supply and consumption is regulated in most European countries. Other drugs such as cannabis, ecstasy, cocaine and heroin are more commonly illegal.

Despite the fact that some drugs are illegal, trade in them is a multi-billion pound global business. This trade can be understood by using the same economic models and principles that explain trade in legal goods and services. There are also occasions when legal drugs are prohibited and illegal drugs are legalised. For example, alcohol has been prohibited during wartime and cannabis is legally available in the Netherlands. We can use our models to look at the economic impact of different regulation and control systems.

As you study the market for drugs, remember that economics tries to answer questions about how markets work. It neither condones nor condemns the activities it seeks to explain. What you learn about the markets for illegal goods is one input into developing your opinion. It is not a substitute for your moral judgements. What follows is an analysis of how markets for prohibited goods work and not an argument about whether they ought to be regulated or prohibited.

To study the market for prohibited goods, we're first going to examine the prices and quantities that would prevail if these goods were not prohibited. Next, we'll see how prohibition works. Then we'll see how a tax might be used to limit the consumption of these goods.

A Free Market for Drugs

Figure 6.8 shows a market for a drug. The demand curve, D, shows that, other things remaining the same, the lower the price of the drug, the larger is the quantity demanded. The supply curve, S, shows that, other things remaining the same, the lower the price of the drug, the smaller is the quantity supplied. If the drug were not prohibited or regulated, the quantity bought and sold would be Q_c and the price would be P_c.

Prohibiting a Drug

When a good is prohibited, the cost of trading in the good increases. By how much the cost increases and on whom the cost falls depend on the penalties for breaking the law and the effectiveness with which the law is enforced. The larger the penalties and the more effective the policing, the higher are the costs to traders. Fines impose a direct cost but prison sentences involve the opportunity cost of lost earnings and discomfort. Penalties may be imposed on sellers, buyers, or both.

Penalties on Sellers   Drug dealers in the United Kingdom face fines and prison sentences if their activities are detected. For example, a cannabis dealer would probably serve a 1.5 year prison term, whereas a heroin dealer would serve a 2.5 year prison term on average. These penalties are part of the cost of supplying illegal drugs and they lead to a decrease in supply – a leftward shift in the supply curve. To determine the new supply curve, we add the cost of breaking the law to the minimum price that drug dealers are willing to accept. In Fig. 6.8, the cost of breaking the law by selling drugs (CBL) is added to the minimum price that dealers will accept and the supply curve shifts leftward to $S + CBL$. If penalties are imposed only on sellers, the market moves from point c to point a. The price increases and the quantity bought decreases.

FIGURE 6.8

The Market for a Prohibited Good

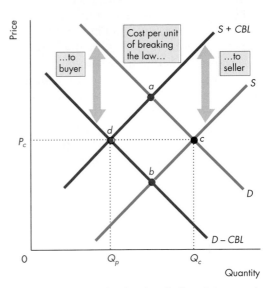

The demand curve for the drug is D and the supply curve is S. With no prohibition or regulation, the quantity consumed is Q_c at a price of P_c – point c. If selling the drug is illegal, the cost of breaking the law (CBL) is added to the other costs and supply decreases to $S + CBL$. The price rises and the quantity consumed decreases – point a. If buying the drug is illegal, the cost of breaking the law is subtracted from the maximum price that buyers are willing to pay, and demand decreases to $D - CBL$. The price falls and the quantity consumed decreases – point b.

If both buying and selling are illegal both the supply curve and the demand curve shift – the quantity consumed decreases even more, but (in this example) the price remains at its unregulated level – point d.

Penalties on Buyers   In the United Kingdom, it is also illegal to possess drugs such as cannabis, cocaine and heroin for personal consumption. The penalty for illegal possession of cannabis is usually a fine and prison sentences are rarely more than 3 months, whereas the penalty for illegal possession of heroin is usually a 9 month prison sentence. Penalties for possession fall on buyers and the cost of breaking the law must be subtracted from the value of the good to determine the maximum price buyers are willing to pay. Demand decreases and the demand curve shifts leftward. In Fig. 6.8, the demand curve shifts to $D - CBL$. If penalties are imposed only on buyers, the market moves from point *c* to point *b*. The price and the quantity bought decrease.

Penalties on Both Sellers and Buyers   If penalties are imposed on sellers *and* buyers, both supply and demand decrease and both the supply curve and demand curve shift. In Fig. 6.8, the costs of breaking the law are the same for both buyers and sellers, so both curves shift leftward by the same amounts. The market moves to point *d*. The price remains at the competitive market price but the quantity bought decreases to Q_p.

The larger the penalty and the greater the degree of law enforcement, the larger is the decrease in demand and/or supply and the greater is the shift of the demand and/or supply curve. If the penalties are heavier on sellers, the price will rise above P_c, and if the penalties are heavier on buyers, the price will fall below P_c. In the United Kingdom, the penalties on sellers are larger than those on buyers. As a result, the decrease in supply is much larger than the decrease in demand. The quantity of drugs traded decreases and the price increases, compared with an unregulated market.

With high enough penalties and effective law enforcement, it is possible to decrease demand and/or supply to the point at which the quantity bought is zero. But in reality, such an outcome is unusual. It does not happen in the case of illegal drugs. The key reason is the high cost of law enforcement and insufficient resources for the police and customs officers to achieve effective enforcement. Because of this, some people suggest that drugs (and other illegal goods) should be legalized but regulated. In particular, legalized drugs could be taxed at a high rate in the same way that legal drugs such as alcohol are taxed. You can read about the problems of setting taxes on alcohol in the European Union in *Reading Between the Lines* on pp. 140–141. How would such an arrangement work?

Legalizing and Taxing Drugs

Figure 6.9 shows what happens if a drug is legalized and taxed. With no tax, the quantity of the drug is Q_c and the price is P_c. Now suppose that the drug is taxed so that the market quantity is the same as when it was illegal. The tax added to the supply price shifts the supply curve to $S + tax$. Equilibrium

FIGURE 6.9

Legalizing and Taxing Drugs

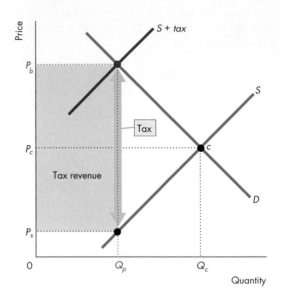

Drugs are legalized but taxed at a high rate. The tax added to the supply price shifts the supply curve from S to $S + tax$. The quantity bought decreases to Q_p, the price paid by consumers increases to P_b, and the price received by suppliers decreases to P_s. The government collects a tax revenue equal to the blue shaded area.

occurs at a quantity of Q_p. The price paid by consumers increases to P_b and the price received by suppliers decreases to P_s. The government collects a tax revenue equal to the blue area in the figure.

Illegal Trading to Evade the Tax   An extremely high tax rate would probably be needed to keep drug consumption at the level in the market before legalisation. High taxes would lead many drug dealers and consumers to evade the tax so that tax revenue would fall short of the area highlighted in Fig. 6.9. This problem can be reduced by requiring sellers to have a licence, as in the case of alcohol and tobacco. Tax evaders would also face the cost of breaking the tax law. If the penalty for tax law violation is severe and the law is as effectively policed as drug dealing laws, then a regulated market could achieve a similar result to prohibition. The quantity of drugs consumed in a regulated market would depend on the penalties for law breaking and on the way in which the penalties are assigned to buyers and sellers.

Some Pros and Cons of Taxes versus Prohibition So which works more effectively, prohibition or taxing? The comparison we've just made suggests that the two methods can be made to be equivalent if the taxes and penalties are set at the appropriate levels. But there are some other differences.

In favour of taxes and against prohibition is the fact that the tax revenue can be used to make law enforcement more effective. Some economists argue that a great deal of inner city crime is caused by the prohibition of drugs – burglaries, muggings, shootings and money laundering. Legalization would reduce the social and policing costs associated with this crime. Tax revenue can also be used to run a more effective education campaign against drugs. In favour of prohibition and against taxes is the fact that a prohibition sends a strong signal that may influence preferences, decreasing the demand for drugs. Also, some people intensely dislike the idea of the government profiting from trade in harmful substances.

R E V I E W

◆ Penalizing sellers of an illegal good increases the cost of selling the good and decreases supply and market quantity.

◆ Penalizing buyers of an illegal good decreases the willingness to pay for the good and decreases demand and market quantity.

◆ The price of an illegal good increases if penalties on sellers are higher than those on buyers and the price decreases if penalties on buyers are higher than those on sellers.

◆ Prohibition and taxation generate law enforcement costs but taxation generates revenue.

◆ Taxing a good at a sufficiently high rate can achieve the same consumption level as prohibition.

Stabilizing Farm Revenue

Freak gale force storms in 1993 wiped out many crops. Farm output fluctuates a great deal because of fluctuations in the weather. How do changes in farm output affect farm prices and farm revenues? And how might farm revenues be stabilized? The answers to these questions depend on how the markets for agricultural goods are organized. We'll begin by looking at an unregulated agricultural market.

An Unregulated Agricultural Market

Figure 6.10 illustrates the unregulated European market for wheat. In both parts the demand curve for wheat is D. Once farmers have harvested their crop, they have no control over the quantity supplied and supply is inelastic along a *momentary supply curve*. In normal climate conditions, the momentary supply curve is MS_0 (in both parts of the figure) – the price is £100 a tonne, the quantity produced is 4 million tonnes, and farm revenue is £400 million (dark blue and red areas).

Suppose the opportunity cost to farmers of producing wheat is also £400 million. Then in normal conditions, farmers just cover their opportunity cost.

Poor Harvest What happens to the price of wheat and the revenue of farmers when there is a poor harvest? These questions are answered in Fig. 6.10(a). Supply decreases and the momentary supply curve shifts leftward to MS_1 where 3 million tonnes of wheat are produced. With a decrease in supply, the price increases to £150 a tonne. But notice farm revenue *increases* to £450 million (light and dark blue areas). On average, farmers are now making a profit in excess of their opportunity cost.

A decrease in supply will increase the price and farm revenues because the demand for wheat is *inelastic*. The percentage decrease in the quantity demanded is less than the percentage increase in price. You can verify this fact by noticing in Fig. 6.10(a) that the increase in revenue from the higher price (£150 million light blue area) exceeds the decrease in revenue from the smaller quantity (£100 million red area).

Although total farm revenue increases when there is a poor harvest, some farmers, whose entire crop is wiped out, suffer a fall in revenue. Others, whose crop is unaffected, make an enormous gain.

Bumper harvest   Figure 6.10(b) shows what happens when there is a bumper harvest. Now, supply increases to 5 million tonnes and the momentary supply curve shifts rightward to MS_2. With the increased quantity supplied, the price falls to £50 a tonne. Farm revenues also decline – to £250 million because the demand for wheat is inelastic. To see this, notice in Fig. 6.10(b) that the decrease in revenue from the lower price (£200 million light blue area) exceeds the increase in revenue from the increase in the quantity sold (£50 million red area).

Elasticity of Demand   What happens if the demand for wheat is elastic? The price fluctuations go in the same directions as when demand is inelastic, but revenues fluctuate in the opposite directions. Bumper harvests increase revenue and poor harvests decrease it. In fact the demand for most agricultural goods is inelastic, and our inelastic example is the relevant one.

Because farm prices fluctuate, institutions have evolved to stabilize them. There are two types of institutions:

◆   Speculative markets in stocks
◆   Price support policy

Speculative Markets in Stocks

Many goods, including a wide variety of agricultural goods, can be stored. These **stocks** of goods – or stores – provide a cushion between production and consumption. If production decreases, goods can be sold from stocks; if production increases, goods can be put into stocks.

In a market that has stocks, the quantity produced is not the same as the quantity supplied. The quantity supplied exceeds the quantity produced when goods are sold from stocks. The quantity supplied is less than the quantity produced when goods are put into stocks. The supply curve, therefore, depends on the behaviour of stock holders who keep stocks. Let's see how they behave.

The Behaviour of Stock Holders   Stock holders speculate. They hope to buy goods and put them into stores when the price is low, and sell them from stores when the price is high. They make a profit or incur a loss equal to their selling price minus their

FIGURE 6.10

Harvests, Farm Prices and Farm Revenue

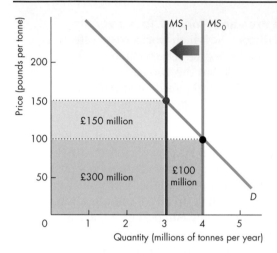

(a) Poor harvest: revenue increases

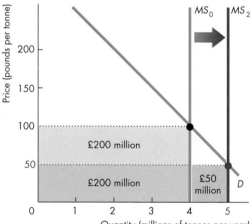

In both parts, the demand curve for wheat is *D*. In normal times, the momentary supply curve is MS_0, and 4 million tonnes are sold for £100 a tonne. In part (a), a poor growing season decreases supply, shifting the momentary supply curve to MS_1. The price increases to £150 a tonne and farm revenue *increases* from £400 million to £450 million – the increase in revenue from the higher price (£150 million light blue area) exceeds the decrease in revenue from the smaller quantity (£100 million red area). In part (b), a bumper harvest increases supply, shifting the momentary supply curve to MS_2. The price decreases to £50 a tonne and farm revenue *decreases* to £250 million – the decrease in revenue from the lower price (£200 million light blue area) exceeds the increase in revenue from the increase in the quantity sold (£50 million red area).

buying price and minus the cost of storage.[1]

But how do stock holders know if the price is high or low? First, stock holders must make their best forecast of future prices. If the current price is above the forecast future price, they sell goods from stores. If the current price is below the forecast future price, they buy goods to put into stores. This activity makes the supply curve perfectly elastic at the future price forecast by stock holders.

Let's work out what happens to price and quantity in a market in which stocks are held when production fluctuates. Let's look again at the wheat market.

Fluctuations in Production   In Fig. 6.11 the demand curve for wheat is D. Stock holders forecast the future price to be £100 a tonne. The supply curve is S – supply is perfectly elastic at the forecast price. Production fluctuates between Q_1 and Q_2.

When production fluctuates and there are no stocks, the price and the quantity fluctuate. We saw this result in Fig. 6.10. But if there are stocks, the price does not fluctuate. When production is low, at Q_1 or 3 million tonnes, stock holders sell 1 million tonnes from stores and the quantity bought by consumers is 4 million tonnes. The price remains at £100 a tonne. When production is high, at Q_2 or 5 million tonnes, stock holders buy 1 million tonnes and consumers continue to buy 4 million tonnes. Again, the price remains at £100 a tonne.

Stores in Reality   The model of a market with stores that we've just reviewed is the simplest possible. But it shows how stocks and stock holders' expectations about future prices reduce price fluctuations. In the above example, the price fluctuations are entirely eliminated. But when storage costs are high or when stocks become almost depleted, price fluctuations do occur, but they are smaller than those occurring in a market without stocks.

Farm Revenue   Even if stock speculation succeeds in stabilizing prices, it does not stabilize farm revenue. With the price stabilized, farm revenue

[1] We will suppose that the cost of storage is so small that we can ignore it. This assumption, though not essential, helps us to see the effects of stock holders' decisions on prices.

FIGURE 6.11

How Stocks Limit Price Changes

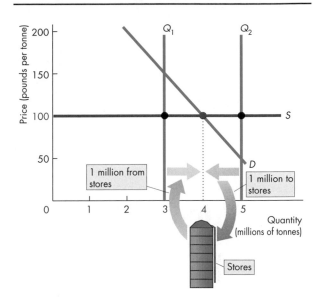

Stock holders supply goods from stores if the price rises above £100 per tonne and take wheat into stores if the price falls below £100 per tonne, making supply perfectly elastic along the supply curve S. When production decreases to Q_1, 1 million tonnes are supplied from store; when production increases to Q_2, 1 million tonnes are added to store. The price remains constant at £100 per tonne.

fluctuates as production fluctuates. Let's look at how farm revenues can be stabilized by an agricultural price support policy.

Agricultural Price Support Policy

In every country, the government intervenes in agricultural markets. The most extensive example is the **Common Agricultural Policy** (CAP) of the European Union. The CAP was set up in 1957 to make sure the bad experiences of war-time shortages and low farm incomes would not be repeated.

The CAP takes the form of price floors set above the equilibrium price – similar to the minimum wage that we studied earlier – and above the production cost of efficient farms. This is achieved by setting a tariff on agricultural products from outside the European Union. Let's look at the CAP's price

A Taxing Problem

The Essence of the Story

THE GUARDIAN, 27 JULY 1996

Alcohol ruling proves hard to swallow

Jon Henley

The Finnish government...finance minister Sauli Niinisto admitted this week he may have difficulty balancing the country's 1997 budget if the European Commission continues to insist that Finland lift its tough restrictions on personal alcohol imports.

If the curbs are eased,...Finland's punitive alcohol duties – which account for 9 per cent of all tax revenue – will almost certainly have to be lowered, significantly denting government income....

Dedicated Finnish drinkers, thousands of whom travel daily to neighbouring Sweden on 'booze cruises' to take advantage of duty-free prices, are allowed to import 15 litres of beer, 5 litres of wine and 1 litre of spirits from any EU country without paying extra tax.

The Commission wants those limits raised to 30 litres, 18 litres and 3 litres respectively by January, and brought fully in line with the rest of the EU by 1999.

'That would be almost bound to prompt a major reduction in alcohol taxes – and therefore alcohol prices – in Finland,' one of the country's leading daily newspapers, *Ilta-Sanomat*, said gleefully.

'Prices would have to be cut near to Danish or German levels to prevent a veritable stampede to the continent.'...

Finns currently pay an extra £2.50 in duty on every litre of wine they buy, while the price of a standard bottle of spirits can be 87 per cent pure tax.

By contrast, seven of the EU's 15 member states charge no fixed tax on wine at all, and the average duty on a bottle of spirits is about half Finland's rate.

Pruning booze prices to Danish levels – a fall of about 30 per cent – would nearly halve alcohol tax revenue, *Ilta-Sanomat* estimated, while a reduction to German levels would cut revenues by 85 per cent.

But the Finnish government has not given up yet. Talks are under way with the Commission, and the case may yet end up in the European Court of Justice.

Exorbitant alcohol prices, the government has repeatedly argued, are needed to protect the Finns from themselves. Lowering them to the same level as Germany could produce a 100 per cent increase in consumption, it claims, with some gruesome social consequences....

■ All restrictions on EU cross-border shopping for alcohol were removed in 1993, providing the goods were not for resale.

■ If you live in a high-tax country, you can now buy as much alcohol as you like in low-tax countries and bring it home without paying any additional tax.

■ Although Finland has been allowed to retain some restrictions since joining the European Union in 1995, the European Commission wants to raise the limits by January 1997 and eventually remove them altogether.

■ Finns currently find it worthwhile to travel to Sweden, Denmark and Germany regularly to buy alcohol – and avoid the highest tax rates in Europe.

■ Relaxing the restrictions will encourage more Finns to buy alcohol abroad, slashing domestic revenue – 9 per cent of Finnish revenue comes from alcohol.

Economic Analysis

■ Figure 1 shows the Finnish market for wine. The demand curve is D_0 and the supply curve without tax is S_0.

■ In 1996, Finns paid a tax of £2.50 per litre of wine. The tax decreases the supply curve – shifting it leftward – to $S_0 + tax_1$. The vertical distance between the two supply curves equals the tax – £2.50. Finns buy 2 million litres of wine in Finland and pay £5.50 per litre. Government revenue is £5 million (2 million × £2.50) – the green shaded area.

■ The current restrictions allow Finns to bring home 5 litres of wine per trip when visiting other countries. The Danish price of wine is 30 per cent lower than the price of wine in Finland – £3.85 a bottle. Five litres of wine in Finland cost £27.50 and £19.25 in Denmark. Finns will find it worthwhile to shop in Denmark for wine providing the cost of travel and their time does not exceed £8.25 per trip.

■ The European Commission wants Finnish restrictions on imports of wine relaxed to 18 litres by 1997 and eventually removed. If taxes stay the same in Finland, shopping trips to Denmark are more attractive. The demand for wine in Finland decreases – shifting leftward – to D_1 in Fig. 1. The price of wine falls to £5.20, but the quantity falls to 1 million litres. Finnish government revenue is halved at £2.5 million – the hatched area.

■ Removing restrictions will push demand back further – reducing revenue to zero. To avoid this, the Finnish government must cut tax and price towards the Danish level.

■ Figure 2 shows the impact of cutting tax to £1 per litre. The supply schedule increases – shifting rightward to $S_0 + tax_2$. Price is reduced to £4.20 and quantity increases to 3 million litres. Revenue falls to £3 million pounds – the hatched area. At this price, fewer Finns find it worthwhile to shop in Denmark for wine even when restrictions are lifted.

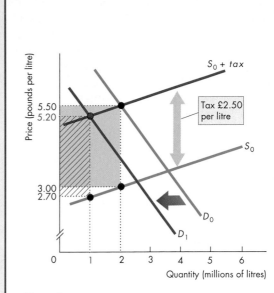

Figure 1

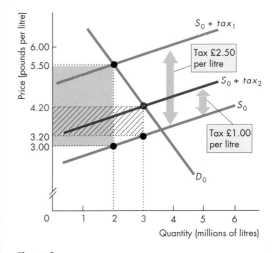

Figure 2

support mechanism for wheat shown in Fig. 6.12 to see how the price support mechanism works.

The demand schedule for wheat is *D* and the supply schedule for wheat is *S*. Without any agricultural policy the market price would be £80 a tonne and 4 million tonnes of wheat would be bought and sold. Let's assume this is also the world price per tonne. But £80 a tonne will not provide sufficient revenue for farmers. To maintain farm revenues, the European Union must set the price for a tonne of wheat higher than the market price. This is called the target price and is set at £100 a tonne in Fig. 6.12. Because the world price of £80 a tonne is now lower than the European Union's target price, cheap imports could flood in and force the EU price down again. So, to make imported wheat sell at the same price as EU wheat, a levy of £20 a tonne is imposed on imports – the difference between the world price and the target price. But at £100 a tonne there is an excess supply of 4 million tonnes of wheat in the EU market and the price will tend to fall. To avoid this, the European Union must buy up the excess wheat and put it into store.

So what happens to the store of wheat? In times of shortage, the European Union can sell off its stocks. But if the target price is consistently above the equilibrium price, the European Union buys more than it sells and ends up with mountains of wheat, beef and butter and lakes of wine! The cost of buying and storing agricultural goods falls on tax payers and the main gainers are the large, efficient farms. As a result, the European Union has begun to reform the CAP – reducing target prices and levies, and introducing direct income support payments to farmers. EU agricultural markets are now more open to world competition and the mountains of butter and lakes of wine are smaller.

FIGURE 6.12

The European Union's Agricultural Price Support System

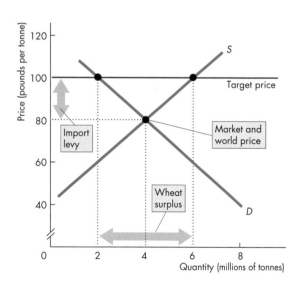

Without a price support system, the EU price of wheat would be £80 a tonne, the same as the world price. To increase farm revenues, the European Union's Common Agricultural Policy sets a target price for wheat, higher than the world price, at £100 a tonne. It imposes a levy of £20 a tonne on all imported wheat to stop cheaper imports reducing the EU target price. The policy causes a surplus at the target price which must be bought up and stored.

R E V I E W

◆ The demand for most farm goods is inelastic.

◆ With no stores, a poor harvest (a decrease in supply) increases price and increases farm revenue and a bumper harvest (an increase in supply) decreases price and decreases farm revenue.

◆ Stock holders speculate by trying to buy at a low price and sell at a high price. Successful speculation reduces price fluctuations.

◆ Farm price support policies limit price fluctuations but usually create surpluses.

◆ ◆ ◆ ◆ We've now completed our study of demand and supply and its applications. You've seen how this model enables us to make predictions about prices and quantities bought and sold and also how it enables us to understand a wide variety of markets and situations. We're now going to start digging a bit more deeply into people's economic choices, and in the next section we'll study the economic choices of households.

SUMMARY

Housing Markets and Rent Ceilings

A decrease in the supply of housing decreases short-run supply and increases equilibrium rents. Higher rents increase the quantity of housing supplied in the short run and stimulate building activity, which increases supply in the long run. Rents decrease and the quantity of housing increases.

If a rent ceiling prevents rents from increasing, there is no inducement to increase the quantity supplied in the short run or the long run. As a result, the quantity of housing is less than it would be in an unregulated market. People spend time searching for housing and the cost of housing, including the value of the time spent searching, exceeds the cost in an unregulated market. (pp. 124–127)

The Labour Market and Minimum Wages

A decrease in the demand for unskilled labour lowers the wage and reduces employment. The lower wage encourages people to quit the unskilled market and to acquire skills. As they do so, the short-run supply of unskilled labour decreases. The wage rises gradually to its original level and employment decreases.

If the government imposes a minimum wage above the equilibrium wage, a decrease in the demand for labour will result in an increase in unemployment and an increase in the amount of time spent searching for a job. Minimum wages bite hardest on people having the fewest skills (pp.127–130)

Taxes

When a good or service is taxed, it is usually offered for sale at a higher price than if it is not taxed. Usually, the quantity bought decreases and the price increases but by less than the amount of the tax. The tax is paid partly by the buyer and partly by the seller. The portion of the tax paid by the buyer and by the seller depends on the elasticity of supply and the elasticity of demand. The more elastic the supply and the less elastic the demand, the greater is the price increase, the smaller is the quantity decrease, and the larger is the portion of the tax paid by the buyer. But if supply is perfectly inelastic or demand is perfectly elastic, the seller pays the entire tax. If supply is perfectly elastic or demand is perfectly inelastic, the buyer pays the entire tax. (pp. 130–134)

Markets for Prohibited Goods

Other things remaining the same, the lower the price of illegal drugs, the larger is the quantity of drugs demanded, and the higher the price, the larger is the quantity of drugs supplied. Penalties on sellers of an illegal good increase the cost of selling the good and decrease its supply. Penalties on buyers decrease their willingness to pay and decrease the demand for the good. The higher the penalties and the more effective the law enforcement, the smaller is the quantity bought. The price is higher or lower than the unregulated price, depending on whether penalties on sellers or buyers are higher. Effective law enforcement and high enough penalties will decrease demand and supply to the point at which the good disappears.

A tax set at a sufficiently high rate will also decrease drug consumption, but there will be a tendency for the tax to be evaded. If the penalty for tax law violation is severe and the law is as effectively policed as drug dealing laws, the quantity of drugs consumed will remain at the prohibition level but the tax revenue will be lower than it would be without the tax evasion. Tax revenue from a drug tax could be used to make law enforcement more effective and to pay for a campaign against drugs. But prohibiting drugs sends a signal that may influence preferences, decreasing the demand for drugs. (pp. 134–137)

Stabilizing Farm Revenue

Farm revenues fluctuate because crop yields vary as climatic conditions fluctuate. The demand for most farm goods is inelastic, so a decrease in supply increases the price and increases farm revenue while an increase in supply decreases the price and decreases farm revenue. Stock holders and government agencies act to stabilize farm prices and revenues.

Stock holders buy at a low price and sell at a high price. As a result, supply is perfectly elastic at the future price expected by stock holders. When production is low, stock holders sell from stores, preventing the price from rising. When production is high, stock holders buy, preventing the price from falling. Agricultural price support policies set price floors above the equilibrium price that create persistent surpluses. (pp. 137–142)

KEY ELEMENTS

Key Terms

Black market, 126
Common Agricultural Policy, 139
Minimum wage law, 128
Price ceiling, 124
Rent ceiling, 125
Search activity, 126
Stocks, 138

Key Figures

Figure 6.1   The Gelderland Housing Market in
              1995, 125

Figure 6.2   A Rent Ceiling, 126
Figure 6.3   A Market for Unskilled Labour, 128
Figure 6.4   Minimum Wages and Unemployment,
              129
Figure 6.5   The Sales Tax, 131
Figure 6.8   The Market for a Prohibited Good,
              135
Figure 6.9   Legalizing and Taxing Drugs, 136
Figure 6.10   Harvests, Farm Prices and Farm
              Revenue, 138
Figure 6.11   How Stocks Limit Price Changes, 139
Figure 6.12   The European Union's Agricultural
              Price Support System, 142

REVIEW QUESTIONS

1 Describe what happens to the rent and to the quantity of housing available if a disaster such as a flood suddenly and unexpectedly reduces the supply of housing. Trace the evolution of the rent and the quantity of housing rented over time.

2 In the situation described in Question 1, how will things be different if a rent ceiling is imposed?

3 Describe what happens to the price and quantity in a market in which there is an increase in supply. Trace the evolution of the price and quantity in the market over time.

4 Describe what happens to the price and quantity in a market in which there is an increase in demand. Trace the evolution of the price and quantity in the market over time.

5 Describe what happens to the wage rate and quantity of labour employed when there is an increase in demand for labour. Trace the evolution of the wage rate and employment over time.

6 In the situation described in Question 5, what would happen if a minimum wage was introduced?

7 Why might a minimum wage create unemployment?

8 When government regulation prevents a price

from changing, what forces come into operation to achieve an equilibrium?

9 How does the imposition of a sales tax on a good influence the supply of and demand for that good? How does it influence the price of the good and the quantity bought?

10 How does prohibiting the sale of a good affect the demand for and supply of the good? How does it affect the price of the good and the quantity bought?

11 How does prohibiting the consumption of a good affect the demand for and supply of the good? How does it affect the price of the good and the quantity bought?

12 Explain the alternative ways in which the consumption of harmful drugs can be controlled. What are the arguments for and against each method?

13 Why do farm revenues fluctuate?

14 Do farm revenues increase or decrease when there is a bumper crop? Why?

15 Explain why speculation can stabilize the price of a storable commodity, but not the revenues of the producers.

16 How does the European Union support agricultural prices? What is the effect of this type of price support?

PROBLEMS

1 You have been given the following information about the market for rented one-bedroom flats in your town:

Rent (pounds per month)	Quantity demanded	Quantity supplied
100	20,000	0
150	15,000	5,000
200	10,000	10,000
250	5,000	15,000
300	2,500	20,000
350	1,500	25,000

  a What is the equilibrium rent?
  b What is the equilibrium quantity of rented housing?

2 Now suppose that a rent ceiling of £150 a month is imposed in the housing market described in Problem 1.

  a What is the quantity of housing demanded?
  b What is the quantity of housing supplied?
  c What is the excess quantity of housing demanded?
  d What is the maximum price that demanders will be willing to pay for the last unit available?
  e Suppose that the average wage rate is £10 an hour. How many hours a month will a person spend looking for housing?

3 The demand for and supply of teenage labour are as follows:

Wage rate (pounds per hour)	Hours demanded	Hours supplied
2	3,000	1,000
3	2,500	1,500
4	2,000	2,000
5	1,500	2,500
6	1,000	3,000

  a What is the equilibrium wage rate?
  b What is the level of employment?
  c What is the level of unemployment?
  d If the government imposes a minimum wage of £3 an hour for teenagers, how many hours do teenagers work?
  e If the government imposes a minimum wage of £5 an hour for teenagers, what are the employment and unemployment levels?
  f If there is a minimum wage of £5 an hour and demand increases by 500 hours, what is the level of unemployment?

4 The following table illustrates three supply curves for train travel:

Price (pence per passenger mile)	Quantity supplied (billions of passenger miles)		
	Momentary	Short-run	Long-run
10	500	300	100
20	500	350	200
30	500	400	300
40	500	450	400
50	500	500	500
60	500	550	600
70	500	600	700
80	500	650	800
90	500	700	900
100	500	750	1,000

  a If the price is 50 pence a passenger mile, what is the quantity supplied in:
    1 The long run?
    2 The short run?
  b Suppose that the price is initially 50 pence, but that it then rises to 70 pence. What will be the quantity supplied:
    1 Immediately following the price rise?
    2 In the short run?
    3 In the long run?

5 Suppose that the supply of train travel is the same as in Problem 4. The following table gives two demand schedules – original and new:

Price (pence per passenger mile)	Quantity demanded (billions of passenger miles)	
	Original	New
10	10,000	10,300
20	5,000	5,300
30	2,000	2,300
40	1,000	1,300
50	500	800
60	400	700
70	300	600
80	200	500
90	100	400
100	0	300

a What is the original equilibrium price and quantity?
b After the increase in demand has occurred, what is:
  1 The momentary equilibrium price and quantity?
  2 The short-run equilibrium price and quantity?
  3 The long-run equilibrium price and quantity?

6 The short-run and long-run demand for train travel is as follows:

Price (pence per passenger mile)	Quantity demanded (billions of passenger miles)	
	Short-run	**Long-run**
10	700	10,000
20	650	5,000
30	600	2,000
40	550	1,000
50	500	500
60	450	400
70	400	300
80	350	200
90	300	100
100	250	0

The supply of train travel is the same as in Problem 4.

a What is the long-run equilibrium price and quantity of train travel?
b Serious floods destroy one-fifth of the trains and train tracks. Supply falls by 100 billion passenger miles. What happens to the price and the quantity of train travel in:
  1 The short run?
  2 The long run?

7 The following are the demand and supply schedules for chocolate cakes:

Price (pence per cakes)	Quantity demanded (millions per day)	Quantity supplied
90	1	7
80	2	6
70	3	5
60	4	4
50	5	3
40	6	2

a If there is no tax on cakes, what is their price and how many are produced and consumed?
b If a tax of 20 pence a cake is introduced, what happens to the price of a cake and the quantity produced and consumed?
c How much tax does the government collect and who pays it?

8 Calculate the elasticity of demand in Fig. 6.10 when the price of wheat is £300 a tonne. Does its magnitude imply that farm revenues fluctuate in the same direction as price fluctuations or in the opposite direction?

9 On Turtle Island, the government is considering ways of stabilizing farm prices and farm revenues. Currently the egg market is competitive, and the demand and supply of eggs are as follows:

Price (pounds per dozen)	Quantity demanded (dozens per week)	Quantity supplied
1.20	3,000	500
1.30	2,750	1,500
1.40	2,500	2,500
1.50	2,250	3,500
1.60	2,000	4,500

a Calculate the competitive equilibrium price and quantity bought and sold.
b The government introduces a floor price of £1.50 a dozen. Calculate the market price, the quantity of eggs bought and sold, and farm revenues. Calculate the surplus of eggs.
c Calculate the amount the government must spend on eggs to maintain the floor price.

10 Read the article in *Reading Between the Lines* on pp.140–141 again and then answer the following questions:

a Explain why the Finnish government is reluctant to reduce the restriction on personal imports of wine to 18 litres per person per trip.
b Use a diagram to show why removing all restrictions on personal imports of wine might reduce the tax on wine in Finland.

Part 2
MARKETS FOR GOODS AND SERVICES

TALKING WITH
ALFRED STEINHERR

Professor Steinherr graduated in Economics at the University of Lausanne, Switzerland and later obtained his PhD at Cornell University, USA. He has had extensive teaching experience as Professor of Economics at the Université Catholique de Louvain in Belgium and as visiting Professor at Johns Hopkins University (Bologna), Drew University (Brussels) and the College of Europe (Bruges). In 1979, he joined the International Monetary Fund as Senior Economist, and in 1981 he became Adviser to the European Commission. Professor Steinherr is currently Chief Economist and Director General at the European Investment Bank. He has published widely on finance and economies in transition, including a recent book written with Daniel Gros called *Winds of Change: Economic Transition in Central and Eastern Europe*, Addison Wesley Longman, 1996, and his latest book *Derivatives: The Wild Beast of Finance*, Wiley, 1997.

Why did you specialize in economics?

Once out of high school I didn't know what to study, so I embarked on three degrees: maths, comparative literature and, to be practical, economics. Economics was the least interesting subject, given the way it was taught at the time. I wasn't good enough in maths to reach the top and teaching literature didn't seem very exciting. So I went on to do a PhD in economics and in graduate school, with its more rigorous approach, I started to identify with economics. I also benefited from my previous training: maths is extremely helpful in economics and being able to write is not a disadvantage either.

Nowadays, economics students interested in a career in banking often ask me what courses they should take to best prepare their career chances: bank management? financial institutions? They look at me incredulously when I reply: the most abstract, theoretical economics courses possible. Knowledge specific to a particular activity can be learned on the job, but not the basic way of thinking about economic and financial issues, nor the technical know-how.

What do you think your role is as an independent economist?

Decision makers – politicians or

managers – are often faced with problems that are hard to handle without the help of a well-structured economic framework. My role as economic adviser is to provide that framework for complex decisions. For example, what are the implications of a single European currency for the configuration of the European capital market, the European banking industry and, hence, the future role of the bank that employs me?

What are the main (micro) principles of economics that you apply in your work?

An important assumption in finance and economics is that people do the best they can when taking actions; they are 'rational' in relation to the information to which they have access and the objectives they have set for themselves. Not only in buying goods, but in all walks of life, people act 'economically': deciding when to enter or leave a marriage, or how much education they wish to pursue.

Another important principle in any economic problem is to separate clearly the variables of choice under our control from those of the environment (state variables). The first are determined by a decision process, the second define the initial conditions in which such decisions are made. State variables evolve slowly, much more slowly than

market data, such as prices, that contain the rest of the information available for decision making.

Experience shows that good economics can already be usefully applied to accounting, which is the basis for rational decision making. In particular, good accounting of the risks to which an enterprise is exposed requires serious economics and good statistics.

Do you think that markets are a good way to allocate resources in general?

Markets do not represent anything but the sum of individuals confronting their supplies and demands. As such, what matters is how well individuals are able to decide what is best for them in order to fulfil their desire to sell or purchase goods and services. How well they are able to decide depends on how well the price system is able to convey the information about the value that participants assign to a good. The price system is the coordinating device of the 'market'. If it is free to fluctuate to integrate new information, then the market allocation is the best there can be. Regulations can affect this free confrontation of supplies and demands through price adjustments. Participants, such as some types of monopolies, can also interfere with the market allocation by deciding unilaterally on the outcome of the market process.

In these cases, the 'market' allocation is not optimal, but is it really what we call a market allocation any more?

> '*Decision-makers – politicians or managers – are often faced with problems that are hard to handle without the help of a well structured economic framework.*'

Of course, markets do not exist in frictionless space and must be supported by some sort of infrastructure: appropriate laws, regulation, or physical infrastructure. Air traffic requires airports, air traffic controls, safety regulations, and so on. Some of this infrastructure is best provided by the state, some by private organizations. Extreme liberals would contest that the state may fulfil some of these functions better than private firms, but this is still an open debate.

The importance of markets has also been demonstrated by the privatization of government activities. Privatizing a monopoly has had limited positive effects (a private monopoly overcharges as much as a public monopoly), whereas big gains have resulted from introducing competition.

To what extent is the basic economic theory of markets helpful in understanding our economy?

This is the key. Of course, basic theory makes many simplifying assumptions, such as perfect competition, or monopoly, which are extreme models. As such they are still useful benchmarks, even if most real-world markets are organized differently. Only recently has game theory thrown light on various forms of imperfect competition, where competitors dispose of different information sets. Results are not generally easily compared and are specific to precise situations, so basic theory is a good and useful start, but its simplicity can, at times, be misleading. A concrete example is the prediction that with perfect

'All economists can agree that the noblest task of the profession is to elaborate ever better institutional designs.'

competition, free trade is best. Where producers use research and development (R&D) to differentiate their products, some protection can lead to more R&D activity and a larger number of products available.

How do institutions affect the way that markets work?

Institutions are extremely important. A 'market' is an institution, but usually we think of governments, trade unions, and so on. All economists can agree that the noblest task of the profession is to elaborate ever better

institutional designs. Here is an example. The Central Bank is the institution that issues money and regulates the money supply. However, the way it accomplishes its job determines the inflation rate and, hence, implicit income redistributions. It can make the planned allocation of resources easier or more complicated, and it can influence the rate of interest and, hence, savings and investment. Its actions determine whether banks or savers succeed or fail and, hence, determine confidence in bank accounts.

Which institutions have the most impact on the market system in the United Kingdom and why?

I would say government (including the Central Bank) at various levels, from the local level to the European Commission. However, in some continental European countries, trade unions are extremely important. While the stock exchanges are major institutions for resource allocation

'Of course, markets do exist in frictionless space and must be supported by some sort of infrastructure: appropriate laws, regulation, or physical infrastructure.'

goods (defence), infrastructure (just imagine private toll roads in a city!), laws and their enforcement (rather than enforcement by the mob), and a social safety network (that's the fraternity part of the French Revolution's *liberté, égalité, fraternité*).

Do you think there is a role for markets in the provision of welfare? If so, what and why/why not?

There certainly is. Markets always exist, even when you can't see them. Unemployment benefits can push part-time jobbers into the black economy. Markets offer insurance and pensions and ways to save and invest for retirement. The professional risks and the risk of losing a job are effectively incorporated in employment contracts. Countries such as Chile or Singapore that support pension schemes with favourable tax treatment and invest contributions in productive assets have achieved high saving rates (pension contributions are mandatory), high investment rates and high growth rates.

Some state investment is justified because individuals do not have identical starting conditions and chance works both ways. But it is important to rely as much as possible on market mechanisms and on interventions that do not distort, or distort as little as possible, the incentives of individuals.

'*In all countries the quality and extent of education are major factors for the long run growth potential of the economy. Schools and universities... play a major economic role and should be subject to economic analysis*'

in the United Kingdom, it would be easy to extend this list. In all countries the quality and extent of education are major factors for the long-run growth potential of the economy. Schools and universities are institutions (some private, most public) that play a major economic role and should be subject to economic analysis.

What is the role of government in a mixed economy?

All economies are mixed and without government there would not be much of an economy. Government needs to coordinate activities (to drive on the left, or on the right hand side), maintain a competitive economy open to the world market, provide public

CHAPTER

7

UTILITY AND DEMAND

After studying this chapter you will be able to:

◆ Explain the connection between individual demand and market demand

◆ Define total utility and marginal utility

◆ Explain the marginal utility theory of consumer choice

◆ Use the marginal utility theory to predict the effects of changing prices

◆ Use the marginal utility theory to predict the effects of changing income

◆ Define and calculate consumer surplus

◆ Explain the paradox of value

W E NEED WATER TO LIVE, BUT WE USE DIAMONDS MAINLY FOR DECORATION. IF THE benefits of water far outweigh the benefits of diamonds, why, then, does water cost practically nothing while diamonds are very expensive? ◆ When OPEC restricted its sale of oil in 1973, it created a dramatic rise in price, but people continued to use almost as much oil as they had before. Our demand for oil was price inelastic. But why? ◆ When the CD player was introduced in 1983, it was sold at a relatively high price and consumers didn't buy many. Since then the price has decreased dramatically, and many households have bought one. Our demand for CD players is price elastic. What makes the demand for some things price elastic while the demand for others is price inelastic? ◆ Over the past 40 years, the real value of incomes in the UK has risen. Over the same period, expenditure on cars has increased from less than 1 per cent of total spending to 15 per cent, while expenditure on

Water, Water, Everywhere

food has fallen from 25 per cent of total expenditure to just 14 per cent today. Thus the proportion of income spent on cars has increased and the proportion spent on food has decreased. Why, as incomes rise, does the proportion of income spent on some goods rise and on others fall?

◆ ◆ ◆ ◆ In the last three chapters, we've seen that demand in any market has an important effect on the price of a good. But what shapes market demand? This chapter examines market demand by looking at individual behaviour and its influence on demand. It explains why demand is elastic for some goods and inelastic for others. It also explains why the prices of some things, such as diamonds and water, are so out of proportion to their total benefits.

Individual Demand and Market Demand

The relationship between the total quantity demanded in a market and the price of a good is called **market demand.** And the relationship between the quantity demanded of a good by an individual and its price is called **individual demand**. The market demand is simply the sum of all the individual demands.

The table in Fig. 7.1 illustrates the relationship between individual demand and market demand. In this example we will assume that Lisa and John are the only people. The market demand is the total demand of Lisa and John. At £3 a cinema ticket, Lisa demands 5 films a month and John demands 2 films, so that the total quantity demanded in the market is 7 films a month. Figure 7.1 illustrates the relationship between individual and market demand curves. Lisa's and John's demand curves for films, shown in parts (a) and (b), sum *horizontally* to give the market demand curve in part (c).

The market demand curve is the horizontal sum of the individual demand curves formed by adding the quantities demanded by each individual at each price.

We're going to investigate what shapes market demand by looking at what shapes individual demand. We will do this by studying how an individual makes consumption choices.

FIGURE 7.1

Individual and Market Demand Curves

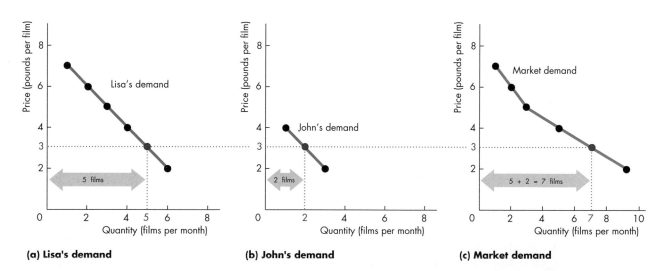

(a) Lisa's demand **(b) John's demand** **(c) Market demand**

Price of a cinema ticket (pounds)	Quantity of films demanded		
	Lisa	**John**	**Market**
7	1	0	1
6	2	0	2
5	3	0	3
4	4	1	5
3	5	2	7
2	6	3	9

The table and the figure illustrate how the quantity of films demanded varies as the price of a cinema ticket varies. In the table, the market demand in the final column is the sum of the individual demands. For example, at a price of £3, Lisa demands 5 films and John demands 2 films, so the total quantity demanded in the market is 7 films per month. In the figure, the market demand curve is the horizontal sum of the individual demand curves. Thus when the price is £3, the market demand curve shows the quantity demanded as the sum of Lisa and John's demands – 7 films.

Individual Consumption Choices

An individual's consumption choices are determined by many factors, and we can model the impact of these factors using two new concepts:

◆ Budget line
◆ Preferences

Budget Line

In this model of individual consumption, choices are constrained by income and by the prices of goods and services. We will assume that each individual has a given amount of income to spend, that everyone consumes all the goods they purchase within the relevant time period, and that individuals cannot influence the prices of the goods and services they buy. People take prices as given.

The limits to individual consumption choices are described by a *budget line*. To make the concept of the individual's budget line as clear as possible, we'll consider a simplified example of one individual – Lisa – and her choice. Lisa has an income of £30 a month to spend. She spends her income on two goods – cinema films and cola. Cinema tickets cost £6 each; cola costs £3 for a six-pack. If Lisa spends all of her income, she will reach the limits to her consumption of films and cola.

In Fig. 7.2, each row of the table shows affordable ways for Lisa to see cinema films and buy cola packs. Row *a* indicates that she can buy 10 six-packs of cola and see no films. You can see that this combination exhausts her monthly income of £30. Row *f* says that Lisa can see 5 films and drink no cola – another combination that exhausts the £30 available. Each of the other rows in the table also exhausts Lisa's income. (Check that each of the other rows costs exactly £30.) The numbers in the table define Lisa's maximum consumption possibilities of films and cola. These consumption possibilities are graphed as points *a* to *f* in Fig. 7.2.

Lisa's budget line is a constraint on her choices. It marks the boundary between what is affordable and what is unaffordable. She can afford all the points on the line and inside it. She cannot afford points outside the line. The constraint on her consumption depends on prices and on her income, and the constraint changes when prices and her income change.

FIGURE 7.2
Consumption Possibilities

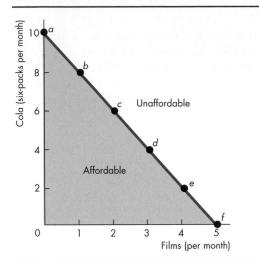

	Expenditure			
	Films		Cola	
Possibility	Quantity	Expenditure (pounds)	Quantity (six-packs)	Expenditure (pounds)
a	0	0	10	30
b	1	6	8	24
c	2	12	6	18
d	3	18	4	12
e	4	24	2	6
f	5	30	0	0

Six possible ways of allocating £30 to films and cola are shown as the rows *a* to *f* in the table. For example, Lisa can see 2 cinema films and buy 6 six-packs (row *c*). Each row shows the combinations of film and cola that cost £30. These possibilities are points *a* to *f* in the figure. The line through those points is a boundary between what Lisa can afford and cannot afford. Her choices must lie inside the orange area or along the line *af*.

Preferences and Utility

How does Lisa divide her £30 between these two goods? The answer depends on her likes and dislikes – or her **preferences**. Economists use the concept of utility to describe preferences. The benefit or satisfaction that a person gets from the consumption of a good or service is called **utility.** But what exactly is utility and in what units can we measure it? Utility is an abstract concept and its units are arbitrary.

Temperature – an Analogy Temperature is an abstract concept and the units of temperature are arbitrary. You know when you feel hot and you know when you feel cold. But you can't *observe* temperature. You can observe water turning to steam if it is hot enough or turning to ice if it is cold enough. You can construct an instrument, called a thermometer, that can help you to predict when such changes will occur. The scale on the thermometer is what we call temperature. But the units in which we measure temperature are arbitrary. For example, we can accurately predict that when a Celsius thermometer shows a temperature of 0 degrees, water will turn to ice. But the units of measurement do not matter because this same event also occurs when a Fahrenheit thermometer shows a temperature of 32 degrees.

The concept of utility helps us make predictions about consumption choices in much the same way that the concept of temperature helps us make predictions about physical phenomena. It has to be admitted, though, that the marginal utility theory is not as precise as the theory that enables us to predict when water will turn to ice or steam.

Let's now see how we can use the concept of utility to describe preferences.

Total Utility

Total utility is the total benefit or satisfaction that a person gets from the consumption of goods and services. Total utility depends on the person's level of consumption – more consumption generally gives more total utility. Table 7.1 shows Lisa's total utility from consuming different quantities of cinema films and cola. If she does not go to the cinema, she gets no utility from seeing films. If she goes once a month, she gets 50 units of utility. As the number of visits in a month increases, her total utility increases so that if she sees 10 films a month, she gets 250 units of total utility. The other part of the table shows Lisa's total utility from cola. If she drinks no cola, she gets no utility from cola. As the amount of cola she drinks rises, her total utility increases.

Marginal Utility

Marginal utility is the change in total utility resulting from a one-unit increase in the quantity of a good consumed. The table in Fig. 7.3 shows the calculation of Lisa's marginal utility from seeing

TABLE 7.1

Lisa's Total Utility from Films and Cola

Films		Cola	
Quantity per month	**Total utility**	**Quantity (six-packs per month)**	**Total utility**
0	0	0	0
1	50	1	75
2	88	2	117
3	121	3	153
4	150	4	181
5	175	5	206
6	196	6	225
7	214	7	243
8	229	8	260
9	241	9	276
10	250	10	291
11	256	11	305
12	259	12	318
13	261	13	330
14	262	14	341

films. When her consumption of films increases from 4 to 5 a month, her total utility from films increases from 150 units to 175 units. Thus for Lisa, the marginal utility of seeing a fifth film each month is 25 units. Notice that marginal utility appears midway between the quantities of consumption. It does so because it is the *change* in consumption from 4 to 5 films that produces the *marginal* utility of 25 units. The table displays calculations of marginal utility for each level of film consumption.

Figure 7.3(a) illustrates the total utility that Lisa gets from seeing films. As you can see, the more films Lisa sees in a month, the more total utility she gets. Part (b) illustrates her marginal utility. This graph tells us that as Lisa sees more films, the marginal utility that Lisa gets from seeing films decreases. For example, her marginal utility from the first film is 50 units, from the second 38 units, and from the third 33 units. We call this decrease in marginal utility as the consumption of a good increases the principle of **diminishing marginal utility**.

Marginal utility is positive but diminishes as the consumption of a good increases. Why does marginal utility have these two features? In Lisa's case, she likes films, and the more she sees the better. That's why marginal utility is positive. The benefit

FIGURE 7.3

Total Utility and Marginal Utility

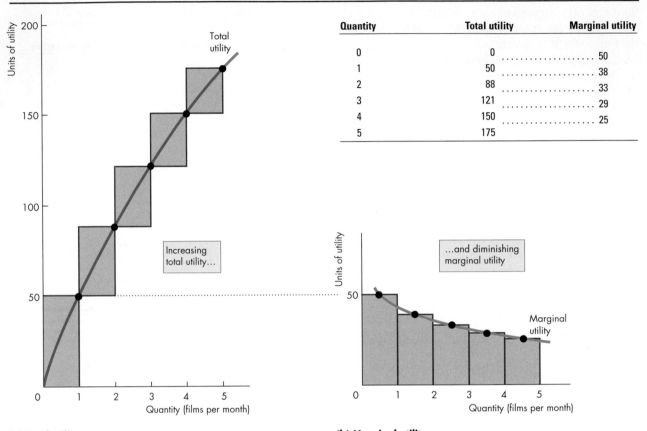

Quantity	Total utility	Marginal utility
0	0	
		50
1	50	
		38
2	88	
		33
3	121	
		29
4	150	
		25
5	175	

(a) Total utility

(b) Marginal utility

The table shows that as Lisa's consumption of films increases, so does the total utility she derives from films. The table also shows her marginal utility – the change in utility resulting from the last film seen. Marginal utility declines as consumption increases. The figure graphs Lisa's total utility

and marginal utility from films. Part (a) shows her total utility. It also shows the extra utility she gains from each additional film – her marginal utility. Part (b) shows how Lisa's marginal utility from films diminishes by placing the bars shown in part (a) side by side as a series of declining steps.

that Lisa gets from the last film seen is its marginal utility. To see why marginal utility diminishes, think about how you'd feel in the following two situations. In one, you've just been studying for 15 evenings in a row. An opportunity arises to see a new film. The utility you get from that film is the marginal utility from seeing one film in a month. In the second situation, you've been on a cinema binge. For the past 15 nights, you have not even seen an assignment or test. You are up to your eyeballs in films. You are happy enough to go to a film on yet one more night. But the thrill that you get out of that sixteenth film in 16 days is not very large. It is the marginal utility of the sixteenth film in a month.

REVIEW

◆ Consumers are constrained in what they can afford by their incomes and by the prices of the things they buy.

◆ Consumers' preferences can be described by using the concept of utility and marginal utility theory is based on two assumptions: the greater the quantity of a good consumed, the higher is the total utility from consuming that good; and as the quantity of a good consumed increases, the marginal utility from consuming that good decreases.

Maximizing Utility

Individual income and prices limit the utility an individual can obtain from consumption. The key assumption of marginal utility theory is that, taking into consideration the income available for spending and the prices people face, individuals consume the quantities of goods and services that maximize total utility. The assumption of **utility maximization** is a way of expressing the fundamental economic problem. People's wants exceed the resources available to satisfy these wants, so they must make hard choices. In making choices, they try to get the maximum attainable benefit – they try to maximize total utility.

Let's model Lisa's choice to see how she allocates her spending between cinema films and cola to maximize her total utility. Lisa makes her choice knowing cinema tickets cost £6 each, cola costs £3 a six-pack, and she has £30 a month to spend.

The Utility-maximizing Choice

The most direct way of calculating how Lisa spends her money if she maximizes her total utility is by making a table like the one shown in Table 7.2. This table shows the same affordable combinations of films and cola that you can find on her budget line in Fig. 7.2. The table records three things: first, the number of cinema films seen and the total utility derived from them (the left side of the table); second, the number of six-packs of cola consumed and the total utility derived from them (the right side of the table); and third, the total utility derived from both films and cola (the centre column of the table).

The first row of Table 7.2 records the situation if Lisa does not go to the cinema but buys 10 six-packs. In this case, she gets no utility from films and 291 units of total utility from cola. Her total utility from films and cola (the centre column) is 291 units. The rest of the table is constructed in the same way.

The consumption of films and cola that maximizes Lisa's total utility is highlighted in the table. When Lisa consumes 2 films and 6 six-packs of cola, she gets 313 units of total utility. This is the best Lisa can do given that she has only £30 to spend and given the prices of cinema tickets and six-packs. If she buys 8 six-packs of cola, she can see only 1 film and gets 310 units of total utility, 3 fewer than the maximum attainable. If she sees 3 films and drinks only 4 six-packs, she gets 302 units of total utility, 11 fewer than the maximum attainable.

TABLE 7.2

Lisa's Utility-maximizing Combinations of Films and Cola

Films		Total utility from films and cola	Cola	
Quantity	Total utility		Total utility	Quantity
0	0	291	291	10
1	50	310	260	8
2	88	313	225	6
3	121	302	181	4
4	150	267	117	2
5	175	175	0	0

We've just described a consumer equilibrium. A **consumer equilibrium** is a situation in which a consumer has allocated his or her income in the way that maximizes total utility.

In finding Lisa's consumer equilibrium, we measured her *total* utility from the consumption of films and cola. There is a better way of determining a consumer equilibrium, which does not involve measuring total utility at all. Let's look at this alternative.

Equalizing Marginal Utility per Pound Spent

Another way to find out the allocation that maximizes a consumer's total utility is to make the marginal utility per pound spent on each good equal for all goods. The **marginal utility per pound spent** is the marginal utility obtained from the last unit of a good consumed divided by the price of the good. For example, Lisa's marginal utility from consuming the first film is 50 units of utility. The price of a cinema ticket is £6, which means that the marginal utility per pound spent on films is 50 units divided by £6, or 8.33 units of utility per pound.

Total utility is maximized when all the consumer's income is spent and when the marginal utility per dollar spent is equal for all goods.

Lisa maximizes total utility when she spends all her income and consumes films and cola such that

$$\frac{\text{Marginal utility of seeing a film}}{\text{Price of a cinema ticket}} = \frac{\text{Marginal utility of a six-pack of cola}}{\text{Price of a six-pack of cola}}$$

Call the marginal utility from films MU_f, the marginal utility from cola MU_c, the price of a cinema ticket P_f, and the price of cola P_c. Then Lisa's utility is maximized when she spends all her income and when

$$\frac{MU_f}{P_f} = \frac{MU_c}{P_c}$$

Let's use this formula to find Lisa's utility-maximizing allocation of her income.

Table 7.3 sets out Lisa's marginal utilities per pound spent for both films and cola. For example, in row *b* Lisa's marginal utility from films is 50 units and, since cinema tickets cost £6 each, her marginal utility per pound spent on films is 8.33 units per pound (50 units divided by £6). Each row contains an allocation of Lisa's income that uses up her £30. You can see that Lisa's marginal utility per pound spent on each good, like marginal utility itself, decreases as consumption of the good increases.

Total utility is maximized when the marginal utility per pound spent on films is equal to the marginal utility per pound spent on cola, possibility *c*, where Lisa consumes 2 films and 6 six-packs – the same allocation as we calculated in Table 7.2.

Figure 7.4 shows why the rule 'equalize marginal utility per pound spent on all goods' works. Suppose that instead of consuming 2 films and 6 six-packs (possibility *c*), Lisa consumes 1 film and 8 six-packs (possibility *b*). She then gets 8.33 units of utility from the last pound spent on films and 5.67 units from the last pound spent on cola. In this situation Lisa can increase her total utility by spending less on cola and more on films. If she spends a pound less on cola and a pound more on films, her total utility from cola decreases by 5.67 units and her total utility from films increases by 8.33 units. Lisa's total utility increases by 2.66 units (a gain of 8.33 minus a loss of 5.67) if she spends less on cola and more on films.

Or, suppose that Lisa consumes 3 films and 4 six-packs (possibility *d*). In this situation, her marginal utility from the last pound spent on films is less than her marginal utility from the last pound spent on cola. Lisa can now increase her total utility by spending less on films and more on cola.

The Power of Marginal Analysis The method we've just used to maximize Lisa's utility is an example of the power of *marginal analysis*. By comparing the marginal gain from having more of

TABLE 7.3

Maximizing Utility by Equalizing Marginal Utilities per Pound Spent

	Films (£6 per ticket)			Cola (£3 per six-pack)		
	Quantity	Marginal utility per pound spent	Marginal utility	Quantity (six-packs)	Marginal utility	Marginal utility per pound spent
a	0	0		10	15	5.00
b	1	50	8.33	8	17	5.67
c	2	38	6.33	6	19	6.33
d	3	33	5.50	4	28	9.33
e	4	29	4.83	2	42	14.00
f	5	25	4.17	0	0	

one good with the marginal loss from having less of another good, Lisa is able to ensure that she gets the maximum attainable utility.

In the example, Lisa consumes at the point at which the marginal utility per pound spent on films and cola are equal. Because we buy goods and services in indivisible lumps, the numbers don't always work out so precisely. But the basic approach always applies. The rule to follow is simple: if the marginal utility per pound spent on films exceeds the marginal utility per pound spent on cola, see more films and drink less cola; if the marginal utility per pound spent on cola exceeds the marginal utility per pound spent on films, drink more cola and see fewer films.

More generally, our model of behaviour says that if the marginal gain from an action exceeds the marginal loss, take the action. You will meet this principle time and again in your study of economics. And you will find yourself applying this model every time you make your own economic choices. You will find an example of how marginal analysis can be used to explain consumer reactions to new innovations in the food industry in *Reading Between the Lines* on pp. 166–167.

Units of Utility In calculating the utility-maximizing allocation of income in Table 7.3 and Fig. 7.4 we have not used the concept of total utility at all. All the calculations have used marginal utility and price. By making the marginal utility per pound spent equal for both goods, we know that Lisa has maximized her total utility.

FIGURE 7.4

Equalizing Marginal Utility per Pound Spent

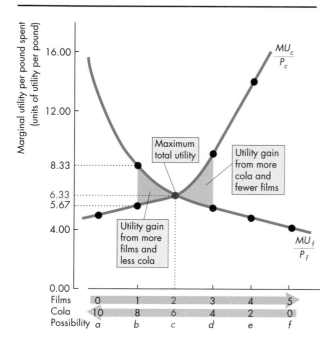

If Lisa consumes 1 cinema film and 8 six-packs of cola (possibility *b*) she gets 8.33 units of utility from the last pound spent on films and 5.67 units of utility from the last pound spent on cola. She can get more total utility if she sees one more film. If she consumes 4 six-packs and sees 3 films (possibility *d*) she gets 5.50 units of utility from the last pound spent on films and 9.33 units of utility from the last dollar spent on cola. She can get more total utility by seeing one fewer film. When Lisa's marginal utility per pound spent on both goods is equal, her total utility is maximized.

This way of viewing maximum utility is important; it means that the units in which utility is measured do not matter. We could double or halve all the numbers measuring utility, or multiply or divide them by any other positive number. None of these transformations of the units used to measure utility makes any difference to the outcome. It is in this respect that utility is analogous to temperature. Our prediction about the freezing of water depends on the model or concept of temperature, not on the temperature scale; our prediction about maximizing utility depends on our model of choice, not on the units of utility.

REVIEW

◆ Individuals make consumption choices that maximize total utility.

◆ They do so by spending all their available income and by making the marginal utility per pound spent on each good equal.

◆ When marginal utilities per pound spent are equal for all goods, a consumer cannot reallocate spending to get more total utility.

Predictions of Marginal Utility Theory

Let's now use marginal utility theory and our model of choice to make some predictions. What happens to Lisa's consumption of films and cola when their prices change and when her income changes?

A Fall in the Price of Cinema Tickets

To determine the effect of a change in price on consumption requires three steps. First, determine the combinations of films and cola that can be bought at the new prices. Second, calculate the new marginal utilities per pound spent. Third, determine the consumption of each good that makes the marginal utility per pound spent on each good equal and that just exhausts the money available for spending.

Table 7.4 shows the combinations of films and cola that exactly exhaust Lisa's £30 of income when cinema tickets cost £3 each and cola costs £3 a six-pack. Her preferences do not change when prices change, so her marginal utility schedule remains the same as that in Table 7.3. But now we divide her marginal utility from films by £3, the new price of a cinema ticket, to get the marginal utility per pound spent on films.

What is the effect of the fall in the price of a cinema ticket on Lisa's consumption? You can find the answer by comparing her new utility-maximizing allocation (Table 7.4) with her original allocation (Table 7.3). Lisa responds to a fall in the price of a cinema ticket by seeing more films (up from 2 to 5 a month) and drinking less cola (down from 6 to 5 six-packs a month). That is, Lisa substitutes films

TABLE 7.4

How a Change in Price of Films Affects Lisa's Choices

Films (£3 per ticket)		Cola (£3 per six-pack)	
Quantity	Marginal utility per pound spent	Quantity (six-packs)	Marginal utility per pound spent
0		10	5.00
1	16.67	9	5.33
2	12.67	8	5.67
3	11.00	7	6.00
4	9.67	6	6.33
5	8.33	5	8.33
6	7.00	4	9.33
7	6.00	3	12.00
8	5.00	2	14.00
9	4.00	1	25.00
10	3.00	0	

FIGURE 7.5

A Fall in the Price of Cinema Tickets

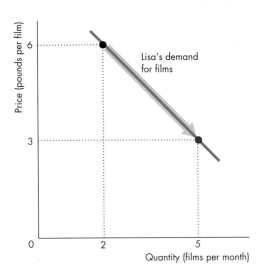

(a) Films

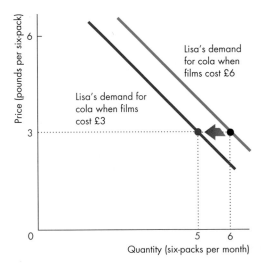

(b) Cola

When the price of cinema tickets falls and the price of cola remains constant, the quantity of films demanded by Lisa increases and in part (a), Lisa moves along her demand curve for films. Also, Lisa's demand for cola decreases and in part (b), her demand curve for cola shifts leftward.

for cola when the price of a cinema ticket falls. Figure 7.5 illustrates these effects. In part (a) a fall in the price of cinema tickets produces a movement along Lisa's demand curve for films and in part (b) it shifts her demand curve for cola.

A Rise in the Price of Cola

Table 7.5 shows the combinations of films and cola that exactly exhaust Lisa's £30 of income when cinema tickets cost £3 each and cola costs £6 a six-pack. Now we divide her marginal utility from cola by £6, the new price of a six-pack, to get the marginal utility per pound spent on cola.

The effect of the rise in the price of cola on Lisa's consumption is seen by comparing her new utility-maximizing allocation (Table 7.5) with her previous allocation (Table 7.4). Lisa responds to a rise in the price of cola by drinking less cola (down from 5 to 2 six-packs a month) and seeing more films (up from 5 to 6 a month). That is, Lisa substitutes films for cola when the price of cola rises. Figure 7.6 illustrates these effects. In part (a) a rise in the price of cola produces a movement along Lisa's demand curve for cola and in part (b) it shifts her demand curve for films.

TABLE 7.5

How a Change in the Price of Cola Affects Lisa's Choices

Films (£3 per ticket)		Cola (£6 per six-pack)	
Quantity	Marginal utility per pound spent	Quantity (six-packs)	Marginal utility per pound spent
0		5	4.17
2	12.67	4	4.67
4	9.67	3	6.00
6	7.00	2	7.00
8	5.00	1	12.50
10	3.00	0	

Marginal utility theory predicts these two results: when the price of a good rises, the quantity demanded of that good decreases; if the price of one good rises, the demand for another good that can serve as a substitute increases. Does this sound familiar? It should. These predictions of marginal

utility theory correspond to the assumptions that we made about consumer demand in Chapter 4. There we *assumed* that the demand curve for a good sloped downward, and we *assumed* that a rise in the price of a substitute increased demand.

We have now seen that marginal utility theory predicts how the quantities of goods and services that people demand respond to price changes. The theory helps us to understand both the shape and the position of the demand curve. It also helps us to understand how the demand curve for one good shifts when the price of another good changes. Marginal utility theory also helps us to understand one further thing about demand – how it changes when income changes.

Let's study the effects of a change in income on consumption.

A Rise in Income

Let's suppose that Lisa's income increases to £42 a month and that cinema tickets cost £3 each and a six-pack costs £3 (as in Table 7.4). In Table 7.4, we saw that with these prices and with an income of £30 a month, Lisa sees 5 films and consumes 5 six-packs a month. We want to compare this

FIGURE 7.6

A Rise in the Price of Cola

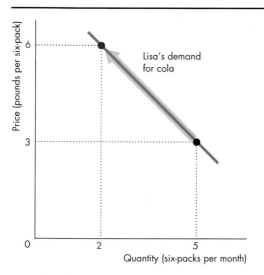

(a) Cola

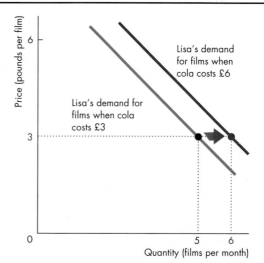

(b) Films

When the price of cola rises and the price of cinema tickets remains constant, the quantity of cola demanded by Lisa decreases and in part (a), Lisa moves along her demand

curve for films. Also, Lisa's demand for films increases and in part (b), her demand curve for films shifts to the right.

consumption of films and cola with Lisa's consumption at an income of £42. The calculations for the comparison are shown in Table 7.6. With £42, Lisa can see 14 films a month and drink no cola or drink 14 six-packs a month and see no films or any combination of the two goods as shown in the rows of the table. We calculate the marginal utility per pound spent in exactly the same way as we did before and find the quantities at which the marginal utilities per pound spent on films and on cola are equal. With an income of £42, the marginal utility per pound spent on each good is equal when Lisa sees 7 films and drinks 7 six-packs of cola a month.

By comparing this situation with that in Table 7.4, we see that with an additional £12 a month, Lisa drinks 2 more six-packs and sees 2 more films. This response arises from Lisa's preferences, as described by her marginal utilities. Different preferences produce different quantitative responses. But for normal goods, a higher income always brings a larger consumption of all goods. For Lisa, cola and films are normal goods. When her income increases, Lisa buys more of both goods.

You have now completed your study of marginal utility theory and Table 7.7 summarizes the key assumptions, implications and predictions of the theory.

Marginal Utility and the Real World

Marginal utility theory can be used to answer a wide range of questions about the real world. The theory can also be used to interpret some of the facts set out at the beginning of this chapter – for example, why the demand for CD players is price elastic and the demand for oil is price inelastic. Elasticities of demand are determined by preferences – by how rapidly marginal utility diminishes.

The marginal utility of CD players diminishes more rapidly than the marginal utility of oil. One CD player yields much more marginal utility than a second CD player. In contrast, the marginal utility of a second and third and fourth litre of oil (or of petrol derived from oil) is almost as large as the marginal

TABLE 7.6

Lisa's Choices with an Income of £42 a Month

Films (£3 per ticket)		Cola (£6 per six-pack)	
Quantity	Marginal utility per pound spent	Quantity (six-packs)	Marginal utility per pound spent
0		14	3.67
1	16.67	13	4.00
2	12.67	12	4.33
3	11.00	11	4.67
4	9.67	10	5.00
5	8.33	9	5.33
6	7.00	8	5.67
7	6.00	7	6.00
8	5.00	6	6.33
9	4.00	5	8.33
10	3.00	4	9.33
11	2.00	3	12.00
12	1.00	2	14.00
13	0.67	1	25.00
14	0.33	0	

TABLE 7.7

Marginal Utility Theory

ASSUMPTIONS

◆ A consumer derives utility from the goods consumed.

◆ Each additional unit of consumption yields additional utility; marginal utility is positive.

◆ As the quantity of a good consumed increases, marginal utility decreases.

◆ A consumer's aim is to maximize total utility.

IMPLICATION

Utility is maximized when all the available income is spent and when the marginal utility per pound spent is equal for all goods.

PREDICTIONS

◆ Other things remaining the same, the higher the price of a good, the lower is the quantity bought (the law of demand).

◆ The higher the price of a good, the higher is the consumption of substitutes for that good.

◆ The higher the consumer's income, the greater is the quantity demanded of normal goods.

utility of the first litre. If marginal utility diminishes rapidly, a small change in the quantity bought brings a big change in the marginal utility per pound spent. So it takes a big price change to bring a small quantity change – demand is inelastic. Conversely, if marginal utility diminishes slowly, even a large change in the quantity bought brings a small change in the marginal utility per pound spent. So it takes only a small price change to bring a large quantity change – demand is elastic.

But the marginal utility theory can do much more than explain *consumption* choices. It can be used to explain *all* individual choices. One of these choices, the allocation of time between work in the home, office, or factory and leisure is the theme of *Economics in History* on pp. 194–195.

R E V I E W

◆ When the price of a good falls and the prices of other goods remain the same, consumers increase their consumption of the good whose price has fallen and decrease their demands for other goods.

◆ These changes result in a movement along the demand curve for the good whose price has changed and a shift in the demand curves for other goods whose prices have remained constant.

◆ When a consumer's income increases, the consumer can afford to buy more of all goods and the quantity bought increases for all normal goods.

Criticisms of Marginal Utility Theory

Marginal utility theory helps us to understand the choices people make, but there are some criticisms of this theory. Let's look at them.

Utility Can't be Observed or Measured

Agreed – we can't observe utility. But we do not need to observe it to use it. We can and do observe the quantities of goods and services that people consume, the prices of these goods and services, and people's incomes. Our goal is to understand the consumption choices that people make and to predict the effects of changes in prices and incomes on these choices. To make such predictions, we *assume* that people derive utility from their consumption, that more consumption yields more utility, that marginal utility diminishes and that people attempt to **maximize total utility**. From these assumptions, we model choice and make predictions about the directions of change in consumption when prices and incomes change. As we've already seen, the actual numbers we use to express utility do not matter. Consumers maximize total utility by making the marginal utility per pound spent on each good equal. As long as we use the same scale to express utility for all goods, we'll get the same answer regardless of the units on our scale. In this regard, utility is similar to temperature – water freezes when it's cold enough, and that occurs independently of the temperature scale used.

'People aren't that Smart'

Some critics maintain that marginal utility theory must be wrong because it assumes that people are super-computers, or at least mathematicians. It implies, such critics say, that people look at the marginal utility of every good at every different quantity they might consume, divide these numbers by the prices of the goods, and then find the quantities at which the marginal utility per pound spent is the same for each good.

This criticism of marginal utility theory confuses the actions of people in the real world with those of people in a model economy. A model economy is no more an actual economy than a model railway is an actual railway. The people in our model perform the calculations that we have just described. People in the real world simply decide which is the best deal available. In doing so, they implicitly do the calculations that economists do explicitly. We observe people's consumption choices, not their mental gymnastics. The marginal utility theory says that the consumption patterns we observe in the real world are similar to those implied by a model in which people do compute the quantities of goods that maximize total utility. We test how closely the model resembles reality by checking the predictions of the model against observed consumption choices.

Marginal utility theory also has some broader implications that provide an interesting way of testing its usefulness. Let's examine two of these.

Implications of Marginal Utility Theory

We all love bargains – paying less for something than its usual price. One implication of the marginal utility theory is that we almost always get a bargain when we buy something. That is, we place a higher total value on the things we buy than the amount that it costs us. Let's see why.

Consumer Surplus and the Gains from Trade

People can gain by specializing in the production of the things in which they have a comparative advantage and then trading with each other. These gains are explored in Chapter 3. Marginal utility theory gives us a way of measuring the value to consumers of the gains from trade.

For Lisa to see films and drink cola, she exchanges her income for them. Does Lisa profit from this exchange? Are the pounds she has to give up worth more or less than the films and cola are worth to her? As we are about to discover, the principle of diminishing marginal utility guarantees that Lisa and everyone else get more value from the things they buy than the amount of money they give up in exchange.

Calculating Consumer Surplus

The **value** a consumer places on a good is the maximum amount that the person would be willing to pay for it. The amount actually paid for a good is its price. **Consumer surplus** is the difference between the value of a good and its price. When people can buy any chosen quantity of a good at a given price, diminishing marginal utility guarantees that a consumer always makes some consumer surplus. To understand why, let's look again at Lisa's consumption choices.

As before, let's assume that Lisa has £30 a month to spend, that cinema tickets cost £3 each, and that she sees 5 films each month. Now let's look at Lisa's demand curve for films, shown in Fig. 7.7(a). We can see from Lisa's demand curve that if she were able to see only 1 film a month she would be willing to pay £7 to see it. She would be willing to pay £6 to see a second film, £5 to see a third, and so on.

Luckily for Lisa, she has to pay only £3 for each film she sees – the market price of a cinema ticket.

FIGURE 7.7

Consumer Surplus

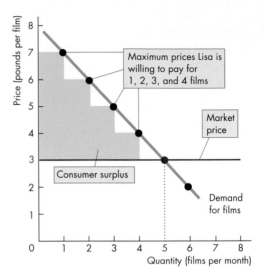

(a) Lisa

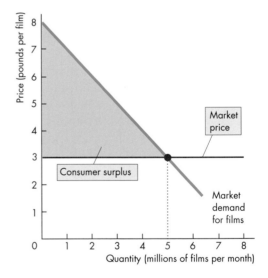

(b) Market

In part (a), Lisa is willing to pay £7 to see the first film, £6 for the second, £5 for the third, £4 for the fourth and £3 for the fifth. She pays £3 for each ticket and has a consumer surplus on the first four films she sees equal to £10 (£4 + £3 + £2 + £1). In part (b), the entire market has a consumer surplus shown by the green triangle. Its value is £12.5 million (the area of the triangle is equal to its base – 5 million films a month, multiplied by its height – £5 a film, divided by 2).

Although she values the first film she sees in a month at £7, she pays only £3, which is £4 less than she would be willing to pay. The second film she sees in a month is worth £6 to her. The difference between the value she places on the film and what she has to pay is £3. The third film she sees in a month is worth £5 to her, which is £2 more than she has to pay for it, and the fourth film is worth £4, which is £1 more than she has to pay for it. You can see this progression in Fig. 7.7(a), which highlights the difference between the price she pays (£3) and the higher value she places on the first, second, third and fourth films. These differences are a gain to Lisa. Let's calculate her total gain.

The total amount that Lisa is willing to pay for the 5 films that she sees is £25 (the sum of £7, £6, £5, £4 and £3). She actually pays £15 (5 films multiplied by £3). The extra value she receives from the films is therefore £10. This amount is the value of Lisa's consumer surplus. From seeing 5 films a month, she gets £10 worth of value in excess of what she has to spend to see them.

Suppose there are 1 million consumers similar to, but not quite identical to Lisa. Some are willing to pay £8 for the first film. At £7.99, yet more films are demanded. As the price falls a penny at a time, the quantity of films demanded increases. For the market as a whole, the consumer surplus is the entire area under the demand curve and above the market price line as shown in Fig. 7.7(b). The consumer surplus in this case is the entire triangle below the demand curve and above the price. Its magnitude can be calculated as the area of the triangle. The area equals the base (5 million films) multiplied by the height (£5 a film – £8 minus £3) divided by 2, that is, £12.5 million.

Let's now look at another implication of the marginal utility theory.

The Paradox of Value

More than 200 years ago, Adam Smith posed a paradox that we also raised at the start of this chapter. Water, which is essential to life itself, costs little, but diamonds, which are useless compared with water, are expensive. Why? Adam Smith could not solve the paradox. Not until the theory of marginal utility had been developed could anyone give a satisfactory answer.

You can solve Adam Smith's puzzle by distinguishing between *total* utility and *marginal* utility. The total utility that we get from water is enormous. But remember, the more we consume of something, the smaller is its marginal utility. We use so much water that the marginal utility – the benefit we get from one more glass of water – diminishes to a tiny value. Diamonds, on the other hand, have a small total utility relative to water, but because we buy few diamonds, they have a high marginal utility.

When an individual has maximized total utility, he or she has allocated his or her budget in the way that makes the marginal utility per pound spent equal for all goods. That is, the marginal utility from a good divided by the price of the good is equal for all goods. This equality of marginal utilities per pound spent holds true for diamonds and water. Diamonds have a high price and a high marginal utility. Water has a low price and a low marginal utility. When the high marginal utility of diamonds is divided by the high price of diamonds, the result is a number that equals the low marginal utility of water divided by the low price of water. The marginal utility per pound spent is the same for diamonds as for water.

◆ ◆ ◆ ◆ We've now completed our study of the marginal utility theory of consumption. We've used that theory to examine how one individual – Lisa – allocates her income between the two goods that she consumes – films and cola. We've also seen how the theory can be used to resolve the paradox of value. Furthermore, we've seen how the theory can be used to explain our real-world consumption choices. ◆ In the next chapter, we're going to study an alternative theory of individual behaviour. To help you see the connection between the marginal utility theory of this chapter and the more modern theory of consumer behaviour of the next chapter, we'll continue with the same example. We'll meet Lisa again and discover another way of understanding how she gets the most out of her £30 a month.

Utility Theory:
Preferring Pea Protein

The Essence of the Story

THE FINANCIAL TIMES, 2 AUGUST 1996

Matter of taste

Vanessa Houlder

Lucas Ingredients has…a new meat substitute…which contains …pea protein and wheat gluten. …The product, called Arrom (Latin for 'fields of grain'), is aimed at a fast-growing market.

Food scares and the desire for a more healthy diet have prompted nearly half of Britons to cut back their meat consumption. …The UK market for vegetarian foods has grown by 83 per cent in the last five years to £388m.

…Lucas believes that products made from Arrum will successfully compete on taste with its direct rivals – other non-branded products based on soya and gluten. …Arrum has a bland taste that can be doctored to taste like meat with the addition of flavourings. It can also be made to look like meat with the addition of suitable colourings.

But the challenge in making a meat substitute concerns its texture, as well as its taste and appearance. The key to mimicking the texture of chicken or beef lies in the correct degree of fibre formation: too much, and it gets too tough; too little, and it falls apart in the mouth.…

The goal that Lucas set itself was to identify the raw materials required to make a texture with the same 'eating characteristics' as chicken. To do this they wired up volunteers' cheek muscles, so they could monitor the amount of work they were doing to eat a piece of Arrum. …The cheek muscles have to put similar amounts of work into eating Arrum and chicken. It takes 6.1 seconds and 10 chews to eat a piece of meat analogue, compared with 5.4 seconds and 9 chews to eat a piece of chicken.

Its tests showed that Arrum is 26 per cent protein, compared with meat which is 20 per cent protein. It has a fat-to-calorie ratio of 11 per cent, compared with 54 per cent for beef and 32 per cent for chicken.

…Roger Whitehead, director of the Medical Research Council's Dunn Nutrition Laboratory, is enthusiastic about Arrum, which he has tasted in steak pie, lasagne and curries. He thinks it tastes good, it has 'appropriate mouth feel', it is flexible, it has intrinsically low fat and – unlike many of its rivals – it is made from natural, home-grown products.

■ Lucas Ingredients has discovered a new pea protein-based meat substitute.

■ Food scares and a trend towards healthier diets have led nearly half the population to cut their meat consumption.

■ The UK market for vegetarian foods has grown by 83 per cent in the past five years.

■ The makers have deliberately made the new meat substitute appeal to existing meat eaters. It looks, feels and chews like chicken.

■ It also provides more protein than chicken and has only one-third of the fat per calorie of chicken. It also tastes good in comparison with other meat substitutes.

Economic Analysis

■ Meat eaters allocate their budget for protein, when shopping, among different meats and meat substitutes.

■ They maximize their total utility by making the marginal utility per pound spent on meats equal to the marginal utility per pound spent on meat substitutes. That is:

$$\frac{Mum}{Pm} = \frac{MUs}{Ps}$$

■ Figure 1 shows the marginal utility of meat per pound as MUm_0/Pm_0 and the marginal utility of meat substitute per pound as MUs_0/Ps_0 for one consumer.

■ The consumer maximizes utility by setting MUm/Pm equal to MUs/Ps and eats 15 kilograms of meat and 5 kilograms of meat substitute a year.

■ Food scares and a preference for healthier diets reduce the marginal utility of meat per pound spent (if income and prices remain the same) and the curve falls to MUm_1/Pm_1. Our consumer gains more utility by cutting meat consumption to 10 kilograms and increasing meat substitute consumption to 10 kilograms a year.

■ A better-quality substitute for meat raises the marginal utility of meat substitutes per pound to MUs_1/Ps_1 in Fig. 2, cutting meat consumption further and increasing meat substitute consumption (if income and prices remain the same). If the consumer substitutes the new meat substitute for existing substitutes, meat consumption will not fall further.

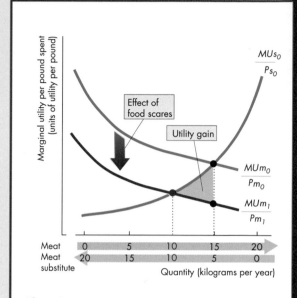

Figure 1

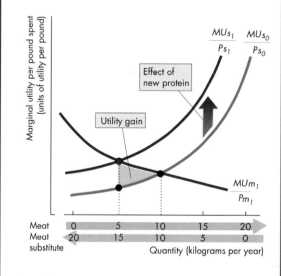

Figure 2

SUMMARY

Individual Demand and Market Demand

Individual demand is the relationship between the price of a good and the quantity demanded by a single individual. Market demand is the sum of all individual demands and the market demand curve is found by summing horizontally all the individual demand curves. (p. 153)

Individual Consumption Choices

The marginal utility theory explains how people divide their spending among goods and services. The theory is based on a model that assumes certain characteristics about the consumer. The consumer derives utility from the goods consumed and the consumer's total utility increases as consumption of the good increases. The change in total utility resulting from a one-unit increase in the consumption of a good is called marginal utility. Marginal utility declines as consumption increases. (pp. 154–156)

Maximizing Utility

The consumer's goal is to maximize total utility, given the income available to be spent and the prices of the goods and services bought. Utility is maximized when all the available income is spent and when the marginal utility per pound spent on each good is equal. (pp. 157–159)

Predictions of Marginal Utility Theory

Marginal utility theory predicts how prices and income affect the amounts of each good consumed. First, it predicts the law of demand. That is, other things remeining the same, the higher the price of a good, the lower is the quantity demanded of that good. Second, it predicts that, other things remaining the same, the higher the consumer's income, the greater is the consumption of all normal goods. (pp. 159–163)

Criticisms of Marginal Utility Theory

Some people criticize marginal utility theory because utility cannot be observed. But utility does not need to be observed to be used. Marginal utility theory predicts that the ratio of marginal utility to price is equal for all goods. Any arbitrary units can be used to represent utility.

Another criticism of marginal utility theory is that consumers can't be as smart as the theory implies. In fact, the theory makes no predictions about the thought processes of consumers. It only makes predictions about their actions and assumes that people spend their income in what seems to them to be the best possible way. (p. 163)

Implications of Marginal Utility Theory

Marginal utility theory implies that when we buy goods and services we usually get more value for our expenditure than the money we spend. We benefit from consumer surplus, which is equal to the difference between the maximum amount that we are willing to pay for a good and the price that we actually pay.

Marginal utility theory resolves the paradox of value. When we talk loosely about value, we are thinking of *total* utility. But price is related to *marginal* utility. A good such as water, which we consume in large amounts, has a high total utility but a low marginal utility while a good such as diamonds, which we consume in small amounts, has a low total utility and a high marginal utility. (pp. 164–165)

KEY ELEMENTS

Key Terms

Consumer equilibrium, 157
Consumer surplus, 164
Diminishing marginal utility, 155
Individual demand, 153
Marginal utility, 155
Marginal utility per pound spent, 157

Market demand, 153
Maximize total utility, 163
Preferences, 154
Total Utility, 155
Utility, 154
Utility maximization, 157
Value, 164

◆ **Key Figures and Table**

Figure 7.1   Individual and Market Demand
                 Curves, 153
Figure 7.2   Consumption Possibilities, 154
Figure 7.3   Total Utility and Marginal Utility, 156
Figure 7.4   Equalizing Marginal Utility per Pound
                 Spent, 159

Figure 7.5   A Fall in the Price of Cinema Tickets,
                 160
Figure 7.6   An Rise in the Price of Cola, 161
Figure 7.7   Consumer Surplus, 164
Table 7.7   Marginal Utility Theory, 162

REVIEW QUESTIONS

1 What is the relationship between individual
demand and market demand?

2 How do we construct a market demand curve
from individual demand curves?

3 What do we mean by utility?

4 Distinguish between total utility and marginal
utility.

5 How does marginal utility change as the level of
consumption of a good changes?

6 Susan is a consumer. When is Susan's utility
maximized?

   a When she has spent all her income?

   b When she has spent all her income and marginal utility is equal for all goods?

   c When she has spent all her income and the
marginal utility per pound spent is equal for
all goods?

   Explain your answers.

7 What does the marginal utility theory predict
about the effect of a change in price on the
quantity of a good consumed?

8 What does the marginal utility theory predict
about the effect of a change in the price of one
good on the consumption of another good?

9 What does the marginal utility theory predict
about the effect of a change in income on consumption of a good?

10 How would you answer someone who says that
the marginal utility theory is useless because
utility cannot be observed?

11 How would you respond to someone who tells
you that the marginal utility theory is useless
because people are not smart enough to compute a consumer equilibrium in which the
marginal utility per pound spent is equal for all
goods?

12 What is consumer surplus? How is consumer
surplus calculated?

13 What is the paradox of value? How does the
marginal utility theory resolve it?

PROBLEMS

1 Shirley's demand for books is given by the following:

Price (pounds per book)	Quantity (books per month)
1	12
2	9
3	6
4	3
5	1

   a Draw a graph of Shirley's demand for books.

Daniel also likes books. His demand for books
is given by the following:

Price (pounds per book)	Quantity (books per month)
1	6
2	5
3	4
4	3
5	2

   b Draw a graph of Daniel's demand curve.

   c If Shirley and Daniel are the only two

individuals, construct the market demand curve for books.

d Draw a graph of the market demand for books.

e Draw a graph to show that the market demand curve is the horizontal sum of Shirley's demand curve and Daniel's demand curve.

2 Calculate Lisa's marginal utility from cola from the numbers given in Table 7.1. Draw two graphs, one of her total utility and the other of her marginal utility from cola. Make your graphs look similar to those in Fig. 7.3.

3 Max enjoys windsurfing and snorkelling. He obtains the following utility from each of these sports:

Half-hours per month	Utility from windsurfing	Utility from snorkelling
1	60	20
2	110	38
3	150	53
4	180	64
5	200	70
6	206	75
7	211	79
8	215	82
9	218	84

a Draw graphs showing Max's utility from windsurfing and from snorkelling.

b Compare the two utility graphs. Can you say anything about Max's preferences?

c Draw graphs showing Max's marginal utility from windsurfing and from snorkelling.

d Compare the two marginal utility graphs. Can you say anything about Max's preferences?

4 Max has £35 to spend. Equipment for windsurfing rents for £10 a half-hour while snorkelling equipment rents for £5 a half-hour. Use this information together with that given in Problem 3 to answer the following questions:

a What is the marginal utility per pound spent on snorkelling if Max snorkels for:
1 Half an hour?
2 One and a half hours?

b What is the marginal utility per pound spent on windsurfing if Max windsurfs for:
1 Half an hour?
2 One hour?

c How long can Max afford to snorkel if he windsurfs for:

1 Half an hour?
2 One hour?
3 One and a half hours?

d Will Max choose to snorkel for one hour and windsurf for one and a half hours?

e How long will Max choose to windsurf and to snorkel?

5 Max's sister gives him £20 to spend on his leisure pursuits, so he now has £55 to spend. How long will Max now windsurf and snorkel?

6 If Max has only £55 to spend and the rent on windsurfing equipment decreases to £5 a half-hour, how will Max now spend his time windsurfing and snorkelling?

7 Does Max's demand curve for windsurfing slope downward or upward?

8 Max takes a Club Med holiday, the cost of which includes unlimited sports activities – including windsurfing, snorkelling and tennis. There is no extra charge for any equipment. Max decides to spend a total of three hours each day on windsurfing and snorkelling.

a What is Max's opportunity cost of windsurfing?

b What is Max's opportunity cost of snorkelling?

c How does Max allocate his three hours between windsurfing and snorkelling?

9 Sara's demand for windsurfing is given by:

Price (pounds per half-hour)	Time windsurfing (half-hours per month)
12.50	8
15.00	6
17.50	4
20.00	2

a If windsurfing costs £17.50 a half-hour, what is Sara's consumer surplus?

b If windsurfing costs £12.50 a half-hour, what is Sara's consumer surplus?

10 Read the article in *Reading Between the Lines* on pp. 166–167 again then:

a Look at Fig. 1 on p.167 and explain why consumers on average would not choose to eat 15 kilograms of meat and 5 kilograms of meat substitute a year.

b Explain the impact on consumer preferences of introducing a healthier meat substitute protein that tastes as good as meat.

CHAPTER 8

POSSIBILITIES, PREFERENCES AND CHOICES

After studying this chapter you will be able to:

◆ Calculate and graph a household's budget line

◆ Work out how the budget line changes when prices or income change

◆ Make a map of preferences by using indifference curves

◆ Explain the choices that households make

◆ Predict the effects of price and income changes on consumption choices

L IKE THE CONTINENTS FLOATING ON THE EARTH'S MANTLE, OUR SPENDING PATTERNS change steadily over time. Goods such as home videos and microwave chips now appear on our shopping lists while 78 rpm gramophone records and horse-drawn carriages have disappeared. ◆ But these surface disruptions obscure deeper and slower changes in our spending. We spend a smaller percentage of our income today on food and clothing than we did in 1950. At the same time, the percentage of our income spent on fuel, housing and cars has grown steadily. Why does consumer spending change over the years? How do people react to changes in income and changes in the prices of the things they buy? ◆ Similar subterranean movements govern the way we spend our time. For example, the average working week has fallen steadily from 70 hours a week in the nineteenth century to 38 hours a week today. Although the average working week is now much shorter than it once was, far more

Subterranean Movements

people now have jobs. This change has been especially dramatic for women. Why has the average working week declined? And why do more women work?

◆ ◆ ◆ ◆ In Chapter 1, Fig. 1.2, we created a simple model of the economy with three economic decision makers: households, firms and governments. In this chapter we are going to study a model of household choice that predicts the effects of changes in prices and incomes on what households buy, how much work they do, and how much they borrow and lend. As a household is just a group of individuals living together as a single decision-making unit, we will assume our household acts as if it were an individual. In this way we can use our model of individual choice from Chapter 7.

Consumption Possibilities

Consumption choices are limited by income and by prices. A household has a given amount of income to spend and cannot influence the prices of the goods and services it buys. It takes prices as given. The limits to a household's consumption choices are described by its **budget line**.

To make the concept of the household's budget line clear, we'll consider a concrete example – the household of Lisa[1], where Lisa is the only individual in her household. She has an income of £30 a month to spend. She consumes two goods – cinema films and cola. Cinema tickets cost £6 each; cola costs £3 for a six-pack. If Lisa spends all of her income, she will reach the limit of her consumption of films and cola.

Figure 8.1 shows Lisa's household budget line, which is the same as Lisa's individual budget line shown in Fig. 7.2 in Chapter 7. Each row of the table in Fig. 8.1 shows an affordable way for Lisa to consume films and cola which just exhausts her monthly income of £30. The numbers in the table define Lisa's household consumption possibilities. We can graph these consumption possibilities as points *a* to *f* in Fig. 8.1.

Divisible and Indivisible Goods Some goods – called divisible goods – can be bought in any quantity desired. Examples are petrol and electricity. We can best understand the model of household choice we're about to study if we assume that all goods and services are divisible. For example, Lisa can consume a half a film a month *on the average* by seeing one film every two months. When we think of goods as being divisible, the consumption possibilities are not just the points *a* to *f* shown in Fig. 8.1, but these points plus all the intermediate points that form the line running from *a* to *f*. Such a line is a budget line.

Lisa's budget line is a constraint on her choices. She can afford all the points on the line and inside

---

[1] If you have read the preceding chapter on marginal utility theory, you have already met Lisa. This tale of her thirst for cola and zeal for films will sound familiar to you – up to a point. But in this chapter we're going to use a different method for representing preferences – one that does not require us to resort to the idea of utility.

FIGURE 8.1

The Budget Line

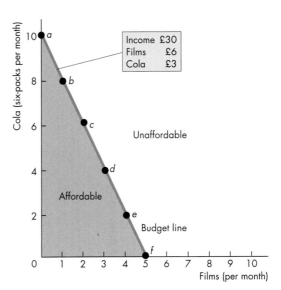

Income	£30
Films	£6
Cola	£3

Consumption possibility	Films (per month)	Cola (six-packs per month)
a	0	10
b	1	8
c	2	6
d	3	4
e	4	2
f	5	0

Lisa's budget line shows the boundary between what she can and cannot afford. Each row of the table lists Lisa's affordable combinations of cinema tickets and cola when her income is £30, the price of cola is £3 a six-pack, and the price of a ticket is £6. For example, row *a* tells us that Lisa exhausts her £30 income when she buys 10 six-packs and sees no films. The figure graphs Lisa's budget line. Points *a* to *f* on the graph represent the rows of the table. For divisible goods, the budget line is the continuous line *af*. To calculate the equation for Lisa's budget line, start from the fact that expenditure equals income. That is:

$$(£3 \times Q_c + £6 \times Q_f) = £30$$

Divide by £3 to obtain:

$$Q_c + 2Q_f = 10$$

Subtract $2Q_f$ from both sides to obtain:

$$Q_c = 10 - 2Q_f$$

it. She cannot afford points outside the line. The constraint on her consumption depends on prices and her income, and the constraint changes when prices or her income change. Let's see how by studying an equation that describes her consumption possibilities.

The Budget Equation

We can describe the budget line by using a *budget equation*. The budget equation starts with the fact that:

$$\text{Expenditure} = \text{Income}$$

In Lisa's case, expenditure and income equal £30 a week.

Expenditure is equal to the sum of the price of each good multiplied by the quantity bought. For Lisa,

$$\text{Expenditure} = \quad \text{Price of cola} \times \text{Quantity of cola}$$
$$+ \text{Price of a cinema ticket}$$
$$\times \text{quantity of films}$$

Call the price of cola P_c, the quantity of cola Q_c, the price of a cinema ticket P_f, the quantity of films Q_f, and income Y. Using these symbols, Lisa's budget equation is:

$$P_c \times Q_c + P_f \times Q_f = Y$$

Using the prices Lisa faces, £3 for a six-pack and £6 for a cinema ticket, and Lisa's income, £30, we get:

$$£3 \times Q_c + £6 \times Q_f = £30$$

Lisa can choose any quantities of cola (Q_c) and films (Q_f) that satisfy this equation. To express the relationship between these quantities, we rearrange the equation so that it describes Lisa's budget line. To do so, divide both sides of the equation by the price of cola (P_c) to get:

$$Q_c + \frac{P_f}{P_c} \times Q_f = \frac{Y}{P_c}$$

Now subtract the term $P_f / P_c \times Q_f$ from both sides of this equation to give:

$$Q_c = Y - \frac{P_f}{P_c} \times \frac{Q_f}{P_c}$$

For Lisa, income (Y) is £30, the price of a cinema ticket (P_f) is £6 and the price of a six-pack (P_c) is £3. So Lisa must choose the quantities of films and cola to satisfy the equation:

$$Q_c = \frac{£30}{£3} - \frac{£6}{£3} \times Q_f$$

or

$$Q_c = 10 - 2 \times Q_f$$

This equation tells us how Lisa's consumption of cola (Q_c) varies as her consumption of films (Q_f) varies. To interpret the equation, go back to the budget line of Fig. 8.1 and check that the equation you've just derived gives you the results of that budget line. Begin by setting Q_f, the quantity of films, equal to zero. In this case, the budget equation tells us that Q_c, the quantity of cola, is Y/P_c, which is £30/£3, or 10 six-packs. This combination of Q_f and Q_c is the same as that shown in row a of the table in Fig. 8.1. Setting Q_f equal to 5 makes Q_c equal to zero (row f of the table in Fig. 8.1). Check that you can derive the other rows.

The budget equation contains two variables chosen by the household (Q_f and Q_c) and two variables (Y/P_c and P_f/P_c) that the household takes as given. Let's look more closely at these variables.

Real Income   A household's **real income** is the maximum quantity of a good that the household can afford to buy. In the budget equation, real income is Y/P_c. This quantity is the maximum number of six-packs that Lisa can buy and is Lisa's real income in terms of cola. It is equal to her money income divided by the price of cola. Lisa's income is £30 and the price of cola is £3 a six-pack, so her real income in terms of cola is 10 six-packs. In Fig. 8.1, real income is the point at which the budget line intersects the y-axis.

Relative Price   A **relative price** is the price of one good divided by the price of another good. In Lisa's budget equation, the variable (P_f/P_c) is the relative price of a film in terms of cola. For Lisa, P_f is £6 a film and P_c is £3 a six-pack, so P_f/P_c is equal to 2 six-packs per film. That is, to see one more film, Lisa must give up 2 six-packs.

You've just calculated Lisa's opportunity cost of a film. Recall that the opportunity cost of an action is the best alternative forgone. For Lisa to see 1 more film a month, she must forgo 2 six-packs. You've also calculated Lisa's opportunity cost of cola. For Lisa to consume 2 more six-packs a month, she must give up seeing 1 film. So her opportunity cost of 2 six-packs is 1 film.

The relative price of a film in terms of cola is the

magnitude of the slope of Lisa's budget line. To calculate the slope of the budget line, recall the formula for slope (introduced in Chapter 2): slope equals the change in the variable measured on the y-axis divided by the change in the variable measured on the x-axis as we move along the line. In Lisa's case (Fig. 8.1), the variable measured on the y-axis is the quantity of cola and the variable measured on the x-axis is the quantity of films. Along Lisa's budget line, as cola decreases from 10 to 0 six-packs, films increase from 0 to 5. Therefore the slope of the budget line is 10 six-packs divided by 5 films, or 2 six-packs per film. The magnitude of this slope is exactly the same as the relative price we've just calculated. It is also the opportunity cost of a film.

A Change in Prices   When prices change, so does the budget line. The lower the price of the good measured on the horizontal axis, other things remaining the same, the flatter is the budget line. For example, if the price of a cinema ticket falls to £3, real income in terms of cola does not change but the relative price of seeing a film falls. The budget line rotates outward and becomes flatter as shown in Fig. 8.2(a). The higher the price of the good measured on the horizontal axis, other things remaining the same, the steeper is the budget line. For example, if the price of a cinema ticket rises to £12, the relative price of seeing a film increases. The budget line rotates inward and becomes steeper as shown in Fig. 8.2(a).

A Change in Income   A change in *money* income changes real income but does not change relative prices. The budget line shifts, but its slope does not change. The bigger a consumer's money income, the bigger is real income and the farther to the right is the budget line. The smaller a consumer's money income, the smaller is real income and the farther to the left is the budget line. The effect of a change in income on Lisa's budget line is shown in Fig. 8.2(b). The initial budget line is the same one that we began with in Fig. 8.1 when Lisa's income is £30. A new budget line shows how much Lisa can consume if her income falls to £15 a month. The new budget line is parallel to the old one but closer to the origin. The two budget lines are parallel – have the same slope – because the relative price is the same in both cases. The new budget line is closer to the origin than the initial one because Lisa's real income has decreased.

FIGURE 8.2

Changes in Prices and Income

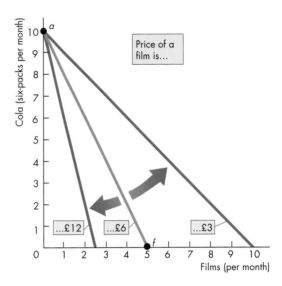

(a) A change in price

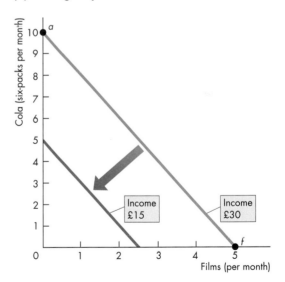

(b) A change in income

In part (a), the price of a cinema ticket changes. A fall in the price from £6 to £3 rotates the budget line outward and makes it flatter. A rise in the price from £6 to £12 rotates the budget line inward and makes it steeper. In part (b), income falls from £30 to £15 while prices remain constant. The budget line shifts leftward but its slope does not change.

R E V I E W

◆ The budget line describes the limits to a house-hold's consumption, which depends on its income and the prices of the goods that it buys.

◆ The position of the budget line depends on real income and its slope depends on the relative price.

◆ A change in the price of one good changes the relative price and changes the slope of the budget line. If the price of the good measured on the horizontal axis rises, the budget line becomes steeper.

◆ A change in income changes real income and shifts the budget line but its slope does not change. An increase in income shifts the budget line outward.

We've studied the limits to what a household can consume. Let's now see how we can describe the household's preferences.

Preferences and Indifference Curves

Preferences are a person's likes and dislikes. A key assumption about preferences is that they do not depend on prices or income. The things you like and dislike do not depend on what you can afford. When a price changes, or when your income changes, you make a new choice, but the preferences that guide that choice don't change. We are going to discover a neat idea – that of drawing a map of a person's preferences.

A preference map is based on the intuitively appealing assumption that people can sort all the possible combinations of goods they might consume into three groups: preferred, not preferred and indifferent. To make this idea more concrete, let's ask Lisa to tell us how she ranks various combinations of films and cola. Figure 8.3 illustrates part of her answer.

Lisa tells us that she currently consumes 2 films and 6 six-packs a month at point *c* in Fig. 8.3. She then lists all the combinations of films and cola that she regards as equally acceptable to her

FIGURE 8.3

Mapping Preferences

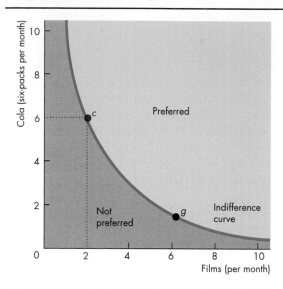

If Lisa consumes 6 six-packs of cola and sees 2 films, she consumes at point *c*. Lisa can compare all other possible combinations of cola and films to point *c*. She can rank them on the scale preferred, not preferred, or indifferent to point *c*. The boundary between points that she prefers to point *c* and those to which *c* is preferred is an indifference curve. Lisa is indifferent between points such as *g* and *c* on the indifference curve. She prefers any point above the indifference curve (yellow area) to any point on it, and she prefers any point on the indifference curve to any point below it (grey area).

as her current consumption. Let's draw a graph of these combinations in Fig. 8.3. When we plot the combinations of films and cola that Lisa tells us she likes just as much as the combination at point *c*, we get the green curve in Fig. 8.3. This curve is the key element in a map of preferences and is called an indifference curve.

An **indifference curve** is a line that shows combinations of goods among which a consumer is indifferent. The indifference curve in Fig. 8.3 tells us that Lisa is just as happy to consume 2 films and 6 six-packs a month at point *c* as to consume the combination of films and cola at point *g* or at any other point along the curve.

Lisa goes on to tell us that starting from any combination of films and cola, she prefers to have more films and no less cola, or more cola and no fewer films. We can interpret Lisa as saying that the indifference curve defines the boundary between combinations of goods that she prefers and combinations that she does not prefer to those on the indifference curve. Lisa prefers any combination in the yellow area above the indifference curve to any combination along the indifference curve. And she prefers any combination on the indifference curve to any combination in the grey area below the indifference curve.

The indifference curve shown in Fig. 8.3 is just one of a whole family of such curves. This indifference curve appears again in Fig. 8.4. It is labelled I_1 and passes through points c and g. Two other indifference curves are I_0 and I_2. Lisa prefers any point on indifference curve I_2 to any point on indifference curve I_1, and she prefers any point on I_1 to any point on I_0. We refer to I_2 as being a higher indifference curve than I_1 and I_1 as being higher than I_0.

Indifference curves never intersect each other. To see why, consider indifference curves I_1 and I_2 in Fig. 8.4. We know that Lisa prefers point j to point c. We also know that Lisa prefers any point on indifference curve I_2 to any point on indifference curve I_1. If these indifference curves did intersect, Lisa would be indifferent between the combination of goods at the intersection point and combinations c and j. But we know that Lisa prefers j to c, so there cannot be an intersection point. Hence the indifference curves never intersect.

A preference map consists of a series of indifference curves. The indifference curves shown in Fig. 8.4 are only a part of Lisa's household preference map. Her entire map consists of an infinite number of indifference curves; each one slopes downward and none of them intersect. They resemble the contour lines on a map that measures the height of a mountain. An indifference curve joins points representing combinations of goods among which a consumer is indifferent in much the same way that contour lines on a map join points of equal height above sea level. By looking at the shape of the contour lines on a map, we can draw conclusions about the terrain. In the same way, by looking at the shape of a person's indifference curves we can draw conclusions about preferences. But interpreting a preference map requires a bit of work. It also requires some way of describing the shape of the indifference curves. In the next two sections, we'll learn how to 'read' a preference map.

Marginal Rate of Substitution

The **marginal rate of substitution** (or *MRS*) is the rate at which a person will give up good y (the good measured on the y-axis) in order to get more of good x (the good measured on the x-axis) and at the same time remain indifferent. The marginal rate of substitution is measured from the slope of an indifference curve. If the indifference curve is steep, the marginal rate of substitution is high. The person is willing to give up a large quantity of good y in exchange for a small quantity of good x while remaining indifferent. If the indifference curve is flat, the marginal rate of substitution is low. The person is willing to give up only a small amount of good y in exchange for a large amount of good x to remain indifferent.

Figure 8.5 shows you how to calculate the marginal rate of substitution. The curve labelled I_1 is

FIGURE 8.4

A Preference Map

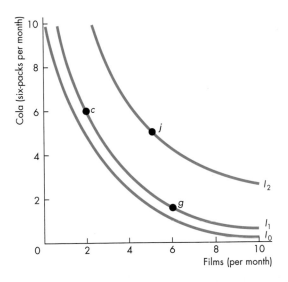

A preference map consists of an infinite number of indifference curves. Here we show just three – I_0, I_1, and I_2 – which are part of Lisa's preference map. Each indifference curve shows points among which Lisa is indifferent. For example, she is indifferent between point c and point g on indifference curve I_1. But she prefers points on a higher indifference curve to points on a lower indifference curve. For example, Lisa prefers point j to point c or g so she prefers any point on indifference curve I_2 to any point on indifference curve I_1.

FIGURE 8.5

The Marginal Rate of Substitution

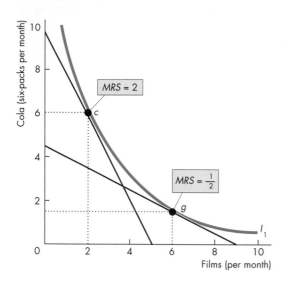

The magnitude of the slope of an indifference curve is called the marginal rate of substitution, *MRS*. The marginal rate of substitution tells us how much of one good a person is willing to give up to gain more of another good, while remaining indifferent. The marginal rate of substitution at point *c* is 2; at point *g* it is ¹/₂.

one of Lisa's indifference curves. Suppose that Lisa drinks 6 six-packs and watches 2 films at point *c* in the figure. Her marginal rate of substitution is calculated by measuring the absolute magnitude of the slope of the indifference curve at point *c*. To measure this magnitude, place a straight line against, or tangent to, the indifference curve at point *c*. The slope of that line is the change in the quantity of cola divided by the change in the quantity of films as we move along the line. As cola consumption decreases by 10 six-packs, film consumption increases by 5. So at point *c* Lisa is willing to give up cola for films at the rate of 2 six-packs per film. Her marginal rate of substitution is 2.

Now, suppose that Lisa consumes 6 films and 1¹/₂ six-packs at point *g* in Fig. 8.5. What is her marginal rate of substitution at this point? The answer is found by calculating the absolute magnitude of the slope of the indifference curve at point *g*. That slope is the same as the slope of the tangent to the indifference curve at point *g*. Here, as cola consumption decreases by 4.5 six-packs, film consumption

increases by 9. So at point *g* Lisa is willing to give up cola for films at the rate of ¹/₂ a six-pack per film. Her marginal rate of substitution is ¹/₂.

Notice that if Lisa drinks a lot of cola and does not see many films (point *c*), her marginal rate of substitution is large. If she watches a lot of films and does not drink much cola (point *g*), her marginal rate of substitution is small. This feature of the marginal rate of substitution is the central assumption of the theory of consumer behaviour and is referred to as the diminishing marginal rate of substitution. The assumption of **diminishing marginal rate of substitution** is a general tendency for the marginal rate of substitution to diminish as the consumer moves along an indifference curve, increasing consumption of good *x* and decreasing consumption of good *y*.

Your Own Diminishing Marginal Rate of Substitution   You might be able to appreciate why we assume the principle of a diminishing marginal rate of substitution by thinking about your own preferences for films and cola. Suppose you consume 10 six-packs of cola a month and see no films. How many six-packs are you willing to give up in exchange for seeing 1 film a month? Your answer to this question is your marginal rate of substitution between cola and films when you see no films. For example, if you are willing to give up 4 six-packs to see 1 film, your marginal rate of substitution of cola for films is 4.

Now suppose that you consume 6 six-packs and see 1 film a month. How many six-packs are you now willing to give up to see 2 films a month? Your answer to this question is your marginal rate of substitution between cola and films when you consume 1 film a month. If your answer is a smaller number than when you see no films, your preferences display a diminishing marginal rate of substitution between cola and films. The greater the number of films you see, the smaller is the quantity of cola you are willing to give up to see one additional film.

The shape of the indifference curves incorporates the principle of the diminishing marginal rate of substitution because the curves are bowed towards the origin. The tightness of the bend of an indifference curve tells us how willing a person is to substitute one good for another while remaining indifferent. Let's look at some examples that will clarify this point.

Degree of Substitutability

Most of us would not regard films and cola as being close substitutes for each other. We probably have some fairly clear ideas about how many films we want to see each month and how many cans of cola we want to drink. Nevertheless, to some degree, we are willing to substitute between these two goods. No matter how big a cola freak you are, there is surely some increase in the number of films you can see that will compensate you for being deprived of a can of cola. Similarly, no matter how addicted you are to films, surely some number of cans of cola will compensate you for being deprived of seeing one film. A person's indifference curves for films and cola might look something like those shown in Fig. 8.6(a).

Close Substitutes   Some goods substitute so easily for each other that most of us do not even notice which we are consuming. A good example concerns different brands of personal computers. Dell, Compaq and Elonex are all clones of the IBM

PC – but most of us can't tell the difference between the clones and the IBM. The same holds true for marker pens. Most of us don't care whether we use a marker pen from the university bookshop or the local supermarket. When two goods are perfect substitutes for each other, their indifference curves are straight lines that slope downward, as Fig. 8.6(b) illustrates. The marginal rate of substitution between perfect substitutes is constant.

Complements   Some goods cannot substitute for each other at all. Instead they are complements. The complements in Fig. 8.6(c) are left and right running shoes. Indifference curves of perfect complements are L-shaped. For most of us, one left running shoe and one right running shoe are as good as one left shoe and two right ones. Two of each is preferred to one of each, but two of one and one of the other is no better than one of each.

The extreme cases of perfect substitutes and perfect complements shown here don't often hap-

---

FIGURE 8.6

The Degree of Substitutability

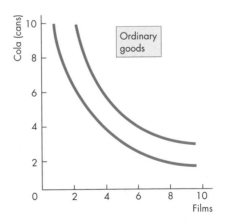

(a) Ordinary goods

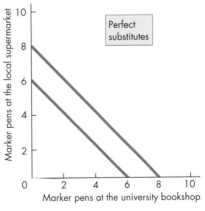

(b) Perfect substitutes

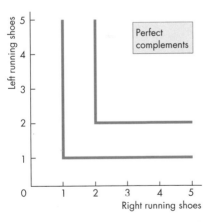

(c) Perfect complements

The shape of the indifference curves reveals the degree of substitutability between two goods. Part (a) shows the indifference curves for two ordinary goods: films and cola. To consume less cola and remain indifferent, one must see more films. The number of films that compensates for a reduction in cola increases as less cola is consumed. Part (b) shows the indifference curves for two perfect substi-

tutes. For the consumer to remain indifferent, one fewer marker pen from the local supermarket must be replaced by one extra marker pen from the university bookshop. Part (c) shows two perfect complements – goods that cannot be substituted for each other at all. Two left running shoes with one right running shoe is no better than one of each. But two of each is preferred to one of each.

pen in reality. They do, however, illustrate that the shape of the indifference curve shows the degree of substitutability between two goods. The more any pair of goods become close substitutes, the less bowed the indifference curves and the more the indifference curves look like straight lines. A high degree of substitutability means that the marginal rate of sustitution falls less quickly. The more any pair of goods become poor substitutes for each other, or become complementary, the more the indifference curves become bowed and tightly curved. At the extreme, the indifference curves become 'L' shaped like those shown in Figure 8.6(c). A low degree of sustitutability, or a high degree of complementarity, means that the marginal rate of sustitution falls more quickly.

The degree of substitutability between two goods might fall if consumers gain information which changes their preferences. The impact of public information about the extent of BSE infection in dairy cattle in the United Kingdom reduced the degree of substitutability between beef and other meats. You can read about this in *Reading Between the Lines* on pp. 186–187.

REVIEW

◆ Preferences are a person's likes and dislikes between any pair of goods which can be represented by a preference map.

◆ A preference map consists of an infinite number of indifference curves. Indifference curves slope downward, bow toward the origin, and do not intersect each other.

◆ The magnitude of the slope of an indifference curve is called the marginal rate of substitution. The marginal rate of substitution diminishes as a person consumes less of the good measured on the y-axis and more of the good measured on the x-axis.

◆ The degree of substitutability between any pair of goods is shown by the shape of the indifference curves.

The two components of the model of household choice are now in place: the budget line and the preference map. We will use these components to work out the consumer's choice.

The Household's Consumption Choice

We are now going to bring Lisa's budget line and indifference curves together to model her best affordable choice of films and cola. What are the quantities of films and cola that Lisa *chooses* to consume? In Fig. 8.7 you can see her budget line from Fig. 8.1 and her indifference curves from Fig. 8.4. First focus on point h on indifference curve I_0. Point h is on Lisa's budget line, so we know that she

---

FIGURE 8.7

The Best Affordable Point

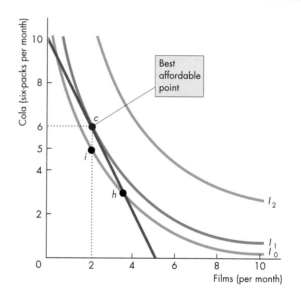

Lisa's best affordable point is c. At that point, she is on her budget line and so spends her entire income on the two goods. She is also on the highest attainable indifference curve. Higher indifference curves (such as I_2) do not touch her budget line, so she cannot afford any point on them. At point c, the marginal rate of substitution (the magnitude of the slope of the indifference curve) equals the relative price of a film (the magnitude of the slope of the budget line). A point such as h on the budget line is not Lisa's best affordable point because at that point she is willing to give up seeing more films in exchange for cola than she has to. She can move to point i, which she regards as being just as good as point h and which leaves her with some unspent income. She can spend that income and move to c, a point that she prefers to point i.

can afford it. But does she choose this combination of films and cola over all the other affordable combinations? No, she does not. To see why not, consider point c, where she consumes 2 films and 6 six-packs. Point c is also on Lisa's budget line, so we know she can afford to consume at this point. But point c is on indifference curve I_1, a higher indifference curve than I_0. Therefore we know that Lisa prefers point c to point h.

Is there any affordable point that Lisa prefers to point c? There is not. All Lisa's other affordable consumption points – all the other points on or below her budget line – lie on indifference curves that are below I_1. Indifference curve I_1 is the highest indifference curve on which Lisa can afford to consume.

Let's look more closely at Lisa's best affordable choice.

Properties of the Best Affordable Point

The best affordable point – point c in this example – has two properties. It is:

◆ On the budget line
◆ On the highest attainable indifference curve

On the Budget Line   The best affordable point is *on* the budget line. If Lisa chooses a point inside the budget line, she will have an affordable point on the budget line at which she can consume more of both goods. Lisa prefers that point to the one inside the budget line. The best affordable point cannot be outside the budget line because Lisa cannot afford such a point.

On the Highest Attainable Indifference Curve
The chosen point is on the highest attainable indifference curve. At this point, the indifference curve has the same slope as the budget line. Stated another way, the marginal rate of substitution between the two goods (the magnitude of the slope of the indifference curve) equals their relative price (the magnitude of the slope of the budget line).

To see why this condition describes the best affordable point, consider point h in Fig. 8.7, which Lisa regards as inferior to point c. At point h, Lisa's marginal rate of substitution is less than the relative price – indifference curve I_0 is flatter than Lisa's budget line. As Lisa gives up films for cola and moves up indifference curve I_0, she moves inside her budget line and has some money left over. She can move to point i, for example, where she consumes 2

films and 5 six-packs and has £3 to spare. She is indifferent between the combination of goods at point i and at point h. But she prefers point c to point i, since at c she has more cola than at i and sees the same number of films.

By moving along her budget line from point h towards point c, Lisa passes through a number of indifference curves (not shown in the figure) located between indifference curves I_0 and I_1. All of these indifference curves are higher than I_0 and therefore any point on them is preferred to point h. Once Lisa gets to point c, she has reached the highest attainable indifference curve. If she keeps moving along the budget line, she will start to encounter indifference curves that are lower than I_1.

REVIEW

◆ Affordable combinations of goods lie on or inside the consumer's budget line.

◆ The consumer's preferences are described by indifference curves.

◆ The consumer's best affordable allocation of income occurs when all income is spent (on the budget line) and when the marginal rate of substitution (the magnitude of the slope of the indifference curve) equals the relative price (the magnitude of the slope of the budget line).

We will now use this model of household choice to make some predictions about changes in consumption patterns when income and prices change.

Predicting Consumer Behaviour

Let's examine how consumers respond to changes in prices and income. We'll start by looking at the effect of a change in price. By studying the effect of a change in price on a consumer's choice, holding all other things constant, we are able to derive a consumer's demand curve.

A Change in Price

The effect of a change in price on the quantity of a good consumed is called the **price effect**. We will use Fig. 8.8(a) to work out the price effect of a fall in the price of a cinema ticket. We start with tickets costing £6 each, cola costing £3 a six-pack, and with Lisa's income at £30 a month. In this situation, she consumes at point c, where her budget line is tangent to her highest attainable indifference curve, I_1. She consumes 6 six-packs and 2 films a month.

Now suppose that the price of a cinema ticket falls to £3. We've already seen how a change in Fig. 8.2(a) affects the budget line. With a lower price of a ticket, the budget line rotates outward and becomes flatter. On the new budget line in Fig.8.8(a), Lisa's best affordable point is j, where she consumes 5 films and 5 six-packs of cola. As you can see, Lisa drinks less cola and sees more films now that films cost less. She reduces her cola consumption from 6 to 5 six-packs, and increases the number of films she sees from 2 to 5 a month. Lisa substitutes films for cola when the price of a cinema ticket falls, and the price of cola and her income remain constant.

The Demand Curve

A demand curve graphs the relationship between the quantity demanded of a good and its price, holding constant all other influences on buying plans. In Chapter 4, we asserted that the demand curve slopes downward and that it shifts when the consumer's income changes, or when the price of another good changes. We can now derive a demand curve from a consumer's budget line and indifference curves. By doing so, we can see that the law of demand and the downward-sloping demand curve are consequences of the consumer choosing his or her best affordable combination of goods.

Let's derive Lisa's demand curve for films. We do so by lowering the price of a cinema ticket and finding her best affordable point at different prices. We just did this for two ticket prices in Fig. 8.8(a). Fig. 8.8(b) highlights these two prices and two points that lie on Lisa's demand curve for films. When the price of a cinema ticket is £6, Lisa sees 2 films a month at point a. When the price falls to £3, she increases the number of films she sees to 5 a month at point b. The entire demand curve is made up of these two points plus all the other points that tell us Lisa's best affordable consumption of films at each ticket price – more than £6, between £6 and £3, and less than £3 – given the price of cola and Lisa's income. As you can see, Lisa's demand curve for films slopes downward – the lower the price of a

FIGURE 8.8

Price Effect and Demand Curve

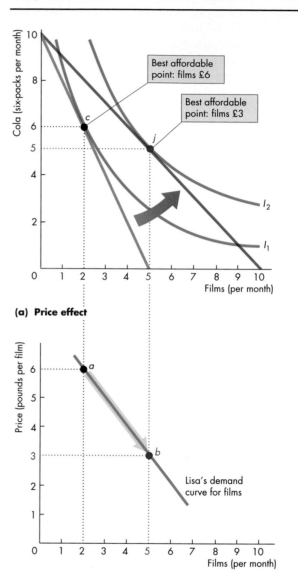

(a) Price effect

(b) Demand curve

Initially, Lisa consumes at point c (part a). If the price of a cinema ticket falls from £6 to £3, she consumes at point j. The increase in films from 2 to 5 per month and the decrease in cola from 6 to 5 six-packs is the price effect. When the price of a cinema ticket falls, Lisa sees more films. She also consumes less cola. Part (b) shows Lisa's demand curve for films. When the price of a ticket is £6, she sees 2 a month, at point a. When the price of a ticket falls to £3, she sees 5 a month, at point b. Lisa's demand curve traces out her best affordable quantity of films as the price of a cinema ticket varies.

cinema ticket, the more films she watches each month. This is the law of demand.

Next, let's examine how Lisa adjusts her consumption when her income changes.

A Change in Income

The effect of a change in income on consumption is called the **income effect.** Let's work out the income effect by examining how consumption changes when income changes and prices remain constant. Figure 8.9(a) shows the income effect when Lisa's income falls. With an income of £30 and with a cinema ticket costing £3 and cola £3 a six-pack, she consumes at point j – 5 films and 5 six-packs. If her income falls to £21, she consumes at point l – 4 films and 3 six-packs. Thus when Lisa's income falls, she consumes less of both goods[2].

The Demand Curve and the Income Effect   A change in income leads to a shift in the demand curve, as shown in Fig. 8.9(b). With an income of £30, Lisa's demand curve is D_0, the same as in Fig. 8.8. But when her income falls to £21, she plans to see fewer films at each price, so her demand curve shifts leftward to D_1.

Substitution Effect and Income Effect   We've now worked out the effects of a change in the price of a cinema ticket and the effects of a change in Lisa's income on her consumption of films and cola. We've discovered that when her income increases, she increases her consumption of both goods. Films and cola are *normal goods*. When the price of a cinema ticket falls, Lisa increases her consumption of films and decreases her consumption of cola. A fall in the price of a normal good leads to an increase in the consumption of that good, as well as to a decrease in the consumption of the substitutes for that good. To see why these changes in spending patterns occur when there is a change in price, we separate the price effect into two parts. One part is called the substitution effect; the other part is called the income effect.

---

[2] For Lisa, films and cola are *normal* goods. When her income falls, she consumes less of both goods and when her income rises, she consumes more of both goods. Some goods are *inferior* goods. When income rises, the consumption of an *inferior* good decreases. Try to draw some indifference curves that illustrate an inferior good.

FIGURE 8.9

Income Effect and Change in Demand

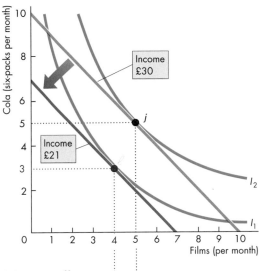

(a) Income effect

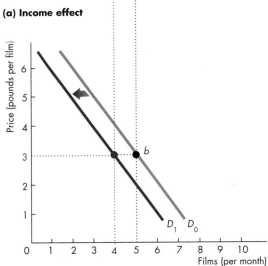

(b) Demand curve

A change in income shifts the budget line and changes consumption. In part (a), when Lisa's income decreases, she consumes less of both films and cola. In part (b), when Lisa's income decreases, her demand curve for films shifts leftward. Lisa's demand for films decreases because she will now see fewer films at each price.

Figure 8.10 illustrates the price effect and its separation into a substitution effect and an income effect. Part (a) shows the price effect that you've already worked out in Fig. 8.8. Let's see how that price effect comes about, first by isolating the substitution effect.

Substitution Effect The **substitution effect** is the effect of a change in price on the quantities consumed when the consumer (hypothetically) remains indifferent between the original and the new combinations of goods consumed. To work out Lisa's substitution effect, we have to imagine that when the price of a cinema ticket falls, Lisa's income also decreases by an amount that is just enough to leave her on the same indifference curve as before.

Figure 8.10(b) illustrates the substitution effect. When the price of a cinema ticket falls from £6 to £3, let's suppose (hypothetically) that Lisa's income decreases to £21. What's special about £21? It is the income that is just enough, at the new price of a ticket, to keep Lisa's best affordable point on the same indifference curve as her original consumption point c. Lisa's budget line in this situation is the light orange line shown in Fig. 8.10(b). With the new price of a cinema ticket and the new lower income, Lisa's best affordable point is l on indifference curve I_1. The move from c to l isolates the substitution effect of the price change. The substitution effect of the fall in the price of a cinema ticket is an increase in the consumption of films from 2 to 4 and a decrease in the consumption of cola. The direction of the substitution effect never varies; when the relative price of a good falls, the consumer substitutes more of that good for the other good.

Income Effect To calculate the substitution effect, we gave Lisa a £9 pay cut. Now let's give Lisa her £9 back. The £9 increase in income shifts Lisa's budget line outward, as shown in Fig. 8.10(c). The slope of the budget line does not change because both prices remain constant. This change in Lisa's budget line is similar to the one illustrated in Fig. 8.9, where we study the effect of income on consumption. As Lisa's budget line shifts outward, her consumption possibilities expand and her best affordable point becomes j on indifference curve I_2. The move from l to j isolates the income effect of the price change. In this example, as Lisa's income increases, she increases

her consumption of both films and cola. For Lisa, films and cola are normal goods.

Price Effect Figure 8.10 shows how the price effect in part (a) is broken into two effects, the substitution effect in part (b) and the income effect in part (c). In part (b), Lisa is indifferent between the two situations. Her income falls at the same time as the price of a cinema ticket falls and she substitutes films for cola. The substitution effect always works in the same direction – the consumer slides along an indifference curve to buy more of the good whose relative price has fallen and less of the good whose relative price has risen. In part (c), prices are constant and Lisa's income returns to its original level. The direction of the income effect depends on whether the good is normal or inferior. By definition, normal goods are ones whose consumption increases as income increases. For Lisa, films and cola are normal goods because the income effect increases their consumption. Both the income effect and the substitution effect increase Lisa's consumption of films.

The arrows in parts (b) and (c) of Fig. 8.10 show the substitution and income effects of a price change. The move from point c to point l in part (b) is the substitution effect, and the move from point l to point j in part (c) is the income effect. For films, the income effect reinforces the substitution effect with the result that Lisa increases her consumption of films. For cola, the substitution effect and the income effect work in opposite directions with the result that Lisa decreases her consumption of cola.

The example that we have just studied is that of a change in the price of a normal good. The effect of a change in the price of an inferior good is different. Recall that an inferior good is one whose consumption decreases as income increases. For an inferior good, the income effect is negative. Thus for an inferior good a lower price does not always lead to an increase in the quantity demanded. The lower price has a substitution effect that increases the quantity demanded. But the lower price also has a negative income effect, which reduces the demand for the inferior good. Thus the negative income effect offsets the substitution effect to some degree. Even so, the substitution effect usually dominates so that the quantity demanded rises when the price falls – confirming the law of demand.

FIGURE 8.10

Price Effect, Substitution Effect and Income Effect

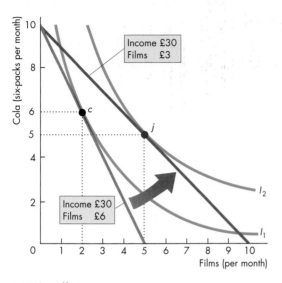

(a) Price effect

(b) Substitution effect

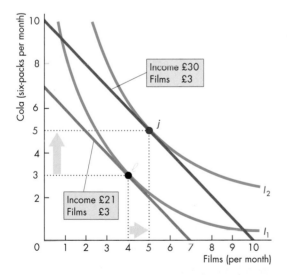

(c) Income effect

The price effect can be separated into a substitution effect and an income effect. Part (a) shows the price effect and it is the same as Fig. 8.8(a).

To calculate the substitution effect (part b), when the price of a cinema ticket falls, decrease Lisa's income so that her best affordable point remains on her original indifference curve. The substitution effect of the price change is the move from *c* to *ℓ*.

To calculate the income effect (part c), restore Lisa's income to its original level. The increase in income shifts the budget line outward and the quantities of films and cola consumed increase. The income effect of the price change is the move from *ℓ* to *j*.

Reading Between the Lines on pp 186–187 shows the income and substitution effects of the UK BSE crisis.

Giffen Goods   It has been suggested that some goods defy the law of demand – the quantity demanded increases when price increases. In fact, they are the exception that proves the rule. These

goods have become known as 'Giffen' goods, named after a nineteenth century economist who suggested the quantity of potatoes demanded increased as the price of potatoes increased during the Irish potato famine. Cases where the income effect is negative *and* stronger than the substitution effect are extremely rare. They arise when the total expenditure on a good is a high

Indifference Curves:
BSE and Beef

The Essence of the Story

THE FINANCIAL TIMES, 21 MARCH 1996

Meat industry braced for dramatic drop in demand

Deborah Hargreaves

The meat industry was bracing itself for a dramatic drop in consumer demand for beef yesterday following the government's admission that there is a probable link between bovine spongiform encephalopathy (BSE or 'mad cow disease') and its human equivalent, Creutzfeldt-Jakob disease....

Beef sales had only just begun to recover from the previous BSE scare just before Christmas when consumption dropped by 20 per cent. In the month up to March 10, beef sales were 13 per cent below the same period last year at around 20,000 tonnes.

The statements about a possible link between BSE and Creutzfeldt-Jakob disease, which is incurable and causes death in humans, could prove ruinous for some of Britain's beef farmers.

Cattle prices had only just begun to recover from a 15 to 20 per cent drop in December. 'I'm expecting to see £80 wiped fairly quickly off the price of an animal that would usually sell for around £840,' said Mr Wood....

The Consumers' Association said the public remained to be convinced that beef was safe....

Consumers have turned against eating beef in a trend against red meat over the past 15 years – and this has been exacerbated by BSE scares. Annual beef consumption has dropped from 21kg per person in 1980 to 15 kg last year. ...

■ In March 1996, the UK government announced a probable link between BSE (bovine spongiform encephalopathy) and its human equivalent, Creutzfeldt-Jakob disease.

■ The announcement came just five months after the previous BSE crisis in November 1995 when beef consumption fell by 20 per cent.

■ During the previous crisis, the fall in consumer demand cut cattle prices by 20 per cent. Farmers are expecting the price of an animal to be cut by 10 per cent after the most recent announcement.

■ BSE beef scares change consumer preferences. Annual beef consumption fell from 21 kilograms per person in 1980 to 15 kilograms in 1995.

Economic Analysis

■ Figure 1 shows indifference curves for beef and white meat before the scare, labelled I_{Nov95}, and just after the scare, I_{Dec95}, and the budget line, A.

■ Before the scare, beef and white meat were good substitutes – the indifference curve does not bow much. After the scare, white meat is preferred to beef – the indifference curve moves and is more bowed.

■ Annual beef consumption fell from 15 kilograms per person to 12 kilograms after the scare, while annual white meat consumption increased.

■ Figure 2 shows the impact in the beef market. Demand for beef before the scare is D_{Nov} and supply is S. Price is P_0 and quantity traded is 23,000 tonnes.

■ As preferences shift from beef to white meat, demand for beef falls to D_{Dec}. There is excess supply of 5,000 tonnes at price P_0, forcing retailers to slash the price of beef to P_1, and quantity falls to 20,000 tonnes.

■ Figure 3 shows the beef price cut makes the budget line less steep, moving from A to B. With the new shaped preferences, consumer choice moves from point a to point c – consumption of both beef and white meat increases.

■ Assuming both beef and white meat are normal goods, the income effect, a to b, increases consumption of white meat, but beef is now relatively cheaper and the substitution effect, b to c, increases beef consumption, but to less than the pre-scare levels.

■ The March scare will have a similar effect, cutting overall beef consumption further.

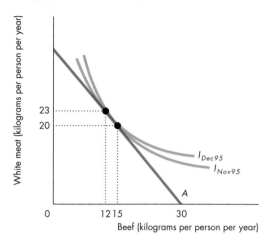

Figure 1

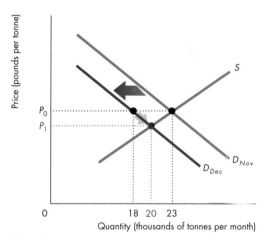

Figure 2

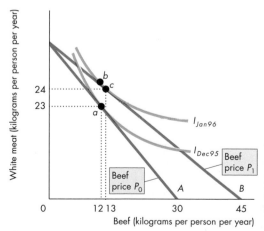

Figure 3

proportion of total income – as in the potato famine example. They do not defy the law of demand because it is based on preference theory which allows for these exceptions. The law of demand holds for all normal goods and for inferior goods, providing they account for a small proportion of total expenditure.

Back to the Facts

We started this chapter by observing how consumer spending has changed over the years. We can use the indifference curve model to explain those changes. Spending patterns are interpreted as being the best choices households can make, given their preferences and incomes and given the prices of the goods they consume. Changes in prices and incomes lead to changes in the best affordable choice and change consumption patterns. Sometimes, of course, prices change because taxes change (which we studied in Chapter 6, pp. 130-134).

Models based on the same ideas that you've studied here are used to explain the actual changes that occur and to measure the response of consumption to changes in prices and in income – the price elasticity and income elasticity of demand. You met some measures of these elasticities in Chapter 5. Most of those elasticities were measured by using the model that we've studied here (but models that have more than two goods).

The model of household choice can do much more than explain consumption choices. It can be used to explain a wide range of other household choices. Let's look at some of these.

Other Household Choices

Households make many choices other than those about how to spend their income on the various goods and services available. We can use the model of consumer choice to understand many other household choices. Some of these are discussed in *Economics in History* on pp. 194–195. Here we'll study two key choices:

◆ How much labour to supply

◆ How much income to save

Labour Supply

Every week, we allocate our 168 hours between working – called *labour* – and all other activities – called *leisure*. How do we decide how to allocate our time between labour and leisure? We can answer this question by using the theory of household choice.

The more hours we spend on leisure, the smaller is our income. The relationship between leisure and income is described by an *income–time budget line*. Figure 8.11 shows Lisa's income–time budget line. If Lisa devotes the entire week to leisure – 168 hours – she has no income and is at point *z*. By supplying labour in exchange for a wage, she can convert hours into income along the time–budget line. The slope of that line is determined by the hourly wage rate. If the wage rate is £2 an hour, Lisa faces the lowest budget line. If she worked for 68 hours a week, she would make an income of £136 a week. If the wage rate is £4 an hour, she faces the middle budget line. If the wage rate is £6 an hour, she faces the highest budget line. Lisa buys time by not supplying labour and by forgoing income. The opportunity cost of an hour of leisure is the hourly wage rate forgone.

Let's assume Lisa is a student who has some time available for part-time work. She must choose

---

FIGURE 8.11

The Income–Time Budget Line

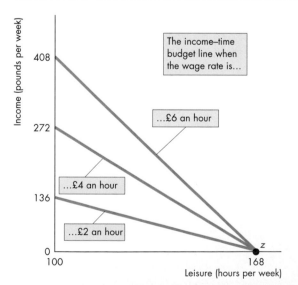

Time can be converted into income by working for a wage. If no work is done, the household has 168 hours of leisure per week and no income, at point *z*. The higher the wage rate, the steeper is the income–time budget line.

a point on a time–budget line. That is, she must choose how many hours of labour to supply. We can study this choice by looking at Lisa's indifference curves. Income and leisure are goods, just like films and cola, and Lisa has indifference curves for income and leisure.

Figure 8.12(a) shows Lisa's indifference curves for income and leisure. The magnitude of the slope of an indifference curve tells us Lisa's marginal rate of substitution – the rate at which she is willing to give up income to get one more hour of leisure, while remaining indifferent.

Lisa chooses her best attainable point. This choice of income and time allocation is just like her choice of films and cola. She gets onto the highest possible indifference curve by making her marginal rate of substitution between income and leisure equal to her wage rate. The choice depends on the wage rate Lisa can earn. At a wage rate of £2 an hour, Lisa chooses point *a* and works 20 hours a week (168 minus 148) for an income of £40 a week.

At a wage rate of £4 an hour, she chooses point *b* and works 35 hours a week (168 minus 133) for an income of £140 a week. At a wage rate of £6 an hour, she chooses point *c* and works 30 hours a week (168 minus 138) for an income of £180 a week.

Figure 8.12(b) shows Lisa's choices of hours to work at different wage rates in the form of her labour supply curve. This curve shows that as the wage rate increases from £2 an hour to £4 an hour, Lisa increases the quantity of labour supplied from 20 hours a week to 35 hours a week. But when the wage rate increases to £6 an hour, she decreases her quantity of labour supplied to 30 hours a week.

Lisa's supply of labour is similar to that described for the economy as a whole at the beginning of this chapter. As wage rates have increased, work hours have decreased. At first, this pattern seems puzzling. We've seen that the hourly wage rate is the opportunity cost of leisure. So a higher wage rate means a higher opportunity

FIGURE 8.12

The Supply of Labour

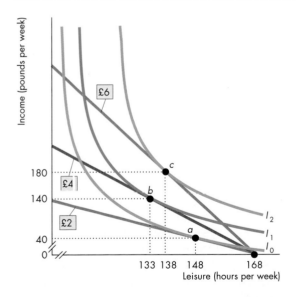
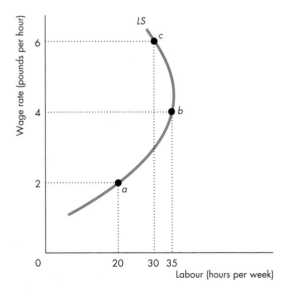

In part (a), at a wage rate of £2 an hour, Lisa takes 148 hours of leisure (works 20 hours) a week at point *a*. If the wage rate increases from £2 to £4, she decreases her leisure to 133 hours (increases her work to 35 hours) a week at point *b*. But if the wage rate increases from £4 to £6, Lisa *increases* her leisure to 138 hours (*decreases* her work to 30 hours) a week at point *c*.

Part (b) shows Lisa's labour supply curve – the change in Lisa's hours of work as the wage rate changes. Lisa's labour supply curve slopes upward between points *a* and *b* and then bends back between points *b* and *c*. The reason is that leisure is a normal good and at a high enough wage rate, the positive income effect of a higher wage rate outweighs the negative substitution effect.

cost of leisure. This fact on its own leads to a decrease in leisure and an increase in work hours. But instead, we've cut our work hours. Why? Because our incomes have increased. As the real wage rate increases, real incomes increase, so people demand more of all normal goods. Leisure is a normal good, so as incomes increase, people demand more leisure.

The higher wage rate has both a *substitution effect* and an *income effect*. The higher wage rate increases the opportunity cost of leisure and so leads to a substitution effect away from leisure. The higher wage rate increases income and so leads to an income effect towards more leisure.

This theory of household choice can explain the facts about work patterns described at the beginning of this chapter. First, it can explain why the average working week has fallen steadily from 70 hours a week in the nineteenth century to 35 hours a week today. The reason is that as wage rates have increased, although people have substituted work for leisure, they have also decided to use their higher incomes in part to consume more leisure. Second, the theory can explain why more women now have jobs in the labour market. The reason is that increases in their wage rates and improvements in their job opportunities have led to a substitution effect away from working at home and towards working in the labour market.

Let's now see how the theory of household choice explains the saving decision.

Saving

Each year, we allocate our income between consumption and saving. By saving, we decrease our *current* consumption and increase our *future* consumption. The choice of how much to consume and how much to save can also be understood by using the same model of household choice that explains the allocation of income to films and cola.

The more we spend on current consumption, the less we can spend on future consumption. The relationship between current consumption and future consumption is described by a *lifetime budget line*. Figure 8.13 shows two possible lifetime budget lines for Lisa when she has qualified. Lisa earns £20,000 a year in her working years; she can consume her entire income each year and save nothing for her retirement at point z. The slope of the lifetime budget line depends on the interest rate. Other things

remaining the same, the higher the interest rate, the steeper is the lifetime budget line. This means that the higher the interest rate, the larger is the amount of future consumption that can be done with a given amount of saving. Along the light orange budget line, the interest rate is 50 per cent compounded to Lisa's retirement. (An annual interest rate of 1.6 per cent compounds to 50 per cent over 25 years.) Along this lifetime budget line, if Lisa decreases her consumption while she is working by £1 (if she saves £1), she can spend an additional £1.50 after she retires. Along the dark orange line, the interest rate is 100 per cent compounded to Lisa's retirement. (An annual interest rate of 3 per cent compounds to 100 per cent over 25 years.) Along this budget line, if Lisa decreases her consumption in her working years by £1, she can spend an additional £2 after she retires.

Lisa must choose a point on her lifetime budget line. If she spends her entire income each year while she is working, she has nothing to spend when she retires and is at point z in Fig. 8.13. By decreasing current consumption, Lisa can increase future consumption along the lifetime budget line. For example, along the light orange lifetime budget line, by saving $8,000, Lisa moves to point a, at which she consumes £12,000 a year while she is working and also £12,000 a year after she retires. Lisa has smoothed out her consumption over her life.

The choice that Lisa makes depends on her preferences. And her preferences are represented by indifference curves for current consumption and future consumption. These indifference curves are similar to those for any pair of goods – films and cola or leisure and income.

Lisa chooses the amount of consumption and saving by making the marginal rate of substitution between current and future consumption equal to the interest rate. Suppose that when the interest rate is 50 per cent, Lisa choses point a. She has a current income of £20,000 a year, she consumes £12,000 and saves $8,000. What happens to Lisa's consumption and saving if the interest rate rises? A rise in the interest rate rotates the budget line outward as shown in the figure. With a higher interest rate, the opportunity cost of current consumption increases. So Lisa substitutes future consumption for current consumption. But the higher interest rate expands Lisa's consumption possibilities in both the current and the future periods. This increase in her consumption possibilities creates an *income effect* which leads to an increase in both

FIGURE 8.13

The Saving Decision

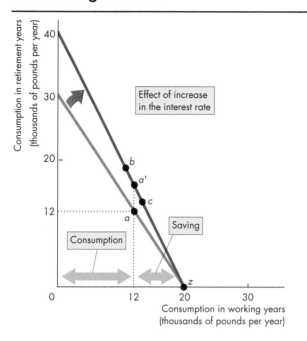

During her working years, Lisa earns £20,000 a year. If she consumes all her income, her consumption when she retires is zero at point *z*. By saving, Lisa can make her retirement consumption equal to her working years consumption at point *a*. An increase in the interest rate increases Lisa's current and future consumption possibilities. The substitution effect of the higher interest rate induces an increase in saving, but the income effect of the higher interest rate induces a decrease in saving. Depending on her preferences, Lisa might move to point *a'* (no change in saving), *b* (an increase in saving), or *c* (a decrease in saving).

current and future consumption.

The outcome for current consumption and saving is ambiguous. If the income effect is smaller than the substitution effect, Lisa moves to *b*. Here, current consumption decreases, saving increases and future consumption increases. If the income effect is larger than the substitution effect, Lisa moves to *c*. Here, current consumption increases, saving decreases and future consumption increases. If the income effect offsets the substitution effect, Lisa moves to *a'*. Here, current consumption and saving remain constant and future consumption increases.

If Lisa is an average consumer, she will move from *a* to *b* when the interest rate rises. That is, the

substitution effect will outweigh the income effect. But the interest rate effect on saving appears to be small.

We've now completed our study of household choices. We've seen how we can derive a demand curve from a model of household choice. And we've seen that the demand curve obeys the law of demand: other things remaining the same, when the price of a good falls the quantity demanded of that good increases We've also seen how the model of household choice can be applied to a wide range of other choices, including the supply of labour and saving. So how does indifference curve theory fit with the marginal utility theory we explored in Chapter 7? They are two ways of saying the same thing. Let's see why.

Marginal Utility and Indifference Curves

Each theory of choice describes consumer's preferences. Marginal utility theory describes preferences in terms of the utility derived from consumption, and indifference curve theory uses indifference curves to represent preferences. You can understand how the two models relate to each other by thinking of an indifference curve as connecting points of equal utility. If Lisa is indifferent between consuming 2 films and 6 six-packs of cola or 6 films and 2 six-packs of cola, we are also saying she gets equal utility from the two choices.

You can see the connection between utility and indifference curves by looking at the two parts of Fig. 8.14. Part (a) has three dimensions – the quantity of cola, the quantity of films and the level of total utility.

Part (b) has just two dimensions – the quantities of cola and films consumed. In part (a), the utility that Lisa gets from cola alone (with no films) appears as the right-hand yellow line. It shows that as Lisa's consumption of cola rises, so does the total utility she gets from cola. Lisa's total utility from films, which appeared in Fig. 7.3, appears here as the left-hand yellow line. It shows that as Lisa's consumption of films increases, so does the total utility she gets from films. Lisa's indifference curve for films and cola is the blue line in part (b). But it also appears in part (a) as the blue contour line which maps points of equal utility. Points *c* and *d* in part (a) are the same as points *c* and *d* in part (b). Viewed in this way, an indifference curve can be interpreted as a contour curve that measures equal levels of total utility.

FIGURE 8.14

Utility and Indifference Curves

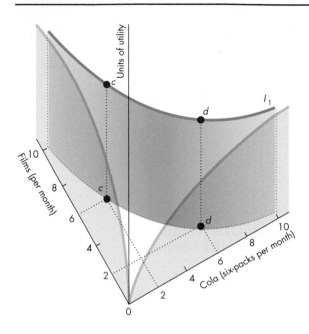

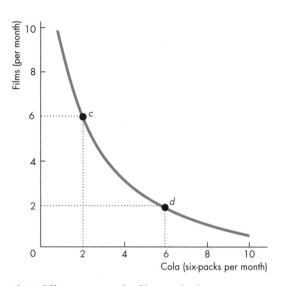

(a) Total utility from films and cola

(b) Indifference curve for films and cola

Part (a) shows the total utility received from films when no cola is consumed (left-hand yellow curve) and the total utility received from cola when no films are seen (right-hand yellow curve). It also shows an indifference curve as a contour that maps all the choices that give equal (constant) utility – the blue curve.

Part (b) shows an indifference curve for films and cola. It is the same as the blue curve in part (a). Points c and d represent the same choices and utility as in part (a). The indifference curve in part (b) is what you would see if you looked straight down on top of the three-dimensional diagram shown in part (a).

We can work either with total utility curves, as we did in Chapter 7, or with indifference curves, as we did in this chapter. They each give the same answer. A mathematical interpretation of this equivalence is set out in Box 8.1. So why do we have two theories? Is one better than the other?

Differences between Theories of Choice

The key difference between our two models of consumer choice is that we do not need to use the concept of utility in the indifference curve approach. We merely have to talk about preferences between different pairs of goods. We have to say whether the consumer prefers one combination to another or is

indifferent between the two combinations. We don't have to say anything about *how* the consumer makes such evaluations. This means we don't have to find a measure for utility to make comparisons of utility between individuals. Most economists agree that the indifference curve theory is better for these reasons.

◆ ◆ ◆ ◆ In the chapters that follow, we're going to study the choices made by firms. We'll see how, in the pursuit of profit, firms make choices governing the supply of goods and services and the demand for factors of production (inputs). After completing these chapters, we'll then bring the analysis of households and firms together and study their interactions in markets for goods and services and factors of production.

SUMMARY

Consumption Possibilities

The budget line shows the limits to a household's consumption given its income and the prices of goods. The budget line is the boundary between what the household can and cannot afford.

The point at which the budget line intersects the y-axis is the household's real income in terms of the good measured on that axis. The magnitude of the slope of the budget line is the relative price of the good measured on the x-axis in terms of the good measured on the y-axis.

A change in price changes the slope of the budget line. The lower the price of the good measured on the x-axis, the flatter is the budget line. A change in income shifts the budget line (rightward for an increase and leftward for a decrease) but does not change its slope. (pp. 173–176)

Preferences and Indifference Curves

A consumer's preferences can be represented by indifference curves. An indifference curve joins all the combinations of goods among which the consumer is indifferent. A consumer prefers any point above an indifference curve to any point on it and any point on an indifference curve to any point below it. Indifference curves bow towards the origin.

The magnitude of the slope of an indifference curve is called the marginal rate of substitution. A key assumption is that the marginal rate of substitution diminishes as consumption of the good measured on the y-axis decreases and consumption of the good measured on the x-axis increases. (pp. 176–180)

The Household's Consumption Choice

A household consumes at its best affordable point. Such a point is on the budget line and on the highest attainable indifference curve. At that point the indifference curve and the budget line have the same slope – the marginal rate of substitution equals the relative price. (pp.180–181)

Predicting Consumer Behaviour

The change in the quantity bought that results from a change in the price of a good is called the price effect. Other things remaining the same, when the price of a good falls a household buys more of that good. The change in the quantity bought that results from a change in income is called the income effect. Other things remaining the same, when income increases, a household buys more of all (normal) goods.

The price effect can be divided into a substitution effect and an income effect. The substitution effect is calculated as the change in consumption resulting from the change in price accompanied by a (hypothetical) change in income that leaves the consumer indifferent between the original situation and the new situation. The substitution effect of a price change always results in an increase in consumption of the good whose relative price has decreased. The income effect of a price change is the effect of (hypothetically) restoring the consumer's original income but keeping the price of the good constant at its new level. For a normal good, the income effect reinforces the substitution effect. For an inferior good, the income effect offsets the substitution effect. (pp. 181–188)

Other Household Choices

The indifference curve model of household choice enables us to understand how a household allocates its time between leisure and work and its lifetime resources between current consumption and future consumption. (pp. 188–192)

'Economy is the art of making the most of life.'

George Bernard Shaw, MAN AND SUPERMAN

Understanding Human Behaviour

THE ISSUES AND IDEAS

The economic analysis of human behaviour, in the family, the workplace, the markets for goods and services, the markets for labour services and financial markets, is based on the idea that our behaviour can be understood as a response to scarcity. Everything we do can be understood as a choice that maximizes utility subject to the constraints imposed by our limited resources and technology. If people's preferences are stable in the face of changing constraints, then we have a chance of predicting how they will respond to an evolving environment.

The incredible change that has occurred over the past 100 years in the way women allocate their time can be explained as the consequence of changing constraints. Technological advances have equipped the nation's factories with machines that have increased the productivity of both women and men, thereby raising the wages they can earn. The increasingly technological world has increased the return to education for both women and men and has led to a large increase in the number of both sexes staying in full-time school and college education. And, equipped with a wide array of gadgets and machines that cut the time of household jobs, an increasing proportion of women have joined the work-force.

This economic view might not be correct, but it is a powerful one. And if it is correct, the changing attitudes towards women are a consequence, not a cause, of their economic advancement.

THEN ...

Economists explain people's actions as the consequence of choices that maximize utility subject to constraints. In the 1890s, fewer than 20 per cent of women chose paid employment and most of those who did had low-paying and unattractive jobs. The other 80 per cent of women chose unpaid work in the home. What were the constraints that led to these choices?

... AND NOW

By 1995, more than 60 per cent of women were in the work-force and, although many had low-paying jobs, more and more women were found in the professions and in executive positions. What brought about this dramatic change compared with 100 years earlier? Was it a change in preferences or a change in the constraints that women face?

THE ECONOMISTS: BENTHAM, JEVONS AND BECKER

William Stanley Jevons

Many economists have contributed to our understanding of human behaviour, but three stand out from the rest. They are Jeremy Bentham (1748–1832), William Stanley Jevons (1835–1882), and Gary Becker (1930–). Bentham, who lived in London (and whose embalmed body is preserved to this day in a glass cabinet in the University of London), was the first to use the concept of utility to explain and prescribe human choices. The distinction between explanation and prescription was not a sharp one in Bentham's day. He was one of the first to propose pensions for retired people, guaranteed employment, minimum wages, and social benefits such as free education and free medical care.

Jeremy Bentham

Jevons's main claim to fame in his own day was his proposal – wrong as it turned out – that economic fluctuations are caused by sun spots. He was a co-discoverer of the concept of *marginal utility*, and it was he who developed the theory explained in this chapter.

Gary Becker teaches both economics and sociology at the University of Chicago. He used the ideas of Bentham and Jevons to explain a wide range of human choices, including the choices made by women about how many children to bear and how much and what type of work to do.

K E Y   E L E M E N T S

Key Terms

Budget line, 173
Diminishing marginal rate of substitution, 178
Income effect, 183
Indifference curve, 176
Marginal rate of substitution, 177
Price effect, 181
Real income, 174
Relative price, 174
Substitution effect, 184

◆ Key Figures

Figure 8.1   The Budget Line, 173
Figure 8.2   Changes in Prices and Income, 175
Figure 8.4   A Preference Map, 177
Figure 8.5   The Marginal Rate of Substitution. 178
Figure 8.7   The Best Affordable Point, 181
Figure 8.8   Price Effect and Demand Curve, 182
Figure 8.9   Income Effect and Change in
               Demand, 183
Figure 8.10   Price Effect, Substitution Effect and
               Income Effect, 185

R E V I E W   Q U E S T I O N S

1   What determines the limits to a household's consumption choices?

2   What is the budget line?

3   What determines the intercept of the budget line on the y-axis?

4   What determines the slope of the budget line?

5   If the price of books is £5 each and the price of CDs is £10 each and you have £50 to spend on books and CDs, write a mathematical equation for the budget line.

6   What happens to the equation in review question 5 if your income rises to £60?

7   What happens to the equation in review question 5 if the price of CDs falls to £5?

8   What is an indifference curve?

9   What do all the points on an indifference curve have in common?

10   Why do individuals prefer to be on a higher indifference curve?

11   What is the marginal rate of substitution?

12   What determines the shape of an indifference curve?

13   What is meant by diminishing rate of marginal substitution?

14   What two conditions are satisfied when a consumer makes the best affordable consumption?

15   What is the effect of a change in income on consumption?

16   What is the effect of a change in price on consumption?

17   What is the price effect?

18   Define the income effect of a price change.

19   Distinguish between the income effect and the substitution effect of a price change.

20   What is the opportunity cost of leisure?

21   What is the effect of reducing the wage rate on the opportunity cost of leisure?

22   Why might the labour supply curve bend backward?

23   What is the opportunity cost of current consumption?

24   What is the effect of decreasing the interest rate on the budget line between current and future consumption?

25   What is the effect of decreasing the interest rate on the substitution and income effect?

PROBLEMS

1 Sara has an income of £12 a week. Pizzas costs £3 each and beer costs £3 a bottle.

a What is Sara's real income in terms of beer?

b What is her real income in terms of pizzas?

c What is the relative price of beer in terms of pizzas?

d What is the opportunity cost of a bottle of beer?

e Calculate the equation for Sara's budget line (placing pizzas on the left side).

f Draw a graph of Sara's budget line with beer on the x-axis.

g In Problem (g), what is the slope of Sara's budget line? What is it equal to?

2 Sara's income and the prices she faces are the same as in Problem 1. Her preferences are shown by her indifference curves in the figure.

a What are the quantities of pizzas and beer that Sara buys?

b What is Sara's marginal rate of substitution of pizzas for beer at the point at which she consumes?

3 Now suppose that in the situation described in Problem 2, the price of beer halves to £1.50 per can and the price of pizzas and Sara's income remain constant.

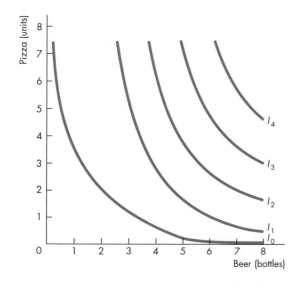

a Find the new quantities of beer and pizzas that Sara buys.

b Find two points on Sara's demand curve for beer.

c Find the substitution effect of the price change.

d Find the income effect of the price change.

e Is beer a normal good or an inferior good for Sara?

f Is pizza a normal good or an inferior good for Sara?

4 Gerry buys cakes that cost £1 each and comic books that cost £2 each. Each month Gerry buys 20 cakes and 10 comic books. He spends all of his income. Next month the price of cakes will fall to 50 pence, but the price of a comic book will rise to £3.

a Will Gerry be able to buy 20 cakes and 10 comic books next month?

b Will he want to?

c If he changes his consumption, which good will he buy more of and which less?

d Which situation does Jerry prefer: cakes at £1 and comic books at £2 or cakes at 50 pence and comic books at £3?

e When the prices change next month will there be an income effect and a substitution effect at work or just one of them? If there is only one effect at work, which one will it be?

5 Now suppose that in the situation described in Problem 4, the prices of cakes and comic books next month remain at £1 and £2 respectively. Gerry gets a pay rise of £10 a month. He now buys 16 comic books and 18 cakes. For Gerry are cakes and comic books normal goods or inferior goods?

6 Jane is a student. She has worked out that she can spend £50 on recorded music tapes and CDs this term. If tapes cost £5 and CDs cost £10:

a Write out an equation for the budget line between tapes and CDs.

b Draw the budget line as a graph.

7 If Jane chooses to buy 6 tapes this term on the basis of the information in Problem 6:

 a How much does she spend on CDs this term?

 b How many CDs does she buy this term?

 c Draw an indifference curve on your graph of the budget from Problem 6 to illustrate the choice between tapes and CDs which maximizes Jane's utility.

 d What is Jane's marginal rate of substitution between tapes and CDs at her preferred choice?

8 Suppose Jane's grandmother sends her a cheque for £20 for her birthday. Jane decides to spend this on tapes or CDs.

 a Draw the new budget line on your graph from Problem 6.

 b Assuming tapes and CDs are both normal goods, draw another indifference curve on the graph to illustrate the choice of tapes and CDs which maximizes Jane's utility.

 c How much does Jane spend on CDs when she includes her birthday money?

 d What is the substitution and income effect of her birthday money on tapes?

9 Jane now has £70 to spend on tapes and CDs this term. But when she goes shopping, she finds the price of tapes has risen to £10:

 a Write an equation for Jane's new budget line.

 b Draw Jane's new budget line on a graph.

 c Assuming Jane's preferences have not changed, how many CDs does she buy this term?

 d What is Jane's marginal rate of substitution between tapes and CDs at her preferred choice?

10 Study the *Reading Between the Lines* on pp. 186–187 and then;

 a Explain what happens to consumers' marginal rate of substitution between beef and white meat as a result of the BSE beef crisis in November.

 b Describe the effect on consumer choice between beef and white meat of the March 1996 announcement of a link between BSE and its human equivalent.

 c Explain why the price of beef is likely to fall after this announcement.

 d If the price of beef falls and the price of white meat remains the same, why does the amount of beef consumed in the United Kingdom rise?

11 Turn back to pp. 194–195 and read the material on *Economics in History.* Then answer the following questions:

 a What is the role of technology in explaining women's increased participation in the work-force over the past 100 years?

 b Use a diagram similar to Fig. 8.11 to illustrate your answer to part (a) of this question.

 c Gary Becker would argue that the decision to have a baby like the decision to join the work-force, can be modelled by utility maximizing behaviour. According to this model, what benefits and costs do you think parents would take into account in the decision to start a family?

 d On the basis of your experience and the economics you have studied, do you think that family decisions are in any part economic decisions? Explain your answer.

BOX 8.1   TWO THEORIES OF CHOICE

In the marginal utility theory of Chapter 7, the consumer maximizes utility by dividing the available income among different goods and services so that the marginal utility per pound spent on each is equal. In Lisa's case, she maximizes utility by making the marginal utility of a pound spent on cola (MU_c/P_c) equal to the marginal utility of a pound spent on cinema tickets (MU_f/P_f). Her choice of cola and films is given by:

$$\frac{MU_c}{P_c} = \frac{MU_f}{P_f} \qquad (1)$$

In the indifference curve theory of Chapter 8, the best consumption point for our example is chosen by making the marginal rate of substitution between cola and cinema (MRS) equal to their relative price (P_c/P_f). Lisa's choice is given by:

$$MRS = \frac{P_c}{P_f} \qquad (2)$$

In Chapter 8, we learned how to calculate the marginal rate of substitution as the magnitude of the slope of the indifference curve. The marginal rate of substitution is, therefore, the absolute value of the ratio of the change in the quantity of films to the change in the quantity of cola, such that Lisa remains indifferent. 'Indifference' in the indifference curve theory means the same thing as 'constant total utility' in the marginal utility theory. The two situations that derive the same utility are two situations between which Lisa is indifferent. The marginal rate of substitution, therefore, is the absolute value of the ratio of the change in the consumption of films to the change in the consumption of cola, holding total utility constant. But, according to the utility theory, when consumption changes total utility changes. The change in total utility (ΔTU) – where Δ stands for 'change in' – is given by:

$$\Delta TU = MU_c \times \Delta Q_c + MU_f \times \Delta Q_f \qquad (3)$$

If Lisa is indifferent, the change in total utility must be zero. So setting Equation 3 = 0 gives:

$$\Delta TU = MU_c \times \Delta Q_c + MU_f \times \Delta Q_f = 0$$

Taking one half of the terms to the right-hand side gives:

$$MU_f \times \Delta Q_f = -MU_c \times \Delta Q_c \qquad (4)$$

If we divide both sides of Equation 4 by ΔQ_c and MU_f, we get:

$$\frac{\Delta Q_f}{\Delta Q_c} = -\frac{MU_c}{MU_f} \qquad (5)$$

Equation 5 shows the change in films divided by the change in cola, while holding total utility constant or, equivalently, while staying on the same indifference curve. Therefore the absolute value of this ratio is the marginal rate of substitution given by:

$$MRS = \frac{MU_c}{MU_f} \qquad (6)$$

You can now see the connection between the two theories. The utility theory says that Lisa chooses her consumption from:

$$\frac{MU_c}{P_c} = \frac{MU_f}{P_f} \qquad (7)$$

The indifference curve theory says that Lisa chooses her consumption from:

$$MRS = \frac{P_c}{P_f} \qquad (8)$$

Substituting Equation 6 into Equation 8 gives:

$$\frac{MU_c}{MU_f} = \frac{P_c}{P_f} \qquad (9)$$

All that you now have to do is to notice that you can manipulate the marginal utility condition by dividing both sides by MU_f and multiplying both sides by P_c. You end up with Equation 2 – the equation indifference curve theory uses to characterize the consumer's best affordable choice.

Equivalently, you can go the other way and start with the indifference curve equation. Multiply both sides by MU_f and divide both sides by P_c and you arrive at the condition for maximizing utility. Thus the condition for maximizing utility, according to the marginal utility theory, and the condition for choosing the best affordable consumption point, according to the indifference curve theory, are equivalent to each other.

The Market Incentive

Whichever theory we use, how does the market system give someone like Lisa the right signals to make the most efficient choice? Does she need to know where all her indifference curves really are? Let's take a closer look at how Lisa makes her choice. To make things simple, we'll assume that Lisa has been given 3.5 cinema tickets (7 over the last two months) and 3 cola six-packs this month. She can change the amount of cola and films that she has by bartering with her friends.

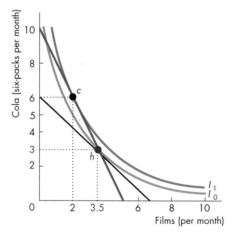

Figure B8.1 shows Lisa is at point h. She maximizes her utility by comparing the relative price of films to cola against her own evaluation of her current consumption at h, her MRS. We'll assume that the barter price is the same ratio as the real market price – a cinema ticket is £6 and a cola six-pack is £3. We know that the ratio of prices is the slope of the budget line. The slope of the budget line is:

$$\frac{\Delta c}{\Delta f} = \frac{10}{5} = \frac{2}{1} = \frac{P_f}{P_c} = \frac{£6}{£3}$$

So 1 film can be traded for 2 cola six-packs and 1 cola six-pack can be traded for 1/2 a film. Lisa's MRS is the absolute slope of her indifference curve at h. Drawing a tangent at h:

$$\frac{\Delta c}{\Delta f} = \frac{6}{6.7} = \frac{0.9}{1}$$

Lisa values 1 film at 0.9 cola six-packs and 1 cola six-pack at 1.1 films. She gives up one film, valued at 0.9 cola six-packs, and some friends offer her 2 cola six-packs in return. She gains 2 cola six-packs worth 2.2 films (2×1.1 films) to her. By giving up 1 film she gets the equivalent of 2.2 films back. Who wouldn't make that exchange?

All Lisa needs to know is the market price and her own feelings about the amount she currently has of cola and films. She will continue to barter along her budget line so long as her MRS < 2, other things being the same. As she swaps more films for cola, her MRS will rise. She stops bartering when the ratio of prices is equal to her MRS. This occurs at point c, when she will have reaped all the possible gains from trade with her friends.

In a barter market, people whose MRS < P_f / P_c create the demand for films, D_f, and people whose MRS > P_f / P_c create the supply of films, S_f. If $D_f > S_f$, P_f / P_c rises. If $D_f < S_f$, P_f / P_c falls. Eventually, individual choice and changing market prices bring the market to an equilibrium.

CHAPTER

9

ORGANIZING PRODUCTION

After studying this chapter you will be able to:

◆ Explain what a firm is and describe the economic problems that all firms face

◆ Define and explain the principal–agent problem

◆ Describe and distinguish between different forms of business organization

◆ Explain how firms raise the funds to finance their operations

◆ Calculate a firm's opportunity cost and economic profit

◆ Explain why firms coordinate some economic activities and markets coordinate others

O N A JULY DAY IN 1977, A TINY NEW FIRM WAS BORN THAT GREW INTO A GIANT – Apple Computer. But that day was not unusual. Every day a new successful firm is born. Apple began its life when two students at Stanford University in the United States produced the world's first commercially successful personal computer in a garage. From that modest start, Apple has grown into one of the world's multinational giants. But most new firms remain small, like family restaurants and corner shops. Although three-quarters of all firms are operated by their owners, as Apple once was, giant corporations now account for the majority of direct investment and trade in Europe. What are the different forms a firm can take? Why do some remain small while others become giants? Why are most firms owner-operated? ◆ Firms spend millions of pounds on buildings and production lines and on developing and marketing new products. How does a firm get the funds needed to pay for all

An Apple a Day

these activities? What do investors expect in return when they put funds into a firm? And how do we measure a firm's economic health? ◆ Most of the components of an IBM personal computer are made by other firms such as Microsoft, which created the operating system. Microsoft has now outgrown IBM, and its products such as DOS and Windows have become household names all over the world. Why doesn't IBM make its own computer components? Why didn't it create its own operating system? Why did it leave these activities to other firms? How do firms decide what to make themselves and what to buy in the marketplace from other firms?

◆ ◆ ◆ ◆ In this chapter, we are going to learn about firms and the choices they make to cope with scarcity. We begin by studying the economic problems and choices that all firms face.

The Firm and its Economic Problem

A **firm** is an institution that hires factors of production and that organizes those factors to produce and sell goods and services. There are 2.8 million firms in the United Kingdom, and they differ enormously in size and in the scope of what they do. Despite this diversity, each firm faces the same fundamental economic problem. How can it get the most out of the scarce resources it has under its control? For the majority of firms, this means making the maximum possible profit. For every firm, whether it is motivated by profit or some other goal, getting the most out of its resources means operating efficiently. A firm is efficient when it produces its output at the lowest possible cost.

In this chapter and in Chapters 10 to 13 we're going to study what decisions a firm must must take to be efficient. We'll see how to predict a firm's behaviour by working out its efficient response to a change in circumstances. Before we start, let's look at the main forms of organizing business which apply throughout Europe and North America.

The Main Types of Firms

The three main types of firms are:

◆ Proprietorship
◆ Partnership
◆ Company

The form of organization influences the management structure of a firm. It determines how factors of production are paid, how much tax its owners pay, who receives its profits and who is liable for its debts if it goes out of business.

Proprietorship A *proprietorship* is a firm with a single owner – the proprietor – who has unlimited liability for the business. *Unlimited liability* is the legal responsibility for all the debts of a firm up to an amount equal to the entire wealth of the owner. If a proprietorship cannot pay its debts, the personal property of the owner can be claimed by those to whom the firm owes money. Corner shops, self-employed computer programmers, window cleaners and many small businesses are all examples of proprietorships.

The proprietor makes the management decisions and is the firm's sole residual claimant. A firm's *residual claimant* is the person who receives the firm's profits and is responsible for its losses. The profits of a proprietorship are part of the income of the owner and are taxed as personal income.

Partnership A *partnership* is a firm with two or more owners who have unlimited liability for the business. Partners must agree on an appropriate management structure and on how to divide the firm's profits among themselves. As in a proprietorship, the profits of a partnership are taxed as the personal income of the owners. But each partner is legally liable for all the debts of the partnership (only limited by the wealth of an individual partner). Liability for the full debts of the partnership is called *joint unlimited liability*. Most solicitors, consultancies and accounting firms are set up as partnerships.

Companies and corporations A **company** is a firm owned by one or more limited liability shareholders. *Limited liability* means the owners have legal liability only for the value of their initial investment. This limitation of liability means that if the company becomes bankrupt, the owners of the company, unlike the owners of a proprietorship or a partnership, cannot be forced to use their personal wealth to pay the company's debts. A large-scale limited liability company is often called a **corporation.**

Some small companies, no bigger than a proprietorship, have just one main owner and are managed in the same way as a proprietorship. Larger corporations have elaborate management structures headed by a board of directors, executive officers and senior managers responsible for such areas as production, finance, marketing and research. These senior managers are in turn served by a series of specialist managers. Each layer in the management structure knows enough about what happens in the layer below it to exercise control, but the entire management consists of specialists who concentrate on a narrow aspect of the corporation's activities.

Large corporations are organized in one of two ways:

◆ Unitary divisional form (U-form)
◆ Multi-divisional form (M-form)

In the U-form system, the directors appoint managers to run separate divisions specializing in a function of business organization – finance, production and marketing, for example. Each division will deal with all the goods and services the company produces. In the M-form system, the corporation is split into a series of miniature U-form companies.

Figure 9.1 compares the U-form with the M-form structure for a motor vehicle corporation such as Ford (UK). Each vehicle type is allocated to a separate division, serviced by its own U-form structure underneath. There is also a separate executive office to develop general strategy and overall finance.

FIGURE 9.1

Corporate Structure

(a) The U-form Corporation

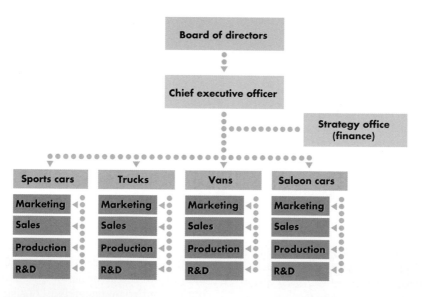

(b) The M-form Corporation

Large companies can be set up in a unitary divisional (U-form) structure or in a multi-divisional (M-form) structure. The functional divisions work on all the different goods and services produced by the firm in a U-form structure. In an M-form structure, each good (or service) produced is allocated to a division and is serviced by a miniature U-form company beneath it. Only the main project finance and strategy function is common to all divisions.

The M-form structure is now the most common structure for large, complex corporations. The growth of multinational corporations (MNCs) or transnational corporations (TNCs) in the 1960s in particular promoted this form of organization. In a TNC, production in each country is allocated to a separate division as in Ford (US) and Ford (UK). The divisions are free to trade and compete with each other and with other firms. There are approximately 38,000 TNCs trading throughout the world, most of which are based in Europe, the United States and Japan. Although TNCs represent only a small proportion of the total number of firms, they generate the majority of international trade and investment.

A company receives its financial resources from its owners – the shareholders – and by borrowing. A *share* is a certificate of ownership. When you see the letters plc (public limited company) after a company name in the United Kingdom, it means the company can raise funds by selling its shares in stock markets like the London Stock Exchange. When you see the abbreviation Ltd (private limited company) after a company name, it means that the shares can only be sold privately. Companies sometimes borrow from banks, but they can also borrow directly from households by issuing bonds – loans on which they pay a fixed amount of interest.

If a company makes a profit, the residual claimants to that profit are the shareholders who receive dividends. If a company becomes bankrupt, the residual loss is absorbed by the banks and the company's other creditors. The shareholders are responsible for the company's debt only up to the value of their initial investment – that's the purpose of limited liability.

Company profits are taxed in addition to the incomes of its shareholders – so corporate profits are taxed twice. After a company has paid tax on its profits, the shareholders themselves pay taxes on the income they receive as dividends on shares and bonds. They also pay tax on capital gains when they sell a share (or bond). A **capital gain** is the income received by selling a share (or a bond) for a higher price than the price paid for it. Company shares generate capital gains when a company retains some of its profit and reinvests it in profitable activities instead of paying dividends. So even retained earnings are effectively taxed twice.

The Relative Importance of Different Sizes of Firms

The total number of businesses in the United Kingdom increased from 1.9 million to 2.8 million between 1979 and 1993. This was largely owing to an increase in the number of one-person and two-person businesses – many of them family businesses. Over 50 per cent of employees in the private sector are employed in small businesses with fewer than 100 employees. The majority of single proprietorships and partnerships are small firms of this type.

Figure 9.2(a) shows the proportion of employment in small firms in 1991 in different sectors of the UK economy. The majority of employment in the services, construction and agriculture sectors is in small firms – mainly single proprietorships and partnerships. By contrast, limited companies are the main employers in the manufacturing sector. The majority are medium sized – employing between 100 and 150 people – and the minority are large – employing more than 150 people. Part (b) shows the importance of firms of different sizes in the UK manufacturing sector. Small firms have become increasingly more important in manufacturing since 1973. Medium-sized firms represent the dominant group, accounting for over 45 per cent of manufacturing employment in 1993. Large corporations are becoming less important in manufacturing.

Now we know which types of firms are operating, let's look at their goals and how they differ.

It is easy to think that all firms aim to be efficient and maximize profits. Although firms strive to be efficient, they operate in a hostile environment and two pervasive facts of life make the profit maximizing decision difficult. They are:

◆ Uncertainty about the future

◆ Incomplete information

Uncertainty About the Future

Management is about planning and strategic thinking. This means making decisions today about what to do tomorrow. Even if managers base every decision on the presumption that it will make the maximum possible contribution to the firm's profits – expectations often turn out to be wrong. The main reason is that a firm must commit itself to a project and spend huge amounts on it *before* it

FIGURE 9.2

Relative Importance of Firms by Size ◆

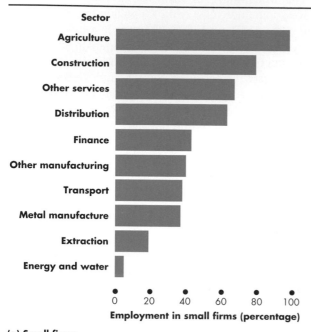

(a) Small firms

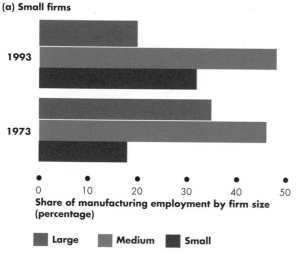

(b) Share of firms

Small firms employing fewer than 100 employees dominate the service, construction and agriculture sectors as shown in part (a). Medium-sized firms – employing between 100 and 150 people – and large firms – employing more than 150 people – dominate the manufacturing sector. Part (b) shows that small firms are also becoming increasingly important in manufacturing over time at the expense of large firms.

Source: *Competitiveness, Forging Ahead*, 1995, House of Commons Papers, Cmnd 2867, London, HMSO.

knows whether it will be able to sell enough output at a high enough price to cover its outlays. For example, 30 years ago French and British aircraft makers spent several years and millions of pounds building a supersonic transatlantic passenger plane – the Concorde. They expected to be able to sell enough of these technologically sophisticated aircraft to recover their costs. It turned out that too few people valued the Concorde's extra speed for it to generate sales revenues equal to its cost. On a smaller scale, millions of people try their luck at opening coffee shops and other small businesses by estimating future demand and costs. If they need to borrow the initial capital, lenders will scrutinize their business plans and forecasts carefully. However, many of them turn out to be too optimistic – revenue falls short of the cost – and the business fails.

The fact that uncertainty exists has led to the development of many ingenious devices for limiting and spreading risk, including different types of corporate structures. We'll look at some of these later in this chapter and in more detail in Chapter 17.

Incomplete Information

The future is not the only unknown. Firms have limited information even about the past and present. It is simply not possible for a firm's owners and managers to know everything that is relevant to the efficient operation of their business. Firms do not know all the possible suppliers of inputs and all the available prices. In particular, firms do not always know the productivity of their employees. What did Cedric Brown, the former chief executive officer (CEO), really do for British Gas? Did his actions warrant raising his pay package to £492,602 in 1994 – a 71 per cent rise? These questions cannot be answered with certainty, even long after the event. Yet companies like British Gas must put CEOs in charge of operations and give them *incentives* to succeed, even when the contribution they make cannot be measured directly.

Similarly, some workers are more productive than others and it is often difficult for managers to know who is productive and who is not. Did sales fall last month because the sales-force took things easy or because of a general fall in demand for the product? Again, firms must devise incentives to motivate their sales-force.

A rich variety of institutions, contractual relationships and compensation schemes have been devised in business organizations to raise efficiency and avoid the problems of limited information. Let's look at this problem in more detail.

The Principal–Agent Problem

Because of uncertainty and incomplete information, firms do not simply demand factors of production and pay for them as if they were buying toothpaste in a supermarket. Instead, they enter into contracts and devise compensation packages that strengthen the incentives to raise productivity and spread risks. These contracts and compensation packages are called agency relationships and they are an attempt to solve what is called the principal–agent problem. The **principal–agent problem** in a firm is to devise compensation rules that induce an agent to act in the best interest of a principal. For example, the relationship between the shareholders of British Gas and its managers is an agency relationship. The shareholders (the principals) want the managers (agents) to act in the shareholders' best interest. Another example of an agency relationship is that between Microsoft Corporation (a principal) and its programmers working on the next version of Windows (agents). Microsoft wants the programmers to work in the best interest of the firm.

We have already seen that some forms of business organization are complex. There is a long chain of interests in large companies from the shareholders, through the board of directors, to divisional and functional managers, and through to production workers. This generates two principal–agent problems.

First, the owners of modern large companies have become separated from the managers who control decision making. The *separation of ownership from control* is a problem if managers pursue different goals from shareholders. For example, the goal of a shareholder (a principal) is to maximize the firm's profit. But the firm's profit depends on the actions of its managers (agents), who may have their own goals.

Second, it is more difficult for managers (principals) to monitor their work-force (agents) closely in complex organizations. This monitoring and motivation problem raises costs and reduces profits.

Why might managers and employees have different goals from shareholders? Is there any reason to believe that managers do not seek efficiency and profit maximization? We can use our model of utility maximization to explain this. If managers are rational utility maximizers, their utility will increase as they get more power, prestige and pay. The best way to increase utility is to maximize sales or the size of the division that they run because power, prestige and pay tend to increase with sales and division size. If managers divert some of the profits into expanding their division and increasing their pay, less profit will be available to shareholders.

Workers are also rational utility maximizers, but their utility falls as they do more work for a given weekly wage. So workers (agents) might do less work if they are not closely monitored by their managers (principals). Business organizations have devised a number of innovative schemes to reduce the principal–agent problem, thus increasing efficiency. Let's look at these more closely.

Coping with the Principal–Agent Problem

The perfect incentive scheme does not exist. Agents, whether they are managers or workers, can pursue their own goals and often impose costs on a principal. The principal–agent problem cannot be solved just by giving orders and having them obeyed. In most firms, it isn't possible for the shareholders to monitor the managers, or even for the managers to monitor the workers. To achieve their goal, the firm's owners (principals) must find a way to induce the managers (agents) to pursue the maximum possible profit, and the managers (principals) must induce the workers (agents) to work efficiently. Each principal does this by creating incentives to persuade each agent to work in the interests of the principal. The four main ways of coping with the principal–agent problem are:

◆ Ownership
◆ Incentive pay
◆ Long-term contracts
◆ Internal restructuring

Ownership Giving a manager or worker ownership (or part-ownership) of a business is a way of improving job performance and increasing a firm's profits. The manager (agent) becomes more like the owner (principal) and profit maximization will become a more important management goal. Part-ownership schemes for senior managers are quite common, but they are less common for workers – only 100 such schemes exist in the United Kingdom. The two largest UK employee share ownership schemes are run by Baxi Partnership Ltd, which makes heating systems, and Tullis Russell Group, which makes paper. Both companies belonged to the same family firm, which decided to distribute over 50 per cent of the shares to employees to raise motivation and profitability.

Incentive pay   Incentive pay schemes are very common. Most middle managers are assessed annually against a wide variety of performance criteria. If they work on a performance related pay scheme, their pay increments will be based on their performance in the previous year. In addition, many companies reward managers and workers by offering separate bonuses for meeting production or sales targets. These types of incentive pay schemes help to focus the goals of all employees on profit maximization, reducing the principal–agent problem.

Long-term contracts   Long-term contracts are another way of coping with the principal–agent problem because they tie the long-term fortunes of managers and workers (agents) to the success of the principal(s) – the owner(s) of the firm.

Internal restructuring   Monitoring and motivating your work-force is easier in a small organization where the owner is also the manager and knows all the staff personally. In a large company, the flow of information can be slow and misleading. The U-form structure is useful because its functional form generates savings from staff specialization. The CEO can hire specialist accountants, marketing staff and engineers, who spread their specialist knowledge across all the products. But there comes a point when the CEO can no longer tell which product is doing well and which should be discontinued. Each divisional manager is recommending a strategy to protect his or her own division.

A major benefit of the M-form structure is the separate strategy office whose staff can look dispassionately at the information on divisions. Divisional managers are made to compete for project bids to raise profits and division managers are moved from division to division to reduce empire building. This form of restructuring reduces the costs of monitoring and increases manager motivation to maximize profits. Another form of

restructuring is to allocate projects to teams that can compete across divisions. Ford have used new communications technology to introduce team work systems that not only span national boundaries but also car model types, as well as divisions.

Part of the reason why incentive schemes and restructuring raise efficiency lies in the difference between principals and agents in their attitude to risk. In general, principals (shareholders) are less risk averse than agents (employees). Shareholders can spread the risk of poor performance by employees by holding many shares in many firms. Employees are more risk averse about a low future income because they have one main source of income – their salary. In an uncertain environment with poor information, incentive schemes and restructuring pool these risks and raise efficiency. For example, incentive schemes raise profitability but expose more risk averse employees to greater variability of future income. An employee may work much harder but fail to get a pay increase if output does not rise. Output is affected by many things which employees cannot control – market demand, the efforts of colleagues and local suppliers. So to be efficient, an incentive scheme must balance the cost of exposing the agent to higher risk against the benefit of reducing risk for the principal. We'll look at risk again in more detail in Chapter 17.

The principal–agent problem seems to be mainly a problem of larger firms. So why isn't all production organized by single proprietors and partnerships? The answer lies in the balance of the benefits of size against the costs of monitoring and control.

The Pros and Cons of the Different Types of Firms

Why do large companies dominate trade? Why do the other types of businesses survive? Why are proprietorships and partnerships more prominent in some sectors? The answer to these questions lies in the pros and cons of the different types of business organizations that are summarized in Table 9.1. Each firm type has its disadvantages, which explains why it has not driven out the other two. Companies dominate because most businesses use a large amount of capital. Proprietorships and partnerships operate where flexibility in decision making is critical.

TABLE 9.1

The Pros and Cons of Different Types of Firms

Type of firm	Pros	Cons
Proprietorship	◆ Easy to set up ◆ Simple decision making ◆ Profits taxed only once as owner's income	◆ Bad decisions not checked by need for consensus ◆ Owner's entire wealth at risk ◆ Firm dies with owner ◆ Capital is expensive ◆ Labour is expensive
Partnership	◆ Easy to set up ◆ Diversified decision making ◆ Can survive withdrawal of partner ◆ Profits taxed only once as owners' incomes	◆ Achieving consensus may be slow and expensive ◆ Owners' entire wealth at risk ◆ Withdrawal of partner may create capital shortage ◆ Capital is expensive
Corporation	◆ Owners have limited liability ◆ Large-scale, low-cost capital available ◆ Professional management not restricted by ability of owners ◆ Perpetual life ◆ Long-term labour contracts cut labour costs	◆ Complex management structure can make decisions slow and expensive ◆ Profits taxed twice as company profit and as shareholders' income

---

REVIEW

◆ A firm is an institution that hires factors of production and organizes the production and sale of goods and services.

◆ Firms strive to be efficient and most firms aim to maximize profit, but they face uncertainty and have incomplete information. To cope with these problems, firms enter into relationships – agency relationships – with owners, managers, workers and other firms and devise efficient legal structures and compensation schemes.

◆ Each main type of firm – proprietorship, partnership and company – has its advantages and disadvantages, and each plays a role in every sector of the economy.

Business Finance

Every year firms raise billions of pounds to enable them to buy capital equipment and to finance their stocks of goods. For example, an airline may raise hundreds of millions of pounds to buy a bigger fleet of jets. A steel manufacturer may raise hundreds of millions of pounds to build a new plant. A software producer may raise millions of pounds to pay programmers to develop a new computer game. Let's see how firms raise funds.

How Firms Raise Funds

All firms get some of their funds from their owners. The owner's stake in a business is called **equity**. Firms also borrow some of the funds they need from banks. Proprietorships and partnerships raise additional funds by borrowing from friends. The more permanent structure of companies gives them two ways of raising large amounts of money that are not generally available to households and proprietorships and partnerships. They are:

◆ Selling shares
◆ Selling bonds

Selling Shares

One major way in which a company can raise funds is by selling shares. A **share** is a long term debt certificate issued by a company, which can never be repaid. Funds raised in this way are the company's *equity* because the shareholders of a company are its owners. They have bought shares of the company's stock. PLCs can sell new issues of their shares and current owners can sell their existing shares on the stock exchange. A *stock exchange* is an organized market for trading in shares. There are stock markets in many major European cities, and the London Stock Exchange is one of the biggest stock exchanges in the world.

Figure 9.3 shows an example of a firm raising funds by selling stock. In June 1996, Monument Oil

and Gas (Holdings) PLC, a gas and oil exploration company, announced the issue of 800 million shares at 25 pence a share to raise £200 million. There is no obligation for a firm to make dividend payments to its shareholders just because it raises funds by selling stock. But shareholders expect a dividend or a capital gain – otherwise no one will buy the shares.

Selling Bonds

A **bond** is a legally enforceable debt obligation to pay specified amounts of money at specified future dates. Usually a bond specifies that a certain amount of money called the *redemption value* of the bond will be paid at a certain future date called the *maturity date*. In addition, another amount will be paid each year between the date of sale of the bond and the maturity date. The amount of money paid each year is called the *dividend payment*.

An example of bond financing is shown in Fig. 9.4. The Halifax Building Society announced the issue of £200 million of bonds (called subordinated variable rate notes) in June 1996. The bonds mature over a period of 12 years and carried an interest rate of 6.275 per cent for the three-month period ending on 27 September, 1996.

FIGURE 9.3

Selling Shares

MONUMENT OIL AND GAS (HOLDINGS) PLC

(Incorporated in England and Wales under the Companies Act 1985 with registration no. 3211318)

Introduction
of up to
800,000,000 Ordinary Shares of 25 pence each
and
admission to listing on the
London Stock Exchange

Share capital following the introduction

Authorised			Issued and fully paid	
Nominal Value	Number		Nominal Value	Number
£200,000,000	800,000,000	Ordinary Shares of 25 pence each	£167,018,021	668,072,083

(Assuming no elections under the mix and match provisions of the Scheme of Arrangement)

Monument's principal business is in the exploration for
and production of oil and gas.

Monument Oil and Gas (Holding) PLC	NatWest Wood Mackenzie & Co. Limited
80 Petty France	135 Bishopsgate
London SW1H 9EX June 25, 1996	London EC2M 3XT

A share in a company entitles its holder to vote at share-holders' meetings, to participate in the election of directors and to a dividend (if the directors vote to pay one). Monument Oil and Gas (Holdings) PLC, an oil and gas exploration company, announced the issue of 800 million shares at 25 pence each, to raise £200 million of additional funds.

FIGURE 9.4

Selling Bonds

Halifax Building Society

(Incorporated in England under the Building Societies Act 1986)

Issue of up to an aggregate of
£200,000,000
Subordinated Variable Rate Notes
with a maturity of 12 years

(Formerly Subordinated Variable Rate Notes issued by
Leeds Permanent Building Society)

Notice is hereby given that the three months interest period from June 27, 1996 to September 27, 1996 (92 days) the Subordinated Notes will carry an interest rate of 6.275%. The interest payable on September 27, 1996 for the Subordinated Notes will be £157.73.

By: The Chase Manhattan Bank, N.A.
London, Principal Paying Agent   CHASE
July 1, 1996

A bond is an obligation to make a stated dividend payment and a redemption payment on a given date. The Halifax Building Society announced an issue of 12-year bonds to raise £200 million. It promised to pay an interest rate of 6.275 per cent for the three-month period ending on 27 September, 1996.

When it makes a financing decision, a firm tries to minimize its cost of funds. If it can raise funds by selling bonds at a lower cost than from any other source, that is the method of financing it chooses. But how does it decide how much to borrow? To answer this question, we need to understand a key principle of business and personal finance.

Discounting and Present Value

When a firm raises funds, it receives money in the current period and takes on an obligation to make a series of payments in *future* periods. But a firm also raises funds, because it plans to use them to generate a future net inflow of cash from its business operations.

To decide whether to borrow and how much to borrow, a firm must somehow compare money today with money in the future. If you are given a choice between a pound today and a pound a year from today, you will choose a pound today. A pound today is worth more to you than a pound in the future because you can invest today's pound to earn interest. The same is true for a firm. To compare an amount of money in the future with an amount of money in the present, we calculate the present value of the future amount of money. The **present value** of a future amount of money is the amount which, if invested today, will grow to be as large as that future amount, taking into account the interest that it will earn. Let's express this idea with an equation:

Future amount = Present value + Interest income

But the interest income is equal to the present value multiplied by the interest rate, r, so

Future amount = Present value + ($r \times$ Present value)

or,

Future amount = Present value $\times (1 + r)$

If you have £100 today and the interest rate is 10 per cent a year ($r = 0.1$), one year from today you will have £110, the original £100 plus £10 interest. Check that the above formula delivers that answer: £100 $\times$ 1.1 = £110.

The formula that we have just used calculates a future amount from the present value and an interest rate. To calculate the present value, we just work backwards. Instead of multiplying the present value by $(1 + r)$, we divide the future amount by $(1 + r)$. That is,

$$\text{Present value} = \frac{\text{Future amount}}{(1 + r)}$$

You can use this formula to calculate present value. Calculating present value is called discounting. **Discounting** is the conversion of a future amount of money to its present value. Let's check that we can use the present value formula by calculating the present value of £110 one year from now when the interest rate is 10 per cent a year. You'll be able to guess that the answer is £100 because we just calculated that £100 invested today at 10 per cent a year becomes £110 in one year. Thus it follows immediately that the present value of £110 in one year's time is £100. But let's use the formula. Putting the numbers into the above formula we have

$$\begin{aligned}
\text{Present value} \quad &= \frac{£110}{(1 + 0.1)} \\
&= \frac{£110}{(1.1)} \\
&= £100
\end{aligned}$$

Calculating the present value of an amount of money one year from now is the easiest case. But we can also calculate the present value of an amount any number of years in the future. As an example, let's see how we calculate the present value of an amount of money available two years from now.

Suppose that you invest £100 today for two years at an interest rate of 10 per cent a year. The money will earn £10 in the first year, which means that by the end of the first year you will have £110. If the interest of £10 is invested, then the interest earned in the second year will be a further £10 on the original £100 plus £1 on the £10 interest. Thus the total interest earned in the second year will be £11. The total interest earned overall will be £21 (£10 in the first year and £11 in the second year). After two years, you will have £121. From the definition of present value, you can see that the present value of £121 two years hence is £100. That is, £100 is the present amount which, if invested at 10 per cent interest, will grow to £121 two years from now.

To calculate the present value of an amount of money two years in the future we use the formula

$$\text{Present value} = \frac{\text{Amount of money in future}}{(1 + r)^2}$$

Let's check that the formula works by calculating

the present value of £121 two years in the future when the interest rate is 10 per cent a year. Putting these numbers into the formula gives

$$\text{Present value} \ = \frac{£121}{(1+0.1)^2}$$

$$= \frac{£121}{(1.1)^2}$$

$$= \frac{£121}{1.21}$$

$$= £100$$

We can calculate the present value of an amount of money any number of years in the future by using a formula based on the two that we've already used. The general formula is

$$\text{Present value} = \frac{\text{Money available } n \text{ years in future}}{(1+r)^n}$$

For example, if the interest rate is 10 per cent a year, £100 to be received 10 years from now has a present value of £38.55. That is, if £38.55 is invested today at an interest rate of 10 per cent, it will accumulate to £100 in 10 years. (You might check this calculation on your pocket calculator.)

Present Value and Marginal Analysis

Firms use the concept of present value to make their financing decisions. But they use it together with another fundamental principle, marginal analysis. In making any decision, only the additional benefit – *marginal benefit* – and additional cost – *marginal cost* – resulting from that decision are relevant. By evaluating the marginal benefit and marginal cost of borrowing, a firm is able to maximize its profit. Marginal benefit minus marginal cost is net benefit, and the present value of net benefit is called *net* present value.

The firm decides how much to borrow by calculating the net present value of borrowing one additional pound – the marginal pound borrowed. If the present value of the marginal pound borrowed is positive, then the firm increases its profit by increasing the amount it borrows. If the present value of the marginal pound borrowed is negative, then the firm increases its profit by *decreasing* its borrowing. When the present value of the marginal pound borrowed is zero, then the firm is maximizing its profit.

◆ Firms finance capital equipment purchases by selling bonds – promises of a fixed income independent of the firm's profit – and selling shares – opportunities to share in the firm's profit.

◆ Firms borrow if doing so increases the net present value of their cash flow.

We've seen how firms pursue maximum profits by establishing appropriate types of business organizations and by raising funds in the most profitable way. But how do firms measure their performance? How do they calculate their costs and profits? These are the questions we now study.

Opportunity Cost and Economic Profit

A firm's *opportunity cost* of producing a good is the best alternative action that the firm forgoes to produce it. Equivalently, it is the firm's best alternative use for the factors of production it employs to produce a good. Opportunity cost is a real alternative forgone. But so that we can compare the opportunity cost of one action with that of another action, we often express opportunity cost in units of money. Even though we sometimes express opportunity cost in money units, it is the real alternative forgone and not the money value of that alternative.

A firm's opportunity cost of production has two components:

1. Explicit costs
2. Implicit costs

Explicit costs are paid directly in money – *money costs*. Implicit costs (measured in units of money) are opportunities forgone but not paid for directly in money. It is easy to measure explicit costs but harder to measure implicit costs.

A firm incurs explicit costs when it pays for a factor of production at the same time as it uses it. The money cost is the amount paid for the factor of production, but this same amount could have been spent on something else, so it is also the opportunity cost (expressed in pounds) of using this factor of production. For example, if a pizza restaurant hires a waiter, the wages paid are both the money cost and the opportunity cost of hiring the waiter – the firm pays the waiter at the same time as it uses the services of the waiter. Labour is the factor of production whose money cost typically equals its opportunity cost.

A firm incurs implicit costs when it uses the following factors of production:

◆ Capital
◆ Stocks
◆ Owner's resources

Cost of Capital

The cost of using capital equipment is an implicit cost because a firm usually buys its equipment – lays out some money – and then uses the equipment over a future period. For example, Ford (UK) buys an assembly line, pays for it this year and uses it for several years. What is the opportunity cost of using capital equipment bought several years earlier? This opportunity cost has two components:

◆ Depreciation
◆ Interest

Depreciation **Economic depreciation** is the change in the market price of a capital asset over a given period. It is calculated as the market price of the capital at the beginning of the period minus its market price at the end of the period. For example, suppose that British Airways has a Boeing 747 jumbo jet that it could have sold on 31 December, 1994 for £5 million. Suppose also that it could sell the same aircraft on 31 December 1995 for £4 million. The £1 million fall in the market value is an implicit cost of using the aircraft during 1995. Notice that the original cost of the aircraft is not directly relevant to this calculation.

Economic depreciation occurs for a variety of reasons. The most common is that an older piece of equipment has a shorter future life, and it is often more costly to maintain in good working order. But economic depreciation also occurs simply because a piece of equipment has become obsolete. It still works well and might do so for many years, but there is something new that works even better. For

example, suppose your university library bought some new photocopiers on 1 January 1996 which it expected to operate for three years. Then, during 1996, a faster photocopier became available and the market price of the slower copiers fell by 90 per cent. This 90 per cent price fall is the opportunity cost of using the photocopiers in 1996. Even though the copiers are new and still work well, their economic depreciation – and opportunity cost – during 1996 is large.

Sunk Cost A **sunk cost** is the *past economic depreciation* of a capital asset (building, plant, or equipment). When the asset was purchased, an opportunity was forgone. But that past forgone opportunity is a bygone. The opportunity cannot be retrieved. Sunk cost is not an *opportunity cost*. In the photocopier example, your university library incurred a high opportunity cost during 1996 when the market price of its slow copiers fell. But as the library's planners look forward to 1997, the fall in the value of its photocopiers in 1996 is a sunk cost. The opportunity cost of using the copiers during 1997 does *not* include that fall in value.

Accounting Depreciation Accountants measure depreciation, but they no not usually measure *economic depreciation*. Instead, they assess this fall in the value of a capital asset by applying a conventional depreciation rate to the original purchase price. The conventions used are based on standardized accounting schedules. For buildings, a conventional depreciation period is 20 years. Thus if a firm buys a new office building for £100,000, its accounts show one-twentieth of that amount, £5,000, as a cost of production each year. At the end of the first year, the firm's accounts record the value of the building as £95,000 (the original cost minus the £5,000 depreciation). Different depreciation rates are used for different types of capital. For example, for cars and computers, the conventional depreciation period is three years.

These accounting measures of depreciation do not measure economic depreciation and are not a correct measure of the depreciation component of the opportunity cost of using capital.

Interest The funds used to buy a capital asset could have been used for some other purpose. In their next best alternative use, they would have yielded a return – an interest income. This forgone interest is part of the opportunity cost of using the capital asset. And it is an opportunity cost regardless of whether a firm borrows the funds it uses to buy its capital (its buildings, plant and equipment). To see why, think about two cases: the firm borrows or uses its previous earnings.

If a firm borrows the money, then it makes an explicit interest payment, so the interest cost is an explicit cost. If the firm uses its own funds, then the opportunity cost is the amount that could have been earned by allocating those funds to their best alternative use. Suppose the best alternative is for the firm to put the money in a bank deposit. The bank deposit interest forgone is the opportunity cost of buying and using the capital asset.

Implicit Rental Rate   To measure the opportunity cost of using capital (buildings, plant and equipment), we calculate the sum of economic depreciation and interest costs. This opportunity cost is the income that the firm forgoes by using the assets itself and not renting them to another firm instead. The firm actually rents the assets to itself. When a firm rents assets to itself, it pays an **implicit rental rate** for their use.

People commonly rent houses, flats, cars, televisions, VCRs and videotapes. Firms commonly rent photocopiers, earth-moving equipment, satellite launching services, and so on. If a piece of equipment is rented, a pound payment called an *explicit* rental rate is made. If a piece of equipment is bought and used by its owner rather than rented to someone else, an *implicit* rental rate is paid. The owner–user of a piece of equipment could have rented the equipment to someone else instead. The income forgone is the opportunity cost of using the equipment. That opportunity cost is the implicit rental rate.

In the absence of transactions costs, explicit rental rates and implicit rental rates are equal. This equality is brought about by market forces. If renting had a lower opportunity cost than buying, everyone would want to rent and no one would want to buy. So renters would not be able to find anyone to rent from and the (explicit) rental rate would rise. If renting had a higher opportunity cost than buying, everyone would want to buy and no one would want to rent. So owners would not be able to find anyone to rent to and the (explicit) rental rate would fall. Only when the opportunity

cost of renting and buying are equal – when the explicit rental rate and the implicit rental rate are equal – can renters and owners find enough people to do business.

Cost of Stocks

The opportunity cost of using an item from stocks is its current replacement cost. If an item is taken out of stocks, it will have to be replaced by a new item. The cost of that new item is the opportunity cost of using the item taken from stocks.

Stocks are stores of raw materials, semi-finished goods and finished goods held by firms. Some firms carry small stocks and some have stocks that turn over quickly. In such cases, the money cost of using an item from stocks and its opportunity cost are the same. When a production process requires stocks to be held for a long time, the two costs might differ.

To measure the cost of using stocks, accountants frequently use a money cost method called FIFO, which stands for 'First In, First Out'. This method of calculating the cost of an item taken from stocks assumes that the first item placed into stocks is the first one taken out. An alternative accountant's measure is called LIFO, which stands for 'Last In, First Out'. The opportunity cost of an item taken from stocks is the cost of replacing it. If prices are constant over long periods of time, FIFO and LIFO measure opportunity cost. But if prices are changing, FIFO is not a measure of opportunity cost, although LIFO is a good approximation to it if the price most recently paid is similar to the price paid to replace the used item.

Cost of Owner's Resources

The owner of a firm often puts a great deal of time and effort into organizing the firm. But the owner could have worked at some other activity and earned a wage. The opportunity cost of the owner's time spent working for the firm is the wage income forgone by not working in the best alternative job.

In addition to supplying labour to the firm, its owner also supplies *entrepreneurial ability* – the factor of production that organizes the business, makes business decisions, innovates and bears the risk of running the business. These activities would not be undertaken without the expectation of a return. The expected return for supplying entrepreneurial ability is called **normal profit.** Normal profit is part of a firm's opportunity cost because it is the cost of a forgone alternative. The forgone alternative is running another firm.

Usually, the owner of a firm withdraws cash from the business to meet living expenses. Accountants regard such withdrawals of cash as part of the owner's profit from the business, rather than as part of the opportunity cost of the owner's time and entrepreneurial ability. But to the extent that they compensate for wages forgone and risk, they are part of the firm's opportunity cost.

Economic Profit

What is the bottom line – the profit or loss of the firm? A firm's **economic profit** is equal to its total revenue minus its opportunity cost. Its opportunity cost is the explicit and implicit cost of the best alternative actions forgone, including normal profit.

Economic profit is not the same as what accountants call profit. For the accountant, a firm's profit is equal to its total revenue minus its money cost and its conventional depreciation.

An Example

To help you get a clearer picture of the concepts of a firm's opportunity cost, normal profit, and economic profit, we'll look at a concrete example. And we'll contrast the economic concepts of cost and profit with the accounting concepts.

Mike owns Mike's Bikes – a shop that sells bikes. His revenue, cost and profit appear in Table 9.2. The accountant's cost calculations are on the left side and the economist's opportunity cost calculations are on the right.

Mike sold £300,000 worth of bikes during the year. This amount appears as his total revenue. The wholesale cost of bikes was £150,000, he bought

---

TABLE 9.2

Mike's Mountain Bikes, Revenue, Cost and Profit Statement

The accountant			The economist		
Item	**Amount**		**Item**	**Amount**	
Total revenue	£300,000		Total revenue	£300,000	
Costs:			Costs:		
Wholesale cost of bikes	150,000		Wholesale cost of bikes	150,000	
Utilities and other services	20,000		Utilities and other services	20,000	
Wages	50,000		Wages	50,000	
Depreciation	22,000		Fall in market value of assets[1]	10,000	
			Mike's wages (implicit)[2]	40,000	
Bank interest	12,000		Bank interest	12,000	
			Interest on Mike's money invested in firm (implicit)[3]	11,500	
			Normal profit (implicit)[4]	6,000	
Total cost	£254,000		Opportunity cost	£299,500	
Profit	£46,000		Economic profit	£500	

Notes

[1] The fall in the market value of the assets of the firm gives the opportunity cost of not selling them one year ago. That is part of the opportunity cost of using them for the year.

[2] Mike could have worked elsewhere for £40 an hour, but he worked 1,000 hours on the firm's business, which means that the opportunity cost of his time is £40,000.

[3] Mike has invested £115,000 in the firm. If the current interest rate is 10 per cent a year, the opportunity cost of those funds is £11,500.

[4] Mike could avoid the risk of running his own business and he would be unwilling to take on the risk for a return of less than £6,000. This is his *normal profit*. (The magnitude of normal profit is assumed.)

$20,000 worth of utilities and other services, and paid out $50,000 in wages to his mechanic and sales assistant. Mike also paid $12,000 in interest to the bank. All of the items just mentioned appear in both the accountant's statement and the economist's statement. The remaining items differ between the two statements and some notes at the foot of the table explain the differences.

The accountant's depreciation calculation is based on conventional life assumptions for Mike's capital. The economist calculates the cost of Mike's time, funds invested in the firm and risk-bearing, and also calculates economic depreciation. The accountant says Mike's costs are $254,000 and his profit is $46,000. In contrast, the economist says that Mike's year in business had an opportunity cost of $299,500 and yielded an economic profit of $500.

The accountant's calculation of Mike's profit does not tell Mike his economic profit because it omits some components of opportunity cost and measures others incorrectly. The economist's measure of economic profit tells Mike how his business is doing compared with what he can normally except. Any positive economic profit is good news for Mike because his normal profit – the normal return to his entrepreneurial ability – is part of the opportunity cost of running his business. *Reading Between the Lines* on pp 220–221 explores an example of the difference between economic and accounting cost.

R E V I E W

◆ A firm's economic profit is equal to its total revenue minus its opportunity cost of production.

◆ Opportunity cost differs from money cost. Money cost measures cost as the money spent to hire inputs. Opportunity cost measures cost as the value of the best alternative forgone.

◆ The main differences between money cost and opportunity cost arise from the cost of capital and stocks and the cost of the resources supplied directly by the owner. Normal profit is part of opportunity cost.

We are interested in measuring the opportunity cost of production, not for its own sake, but so that we can compare the efficiency of alternative methods of production. What do we mean by efficiency?

Economic Efficiency

How does a firm choose among alternative methods of production? What is the most efficient way of producing? There are two concepts of efficiency: technological efficiency and economic efficiency. **Technological efficiency** occurs when it is not possible to increase output without increasing inputs. **Economic efficiency** occurs when the cost of producing a given output is as low as possible.

Technological efficiency is an engineering matter. Given what is technologically feasible, something can or cannot be done. Economic efficiency depends on the prices of the factors of production. Something that is technologically efficient may not be economically efficient. But something that is economically efficient is always technologically efficient. Let's study technological efficiency and economic efficiency by looking at an example.

Suppose that there are four methods of making TV sets:

a *Robot production.* One person monitors the entire computer-driven process.

b *Production line.* Workers specialize in a small part of the job as the emerging TV set passes them on a production line.

c *Human production.* Workers specialize in a small part of the job but walk from bench to bench to perform their tasks.

d *Hand-tool production.* A single worker uses a few hand tools to make a TV set.

Table 9.3 sets out the amount of labour and capital required to make 10 TV sets a day by each of

---

TABLE 9.3

Four Ways of Making 10 TV Sets a Day

Method		Quantities of inputs	
		Labour	Capital
a	Robot production	1	1,000
b	Production line	10	10
c	Human production	100	10
d	Hand-tool production	1,000	1

these four methods. Are all of these alternative methods technologically efficient? By inspecting the numbers in the table you will be able to see that method c is not technologically efficient. It requires 100 workers and 10 units of capital to produce 10 TV sets. Those same 10 TV sets can be produced by method b with 10 workers and the same 10 units of capital. Therefore method c is not technologically efficient.

Are any of the other methods not technologically efficient? The answer is no: each of the other three methods is technologically efficient. Method a uses less labour and more capital than method b, and method d uses more labour and less capital than method b.

What about economic efficiency? Are all three methods economically efficient? To answer this question, we need to know the labour and capital costs. Let's suppose that labour costs £75 per person–day and that capital costs £250 per machine–day. Recall that economic efficiency occurs with the least expensive production process. Table 9.4 calculates the costs of using the four different methods of production. As you can see, the least expensive method of producing a TV set is b. Method a uses less labour but more capital. The combination of labour and capital needed by method a costs much more than in method b. Method d, the other technologically efficient method, uses much more labour and hardly any capital. Like method a, it costs far more to make a TV set using method d than method b.

Method c is technologically inefficient. It uses the same amount of capital as method b but 10 times as much labour. It is interesting to notice that although method c is technologically inefficient, it costs less to produce a TV set using method c than it does using methods a and d. But method b dominates method c. Because method c is not technologically efficient, there is always a lower-cost method available. That is, a technologically inefficient method is never economically efficient.

A firm that does not use the economically efficient method of production makes a smaller profit. Natural selection favours firms that choose the economically efficient method of production and goes against firms that do not. In extreme cases, an inefficient firm may go bankrupt or be taken over by another firm that can see the possibilities for lower cost and greater profit. Efficient firms will be stronger and better able to survive temporary adversity than inefficient ones.

Firms and Markets

At the beginning of this chapter, we defined a firm as an institution that hires factors of production and organizes them to produce and sell goods and services. To organize production, firms coordinate the economic decisions and activities of many individuals. But firms are not the only coordinators of economic decisions. As we learned in Chapter 4, markets also coordinate decisions. By adjusting prices, markets make the decisions of buyers and sellers consistent – make the quantities demanded equal to the quantities supplied of the many different goods and services.

An example of market coordination is the production of a rock concert. A promoter hires a stadium, some stage equipment, audio and video

TABLE 9.4

Costs of Four Ways of Making 10 TV Sets a Day

Method	Labour cost (£75 per day)		Capital cost (£250 per day)		Total cost	Cost per TV set
a	£75	+	£250,000	=	£250,075	£25,007.50
b	750	+	2,500	=	3,250	325.00
c	7,500	+	2,500	=	10,000	1,000.00
d	75,000	+	250	=	75,250	7,525.00

recording engineers and technicians, some rock groups, a superstar, a publicity agent and a ticket agent – all market transactions – and sells tickets to thousands of rock fans, audio rights to a recording company and video and broadcasting rights to a television network - another set of market transactions. If rock concerts were produced like cornflakes, the firm producing them would own all the capital used (stadiums, stage, sound and video equipment) and would employ all the labour needed (singers, engineers, sales persons, and so on).

What determines whether a firm or markets coordinate a particular set of activities? Why is the production of cornflakes coordinated by a firm and the production of a rock concert coordinated by markets? The answer is cost. Taking account of the opportunity cost of time as well as the costs of the other inputs, people use the method that costs least. In other words, they use the economically efficient method.

Firms coordinate economic activity when they can perform a task more efficiently than markets. In such a situation, it is profitable to set up a firm. If markets can perform a task more efficiently than a firm, people will use markets, and any attempt to set up a firm to replace such market coordination will be doomed to failure.

Why Firms?

There are four key reasons why, in many instances, firms are more efficient than markets as coordinators of economic activity. Firms achieve:

◆ Lower transactions costs

◆ Economies of scale

◆ Economies of scope

◆ Economies of team production

Transactions Costs   The idea that firms exist because there are activities in which they are more efficient than markets was first suggested by a University of Chicago economist and Nobel Laureate, Ronald Coase[1]. Coase focused on the

---

[1] Ronald H. Coase 'The Nature of the Firm', *Economica*, (November 1937) 386–405.

firm's ability to reduce or eliminate transactions costs. **Transactions costs** are the costs arising from finding someone with whom to do business, of reaching an agreement about the price and other aspects of the exchange, and of ensuring that the terms of the agreement are fulfilled. *Market* transactions require buyers and sellers to get together and to negotiate the terms and conditions of their trading. Sometimes lawyers have to be hired to draw up contracts. A broken contract leads to still more expenses. A *firm* can lower such transactions costs by reducing the number of individual transactions undertaken.

Consider, for example, two ways of getting your creaking car fixed.

Firm coordination. You take the car to the garage. Parts and tools as well as the mechanic's time are coordinated by the garage owner and your car gets fixed. You pay one bill for the entire job.

Market coordination. You hire a mechanic who diagnoses the problems and makes a list of the parts and tools needed to fix them. You buy the parts from the local breaker's yard and rent the tools from ABC Rentals. You hire the mechanic again to fix the problems. You return the tools and pay your bills – wages to the mechanic, rental to ABC and the cost of the parts used to the breaker.

What determines the method that you use? The answer is cost. Taking account of the opportunity cost of your own time as well as the costs of the other inputs that you'd have to buy, you will use the method that costs least. In other words, you will use the economically efficient method.

The first method requires that you undertake only one transaction with one firm. It's true that the firm has to undertake several transactions – hiring the labour and buying the parts and tools required to do the job. But the firm doesn't have to undertake those transactions simply to fix your car. One set of such transactions enables the firm to fix hundreds of cars. Thus there is an enormous reduction in the number of individual transactions that take place if people get their cars fixed at the garage rather than going through an elaborate sequence of market transactions.

Economies of Scale   When the cost of producing a unit of a good falls as its output rate increases, **economies of scale** exist. Many industries experience economies of scale; car manufacturing is an example. One firm can produce 4 million cars a year at a lower cost per car than 200 firms each producing 20,000 cars a year. Economies of scale arise from specialization and the division of labour that can be reaped more effectively by firm coordination rather than market coordination.

Economies of Scope   Economies which are derived from the size of the firm rather than the amount of plant or machinery available are called **economies of scope**. Today's large companies face high costs when developing, financing and marketing a new good – costs which must be recouped from sales of the new product. The bigger a firm's potential volume of sales, the less each unit sold of a new good must contribute to its development costs. So the price of a new good produced by a large firm, which already has a large-scale sales-force and retail outlets, will be less than a similar product launched by a smaller firm.

Team Production   A production process in which a group of individuals each specializes in mutually supportive tasks is *team production*. Sport provides the best example of team activity. Some team members specialize in striking and some in defending, some in speed and some in strength. The production of goods and services offers many examples of team activity. For example, production lines in car plants and TV manufacturing plants work most efficiently when individual activity is organized in teams, each specializing in a small task. You can also think of an entire firm as being a team. The team has buyers of raw materials and other inputs, production workers and sales persons. There are even specialists within these various groups. Each individual member of the team specializes, but the value of the output of the team and the profit that it earns depend on the coordinated activities of all the team's members. The idea that firms arise as a consequence of the economies of team production was first suggested by Armen Alchian and Harold

Demsetz of the University of California at Los Angeles[2].

Because firms can economize on transactions costs, reap economies of scale and scope, and organize efficient team production, it is firms rather than markets that coordinate most of our economic activity. Reductions in transactions costs explain why Ford, which started hand-building cars in the early 1900s, created a U-form structured company based on production line technology. But there are limits to the economic efficiency of firms. If a firm becomes too big or too diversified in the things that it seeks to do, the cost of management and monitoring per unit of output begins to rise and, at some point, the market becomes more efficient at coordinating the use of resources. This explains why Ford restructured into a global M-form TNC, effectively creating a set of smaller, more independent companies. It also explains why companies such as Hanson Trust target segments of large, ailing TNCs to run as separate, more profitable companies.

Sometimes firms enter into long-term relationships with each other that effectively cut out ordinary market transactions and make it difficult to see where one firm ends and another begins. For example, when Rover became part of BMW, it had a   long-term relationship with Honda as a supplier of gearboxes. These long-term relationships are also common between supermarkets and manufacturers. Famous cereal manufacturers produce supermarket own-label brands as well as their own more established brands.

◆ ◆ ◆ ◆ In this chapter we examined why different firms exist, their objectives and how they cope with the problems of uncertainty and limited information. We have used our concepts of marginal decisions and opportunity costs to explain the decisions that firms make. In the next chapter, we are going to study more choices of firms. We will study their production decisions, how they minimize cost, and how they choose the amounts of labour and capital to employ.

---

[2] Armen Alchian and Harold Demsetz, 'Production, Information Costs, and Economic Organization', *American Economic Review* (December 1972) 57, 5 777–795.

Cutting Costs with Old Technology

The Essence of the Story

THE TIMES, 13 MAY 1992

Horsepower pulls ahead of tractors

David Young

THE two newest members of Bracknell Forest Borough Council gardening department will clock on for the first time next Monday to be rewarded for an eight hour shift with a handful of carrots, a bale of hay and a bucket of oats.

The council in Berkshire has gone green. Instead of spending £20,000 or more to replace a worn-out tractor, it has bought two £4,000 Shire horses who will pull trailers around the town's gardens, and lug tankers used for watering its hanging baskets. Their working life could span 15 years, double the average tractor's. The council will save on a road fund licence and the insurance premiums will be lower.

Alan Stanton, environmental health officer, said: 'We looked at the figures very closely and, on the economics, are in favour of the horses. We have drawn on the experience of other horse users, such as the brewers, who have found them to be more economical for local work than lorries.'

Several authorities are considering heavy horses. Aberdeen has bought 14 Clydesdales for the parks department, Luton, whose fortunes owe much to the international combustion engine, has bought a Shire horse. Bradford, West Yorkshire, uses three to pull flower-watering machines, street-cleaning equipment and mowers at its industrial museum.

Winning ride: research for the Shire Horse Society shows that, in most cases, horsepower can work out cheaper than motor power, with horses also earning unquantifiable amounts of goodwill for their users. The society can provide figures which show that horses win over lorries by a short neck when used for local journeys during an eight-hour day. In addition, each horse produces £45 worth of manure each year.

How the Costs Compare

Two Horses	£8,000	Lorry	£14,400
Stabling	£2,223	Garaging	£1,332
Insurance	£216	Insurance	£270
Tax	Nil	Tax	£427
Wages	£12,600	Wages	£10,800
Keep	£3,481	Fuel	£792
Depreciation	£436	Depreciation	£2,876
Maintenance	£540	Maintenance	£2,605
		Tyres	£243

All costs are based on 1981 prices supplied by The Shire Horse Society (adjusted to 1991 prices)

- Bracknell Forest Borough Council has replaced a worn-out tractor with two shire horses rather than a new tractor.

- The attractions to the council of doing this are economic: two horses have lower running costs than a tractor.

- Data from the Shire Horse Society suggests that the cost of purchasing and maintaining two horses is about a fifth lower than that for a lorry.

- The working life of a horse is twice that of a tractor.

- Moreover, the two horses would produce manure worth £90 a year which could be sold or used in the council's gardens.

- Horse-drawn vehicles are slower than tractors and lorries, but for tasks where time and distance are not important factors, horses cost less.

Economic Analysis

■ A number of councils have identified tasks for which shire horses could be employed more cheaply than tractors and other mechanical alternatives.

■ The data from the Shire Horse Society indicates a number of areas where costs for two horses are lower than the cost of a lorry.

■ The initial purchase cost of two horses is lower than that of one lorry and the depreciation of horses is also significantly lower. These differences are further amplified by the councils' prediction that two horses will have twice the operational life of a lorry.

■ All other figures for the annual running costs indicate that it will cost the councils about the same to operate two horses as to operate one lorry.

■ By changing the technology employed, the councils are able to make economic efficiency gains by lowering the costs of producing the same output.

■ The figure compares the costs for two horses with those for a lorry.

Costs of Horse and Lorry

Accountant's costs		
Item	Two horses	Lorry
Purchase	£8,000	£14,400
Depreciation	£436	£2,876
Housing	£2,223	£1,332
Insurance	£216	£270
Tax	£0	£427
Fuel	£3,487	£792
Maintenance	£540	£2,605
Tyres	£0	£243
Totals	£14,902	£22,945

Economist's opportunity costs		
Item	Two horses	Lorry
Purchase price	£8,000	£14,400
less		
Market value at year end	£7,000	£10,000 (assumed)
equals		
Economic depreciation	£1,000	£4,400
Interest (at 5% pa)	£400	£720
Housing	£2,223	£1,332
Insurance	£216	£270
Tax	£0	£427
Fuel	£3,487	£792
Maintenance	£540	£2,605
Tyres	£0	£243
Totals	£7,866	£10,789

SUMMARY

The Firm and its Economic Problem

Firms hire and organize factors of production to produce and sell goods and services. The main types of firms are: proprietorships, partnerships and companies. Proprietorships are easy to set up and they face lower taxes than corporations, but they are riskier and face higher costs of capital and labour. Partnerships can draw on diversified expertise, but they can also involve decision conflicts. Companies have limited liability so they can obtain large-scale capital at relatively low cost. They can hire professional management, but complex management structures can slow down decisions. Company profits are taxed twice – as company profit and as shareholder income.

Firms strive to be efficient – to produce output at the lowest possible cost and to maximize profit. Uncertainty and incomplete information place limits on what a firm can attain. To operate efficiently, a firm's owners (principals) must induce its managers (agents) to pursue the maximum possible profit. And the managers (principals) must induce the workers and other firms (agents) to work efficiently. But incentive schemes are imperfect and firms constantly strive to find ways of improving performance and increasing profits. (pp. 203–209)

Business Finance

Firms get funds from their owners and from the sale of shares and bonds. When a firm raises funds, it receives money in the current period and takes on an obligation to make a series of payments in future periods. It compares money received today with money paid out in the future by calculating the present value of the future payments by using the formula:

$$\text{Present value} = \frac{\text{Money } n \text{ years in future}}{(1 + r)^n}$$

A firm decides how much to borrow by calculating the net present value of borrowing one additional pound – the marginal pound borrowed. It increases its borrowing up to the point at which the present value of the marginal pound borrowed is zero. At this amount of borrowing, the firm is maximizing its profit. (pp. 209–212)

Opportunity Cost and Economic Profit

Economic profit is calculated as total revenue minus opportunity cost. The opportunity cost has two components: explicit costs and implicit costs Explicit costs are paid directly in money – money costs. Implicit costs (measured in units of money) are opportunities forgone but not paid for directly in money. A firm's implicit costs arise from its use of capital, stocks and resources provided by its owner.

The opportunity cost of capital is made up of economic depreciation – the change in the market price of a capital asset over a period plus the interest on the funds used to buy capital. Interest is an opportunity cost even if the funds used are not borrowed. Interest is forgone on an alternative investment. The opportunity cost of using capital is the sum of economic depreciation and interest and is an implicit rental rate. Past economic depreciation of a capital asset is not a current opportunity cost. It is a sunk cost – a bygone. The opportunity cost of using an item from stock is its current replacement cost. The opportunity cost of the resources supplied by a firm's owner are the wages forgone by not working in the best alternative job and normal profit. (pp. 212–216)

Economic Efficiency

There are two concepts of efficiency: technological efficiency and economic efficiency. A method of production is technologically efficient when to produce a given output, it is not possible to use less of a factor of production without at the same time using more of another. A method of production is economically efficient when the cost of producing a given output is as low as possible. Economic efficiency requires technological efficiency. Economically efficient firms have a better chance of surviving than do inefficient ones. (pp. 216 –217)

Firms and Markets

Firms coordinate economic activities when they can achieve lower costs than coordination through markets. Firms can economize on transactions costs and achieve the benefits of economies of scale and of team production. (pp. 217–219)

KEY ELEMENTS

Key Terms

Bond, 210
Capital gain, 205
Company, 203
Corporation, 203
Discounting, 211
Economic depreciation, 213
Economic efficiency, 216
Economic profit, 215
Economies of scale, 219
Economies of scope, 219
Equity, 209
Firm, 203
Implicit rental rate, 214
Normal profit, 215
Present value, 211

Principal–agent problem, 207
Share, 210
Stocks, 214
Sunk cost, 213
Technological efficiency, 216
Transactions costs, 218

◆ Key Figure and Tables

Figure 9.2   Relative Importance of Firms by Size, 206
Table 9.1   The Pros and Cons of Different Types of Firms, 209
Table 9.2   Mike's Mountain Bikes' Revenue, Cost and Profit Statement, 215
Table 9.3   Four Ways of Making 10 TV Sets a Day, 216

REVIEW QUESTIONS

1 What is a firm and what are the economic problems that all firms face?

2 What factors make it difficult for a firm to get the most out of its resources?

3 What are the principal–agency relationships?

4 Why do principal–agency relationships arise?

5 What is the difference between an M-form and a U-form structured firm?

6 What are the main forms of business organization and the advantages and disadvantages of each?

7 What is the most common form of business?

8 What are the main ways in which firms can raise funds?

9 Describe and contrast a bond and a share.

10 What do we mean by net present value?

11 What determines the value of a bond?

12 Distinguish between money cost and opportunity cost.

13 What are the main items of opportunity cost and opportunity cost that don't get counted as part of money cost?

14 Explain how a firm uses marginal analysis when it makes a financial decision.

15 Distinguish between profit as defined by accountants, normal profit and economic profit.

16 Distinguish between implicit costs and explicit costs.

17 Distinguish between technological efficiency and economic efficiency.

18 Why do firms, rather than markets, coordinate such a large amount of economic activity?

PROBLEMS

1 Soap Bubbles PLC has a bank loan of £1 million on which it is paying an interest rate of 10 per cent a year. The firm's financial adviser suggests paying off the loan by selling bonds. To sell bonds valued at £1 million, Soap Bubbles must offer the following deal: one year from today, pay the bondholders £9 for each £100 of bonds; two years from today, redeem the bonds for £114 per £100 of bonds.

  a Does it pay Soap Bubbles to sell the bonds to repay the bank loan?

  b What is the present value of the profit or loss that would result from repaying the bank loan and selling the bonds?

2 One year ago, Jack and Jill set up a vinegar bottling firm (called JJVB).

◆ Jack and Jill put £50,000 of their own money into the firm.

◆ They bought equipment for £30,000 and an inventory of bottles and vinegar for £15,000.

◆ They hired one employee to help them for an annual wage of £20,000.

◆ JJVB's sales for the year were £100,000.

◆ Jack gave up his previous job, at which he earned £30,000, and spent all his time working for JJVB.

◆ Jill kept her old job, which paid £30 an hour, but gave up 10 hours of leisure each week (for 50 weeks) to work for JJVB.

◆ The cash expenses of JJVB were £10,000 for the year.

◆ The stock at the end of the year was worth £20,000.

◆ The market value of the equipment at the end of the year was £28,000.

◆ JJVB's accountant depreciated the equipment by 20 per cent a year.

  a Construct JJVB's profit and loss account as recorded by its accountant.

  b Construct JJVB's profit and loss account based on opportunity cost rather than money cost concepts.

3 There are three methods of completing your income tax return: using a personal computer, using a pocket calculator, or using a pencil and paper. With a PC, you complete the task in an hour; with a pocket calculator, it takes 12 hours; and with a pencil and paper, it takes two days. The PC and its software cost £1,000, the pocket calculator costs £10, and the pencil and paper cost £1.

  a Which, if any, of the above methods is technologically efficient?

  b Suppose that your wage is £5 an hour. Which of the above methods is economically efficient?

  c Suppose your wage is £50 an hour. Which of the above methods is economically efficient?

  d Suppose your wage is £500 an hour. Which of the above methods is economically efficient?

4 Study *Reading Between the Lines* on pp. 220–221.

  a Identify the main factors which make two horses cheaper to run than a lorry.

  b Explain the difference between the opportunity cost and the accounting cost of two horses compared to one lorry.

  c Explain why using two horses rather than one lorry is economically efficient.

CHAPTER

10

OUTPUT
AND
COSTS

After studying this chapter you will be able to:

◆ Explain what limits the profitability of a firm

◆ Explain the relationship between a firm's output and its costs

◆ Derive a firm's short-run cost curves

◆ Explain how cost changes when a firm's plant size changes

◆ Derive a firm's long-run average cost curve

L ARGE SIZE DOES NOT GUARANTEE SURVIVAL IN BUSINESS. WHILE SOME OF Europe's large corporations – such as Shell and BMW – have been operating for many years, most of their contemporaries from 30 years ago have disappeared. But remaining small does not guarantee survival either. Every year, millions of small businesses close down. Phone a random selection of restaurants and plumbers from last year's Yellow Pages and see how many have vanished. So what does a firm have to do to be one of the survivors? ◆ Firms differ in lots of ways – from the local corner shop to multinational giants producing high-tech goods. But regardless of their size or what they produce, all firms must decide how much to produce and how to produce it. How do firms make these decisions? ◆ Most European car makers can produce far more cars than they can sell. Why do car makers have expensive equipment lying around that isn't fully used? Many electric utilities in the United Kingdom don't have enough production equipment on hand to meet demand on the coldest and hottest days and have to buy power from the central pool. Why don't such firms have a bigger production plant so that they can supply the market themselves?

Survival of the Fittest

◆ ◆ ◆ ◆ We are going to answer these questions in this chapter. To do so, we are going to model the economic decisions of a small, imaginary firm – Neat Knits Ltd, a producer of knitted jumpers. The firm is owned and operated by Sam. By studying Neat Knits' economic problems and the way Sam solves them, we will be able to get a clear view of the problems that face all firms. We will be able to understand and predict the behaviour of small firms as well as the giants.

The Firm's Objective and Constraints

The first step in modelling a firm's behaviour is to start by describing a firm's objective – what it is trying to achieve.

The Objective: Profit Maximization

We will assume that the firm that we will study has a single objective: profit maximization. *Profit maximization* means striving for the largest possible profit. A firm that seeks the largest possible profit is one that tries to use its scarce resources efficiently. And a firm that maximizes profit has the best chance of surviving in a competitive environment and of avoiding being taken over by another firm.

Two types of constraints limit the profit a firm can make. They are:

♦ Market constraints
♦ Technology constraints

Market Constraints

A firm's market constraints are the conditions under which it can buy its inputs and sell its output. On the output side, people have a limited demand for each good or service and will buy additional quantities only at lower prices. On the input side, people have a limited supply of the factors of production that they own and will supply additional quantities only at higher prices.

We'll study these market constraints on firms in Chapters 11–16. Neat Knits, the firm that we'll study in this chapter, is small and cannot influence the prices at which it sells its output or buys its inputs. For such a firm, the market constraints are a given set of market prices.

Technology Constraints

Firms combine inputs – factors of production like capital and labour – to produce output. A firm's technology constraints are the limits to the quantity of output that can be produced from given quantities of inputs. To maximize profit, a firm chooses a *technologically efficient* method of production. This means it does not use more inputs than necessary to produce its chosen output. Equivalently, it does not waste resources. But a firm must also choose how to combine its inputs – its technique. It must choose the *economically efficient* technique – the combination of inputs that produces its chosen output at the lowest possible cost (see Chapter 9, pp. 216–217). This might be a labour-intensive technique which uses relatively more labour than capital, or a capital-intensive technique which uses relatively more capital than labour.

The possibilities open to a firm depend on the length of the planning period over which it is making its decisions. A firm that wants to change its output overnight has fewer options than one that plans to change its output several months in the future. In studying the way a firm's technology constrains its actions, we distinguish between two planning horizons: the short run and the long run.

The Short Run and the Long Run

The **short run** is a period of time in which the quantity of at least one input is fixed and the quantities of the other inputs can be varied. The **long run** is a period of time in which the quantities of all inputs can be varied. Inputs whose quantity can be varied in the short run are called *variable inputs*. Inputs whose quantity cannot be varied in the short run are called *fixed inputs*.

There is no specific time that can be marked on the calendar to separate the short run from the long run. In some cases, such as a photocopying service, the short run is a month or two. New premises can be rented and new machines installed quickly. In other cases, for example an electricity power company, the short run is several years. Bigger power generators take several years to build.

Let's go back to our small company, Neat Knits. It has a fixed amount of capital – knitting machines – so to vary its output in the short run it must vary the quantity of labour employed. For Neat Knits, the knitting equipment is the fixed input and labour is the variable input. In the long run, Neat Knits can vary the quantity of both inputs – knitting machines and labour employed.

Let's look more closely at the short-run technology constraint.

Short-run Technology Constraint

To increase output in the short run, a firm must increase the quantity of a variable input. To make a decision about the quantity of a variable input to use, the firm must calculate the effect on output of making a small change – a marginal change – in the quantity of the variable input used, when the fixed inputs remain unchanged. To make such a calculation, the firm uses its short-run technology constraint. A firm's short-run technology constraint can be described using three related concepts:

◆ Total product
◆ Marginal product
◆ Average product

Total Product

The total output produced with a given quantity of a fixed input is called **total product.** The *total product curve* shows the maximum output attainable with a given amount of capital as the amount of labour employed is varied. Equivalently, the relationship between total product and the amount of labour employed can be described by a schedule that lists the amounts of labour required with the given amount of capital to produce given amounts of output. Neat Knits' total product schedule and curve are shown in Fig. 10.1. Labour is the variable input used with 1 machine. As you can see, when employment is zero, no jumpers are knitted. As employment increases, so does the number of jumpers knitted. Neat Knits' total product curve with 1 machine, *TP*, is based on the schedule in the figure. Points *a* to *f* on the curve correspond to the same rows in the table.

The total product curve is similar to the *production possibility frontier* (explained in Chapter 3). It separates the attainable output levels from those that are unattainable. All the points that lie above the curve are unattainable. Points that lie below the curve, in the orange area, are attainable. But they are inefficient – they use more labour than is necessary to produce a given output. Only the points *on* the total product curve are technologically efficient.

FIGURE 10.1

Total Product

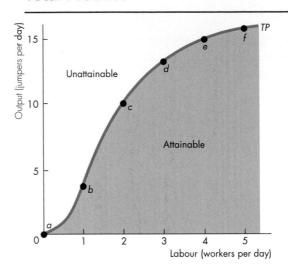

	Labour (workers per day)	Output (jumpers per day)
a	0	0
b	1	4
c	2	10
d	3	13
e	4	15
f	5	16

The table shows how many jumpers Neat Knits can produce when it uses 1 knitting machine and different amounts of labour. For example, using 1 knitting machine, 2 workers can produce 10 jumpers a day (row *c*). The total product curve, *TP*, is based on these data. Points *a* to *f* on the curve correspond to the rows of the table. The total product curve separates the attainable output from the unattainable output.

Marginal Product

The **marginal product** of an input is the increase in total product divided by the increase in the quantity of the input employed, when the quantity of all other inputs is constant. For example, the marginal product of labour is the increase in total product divided by the increase in the quantity of labour employed, when the quantity of capital is constant. Equivalently, it is the change in total product resulting from a 1-unit increase in the quantity of labour employed.

Table 10.1 shows the calculation of Neat Knits' marginal product of labour with 1 machine. For example, when the quantity of labour increases from 2 to 3 workers, total product increases from 10 to 13 jumpers. The change in total product – 3 jumpers – is the marginal product of going from 2 to 3 workers.

Figure 10.2 illustrates Neat Knits' marginal product of labour with 1 machine. Part (a) reproduces the total product curve that you met in Fig. 10.1. Part (b) shows the marginal product curve, *MP*. In part (a), the height of the orange bars illustrate the marginal product of labour. Marginal product is also measured by the slope of the total product curve. Recall that the slope of a curve is the change in the value of the variable measured on the *y*-axis – output – divided by the change in the variable measured on the *x*-axis – labour input – as we move along the curve. A 1-unit increase in

FIGURE 10.2

Marginal Product

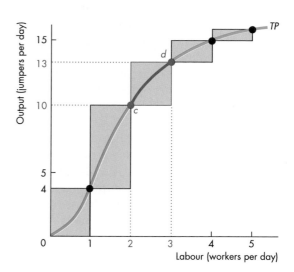

(a) Total product

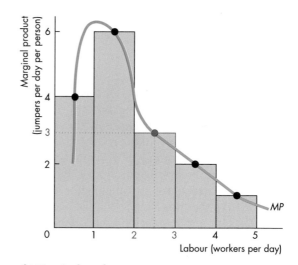

(b) Marginal product

Marginal product is illustrated in both parts of the figure by the orange bars. The height of each bar indicates the size of the marginal product. For example, when labour increases from 2 to 3, marginal product is the orange bar whose height is 3 jumpers. (Marginal product is shown midway between the labour inputs to emphasize that it is the result of *changing* inputs – moving from one level to the next.) The steeper the slope of the total product curve (*TP*) in part (a), the larger is marginal product (*MP*) in part (b). Marginal product increases to a maximum (when 1 worker is employed in this example) and then declines – diminishing marginal product.

TABLE 10.1

Calculating Marginal Product and Average Product

	Labour (workers per day)	Output (jumpers per day)	Marginal product (jumpers per day)	Average product (jumpers per worker)
a	0	0		
			·········· 4	
b	1	4		4.00
			·········· 6	
c	2	10		5.00
			·········· 3	
d	3	13		4.33
			·········· 2	
e	4	15		3.75
			·········· 1	
f	5	16		3.20

Marginal product of an input is the change in total product resulting from a 1-unit increase in an input. For example, when labour increases from 2 to 3 workers a day (row *c* to row *d*), total product increases from 10 to 13 jumpers a day. The marginal product of going from 2 to 3 workers is 3 jumpers.

Average product of an input is total product divided by the quantity of an input employed. For example, 3 workers produce 13 jumpers a day, so the average product of 3 workers is 4.33 jumpers per worker.

labour input, from 2 to 3 workers, increases output from 10 to 13 jumpers, so the slope from point *c* to point *d* is 3, the same as the marginal product that we've just calculated.

We've calculated the marginal product of labour for a series of unit increases in the amount of labour. But labour is divisible into smaller units than one person. It is divisible into hours and even minutes. By varying the amount of labour in the smallest imaginable units, we can draw the marginal product curve shown in Fig. 10.2(b). The *height* of this curve measures the *slope* of the total product curve at a point. The total product curve in part (a) shows that an increase in employment from 2 to 3 workers increases output from 10 to 13 jumpers (an increase of 3). The increase in output of 3 jumpers appears on the vertical axis of part (b) as the marginal product of going from 2 to 3 workers. We plot that marginal product at the midpoint between 2 and 3 workers. Notice that marginal product shown in Fig. 10.2(b) reaches a peak at 1 unit of labour and at that point marginal product is more than 6. The peak occurs at 1 unit of labour because the total product curve is steepest at 1 unit of labour.

Average Product

The **average product** of an input is equal to total product divided by the quantity of the input employed. Average product tells us how productive, on the average, a factor of production is. Table 10.1 shows Neat Knits' average product of labour with 1 machine. For example, 3 workers can knit 13 jumpers a day, so the average product of labour is 13 divided by 3, which is 4.33 jumpers per worker.

Figure 10.3 illustrates Neat Knits' average product of labour, *AP*, and marginal product of labour, *MP*, and shows the relationship between average product and marginal product. Points *b* to *f* on the average product curve are plotted from the same rows in Table 10.1. Average product increases from 1 to 2 workers (its maximum value is at point *c*) but then decreases as yet more workers are employed. Notice that average product is largest when average product and marginal product are equal. That is, the marginal product curve cuts the average product curve at the point of maximum average product. For employment levels at which marginal product is less than average product, average product is decreasing.

The relationships between the average and marginal product curves that you've just seen are a general feature of the relationship between the

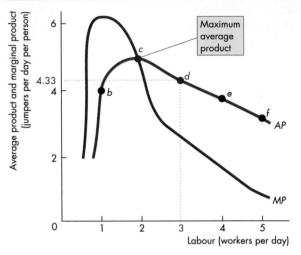

The figure shows the average product of labour, *AP*, and the marginal product of labour, *MP*, and the relationship between the shape of the two curves. With 1 worker per day, marginal product exceeds average product, so average product is increasing. With 2 workers per day, marginal product equals average product, so average product is at its maximum. With more than 2 workers per day, marginal product is less than average product, so average product is decreasing.

average and marginal values of any variable. Let's look at a familiar example.

Marginal Marks and Average Marks

Sam is also a part-time student who takes one course per term. (He's too busy at the jumper factory to do more than one course.) Figure 10.4 shows Sam's performance over five terms. He gains a mark of 50 per cent in his first exam for calculus. This is his marginal mark and it is his average mark as it is the first course taken. Sam takes French in the second term and gets 60 per cent in the exam. As French is Sam's marginal course, his marginal mark is 60 per cent, but his average mark rises to 55 per cent, the average of 50 and 60. His average mark rises because his marginal mark is greater than his previous average mark – it pulls his average up. In the third term, Sam takes economics, his best subject. His marginal mark is 70 per cent, which is higher than his previous average. His marginal mark pulls his average up, this time

FIGURE 10.4

Marginal Mark and Average Mark

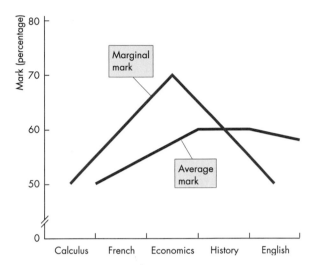

Sam's first course is calculus for which he gets 50 per cent. His marginal grade is 50 per cent and his average is 50 per cent. He then gets 60 per cent for French, which pulls his average up to 55 per cent. Next he gets 70 per cent for economics, which pulls his average up again to 60 per cent. On his next course, history, he gets 60 per cent, which maintains his average. Then his mark drops to 50 per cent for English. This marginal mark is below his previous average and so it pulls his average down.

to 60 per cent, the average of 50, 60 and 70. In the fourth term, Sam takes history. Unfortunately, he achieves only 60 per cent in the exam. This time, his marginal mark is equal to his previous average – so his average does not change. In the fifth term, Sam takes English but achieves only 50 per cent in the exam. This time his marginal mark is below his previous average, and drags his average down to 55 per cent, the average of 50, 60, 70, 60, and 50 per cent.

This example of an everyday relationship between marginal and average values agrees with the relationship between marginal and average product that we have just discovered. Sam's average mark increases when the mark on the last course taken, the marginal mark, exceeds his previous average. The average mark falls when the mark on the marginal course is below his previous average. His average mark is constant (it neither increases nor decreases) when the mark for the marginal course equals his previous average.

The Shapes of the Product Curves

Now let's get back to studying production. The total, marginal and average product curves are different for different firms and different types of goods. BMW's product curves are different from those of your local supermarket, which in turn are different from those of Sam's jumper factory. But the shapes of the product curves are similar, because almost every production process incorporates two features:

◆ Increasing marginal returns initially

◆ Diminishing marginal returns eventually

Increasing Marginal Returns **Increasing marginal returns** occur when the marginal product of an additional worker exceeds the marginal product of the previous worker. If Sam employs just one worker at Neat Knits, that person has to learn all the different aspects of jumper production, running the knitting machines, fixing breakdowns, packaging and mailing jumpers, buying and checking the type and colour of the wool. All of these tasks have to be done by that one person. If Sam employs a second person, the two workers can specialize in different parts of the production process. As a result, two workers produce more than twice as much as one. The marginal product of the second worker is greater than the marginal product of the first worker. Marginal returns are increasing.

Diminishing Marginal Returns Increasing marginal returns do not always occur, but all production processes eventually reach a point of diminishing marginal returns. **Diminishing marginal returns** occur when the marginal product of an additional worker is less than the marginal product of the previous worker. If Sam employs a third worker, output increases but not by as much as it did when he added the second worker. In this case, after two workers are employed, all the gains from specialization and the division of labour have been exhausted. By employing a third worker, the factory produces more jumpers, but the equipment is being operated closer to its limits. There are even times when the third worker has nothing to do because the plant is running without the need for further attention. Adding yet more and more workers continues to increase output but by successively smaller amounts. Marginal returns are diminishing.

This phenomenon is such a pervasive one that it is called "the law of diminishing returns". The **law of diminishing returns** states that:

> As a firm uses more of a variable input, with a given quantity of fixed inputs, the marginal product of the variable input eventually diminishes.

Because marginal product eventually diminishes, so does average product. Recall that average product decreases when marginal product is less than average product. If marginal product is diminishing it must eventually become less than average product and, when it does so, average product begins to decline.

◆ Three curves – total product, marginal product and average product – show how the output rate of a firm varies as the variable input – labour – varies with fixed capital.

◆ Initially, as the labour input increases, marginal product and average product might increase.

◆ But as the labour input increases further, first marginal product and later average product decline.

◆ When marginal product exceeds average product, average product increases; when marginal product is less than average product, average product decreases; and when marginal product and average product are equal, average product is at its maximum.

Why does Sam care about Neat Knits total product, marginal product and average product, and whether marginal product and average product are increasing or decreasing? He cares because the product curves influence costs and the way costs change with the quantity of jumpers produced.

Short-run Cost

To produce more output in the short run, a firm must employ more labour. But if the firm employs more labour, its costs increase. Thus to produce more output, a firm must increase its costs. Let's study Neat Knits' costs to see how a firm's costs change with the level of production.

Neat Knits is a small firm and we'll assume that it cannot influence the prices it pays for its inputs. Given the prices of its inputs, Neat Knits' lowest attainable cost of production for each output level is determined by its technology constraint. Let's see how.

Total Cost

A firm's **total cost** is the sum of the costs of all the inputs it uses in production. It includes the cost of renting land, buildings and equipment, the wages paid to the firm's work-force and normal profit. Total cost is divided into two categories: fixed cost and variable cost.

A **fixed cost** is the cost of a fixed input. Because the quantity of a fixed input does not change as output changes, a fixed cost is a cost that is independent of the output level. For example, BMW can change its output of cars without changing the amount it spends on advertising. The cost of advertising is a fixed cost.

A **variable cost** is a cost of a variable input. Because to change its output a firm must change the quantity of variable inputs, a variable cost is a cost that varies with the output level. For example, to produce more cars, BMW must run its assembly lines for longer hours and hire more labour. The cost of this labour is a variable cost.

Total fixed cost is the total cost of the fixed inputs. **Total variable cost** is the total cost of the variable inputs. We call total cost TC, total fixed cost TFC and total variable cost TVC. The total cost of production is the sum of total fixed cost and total variable cost. That is,

$$TC = TFC + TVC$$

Table 10.2 shows Neat Knits' total cost and its division into total fixed cost and total variable cost. Neat Knits has 1 knitting machine and this is its fixed input. To produce more jumpers Sam must employ more labour, and the first two columns of the table show how many jumpers can be produced at each level of employment. This is Neat Knits' technology constraint.

Neat Knits rents its knitting machine for £25 a day. This amount is its total fixed cost. It employs workers at a wage rate of £25 a day and its total variable cost is equal to the total wage bill. For example, if Neat Knits employs 3 workers, its total variable cost is (3 × £25), which equals £75. Total cost is the sum of total fixed cost and total variable

TABLE 10.2

Calculating a Firm's Costs

Labour	Output	Total fixed cost (*TFC*)	Total variable cost (*TVC*)	Total cost (*TC*)	Marginal cost (*MC*)	Average fixed cost (*AFC*)	Average variable cost (*AVC*)	Average total cost (*ATC*)
(workers per day)	(jumpers per day)	(pounds per day)				(pounds per jumper)		
0	0	25	0	25		–	–	–
					6.25			
1	4	25	25	50		6.25	6.25	12.50
					4.17			
2	10	25	50	75		2.50	5.00	7.50
					8.33			
3	13	25	75	100		1.92	5.77	7.69
					12.50			
4	15	25	100	125		1.67	6.00	78.33
					25.00			
5	16	25	125	150		1.56	7.81	9.38

cost. For example, when Neat Knits employs 3 workers, its total cost is £100 – total fixed cost of £25 plus total variable cost of £75.

Marginal Cost

A firm's **marginal cost** is the increase in its total cost divided by the increase in its output. Equivalently, it is the change in total cost that results from a unit increase in output. For example, when output increases from 10 to 13 jumpers, total cost increases from £75 to £100. The change in output is 3 jumpers and the change in total cost is £25. The marginal cost of one of these 3 jumpers is (£25 ÷ 3), which equals £8.33.

Notice that when Neat Knits hires a second worker, marginal cost decreases but when a third, fourth and fifth worker are employed, marginal cost successively increases. Marginal cost eventually increases because each additional worker produces a successively smaller addition to output – *the law of diminishing returns*. The law of diminishing returns means that each additional worker produces a successively smaller addition to output. So to get an additional unit of output, ever more workers are required. Because more workers are required to produce one additional unit of output, the cost of the additional output – marginal cost – must eventually increase.

Average Cost

Average cost is the cost per unit of output. There are three average costs:

1. Average fixed cost
2. Average variable cost
3. Average total cost

Average fixed cost (*AFC*) is total fixed cost per unit of output. **Average variable cost** (*AVC*) is total variable cost per unit of output. **Average total cost** (*ATC*) is total cost per unit of output. The average cost concepts are calculated from the total cost concepts as follows:

$$TC = TFC + TVC$$

Divide each total cost term by the quantity produced, Q, to give:

$$\frac{TC}{Q} = \frac{TFC}{Q} + \frac{TVC}{Q}$$

or,

$$ATC = AFC + AVC$$

Average total cost equals average fixed cost plus average variable cost.

Table 10.2 shows the calculation of average total cost. For example, when output is 10 jumpers, average fixed cost is (£25 ÷ 10), which equals £2.50,

FIGURE 10.5

Short-run Costs

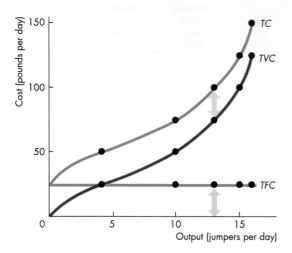

(a) Total costs

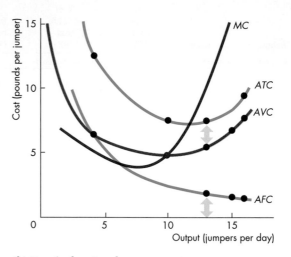

(b) Marginal cost and average costs

The short-run costs are calculated in Table 10.2 and illustrated in the graphs. Part (a) shows the total cost curves. Total cost (*TC*) increases as output increases. Total fixed cost (*TFC*) is constant – it graphs as a horizontal line – and total variable cost (*TVC*) increases in a similar way to total cost. The vertical distance between the total cost curve and the total variable cost curve is total fixed cost.

Part (b) shows the average and marginal cost curves. Average fixed cost (*AFC*) decreases as output increases. The average total cost curve (*ATC*) and average variable cost curve (*AVC*) are U-shaped. The vertical distance between these two curves is equal to average fixed cost. The marginal cost curve (*MC*) is also U-shaped. It intersects the average variable cost curve and the average total cost curve at their minimum points.

average variable cost is ($50 ÷ 10), which equals $5.00, and average total cost is ($75 ÷ 10), which equals $7.50. Equivalently, average total cost is equal to average fixed cost ($2.50) plus average variable cost ($5.00).

Short-run Cost Curves

Figure 10.5(a) illustrates Neat Knits' short-run costs as the total cost curves. Total fixed cost is a constant $25. It appears in the figure as the horizontal green curve *TFC*. Total variable cost and total cost both increase with output. They are graphed as the purple total variable cost curve (*TVC*) and the blue total cost curve (*TC*). The vertical distance between those two curves is equal to total fixed cost – as indicated by the arrows. Because total fixed cost is a constant $25, the distance between the purple total variable cost curve and the blue total cost curve is a constant $25. Use your ruler to check that the distance is a constant $25.

Figure 10.5(b) shows the average cost curves. The green average fixed cost curve (*AFC*) slopes downward. As output increases, the same constant fixed cost is spread over a larger output. When Neat Knits produces 4 jumpers, average fixed cost is $6.25; when total product increases to 16 jumpers, average fixed cost decreases to $1.56.

The blue average total cost curve (*ATC*) and the purple average variable cost curve (*AVC*) are U-shaped. The vertical distance between the average total cost and average variable cost curves is equal to average fixed cost – as indicated by the arrows. That distance shrinks as output increases because average fixed cost declines with increasing output.

Figure 10.5(b) also illustrates the marginal cost curve. It is the red curve *MC*. This curve is also U-shaped. The marginal cost curve intersects the average variable cost and the average total cost curve at their minimum points. That is, when

TABLE 10.3

A Compact Glossary of Costs

Term	Symbol	Equation	Definition
Fixed cost			Cost that is independent of the output level
Variable cost			Cost that varies with the output level
Total fixed cost	TFC		Cost of the fixed inputs (equals their number times their unit price)
Total variable cost	TVC		Cost of the variable inputs (equals their number times their unit price)
Total cost	TC	$TC = TFC + TVC$	Cost of all inputs (equals fixed costs plus variable costs)
Output (total product)	TP		Output produced
Marginal cost	MC	$MC = \Delta TC \div \Delta TP$	Change in total cost resulting from a one-unit increase in total product (equals the change in total cost divided by the change in total product)
Average fixed cost	AFC	$AFC = TFC \div TP$	Total fixed cost per unit of output (equals total fixed cost divided by total product)
Average variable cost	AVC	$AVC = TVC \div TP$	Total variable cost per unit of output (equals total variable cost divided by total product)
Average total cost	ATC	$ATC = AFC + AVC$	Total cost per unit of output (equals average fixed cost plus average variable cost)

marginal cost is less than average cost, average cost is decreasing, and when marginal cost exceeds average cost, average cost is increasing. This relationship holds for both the *ATC* and the *AVC* curves and is just another example of the relationship you saw in Fig. 10.4 for Sam's course marks.

Why the Average Total Cost Curve is U-Shaped

Average total cost, *ATC,* is the sum of average fixed cost, *AFC,* and average variable cost, *AVC*. So the shape of the *ATC* curve combines the shapes of the *AFC* and *AVC* curves. The U-shape of the average total cost curve arises from the influence of two opposing forces:

1. Spreading fixed cost over a larger output
2. Eventually diminishing returns

When output increases, the firm spreads its fixed costs over a larger output and its average fixed cost decrease – its average fixed cost curve slopes downward.

When output increases, diminishing returns eventually set in. That is, to produce an additional unit of output, ever larger amounts of labour are

required. So average variable cost eventually increases and the firm's *AVC* curve eventually slopes upward.

The shape of the average total cost curve combines these two effects. Initially, as output increases, both average fixed cost and average variable cost decrease, so average total cost decreases and the *ATC* curve slopes downward. But as output increases further and diminishing returns set in, average variable cost begins to increase. Eventually, average variable cost increases more quickly than average fixed cost decreases, so average total cost increases and the *ATC* curve slopes upward. At the output level at which declining average fixed cost offsets increasing average variable cost, average total cost is constant and at its minimum.

Cost Curves and Product Curves

A firm's cost curves are determined by its technology and its product curves. Figure 10.6 shows the links between the product curves and the cost curves. The upper part of the figure shows the average product curve and the marginal product curve – like those in Fig. 10.3. The lower part of the figure shows the average variable cost curve and the marginal cost curve – like those in Fig. 10.5(b).

Notice that at over the output range in which marginal product and average product are rising, marginal cost and average variable cost are falling. Then, at the point of maximum marginal product, marginal cost is a minimum. At output levels above this point, marginal product diminishes and marginal cost increases. But there is an intermediate range of output over which average product is still rising and average variable cost is falling. Then an output is reached at which average product is a maximum and average variable cost is a minimum. At outputs above this level, average product diminishes and average variable cost increases.

Shifts in the Cost Curves

The position of a firm's short-run cost curves depend on technology, described by its product curves, and by the prices it pays for its factors of production. If technology changes or if factor prices change, the firm's costs change and its cost curves shift. You can read about the effects of new technology on oil-refining costs in *Reading Between the Lines* on pp. 242–243.

A technological change that increases productivity shifts the product curves upward and shifts the cost curves downward. For example, advances in robotic production techniques have increased productivity in the car industry. As a result, the product curves of BMW, Renault and Volvo have shifted upward and their cost curves have shifted downward. But the relationships between their product curves and cost curves have not changed. The curves are still linked in the way shown in Fig. 10.6.

An increase in factor prices increases costs and shifts the cost curves. But the way the curves shift depends on which factor prices change. A change in rent or some other component of *fixed* cost shifts the fixed cost curves (*TFC* and *AFC*) and the total cost curve (*TC*) upward, but leaves the variable cost curves (*AVC* and *TVC*) and the marginal cost curve (*MC*) unchanged. A change in wages or some other component of *variable* cost shifts the variable curves (*TVC* and *AVC*), the total cost curve (*TC*) and the marginal cost curve (*MC*) upward, but leaves the fixed cost curves (*AFC* and *TFC*) unchanged.

We've studied the way costs change when a firm changes its output by changing the quantity of labour it employs in a fixed plant. All the concepts that you've met are summarized in a

FIGURE 10.6

Product Curves and Cost Curves

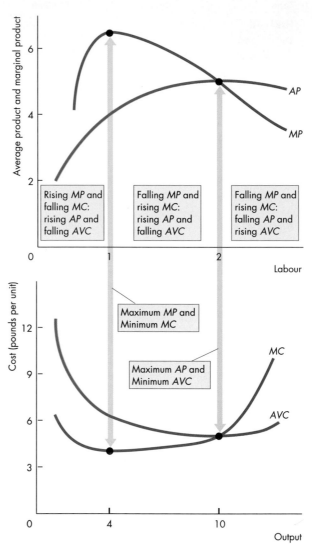

A firm's cost curves are linked to its product curves. Over the range of rising marginal product, marginal cost is falling. When marginal product is a maximum, marginal cost is a minimum. Over the range of rising average product, average variable cost is falling. When average product is a maximum, average variable cost is a minimum. Over the range of diminishing marginal product, marginal cost is rising. And over the range of diminishing average product, average variable cost is rising.

compact glossary in Table 10.3. But what happens if the firm changes its plant? Let's answer this question by seeing what happens if Neat Knits installs more knitting machines.

◆ Tables 10.2 and Figures 10.5 and 10.6 define the key concepts and explain the key relationships between short-run cost and output.

◆ Marginal cost eventually increases because of diminishing returns – each additional worker produces a successively smaller addition to output.

◆ Average fixed cost decreases because as output increases, fixed costs are spread over a larger output.

◆ The average total cost curve is U-shaped because it combines the influences of falling average fixed cost and eventually diminishing returns.

Plant Size and Cost

We have studied how the cost of production varies for a given jumper plant when different quantities of labour are used. We are now going to see how the cost of production varies when both plant size – the number of machines – and the quantity of labour are varied. That is, we are going to study a firm's long-run costs. **Long-run cost** is the cost of production when a firm uses the economically efficient quantity of labour and plant size.

The behaviour of long-run cost depends on the firm's production function. A **production function** is the relationship between the maximum output attainable and the quantities of *all* inputs used.

The Production Function

Figure 10.7 shows Neat Knits' production function. The table lists the total product for four different plant sizes and five different quantities of labour. The numbers for Plant 1 are for the jumper factory whose short-run product and cost curves we've just studied. The other three plants have 2, 3 and 4 machines. If Sam doubles the plant size to 2 knitting machines, the various amounts of output that labour can produce are shown in the third column of the table. The other two columns show the outputs of yet larger plants.

The numbers in the table are graphed as the four total product curves in Fig. 10.7. Each total product curve has the same basic shape, but the larger the number of knitting machines, the larger is the number of jumpers knitted each day by a given number of workers.

FIGURE 10.7

The Production Function

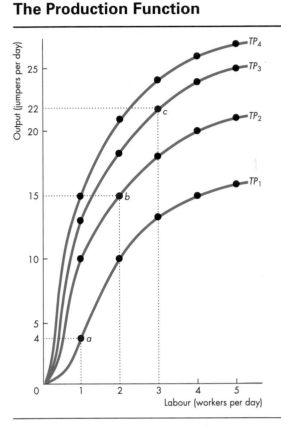

Labour	Output (jumpers per day)			
(workers per day)	Plant 1	Plant 2	Plant 3	Plant 4
1	4	10	13	15
2	10	15	18	21
3	13	18	22	24
4	15	20	24	26
5	16	21	25	27
Knitting machines (number)	1	2	3	4

The table shows the short-run total product data for four plant sizes with different numbers of machines. These numbers are graphed as the total product curves, TP_1, TP_2, TP_3 and TP_4. The bigger the plant, the larger is the total product for any given amount of labour employed. But each total product curve displays diminishing marginal product. The highlighted numbers show what happens. If Neat Knits doubles its scale from 1 machine and 1 worker to 2 machines and 2 workers, its output more than doubles – increasing returns to scale are shown between *a* and *b*. But increasing the scale again from 2 workers and 2 machines to 3 workers and 3 machines or to 4 workers and 4 machines increases output by a smaller percentage than the increase in inputs – decreasing returns to scale are shown from *b* to *c*.

Diminishing Returns

Diminishing returns occur in all four plants as the labour input increases. You can check that fact by doing similar calculations for the larger plants to those you've already done for a plant with one machine. Regardless of the plant size, as the labour input increases, its marginal product (eventually) decreases.

Diminishing Marginal Product of Capital Just as we can calculate the marginal product of labour for each plant size, we can also calculate the marginal product of capital for each quantity of labour. The *marginal product of capital* is the change in total product divided by the change in capital employed when the amount of labour employed is constant. Equivalently, it is the change in output resulting from a one-unit increase in the quantity of capital employed. For example, if Neat Knits employs 3 workers and increases the number of machines from 1 to 2, output increases from 13 to 18 jumpers a day. The marginal product of capital is 5 jumpers a day. The marginal product of capital diminishes, just like the marginal product of labour. For example, if with 3 workers Neat Knits increases the number of machines from 2 to 3, output increases from 18 to 22 jumpers a day. The marginal product of the third machine is 4 jumpers a day, down from 5 jumpers a day for the second machine.

The law of diminishing returns tells us what happens to output when a firm changes one input, either labour or capital, and holds the other input constant. But what happens to a firm's output if it changes both labour and capital?

Returns to Scale

A change in scale occurs when there is an equal percentage change in the use of all the firm's inputs. For example, if Neat Knits has been employing one worker and has one knitting machine and then doubles its use of both inputs (to use two workers and two knitting machines), the scale of the firm will double. **Returns to scale** are the increases in output that result from increasing all inputs by the same percentage. There are three possible cases:

- Constant returns to scale
- Increasing returns to scale
- Decreasing returns to scale

Constant Returns to Scale **Constant returns to scale** occur when the percentage increase in a firm's output is equal to the percentage increase in its inputs. If constant returns to scale are present and a firm doubles all its inputs, its output exactly doubles. Constant returns to scale occur if an increase in output is achieved by replicating the original production process. For example, BMW can double its production of its 5-series by doubling its production facility for those cars. It can build an identical production line and hire an identical number of workers. With the two identical production lines, BMW produces exactly twice as many cars.

Increasing Returns to Scale **Increasing returns to scale** occur when the percentage increase in output exceeds the percentage increase in inputs. If increasing returns to scale are present and a firm doubles all its inputs, its output more than doubles. Increasing returns to scale occur in production processes where increased output enables a firm to increase the division of labour and to use more specialized labour and capital. For example, if BMW produces only 100 cars a week, each worker and each machine must be capable of performing many different tasks. But if it produces 10,000 cars a week, each worker and each piece of equipment can be highly specialized. Workers specialize in a small number of tasks at which they become highly proficient. BMW might use 100 times more capital and labour, but the number of cars produced increases by more than a hundredfold. In this case, BMW experiences increasing returns to scale. Another source of increasing returns is technological. A doubling of the surface area of an oil pipe (a doubling of inputs), more than doubles the volume of oil that can flow through the pipe.

Decreasing Returns to Scale **Decreasing returns to scale** occur when the percentage increase in output is less than the percentage increase in inputs. If decreasing returns to scale are present and a firm doubles all its inputs, its output less than doubles. Decreasing returns to scale occur in all production processes at some output rate, but may not appear until a very large output rate is achieved. The most common source of decreasing returns to scale is the increasingly complex management and organizational structure required to control a large international firm. The larger the organization, the larger are the number of layers in the management pyramid and the greater are the costs of monitoring and maintaining control of the production and marketing process.

Returns to Scale at Neat Knits   Neat Knits' production possibilities, set out in Fig. 10.7, display both increasing returns to scale and decreasing returns to scale. If Sam has 1 knitting machine and employs 1 worker, his factory will produce 4 jumpers a day at point a. If he doubles the firm's inputs to 2 knitting machines and 2 workers, the factory's output increases almost fourfold to 15 jumpers a day at point b. If he increases the firm's inputs by another 50 per cent to 3 knitting machines and 3 workers, output increases to 22 jumpers a day at point c – an increase of less than 50 per cent. Doubling Neat Knits' scale from 1 to 2 units of each input gives rise to increasing returns to scale from point a to point b, but the further increase from 2 to 3 units of each input gives rise to decreasing returns to scale from point b to point c.

Whether a firm experiences increasing, constant, or decreasing returns to scale affects its long-run costs. Let's see how.

Short-run Cost and Long-run Cost

The cost curves in Fig. 10.5 apply to a plant with 1 knitting machine. There is a set of short-run cost curves like those shown in Fig. 10.5 for each different plant size. Let's look at the short-run costs for the four plants set out in Fig. 10.7 and see how plant size affects the cost curves.

We've already studied the costs of a plant with 1 knitting machine. We'll call the average total cost curve for that plant ATC_1 in Fig. 10.8. The average total cost curve for larger plants (with 2, 3 and 4 knitting machines respectively) are also shown in Fig. 10.8 as ATC_2 (for 2 machines), ATC_3 (for 3 machines) and ATC_4 (for 4 machines). The average total cost curve for each plant size has the same

---

FIGURE 10.8

Short-run and Long-run Costs

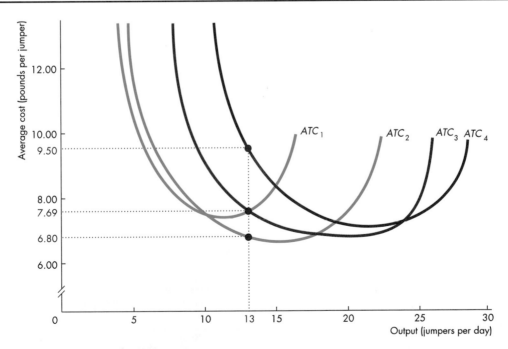

The figure shows short-run average total cost curves for four different plants. Neat Knits can produce 13 jumpers a day with 1 knitting machine on ATC_1 or with 3 knitting machines on ATC_3 for an average cost of £7.69 per jumper. It can produce the same number of jumpers by using 2 knitting machines on ATC_2 for £6.80 per jumper or with 4 machines on ATC_4 for £9.50 per jumper. If Neat Knits produces 13 jumpers a day, the least-cost method of production – the long-run method – is with 2 machines on ATC_2.

basic U-shape. And because larger plants produce larger outputs with the same amount of labour, the ATC curves for successively larger plants lie farther to the right. Which of these cost curves Neat Knits operates on depends on its plant size. For example, if Neat Knits has 1 machine, then its average total cost curve is ATC_1 and it costs £7.69 per jumper to knit 13 jumpers a day. But Neat Knits can produce 13 jumpers a day with any of these four plant sizes. If it uses 2 machines, the average total cost curve is ATC_2 and the average total cost of a jumper is £6.80. If it uses 4 machines, the average total cost curve is ATC_4, and the average total cost of a jumper is £9.50. If Neat Knits wants to produce 13 jumpers a day, the economically efficient plant size is 2 machines – the one with the lowest average total cost of production.

The Long-run Average Cost Curve

The *long-run average cost curve* traces the relationship between the lowest attainable average total cost and output when both capital and labour inputs can be varied. This curve is illustrated in Fig. 10.9 as $LRAC$. It is derived directly from the short-run average total cost curves that we have just reviewed in Fig. 10.8. As you can see, ATC_1 has the lowest average total cost for all output rates up to 10 jumpers a day. ATC_2 has the lowest average total cost for output rates between 10 and 18 jumpers a day. ATC_3 has the lowest average total cost for output rates between 18 and 24 jumpers a day. And ATC_4 has the lowest average total cost for output rates in excess of 24 jumpers a day. The segment of each of the four average total cost curves for which that plant has the lowest average total cost is shown as dark blue in Fig. 10.9. The scallop-shaped curve made up of these four segments is the long-run average cost curve.

Neat Knits will be on its long-run average cost curve if it does the following: to produce up to 10 jumpers a day it uses 1 machine; to produce between 11 and 18 jumpers a day it uses 2 machines; to produce between 19 and 24 jumpers it uses 3 machines;

FIGURE 10.9

The Long-run Average Cost Curve

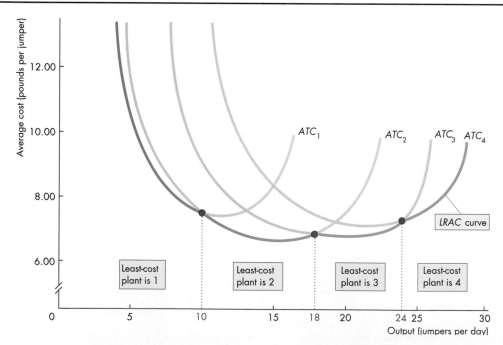

The figure shows the construction of the long-run average cost curve. The curve traces the lowest attainable costs of production at each output when both capital and labour inputs are varied. On the long-run average cost curve,

Neat Knits uses 1 machine to produce up to 10 jumpers a day, 2 machines to produce between 11 and 18 jumpers a day, 3 machines to produce between 19 and 24 jumpers a day, and 4 machines to produce more than 24 jumpers a day.

and, finally, to produce more than 24 jumpers it uses 4 machines. Within these ranges, Neat Knits varies its output by varying only the amount of labour employed.

Economies and Diseconomies of Scale

Economies of scale are present when, as output increases, long-run average cost decreases. When economies of scale are present, the *LRAC* curve slopes downward. Neat Knits experiences economies of scale for outputs up to 15 jumpers a day. **Diseconomies of scale** are present when, as output increases, long-run average cost increases. When diseconomies of scale are present, the *LRAC* curve slopes upward. At outputs greater than 15 jumpers a day, Neat Knits experiences diseconomies of scale. Between the regions of economies of scale and diseconomies of scale, at an output of 15 jumpers a day, Neat Knits' long-run average cost is at a minimum.

Neat Knits' long-run average cost curve has two special features that are not always found. First, Neat Knits can adjust its plant size only in big jumps by adding another knitting machine per day. In general, we can imagine varying the plant size in smaller increments by adding another knitting machine for part of a day so that there is an infinite number of plant sizes. In such a situation, there is an infinite number of short-run average total cost curves, one for each plant size. Second, Neat Knits' long-run average cost curve is U-shaped – it slopes either downward (economies of scale) or upward (diseconomies of scale). In contrast, many production processes have been shown to have constant long-run average cost over some intermediate range of output. The long-run average cost curve is horizontal over this range.

Figure 10.10 illustrates this situation. Here there is an infinite number of plant sizes so the long-run average cost curve is smooth, not scalloped like Neat Knits'. For outputs up to Q_1, there are economies of scale and long-run average cost is decreasing. For outputs that exceed Q_2, there are diseconomies of scale and long-run average cost is increasing. And for outputs between Q_1 and Q_2, long-run average cost is constant.

To keep the figure clear, only two of the infinite number of short-run average total cost curves, $SRAC_a$ and $SRAC_b$, are shown. Each short-run average total cost curve touches the long-run average cost curve, *LRAC*, at a single point – at a unique level of output. Thus for each output, there is a unique, economically efficient plant size. The short-run

FIGURE 10.10

FIGURE 10.10
Economies of Scale

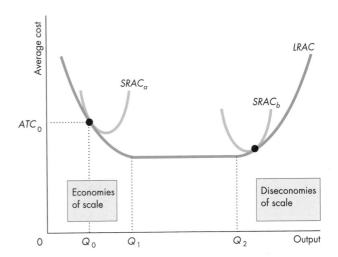

If capital can be varied in small units, there is an infinitely large number of plant sizes and an infinitely large number of short-run average total cost curves. Each short-run average total cost curve touches the long-run average cost curve at a single point. For example, the short-run average total cost curve ($SRAC_a$) touches the long-run average cost curve (*LRAC*) at the output rate Q_0 and average total cost ATC_0. For outputs up to Q_1, there are economies of scale; for outputs between Q_1 and Q_2, there are constant costs; and for outputs greater than Q_2, there are diseconomies of scale. For firms that face constant factor prices, economies of scale and returns to scale are linked. For outputs up to Q_1, there are increasing returns to scale; for outputs between Q_1 and Q_2, there are constant returns to scale; and for outputs greater than Q_2, there are decreasing returns to scale.

average total cost curve $SRAC_a$ is for the plant that can produce the output rate Q_0 at minimum average total cost, ATC_0.

The first time the long-run average cost curve appeared in print, it was drawn incorrectly. Take a look at *Economics in History* (pp. 256–257) to see why. You will understand the connection between the short-run and long-run average cost curves more thoroughly after you have studied that material.

Returns to Scale and Economies of Scale

A firm can experience economies (or diseconomies) of scale for two reasons:

Output and Costs: Oil Refining

The Essence of the Story

THE FINANCIAL TIMES, 12 JANUARY 1996

A very refined dilemma

David Lascelles

The chronic overcapacity of the refining industry, particularly in ... Europe, has depressed oil company profits for years. ...Yesterday, BP announced plans to shut down or sell three refineries in the US and Europe, cutting its refinery capacity by nearly a third but also reducing losses by up to $200m a year.

The overcapacity that triggered BP's action has several causes....

❑ The technology is widely available so that entry barriers are low;

❑ Shortages created by the Gulf war in 1991 triggered a rush to build new refineries, particularly in the Far East;

❑ Improvements in technology allow existing operators to squeeze more and more out of their plants. Global capacity grows by the equivalent of four average-sized refineries a year for this reason alone....

At the same time, oil companies have had to come to terms with...falling transport costs. These have improved the fluidity of the world refined products market and ensured that regional shortages are quickly supplied.

As a result, margins in the refining business have been falling for several years. ...The 1995 margin in Europe of $1.40 a barrel was down a third on 1994....

Last year Mobil, the second-largest US company, shut its German refinery at Wörth and rationalised two refineries in the UK and France. It had previously sold or shut several smaller European refineries....

According to Mobil, the market needs to lose between 800,000 and 900,000 barrels a day of capacity to return to equilibrium. BP's cuts would remove at most 400,000 b/d.

Mr Jeremy Hudson, an oil analyst at Salomon Brothers, calculates that returns from oil refining are so low – or in many cases negative – that large companies will be unable to cover their cost of capital under foreseeable market conditions. He predicts BP's move could actually force other companies to follow suit....

■ The oil refining industry operates with excess capacity in Europe – its refineries can produce far more oil than can be sold in the world market.

■ BP plans to close one of its refineries and sell two others, cutting industry output by 400,000 barrels per day.

■ Improvements in technology have increased the capacity of existing refineries and world production of refined oil is growing by the equivalent of four refineries a year – without any being built.

■ Other factors raising capacity include lower transport costs, which reduce the need for local refineries, new suppliers and the Gulf war. Other refineries will have to close if the industry is to remain profitable.

Economic Analysis

■ Excess capacity means that individual refineries are not operating at minimum average total cost. This is a common problem in manufacturing.

■ Figure 1 shows the short-run average total cost curve (ATC_{95}) for one of BP's refineries in 1995. The refinery operates efficiently at average total cost ATC_1 and produces 400,000 barrels a day.

■ Let's assume BP has six refineries and the maximum demand for BP's refined oil is 2.4 million barrels a day.

■ Each refinery could lower its costs to ATC_{min} and produce 460,000 barrels a day without any new technology or plant, but market demand limits each refinery's output to 400,000 barrels a day.

■ Technological developments in 1996 mean BP's existing refineries can produce more at lower cost, shifting the average total cost curve to ATC_{96}.

■ Each refinery could produce 500,000 barrels a day at the lower average cost ATC_2, but output remains constrained to 400,000 barrels a day by market demand.

■ Figure 2 shows the impact of BP's decision to close one refinery and sell two others on the long-run average cost curve, $LRAC$.

■ Facing the same total demand, BP can now increase output in its three remaining refineries from 400,000 to 500,000 barrels a day, reaping economies of scale.

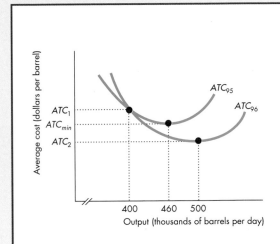

Figure 1

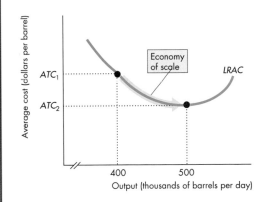

Figure 2

1. Factor prices might change with scale

2. Returns to scale

A small firm might pay a higher price for its inputs than a large firm. For example, a large farmer can buy seeds and fertilizer in bulk for a lower price than a small farmer who buys in small batches. In this case, as scale increases, average cost decreases – there are economies of scale. The opposite case might also arise. A small firm might be able to buy its inputs for a lower price than a large firm. For example, a small car-hire firm might operate with part-time labour, while a large firm must hire full-time labour and operate for 24 hours a day. The large firm pays a much higher wage rate and possibly faces a diseconomy of scale.

But most firms face the same factor prices and are price takers. Even in this case, there are economies and diseconomies of scale. But they arise from the firm's production function and from its returns to scale. With constant factor prices, economies of scale occur – the *LRAC* curve is downward-sloping – when there are increasing returns to scale. Diseconomies of scale occur – the *LRAC* curve is upward-sloping – when there are decreasing returns to scale. And constant average costs occur – the *LRAC* curve is horizontal – when there are constant returns to scale.

To see why returns to scale and economies of scale are linked, think about what happens if a firm doubles all its inputs. Because its inputs double, total cost also doubles. If the firm has constant returns to scale output doubles, so average cost is constant. If the firm has increasing returns to scale output more than doubles, so average cost falls. If the firm has decreasing returns to scale output less than doubles, so average cost rises.

You've now studied the principles of long-run cost. Let's use what you've learned to answer some questions about real businesses.

Producing Cars and Generating Electric Power

At the beginning of this chapter, we noted that most car makers can produce far more cars than they can sell. We posed the question: why do car makers have expensive equipment lying around that isn't fully used? You can see the answer in Fig. 10.10. Car

producers experience economies of scale. The minimum cost of production occurs on a short-run average total cost curve that looks like $SRAC_a$.

We also noted that many electric utilities don't have enough production equipment on hand to meet demand on the coldest and hottest days and have to buy power from other producers. You can now see why this occurs and why they don't build a bigger plant. Power producers experience diseconomies of scale. They have short-run average total cost curves like $SRAC_b$. If they had larger plants, their average total costs of producing their normal output would increase.

Long-run Costs are Variable Costs   For short-run costs, we distinguish between fixed costs and variable costs. We do not make this distinction for long-run costs. All inputs vary in the long run, so there are only variable costs. The long-run average cost curve is also the long-run average variable cost curve.

There is a long-run marginal cost curve that goes with the long-run average cost curve. The relationship between the long-run average cost curve and the long-run marginal cost curve is similar to that between the short-run average total cost curve and the short-run marginal cost curve. When long-run average cost is decreasing, long-run marginal cost is less than long-run average cost. When long-run average cost is increasing, long-run marginal cost exceeds long-run average cost. And when long-run average cost is constant, long-run marginal cost is equal to long-run average cost.

◆ ◆ ◆ ◆ We've now studied the way in which a firm's costs vary as the firm changes its inputs and its output. We've seen that diminishing marginal product gives rise to increasing marginal and average costs. We've also seen how the long-run cost curve takes its shape from economies and diseconomies of scale – long-run average cost decreases as output increases with economies of scale, and long-run average cost increases as output increases with diseconomies of scale. ◆ Our next task is to study the interactions of firms and households in markets for goods and services and see how prices, output levels and profits are determined.

The Firm's Objective and Constraints

Firms aim to maximize profit. To do so, they try to use their scarce resources efficiently. Profit is constrained by the market and by technology. The market constrains profit because people have limited demands for each good or service and a limited supply of each factor of production. They buy additional quantities only at lower prices and supply additional quantities of factors only at higher prices. Technology constrains profit because the maximum quantity that can be produced depends on the quantities of inputs – factors of production – employed. To maximize profit, a firm chooses a technologically efficient method of production. The actions a firm can take depend on its planning horizon. In the short run, the quantity of at least one input – usually capital – is fixed and the quantities of the other inputs – usually labour – can be varied. In the long run, the quantities of all inputs can be varied. (pp. 227–227)

Short-run Technology Constraint

A firm's short-run technology constraint determines how much additional output can be produced by a given increase in its variable input. It is described by a total product curve. Like the *production possibility frontier* (explained in Chapter 3), the total product curve separates attainable output levels from unattainable output levels.

The *slope* of the total product curve is the marginal product of labour. Initially, marginal product increases as the quantity of labour increases. But eventually, marginal product diminishes. Average product – output per worker – also increases initially and eventually diminishes. Average product increases when marginal product exceeds average product. Average product decreases when marginal product is less than average product. And average product is at a maximum and constant when marginal product equals average product. (pp. 228–232)

Short-run Cost

Total cost is divided into total fixed cost and total variable cost. As output increases, total cost increases because total variable cost increases. A firm's average costs and marginal cost depend on how much it produces. Average fixed cost decreases as output increases. Average variable cost, average total cost and marginal cost are U-shaped – at small output levels they decline as output increases. They pass through a minimum point, which occurs at a different output for each cost, and then eventually increase as output increases. When marginal cost is less than average cost, average cost is decreasing. When marginal cost equals average cost, average cost is at its minimum. And when marginal cost exceeds average cost, average cost is increasing.

Average cost is linked to average product. At the output level at which average product is at a maximum, average variable cost is at a minimum. The output range over which average product is increasing, average variable cost is decreasing, and the output range over which average product is decreasing, average variable cost is increasing.

Marginal cost is linked to marginal product. At the output level at which marginal product is at a maximum, marginal cost is at a minimum. The output range over which marginal product is increasing, marginal cost is decreasing, and the output range over which marginal product is decreasing, marginal cost is increasing. (pp. 232–237)

Plant Size and Cost

Long-run cost is the cost of production when all inputs – labour as well as plant and equipment – have been adjusted to their economically efficient levels. The behaviour of long-run cost depends on the firm's production function, the relation of output to costs. As a firm uses more labour while holding capital constant, it eventually experiences diminishing returns. When it uses more capital while holding labour constant, it also eventually experiences diminishing returns. When the firm increases all its inputs in equal proportions, it experiences returns to scale. Returns to scale can be constant, increasing, or decreasing.

There is a set of short-run cost curves for each different plant size. There is one least-cost plant for each output. The larger the output, the larger

CHAPTER
11

COMPETITION

After studying this chapter you will be able to:

◆ Define perfect competition

◆ Explain how price and output are determined in a competitive industry

◆ Explain why firms sometimes shut down temporarily and lay off workers

◆ Explain why firms enter and leave an industry

◆ Predict the effects of a change in demand and of a technological advance

◆ Explain why perfect competition is efficient

P ERSONAL COMPUTERS ARE BIG BUSINESS IN EUROPE. MILLIONS OF PCS ARE bought and sold each year in a multibillion pound market. Competition in supply is strong. National names such as Elonex and Gateway compete with international contenders such as Dell and IBM. New firms enter and try their luck while other firms are squeezed out of the industry. How does competition affect prices and profits? What causes some firms to enter an industry and others to leave it? What are the effects on profits and prices of new firms entering and old firms leaving an industry? ◆ In 1995, 16 million people were unemployed in the European Union. Of these, a large proportion were unemployed because they had been laid off by firms seeking to trim their costs and avoid bankruptcy. PC suppliers, ice cream producers and firms in almost every sector of the economy laid off workers in 1994. Why do firms lay off workers? When

Rivalry in Personal Computers

will a firm temporarily shut down, laying off its workers? ◆ Over the past few years, there has been a dramatic fall in the prices of PCs. For example, a slow 286 computer cost almost £3,000 a few years ago and a much faster P125 costs only £1,500 today. What goes on in an industry when the price of its output decreases sharply? What happens to the profits of the firms producing such goods?

◆ ◆ ◆ ◆ Computers, like most other goods, are produced and supplied by more than one firm and these firms compete with each other. In order to study competitive markets, we are going to build a model of a market in which competition is as fierce and extreme as possible. We call this case perfect competition.

Perfect Competition

Perfect competition is an extreme form of competition that arises when:

◆ There are many firms, each selling an identical product.

◆ There are many buyers.

◆ There are no restrictions on entry into the industry.

◆ Firms in the industry have no advantage over potential new entrants.

◆ Firms and buyers are completely informed about the prices of the products of each firm in the industry.

An industry can have a large number of firms only if the demand for its product is large relative to the minimum efficient scale of producing it. Minimum efficient scale is the output level at which average total cost is at a minimum. For example, the worldwide demand for wheat, rice and other basic grains is many thousands of times larger than the output that can be produced by a single farm at minimum average cost.

The conditions that define perfect competition imply that no individual firm can influence the price at which it sells its output. Firms in perfect competition are said to be price takers. A **price taker** is a firm that cannot influence the price of a good or service.

The key reasons why a perfectly competitive firm is a price taker are that it produces a tiny fraction of the total output of a particular good and buyers are well informed about the prices of other firms. Imagine for a moment that you are a carrot farmer in East Anglia in the United Kingdom. You have a thousand acres under cultivation – which sounds like a lot. But when you take a drive around East Anglia you see thousands more acres like yours full of carrots. Your thousand acres is just a drop in an ocean of carrots.

Nothing makes your carrots any better than any other farmer's, and all the buyers of carrots know the price at which they can do business. If everybody else sells their carrots for 50 pence a kilogram, and you want 60 pence, why would people buy from you? They can simply go to the next farmer, and the one after that, and the next, and buy all they need for 50 pence a kilogram. You are a price taker.

A price-taking firm faces a demand curve that is perfectly elastic.

The market demand for carrots is not perfectly elastic. The market demand curve is downward-sloping, and its elasticity depends on the substitutability of carrots for other vegetables such as parsnips, cabbage and peas. The demand for carrots from farm A is perfectly elastic because carrots from farm A are a *perfect substitute* for carrots from farm B.

Perfect competition does not occur frequently in the real world. But competition in many industries is so fierce that the model of perfect competition we're about to study is of enormous help in predicting the behaviour of the firms in these industries. Assembling and retailing PCs, ice cream making, producing all kinds of agricultural goods, fishing, wood pulping and paper milling, the manufacture of paper cups and plastic shopping bags, photo-processing, plant growing and retailing, plumbing, painting and dry cleaning are all examples of industries that are highly competitive.

Profit and Revenue

The goal of a firm is to maximize profit, which is the sum of normal profit and economic profit. **Normal profit** is the return that a firm's owner could obtain in the best alternative business. So it is a forgone alternative or *opportunity cost* and part of the firm's total cost. **Economic profit** is equal to total revenue minus total cost.

Total revenue is the value of a firm's sales. It equals the price of the firm's output multiplied by the number of units of output sold (price × quantity). **Average revenue** is total revenue divided by the total quantity sold – revenue per unit sold. Because total revenue equals price multiplied by quantity sold, average revenue (total revenue divided by quantity sold) equals price. **Marginal revenue** is the change in total revenue divided by the change in quantity. That is, marginal revenue is the change in total revenue resulting from a one-unit increase in the quantity sold. In the case of perfect competition, the price remains constant when the quantity sold changes. So the change in total revenue resulting from a one-unit increase in the quantity sold equals price. Therefore, in perfect competition, marginal revenue equals price and marginal revenue does not vary with quantity.

An example of these revenue concepts is set out for Neat Knits Ltd in Fig. 11.1. The table shows three different quantities of jumpers sold. For a price taker, as the quantity sold varies, the price stays constant – in this example at £25. Total revenue is equal to price multiplied by quantity. For example, if Neat Knits sells 8 jumpers, total revenue is 8 times £25, which equals £200. Average revenue is total revenue divided by quantity. Again, if Neat Knits sells 8 jumpers, average revenue is total revenue (£200) divided by quantity (8), which equals £25. Marginal revenue is the change in total revenue resulting from a 1-unit change in quantity. For example, when the quantity sold increases from 8 to 9, total revenue increases from £200 to £225, so marginal revenue is £25. (Notice that in the

table, marginal revenue appears *between* the lines for the quantities sold. This arrangement presents a visual reminder that marginal revenue results from the *change* in the quantity sold.)

Suppose that Neat Knits is one of a thousand similar small producers of jumpers. Figure 11.1(a) shows the demand and supply curves for the entire jumper industry. Demand curve *D* intersects supply curve *S* at a price of £25 and a quantity of 9,000 jumpers. Figure 11.1(b) shows Neat Knits' demand curve. Because the firm is a price taker, its demand curve is perfectly elastic – the horizontal line at £25. The figure also illustrates Neat Knits' total, average and marginal revenues, calculated in the

FIGURE 11.1

Demand, Price and Revenue in Perfect Competition

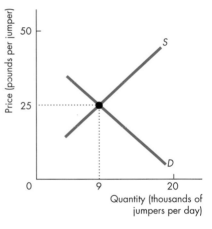

(a) Jumper industry

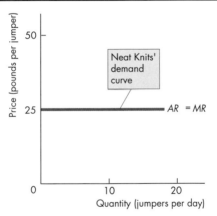

(b) Neat Knits' demand, average revenue and marginal revenue

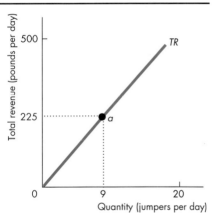

(c) Neat Knits' total revenue

Quantity sold (Q) (jumpers per day)	Price (P) (pounds per jumper)	Total revenue (TR = P × Q) (pounds)	Average revenue (AR = TR/Q) (pounds per jumper)	Marginal revenue (MR = ΔTR/ΔQ) (pounds per jumper)
8	25	200	25	
				25
9	25	225	25	
				25
10	25	250	25	

In perfect competition, price is determined where the industry demand and supply curves intersect. Such an equilibrium is illustrated in part (a) where the price is £25 and 9,000 jumpers are bought and sold. Neat Knits, a perfectly competitive firm, faces a fixed price, £25 in this example, regardless of the quantity it produces. The table calculates Neat Knits' total revenue, average revenue and marginal revenue. For example, when 9 jumpers are sold, total revenue is £225 and average revenue is £25. When sales increase from 9 jumpers to 10 jumpers, marginal revenue equals £25. The demand curve faced by Neat Knits is perfectly elastic at the market price and is shown in part (b) of the figure. Neat Knits' demand curve is also its average revenue curve and marginal revenue curve (AR = MR). Neat Knits' total revenue curve (TR) is shown in part (c). Point a on the total revenue curve corresponds to the second row of the table.

table. The average revenue curve and marginal revenue curve are the same as the firm's demand curve. That is, the firm's demand curve tells us the revenue per jumper sold and the change in total revenue that results from selling one more jumper. Neat Knits' total revenue curve (part c) shows the total revenue for each quantity sold. For example, when Neat Knits sells 9 jumpers, total revenue is £225 (point *a*). Because each additional jumper sold brings in a constant amount – in this case £25 – the total revenue curve is an upward-sloping straight line.

The Firm's Decisions in Perfect Competition

Firms in a perfectly competitive industry face a given market price and have the revenue curves that you've just studied. These revenue curves summarize the market constraint faced by a perfectly competitive firm.

Firms also have a technology constraint, which is described by the product curves (total product, average product and marginal product) that you studied in Chapter 10. The technology available to the firm determines its costs, which are described by the cost curves (total cost, average cost and marginal cost) that you also studied in Chapter 10.

The task of the competitive firm is to make the maximum profit possible, given the constraints it faces. To achieve this objective, a firm must make four key decisions, two in the short run and two in the long run.

Short-run Decisions　The short run is a timeframe in which each firm has a given plant and the number of firms in the industry is fixed. But many things can change in the short run and the firm must react to these changes. For example, the price for which the firm can sell its output might have a seasonal fluctuation, or it might be affected by general business fluctuations.

The firm must react to such short-run price fluctuations and decide:

1. Whether to produce or to temporarily shut down
2. If the decision is to produce, what quantity to produce

Long-run Decisions　The long run is a timeframe in which each firm can change the size of its plant and can decide whether to enter or leave an industry. So in the long run, both the plant size of each firm and the number of firms in the industry can change. Many additional things can change in the long run to which the firm must react. For example, the demand for a good can permanently fall. Or a technological advance can change an industry's costs.

The firm must react to such long-run changes and decide:

1. Whether to increase or decrease its plant size
2. Whether to stay in the industry or leave it

The Firm and the Industry in the Short Run and the Long Run　To study a competitive industry, we begin by looking at an individual firm's short-run decisions. We then see how the short-run decisions of all the firms in a competitive industry combine to determine the industry price, output and economic profit. Then we turn to the long run and study the effects of long-run decisions on the industry price, output and economic profit.

All the decisions we study are driven by the single objective: to maximize profit.

Profit-maximizing Output

A perfectly competitive firm cannot influence profit by choosing a price. But it can maximize profit in the short run by choosing its output level. One way of finding the profit-maximizing output is to study a firm's total revenue and total cost curves and to find the output level at which total revenue exceeds total cost by the largest amount. Figure 11.2 shows you how to do this for Neat Knits. The table lists Neat Knits' revenue and total cost at different outputs, and part (a) of the figure shows Neat Knits' total revenue and total cost curves. These curves are graphs of the numbers shown in the first three columns of the table. The total revenue curve (*TR*) is the same as that in Fig. 11.1(c). The total cost curve (*TC*) is similar to the one that you met in Chapter 10. As output increases, so does total cost.

Economic profit equals total revenue minus total cost. The fourth column of the table in Fig. 11.2 shows Neat Knits' economic profit and part (b) of the figure illustrates these numbers as Neat Knits's profit curve. This curve shows that Neat Knits makes an economic profit at outputs greater than 4 and fewer than 12 jumpers a day. At outputs of fewer than 4 jumpers a day, Neat Knits incurs a loss. It also

FIGURE 11.2

Total Revenue, Total Cost and Profit

Quantity (Q) (jumpers per day)	Total revenue (TR) (pounds)	Total cost (TC) (pounds)	Economic profit (TR − TC) (pounds)
0	0	22	−22
1	25	45	−20
2	50	66	−16
3	75	85	−10
4	100	100	0
5	125	114	11
6	150	126	24
7	175	141	34
8	200	160	40
9	225	183	42
10	250	210	40
11	275	245	30
12	300	300	0
13	325	360	−35

(a) Revenue and cost

(b) Economic profit and loss

The table lists Neat Knits' total revenue, total cost and economic profit. Part (a) graphs the total revenue and total cost curves. Economic profit is seen in part (a) as the blue area between the total cost and total revenue curves. The maximum economic profit, £42 a day, occurs when 9 jumpers are produced – where the vertical distance between the total revenue and total cost curves is at its largest. At outputs of 4 jumpers a day and 12 jumpers a day, Neat Knits makes zero economic profit – these are break-even points. At outputs fewer than 4 and greater than 12 jumpers a day, Neat Knits incurs a loss. Part (b) of the figure shows Neat Knits' profit curve. The profit curve is at its highest when profit is at a maximum and cuts the horizontal axis at the break-even points.

incurs a loss if output exceeds 12 jumpers a day. At outputs of 4 jumpers and 12 jumpers a day, total cost equals total revenue and Neat Knits' economic profit is zero. An output at which total cost equals total revenue is called a *break-even point*. Because normal profit is part of total cost, a firm makes normal profit at a break-even point.

Neat Knits' economic profit, calculated in the final column of the table, is graphed in part (b) of the figure. Notice the relationship between the total revenue, total cost and profit curves. Economic profit is measured by the vertical distance between the total revenue and total cost curves. When the total revenue curve in part (a) is above the total cost curve, between 4 and 12 jumpers, the firm is making an economic profit and the profit curve in part (b) is above the horizontal axis. At the break-even point, where the total cost and total revenue curves intersect, the profit curve intersects the horizontal axis.

The profit curve is at its highest when the distance between *TR* and *TC* is greatest. In this example, profit maximization occurs at an output of 9 jumpers a day. At this output, Neat Knits' economic profit is £42 a day.

Marginal Analysis

Another way of finding the profit-maximizing output is to use *marginal analysis*. To use marginal analysis, a firm compares its marginal cost, *MC*, with its marginal revenue, *MR*. As we have seen, marginal revenue in perfect competition is constant and marginal cost increases as output increases. If marginal revenue exceeds marginal cost (if *MR > MC*), then the extra revenue from selling one more unit exceeds the extra cost incurred to produce it, so profit increases if output increases. If marginal revenue is less than marginal cost (if *MR < MC*), then the extra revenue from selling one more unit is less than the extra cost incurred to produce it, so profit increases if output *decreases*. If marginal revenue equals marginal cost (if *MR = MC*), profit is maximized. The rule *MR = MC* is a prime example of marginal analysis. Let's check that this rule works to find the profit-maximizing output by returning to Sam's jumper factory.

Look at Fig. 11.3. The table records Neat Knits' marginal revenue and marginal cost. Focus on the highlighted rows of the table. If output increases from 8 jumpers to 9 jumpers, marginal revenue is £25 and marginal cost is £23. Because marginal revenue exceeds marginal cost, profit increases. The last column of the table shows that profit increases from £40 to £42, an increase of £2. This profit from the ninth jumper is shown as the blue area in the figure.

If output increases from 9 jumpers to 10 jumpers, marginal revenue is still £25, but marginal cost is £27. Because marginal revenue is less than marginal cost, profit decreases. The last column of the table shows that profit decreases from £42 to £40. This loss from the tenth jumper is shown as the red area in the figure.

Neat Knits maximizes profit by producing 9 jumpers a day, the quantity at which marginal revenue equals marginal cost.

Economic Profit in the Short Run

In the short run, when a firm has set its marginal cost equal to its marginal revenue and maximized profit, it might make an economic profit, break even (making normal profit), or incur an economic loss. Maximizing profit is not the same as making a profit. To determine which of these three possible outcomes occurs, we need to compare the firm's total revenue and total cost. Alternatively, we can compare price with average total cost. If price exceeds

FIGURE 11.3

Marginal Revenue, Marginal Cost and Profit-maximizing Output

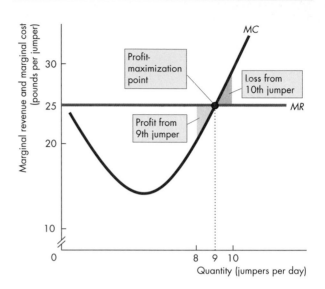

Quantity (*Q*) (jumpers per day)	Total revenue (*TR*) (pounds)	Marginal revenue (*MR*) (pounds per jumper)	Total cost (*TC*) (pounds)	Marginal cost (*MC*) (pounds per jumper)	Economic profit (*TR−TC*) (pounds)
7	175		141		34
		 25		 19	
8	200		160		40
		 25		 23	
9	225		183		42
		 25		 27	
10	250		210		40
		 25		 35	
11	275		245		30

Another way of finding the profit-maximizing output is to determine the output at which marginal revenue equals marginal cost. The table shows that if output increases from 8 to 9 jumpers, marginal cost is £23, which is less than the marginal revenue of £25. If output increases from 9 to 10 jumpers, marginal cost is £27, which exceeds the marginal revenue of £25. The figure shows that marginal cost and marginal revenue are equal when Neat Knits produces 9 jumpers a day. If marginal revenue exceeds marginal cost, an increase in output increases profit. If marginal revenue is less than marginal cost, an increase in output decreases profit. If marginal revenue equals marginal cost, economic profit is maximized.

average total cost, a firm makes an economic profit. If price equals average total cost, a firm breaks even – makes a normal profit. If price is less than average total cost, a firm incurs an economic loss. But the economic loss incurred is its minimum possible loss. Profit maximization implies loss minimization. Let's look more closely at these three possible outcomes for a firm.

Three Possible Profit Outcomes Figure 11.4 shows the three possible profit outcomes in the short run. In part (a), price exceeds average total cost and Neat Knits makes an economic profit. Price and marginal revenue are £25 a jumper and the profit-maximizing output is 9 jumpers a day. Neat Knits' total revenue is £225 a day (9 × £25). Average total cost is £20.33 a jumper and total cost is £183 a day (9 × £20.33). Neat Knits' economic profit is £42 a day. Economic profit equals total revenue minus total cost, which is £225 – £183 or £42 a day. Economic profit also equals economic profit per jumper, which is £4.67 (£25.00 – £20.33), multiplied by the number of jumpers (£4.67 × 9 = £42). The blue rectangle in the figure shows this economic profit. The height of the rectangle is profit per jumper, £4.67, and the length is the quantity of jumpers produced, 9 a day,

so the area of the rectangle measures Neat Knits' economic profit of £42 a day.

In part (b), price equals average total cost and Neat Knits breaks even – makes normal profit and zero economic profit. Price and marginal revenue are £20 a jumper and the profit-maximizing output is 8 jumpers a day. At this output, average total cost is at its minimum.

In part (c), price is less than average total cost and Neat Knits incurs an economic loss. Price and marginal revenue are £17 a jumper and the profit-maximizing (loss-minimizing) output is 7 jumpers a day. Neat Knits' total revenue is £119 a day (7 × £17). Average total cost is £20.14 a jumper and total cost is £141 a day (7 × £20.14). Neat Knits' economic loss is £22 a day. Economic loss equals total revenue minus total cost, which is £119 – £141 = –£22 a day. The economic loss, £22, also equals economic loss per jumper, £3.14 (£20.14 – £17.00), multiplied by the number of jumpers (£3.14 × 7 = £22). The red rectangle in the figure shows this economic loss. The height of the rectangle is economic loss per jumper, £3.14, and the length is the quantity of jumpers produced, 7 a day, so the area of the rectangle measures Neat Knits' economic loss of £22 a day.

FIGURE 11.4

Three Possible Profit Outcomes in the Short Run

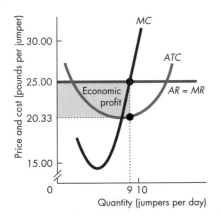
(a) Economic profit

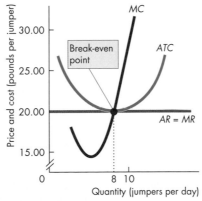
(b) Normal profit

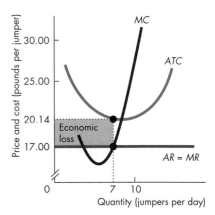
(c) Economic loss

In the short run, firms might make an economic profit, break even (making a normal profit), or incur a loss. If the market price is higher than the average total cost of producing the profit-maximizing output, the firm makes an economic profit (part a). If price equals minimum average total cost, the firm breaks even and makes a normal profit (part b). If the price is below minimum average total cost, the firm incurs an economic loss (part c). The firm's economic profit is shown as the blue rectangle and the firm's economic loss is the red rectangle.

The Firm's Short-run Supply Curve

A perfectly competitive firm's supply curve shows how the firm's profit-maximizing output varies as the market price varies, other things remaining the same. Figure 11.5 shows you how to derive Neat Knits' entire supply curve. Part (a) shows Neat Knits' marginal cost and average variable cost curves and part (b) shows its supply curve. Let's look at the link between the marginal cost and average variable cost curves and the supply curve.

Temporary Plant Shutdown A firm can avoid only variable costs. Fixed costs are incurred even at zero output, and a firm that shuts down and produces no output incurs a maximum loss equal to its total fixed cost. If the price falls below average variable cost, the firm's profit-maximizing action is to shut down temporarily, lay off its workers and produce nothing. A firm's **shutdown point** is the level of output and price where the firm is just covering its total *variable* cost incurring a loss equal to its total fixed cost. If a firm did produce and sell its output for less than its average variable cost, its loss would exceed its total fixed cost. Such a firm would not be maximizing profit (minimizing loss).

The shutdown point is shown in Fig. 11.5(a). When the marginal revenue curve is MR_0, price is £17 and the firm produces 7 jumpers a day at the shutdown point s. If the price falls just a penny below £17, profit is maximized (loss is minimized) by producing nothing.

Production Decisions If the price is above minimum average variable cost, Neat Knits maximizes profit by producing the output at which marginal cost equals price. We can determine the quantity produced at each price from the marginal cost curve. At a price of £25, the marginal revenue curve is MR_1 and Neat Knits maximizes profit by producing 9 jumpers. At a price of £31, the marginal revenue curve is MR_2 and Neat Knits produces 10 jumpers.

The Supply Curve The supply curve is shown in Fig. 11.5(b). In the range of prices that exceed minimum average variable cost, the supply curve is the same as the marginal cost curve above the shutdown point (s). At prices below minimum average variable cost, Neat Knits shuts down and produces nothing. Its supply curve runs along the vertical axis. At a price of £17, Neat Knits is indifferent between shutting down and producing 7 jumpers a day. Either way, it incurs a loss of £25 a day.

FIGURE 11.5

Neat Knits' Supply Curve

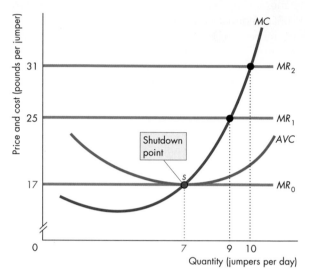

(a) Marginal cost and average variable cost

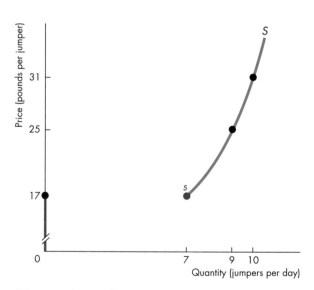

(b) Neat Knits' supply curve

Part (a) shows Neat Knits' profit-maximizing output at each market price. At £25 a jumper, Neat Knits produces 9 jumpers. At £17 a jumper, Neat Knits produces 7 jumpers. At any price below £17 a jumper, Neat Knits produces nothing as Neat Knits' shutdown point is s. Part (b) shows Neat Knits' supply curve – the number of jumpers Neat Knits will produce at each price. Neat Knits' supply curve is made up of its marginal cost curve (part a) at all points above the average variable cost curve, and the vertical axis at all prices below minimum average variable cost.

REVIEW

◆ In perfect competition, a firm is a price taker and its marginal revenue equals the market price.

◆ If price exceeds average variable cost, a firm maximizes profit by producing the output at which marginal cost equals marginal revenue (equals price). The lowest price at which a firm produces is equal to its minimum average variable cost.

◆ If price falls below minimum average variable cost, the firm stops producing and incurs an economic loss equal to its total fixed cost.

◆ In the short run, a firm can make an economic profit, break even (make zero economic profit and earn normal profit), or incur an economic loss. The maximum economic loss that a firm incurs is equal to its total fixed cost.

So far, we have seen that the firm's profit-maximizing actions depend on the market price. But how is the market price determined? Let's find out.

Output, Price and Profit in the Short Run

To determine the market price and the quantity bought and sold in a perfectly competitive market, we need to study how market demand and market supply interact. We begin this process by studying a perfectly competitive market in the short run.

Short-run Industry Supply Curve

The **short-run industry supply curve** shows how the quantity supplied by the industry varies as the market price varies when the plant size of each firm and the number of firms in the industry remain the same. The quantity supplied by the industry at a given price is the sum of the quantities supplied by all firms in the industry at that price. To construct the industry supply curve, we sum horizontally the supply curves of the individual firms. Let's see how we do that.

Suppose that the competitive jumper industry consists of 1,000 firms exactly like Neat Knits. The relationship between a firm's supply curve and the

industry supply curve, for this case, is illustrated in Fig. 11.6. Each of the 1,000 firms in the industry has a supply schedule like Neat Knits', set out in the table. At a price below £17, every firm in the industry will shut down production so that the industry will supply nothing. At £17, each firm is indifferent between shutting down and producing 7 jumpers. Because each firm is indifferent, some firms will produce and others will shut down. Industry supply can be anything between 0 (all firms shut down) and 7,000 (all firms producing 7 jumpers a day each). Thus at £17, the industry supply curve is horizontal – it is perfectly elastic. As the price rises above £17,

---

FIGURE 11.6

Industry Supply Curve

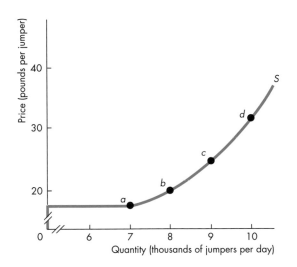

	Price (pounds) per jumper)	Quantity supplied by Neat Knits (jumpers per day)	Quantity supplied by industry (jumpers per day)
a	17	0 or 7	0 to 7,000
b	20	8	8,000
c	25	9	9,000
d	31	10	10,000

The industry supply schedule is the sum of the supply schedules of all individual firms. An industry that consists of 1,000 identical firms will supply a quantity 1,000 times as large as that of the individual firm (see table). The industry supply curve is S. Points a, b, c and d correspond to the rows of the table. At the shutdown price of £17, each firm produces either 0 or 7 jumpers per day. The industry supply curve is perfectly elastic at the shutdown price.

each firm increases its quantity supplied and the quantity supplied by the industry also increases, but by 1,000 times that of each individual firm.

The supply schedules set out in the table form the basis of the industry supply curve in Fig. 11.6. At each price, the quantity supplied by the industry is 1,000 times the quantity supplied by a single firm. At a price of £17 a jumper, a firm supplies either nothing or 7 jumpers a day, so the industry supplies any quantity between zero and 7,000 jumpers. The industry supply curve is perfectly elastic over that range.

Short-run Equilibrium

Market price and industry output are determined by industry demand and supply. Figure 11.7(a) shows three different possible short-run equilibrium positions in a perfectly competitive market. The industry supply curve is S and the industry demand curve is D_1, the equilibrium price is £25 and industry output is 9,000 jumpers a day. If the demand curve is D_2, the price is £20 and industry output is 8,000 jumpers a day. If the demand curve is D_3, the price is £17 and industry output is 7,000 jumpers a day.

Figure 11.7(b) shows the situation facing each of the 1,000 individual firms. With demand curve D_1, the price is £25 a jumper, so each firm produces 9 jumpers a day and makes an economic profit (the blue rectangle); if the demand curve is D_2, the price is £20 a jumper, so each firm produces 8 jumpers a day and makes zero economic profit (normal profit); and if the demand curve is D_3, the price is £17 a jumper, so each firm produces 7 jumpers a day and incurs a loss (the red rectangle).

If the demand curve shifts farther leftward than D_3, the price remains constant at £17 because the industry supply curve is horizontal at that price. Some firms continue to produce 7 jumpers a day and others shut down. Firms are indifferent between these two activities and, whichever they choose, they incur a loss equal to total fixed cost. The number of firms continuing to produce is just enough to satisfy the market demand at a price of £17.

FIGURE 11.7

Three Short-run Equilibrium Positions for a Competitive Industry

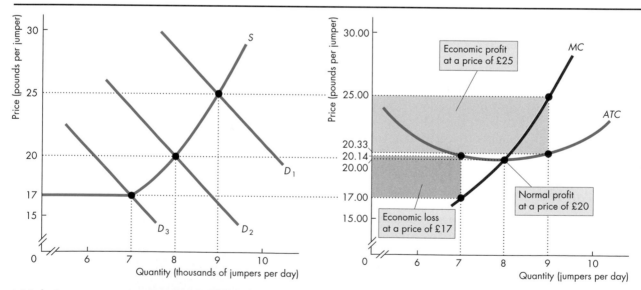

(a) Industry

(b) Firm

In part (a), the competitive jumper industry's supply curve is S. If demand is D_1, the price is £25 and the industry produces 9,000 jumpers. If demand is D_2, the price is £20 and industry output is 8,000 jumpers. If demand is D_3, the price is £17 and industry output is 7,000 jumpers.

In part (b), when the price is £25, an individual firm is making an economic profit; when the price is £20, it is breaking even (making normal profit), and when the price is £17 it is incurring an economic loss.

In the short-run, the number of firms and plant size of each firm is fixed. In the long run, each of these features of an industry can change. Also, as you are about to discover, there are forces at work that will disturb some of the short-run situations we've just examined. Let's now look at the forces that operate in the long run.

Output, Price and Profit in the Long Run

In short-run equilibrium, a firm might make an economic profit, incur an economic loss, or break even (make normal profit). Although each of these three situations is a short-run equilibrium, only one of them is a long-run equilibrium. To see why, we need to examine the forces at work in a competitive industry in the long run.

In the long run, an industry adjusts in two ways: the number of firms in the industry changes and firms change the scale of their plants. The number of firms in an industry changes as a result of entry and exit. *Entry* is the act of setting up a new firm in an industry. *Exit* is the act of a firm leaving an industry. Let's first see how economic profit and loss trigger entry and exit.

Economic Profit and Economic Loss as Signals

An industry in which firms are making an economic profit attracts new entrants; one in which firms are incurring an economic loss induces exits; and an industry in which firms are making normal profit (zero economic profit) induces neither entry nor exit. Thus economic profit and economic loss are the signals to which firms respond in making entry and exit decisions.

Temporary economic profits and temporary losses that are random, like the winnings and losses at a casino, do not trigger entry or exit. But the prospect of persistent economic profit or loss does.

Entry and exit influence market price, the quantity produced and economic profit. The immediate effect of entry and exit is to shift the industry supply curve. If more firms enter an industry, the industry supply curve shifts rightward: supply increases. If firms exit an industry, the industry supply curve shifts leftward: supply falls. Let's see what happens when new firms enter an industry.

The Effects of Entry

Figure 11.8 shows the effects of entry. Suppose that the demand curve for jumpers is D and the industry supply curve is S_A, so jumpers sell for £23 and 7,000 jumpers are being produced. Firms in the industry are making an economic profit. Some new firms enter the industry. As they do so, the industry supply curve shifts rightward to S_0. With the greater supply and unchanged demand, the market price falls from £23 to £20 a jumper and the quantity produced increases from 7,000 to 8,000 jumpers a day.

As the price falls, Neat Knits and every other firm in the industry moves down along its supply curve and decreases output. That is, for each existing firm in the industry, the profit-maximizing output decreases. Because the price falls and each firm sells less, economic profit decreases. When the price falls to £20, economic profit disappears and each firm makes a normal profit.

FIGURE 11.8

Entry and Exit

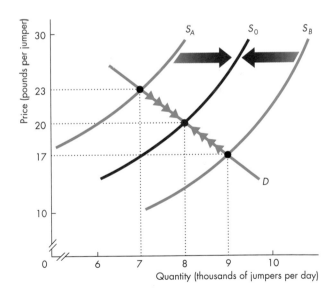

When new firms enter the jumper industry, the industry supply curve shifts rightward, from S_A to S_0. The equilibrium price falls from £23 to £20, and the quantity produced increases from 7,000 to 8,000 jumpers. When firms exit the jumper industry, the industry supply curve shifts leftward, from S_B to S_0. The equilibrium price rises from £17 to £20, and the quantity produced decreases from 9,000 to 8,000 jumpers.

You have just discovered a key proposition:

As new firms enter an industry, the price falls and the economic profit of each existing firm decreases.

A good example of this process has occurred in the last few years in the personal computer industry. When IBM introduced its first personal computer in the early 1980s, there was little competition and the price of PCs gave IBM a big profit. But new firms such as Amstrad, Dell, Elonex and a host of others soon entered the industry with machines technologically identical to the IBM PC. In fact, they were so similar that they came to be called 'clones'. The massive wave of entry into the personal computer industry shifted the supply curve rightward and lowered the price and the economic profit for all firms.

Let's now see what happens when firms leave an industry.

The Effects of Exit

Figure 11.8 shows the effects of exit. Suppose that the demand curve is D and the supply curve is S_B, so the market price is £17 and 9,000 jumpers are being produced. Firms in the industry are incurring an economic loss. As firms leave the industry, the supply curve shifts leftward to S_0. With the decrease in supply, industry output decreases from 9,000 to 8,000 jumpers and the price rises from £17 to £20.

As the price rises, Neat Knits and every other firm in the industry moves up along its supply curve and increases output. That is, for each existing firm in the industry, the profit-maximizing output increases. Because the price rises and each firm sells more, economic loss decreases. When the price rises to £20, economic loss disappears and each firm makes a normal profit.

You have just discovered a second key proposition:

As firms leave an industry, the price rises and so do the economic profits of the remaining firms.

An example of a firm leaving an industry is Escom UK – the United Kingdom's largest high street specialist computer chain in 1996. Escom's German parent company, Escom AG, also went bankrupt after making losses of £76 million in 1995. Escom entered the UK market in 1993, and expanded in

1995 when it took over 231 Rumbelows shops. Its agressive price-cutting strategy did not generate sufficient revenue as other retailers also reduced their prices. Profit margins in the industry were squeezed. Escom eventually exited the industry because it made persistent economic losses. When it exited the industry, it had already closed down many of its outlets. This decrease allowed the remaining retailers to break even or regain some economic profit. You can read about the effects of entry and exit on the container shipping industry in *Reading Between the Lines*, pp. 278–279.

Long-run Equilibrium

Long-run equilibrium occurs in a competitive industry when firms are earning normal profit and economic profit is zero. If the firms in a competitive industry make an economic profit, new firms enter the industry and the supply curve shifts rightward. As a result, the market price falls and so does economic profit. Firms continue to enter and economic profit continues to decrease as long as the industry is earning positive economic profits. Only when the economic profit has been eliminated and normal profit is being made do firms stop entering.

If the firms in a competitive industry incur an economic loss, some of the firms exit the industry and the supply curve shifts leftward. As a result, the market price rises and the industry's economic loss shrinks. Firms continue to leave and economic loss shrinks as long as the industry is incurring an economic loss. Only when the economic loss has been eliminated and normal profit is being made do firms stop exiting.

So, in long-run equilibrium in a competitive industry, firms neither enter nor exit the industry.

Let's now examine the second way in which the competitive industry adjusts in the long run – by existing firms changing their plant size.

Changes in Plant Size

A firm changes its plant size if, by doing so, its profit increases. Figure 11.9 shows a situation in which Neat Knits can increase its profit by increasing its plant size. With its current plant, Neat Knits' marginal cost curve is MC_0 and its short-run average total cost curve is $SRAC_0$. The market price is £25 a jumper, so Neat Knits' marginal revenue curve is

FIGURE 11.9

Plant Size and Long-run Equilibrium

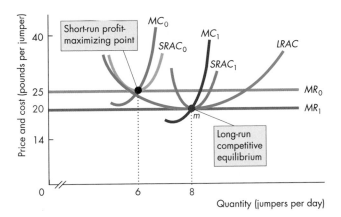

Initially, Neat Knits' plant has marginal cost curve MC_0 and short-run average total cost curve $SRAC_0$. The market price is £25 a jumper and Neat Knits' marginal revenue is MR_0. The short-run profit-maximizing quantity is 6 jumpers a day. Neat Knits can increase its profit by increasing its plant size. If all firms in the jumper industry increase their plant sizes, the short-run industry supply increases and the market price falls.

In long-run equilibrium, a firm operates with the plant that minimizes its average cost. Here, Neat Knits operates the plant with short-run marginal cost MC_1 and short-run average total cost $SRAC_1$. Neat Knits is also on its long-run average cost curve $LRAC$ and produces at point m. Output is 8 jumpers a day and average total cost equals the price of a jumper at £20.

MR_0 and Neat Knits maximizes profit by producing 6 jumpers a day.

Neat Knits' long-run average cost curve is $LRAC$. By increasing its plant size – installing more knitting machines – Neat Knits can move along its long-run average cost curve. As Neat Knits increases its plant size, its short-run marginal cost curve shifts rightward.

Recall that a firm's short-run supply curve is linked to its marginal cost curve. As Neat Knits' marginal cost curve shifts rightward, so does its supply curve. If Neat Knits and the other firms in the industry increase their plants, the short-run industry supply curve shifts rightward and the

market price falls. The fall in the market price limits the extent to which Neat Knits can profit from increasing its plant size.

Figure 11.9 also shows Neat Knits in a long-run competitive equilibrium. This situation arises when the market price has fallen to £20 a jumper. Marginal revenue is MR_1, and Neat Knits maximizes profit by producing 8 jumpers a day. In this situation, Neat Knits cannot increase its profit by changing its plant size. It is producing at minimum long-run average cost (point m on $LRAC$).

Because Neat Knits is producing at minimum long-run average cost, it has no incentive to change its plant size. Either a bigger plant or a smaller plant has a higher long-run average cost.

If all firms in the jumper industry are in the situation described in Fig. 11.9, the industry is in long-run equilibrium. No firm has an incentive to change its plant size. Also, because each firm is making zero economic profit (normal profit), no firm has an incentive to enter the industry or to leave it.

R E V I E W

Long-run competitive equilibrium is described by three conditions:

◆ Firms maximize short-run profit by producing the quantity that makes marginal cost equal to marginal revenue and price.

◆ Economic profits are zero, so no firm has an incentive to enter or to leave the industry.

◆ Long-run average cost is at a minimum, so no firm has an incentive to change its plant size.

We've seen how economic loss triggers exit, which eventually eliminates the loss, and we've seen how economic profit triggers entry, which eventually eliminates the profit. In the long run, normal profit is earned. But a competitive industry is rarely in a long-run equilibrium. It is restlessly evolving towards such an equilibrium and the conditions the industry faces are constantly changing. The two most persistent sources of change are in tastes and technology. Let's see how a competitive industry reacts to such changes.

Changing Tastes and Advancing Technology

Increased awareness of the health hazard of smoking has caused a decrease in the demand for tobacco and cigarettes. The development of cheap cars and air travel has caused a huge decrease in the demand for long-distance trains and buses. Solid-state electronics have caused a large decrease in the demand for TV and radio repair. The development of good quality budget clothing has decreased the demand for sewing machines. What happens in a competitive industry when there is a permanent decrease in the demand for its products?

The development of the microwave oven has produced an enormous increase in demand for paper, glass and plastic cooking utensils, and for plastic wrap. The demand for almost all products is steadily increasing as a result of increasing population and increasing incomes. What happens in a competitive industry when the demand for its product increases?

Advances in technology are constantly lowering the costs of production. New biotechnologies have dramatically lowered the costs of many food and pharmaceutical products. New electronic technologies have lowered the cost of producing just about every good and service. What happens in a competitive industry when technological change lowers its production costs?

Let's use the theory of perfect competition to answer these questions.

A Permanent Change in Demand

Figure 11.10(a) shows an industry that initially is in long-run competitive equilibrium. The demand

---

FIGURE 11.10

A Decrease in Demand

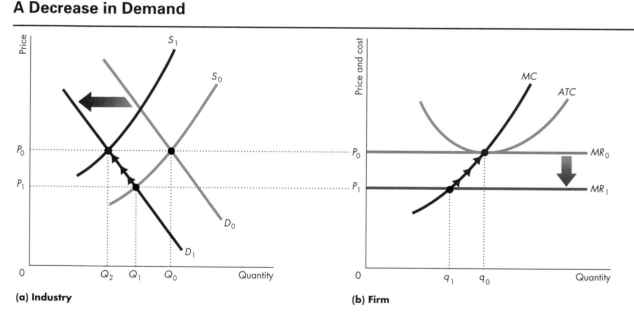

(a) Industry

(b) Firm

An industry starts out in long-run competitive equilibrium. Part (a) shows the industry demand curve D_0 and the industry supply curve S_0, the equilibrium quantity Q_0 and the market price P_0. Each firm sells at price P_0, so its marginal revenue curve is MR_0 in part (b). Each firm produces q_0 and makes a normal profit. Demand decreases from D_0 to D_1 (part a). The equilibrium price falls to P_1, each firm decreases its output to q_1 (part b) and industry output decreases to Q_1 (part a). In this new situation,

firms are incurring losses and some firms leave the industry. As they do so, the industry supply curve gradually shifts leftward, from S_0 to S_1. This shift gradually raises the industry price from P_1 back to P_0. While the price is below P_0, firms are incurring losses and some leave the industry. Once the price has returned to P_0, each firm makes a normal profit. Firms have no further incentive to leave the industry. Each firm produces q_0 and industry output is Q_2.

curve is D_0, the supply curve is S_0, the market price is P_0 and industry output is Q_0. Figure 11.10(b) shows a single firm in this initial long-run equilibrium. The firm produces q_0 and makes a normal profit and zero economic profit.

Now suppose that demand decreases and the demand curve shifts leftward to D_1, as shown in part (a). The price falls to P_1 and the quantity supplied by the industry decreases from Q_0 to Q_1 as the industry slides down its short-run supply curve S_0. Part (b) shows the situation facing a firm. Price is now below minimum average total cost so the firm incurs an economic loss. But to keep its loss to a minimum, the firm adjusts its output to keep price equal to marginal cost. At a price of P_1 each firm produces an output of q_1.

The industry is now in short-run equilibrium but not long-run equilibrium. It is in short-run equilibrium because each firm is maximizing profit. But it is not in long-run equilibrium because each firm is incurring an economic loss – its average total cost exceeds the price.

In this situation, some firms leave the industry. As they do so, short-run industry supply decreases and the supply curve shifts leftward. As supply decreases, the price rises. At each higher price a firm's profit-maximizing output is greater, so those remaining in the industry increase their output as the price rises. Each slides up its marginal cost or supply curve (part b). That is, as firms exit the industry, industry output decreases but the output of the firms that remain in the industry increases. Eventually, enough firms leave the industry for the supply curve to have shifted to S_1 (part a). At this time, the price has returned to its original level, P_0. At this price, the firms remaining in the industry produce q_0, the same quantity as they produced before the decrease in demand. Because firms are now making normal profits and zero economic profit, no firm wants to enter or exit the industry. The industry supply curve remains at S_1 and industry output is Q_2. The industry is again in long-run equilibrium.

The difference between the initial long-run equilibrium and the final long-run equilibrium is the number of firms in the industry. A permanent decrease in demand has decreased the number of firms. Each remaining firm produces the same output in the new long-run equilibrium as it did initially and earns a normal profit. In the process of moving from the initial equilibrium to the new

one, firms that remain in the industry incur losses.

The market for mainframe computers is one that has experienced a decrease in demand in recent years. As personal computers have become faster and cheaper, more and more data processing has been done on people's desktops rather than in big computer laboratories. The effects of this decrease in demand have been similar to those we have just studied.

We've just worked out how a competitive industry responds to a permanent *decrease* in demand. A permanent increase in demand triggers a similar response, except in the opposite direction. The increase in demand brings a higher price, profit and entry. Entry increases supply and eventually lowers the price to its original level.

We've now studied the effects of a permanent change in taste that brings a permanent change in demand for a good. We began and ended in a long-run equilibrium and examined the *process* that gets a market from one equilibrium to another. It is this process that describes the real world, not the equilibrium points.

One feature of the predictions that we have just generated seems odd: in the long run, regardless of whether demand increases or decreases, the price returns to its original level. Is this outcome inevitable? In fact, it is not. It is possible for the long-run equilibrium price to remain the same, rise, or fall.

External Economies and Diseconomies

Whether the long-run equilibrium price remains the same, rises, or falls depends on external economies and external diseconomies. **External economies** are factors beyond the control of an individual firm that lower its costs as *industry* output increases. **External diseconomies** are factors outside the control of a firm that raise its costs as industry output increases. With no external economies or external diseconomies, a firm's costs remain constant as industry output changes.

Figure 11.11 illustrates these three cases and introduces a new supply concept, the long-run industry supply curve. A **long-run industry supply curve** shows how the quantity supplied by an industry varies as the market price varies after all the possible adjustments have been made, including changes in plant size and changes in the number of firms in the industry.

FIGURE 11.11

Long-run Changes in Price and Quantity

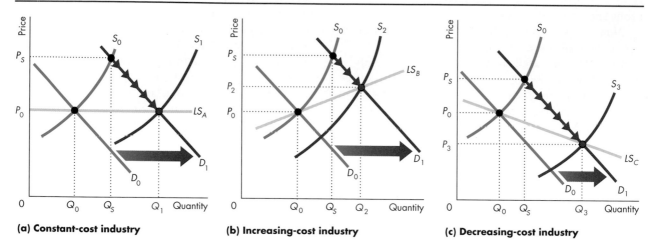

(a) Constant-cost industry   **(b) Increasing-cost industry**   **(c) Decreasing-cost industry**

Three possible long-run changes in price and quantity are illustrated. When demand increases from D_0 to D_1, entry occurs and the industry supply curve shifts from S_0 to S_1. In part (a), the long-run supply curve LS_A is horizontal. The quantity increases from Q_0 to Q_1 and the price remains constant at P_0. In part (b), the long-run supply curve is LS_B; the price increases to P_2 and the quantity increases to Q_2. This case occurs in industries with external diseconomies. In part (c), the long-run supply curve is LS_C; the price decreases to P_3 and the quantity increases to Q_3. This case occurs in an industry with external economies.

Part (a) shows the case we have just studied – no external economies or diseconomies. The long-run industry supply curve (LS_A) is perfectly elastic. In this case, a permanent increase in demand from D_0 to D_1 has no effect on the price in the long run. The increase in demand brings a temporary increase in price to P_S, and a short-run quantity increase from Q_0 to Q_S. Entry increases short-run supply from S_0 to S_1, which lowers the price to its original level, P_0, and increases the quantity to Q_1.

Part (b) shows the case of external diseconomies. In this case, the long-run supply industry curve (LS_B) slopes upward. A permanent increase in demand from D_0 to D_1 increases the price in both the short run and the long run. As in the previous case, the increase in demand brings a temporary increase in price to P_S, and a short-run quantity increase from Q_0 to Q_S. Entry increases short-run supply from S_0 to S_1, which lowers the price to P_2 and increases the quantity to Q_2.

One source of external diseconomies is congestion. The airline industry provides a good illustration. With bigger airline industry output, there is more congestion of both airports and airspace, which results in longer delays and extra waiting time for passengers and aircraft. These external diseconomies mean that as the output of air travel services increases (in the absence of technological advances), average cost increases. As a result, the long-run supply curve is upward-sloping. So a permanent increase in demand brings an increase in quantity and a rise in the price. Technological advances decrease costs and *shift* the long-run supply curve downward. So even an industry that experiences external diseconomies might have falling prices over the long run.

Part (c) shows the case of external economies. In this case, the long-run industry supply curve (LS_C) slopes downward. A permanent increase in demand from D_0 to D_1, increases the price in the short run and lowers it in the long run. Again, the increase in demand brings a temporary increase in price to P_S, and a short-run quantity increase from Q_0 to Q_S. Entry increases short-run supply from S_0 to S_3, which lowers the price to P_3 and increases the quantity to Q_3.

One of the best examples of external economies is the growth of specialist support services for an industry as it expands. As farm output increased in the nineteenth and early twentieth centuries, the services available to farmers expanded and their costs fell. For example, markets developed in farm machinery and fertilizers that lowered farm costs. Farms enjoyed the benefits of external economies. As a consequence, as the demand for farm products increased, the quantity produced increased but the price fell.

Over the long term, the prices of many goods and services have fallen, not because of external economies but because of technological change. Let's now study this influence on a competitive market.

Technological Change

Industries are constantly discovering lower-cost techniques of production. Most cost-saving production techniques cannot be implemented, however, without investing in new plant and equipment. As a consequence, it takes time for a technological advance to spread through an industry. Some firms whose plants are on the verge of being replaced will be quick to adopt the new technology, while other firms whose plants have recently been replaced will continue to operate with an old technology until they can no longer cover their average variable cost. Once average variable cost cannot be covered, a firm will scrap even a relatively new plant (embodying an old technology) in favour of a plant with a new technology.

New technology allows firms to produce at a lower cost and to make a larger profit than the existing technology. As a result, as firms adopt a new technology, their cost curves shift downward. With lower costs, firms are willing to supply a given quantity at a lower price or, equivalently, they are willing to supply a larger quantity at a given price. In other words, supply increases and the supply curve shifts rightward. With a given demand, the quantity produced increases and the price falls.

Two forces are at work in an industry undergoing technological change. Firms that adopt the new technology make an economic profit. So there is entry by new-technology firms. Firms that stick with the old technology incur economic losses. They either exit the industry or switch to the new technology.

As old-technology firms disappear and new-technology firms enter, the price falls and the quantity produced increases. Eventually, the industry arrives at a long-run equilibrium in which all the firms use the new technology, produce at minimum long-run average cost and make zero economic profit (a normal profit). Because in the long run competition eliminates economic profit, technological change

brings only temporary gains to producers. But the lower prices and better products that technological advances bring are permanent gains for consumers.

The process that we've just described is one in which some firms experience economic profits and others experience economic losses. It is a period of dynamic change for an industry. Some firms do well and others do badly. Often the process has a geographical dimension – the expanding new-technology firms bring prosperity to the 'rust-belt' regions where traditional industries have gone into decline. Sometimes the new-technology firms are in a foreign country, while the old-technology firms are in the domestic economy. Scotland's 'silicon glen' is an example of a high-tech industry which has located in a traditionally agricultural area. The information revolution of the 1990s has produced many examples of changes like these. Technological advances are not confined to the information industry. Even milk production is undergoing a major technological change, which arises from the use of hormones in cattle.

R E V I E W

◆ A fall in demand in a competitive industry brings a fall in price, economic loss and exit. Exit decreases supply, which brings a rise in price. In the long run, enough firms exit for those remaining to make a normal profit.

◆ A rise in demand in a competitive industry brings a rise in price, economic profit, and entry. Entry increases supply, which brings a fall in price. In the long run, enough firms enter to compete away the economic profit and leave firms making a normal profit.

◆ A new technology lowers costs, increases supply, and lowers price. New-technology firms make an economic profit and enter. Old-technology firms incur an economic loss and exit. In the long run, all firms adopt the new technology and make normal profits.

You've now studied how a competitive market works and have used the model of perfect competition to interpret and explain a variety of aspects of real-world economic behaviour. The last topic that we'll study in this chapter is efficiency in our model of perfect competition.

Competition and Efficiency

I s perfect competition efficient? To answer this question, we need to describe the conditions that prevail when efficiency has been achieved.

Allocative Efficiency

Allocative efficiency occurs when no resources in the economy are wasted. It is a point where society's welfare is maximized. If someone can be made better off – gain more utility – without making someone else worse off, resources are being wasted, and efficiency has not been achieved. To achieve allocative efficiency, three conditions must be satisfied. They are:

1. Producer efficiency
2. Consumer efficiency
3. Exchange efficiency

   Producer efficiency occurs when firms cannot decrease the cost of producing a given output by changing the factors of production used. An individual firm achieves producer efficiency if it produces at a point on its marginal cost curve, or equivalently, on its supply curve. An industry achieves producer efficiency if it produces at a point on the industry supply curve. If all firms in all industries minimize cost, the economy is at a point on its *production possibility frontier* (see Chapter 3, pp. 48–50).

   Consumer efficiency occurs when consumers cannot make themselves better off – they cannot increase their utility by reallocating their budgets. Consumer efficiency is achieved at all points along a demand curve.

   Exchange efficiency occurs when the price at which trade takes place equals marginal social cost and also equals marginal social benefit. **Marginal social cost** is the full cost to society of producing one additional unit of output. **Marginal social benefit** is the full benefit to society from one additional unit of consumption. Society's welfare is the sum of total social benefit minus total social cost to all individuals, whether they are producers or consumers. Total social welfare is maximized with allocative efficiency.

   Figure 11.12(a) illustrates allocative efficiency. The marginal social benefit curve is *MSB* and the marginal social cost curve is *MSC*. If output is 1

unit, *MSC* at £10 is less than *MSB* at £70, and producers could supply more for less than the value people place on additional output. This means resources are being wasted and total social welfare (*TSW*) is not maximized. The value of *TSW* at each unit of output is shown in part (b). The addition to *TSW* is total social benefit for each unit (blue plus red area) minus total social cost for each unit (red area), shown in part (a). Let's see why. If output is 2 units, *MSB* is £60 and *MSC* is £20, adding a further £40 (£60–£20) to *TSW*. So producing the second unit increases *TSW* from £60 to £100 (£60 + £40).

   At the allocatively efficient quantity and price, the marginal benefit to society of the last unit produced exactly equals the marginal cost to society of the last unit. If output is 4 units and price is £40 a unit as shown in part (a), allocative efficiency is achieved – no resources are wasted – and total social welfare shown in part (b) is at its highest level at £130. The market could not reallocate resources through trade, production and consumption in any way that would make at least one person better off without making anyone else worse off. Allocative efficiency is also known as **Pareto efficiency**.

Market Failure

The three types of efficiency required for allocative efficiency can only occur if markets work perfectly. There must be a market for every imaginable good or service, these markets must generate appropriate prices, and people must be able to buy and sell without any additional costs. In reality, most markets don't work perfectly. The kinds of problems which prevent markets working perfectly are called **market failure**. As we will see in Part 4, market failure problems can be used to explain different types of government policy. There are five main types of market failure.

1. Limited information and uncertainty
2. Poor definition of property rights
3. External costs and external benefits
4. Monopoly power
5. Public goods

   We've already discussed some of the problems caused by **limited information and uncertainty** in Chapter 9. We saw that incomplete information led firms to devise agency relationships to resolve the *principal–agent* problem. Firms enter into

FIGURE 11.12

Allocative Efficiency

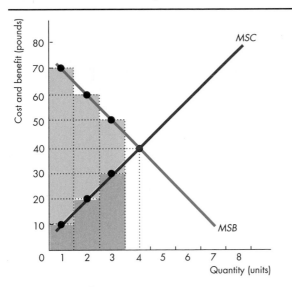

(a) Allocative efficiency

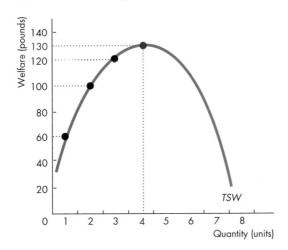

(b) Maximizing welfare

Allocative efficiency requires producer efficiency, consumer efficiency and exchange efficiency. Exchange efficiency occurs when 4 units are produced, where marginal social cost (*MSC*) equals marginal social benefit (*MSB*) as shown in part (a). If the second unit is produced, *MSB* is greater than *MSC* – total social welfare (*TSW*) increases but is not maximized as shown in part (b). *TSW* is total social benefit minus total social cost. Producing the second unit raises *TSW* to £100 – an increase of £40 (£60–£20). Allocative efficiency only occurs at 4 units of output and a price of £40 a unit where *MSB* = *MSC*. At this point no resources are wasted and total social welfare is maximized at £130.

contracts and offer compensation packages to their employees to strengthen incentives and raise productivity when information about the actions of the agent are limited. The principal–agent problem can also be used to explain different structures for firms. We used another form of limited information, *transaction costs*, to explain why organizing production within a firm can be more efficient than individuals trading in many markets. Uncertainty is a situation where more than one event can happen in the future but we don't know which one. If we are particularly averse to some events, such as our house burning down, we can avoid the costs of uncertainty by taking out insurance. We'll look at the problems of uncertainty in more detail in Chapter 17.

If ownership of goods and resources was in doubt, the market system would not work. We call this problem **poor definition of property rights**. If there was no clear system of individual or company ownership, you could not righfully buy or sell a resource or product in a market. That is why a legal system is needed to help market systems work properly. An example faced by many companies is the ownership of new technology that they have developed. Once the technology is used to produce a good, anyone can copy it and the benefits of the research and development needed to create the technology are lost to the company. That is why we have a system of patents to protect the returns on investment in new technology. We will look at patents again in Chapter 20. This problem of poor definition of property rights is linked to the next type of market failure.

External costs are costs not borne by the producer or consumer but by other members of society. Pollution and road traffic accidents are examples. **External benefits** are benefits accruing to people other than the buyer of a good. These include the pleasure we get from well-designed buildings and beautiful works of art in public galleries. Producing energy and well-designed buildings also produces other goods and services – pollution and pleasure – that people suffer or enjoy without payment. External costs and benefits are not priced because they are goods and services that do not have a market – often because property rights are poorly defined. As a result, resources are used inefficiently. We'll look at external costs, environmental problems and policy again in Chapter 20.

Monopoly power is created when there are barriers to entry into a market. Economic profit in perfect competition will remain if new firms cannot

Competition:
The Market for
Container Lines

The Essence of the Story

THE FINANCIAL TIMES, 28 NOVEMBER 1996

Congestion in the world's sea lanes

Charles Batchelor

P&O and Maersk are among the stronger participants in the con-...tainer sector...but cut-throat competition is forcing change on long-established alliances and ways of doing business....

Containers carry 17 per cent of the world's sea-borne tonnage but closer to 60 per cent of sea-borne trade by value, according to *Containerisation International*, a trade journal.

After being introduced in the 1970s, containers rapidly became the standard method of moving high-value items such as consumer electronics, garments or vehicle parts, because of the protection they provided against damage and theft and the ease of handling on the quayside.

Now, with little scope for the shipping lines to push up rates of hire, the rival groups are engaged in a fierce battle for market share which has depressed returns.

NatWest Securities expects demand for container shipments to grow by 7–8 per cent a year over the next two to three years but capacity will also increase by 7 per cent a year.

'No real money has been made by the container shipping companies in the 1980s or the 1990s,' commented an analyst at Drewry, a consultancy....

Pressure on the long-established European and US lines has been increased by the rapid growth of Asian competitors such as Evergreen of Taiwan, Hanjin Shipping of South Korea and Cosco of China....

The commercial pressures on the industry have been compounded by the decline of the traditional 'conferences' – agreements between the shipping lines to set cargo rates and capacity levels on important routes.

Conferences have fallen foul of increasingly vigilant regulators, who have seen them as unfair restraints on free trade....

Joint purchasing is just one strand in a policy of tight control of costs which the lines have been forced to adopt. 'We have to cut costs because rates won't go up,' said Lord Sterling, chairman of P&O....

Savings are also being achieved by increases in the size of container vessels. Maersk...has moved in recent years from operating ships capable of carrying 3,500 twenty-foot equivalent (teu) containers to just 5,000 teu. P&O is negotiating with ship-building yards to order ships capable of carrying 6,000 teu and more.

Technology is also playing a role. The larger lines make use of sophisticated computer systems to locate the position of containers on the quayside and in the ship so that loading and unloading can be carried out efficiently. Tracking systems allow the progress of containers around the world to be monitored.

'The companies are running hard to stand still,' commented the Drewry analyst....

■ Containers were introduced in the 1970s and now move 17 per cent of the world's sea-borne tonnage but almost 60 per cent of sea-borne trade by value.

■ Fierce competition and new entrants from Asia have kept rates of hire low, but demand and capacity are set to rise.

■ Container firms have been making minimal profits in the 1980s and 1990s.

■ Regulators have restricted the use of traditional agreements among firms which set cargo rates and capacity levels.

■ Container firms are now cutting costs, introducing new technology and increasing ship capacity to survive.

Economic Analysis

■ Strong regulation has removed collusive practices – making the industry highly competitive. Container firms must now act as price takers.

■ Figure 1 shows a container firm in a competitive environment. The firm's marginal cost is MC_0, average total cost ATC_0, and marginal revenue is MR_0.

■ Firms maximize profits by setting MR equal to MC and shipping 100,000 twenty-foot equivalent (teu) containers a month at price P_0. Container firms are still making some abnormal profit – the blue shaded area.

■ Figure 2 shows the market before entry by new firms. Demand is D_0, supply is S_0 and the equilibrium price and quantity are P_0 and Q_0. New entrants increase supply and shift the

supply curve rightward to S_1. Price falls to P_1 and quantity rises to Q_1.

■ Figure 1 shows that at price P_1, container firms make no abnormal profit as marginal revenue falls to MR_1. Each firm ships 90 teu per month.

■ Figure 3 shows the impact of achieving economies of scale through increasing capacity and introducing new technology. Average total costs fall from ATC_0 to ATC_1 and marginal costs fall from MC_0 to MC_1, and firms now ship 150,000 teu containers per month.

■ Abnormal profits are regained (blue shaded area), but new entrants will continue to force down price and abnormal profit towards the long-run equilibrium at 200,000 teu per month.

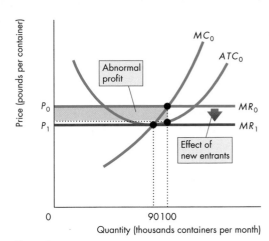

Figure 1

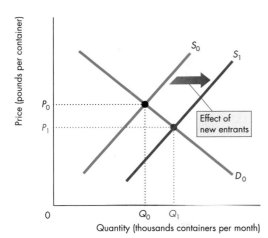

Figure 2

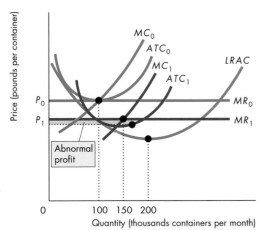

Figure 3

Reading Between the Lines

enter a market at low cost to increase supply and cut market price. In the long run, firms will not be producing at the point where average cost is minimized. Typical examples of barriers to entry are those caused by high cost of advertising and patents on new technology. We examine these problems in more detail in the next chapter and in Chapter 19.

Public goods are the type of goods and services that the market sector will not supply. These goods and services have special characteristics. In particular, the marginal cost of providing an extra unit is close to zero as in the case of national defence. This makes supply by private firms unprofitable. But if the goods and services are not supplied, the benefits from consumption are lost. The argument that governments should supply these goods is set out in Chapter 18.

Efficiency of Perfect Competition

Perfect competition delivers allocative efficiency if there is no market failure. In such a case, all the benefits and costs are taken into account. The marginal social benefit curve is the same as the industry demand curve and the marginal social cost curve is the same as the industry supply curve. Private benefits and costs are the same as social benefits and costs. If there is no market failure with perfect competition, price and quantity are determined at the point of intersection of the demand and supply curves. This is also the allocatively efficient price and quantity shown in Fig. 11.12 which maximizes social welfare.

Adam Smith believed that competitive markets were efficient because each participant in the market was 'led by an invisible hand to promote an end (an efficient allocation of resources) which was no part of his intention'. You can see the invisible hand at work in the cartoon. When there is no demand for ice cream but there is a demand for shade, the ice cream vendor temporarily exits the ice cream market and enters the sunshade market. A transaction occurs that makes two people better off.

◆ ◆ ◆ ◆ We have now completed our study of the model of perfect competition. It has given us a

Drawing by M. Twohy; © 1988 The New Yorker Magazine, Inc.

clear insight into the way that firms make choices when competition is strong and firms have little influence over price. However, perfect competition is not an appropriate model for every market and our next task is to study markets where there is a significant amount of market failure. We'll start by studying a model where firms have the power to influence prices by restricting output. We study the simplest case, monopoly, in the next chapter and other cases, monopolistic competition and oligopoly, in Chapter 13.

SUMMARY

Perfect Competition

Perfect competition occurs in a market in which a large number of firms produce an identical good; there are many buyers; there are no restrictions on entry and exit; and all firms and buyers are fully informed about the prices charged by each firm. Each firm sells its good for the same price – the market price. It chooses how much to produce, whether to shut down temporarily, its scale, and whether to leave an industry permanently.

The firm's choices are motivated by its desire to maximize profit. By maximizing profit, the firm can make an economic profit – a normal profit – or an economic loss depending on market price. If price is low enough, the firm maximizes profit by temporarily shutting down and laying off its workers. When price equals minimum average variable cost, the firm incurs a loss equal to its total fixed costs whether it produces the profit-maximizing output or shuts down.

The firm's supply curve is the upward-sloping part of its marginal cost curve above minimum average variable cost and runs along the vertical axis at all prices below minimum average variable cost. (pp. 260–267)

Output, Price and Profit in the Short Run

The short-run industry supply curve shows how the total quantity supplied in the short run by all the firms in an industry varies as the market price varies. The market price is such that the quantity supplied and the quantity demanded are equal. Each firm takes the market price as given and chooses the output that maximizes profit. In short-run equilibrium, each firm can make an economic profit, an economic loss, or it can break even. (pp. 267–269)

Output, Price and Profit in the Long Run

If the firms in an industry make economic profits, new firms enter the industry and existing firms might increase their plant size. If the firms in an industry incur economic losses, some firms will leave the industry and the remaining firms might decrease their plant size. Entry and exit and changes in plant size shift the short-run industry supply curve. Entry decreases the economic profit of existing firms and exit increases the economic profit of existing firms (or decreases their losses).

Long-run competitive equilibrium occurs when each firm maximizes profit (marginal revenue equals marginal cost); economic profit is zero (normal profit is earned), so that there is no entry or exit; and each firm produces at the point of minimum long-run average cost, so it has no incentive to change its plant size. (pp. 269–271)

Changing Tastes and Advancing Technology

In a perfectly competitive market, a permanent decrease (increase) in demand leads to a smaller (larger) industry output and a smaller (larger) number of firms in the industry. If there are no external economies or diseconomies, the market price remains constant in the long run as demand changes. If there are external economies, price falls in the long run as demand increases. If there are external diseconomies, price increases in the long run as demand increases.

New technology increases the industry supply, and in the long run the market price falls and the quantity sold increases. Firms that are slow to change make losses and eventually go out of business. Firms that are quick to change make economic profits initially, but eventually they will make zero economic profit. (pp. 272–275)

Competition and Efficiency

Allocative efficiency occurs when no one can be made better off without making someone else worse off. Three conditions for allocative efficiency – producer efficiency, consumer efficiency and exchange efficiency – occur in perfect competition when there is no market failure. It is this situation that Adam Smith was describing when he talked of the economy being led by an 'invisible hand'.

There are five market failure obstacles to the achievement of allocative efficiency in perfect competition – poor information and uncertainty, poor definition of property rights, external costs and benefits, monopoly power and public goods. (pp. 276–280)

K E Y   E L E M E N T S

Key Terms

Allocative efficiency, 276
Average revenue, 260
Consumer efficiency, 276
Economic profit, 260
Exchange efficiency, 276
External benefits, 277
External costs, 277
External diseconomies, 273
External economies, 273
Limited information and uncertainty, 276
Long-run industry supply curve, 273
Marginal revenue, 260
Marginal social benefit, 276
Marginal social cost, 276
Market failure, 276
Monopoly power, 277
Normal profit, 260
Pareto efficiency, 276
Perfect competition, 260

Poor definition of property rights, 277
Price taker, 260
Producer efficiency, 276
Public goods, 280
Short-run industry supply curve, 267
Shutdown point, 266
Total revenue, 260

◆ Key Figures

Figure 11.2   Total Revenue, Total Cost and Profit, 263
Figure 11.3   Marginal Revenue, Marginal Cost and Profit-maximizing Output, 264
Figure 11.5   Neat Knits' Supply Curve, 266
Figure 11.6   Industry Supply Curve, 267
Figure 11.9   Plant Size and Long-run Equilibrium, 271
Figure 11.12   Allocative Efficiency, 277

R E V I E W   Q U E S T I O N S

1 What are the main features of a perfectly competitive industry?

2 Why can't a perfectly competitive firm influence the industry price?

3 List the three key decisions that a firm in a perfectly competitive industry has to make in order to maximize profit.

4 Why is marginal revenue equal to price in a perfectly competitive industry?

5 When will a perfectly competitive firm temporarily stop producing?

6 What is the connection between the supply curve and marginal cost curve of a perfectly competitive firm?

7 What is the relationship between a firm's supply curve and the short-run industry supply curve in a perfectly competitive industry?

8 When will firms enter an industry and when will they leave it?

9 What happens to the short-run industry supply curve when firms enter a competitive industry?

10 What is the effect of entry on the price and quantity produced?

11 What is the effect of entry on economic profit?

12 Trace the effects of a permanent increase in demand on price, quantity sold, number of firms and economic profit.

13 Trace the effects of a permanent decrease in demand on price, quantity sold, number of firms and economic profit.

14 Under what circumstances will a perfectly competitive industry have:
   a A perfectly elastic long-run supply curve?
   b An upward-sloping long-run supply curve?
   c A downward-sloping long-run supply curve?

15 What is allocative efficiency and under what circumstances docs it arise?

PROBLEMS

1 Pat's Pottery is a price taker. It has the following hourly costs:

Output (glazed pots per hour)	Total cost (pounds per hour)
0	10
1	21
2	30
3	41
4	54
5	79
6	96

a If glazed pots sell for £14, what is Pat's profit-maximizing output per hour? How much economic profit does she make?
b What is Pat's shutdown point?
c Derive Pat's supply curve.
d What range of prices will cause Pat to leave the craft pottery industry?
e What range of prices will cause other firms with costs identical to Pat's to enter the industry?
f What is the long-run equilibrium price of glazed pots?

2 Why have the prices of pocket calculators and VCRs fallen?

3 What has been the effect of an increase in world population on the wheat market and the individual wheat farmer?

4 The market demand schedule for pop CD's is as follows:

Price (pounds per CD)	Quantity demanded (CDs per week)
3.65	500,000
4.40	475,000
5.20	450,000
6.00	425,000
6.80	400,000
7.60	375,000
8.40	350,000
9.20	325,000
10.00	300,000
10.80	275,000
11.60	250,000
12.40	225,000
13.20	200,000
14.00	175,000
14.80	150,000

The market is perfectly competitive and each firm has the same cost structure described by the following table:

Output (CDs per week)	Marginal cost	Average variable cost (pounds per CD)	Average total cost
150	6.00	8.80	15.47
200	6.40	7.80	12.80
250	7.00	7.00	11.00
300	7.65	7.10	10.43
350	8.40	7.20	10.06
400	10.00	7.50	10.00`
450	12.40	8.00	10.22
500	12.70	9.00	11.00

There are 1,000 firms in the industry.

a What is the market price?
b What is the industry's output?
c What is the output of each firm?
d What is the economic profit of each firm?
e What is the shutdown point?
f What is the long-run equilibrium price?
g What is the number of firms in the long run?

5 The same demand conditions as those in Problem 5 prevail and there are still 1,000 firms in the industry, but fixed costs increase by £980.

a What is the short-run profit-maximizing output for each firm?
b Do firms enter or exit the industry in the long run?
c What is the new long-run equilibrium price?
d What is the new long-run equilibrium number of firms in the industry?

6 Study *Reading Between the Lines* on pp 278–279 and then answer the following questions :

a Why did shipping prices fall when the new Asian competitors entered the industry?
b Why did the Asian competitors enter the industry?
c The impact of introducing larger ships and new technology on the industry.

CHAPTER 12

MONOPOLY

After studying this chapter you will be

◆ Define monopoly and explain the conditions under which it arises

◆ Distinguish between legal monopoly and natural monopoly

◆ Explain how a monopoly determines its price and output

◆ Define price discrimination and explain why it leads to a bigger profit

◆ Compare the performance of a competitive and a monopolistic industry

◆ Define rent seeking and explain why it arises

◆ Explain the conditions under which monopoly is more efficient than competition

W E'VE TALKED A LOT ABOUT FIRMS THAT WANT TO MAXIMIZE PROFIT. BUT are all firms really so intent on maximizing profit? After all, you have probably been offered a student's discount at some book-shops, theatres and record shops. Airlines often give a discount for buying a ticket in advance and rail companies offer discounts for student travel. Are all these firms simply being generous? Are they throwing money away? Or perhaps the perfectly competitive model does not apply in all cases. ◆ When you buy water, you don't shop around. You buy from your water utility, which is your only available sup-plier. If you live in Leeds and want a water supply, you only have one option: buy from Yorkshire Water. These are examples of a single pro-ducer of a good or service controlling its supply. Such firms are obviously not like firms in perfectly competi-tive industries. They don't face a market-determined price. They can choose the price they charge. How do such firms behave? How do they choose the quantity to produce and the price at which to sell it? How does their behaviour compare with firms in perfectly competitive industries? Do such firms charge prices that are too high and that damage the interests of consumers? Do such firms bring any benefits?

The Profits of Generosity

◆ ◆ ◆ ◆ In this chapter we are going to build a model of a monopoly supplier. We will use this model to study markets in which an individual firm can influence the quantity of goods supplied and can also determine price. We can then compare the performance and efficiency of a monopoly market with our model of a competitive market.

How Monopoly Arises

A **monopoly** is an industry that produces a good or service for which no close substitute exists and in which there is one supplier that is protected from competition by a barrier preventing the entry of new firms. The lack of close substitutes and the barriers to entry are the reasons why monopoly is a form of market failure. Monopolies can operate locally, nationally or globally. The supplier of electricity is an example of a local monopoly, where the barriers to entry are restricted to a geographic region. The UK Post Office is an example of a national monopoly. Microsoft Corporation, the software developer that created the PC operating system DOS, is an example of a global monopoly.

No Close Substitutes

The first key feature of a monopoly is that it has no close substitutes. If a good does have a close substitute, even though only one firm produces it, that firm effectively faces competition from the producers of substitutes. Electricity supplied by a local public utility is an example of a good that does not have close substitutes. While mains gas and oil are substitutes for domestic heating, there is no realistic substitute for domestic electrical appliances.

Innovation and technological change create new products and services. Some of these are substitutes for existing products and so weaken existing monopolies. For example, the spread of international courier services such as DHL, the development of the fax machine and e-mail, have weakened the first-class letter monopoly of the UK Post Office. Advances in telecommunications technology have weakened British Telecommunication's telephone monopoly. In particular, cellular telephones have begun to undermine the monopoly in local calls.

Other new products have few substitutes and so create new monopolies. The development of the computer has created monopolies, the most obvious of which is Microsoft's PC operating system – DOS. Similarly, research in the pharmaceuticals industry is constantly creating new monopolies in drugs.

Barriers to Entry

The second key feature of a monopoly is the existence of barriers preventing the entry of new firms. **Barriers to entry** are legal or natural impediments protecting a firm from competition from potential new entrants.

Legal Barriers to Entry   Legal barriers to entry create legal monopoly. A **legal monopoly** is a market in which competition and entry are restricted by the granting of a franchise, licence, patent or copyright, or in which a firm has acquired ownership of a significant proportion of a key resource.

A *monopoly franchise* is an exclusive right granted to a firm to supply a good or service. An example of a monopoly franchise is the UK Post Office, which has been granted the exclusive right to provide some letter-carrying services.

A *government licence* controls entry into particular occupations, professions and industries. Government licensing in the professions is the most common example of this type of barrier to entry. For example, a licence is required to practise medicine, law and dentistry among many other professional services. Licensing need not create monopoly, but it does restrict competition. When a new TV channel is offered for franchise, the successful bidder gains a licence to broadcast for a limited period. In this case, it confers a monopoly on the channel broadcaster. Where the number of channels is restricted, competition in broadcasting will be limited.

A **patent** is an exclusive right granted to the inventor of a product or service. A *copyright* is an exclusive right granted to the author or composer of a literary, musical, dramatic, or artistic work. Patents and copyrights are valid for a limited time period that varies from country to country. In the United Kingdom, a patent is valid for 16 years. Patents protect inventors by creating a property right and thereby encourage invention by preventing others from copying an invention until sufficient time has elapsed for the inventor to have reaped some benefits. They also stimulate *innovation* – the use of new inventions – by increasing the incentives for inventors to publicize their discoveries and offer them for use under licence.

In some industries, the government does not grant a legal monopoly, but a single firm acquires ownership of a significant proportion of a key resource. A past example of this type of monopoly is Alcoa, an aluminium producer that controlled a large proportion of the sources of supply of aluminium during the 1930s. A modern example is DeBeers, a South African firm that controls some 95 per cent of the world's supply of natural diamonds.

Natural Barriers to Entry   Natural barriers to entry give rise to natural monopoly. **Natural monopoly** occurs when one firm can supply the entire market at a lower price than two or more firms can. This situation arises when demand limits sales to a quantity at which economies of scale exist. Figure 12.1 shows such a situation. Here the demand curve for electric power is D and the average total cost curve is ATC. Because average total cost decreases as output increases, economies of scale prevail over the entire length of the ATC curve. One firm can produce 4 million kilowatt-hours at 5 pence a kilowatt-hour. At this price, the quantity demanded is 4 million kilowatt-hours. So if the price was 5 pence, one firm could supply the entire market. If two firms shared the market, it would cost each of them 10 pence a kilowatt-hour to produce a total of 4 million kilowatt hours. If four firms shared the market, it would cost each of them 15 pence a kilowatt-hour to produce a total of 4 million kilowatt hours. So in conditions like those shown in Fig. 12.1, one firm can supply the entire market at a lower cost than two or more firms can. Electricity generating utilities are an example of natural monopoly. Another example is natural gas distribution.

Most monopolies in the real world, whether legal or natural, are regulated in some way by government or by government agencies. We will study such regulation in Chapter 19. Here we will study unregulated monopoly for two reasons. First, we can better understand why governments regulate monopolies and the effects of regulation if we also know how an unregulated monopoly behaves. Second, even in industries with more than one producer, firms often have a strong degree of monopoly power, arising from locational advantages or from differences in product quality protected by patents. The theory of monopoly sheds light on the behaviour of many of these firms and industries.

We begin by studying the behaviour of a single-price monopoly. A *single-price monopoly* is a monopoly that charges the same price for each and every unit of its output. How does a single-price monopoly determine the quantity to produce and the price to charge for its output?

Single-price Monopoly

The starting point for understanding how a single-price monopoly chooses its price and output is to work out the relationship between the demand for the good produced by the monopoly and the monopoly's revenue.

Demand and Revenue

Because in a monopoly there is only one firm, the demand curve facing that firm is the industry demand curve. Let's look at an example of a local monopoly: Cut and Dry, the only hairdressing salon in a 15 mile radius in a small town in North Yorkshire. The demand schedule that the owner faces is set out in Table 12.1. At a price of £20, Cut and Dry sells no haircuts. The lower the price, the more haircuts per hour it can sell. For example, at a price of £12, consumers demand 4 haircuts per hour (row e), and at

FIGURE 12.1

Natural Monopoly

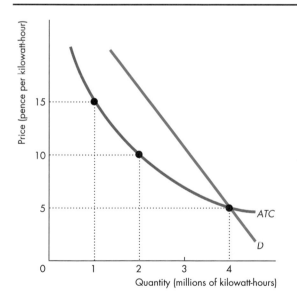

The demand curve for electric power is D and the average total cost curve is ATC. Economies of scale exist over the entire ATC curve. One firm can produce a total output of 4 million kilowatt-hours at a cost of 5 pence a kilowatt-hour. This same total output costs 10 pence a kilowatt-hour with two firms and 15 pence a kilowatt-hour with four firms. So one firm can meet the demand in this market at a lower cost than two or more firms can and the market is a natural monopoly.

a price of £4, they demand 8 haircuts per hour (row i).

Total revenue (*TR*) is the price (*P*) multiplied by the quantity sold (*Q*). For example, in row d, Cut and Dry sells 3 haircuts at £14 each, so total revenue is £42. *Marginal revenue* (*MR*) is the change in total revenue (ΔTR) resulting from a 1-unit increase in the quantity sold. For example, if the price falls from £18 (row b) to £16 (row c), the quantity sold increases from 1 to 2 haircuts. Total revenue rises from £18 to £32, so the change in total revenue is £14. Because the quantity sold increases by 1 haircut, marginal revenue equals the change in total revenue and is £14. When recording marginal revenue, it is written between the two rows to emphasize that marginal revenue relates to the *change* in the quantity sold.

Figure 12.2 shows the demand curve (*D*) for the Cut and Dry salon. Each row of Table 12.1 corresponds to a point on the demand curve. For example, row d in the table and point d on the demand curve tell us that at a price of £14, it sells 3

TABLE 12.1

A Single-price Monopoly's Revenue

	Price *P* (pounds per haircut)	Quantity demanded *Q* (haircuts per hour)	Total revenue *TR* = *P* × *Q* (pounds)	Marginal revenue *MR* = $\Delta TR/\Delta Q$ (pounds per haircut)
a	20	0	0	
				 18
b	18	1	18	
				 14
c	16	2	32	
				 10
d	14	3	42	
				 6
e	12	4	48	
				 2
f	10	5	50	
				.... −2
g	8	6	48	
				.... −6
h	6	7	42	
				.... −10
i	4	8	32	
				.... −14
j	2	9	18	
				.... −18
k	0	10	0	

The table shows Cut and Dry's demand schedule – the number of haircuts demanded per hour at each price. Total revenue (*TR*) is price multiplied by quantity sold. For example, row c shows that when the price is £16 a haircut, two haircuts are sold for a total revenue of £32. Marginal revenue (*MR*) is the change in total revenue resulting from a 1-unit increase in the quantity sold. For example, when the price falls from £16 to £14 a haircut, the quantity sold increases from 2 to 3 haircuts and total revenue increases by £10. The marginal revenue of the third haircut is £10. Total revenue rises to row f, where 5 haircuts are sold for £10, and it falls thereafter. In the output range over which total revenue is increasing, marginal revenue is positive; in the output range over which total revenue is decreasing, marginal revenue is negative.

FIGURE 12.2

Demand and Marginal Revenue for a Single-price Monopoly

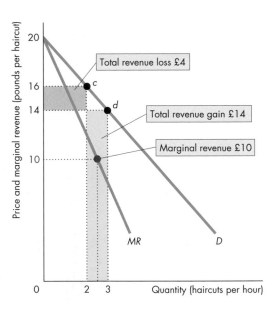

The monopoly demand curve (*D*) is based on the numbers in Table 12.1. At a price of £16 a haircut, Cut and Dry sells 2 haircuts an hour. If the price is cut to £14, 3 haircuts an hour are sold. The sale of the third haircut brings a revenue gain of £14 (the price charged for the third haircut). But there is a revenue loss of £4 (£2 per haircut) on the initial 2 haircuts that could have been sold for £16 each. The marginal revenue (extra total revenue) from the third haircut is the difference between the revenue gain and the revenue loss – £10. The marginal revenue curve (*MR*) shows the marginal revenue at each level of sales. Marginal revenue is lower than price.

haircuts. The figure also shows the marginal revenue curve (MR). Notice that the marginal revenue curve is below the demand curve. That is, at each level of output marginal revenue is less than price. Why is marginal revenue less than price? It is because when the price is lowered to sell one more unit, there are two opposing effects on total revenue. The lower price results in a revenue loss and the increased quantity sold results in a revenue gain. For example, at a price of £16, the salon sells 2 haircuts (point c). If the price is reduced to £14, it sells 3 haircuts and revenue increases by £14 on the third haircut. But if all haircuts are sold at the same price, the salon receives only £14 on the first two as well – £2 less than before. As a result, the salon loses £4 of revenue on the first 2 haircuts. This is deducted from the revenue gain of £14. Marginal revenue – the difference between the revenue gain and the revenue loss – is £10.

Figure 12.3 shows the demand curve, marginal revenue curve (MR) and total revenue curve (TR) for the Cut and Dry salon, and illustrates the connections between them. Again, each row in Table 12.1 corresponds to a point on the curves. For example, row d in the table and point d on the graphs tell us that when 3 haircuts are sold for £14 each (part a) total revenue is £42 (part b). Notice that as the quantity sold increases, total revenue rises to a peak of £50 (point f) and then declines. To understand the behaviour of total revenue, notice what happens to marginal revenue as the quantity sold increases. Over the range 0–5 haircuts, marginal revenue is positive. When more than 5 haircuts are sold, marginal revenue becomes negative. The output range over which marginal revenue is positive is the same as that over which total revenue is rising. The output range over which marginal revenue is negative is the same as that over which total revenue declines. When marginal revenue is 0, total revenue is at a maximum.

Revenue and Elasticity

The elasticity of demand is the percentage change in the quantity demanded divided by the percentage change in price. If a 1 per cent decrease in price results in a greater than 1 per cent increase in the quantity demanded, the elasticity of demand, is greater than 1 and demand is *elastic*. If a 1 per cent decrease in price results in a less than 1 per cent increase in the quantity demanded, the elasticity of demand is less than 1 and demand is *inelastic*. If a 1 per cent decrease in price results in a 1 per cent increase in the quantity demanded, the elasticity of

demand is 1 and demand is *unit elastic*.

The elasticity of demand influences the change in total revenue. If demand is elastic total revenue increases when the price decreases. The reason is that the positive effect on revenue from an increase in the quantity sold outweighs the negative effect from a lower price. If demand is inelastic total revenue decreases when the price decreases. In this case, the positive effect on revenue from an increase in the quantity sold is outweighed by the negative effect from a lower price. If demand is unit elastic total revenue does not change when the price changes. In this case, the positive effect on revenue from an increase in the quantity sold is offset by an equal negative effect from a lower price. (Chapter 5, pp. 106–107, explains the relationship between revenue and elasticity more fully.)

The output range over which total revenue increases when the price decreases is the same as the range where marginal revenue is positive – shown in Fig. 12.3. This is also the output range where demand is elastic – where the elasticity of demand is greater than 1. The output range over which total revenue decreases when price decreases is the same as the range where marginal revenue is negative. This is also the output range where demand is inelastic – where the elasticity of demand is less than 1. The output at which total revenue remains constant when the price decreases is where marginal revenue is zero. Thus the output at which marginal revenue is zero is also the output at which demand is unit elastic – at which the elasticity of demand is 1.

The relationship that you have just discovered implies that a profit-maximizing monopoly never produces an output in the inelastic range of its demand curve. If it did so, marginal revenue would be negative – each additional unit sold would lower total revenue. In such a situation, profit increases if the firm charges a higher price and produces a smaller quantity. The reason is that its total revenue rises and its total cost falls as it produces less. But exactly what price and quantity does a profit-maximizing monopoly choose?

Price and Output Decision

To determine the output level and price that maximize a monopoly's profit, we need to study the behaviour of both revenue and costs as output varies. A monopoly faces the same types of technology and cost constraints as a competitive firm. But it faces a different market constraint. The competitive firm is a price taker, whereas the monopoly's

FIGURE 12.3

A Single-price Monopoly's Revenue Curves

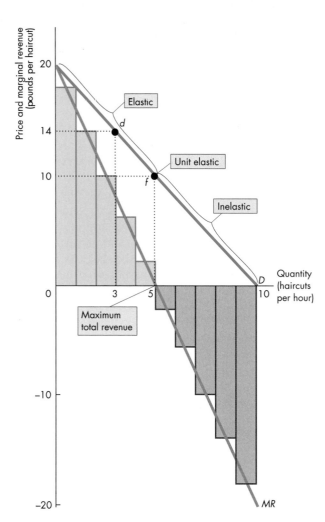

(a) Demand and marginal revenue curves

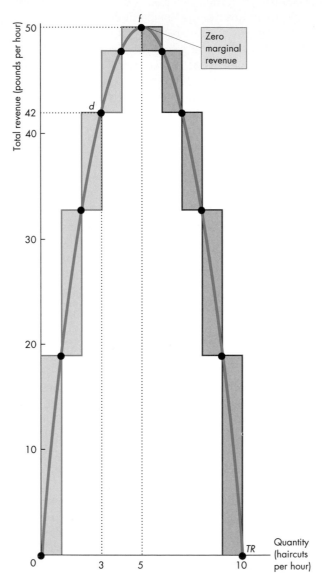

(b) Total revenue curve

Cut and Dry's demand curve (*D*) and marginal revenue curve (*MR*), shown in part (a), and total revenue curve (*TR*), shown in part (b), are based on the numbers in Table 12.1. For example, at a price of £14, the salon sells 3 haircuts an hour (point *d* in part (a)) for a total revenue of £42 (point *d* in part (b)). Over the range 0–5 haircuts an hour, total revenue is increasing and marginal revenue is positive, as

shown by the blue bars. Over the range 5–10 haircuts an hour, total revenue declines – marginal revenue is negative, as shown by the red bars. Over the range of output for which marginal revenue is positive, demand is elastic. At the level of output at which marginal revenue is zero, demand is unit elastic. Over the range of output for which marginal revenue is negative, demand is inelastic.

production decision influences the price it receives. Let's see how.

The revenue for the Cut and Dry salon studied in Table 12.1 and Figs 12.2 and 12.3 is shown again in Table 12.2. The table also contains information on the salon's costs and economic profit. Total cost (TC) rises as output increases and so does total revenue (TR). Economic profit equals total revenue minus total cost. As you can see in the table, the maximum profit (£12) occurs when the salon sells 3 haircuts for £14 each. Selling 2 haircuts for £16 each or 4 haircuts for £12 each would mean less economic profit at only £8.

You can see why 3 haircuts is the profit-maximizing output by looking at the marginal revenue and marginal cost columns. When the salon increases output from 2 to 3 haircuts, the marginal revenue is £10 and the marginal cost is £6. Profit increases by the difference – £4 an hour. If the salon increases output yet further, from 3 to 4 haircuts, marginal revenue is £6 and marginal cost is £10. In this case, marginal cost exceeds marginal revenue by £4, so profit decreases by £4 an hour. When marginal revenue exceeds marginal cost, profit increases if output increases. When marginal

cost exceeds marginal revenue, profit increases if output decreases. When marginal cost and marginal revenue are equal, profit is maximized.

The information set out in the table is shown graphically in Fig. 12.4. Part (a) shows the Cut and Dry salon's total revenue curve (TR) and total cost curve (TC). Economic profit is the vertical distance between TR and TC. Profit is maximized at 3 haircuts an hour – economic profit is £42 minus £30, or £12.

Figure 12.4(b) shows the salon's demand curve (D) and the marginal revenue curve (MR) along with the marginal cost curve (MC) and average total cost curve (ATC). To maximize profit, a monopolist, like a competitive firm, sets marginal cost equal to marginal revenue. In the case of the Cut and Dry salon, marginal cost equals marginal revenue when output is 3 haircuts a day. But for a monopoly, price is greater than marginal cost. To find the price, the monopolist uses the demand curve. In the case of the Cut and Dry salon, the price at which it can sell 3 haircuts a day is £14 a cut.

A firm maximizes profit when marginal cost equals marginal revenue. But whether the maximum profit is an economic profit, normal profit (zero economic profit), or an economic loss depends on

TABLE 12.2

A Monopoly's Output and Price Decision

Price (P) (pounds per haircut)	Quantity demanded (Q) (haircuts per hour)	Total revenue (TR = P × Q) (pounds)	Marginal revenue (MR = ΔTR/ΔQ) (pounds per haircut)	Total Cost (TC) (pounds)	Marginal cost (MC = ΔTC/ΔQ) (pounds per haircut)	Profit (TR − TC) (pounds)
20	0	0		20		−20
			18		1	
18	1	18		21		−3
			14		3	
16	2	32		24		+8
			10		6	
14	3	42		30		+12
			6		10	
12	4	48		40		+8
			2		15	
10	5	50		55		−5

The table adds information about total cost (TC), marginal cost (MC) and economic profit to the information on demand and revenue in Table 12.1. Total profit ($TR − TC$) equals total revenue (TR) minus total cost (TC). Profit is maximized at a price of £14 when 3 haircuts are sold – the row highlighted in red. Total revenue is £42, total cost is £30 and economic profit is £12 (£42 − £30).

FIGURE 12.4

A Single-price Monopoly's Output and Price

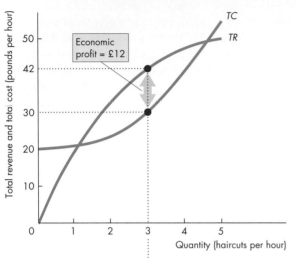

(a) Total revenue and total cost curves

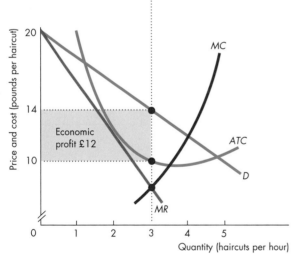

(b) Demand and marginal revenue and cost curves

This figure graphs the numbers in Table 12.2. The vertical distance between total revenue (*TR*) and total cost (*TC*) in part (a) determines the maximum economic profit output. Maximum profit occurs at 3 haircuts an hour. In part (b), economic profit is maximized where marginal cost (*MC*) equals (*MR*). The monopoly sells its profit-maximizing output for the highest price that buyers are willing to pay, which is determined by the demand curve (*D*). In this case, that price is £14. The monopoly's economic profit is illustrated in part (b) by the blue rectangle. That economic profit is £12 – the profit per haircut (£4) multiplied by 3 haircuts.

price and average total cost. If price exceeds average total cost, an economic profit is made. If price equals average total cost, zero economic profit is made, and if price is less than average total cost, an economic loss is incurred.

When the Cut and Dry salon produces 3 haircuts an hour, the average total cost is £10 (read from the *ATC* curve) and the price is £14 (read from the *D* curve). The profit per haircut is £4 (£14 minus £10). The economic profit is indicated by the blue rectangle, which equals the profit per haircut (£4) multiplied by the number of haircuts (3), making a total of £12.

The salon makes a positive economic profit. But suppose that the owner of the salon rents the premises. If the rent is increased by £12 an hour, the fixed cost increases by £12 an hour. The marginal cost and marginal revenue don't change, so her profit-maximizing output remains at 3 haircuts an hour. However, profit has fallen by £12 an hour to zero. If the salon owner pays more than an additional £12 an hour for the shop lease, the salon makes an economic loss. If this situation was permanent, the owner would go out of business. But entrepreneurs are a hardy lot, and it might pay to find another shop where the rent is lower.

If firms in a perfectly competitive industry are making a positive economic profit, new firms enter. This does not happen in a monopolistic industry. Barriers to entry prevent new firms from entering. So in a monopolistic industry, a firm can make a positive economic profit and continue to do so indefinitely. Sometimes that profit is large, as in the international diamond business.

R E V I E W

◆ A single-price monopoly maximizes profit, like all other firms, by producing an output at which marginal cost equals marginal revenue.

◆ At the profit-maximizing output, the monopoly charges the price that consumers are willing to pay, which is determined by the demand curve.

◆ Because in a monopoly price exceeds marginal revenue, price also exceeds marginal cost.

◆ A monopoly can make a positive economic profit even in the long run because barriers prevent the entry of new firms.

Price Discrimination

Price discrimination is the practice of charging some customers a lower price than others for an identical good or of charging an individual customer a lower price on a large purchase than on a small one, even though the cost of servicing all customers is the same. An example of price discrimination is the practice of charging children or students a lower price than others to travel by train. Another example is the common practice of hairdressers giving discounts to senior citizens and students. Price discrimination can be practised in varying degrees. *Perfect price discrimination* occurs when a firm charges a different price for each unit sold and charges each consumer the maximum price that he or she is willing to pay for the unit. Although perfect price discrimination does not happen in the real world, it shows the limit to which price discrimination can be taken.

Not all price *differences* imply price discrimination. In many situations, goods that are similar but not identical have different costs and sell for different prices *because* they have different costs. For example, the marginal cost of producing electricity depends on the time of day. If an electric power company charges a higher price for consumption between 7.00 and 9.00 in the morning and between 4.00 and 7.00 in the evening than it does at other times of the day, this practice is not called price discrimination. Price discrimination charges varying prices to consumers, not because of differences in the cost of producing the good, but because of differences in consumers' elasticities of demand for the good.

At first sight, it appears that price discrimination contradicts the assumption of profit maximization. Why would British Rail give a student discount? Why would a hairdresser charge students and senior citizens less? Aren't these producers losing profit by being so generous?

Deeper investigation shows that far from losing profit, price discriminators actually make a bigger profit than they would otherwise. Thus a monopoly has an incentive to try to find ways of discriminating among groups of consumers and charging each group the highest possible price. Some people may pay less with price discrimination, but others pay more. How does price discrimination bring in more total revenue?

Price Discrimination and Total Revenue

The total revenue received by a single-price monopoly equals the quantity sold multiplied by the single price charged. Let's look at the relationship between total revenue and price discrimination using our hair salon example. Figure 12.5 shows the demand curve, D, for Cut and Dry Salon haircuts, and the shaded areas show total revenue. Suppose that the Cut and Dry salon sells 4 haircuts for a single price of £12 each. The area of the blue rectangle shows total revenue is £48 – the quantity sold, 4 haircuts, multiplied by the price of a haircut, £12.

FIGURE 12.5

Total Revenue and Price Discrimination

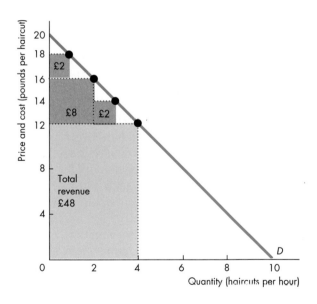

If Cut and Dry sells 4 haircuts for the same price – £12 each – total revenue is £48, as shown by the blue rectangle. If the salon charges two prices – £16 each for the first 2 haircuts and £12 each for the next 2 – total revenue will be £56 (the blue rectangle plus the the red rectangle). If the salon charges four different prices – £18 for the first haircut, £16 for the second haircut, £14 for the third haircut and £12 for the fourth haircut – total revenue will be £60 (the blue rectangle plus the red rectangle plus the two orange areas). The more finely a monopoly can price discriminate, the larger is its total revenue from a given level of sales.

Now suppose that the salon can discriminate between its customers so that it can sell some haircuts for one price and some for another, higher price. If the first 2 haircuts are sold for £16 each and then 2 more are sold for the original price, £12, the salon makes greater total revenue than when it charged a single price. The salon gets the extra revenue earned on the first 2 haircuts (the area of the red rectangle) added to the original revenue (the blue rectangle). Total revenue is now £56 (£48 + £8).

What would happen if the salon could find a way to perfectly discriminate among customers by selling each haircut for the maximum possible price each customer is willing to pay? Let's look again at Fig. 12.5. The first haircut sells for £18, the next for £16, the third for £14 and the fourth for £12. Total revenue is £60 – the blue area plus the red area plus the two orange areas, £12 more than if it sold all four haircuts for the single price of £12.

So how many haircuts will the perfectly discriminating salon sell? To answer this question, we must look at the marginal cost of each haircut relative to the price charged. Fig. 12.4(b) showed that the maximum profit for the single price monopolist is £12, when 3 haircuts are sold for £14 each. The perfectly price discriminating monopolist earns an extra £4 on the first haircut sold at £18, an extra £2 on the second haircut sold at £16, and no extra profit on the third haircut sold at £14. But unlike the single price monopolist it can also earn extra profit on the fourth haircut sold at £12, as Table 12.2 shows the marginal cost of selling the fourth haircut is only £10. The output and profit of the perfectly price discriminating monopolist exceeds that of the single price monopolist because it earns greater revenue for the same level of cost.

Price Discrimination and Consumer Surplus

Demand curves slope down because the value that an individual places on a good falls as the quantity consumed of that good increases. When all the units consumed can be bought for a single price, consumers benefit. We call this benefit *consumer surplus*. (If you need to refresh your understanding of consumer surplus, flip back to Chapter 7, p. 164.) Price discrimination can be seen as an attempt by a monopoly to capture the consumer surplus (or as much of the surplus as possible) for itself.

Discriminating among Units of a Good

One form of price discrimination charges each single buyer a different price on each unit of a good bought. An example of this type of discrimination is a discount for bulk buying. The larger the order, the larger is the discount – and the lower is the price. This type of price discrimination works because each individual's demand curve slopes downward. Some discounts for bulk arise from lower costs of production for greater bulk. In these cases, such discounts are not price discrimination.

To extract every pound of consumer surplus from every buyer, a monopolist would have to offer each individual customer a separate price schedule based on that customer's own demand curve. Clearly such price discrimination cannot be carried out in practice because a firm does not have enough information about each consumer's demand curve.

Discriminating among Individuals

Even when it is not possible to charge each individual a different price for each unit bought, it may still be possible to discriminate among individuals. This possibility arises from the fact that some people place a higher value on consuming one more unit of a good than do other individuals. By charging such an individual a higher price, the producer can obtain some of the consumer surplus that would otherwise accrue to its customers.

Discriminating between Groups

Price discrimination often takes the form of discriminating between different groups of consumers on the basis of age, employment status, or some other easily distinguished characteristic. This type of price discrimination works only if each group has a different price elasticity of demand for the product. But this situation is a common one. For example, the elasticity of demand for haircuts is lower for business people than for students, and the elasticity of demand for air travel is lower for business travellers than for holiday-makers. Let's see how an airline exploits the differences in demand by business travellers and holiday-makers and increases its profit by price discriminating.

Global Air has a monopoly on an exotic route. Figure 12.6(a) shows the demand curve (*D*) and the marginal revenue curve (*MR*) for travel on this route. It also shows Global Air's marginal cost curve (*MC*). Marginal cost is constant, and fixed cost is zero[1]. Global Air is a single-price monopoly and maximizes its profit by producing the output at which marginal revenue equals marginal cost. This output is 10,000 trips a year. The price at which Global can sell 10,000 trips is £1,500 per trip. Global Air's total revenue is £15 million a year. Its total cost is £10 million a year, so its economic profit is £5 million a year, as shown by the blue rectangle in part (a).

_____

[1] The more usual case in which marginal cost increases when output increases (such as Cut and Dry's) is harder to analyse. All the key principles are shown by this special situation in which marginal cost is constant.

Global is struck by the fact that most of its customers are business travellers. Global knows that its exotic route is ideal for holidays, but it also knows that to attract more holiday-makers, it must offer a lower fare than £1,500. At the same time, Global knows that if it cuts the fare, it will lose revenue on its business travellers. So Global decides to price discriminate between the two groups.

Global's first step is to determine the demand curve of business travellers and the demand curve of holiday-makers. The market demand curve *D* (in Fig. 12.6a) is the horizontal sum of the demand curves for these two types of travellers (see Chapter 7, pp. 153). Global determines that the demand curve for business travel is D_B in Fig. 12.6(b) and the demand curve for holiday-makers is D_H in Fig. 12.6(c). At the single fare of £1,500, the 10,000 trips that Global sells is made up of 6,000 to business travellers and 4,000 to holiday-makers. At £1,500 a trip, business travellers buy more trips than holiday-makers – but

FIGURE 12.6

A Single-price Monopoly

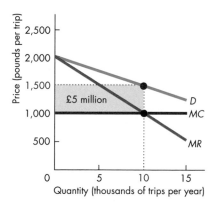

(a) All travellers

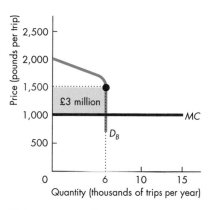

(b) Business travellers

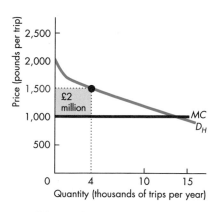

(c) Holiday-makers

Part (a) shows the demand curve (*D*), marginal revenue curve (*MR*) and marginal cost curve (*MC*), for a route on which Global Airlines has a monopoly. As a single-price monopoly, Global maximizes profit by selling 10,000 trips a year (the quantity at which *MC* = *MR*) at a fare of £1,500 a trip. Its profit is £5 million, which is shown by the blue rectangle in part (a). The demand curve in part (a) is the horizontal sum of the demand curves for business travel (D_B) in part (b) and for holiday travel (D_H in part (c). Global sells 6,000 trips to business travellers for a profit of £3 million and 4,000 trips to holiday-makers for a profit of £2 million.

at this price, the demand for business travel is much less elastic than holiday travel. As the price decreases below £1,500, the demand for business travel becomes perfectly inelastic while the demand for holiday travel is more elastic.

Profiting by Price Discrimination

Global uses the profit-maximization rule: produce the quantity at which marginal revenue equals marginal cost and set the price at the level the consumer is willing to pay. But now that Global has separated its market into two parts, it has two marginal revenue curves. Global's marginal revenue curve for business travel is MR_B as shown in Fig. 12.7(a) and its marginal revenue curve for holiday travel is MR_H as shown in Fig. 12.7(b).

In Fig. 12.7(a), marginal revenue from business travel equals marginal cost of £1,000 at 5,000 trips a year. The price that business travellers are willing

to pay for this quantity of trips is £1,700 a trip, up £200 on the current price. In Fig. 12.7(b), marginal revenue from holiday travel equals marginal cost of £1,000 at 7,000 trips a year. The price that holiday-makers are willing to pay for this quantity of trips is £1,350 a trip, *down* £150 on the current price.

If Global can charge its business travellers a fare of £1,700 and its holiday-makers a fare of £1,350, it can increase its sales from 10,000 to 13,000 trips a year and can increase its economic profit from £5 million to £5.95 million a year. On business travellers, it can make £3.5 million a year, which is £700 per trip on 5,000 trips. This economic profit is shown by the blue rectangle in Fig. 12.7(a). On holiday-makers, Global can make £2.45 million a year, which is £350 per trip on 7,000 trips. The blue rectangle in Fig. 12.6(b) illustrates this economic profit.

How can Global get its business travellers to pay £1,700? If it offers fares to holiday-makers for £1,350, won't business travellers claim to be on holiday to

FIGURE 12.7

Global's Price Discriminating Strategy

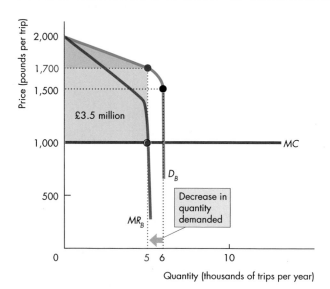

(a) Business travellers

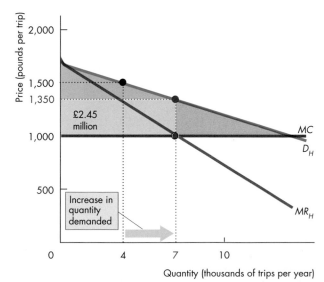

(b) Holiday-makers

The marginal revenue curve for business travel is (MR_B) in part (a) and for holiday travel is (MR_H) in part (b). Profit is maximized by making marginal revenue equal to marginal cost for each type of travel. By increasing the fare for business travel (part a) to £1,700 and by cutting the fare for

holiday travel (part b) to £1,350, Global increases its economic profit. It now makes £3.5 million on business travel (the blue rectangle in part (a)) and £2.45 million on holiday travel (the blue rectangle in part (b)). Total profit is £5.95 million, up £950,000 on its single-price strategy.

get the lower fare? Not with the deal that Global comes up with.

Global has noticed that its business travellers never make reservations more than three weeks in advance. It conducts a survey, which reveals that these travellers never know more than a month in advance when they will need to travel. Its survey also reveals that holiday-makers always know at least a month in advance of their travel plans. So Global offers a deal to all travellers. The basic fare is increased from £1,500 to £1,700. But if a traveller buys a non-refundable ticket one month in advance of the date of travel, the fare is discounted by £350 to £1,350. By price discriminating between business travellers and holiday-makers, Global increases the quantity of trips sold from 10,000 to 12,000 and increases its profit by £950,000 a year.

More Perfect Price Discrimination

Global can do even better. Some of the business travellers are willing to pay more than £1,700 a trip – their consumer surplus is shown by the green triangle in Fig. 12.7(a). Most holiday-makers, paying £1,350 a trip, are also willing to pay more – their consumer surplus is shown by the green triangle in Fig. 12.7(b). Some potential holiday-makers are not willing to pay £1,350, but are willing to pay at least £1,000. With a marginal cost of £1,000 a trip, there is a consumer surplus for potential holiday-makers, as shown by the orange triangle in Fig. 12.7(b).

Global gets creative. It comes up with a host of special deals. For higher prices, it offers priority reservations and frills to business travellers. (These deals don't change Global's marginal cost.) It refines the list of restrictions on its discount fares and creates many different fare categories, the lowest of which has lots of restrictions but is £1,000 a trip.

The quantity of seats sold increases until Global is selling 20,000 trips year – 6,000 to business travellers at various prices between £1,500 and almost £2,000 and 14,000 to holiday-makers at prices ranging between £1,000 and £1,700 a trip. Global is now almost a perfect price discriminator – capturing virtually the entire consumer surplus as profit.

Price Discrimination in Practice

You can now see why price discrimination is profitable. Global's special offer – 'Normal fare, £1,700, 30-day advance purchase special, £1,300' – is no generous gesture. It is profit-maximizing behaviour. The model of price discrimination that you have just studied explains a wide variety of familiar pricing practices where firms have the ability to set prices, even if they are not pure monopolies.

For example, real airlines, not just the imaginary Global that we've just studied, offer lower fares for advance-purchase tickets than for last-minute travel. Last-minute travellers usually have a lower elasticity of demand, while holiday-makers who can plan ahead have a higher elasticity of demand. Retail shops of all kinds hold seasonal 'sales' when they reduce their prices, often by substantial amounts. These 'sales' are a form of price discrimination. Each season, the newest fashions carry a high price tag but retailers do not expect to sell all their stock at such high prices. At the end of the season, they sell off what is left at a discount. These stores discriminate between buyers who have an inelastic demand (for example, those who want to be instantly fashionable) and buyers who have a more elastic demand (for example, those who pay less attention to up-to-the-minute fashion and more attention to price).

Limits to Price Discrimination

If price discrimination is profitable, why don't more firms do it? Why doesn't every air passenger have a separately discounted ticket? What are the limits to price discrimination?

Profitable price discrimination can take place only under certain conditions. First, it is possible to price discriminate only if the good cannot be resold. If a good can be resold, then customers who get the good for the low price can resell it to someone willing to pay a higher price. Price discrimination breaks down. It is for this reason that price discrimination usually occurs in markets for services rather than in markets for storable goods. One major exception, price discrimination in the sale of fashion clothes, works because at the end of the season when the clothes go on sale, fashion-conscious people are looking for next season's fashions. People buying on sale have no one to whom they can resell the clothes at a higher price.

Second, a price-discriminating monopoly must be able to identify groups with different elasticities of demand. The characteristics used for discrimination must also be within the law. These requirements usually limit price discrimination to cases based on age, employment status, or the timing of the purchase.

◆ Price discrimination can increase a monopoly's profit.

◆ By charging the highest price for each unit of the good that each person is willing to pay, a monopoly perfectly price discriminates and captures all of the consumer surplus.

◆ Most price discrimination takes the form of discriminating among different groups of customers with different elasticities of demand.

◆ People with a lower elasticity of demand pay a higher price, and people with a higher elasticity of demand pay a lower price.

◆ A price-discriminating monopoly produces a larger output than a single-price monopoly.

Comparing Monopoly and Competition

We have now studied a variety of ways in which firms and households interact in markets for goods and services. In Chapter 11, we saw how perfectly competitive firms behave and discovered the price and output at which they operate. In this chapter, we have studied the price and output of a single-price monopoly and a monopoly that price discriminates. How do the quantities produced, prices and profits of these different types of firms compare with each other?

To answer this question, let's imagine an industry made up of a large number of identical competitive firms. We can work out what the price charged and quantity produced will be in that industry. Then we can imagine that a single firm buys out all the individual firms and creates a monopoly. We will then work out the price charged and quantity produced by the monopoly, first when it charges a single price and second when it price discriminates.

Price and Output

Look carefully at Fig. 12.8. The industry demand curve is D and the industry supply curve is S. In perfect competition, the market equilibrium occurs

where the supply curve and the demand curve intersect. The quantity produced by the industry is Q_C and the price is P_C.

Each firm takes the price P_C and maximizes its profit by producing the output at which its own marginal cost equals the price. Because each firm is a small part of the total industry, there is no incentive for any firm to try to manipulate the price by varying its output.

Now suppose that this industry is taken over by a single firm. No changes in production techniques occur, so the new combined firm has identical costs

FIGURE 12.8

Monopoly and Competition Compared

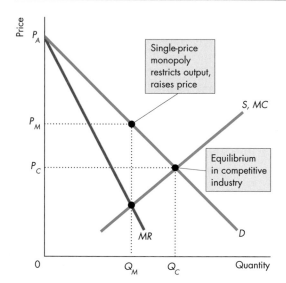

A competitive industry has a demand curve D and a supply curve S. Equilibrium occurs where the quantity demanded equals the quantity supplied at quantity Q_C and price P_C. If all the firms in the industry are taken over by a single producer that sells the profit-maximizing output for a single price, marginal revenue is MR and the competitive industry supply curve, S, becomes the monopoly's marginal cost curve, MC. The monopoly produces the output at which marginal revenue equals marginal cost. A single-price monopoly produces Q_M and sells that output for the price P_M. A perfectly price-discriminating monopoly produces Q_C and charges a different price for each unit sold. The prices charged range from P_A to P_C.

Monopoly restricts output and raises the price. But the more perfectly a monopoly can price discriminate, the closer its output gets to the competitive output.

to the original separate firms. The new single firm recognizes that by varying output it can influence price. It also recognizes that its marginal revenue curve is MR. To maximize profit, the firm chooses an output at which marginal revenue equals marginal cost.

But what is the monopoly's marginal cost curve? To answer this question, you need to recall the relationship between the marginal cost curve and the supply curve of a competitive firm. The supply curve of an individual competitive firm is its marginal cost curve above minimum average variable cost. The industry supply curve is the industry's marginal cost curve. (The supply curve has also been labelled MC to remind you of this fact.) Therefore, when the industry is taken over by a single firm, that firm's marginal cost curve is the same as what used to be the competitive industry's supply curve.

We have seen that a competitive industry always operates at the point of intersection of its supply and demand curves. In Fig. 12.8, this is the point at which price is P_C and the industry produces the quantity Q_C. In contrast, the single-price monopoly maximizes profit by restricting output to Q_M, where marginal revenue equals marginal cost. Because the marginal revenue curve is below the demand curve, output Q_M will always be smaller than output Q_C. The monopoly charges the price for which output Q_M can be sold, and that price, which is determined by the demand curve, is P_M. We have just established a key proposition:

> Compared with a perfectly competitive industry, a single-price monopoly restricts its output and charges a higher price.

If a monopoly can perfectly price discriminate, it will charge a different price on each unit sold and increase output to Q_C. The highest price charged is P_A and the lowest price charged is P_C, the price in a competitive market. The price P_A is the highest that is charged because at yet higher prices nothing can be sold. The price P_C is the lowest price charged because when a monopoly perfectly price discriminates, its marginal revenue curve is the same as the demand curve and at prices below P_C marginal cost exceeds marginal revenue. We have just established a second key proposition:

> The more perfectly the monopoly can price discriminate, the closer its output gets to the competitive output.

We've seen how the output and price of a monopoly compare with those in a competitive industry. Let's now compare the efficiency of the two types of markets.

Allocative Efficiency

Except for the case of a perfect price-discriminating monopoly, monopoly is a form of market failure and is less efficient than competition. Market failure prevents some of the gains from trade from being achieved. To see why, look at Fig. 12.9. The maximum price that consumers are willing to pay for each unit is shown by the demand curve. This price measures the *value* of the good to the consumer. The difference between the value of a good and its price is **consumer surplus.** (See Chapter 7, p. 164, for a more detailed explanation of consumer surplus.)

Under perfect competition (part a), consumers pay P_C for each unit bought and obtain a consumer surplus represented by the green triangle. A single-price monopoly (part b) restricts output to Q_M and sells that output for P_M. Consumer surplus is decreased to the smaller green triangle. Consumers lose partly by having to pay more for what is available and partly by getting less of the good. But is the consumers' loss equal to the monopoly's gain? Is there simply a redistribution of the gains from trade and hence no loss in overall efficiency? A closer look at Fig. 12.9(b) will convince you that there is a reduction in the gains from trade. It is true that some of the loss in consumer surplus does accrue to the monopoly – the monopoly gets the difference between the higher price (P_M) and P_C on the quantity sold (Q_M). So the monopoly has taken the blue rectangle part of the consumer surplus. This portion of the loss of consumer surplus is not a loss to society and hence not a loss of efficiency. It is a redistribution from consumers to the monopolist.

But where is the rest of the consumer surplus? The answer is that because output has been restricted, it is lost. But more than that has been lost. The total loss resulting from the lower monopoly output (Q_M) is the grey triangle in Fig. 12.9(b). The part of the grey triangle above P_C is the loss of consumer surplus and the part of the triangle below P_C is a loss to the producer – a loss of producer surplus. **Producer surplus** is the difference between a producer's revenue and the opportunity cost of production. It is calculated as the sum of the differences between price and the marginal cost of producing each unit of output. Under competitive

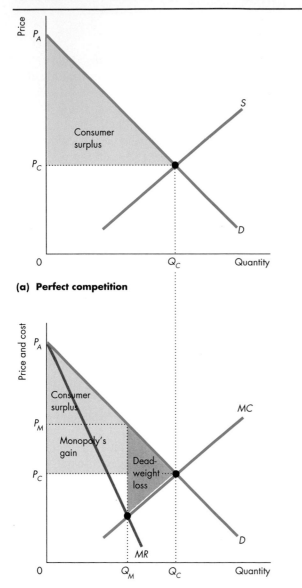

FIGURE 12.9

Allocative Inefficiency of Monopoly

(a) Perfect competition

(b) Monopoly

In perfect competition (part a), quantity is Q_C, price is P_C and consumer surplus is the green triangle. With free entry, firms' economic profits in long-run equilibrium are zero. Consumer surplus is maximized. Under a single-price monopoly (part b), output is restricted to Q_M and the price increases to P_M. Consumer surplus is reduced to the smaller green triangle. The monopoly takes the blue rectangle for itself, but the grey triangle is a deadweight loss. Part of the deadweight loss (above P_C) is a loss of consumer surplus, and part (below P_C) is a loss of producer surplus.

conditions, the producer sells the output between Q_M and Q_C for a price of P_C. The marginal cost of producing each extra unit of output through that range is shown by the marginal cost (supply) curve. Thus the vertical distance between the marginal cost curve and price represents a producer surplus. Part of the producer surplus is lost when a monopoly restricts output to less than its competitive level.

The grey triangle, which measures the total loss of both consumer and producer surplus, is called the deadweight loss. **Deadweight loss** measures the loss of allocative efficiency as the reduction in consumer and producer surplus resulting from a restriction of output below its efficient level. A monopoly's reduced output and higher price results in the monopoly capturing some of the consumer surplus. It also results in the elimination of the producer surplus and the consumer surplus on the output that a competitive industry would have produced but that the monopoly does not. Deadweight loss measures the degree of market failure or allocative inefficiency created by a monopoly. *Reading Between the Lines* on pp 304–305 explores the efficiency loss arising from monopoly pricing in a suspected European cartel.

Usually a monopoly produces an output well below that at which average total cost is at a minimum. It has far more capacity than it uses. But even if a monopoly produces the quantity at which average total cost is a minimum, which it might, the consumer does not have the opportunity of buying the good at that price. The price paid by the consumer always exceeds marginal cost.

We have seen that a single-price monopoly creates a deadweight loss by restricting output. What is the deadweight loss if the monopoly practises perfect price discrimination? The answer is zero. A perfect price discriminator produces the same output as the competitive industry. The last item sold costs P_C, the same as its marginal cost. Thus from the point of view of allocative efficiency, a perfect price-discriminating monopoly achieves the same result as perfect competition.

Redistribution

Under perfect competition, the consumer surplus is the green triangle in Fig. 12.9(a) and the long-run equilibrium economic profit is zero. We've just seen that the creation of monopoly reduces consumer surplus and may lead to a deadweight loss. But what happens to the distribution of surpluses between producers and consumers? The answer is that the monopoly always wins. In the case of a single-price monopoly (Fig. 12.9b), the monopoly gains the blue rectangle at the expense of the consumer, but it loses part of its producer surplus – its share of the deadweight loss. This loss reduces its gain. But there is always a net gain for the monopoly and a net loss for the consumer. We also know that because there is a deadweight loss, the consumer loses more than the monopoly gains.

In the case of a perfect price-discriminating monopoly, there is no deadweight loss but there is an even larger redistribution of the gains from trade away from consumers to the monopoly. In this case, the monopoly captures the entire consumer surplus, the green triangle in Fig. 12.9(a).

It is because it creates a deadweight loss that monopoly is inefficient. It imposes a cost on society. This cost might be avoided by the break-up of a monopoly and a considerable amount of law and regulation, which is described and explained in Chapter 19, is directed at this problem.

REVIEW

◆ The creation of a monopoly results in a redistribution of economic gains away from consumers and to the monopoly producer.

◆ If a monopoly can perfectly price discriminate, it produces the same output as a competitive industry and achieves allocative efficiency, but it captures the entire consumer surplus.

◆ A monopoly cannot usually perfectly price discriminate, so it restricts output below the level that a competitive industry would produce and creates a deadweight loss. The monopoly creates allocative inefficiency – the consumers' loss exceeds the monopoly's gain.

Rent Seeking

The activity of creating a monopoly from which an economic profit can be made is called **rent seeking.** The term 'rent seeking' is used because 'rent' (or 'economic rent') is another name for consumer surplus plus producer surplus. We've seen that a monopoly makes its economic profit by diverting part of the consumer surplus to itself. Thus the pursuit of an economic profit by a monopolist is rent seeking. It is the attempt to capture some consumer surplus.

Rent seeking is a profitable activity and one that is widely pursued. It is profitable because a monopoly can make an economic profit in the long run, while a firm in a competitive industry can hope to make an economic profit only in the short run. In a competitive industry, freedom of entry brings new firms and results in economic profit being competed away. In a monopoly industry, barriers to entry prevent this process. Because a monopoly can make an economic profit in the long run, there is an incentive to acquire a monopoly – to rent seek. What do rent seekers do?

One form of rent seeking is the searching out of existing monopoly rights that can be bought for a lower price than the monopoly's economic profit – that is, seeking to acquire existing monopoly rights. There are many examples of this type of rent-seeking activity. One that is well known is the purchase of taxi licences. In most cities, taxis are regulated. The city restricts both the fares and the number of taxis that are permitted to operate. Operating a taxi results in economic profit or rent. A person who wants to operate a taxi must buy the right to do so from someone who already has that right.

But buying an existing monopoly does not assure an economic profit. The reason is that there is freedom of entry into the activity of rent seeking. Rent seeking is like perfect competition. If an economic profit is available, a new entrant will try to get some of it. Competition among rent seekers pushes the price that must be paid for a monopoly right up to the point at which only a normal profit can be made by operating the monopoly. The economic profit – the rent – goes to the person who created the monopoly in the first place. For example, competition for the right to operate a taxi in UK cities leads to a price of more than £10,000, which is sufficiently high to eliminate long-run economic profit for the taxi operator. But the person who acquired the right in the first place collects the economic rent. This type of rent seeking transfers wealth from the buyer to the seller of the monopoly.

Although a great deal of rent-seeking activity involves searching out existing monopoly rights that can be profitably bought, most of it is devoted to the creation of monopoly. This type of legitimate rent-seeking activity takes the form of lobbying and seeking to influence the political process. Such influence is sometimes sought by making political contributions in exchange for legislative support or by indirectly seeking to influence political outcomes through publicity in the media or more direct contacts with politicians and bureaucrats. An example would be the donations to political parties that the alcohol and tobacco companies make in an attempt to avoid a tightening of legislation on activities such as advertising and licensing, which might affect their profits.

This type of rent seeking is a costly activity that uses up scarce resources. In aggregate, firms spend millions of pounds lobbying Parliament in the pursuit of licences and laws that create barriers to entry and establish a monopoly right. Everyone has an incentive to rent seek, and because there are no barriers to entry into the rent-seeking activity, there is a great deal of competition for new monopoly rights.

What determines the value of the resources that a person will use to obtain a monopoly right? The answer is the monopoly's economic profit. If the value of resources spent trying to create a monopoly exceeds the monopoly's economic profit, the result is an economic loss. But as long as the value of the resources used to create a monopoly falls short of the monopoly's economic profit, there is an economic profit to be earned. With no barrier to entry into rent seeking, the value of the resources used up in rent seeking equals the monopoly's economic profit.

Because of rent seeking, monopoly imposes social costs that exceed the deadweight loss that we calculated earlier. To calculate that cost, we must add to the deadweight loss the value of resources used in rent seeking. That amount equals the monopoly's entire economic profit, because that is the value of the resources that it pays to use in rent seeking. Thus the social cost of monopoly is the deadweight loss plus the monopoly's economic profit.

Gains from Monopoly

So far, compared with perfect competition, monopoly has come out in a pretty bad light. If monopoly is so bad, why do we put up with it? Why don't we have laws that crack down on monopoly so hard that it never rears its head? We do indeed have laws that limit monopoly power (see Chapter 19). We also have laws that regulate these monopolies that exist. But monopoly is not all bad. Let's look at its potential advantages and some of the reasons for its existence.

The main reasons why monopoly might have some advantages are:

◆ Economies of scale and economies of scope
◆ Incentives to innovate

Economies of Scale and Scope   A firm experiences *economies of scale* when an increase in its production of a good or service brings a decrease in the average total cost of producing it – see Chapter 10, pp. 241–244. **Economies of scope** arise when an increase in the *range of goods produced* brings a decrease in average total cost. Economies of scope occur when highly specialized (and usually expensive) technical inputs can be shared by different goods. For example, McDonald's can produce both hamburgers and chips at an average total cost that is lower than what it would cost two separate firms to produce the same goods because hamburgers and chips share the use of specialized food storage and preparation facilities. Firms producing a wide range of products can hire specialist computer programmers, designers and marketing experts whose skills can be used across the product range, thereby spreading their costs and lowering the average total cost of production of each of the goods.

Large-scale firms that have control over supply and can influence price – and that therefore behave like the monopoly firm that we've been studying in this chapter – can reap these economies of scale and scope; small, competitive firms cannot. As a consequence, there are situations in which the comparison of monopoly and competition that we made earlier in this chapter is not a valid one. Recall that we imagined the takeover of a large number of competitive firms by a single monopoly firm. But we also assumed that the monopoly would use exactly the same technology as the small firms and have the same costs. But if one large firm can reap economies of scale and scope, its marginal cost curve will lie below the supply curve of a competitive industry made up of thousands of small firms. It is possible for such economies of scale and scope to be so large as to result in a higher output and lower price under monopoly than a competitive industry would achieve.

Figure 12.10 illustrates such a situation. Here, the demand curve and the marginal revenue curve are the same regardless of whether the industry is a competitive one or a monopoly. With a competitive industry, the supply curve is S, the quantity produced is Q_C and the price is P_C. With a monopoly that can exploit economies of scale and scope, the marginal cost curve is MC_M. The monopoly maximizes profit by producing the output (Q_M) at which marginal revenue equals marginal cost. The price that maximizes profit is P_M. By exploiting a superior technology not available to each of the large number of small firms, the monopoly is able to achieve a higher output and lower price than the competitive industry.

There are many examples of industries in which economies of scale are so significant that they lead to an outcome similar to that shown in Fig. 12.10. Public utilities such as gas, electric power, water and rubbish collection are all such cases. There are also many examples where a combination of

economies of scale and economies of scope arise. These include the brewing of beer, the manufacture of refrigerators, other household appliances and pharmaceuticals, and the refining of petroleum.

Incentives to Innovate

Innovation is the first-time application of new knowledge in the production process. Innovation may take the form of developing a new product or a lower-cost way of making an existing product. Controversy has raged among economists over whether large firms with monopoly power or small competitive firms lacking such monopoly power are the most innovative. It is clear that some temporary monopoly power arises from innovation. A firm that develops a new product or process and patents it obtains an exclusive right to that product or process for the term of the patent.

But does the granting of a monopoly, even a temporary one, to an innovator increase the pace of innovation? One line of reasoning suggests that it does. With no protection, an innovator is not able to enjoy the profits from innovation for long. Thus the incentive to innovate is weakened. A contrary argument is that monopolies can afford to be lazy while competitive firms cannot. Competitive firms must strive to innovate and cut costs even though they know that they cannot hang on to the benefits of their innovation for long. But that knowledge spurs them on to greater and faster innovation.

A matter such as this one cannot be resolved by listing arguments and counter-arguments. It requires a careful empirical investigation. Many such investigations have been conducted. But the evidence that they bring to bear on this question is mixed. They show that large firms do much more research and development than do small firms. They also show that large firms are significantly more prominent at the development end of the research and development process. But measuring research and development is measuring the volume of inputs into the process of innovation. What matters is not input but output. Two measures of the output of research and development are the number of patents and the rate of productivity growth. On these measures, there is no clear evidence that big is best. But there is a clear pattern in the process of diffusion of technological knowledge. After innovation, a new process or product spreads gradually through the industry.

FIGURE 12.10

When Economies of Scale and Scope Make Monopoly More Efficient

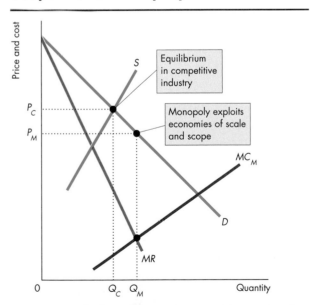

In some industries, economies of scale and economies of scope result in the monopoly's marginal cost curve (MC_M) lying below the competitive industry supply curve (S). In such a case, it is possible that the single-price monopoly output (Q_M) exceeds the competitive output (Q_C) and that the monopoly price (P_M) is below the competitive price (P_C).

Monopoly in Action: Investigating a Heating Pipe Cartel

The Essence of the Story

THE FINANCIAL TIMES, 12 MARCH 1996

Brussels digs for evidence of heating pipe cartel

William Lewis and Hugh Carnegy

The European Commission is examining the operation of a ... suspected tightly knit cartel within the district heating pipe manufacturing industry, which has a total annual turnover in Europe of about £600m....

Organised price fixing, deals to carve up market share and intimidation are all methods which Brussels suspects have regularly been used to enforce, or attempt to enforce, the cartel in a number of European countries.... Six companies are suspected of being members of the cartel....

The chief victim of the suspected cartel in recent years is understood to be Powerpipe, an independent, privately owned company based outside Gothenburg....

The investigators believe that suspected cartel members subjected Powerpipe to reprisals after the award of the contract... in March 1995....

Investigators suspect that in retaliation, cartel members 'possibly threatened a collective boycott on Powerpipe's suppliers and customers, in order for them to break their business connections with Powerpipe', a letter written by the Commission states.

Further allegations of boycotts came last year in Denmark where...prices for district heating contracts have at times been as much as 50 per cent higher than in neighbouring Sweden, despite both markets being served by many of the same companies....

It is understood there were more than 20 cases in Germany where contracts worth more than DM100,000 had been divided up by the suspected cartel....

At different times in different markets, relationships between the suspected cartel members break down, leading to price wars....

A steady price trend in Denmark was suddenly broken two years ago after Isoplus came into the market for the first time and prices fell by up to 40 per cent. Within a year, prices were back to 1993 levels....Evidence indicates that...efforts have been made to stabilise the operation of 'the circle' across Europe in an effort to cut out the incidence of such occasional infighting.

■ The European Commission began an investigation into an alleged cartel in the European heating market in 1996, known to its members as 'The Circle'.

■ A Swedish–Swiss engineering multinational and five other European companies are suspected of forming a price-fixing and market-rigging cartel spanning operations in Germany, the Netherlands, Austria, Sweden and Denmark.

■ One independent Swedish company, Powerpipe, has tried to compete against the cartel, but argues it has suffered reprisals – a collective boycott of its customers and suppliers.

■ The cartel appears particularly effective in Denmark where prices are 50 per cent higher than in neighbouring Sweden, although both countries are served by the same companies.

■ The cartel must reach an agreement with each new entrant to avoid competition erupting into price wars.

Economic Analysis

■ A successful cartel operates as one firm in the industry — a monopoly.

■ Figure 1 shows that the cartel faces the downward-sloping European district heating industry demand curve, D. The average total cost for the combination of firms is ATC, marginal cost is MC and marginal revenue is MR.

■ To maximize profits, the cartel sets price at P_m, where MR equals MC, generating an economic profit shown by the blue area. The quantity of pipes supplied, Q_0, and a hypothetical economic profit of £5 million, is shared between the cartel members.

■ Figure 2 shows the impact of the cartel action in Denmark and the effect on consumer surplus. The demand for district heating in Denmark is D_0, marginal revenue is MR_0 and marginal cost is MC_0.

■ If Powerpipe and other competitors undermine the cartel, a price war forces prices down to the competitive level, P_C, and the quantity of pipes supplied increases to Q_C. Consumer surplus is maximized (the areas shaded green, blue and red).

■ If the cartel reaches an agreement with new entrants or forces new entrants out of the Danish market, a monopoly is maintained. Price rises by 50 per cent to P_m and quantity supplied falls to Q_m, and some consumer surplus is transferred to the cartel (blue area).

■ Cartels are illegal under European law because they are inefficient — some consumer and producer surplus is lost in the deadweight loss (red plus grey area).

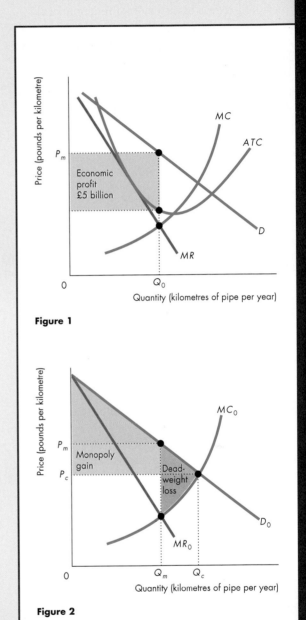

Figure 1

Figure 2

Whether an innovator is a small firm or a large firm, large firms jump on the bandwagon more quickly than do the remaining small firms. Thus large firms speed the process of diffusion of technological advances.

In determining public policy towards monopoly (discussed in Chapter 19), laws and regulations are designed that balance the gains from monopoly (economies of scale and scope and innovation) against the deadweight loss and redistribution that they also generate.

◆ ◆ ◆ ◆ We've now studied two models of market structure – perfect competition and monopoly.

We've discovered the conditions under which perfect competition achieves allocative efficiency and we've compared the efficiency of competition with that of monopoly. ◆ Although there are examples of markets in the European economies that are highly competitive or highly monopolistic, the markets for most goods and services lie somewhere between these two extremes. In the next chapter, we're going to study this middle ground between monopoly and competition. We're going to discover that many of the lessons that we learned from these two extreme models are still relevant and useful in understanding behaviour in real-world markets.

S U M M A R Y

How Monopoly Arises

A monopoly is an industry in which there is a single supplier of a good, service, or resource. Monopoly arises because of barriers to entry that prevent competition. Barriers to the entry of new firms may be legal or natural. Legal barriers take the form of public franchise, government licence, patent, copyright, or when a single firm has significant control of a resource. Natural barriers exist when economies of scale are so large that a single firm can supply an entire market at a lower average total cost than can several firms or when set-up costs are large. (pp. 286–287)

Single-price Monopoly

A single-price monopoly is a firm that charges the same price for each unit of output. The monopoly's demand curve is the market demand curve for the good. For a single-price monopoly, marginal revenue is less than price. Total revenue rises at first, but above some output level it begins to decline. When total revenue is rising, marginal revenue is positive. When total revenue is falling, marginal revenue is negative. When total revenue is a maximum, marginal revenue is zero. When marginal revenue is positive (total revenue rising), the elasticity of demand is greater than 1. The elasticity of demand equals 1 when marginal revenue is zero.

A monopoly's technology and costs behave in a way similar to those of any other type of firm. The monopoly maximizes profit by producing the output that makes marginal revenue equal to marginal cost and by charging the maximum price that consumers are willing to pay for that output. The price charged always exceeds marginal cost. (pp. 287–292)

Price Discrimination

Price discrimination is the practice of charging some consumers a higher price than others for an identical item or charging an individual customer a higher price on a small purchase than on a large one. Price discrimination is an attempt by the monopoly to convert consumer surplus into economic profit. Perfect price discrimination extracts all the consumer surplus. Such a monopoly charges a different price for each unit sold and obtains the maximum price that each consumer is willing to pay for each unit bought. With perfect price discrimination, the monopoly's marginal revenue curve is the same as its demand curve and the monopoly produces the same output as would a perfectly competitive industry.

A monopoly can discriminate between different groups of customers on the basis of age, employment status, or other distinguishable characteristics. Such price discrimination increases the monopoly's economic profit if each group has a different elasticity of demand for the product. To maximize profit with price discrimination, the monopoly produces an output such that marginal cost equals marginal revenue, but then charges each group the maximum price that it is willing to pay. These prices will be different.

Price discrimination can be practised only when it is impossible for a buyer to resell the good and when consumers with different elasticities can be identified. (pp. 293–298)

Comparing Monopoly and Competition

If a monopoly takes over all the firms in a perfectly competitive industry and if the technology and input prices in the industry remain unchanged, the monopoly charges a higher price and produces a lower quantity than would prevail in a perfectly competitive industry. If the monopoly can perfectly price discriminate, it produces the competitive quantity and sells the last unit for the competitive price.

A single-price monopoly is less efficient than competition because it prevents some of the gains from trade from being achieved. It captures part of consumer surplus, by restricting output and creating a deadweight loss. The more a monopoly can price discriminate, the smaller is the deadweight loss, the larger is the economic profit and the smaller is the consumer surplus.

Monopoly imposes costs that equal its deadweight loss plus the cost of the resources devoted to rent seeking – searching out profitable monopoly opportunities. At most, the resources used in rent seeking are equal in value to the economic profit that the monopoly might attain. As a result, the maximum cost of monopoly equals its deadweight loss plus its economic profit.

A monopoly can be more efficient than a competitive industry if available economies of scale and scope are so large that the monopoly's output is higher and its price lower than those that would arise with a large number of firms. There are also situations in which monopoly may be more innovative than competition, resulting in a faster pace of technological change. (pp. 298–306)

KEY ELEMENTS

Key Terms

Barriers to entry, 286
Consumer surplus, 299
Deadweight loss, 300
Economies of scope, 302
Legal monopoly, 286
Monopoly, 286
Natural monopoly, 287
Patent, 286
Price discrimination, 293
Producer surplus, 299
Rent seeking, 301

◈ Key Figures

Figure 12.2   Demand and Marginal Revenue for a Single-price Monopoly, 288
Figure 12.3   A Single-price Monopoly's Revenue Curves, 290
Figure 12.4   A Single-price Monopoly's Output and Price, 292
Figure 12.8   Monopoly and Competition Compared, 298

REVIEW QUESTIONS

1 What is a monopoly? What are some examples of monopoly in your region?

2 How does monopoly arise?

3 Distinguish between a legal monopoly and a natural monopoly. Give examples of each type.

4 Explain why marginal revenue is always less than price for a single-price monopoly.

5 Why does a monopoly's economic profit increase as output increases initially but eventually decrease when output gets too big?

6 Does a single-price monopoly operate on the inelastic part of its demand curve? Explain why it does or does not.

7 Explain how a single-price monopoly chooses its output and price.

8 Can any monopoly price discriminate? If yes, why? If no, why not?

9 Explain why a single-price monopoly produces a smaller output than an equivalent competitive industry.

10 Is a single-price monopoly as efficient as competition?

11 What is deadweight loss?

12 Show graphically the deadweight loss under perfect price discrimination.

13 As far as allocative efficiency is concerned, is a single-price monopoly better or worse than perfect price discrimination? Why?

14 Monopoly redistributes consumer surplus. Explain why the consumer loses more under perfect price discrimination than under single-price monopoly.

15 Explain why people indulge in rent-seeking activities.

16 When taking account of the cost of rent seeking, what is the social cost of monopoly?

17 What are economies of scale and economies of scope? What effects, if any, do they have on allocative efficiency of monopoly?

PROBLEMS

1 Cool Condiments, a single-price monopoly, faces the following demand schedule for bottled balsamic vinegar:

Price (pounds per bottle)	Quantity demanded (bottles)
10	0
8	1
6	2
4	3
2	4
0	5

a Calculate the company's total revenue schedule.

b Calculate its marginal revenue schedule.

c At what price is the elasticity of demand equal to 1?

2 Cool Condiments has the following total cost:

Quantity produced (bottles)	Total cost (pounds)
0	1
1	3
2	7
3	13
4	21
5	31

Calculate the profit-maximizing levels of

a Output

b Price

c Marginal cost

d Marginal revenue

e Economic profit

3 Suppose that Cool Condiments can perfectly price discriminate. Calculate its profit-maximizing

a Output
b Total revenue
c Economic profit

4 What is the maximum price that someone would be willing to pay the company for a licence to operate its balsamic vinegar cellars?

5 Two demand schedules for round-trip flights between London and New York are set out below. The schedule for weekday travellers is for those making round-trips on weekdays and returning within the same week. The schedule for weekend travellers is for those who stay over the weekend. (The former tend to be business travellers and the latter holiday and pleasure travellers.)

Weekday travellers		Weekend travellers	
Price (pounds per roundtrip)	Quantity demanded (thousands of roundtrips)	Price (pounds per roundtrip)	Quantity demanded (thousands of roundtrips)
1,500	0	750	0
1,250	5	500	5
1,000	10	250	10
750	15	0	15
500	15		
250	15		

The marginal cost of a round-trip is £500. If a single-price monopoly airline controls the London–New York route, use a graph to find out the following:

a What price is charged?
b How many passengers travel?
c What is the consumer surplus for weekday travellers?
d What is the consumer surplus for weekend travellers?

6 Barbara runs a cafe in the Scottish Highlands, miles from anywhere. She has a monopoly and faces the following demand schedule for meals:

Price (pounds per meal)	Quantity demanded (meals per week)
1.00	160
1.50	140
2.00	120
2.50	100
3.00	80
3.50	60
4.00	40
4.50	20
5.00	0

Barbara's marginal cost and average total cost are a constant £2 per meal.

a If Barbara charges all customers the same price for a meal, what price is it?
b What is the consumer surplus of all the customers who buy a meal from Barbara?
c What is the producer surplus?
d What is the deadweight loss?

7 Barbara discovers that some of the people stopping for meals are truck drivers and some of them are tourists. She estimates that the demand schedules for the two groups are:

Price (pounds per meal)	Quantity demanded (meals per week)	
	Truck Drivers	Tourists
1.00	70	90
1.50	65	75
2.00	60	60
2.50	55	45
3.00	50	30
3.50	45	15
4.00	40	0
4.50	20	0
5.00	0	0

If Barbara price discriminates between the two,

a What price does she charge truck drivers?
b What price does she charge tourists?
c What is her output per week and is it higher, lower, or the same as when she did not price discriminate?
d What is her weekly economic profit and is it higher, lower, or the same as when she did not price discriminate?
e What is the consumer surplus for truck drivers?
f What is the consumer surplus for tourists?

8 Study *Reading Between the Lines* on pp. 304–305 and then:
a Describe the alleged strategy of the six European domestic heating pipe companies.
b Explain the impact on consumer surplus of the formation of a cartel in the European domestic heating pipe industry.
c Explain why the European Commission is investigating the alleged cartel.

CHAPTER
13

MONOPOLISTIC
COMPETITION
AND
OLIGOPOLY

**After studying this chapter
you will be able to:**

◆ Describe and distinguish among
   market structures that lie between
   perfect competition and monopoly

◆ Define monopolistic competition and
   oligopoly

◆ Explain how price and output are
   determined in a monopolistically
   competitive industry

◆ Explain why the price may be sticky
   in an oligopoly industry

◆ Explain how price and output are
   determined when there is one
   dominant firm and several small
   firms in an industry

◆ Use game theory to make
   predictions about price wars and
   competition among small numbers
   of firms

EVERY WEEK, WE RECEIVE A NEWSPAPER STUFFED WITH SUPERMARKET FLIERS describing this week's 'specials', providing coupons and other enticements. They are all designed to persuade us that Tesco, Safeway, Sainsbury's, Waitrose, Morrison's, Kwik Save, and Aldi have the best deals in town. One claims the lowest price, another the best brands, yet another the best value for money even if its prices are not the lowest. How do firms locked in such fierce competition set their prices, pick their goods and services and choose the quantities to produce? How are the profits of such firms affected by the actions of other firms? ◆ Until recently, only one firm made the chips that drive IBM and compatible PCs – Intel Corporation. During 1994, the prices of powerful personal computers based on Intel's fast 486 and Pentium chips collapsed. The reason: Intel suddenly faced competition from new chip producers. The

Fliers and War Games

price of Intel's Pentium processor, set at more than £1,500 when it was launched in 1993, fell to less than £350 by spring 1995, and the price of Pentium-based computers fell to less than £1,500. How did competition among a small number of chip makers bring such a rapid fall in the price of chips and computers?

◆ ◆ ◆ ◆ The theories of monopoly and perfect competition do not predict the kind of behaviour just described. There are no fliers and coupons, best brands, or price wars in perfect competition because each firm produces an identical product and is a price taker. Similarly, there are none in monopoly because each monopoly firm has the entire market to itself. To understand coupons, fliers and price wars, we need the more complex models explained in this chapter.

Varieties of Market Structure

We have studied two types of market structure – perfect competition and monopoly. In perfect competition, a large number of firms produce identical goods and there are no barriers to the entry of new firms into the industry. In this situation, each firm is a price taker and, in the long run, there is no economic profit. In monopoly, there is just one firm in the industry which is protected by barriers, preventing the entry of new firms. The firm sets its price to maximize profit and might enjoy economic profit even in the long run.

Many real-world industries are not well described by the models of perfect competition and monopoly because they lie between the two cases. Two other market models have been developed to study the industries that lie between perfect competition and monopoly. They are:

1. Monopolistic competition

2. Oligopoly

Monopolistic competition is a market structure in which a large number of firms compete with each other by making similar but slightly different products. Making a product slightly different from the product of a competing firm is called **product differentiation**. Because of product differentiation, a monopolistically competitive firm has an element of monopoly power. The firm is the sole producer of the particular version of the good in question. For example, in the breakfast cereal market, only Weetabix Ltd makes Weetabix and only the Kellogg Company makes All Bran. Differentiated products are not necessarily different in an objective sense. For example, there are many cereals which are similar to Weetabix and All Bran in shape, content and production. Many supermarkets sell their own brands of these cereals under different names. The differences are mainly in the packaging and name. What matters is that consumers perceive products to be different.

In some markets, there are few firms but entry and exit is so easy that competition from *potential* new firms is fierce. A market in which potential entry is free is called a **contestable market**. Even if there are some small costs to entry and exit, a market can still be highly contestable. An example of a virtually contestable market is that of local private bus routes. Firms can easily switch their buses from one route to another with virtually no entry and exit costs. Contestable markets can also be studied using the model of monopolistic competition.

Oligopoly is a market structure in which a small number of producers compete with each other. There are hundreds of examples of oligopolistic industries. Computer software, aircraft and car manufacture are but a few. In some oligopolistic industries, each firm produces an almost identical product. In others, products are differentiated. For example, oil and petrol are essentially the same whether they are made by Shell or Esso. But in the European car market, the Volkswagen Golf is a differentiated commodity from the Renault 5 or Peugeot 205.

Measures of Concentration

In order to tell which of our market models best describes a particular industry, and hence how much market power firms in the industry might have, economists use measures of industrial concentration. Industrial concentration measures the proportion of output or employment accounted for by a specified number of the largest firms in the industry. The most commonly used measure is the five-firm concentration ratio, but there is no reason why a three- or four-firm ratio could not be used.

Five-firm concentration ratio The **five-firm concentration ratio** is the percentage of the industry's output accounted for by the five firms with the largest output in the industry. Output could be measured by volume or the value of sales. The range of the concentration ratio is from almost zero for perfect competition to 100 for monopoly. This ratio is the main measure used to assess market structure.

Table 13.1 sets out two hypothetical concentration ratio calculations, one for shoe manufacturing and one for egg farming. In this example, there are 15 firms in the shoe manufacturing industry. The largest five have 81 per cent of the sales of the industry, so the five-firm concentration ratio for that industry is 81 per cent. In the egg industry, with 1,005 firms, the top five firms account for only 0.8 per cent of total industry sales. In this case, the five-firm concentration ratio is 0.8 per cent.

The idea behind calculating five-firm concentration ratios is to get information about the degree of competitiveness of a market. A low concentration ratio indicates a high degree of competition, and a high concentration ratio indicates an absence of competition. In the extreme case of monopoly, the

TABLE 13.1

Concentration Ratio Calculations (hypothetical)

Shoemakers		Egg farmers	
Firm	**Sales (£ million)**	**Firm**	**Sales (£ million)**
Lace-up plc	250	Bills's	0.9
Finefoot plc	200	Sue's	0.7
Easyfit plc	180	Jane's	0.6
Comfy plc	120	Tom's	0.4
Loafers plc	70	Jill's	0.2
Top 5 sales	820	Top 5 sales	2.8
Other 10 firms	190	Other 1,000 firms	349.2
Industry sales	1,010	Industry sales	352.0

Five-firm concentration ratios:

Shoemakers: $\dfrac{820}{1,010} = 81\%$

Printers: $\dfrac{2.80}{352} = 0.8\%$

concentration ratio is 100 per cent as the largest (and only) firm makes the entire industry sales. Between these extremes, the five-firm concentration ratio is regarded as being a useful indicator of the likelihood of collusion among firms in an oligopoly. If the ratio exceeds 60 per cent, it is likely that firms in that industry will have a high degree of market power. They are likely to collude and behave like a monopolist. If the ratio is less than 40 per cent, it is likely that the firms will compete effectively. Between the ratios of 40 and 60 per cent, the industries have oligopolistic and monopolistic competitive structures. But the degree of market power for firms in these industries is likely to be limited by some form of competition.

Limitations of Concentration Measures

Although concentration ratios are useful, they have some limitations. They must be supplemented by other information to determine the structure of an industry and the degree of market power of firms in that industry. The three key problems are:

◆ The geographical scope of the market

◆ Barriers to entry and firm turnover

◆ The correspondence between a market and an industry

Geographical Scope of Market   Concentration ratio data are based on a national view of the market.

Many goods are sold on a national market, but some are sold on a regional market and some on a global one. The brewing industry is a good example of one in which the local market is more relevant than the national market. Thus although the national concentration ratio for brewers is in the middle range, there is nevertheless a high degree of concentration in the brewing industry in most regions. The automobile industry is an example of one for which there is a global market. Thus although the largest five car producers in the United Kingdom account for 80 per cent of all cars sold by UK producers, they account for a smaller percentage of the total UK car market, which includes imports, and an even smaller percentage of the global market for cars.

Barriers to Entry and Turnover   Measures of concentration do not indicate the severity of any barriers to entry in a market. Some industries, for example, are highly concentrated but their markets have virtually free entry and a high turnover of firms. A good example is the market for local restaurants. Many small towns have few restaurants, but there are few restrictions on entering the restaurant industry. So firms enter and exit with great regularity.

Even if the turnover of new firms in a market is limited, an industry might be competitive because of potential entry. This will be the case if the market is *highly contestable*. Table 13.2 summarizes

TABLE 13.2

Market Structure

Characteristics	Perfect competition	Monopolistic competition	Contestable	Oligopoly	Monopoly
Number of firms in industry	Many	Many	Few	Few	One
Product	Identical	Differentiated	Differentiated	Either identical or differentiated	No close substitutes
Barriers to entry	None	None	None	Scale and scope economies	Scale and scope or legal barriers
Firm's control over price	None	Some	Some	Considerable	Considerable or regulated
Concentration ratio (0–100)	0	Low	Low	High	100
Examples	Agricultural goods	Corner shops, bread, car mechanics	Local restaurants, buses	Washing powders, disposable nappies	Local water utility, postal letter service

the characteristics of different market structures and their concentration ratios.

Market and Industry The classifications used to calculate UK concentration ratios allocate every firm in the economy to a particular industry. But markets for particular goods do not usually correspond to these industries.

The main problem is that markets are often narrower than industries. For example, the basic industrial chemicals industry, which has a medium concentration ratio, operates in many separate markets for individual products (tobacco and cement), each one of which has few substitutes. So this industry, which looks relatively competitive, operates in some monopolistic markets.

Another problem arises from the fact that firms make many products. For example, the tobacco firms also operate in insurance. The privatized water companies operate hotels and printing works. The value of sales for each firm can overestimate their contribution to the industry to which they have been assigned.

If concentration ratios are combined with information about the geographical scope, barriers to entry and the extent to which large, multi-product firms straddle a variety of markets, they can provide a basis for classifying industries. The less concentrated an industry and the lower its barriers to entry, the more closely it approximates the perfect competition case. The more concentrated an

industry and the higher the barriers to entry, the more it approximates the monopoly case.

Concentration in the UK Economy

Concentration ratios for the United Kingdom can be derived from the regular census of manufacturing companies known as the Census of Production. The census is undertaken every year and provides information on the sales, employment and structure of every manufacturing firm in the United Kingdom. Figure 13.1 shows a selection of the five-firm concentration ratio calculations using sales data. As you can see, some industries such as plastics, printing, metal foundries and wool have low concentration ratios – implying firms in these industries are competitive. At the other extreme are industries with high concentration ratios such as tobacco, man-made fibres, wines and ciders, and motor vehicles. These industries appear to have a high degree of monopoly power. Medium concentration ratios are found in industries like mineral oils, water supply and basic chemicals. Firms in these industries have a limited amount of market power.

Market structures in the UK

The majority of markets for goods and services in Europe are highly competitive and only a few markets are monopolized. For example, more than 70 per cent by value of UK goods and services are

FIGURE 13.1

Some Concentration Measures in the United Kingdom

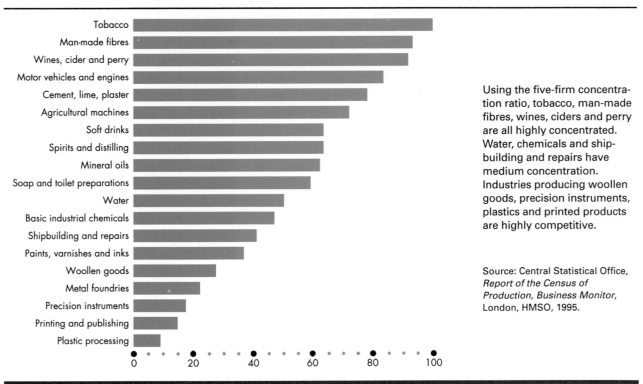

Using the five-firm concentration ratio, tobacco, man-made fibres, wines, ciders and perry are all highly concentrated. Water, chemicals and shipbuilding and repairs have medium concentration. Industries producing woollen goods, precision instruments, plastics and printed products are highly competitive.

Source: Central Statistical Office, *Report of the Census of Production, Business Monitor*, London, HMSO, 1995.

traded in highly competitive markets. Where pure monopoly does arise it is usually in the public services although this has declined with privatization. But monopoly power can still be strong in markets like telecommunications when privatization attracts few new entrants. Less than 6 per cent of the value of goods and services traded in the UK are in highly monopolized markets. Oligopoly is more common in manufacturing than in the services sector, but more than 55 per cent of UK manufacturing industries have a concentration ratio of less than 40 per cent.

The overall level of concentration across an economy can be measured by the proportion of total output accounted for by the largest 100 firms. Figure 13.2 shows the UK aggregate concentration ratio in manufacturing since 1949. Aggregate concentration increased in the post-war period indicating an increase in market power, but it levelled off in the 1970s and 1980s and has fallen in recent years. The increase in concentration resulted from several waves of merger activity and

the growth of transnational corporations serving new global markets. This is not surprising given the growth in world trade, and advances in telecommunications and low-cost transport. So although the United Kingdom's national aggregate concentration has increased, many of its markets are now globalized and highly competitive.

Monopolistic Competition

Monopolistic competition arises in an industry in which:

1. A large number of firms compete with each other.
2. Each firm produces a differentiated product, which is a close but not a perfect substitute for the products of the other firms.
3. Firms are free to enter and exit.

FIGURE 13.2

Concentration in Manufacturing

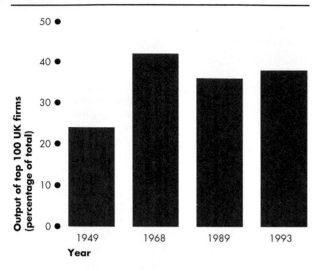

The output of the top 100 manufacturing firms as a percentage of total UK output in manufacturing is a measure of concentration in the manufacturing sector. The concentration ratio as a percentage increased from 22 per cent in 1949 to 43 per cent in 1968, indicating an increase in market power in manufacturing. Concentration has declined since then. The ratio fell to 35 per cent in 1989 and increased slightly in 1993.

Source: Central Statistical Office, *Report of the Census of Production*, *Business Monitor*, London, HMSO, 1995.

Local corner shops and bakers, family restaurants, service garages and makers of running shoes are all examples of firms that operate in monopolistic competition. In monopolistic competition, as in perfect competition, the industry consists of a large number of firms and each firm supplies a small part of the total industry output. Because each firm is small, no one firm can effectively influence what other firms do. If one firm changes its price, this action has no effect on the actions of the other firms.

Unlike perfect competition and like monopoly, a firm in monopolistic competition faces a downward-sloping demand curve. The reason is that the firm's product is differentiated from the products of its competitors. Some people will pay more for one variety of the product, so when its price rises, the quantity demanded falls but it does not (necessarily) fall to zero. For example, Adidas, Asics, New Balance, Nike, Puma and Reebok all make differentiated running shoes, as do many other firms. Other things remaining the same, if the price of Adidas running shoes rises and the prices of the other shoes remain constant, Adidas sells fewer shoes and the other producers sell more. But Adidas shoes don't disappear from the market unless the price rises by a large amount. Because a firm in monopolistic competition faces a downward-sloping demand curve it maximizes profit by choosing both its price and its output.

Like competition and unlike monopoly, in monopolistic competition there is free entry and free exit. As a consequence, a firm in monopolistic competition cannot make an economic profit in the long run. When economic profit is being made, new firms enter the industry. This entry lowers prices and eventually eliminates economic profit. When economic losses are incurred, some firms leave the industry. This exit increases prices and profits and eventually eliminates the economic loss. In long-run equilibrium, firms neither enter nor leave the industry, and the firms in the industry make zero economic profit – earn a normal profit.

Price and Output in Monopolistic Competition

Figure 13.3 shows how price and output are determined by a firm in a monopolistically competitive industry. Part (a) deals with the short run and part (b) the long run. Let's concentrate initially on the short run. The demand curve D is the demand curve for the firm's own variety of the product. For example, it is the demand for Disprin rather than for aspirin in general; or for McDonald's hamburgers rather than for hamburgers in general. The curve MR is the marginal revenue curve associated with the demand curve. The figure also shows the firm's average total cost (ATC) and marginal cost (MC). The firm maximizes profit in the short run by producing output Q_S, where marginal revenue equals marginal cost, and charging the price P_S. The firm's average total cost is C_S and the firm makes a short-run economic profit, as measured by the blue rectangle.

So far, the monopolistically competitive firm looks just like a monopoly. It produces the quantity at which marginal revenue equals marginal cost and then charges the price that buyers are willing to pay for that quantity, determined by the demand curve. The key difference between monopoly and monopolistic competition lies in what happens next.

There is no restriction on entry in monopolistic

FIGURE 13.3

Monopolistic Competition

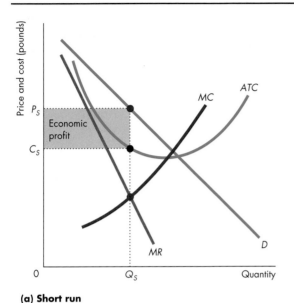

(a) Short run

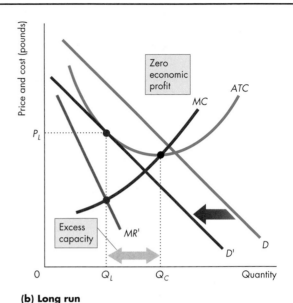

(b) Long run

In monopolistic competition, because it produces a differentiated product, a firm faces a downward-sloping demand curve. Part (a) shows the short run. Profit is maximized where marginal revenue equals marginal cost. In the short run profit is maximized by producing the quantity Q_S and selling it for the price P_S. Average total cost is C_S, and the firm makes an economic profit represented by the blue rectangle. Economic profit encourages new entrants in the

long run. Part (b) shows the long-run outcome. The entry of new firms decreases each firm's demand and the demand curve and marginal revenue curve shift leftward. When the demand curve has shifted from D to D', the marginal revenue curve is MR' and the firm is in a long-run equilibrium. The output that maximizes profit is Q_L and the price is P_L. In long-run equilibrium, economic profit is zero and there is no further entry. Each firm has excess capacity.

competition so economic profit attracts new entrants. As new firms enter the industry, the firm's demand curve and marginal revenue curve start to shift leftward. At each point in time, the firm maximizes its short-run profit by producing the quantity at which marginal revenue equals marginal cost, and by charging the price that buyers are willing to pay for this quantity. But as the demand curve shifts leftward, the profit-maximizing quantity and price fall.

Figure 13.3(b) shows the long-run equilibrium. The firm produces Q_L and sells it at a price of P_L. In this situation, the firm is making a zero economic profit. Average total cost equals price. There is no incentive for firms to enter or exit.

Excess Capacity   A firm's *capacity* output is the output produced when average total cost is at its minimum point – the output at the bottom of the U-shaped *ATC* curve. In monopolistic competition, in

the long run, firms always have *excess capacity*. That is, they produce less output than that which minimizes average total cost. As a consequence, the consumer pays more than the minimum average total cost. This result arises from the fact that the firm faces a downward-sloping demand curve. The demand curve slopes down because of product differentiation – because one firm's product is not a perfect substitute for another firm's product. Thus it is product differentiation that produces excess capacity.

You can see the excess capacity in monopolistic competition all around you. Family restaurants (except for the truly outstanding ones) almost always have a few empty tables. You can always get a pizza delivered in less than 30 minutes and many local service garages will offer an exhaust emission test on the spot without an appointment. It is rare for the bakery to have no leftover bread and cakes at the end of the day.

Efficiency of Monopolistic Competition

When we studied a perfectly competitive industry, we discovered that in some circumstances such an industry achieves allocative efficiency. A key feature of allocative efficiency is that price equals marginal cost. Recall that price measures the value placed on the last unit bought by the consumer and marginal cost measures the firm's opportunity cost of producing the last unit. We also discovered that monopoly is allocatively inefficient because it restricts output below the level at which price equals marginal cost. As we have just discovered, monopolistic competition shares this feature with monopoly. Even though there is zero economic profit in long-run equilibrium, the monopolistically competitive industry produces an output at which price equals average total cost but exceeds marginal cost.

Because price exceeds marginal cost, monopolistic competition, like monopoly, is allocatively inefficient. The marginal cost of producing one more unit of output is less than the marginal benefit to the consumer – the price the consumer is willing to pay. But the inefficiency of monopolistic competition arises from product differentiation – product variety. This variety is valued by consumers, but it is only achievable if firms make differentiated products. So the loss in allocative efficiency that occurs in monopolistic competition must be weighed against the gain of greater product variety.

Product Innovation

Another source of gain from monopolistically competitive industries is product innovation. Monopolistically competitive firms are constantly looking for new products that will provide them with a competitive edge, even if only temporarily. A firm that manages to introduce a new and differentiated variety will temporarily face a steeper demand curve than before and will be able temporarily to increase its price. New firms that make close substitutes for the new product will enter and eventually compete away the economic profit arising from this initial advantage.

Selling Costs

A large and increasing proportion of the prices we pay goes to cover the cost of selling the good, not the cost of making it. When you visit a major shopping centre, you see window displays, promotional gimmicks, indoor gardens and waterfalls. The costs of these items are just a part of selling costs. Others costs arise from the production of glossy catalogues and brochures, magazine and television advertising, and from the salaries, air fares, and hotels bills of sales staff. All these costs are incurred because monopolistically competitive firms strive to differentiate their products from those of other firms. Some product differentiation is achieved by designing and introducing products that are actually different from those of the other firms in the industry. But firms also attempt to differentiate the consumer's perception of the product through marketing and advertising. Whatever the source, these costs increase a monopolistically competitive firm's costs above those of a competitive firm or a monopoly, which do not generate selling costs.

To the extent that selling costs provide consumers with services that are valued and with information about the precise nature of the differentiation of products, they serve a valuable purpose to the consumer and enable a better product choice to be made. But the opportunity cost of the additional services and information must be weighted against the gain to the consumer.

The bottom line on the question of allocative efficiency of monopolistic competition is ambiguous. In some cases, the gains from extra product variety unquestionably offset the selling costs and the extra cost arising from excess capacity. The tremendous varieties of books and magazines, of clothing, food and drink are examples of such gains. It is less easy to see the gains from being able to buy brand-name drugs and cleaning products that have a chemical composition identical to a generic alternative. But some people willingly pay more for the brand-name alternative.

Contestable Markets

In a contestable market, potential entry is so easy that the firms in the market, even if few in number, must behave in a way that deters entry. To prevent entry, the firms in the market set a price and produce a quantity that leaves zero economic profit for new entrants. This price is determined by the minimum average cost of the potential entrant. The lower the costs of entry and exit, the closer are the price and quantity to those in perfect competition.

◆ In monopolistic competition, a large number of firms compete with each other but, because each firm produces a differentiated product, it faces a downward-sloping demand curve.

◆ Economic profit stimulates entry.

◆ In long-run equilibrium, price equals average total cost but exceeds marginal cost, and the quantity produced is less than that which minimizes average total cost.

◆ The cost of monopolistic competition is excess capacity and high advertising expenditure; the gain is a wide product variety and valuable information to the consumer.

We've looked at monopolistic competition and seen how profit triggers entry, competing away all economic profit in the long run. We're now going to look at a completely different market type – oligopoly – where excess profits might be maintained.

Oligopoly

In oligopoly, a small number of producers compete with each other. The quantity sold by any one producer depends on that producer's price *and* the prices and quantities sold by the other producers. Each firm must take into account the effects of its own actions on the actions of other firms.

To see the interplay between prices and sales, suppose you run one of the three service garages in a small town. If you lower the price you charge for an hour's work and your two competitors don't lower theirs, you will get more hours of work, but the other two firms will get less work. In such a situation, the other firms are likely to lower their prices too. If they do cut their prices, hours of work and profits will fall again. So before deciding to cut your price, you try to predict how the other firms will react and you attempt to calculate the effects of those reactions on your own profit.

A variety of models have been developed to explain the determination of price and quantity in oligopoly markets, and no one theory has been found that can explain all the different types of behaviour that we observe in such markets. The models fall into two broad groups: traditional models and game theory models. We'll look at examples of both types, starting with two traditional models.

The Kinked Demand Curve Model

The kinked demand curve model is a model of oligopoly based on assumptions about the beliefs of each firm concerning the reactions of another firm (or firms) to its own actions. These beliefs are:

1. If I increase my price, I will be on my own – others will not follow me.

2. If I decrease my price, so will everyone else.

Figure 13.4 shows a demand curve, D, that reflects these beliefs. The demand curve has a kink occurring at the current price, which is P. At prices above P, the demand curve is relatively elastic. It reflects the belief that if the firm raises its price above P, its price will be higher than the price of the other firms. So the quantity demanded will fall by a relatively large amount. At prices below P, the demand curve is less elastic. It reflects the belief that if the firm lowers its price, the other firms will lower their prices too. So the quantity demanded will increase by a relatively small amount.

The kink in demand curve D creates a break in the marginal revenue curve (MR). To maximize profit, the firm produces the quantity that makes marginal cost and marginal revenue equal. But that output, Q, is where the marginal cost curve passes through the discontinuity in the marginal revenue curve – the gap ab. If marginal cost fluctuates between a and b, an example of which is shown in the figure with the marginal cost curves MC_0 and MC_1, the firm will change neither its price nor its quantity of output. Only if marginal cost fluctuates outside the range ab will the firm change its price and quantity produced.

Thus the kinked demand curve model predicts that price and quantity will be insensitive to small cost changes, but will respond if cost changes are large enough. But there are two problems with the kinked demand curve model:

1. It does not tell us how the price, P, is determined.

2. It does not tell us what happens if firms discover that their belief about the demand curve is incorrect.

FIGURE 13.4

The Kinked Demand Curve Model

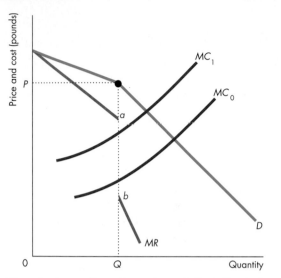

The price in an oligopoly market is *P*. Each firm believes it faces the demand curve *D*. At prices above *P*, demand is highly elastic because the firm believes that its price increases will not be matched by other firms. At prices below *P*, demand is less elastic because the firm believes its price cuts will be matched. Because the demand curve is kinked, the marginal revenue curve, *MR*, has a break *ab*. Profit is maximized by producing *Q*. Marginal cost changes inside the range *ab* leave the price and quantity unchanged.

Suppose, for example, that marginal cost increases by enough to cause the firm to increase its price and that all firms experience the same increase in marginal cost so they all increase their prices together. Each firm bases its action on the belief that other firms will not match its price increase, but that belief is incorrect. The firm's beliefs are inconsistent with reality, and the demand and marginal revenue curves which summarize those beliefs (such as those in Fig. 13.4) are not the correct ones for the purpose of calculating the new profit-maximizing price and output. A firm that bases its actions on beliefs that are wrong does not maximize profit and might well end up incurring an economic loss leading to its eventual exit from the industry.

The kinked demand curve model is an attempt to understand price and output determination in an oligopoly in which the firms are of similar size. Another traditional model deals with the case in which firms differ in size and one firm dominates the industry.

Dominant Firm Oligopoly

A dominant firm oligopoly arises when one firm – the dominant firm – has a substantial cost advantage over the other firms and produces a large part of the industry output. The dominant firm sets the market price and the other firms are price takers. An example of a dominant firm oligopoly is a large petrol retailer or a big video rental company that dominates its market in a particular city.

To see how a dominant firm oligopoly works, suppose that 11 firms operate petrol stations in a city. Big-G is the dominant firm. It sells 50 per cent of the city's petrol. The other firms are small and each sells 5 per cent of the city's petrol.

Figure 13.5 shows the market for petrol in this city. In part (a), the demand curve *D* tells us how the total quantity of petrol demanded in the city is influenced by its price. The supply curve S_{10} is the supply curve of the 10 small suppliers. These firms are price takers.

Part (b) shows the situation facing Big-G, the dominant firm. Big-G's marginal cost curve is *MC* and it faces the demand curve for petrol *XD*. *XD* is found by working out the amount of excess demand arising from the rest of the market. It graphs the difference between the quantity demanded and the quantity supplied in the rest of the market at each price. Thus, for example, at a price of 50 pence a litre, the distance *ab* in part (a) measures the excess quantity demand in the rest of the market. That same distance *ab* at the price 50 pence a litre in part (b) provides us with one point, point *b*, on Big-G's demand curve, *XD*.

If the city petrol market was perfectly competitive, Big-G would be willing to supply petrol at the prices indicated by its marginal cost curve. The city market would operate at the point of intersection of Big-G's marginal cost curve and its demand curve. But Big-G can do better for itself than that. Because it controls 50 per cent of the city's petrol market it can restrict its sales, decreasing the amount of petrol available and increasing its price.

To maximize its profit, Big-G operates like a monopoly. It takes the excess demand curve as its demand curve and then calculates its marginal revenue curve – the extra revenue obtained from selling one more litre of petrol. It then sells the quantity that makes its marginal revenue equal to its marginal cost. Thus it sells 10,000 litres of petrol for

FIGURE 13.5

A Dominant Firm Oligopoly

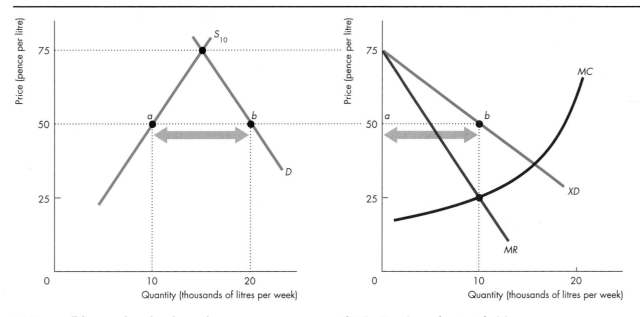

(a) Ten small firms and market demand

(b) Big-G's price and output decision

The demand curve for petrol in a city is *D* in part (a). There are 10 small competitive firms which together have a supply curve of S_{10}. In addition, there is one large firm, Big-G, shown in part (b). Big-G faces the demand curve, *XD*, determined as market demand *D* minus the supply of the other firms S_{10} – the demand that is not satisfied by the

small firms. Big-G's marginal revenue is *MR* and marginal cost is *MC*. Big-G sets its output to maximize profit by equating marginal cost, *MC*, and marginal revenue, *MR*. This output is 10,000 litres. The price at which Big-G can sell this quantity is 50 pence a litre. The other 10 firms take this price and each firm sells 1,000 litres.

50 pence a litre. This price and quantity of sales gives Big-G the biggest possible profit. The 10 small firms are price takers, so they take the price of 50 pence a litre and behave competitively. The quantity of petrol demanded in the entire city at 50 pence a litre is 20,000 litres, as shown in part (a). Of this amount, 10,000 litres are sold by Big-G and 10,000 litres are sold by the 10 small firms which sell 1,000 litres each.

R E V I E W

◆ In the kinked demand curve model, the firm believes that a price cut will be matched by other firms but a price rise will not. The firm faces a demand curve with a kink at the current price and quantity and a marginal revenue curve with a break in it. Price is sticky.

◆ In the dominant firm model, the dominant firm acts like a monopoly and sets its price. The other firms take this price and act like competitive firms.

The dominant firm model of oligopoly works for markets in which there is a producer that has a cost advantage over all the other firms. But the model doesn't explain why the dominant firm has a cost advantage or what happens if some of the smaller firms acquire the same technology and costs as the dominant firm. Also it does not predict prices and quantities in markets in which firms are of similar size. The kinked demand curve model attempts to deal with this alternative case. But, as we've seen, that model has some weaknesses.

The weaknesses of traditional theories of oligopoly and a widespread dissatisfaction with them is one of the main forces leading to the development of new oligopoly models based on game theory.

Game Theory

Game theory is a method of analysing *strategic behaviour* – behaviour that takes into account the expected behaviour of others and the mutual recognition of interdependence. Game theory was invented by John von Neumann in 1937 and extended by von Neumann and Oskar Morgenstern in 1944. Today it is a major research field in economics.

Game theory seeks to understand oligopoly as well as political and social rivalries by using a method of decision analysis specifically designed to understand games of all types, including the familiar games of everyday life. We will begin our study of game theory, and its application to the behaviour of firms, by considering those familiar games.

Familiar Games: What They Have in Common

What is a game? At first thought, the question seems silly. After all, there are many different games. There are ball games and board games, games of chance and games of skill. What do games of such diversity and variety have in common? In answering this question, we will focus on those features of games that are relevant for game theory and for analysing oligopoly as a game. All games have three things in common:

♦ Rules
♦ Strategies
♦ Payoffs

Let's see how these common features of games apply to a game called 'the prisoners' dilemma.' This game, it turns out, captures some of the essential features of oligopoly and it gives a good illustration of how game theory works and how it leads to predictions about the behaviour of the players.

The Prisoners' Dilemma

John and Bob have been caught red-handed stealing a car. Facing airtight cases, they will receive a sentence of two years each for their crime. During her interviews with the two prisoners, the arresting police officer begins to suspect that she has stumbled on the two people who were responsible for a multimillion-pound bank robbery some months

earlier. But she also knows that this is just a suspicion. The police officer cannot charge the suspects of the greater crime unless she can get each of them to confess to it. She decides to adopt a new interview procedure but must get agreement from her superior. She explains to her superior that the new procedure can be represented by a game with the following rules.

Rules Each prisoner (player) is placed in a separate room and there is no communication between them. Each is told that he is suspected of having carried out the bank robbery and that if both he and his accomplice confess to the larger crime, each will receive sentences of 3 years; if he alone confesses and his accomplice does not, he will receive an even shorter sentence of 1 year while his accomplice will receive a 10-year sentence.

Strategies In game theory, as in ordinary games, **strategies** are all the possible actions of each player. The strategies in the prisoners' dilemma game are very simple. Each prisoner (player) can do only one of two things:

1. Confess to the bank robbery.

2. Deny having committed the bank robbery.

Payoffs Because there are two players, each with two strategies, there are four possible outcomes.

1. Neither player confesses.

2. Both players confess.

3. John confesses but Bob does not.

4. Bob confesses but John does not.

Each prisoner can work out exactly what will happen to him – his *payoff* – in each of these four situations. We can tabulate the four possible payoffs for each of the prisoners in what is called a payoff matrix for the game. A **payoff matrix** is a table that shows the payoffs for every possible action by each player for every possible action by each other player.

Table 13.3 shows a payoff matrix for John and Bob. The squares show the payoffs for each prisoner – the red triangle in each square shows John's and the blue triangle Bob's. If both prisoners confess (top left), they each get a prison term of 3 years. If Bob confesses but John denies (top right), John gets a 10-year sentence and Bob gets a 1-year sentence. If John confesses and Bob

TABLE 13.3

Prisoners' Dilemma Payoff Matrix

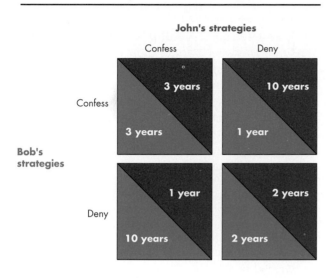

John's strategies

Each square shows the payoffs for the two players, John and Bob, for each possible pair of actions. In each square, John's payoff is shown in the red triangle and Bob's in the blue triangle. For example, if both confess, the payoffs are in the top left square. John reasons as follows: if Bob confesses, it pays me to confess because then I get 3 years rather than 10. If Bob denies, it pays me to confess because then I get 1 year rather than 2. Regardless of what Bob does, it pays me to confess. John 's dominant strategy is to confess. Bob reasons similarly: if John confesses, it pays me to confess and get 3 years rather than 10. If John denies, it pays me to confess and get 1 year rather than 2. Bob's dominant strategy is to confess. Since each player's dominant strategy is to confess, the equilibrium of the game is for both players to confess and each to get 3 years.

denies (bottom left), John gets a 1-year sentence and Bob gets a 10-year sentence. Finally, if both of them deny (bottom right), neither can be convicted of the bank robbery charge but both are sentenced for the car theft – a 2-year sentence.

The Dilemma   The dilemma is seen by considering the consequences of confessing and not confessing. Each prisoner knows that if he and his accomplice remain silent about the bank robbery, they will only be sentenced to 2 years for stealing the car. But neither prisoner has any way of knowing that his accomplice will remain silent and refuse to confess. Each knows that if the other confesses

and he denies, the other will receive only a 1-year sentence while the one denying will receive a 10-year sentence. Each poses the following questions: should I deny and rely on my accomplice to deny so that we may both get only 2 years? Or should I confess in the hope of getting just 1 year (providing my accomplice denies), but knowing that if my accomplice does confess we will both get 3 years in prison? Resolving the dilemma involves finding the equilibrium for the game.

Equilibrium   The equilibrium of a game is called a Nash equilibrium; it is so named because it was first proposed by John Nash. A **Nash equilibrium** occurs when player A takes the best possible action given the action of player B, and player B takes the best possible action given the action of player A. In the case of the prisoners' dilemma, the equilibrium occurs when John makes his best choice given Bob's choice, and when Bob makes his best choice given John's choice.

The prisoners' dilemma is a game that has a special kind of Nash equilibrium called a dominant strategy equilibrium. A *dominant strategy* is a strategy that is the same regardless of the action taken by the other player. In other words, there is a unique best action regardless of what the other player does. A **dominant strategy equilibrium** occurs when there is a dominant strategy for each player. In the prisoners' dilemma, no matter what Bob does, John's best strategy is to confess; and no matter what John does, Bob's best strategy is to confess. Thus our police officer has shown her superior that the equilibrium of the prisoners' dilemma is that each player confesses. To see why each player confesses, let's consider again their strategies and the payoffs from the alternative courses of action.

Look at the situation from John's point of view. John realizes that his outcome depends on the action Bob takes. If Bob confesses, it pays John to confess also, for in that case, he will be sentenced to 3 years rather than 10 years. But if Bob does not confess, it still pays John to confess for in that case he will receive 1 year rather than 2 years. John reasons that regardless of Bob's action, his own best action is to confess.

The dilemma from Bob's point of view is identical to John's. Bob knows that if John confesses, he will receive 10 years if he does not confess or 3 years if he does. Therefore if John confesses, it pays Bob to confess. Similarly, if John does not confess, Bob will receive 2 years for not confessing and 1 year if he confesses. Again, it pays Bob to confess. Bob's best action, regardless of John's action, is to confess.

Each prisoner sees that regardless of what the other prisoner does, his own best action is to confess. Because each player's best action is to confess, each will confess, each will get a 3-year prison term, and the police officer has solved the bank robbery. This is the equilibrium of the game.

A Bad Outcome For the prisoners, the equilibrium of the game, with each confessing, is not the best outcome. If neither of them confesses, each will get only 2 years for the lesser crime. Isn't there some way in which this better outcome can be achieved? It seems that there is not, because the players cannot communicate with each other since they are interviewed separately. Each player can put himself in the other player's place, and so each player can figure out that there is a dominant strategy for each of them. The prisoners are indeed in a dilemma. Each knows that he can serve 2 years only if he can trust the other not to confess. But each prisoner also knows that it is not in the best interest of the other not to confess. Thus each prisoner knows that he has to confess, thereby delivering a bad outcome for both.

Let's now see how we can use the ideas we've just developed to understand price fixing, price wars and the behaviour of firms in oligopoly.

Oligopoly Game

To understand how an oligopoly game works, it is revealing to study a special case of oligopoly called duopoly. **Duopoly** is a market structure in which there are two producers of a commodity competing with each other. There are few cases of duopoly on a national and international scale but many cases of local duopolies, such as, two car rental firms, or two university bookshops. But the main reason for studying duopoly is not its 'realism'. It is the fact that it captures all the essential features of oligopoly and yet is more manageable to analyse and understand.

To study a duopoly game, we're going to build a model of a duopoly industry. Suppose that only two firms, Trick and Gear, make a particular kind of electric switchgear. We will make predictions about the prices charged and the outputs produced by each of the two firms by constructing a duopoly game. To set out the game, we need to specify the strategies of the players and the payoff matrix.

We will suppose that the two firms enter into a collusive agreement. A **collusive agreement** is an agreement between two (or more) producers to restrict output in order to raise prices and profits. Such an agreement is illegal in the United Kingdom and under EU rules and is undertaken in secret. A group of firms that has entered into a collusive agreement to restrict output and increase prices and profits is called a **cartel**. The strategies that firms in a cartel can pursue are to:

1. Comply
2. Cheat

Complying simply means sticking to the agreement. Cheating means breaking the agreement in a manner designed to benefit the cheating firm.

Because each firm has two strategies, there are four possible combinations of actions for the two firms:

◆ Both firms comply.
◆ Both firms cheat.
◆ Trick complies and Gear cheats.
◆ Gear complies and Trick cheats.

We need to work out the payoffs to each firm from each of these four possible sets of actions. To do that we need to explore the costs and demand conditions in the industry.

Cost and Demand Conditions

The cost of producing switchgears is the same for both Trick and Gear. The average total cost curve (*ATC*) and the marginal cost curve (*MC*) for each firm are shown in Fig. 13.6(a). The market demand curve for switchgears (*D*) is shown in Fig. 13.6(b). Each firm produces an identical switchgear product, so one firm's switchgear is a perfect substitute for the other's. The market price of each firm's product, therefore, is identical. The quantity demanded depends on that price – the higher the price, the lower is the quantity demanded.

Notice that in this industry, there is room for only two firms. For each firm the *minimum efficient scale* of production is 3,000 switchgears a week. When the price equals the average total cost of production at the minimum efficient scale, total industry demand is 6,000 switchgears a week. If there were only one firm in the industry, it would make an economic profit and stimulate entry. If there were three firms, at least one of them would incur an economic loss and exit. Thus the number of firms that an industry can sustain depends on the relationship between cost and the industry's demand conditions.

In the model industry that we're studying here, the particular cost and demand conditions assumed are designed to generate an industry in which two firms can survive in the long run. In real-world oligopoly and duopoly, barriers to entry may arise from economies of scale of the type featured in our model industry, but there are other possible barriers as well (as discussed in Chapter 12, pp. 287–288).

Colluding to Maximize Profits

Let's begin by working out the payoffs to the two firms if they collude to make the maximum industry profit by acting like a monopoly. The calculations

that the two firms will perform are exactly the same calculations that a monopoly performs. (You studied these calculations in Chapter 12, pp. 283–292.) The only additional thing that the duopolists have to do is to agree on how much of the total output each of them will produce.

The price and quantity that maximizes industry profit for the duopolists is shown in Fig. 13.7. Part (a) shows the situation for each firm and part (b) for the industry as a whole. The curve labelled MR is the industry marginal revenue curve. The curve labelled MC_I is the industry marginal cost curve if each firm produces the same level of output. That curve is constructed by adding together the outputs of the two firms at each level of marginal cost. That is, at each level of marginal cost, industry output is twice as much as the output of each individual firm. Thus the curve MC_I in part (b) is twice as far to the right as the curve MC in part (a).

To maximize industry profit, the duopolists agree to restrict output to the rate that makes the industry marginal cost and marginal revenue equal.

FIGURE 13.6

Costs and Demand

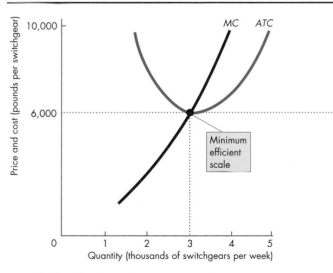

(a) Individual firm

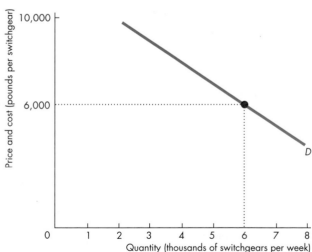

(b) Industry

Part (a) shows the costs facing Trick and Gear, two duopolists which make switchgears. Each firm faces identical costs. The average total cost curve for each firm is *ATC* and the marginal cost curve is *MC*. For each firm the minimum efficient scale of production is 3,000 switchgears a week

and the average total cost of producing that output is £6,000 a unit. Part (b) shows the industry demand curve. At a price of £6,000, the quantity demanded is 6,000 switchgears per week. There is room for only two firms in this industry.

That output rate, as shown in part (b), is 4,000 switchgears a week. The highest price for which the 4,000 switchgears can be sold is £9,000 each. Let's suppose that Trick and Gear agree to split the market equally so that each firm produces 2,000 switchgears a week. The average total cost (*ATC*) of producing 2,000 switchgears a week is £8,000, so the profit per unit is £1,000 and economic profit is £2 million (2,000 switchgears × £1,000 per unit). The economic profit of each firm is represented by the blue rectangle in Fig. 13.7(a).

We have just described one possible outcome for the duopoly game: the two firms collude to produce the monopoly profit-maximizing output and divide that output equally between themselves. From the industry point of view, this solution is identical to a monopoly. A duopoly that operates in this way is indistinguishable from a monopoly. The economic profit that is made by a monopoly is the maximum total profit that can be made by colluding duopolists.

Cheating on a Collusive Agreement

Under a collusive agreement, the colluding firms restrict output to make their joint marginal revenue equal to their joint marginal cost. They set the highest price for which the quantity produced can be sold – a price higher than marginal cost. In such a situation, each firm recognizes that if it cheats on the agreement and raises its output, even though the price will fall below that agreed to, more will be added to its revenue than to its cost, so its profit will increase. Because each firm recognizes this fact, there is a temptation for each firm to cheat. There are two possible cheating situations: one in which one firm cheats and one in which both firms cheat.

One Firm Cheats What is the effect of one firm cheating on a collusive agreement? How much extra profit does the cheating firm make? What happens to the profit of the firm that sticks to the

---

FIGURE 13.7

Colluding to Make Monopoly Profits

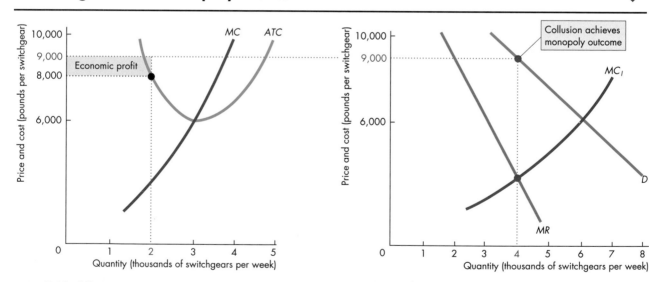

(a) Individual firm

(b) Industry

If Trick and Gear come to a collusive agreement, they can act as a single monopolist and maximize profit. To maximize profit, the firms first calculate the industry marginal cost curve, *MC$_I$* (part b), which is the horizontal sum of the two firms' marginal cost curves, *MC* (part a). Next they calculate the industry marginal revenue, *MR*. They then choose the output rate that makes marginal revenue equal to marginal cost (4,000 switchgears per week). They agree

to sell that output for a price of £9,000, the price at which 4,000 switchgears are demanded.

Each firm has the same costs, so each produces half the total output – 2,000 switchgears per week. Average total cost is £8,000 per unit, so each firm makes an economic profit of £2 million (blue rectangle) – 2,000 switchgears multiplied by £1,000 profit per unit.

agreement in the face of cheating by the other firm? Let's work out the answers to these questions.

There are many different ways for a firm to cheat. We will work out just one possibility. Suppose Trick convinces Gear that there has been a fall in industry demand and that it cannot sell its share of the output at the agreed price. It tells Gear that it plans to cut its price in order to sell the agreed 2,000 switchgears each week. Because the two firms produce a virtually identical product, Gear has no alternative but to match the price cut of Trick.

In fact, there has been no fall in demand and the lower price has been calculated by Trick to be exactly the price needed to sell the additional output that it plans to produce. Gear, though lowering its price in line with that of Trick, restricts its output to the previously agreed level.

Figure 13.8 illustrates the consequences of Trick cheating in this way. Part (a) shows what happens to Gear (the complier); part (b) shows what happens to Trick (the cheat); and part (c) shows what is happening in the industry as a whole.

Suppose that Trick decides to raise output from 2,000 to 3,000 switchgears a week – the output at which average total cost is minimized. It recognizes

that if Gear sticks to the agreement to produce only 2,000 switchgears a week, total output will be 5,000 a week, and given demand in part (c), the price will have to be cut to £7,500 a unit.

Gear continues to produce 2,000 switchgears a week at a cost of £8,000 a unit, and incurs a loss of £500 a unit or £1 million a week. This loss is represented by the red rectangle in part (a). Trick produces 3,000 switchgears a week at an average total cost of £6,000 each. With a price of £7,500, Trick makes a profit of £1,500 a unit and therefore an economic profit of £4.5 million. This economic profit is the blue rectangle in part (b).

We have now described a second possible outcome for the duopoly game – one of the firms cheats on the collusive agreement. In this case, the industry output is larger than the monopoly output and the industry price is lower than the monopoly price. The total economic profit made by the industry is also smaller than the monopoly's economic profit. Trick (the cheat) makes an economic profit of £4.5 million and Gear (the complier) incurs a loss of £1 million. The industry makes an economic profit of £3.5 million. Thus the industry profit is £0.5 million less than the economic profit a monopoly would make. But

FIGURE 13.8

Cheating on a Collusive Agreement

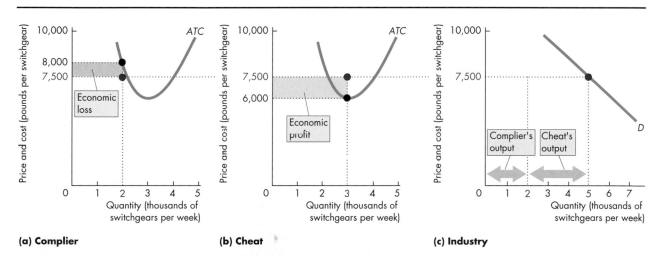

(a) Complier

(b) Cheat

(c) Industry

One firm, shown in part (a), complies with the agreement and produces 2,000 switchgears. The other firm, shown in part (b), cheats on the agreement and increases production to 3,000 switchgears. Given the market demand curve, shown in part (c), and with a total production of 5,000 switchgears a week, the market price falls to £7,500. At this price, the complier in part (a) incurs an economic loss of £1 million (£500 × 2,000 units) shown as the red rectangle. In part (b), the cheat makes an economic profit of £4.5 million (£1,500 × 3,000 units), shown as the blue rectangle.

that profit is distributed unevenly. Trick makes an even bigger profit than it would under the collusive agreement, while Gear incurs a loss.

We have just worked out what happens if Trick cheats and Gear complies with the collusive agreement. There is another similar outcome that would arise if Gear cheated and Trick complied with the agreement. The industry profit and price would be the same but in this case Gear (the cheat) would make an economic profit of £4.5 million and Trick (the complier) would incur a loss of £1 million.

There is yet another possible outcome: both firms cheat on the agreement.

Both Firms Cheat   Suppose that instead of just one firm cheating on the collusive agreement, both firms cheat. In particular, suppose that each firm behaves in exactly the same way as the cheating firm that we have just analysed. Each tells the other that it is unable to sell its output at the going price and that it plans to cut its price. But because both firms cheat, each will propose a successively lower price. So long as price exceeds marginal cost, each firm has an incentive to increase its production – to cheat. Only when price equals marginal cost is there no further incentive to cheat. This situation arises when the price has reached £6,000. At this price, marginal cost equals price. Also price equals minimum average cost. At a price of less than £6,000, each firm incurs a loss. At a price of £6,000, each firm covers all its costs and makes zero economic profit – makes normal profit. Also at a price of £6,000, each firm wants to produce 3,000 switchgears a week, so that the industry output is 6,000 switchgears a week. Given the demand conditions, 6,000 switchgears can be sold at a price of £6,000 each.

The situation just described is illustrated in Fig. 13.9. Each firm, shown in part (a) of the figure, is producing 3,000 switchgears a week, and this output level occurs at the point of minimum average total cost (£6,000 per unit). The market as a whole, shown in part (b), operates at the point at which the demand curve (D) intersects the industry marginal cost curve. This marginal cost curve is constructed as the horizontal sum of the marginal cost curves of the two firms. Each firm has lowered its price and increased its output in order to try to gain an advantage over the other firm. They have each pushed this process as far as they can without incurring economic losses.

We have now described a third possible outcome of this duopoly game – both firms cheat. If both firms cheat on the collusive agreement, the output of each firm is 3,000 switchgears a week and the price is £6,000. Each firm makes zero economic profit.

The Payoff Matrix and Equilibrium

Now that we have described the strategies and payoffs in the duopoly game, let's summarize the strategies and the payoffs in the form of the game's payoff matrix and then calculate the equilibrium.

Table 13.4 sets out the payoff matrix for this game. It is constructed in exactly the same way as the payoff matrix for the prisoners' dilemma in Table 13.3. The squares show the payoffs for the two firms – Gear and Trick. In this case, the payoffs are profits. (In the case of the prisoners' dilemma, the payoffs were losses.)

The table shows that if both firms cheat (top left), they achieve the perfectly competitive outcome – each firm makes zero economic profit. If both firms comply (bottom right), the industry makes the monopoly profit and each firm earns an economic profit of £2 million. The top-right and bottom-left squares show what happens if one firm cheats while the other complies. The firm that cheats collects an economic profit of £4.5 million and the one that complies incurs a loss of £1 million.

This duopoly game is, in fact, the same as the prisoners' dilemma that we examined earlier in this chapter; it is a duopolist's dilemma. You will see this once you have determined what the equilibrium of this game is.

To find the equilibrium, let's look at things from the point of view of Gear. Gear reasons as follows. Suppose that Trick cheats. If we comply with the agreement, we incur a loss of £1 million. If we also cheat, we make zero economic profit. Zero economic profit is better than a £1 million loss, so it will pay us to cheat. But suppose Trick complies with the agreement. If we cheat, we will make a profit of £4.5 million, and if we comply, we will make a profit of £2 million. A £4.5 million profit is better than a £2 million profit so it would again pay us to cheat. Thus regardless of whether Trick cheats or complies, it pays us to cheat. Gear's dominant strategy is to cheat.

Trick comes to the same conclusion as Gear. Therefore both firms will cheat. The equilibrium of this game is that both firms cheat on the agreement. Although there are only two firms in the industry, the price and quantity are the same as in a competitive

FIGURE 13.9

Both Firms Cheat

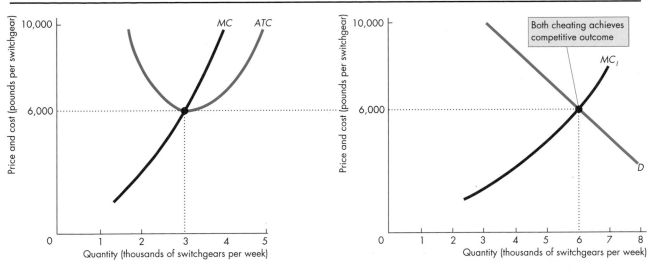

(a) Individual firm

(b) Industry

If both firms cheat by raising their output and lowering the price, the collusive agreement completely breaks down. The limit to the breakdown of the agreement is the competitive equilibrium. Neither firm will want to cut the price below £6,000 (minimum average total cost), for to do so will result in losses. Part (a) shows the situation facing each firm. At a price of £6,000, the firm's profit-maximizing output is 3,000 switchgears per week. At that output rate, price equals marginal cost, and it also equals average total cost. Economic profit is zero. Part (b) describes the situation in the industry as a whole. The industry marginal cost curve (MC_I) – the horizontal sum of the individual firms' marginal cost curves (MC) – intersects the demand curve at 6,000 switchgears per week and at a price of £6,000. This output and price is the one that would prevail in a competitive industry.

industry. Each firm makes zero economic profit.

Although we have done this analysis for only two firms, it would not make any difference (other than to increase the amount of arithmetic) if we were to play the game with three, four, or more firms. In other words, although we have analysed duopoly, the game theory approach can also be used to analyse oligopoly. The analysis of oligopoly is much harder, but the essential ideas that we have learned also apply to oligopoly.

Repeated Games

The first game that we studied, the prisoners' dilemma, was played just once. The prisoners did not have an opportunity to observe the outcome of the game and then play it again. The duopolist game just described was also played only once. In contrast, most real-world duopolists get opportunities to play repeatedly against each other. This fact suggests that real-world duopolists might find some way of learning to cooperate so that their efforts to collude are more effective.

If a game is played repeatedly, one player always has the opportunity to penalize the other player for previous 'bad' behaviour. If Trick refuses to cooperate this week, then Gear can refuse to cooperate next week (and vice versa). If Gear cheats this week, perhaps Trick will cheat next week. Before Gear cheats this week, shouldn't it take account of the possibility of Trick cheating next week?

What is the equilibrium of this more complicated prisoners' dilemma game when it is repeated indefinitely? Actually there is more than one possibility. One is the Nash equilibrium that we have just analysed. Both players cheat with each making zero economic profit forever. In such a situation, it will never pay one of the players to start complying unilaterally, for to do so would result in a loss for that player and a profit for the other. The price and quantity will remain at the competitive levels forever.

But another equilibrium is possible – one in

TABLE 13.4

Duopoly Payoff Matrix

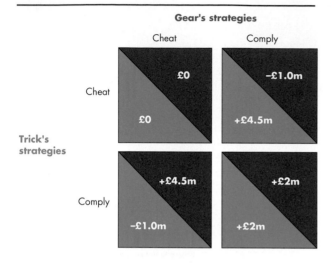

Each square shows the payoffs from a pair of actions. For example, if both firms comply with the collusive agreement, the payoffs are recorded in the square at the bottom right corner of the table. The red triangle shows Gear's payoff and the blue triangle shows Trick's. The equilibrium is a Nash equilibrium in which both firms cheat.

which the players make and share the monopoly profit. How might this equilibrium come about? The key to answering this question is the fact that when a prisoners' dilemma game is played repeatedly, the players have an increased array of strategies. Each player can punish the other player for previous actions.

There are two extremes of punishment. The smallest penalty that one player can impose on the other is what is called 'tit-for-tat'. A *tit-for-tat strategy* is one in which a player cooperates in the current period if the other player cooperated in the previous period, but cheats in the current period if the other player cheated in the previous period. The most severe form of punishment that one player can impose on the other arises in what is called a trigger strategy. A *trigger strategy* is one in which a player cooperates if the other player cooperates, but plays the Nash equilibrium strategy forever thereafter if the other player cheats. Because a tit-for-tat strategy and a trigger strategy are the extremes of punishment – the most mild and most severe – there are evidently

other intermediate degrees of punishment. For example, if one player cheats on the agreement, the other player could punish by refusing to cooperate for a certain number of periods. In the duopoly game between Gear and Trick, a tit-for-tat strategy keeps both players cooperating and earning monopoly profits. Let's see why.

If both firms stick to the collusive agreement in period 1, they make an economic profit of £2 million each. Suppose that Trick contemplates cheating in period 2. The cheating produces a quick £4.5 million profit and inflicts a £1 million loss on Gear. Adding up the profits over two periods of play, Trick comes out ahead by cheating (£6.5 million compared with £4 million if it did not cheat). In the next period Gear will hit Trick with its tit-for-tat response and cheat. Both will make zero economic profit in period 3. If Trick reverts to cooperating, to induce Gear to cooperate in period 4, Gear now makes a profit of £4.5 million and Trick incurs a loss of £1 million. Adding up the profits over four periods of play, Trick would have made more profit by cooperating. In that case, its profit would have been £8 million compared with £5.5 million from cheating and generating Gear's tit-for-tat response.

What is true for Trick is also true for Gear. Because each firm makes a larger profit by sticking with the collusive agreement, both firms do so and the monopoly price, quantity and profit prevail in the industry. This equilibrium is called a **cooperative equilibrium** – an equilibrium resulting from each player responding rationally to the credible threat of the other player to inflict heavy damage if the agreement is broken. For this strategy to be credible, each player must recognize that it is in the interest of the other player to respond with a tit-for-tat. The tit-for-tat strategy is credible because if one player cheats, it clearly does not pay the other player to continue complying. So the threat of cheating in the next period is credible and sufficient to support the monopoly equilibrium outcome.

In reality, whether a cartel works like a one-play game or a repeated game, depends primarily on the number of players and the ease of detecting and punishing cheating. The larger the number of players, the more opportunities there are to cheat and not be detected immediately, so the cartel will work more like a repeated game sequence. *Reading Between the Lines* on pp 334–335 explores a tit-for-tat strategy as part of a repeated game in supermarket pricing.

◆ The rules of the oligopoly game tell us the number of players (firms), the method of calculating the score (economic profit or loss) and the strategies for winning.

◆ The prisoners' dilemma explains the behaviour of a duopoly cartel. If the game is played once, the cartel breaks down, the price is the competitive price and economic profit is zero. If the game is played repeatedly the cartel behaves like a monopoly.

Games and Price Wars

The theory of price and output determination under duopoly can help us understand real-world behaviour and, in particular, price wars. Some price wars can be interpreted as the implementation of a tit-for-tat strategy. We've seen that with a tit-for-tat strategy in place, firms have an incentive to stick to the monopoly price. But fluctuations in market demand lead to fluctuations in the monopoly price. This type of price change can be seen by one firm, mistakenly, to be the result of the other firm cheating. To avoid unnecessary cheating, firms might decide to ignore small reductions in price up to a certain level. If a large change in demand occurs and the price falls below the critical value for one firm, that firm will break the agreement and cut the price further. This triggers a retaliation from the other firm. In this case, a type of price war breaks out. The price war ends only when each firm has satisfied itself that the other is ready to cooperate again. The price war is not damaging to the collusive agreement because it maintains the credibility of the tit-for-tat threat. We often see cycles of price wars and the restoration of collusive agreements. Fluctuations in the world price of oil can be interpreted in this way.

Some price wars arise from the entry of a small number of firms into an industry that had been a monopoly. Although the industry has a small number of firms, the firms are in a prisoners' dilemma and they cannot impose effective penalties for price cutting. The behaviour of prices and outputs in the computer chip industry during 1994 and 1995 can be explained in this way. Until 1994, the market for PC chips was dominated by one firm, Intel Corporation, which was able to make maximum economic profit by producing the quantity of chips at which marginal cost equalled marginal revenue. The price of Intel's chips was set to ensure that the quantity demanded equalled the quantity produced. Then, in 1994 and 1995, with the entry of a small number of new firms, the industry became an oligopoly. If the firms had maintained Intel's price and shared the market, together they could have made economic profits equal to Intel's profit. But the firms were in a prisoners' dilemma. So prices tumbled to competitive levels.

Other Strategic Variables

We have focused here on firms that play a simple game and consider only two possible strategies – complying and cheating, and two variables – price and quantity produced. But the approach that we have used can be extended to deal with a much wider range of choices facing firms. For example, a firm has to decide whether to mount an expensive advertising campaign; whether to modify its product; how reliable to make its product (the more reliable a product, usually, the more expensive it is to produce); whether to price discriminate and, if so, among which groups of customers and to what degree; whether to undertake a large research and development (R&D) effort aimed at lowering production costs; or whether to enter or leave an industry. All of these choices can be analysed by using game theory. The basic method of analysis that you have studied can be applied to these problems by working out the payoff for each of the alternative strategies and then finding the equilibrium of the game.

We'll look at two examples. The first is an R&D game and the second is an entry-deterrence game – a game in which a firm tries to prevent other firms from entering an industry.

An R&D Game

There are two big players in the European disposable nappy market – Procter & Gamble (the maker of Pampers) and Kimberly-Clark (the maker of Huggies). Procter & Gamble has the largest share, but both firms have about one third of the market. The disposable nappy industry is fiercely competitive. When the product was first introduced, it had to be cost-effective in competition against reusable, laundered nappies. A costly research and development effort resulted in the development of machines that could make disposable nappies at a low enough cost to achieve that initial competitive edge. But as the industry has matured, a large number of firms have tried to get into the business and take market share away from the two industry leaders, and the industry leaders themselves have battled against each other to maintain or increase their own market share.

The disposable nappy industry is one in which technological advances that result in small decreases in the average total cost of production can provide an individual firm with an enormous competitive advantage. The current machines can produce disposable nappies at a rate of 3,000 an hour – a rate that represents a tenfold increase on the output rate of just a decade earlier. The firm that develops and uses the least-cost technology gains a competitive edge, undercutting the rest of the market, increasing its market share and increasing its profit. But the research and development effort that has to be undertaken to achieve even small cost reductions is itself very costly. The cost of R&D has to be deducted from the profit resulting from the increased market share that lower costs achieve. If no firm conducts R&D, every firm can be better off, but if one firm initiates the R&D activity, all must.

Each firm is in a research and development dilemma that is similar to the game played by John and Bob. Although the two firms play an ongoing game against each other, it has more in common with the one-play game than a repeated game. The reason is that R&D is a long-term process. Effort is repeated, but payoffs occur only infrequently and uncertainly.

Table 13.5 illustrates the dilemma (with hypothetical numbers) for the R&D game that Kimberly-Clark and Procter & Gamble are playing. Each firm has two strategies: to spend £25 million a year on R&D or to spend nothing on R&D. If neither firm spends on R&D, they make a joint profit of £100 million, £30 million for Kimberly-Clark and £70 million for Procter & Gamble (bottom right square of payoff matrix). If each firm conducts R&D, market shares are maintained but each firm's profit is lower, by the amount spent on R&D (top left square of payoff matrix). If Kimberly-Clark pays for R&D but Procter & Gamble does

not, Kimberly-Clark gains a large part of Procter & Gamble's market. Kimberly-Clark profits and Procter & Gamble loses (top right square of payoff matrix). Finally, if Procter & Gamble invests in R&D and Kimberly-Clark does not, Procter & Gamble gains market share from Kimberly-Clark, increasing its profit, while Kimberly-Clark incurs a loss (bottom left square).

Confronted with the payoff matrix in Table 13.5, the two firms calculate their best strategies. Kimberly-Clark reasons as follows. If Procter & Gamble does not undertake R&D, we make £85 million if we do and £30 million if we do not; therefore it pays to conduct R&D. If Procter & Gamble conducts R&D, we lose £10 million if we don't and make £5 million if we do. Again, R&D pays off. Thus conducting R&D is a dominant strategy for Kimberly-Clark. Doing it pays regardless of Procter & Gamble's decision.

Procter & Gamble reasons similarly. If Kimberly-Clark does not undertake R&D, we make £70 million if we follow suit and £85 million if we conduct R&D. It therefore pays to conduct R&D. If Kimberly-Clark does undertake R&D, we make £45 million by doing the same and lose £10 million by not doing R&D. Again, it pays to conduct R&D. So for Procter & Gamble R&D is also a dominant strategy.

Because R&D is a dominant strategy for both players, it is the Nash equilibrium. The outcome of this game is that both firms conduct R&D. They make lower profits than they would if they could collude to achieve the cooperative outcome of no R&D.

The real-world situation has more players than Kimberly-Clark and Procter & Gamble. There are a large number of other firms sharing a small portion of the market, all of them ready to eat into the market share of Procter & Gamble and Kimberly-Clark. So the R&D effort by these two firms not only serves the purpose of maintaining shares in their own battle, but also helps to keep barriers to entry high enough to preserve their joint market share.

Let's now study an entry-deterrence game in which a firm tries to prevent other firms from entering an industry. Such a game is played in a type of market called a contestable market.

Contestable Markets

A *contestable market* is a market in which one firm (or a small number of firms) operates but in which

TABLE 13.5

Pampers versus Huggies: An R&D Game

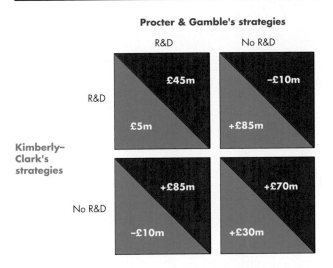

Procter & Gamble's strategies

	R&D	No R&D
R&D	£45m / £5m	−£10m / +£85m
No R&D	+£85m / −£10m	+£70m / +£30m

Kimberly–Clark's strategies

If both firms undertake R&D, their payoffs are those shown in the top left square. If neither firm undertakes R&D, their payoffs are in the bottom right square. When one firm undertakes R&D and the other one does not, their payoffs are in the top right and bottom left squares. The red triangle shows Procter & Gamble's payoff and the blue triangle shows Kimberly-Clark's. The dominant strategy equilibrium for this game is for both firms to undertake R&D. The structure of this game is the same as that of the prisoners' dilemma.

both entry and exit are free so that the firm (or firms) in the market faces perfect competition from *potential* entrants. Examples of contestable markets are routes served by airlines and by private bus companies. These markets are contestable because even though only one or a few firms actually operate on a particular air or bus route, other firms could enter those markets if an opportunity for economic profit arose and could exit those markets if the opportunity for economic profit disappeared. The potential entrance prevents the single firm (or small number of firms) from making an economic profit.

If the five-firm concentration ratio is used to determine the degree of competition, a contestable market appears to be uncompetitive. It looks like an oligopoly or monopoly. But a contestable market behaves as if it were perfectly competitive. You can see why by thinking about a game that we'll call an entry-deterrence game.

Entry-deterrence game   In the entry-deterrence game we'll study, there are two players. One player is Better Bus, the only firm operating on a particular route. The other player is Wanabe Co., a potential entrant. The strategies for Better Bus are to set its price at the monopoly profit-maximizing level or at the competitive (zero economic profit) level. The strategies for Wanabe are to enter and set a price just below that of Better Bus or not to enter.

Table 13.6 shows the payoffs for the two firms. If Wanabe does not enter, Better Bus earns a normal profit by setting a competitive price and earns maximum monopoly profit (a positive economic profit) by setting the monopoly price. If Wanabe does enter and undercuts Better Bus' price, Better Bus incurs an economic loss regardless of whether it sets its price at the competitive or monopoly level. The reason is that Wanabe takes the market with the lower price, so Better Bus incurs a cost but has zero revenue. If Better Bus sets a competitive price, Wanabe earns a normal profit if it does not enter, but incurs an economic loss if it enters and undercuts Better Bus by setting a price that is less than average total cost. If Better Bus sets the monopoly price, Wanabe earns a positive economic profit by entering and a normal profit by not entering.

The Nash equilibrium for this game is a competitive price at which Better Bus earns a normal profit and Wanabe does not enter. If Better Bus raised the price to the monopoly level, Wanabe would enter and by undercutting Better Bus' price would take all the business, leaving Better Bus with an economic loss equal to total cost. Better Bus avoids this outcome by sticking with the competitive price and deterring Wanabe from entering.

Limit Pricing   **Limit pricing** is the practice of charging a price below the monopoly profit-maximizing price and producing a quantity greater than that at which marginal revenue equals marginal cost in order to deter entry. The game that we've just studied is an example of limit pricing, but the practice is more general. For example, a firm can use limit pricing to try to convince potential entrants that its own costs are so low that new entrants will incur an economic loss if they enter the industry. To see how this works, lets go back to Better Bus and Wanabe.

Wanabe knows the current market price but does not know Better Bus' costs and profit. It can infer those costs though. Suppose Wanabe believes that marginal revenue is 50 per cent of

Oligopoly in Action:
Supermarket Loyalty Cards

The Essence of the Story

THE FINANCIAL TIMES, 9 MAY 1996

Annual profits slide at Sainsbury

Christopher Brown-Humes

J. Sainsbury yesterday announced its first fall in underlying profits in 22 years as a public company. But the supermarket group said it aimed to recapture lost market share with new marketing initiatives and a loyalty card.

The group, knocked off top slot by rival Tesco in the last year, said pre-tax pre-exceptional profits fell from £808m to £764m in the year to March 9....

The centrepiece of the fightback will be a loyalty card, reversing the group's staunch opposition to the concept and acknowledging the successes achieved by Tesco and Safeway with their versions....

Sainsbury's market share has slipped from 12.6 per cent to 12.5 per cent, while Tesco's has surged from 12.4 per cent to 13.9 per cent.

Tesco has gained a reputation for being more dynamic and innovative in a mature market, not least because its highly successful Clubcard has attracted 8m users.

Mr David Sainsbury, chairman, admitted the group had made mistakes. He said it had not moved quickly enough to issue a loyalty card in the right form....

■ Competition between major supermarkets is strong. The market leaders are Tesco and Sainsbury.

■ Sainsbury announced its first fall in profits in 22 years in March 1996. Profits fell 5.4 per cent.

■ Both stores engaged in price cutting but when Tesco introduced a loyalty card — shoppers receive cash vouchers for purchases — Sainsbury did not follow.

■ Sainsbury's market share fell and Tesco's market share shot up. The loyalty card attracted 8 million new shoppers.

■ Sainsbury must now follow this innovative move to regain its market share and increase profits.

Economic Analysis

■ Supermarkets operate in an oligopoly market, but the two supermarkets with the biggest market share – Sainsbury and Tesco – act like a duopoly. Each supermarket looks for new strategies to raise market share and profits.

■ Sainsbury made a mistake by not copying Tesco's new strategy in 1995 – introducing a loyalty card. The impact is shown in Fig. 1. Tesco's market share increased, and profits rose by 15 per cent. Sainsbury's market share decreased and profits fell by 5.4 per cent.

■ Table 1 shows the strategy as a loyalty card game. If neither supermarket introduces loyalty cards, market shares are maintained. Each supermarket gains a hypothetical maximum increase in profits of 10 per cent (top left box).

■ Loyalty cards are a form of general price cutting – reducing profit margins. If both supermarkets introduce loyalty cards, they maintain market share but the profit increase is cut to a hypothetical 5 per cent (bottom right box).

■ When Tesco introduced a card, Sainsbury did not follow because it thought in-store price cutting would keep customers. It was wrong. Tesco's profits increased and Sainsbury's profits fell (top right box).

■ Tesco's gain is short-lived as Sainsbury will introduce a card leading to a dominant Nash equilibrium. This strategy game is one of many price-cutting strategies forming a repeated game and tit-for-tat tactics between Tesco and Sainsbury.

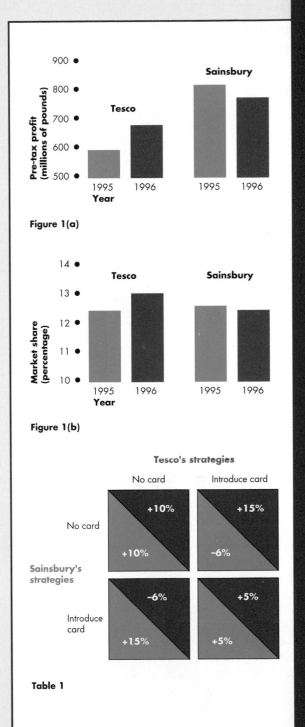

Figure 1(a)

Figure 1(b)

Table 1

TABLE 13.6

Better Bus versus Wanabe: An Entry-deterrence Game

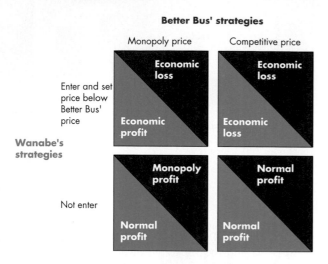

Better Bus is the only firm in a contestable market. If Better Bus sets the monopoly price, Wanabe earns an economic profit by entering and undercutting Better Bus's price and a normal profit by not entering. So if Better Bus sets the price at the monopoly level, Wanabe will enter. If Better Bus sets the competitive price, Wanabe earns a normal profit if it does not enter and incurs an economic loss if it enters. So if Better Bus sets the price at the competitive level, Wanabe will not enter. With entry, Better Bus incurs an economic loss regardless of the price it sets. The Nash equilibrium of this game is for Better Bus to set the competitive price, for Wanabe not to enter, and for both firms to make normal profit.

price. If the price is £100, then Wanabe estimates that marginal revenue is £50. Wanabe might assume that Better Bus is maximizing profit by setting marginal revenue equal to marginal cost. Given this assumption, Wanabe estimates Better Bus' marginal cost to be £50. If Wanabe's marginal cost

is greater than £50, it can't compete with Better Bus, so it will drop the idea of entering this industry. But if its marginal cost is less than £50, it might be able not only to enter the industry, but also to drive Better Bus out.

Recognizing that Wanabe (and other potential entrants) reason in this way, Better Bus might decide to use limit pricing to send a false but possibly believable signal to them. It might cut its price to (say) £80 to make Wanabe believe that its marginal cost is only £40 (50 per cent of £80). The lower Wanabe believes Better Bus' marginal cost to be, the less likely is Wanabe to enter. The strategic use of limit pricing makes it possible, in some situations, for a firm (or group of firms) to maintain a monopoly or collusive oligopoly and limit entry.

◆ ◆ ◆ ◆ We have now studied the four main market structures – perfect competition, monopolistic competition, oligopoly and monopoly – and discovered how prices and output, revenue, cost and economic profit are determined in these industries. We have used the various models to make predictions about behaviour and to assess the efficiency of alternative market structures. ◆ A key element in our analysis of the markets for goods and services is the behaviour of costs. Costs are determined partly by technology and partly by the prices of factors of production. We have treated those factor prices as given. We are now going to see how factor prices are themselves determined. Factor prices interact with the goods market that we have just studied in two ways. First, they determine the firm's production costs. Second, they determine household incomes and therefore influence the demand for goods and services. Factor prices also affect the distribution of income. ◆ The firms that we've been studying in the last four chapters decide *how* to produce; the interactions of households and firms in the markets for goods and services decide *what* will be produced. But the factor prices determined in the markets for factors of production determine *for whom* the various goods and services are produced.

SUMMARY

Varieties of Market Structure

Two market structures lie between monopoly and perfect competition – monopolistic competition and oligopoly. Also, even markets with a small number of firms might be competitive because they are contestable. The degree of market power in an industry can be measured by the five-firm concentration ratio. In the United Kingdom, most industries are effectively competitive, but there are some significant oligopoly and monopoly elements. (pp. 312–315)

Monopolistic Competition

Monopolistic competition occurs when a large number of firms compete with each other by making slightly different products. Under monopolistic competition, each firm faces a downward-sloping demand curve and so has to choose its price as well as its output level. Because there is free entry, in long-run equilibrium zero economic profit is earned. When profit is maximized, with marginal cost equal to marginal revenue, average cost also equals price in the long run. But average cost is not at its minimum point. That is, in monopolistic competition firms operate with excess capacity. Monopolistic competition is inefficient because marginal cost is less than price. But the inefficiency must be weighed against product variety. (pp. 315–319)

Oligopoly

Oligopoly is a situation in which a small number of producers compete with each other and take into account the effects of their own actions on the behaviour of other firms and the effects of the actions of other firms on their own profits.

The kinked demand curve model is based on the assumption that each firm believes its price cuts will be matched by its rivals but its price increases will not be matched. If these beliefs are correct, each firm faces a kinked demand curve for its product, the kink occurring at the current price, and has a break in its marginal revenue curve. To maximize profit, the firm produces the quantity that makes marginal cost and marginal revenue equal, an output level such that the marginal cost curve passes through the break in the marginal revenue curve.

Fluctuations in marginal cost inside the range of the break in marginal revenue have no effect on either price or output.

The dominant firm model of oligopoly assumes that an industry consists of one large firm and a large number of small firms. The large firm acts like a monopoly and sets a profit-maximizing price. The small firms take this price as given and act like perfectly competitive firms. (pp. 319–321)

Game Theory

Game theory is a method of analysing strategic behaviour that focuses on three aspects of a game: rules, strategies and payoffs. Given their payoffs, the players choose strategies and the combined strategies lead to an outcome – the equilibrium of the game. In a classic game called the prisoners' dilemma, two prisoners, each acting in his own best interest, confess to a crime they may not have committed. (pp. 322–324)

Oligopoly Game

An oligopoly with two firms – a duopoly game – can be constructed in which the firms consider colluding to achieve a monopoly profit. The firms may in fact collude, or one may cheat on the collusive agreement to make a bigger profit at the expense of the other firm. Such a game is a prisoners' dilemma. If the game is played only once, the equilibrium is for both firms to cheat. The industry output and price are the same as in perfect competition.

If a game is repeated indefinitely, there is an opportunity for one player to punish another player for previous 'bad' behaviour. In such a situation, a tit-for-tat strategy can produce an equilibrium in which both firms stick to the agreement and the price and output are the same as in a monopoly.

Firms in oligopolistic industries have to make a large number of decisions: whether to enter or leave an industry; how much to spend on advertising; whether to modify their products; whether to price discriminate; whether to undertake research and development. These choices result in payoffs for all the firms in the industry and can be studied by using game theory. (pp. 324–336)

KEY ELEMENTS

Key Terms

Cartel, 324
Collusive agreement, 324
Contestable market, 312
Cooperative equilibrium, 330
Dominant strategy equilibrium, 323
Duopoly, 324
Five-firm concentration ratio, 312
Game theory, 322
Limit pricing, 333
Monopolistic competition, 312
Nash equilibrium, 323
Oligopoly, 312

Payoff matrix, 322
Product differentiation, 312
Strategies, 322

◆ Key Figures and Tables

Figure 13.3 Monopolistic Competition, 317
Figure 13.6 Costs and Demand, 325
Figure 13.7 Colluding to Make Monopoly Profits, 326
Figure 13.9 Both Firms Cheat, 329
Table 13.2 Market Structure, 314
Table 13.4 Duopoly Payoff Matrix, 330

REVIEW QUESTIONS

1 What are the main varieties of market structure? What are the main characteristics of each of those market structures?

2 What is a five-firm concentration ratio? If the five-firm concentration ratio is 90 per cent, what does that mean?

3 Give some examples of UK industries that have a high concentration ratio and of UK industries that have a low concentration ratio.

4 Explain how a firm can differentiate its product.

5 What is the difference between monopolistic competition and perfect competition?

6 Is monopolistic competition efficient? Explain your answer.

7 What is the difference between duopoly and oligopoly?

8 In what circumstances might the dominant firm model of oligopoly be relevant?

9 List the key features that all games have in common with each other.

10 Why might the demand curve facing an oligopolist be kinked, and what happens to a firm's marginal revenue curve if its demand curve is kinked?

11 What is the prisoners' dilemma?

12 What is a dominant strategy equilibrium?

13 What is the essential feature of both duopoly and oligopoly?

14 What are the features of duopoly that make it reasonable to treat duopoly as a game between two firms?

15 What is meant by a repeated game?

16 Explain what a tit-for-tat strategy is.

17 What is a price war? What is the effect of a price war on the profit of the firms in the industry and on the profitability of the industry itself?

18 What is a contestable market? Will a concentration ratio reveal such a market? How does a contestable market operate?

19 What is limit pricing? How might a firm try to use limit pricing to increase its economic profit?

PROBLEMS

1 A monopolistically competitive industry is in long-run equilibrium as illustrated in Fig. 13.3(b). Demand for the industry's product increases, increasing the demand for each firm's output. Using diagrams similar to those in Fig. 13.3, analyse the short-run and long-run effects on price, output and economic profit of this increase in demand.

2 Another monopolistically competitive industry is in long-run equilibrium, as illustrated in Fig. 13.3(b), when it experiences a large increase in wages. Using diagrams similar to those in Fig. 13.3, analyse the short-run and long-run effects on price, output and economic profit of this increase in wages.

3 A firm with a kinked demand curve experiences an increase in its variable cost. Explain the effects on the firm's price, output and economic profit/loss.

4 An industry with one large firm and 100 small firms experiences an increase in the demand for its product. Use the dominant firm model to explain the effects on:

  a The price, output and economic profit of the large firm.
  b The price, output and economic profit of a typical small firm.

5 Describe the game known as the prisoners' dilemma. In describing the game:

  a Make up a story that motivates the game.
  b Work out a payoff matrix.
  c Describe how the equilibrium of the game is arrived at.

6 Consider the following game. There are two players and they are each asked a question. They can answer the question honestly or they can lie. If they both answer honestly, they each receive a payoff of £100. If one answers honestly and the other lies, the liar gains at the expense of the honest player. In that event, the liar receives a profit of £500 and the honest player gets nothing. If they both lie then they each receive a payoff of £50.

  a Describe this game in terms of its players, strategies and payoffs.
  b Construct the payoff matrix.
  c What is the equilibrium for this game?

7 Two firms, Soapy Plc and Suddies Plc, are the only two producers of soap powder. They collude and agree to share the market equally. If neither firm cheats on the agreement, they can each make £1 million profit. If either firm cheats, the cheater can increase its profit to £1.5 million, while the firm that abides by the agreement incurs a loss of £500,000. Neither firm has any way of policing the actions of the other.

  a Describe the best strategy for each firm in a game that is played once.
  b What is the payoff matrix and equilibrium of a game that is played just once?
  c What is the economic profit for each firm if they both cheat?
  e If this duopolist game can be played many times, describe some of the strategies that each firm may adopt.

8 Explain the behaviour of the prices of computer chips in 1994 and 1995 by using the prisoners' dilemma game. Describe the types of strategies that individual firms in the industry have adopted.

9 Use the model of oligopoly to explain why producers of pet foods spend so much on advertising.

10 Read the analysis in *Reading Between the Lines* pp. 334–335 and then:

  a Explain why Sainsbury did not introduce a customer loyalty card at the same time as Tesco.
  b Write a list of competing strategies you think Sainsbury could adopt instead of a customer loyalty card.
  c Explain why both supermarkets end up adopting strategies that reduce their potential profits.

Part 3
MARKETS FOR FACTORS
OF PRODUCTION

TALKING WITH
JOHN HEY

John Hey has a BA from Cambridge and an MSc from Edinburgh and first got excited about economics in his first academic job, as Lecturer in Economics at the University of Durham. After a brief spell at the University of St Andrews, he moved to the University of York in 1975, where he has been ever since, becoming Professor of Economics and Statistics in 1984. In 1986 he took over the editorship of the *Economic Journal* and handed it on 10 years later. He remains on the editorial boards of various other journals. In 1986 he founded with Graham Loomes the Centre for Experimental Economics at the University of York, a leading international centre. Experimental work has increasingly occupied his time, although the basic purpose of his research work is to discover and explore the implications of the ways people take decisions under risk and uncertainty.

Why do you think economics is important and interesting as a subject area?

To use a corny old phrase: 'Because all human life is there'.

This should not be misinterpreted. It is not meant to suggest that economists have the answers to all human problems; nor that what people think is the 'economic solution' to any particular problem is *the* solution to that problem. It is rather that economics provides a unique way of viewing problems, of thinking about them and of analysing them. Like all insightful ideas, the economics way of looking at problems is obvious in retrospect, but nevertheless extremely useful. Economics tells us that in all interesting, important and relevant matters, there is a trade-off problem. Whatever solution is proposed, there are bound to be points for it and points against; for if there were not, the problem would have been trivial in the first instance. The discussion then revolves around the relevant weights for and against the various arguments. Here again economics provides insight, as it makes you ask why some things have more weight than others.

Can economists (as opposed to psychologists) really model the way that people make choices?

If I had been asked this question a decade ago, I would have given a completely different answer than I will today. Ten years ago, economists – or at least the mainstream majority – were hung up on the *rationality* of economic agents and, moreover, had a strong concept of what rationality meant. In those days it was obvious to most economists what rationality was and why ordinary people should be rational in that sense. The past decade has seen a big change, partly as a result of a large amount of psychological and economic experimental evidence, but also because of some interesting new economic theory, which showed that certain kinds of behaviour, hitherto considered irrational, could be regarded as perfectly rational.

Coincidental with this change in attitude has been a dramatic increase in the explanatory power of economics. Interestingly, there is now less divergence between psychologists' stories of how people make choices and economists' stories. This convergence has come about partly through psychologists and economists working together and using each other's tools and techniques. Of course, we should remember that the two disciplines are not always interested in, and addressing, the same issues, but where they are, they are closer together than they were a decade ago. Perhaps more interestingly, the economists' ideas about utility still lie at the core of the new theories of choice.

What are the main economic principles that guide your work?

That economic agents are rational in *some* sense, if not in the strict sense adopted a decade ago; that all of life is a trade-off problem; and that the sole purpose of the whole of economic activity is *exchange* and hence that the ultimate purpose of the economist is to study how exchange is actually carried out and how best it might be carried out. Let me expand on these briefly. That economic agents are rational in some sense is another way of saying that economic behaviour is consistent in some sense – and hence *predictable*; for if it were not, there would be no point in trying to do economics. In essence, this is an assumption shared by all the sciences.

That life is a trade-off problem, I take, as discussed above, as self-evident. That economic activity is driven by a desire to exchange is perhaps less obvious, but equally important and insightful. If all economic agents had identical tastes and identical endowments there would be little scope for exchange and few benefits to be gained from it. But given that tastes are not identical and endowments are not identical then there are large benefits to be gained from trade. To describe how this is done and how best it might be done (where 'best' has to be appropriately defined) is the whole purpose of economics.

The economic models of utility and preferences are often criticized on the basis that they are not realistic. Do you agree with this criticism? How useful are these models?

As I have argued above, things have changed a lot in this respect over the past decade. Economists' views on utility and preferences are now 'more realistic' than they were ten years ago. But having said that, it must be recognized that there is necessarily (in all sciences and not just in economics) a trade-off between the *descriptive power* of our theories and their *predictive power*. The great advantage of the

'...economics provides insight, as it makes you ask why some things have more weight than others.'

earlier theories which made strong assumptions about the rationality of economic agents was that they came up with some strong predictions. It is true that these predictions were not always correct but at least they were strong. The new theories may be correct more often, but they usually make weaker predictions. Ask yourself, for example, what you would prefer: a theory which made tight and specific predictions and was wrong 5% of the time, or a theory which made weak and almost useless predictions and was wrong just 2% of the time? What do you think of the following theory (which is never wrong): 'people do something'?

You have been involved in the development of 'laboratory experiments' to examine people's choices. Can we conduct experiments on people like we do on animals and get sensible answers?

The key difference between animal and human experiments is that you do not treat people like

animals, nor do you need to, nor do you want to. You want to see how people behave in a controlled environment – and you want to see how they behave *as people*. I think the problem lies with those experimentalists who have used animal subjects and tried to infer from those experiments how people behave. I am not sure one can. I have never tried.

How important do you think the game theory and decision-making revolution has been in economics?

I think you need to make a sharp distinction between the two. The notions of rationality in game theory are quite different from those in decision theory. But there has been a revolution in both fields, largely caused by the findings from experimental work of various kinds. Interestingly, what game theory experiments seem to be telling us is that strategic considerations are much less important to ordinary people than economists would have us believe, and perhaps that ordinary people are more sophisticated than the

narrow rationality of game theory suggests. Developments in both fields have made us think much more carefully about what it is we might mean by 'rationality'. This is all for the good.

Can we use experiments to look at how markets determine prices and how market competition and market power work rather than individual choice? If so, how?

There have been an enormous number of experiments on markets – probably many more than on individual choice. Interestingly, markets seem to suggest that the collective rationality of agents is stronger than individual rationality; that the

'...economics should be about explaining the typical behaviour of the typical economic agents in typical situations. The next century should help to define what we should mean by "typical".'

operation of markets themselves imposes an additional rationality on agents. Perhaps I could usefully refer at this stage to the invaluable

Handbook of Experimental Economics, edited by A.E. Roth and J.H. Kagel and published in 1995 by Princeton University Press, which surveys, in an interesting, entertaining and informative fashion, the contribution that experimental economics has made to economic knowledge.

What do you think will be the most important developments in your field of economics in the next century?

I asked the same question of a number of distinguished economists in 1990 and published their responses in the centenary volume of the *Economic Journal* (in 1991), which was published in book form in *A Century of Economics* by Blackwells in 1991.

Little did I think then that I would similarly be put on the same spot six years later! Yet it is an important question. My prediction is that we will see a much stronger interplay between theoretical and empirical – particularly experimental – work over the next century than we have seen over much of the past century (particularly the second half of it).

Experimental work allows us to isolate particular bits of theories and subject them to rigorous and controlled testing. At the same time, I think the expansion of such experimental work will force us to think more carefully about

precisely what it is that economics is concerned about and where the dividing line is between economics and psychology. I do not think that economics should be concerned about explaining the detailed behaviour of each and every economic agent in all possible circumstances. Rather, economics should be about explaining the typical behaviour of the typical economic agents in typical situations. The next century should help to define what we mean by 'typical'.

CHAPTER 14

PRICING AND ALLOCATING FACTORS OF PRODUCTION

After studying this chapter you will be able to:

◆ Explain how firms choose the quantities of labour, capital and land to demand

◆ Explain how households choose the quantities of labour, capital, land and entrepreneurship to supply

◆ Explain how wages, interest, rent and normal profit are determined in competitive factor markets

◆ Explain the concept of economic rent and distinguish between economic rent and transfer earnings

I T MAY NOT BE YOUR BIRTHDAY, AND EVEN IF IT IS CHANCES ARE YOU ARE SPENDING MOST of it working. But at the end of the week or month (or, if you're devoting all your time to college, when you graduate), you will receive the *returns* from your labour. These returns vary a lot. Julie Adams, who spends her working days as a professional nurse, earns a happy return of £8.20 an hour, about £16,000 a year. Cedric Brown, the former chairman of British Gas, made a very happy return of £500,000 a year, more than £200 an hour. Students working at what have been called McJobs – serving fast food, labouring, or cleaning – earn just a few pounds an hour. Why aren't *all* jobs well-paid? ◆ Most of us have little trouble spending our pay. But most of us do manage to save some of what we earn. What determines the amount of saving that people do and the returns they make on that saving? How do the returns on saving influence the allocation of savings across the many industries and activities that use our capital

Many Happy Returns

resources? ◆ Some people receive income from supplying land, but the amount earned varies enormously with its location and quality. For example, an acre of farm land in Devon or Brittany rents for about £1,000 a year while a block of offices in London or Paris rents for several million pounds a year. What determines the rent that people are willing to pay for different blocks of land? Why are rents so enormously high in big cities and so relatively low in the great farming regions of the European Union?

◆ ◆ ◆ ◆ In this chapter we study the markets for factors of production – labour, capital, land and entrepreneurship – and learn how their prices and people's incomes are determined.

FIGURE 14.2

Changes in Demand

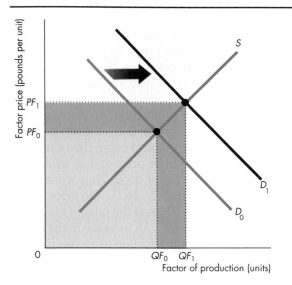

(a) An increase in demand

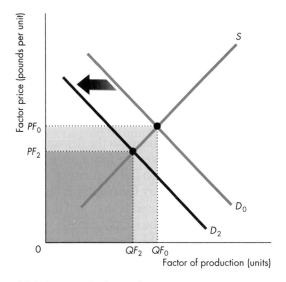

(b) A decrease in demand

An increase in the demand for a factor of production (part a) shifts its demand curve rightward – from D_0 to D_1. The quantity used increases from QF_0 to QF_1 and the price increases from PF_0 to PF_1. The factor income increases, and that income increase is shown by the dark blue area. A decrease in the demand for a factor of production from D_0 to D_2, results in a decrease in the quantity used, from QF_0 to QF_2, and a decrease in the factor price, from PF_0 to PF_2. The decrease in demand results in a decrease in the factor income. That decrease in income is illustrated by the light blue area.

FIGURE 14.3

Factor Income and Demand Elasticity

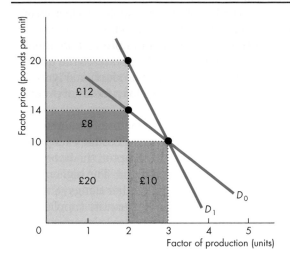

A decrease in the quantity used of a factor of production may result in a decrease or an increase in the factor's income. If the demand curve is D_0 (an elastic demand curve over the relevant range), a decrease in the quantity from 3 to 2 results in a decrease in the factor income from £30 to £28. If the demand curve is D_1 (an inelastic demand curve over the relevant range), a decrease in the quantity from 3 to 2 results in an increase in the factor's income from £30 to £40.

If the demand for the factor is shown by the curve D_0, the decrease in supply results in an increase in the price of the factor but a decrease in the income of those supplying this factor of production. You can see that income decreases by multiplying the factor price by the quantity used. Initially, when the quantity is 3 units and the price is £10, the income earned by the suppliers of this factor of production is £30 (£20 light blue area plus £10 red area). When the quantity decreases to 2 units and the price increases to £14, income decreases by the £10 (red area) but increases by the £8 (dark blue area) for a net decrease of £2 to £28. Over the range of the price change that we've just considered, the demand for the factor is elastic.

Conversely, suppose that the demand for the factor is shown by the curve is D_1. In this case, when the quantity decreases to 2 units, the price increases to £20 a unit. Income increases to £40. The smaller quantity lowers income by £10 (red area), but the higher factor price increases income by £20 (dark blue plus green areas). Over the range of the price change that we've just considered, the demand for the factor is inelastic.

We've just seen how demand and supply in a factor market determine the price, quantity used and income of a factor of production. We're going to spend the rest of this chapter exploring more closely the influences on the demand for and supply of factors of production. We're also going to study the influences on the elasticities of supply and demand for factors. These elasticities are important because of their effects on factor prices and the incomes earned. Let's begin by studying the demand for factors of production.

Demand for Factors

The demand for a factor of production is a derived demand. A **derived demand** is a demand for an item not for its own sake but in order to use it in the production of goods and services. A firm's derived demand for factors depends on the constraints the firm faces – its technology constraint and its market constraint. It also depends on the firm's objective. We will study the behaviour of firms whose objective is to maximize profit.

A firm's demand for factors of production stems from its profit-maximization decision. *What* to produce and *how* to produce it are the questions that the firm must answer in order to make maximum profit. These choices have implications for the firm's demand for factors, which we'll now investigate.

Profit Maximization

In the short-run, a firm's factors of production fall into two categories: variable and fixed. In most industries, the variable factor is labour and the fixed factors are capital (that is, plant, machinery and buildings) and land. A firm makes short-run changes in output by changing the quantity of labour it employs. It makes long-run changes in output by changing the quantities of labour, capital and land it employs.

A profit-maximizing firm produces the output at which marginal cost equals marginal revenue. This principle holds true whether the firm is in a perfectly competitive industry, in monopolistic competition, in oligopoly, or a monopoly. If one more unit of output adds less to total cost than it adds to total revenue, the firm can increase its profit by producing more. A firm maximizes profit by producing the output at which the additional cost of producing one more unit of output equals the additional revenue from selling it.

If we shift our perspective slightly, we can state the condition for maximum profit in terms of the marginal cost of a factor of production and the marginal revenue that factor generates. Let's look at these two concepts.

Marginal Cost of a Factor The marginal cost of a factor of production is the addition to a firm's total cost that results from employing one more unit of a factor. For a firm that buys its factors of production in competitive factor markets, this marginal cost is the price of the factor. That is, in a competitive factor market, each firm is such a small user of the factor that it has no influence on the price it must pay for each unit employed. The firm simply has to pay the going factor price – market wage rate for labour, interest rate for capital and rent for land.

Marginal Revenue Product To maximize profit, a firm must compare the marginal cost of a factor with the marginal revenue that the factor generates, which is called marginal revenue product. **Marginal revenue product** is the change in total revenue resulting from employing one more unit of a factor of production while the quantity of all other factors remains constant.

The concept of *marginal revenue product* sounds a bit like the concept of *marginal revenue* that you have met before. These concepts are indeed related but there is a crucial distinction between the two. Marginal revenue product is the extra revenue generated as a result of employing one extra unit of a factor; marginal revenue is the extra revenue generated as a result of selling one additional unit of output.

Quantity of Factor Demanded To maximize profit, a firm hires the quantity of a factor of production that makes the price of the factor equal to its marginal revenue product. If the marginal revenue product of a factor exceeds its price, the firm can increase its profit by increasing the quantity of the factor employed. If the marginal revenue product of a factor is less than its price, the firm can increase its profit by decreasing the quantity of the factor employed. But if the marginal revenue product of a factor is equal to its price, the firm can only decrease its profit by changing the quantity of the factor employed. At this point, the firm is maximizing profit.

As the price of a factor varies, the quantity demanded of it also varies. The lower the price of a factor, the larger is the quantity demanded of that factor. Let's illustrate this proposition by working through an example – that of labour.

The Firm's Demand for Labour

Labour is a variable factor. A firm can change the quantity of labour it employs in both the short run and the long run. Let's focus first on a firm's short-run demand for labour.

A *total product schedule* describes a firm's short-run technology constraint. The first two columns of Table 14.1 set out the total product schedule for a car wash operated by Max's Wash 'n' Wax. (This total product schedule is similar to the one we studied in Chapter 10, Fig. 10.1.) The numbers tell us how the maximum number of car washes each hour varies as

the amount of labour employed varies. The third column of Table 14.1 shows the *marginal product of labour* – the change in output resulting from a 1-unit increase in the quantity of labour employed.

Max's market constraint is the demand curve for his product. If, in the goods market, a firm is a monopoly or engaged in monopolistic competition or oligopoly, the demand curve for its product is downward-sloping. If a firm is perfectly competitive, the demand curve for its product is perfectly elastic – the firm is a price taker. Assume that the car wash market is perfectly competitive. Max can sell as many washes as he chooses at a constant price of £4 a wash. Given this information, we can calculate Max's total revenue (fourth column) by multiplying the number of cars washed an hour by £4. For example, if 9 cars are washed each hour (row *c*), total revenue is £36.

The fifth column shows the calculation of marginal revenue product of labour – the change in total revenue per unit change in labour. For example, if Max hires a second worker (row *c*), total

---

TABLE 14.1

Marginal Revenue Product at Max's Wash 'n' Wax

	Quantity of labour L (workers)	Output Q (cars washed per hour)	Marginal product $MP = \Delta Q/\Delta L$ (washes per worker)	Total revenue $TR = P \times Q$ (pounds)	Marginal revenue product $MRP = \Delta TR/\Delta L$ (pounds per worker)
a	0	0		0	
			5		20
b	1	5		20	
			4		16
c	2	9		36	
			3		12
d	3	12		48	
			2		8
e	4	14		56	
			1		4
f	5	15		60	

The marginal revenue product of labour is the change in total revenue that results from a unit increase in labour. Max operates in a perfectly competitive car wash market and can sell any quantity of washes at £4 a wash. To calculate marginal revenue product, first work out total revenue.

If Max hires 1 worker (row *b*), output is 5 washes an hour, and total revenue is £20. If he hires 2 workers (row *c*), output is 9 washes an hour and total revenue is £36. By hiring the second worker, total revenue rises by £16 – the marginal revenue product of labour is £16.

revenue increases from £20 to £36, so marginal revenue product of labour is £16.

There is an alternative way of calculating the marginal revenue product of labour. The marginal product of labour tells us how many washes an additional worker produces. Marginal revenue tells us the change in total revenue from selling one more wash. So an additional worker changes total revenue by an amount that equals marginal product multiplied by marginal revenue. That is, marginal revenue product equals marginal product multiplied by marginal revenue. For a perfectly competitive firm, marginal revenue equals price, so marginal revenue product equals marginal product multiplied by price.

To see that this method works, let's use the numbers in Table 14.1. Multiply the marginal product of hiring a second worker – 4 cars an hour – by marginal revenue – £4 a car – and notice that the answer is £16, the same as we have already calculated.

Notice that as the quantity of labour rises, the marginal revenue product of labour falls. When Max hires the first worker, the marginal revenue product of labour is £20. If Max hires a second worker, the marginal revenue product of labour is £16. Marginal

revenue product of labour continues to decline as Max hires more workers.

Marginal revenue product diminishes as Max hires more workers because of the principle of diminishing returns that we first studied in Chapter 10. With each additional worker hired, the marginal product of labour falls and so brings in a smaller marginal revenue product. Because Max's Wash 'n' Wax is a perfectly competitive firm, the price of each additional car wash is the same and brings in the same marginal revenue.

If Max had a monopoly in car washing, he would have to lower his price to sell more washes. In this case, the marginal revenue product of labour diminishes even more quickly than in perfectly competitive conditions. For a monopoly, marginal revenue product diminishes because of diminishing marginal product of labour and also because of diminishing marginal revenue.

The Labour Demand Curve

Figure 14.4 shows how the labour demand curve is derived from the marginal revenue product curve.

FIGURE 14.4

FIGURE 14.4

The Demand for Labour at Max's Wash 'n' Wax

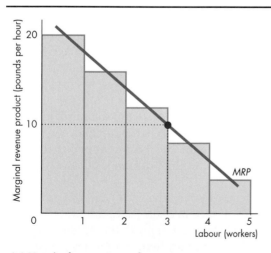

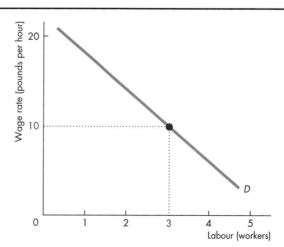

(a) Marginal revenue product

(b) Demand for labour

Max's Wash 'n' Wax operates in a perfectly competitive car wash market and can sell any quantity of washes at £4 a wash. The blue bars in part (a) represent the firm's marginal revenue product of labour. They are based on the numbers in Table 14.1. The orange line is the firm's marginal revenue product of labour curve. (Each point is plotted

midway between the quantity of labour used in its calculation.) Part (b) shows Max's demand for labour curve. This curve is identical to Max's marginal revenue product curve. Max demands the quantity of labour that makes the wage rate, which is the marginal cost of labour, equal to the marginal revenue product of labour.

The *marginal revenue product curve* graphs the marginal revenue product of a factor at each quantity of the factor hired. Figure 14.4(a) illustrates the marginal revenue product curve for workers employed by Max. The horizontal axis measures the number of workers that Max hires and the vertical axis measures the marginal revenue product of labour. The blue bars show the marginal revenue product of labour as Max employs more workers. These bars correspond to the numbers in Table 14.1. The curve *MRP* is Max's marginal revenue product curve.

The firm's demand for labour curve is based on its marginal revenue product curve. You can see Max's demand for labour curve (*D*) in Fig. 14.4(b). The horizontal axis measures the number of workers hired – the same as part (a). The vertical axis measures the wage rate in pounds per hour. The demand for labour curve is exactly the same as the firm's marginal revenue product curve. For example, when Max employs 3 workers an hour, his marginal revenue product is £10 an hour, as in Fig. 14.4(a); and at a wage rate of £10 an hour, Max hires 3 workers an hour, as in Fig. 14.4(b).

Why is the demand for labour curve identical to the marginal revenue product curve? Because the firm hires the profit-maximizing quantity of labour. If the cost of hiring one more worker – the wage rate – is less than the additional revenue that the worker brings in – the marginal revenue product of labour – then the firm can increase its profit by employing one more worker. Conversely, if the cost of hiring one more worker is greater than the additional revenue that the worker brings in – the wage rate exceeds the marginal revenue product – then the firm can increase its profit by employing one fewer worker. But if the cost of hiring one more worker is equal to the additional revenue that the worker brings in – the wage rate equals the marginal revenue product – then the firm cannot increase its profit by changing the number of workers it employs. The firm is making the maximum possible profit. This situation occurs when the wage rate equals the marginal revenue product of labour. Thus the quantity of labour demanded by the firm is such that the wage rate equals the marginal revenue product of labour.

Table 14.2 is a compact glossary of the factor market terms that you've just learned.

TABLE 14.2

Compact Glossary of Factor Market Terms

Factors of production	Labour, capital, land and entrepreneurship
Factor prices	Wage – price of labour; interest – price of capital; rent – price of land; normal profit – price of entrepreneurship
Marginal product	Output produced by last unit of factor hired; for example, the marginal product of labour is additional output produced by employing one more person
Marginal revenue	Revenue resulting from selling one additional unit of output
Marginal revenue product	Revenue resulting from hiring one additional unit of a factor of production, for example, marginal revenue product of labour is the additional revenue resulting from selling the output produced by employing one more person

Two Conditions for Profit Maximization

When we studied firms' output decisions, we discovered that a condition for maximum profit is that marginal revenue equals marginal cost. We've now discovered another condition for maximum profit – marginal revenue product of a factor equals the factor's price. These two conditions are equivalent to each other as Table 14.3 shows. When a firm produces the output that maximizes profit, marginal revenue equals marginal cost and the firm's technological and market constraints imply that the firm is employing the amount of labour that makes the marginal revenue product of labour equal to the wage rate.

We have just derived the law of demand as it applies to the labour market. We've discovered that the same principles that apply to the demand for goods and services apply here as well. The demand for labour curve slopes downward. Other things remaining the same, the lower the wage rate (the price of labour), the greater is the quantity of labour demanded. Let's now study the influences that change in the demand for labour and shift in the demand for labour curve.

TABLE 14.3

Two Conditions for Maximum Profit

SYMBOLS

Marginal product	MP
Marginal revenue	MR
Marginal cost	MC
Marginal revenue product	MRP
Factor price	PF

TWO CONDITIONS FOR MAXIMUM PROFIT

1. $MR = MC$ 2. $MRP = PF$

EQUIVALENCE OF CONDITIONS

1. $MRP/MP = MR$ $=$ $MC = PF/MP$

Multiply by MP Multiply by MP
to give   to give

$MRP = MR \times MP$ $MC \times MP = PF$

Flipping the   Flipping the
equation over   equation over

2. $MR \times MP = MRP$ $=$ $PF = MC \times MP$

Marginal revenue product (*MR*) equals marginal cost (*MC*), and marginal revenue product (*MRP*) equals the price of the factor (*PF*). The two conditions for maximum profit are equivalent because marginal revenue product (*MRP*) equals marginal revenue (*MR*) multiplied by marginal product (*MP*), and the factor price (*PF*) equals marginal cost (*MC*) multiplied by marginal product (*MP*).

Changes in the Demand for Labour

The position of a firm's demand for labour curve depends on three factors:

1. The price of the firm's output
2. The prices of other factors of production
3. Technology

Because the firm's demand for labour is a derived demand, the amount of labour a firm plans to hire depends on the price of the firm's output. The higher the price of a firm's output, the greater is the quantity of labour demanded by the firm,

other things remaining the same. The price of output affects the demand for labour through its influence on marginal revenue product. A higher price for the firm's output increases marginal revenue which, in turn, increases the marginal revenue product of labour. A change in the price of a firm's output leads to a shift in the firm's demand for labour curve. If the output price increases, the demand for labour increases.

The other two influences on the demand for labour have their main effects not in the short run but in the long run. The *short-run demand for labour* is the relationship between the wage rate and the quantity of labour demanded when the firm's capital is fixed and labour is the only variable factor. The *long-run demand for labour* is the relationship between the wage rate and the quantity of labour demanded when all factors can be varied. A change in the relative price of factors of production – such as the relative price of labour and capital – leads to a substitution away from the factor whose relative price has increased and towards the factor whose relative price has decreased. Thus if the price of using capital decreases relative to that of using labour, the firm substitutes capital for labour, increasing the quantity of capital demanded and decreasing its demand for labour.

Finally, a new technology that influences the marginal product of labour also affects the demand for labour. For example, the development of electronic telephones with memories and a host of clever features decreased the marginal product of telephone operators and so decreased the demand for telephone operators. This same technological change increased the marginal product of telephone engineers and so increased the demand for telephone engineers. Again, these effects are felt in the long run when the firm adjusts all its factors and incorporates new technologies into its production process.

As we saw earlier, Fig. 14.2 illustrates the effects of a change in the demand for a factor. If that factor is labour, then Fig. 14.2 shows the effects of a change in the demand for labour on the wage rate and the quantity of labour hired. But we can now say why the demand for labour curve shifts. For example, an increase in the price of the firm's output, an increase in the price of capital, or a technological change that increases the marginal product of labour shifts the demand for labour curve from D_0 to D_1 in Fig. 14.2(a). Conversely, a decrease in the price of the firm's output, a decrease in the price of capital, or a technological change that lowers the marginal product of labour shifts the demand curve for labour from D_0 to D_2 in Fig. 14.2(b).

Table 14.4 summarizes the influences on a firm's demand for labour.

You can read about Newcastle United's demand for top strikers in *Reading Between the Lines* on pp. 360–361.

Market Demand

So far we've studied only the demand for labour by an individual firm. Let's now look at the market demand. The market demand for a factor of production is the total demand for that factor by all firms. Thus the concept of the market demand for labour curve is exactly like the concept of the market demand curve for a good or service. The market demand curve for labour, like other market services, is obtained by adding together the quantities of labour demanded by all firms at each wage rate.

Elasticity of Demand for Labour

The elasticity of demand for labour measures the responsiveness of the quantity of labour demanded

to the wage rate. We calculate this elasticity in the same way that we calculate a price elasticity. The elasticity of demand for labour equals the magnitude of the percentage change in the quantity of labour demanded divided by the percentage change in the wage rate.

The demand for labour is less elastic in the short run, when only labour can be varied, than in the long run, when labour and other factors can be varied. The elasticity of demand for labour depends on:

◆ The labour intensity of the production process

◆ How rapidly the marginal product of labour diminishes

◆ The elasticity of demand for the product

◆ The substitutability of capital for labour

Labour Intensity   A labour-intensive production process is one that uses a lot of labour and little capital – a process that has a high ratio of labour to capital. Home building is an example. The larger the labour – capital ratio, the more elastic is the demand for labour, other things remaining the same. Let's see why.

If wages are 90 per cent of total cost, a 10 per cent increase in the wage rate increases total cost by 9 per cent. Firms will be extremely sensitive to such a large change in total cost. If the wage rate increases, firms will decrease the quantity of labour demanded by a large amount. If wages are 10 per cent of total cost, a 10 per cent increase in the wage rate increases total cost by 1 per cent. Firms will be less sensitive to this increase in cost. If wage rates increase in this case, firms will decrease the quantity of labour demanded by a small amount.

How Rapidly Marginal Product Diminishes
The more rapidly the marginal product of labour diminishes, the less elastic is the demand for labour, other things remaining the same. In some activities marginal product diminishes quickly. For example, the marginal product of one bus driver is high, but the marginal product of a second driver on the same bus is close to zero. In other activities marginal product diminishes slowly. For example, hiring a second window cleaner on a team almost doubles the amount of glass that can be cleaned in an hour – the marginal product of the second window cleaner is almost the same as the first.

The Elasticity of Demand for the Product   The greater the elasticity of demand for the good, the

---

TABLE 14.4

A Firm's Demand for Labour

THE LAW OF DEMAND

The quantity of labour demanded by a firm

Decreases if:	*Increases if:*
◆ The wage rate increases	◆ The wage rate decreases

CHANGES IN DEMAND

A firm's demand for labour

Decreases if:	*Increases if:*
◆ The firm's output price decreases	◆ The firm's output price increases
◆ The prices of other factors decrease	◆ The prices of other factors increase
◆ A technological change decreases the marginal product of labour	◆ A technological change increases the marginal product of labour

larger is the elasticity of demand for the factors of production used to produce it. To see why, think about what happens when the wage rate increases. An increase in the wage rate increases marginal cost and decreases the supply of the good. The decrease in the supply of the good increases the price of the good and decreases the quantity demanded of the good and the factors that produce it. The greater the elasticity of demand for the good, the larger is the decrease in the quantity demanded of the good and so the larger is the decrease in the quantities of the factors of production used to produce it.

The Substitutability of Capital for Labour The substitutability of capital for labour influences the long-run elasticity of demand for labour but not the short-run elasticity. In the short run, capital is fixed. In the long run, capital can be varied, and the more easily capital can be substituted for labour in production, the more elastic is the long-run demand for labour. For example, it is fairly easy to substitute robots for assembly-line workers in car factories and automatic picking machines for labour in vineyards and orchards. At the other extreme, it is difficult (though not impossible) to substitute robots for newspaper reporters, bank loan officers and teachers. The more readily capital can be substituted for labour, the more elastic is the firm's demand for labour in the long run.

R E V I E W

◆ A firm chooses the quantity of labour to hire so that its profit is maximized.

◆ Profit is maximized when the marginal revenue product of labour equals the wage rate.

◆ The marginal revenue product of labour curve is the firm's demand for labour curve. The lower the wage rate, the greater is the quantity of labour demanded.

◆ The short-run elasticity of demand for labour depends on the labour intensity of production, how rapidly marginal product diminishes and the elasticity of demand for the product. The long-run elasticity of demand for labour depends on these three conditions and on how easily capital can be substituted for labour.

Supply of Factors

The supply of factors is determined by the decisions of households. Households allocate the factors of production that they own to their most rewarding uses. The quantity supplied of any factor of production depends on its price. Usually, the higher the price of a factor of production, the larger is the quantity supplied. There is a possible exception to this general law of supply concerning the supply of labour. It arises from the fact that people have preferences about how they use their time.

Let's examine household factor supply decisions, beginning with the supply of labour.

Supply of Labour

A household chooses the number of hours per week of labour to supply as part of its time allocation decision. Time is allocated between two broad activities:

1. Market activity
2. Non-market activity

Market activity is the same thing as supplying labour. **Non-market activity** consists of everything else: leisure, non-market production activities including education and training, shopping, cooking and other activities in the home. The household obtains a return from market activity in the form of a wage. Non-market activities generate a return in the form of goods and services produced in the home, a higher future income, or leisure, which is valued for its own sake and which is classified as a good.

In deciding how to allocate its time between market activity and non-market activity, a household weighs the returns that it can get from the different activities. We are interested in the effects of the wage rate on the household's allocation of its time and on how much labour it supplies.

Wages and Quantity of Labour Supplied To induce a household to supply labour, it must be offered a high enough wage rate. Non-market activities are valued by households either because the time is used in some productive activity or because of the value they attach to leisure. In order for it to be worthwhile to supply labour, a household has to be offered a wage rate that is at least equal to the value it places on the last hour it spends in non-market activities. This wage rate – the lowest one for which a household will supply labour to the market – is called its **reservation wage**. At wage rates below the reservation wage, the household supplies no labour. Once the wage rate reaches the reservation wage, the household begins to supply labour. As the wage rate rises above the reservation wage, the household varies the quantity of labour that it supplies. But a higher wage rate has two off-setting effects on the quantity of labour supplied – a *substitution effect* and an *income effect*.

Substitution Effect   Other things remaining the same, the higher the wage rate, the more time people allocate to market activity and the less they allocate to non-market activities. Suppose, for example, that the market price of a duvet cleaning laundry service is £10 an hour. If the wage rate available to a household is less than £10 an hour, the household will provide its own laundry service – a non-market activity. If the household's wage rate rises above £10 an hour, it will be worthwhile for the household to work more hours and use part of its income to buy laundry services. The higher wage rate induces a switch of time from non-market activities to market activities.

Income Effect   The higher the household's wage rate, the higher is its income. A higher income, other things remaining the same, induces a rise in demand for most goods. Leisure, a component of non-market activity, is one of these goods. Because an increase in income creates an increase in the demand for leisure, it also creates a decrease in the amount of time allocated to market activities and, therefore, to a fall in the quantity of labour supplied.

Backward-bending Household Supply of Labour Curve   The substitution effect and the income effect operate in opposite directions. The higher the wage rate, the higher is the quantity of labour supplied via the substitution effect, but the lower is the quantity of labour supplied via the income effect. At low wage rates, the substitution effect is larger than the income effect. As the wage rate rises, the household supplies more labour. But as the wage rate continues to rise, there comes a point at which the substitution effect and the income effect just offset each other. At that point, a change in the wage rate has no effect on the quantity of labour supplied. If the wage rate continues to

rise, the income effect begins to dominate the substitution effect and the quantity of labour supplied declines. The household's supply of labour curve does not slope upward throughout its entire length but begins to bend back on itself. It is called a backward-bending supply curve.

Three individual household labour supply curves are shown in Fig. 14.5(a). Each household has a different reservation wage. Household A has a reservation wage of £1 an hour, household B of £4 an hour and household C of £7 an hour. Each household's labour supply curve is backward-bending.

Market Supply   The quantity of labour supplied to the entire market is the total quantity supplied by all households. The market supply of labour curve is the sum of the supply curves of all the individual households. Figure 14.5(b) shows the market supply curve (S_M) derived from the supply curves of the three households (S_A, S_B, S_C) in Fig. 14.5(a). At wage rates of less than £1 an hour, the three households do only non-market activities such as laundry and cooking, and they do not supply any market labour. The household most eager to supply market labour has a reservation wage of £1 an hour. As the wage rate rises from £1 to £4 an hour, household A increases the quantity of labour that it supplies to the market. The reservation wage of household B is £4 an hour, so as the wage rate rises above £4 an hour, the quantity of labour supplied in the market is the sum of the labour supplied by households A and B. When the wage rate reaches £7 an hour, household C begins to supply some labour to the market. At wage rates above £7 an hour, the quantity supplied in the market is equal to the sum of the quantities supplied by the three households.

Notice that the market supply curve S_M, like the individual household supply curves, eventually bends backward. But the market supply curve has a long upward-sloping section. The reason why the market supply curve slopes up for such a long stretch is that the reservation wage rates of individual households are not equal and at higher wage rates additional households reach their reservation wage and so begin to supply labour.

Although the market supply curve eventually bends backward, no real-world wage rate is so high that the economy operates on the backward-bending portion of its labour supply curve. But many individual households are on the backward-bending portion of their own labour supply curve. Thus as wage rates rise, some people allocate fewer hours

FIGURE 14.5

The Supply of Labour

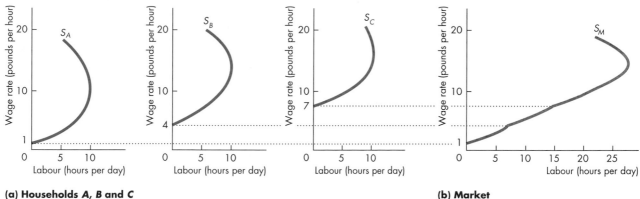

(a) Households A, B and C

Part (a) shows the labour supply curves of three house-holds (S_A, S_B, and S_C). Each household has a reservation wage below which it will supply no labour. As the wage rises above the reservation wage, the quantity of labour supplied rises to a maximum. If the wage continues to rise, the quantity of labour supplied begins to decline. Each

(b) Market

household's supply curve eventually bends backward.

Part (b) shows how, by adding together the quantities of labour supplied by the individual households at each wage rate, we derive the market supply curve of labour (S_M). The market supply curve also eventually bends backward, but has a long upward-sloping region before it bends backward.

to market activity. But higher wage rates induce those workers who are on the upward-sloping part of their labour supply curve to supply more hours and induce additional households into market activity. The response of these workers to higher wage rates dominates that of those whose work hours decline as wage rates rise. Therefore, for the economy as a whole, the labour supply curve slopes upward. For this reason, we will restrict our attention to the upward-sloping part of the labour supply curve in Fig. 14.5(b).

Supply to Individual Firms   We've studied the labour supply decisions of individual households and seen how these decisions add up to the total market supply. But how is the supply of labour to each individual firm determined? The answer to this question depends on the degree of competitiveness in the labour market. In a perfectly competitive labour market, each firm faces a perfectly elastic supply of labour. That is, the firm can hire any quantity of labour at the going market wage rate. This situation arises because the individual firm is such a small part of the total labour market that it has no influence on the wage rate.

Some labour markets are non-competitive in the sense that firms can and do influence the price of the labour that they hire. In these cases, firms face an upward-sloping supply of labour curve. The

more labour they wish to employ, the higher is the wage rate they have to offer. We examine how this type of labour market operates in Chapter 15.

R E V I E W

◆ At wage rates above the household's reservation wage, the household supplies labour to the market.

◆ An increase in the wage rate has a substitution effect (less leisure and more work) and an income effect (more leisure and less work).

◆ At low wage rates, the substitution effect is the more powerful and the labour supply curve slopes upward. At high wage rates, the income effect is the more powerful and the labour supply curve bends backward.

◆ The market supply of labour curve is the sum of the supply curves of individual households and is upward-sloping.

◆ The supply of labour curve faced by each individual firm depends on the degree of competitiveness of the labour market.

◆ In a perfectly competitive labour market, each firm faces a perfectly elastic supply curve.

Supply of Capital

The supply of capital is more indirect than the supply of labour. It is determined by households' saving decisions. If households supplied capital in the same direct way that they supply labour, then all the buildings, machines and other equipment would be owned by households and rented to firms. In fact, most capital is owned by firms, which in effect rent it to themselves. Households supply the funds, called **financial capital**, that firms use to buy capital. Households lend some of these funds to firms by buying their stocks and bonds and by making deposits in banks, which the banks lend to firms. Households also lend funds to firms in the form of retained earnings – profits that have not been paid out to the firms' owners, their stockholders. The total amount of capital that firms can acquire and use depends on the total quantity of financial capital. This quantity is a *stock* – a quantity at a point in time. The stock of financial capital depends on the amounts that households have saved in previous years. Saving is a *flow* – a quantity per year – that adds to the stock of financial capital.

The most important factors determining a household's saving are:

◆ Current income and expected future income
◆ The interest rate

Current and Expected Future Income A household with a current income that is low compared with its expected future income saves little and might even have negative saving. A household with a current income that is high compared with its expected future income saves a great deal in the present in order to be able to consume more in the future. The stage in the household's life cycle is the main factor influencing whether current income is high or low compared with expected future income. Young households typically have a low current income compared with their expected future income, while older working households have a high current income relative to their expected future income. The consequence of this pattern in income over the life cycle is that young people have negative saving and older working people have positive saving. Thus the young incur debts (such as consumer credit) to acquire durable goods and to consume more than their income, while older working people save and accumulate assets (often in the form of pension and life insurance arrangements)

to provide for their retirement years.

The Interest Rate The interest rate is the opportunity cost of consuming in the current year rather than in the following year. If the interest rate is 10 per cent a year, £100 consumed in the current year costs £110 of consumption in the following year. So by consuming £100 in the current year rather than in the following year, consumption falls by £10 or 10 per cent of current consumption. Equivalently, £100 saved (not consumed) in the current year brings the possibility of increasing consumption by £110 in the following year – a net increase in consumption of £10 or 10 per cent.

Other things remaining the same, the higher the interest rate, the greater is the amount of saving and the greater is the quantity of capital supplied. With a high interest rate, people have a strong incentive to cut consumption and increase their saving in order to take advantage of the high returns available. With a low interest rate, people have only a weak incentive to cut their consumption and save.

The Supply Curve of Capital

The quantity of capital supplied in the market is the sum of the quantities supplied by all the individual households. The market supply curve of capital shows how the quantity of capital supplied varies as the interest rate varies. In the short-run, the supply of capital is inelastic and might even be zero-elastic. Such a case is illustrated in Fig. 14.6 as the vertical supply curve *SS*. The reason is that households find it difficult to change their consumption plans quickly in response to changes in the interest rate. But given sufficient time to make the necessary substitutions, they do respond to a change in the interest rate. As a result, the long-run supply of capital is much more elastic. Such a case is illustrated in Fig. 14.6 by the supply curve *LS*.

Supply to Individual Firms In the short run a firm can vary its labour but not its capital. Thus in the short run, the firm's supply of capital is fixed. It has a specific set of capital assets. For example, a car manufacturer has a production assembly line; a laundry has a number of washing machines and dryers; the university print shop has a number of photocopying and other printing machines. These pieces of capital cannot be quickly disposed of or added to.

FIGURE 14.6

Short-run and Long-run Supply of Capital

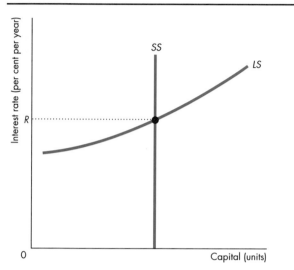

The long-run supply of capital (*LS*) is highly elastic. In the long run, if the interest rate is above *R*, households increase their saving and the quantity of capital supplied increases. Also in the long run, if the interest rate is below *R*, households decrease their saving and the quantity of capital supplied decreases. The short-run supply of capital (*SS*) is inelastic (perfectly inelastic in the figure). In the short run, there is a fixed amount of capital and this quantity cannot be varied, no matter what the interest rate is.

In the long run a firm can vary all its factors – capital as well as labour. A firm operating in a competitive capital market can obtain any amount of capital it chooses at the going market interest rate. Thus it faces a perfectly elastic supply of capital.

The fact that the short-run supply of capital is inelastic and the long-run supply of capital is elastic means that interest rates can differ across industries in the short run, but these differences become small or disappear in the long run.

Let's complete our analysis of the supply of factors of production by examining the supply of land.

Supply of Land

Land is the stock of natural resources and its aggregate quantity supplied cannot be changed by any individual decisions. Individual households can vary the amount of land they own, but whatever land is acquired by one household is sold by another so

that the aggregate quantity of land supplied of any particular type and in any particular location is fixed regardless of the decisions of any individual household. This fact means that the supply of each particular piece of land is perfectly inelastic. Figure 14.7 illustrates such a supply. Regardless of the rent available, the quantity of land supplied in London's Westminster area is a fixed number of square metres.

Expensive land can be, and is, used more intensively than inexpensive land. For example, high-rise buildings enable land to be used more intensively. However, to use land more intensively, it has to be combined with another factor of production – capital. Increasing the amount of capital per block of land does not change the supply of land itself. But it does enable land to become more productive. A rising price of land strengthens the incentive to find ways of increasing its productivity. These issues are explored more fully in *Economics in History* on pp. 368–369.

Although the supply of each type of land is fixed and its supply is perfectly inelastic, each individual firm, operating in competitive land markets, faces an elastic supply of land. For example, Oxford

FIGURE 14.7

The Supply of Land

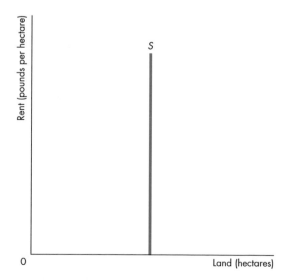

The supply of a given piece of land is perfectly inelastic. No matter what the rent, no more land than exists can be supplied.

Factor Income in Football

The Essence of the Story

THE FINANCIAL TIMES, 30 JULY 1996

Newcastle sign Alan Shearer for record £15m fee

Patrick Harverson and Chris Tighe

Newcastle United yesterday smashed the world football transfer fee by acquiring England's star striker Alan Shearer from Blackburn Rovers for £15m....

In almost doubling the previous UK transfer record – Stan Collymore's £8.5m move from Nottingham Forest to Liverpool last year – Newcastle are betting that Shearer's goal-scoring feats will lead to triumphs in the English league and European competition, where success can earn a club up to £10m in television fees and prize money.

The deal also underlined the remarkable new-found wealth of the top English football clubs.... Rapid growth in revenues from television fees, merchandising sales, gate receipts and sponsorship is behind the affluence.

Newcastle beat the previous world transfer record of £13m paid by both AC Milan of Italy for Gianluigi Lentini in 1992 and by Barcelona of Spain for Brazil's Ronaldo this summer....

Shearer, born in Newcastle, scored 31 goals in the Premier league last season, making him the first player in English football to score more than 30 goals in three consecutive seasons. He was also top scorer in this summer's Euro 96 championship. His estimated salary at Newcastle will be £1.5m a year.

Last year the club spent £13.5m on strikers Les Ferdinand and Faustino Asprilla, and is expected to sell one or both before the beginning of the season....

■ Newcastle United Football Club paid a record £15 million for a star striker, Alan Shearer, in July 1996.

■ The transfer fee nearly doubled the previous UK payment for Stan Collymore in 1995 and beats the world record fee of £13 million paid by AC Milan for Lentini and by Barcelona for Ronaldo.

■ Shearer is the first English footballer to score 30 goals or more in three consecutive seasons. His salary will be £1.5 million.

■ Newcastle hope Shearer's skills will boost annual revenue by £10 million through extra television fees and prize money, and entry to European club competitions.

Economic Analysis

■ Top-class strikers are a factor of production for football clubs. Demand for top-class strikers is derived from their marginal revenue product (*MRP*).

■ Figure 1 shows Newcastle United's marginal revenue product, *MRP*, for top-class strikers in 1995. *MRP* equals the club's demand for top strikers, *D*.

■ The club pays the going factor price for strikers, £8.5 million, in a competitive factor market. To maximize profits, Newcastle United buys additional strikers up to the point where *MRP* equals factor price at Q_0.

■ Figure 2 shows the UK market for top-scoring players in 1995. High scoring raises the marginal revenue product for top strikers and leads to a high demand, D_{95}.

■ The number of top-scoring strikers is limited, leading to low, inelastic supply, S_0. The market price for top strikers is £8.5 million and the market quantity is low, Q_0.

■ The development of satellite sports programmes and new BSkyB contracts increased demand for top strikers in 1996 to D_{96} in Fig. 2. The factor price of top scorers rises to £13 million. Quantity rises slightly to Q_1, as one or two good scorers try harder to become top strikers.

■ As supply is highly inelastic, most of Shearer's income will be economic rent. Shearer is paid more than the market price because his unique scoring record raises his individual *MRP*.

■ If Newcastle United has miscalculated Shearer's projected *MRP* for 1997, revenues won't cover costs and the club will make a loss.

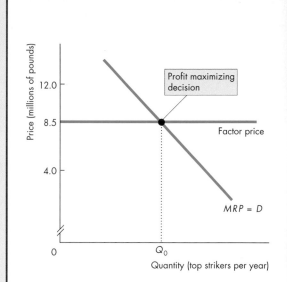

Figure 1

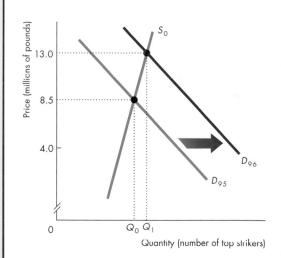

Figure 2

Street in London has a fixed amount of land, but Waterstones, a bookshop, could rent some space from John Lewis, a department store. Each firm can rent the quantity of land that it demands at the going rent, which is determined in the marketplace. Thus provided land markets are highly competitive, firms are price takers in these markets, just as they are in the markets for other factors of production.

R E V I E W

◆ The supply of capital is determined by households' saving decisions.

◆ Other things remaining the same, the higher the interest rate, the greater is the amount of capital supplied. The supply of capital to individual firms is inelastic in the short run but perfectly elastic in the long run.

◆ The supply of land is fixed – is perfectly inelastic. But the supply of land to individual firms is elastic.

We've now seen how demand and supply in factor markets determine incomes, and we've probed more deeply into the influences on the demand for and supply of factors of production. Let's now use what we've learned to see why some factors of production earn high incomes and others earn low ones. Let's also learn about economic rent and transfer earnings.

Incomes, Economic Rent and Transfer Earnings

We saw at the beginning of this chapter, in Figs 14.1, 14.2 and 14.3, that the price of a factor of production and the quantity of it used are determined by the interaction of demand and supply. We've seen that demand is determined by marginal productivity and supply is determined by the resources available and by households' choices about their use. The interaction of demand and supply in factor markets determines who receives a large income and who receives a small income.

Large and Small Incomes

Why does the director of a large corporation earn a large income? It must be because such a person has a high marginal revenue product. This is reflected in the demand curve for his or her services. The supply of people with the combination of talents needed for this kind of job is also small and this is reflected in the supply curve. Equilibrium occurs at a high wage rate and a small quantity employed.

Why do McJobs pay low wages? It is because they have a low marginal revenue product – reflected in the demand curve – and there are many households able and willing to supply their labour for these jobs. Equilibrium occurs at a low wage rate and large quantity employed.

If the demand for news readers increases, their incomes increase by a large amount and the number of news readers barely changes. If the demand for workers in McJobs increases, the number of people doing these jobs increases by a large amount and the wage rate barely changes.

You can get a further insight into people's incomes by learning about the distinction between economic rent and transfer earnings..

Economic Rent and Transfer Earnings

The total income of a factor of production is made up of its economic rent and its transfer earnings. **Economic rent** is an income received by the owner of a factor over and above the amount required to induce that owner to offer the factor for use. Any factor of production can receive an economic rent. The income required to induce the supply of a factor of production is called **transfer earnings**. Transfer earnings are the opportunity cost of using a factor of production – the value of the factor in its next best use.

Figure 14.8 illustrates the concepts of economic rent and transfer earnings. The figure shows the market for a factor of production. It could be *any* factor of production – labour, capital, land or entrepreneurship. The demand curve for the factor of production is D and its supply curve is S. The factor price is PF and the quantity of the factor used is QF. The income of the factor is the sum of the yellow and green areas. The yellow area below the supply curve measures transfer earnings and the green area below the factor price but above the supply curve measures economic rent.

To see why the area below the supply curve

measures transfer earnings, recall that a supply curve can be interpreted in two different ways. One interpretation is that a supply curve indicates the quantity supplied at a given price. But the alternative interpretation of a supply curve is that it shows the minimum price at which a given quantity is willingly supplied. If suppliers receive only the minimum amount required to induce them to supply each unit of the factor of production, they will be paid a different price for each unit. The prices will trace the supply curve and the income received is entirely transfer earnings – the yellow area in Fig. 14.8.

The concept of economic rent is similar to the concept of consumer surplus that you met in Chapter 7, pp. 164–165. Remember that consumer surplus is the difference between the price the household pays for a good and the maximum price it would be willing to pay, as indicated by the demand curve. In a parallel sense, economic rent is the difference between the factor price a household actually receives and the minimum factor price at which it would be willing to supply a given amount of a factor of production.

Economic rent is not the same thing as *rent*. Rent is the price paid for the services of land. Economic rent is a component of the income received by any factor of production.

The portion of the income of a factor of production that consists of economic rent depends on the elasticity of the supply of the factor of production. When the supply of a factor of production is perfectly inelastic, its entire income is economic rent. Most of Madonna's income is economic rent. Also, a large part of the income of an international football player is economic rent. When the supply of a factor of production is perfectly elastic, none of its income is economic rent. Most of the income of a babysitter is transfer earnings. In general, when the supply curve is neither perfectly elastic nor perfectly inelastic (like that illustrated in Fig. 14.8), some part of the factor income is economic rent and the other part transfer earnings.

Figure 14.9 illustrates the three possibilities. Part (a) of the figure shows the market for a particular parcel of land in London. The land is fixed in size at L hectares. Therefore the supply curve of the land is vertical – perfectly inelastic. No matter what the rent on the land is, there is no way of increasing the quantity that can be supplied.

The demand for that block of land is determined by its marginal revenue product. The marginal revenue product in turn depends on the uses to which the land can be put. In a central business district such as Canary Wharf, the marginal revenue product is high because a large number of people are concentrated in that area, making it a prime place for conducting business. Suppose that the marginal revenue product of this block of land is shown by the demand curve in Fig. 14.9(a). Then it commands a rent of R. The entire income accruing to the owner of the land is the green area in the figure. This income is economic rent. The rent charged for this piece of land depends entirely on its marginal revenue product – on the demand curve. If the demand curve shifts rightward, the rent rises. If the demand curve shifts leftward, the rent falls. The quantity of land supplied remains constant at L.

Is wine expensive in Canary Wharf because land rents are high, or are land rents high because people in Canary Wharf are willing to pay a high price for wine? If you asked wine bar owners in Canary

FIGURE 14.8

Economic Rent and Transfer Earnings

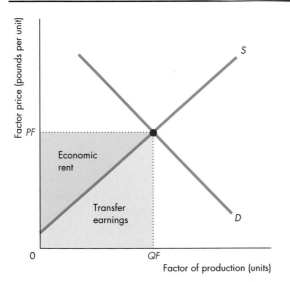

The total income of a factor of production is made up of its economic rent and its transfer earnings. Transfer earnings are measured by the yellow area under the supply curve, and economic rent is measured by by the green area above the supply curve and below the factor price.

FIGURE 14.9

Economic Rent and Supply Elasticity

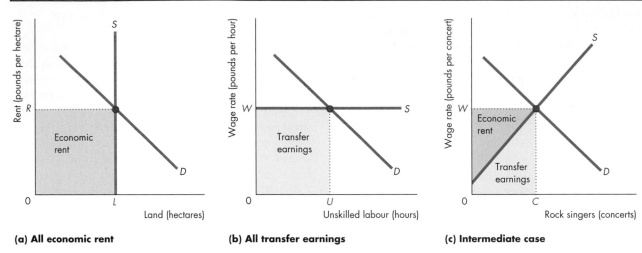

(a) All economic rent **(b) All transfer earnings** **(c) Intermediate case**

When the supply of a factor of production is perfectly inelastic (the supply curve is vertical) as in part (a), the entire factor income is economic rent. When the supply of the factor of production is perfectly elastic, as in part (b), the factor's entire income is transfer earnings. When a fac-

tor supply curve slopes upward, as in part (c), part of the factor income is economic rent and part is transfer earnings. Land is the example shown in part (a); unskilled labour in poor countries such as India and China in part (b); and rock singers in part (c).

Wharf this question, the answer you would get is that they charge a high price for wine because the rent they pay for the land is so high. But this is only part of the answer. The rent is high because the wine bar's marginal revenue product of that land is high. That is, the rent of a Canary Wharf site is determined by the demand for it, and that demand, in turn, is determined by its marginal revenue product. Land has a high marginal revenue product because someone is willing to pay a high price to use the land.

Figure 14.9(b) shows the market for a factor of production that is in perfectly elastic supply. An example of such a market might be that for unskilled labour in a poor country such as India or China. In these countries, large amounts of labour flock to the cities and are available for work at the going wage rate (in this case, W). Thus in these situations, the supply of labour is almost perfectly elastic. The entire income earned by this labour is transfer earnings. They receive no economic rent.

Figure 14.9(c) shows the market for rock singers. To induce rock singers to sing at a larger number of concerts, a higher income has to be offered – the supply curve of rock singers is

upward-sloping. The demand curve – measuring the marginal revenue product of the rock singer – is labelled D in the figure. Equilibrium occurs where the rock singer receives a wage of W and sings in C concerts. The green area above the rock singer's supply curve is economic rent and the yellow area below the supply curve is the rock singer's transfer earnings. If the rock singer is not offered at least the amount of the transfer earnings, then the singer will withdraw from the rock concert market and perform other alternative activities, such as recording CDs or teaching singing.

◆ ◆ ◆ ◆ We've now studied the markets for factors of production, the returns to these factors and how demand and supply determine factor prices and factor incomes. We've seen the role of the factor's marginal revenue product in determining why some factors receive large incomes and others receive small incomes. Finally, we've distinguished between economic rent and transfer earnings. ◆ In the next chapter, we're going to examine labour markets more closely and explain differences in wage rates among skilled and unskilled workers, males and females, and racial and ethnic minorities.

SUMMARY

Factor Prices and Incomes

The factors of production – labour, capital, land and entrepreneurship – earn a return – wages, interest, rent and normal profit. Labour is the largest source of income. Factor prices are determined by the demand for and supply of factors of production. Incomes are determined by the prices of factors of production and the quantities used. An increase (decrease) in the demand for a factor of production increases (decreases) the factor's price and income. An increase (decrease) in supply increases (decreases) the quantity used of a factor of production but decreases (increases) its price. Whether an increase in supply leads to an increase or decrease in the income of a factor of production depends on the elasticity of demand for the factor. When elasticity of demand is greater (less) than 1, an increase in supply leads to an increase (decrease) in the factor's income. (pp. 346–349)

Demand for Factors

A firm's demand for a factor stems from its attempt to maximize profit. The change in total revenue generated by hiring one more unit of a factor is called the marginal revenue product of the factor. A firm maximizes profit by hiring the quantity of a factor of production that makes the marginal revenue product of the factor equal the factor's price. A firm's demand curve for a factor is exactly the same as that factor's marginal revenue product curve.

Firms can vary the amount of labour hired in both the short run and the long run. The short-run elasticity of demand for labour depends on the labour intensity of the production process, on how rapidly the marginal product of labour diminishes and on the elasticity of demand for the firm's product. The long-run elasticity of demand for labour depends on these three conditions and on the ease with which capital can be substituted for labour in the long run. The market demand for labour is the sum of the demands by each individual firm. (pp. 349–355)

Supply of Factors

The supply of factors is determined by households' decisions on the allocation of their time and the division of their income between consumption and saving. Each household compares the wage rate that can be earned with the value of its time in other non-market activities. At wage rates below its reservation wage, the household supplies no labour. At wage rates above the household's reservation wage, the quantity of labour supplied rises as long as the substitution effect of the higher wage rate is larger than the income effect. As the wage rate continues to rise, the income effect, which leads to more time taken for leisure, becomes larger than the substitution effect, and the quantity of labour supplied by the household falls.

The market supply curve of labour is the sum of the supply curves of all households. Unlike the household's labour supply curve, the market supply curve slopes upward over a large range of wages.

Households supply capital by saving. Saving increases as the interest rate increases. The supply of capital to an individual firm is highly inelastic in the short run but highly elastic in the long run. The supply of land is fixed and independent of its rent. (pp. 355–362)

Incomes, Economic Rent and Transfer Earnings

In a competitive factor market, the intersection of the demand and supply curves determines the factor price and quantity used. High (low) factor prices occur for factors of production that have a high (low) marginal revenue product and a low (high) supply.

Economic rent is that part of the income received by a factor owner over and above the amount needed to induce the owner to supply the factor of production for use. The rest of a factor's income is transfer earnings or opportunity costs. When the supply of a factor is perfectly inelastic, its entire income is made up of economic rent. Factors that have a perfectly elastic supply receive only transfer earnings. In general the supply curve of a factor is upward-sloping, and part of its income received is transfer earnings (below the supply curve) and part is economic rent (above the supply curve but below the factor price). (pp. 362–364)

KEY ELEMENTS

Key Terms

Derived demand, 349
Economic rent, 362
Financial capital, 358
Marginal revenue product, 349
Market activity, 355
Non-market activity, 355
Reservation wage, 356
Transfer earnings, 362

◆ Key Figures and Tables

Figure 14.1   Demand and Supply in a Factor
            Market, 347
Figure 14.2   Changes in Demand, 348
Figure 14.4   The Demand for Labour at Max's
            Wash 'n' Wax, 351
Figure 14.8   Economic Rent and Transfer
            Earnings, 363
Table 14.2   A Compact Glossary of Factor Market
            Terms, 352
Table 14.3   Two Conditions for Maximum Profit,
            353
Table 14.4   A Firm's Demand for Labour, 354

REVIEW QUESTIONS

1 Explain what happens to the price of a factor of production and its income if the following occurs:

   a There is an increase in demand for the factor.
   b There is an increase in supply of the factor.
   c There is a decrease in demand for the factor.
   d There is a decrease in supply of the factor.

2 Explain why the effect of a change in supply of a factor on a factor's income depends on the elasticity of demand for the factor.

3 Define marginal revenue product and distinguish between marginal revenue product and marginal revenue.

4 Why does marginal revenue product decline as the quantity of a factor employed increases?

5 What is the relationship between the demand curve for a factor of production and its marginal revenue product curve? Why?

6 Show that the condition for maximum profit in the product market – marginal cost equals marginal revenue – is equivalent to the condition for maximum profit in the factor market – marginal revenue product equals marginal cost of factor (equals factor price in a competitive factor market).

7 Review the main influences on the demand for a factor of production – the influences that shift the demand curve for a factor.

8 What determines the short-run and the long-run elasticity of demand for labour?

9 What determines the supply of labour?

10 Why might the supply of labour curve bend backward at a high enough wage rate?

11 What determines the supply of capital?

12 Define economic rent and transfer earnings and distinguish between these two components of income.

13 Suppose that a factor of production is in perfectly inelastic supply. If the marginal revenue product of the factor decreases, what happens to its price, quantity used, income, transfer earnings and rent of the factor?

PROBLEMS

1 Wanda owns a fish shop and employs students to pack the fish. Students can pack the following amounts of fish in an hour:

Number of students	Quantity of fish (kilograms)
1	20
2	50
3	90
4	120
5	145
6	165
7	180
8	190

a Draw the average and marginal product curves of these students.

b If Wanda can sell her fish for 50 pence a kilogram, draw the average and marginal revenue product curves.

c Draw Wanda's demand for labour curve.

2 The price of fish falls to 33 pence a kilogram, and fish packers' wages remain at £7.50 an hour.

a What happens to Wanda's average and marginal product curves?

b What happens to her average and marginal revenue product curves?

c What happens to her demand for labour curve?

d What happens to the number of students that she hires?

3 Fish packers' wages increase to £10 an hour but the price of fish remains at 50 pence a kilogram.

a What happens to Wanda's average and marginal revenue product curves?

b What happens to her demand curve for labour?

c How many packers does Wanda hire?

4 Using the information provided in Problem 4, calculate Wanda's marginal revenue and marginal cost, marginal revenue product and marginal cost of labour. Show that when Wanda is making maximum profit, marginal cost equals marginal revenue and marginal revenue product equals the marginal cost of labour.

5 You are given the following information about the labour market in an isolated town in the Amazon rain forest. Everyone works for logging companies, but there are many logging companies in the town. The market for logging workers is perfectly competitive. The town's labour supply is given as follows:

Wage rate (cruzeiros per hour)	Quantity of labour supplied (hours)
200	120
300	160
400	200
500	240
600	280
700	320
800	360

The market demand for labour from all the logging firms in the town is as follows:

Wage rate (cruzeiros per hour)	Quantity of labour demanded (hours)
200	400
300	360
400	320
500	280
600	240
700	200
800	160

a What is the competitive equilibrium wage rate and the quantity of labour employed?

b What is total labour income?

c How much of that labour income is economic rent and how much is transfer earnings? (You may find it easier to answer this question by drawing graphs of the demand and supply curves and then finding the economic rent and transfer earnings as areas on the graph in a manner similar to what was done in Fig. 14.8.)

6 Study *Reading Between the Lines* on pp. 360–361 and answer the following questions:

a What determines a football club's demand for top class strikers?

b How does a profit-maximizing football club determine the number of top class strikers to buy each year?

c Explain the likely impact on strikers' transfer fees of introducing new satellite sports programmes.

*'Men, like all animals, naturally multiply in
proportion to the means of their subsistence.'*

Adam Smith, THE WEALTH OF NATIONS

Running Out of Resources?

THE ISSUES AND IDEAS

Is there a limit to economic growth, or can we expand production and population without effective limit? One of the most influential answers to these questions was given by Thomas Robert Malthus in 1798. He believed that population, unchecked, would grow at a geometric rate – 1, 2, 4, 8, 16 ... – while the food supply would grow at an arithmetic rate – 1, 2, 3, 4, 5 .... To prevent the population from outstripping the available food supply, there would be periodic wars, famines and plagues. In Malthus's view, only a change in the moral code by which people live could prevent such periodic disasters.

As industrialization proceeded through the nineteenth century, Malthus's idea came to be applied to all natural resources, especially those that are exhaustible. A modern day Malthusian, ecologist Paul Ehrlich, believes that we are sitting on a 'population bomb' and that the government must limit both population growth and the resources that may be used each year.

In 1931, Harold Hotelling developed a theory of natural resources with different predictions from those of Malthus. The Hotelling Principle is that the relative price of an exhaustible natural resource will rise steadily, bringing a decline in the quantity used and an increase in the use of substitute resources.

Julian Simon, a contemporary economist, has challenged both the Malthusian gloom and the Hotelling Principle. He believes that *people* are the 'ultimate resource' and predicts that a rising population *lessens* the pressure on natural resources. A bigger population provides a larger number of resourceful people who can work out more efficient ways of using scarce resources. As these solutions are found, the prices of exhaustible resources actually fall. To demonstrate his point, in 1980 Simon bet Ehrlich that the prices of five metals – copper, chrome, nickel, tin and tungsten – would fall during the 1980s. Simon won the bet!

THEN ...

No matter whether it is agricultural land, an exhaustible natural resource, or the space in the centre of Manchester and no matter whether it is 1995 or, as shown here, 1914, there is a limit to what is available, and we persistently push against that limit. Economists see urban congestion as a consequence of the value of doing business in the city centre relative to the cost. They see the price mechanism, bringing ever higher rents and prices of raw materials, as the means of allocating and rationing scarce natural resources. Malthusians, in contrast, explain congestion as the consequence of population pressure, and they see the solution as population control.

In Tokyo, the pressure on space is so great that in some residential neighbourhoods, a parking space costs £1,000 a month. To economize on this expensive space – and to lower the cost of car ownership and hence boost car sales – Honda, Nissan and Toyota, three of Japan's big car producers, have developed a parking machine that enables two cars to occupy the space of one. The most basic of these machines costs just £7,500, less than 6 months' worth of parking fees.

THE ECONOMISTS: THOMAS ROBERT MALTHUS AND HAROLD HOTELLING JR

Thomas Robert Malthus

Thomas Robert Malthus (1766–1834), an English parson and professor, was an extremely influential social scientist. In his best-selling *Essay on the Principle of Population*, published in 1798, he argued that population growth would outstrip food production. Modern-day Malthusians believe that his basic idea was right and that it applies to all natural resources.

The most profound work on the economics of natural resources is that of Harold Hotelling (1895–1973). Hotelling worked as a journalist, schoolteacher and mathematical consultant before becoming an economics professor at Columbia University. He explained how the price mechanism allocated exhaustible resources, making them progressively more expensive. Their higher price encourages the development of new technologies, the discovery of new sources of supply and the development of substitutes.

Harold Hotelling Jr

CHAPTER 15

LABOUR
MARKETS

After studying this chapter you will be able to:

◆ Explain why skilled workers earn more, on the average, than unskilled workers

◆ Explain why university graduates earn more, on the average, than school leavers

◆ Explain why union workers earn higher wages than non-union workers

◆ Explain why, on the average, men earn more than women and whites earn more than minorities

◆ Predict the effects of equal pay and equal worth laws

A S YOU WELL KNOW, STUDYING IS NOT A PARTY. THOSE EXAMS AND PROBLEM-sets require a lot of time and effort. Are they worth the sweat that goes into them? What is the payoff? Is it sufficient to make up for the years of tuition, rents and lost wages? (You could, after all, be working now instead of slogging through this economics course.) ◆ Many workers belong to trade unions. Usually, union workers earn a higher wage than non-union workers in comparable jobs. Why? How are unions able to get higher wages for their members than non-union workers? ◆ Among the most visible and persistent differences in earnings are those between men and women and between whites and ethnic minorities. Women, on the average, earn hourly incomes that are 78 per cent of men's incomes in the United Kingdom. Non-white workers, on the average, earn hourly incomes that are 92 per cent of white workers' incomes in the United

The Sweat of Our Brows

Kingdom. Why do minorities and women so consistently earn less than white men? Is it because of discrimination and exploitation? Or is it because of economic factors? Or is it a combination of the two? ◆ Equal pay legislation was introduced in the United Kingdom in 1970. Since 1976, the law has required men and women who perform similar tasks to be paid the same rate. Does this type of legislation bring economic help to women and minorities?

◆ ◆ ◆ ◆ In this chapter, we answer these questions by continuing our study of labour markets. We begin by extending the competitive labour market model developed in Chapter 14 to analyse the effects of education and training on wages. We then study differences in union and non-union wages and in pay among men, women and minorities. Finally, we analyse the effects of equal pay legislation.

Skill Differentials

Differences in earnings between workers with varying levels of education and training can be explained using a model of competitive labour markets. In the real world, there are many different levels and varieties of education and training. To keep our analysis as clear as possible, we'll study a model economy in which there are just two different levels that result in two types of labour, what we will call skilled labour and unskilled labour. We'll study the demand for and supply of these two types of labour and see why there is a difference in their wages and what determines that difference. Let's begin by looking at the demand for the two types of labour.

The Demand for Skilled and Unskilled Labour

Skilled workers can perform a wide variety of tasks that unskilled workers would perform badly or perhaps could not even perform at all. Imagine an untrained, inexperienced person performing surgery or piloting an airplane. Skilled workers have a higher marginal revenue product than unskilled workers. As we learned in Chapter 14, the demand for labour curve is derived from the marginal revenue product curve. Other things remaining the same, the higher the marginal revenue product of labour, the greater is the demand for labour.

Figure 15.1(a) shows the demand curves for skilled and unskilled labour. At any given level of employment, firms are willing to pay a higher wage to a skilled worker than to an unskilled worker. The gap between the two wages is the difference between the marginal revenue products of a given number of skilled and unskilled workers. This difference is the marginal revenue product of skill. For example, at an employment level of 2,000 hours, firms are willing to pay $12.50 for a skilled worker and only $5 for an unskilled worker. The difference in the marginal revenue product of the two workers is $7.50 an hour. Thus the marginal revenue product of skill is $7.50 an hour.

The Supply of Skilled and Unskilled Labour

Skills are costly to acquire. Furthermore, a worker usually pays the cost of acquiring a skill before benefiting from a higher wage. For example, attending university usually leads to a higher income, but the higher income is not earned until after graduation. These facts imply that the acquisition of a skill is an investment. To emphasize the investment nature of acquiring a skill, we call that activity an investment in human capital. **Human capital** is the accumulated skill and knowledge that individuals acquire through learning, training, work and life experiences.

The opportunity cost of acquiring a skill includes actual expenditures on such things as tuition and room and board, and also costs in the form of lost or reduced earnings while the skill is being acquired. When a person studies full time, that cost is the total earnings forgone. However, some people acquire skills on the job. Such skill acquisition is called on-the-job training. Usually a worker undergoing on-the-job training is paid a lower wage than one doing a comparable job but not undergoing training. In such a case, the cost of acquiring the skill is the difference between the wage paid to a person not being trained and that paid to a person being trained.

Supply Curves of Skilled and Unskilled Labour

The position of the supply curve of skilled workers reflects the cost of acquiring the skill. Figure 15.1(b) shows two supply curves, one for skilled workers and the other for unskilled workers. The supply curve for skilled workers is S_S and for unskilled workers S_U.

The skilled worker's supply curve lies above the unskilled worker's supply curve. The vertical distance between the two supply curves is the compensation that skilled workers require for the cost of acquiring the skill. For example, suppose that the quantity of unskilled labour supplied is 2,000 hours at a wage rate of $5 an hour. This wage rate compensates the unskilled workers purely for their time on the job. Consider next the supply of skilled workers. To induce 2,000 hours of skilled labour to be supplied, firms must pay a wage rate of $8.50 an hour. This wage rate for skilled labour is higher than that for unskilled labour because skilled labour must be compensated not only for the time on the job but also for the time and other costs of acquiring the skill.

Wage Rates of Skilled and Unskilled Labour

To work out the wage rates of skilled and unskilled labour, all we have to do is bring together the effects of skill on the demand and supply of labour. Figure 15.1(c) shows the demand curves and the supply curves for skilled and unskilled labour. These curves are exactly the same as those plotted in parts (a) and (b). Equilibrium occurs in the market for unskilled labour where the supply and demand curves for unskilled labour intersect. The equilibrium wage rate is £5 an hour and the quantity of unskilled labour employed is 2,000 hours. Equilibrium in the market for skilled workers occurs where the supply and demand curves for skilled workers intersect. The equilibrium wage rate is £10 an hour and the quantity of skilled labour employed is 3,000 hours.

As you can see in part (c), the equilibrium wage rate of skilled labour is higher than that of unskilled labour. There are two reasons why this occurs. First, skilled labour has a higher marginal revenue product than unskilled labour, so at a given wage rate the demand for skilled labour is greater than the demand for unskilled labour; second, skills are costly to acquire so that at a given wage rate the

supply of skilled labour is less than the supply of unskilled labour. The wage differential (in this case £5 an hour) depends on both the marginal revenue product of the skill and the cost of acquiring it. The higher the marginal revenue product of the skill, the larger is the vertical distance between the demand curves for skilled and unskilled labour. The more costly it is to acquire a skill, the larger is the vertical distance between the supplies of skilled and unskilled labour. The higher the marginal revenue product of the skill and the more costly it is to acquire, the larger is the wage differential between skilled and unskilled workers.

UK MPs voted themselves a 26 per cent pay rise in July 1996, raising their salaries to £43,000 a year. They argued that their pay did not reflect differentials seen in the private sector. The increase would reward the high level of marginal revenue product from the specialist skills needed by an MP and the high cost of gaining those skills – an alternative

---

FIGURE 15.1

Skill Differentials

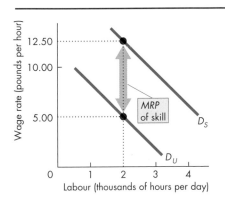

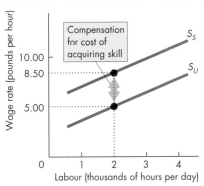

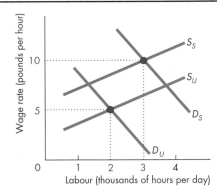

(a) Demand for skilled and unskilled labour

(b) Supply of skilled and unskilled labour

(c) Markets for skilled and unskilled labour

Part (a) illustrates the marginal revenue product of skill. Unskilled workers have a marginal revenue product that gives rise to the demand curve marked D_U. Skilled workers have a higher marginal revenue product than unskilled workers. Therefore the demand curve for skilled workers, D_S, lies to the right of D_U. The vertical distance between these two curves is the marginal revenue product of the skill.

Part (b) shows the effects of the cost of acquiring skills on the supply curves of labour. The supply curve for unskilled workers is S_U. Skilled workers have to incur costs in order to acquire their skills. Therefore they would only supply labour services at a wage rate that exceeds that of unskilled labour. The supply curve for skilled workers is S_S.

The vertical distance between these two curves is the required compensation for the cost of acquiring a skill.

Part (c) shows the determination of the equilibrium levels of employment and the skilled/unskilled wage differential. Unskilled workers earn a wage rate of £5 an hour, at which the quantities demanded and supplied of unskilled workers are equal. The employment level of unskilled workers is 2,000 hours. Skilled workers earn the wage rate £10 an hour where the quantities demanded and supplied of skilled workers are equal. The employment level of skilled workers is 3,000 hours. Wages for skilled workers are always greater than those for unskilled workers.

'I earn too much to kiss babies'

© Jeremy Banks, *Financial Times*, 27 May 1996

FIGURE 15.2

Education, Age and Real Earnings

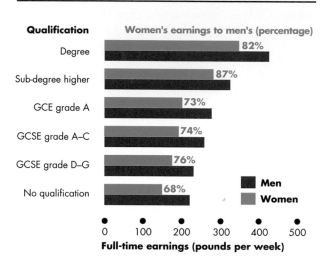

(a) Qualifications and earnings for men and women

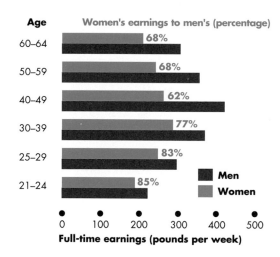

(b) Age and earnings for men and women

career forgone. Of course, not all of the duties of an MP require a great deal of skill as you can see from the cartoon.

Do Education and Training Pay?

There are large and persistent differences in earnings based on the degree of education and training. An indication of those differences in the United Kingdom can be seen in part (a) of Fig. 15.2. It shows that the higher the level of education, other things remaining the same, the higher are earnings for both men and women. The percentages indicate women's earnings as a percentage of men's earnings. Men earn more than women on average at all qualification levels but the gap between men's and women's earnings is lower at higher levels of qualifications. Most people finish their education by the time they are 25, so do earnings increase with age? The link between age and earnings is shown in part (b) of Fig. 15.2. You can see that earnings rise with age up to middle age and then decline. Men earn more than women in all age groups but the gap is greatest between the ages of 40 and 49. This is because age is also correlated with experience and the degree of on-the-job training up to middle age. The gap between men's and women's earnings increases because women take periods away from work to raise children, reducing their years of experience and on-the-job training in middle age.

We can see from part (a) of Fig. 15.2 that going through school, university and postgraduate education leads to higher incomes. But do they pay in the

Part (a) shows full-time weekly earnings for men and women in 1993 by qualification. Earnings increase with the amount of education for men and women. The gap between men's and women's earnings declines with higher levels of qualifications. Part (b) shows full-time weekly earnings for men and women in full-time work in 1995 by age. Men earn more than women at all ages but the gap widens with age up to middle age. Beyond that age, earnings decrease for both men and women more equally.

Source: (a) Office of Population Censuses and Surveys, *General Household Survey, 1993*, London, HMSO, 1995. (b) Department of Employment, 'Labour Force Survey', *Employment Gazette*, March 1996.

sense of yielding a higher income that compensates for the cost of education and for the delay in the start of earnings? For most people, college or university does pay. Rates of return have been estimated to be in the range of 5–10 per cent a year after allowing for inflation, which suggests that a university degree is a better investment than almost any other.

Education is an important source of earnings differences. But there are others. One is the activities of trade unions. Let's see how unions affect wages and why, on the average, union wages exceed non-union wages.

Union–Non-union Wage Differentials

A union is an organized group of workers who aim to increase wages and influence other job conditions. A union acts in the labour market like a monopolist in the product market. The union seeks to restrict competition and, as a result, increases the price at which labour is traded. A compact glossary on labour relations can be found in Table 15.1.

There are two main types of unions: trade (or craft) unions and industrial unions. A **trade union** is a group of workers who have similar skills, but may work in many different firms and in different industries. This is the most common type of union in the United Kingdom. Because of this, a large-scale employer may have to deal with many unions at a time during negotiation. An **industrial union** is a group of workers who have a variety of skills and job types but work for the same firm or industry. Industrial unions are most commonly found in the United States and in Germany. They allow an industry-wide agreement to be made through negotiation with just one union.

A union can be organized as an open shop or a closed shop. An *open shop* is an arrangement in which workers can be employed without joining the union – there is no union restriction on who can work in the 'shop'. In an open shop, non-union members may belong to other professional organizations and are not represented by the union. However, non-union staff usually receive the same benefits as union staff after a dispute, even if they have not participated in any action. A closed shop is an arrangement in which only union members can be employed by a firm. This arrangement was pre-

TABLE 15.1

A Compact Glossary on Labour Relations

Arbitration	When parties to a dispute accept the determination of wages and other employment conditions by a third party (an arbitrator)
Collective bargaining	Negotiations between representatives of employers and unions on wages and conditions
Corporatist bargaining	Collective bargaining at the national level between unions and employer federations, with government, for national wages and conditions
Decentralized bargaining	Collective bargaining, at the local level between unions and employers, for local wages and conditions
Employer federation	An organization of employer representatives which provides a service to its members and acts as the national voice of employers. The Confederation of British Industries is an example
Industrial union	An organized group of workers with different skills and job types that attempts to increase wages and improve conditions for its members within that industry
Lockout	When a firm will not allow its employees access to the workplace
Trade union	An organized group of workers with similar skills and job types that attempts to increase wages and improve conditions for its members in that trade
Open shop	A place of work that has no union restriction on who can work in it; here, the union bargains for its members but not for non-members
Strike	When a group of employees refuse to work under the exisiting conditions
Union federation	An organization of union representatives which provides a service to its members and acts as the national voice of unions. The Trades Union Congress is an example

ferred by unions as it strengthened the power of the union in a dispute with employers. Closed shops virtually disappeared in the United Kingdom as a result of the 1980 Employment Act.

Unions negotiate with employers or their representatives in a process called **collective bargaining.** Countries like the United Kingdom use a process of *decentralized bargaining*, where individual employers and local union representatives negotiate local wages and conditions. Countries like Sweden adopt a *corporatist bargaining* process. In this process, the government brings employer and union representatives together at the national level to negotiate national wage structures and conditions. The parties in corporatist bargaining are employer federations, union federations and government. Federations have affiliated members and aim to represent their views to the public and in national negotiation, as well as providing information services to their members. The Confederation of British Industries (CBI) is the main employer federation and the Trades Union Congress (TUC) is the union federation in the United Kingdom.

The main weapons available to the union and the employer in collective bargaining are the strike and the lockout. A *strike* is a group decision to refuse to work under prevailing conditions. A *lockout* is a firm's refusal to operate its plant and pay its workers. Each party uses the threat of a strike or a lockout to try to get an agreement in its own favour. Sometimes when the two parties in the collective bargaining process cannot agree on the wage rate and other conditions of employment, they agree to submit their disagreement to binding arbitration. *Arbitration* is a process in which a third party – an arbitrator – determines wages and other employment conditions on behalf of the negotiating parties. The decision of the arbitrator may be binding or subject to voluntary agreement.

There are about 243 unions in the United Kingdom. The smallest has fewer than 100 members and the largest, Unison, the public sector union, has nearly 1.4 million members. Most of the larger unions are members of the TUC. Figure 15.3 shows that the number of unions in the United Kingdom has declined during this century. At its peak, in 1921, there were more than 1,300 separate unions. Union membership, by contrast, has increased over most of this century. It was at its highest in the United Kingdom in 1979, when more than a half the labour force, 13.3 million people, were members of trade unions. Since then, there has been a steady decline

in union membership to its current level of 8.3 million members. There are two main reasons for the recent decline in membership. The first is the decline in the proportion of total employment of the traditional industries such as shipbuilding, coal and steel on which the union movement developed. New jobs have been created in the expanding services sectors, but many of these are part-time and taken up by women. Part-timers and women did not believe unions served their interests in the past. The second is the impact of technology on production processes. Robotics and computer-controlled production have cut employment and reduced the power of union members to halt production in a dispute. The introduction of flexible work practices and no-union agreements have also undermined traditional union practices.

Professional associations are not unions in a legal sense, but they act like unions. A *professional association* is an organized group of professional workers such as doctors, lawyers and accountants (an example is the British Medical Association – BMA). Professional associations control entry into the professions and license practitioners, ensuring the adherence to minimum standards of competence. They also influence the level of wages and conditions for their members.

Unions' Objectives and Constraints

A union has three broad objectives that it strives to achieve for its members:

1. To increase compensation
2. To improve working conditions
3. To expand job opportunities

Each of these objectives contains a series of more detailed goals. For example, in seeking to increase the compensation of its members, a union operates on a variety of fronts: wage rates, fringe benefits, retirement pay and such things as holiday allowances. In seeking to improve working conditions, a union is concerned with occupational health and safety as well as the environmental quality of the workplace. In seeking to expand job opportunities, a union tries to obtain greater job security for existing union members and to find ways of creating additional jobs for them.

A union's ability to pursue its objectives is restricted by two sets of constraints – one on the supply side and the other on the demand side of

FIGURE 15.3

Union Numbers and Union Membership

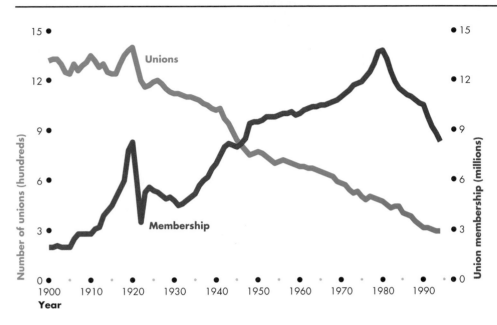

The number of unions in the United Kingdom has declined steadily over this century, peaking in the early 1920s when there were more than 1,300 individual unions compared with just 243 in 1994. By contrast, union membership increased steadily to a peak in 1979 with 13.3 million, but then declined to its current level of 8.3 million members. The number of unions has declined as smaller unions have merged, and the largest seven unions now account for 59 per cent of union membership.

Source: Central Statistical Office, *Labour Market Trends*, p. 50, London, HMSO, February 1996.

the labour market. On the supply side, the union's activities are limited by how well it can restrict non-union workers from offering their labour in the same market. The larger the fraction of the workforce controlled by the union, the more effective the union can be. If the union is unable to restrict entry, such as in the market for bar and nightclub staff, it cannot have any effect. At the other extreme, unions in the construction industry can influence the number of people obtaining skills as electricians, plasterers and carpenters, and so can better pursue their goals. Those best able to restrict supply are the professional associations for such groups as doctors, lawyers and accountants. These groups control the number of qualified workers by controlling either the examinations that new entrants must pass or entrance into professional degree programmes.

On the demand side of the labour market, the constraint facing a union is the fact that it cannot force firms to hire more labour than the quantity that maximizes their profits. Anything that increases the wage rate or other employment costs decreases the quantity of labour demanded. Unless the union can take actions that shift the demand curve for the

labour that it represents, it has to accept the fact that a higher wage rate can be obtained only at the price of lower employment. For this reason, unions try to make the demand for their union labour inelastic as well as to increase the demand for it. Some of the methods employed by unions are:

1. To encourage import restrictions
2. To support minimum wage laws
3. To increase demand for the good produced
4. To increase the marginal product of union members

One of the best examples of import restrictions in the United Kingdom is the support by the National Union of Mineworkers for restrictions on imports of foreign coal. Unions support minimum wage laws in order to increase the cost of employing unskilled labour. An increase in the wage rate of unskilled labour leads to a decrease in the quantity demanded of unskilled labour and to an increase in demand for skilled union labour, a substitute for unskilled labour. An increase in the demand for the good produced increases the demand for union labour because the demand for labour is a derived demand. Good examples are attempts by textiles and car unions to encourage their own workers as well as the public to buy British. Increasing the marginal product of union members directly shifts the demand curve for their services. Unions use apprenticeship, training and professional certification to increase the marginal product of their members.

Unions in a Competitive Labour Market

When a union operates in an otherwise competitive labour market, it seeks to increase wages and other compensation and to limit employment reductions by increasing demand for the labour of its members.

Figure 15.4 illustrates a labour market. The demand curve is D_C and the supply curve is S_C. If

FIGURE 15.4

A Union in a Competitive Labour Market

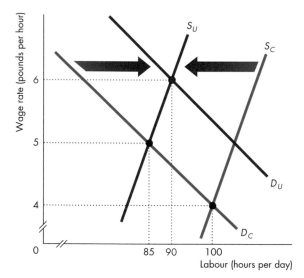

In a competitive labour market, the demand curve is D_C and the supply curve is S_C. Competitive equilibrium occurs at a wage rate of £4 an hour with 100 hours employed. By restricting employment below its competitive level, the union shifts the supply of labour to S_U. If the union can do no more than that, the wage rate will increase to £5 an hour, but employment will fall to 85 hours. If the union can increase the demand for labour (by increasing the demand for the good produced by the union members or by raising the price of substitute labour) and shift the demand curve to D_U, then it can increase the wage rate still more to £6 an hour and achieve employment of 90 hours.

the market is a competitive one with no union, the wage rate is £4 an hour and 100 hours of labour will be employed. Suppose that a union is formed to organize the workers in this market and that the union has sufficient control over the supply of labour to be able to artificially restrict that supply below its competitive level – to S_U. If that is all the union does, employment will fall to 85 hours of labour and the wage rate will rise to £5 an hour. If the union can also take steps that increase the demand for labour to D_U, it can achieve an even bigger increase in the wage rate with a smaller fall in employment. By maintaining the restricted labour supply at S_U, the union increases the wage rate to £6 an hour and achieves an employment level of 90 hours of labour.

Because a union restricts the supply of labour in the market in which it operates, its actions increase the supply of labour in non-union markets. Those who can't get union jobs must look elsewhere for work. This increase in supply in non-union markets lowers the wage rate in those markets and further widens the union–non-union differential. But low non-union wages decrease the demand for union labour and limit the increase in wages that unions can achieve. For this reason, unions are strong supporters of minimum wage laws that keep non-union wages high and limit the incentive to use non-union labour.

Let's now turn our attention to the case in which employers have considerable influence in the labour market.

Monopsony

A **monopsony** is a market structure in which there is just a single buyer. With the growth of large-scale production over the last century, large organisations such as coal mines, steel and textile mills, and car manufacturers became the major employer of labour in some regions, and in some places a single firm employed almost all the labour. Such a firm has some monopsony power.

A monopsony can make a bigger profit than a group of firms that have to compete with each other for their labour. Figure 15.5 illustrates how a monopsony operates. The monopsony's marginal revenue product curve is *MRP*. This curve tells us the extra revenue from selling the output produced by the last hour of labour hired. The curve labelled *S* is the supply curve of labour. This curve tells us how many hours are supplied at each wage rate. It also tells us the minimum wage that is acceptable at each level of labour supplied.

In deciding how much labour to hire, the monopsony recognizes that to hire more labour it must pay a higher wage or, equivalently, by hiring less labour the monopsony can get away with paying a lower wage. The monopsony takes account of this fact when calculating its marginal cost of labour. The marginal cost of labour is shown by the curve *MCL*. The relationship between the marginal cost of labour curve and the supply curve is similar to the relationship between the marginal cost and average total cost curves that you studied in Chapter 10. The supply curve is like the average total cost of labour curve. For example, in Fig. 15.5 the firm can hire 50 hours of labour at £5 an hour, so its average total cost is £5 an hour. The total cost of labour is £5 an hour multiplied by 50 hours, which equals £250 an hour. But suppose that the firm hires slightly less than 50 hours of labour, say 49 hours. The wage rate at which 49 hours of labour can be hired is just below £4.90 an hour. The firm's total labour cost is £240. Hiring the fiftieth hour of labour increases the total cost of labour from £240 to £250, which is £10. The curve *MCL* shows the £10 marginal cost of hiring the fiftieth hour of labour.

To calculate the profit-maximizing quantity of labour to hire, the firm sets the marginal cost of labour equal to the marginal revenue product of labour. That is, the firm wants the cost of the last worker hired to equal the extra revenue brought in. In Fig. 15.5, this outcome occurs when the monopsony employs 50 hours of labour. What is the wage rate that the monopsony pays? To hire 50 hours of labour, the firm must pay £5 an hour, as shown by the supply of labour curve. The marginal revenue product of labour, however, is £10 an hour, which means that the firm makes an economic profit of £5 on the last hour of labour that it hires. Each worker is paid £5 an hour.

Compare this outcome with that in a competitive labour market. If the labour market shown in Fig. 15.5 were competitive, equilibrium would occur at the point of intersection of the demand curve and the supply curve. The wage rate would be £7.50 an hour and 75 hours of labour a day would be employed. So, compared with a competitive labour market, a monopsony decreases both the wage rate and the level of employment.

The ability of a monopsony to lower the wage rate and employment level and make an economic profit depends on the elasticity of labour supply.

FIGURE 15.5

A Monopsony Labour Market

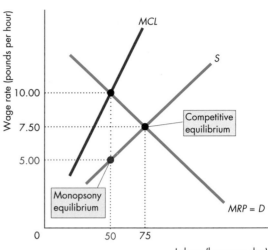

A monopsony is a market structure in which there is a single buyer. A monopsony in the labour market which has a marginal revenue product curve *MRP* faces a labour curve *S*. The marginal cost of labour curve is *MCL*. Profit is maximized by making the marginal cost of labour equal to marginal revenue product. The monopsony hires 50 hours of labour and pays the lowest wage for which that labour will work, £5 an hour.

If a union enters the market, it will attempt to increase the wage rate to above £5 an hour. If the union is all powerful, the highest wage it can achieve is £10 an hour. If the union and the firm are equally powerful they will bargain and agree to a wage rate of £7.50 an hour – the wage rate that equally splits the difference between marginal revenue product and the lowest wage for which labour will work.

The more elastic the supply of labour, the less opportunity a monopsony has to cut wages and employment and make an economic profit.

Monopsony Tendencies   With today's low costs of transport, it is unlikely that many pure monopsonies remain. Workers can easily commute long distances to a job, and so for most people there is not just one potential employer. But some firms do have a monopsony tendency. That is, while they are not pure monopsonies, they face an upward-sloping supply of labour curve and their marginal cost of labour exceeds the wage rate. Monopsony tendencies arise in isolated communities in which a single firm is the main employer. But in such situations there is also, usually, a union. Let's see how a union interacts with a monopsony.

Monopsony and Unions   When we studied monopoly in Chapter 12, we discovered that a single seller in a market is able to determine the price in that market. We have just studied monopsony – a market with a single buyer – and discovered that in such a market the buyer is able to determine the price. Suppose that a union starts to operate in a monopsony labour market. A union is like a monopoly. It controls the supply of labour and acts like a single seller of labour. If the union (monopoly seller) faces a monopsony buyer, the situation is one of **bilateral monopoly**. In bilateral monopoly, the wage rate is determined by bargaining between the two sides. Let's study the bargaining process.

In Fig. 15.5, if the monopsony is free to determine the wage rate and the level of employment, it hires 50 hours of labour for a wage rate of £5 an hour. But suppose that a union represents the workers and can, if necessary, call a strike. Also suppose that the union agrees to maintain employment at 50 hours, but seeks the highest wage rate the employer can be forced to pay. That wage rate is £10 an hour. That is, the wage rate equals the marginal revenue product of labour. It is unlikely that the union will get the wage rate up to £10 an hour. But it is also unlikely that the firm will keep the wage rate down to £5 an hour. The monopsony firm and the union will bargain over the wage rate and the result will be an outcome between £10 an hour (the maximum that the union can achieve) and £5 an hour (the minimum that the firm can achieve).

The actual outcome of the bargaining depends on the costs that each party can inflict on the other as a result of a failure to agree on the wage rate. The firm can shut down the plant and lock out its workers, and the workers can shut down the plant by striking. Each party knows the strength of the other and knows what it will lose if it does not agree to the demands of the other. If the two parties are equally strong, and they realize it, they will split the difference and agree to a wage rate of £7.50 an hour. If one party is stronger than the other – and both parties know it – the agreed wage will favour the stronger party. Usually, an agreement is reached without a strike or a lockout. The threat – the knowledge that such an event can occur – is usually enough to bring the bargaining parties to an agreement. When strikes or lockouts do occur, it is usually because each party has misjudged the costs the other can inflict.

Monopsony has an interesting implication for the effects of minimum wage laws. Let's now study these effects.

Monopsony and the Minimum Wage

A **minimum wage** that exceeds the equilibrium wage in a competitive labour market decreases employment (see Chapter 6, pp. 127–130). A minimum wage in a monopsony labour market can *increase* both the wage rate and employment. Let's see how.

Minimum Wages and Monopsony   Suppose that the labour market is that shown in Fig. 15.6 and that the wage rate is £5 an hour with 50 hours of labour employed. The government now passes a minimum wage law that prohibits anyone from hiring labour for less than £7.50 an hour. Firms can hire labour for £7.50 an hour or more but not for less than that wage. The monopsony in Fig. 15.6 now faces a perfectly elastic supply of labour at £7.50 an hour up to 75 hours. Above 75 hours, a higher wage than £7.50 an hour must be paid to hire additional hours of labour. Because the wage rate is a fixed £7.50 an hour up to 75 hours, the marginal cost of labour is also constant at £7.50 up to 75 hours. Beyond 75 hours, the marginal cost of labour rises above £7.50 an hour. To maximize profit, the monopsony sets the marginal cost of labour equal to its marginal revenue product. That is, the monopsony hires 75 hours of labour at £7.50 an hour. The minimum wage law has made the supply of labour perfectly elastic and made the marginal cost of labour the same as the wage rate up to 75 hours. The law has not affected the supply of labour curve or the marginal cost of labour at employment levels above 75 hours. The minimum wage law has succeeded in raising the wage rate by £2.50 an hour and raising the amount of labour employed by 25 hours.

The Scale of Union–Non-union Wage Differentials

We have seen that unions can influence the wages of their members partly by restricting the supply of labour and partly by increasing the demand for labour. How much of a difference to wage rates do unions make in practice? How big is the union mark-up over non-union wages?

Estimates of the union mark-up in the United Kingdom suggest that it was about 3.8 per cent in the

FIGURE 15.6

Minimum Wage in Monopsony

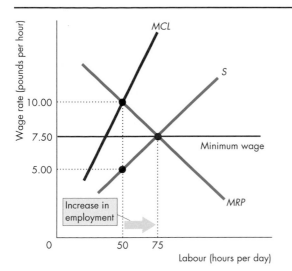

In a monopsony labour market the wage rate is £5 an hour. If a minimum wage law increases the wage rate to £7.50 an hour, employment increases to 75 hours.

early 1960s but increased steadily to a peak of 8.8 per cent in 1982. Since then the mark-up has remained positive but has decreased to between 5 and 6 per cent. It is not clear that all of this mark-up is a result of union activities. In times of high unemployment, union workers lose their jobs and add to the non-union labour supply. This reduces wages in the non-union sector and increases the mark-up. Also, in some industries, union wages are higher than non-union wages because union members do jobs that involve greater skill. Even without a union, those who perform such tasks receive a higher wage.

R E V I E W

◆ Differences in earnings based on skill or education level arise because skilled labour has a higher marginal revenue product than unskilled labour and because skills are costly to acquire.

◆ Union workers have higher wage rates than non-union workers because a union is able to control the supply of labour and, indirectly, influence the marginal revenue product of its members.

Wage Differentials Between Sexes and Races

W e have already seen from Fig. 15.2 that men earn more than women across all age groups and qualification levels. White male workers earn more on average than all other workers whatever their gender or race. White male full-time workers earned £8 an hour on average in 1994, 12 per cent more than men from ethnic minorities. While white female full-time workers earned more than their female ethnic minority counterparts, the differential was much smaller than for men.

Why do these differentials exist? Do they arise because there is discrimination against women and members of minority races, or is there some other explanation? These controversial questions generate an enormous amount of passion. It is not our intention to make you angry, but that may happen as an unintended consequence of this discussion. The objective of this section is to show you how to use economic analysis to address controversial and emotionally charged issues.

We are going to examine four possible explanations for these earnings differences:

1. Job types
2. Discrimination
3. Human capital differences
4. Degrees of specialization

Job Types

Some of the difference in men's and women's wages arises from the fact that men and women do different jobs and, for the most part, men's jobs are better paid than women's jobs. But there are increasing numbers of women entering areas that were traditionally the preserve of men. This trend is particularly clear in professions such as architecture, medicine, management, law and accounting. The percentage of total enrolments in university courses in these subjects for women has increased from less than 20 per cent in 1970 to 50 per cent in some cases, such as medicine, today. Women are also increasingly seen as bus drivers, police officers and construction workers, all jobs that traditionally were done mainly by men.

The pattern of occupational structures over time is shown in Fig. 15.7. One reason why men have earned more than women on the average is that a higher proportion of men had higher-paid work in professional or senior managerial jobs and skilled work. As a result, a smaller proportion of men had poorly paid unskilled work. However, the pattern is changing. A growing proportion of women now have higher-paid managerial jobs compared with 1975. As a result, a smaller proportion of women than men now have low-paid skilled or unskilled work. This has had an impact – reducing the gap between men's and women's earnings since 1975.

But there are many situations in which women and minorities earn less than white men, even when they do essentially the same job. One possible reason is that women and minorities are discriminated against. Let's see how discrimination might affect wage rates.

Discrimination

To see how **discrimination** can affect earnings, let's look at a simple model to examine an example – the market for investment advisers. Suppose that there are two groups of investment advisers who are identical in their skills at picking good investments. One group consists of black females and the other of white males. Figure 15.8(a) shows the supply curve of black females, S_{BF}, and Fig. 15.8(b) shows the supply curve of white males, S_{WM}. These supply curves are identical. The marginal revenue product of investment advisers, whether they are black female or white male, is also identical, as shown by the two curves labelled *MRP* in parts (a) and (b). (Their revenues are the fees their customers pay for investment advice.)

Suppose that everyone in this society is free of prejudice about race and sex. The market for black female investment advisers determines a wage rate of £40,000 a year, and there are 2,000 black female investment advisers. The white male investment adviser market also determines a wage rate of £40,000 a year, and there are 2,000 white male investment advisers.

In contrast to the situation just described, suppose that the customers of investment houses are prejudiced against women and against members of racial minorities. The two types of investment advisers are equally able, as before, but the degree of prejudice is so strong that the customers are not willing to pay as much for investment advice given by a black female as they will pay for advice from a white male. Because of the differences in the amounts that

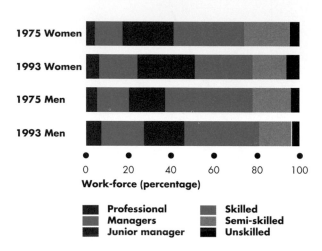

FIGURE 15.7

Occupational Differences

1975 Women

1993 Women

1975 Men

1993 Men

0   20   40   60   80   100

Work-force (percentage)

■ **Professional**   ▨ **Skilled**
▨ **Managers**   ▨ **Semi-skilled**
▨ **Junior manager**   ■ **Unskilled**

In 1975 a higher proportion of men had higher-paid work in professional or senior managerial jobs and skilled work than women. A smaller proportion of men had poorly paid unskilled work. By 1993, a larger proportion of women had higher-paid managerial jobs and a smaller proportion of women than men had low-paid skilled or unskilled work. This has reduced the gap between men's and women's earnings since 1975.

Source: Office of Population Censuses and Surveys, *General Household Survey, 1993*, London, HMSO, 1995.

people are willing to pay, based purely on their prejudices, the marginal revenue products of the two groups are different. The ability of the two groups is the same but the value that prejudiced consumers place on their outputs is not the same. Suppose that the marginal revenue product of black females, when discriminated against, is the line labelled $MRP_{DA} - DA$ standing for discriminated against. Suppose that the marginal revenue product of white males, the group discriminated in favour of, is $MRP_{DF} - DF$ standing for discriminated in favour of. Given these marginal revenue product curves, the markets for the two groups of investment advisers will now determine very different wages and employment levels. Black females will earn £20,000 a year and only 1,000 will work as investment advisers. White males will earn £60,000 a year and 3,000 of them will work as investment advisers. Thus, purely on the basis of the prejudice of the demanders of investment advice, black women will earn one-third of the wages of

FIGURE 15.8

Discrimination

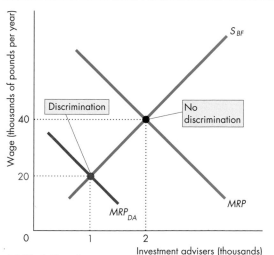

(a) Black females

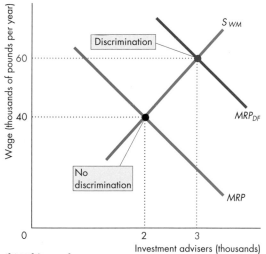

(b) White males

The supply curve for black female investment advisers is S_{BF} in part (a), and the supply curve for white male investment advisers is S_{WM} in part (b). If the marginal revenue product of both groups of investment advisers is MRP (the same curve in each part), then the equilibrium wage rate for each group is £40,000 a year and 2,000 of each type of adviser are employed. If there is discrimination against blacks and women, the marginal revenue product curve is to the left of the original curve. It is the curve labelled MRP_{DA} – DA standing for discriminated against. There is discrimination in favour of white males, so their marginal revenue product curve is MRP_{DF} – DF standing for discriminated in favour of. The wage rate for black women falls to £20,000 a year and only 1,000 are employed. The wage rate for white males increases to £60,000 a year and 3,000 are employed.

white men, and three-quarters of all investment advisers will be white men and only one-quarter will be black women.

We've just examined a hypothetical example of how prejudice can produce differences in earnings. Economists disagree about whether prejudice actually causes wage differentials, and one line of reasoning suggests that it does not. In the example, the customers who buy from white men pay a higher service charge for investment advice than the customers who buy from black women. This price difference acts as an incentive to limit discrimination and encourages people who are prejudiced to buy from the people whom they are prejudiced against. This force could be so strong as to eliminate the effects of discrimination altogether. Suppose, as is true in manufacturing, that a firm's customers never meet its workers. If a manufacturing firm discriminated against women or minorities, it would not be able to compete with firms which hired these groups. So only those firms that do not discriminate are able to survive in a competitive industry. This line of reasoning suggests a test for discrimination. Customers who discriminate against women and minorities must pay a higher price for the services they buy from white males than the prices paid by those willing to buy from women and minorities. And firms that discriminate must make lower profit than those that do not.

But while you can recognize prejudice when you see it, you cannot easily measure it objectively. The model we've studied shows that sex and race differentials might come from prejudice. But without a way of directly measuring prejudice, we cannot test that model in a completely convincing way to see whether it is true.

We need to make another point as well. Our model of prejudice, like all economic models, is in an equilibrium, albeit an unhappy one. But simply because a model is in equilibrium does not mean that such a real situation is either desirable or inevitable. Economic theory makes predictions about the way things will be, not moral statements about the way things ought to be. Policies designed to bring equal wages and employment prospects to women and minorities can be devised. But to be successful, such policies must be based on careful economic analysis. Good intentions are not enough to bring about equality.

A further source of wage rate differences lies in differences in human capital. Let's now examine the effects of human capital on wage rates.

Pay Differentials between Men and Women

The Essence of the Story

THE FINANCIAL TIMES, 17 JULY 1995

Women win when it comes to rises

Richard Donkin

Women executives have received higher pay awards than men in the past year, a report says today, ...which analyses pay awards of just over 4,500 executives in 300 companies. It says male executives had median pay rises of 4.1 per cent compared with 3.5 per cent in the previous 12 months. Women had median increases of 5 per cent compared with 4.1 per cent.

'A number of employers have made conscious attempts to bring women's pay more in line with men's and some companies have accelerated the promotion opportunities for female high-flyers, recognising an imbalance in the male/female ratio at management level,' said Mr Andy Christie, remuneration director at Sedgwick Noble Lowndes.

The high awards for women 'may simply reflect that they are performing better than men', he said.

In spite of the evidence of more generous awards for women, it seems to be making little difference to pay differentials. Male departmental managers received an average base salary of £38,571, while women at the same level received £35,199 on average, a 10 per cent gap.

The differential increases as jobs become more senior. A man at the level of function head could expect to earn £48,145 on average where a woman in the same job would get 15 per cent less.

Mr Christie suggested the reason for continuing higher differentials was that women entering senior management tended to come from a lower pay base.

■ Female executives received higher pay rises than men for the second year running in 1995 according to a new survey of 4,500 executives.

■ Female executives had median pay rises of 5 per cent in 1995 compared with just 4.1 per cent for male executives.

■ Some companies have made a deliberate effort to close the gender gap in executive pay, but another reason may be that women are simply performing better than men.

■ Despite the higher pay rises for females, male departmental managers receive 10 per cent more and male senior executives receive 15 per cent more than their female counterparts. This may be because women enter management with a lower pay base.

Economic Analysis

■ Figure 1 shows the continuing difference in male and female salaries may be explained by differences in skill levels when entering management.

■ The demand for male executives, D_M, is higher than the demand for female executives, D_F, reflecting a higher skill level and hence marginal revenue product (MRP) for male executives.

■ For the same quantity of labour hours hired per year, Q_0, males receive higher salaries than females.

■ Figure 2 shows that the higher rise in female executive pay in 1995 may be because of better performance and rising skills relative to males.

■ In part (a), male executives' performance rises from MRP_{M94} to MRP_{M95}, and their salaries rise 4.1 per cent to £38,571. In part (b), female executives' performance rises further from MRP_{F94} to MRP_{F95}, leading to a 5 per cent rise in salary to £35,199.

■ Salary differentials may be caused by discrimination as shown in Fig. 3. If the supply of male and female executives is the same, the combined supply is S_C and the combined MRP is MRP_C. 200,000 hours of executive labour are hired, 100,000 male and 100,000 female hours at the same salary of £36,500.

■ With discrimination, the MRP is higher for males and lower for females, so that 150,000 hours of male time is hired at a salary of £38,000, and only 50,000 hours of female time is hired at a salary of £35,000.

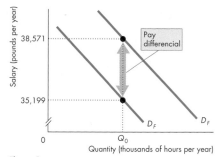

Figure 1

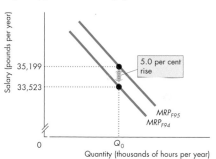

Figure 2(a) Male executive pay

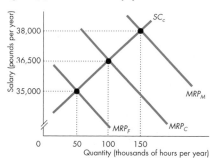

Figure 2(b) Female executive pay

Figure 3

Human Capital Differences

Wages are compensation in part for time spent on the job and in part for the cost incurred in acquiring skill – *human capital*. The more human capital a person possesses, the more that person earns, other things remaining the same. It is impossible to measure human capital precisely but there are some rough indicators. The three most useful indicators are:

1. Years of schooling
2. Years of work experience
3. Number of job interruptions

Years of work experience and job interruptions are interrelated, as we saw in Fig. 15.2. For people of a given age and given amount of schooling, a person who has had fewer job interruptions has usually had more years of work experience. But interruptions to a career disrupt and reduce the effectiveness of job experience, slow down the accumulation of human capital, and even sometimes result in the depreciation of human capital through its lack of use. Historically and today, job interruptions are more serious for women than for men. Traditionally, women's careers have been interrupted for bearing and rearing children. It is estimated that women give up £200,000 of income, on the average, over their working lives rearing two children at home. This factor is a possible source of lower wages, on the average, for women. But just as education differences are virtually disappearing, so career interruptions for women are becoming less common. Maternity leave and day-care facilities are providing an increasing number of women with uninterrupted employment that makes their human capital accumulation more similar to that of men.

Thus it seems that human capital differences possibly can account for earnings differentials among races and sexes in the past and some of the differentials that still remain. The trends, however, suggest that wage differentials from this source will eventually disappear.

There is one final source of earnings differences that is likely to affect women's incomes adversely: the relative degree of specialization of women and men.

Degrees of Specialization

People undertake two kinds of production activities. They supply labour services to the market (market activities) and they undertake household production (non-market activities). *Household production* creates goods and services to be consumed within the household rather than to be supplied to the market. Such activities include cooking, cleaning, minor repair work, education, shopping and various organizational services such as arranging holidays and leisure activities. Bearing and rearing children is another important non-market activity.

In Chapter 3, we discovered that people can gain from specializing in particular activities and trading their output with each other. Specialization and the gains from trade do not operate exclusively in the marketplace. They also operate within the household and among its members. It is not uncommon for each member of a household to specialize in a limited range of activities. For example, one does the shopping and cleaning while another does laundry and prepares meals. Specialization in bearing children is a biological necessity, although rearing them is not.

Consider, for example, a household that has two members – Bob and Sue. Bob and Sue have to decide how they will allocate their time between various non-market household production activities and market activity. One solution is for Bob to specialize in market activity and Sue to specialize in non-market activity. Another solution is to reverse the roles so that Sue specializes in market activity and Bob in non-market activity. Alternatively, one or both of them can become diversified, doing some market and some non-market activity. A completely egalitarian allocation will mean they share the non-market tasks equally and each devote the same amount of time and energy to market activity. But unequal allocations of time are also possible with one of the household members specializing in market activity and the other being diversified.

In deciding which of the many alternative time allocations to choose, Bob and Sue will take into consideration their plans for having children. The particular allocation chosen by Bob and Sue will depend on their preferences and on the market earning potential of each of them. An increasing number of households are choosing the egalitarian allocation with each person diversified between non-market household production and market activity. Most households, however, still choose an allocation in which Bob almost fully specializes in market activity and Sue covers a greater diversity of tasks in both the job market and the household.

What are the effects of this common assignment of market and non-market tasks? Although there will always be exceptions, on the average, it seems likely that if Bob specializes in market production and Sue diversifies between market and non-market production, Bob will have higher earning potential in the marketplace than Sue. If Sue is devoting a great deal of productive effort to ensuring Bob's mental and physical well-being, the quality of Bob's market labour will be higher than if he were undertaking his household production tasks on his own. If the roles were reversed, Sue would be able to supply market labour capable of earning more than Bob.

Economists have attempted to test whether the degree of specialization can account for earnings differentials between the sexes. They do this by examining the wages of men and women where, as far as possible, the degree of specialization is held constant. If the degree of specialization is an important factor influencing a person's wage, then we expect men and women of identical ages and educational backgrounds in identical occupations will be paid different wages depending on whether they are single, married to a spouse who specializes in household production, or married to a spouse who works. If single men and women live alone, are equally specialized in household market production, have the same amounts of human capital and do similar jobs, then we expect they will be paid the same wage. To make non-market factors as similar as possible, economists have studied two groups: 'never-married' men and 'never-married' women.

The available evidence suggests that, on the average, when they have the same amount of human capital – measured by years of schooling, work experience and career interruptions – the wages of these two groups are not identical but the difference between them is much closer than the difference between average wages for men and women. Women are paid, on the average, about 78 per cent of the wage rates of men. When allowance is made for degree of specialization and human capital, this wage differential comes down to between 5 and 10 per cent, by some estimates. Some economists suspect the remaining discrepancy stems from discrimination against women, although the difficulty of measuring such discrimination makes this hypothesis hard to test. We explore the issue of wage differentials and discrimination between male and female executives in *Reading Between the Lines* on pp 384–385.

Because labour markets do not seem to treat everyone in the same way, governments intervene in these markets to modify the wages and employment levels that they determine. One potentially far-reaching intervention is equal pay laws. Let's see how these laws work.

Equal Pay and Equal Worth Laws

The Equal Pay Act of 1970, the Sex Discrimination Act of 1975 and the Race Discrimination Act of 1980 were designed to promote *equal pay* and equality of opportunity between men and women and between people of different ethnic origin. They are attempts to remove the most blatant forms of discrimination between men and women and whites and minorities. But many people believe that these acts do not go far enough. In their view, getting paid the *same* wage for doing the *same* job is just the first tiny step that has to be taken. What the law should state is that jobs of *equal worth* receive the same wages regardless of whether they are done by men or women or by blacks or whites. Paying the same wage for different jobs that are judged to be comparable is called **equal pay for equal worth**.

Advocates of equal worth laws argue that wages should be determined by analysing the characteristics of jobs and determining their worth on objective grounds. However, such a method of determining wage rates does not achieve the objectives sought by supporters of wage equality. Let's see why.

Figure 15.9 shows two markets: that for oil rig operators in part (a) and that for school teachers in part (b). The marginal revenue product curves (MRP_R and MRP_T) and the supply curves (S_R and S_T) are shown for each type of labour. Competitive equilibrium generates a wage rate W_R for oil rig operators and W_T for teachers.

Suppose that the knowledge and skills required in these two occupations – the mental and physical demands, the responsibilities and the working conditions – result in a judgement that these two jobs are of equal worth. The wage rate that is judged to apply to each of them is W_C, and the courts enforce this wage rate. What happens?

FIGURE 15.9

The Problem with Equal Worth

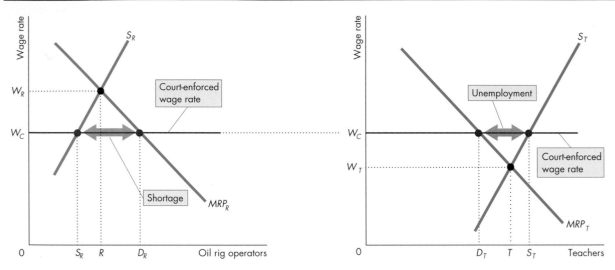

(a) Market for oil rig operators

(b) Market for teachers

The demand for and supply of oil rig operators, MRP_R and S_R, are shown in part (a), and those for school teachers, MRP_T and S_T, in part (b). The competitive equilibrium wage rate for oil rig operators is W_R, and that for teachers is W_T. If an evaluation of the two jobs finds that they have equal worth and rules that the wage rate W_C be paid to both types of workers, there is an excess of demand for oil rig operators

and an excess supply of teachers. There are $S_T - D_T$ teachers unemployed and a shortage of $D_R - S_R$ oil rig operators. Oil producers search for other labour-saving ways of producing oil (that are more expensive) and teachers search for other jobs (that are less desirable to them and probably less well paid).

First, there is a shortage of oil rig operators. Oil rig companies are able to hire only S_R workers at the wage rate W_C. They cut back their production or build more expensive labour-saving oil rigs. Second the number of teachers employed decreases. But this decrease occurs because school governors demand fewer teachers. At the higher wage W_C, school governors demand only D_T teachers. The quantity of teachers supplied is S_T and the difference between S_T and D_T is the number of unemployed teachers looking for jobs. These teachers eventually accept non-teaching jobs (which they don't like as much as teaching jobs), and probably at a lower rate of pay than that of teachers.

Thus equal worth laws may have serious and costly unintended consequences.

R E V I E W

◆ Wage differences might arise from differences in the types of jobs done, discrimination and differences in human capital.

◆ Wage differences might also arise from differences in the degree of specialization.

◆ Equal worth laws cannot, themselves, eliminate wage differences.

◆ Wage differences will be reduced only if differences in actual and perceived marginal revenue product are reduced.

◆ ◆ ◆ ◆ In this chapter, we extended and applied the factor market model to understand a variety of phenomena in labour markets such as wage differentials. In the next chapter, we apply and extend the factor market model to deal with markets for capital and for natural resources.

SUMMARY

Skill Differentials

Skill differentials arise partly because skilled labour has a higher marginal product than unskilled labour and partly because skills are costly to acquire. The higher marginal product of skilled workers results in a higher marginal revenue product. Because the demand for labour curve is derived from the marginal revenue product curve, the higher the marginal revenue product of skilled labour, the greater is the demand for skilled labour.

Skills are costly to acquire because households have to invest in human capital to become skilled. Investment sometimes means direct payments such as tuition and other training fees and sometimes means working for a lower wage during on-the-job training. Because skills are costly to acquire, households supply skilled labour on terms that compensate them for both the time spent on the job and the costs of acquiring the skills. Thus the supply curve of skilled labour lies above the supply curve of unskilled labour.

Wage rates of skilled and unskilled labour are determined by demand and supply in the two labour markets. The equilibrium wage rate for skilled labour exceeds that for unskilled labour. The difference in wages reflects the higher marginal product of skill and the cost to acquire skill. (pp. 372–375)

Union–Non-union Wage Differentials

Labour unions influence wages by controlling the supply of labour. In competitive labour markets, unions obtain higher wages only at the expense of lower employment. Unions in competitive industries also influence the marginal revenue product of their members by supporting import restrictions, minimum wages and immigration restrictions, by increasing demand for the good they produce, and by increasing the marginal productivity of their members.

In a monopsony – a market in which there is a single buyer – a union can increase the wage rate without sacrificing employment. Bilateral monopoly occurs when the union is a monopoly seller of labour, the firm is a monopsony buyer of labour and the wage rate is determined by bargaining between the two parties. Also, in a monopsony a minimum wage law can increase both the wage rate and the level of employment.

In practice, union workers earn an estimated 5–6 per cent more than comparable non-union workers. (pp. 375–381)

Wage Differentials Between Sexes and Races

Earnings differentials between men and women and between whites and minorities arise from differences in types of jobs, discrimination, differences in human capital and differences in degree of specialization.

Well-paid jobs such as those in the legal, medical and other professions, and in higher ranks of management are more likely to be held by white men than by women and minorities. Women and minorities are more likely to be discriminated against than white males, but discrimination is hard to measure objectively. Historically, white males have had more human capital than other groups, but human capital differences arising from schooling differences have been falling and have almost been eliminated. Differentials based on work experience have kept women's pay below that for men because women's careers have traditionally been interrupted more frequently than those of men, resulting on the average in a smaller accumulation of human capital. This difference is less important today than in the past.

Differentials arising from different degrees of specialization are probably important and may persist. Men have traditionally been more specialized in market activity, on the average, than women. Women have traditionally undertaken both non-market, household production activities as well as market activities. Attempts to test for the importance of the degree of specialization suggest that it is an important source of the difference between the earnings of men and women. (pp. 381–387)

Equal Pay and Equal Worth Laws

Equal worth laws would determine wages by using objective characteristics rather than what the market will pay to assess the value of different types of jobs. Determining wages through equal worth will result in a decrease in the number of people employed in those jobs on which the market places a lower value and shortages of those workers that

the market values more highly. Thus the attempt to achieve equal wages for comparable work has costly, unintended consequences. (pp. 387–388)

K E Y E L E M E N T S

Key Terms

Bilateral monopoly, 380
Collective bargaining, 376
Discrimination, 382
Equal pay for equal worth, 387
Human capital, 372
Industrial union, 375
Minimum wage, 380
Monopsony, 378
Trade union, 375

 ## Key Figures and Table

Figure 15.1 Skill Differentials, 373
Figure 15.4 A Union in a Competitive Labour Market, 378
Figure 15.8 Discrimination, 383
Table 15.1 A Compact Glossary on Labour Relations, 375

R E V I E W Q U E S T I O N S

1 Explain why skilled workers are paid more than unskilled workers.

2 Explain why the demand curve for high-skilled workers lies to the right of the demand curve for low-skilled workers.

3 Explain why the demand curve for high-skilled workers lies to the left of the supply curve for low-skilled workers.

4 What is the influence of education and on-the-job training on earnings?

5 Explain why skilled workers are paid more than low-skilled workers.

6 What are the main types of trade unions?

7 What is corporatist bargaining and how does it differ from decentralized bargaining?

8 What are the main weapons available to a union and to employers.

9 How does a union try to influence wages?

10 What can a union do in a competitive labour market?

11 How might a union increase the demand for its members' labour?

12 Explain why the elasticity of supply of labour influences how much the union can raise the wage rate paid to union members.

13 What is a monopsony?

14 Explain why the supply of labour facing a monopsony is not the marginal cost of labour.

15 Explain why a monopsony maximizes its profit by paying labour a wage rate that is less than the marginal revenue product of labour.

16 Under what circumstances will the introduction of a minimum wage increase employment?

17 Describe the differences in male and female earnings in the United Kingdom today?

18 What are the main reasons for the existence of sex and race differentials in earnings?

19 How would equal worth laws work?

20 What are the predicted effects of equal worth laws?

PROBLEMS

1 The demand for and supply of unskilled labour is given by the following schedules:

Hourly wage rate (pounds per hour)	Quantity supplied (hours)	Quantity demanded (hours)
9	9,000	1,000
8	8,000	2,000
7	7,000	3,000
6	6,000	4,000
5	5,000	5,000
4	4,000	6,000
3	3,000	7,000
2	2,000	8,000

  a What is the wage rate of unskilled labour?
  b What is the quantity of unskilled labour employed?

2 The workers in Problem 1 can be trained to obtain a skill – and their marginal productivity doubles. (The marginal product at each employment level is twice the marginal product of an unskilled worker.) The compensation for the cost of acquiring skill adds £2 an hour to the wage that must be offered to attract skilled labour.

  a What is the wage rate of skilled labour?
  b What is the quantity of skilled labour employed?

3 Suppose that skilled workers in Problem 1 become unionized and the union restricts the amount of high-skilled labour to 5,000 hours.

  a What is the wage rate of skilled workers?
  b What is the wage differential between low-skilled and high-skilled workers?

4 If in Problem 1, the government introduces a minimum wage rate of £6 an hour for low-skilled workers

  a What is the wage rate paid to low-skilled workers?
  b How many hours of low-skilled labour gets hired each day?

5 Look again at the information in Fig.15.2 of this chapter. Use diagrams similar to those in Fig.15.1 to explain the fact that both men and women with a degree earn more on average than both men and women with no qualifications.

6 Look again at the cartoon on p 374 of this chapter. What is implied about the marginal revenue products associated with the range of skills demanded of an MP?

7 Following on from Problem 6, if an MP is required to have a wide range of skills with different marginal revenue products, which of the following do you think the wage rate should reflect:

  a The highest level of skill – if so why?
  b The average level of skill – if so why?
  c The lowest level of skill – if so why?

8 In a small, isolated town in Yorkshire, the only firm hiring workers is a cloth manufacturer. The firm's demand for labour and the town's supply of labour are as follows:

Wage rate (pounds per hour)	Quantity supplied (hours per day)	Quantity demanded (hours per day)
1	20	220
2	40	200
3	60	180
4	80	160
5	100	140
6	120	120
7	140	100
8	160	80
9	180	60
10	200	40

  a Draw both the supply of labour and the marginal revenue product of labour on the same graph.
  b Write down the total cost of labour for each level of supply.
  c What is the wage rate?
  d How much labour does the firm hire?
  e How much labour does the firm hire?
  f What would the wage rate be if there was a competitive labour market in the town?

9 The people from the town in Problem 8 form a union. The union and the firm agree that the level of employment will not change and the union gets the highest wage rate acceptable to the firm. What is that wage rate?

10 In Problem 8, the government imposes a minimum wage rate at the competitive equilibrium wage.

  a What is the impact of the minimum wage law on the supply of labour below the minimum wage?

  b What is the impact of the minimum wage law on the supply of labour above the minimum wage?

  c By how much has the amount of labour employed increased?

  d By how much has the wage rate risen?

11 A nationwide investigation determines that on the basis of equal worth, a loom operator should be paid £7 an hour. In the cloth making village in Problem 4 and before the union described in Problem 5 is formed:

  a What is the actual hourly wage rate paid?

  b How much labour does the cloth manufacturer hire at this wage?

  c How much labour is unemployed?

12 Read the story in *Reading Between the Lines* on pp 384–385 and then:

  a Give reasons as to why female departmental managers and female executives are paid less than their male counterparts.

  b Explain why female executives received higher pay rises than their male counterparts in 1994 and 1995.

CHAPTER

16

CAPITAL
AND
NATURAL
RESOURCE
MARKETS

After studying this chapter you will be able to:

◆ Describe the structure of capital markets today

◆ Explain how the demand for and supply of capital are determined

◆ Explain how interest rates and share prices are determined and why share prices fluctuate

◆ Explain how the prices of natural resources are determined

◆ Explain how markets regulate the pace at which we use exhaustible resources such as oil

◆ Explain the difference between man-made and natural capital resources

PANIC FILLED THE CAVERNOUS NEW YORK STOCK EXCHANGE ON MONDAY, 19 October, 1987. It had taken five years, from August 1982, for the average price of shares to climb 200 per cent. But on that single day, share prices in New York fell an unprecedented 22 per cent. The crash sparked off similar responses in European stock markets – a fall of 4.6 per cent in Paris, 7.0 per cent in Frankfurt and 10.8 per cent in London – as well as in stock markets as distant as Tokyo. Why does the stock market boom for several years and then crash suddenly and spectacularly? ◆ The European and New York Stock Exchanges are just a part of the worldwide capital market. Every year, trillions of pounds flow through these markets. People's savings are channelled through banks, insurance companies and stock exchanges and end up financing the purchases of capital such as machinery, factory and office buildings, cars and homes. How does a pound saved and placed on deposit

Boom and Bust

in a bank enable BMW to open a new car manufacturing plant? ◆ Many of our natural resources are exhaustible and yet we are using them up at a rapid rate. Every year, we burn trillions of cubic metres of natural gas, billions of litres of petrol and millions of tonnes of coal. We extract bauxite to make aluminium and iron ore to make steel. Aren't we one day going to run out of these and other natural resources? How are their prices determined? Do their prices rise to encourage conservation, or does the market need help to ensure that we do not run out of nature's exhaustible resources?

◆ ◆ ◆ ◆ In this chapter, we study the markets for man-made and natural capital. We'll find out what determines the amount of saving and investment and how interest rates and share prices are determined. We'll also see how market forces and the price mechanism encourage the conservation and discovery of exhaustible natural resources.

The Structure of Capital Markets

Capital assets are things of value owned by households, firms or government. Capital assets come in many forms. Financial assets are simply claims against another household, firm or government as a result of a loan – a form of IOU. Physical assets are goods used in the production process – goods such as plant, machinery, buildings and stocks. Natural assets are the world's stock of natural resources – such as coal, the air and oil reserves – which are also used in production and consumption. The wealth of a household, a firm or a government is the sum of the assets owned minus any debt outstanding. Firms and governments increase or run down their wealth by changing the amount of capital they own through their activities in capital markets.

Capital markets are the channels through which household savings flow into firms and governments. They are markets for financial capital assets. Firms and governments use the financial resources they obtain in capital markets to buy physical and natural capital goods. Physical and natural capital goods are bought and sold, or rented. The markets in which capital goods are bought, sold and rented *are not* capital markets. They are goods markets and factor rental markets. These markets coordinate the decisions of producers and buyers, and of owners and renters of capital goods. In these markets, the forces of demand and supply, which you first met in Chapter 4, determine the prices and quantities of the various capital goods.

Capital markets coordinate the saving plans of households, which determine the supply of capital funds, and the investment plans of firms, which determine the demand for capital funds. The price of capital funds is the interest rate, which adjusts to make the quantity of capital funds supplied equal to the quantity demanded.

The three main types of capital fund markets are:

◆ Stock markets
◆ Bond markets
◆ Loan markets

Stock Markets

A **stock market** is a market in which company shares are traded. Shares are long-term assets issued by firms which are never repaid (see Chapter 9). So savers use stock markets to buy shares or to sell shares if they need to turn these long-term assets into more liquid assets – cash. Many major cities of the world have long-established stock markets which specialize in trading the shares of tens of thousands of domestic and foreign companies. The most famous are in New York, London, Paris, Frankfurt, Tokyo and Toronto. In recent years, new stock markets have begun to operate in Europe as well as in Shanghai, Taipei, Bangkok, Seoul and other centres in the emerging market economies of East Asia.

If you want to buy or sell shares on a stock exchange, you must give an instruction to a *broker*, who in turn places a buy or sell order with a *specialist*, who deals in the shares you want to trade. The specialist, who works on the *floor* of the stock exchange, continuously monitors demand and supply and tries to keep the price of the share at the level at which the quantity demanded equals the quantity supplied.

Bond Markets

A **bond market** is a market in which the bonds or debentures of corporations and governments are traded. The distinction between a share and a bond is described in Chapter 9, p. 210. A share is never repaid, but shareholders receive a periodic payment or dividend, which fluctuates with the firm's economic profit. Bonds have a redemption value and maturity date when they will be repaid, and the bondholder receives a fixed periodic interest payment before the bond matures. Bond markets, like stock markets, are located in all the major financial centres, and brokers in these markets strive to maintain a balance between the quantities of bonds demanded and supplied.

Loan Markets

A **loan market** is a market in which households and firms make and receive loans. Loans markets are operated by **financial intermediaries**, institutions that receive deposits and make loans. The best-known financial intermediaries are commercial banks and building societies. When you make a deposit in a bank as part of your saving, you make a loan to the bank and the bank uses the funds it receives from depositors to make loans to businesses and households.

The Flows of Funds

Figure 16.1 shows the main flows of funds through the capital markets that we've just described. Households save part of their incomes and supply *financial capital.* Firms and governments demand

FIGURE 16.1

Capital Market Flows

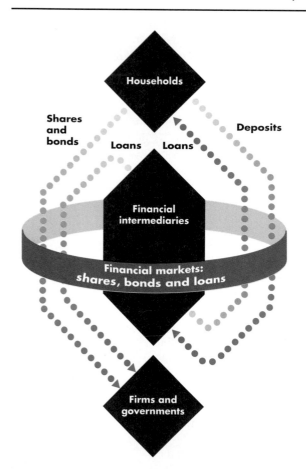

Households supply *financial* capital to firms and governments, and firms and governments use financial capital to buy *physical* capital. Households purchase shares and bonds and make deposits in financial intermediaries. Financial intermediaries lend to households, firms and governments. These flows are shown by the green dotted lines.

financial capital and use it to buy *physical* and *natural capital goods.* Financial intermediaries facilitate these transactions in the markets for shares, bonds and loans. The green dotted lines in the figure illustrate the financial transactions. Households use their saving to buy shares or bonds issued by firms and governments and to make deposits with financial intermediaries. Financial intermediaries make loans to households and firms and governments.

Let's begin to learn how capital markets work by building a model of capital markets. We'll start by studying the demand for capital funds – financial capital. To simplify our model we will consider the decision to invest in physical capital by firms.

The Demand for Capital

A firm's demand for *financial* capital stems from its demand for *physical* capital, and the amount that a firm plans to *borrow* in a given time period is determined by its planned *investment.*

Capital, Investment and Depreciation

Capital is a *stock* – the quantity of previously manufactured goods in existence at a given time that are used to produce other goods and services. Gross investment is a *flow* – the purchase of new capital goods during a given period. Investment – new capital – is added to the capital stock. Capital is like the water stored in a major reservoir at a given point in time and gross investment is like the water flowing into the reservoir from local rivers during a given period. The inflow adds to the stock of water stored in the reservoir. Depreciation is another flow. It measures the amount of existing capital that wears out in a given period. Depreciation is like the water flowing out of the reservoir for use by households and firms. This outflow decreases the stock of water in the reservoir. The change in the capital stock during a given period is called *net investment* and equals gross investment minus depreciation. Similarly, the change in the stock of water in the reservoir equals the inflow minus the outflow.

Investment Decisions

To decide how much to invest and borrow, a firm decides on the size of its capital stock. This decision, like a firm's decision about the amount of other factors of production to employ, is driven by its attempt to maximize profit.

As a firm increases the quantity of capital employed, other things remaining the same, the marginal revenue product of capital eventually diminishes. To find the amount of capital goods that will maximize profit, a firm employs capital up to the point where the marginal revenue product of capital is equal to the price of using capital. The price of using capital is the interest rate. So a firm increases the quantity of capital employed until the additional revenue generated by using one extra unit of capital equals the interest rate.

The easiest way to see that the interest rate is the price of using capital is to think about capital that is rented. If a firm rents a computer from Computerland, it pays an annual rental rate. This rental rate gives Computerland a rate of return equal to the interest rate. If Computerland made a return less than the interest rate, it would sell some computers and buy some shares or bonds that yield an interest rate higher than that on computers. If Computerland made a return greater than the interest rate, it would buy more computers and sell some shares or bonds that have an interest rate lower than that on computers.

But most capital is not rented. Firms *buy* buildings, plant and equipment and operate them for several years. To decide how much capital equipment to buy, the firm compares the price to be paid here and now for the equipment with the expected returns – the future flow of marginal revenue product – that the equipment will generate over its life. The interest rate is still the price of using capital, even when it is bought rather than rented. The reason is that to decide how much capital to buy, the firm must convert a stream of *future* marginal revenue product into a *present value* so that it can be directly compared with the price of a new piece of capital equipment. Chapter 9 (pp. 211–212) explains the concept of present value and you might like to review those pages before moving on.

The Net Present Value of a Computer

Let's see how a firm decides how much capital to buy by calculating the present value of a new computer. Table 16.1 summarizes the data. Tina runs Taxfile plc, a firm that sells advice to taxpayers. Tina is considering buying a new high-power computer workstation that costs £10,000 in total. The worksta-

---

TABLE 16.1

Net Present Value of an Investment – Taxfile plc

(a) Data

Price of workstation	£10,000
Life of workstation	2 years
Marginal revenue product	£5,900 at end of each year
Interest rate	4% a year

(b) Present value of the flow of marginal revenue product:

$$PV = \frac{MRP_1}{(1+r)} + \frac{MRP_2}{(1+r)^2}$$

$$= \frac{£5,900}{1.04} + \frac{£5,900}{(1.04)^2}$$

$$= £5,673 + £5,455$$

$$= £11,128$$

(c) Net present value of investment:

$$NPV = PV \text{ of Marginal revenue product} - \text{Cost of workstation}$$

$$= £11,128 - £10,000$$

$$= £1,128$$

---

tion has a life of two years, after which it will be worthless. If Tina buys the workstation, she will pay out £10,000 now and she expects to generate business that will bring in an additional £5,900 at the end of each of the next two years.

To calculate the present value, *PV*, of the marginal revenue product of a new computer, Tina uses the formula

$$PV = \frac{MRP_1}{(1+r)} + \frac{MRP_2}{(1+r)^2}$$

Here, MRP_1 is the marginal revenue product received by Tina at the end of the first year. It is converted to a present value by dividing it by $(1+r)$. The term MRP_2 is the marginal revenue product received at the end of the second year. It is converted to a present value by dividing it by $(1+r)^2$. Table 16.1(b) puts Tina's numbers into the present value formula and calculates the present value of the marginal revenue product of a workstation.

The first calculation in Table 16.1 is for the case in which Tina can borrow or lend at an interest rate of 4 per cent a year. The present value (*PV*) of £5,900 one year in the future is £5,900 divided by

1.04 (4 per cent as a proportion is 0.04). The present value of £5,900 two years in the future is £5,900 divided by $(1.04)^2$. Working out these two present values and then adding them gives Tina the present value of the future stream of marginal revenue products, which is £11,128.

Tina's Decision to Buy Tina decides whether to buy the workstation by comparing the present value of its stream of marginal revenue product with its purchase price. She makes this comparison by calculating the net present value (*NPV*) of the computer. **Net present value** is the present value of the future return – the future stream of marginal revenue product generated by the capital minus the cost of buying the capital. If net present value is positive, the firm should buy additional capital. If net present value is negative, the firm should not buy additional capital. Table 16.1(c) shows the calculation of Tina's net present value of a workstation. The net present value is £1,128 – greater than zero – so Tina buys the workstation.

Tina can buy any number of workstations that cost £10,000 and have a life of two years. But like all other factors of production, capital is subject to diminishing marginal returns. The greater the amount of capital employed, the smaller is its marginal revenue product. So if Tina buys a second workstation or a third one, she gets successively smaller marginal revenue products from the additional workstations.

Table 16.2(a) sets out Tina's marginal revenue products for one, two and three workstations. The marginal revenue product of one computer workstation (the case just reviewed) is £5,900 a year. The marginal revenue product of a second workstation is £5,600 a year, and the marginal revenue product of a third computer is £5,300 a year. Table 16.2(b) shows the calculations of the present values of the marginal revenue products of the first, second and third computers workstations.

You've seen that with an interest rate of 4 per cent a year, the net present value of one workstation is positive. At an interest rate of 4 per cent a year, the present value of the marginal revenue product of a second workstation is £10,562, which exceeds its price by £562. So Tina buys a second computer workstation. But at an interest rate of 4 per cent a year, the present value of the marginal revenue product of a third workstation is £9,996, which is £4 less than the price of the computer. So Tina does not buy a third workstation.

TABLE 16.2

Taxfile's Investment Decision

(a) Data

Price of workstation	£10,000
Life of workstation	2 years

Marginal revenue product:

Using 1 workstation	£ 5,900 a year
Using 2 workstations	£ 5,600 a year
Using 3 workstations	£ 5,300 a year

(b) Present value of the stream of marginal revenue product

If *r* = 0.04 (4% a year)

Using 1 workstation: $PV = \dfrac{£5,900}{1.04} + \dfrac{£5,900}{(1.04)^2} = £11,128$

Using 2 workstations: $PV = \dfrac{£5,600}{1.04} + \dfrac{£5,600}{(1.04)^2} = £10,562$

Using 3 workstations: $PV = \dfrac{£5,300}{1.04} + \dfrac{£5,300}{(1.04)^2} = £9,996$

If *r* = 0.08 (8% a year):

Using 1 workstation: $PV = \dfrac{£5,900}{1.08} + \dfrac{£5,900}{(1.08)^2} = £10,521$

Using 2 workstations: $PV = \dfrac{£5,600}{1.08} + \dfrac{£5,600}{(1.08)^2} = £9,986$

If *r* = 0.12 (12% a year):

Using 1 workstation: $PV = \dfrac{£5,900}{1.12} + \dfrac{£5,900}{(1.12)^2} = £9,971$

A Change in the Interest Rate We've seen that at an interest rate of 4 per cent a year, Tina buys two computer workstations but not three. Suppose that the interest rate is 8 per cent a year. In this case, the present value of the first computer is £10,521 (see Table 16.2b), so Tina still buys one workstation because it has a positive net present value. At an interest rate of 8 per cent a year, the net present value of the second workstation is £9,986, which is less than £10,000, its price. So, at an interest rate of 8 per cent a year, Tina buys only one computer workstation.

Suppose that the interest rate is even higher at 12 per cent a year. In this case, the present value of the marginal revenue product of one workstation is £9,971 (see Table 16.6(b)). At this interest rate, Tina buys no computer workstations.

These calculations trace Taxfile's demand schedule for capital. They show the number of computer workstations demanded – and the value of funds – at each interest rate. Other things remaining the same, the higher the interest rate, the smaller is the quantity of *physical* capital demanded. But to finance the purchase of physical capital, firms demand financial capital. So the higher the interest rate, the smaller is the quantity of *financial* capital demanded.

Demand Curve for Capital

A firm's demand curve for capital shows the relationship between the quantity of capital demanded and the interest rate, other things remaining the same. Figure 16.2 illustrates Taxfile's demand for computer workstations (D_F). Points a, b and c correspond to the example that we have just worked through. At an interest rate of 12 per cent a year,

FIGURE 16.2

A Firm's Demand for Capital

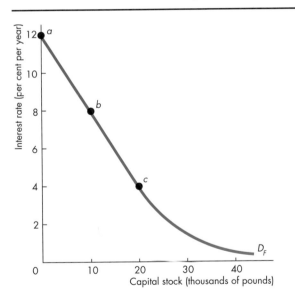

Taxfile demands capital (workstations) until the present value of the stream of marginal revenue product of workstations equals the price of a workstation. The present value depends on the interest rate. The lower the interest rate, the larger is the number of workstations demanded. At an interest rate of 12 per cent a year, Taxfile demands no workstations (point *a*). At an interest rate of 8 per cent a year, the firm demands 1 workstation worth £10,000 (point *b*). At an interest rate of 4 per cent a year, the firm demands 2 workstations worth £20,000 (point *c*). If workstations of different types (fractions of a £10,000 unit) can be bought a demand curve that passes through points *a*, *b* and *c* is generated.

Tina buys no workstations – point a. At an interest rate of 8 per cent, she buys 1 workstation worth £10,000 – point b. At an interest rate of 4 per cent, she buys 2 workstations worth £20,000 – point c.

We've considered only one type of computer workstation – one that costs £10,000. But Tina can buy different types, the power of which can be expressed as a multiple or fraction of a £10,000 workstation. For example, there may be a £5,000 computer workstation that has half the power of a £10,000 workstation. There may also be a network that costs £12,500 and has one and a quarter times the power of a £10,000 workstation. If we consider all the different types of workstations that Tina can buy, we generate not just the three points, a, b and c, but an entire demand curve like that shown in Fig. 16.2. This demand curve shows the quantity of capital (workstations) demanded by Taxfile at different rates of interest, other things remaining the same.

The Market Demand for Capital

The market demand curve for capital is the horizontal sum of all the individual firm's demand curves. Figure 16.3 shows the market demand curve, which like the firm's demand curve slopes downward. When the interest rate rises, other things remaining the same, the quantity of capital demanded decreases along the demand curve. Figure 16.3 shows such a change by the movement along demand curve D_0.

Changes in the Demand for Capital   The main influences on the demand for capital are:

1. Population growth
2. Technological change

   Population growth brings a steady increase in the demand for capital. Technological change brings fluctuations in the demand for capital. Technological change increases the demand for some types of physical capital and decreases the demand for other types. For example, the development of diesel engines for railway transport decreased the demand for steam engines and increased the demand for diesel engines. In this case, the railway industry's overall demand for capital did not change much. In contrast, the development of desktop computers increased the demand for office computing equipment, decreased the demand for electric typewriters and increased

FIGURE 16.3

The Demand for Capital

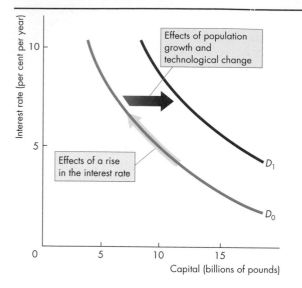

Other things remaining the same, the quantity of capital demanded decreases as the interest rate rises and there is a movement along the demand curve for capital. An increase in population and advances in technology increase the demand for capital and shift the demand curve rightward.

the overall demand for capital in the office. Figure 16.3 shows such fluctuations in demand by a shift in the demand curve from D_0 to D_1.

R E V I E W

◆ Firms' profit-maximization decisions determine the demand for capital – both physical and financial.

◆ The quantity of capital demanded depends on the marginal revenue product of capital and the interest rate.

◆ The higher the interest rate, the smaller is the present value of the future stream of marginal revenue product and the smaller is the quantity of capital demanded.

◆ The demand for capital grows as population grows and fluctuates as technology changes.

The Supply of Capital

The quantity of capital supplied results from people's saving decisions. Saving is a *flow*, which equals income minus consumption. The current market value of a household's past saving, together with any inheritances it has received, is the household's **wealth**, which is a *stock*. Households hold their wealth as financial capital such as shares, bonds and bank deposits, and as physical capital such as houses, cars and other consumer durable goods. The wealth that households hold as financial capital is used by firms and governments to finance the purchase of physical and natural capital. So for the economy, wealth also equals the value of physical capital and natural capital – the total value of the physical and natural capital of households, firms and government.

Portfolio Choices   A household's decision about how to hold its wealth is called a *portfolio choice*. In everyday language, we often refer to the purchase of shares and bonds as investment. That everyday use of the word 'investment' can cause confusion in economic analysis. *Investment* in economic analysis is the purchase of new physical capital by firms and households. To avoid this confusion, we use the term 'portfolio choice' to refer to the choices that households make in allocating their wealth across the various financial assets available to them.

The Saving Decision

Three main factors determine saving. They are:

◆ Income

◆ Expected future income

◆ Interest rate

Income   Saving is the act of converting *current* income into *future* consumption. Usually, the higher a household's income, the more it plans to consume both in the present and in the future. But to increase future consumption, the household must save. So, other things remaining the same, the higher a household's income, the more it saves.

Expected Future Income   Because a major reason for saving is to increase future consumption, the amount that a household saves depends not only on its current income but also on its *expected future income*. If a household's current income is high and its expected future income is low, it will have a high level of saving. But if its current income is low and its expected future income is high, it will have a low (perhaps even negative) level of saving.

Young people (especially students) usually have low current incomes compared with their expected future income. To smooth out their lifetime consumption, they consume more than they earn and incur debts. Such people have a negative amount of saving. In middle age, most people's incomes reach their peak. At this stage in life, saving is at its maximum. After retirement, people spend part of the wealth they have accumulated during their working lives.

Interest Rate   A pound saved today grows into a pound plus interest tomorrow. The higher the interest rate, the greater is the future value of a pound saved today. Thus, the higher the interest rate, the greater is the opportunity cost of current consumption. Interest rates have two influences on saving. They are:

◆ Substitution effect
◆ Income effect

Substitution Effect   Because a higher interest rate increases the future return from today's saving and increases the opportunity cost of current consumption, it stimulates saving. It encourages people to economize on current consumption and take advantage of the higher interest rate. That is, the substitution effect of interest rates on saving is positive. Other things remaining the same, the higher the interest rate, the greater is the quantity of saving.

Income Effect   A change in the interest rate changes a household's future income. Other things remaining the same, as a household's income increases so too does its consumption. But the effect of a change in the interest rate on a household's income depends on whether the household is a net borrower or a net lender. For a net lender, an increase in interest rates increases income, so it increases saving. The income effect reinforces the substitution effect and a higher interest rate results in increased saving. For a net borrower, an increase in interest rates decreases income and decreases saving (and consumption). In this case, the income effect of a higher interest rate works in a direction opposite to that of the substitution effect and sav-

ing might increase or decrease depending on the relative strengths of the substitution effect and the income effect.

For individual households that are net borrowers, the effect of a change in the interest rate on saving is ambiguous, but for households that are net lenders, and for the economy as a whole, there is no ambiguity. Other things remaining the same, the higher the interest rate, the greater is the flow of saving in a given period and the greater is the stock of financial capital supplied.

Supply Curve of Capital

The quantity of capital supplied is the total value of accumulated saving – wealth. Remember that for the economy, wealth is the sum of all physical and natural capital. Figure 16.4 shows the supply curve of capital – the relationship between the quantity of capital supplied and the interest rate, other things remaining the same. An increase in the interest rate brings an increase in the quantity of capital supplied and a movement along the supply curve, as shown along the supply curve S_0. The supply curve

FIGURE 16.4

The Supply of Capital

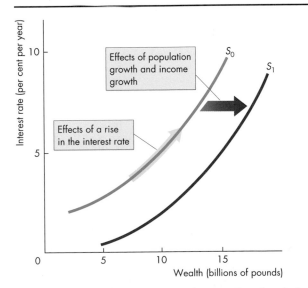

Other things remaining the same, the quantity of capital supplied increases as the interest rate rises and there is a movement along the supply curve for capital. An increase in population and rising incomes increase the supply of capital and shift the supply curve rightward.

is inelastic in the short run, but probably quite elastic in the long run. The reason is that in any given year, the total amount of saving is small relative to the stock of wealth. So even a large change in the amount of saving brings only a small change in the supply of capital.

Changes in the Supply of Capital   A change in any influence on saving, other than the interest rate, changes the amount of saving and shifts the supply curve of capital. The main influences on the supply of capital are income and its distribution and the size and age distribution of the population.

Other things remaining the same, an increase in income or an increase in the population bring an increase in the supply of capital. Also, other things remaining the same, the more unequally income is distributed, the higher is the saving rate. The reason is that low-income and middle-income families have low saving rates, while high-income families have high saving rates. So the larger the proportion of total income earned by the highest-income families, the greater is the amount of saving. Finally, and again other things remaining the same, the larger the proportion of middle-aged people, the higher is the saving rate. The reason is that middle-aged people do most of the saving as they build up a pension fund to provide an income in their retirement.

Any one of the factors that increases the supply of capital shifts the supply curve of capital rightward, as shown in Fig. 16.4, where the supply curve shifts from S_0 to S_1.

R E V I E W

◆ The quantity of capital supplied is determined by saving decisions.

◆ Other things remaining the same, the higher the interest rate, the larger is the quantity of capital supplied.

◆ The supply of capital changes as a result of changes in the level of income and in the population and its age composition. Income growth and population growth bring a steady increase in the supply of capital.

Now that we have studied the demand for and supply of capital, we can bring these two sides of the

capital market model together and study the determination of interest rates and asset prices. We'll then be able to answer some of the questions posed at the beginning of this chapter about the stock market and understand the forces that produce stock market booms and crashes.

Interest Rates and Share Prices

Saving plans and investment plans are coordinated through capital markets. Interest rates, share prices and bond prices adjust to make these plans compatible. We are now going to study the way in which these market forces work. We are also going to discover what determines the stock market value of a firm.

Two Sides of the Same Coin

Interest rates and share (and bond) prices can be viewed as two sides of the same coin. We'll look first at interest rates, then at prices and lastly at the connection between them. The rate of return earned on a share is the dividend paid out on the share, expressed as a percentage of the price of the share. The rate of return earned on a bond is the dividend payment of the bond, expressed as a percentage of the price of the bond. So, to calculate the rate of return on a share (or bond), we divide the earnings of the share (or bond) by its price. For example, if Taxfile pays a dividend of £5 a share and if the price of a share is £50, then the rate of return is 10 per cent (£5 divided by £50, expressed as a percentage). If Taxfile's dividend is £5 and the share price is £100, then the rate of return is 5 per cent.

These calculations show that for a given amount of earnings, the higher the price of a share, the lower is its rate of return. This connection between the price of a share and its rate of return – or interest rate – means that we can study the market forces in capital markets as simultaneously determining interest rates (rates of return) and share and bond prices. We will first look at capital market equilibrium in terms of interest rate (or rate of return) determination and then in terms of the stock market value of a firm.

Equilibrium Interest Rate

Figure 16.5 shows the capital market. The horizontal axis measures the total quantity of capital. Notice that the axis is labelled 'Capital stock and wealth'. This label emphasizes the fact that the value of the capital stock and wealth are equivalent. The vertical axis measures the interest rate. The demand curve is D, and the supply curve is S. Capital market equilibrium occurs where the quantity of capital supplied equals the quantity of capital demanded. In Fig. 16.5, this equilibrium is at an interest rate of 5 per cent a year and £10 billion of capital is supplied and demanded.

The market forces that bring about this equilibrium are the same as those that we studied in the markets for goods and services. If the interest rate exceeds 5 per cent a year, the quantity of financial capital demanded is less than the quantity supplied. There is a surplus of funds in the capital market. In such a situation, as lenders compete to make loans, interest rates fall. The quantity of financial

capital demanded increases as firms increase their borrowing and buy more capital goods. The interest rate continues to fall until lenders are able to lend all the funds they wish at that interest rate.

Conversely, if the interest rate is below 5 per cent a year, the quantity of financial capital supplied is less than the quantity demanded. There is a shortage of funds in the capital market. Borrowers are unable to borrow all the funds they wish so they offer a higher interest rate. Interest rates increase until there are no unsatisfied borrowers. In either case, the interest rate converges on 5 per cent a year, the equilibrium interest rate.

The institutions that specialize in trading in financial capital markets – banks, insurance companies and building societies – handle millions of pounds of business every day and maintain a near continuous equality between the quantity of capital demanded and the quantity supplied. These same competitive forces ensure that the interest rate is the same in all parts of the capital market, both across the regions of the country and around the world.

The interest rate determined in Fig. 16.5 is the *average* interest rate. Interest rates on individual assets will be distributed around this average, based on the relative degree of riskiness of individual assets. An asset with a high degree of risk will earn an interest rate that exceeds the average and a safe asset will earn an interest rate that is below the average. The riskier asset earns a higher interest rate to compensate for the higher risk. For example, if the average interest rate is 5 per cent a year as shown in Fig. 16.5, the interest rate on a bank deposit (a safer asset) might be 3 per cent a year and that on a company share (a riskier asset) might be 8 per cent a year.

We've now seen how interest rates (rates of return) are determined. Let's look at the other side of the coin – share (and bond) prices. To do so, we'll look at the stock market value of a firm.

Stock Market Value of a Firm

What determines the price of a firm's shares? The price of a firm's shares depends on the dividends the firm is expected to pay and on the interest rate. To see why, suppose that Pronto, a printing firm, is expected to pay a dividend of £10 a share in each future year and that the interest rate is 10 per cent a year. The price of Pronto's shares will be £100 a share. At this price, Pronto's shares yield a return of 10 per cent a year – the interest rate. If Pronto's shares could be bought for less than £100 each, its

---

FIGURE 16.5

Capital Market Equilibrium

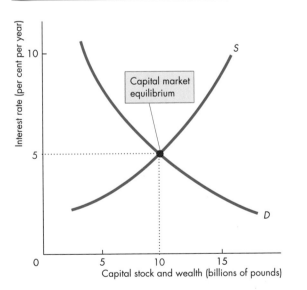

Capital market equilibrium occurs when the interest rate is such that the quantity of capital demanded equals the quantity of capital supplied. The demand curve is D and the supply curve is S. These curves intersect at an interest rate of 5 per cent a year and a capital stock of £10 billion.

expected rate of return would exceed 10 per cent. In this case, people would buy Pronto's shares and the price would rise. If Pronto's shares cost more than £100 each, its expected rate of return would be less than 10 per cent a year. In this case, people would sell Pronto's shares and the price would fall. Only when Pronto's shares cost £100 each and the rate of return is 10 per cent – the same as the current interest rate – do people neither buy nor sell the shares. So only when Pronto's share price is £100 does the price remain constant. Thus if a firm is expected to pay a dividend of £10 a share and if the interest rate is 10 per cent a year, the price of the firm's shares will be £100 each. The stock market value of the firm equals the price of a share multiplied by the number of shares.

The price of a firm's shares increases if the expected dividend increases or if the interest rate falls. For example, if Pronto becomes more profitable and is expected to pay a dividend of £20 a share in each future year and the interest rate remains at 10 per cent a year, the price of Pronto's shares will rise to £200 each. And if Pronto is expected to pay a dividend of £10 a share each future year but the interest rate falls to 5 per cent a year, the price of Pronto's shares will also rise to £200 each.

Price–Earnings Ratio

A commonly used measure to describe the performance of a firm's shares is its price-earnings ratio. A *price–earnings ratio* is the current price of a share divided by the most recent year's profit per share. In 1996, the average price–earnings ratio of the shares that formed the UK FT-SE 100 was 14.5. What determines a price–earnings ratio? Why, in April 1996, was the average price–earnings ratio in the water utilities industry only 8.63 while the average price–earnings ratio in the oil extraction industry was 37.98?

The higher a firm's *expected future* dividend, the higher is the *current* price of its shares. Because the firm's price–earnings ratio is the ratio of its current price to its *current* profit, its price–earnings ratio depends on its expected future profit relative to its current profit. When expected future profit is high relative to current profit, the price–earnings ratio is high. Fluctuations in the price–earnings ratio arise from fluctuations in expected future profit relative to current profit.

Stock Market Volume and Prices

Sometimes share prices rise or fall with little trading taking place. At other times, they rise or fall with an enormous volume of trading. On yet other occasions, there is little change in share prices but an enormous volume of trading. What determines the volume of shares traded?

We've seen that share prices rise and fall because of changes in expectations of future dividends and changes in interest rates. Suppose expected future dividends increase and suppose the source of this expectation is so obvious that everyone can see it. Everyone agrees that a firm's earnings are going to be higher in the future. In this situation, the price of the firm's shares rises but no one buys or sells shares. Shareholders are happy with the shares they already hold and the price rises to make the new expected dividend provide an interest rate equal to that available on other assets.

Conversely, suppose an event occurs that changes expectations about this firm's future dividends but is difficult to interpret. Some people believe that dividends will increase and others believe that they will decrease. Call the first group optimists and the second group pessimists. The optimists will buy the shares of this firm and the pessimists will sell them. The price will not necessarily change but a large volume of shares will be traded. What increases the volume traded is the disagreement, not the event that triggered the change in expected profitability. A large volume of shares traded on the stock market implies a large amount of disagreement. Large price changes with small volumes traded imply a great deal of agreement that something fundamental has changed. A large volume traded with hardly any price change means that the underlying changes are difficult to interpret: some people predict that things will move in one direction while others predict the opposite.

Takeovers and Mergers

The theory of capital markets that you've now studied can be used to explain why takeovers and mergers occur. A **takeover** is the purchase of the shares of one firm by another firm. A takeover occurs when the stock market value of a firm is less than the present value of the expected future profits from operating the firm. For example, suppose that Taxfile plc has a stock market value of £120,000. If the present value of its expected future profit is £150,000, someone will have an incentive to take over the firm. Takeover activity affects the price of a firm, and often the threat of a takeover drives the price to the point at which the takeover is no longer profitable.

But a takeover does occur if the profitability of the firm taken over is expected to be larger after the takeover than it was before. One recent example that illustrates this possibility is the takeover of Rover by BMW. Rover had a range of cars that would extend the product base of BMW's prestige range. BMW had a wider European market of distributors through which it could sell the Rover range. As a result, BMW believed it could operate Rover more profitably than Rover could operate on its own. So BMW was willing to offer a higher price for Rover's shares than the current market value.

A **merger** is the combining of the assets of two firms to form a single, new firm. Mergers take place when two firms perceive that by combining their assets, they can increase their combined stock market values. For example, in the United Kingdom Lloyds Bank and the Trustee Savings Bank (TSB) announced a merger in 1995 designed to generate economies of scale in administration and raise profitability. In 1996, the new merged company proposed to close one of the original head offices, shedding 500 jobs through early retirement and voluntary redundancy to reduce administration costs.

R E V I E W

- An interest rate is the income earned on a share (or bond) expressed as a percentage of the price of the share (or bond).
- For a given dividend, as the price of a share (or bond) increases, its interest rate decreases.
- The average interest rate and share (or bond) price makes the quantity of capital supplied equal to the quantity demanded.
- The stock market value of a firm fluctuates because its expected dividend fluctuates. The price–earnings ratio fluctuates because current profit relative to expected future profit changes.
- Takeovers and mergers occur when they lead to an increase in stock market value.

The lessons that we've just learned about capital markets have wider application than explaining fluctuations in the stock market. They also help us to understand how natural resource markets work. Let's now examine these important markets.

Natural Resource Markets

Natural resources are the non-produced factors of production. They can be considered as natural rather than man-made capital goods. Natural resources fall into two categories: exhaustible and non-exhaustible. **Exhaustible natural resources** are natural resources that can be used only once and that cannot be replaced once used. Examples of exhaustible natural resources are coal, natural gas and oil – the so-called hydrocarbon fuels. **Non-exhaustible natural resources** are natural resources that can be used repeatedly without depleting the potential stock available for future use. Examples of non-exhaustible natural resources are land, seas, rivers, lakes, rain and sunshine. Plants and animals are also examples of non-exhaustible natural resources. By careful management, harvesting and farming, more of these natural resources can be produced to replace those used up in production and consumption activities.

Natural resources, like other capital, have two important economic dimensions – a stock dimension and a flow dimension. The stock of each natural resource is determined by nature and by the previous rate of use of the resource. The flow of a natural resource is the rate at which it is being used. This flow is determined by human choices, and these choices determine whether a given stock of natural resources is used up quickly, slowly, or not at all. In studying natural resource markets, we'll begin by considering a model of the stock dimension of a natural resource.

Supply and Demand in a Natural Resource Market

The stock of a natural resource supplied is the amount of the resource in existence. For example, the stock of oil supplied is the total volume of oil lying beneath the earth's surface. This amount is fixed independently of the price of the resource. Its supply is perfectly inelastic.

The actual stock supplied is not the same as the known (or proven) quantity. The known quantity of a natural resource is smaller than the actual stock and the known quantity can increase, despite the fact that the resource is being used up. The known quantity of a natural resource increases for two reasons. First, advances in technology enable ever less accessible resources to be discovered. Second, as the price of a natural resource rises, other things remaining the same, the incentive to widen the search for additional reserves is strengthened. Both of these factors operated to double the known reserves of oil between 1970 and 1995. During this same period, the quantity of oil consumed exceeded the 1970 known reserves.

Demand for a Stock   The stock of a natural resource demanded is determined by the *expected* rate of return or expected interest rate from holding the stock. The reason is that firms buy stocks of natural resources as an alternative to buying shares, bonds, or physical capital, and they do so in the expectation of making a return.

The expected interest rate from owning the stock of a natural resource is determined by two factors:

1. The rate of economic profit available from extracting and selling the stock.
2. The rate at which the price of the resource is expected to rise.

If the market for the extracted resource is competitive, firms just make a normal profit on their extraction activity, so the return from holding a natural resource comes from increases in the price of the resource. The faster the price of a natural resource increases, the higher is the return from owning that natural resource. Because firms don't know the future, they must forecast this interest rate and the forecasted or *expected* interest rate is equal to the *expected* percentage increase in the price of the resource.

Market Equilibrium for the Stock of Natural Resources   Equilibrium occurs in the market for the stock of a natural resource when the price of the resource is *expected* to rise at a rate equal to the interest rate on similarly risky shares and

bonds. This proposition is called the **Hotelling Principle**[1].

The price of a natural resource is expected to grow at a rate equal to the interest rate on similarly risky shares and bonds because it makes the expected interest rate on the natural resource equal to the interest rate on these other comparably risky assets. Firms look for the highest returns they can find, holding risk constant. So if the expected interest rate on a stock of a natural resource exceeds that on similarly risky shares and bonds, firms buy the stocks of natural resources and sell shares and bonds. Conversely, if the expected interest rate on a natural resource is less than that on similarly risky shares and bonds, firms buy shares and bonds and sell stocks of natural resources.

Equilibrium occurs in the market for the stock of a natural resource when prices and expectations about future prices for the stock have adjusted to make the *expected* interest rate earned on the natural resource equal to the interest rate on similarly risky stocks and bonds.

Supply and demand in the market for the stock of a natural resource determine the interest rate from owning that stock and the future *expected rate of change* of the price. But what determines the *current price* of the resource? To determine the current price of a natural resource, we must extend our model of the demand for and supply of the stock of the resource to include the demand for its use.

Current Price of a Natural Resource

To determine the current price of a natural resource, we must consider the influences on the demand for the use of the natural resource. Then our model will show the equilibrium that emerges from the interaction of the demand for the use of the resource – the demand for a *flow* – with the demand to own the natural resource – the demand for a *stock*.

---

[1] The Hotelling Principle, discovered by Harold Hotelling, first appeared in 'Economics of Exhaustible Resources', *Journal of Political Economy* (April 1931), **39**, 137–175.

Demand for the Use of a Natural Resources

Figure 16.6(a) shows the demand curve, D, for the flow of a natural resource for use in production. The demand curve for this service is determined in the same way as for any other factor of production. A firm in a perfectly competitive market maximizes profit by using the quantity of a natural resource that makes the marginal revenue product of the resource equal to its price. Marginal revenue product diminishes as the quantity of the resource used increases so the lower the price of a resource, the greater is the quantity demanded for use in production.

For any resource, there is a price that is so high that no one uses it. The price at which no one uses a natural resource is called the **choke price**. It is the price at which the demand curve touches the price axis. In Fig. 16.6(a), the choke price is £144 a tonne. Everything has substitutes and an opportunity cost – at a high enough price, only a substitute will be used. For example, we do not have to put soft drinks in aluminium cans if the price of aluminium is high; we can use plastic instead. We do not have to generate electric power with coal, oil, or uranium; we can use solar or tidal energy instead. The natural resources that we *do* use are the least expensive alternative available at the time they are used – with the lowest opportunity cost. If the price of aluminium increased, soft drinks producers would substitute plastic or glass bottles for aluminium cans. If the price of aluminium reached the choke price, only plastic or glass bottles would be used and the aluminium can would disappear.

Equilibrium Stock and Flow

The price of a natural resource and its rate of use depend on three things:

1. The interest rate
2. The demand for the flow of the resource
3. The stock of the resource

Figure 16.6 shows how these things combine to determine the price and rate of use of a natural resource. We start at the time the resource becomes depleted and work backwards. When the resource is depleted the quantity supplied is zero, so the quantity demanded must also be zero. The price that makes the quantity demanded zero is the choke price. So at the end of the life of a resource,

FIGURE 16.6

The Market for an Exhaustible Natural Resource

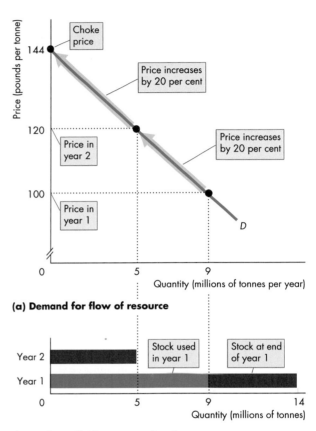

(a) Demand for flow of resource

(b) Stock available at start of each year

In part (a) at a price below £144 a tonne – the *choke price* – the quantity demanded is positive and the lower the price, the larger is the quantity demanded. In part (b) the initial stock of the resource is 14 million tonnes. The interest rate is 20 per cent a year. The current price is £100, which is determined by working backwards from the choke price. Starting from £100, the price rises by 20 per cent a year to reach the choke price in two years. The demand curve (D) tells us that the quantity demanded (used) in the first year is 9 million tonnes and the quantity used in the second year is 5 million tonnes, so the remaining stock is exhausted after two years.

its price equals the choke price. In Fig. 16.6, this price is £144.

The price of a natural resource must be expected to rise at a rate equal to the interest rate.

Given this fact, the price in the year before the resource is depleted must be less than the choke price by a percentage amount determined by the interest rate. In Fig. 16.6, the interest rate is 20 per cent a year, so the price in the year before depletion is £120. A 20 per cent price rise takes the price to the choke price of £144 the following year. We now repeat this type of calculation. The price two years before depletion is yet lower and in the example is £100. A 20 per cent increase on £100 takes the price to £120 in the following year and to £144 in two years.

We repeat this calculation for as many years as necessary until the accumulated flow of the resource used up, which is determined by the demand curve and the sequence of prices we've calculated, just exhausts the current stock of the resource. In Fig. 16.6, the stock is exhausted in only two years. (This short life lets you see the principles more clearly.) To see that the stock depletes after two years, notice that the stock available initially is 14 million tonnes. In year 2, the last year the resource is used when the price is £120, the flow of quantity used is 5 million tonnes. In year 1, the year earlier when the price is £100, the flow of quantity used is 9 million tonnes. These two amounts, 5 million tonnes plus 9 million tonnes exhaust the stock available of 14 million tonnes. So the price of this natural resource starts at £100 this year and rises by 20 percent a year for two years until it reaches its choke price of £144 a tonne, when it is depleted.

The higher the interest rate, the lower is the current price of a natural resource. You can see this fact by recalling that the price must end up at the choke price. If the price is to rise more quickly and end up at the same price, it must start out from a lower price. But starting from a lower price means that the resource is used up at a faster rate.

The greater the marginal revenue product of the natural resource – the larger the demand for the flow of the natural resource – the higher is the current price of the resource. A greater marginal revenue product means that the demand curve for the resource lies farther to the right and that the choke price is higher. A higher current price is necessary to decrease the quantity of the resource demanded and ensure that the available quantity equals the quantities demanded over the remaining years of the life of the resource.

The larger the initial stock of the natural resource, the lower is the current price. If the known stock increases, more of the resource must be used up before the choke price is reached. To induce an increase in the amount used, the price of the resource must fall. You can read about the factors which affect the price of natural forest wood in *Reading Between the Lines* on pp. 410–411.

Expected Prices and Actual Prices

Equilibrium in the market for a natural resource determines the current price of the resource and the *expected* rate of change of its future price. But the actual price rarely follows the path predicted by the Hotelling Principle. Figure 16.7 shows that the prices of metals have tended to fall, rather than rise as predicted by the Hotelling Principle. This fact was the basis of a famous wager between a conservationist and an economist – see *Economics in History* on pp. 368–369. Why do natural resource prices fluctuate and sometimes even fall rather than follow their expected path and increase over time?

FIGURE 16.7

Falling Metal Prices

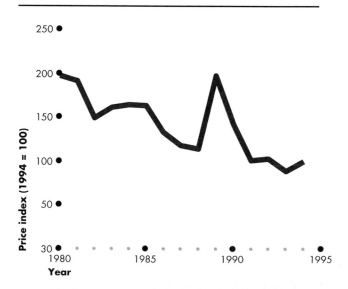

The prices of metals (here an average of the prices of copper, lead and zinc) have tended to fall over time, not rise as expected by the Hotelling Principle. The reason is that advances in technology have decreased the cost of extracting resources and greatly increased the exploitable known reserves.

Source: *Annual Abstract of Statistics,* 1995 Central Statistical Office, London, HMSO.

The price of a natural resource depends on uncertain events in the future. It depends on expectations about the future interest rate, the demand for the use of the resource and the size of the known stock, which in turn depends on the technologies and costs of extracting it. Natural resource markets are constantly being bombarded by new information that leads to new expectations. New information about the stock of a resource or the technologies available for its use or extraction can lead to sudden and perhaps quite large changes in the price of a natural resource.

All of these forces have been at work in many of the markets for exhaustible natural resources in recent years. The market for oil illustrates these effects very well. The discovery of new sources of supply and of new extraction technologies has resulted in previously unforeseen increases in the known stock of oil. The development of energy-efficient automobile and aircraft engines has slowed the growth in the quantity of oil used for transport to below the level expected in the early 1970s. The combination of these factors has led to a fall in the price of oil. Fluctuations in the price around this trend have been caused by fluctuations in interest rates.

An additional force leading to price changes in natural resource markets in general and in the oil market in particular is the degree of competitiveness. The model market that we have been studying is a perfectly competitive one. But the real-world market for oil has been dominated by the OPEC cartel, an oligopoly similar to that analysed in Chapter 13 (pp. 320–321). The declining power of the OPEC cartel contributed significantly to the decline in the price of oil during the 1980s.

Conservation and Doomsday

The theory of the price of a natural resource and its expected change over time has important implications for the popular debate about the use of natural resources. Many people fear that we are using the earth's exhaustible natural resources at such a rapid pace that we will eventually (and perhaps in the not distant future) run out of sources of energy and other crucial raw materials. They urge a slowing down in the rate at which we use exhaustible natural resources so that the limited stocks available today will last longer.

This topic is an emotional one and generates passionate debate. It is also a matter that involves economic issues, which can be understood using the economic model of a depletable natural resource that you have just studied.

The economic analysis of an exhaustible natural resource market predicts that doomsday – the using up of the entire stock of a natural resource – will eventually arise if our use of natural resources is organized in competitive markets. The economic model also implies that a competitive market will provide an automatic conservation programme arising from the steadily rising price. As the stock of a natural resource gets closer and closer to depletion, its price gets closer to the choke price – the price at which no one wants to use the resource any more. Each year, as the price rises, the quantity demanded of the flow declines and the search for alternatives increases.

But what if the resource gets completely used up? Don't we then have a real problem? We have the problem of scarcity but in no more acute a form than we had it before. Everything has substitutes. The resource that is no longer available was used because it was more efficient to use it than some alternative. For example, it is more efficient to generate electricity today by using coal and oil rather than solar power. It is efficient to stop using an exhaustible resource only when a lower-cost alternative is available. This substitution might occur before the resource is depleted or at the same time as it becomes depleted. So the market economy handles the depleting stocks of natural resources by persistently forcing up their prices. Higher prices cause us to ration our use and eventually drive the quantity demanded of the flow to zero. This happens when the supply of the stock disappears.

But will a competitive market lead us to use our scarce exhaustible natural resources at an efficient rate? Perfectly competitive markets for goods and services achieve allocative efficiency if there is no market failure – full information, no external costs and benefits, and no uncertainty. (The allocative efficiency of a perfectly competitive market is explained in Chapter 11, pp. 276–280.) The same proposition applies to markets for natural resources. If there is no market failure arising from the use of a natural resource, then the rate of its use determined in a perfectly competitive exhaustible natural resource market is the efficient rate of use.

But let's look at an example of the impact of market failure when external costs arise from the

Limited World Wood Supply

The Essence of the Story

THE FINANCIAL TIMES, 28 FEBRUARY 1996

Wood supply's stunted growth

Bernard Simon and Christopher Brown-Humes

Is the world's forest industry running out of wood?... The spectre of wood shortages was widely cited as one factor behind galloping pulp and paper prices between early 1994 and last summer. Northern bleached softwood kraft pulp, the industry's benchmark product, soared from $390 (£253) to a peak of $1,000 (£649) a tonne....

Robert Hagler, a Virginia-based consultant, told a *Pulp and Paper Week* conference last summer that 'a sharp divergence between the volume of timber that is "physically available" for industrial purposes, and the volume that will "actually" be available has emerged'.

The trend is especially evident in North America. Pressure from environmental groups has led governments to tighten forestry practices and set aside tracts of forests as parks and wildlife reserves. For example, British Columbia is doubling the area of protected forest to 12 per cent of the province's land area.

Hagler says: 'Despite physical surpluses, the availability of timber for industrial purposes is extremely limited ... It would seem that North America will begin to experience the realities of a limited resource environment.'

The alternatives for the forestry industry are few. High transport costs are likely to put Siberia's vast forests out of commercial reach for years to come. The steady expansion of peasant farmland has shrunk tropical hardwood forests in developing countries such as Indonesia, Haiti and Mozambique. Pessimists also point to rising demand for wood and paper products in fast-growing economies, such as China and India, which could further increase the pressure on supplies.

However, the forestry industry has been remarkably resourceful. Plantations have to a significant extent replaced old-growth forests as a raw material source.... The forestry industry has succeeded in substituting plentiful wood species for those in diminishing supply....

Paper mills and building material suppliers have also found new raw materials. Oriented strand-board, used for timber housing and made from low-grade species such as aspen and poplar, has become increasingly popular. The proportion of waste paper recovered for recycling has risen in the past decade from 31 per cent of global consumption to 42 per cent.

However, the industry's ingenuity in finding untapped resources may not be enough to eliminate fibre shortages entirely. According to Hagler, the stage has been reached where 'we can define limits on available supply, and recognise that, in many regions of the world, expansion of capacity will be difficult, if not impossible, for the first time in modern history'.

The implication is that wood prices are on a long-term upward trend, spurring even greater use of substitutes, such as steel and plastics in building materials, and recycled paper, straw and hemp in paper making. ...

■ The price of wood pulp soared in 1994–95 from £253 a tonne to £649 a tonne and the reason is limited wood supply.

■ Natural forests are no longer available for industrial use as governments continue to protect existing forests. North America has virtually no surplus forest and must now treat wood pulp as a limited resource.

■ Other world resources of natural forest have been devastated by agriculture or their value is outweighed by transport costs. Demand is increasing in China and India.

■ But rising prices have expanded investment in plantations for harvesting, technology has aided the use of low-quality pulp in building materials, and straw and hemp in paper making, and more paper is being recycled.

Economic Analysis

■ With a given stock of natural forest in 1994, and no unanticipated changes in demand or technology, we would expect the price of wood pulp from natural forest to rise in line with interest rates according to the Hotelling principle.

■ Figure 1(a) illustrates this principle showing a hypothetical demand for the flow of wood pulp as D_F. At the end of 1993, the price is £253 a tonne and 13 million tonnes are used.

■ Prices should rise by 5 per cent to £294 a tonne in 1996, when 10 million tonnes are used. But the actual price of wood pulp rose above £600 a tonne in 1994 prices.

■ Figure 1(b) shows the initial hypothetical supply of natural forest as 91 million tonnes in 1993. At the rates of use shown in part (a) — 13 + 12 + 11 + 10 and so on — supply is exhausted in 13 years when the choke price of £440 a tonne is reached, all other things remaining the same.

■ Figure 1(c) shows the effect of government forest protection that cuts supply to 42 million tonnes in 1994.

■ At the current annual prices shown in part (a), the stock is exhausted in just three years, before the choke price is reached. Current prices must rise to re-establish equilibrium.

■ Figure 2 shows another reason why actual prices rise. The demand for flow in 1993 is D_{F0} but an increase in the marginal revenue product of natural forest wood pulp in fast-growing economies increases demand to D_{F1}, raising price to £310 a tonne.

■ As we expect, government action has forced a price rise reflecting the scarcity of natural forests, and this rising price has triggered the search for substitutes including cultivating fast-growing plantation forest, straw and hemp.

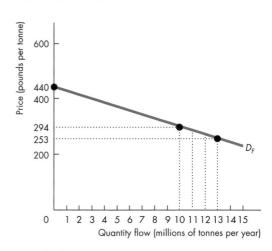

Figure 1(a)

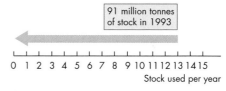

Figure 1(b)

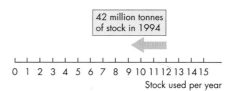

Figure 1(c)

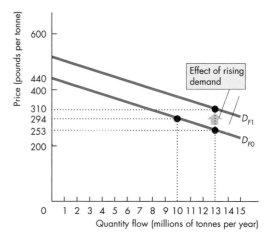

Figure 2

use of a natural resource. For example, if burning hydrocarbon fuels increases the carbon dioxide in the atmosphere and a warming of the earth's atmosphere results – the so-called greenhouse effect – the costs associated with this atmospheric change have to be added to the costs of using oil and coal as fuels. When these costs are taken into account, the allocatively efficient rate of use of these fuels is slower than that resulting from a perfectly competitive market. So efficiency would require a slower rate of use of the resource than that in the competitive market. We examine ways in which government intervention can achieve allocative efficiency in such a situation in Chapter 20 (pp. 499–506). We also look at how uncertainty affects the rate of use of a non-renewable resource in Chapter 17.

Finally, we have suggested that natural capital may be treated as a substitute for man-made capital, and that the total capital stock is a measure of our wealth. If as we deplete our reserves of natural capital we can replace them with man-made capital and human capital, then we will not lose any total wealth or potential for future economic growth. This is the notion of *sustainable economic development*, established at the World Commission on Environment and Development in 1987. It is an important idea because it suggests that current consumption and economic growth need not conflict with the needs of the environment. Let's see why.

If there is no market failure and man-made capital is a good substitute for natural capital, markets will provide future generations with the same total stock of capital, but in a different mix.Our need to use up the stock of natural resources to create more goods and services today, will not restrict the ability of future generations to do the same. If the total stock of wealth is constant, society's total utility or well-being cannot fall, and may even rise despite the fact that we exhaust the stock of some natural resources.

The idea of sustainable development depends on the substitutability of different types of capital. Some economists and ecologists argue that many natural resources cannot be replaced. Certain types of natural capital have critical value because they are essential to the maintenance of the ecosystem and have no close substitutes. The oceans and the atmosphere are examples of natural resources which support life, biodiversity, climatic conditions,

natural beauty and act as an essential waste deposit system. If they are right, sustainable economic development means that we must protect stocks of critical natural resources and not allow the market mechanism to determine their rate of use.

R E V I E W

◆ Natural resources are non-produced factors of production and a form of capital. Firms use stocks of natural resources as an alternative to other forms of investment.

◆ Hotellings principle shows that the price of natural resources should rise over time.

◆ The current price of a natural resource and its rate of use depend on the interest rate, the demand for its use and the level of the stock available.

◆ The smaller the demand for its use and the larger the initial stock, the lower is the current price and final choke price.

◆ The higher the interest rate and the lower the current price, the faster the rate of use.

◆ Perfect competition leads to an efficient use of natural resources, but market failure results in too rapid a rate of depletion.

◆ ◆ ◆ ◆ Looking back over the last three chapters, we have studied the way in which factor markets allocate scarce productive resources – labour, land and capital – and the determination of factor prices and factor incomes. The prices and quantities determined in factor markets in turn determine the distribution of income among individuals and families. That income distribution determines *for whom* goods and services are produced. But that outcome is uncertain. People decide what type of work to do, how much to save and what to do with their savings with no sure knowledge of the incomes they'll receive from their decisions. So we must now study uncertainty and its consequences in a more systematic way. We will discover some of the ways in which uncertainty affects efficiency and how we cope with uncertainty in the next chapter.

SUMMARY

The Structure of Capital Markets

Capital markets – stock markets, bond markets and loan markets – are the channels through which households' savings flow into firms. Households supply financial capital to firms, and firms use financial capital to buy physical capital. Financial intermediaries facilitate capital market transactions. (pp. 395–396)

Demand for Capital

Capital is a stock and investment and depreciation are flows. Gross investment is the purchase of new capital during a given period which adds to the capital stock, and depreciation is the amount of existing capital that wears out in a given period.

The demand for capital is determined by firms' profit-maximization decisions. The quantity of capital demanded by a firm is such that the marginal revenue product of capital equals its opportunity cost – the interest rate. Other things remaining the same, the higher the interest rate, the lower is the present value of the future stream of marginal revenue products, and the smaller is the quantity of capital equipment a firm buys. The lower the interest rate, the greater is the quantity of capital demanded – the demand curve for capital is downward-sloping. The demand curve for capital shifts steadily rightward as a result of population growth and fluctuates because of technological change. (pp. 396–400)

The Supply of Capital

The quantity of capital supplied results from the saving decisions of households. Savings depend on current income and expected future income and on the extent to which households smooth their consumption over their lifetime. Savings also depend on the interest rate. Other things remaining the same, as interest rates rise, the quantity of capital supplied increases – the supply curve of capital is upward-sloping. Changes in the size and the age composition of the population and changes in income shift the supply curve of capital over time. (pp. 400–402)

Interest Rates and Stock Prices

Interest rates and asset prices can be viewed as two sides of the same coin. Interest rates and asset prices adjust to achieve equality between the quantity of capital demanded and the quantity supplied. Interest rates on particular assets are distributed around the average rate according to the degree of riskiness of different types of assets. The price of a firm's shares may be high or low, relative to its current profit, and is indicated by the price–earnings ratio. When people are in agreement about expected future dividends, there is little trading in a firm's stock, but when there is disagreement about the future, trading is heavy. If a firm's stock market value is low, relative to its earnings potential, the firm becomes a takeover target. (pp. 402–405)

Natural Resource Markets

Natural resources are the non-produced factors of production with which we are endowed. The price of a natural resource is determined by the interest rate, its marginal revenue product (which determines the demand for its flow) and the stock of the natural resource (which determines the supply). The price of a natural resource is such that its future price is expected to rise at a rate equal to the interest rate and to reach the choke price at the time at which the resource is exhausted. The actual price is constantly changing to take into account new information. Even though the future price is expected to increase, the actual price often decreases as a result of new information, leading to an increase in the estimate of the remaining stock or to a decrease in the demand for the flow of the resource. (pp. 405–412)

KEY ELEMENTS

Key Terms

Bond market, 395
Choke price, 407
Exhaustible natural resources, 405
Financial intermediary, 395
Hotelling Principle, 406
Loan market, 395
Merger, 405
Natural resources, 405
Net present value, 398
Non-exhaustible natural resources, 405

Stock market, 395
Takeover, 404
Wealth, 400

 **Key Figures**

Figure 16.1   Capital Market Flows, 396
Figure 16.3   The Demand for Capital, 400
Figure 16.4   The Supply of Capital, 401
Figure 16.5   Capital Market Equilibrium, 403

REVIEW QUESTIONS

1 Briefly describe the structure of the capital markets.

2 Distinguish between financial capital and physical capital.

3 Describe the main flow of funds in the capital markets.

4 Distinguish between a stock market, a bond market and a loan market.

5 What is the net present value of an investment?

6 What are the main influences on the demand for capital?

7 Why does the quantity of capital demanded by a firm increase as the interest rate decreases?

8 What are the main factors that change the demand for capital? How do they change the demand curve for capital?

9 What are the influences of the interest rate on the amount of saving and the supply of capital?

10 How does the age structure of the population influence the supply of capital?

11 What is the relationship between the interest rate and the price of a share or bond?

12 How is the interest rate determined?

13 How are share prices and bond prices determined?

14 Distinguish between a takeover and a merger. Explain why takeovers and mergers occur.

15 What is an exhaustible resource? Give some examples.

16 Distinguish between the stock and the flow of an exhaustible natural resource.

17 Explain why the price of an exhaustible natural resource is expected to rise at a rate equal to the interest rate.

18 What determines the price of a natural resource?

19 Why do the prices of some natural resources fall over time?

20 What is meant by sustainable economic development?

PROBLEMS

1 At the end of 1994 a firm had a production plant worth £1,000,000. The plant depreciated during 1995 by 10 per cent. During the same year, the firm also bought new capital equipment for £250,000. What is the value of the firm's stock of capital at the end of 1995? What was the firm's gross investment during 1995? What was the firm's net investment during 1995?

2 You earn £20,000 per year for three years and you spend £16,000 each year. How much do you save each year? What happens to your wealth during this three-year period?

3 What are the different ways in which household saving can finance a firm's investment?

4 A firm is considering buying a new machine. It is estimated that the marginal revenue product of the machine will be £10,000 a year for five years. The machine will have a scrap value at the end of five years of £10,000. The interest rate is 10 per cent a year.

a What is the maximum price that the firm will pay for the machine?

b If the machine costs £40,000, would the firm buy the machine at an interest rate of 10 per cent? What is the highest interest rate at which the firm would buy the machine?

5 Suppose that exploration in Norway reveals a vast stock of natural gas that was previously undreamed of and that exceeds all the currently known stocks in Norway. What do you predict will happen to the world price of natural gas:

a At the moment the news of the discovery breaks?

b Over the following ten years?

c What will happen to the rate of use of natural gas?

6 You've been hired by Greenpeace to make the economic case for conserving the world's stock of copper. Set out your case and anticipate the arguments that an economist opposing you would make.

7 Doomsday is close for zapton, an exhaustible natural resource, the remaining stock of which is 6 million tonnes. The marginal revenue product schedule for zapton is:

Quantity used (millions of tonnes)	Marginal revenue product (pounds per tonne)
0	16.11
1	14.64
2	13.31
3	12.10
4	11.00
5	10.00

The interest rate is 10 per cent a year.

a What is the choke price of zapton?

b What is the current price of zapton?

c If there is no change in the marginal revenue product schedule for zapton, after how many years is its stock exhausted?

8 In Problem 7, a new use is discovered for zapton that increases its marginal revenue   product. Does the:

a Choke price of zapton rise, fall, or remain unchanged?

b Current price of zapton rise, fall, or remain unchanged?

c Number of years to zapton's exhaustion increase, decrease, or remain the same?

9 Read the story in *Reading Between the Lines* on pp. 410–411 again and then answer the following questions:

a Use Hotellings principle to explain why we would expect the price of wood pulp from natural forests to rise in line with interest rates.

b Explain why the price of wood pulp from natural forests increased faster than the rate of interest in 1994.

CHAPTER
17

UNCERTAINTY
AND
INFORMATION

After studying this chapter you will be able to:

◆ Explain how people make decisions when they are uncertain about the consequences

◆ Explain why people buy insurance and how insurance companies make a profit

◆ Explain why buyers search and sellers advertise

◆ Explain how markets cope with private information

◆ Explain how people use financial markets to lower risk

LIFE IS LIKE A LOTTERY. YOU WORK HARD IN COLLEGE AND UNIVERSITY, BUT WHAT will you the payoff be? Will you get an interesting, well-paying job or a miserable, low-paying one? Will you make enough income to buy a house and a car or will you struggle to get by? We've already seen that uncertainty can generate price wars in business in Chapter 13. So how do individuals make a decision when they don't know its consequences? ◆ As you drive across a road junction on a green light, you see a car approaching from the left at high speed. Will it stop or will it drive through the red light? You buy insurance against such a risk, and insurance companies make a profit. Why are we willing to buy insurance at prices that leave insurance companies with a gain? ◆ Buying a new car – or a used car – is fun, but it's also scary. You could get stuck with a bad buy – a lemon. Just about every complicated product you buy could be

Lotteries and Lemons

defective. How do car dealers and retailers induce us to buy what may turn out to be a lemon? ◆ People keep some of their wealth in the bank, some in building societies, some in bonds and some in shares. Some of these ways of holding wealth have a high return and some have a low return. Why does it pay to diversify?

◆ ◆ ◆ ◆ In this chapter, we answer questions such as these, and in doing so we will extend and enrich the more abstract models of markets that we've studied in earlier chapters. We'll begin by explaining how people make decisions when they're uncertain about the consequences. We'll see how it pays to buy insurance and why we use scarce resources to generate and disseminate information.

Uncertainty and Risk

In our economic model of allocative efficiency, we showed that uncertainty was one form of market failure. To remind yourself, go back and read the last section of Chapter 11 again. Does the market have any ways of dealing with the problem of uncertainty? The answer is yes – insurance markets. But before we start to look at these markets and how we make decisions and do business with each other in an uncertain world, we must understand what uncertainty is. We live in a risky world. Is risk the same as uncertainty? Let's begin by defining uncertainty and risk and distinguishing between them.

Uncertainty is a situation in which more than one event may occur, but we don't know which one. Usually, the event that does occur affects our economic well-being. For example, when farmers plant their crops, they are uncertain about the weather during the growing season, but their profits depend on the weather.

To describe uncertainty we use the concept of probability. A *probability* is a number between zero and one that measures the chance of some possible event occurring. A zero probability means the event will not happen. A probability of one means the event will occur for sure – with certainty. A probability of 0.5 means that the event is just as likely to occur as not. An example is the probability of a tossed coin falling heads. In a large number of tosses, about half of them will be heads and the other half tails.

In ordinary speech, risk is the probability of incurring a loss (or some other misfortune). In economics, **risk** is a situation in which more than one outcome may occur, and the *probability* of each possible outcome can be estimated. Probabilities can be measured. For example, the probability that a tossed coin will come down heads is based on the fact that, in a large number of tosses, half are heads and half are tails; the probability that a car driver in London in 1996 will be involved in an accident can be estimated by using police and insurance records of previous accidents; the probability that you will win the jackpot in the national lottery can be estimated by dividing the number of tickets you have bought by the total number of tickets bought – about 1 in 14 million in the United Kingdom.

Some situations cannot be described using probabilities based on past observed events. These situations may be unique events, such as the introduction of a new product. How much will we sell and at what price? Because the product is new, there is no previous experience on which to base a probability. But the question can be answered by looking at past experience with *similar* new products, supported by some judgements. Such judgements are called *subjective probabilities*.

Regardless of whether the probability of some event occurring is measured using actual data or judgements – even guesses – we can use probability to explain the way in which people make decisions in the face of uncertainty. The first step in doing this is to describe how people assess the cost of risk.

Measuring the Opportunity Cost of Risk

Some people are more willing to bear risk than others, but everyone prefers less risk to more, other things remaining the same. We measure people's attitudes towards risk by using their utility of wealth schedules and curves. The **utility of wealth** is the amount of utility a person attaches to a given amount of wealth. The greater a person's wealth, other things remaining the same, the higher is the person's total utility. Not only does greater wealth bring higher total utility, but as wealth increases, each additional unit of wealth increases total utility by a smaller amount. That is, the *marginal utility of wealth diminishes*.

Figure 17.1 sets out Tania's utility of wealth schedule and curve. Each point *a* to *e* on Tania's utility of wealth curve corresponds to the row of the table identified by the same letter. You can see that as her wealth increases, so does her total utility of wealth. You can also see that her marginal utility of wealth diminishes. When wealth increases from $3,000 to $6,000, total utility increases by 20 units, but when wealth increases by a further $3,000 to $9,000, total utility increases by only 10 units.

We can use Tania's utility of wealth curve to measure her *opportunity cost* of risk. The bigger the risk Tania faces, the worse off she is and the less she likes it. To measure Tania's cost of risk, let's see how she evaluates two alternative jobs that involve different amounts of risk.

One job, working as a painter, pays enough for her to save $5,000 by the end of the year, given her living costs. There is no uncertainty about the income from this job and hence no risk. If Tania takes this job, by the end of the summer her wealth will be $5,000. The other job – telesales – involves selling subscriptions to a magazine by phone and is risky. If she takes this job, her wealth at the end of the summer depends entirely on her success at selling. She

FIGURE 17.1

The Utility of Wealth

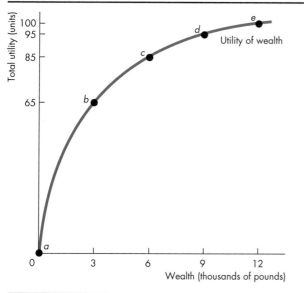

	Wealth (thousands of pounds)	Total utility (units)	Marginal utility (units)
a	0	0	
			65
b	3	65	
			20
c	6	85	
			10
d	9	95	
			5
e	12	100	

The table shows Tania's utility of wealth schedule, and the figure shows her utility of wealth curve. Utility increases as wealth increases, but the marginal utility of wealth diminishes.

might be a good sales person and earn enough to save £9,000, or a poor one earning only enough to save £3,000. Tania has never tried telesales before, so she doesn't know how successful she'll be. She assumes that there is an equal chance – a probability of 0.5 – of saving either £3,000 or £9,000. Which outcome does Tania prefer, £5,000 for sure from the painting job or a 50 per cent chance of either £3,000 or £9,000 from the telesales job?

As people do not know the *actual* outcome when there is uncertainty, they cannot know the actual utility they will get from taking a particular

FIGURE 17.2

Choice under Uncertainty

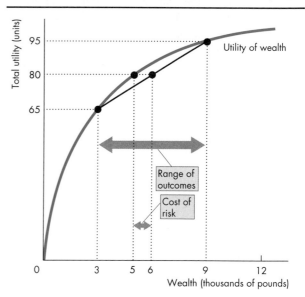

If Tania's wealth is £5,000 and she faces no risk, her utility is 80 units. If she faces an equal probability of having £9,000 or £3,000, her expected wealth is £6,000. But her expected utility is 80 units the same as with £5,000 and no uncertainty. Tania is indifferent between these two alternatives. Tania's extra £1,000 of expected wealth is just enough to offset her extra risk.

action. But it is possible to calculate the utility they *expect* to get. **Expected utility** is the average utility arising from all the possible outcomes. So to choose her summer job, Tania calculates the expected utility arising from painting and telesales. Figure 17.2 shows how she does this.

If Tania takes the painting job, she has £5,000 of wealth and 80 units of utility. There is no uncertainty in this case, so her expected utility equals her actual utility – 80 units. But suppose she takes the telesales job. If she saves £9,000, her utility is 95 units, and if she saves £3,000, her utility is 65 units. Tania's *expected income* is the average of these two outcomes – £6,000 – calculated as (£9,000 × 0.5) + (£3,000 × 0.5). This average is called a *weighted average*, the weights being the probabilities of each outcome (both 0.5 in this case). Tania's *expected utility* is the average of the two possible total utilities – 80 units – calculated as (95 × 0.5) + (65 × 0.5).

Tania chooses the job that maximizes her expected utility. In this case, the two alternatives give the same expected utility – 80 units – so she is indifferent between them. She is equally likely to take either job. The difference between Tania's expected wealth of £6,000 from the risky job and £5,000 from the no-risk job – £1,000 – is just large enough to offset the opportunity cost of taking the risky telesales job.

The calculation that we've just done enables us to measure Tania's cost of risk. The cost of risk is the amount by which expected wealth must be increased to give the same expected utility as a no-risk situation. In Tania's case, the cost of the risk arising from an uncertain income of £3,000 or £9,000 is £1,000.

If the amount Tania can make from painting falls to £3,000, the potential for higher income from the risky job will be more than enough to compensate her for the risk and she will take the risky telesales job. An income of £3,000 for sure gives only 65 units of utility, an amount less than the 80 units expected from the telesales job.

If the amount Tania can make from painting remains at £5,000 and the expected income from telesales also remains constant while its range of uncertainty increases, Tania will take the painting job. To see this conclusion, suppose that good telesales summer staff can save £12,000, and poor ones save nothing. The average saving from telesales is unchanged at £6,000, but the range of uncertainty has increased. Looking at the table in Fig. 17.1 you can see that Tania gets 100 units of utility from a wealth of £12,000 and zero units of utility from a wealth of zero. Thus in this case, Tania's expected utility from telesales is 50 units – calculated as (100 × 0.5) + (0 × 0.5). Because the expected utility from telesales is now less than that from painting, she chooses painting.

Risk Aversion and Risk Neutrality

There is an enormous difference between Richard Branson, who favours more risky ventures for his Virgin empire, and high street bank managers, who favour safe investment ventures. They place a different value on the opportunity cost of risk. Bank managers are much more *risk averse* than is Richard Branson. Tania is also *risk averse*; other things remaining the same, she prefers situations with less risk. The shape of the utility of wealth curve tells us about the person's attitude towards risk – the person's degree of *risk aversion*. The more rapidly the

marginal utility of wealth diminishes, the more the person dislikes risk – the more risk averse that person is. You can see this fact best by considering the case of *risk neutrality*. There is no opportunity cost to risk for a risk-neutral person. Such a person cares only about *expected wealth* and does not mind how much uncertainty there is.

Figure 17.3 shows the utility of wealth curve of a risk-neutral person. It is a straight line and the marginal utility of wealth is constant. If this person has an expected wealth of £6,000, expected utility is 50 units regardless of the range of uncertainty around that average. An equal probability of having £3,000 or £9,000 gives the same expected utility as an equal probability of having £0 or £12,000, which is also the expected utility of £6,000 for certain. Most people are risk averse and their utility of wealth curves look like Tania's. Some, like Richard Branson, are just less risk averse than others. But the case of risk neutrality illustrates the importance and the consequences of the shape of the utility of wealth curve for a person's degree of risk aversion.

FIGURE 17.3

Risk Neutrality

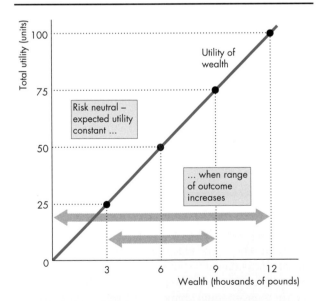

People's dislike of risk implies a diminishing marginal utility of wealth. A (hypothetical) risk-neutral person has a linear utility of wealth curve and a constant marginal utility of wealth. For a risk-neutral person, expected utility does not depend on the range of uncertainty and the cost of risk is zero.

◆ Faced with uncertain outcomes, people take the actions that maximize expected utility.

◆ The opportunity cost of risk can be measured as the amount by which expected wealth must be increased to give the same expected utility as in a no-risk situation.

◆ The opportunity cost of risk depends on the degree of risk aversion. The greater the degree of risk aversion, the greater is the cost of risk.

◆ For a risk-neutral person, risk is costless.

Insurance

One way of reducing the risk we face is to buy insurance. How does insurance reduce risk? Why do people buy insurance? What determines the amount we spend on insurance? Before we answer these questions, let's look at the insurance industry in the United Kingdom today.

Insurance Industry in the United Kingdom

Insurance markets are big business. There are more than 820 authorized insurance companies employing more than 268,000 workers in the United Kingdom. Each household spends about £1,150 each year on private insurance, but it also buys insurance through government taxation – social insurance. The insurance industry takes £90 billion in premiums each year, 65 per cent of which is private insurance.

When we buy private insurance, we enter into an agreement with an insurance company to pay an agreed price – called a *premium* – in exchange for benefits to be paid to us if some specified event occurs. The two main types of private insurance we buy are:

◆ General insurance

◆ Long-term insurance

You can see from Fig. 17.4 that about two-thirds of all private premiums were paid back as claims or benefits in 1994.

FIGURE 17.4

The UK Private Insurance Market

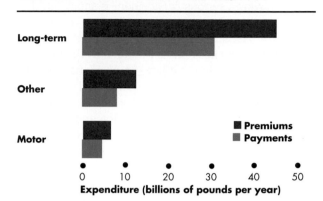

The UK insurance market is mainly in general or long-term insurance. General insurance accounts for about 30 percent of the market and includes car insurance and all other property insurance. Long-term insurance is the bulk of the market and includes both life insurance and pension plans. Insured parties, on the average, get between 66 and 72 per cent of their premiums paid back in claims and benefits.

Source: British Association of Insurers, *Insurance Statistics*, 1995, London.

General Insurance   General insurance reduces the risk of financial loss in the event of accidents, theft or damage. Claims are made for damage and replacement, as well as for injury to individuals. General insurance accounts for about 30 per cent of the market and includes car insurance and all other property insurance. More than 67 per cent of households own their own homes in the United Kingdom. The majority of owner–occupiers insure their buildings against damage by fire and floods, and insure the contents of their homes against theft and damage. This type of insurance makes up the bulk of other property insurance.

Long-term Insurance   Long-term insurance includes life insurance and pension plans. Life insurance reduces the risk of financial loss in the event of death. Pension plans pay a certain income to individuals when they retire. More than 60 per cent of households in the United Kingdom have life insurance, but companies also buy life insurance and pensions for their employees. Figure 17.4 shows that life insurance and pension plan premiums make up the bulk of the United Kingdom's insurance business.

How Insurance Works Insurance works by pooling risks. It is possible and profitable because people are risk averse. The probability of any one person having a serious car accident is small, but the cost of an accident to the person involved is enormous. For a large population, the probability of one person having an accident is the same as the proportion of the population that have an accident. Because this probability can be estimated, the total cost of accidents can be predicted. An insurance company can pool the risks of a large population and share the costs. It does so by collecting premiums from everyone and paying out benefits to those who suffer a loss. If the insurance company does its calculations correctly, it collects at least as much in premiums as it pays out in benefits and operating costs.

To see why people buy insurance and why it is profitable, let's consider an example. Daniel has the utility of wealth curve shown in Fig. 17.5. He owns a car worth £10,000 and that is his only wealth. If there is no risk of his having an accident, his utility will be 100 units. But there is a 10 per cent chance (a probability of 0.1) that he will have an accident within a year. Suppose Daniel does not buy insurance. If he does have an accident his car is worthless, and with no insurance he has no wealth and no utility. Because the probability of an accident is 0.1, the probability of *not* having an accident is 0.9. Daniel's expected wealth, therefore, is £9,000 (£10,000 × 0.9 + £0 × 0.1), and his expected utility is 90 units (100 × 0.9).

FIGURE 17.5

The Gains from Insurance

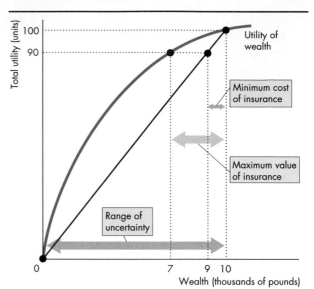

Daniel has a car valued at £10,000 which gives him a utility of 100 units, but there is a 0.1 probability that he will have an accident making his car worthless (wealth and utility equal to zero). With no insurance, his expected utility is 90 units and he is willing to pay up to £3,000 for insurance. An insurance company (with no operating expenses) can offer insurance to Daniel and the rest of the community for £1,000. Hence there is a potential gain from insurance for both Daniel and the insurance company.

TABLE 17.1

Risk Taking versus Insurance

(a) Possible Outcomes

	No accident		Accident	
Probability	0.9		0.1	
	Wealth	**Utility**	**Wealth**	**Utility**
No insurance	£10,000	100	£0	0
Insurance	£8,000	95	£8,000	95

(b) Expected Outcomes

	Expected wealth	Expected utility
No insurance	£10,000 × 0.9 + £0 × 0.1 = £9,000	100 × 0.9 + 0 × 0.1 = 90
Insurance	£8,000 × 0.9 + £8,000 × 0.1 = £8,000	95 × 0.9 + 95 × 0.1 = 95

With no insurance, Daniel's expected wealth is £9,000 and his expected utility is 90 units. If he buys insurance for £2,000, Daniel's expected wealth falls to £8,000, but he has no uncertainty and his expected utility increases to 95 units.

Given his utility of wealth curve, Daniel has 90 units of utility if his wealth is £7,000 and he faces no uncertainty. That is, Daniel's utility of a guaranteed wealth of £7,000 is the same as his utility of a 90 per cent chance of having wealth of £10,000 and a 10 per cent chance of having nothing. If the cost of an insurance policy that pays out in the event of an accident is less than £3,000 (£10,000 – £7,000), Daniel will buy the policy. Thus Daniel has a demand for car insurance at premiums less than £3,000 a year.

Suppose there are lots of people like Daniel, each with a £10,000 car and each with a 10 per cent chance of having an accident within the year. If an insurance company agrees to pay each person who has an accident £10,000, the company will pay out £10,000 to one-tenth of the population, or an average of £1,000 per person. This amount is the insurance company's minimum premium for such insurance. It is less than the value of insurance to Daniel because Daniel is risk averse. He is willing to pay something to reduce the risk he faces.

Now suppose that the insurance company's operating expenses are a further £1,000 and that it offers insurance for £2,000. The company now covers all its costs – the amounts paid out to policyholders for their losses plus the company's operating expenses. Daniel – and all the other people like him – will maximize their utility by buying this insurance. The calculations in Table 17.1 summarize the gain each makes. With no insurance, expected utility is 90 units. But with insurance costing £2,000, utility is 95 units, a gain of 5 units.

REVIEW

◆ We spend £90 million pounds each year on general and long-term insurance cover in the United Kingdom – £1,500 each every year.

◆ Insurance works by pooling risks. Every insured person pays in but only those who suffer a loss are compensated.

◆ Insurance is worth buying and is profitable because people are risk averse and are willing to pay for lower risk.

Much of the uncertainty we face arises from ignorance. We just don't know all the things that could benefit us. Not having full information is another form of market failure. But there are markets for information. If we have to pay for information, we must make decisions about how much information to acquire. Let's now study the choices we make about obtaining information and see how incomplete information affects some of our economic transactions.

Information

We spend a huge quantity of our scarce resources on economic information. **Economic information** includes data on the prices, quantities and qualities of goods and services and factors of production.

In the models of perfect competition, monopoly and monopolistic competition, information was assumed to be free. Everyone has all the information he or she needs. Households are completely informed about the prices of the goods and services they buy and the factors of production they sell. Similarly, firms are completely informed.

In contrast, information is scarce in the real world. If it were not, we wouldn't need the *Financial Times* or the Internet. We wouldn't need to shop around for bargains or spend time looking for a job. The opportunity cost of economic information – the cost of acquiring information on prices, quantities and qualities of goods and services and factors of production – is called **information cost.** It is a form of transactions cost. Let's look at some of the consequences of information cost.

Searching for Price Information

When many firms sell the same good or service, there is a range of prices and buyers want to find the lowest price. But searching takes time and is costly. So buyers must balance the expected gain from further search against the cost of further search. To perform this balancing act, buyers use a decision rule called the *optimal-search rule*, or *optimal-stopping rule*. The optimal-search rule is:

◆ Search for a lower price until the expected marginal benefit of search equals the marginal cost of search.

◆ When the expected marginal benefit from additional search is less than or equal to the marginal cost, stop searching and buy.

To implement the optimal-search rule, each buyer chooses her or his own reservation price. The buyer's **reservation price** is the highest price that the buyer is willing to pay for a good. The buyer will continue to search for a lower price if the lowest price so far found exceeds the reservation price, but will stop searching and buy if the lowest price found is less than or equal to the reservation price. At the buyer's reservation price, the expected marginal benefit of search equals the marginal cost of search.

Figure 17.6 illustrates the optimal-search rule. Suppose you've decided to buy a used Golf GTi. Your marginal cost of search is C per dealer visited and is shown by the horizontal orange line in the figure. This cost includes the value of your time. Your expected marginal benefit of visiting one more dealer depends on the lowest price that you've found. The lower the price you've already found, the lower is your expected marginal benefit of visiting one more dealer, as shown by the blue curve in the figure.

The price at which expected marginal benefit equals marginal cost is your reservation price – £8,000 in the figure. If you find a price below your

reservation price, you stop searching and buy. If you find a price that exceeds your reservation price, you continue to search for a lower price. Individual shoppers differ in their marginal cost of search and so have different reservation prices. As a result, identical items can be found selling for a range of prices.

Buyers are not alone in creating information. Sellers do a lot of it too – in the form of advertising. Let's see what the effects of advertising are.

Advertising

Advertising constantly surrounds us – on television, radio and billboards and in newspapers and magazines – and costs billions of pounds. How do firms decide how much to spend on advertising? Does advertising create information, or does it just persuade us to buy things we don't really want? What does it do to prices?

Advertising for Profit Maximization   A firm's advertising decision is part of its overall profit-maximization strategy. Firms in perfect competition don't advertise because everyone has all the information there is. But firms selling differentiated products in monopolistic competition and firms locked in the struggle of survival in oligopoly advertise a lot.

The amount of advertising undertaken by firms in monopolistic competition is such that the marginal revenue product of advertising equals its marginal cost. The amount of advertising undertaken by firms in oligopoly is determined by the game they are playing. If that game is a *prisoners' dilemma*, they might spend amounts that lower their combined profits but they can't avoid advertising without being wiped out by other firms in the industry.

Persuasion or Information   Much advertising is designed to persuade us that the product being advertised is the best in its class. For example, the Pepsi advertisement tells us that Pepsi is really better than Coke. The Coca-Cola advertisement tells us that Coke is really better than Pepsi. But advertising also informs. It provides information about the quality and price of a good or service.

Does advertising mainly persuade or mainly inform? The answer varies for different goods and different types of markets. Goods whose quality can be assessed *before* they are bought are called *search goods*. Typically, the advertising of search goods mainly informs – gives information about price, quality and location of suppliers. Examples of such goods are petrol, basic foods and household goods. Goods

FIGURE 17.6

Optimal-search Rule

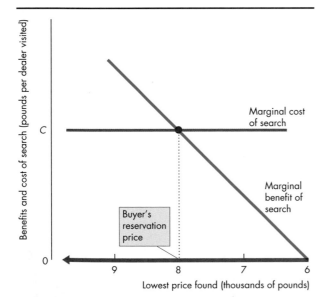

The marginal cost of search is constant at £*C*. As the lowest price found (measured from right to left on the horizontal axis) declines, the expected marginal utility of further search diminishes. The lowest price found at which the marginal cost equals the expected marginal benefit is the reservation price. The optimal-search rule is to search until the reservation price (or lower) is found and then buy at that lowest found price.

whose quality can only be assessed *after* they are bought are called *experience goods*. Typically, the advertising of experience goods mainly persuades – encourages the consumer to buy now and make a judgement later about quality, based on experience with the good. Examples of such goods are cigarettes, alcoholic beverages and perfume.

Because most advertising involves experience goods, it is likely that advertising is more often persuasive rather than merely informative. But persuasive advertising might result in lower prices.

Advertising and Prices   Advertising is costly, but does it increase the price of the good advertised? It might, but two lines of reasoning tell us that advertising can lower prices. The first is that if advertising is informative, it *increases* competition. By informing potential buyers about alternative sources of supply, advertising forces firms to keep their prices low. There is evidence of such effects, especially in retailing. The second is that if advertising enables firms to increase their output and reap economies of scale, it is possible that the price of the good will be lower with advertising than without it, provided competition prevents monopoly pricing. So provided the firm does not become so large that it is able to extract monopoly profits, consumers might benefit from advertising.

We know that advertising would be wasteful and inefficient in perfect competition because there is full information. But if there is incomplete information, we just don't know whether advertising increases or decreases efficiency overall.

R E V I E W

◆ Data on the prices, quantities and qualities of goods and services and factors of production – economic information – is scarce and people economize on its use.

◆ Buyers searching for price information stop when they find their reservation price, the price that makes the expected marginal benefit of search equal the marginal cost of search.

◆ Sellers advertise to inform potential buyers of the good or to persuade them to buy it.

◆ We do not know whether advertising is efficient with imperfect information.

Private Information

So far we have looked at situations in which information is available to everyone and can be bought and sold. But not all situations are like this. For example, someone might have private information. **Private information** is information that is available to one person but too costly for anyone else to obtain. This means that one person has more information than others – *asymmetric information*.

Private information affects many economic transactions. One is your knowledge about your driving. You know much more than your car insurance company does about how carefully or badly you drive. Another is your knowledge about your work effort. You know far more than your employer about how hard you work. Yet another is your knowledge about the quality of your car. You know whether it's a lemon. But the person to whom you are about to sell it does not and can't find out until after he has purchased it from you.

Private information creates two special types of market failure:

1. Moral hazard
2. Adverse selection

Moral hazard exists when one of the parties to an agreement has an incentive, *after the agreement is made*, to act in a manner that brings additional benefits to himself or herself at the expense of the other party. Moral hazard arises because it is too costly for the injured party to monitor the actions of the advantaged party. For example, Jackie hires Matt as a sales person and pays him a fixed wage regardless of his sales. Matt faces a moral hazard. He has an incentive to put in the least possible effort, benefiting himself and lowering Jackie's profits. For this reason, sales people are usually paid by a formula that makes their income higher the greater is the volume (or value) of their sales.

Adverse selection is the tendency for people to enter into agreements in which their private information can be used to their own advantage and to the disadvantage of the less informed party. For example, if Jackie offers sales people a fixed wage, she will attract lazy sales people. Hardworking sales people will prefer *not* to work for Jackie because they can earn more by working for someone who pays by results. The fixed wage contract adversely selects those with private information (knowledge about their work habits), who can use that knowledge to their own advantage and to the disadvantage of the other party.

A variety of devices have evolved that enable markets to work more efficiently in the face of moral hazard and adverse selection. We've just seen one, the use of incentive payments for sales people. Let's look at some more and also see how moral hazard and adverse selection influence three real-world markets:

◆ The market for used cars

◆ The market for loans

◆ The market for insurance

The Market for Used Cars

When a person buys a new car it might turn out to be a lemon. If the car is a lemon it is worth less to the person who bought it and to everyone else than if it has no defects. Does the used car market have two prices reflecting these two values – a low price for lemons and a higher price for cars without defects? It does not. To see why, let's look at a used car market, first with no dealer warranties and second with warranties.

Used Cars without Warranties   To make the points as clearly as possible, we'll make some extreme assumptions. There are just two kinds of cars, lemons and those without defects. A lemon is worth $1,000 both to its current owner and to anyone who buys it. A car without defects is worth $5,000 to its current owner and potential future owners. Whether a car is a lemon is private information to the person who owns it and has spent enough time driving it to discover its quality. Buyers of used cars can't tell whether they are buying a lemon until *after* they have bought the car and learned as much about it as its current owner knows. There are no dealer warranties.

The first thing to notice is that because buyers can't tell the difference between a lemon and a good car, they are willing to pay only one price for a used car. What is that price? Are they willing to pay $5,000, the value of a good car? They are not, because there is at least some probability that they are buying a lemon worth only $1,000. If buyers are not willing to pay $5,000 for a used car, are the owners of good cars willing to sell? They are not, because a good car is worth $5,000 to them, so they

hang on to their cars. Only the owners of lemons are willing to sell – as long as the price is $1,000 or higher. But, reason the buyers, if only the owners of lemons are selling, all the used cars available are lemons so the maximum price worth paying is $1,000. Thus the market for used cars is a market for lemons and the price is $1,000.

Moral hazard exists in the used car market because sellers have an incentive to claim that lemons are good cars. But, given the assumptions in the above description of the used car market, no one believes such claims. Adverse selection exists, so only lemons are actually traded.

The market for used cars is not working well. Good used cars just don't get bought and sold, but people want to be able to exchange good used cars. How can they do so? The answer is by introducing warranties into the market.

Used Cars with Warranties   Car dealers perform two economic functions: they are intermediaries between buyers and sellers and they do car maintenance work (usually on the cars they have sold). The information they get from their car maintenance business is useful in helping them make the market for used cars operate more efficiently than the market for lemons that we've just described.

Buyers of used cars can't tell a lemon from a good car but car dealers can. Sometimes they have as much information about a car's quality as its owner has. For example, they might have regularly serviced the car. They know, therefore, whether they are buying a lemon or a good car and can offer $1,000 for lemons and $5,000 for good cars[1]. But how can they convince buyers that it is worth paying $5,000 for what might be a lemon? The answer is by giving a guarantee in the form of a warranty. The dealer *signals* which cars are good ones and which are lemons. A **signal** is an action taken outside a market that conveys information that can by used by that market. In *Reading Between the Lines* on pp. 432–433 you will see that your degree grade is an example of a signal – a signal to the job market. In the case of the used cars, dealers take actions in the market for car repairs that can be used by the market for cars. For each good car sold, the dealer gives

---

[1] In this example, to keep the numbers simple, we'll ignore dealers' profit margins and other costs of doing business and suppose that dealers buy cars for the same price as they sell them. The principles are the same with dealers' profit margins.

a warranty. The dealer agrees to pay the costs of repairing the car if it turns out to have a defect. Cars with a warranty are good; cars without a warranty are lemons.

Why do buyers believe the signal? It is because the cost of sending a false signal is high. A dealer who gives a warranty on a lemon ends up paying the high cost of repairs – and risks gaining a bad reputation. A dealer who gives a warranty only on good cars has few repair costs and a reputation that gets better and better. It pays to send an accurate signal. It is rational, therefore, for buyers to believe the signal. Warranties break the lemon problem and enable the used car market to function more efficiently. The used car market now has two prices, one for lemons and one for good cars.

The Market for Loans

The market for bank loans is one in which private information plays a crucial role. The quantity of loans demanded by borrowers depends on the interest rate. The lower the interest rate, the greater is the quantity of loans demanded – the demand curve for loans is downward-sloping.

The supply of loans by banks and other lenders depends on the cost of lending. This cost has two parts. One is interest and this interest cost is determined in the market for bank deposits – the market in which the banks borrow the funds that they lend. The other part of the cost of lending is the cost of bad loans – loans that are not repaid – called the default cost. The interest cost of a loan is the same for all borrowers. The default cost of a loan depends on the quality of the borrower.

Suppose that borrowers fall into two classes: low-risk and high-risk. Low-risk borrowers only default on their debts for reasons beyond their control. For example, a firm might borrow to finance a project that fails and be unable to repay the bank. High-risk borrowers take high risks with the money they borrow and frequently default on their loans.

If banks could separate borrowers into the two risk categories, they would supply loans to low-risk borrowers at one interest rate and to high-risk borrowers at a higher interest rate. But banks often have no sure way of knowing whether they are lending to a low-risk or a high-risk borrower.

So the banks must charge a single interest rate to both low-risk and high-risk borrowers. If they offered loans to everyone at the low-risk interest rate, borrowers would face moral hazard and the

banks would attract a lot of high-risk borrowers – adverse selection. Most borrowers would default and the banks would incur economic losses. If the banks offered loans to everyone at the high-risk interest rate, most low-risk borrowers, with whom the banks would like to do profitable business, would be unwilling to borrow.

Faced with moral hazard and adverse selection, banks use *signals* to discriminate between borrowers and they *ration* or limit loans to amounts below the amounts demanded. To restrict the amounts they are willing to lend to borrowers, banks use signals such as length of time in a job, ownership of a home, marital status, age and business record.

Figure 17.7 shows how the market for loans works in the face of moral hazard and adverse selection. The demand for loans is *D,* and the supply is *S*. The supply curve is horizontal – perfectly elastic supply – because it is assumed that banks have access to a large quantity of funds that have a constant marginal cost of *r*. With no loan limits, the

---

FIGURE 17.7

The Market for Loans

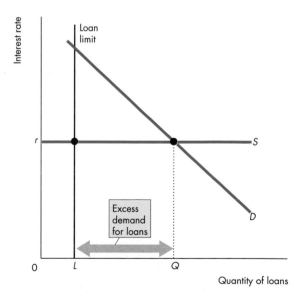

If a bank supplied loans on demand at the going interest rate *r*, the quantity of loans would be *Q*, but most of the loans would be taken by high-risk borrowers. Banks use signals to distinguish between low-risk and high-risk borrowers and they ration loans. Banks have no incentive to increase interest rates and increase the quantity of loans because the additional loans would be to high-risk borrowers.

interest rate is r and the quantity of loans is Q. Because of moral hazard and adverse selection, the banks set loan limits based on signals and restrict the total loans made to L. At the interest rate r, there is an excess demand for loans. A bank cannot increase its profit by making more loans because it can't identify the types of borrowers taking the loans. And because the signals used mean that more high-risk borrowers are unsatisfied than low-risk borrowers, it is likely that any additional lending will be biased towards high-risk (and high-cost) borrowers.

The Market for Insurance

People who buy insurance face a moral hazard problem and insurance companies face an adverse selection problem. The moral hazard problem is that a person with insurance coverage for a loss has less incentive than an uninsured person to avoid such a loss. For example, a business with fire insurance has less incentive to take precautions against fire, such as installing a fire alarm or sprinkler system, than a business with no fire insurance. The adverse selection problem is that people who face greater risks are more likely to buy insurance. For example, a person with a family history of serious illness is more likely to buy life insurance than a person with a family history of good health.

Insurance companies have an incentive to find ways around the moral hazard and adverse selection problems. By doing so, they can lower premiums and increase the amount of business they do. Real-world insurance markets have developed a variety of devices for overcoming or at least moderating these private information problems. Let's see how signals work in markets for insurance by looking at the example of car insurance.

One of the clearest signals a person can give a car insurance company is her or his driving record. Suppose that Daniel is a good driver and rarely has an accident. If he can demonstrate to the insurance company that his driving record is impeccable over a long enough period, then the insurance company will recognize him as a good driver. Daniel will work hard at establishing a reputation as a good driver because he will be able to get his insurance at a lower price.

If all drivers, good and bad alike, can establish good records, then simply having a good record will not convey any information. For the signal to be efficient, it must be difficult for bad drivers to fake low risk by having a good record. The signals used in car insurance are the 'no-claim' bonuses that drivers accumulate when they do not make an insurance claim.

Another device used by insurance companies is the deductible. A deductible is the amount of a loss that the insured party agrees to bear. For example, most insurance policies make the insured party pay the first £50 to £100 worth of damage. The premium varies with the deductible in a significant way. The decrease in the premium is more than proportionate to the increase in the deductible. High-risk people choose policies with low deductibles and high premiums, while low-risk people choose policies with high deductibles and low premiums. The insurance company can profitably do business with both high-risk and low-risk people.

◆ Private information leads to market failure from asymmetric information. This creates the problems of moral hazard and adverse selection.

◆ In markets for cars, loans and insurance, methods such as warranties, loan limits, no-claim bonuses and deductibles have been devised to limit the problems caused by asymmetric information.

Managing Risk in Financial Markets

Risk is a dominant feature of markets for shares and bonds – indeed for any asset whose price fluctuates. One thing people do to cope with risky asset prices is diversify their asset holdings.

Diversification to Lower Risk

The idea that diversification lowers risk is natural. It is just an application of not putting all your eggs into the same basket. How exactly does diversification reduce risk? The best way to answer this question is to consider an example.

Suppose there are two risky projects that you can undertake. Each involves investing £100,000. The two projects are independent of each other, but they each promise the same degree of risk and return.

On each project, you will either make £50,000 or lose £25,000, and the chance that either of these things will happen is 50 per cent. The expected return on each project is (£50,000 × 0.5) − (£25,000 × 0.5), which is £12,500. But because the two projects are completely independent, the outcome of one project in no way influences or is related to the outcome of the other.

Undiversified   Suppose you put all your eggs in one basket – investing the £100,000 in either Project 1 or Project 2. You will either make £50,000 or lose £25,000 and the probability of each of these outcomes is 50 per cent. Your expected return is the average of these two outcomes – an expected return of £12,500. But if only one project is chosen, there is no chance that you will actually make a return of £12,500.

Diversified   Suppose instead that you diversify by putting 50 per cent of your money into Project 1 and 50 per cent into Project 2. (Someone else is putting up the other money in these two projects.) Because the two projects are independent, you now have *four* possible returns. They are:

1. Both projects lose £12,500 and your total loss is £25,000.
2. Project 1 makes £25,000, Project 2 loses £12,500 and your return is £12,500.
3. Project 1 loses £12,500, Project 2 makes £25,000 and your return is £12,500.
4. Both projects make £25,000 and your return is £50,000.

Each of these four possible outcomes is equally probable – each has a 25 per cent chance of occurring. You have lowered the chance that you will earn £50,000, but you have also lowered the chance that you will lose £25,000. And you have increased the chance that you will actually make your expected return of £12,500. By diversifying your portfolio of assets you have reduced its riskiness while maintaining an expected return of £12,500.

If you are risk averse – that is, if your utility of wealth curve looks like Tania's, which you studied earlier in this chapter – you'll prefer the diversified portfolio to the one that is not diversified. That is, your *expected utility* is greater with a diversified set of assets.

Drawing by Roger Beale, *Financial Times Quarterly Review of Personal Finance*, 19–20 July, 1996.

Evidence from empirical studies shows that most people prefer a diversified portfolio as they are risk averse on the average. Of course, even if you are risk averse on the average, you might not be risk averse for all decisions. Providing the majority of your assets are diversified, you might be risk neutral or even risk seeking with a small part of your assets. What do you think is the shape of the utility of wealth schedule for gambling decisions for the man in our cartoon?

A further consequence of risk is the development of markets that enable people to avoid risk – forward and futures markets.

Forward and Futures Markets

Producers are especially concerned about two uncertainties: the price at which they will be able to sell their product and the conditions affecting how much of their product will be produced. Farmers provide a clear illustration of the importance of these two uncertainties. First, when farmers decide how many hectares of wheat to plant, they do not know the price at which the wheat will be sold. Knowing the price of wheat today does not help them make decisions about how much seed to sow today. Today's planting becomes tomorrow's crop, and so tomorrow's price determines how much revenue farmers get from today's sowing. Second, when farmers plant wheat, they do not know what the growing conditions will be. Conditions may be excellent, producing a high yield and a bumper crop, or conditions such as drought and inadequate sunshine may lead to a low crop yield and disaster.

Uncertainty about the future price of a good can arise from uncertainty about its future demand or its future supply. We have just considered some uncertainties about supply. There are also many uncertainties about demand. We know that demand for a good depends on the prices of its substitutes and complements, income, population and preferences. Demand varies as a result of fluctuations in all these influences on buyers' plans. Because these influences *do* fluctuate and are impossible to predict exactly, the level of future demand is always uncertain.

Because people face risks and are willing to pay to lower the risk they bear, markets have developed in which risk can be traded. By trading risks, both the buyers and the sellers of risk gain, making trade more efficient. Let's look at some of these markets.

Forward Markets   Uncertainties about future supply and demand make future prices uncertain. But producers must make decisions today even though they do not know the price at which their output will be sold. In making such decisions, farmers are able to take advantage of special types of markets – forward markets.

A **forward market** is a market in which the seller agrees to deliver and the buyer agrees to take delivery of a specified quantity of a commodity at a specified price and at a specified future date. For example, in the forward market in wheat, a farmer can agree to deliver and a miller can agree to take delivery of 2,000 tonnes of wheat at £5 a tonne 6 months in the future. By entering into such agreements, farmers and millers eliminate the risk of future price fluctuations.

Futures Markets   Forward contracts enable farmers, millers and others engaging in transactions for the future to reduce their risk arising from price variations. But they don't eliminate risk. The person holding the contract stands ready to deliver or take delivery at the agreed price. In some situations it might be extremely costly actually to deliver or take delivery of the goods. For example, suppose the farmer who has agreed to deliver 2,000 tonnes of wheat has a poor harvest and grows only 1,000 tonnes. This farmer could gain by selling a promise to deliver 1,000 tonnes to someone else. Or suppose that the miller who has agreed to buy 2,000 tonnes

of wheat decides to shut down. This miller could gain by selling the promise to take delivery of 2,000 tonnes to someone else. To facilitate exchanges such as these, futures markets have developed. A **futures market** is a market in which contracts for the future delivery of goods are exchanged. These markets function because specialist traders stand ready to buy or sell contracts and make a living from the difference between the price at which they buy and sell.

To decide whether to engage in a forward or futures transaction, specialist traders and producers must make forecasts of future prices. How do they do that?

Rational Expectations

To forecast prices, people use all the relevant information available to them. They use this information to make a forecast that they believe will be right, on the average, and have the smallest possible range of error. If any information is available that can improve a forecast, that information will be used. The forecast that uses all of the relevant information available and that has the least possible error is called a **rational expectation**.

We calculate the rational expectation of a price by using demand and supply. We know that next year's demand and next year's supply determine next year's price. So we forecast the factors that influence demand and supply. Let's work out a rational expectation of the future price of wheat.

To forecast the future price of wheat, we must forecast next year's demand and supply of wheat. The demand for a good depends on the prices of its substitutes and complements, income, population and preferences. The expected demand, therefore, depends on the expected values of these variables. So to form an expectation of the future demand for wheat, it is necessary to forecast the future prices of wheat's substitutes and complements, income, population and current trends that might influence tastes. By taking into account every conceivable piece of available information that helps forecast such variables, farmers – or the specialists from whom they buy forecasts – can form a rational expectation of next year's demand for wheat.

The supply of a good depends on the prices of its substitutes and complements in production, the prices of the resources used to produce the good and the weather. Expected supply depends on the expected values of these variables. So to form an expectation of the future supply of wheat, it is necessary to forecast the future prices of wheat's substitutes and complements in production, the prices of the resources used to produce wheat (the wages of farm workers and the prices of seed and fertilizers) as well as any current trends in weather patterns that might influence growing conditions. By taking into account every available piece of information that helps forecast such variables, farmers can form a rational expectation of the next year's wheat supply.

Figure 17.8 illustrates how to calculate a rational expectation of next year's price of wheat. The horizontal axis measures the quantity expected next year. The vertical axis measures the price expected next year. The curve *ED* is the best forecast available of next year's demand for wheat. The curve *ES* is the best forecast available of next year's supply of wheat. The rational expectation of the price of wheat next year is £3 a tonne – the price at which the expected quantity demanded equals the

---

FIGURE 17.8

A Rational Expectation of Price ◆

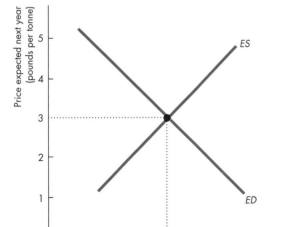

Expected price is determined by expected supply and expected demand. The point where expected demand, *ED*, cuts expected supply, *ES*, determines the rational expectation of the price (£3 a tonne) and quantity (16 billion tonnes).

---

expected quantity supplied. It is a rational expectation because the forecast is based on all the available relevant information. Farmers use the forecast of next year's price to decide how many hectares of wheat to plant today.

What are the implications of rational expectations for the way in which competitive asset markets work? Let's answer this question by looking at the stock market.

The Stock Market The stock market – the market in which the shares of corporations are traded – works like the market we've just examined. If the price of a share today is higher than the expected price tomorrow, people will sell the share. If the price of a share today is less than its expected price tomorrow, people will buy the share. As a result of such trading, today's price equals tomorrow's expected price. Because the actual share price today is equal to the price expected tomorrow, the price embodies all the relevant information that is available about the share. A market in which the actual price embodies all currently available relevant information is called an **efficient market.**

In an efficient market, it is impossible to forecast changes in price. Why? If your forecast is that the price is going to rise tomorrow you will buy now (because the price is low today compared with what you predict it is going to be tomorrow). Your action of buying today is an increase in demand today and increases *today's* price. It's true that your action – the action of a single trader – is not going to make much difference to a huge market like the London Stock Exchange. But if traders in general expect a higher price tomorrow and they all act today on the basis of that expectation, then today's price will rise. It will keep on rising until it reaches the expected future price. For only at that price do traders see no profit in buying more shares today.

There is an apparent paradox about efficient markets. Markets are efficient because people try to make a profit. They seek a profit by buying at a low price and selling at a high price. But the very act of buying and selling to make a profit means that the market price moves to equal its expected future value. Having done that, no one, not even those who are seeking to profit, can *predictably* make a profit. Every profit opportunity seen by traders leads to an action that produces a price change that removes the profit opportunity for others. Even the

Market Signals: A-level Grade Inflation?

The Essence of the Story

THE GUARDIAN, 15 AUGUST 1996

A-levels still pass the test

John Carvel

For the ninth successive year more pupils have passed the exam – and more achieved an A grade. Yet even before pupils have opened the envelope with their individual results, the sceptics were at work. Sir Rhodes Boyson, former education minister and former head teacher, spoke yesterday of an examination system where there was 'no longer any rigour ... the system has gone soft'. Stand by for business and university people to join in the debate today bewailing the decline in the standards of literacy and numeracy....

There are serious questions which need to be asked and disentangled. Hopefully, the official inquiry into A-level results, set up last year to study 'standards over time' and due to report in October, will end what has become an annual debate about the devaluation of the education system's 'gold standard'.

A-level examinations are no longer restricted to an elite. ...Serious researchers have shown a worrying variation in the existing standards: between subjects (with higher standards needed for good grades in maths and science than in arts or humanities), within subjects (with candidates on modular courses in mathematics achieving at least one grade higher than [those] on conventional courses), and between the six different examination boards.

Critics grumble about four specific issues. The 86 per cent of pupils who obtained a pass this year compared to the 70 per cent in the early days of the exam. ...The new modular option under which pupils are awarded 20 per cent for course work, 50 per cent for interim tests with only 30 per cent reserved for the final exam. ...The unlimited number of times students can resit unit tests. ...The degree to which the increase in vocational A-level courses (business studies, photography, media) is eroding standards. But this is misplaced. We need more high quality and challenging vocational courses, not fewer, as our international competitors have demonstrated. This year's Dearing report produced the solution to the shortfall: applied A-levels. The sooner they start, the better.

■ The 1996 UK A-level results showed that the proportion of successful students has increased for the ninth year running.

■ 86 per cent of applicants passed in 1996 compared with the early years of the exam, and the proportion of grade A and B passes increased in 1996.

■ Employers and universities fear that the rise in the number of passes, particularly grade A passes, is a result of grade inflation – a decline in the overall standard – rather than an improvement in student ability.

■ An official inquiry into A-level standards was due to report in October 1996.

Economic Analysis

■ Figure 1 shows the increase in the A-level pass rate for England and Scotland which led employers and universities to worry about grade inflation.

■ Employers and universities use A-level grades as a signal of academic ability and future performance, because they don't have full information about each individual student.

■ Figure 2 shows the labour market for students with A-levels. The supply curve is S, and the marginal revenue product curve is MRP. The wage rate is W and Q students are employed.

■ Let's suppose there are two types of A-level students: the hard-working type with a high MRP, MRP_H, and the lazy type with a low MRP, MRP_L. If employers don't know which type of student they are employing, everyone gets the same wage, W.

■ But employers look for signals because at wage W, profit would be higher if they employed more students of the MRP_H type, and fewer of the MRP_L type.

■ Of course, after a while, employers and universities would eventually be able to distinguish among their students, but the labour market and the university system would be more efficient if this information was available at the point when students are taken on.

■ Figure 3 shows that if A-levels are good market signals – a gold standard – employers pay W_H for highly productive students and employ Q_H. Firms pay W_L for lazy students and employ just Q_L.

■ If more students pass and get high grades because of falling standards, the A-level will no longer act as a good market signal. If the inquiry shows standards are not falling, then employers and universities will be more certain that the pool of hard-working students is increasing.

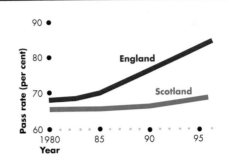

Figure 1 A level results

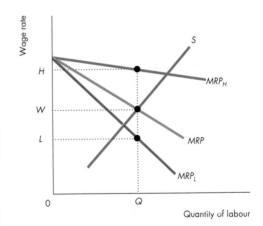

Figure 2 No grading

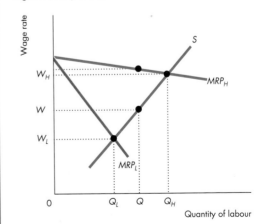

Figure 3 Perfect grading

most unlikely event, such as a meteor sinking and destroying London is taken into account in determining stock market prices.

Thus an efficient market has two features:

1. Its price equals the expected future price and embodies all the available information.

2. There are no forecastable profit opportunities available.

The key thing to understand about an efficient market such as the stock market is that if something can be anticipated it will be, and the anticipation will affect the current price of a share.

Volatility in Stock Prices If the price of a share is always equal to its expected future price, why is the stock market so volatile? The answer must be that expectations themselves are subject to fluctuation. Expectations depend on the information available. As new information becomes available, share traders form new expectations about the future state of the economy and, in turn, new expectations of future share prices. New information comes randomly so prices change randomly.

Expectations about the economy are of crucial importance. Is the economy going to enjoy sustained rapid expansion? Or is it going to suffer a recession? Macroeconomic events, such as expansion and recession, influence share prices. Individual share prices are influenced by technological change, which in turn influences the supply of and demand for particular goods and services. Because new information is being accumulated daily about all these matters, expectations about the future price of a share are constantly being re-evaluated. It is this process of re-evaluation that leads to high volatility in the stock market. As expectations change from being optimistic to being pessimistic, the stock market can plunge many percentage points – as it did dramatically on 19 October 1987. On the other hand, a sustained

period of increasing optimism can produce a long upswing in stock prices. The eight-year run from 1988 to 1996 is an example of such stock market behaviour.

REVIEW

◆ Diversified portfolios reduce risk by combining the rate of returns on independent projects and increasing the chance of making a given rate of return.

◆ Forward markets allow risk averse producers to reduce risk by selling future output at a known price.

◆ Futures markets are used to trade risks in order to reduce the risk arising from future price variations.

◆ A forecast of a future price which uses all the relevant and available information is called a rational expectation. Rational expectations are efficient because they are correct on average and have the smallest forecast error.

◆ The stock market is an example of an efficient market, where today's prices are based on a rational expectation of future prices.

◆ ◆ ◆ ◆ We've studied the way people cope with uncertainty and how markets work when there are market failure problems because of incomplete information. In the following chapters we're going to study some problems of market failure for which markets do not find appropriate solutions. These cases give rise to government intervention in the economy. We'll learn how government actions and programmes modify the outcome of a pure market economy and influence the distribution of income and wealth.

SUMMARY

Uncertainty and Risk

Uncertainty is a form of market failure. It is a state in which more than one event may occur, but we don't know which one. To describe uncertainty we use the concepts of probability and risk. A probability is a number between zero and one that measures the chance of some possible event occurring. Risk is uncertainty with probabilities attached to each possible outcome. When probabilities cannot be measured, they are subjective probabilities.

A person's attitude towards risk, called the degree of risk aversion, is described by a utility of wealth schedule and curve. Faced with uncertainty, people choose the action that maximizes expected utility. (pp. 418–421)

Insurance

We each spend £1,500 every year on insurance. It is one of the most important ways in which we reduce risk. The two main types of insurance are general insurance, including car insurance, and long-term insurance such as life insurance. Insurance works by pooling risks, and it pays people to insure because they are risk averse – they value risk reduction. By pooling risks, insurance companies can reduce the risks people face (from insured activities) and at a low cost in terms of reduced expected wealth. The decrease in risk is valued more than the decrease in wealth and improves market efficiency. (pp. 421–423)

Information

Economic information is data on the prices, quantities and qualities of goods and services and factors of production. Lack of information is a form of market failure. It means that buyers must search for price information – looking for the least-cost source of supply. In doing so, they use the optimal-search rule of searching for a lower price until the expected marginal benefit of search equals the marginal cost of search. There is a reservation price at which the expected marginal benefit of search equals the marginal cost of search. When a price equal to (or less than) the reservation price is found, the search ends and the item is bought.

Sellers advertise, sometimes to persuade and sometimes to inform as part of a profit-maximization strategy. In general advertising increases prices, but can reduce prices by increasing competition and economies of scale. Search activity and advertising can increase market efficiency. (pp 423–425)

Private Information

Private information is one person's knowledge that is too costly for anyone else to discover. The asymmetric information problem leads to moral hazard – the use of private information to the advantage of the informed person and the disadvantage of the uninformed person, and adverse selection – the tendency for the people who accept contracts to be those with private information that can be used to their own advantage and to the disadvantage of the uninformed person or firm. To improve market efficiency, devices like incentive payments, warranties and signals are widely used. (pp. 425–428)

Managing Risk in Financial Markets

Risk can be reduced by diversifying asset holdings, by trading in forward markets, and by trading in futures markets which enables people to take positions in forward markets without taking delivery of goods. Decisions to engage in a forward or futures transaction are based on rational expectations of future prices which uses all the available and relevant information. They are correct, on the average, and have the smallest possible range of forecast error.

Asset markets can be efficient if they determine a price that embodies a rational expectation of the future price. In such markets there are no forecastable price changes or profit opportunities. (pp. 428–434)

KEY ELEMENTS

Key Terms

Adverse selection, 425
Economic information, 423
Efficient market, 431
Expected utility, 419
Forward market, 430
Futures market, 430
Information cost, 423
Moral hazard, 425
Private information, 425
Rational expectation, 430
Reservation price, 423

Risk, 418
Signal, 426
Uncertainty, 418
Utility of wealth, 418

◆ Key Figures

Figure 17.1   The Utility of Wealth, 419
Figure 17.2   Choice under Uncertainty, 419
Figure 17.5   The Gains from Insurance, 422
Figure 17.6   Optimal-search Rule, 424
Figure 17.8   A Rational Expectation of Price, 431

REVIEW QUESTIONS

1 What is the difference between uncertainty and risk?

2 How do we measure a person's attitude towards risk?

3 How do these attitudes vary from one person to another?

4 What is a risk-neutral person and what does such a person's utility of wealth curve look like?

5 What is risk aversion and how could you tell which of two people are the more risk averse by looking at their total utility of wealth curves?

6 Why do people buy insurance and why do insurance companies make a profit?

7 Why is information valuable?

8 What determines the amount of searching you do for a bargain?

9 Why do firms advertise?

10 What are moral hazard and adverse selection, and how do they influence the way markets for loans and insurance work?

11 What is meant by 'buying a lemon' and how does the 'lemon' problem arise?

12 Explain how the used car market works.

13 Why do firms give warranties and guarantees?

14 Why do banks limit the amounts they are willing to lend?

15 How do deductibles make insurance more efficient and enable insurance companies to discriminate between high-risk and low-risk customers?

16 What is the most common form of diversifying assets?

17 How does diversification lower risk?

18 What is the difference between a forward market and a futures market?

19 What is a rational expectation? How is such an expectation arrived at?

20 Why is the stock market described as an efficient market?

PROBLEMS

1 The figure shows Leigh's utility of wealth curve.

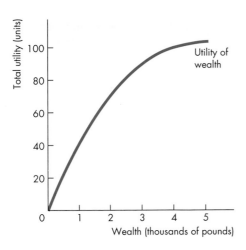

Leigh is offered a job as a salesperson in which there is a 50 per cent chance he wil make £4,000 a month and a 50 per cent chance he will make nothing.

a What is Leigh's expected income from taking this job?

b What is Leigh's expected utility from taking this job?

c What is the certain income another firm have to offer Leigh to persuade him not to take the risky sales job?

2 Jimmy and Julia have the following utility of wealth schedules:

Wealth	Jimmy's utility	Julia's utility
0	0	0
100	200	512
200	300	640
300	350	672
400	375	678
500	387	681
600	393	683
700	396	684

Who is more risk averse, Jimmy or Julia?

3 In Problem 2, suppose that Jimmy and Julia each have £400 and that each see a business project that involves committing their entire £400 to the project. They reckon that the project could return £600 (a profit of £200) with a probability of 0.85, or £200 (a loss of £200) with a probability of 0.15. Who goes for the project and who hangs on to the initial £400?

4 In Problem 3, who is more likely to buy insurance, Jimmy or Julia, and why?

5 There are two independent investment projects: Project 1 is expected to give the investor a wealth of £200 with a probability of 0.5 or a wealth of zero with a probability of 0.5. Project 2 is expected to give a wealth of £300 with a probability of 0.5 or zero with a probability of 0.5.

a Which project would a risk-neutral person invest in?

b How much would Jimmy (from Problem 1) be willing to invest in Project 1? In Project 2?

c How much would Julia (from Problem 1) be willing to invest in Project 1? In Project 2?

6 Study *Reading Between the Lines* on pp. 432–433 and then answer the following questions:

a What do A level results signal about a student and why are these signals needed?

b Why might grade inflation cause problems for students, universities and employers?

c What will happen if the enquiry shows that standards are not falling?

Part 4
MARKETS AND GOVERNMENTS

TALKING WITH JOHN KAY

John Kay is Professor of Management and Director of the School of Management Studies at Oxford University. He was educated at Edinburgh University and Nuffield College, Oxford, and elected to a fellowship in economics at St John's College, Oxford. After teaching economics at Oxford University, he became Director of the Institute for Fiscal Studies and subsequently Professor of Economics at the London Business School. In 1986 he established his own company, London Economics, which sells advice on microeconomics to businesses in the United Kingdom and around the world and now has a staff of 60 economists. He is the author of many books and articles, including *The British Tax System*, now in its fifth edition, and more recently *Foundations of Corporate Success* and *The Business of Economics*.

What are the main economic concepts that guide your work?

The economic concept I now find myself applying every day is the idea of economic rent – the profits firms earn over and above the cost of capital. When I look at a firm, the key question is always: 'What can *this* firm do that its competitors can't – and still can't do even after these competitors realized the benefits it brings?' It's only a distinctive capability that will enable a company to sustain a competitive advantage and make returns above the cost of capital. The concept of economic rent provides the link between the economic analysis of the firm and its business strategy.

When I look at an industry, the question again is always: 'Where are the rents?' What are the scarce factors that determine industry structures, and who is doing well and badly within them? Sometimes these scarce factors are physically scarce, like radio spectrum for broadcasters, or well-placed sites with planning permission for rock concerts. Sometimes they are intangible, like Marks & Spencer's reputation with its customers and relationships with its suppliers. But it's always assets of these kinds that are the main influence on the way an industry is organized, and on how it evolves.

How useful is economics in helping us to understand how firms operate in markets?

Economics is simply the only coherent organizing framework we have for analysing these questions. It gives us a set of tools for understanding how the firm's costs, revenues and profitability relate to each other; and for understanding the strategic interactions between firms. It also gives us models of markets which describe the nature of competition between firms and the range of diversity of products available in them.

> '*...modern microeconomics is increasingly useful in helping us to understand how firms develop and change.*'

Can economics help us to understand how firms develop and change?

One of the strangest things about microeconomic theory is that the firm was neglected for so long. Economists talked about firms, of course, but they never adequately explained the role firms played in economic life, and in most of our models all firms were the same, or differed from each other only in rather trivial ways.

I think much of the blame for that lies with a Marshallian tradition which emphasized the industry and the market as the main units of analysis; and more recently with what came to be called the structure-conduct-performance paradigm, which showed how supply and demand conditions influenced market structure, which in turn determined how the industry behaved. You can easily see two of the consequences of that approach. First, the issue most important to business people is that we can't explain why different firms in the same market environment perform differently. Second, industrial economists focused on issues of public policy, such as anti-trust and regulation, rather than on questions of business policy.

This is why economics is much less used in business than it should be. But things are changing. The economics we do is now much more relevant to issues that concern firms. A lot of recent research is on how markets handle asymmetric information and the kinds of contracts we make; and game theory illustrates how small groups of individuals and firms interact with each other. So modern microeconomics is increasingly useful in helping us to understand how firms develop and change.

To what extent should government regulate the activities of firms and why?

The standard economic case for government regulation of industry is that it should intervene to correct market failures and externalities, where the activities of firms affect other parties – as in pollution, or health and safety. Government should try to restrict the exercise of monopoly power. Government may need to be involved to correct information asymmetry, where markets do not work well because buyers know much less than sellers, as with financial services. Government should set the framework and allow firms to make as much money as they can within that framework.

However, I have come to think that the issues are really more complex than this perspective suggests. Markets function within a social context, and around the world there are many different social contexts within which markets function. The Japanese or the Swiss market economy is very different from that of the United Kingdom or the United States, for example. One of the key roles of government is to understand and influence that social context. By doing so, it can have a wider influence on the way firms act, but it can also achieve many things without having to adopt explicit regulation.

Take financial services, for example. Ten years ago, we seemed to be moving towards a regime in which detailed codes of behaviour were prescribed for all the major sectors of the industry. As long as you were within the rules, you could do as you liked. But this couldn't work, and didn't. The rule book could never be detailed enough, or far-seeing enough, to prohibit anything that you would like to stop. At the same time, it was detailed enough to impose significant burdens on firms and make it harder for them to innovate and respond to customer needs.

A better solution, and the one which has been increasingly adopted, is to acknowledge that the best regulatory mechanism is firms' own concern for their reputation. The advantage of this is that it encourages companies to internalize the process of regulation: as far as possible to decide best practice for themselves. A principal role of government is then to help ensure that reputations are deserved. The various regulatory agencies have been quite effective in exposing the weaknesses of firms, even well-known firms, which have fallen below their own standards. All this involves a more sophisticated view of regulation than the one that simply stresses government as umpire, enforcing the rules.

How can or should we judge the 'success' of the privatization programme?

The objectives of privatization have changed many times. It began as a means of taming public sector trade unions, became a means of reducing public sector borrowing and was then put forward as a route to wider share ownership. But the key test is what it did for the efficiency of the

'*T*wo cheers for the privatisation programme. We are certainly better off than if it hadn't happened. But there are many things which we still need to put right.'

organizations concerned. There is no doubt that the 1980s led to marked improvements in the efficiency of those firms that were publicly owned in 1979. But a careful analysis of the data suggests conclusions that are more complicated than a simple public good, private bad claim.

There are three main findings. First, efficiency – as measured by the rate of growth of productivity – did improve markedly. Second, the change seems to begin about 1983, more or less in line with the date at which the Conservative government came to favour wide-ranging privatization. But third, the improvement seems to have happened in *all* publicly owned firms, whether they were privatized or not.

The gains seem to have more to do with the introduction of competition than any change in ownership as such. The most spectacular performance turnarounds took place in British Steel and British Airways, and these occurred when the companies were publicly owned; in fact the causation ran from efficiency gain to privatization, not the other way around.

So are firms more efficient organizers of production than governments?

Obviously there is no reason in principle why a person or a process should be more efficient under private than public management. The problem has been that the structures of control and accountability which have been traditional in the public sector have not favoured efficiency. Effective management is based on freedom with accountability. By that I mean that you are able to get on with the job but from time to time you are held rigorously to account for your performance. For what are seen as good constitutional and democratic reasons, public sector organization has not usually allowed this. Accountability has amounted to a process of supervision and interference of which the outcome has been that no one is really responsible for the performance of the activities concerned.

Now you could reform all this within the public sector, but that's difficult. It's beginning. But privatization has generally seemed an easier solution.

So has privatization been in the public interest?

Two cheers for the privatization programme. We are certainly better off than if it hadn't happened. But there are many things which we still need to put right.

CHAPTER 18

MARKET
FAILURE
AND
PUBLIC
CHOICE

**After studying this chapter
you will be able to:**

◆ Describe and explain the growth in
the size of government

◆ Explain how government policy
arises from market failure and why
government policy might improve
the performance of the market
economy

◆ Distinguish between public goods
and private goods and explain the
free-rider problem

◆ Explain how the quantity of public
goods is determined

◆ Explain why government chooses to
raise revenue from different sources

◆ Explain why some goods are taxed
at a high rate

I N 1994, THE CENTRAL AND LOCAL GOVERNMENTS IN THE UNITED KINGDOM SPENT £285.7 billion – more than one-third of UK output. In other countries governments spend an even higher proportion of their national output on public sector services. Do we need this much government? Is government, as conservatives sometimes suggest, too big? Or, despite its enormous size, is government too small to do all the things it must attend to? Is government, as liberals sometimes suggest, not contributing enough to economic life? ◆ Government touches many aspects of our lives from birth to death. It supports health care when we're born and our schools, colleges and teachers. It is present throughout our working lives, taxing our incomes and employers, regulating our work environment and paying us benefits when we are unemployed. It is present throughout our retirement, paying us a small income, and when we die, taxing our bequests. Governments also create laws, and provide goods and services such as policing and

Government: Solution or Problem?

national defence. ◆ But the government does not make all our choices. We decide what work to do, how much to save and what to spend our income on. Why does the government participate in some aspects of our lives but not others? What determines the scale on which public services are provided? Is government policy really needed? Can't government services be provided equally well in the private sector?

◆ ◆ ◆ ◆ In this chapter and the next three, we study the interactions of governments and markets. We'll begin by describing the government sector, and explain why governments intervene in markets. We also explain the scale of government and examine whether their services are provided efficiently.

The Government Sector

The size of the government sector can be measured by the share of government expenditure out of total output. The share of government expenditure in the world's major industrialized countries is shown in Fig. 18.1(a). You can see that the size of government is increasing over time. Government expenditure was just 27 per cent of the total output of major industrialized countries in 1960. By 1994, it had risen to a peak of 50 per cent. The only period of a sustained fall in the size of government expenditure in industrialized countries was between 1985 and 1990. But since 1990, the size of government expenditure has increased again.

The UK Government Sector

All European countries have at least two levels of government with different responsibilities. The United Kingdom has only two levels: central and local. In the United Kingdom central government spending accounts for 80 per cent of total government expenditure. Nearly 60 per cent of this is spent by the three biggest government departments – social security, health and defence. Other departments, including transport, agriculture, fisheries and food, and trade and industry, have much smaller budgets. Local government is mainly responsible for school education, personal social services such as care for the elderly, housing and the police. It also provides some local services such as local roads, refuse collection and leisure facilities.

Like most industrial economies, the trend is for the size of the government sector in the United Kingdom to increase over time as Fig. 18.1(b) shows. Government expenditure had increased from just 13 per cent of total output in 1900 to 37 per cent in 1995. The size of the government sector jumped temporarily during World Wars I and II , and then increased steadily over three decades to peak at 47 per cent in 1975. Since then, the size of the government sector has declined to its current level of 37 per cent. By contrast, government expenditure in the United States, Japan and most other European countries continued to rise after 1975. This suggests that the trend for the size of the government sector to increase in the United

FIGURE 18.1

The Size of Government

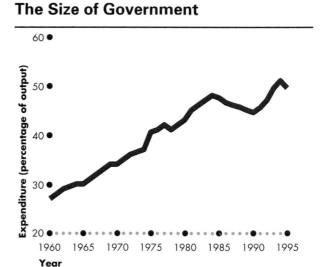

(a) Government expenditure in major industrialized countries

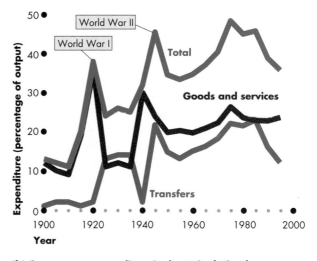

(b) Government expenditure in the United Kingdom

The size of government can be measured by the share of government expenditure out of total output. Part (a) shows how the size of government has grown in all major industrialized economies over the last 35 years. The size of the UK government sector follows a similar upward trend – expenditure peaked in 1975 and then slowly declined to its current level of 37 per cent. The decline in the size of UK government expenditure after 1975 is partly owing to a decrease in transfer payments and partly owing to a decrease in the provision of goods and services – but evidence from other countries suggests this may be a temporary decline.

Source: Central Statistical Office, *Economic Trends*, 1995, London, HMSO.

Kingdom is still present and the recent decline in expenditure may be temporary.

About one-half of government expenditure in the United Kingdom is on the direct provision of goods and services such as education and health. The other half is paid as benefits to individuals with low incomes – as unemployment and sickness benefit, income support and pensions. These benefits are called *transfer payments* as income is *transferred* by taxing one group of people with higher incomes to pay benefits to others who have low incomes. You can see from Fig. 18.1(b) that transfer payments are a more important share of total government expenditure now than they were in 1900 as more people are entitled to state pensions, income support payments and unemployment benefits than before. The early part of the decline in the size of the government sector in the United Kingdom was caused by a reduction in transfer payments and the later part by lower expenditure on goods and services.

The growth of government expenditure understates the growth of government influence on economic life. That influence stems not only from the government's share of expenditure but also from the increasing number of laws and regulations that affect the economic actions of households and firms.

Why does the government sector become an ever larger part of the economy in so many countries? Why has public expenditure as a proportion of the total declined in the United Kingdom in the last few years? We'll discover the answers to these and other questions about government later in this chapter and in the following three chapters. But first let's look at the economic role that government plays.

The Economic Theory of Government

Government economic activity – policy – arises, in part, because market economies do not always achieve an *efficient allocation of resources* – when there is **market failure**. In Chapter 11, we saw that markets will only be allocatively efficient when the extreme assumptions of our basic model hold. When they don't hold, markets will be inefficient and resources will not be allocated efficiently. Market economies will produce

too many of some goods and services and too few of others. Social welfare will not be maximized as the marginal social cost of each good and service will not equal its marginal social benefit.

If we could reallocate resources, it might be possible to make some people better off, while making no one worse off – increasing social welfare. Sometimes, market economies create institutions and devices to improve the efficiency of markets. We've already looked at some – futures markets, stock exchanges and signals. But when this does not happen, some government policy to modify the market is needed to improve market efficiency.

Figure 18.2 shows that government policy has three aims. The first is to implement policies to make markets work more efficiently by reducing

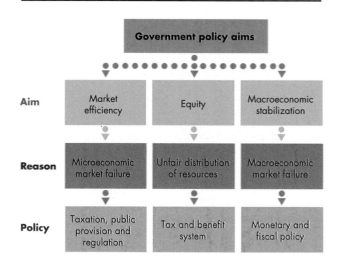

FIGURE 18.2

The Aims of Government Policy

Government policy has three aims. First, governments try to improve efficiency by reducing the impact of microeconomic market failure. They can use a mixture of taxation, public provision and regulation to help individual markets work more efficiently. Second, governments try to improve equity by redistributing incomes and wealth. This can be done by designing an appropriate tax and benefit system which transfers income and wealth, for example, from the rich to the poor. Third, governments try to reduce the impact of uncertainty and limited information on macroeconomic growth by using a mixture of monetary and fiscal policies.

market failure. As we will see in this chapter and following chapters, governments can use a range of policies to achieve this. Second, since market economies do not achieve what most people regard as an *equitable distribution of income*, some government policy is needed to redistribute income and wealth, usually through the tax and benefit system. We will look at these policies in more detail in Chapter 21. Third, market economies are subject to shocks and uncertainty and these can cause macroeconomic problems such as unemployment and inflation, so some government policy is needed to stabilize the economy over time. Macroeconomic policy is examined in Parts 6 and 7 of this book. So let's look at the first issue of market failure and government policy in more detail.

There are five types of microeconomic market failure. They are:

◆ Public goods

◆ Monopoly

◆ Externalities

◆ Incomplete information

◆ Uncertainty

Public Goods

A pure **public good** is a good or service that can be consumed simultaneously by everyone and from which no one can be excluded. The first feature of a public good is called non-rivalry. A good is **non-rival** if consumption of one unit by one person does not decrease available units for consumption by another person. An example of non-rival consumption is watching a television show. A private good, by contrast, is rival. A good is *rival* if consumption of one unit by one person does decrease available units for consumption by another person. An example of rival consumption is eating a burger.

The second feature of a public good is that it is non-excludable. A good is **non-excludable** if it is impossible, or extremely costly, to prevent someone from benefiting from a good who has not paid for it. An example of a non-excludable good is national defence. It would be difficult to exclude a foreign visitor from being defended. A private good, by contrast, is also excludable. A good is *excludable* if it is possible to prevent a person from enjoying the benefits of a good if they have not paid. An example of an excludable good is cable television. Cable

companies can ensure that only those people who have paid the fee receive programmes.

Figure 18.3 classifies goods by these two criteria and gives some examples of goods in each category. Goods in the bottom right hand corner are knows as *pure* public goods. The classic example of a pure public good is a lighthouse. A modern example is national defence. One person's consumption of the security provided by our national defence system does not decrease the amount available for someone else – defence is non-rival. The army cannot select those whom it will protect and those whom it will leave exposed to threats – defence is non-excludable.

Many goods have a public element but are not pure public goods. An example is a motorway. A motorway is non-rival until it becomes congested. One more car on the Paris ring road with plenty of space does not reduce the consumption of road services of anyone else. But once the motorway

FIGURE 18.3

Public Goods and Private Goods

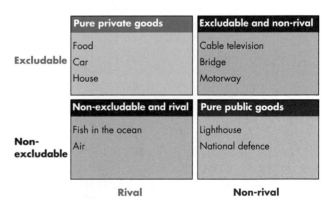

A pure public good (bottom right) is one for which consumption is non-rival and from which it is impossible to exclude a consumer. Pure public goods pose a free-rider problem. A pure private good (top left) is one for which consumption is rival and from which consumers can be excluded. Some goods are non-excludable but are rival (bottom left) and some goods are non-rival but are excludable (top right).

Source: Adapted from and inspired by E. S. Savas, *Privatizing the Public Sector*, Chatham, NJ, Chatham House Publishers Inc, 1982, p. 34.

becomes congested, one extra vehicle lowers the quality of the service available for everyone else – it becomes rival like a private good. Also, users can be excluded from a motorway by toll gates. Another example is fish in the ocean. Ocean fish are rival because a fish taken by one person is not available for anyone else. But ocean fish are non-excludable because it is difficult to stop other countries taking them if they are outside a country's terrritorial limits.

Public goods create a free-rider problem. A **free rider** is a person who consumes a good without paying for it. Public goods create a *free-rider problem* because the quantity of the good that the person is able to consume is not influenced by the amount the person pays for the good. Markets fail to supply a public good because no one has an incentive to pay for it. We'll see how government can help to cope with the free-rider problem later in this chapter. But first let's look at the other sources of government economic activity.

Monopoly

We have already seen in Chapter 12 that *rent seeking* and *monopoly* prevent the allocation of resources from being efficient. Markets fail when monopoly power exists, because it is usually possible to increase profit by restricting output and increasing price. Until a few years ago, for example, British Telecommunications had a monopoly on telephone services and the price of business and domestic telephone services was higher than it is today.

Although some monopolies arise from *legal barriers to entry* – barriers to entry created by governments – a major activity of government is to regulate monopoly and to enforce laws that prevent cartels and other restrictions on competition. When governments privatize government monopolies such as utilities and telecommunications, they must regulate these companies to ensure that their monopoly status does not lead to inefficiency. We study competition and monopoly regulations in Chapter 19.

Externalities

An **externality** is a cost or a benefit arising from an economic transaction that falls on people who do not participate in that transaction. They cannot participate because there is no market for the cost or benefit. For example, when a chemicals factory (legally) dumps its waste into a river and kills the fish, it imposes an externality – in this case, an external cost – on the fisherman who lives downstream. External costs and benefits are not taken into account by the people whose actions create them if there are no markets – and no prices – for these costs and benefits. For example, the chemicals factory does not take the damaging effects on the fish into account when deciding whether to dump waste into the river because there is no market for waste water. When a home owner fills her garden with spring bulbs, she generates an external benefit for all the joggers and walkers who pass by. In deciding how much to spend on this lavish display, she takes into account only the benefits accruing to herself. We study externalities and the way governments and markets cope with them in Chapter 20.

Incomplete Information and Uncertainty

We have already seen in Chapter 17 that markets fail to allocate resources efficiently if there is incomplete information and if the outcome of a decision is uncertain. Of course, utility-maximizing decision makers can buy information, and use signals, stocks and insurance markets to try to increase information and reduce risk. This will improve the efficiency of the market economy and increase social welfare. But there are occasions when these devices do not work. If a drugs company creates a wonderful new drug that cures cancer, it may decide not to market it if it thinks that every other drugs company will be able to analyse the drug and copy it. It has spent a lot of money on research and needs to maintain a high price for the drug to cover its costs. So the benefits for us all may be lost. And no insurance company will provide health insurance for someone who is already diagnosed as having a fatal disease. So some people will never be able to insure themselves. We will look at how government policy can resolve the problems of incomplete information and uncertainty in individual markets in the following three chapters.

Before we look at government policy, we need to understand the arena in which governments operate. To do this we are going to build a model of the 'political marketplace'.

Public Choice and the Political Marketplace

Government is a complex organization made up of millions of individuals, each with their *own* economic objectives. Government policy choices are the outcome of the choices made by these individuals. To analyse these choices, economists have developed a theory of the political activity called **public choice theory**. We can use this theory to build a model of the political marketplace similar to our market models.

The actors in the political marketplace model are:

◆ Voters
◆ Politicians
◆ Bureaucrats

The choices and interactions of these actors are illustrated in Fig. 18.4. Let's look at each in turn.

Voters

Voters are the consumers of the political process. In markets for goods and services, people express their demands by their willingness to pay. In the political marketplace, they express their demands by voting, campaigning, lobbying and making financial contributions. They may do this as individuals or as organizations. Many firms and trade unions make financial contributions to political parties.

Economic models of public choice assume that people support policies that they believe will make them better off and oppose policies that they believe will make them worse off. They neither oppose nor support – they are indifferent towards – policies that they believe have no effect on them. Voters' *perceptions* of policy outcomes are what guide their choices.

Politicians

Politicians are the elected administrators and legislators at all levels of government. Economic models of public choice assume that the objective of a politician is to get elected and to remain in office. Votes, to a politician, are like pounds to a firm. To get enough votes, politicians form coalitions – political parties – to develop policy proposals, which they expect will appeal to a majority of voters.

FIGURE 18.4

The Political Marketplace

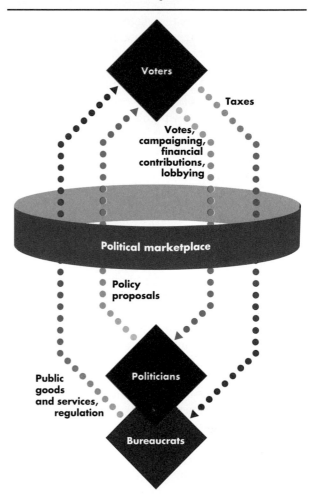

Voters express their demands for policies by voting, election campaigning, making financial contributions to political parties and joining interest groups to lobby government. Politicians propose policies to appeal to a majority of voters. Bureaucrats try to maximize the budgets of their departments or agencies. If voters are well-informed, the political equilibrium is efficient. If voters are rationally ignorant, the cost and provision of public goods exceeds the efficient level.

Bureaucrats

Bureaucrats are employed staff who work in government departments at all levels. They are responsible for enacting government policy. The most senior bureaucrats are hired by politicians. Junior bureaucrats are hired by senior ones.

Economic models of public choice assume that bureaucrats aim to maximize their own utility. To achieve this objective, they try to maximize the budget of the agency or department in which they work. This is because the bigger the budget, the greater is the prestige of the agency or department boss and the larger is the opportunity for promotion for people further down the bureaucratic ladder. To maximize their budgets, bureaucrats devise programmes that they expect will appeal to politicians and they help politicians to sell programmes to voters.

Political Equilibrium

Voters, politicians and bureaucrats make their economic choices to maximize their own objectives. But each group is constrained in two ways: by the preferences of the other groups and by what is technologically feasible. The outcome of the choices of voters, politicians and bureaucrats is the political equilibrium. The **political equilibrium** is a situation in which the choices of voters, politicians and bureaucrats are all compatible and in which no group can improve its position by making a different choice. Two types of political equilibrium are possible: efficient and inefficient. *Public interest* theory predicts that governments make choices that achieve efficiency. *Public choice* theory recognizes the possibility of inefficient outcomes – of *government failure* that parallels the possibility of market failure. We'll now look at these two theories to see which one is the better description of reality.

Let's see how voters, politicians and bureaucrats interact to determine the quantity of public goods.

Public Goods

Why does the government provide public goods and services such as national defence and health services – goods and services that can be consumed simultaneously by everyone and from which no one can be excluded? Why don't we leave the provision of these goods and services to private firms that sell their output in markets? Why don't we buy our national defence from North Pole Protection plc, a private firm that competes for our pounds in the marketplace in the same way that McDonald's and Coca-Cola do? The answer to these questions lies in the *free-rider problem*.

The Free-rider Problem

Suppose that for its effective national defence, a country must launch some communication and surveillance satellites. One satellite can do part of the job required. But the larger the number of satellites deployed, the greater is the degree of security. Satellites are expensive, and to build them resources are diverted from other productive activities. The larger the number of satellites installed, the greater is their marginal cost.

Our task is to work out the number of satellites to install to achieve allocative efficiency. We'll then examine whether private provision can achieve allocative efficiency, and we'll discover that it cannot – that there is a free-rider problem.

Benefits and Costs of Satellites

The benefit provided by a satellite is based on the preferences and beliefs of the consumers of its services. It is the *value* of its services. The value to an individual of a *private* good is the maximum amount that the person is willing to pay for one more unit of the good. The individual's demand curve tells us this value. Similarly, the value to an individual of a *public* good is the maximum amount that the person is willing to pay for one more unit of the good.

To calculate the value a person places on one more unit of a public good, we can use a total benefit curve. *Total benefit* is the total pound value that a person places on a given level of provision of a public good. The greater the quantity of the public good, the larger is a person's total benefit. The increase in total benefit resulting from a one-unit increase in the quantity of a public good is the **marginal benefit**.

Figure 18.5 shows an example of the marginal benefit that arises from defence satellites for a society of just two people, Lisa and Max. Lisa's and Max's marginal benefits are graphed as MB_L and MB_M, respectively, in parts (a) and (b) of the figure. As you can see, the greater the quantity of satellites, the smaller is the marginal benefit for both Lisa and Max. By the time 4 satellites are deployed, Lisa perceives no additional benefits and Max perceives only £10 worth of benefit.

Part (c) of the figure shows the economy's marginal benefit curve, MB (where the economy has only two people, (Lisa and Max). An individual's marginal benefit curve for a public good is similar to the individual's demand curve for a private good.

FIGURE 18.5

Benefits of a Public Good

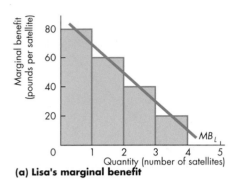

(a) Lisa's marginal benefit

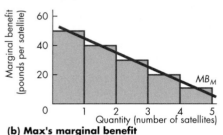

(b) Max's marginal benefit

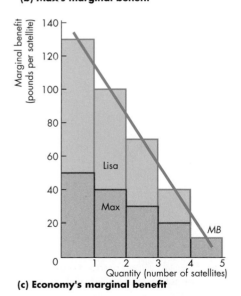

(c) Economy's marginal benefit

The figure shows the marginal benefit for two individuals Lisa and Max and for the whole economy (comprising only Lisa and Max) for different quantities of satellites. The marginal benefit curves are MB_L for Lisa, MB_M for Max and MB for the economy. The marginal benefit to the economy at each quantity of the public good is the sum of the marginal benefits to each individual.

But the economy's marginal benefit curve for a public good is different from the market demand curve for a private good. To obtain the market demand curve for a private good, we add up the quantities demanded by each individual at each price. In other words, we sum the individual demand curves horizontally[1]. In contrast, to find the economy's marginal benefit curve of a public good, we add the marginal benefit of each individual at each quantity provided, as one person's consumption does not reduce the amount available for another. So we sum the individual marginal benefit curves of Lisa and Max vertically. The resulting marginal benefit curve for the whole economy of two people is graphed in part (c) – the curve MB.

In reality, an economy with two people would not buy any satellites – the total benefit falls far short of the cost. But an economy with 50 million people might. To determine the efficient quantity, we need to take cost as well as benefit into account. The cost of a satellite is based on technology and the prices of the factors of production used to produce it. It is an opportunity cost and is derived in the same way as the cost of producing jumpers – explained in Chapter 10. The efficient quantity is the one that maximizes *net benefit* – total benefit minus total cost.

Figure 18.6 illustrates the efficient quantity of satellites. The first three columns of the table show the total and marginal benefits to an economy consisting of 50 million people. The next two columns show the total and marginal cost of producing satellites. The final column shows net benefit. Total benefit, *TB,* and total cost, *TC,* are graphed in part (a) of the figure. Net benefit (total benefit minus total cost) is maximized when the vertical distance between the *TB* and *TC* curves is at its largest, a situation that occurs with 2 satellites. This is the efficient quantity.

Another way of describing the efficient scale uses marginal benefit and marginal cost. The marginal benefit, *MB,* and marginal cost, *MC,* of satellites are graphed in part (b). When marginal benefit exceeds marginal cost, net benefit increases if the quantity produced increases. When marginal cost exceeds marginal benefit, net benefit increases

---

[1] The derivation of the market demand curve from the individual demand curves is explained in Fig. 7.1, p. 153.

FIGURE 18.6

The Efficient Quantity of a Public Good

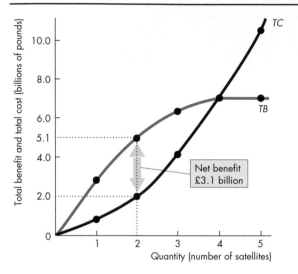

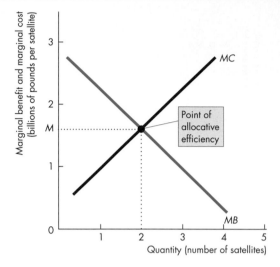

(a) Total benefit and total cost

(b) Marginal benefit and marginal cost

Quantity (number of satellites)	Total benefit (billions of pounds)	Marginal benefit (billions of pounds per satellite)	Total cost (billions of pounds)	Marginal cost (billions of pounds per satellite)	Net benefit (billions of pounds)
0	0		0		0
		3		......0.7	
1	3		0.7		2.3
		......2.1		......1.3	
2	5.1		2		3.1
		......1.2		2	
3	6.3		4		2.3
		......1.0		......3.3	
4	7.3		7.3		0
		0		4	
5	7.3		11		−3.7

Total benefit and total cost are graphed in part (a) as the total benefit curve, *TB*, and the total cost curve, *TC*. Net benefit – the vertical distance between the two curves – is maximized when 2 satellites are installed.

Part (b) shows the marginal benefit curve, *MB*, and marginal cost curve, *MC*. When marginal cost equals marginal benefit, net benefit is maximized and allocative efficiency is achieved.

if the quantity produced decreases. Marginal benefit equals marginal cost at *M* in part (b) with 2 satellites. So making marginal cost equal to marginal benefit maximizes net benefit and determines the allocatively efficient quantity of the public good.

Private Provision

We have now worked out the quantity of satellites that maximizes net benefit. Would a private firm – North Pole Protection plc – deliver that quantity? It would not. To do so, it would have to collect £15 million to cover its costs – or £40 from each of the 50 million people in the economy. But no one would have an incentive to buy his or her 'share' of the satellite system. Each person would reason as follows. The number of satellites provided by North Pole Protection is not affected by my £40. My consumption of other goods will be greater if I free ride and do not pay my share of the cost of the satellite system. If I do not pay and everyone else does, I enjoy the same level of security and can buy more private goods.

If everyone reasons the same way, North Pole Protection has no revenue and can't supply any satellites. The market does not provide the efficient level – two satellites – so private provision is inefficient.

Public Provision

Suppose there are two political parties, the Greys and the Browns, that agree with each other on all issues except satellites. The Greys would like to provide 4 satellites at a cost of £7.3 billion, with benefits of £7.3 billion and a net benefit of zero, as shown in Fig. 18.7. The Browns would like to provide 1 satellite at a cost of £0.7 billion, a benefit of £3 billion and a net benefit of £2.3 billion.

Before campaigning, the two political parties do a 'what-if' analysis. Each party reasons as follows. If each party offers the satellite programme it wants – Greys 4 satellites and Browns 1 satellite – the voters will get a net benefit of £2.3 billion from the Browns, zero net benefit from the Greys, and the Browns will win the election.

Contemplating this outcome, the Greys realize that their party is too grey to get elected. They figure that they must offer net benefits in excess of £2.3 billion if they are to beat the Browns. So they scale back their proposal to 2 satellites. At this level of provision, total cost is £2 billion, total benefit is £5.1 billion and net benefit is £3.1 billion. If the Browns stick with 1 satellite, the Greys will win the election.

But contemplating this outcome, the Browns realize that the best they can do is to match the Greys. They too propose to provide 2 satellites on exactly the same terms as the Greys. If the two parties offer the same number of satellites, the voters are indifferent between the parties. They toss coins to decide their votes and each party receives around 50 per cent of the vote.

The result of the politicians' 'what-if' analysis is that each party offers 2 satellites so regardless of who wins the election, this is the quantity of

FIGURE 18.7

Provision of a Public Good in a Political System

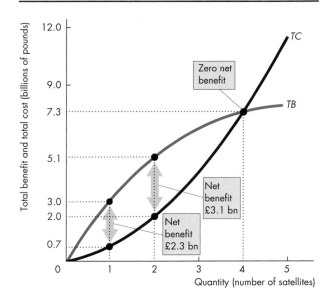

Net benefit is maximized if 2 satellites are installed, with a total benefit of £5.1 billion and a total cost of £2 billion. The Browns would like 1 satellite and the Greys would like 4. But each party recognizes that its only hope of being elected is to provide 2 satellites – the quantity that maximizes net benefit and so leaves no room for the other party to improve on. If voters are well informed about the cost and benefit of a public good, competition between political parties for their votes achieves the efficient outcome.

satellites installed. This quantity is efficient because it maximizes the perceived net benefit of the voters. Thus in this example, competition in the political marketplace results in the efficient provision of a public good. But for this outcome to occur, voters must be well-informed and able to evaluate the alternatives. We'll see below that they do not always have an incentive to do so.

In the example we've just studied, both parties eventually propose identical policies. This is called the principle of minimum differentiation. We have analysed the behaviour of politicians but not that of the bureaucrats who translate the choices of the politicians into programmes. Let's now see how the economic choices of bureaucrats influence the political equilibrium.

The Role of Bureaucrats

We've seen in Figs. 18.6 and 18.7 that 2 satellites at a cost of £2 billion maximize net benefit and that competition between two political parties delivers this outcome. But will the Department of Defence's bureaucrats cooperate?

Suppose the Department of Defence's aim is to maximize the defence budget. To achieve its objective, the department will try to persuade Parliament that 2 satellites cost more than £2 billion. As Fig. 18.8 shows, it will argue if possible that they cost £5.1 billion – the entire benefit. Pressing its position even more strongly, the department will argue for more satellites. It will press for 4 satellites and a budget of £7.3 billion. In this situation, total benefit and total cost are equal and net benefit is zero.

But won't the politicians always control the bureaucracy and keep spending down to the efficient level – the level that maximizes the perceived

net benefits of the voters? We've already seen that when there are two political parties competing for votes, the party that comes closest to maximizing net benefit gets the most votes. Don't these forces of competition for votes dominate the aims of the bureaucrats to ensure that the Department of Defence only gets a budget big enough to provide two satellites – to maximize net benefit?

If voters are well-informed and if their perception of their self-interest is correct, the political party that wins the election does hold the budget to the level that provides the efficient outcome. But there is another possible political equilibrium. It is one based on the principle of voter ignorance and well-informed interest groups.

Voter Ignorance and Well-informed Interest Groups A principle of public choice theory is that it is rational for a voter to be ignorant about an issue unless that issue has a perceptible effect on the voter's income. **Rational ignorance** is the decision *not* to acquire information because the cost of doing so exceeds the expected benefit. For example, each voter knows that he or she can make virtually no difference to the defence policy of the government. Each voter also knows that it would take an enormous amount of time and effort to become even moderately well-informed about alternative defence technologies. So voters remain relatively uninformed. (Though we are using defence policy as an example, the same applies to all aspects of government economic activity.)

All voters are consumers of national defence. But only a few voters are producers of national defence. Those voters who own or work for firms that produce satellites have a direct personal interest in defence because it affects their incomes. Such voters have an incentive to become well-informed about defence issues and to form or join interest groups to lobby government and further their own interests. In collaboration with the Department of Defence's bureaucracy, these voters exert a larger influence than the relatively uninformed voters who only consume defence.

When the rationality of the uninformed voter and special interest groups are taken into account, the political equilibrium provides public goods in excess of the efficient quantity. So in the satellite example, 3 or 4 satellites might be installed rather than the efficient quantity, which is 2 satellites. An efficient outcome is predicted by the public interest

---

FIGURE 18.8

Bureaucratic Overprovision

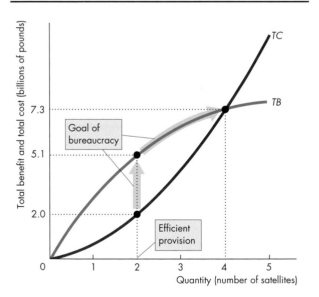

The goal of a bureaucracy is to maximize its budget. A bureau that maximizes its budget will seek to increase cost all the way to the total benefit and to expand output and expenditure as far as possible. Here, the Department of Defence tries to get £2 billion to provide 2 satellites and to increase the quantity of satellites to 4 with a budget of £7.3 billion.

theory and an inefficient overprovision is predicted by the public choice theory.

Why Government is Large and Grows

We saw at the beginning of this chapter that government expenditure has grown over the years. Now that we know how the quantity of public goods is determined, we can explain part of the reason for the growth of government. Government grows in part because the demand for some public goods increases at a faster rate than the demand for private goods. There are two possible reasons for this growth:

◆ Voter preferences
◆ Inefficient overprovision

Voter Preferences The growth of government can be explained by voter preferences in the following way. As voters' incomes increase (as they usually do in most developed economies), the quantity of public goods demanded increases more quickly than income. The *income elasticity of demand* for public goods is greater than one. Many (and the most expensive) public goods are in this category. They include communication systems, such as motorways, airports and air-traffic control, public health, education and defence. If government's did not support increasing expenditure, they would not get elected. So this first reason for government growth seems convincing.

Inefficient Overprovision Inefficient overprovision might explain the *size* of government but not the *growth* of government. It only explains why government might be *larger* than its efficient scale at any point in time. It does, however, explain why governments might introduce mechanisms to make government work more efficiently, resulting in a reduction in the size of the government sector.

Inefficient overprovision is the reason given by the UK government for introducing a range of government department budget cuts and systems to make the bureaucracy more efficient. For example, in 1996, the government announced a 25 per cent cut in the budget for the Department of Social Security to promote efficiency.

Another way to make the government sector more efficient is to privatize the *production* of public goods and services. Government *provision* of a public good (or service) does not automatically imply that a government operated department must *produce* the good (or service). Many government activities have been partly or wholly privatized in the United Kingdom in order to introduce more competition and efficiency. We will look at privatization in more detail in Chapter 19.

Governments can also introduce performance indicators and auditing procedures to create greater public accountability to voters. These have been widely used in the provision of health, education, police and emergency services. The 1991 and 1996 reforms of the UK national health service created a more centralized management structure with a large bureaucracy running new auditing and monitoring procedures, and new standards for accountability. Of course the gains in efficiency may be outweighed by the additional costs of red tape and bureaucracy. The national health service problem is analysed in the article in *Reading Between the Lines* on pp. 458–459.

These mechanisms have reduced the share of government expenditure out of the total in the United Kingdom in the last few years as we saw in Fig. 18.1. But this is a one-off effect. They cannot stop any underlying growth in government expenditure over time. So will government expenditure start to increase again in the United Kingdom, even with a more efficient structure?

Voters Strike Back

If government expenditure grows too large relative to voters' preferences, there is always the possibility of a voter backlash. Governments have to pay for their spending and policies by raising revenue through taxation or borrowing. Higher taxes reduce voters' incomes – reducing voter utility – so governments must balance the increase in voter utility from spending against the decrease in voter utility from taxation.

If governments borrow too much, they will generate inflation and become equally unpopular. When governments fear they will lose the next election as a result of rising public sector expenditure, taxation or inflation, they'll start to cut expenditure. For this reason, governments in the United Kingdom and the United States have tried to reduce taxation by cutting expenditure on welfare services and public goods. You can find examples of similar policies being introduced all over Europe – particularly in Belgium, France, Germany, Italy and Sweden.

> ## REVIEW
>
> ◆ Governments use policies to achieve three goals: reducing inefficiency from market failure, increasing equality and stabilizing the economy to achieve macroeconomic growth.
>
> ◆ There are five types of market failure: public goods, monopoly, externalities, limited information and uncertainty.
>
> ◆ Private provision of a public good creates a free-rider problem and provides less than the efficient quantity of the good.
>
> ◆ Competition between politicians for votes can achieve an efficient quantity of a public good, provided voters are well-informed and bureaucrats do not maximize the size of their own departments.
>
> ◆ The efficient size of government will tend to grow with voters' incomes.

We've now seen how voters, politicians and bureaucrats interact to determine the quantity of public goods and services. But public goods must be paid for with taxes. How does the political marketplace determine the scale and variety of taxes that we pay?

Taxes

Taxes generate the financial resources that governments use to provide voters with public goods and other benefits. For the UK government in 1994, 26 per cent of total revenue came from income tax, 28 per cent from value added tax and excise taxes, and 20 per cent from social security taxes. What factors affect the government's choice of revenue sources?

Taxes and Income

The amounts that people pay in tax and receive in benefits from social security payments depends mainly on their income. Other things remaining the same, the higher a person's income, the greater is the amount of income tax paid and the smaller is the amount of benefit received. So as a rule high-income people prefer to vote for a political party that proposes low benefits and low income tax rates, while low-income people prefer to vote for a political party that proposes high benefits and high income tax rates. Let's build a model of the political marketplace based on the idea that politicians try to find the income tax rate and benefit level that attracts the majority of voters – the median voter theorem.

The Median Voter Theorem   The **median voter theorem** states that political parties will pursue policies that appeal to the median voter. The median member of a population is the one in the middle – one-half of the population lies on one side and one-half on the other. Let's see how the median voter theorem applies to the question of how large the tax and benefit system should be.

Imagine a list of all the possible levels of benefit from government policies and the associated tax rate needed to finance them. We'll assume that the only tax is an income tax to simplify the problem. The list begins with the highest possible level of benefit and tax rate and ends with no benefit and a zero tax rate. We can identify each entry in the list by the tax rate associated with it.

Next imagine arranging all the voters along a line running from A to D, as shown in Fig. 18.9. The voter who favours the highest tax rate (and the highest benefit level) is at A. The voter who favours a zero tax rate (and no benefits) is at D. All the other voters are arranged along the line based on the tax rate (and benefit level) that they favour most. The curve in the figure shows the tax rate favoured by each voter between A and D. The median voter in the example favours a tax rate of 30 per cent.

Suppose that two political parties propose slightly different tax rates. The high-tax party proposes a tax rate of 61 per cent and the low-tax party proposes a tax rate of 59 per cent. Given this choice, all the voters between A and B prefer the higher tax rate and will vote for the high-tax party. All the voters between B and D prefer the lower tax and will vote for the low-tax party. The low-tax party will win the election.

Alternatively, suppose that the high-tax party proposes a tax rate of 11 per cent and the low-tax party proposes a tax rate of 9 per cent. The voters between A and C will vote for the high-tax party and those between B and C will vote for the low-tax party. This time, the high-tax party will win the election.

FIGURE 18.9

Voting for Income Taxes

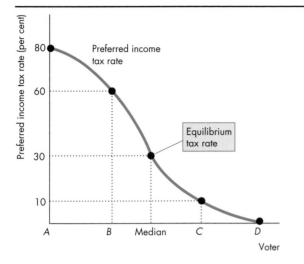

A political party can win an election by proposing policies that appeal to the median voter and to all the other voters on one side of the median. If the median voter favours a policy, that policy will be proposed. In the figure, voters have different preferences concerning the income tax rate (and benefit rate). They are ranked in descending order of their preferred tax – A's preferred tax rate is highest, B's is next highest, and so on.

There are two political parties. If one proposes a 61 per cent tax and the other a 59 per cent tax, the low-tax party will win the election – voters between A and C will vote for the high tax and those between C and B for the low tax. If both parties propose low taxes – 11 per cent and 9 per cent – the high-tax party will win. It will pick up the votes between A and D, leaving only the votes between D and B for the low-tax party. Each party has an incentive to move towards the tax rate preferred by the median voter. At that point, each party picks up half the votes and neither can improve its share.

In either of the two situations we've just examined, the party that wins the election is the one offering a tax rate closest to the tax rate preferred by the median voter. So each party can improve its election performance by moving closer to the median than the other party. But each party has the same incentive, so each moves towards the median. Once the two parties are offering the tax rate favoured most by the median voter, neither can increase its vote by changing its proposal. One party will get the votes between A and the median, and the other party will get the votes between the median and D.

All the voters except those at the median will be dissatisfied – for those between A and the median, the benefits and the tax rate are too low, and for those between D and the median, the benefits and the tax rate are too high. But no political party can propose programmes other than those that can be financed with a 30 per cent tax rate and expect to win the election. If the two parties propose identical programmes and a 30 per cent tax rate, the voters are indifferent and either don't vote or toss a coin to decide which party to vote for.

The median voter theorem implies the principle of minimum differentiation that we've already studied. The policies of different political parties will tend to converge. But this does not mean that all political parties will be identical. They may be aligned to wealthy people or to poor people and will retain a rhetoric which shows this. One party will talk about higher taxes and benefits and the other will talk about cutting taxes and benefits, but neither will actually carry such policies to excess for fear of losing the support of the median voter.

Our discussion so far has focused on income taxes, but 28 per cent of total revenue is drawn from indirect taxes – taxes on expenditure. Let's look now at the factors that determine the level of expenditure taxes and which goods are taxed by governments.

Excise Taxes

An **excise tax** is a tax on the sale of a particular commodity. We'll now study the effects of an excise tax by considering the tax on petrol shown in Fig. 18.10. The demand curve for petrol is D and the supply curve is S. If there is no tax on petrol, its price is 60 pence a litre and 400 million litres of petrol a day are bought and sold.

Now suppose that a tax is imposed on petrol at the rate of 60 pence a litre. If producers are willing to supply 400 million litres a day for 60 pence when there is no tax, then they are willing to supply that same quantity in the face of a 60 pence tax only if the price increases to 120 pence a litre. That is, they want to get the 60 pence a litre they received before, plus the additional 60 pence that they now have to hand over to the government in the form of a petrol tax. As a result of the tax, the supply of petrol decreases and the supply curve shifts leftward. The magnitude of the shift is such that the vertical distance between the original and the new supply curve is the amount of the tax. The new supply curve is the red curve *S + tax*. The new supply curve intersects the demand curve at 300 million litres a day and 110 pence a litre. This situation is the new equilibrium after the imposition of the tax.

Why Excise Tax Rates Vary

Why does government tax petrol, alcohol and tobacco at high rates and some goods not at all? One reason is that taxes create deadweight losses. (You first encountered the concept of deadweight loss when you studied monopoly in Chapter 12, pp. 299–301). A **deadweight loss** is the inefficiency caused by the tax when people substitute cheaper alternatives for the more expensive taxed good. (This is the substitution effect that we met in Chapter 8, p. 184.) It is impossible to avoid deadweight losses from taxes, but they can be minimized by varying the tax rate and the goods taxed. As we'll see, minimizing deadweight loss on excise taxes is also consistent with the median voter theorem.

Minimizing the Deadweight Loss of Taxes

You can see the deadweight loss that taxes create in Fig. 18.10. Without a tax, 400 million litres of petrol a day are consumed at a price of 60 pence a litre. With a 60 pence a litre tax, the price paid by the consumer rises to 110 pence a litre and the quantity consumed declines to 300 million litres a day. The consumer surplus loss arising from the change is shown by the light grey triangle. On the 300 millionth litre bought – the marginal unit bought – the consumer pays 110 pence compared with 60 pence in the absence of a tax. So 50 pence of consumer surplus is lost on this unit. On each successive unit up to the 400 millionth, there is a successively smaller loss of consumer surplus. The total amount of consumer surplus equals the area of the light grey triangle, which is £25 million a day[2].

There is also a loss of producer surplus as shown by the dark grey triangle. On the 300 millionth litre sold – the marginal unit sold – the producer receives 50 pence compared with 60 pence in the absence of a tax. So 10 pence of producer surplus is lost on this unit. On each successive unit up to the 400 millionth, there is a successively smaller loss of

FIGURE 18.10

An Excise Tax

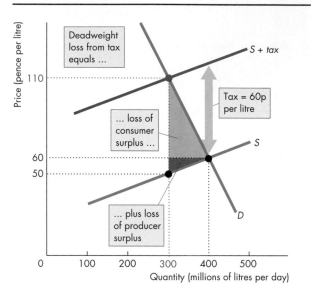

The demand curve for petrol is *D* and the supply curve is *S*. In the absence of any taxes, petrol will sell for 60 pence a litre and 400 million litres a day will be bought and sold. When a tax of 60 pence a litre is imposed, the supply curve shifts upward to become the curve *S + tax*. The new equilibrium price is 110 pence a litre and 300 million litres a day are bought and sold. The excise tax creates a deadweight loss represented by the grey triangle. The tax revenue collected is 60 pence a litre on 300 million litres, which is £180 million a day. The deadweight loss from the tax is £30 million a day. That is, to raise tax revenue of £180 million a day a deadweight loss of £30 million a day is incurred.

producer surplus. The total amount of producer surplus equals the area of the dark grey triangle, which is £5 million pounds a day[3].

The deadweight loss – the sum of consumer and producer surplus lost – is indicated by the two grey triangles in Fig. 18.10. The pound value of that triangle is £30 million a day. But how much revenue is raised by this tax? Since 300 million litres of petrol are sold each day and since the tax is 60 pence a litre, total revenue from the petrol tax is £180 million a day (300 million litres multiplied by 60 pence

---

[2] You can calculate the area of that triangle by using the formula: (base × height)/2. The base is 100 pence, the decrease in quantity. The height is the price increase – 50 pence. Multiplying 100 million litres by 50 pence and dividing by 2 gives £25 million a day.

[3] The base is 100 pence, the decrease in quantity. The height is the price decrease for the producer – 10 pence. Multiplying 100 million litres by 10 pence and dividing by 2 gives £5 million a day.

a litre). Thus to raise tax revenue of £180 million pounds a day using the petrol tax, a deadweight loss of £30 million a day – one-sixth of the tax revenue – is incurred.

One of the main influences on the deadweight loss arising from a tax is the elasticity of demand for the product. As the demand for petrol is fairly inelastic, when a tax is imposed the quantity demanded falls by a smaller percentage than the percentage rise in price. In our example, the quantity demanded falls by 25 per cent but the price increases by 83.33 per cent.

To see the importance of the elasticity of demand, let's consider a different commodity – orange juice. To help make a direct comparison, let's assume that the orange juice market is exactly as big as the market for petrol. Figure 18.11 illustrates this market. The demand curve for orange juice is *D* and the supply curve is *S*. When orange juice is not taxed, the quantity of orange juice traded is 400 million litres a day and the price of orange juice is 60 pence a litre.

Now suppose that the government contemplates abolishing the petrol tax and taxing orange juice instead. The demand for orange juice is more elastic than the demand for petrol. It has many more good substitutes in the form of other fruit juices. The government wants to raise £180 million a day so that its total revenue is not affected by this tax change. The government's economists, armed with their statistical estimates of the demand and supply curves for orange juice that appear in Fig. 18.11, work out that a tax of 90 pence a litre will do the job. This tax will shift the supply curve upward to the curve labelled *S + tax*. This new supply curve intersects the demand curve at a price of 130 pence a litre and at a quantity of 200 million litres a day. The price at which suppliers are willing to produce 200 million litres a day is 40 pence a litre. The government collects the required revenue of £180 million pounds a day – 90 pence a litre on 200 million litres a day.

But what is the deadweight loss in this case? The answer can be seen by looking at the grey triangle in Fig. 18.11. The magnitude of that deadweight loss is £90 million[4]. Notice how much

---

[4] This deadweight loss is calculated in exactly the same way as our previous calculation of the deadweight loss from the petrol tax. The loss of consumer surplus is 200 million litres multiplied by 70 pence, divided by 2, which equals £70 million a day. The loss of producer surplus is 200 million litres multiplied by 20 pence, divided by 2, which equals £20 million a day. The deadweight loss is the sum of the two losses, which equals £90 million a day.

FIGURE 18.11

Why We Don't Tax Orange Juice

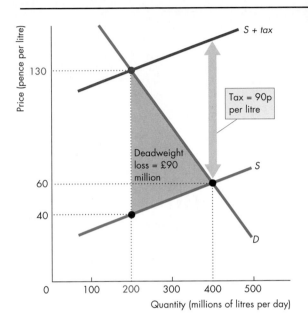

The demand curve for orange juice is *D* and the supply curve is *S*. The equilibrium price is 60 pence a litre and 400 million litres of juice a day are traded. To raise £180 million of tax revenue, a tax of 90 pence a litre will have to be imposed. The introduction of this tax shifts the supply curve to *S + tax*. The price rises to 130 pence a litre and the quantity bought and sold falls to 200 million litres a day. The deadweight loss is represented by the grey triangle and equals £90 million a day. The deadweight loss from taxing orange juice is much larger than that from taxing petrol (Fig. 18.10) because the demand for orange juice is more elastic than the demand for petrol. Items that have a low elasticity of demand are taxed more heavily than items that have a high elasticity of demand.

bigger the deadweight loss is from taxing orange juice than that from taxing petrol. In the case of orange juice, the deadweight loss is one-half of the revenue raised, while in the case of petrol it is only one-sixth. What accounts for this difference? The supply curves and the initial pre-tax prices and quantities were identical in each case. The only difference is the elasticity of demand. In the case of petrol, the quantity demanded falls by only 25 per cent when the price almost doubles. In the case of orange juice, the quantity demanded falls by 50 per cent when the price only slightly more than doubles.

Monitoring Costs in Public Health Care

The Essence of the Story

THE FINANCIAL TIMES, 22 FEBRUARY 1996

Tighter controls start complaints against red tape

Mark Suzman

The 1983 Griffiths report into the NHS said: 'If Florence Nightingale were carrying her lamp through the corridors of the NHS today, she would almost certainly be searching for the people in charge.'...

The statement focused not only on a lack of management but [also] on serious deficiencies in accountability and governance.

Like most other aspects of the health service, those areas have changed dramatically since the reforms. Most notable has been a growing centralisation of decision-making, a process that will be accelerated by the abolition of the regional health authorities in April 1996....

The reforms have transformed a loose conglomeration of different services ... into a much more unified managerial structure....

Much has been done to improve procedures of governance and accountability. ...New standards and guidelines ... have been put in place. A project aimed at tightening audit and monitoring procedures is being piloted....

But most managers ... believe that far too much time is spent by the centre trying to monitor their activities. ...Close scrutiny costs time and money that could be spent on patient services....

Mr Alan Langlands, NHS chief executive, is unperturbed. 'Of course there is a tension between public accountability and running a devolved system,' he says. 'But trusts [have] a framework of accountability as good and as well developed as any in government or the private sector.'...

It seems there is still much to complain about. The Audit Commission found that in 1995 alone there were 181 reported incidences of fraud in the NHS....

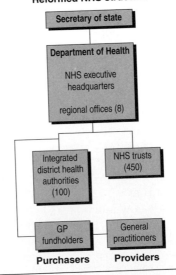

Reformed NHS structure

© The Financial Times. Reprinted with permission.

- The 1983 Griffiths Report on the NHS said there were too few managers and insufficient accountability.

- The 1991 and 1996 reforms created a more centralized management structure in the NHS, with a large management bureaucracy to run the internal market.

- New auditing and monitoring procedures have been introduced together with new standards for accountability.

- But managers now believe that closer monitoring and more red tape costs too much and takes money away from essential health services.

- Despite the reforms, the Audit Commission found 181 reported incidences of fraud within the NHS in 1995.

Economic Analysis

■ The 1991 reforms aimed to improve the accountability of public health care by introducing market pricing, contracting, professional managers and tighter monitoring of management decisions.

■ The figure in the article shows the new structure and the split between purchasers and providers. Providers must now bid and contract with purchasers of services.

■ Before the reforms, each part of the service was produced by a small public bureaucracy whose goal was to maximize its own budget without stating explicit costs of service provision.

■ Figure 1 shows the efficient level of provision of NHS care at Q_E, where the difference between the total benefit, shown by *TB*, and total cost, shown by *TC*, is greatest. We'll assume government provides an efficient quantity.

■ *B* is the maximum voters are prepared to spend on producing the total quantity of health care, Q_E, and budget-maximizing bureaucrats ensure that the total available budget is spent.

■ After the reforms, providers have an incentive to provide poorer-quality services, so more intensive monitoring is needed by a new bureaucracy of managers, who also aim to maximize their budgets.

■ Figure 2 shows that the maximum budget available to the new monitoring bureaucracy is *B* minus *C*. *C* is the now explicit cost of services emerging from the contract and bidding system – evidence of improved accountability.

■ The case for the reforms is that the new monitoring bureaucracy can't expand its budget by much and the total cost of service provision is less with greater accountability.

■ The case against the reforms is that it is more costly to monitor and run the new internal market than to produce it with less accountability.

■ The issue is still being debated and is considered in more detail in Chapter 21. Costs of services have been cut and accountability improved, but the result has been high levels of fraud and an increase of 355 per cent on managers' salaries.

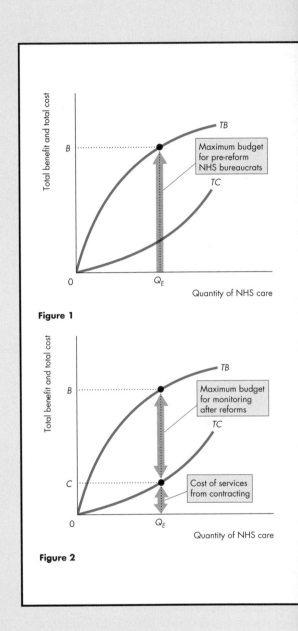

Figure 1

Figure 2

459

You can see why taxing orange juice is not on the political agenda of any of the major parties. Vote-seeking politicians seek out taxes that benefit the median voter. Other things remaining the same, this means that they try to minimize the deadweight loss of raising a given amount of revenue. Equivalently, they tax items with poor substitutes more heavily than items with close substitutes.

Value Added Tax (VAT) was introduced throughout the European Union in 1969 to harmonize the various forms of sales and purchase taxes that were operating in different member states. In the United Kingdom, some goods such as children's clothes and food are still exempt from VAT, so that only 40 per cent of private expenditure is covered by VAT compared to 90 per cent in most other member states. Is there an economic efficiency reason for reducing exemptions? The answer lies in the degree of substitution. The more goods that are subject to VAT, the smaller is the number of tax free goods towards which consumers can switch, and so the smaller the deadweight loss associated with the VAT system as a whole. In fact the UK government argues that the exemptions are needed to relieve poverty. We will be looking at this apparent trade-off between efficiency and fairness again in more detail in Chapter 21.

Compliance and Administration Costs

When any new tax is introduced there will be some additional costs. *Compliance costs* are the costs of ensuring that people do not avoid or evade the tax. *Administration costs* are the costs of running the new tax system, including the wages of tax officials and creating new computer software. Vote-seeking politicians will tend to choose taxes which minimize compliance and administration costs. This will benefit the median voter because it reduces the total amount of revenue needed for any set of benefits. When the UK government decided to fund local government using a per head tax (the Poll tax) rather than a housing tax (Rates), it found that compliance and administration costs increased dramatically. Administration costs increased because more bills and reminders had to be issued as more people pay a per head tax than a household tax. Compliance costs rose because the tax was

unpopular and many people refused to pay, or delayed paying. Court costs were high and the tax rate had to be increased to cover the shortfall from non-payment. Eventually the tax was replaced by another housing tax, the Council tax. Vote-seeking politicians were forced to adopt a more efficient tax with lower costs. Whether a housing tax also has a lower deadweight loss than a per head tax is debatable, but it is likely that the gains from lower compliance and administration costs under the new Council tax outweigh any loss from a higher deadweight loss.

REVIEW

◆ Taxes generate resources for government expenditure and most revenue is derived from income taxes and taxes on goods and services.

◆ Income taxes appeal to the median voter.

◆ Indirect taxes generate a deadweight loss – consumer and producer surplus is lost which is not transferred to government as revenue.

◆ The efficiency of a tax depends on the size of the deadweight loss, which in turn depends on the elasticity of demand.

◆ Minimizing deadweight loss, and administration and compliance costs appeal to the median voter.

◆ ◆ ◆ ◆ We've seen that markets don't always achieve allocative efficiency – that there is market failure. We've looked at one example of how government policy can overcome market failure in the provision of public goods. But we've also seen that bureaucrats can overprovide a public good, creating government failure. Finally, we've seen how the political marketplace can determine the rates of income tax and excise tax, as well as which goods are taxed. In the next three chapters, we are going to look more closely at government policy to overcome other forms of market failure – monopoly, externalities, uncertainty and limited information – as well as the problem of inequality.

SUMMARY

The Government Sector

The trend is for the size of the government sector to increase in all developed economies. The total spending by the government sector equals 37 per cent of total income in the United Kingdom. The biggest departments of government deal with the provision of defence and health services. The government share of the economy has grown over the years, increasing from 13 per cent in 1900 to 47 per cent in 1975 and falling back to 37 per cent by 1995. (pp. 443–444).

The Economic Theory of Government

Government policy is an attempt to cope with problems created by market failure – public goods, monopoly, externalities, uncertainty and limited information. Market failure means that markets do not provide the efficient level of some goods and services. Government can use policies such as public provision, taxation and regulation to improve market efficiency caused by market failure. In addition, governments use the tax and benefit system to make the market allocation of resources more equitable, and use monetary and fiscal policy to stabilize the economy and generate more potential for growth. (pp. 444–446)

Public Choice and the Political Marketplace

To study government policy we use public choice theory. Public choice theory can be used to create a model of the political marketplace in which voters, politicians and bureaucrats interact with each other. Voters are the consumers of the political process and they express their demands through their votes, political campaigning and financial contributions, and by lobbying. Politicians propose policies and their objective is to win elections. Bureaucrats implement policies and their objective is to maximize their own departmental budgets. The outcome of the interaction of voters, politicians and bureaucrats is a political equilibrium which might or might not be efficient. (pp. 447–448)

Public Goods

The efficient level of provision of a public good maximises the value of total benefit minus total cost – where marginal benefit equals marginal cost. The existence of public goods creates a free-rider problem – people have little incentive to pay voluntarily for such goods. If private companies cannot generate any revenue for these goods, they will not supply them and the market allocation will be less than the efficient level of provision.

A government can provide a public good and pay for it with tax revenue to avoid the free-rider problem. People will vote for a political party that proposes to produce a public good on a scale at which total benefit exceeds total cost. Competition between political parties, each of which tries to appeal to the maximum number of voters, will lead both parties to propose the same policies at the efficient level.

Bureaucrats try to maximize their budgets, but they are constrained by voters' preferences. If voters are well-informed, politicians will be elected who propose to provide the efficient quantity of a public good and constrain the size of bureaucrats' budgets. But if voters are rationally ignorant, producer interests may result in voting to support taxes that provide public goods in quantities that exceed those that maximize net benefit. (pp. 448–454)

Taxes

Most government revenue comes from income taxes, value added tax and excise taxes on petrol, alcoholic beverages and tobacco products.

Income taxes appeal to the median voter. Voters with a high income pay for more benefits than they receive and want a lower tax rate. Voters with a low income pay for less benefits than they receive and want a higher tax rate. The tax rate that wins elections is the one that appeals to the median voter.

The imposition of a tax on a good creates a deadweight loss, the size of which depends on the elasticity of demand. High levels of tax are an efficient method of raising revenue if they tax goods with low elasticity of demand. Excise taxes are placed on goods with low elasticity of demand so that the deadweight loss of raising a given amount of tax revenue is minimized. Minimizing the deadweight loss and compliance and administration costs also appeal to the median voter. (pp. 454–460)

KEY ELEMENTS

Key Terms

Bureaucrats, 447
Deadweight loss, 456
Excise tax, 455
Externality, 446
Free rider, 446
Marginal benefit, 448
Market failure, 444
Median voter theorem, 454
Non-excludable, 445
Non-rival, 445
Political equilibrium, 448
Public choice theory, 447
Public good, 445
Rational ignorance, 452

 Key Figures

Figure 18.2   The Aims of Government Policy, 444
Figure 18.5   Benefits of a Public Good, 449
Figure 18.6   The Efficient Quantity of a Public Good, 450
Figure 18.7   Provision of a Public Good in a Political System, 451
Figure 18.8   Bureaucratic Overprovision, 452
Figure 18.9   Voting for Income Taxes, 455
Figure 18.10 An Excise Tax, 456
Figure 18.11 Why We Don't Tax Orange Juice, 457

REVIEW QUESTIONS

1 Describe the growth of the government sector of the UK economy over the past 90 years.

2 What is market failure and from what does it arise?

3 What is a public good? Give three examples.

4 What is the free-rider problem and how does government help overcome it?

5 What is an externality?

6 Describe the three actors in the political marketplace.

7 Describe the economic functions of voters and explain how they make their economic choices.

8 Describe the economic functions of politicians and explain how they make their economic choices.

9 Describe the economic functions of bureaucrats and explain how they make their economic choices.

10 What is meant by political equilibrium?

11 How does the principle of minimum differentiation explain the policy choice of different political parties?

12 Explain why it is likely that the quantity of public goods will exceed the efficient scale.

13 Why is it rational for voters to be ignorant?

14 What is the median voter theorem?

15 What features of political choices does the median voter theorem explain?

P R O B L E M S

1 You are given the following information about a sewage disposal system that a city of 1 million people is considering installing:

Capacity (thousands of litres per day)	Marginal private benefit to one person (pounds)	Total cost (millions of pounds)
0		0
	100	
1		10
	80	
2		30
	60	
3		60
	40	
4		100
	20	
5		150

a What is the capacity that achieves maximum net benefit?

b How much will each person have to pay in taxes in order to pay for the efficient capacity level?

c What are the total and net benefits?

d What is the political equilibrium if voters are well-informed?

e What is the political equilibrium if voters are rationally ignorant and bureaucrats achieve the highest attainable budget?

2 Your local council is contemplating upgrading its system for controlling traffic signals. It reckons that by installing a sophisticated computer with sensing mechanisms at all the major intersections, it can better adjust the timing of the changes in signals and improve the speed of the traffic flow. The bigger the computer the council buys, the better is the job it can do, and the more sensors it installs, the more intersections it can monitor and the faster will be the resulting overall traffic flow. The mayor and the other elected officials who are working on the proposal want to determine the scale and sophistication of the system that will win them the most votes. The city bureaucrats in the traffic department want to maximize the budget. Suppose that you are an economist who is observing this public choice. Your job is to calculate the quantity of this public good that maximizes net benefit – that achieves allocative efficiency.

a What data would you need in order to reach your own conclusions?

b What does the public choice theory predict will be the quantity chosen?

c How could you, as an informed voter, attempt to influence the choice?

3 An economy with 9 groups of people, identified by letters A to I has net benefits from different tax income tax levels as follows:

A	B	C	D	E	F	G	H	I
90	80	70	60	50	0	0	0	0

Suppose there are two political parties competing for office in this community. What income tax rate would the parties propose?

4 You are given the following information about a competitive market for biscuits:

Price (pounds per kilogram)	Quantity demanded (kilograms per month)	Quantity supplied (kilograms per month)
10	0	36
8	3	30
6	6	24
4	9	18
2	12	12
0	15	0

a What are the equilibrium price and quantity bought and sold?

b Suppose that a 10 per cent tax is imposed on biscuits.
   1 What is the new price of biscuits?
   2 What is the new quantity bought and sold?
   3 What is the total amount of tax revenue raised by the government?
   4 What is the deadweight loss?

5 You are given the following information about the market for ball point pens.

Price (pence per week)	Quantity demanded (thousands a week)	Quantity supplied
10	200	0
20	180	30
30	160	60
40	140	90
50	120	120
60	100	140
70	80	160
80	60	180
90	40	200

a Draw the demand and supply curves on a graph.

b What is the equilibrium price and quantity of ball point pens?

c Estimate the value of consumer surplus.

d Estimate the value of producer surplus.

6 Suppose the government decides to impose a tax of 20 pence per pen. Using your graph from Problem 5, answer the following:

a What is the new equilibrium price and quantity of ball point pens?

b How much revenue does the government make?

c Estimate the value of consumer surplus after tax.

d Estimate the value of producer surplus after the tax.

e Estimate the value of the deadweight loss associated with the tax.

7 Suppose the demand for pens in Problem 6 were more elastic.

a Draw an example of a more inelastic demand for pens on your graph from Problem 6. (Draw the line through the original equilibrium point before tax.)

b Using the new demand curve, shade in the area of the deadweight loss when the government imposes a tax of 20 pence per pen.

c Is the deadweight loss larger or smaller with the new, more inelastic demand curve?

d Is government revenue larger or smaller with the new, more inelastic demand curve?

8 Read the story in *Reading Between the Lines* on pp. 458–459 again and then answer the following questions:

a What was the purpose of introducing a split between purchasers and providers in the new NHS structure?

b Why has the government introduced new auditing and monitoring procedures?

c What is the case for the reforms?

d What is the case against the reforms?

CHAPTER
19

REGULATION
AND
PRIVATIZATION

After studying this chapter you will be able to:

◆ Define regulation and monopoly control law

◆ Distinguish between the public interest and capture theories of regulation

◆ Explain how regulation affects prices, outputs, profits and the distribution of the gains from trade between consumers and producers

◆ Explain how monopoly and competition law are applied in the UK and the European Union

◆ Explain the case for public ownership and privatization

◆ Explain how and why privatized organizations are regulated by government

WHEN YOU CONSUME WATER, ELECTRIC POWER, NATURAL GAS, OR telephone services you buy from a regulated local monopoly. Why and how are the industries that produce these goods and services regulated? Do the regulations work in the public interest – the interest of all consumers and producers – or do they serve special interests – the interests – of particular groups of consumers or producers? ◆ Regulation extends beyond monopoly to oligopoly. For example, until 1987, the price of tickets and the routes that airlines could fly throughout Europe were regulated to create a cartel. EU member states have agreed to deregulate airline routes in 1997 to free up access to European routes and promote cut-price tickets. Why do we regulate and then deregulate some industries? ◆ In 1995, the UK Monopolies and Mergers Commission blocked the merger of a regional bus company and a national bus company using monopoly control laws but allowed the merger of two electricity generators with electricity suppliers. What are monopoly control laws and whose interest do they serve? ◆ After 1945, many monopolies, flagship firms and major industries were bought by the government. Since 1979, many of these have been privatized. Why has government bought up firms and industries and then sold them off? Does privatization serve the public interest or the special interests of producers and shareholders?

Public Interest or Special Interest

◆ ◆ ◆ ◆ This chapter studies government regulation of markets for goods and services and identifies who stands to gain and who stands to lose from different types of regulation. It also looks at the economic behaviour of politicians and bureaucrats who supply regulation.

Market Intervention

The government intervenes in monopolistic and oligopolistic markets to influence prices, quantities produced and the distribution of the gains from economic activity. It intervenes in two main ways:

◆ Regulating prices, products and market entry

◆ Controlling monopoly

Regulation

Regulation consists of rules administered by a government agency to influence economic activity by determining prices, product standards and types, and the conditions under which new firms may enter an industry. In order to implement its regulations, the government establishes agencies to oversee the regulations and ensure their enforcement. Price and entry condition regulations are typically applied at the industry level to banking and financial services, telecommunications, gas and electricity suppliers, railways, airlines and buses. Many new UK regulatory agencies such as OFWAT, the water regulator, and OFTEL, the telecommunications regulator, were set up after privatization to regulate prices. Other similar industry-level regulatory organizations exist in most other countries, and EU industries are also regulated by the European Commission.

Regulation is also widely applied at the product level on many agricultural and manufactured products. You need look no further than recent health scares – salmonella in chicken eggs, listeria in cook-chill foods and BSE in dairy cattle – to see the importance of product regulation in any one country. But the European Union has also introduced a wide range of directives to harmonize standards of regulation across its members in order to ensure fair competition. Members states are not allowed to use regulation as a way of protecting home industries from competition.

Since the late 1970s, there has been a tendency in many countries to deregulate the economy. **Deregulation** is the process of removing restrictions on prices, product standards and types, and entry conditions. Deregulation has been introduced where the existing regulation is thought to cause a barrier to entry in a market –

reducing competition. Financial services were substantially deregulated to allow building societies to compete with banks, and restrictions on entry to bus routes were removed to allow new bus companies to enter the market. Deregulating airways has left the United Kingdom with the most liberalized air market in Europe. In 1994, the Deregulation and Contracting Out Act allowed for the amendment and repeal of old regulatory legislation to help reduce industrial administration costs. Recent examples include less paperwork for road hauliers, an end to licensing for employment agencies and simplified accounting for small businesses.

Monopoly Control

Monopoly control law regulates and prohibits certain kinds of market behaviour, such as monopoly and monopolistic practices. Some countries, like the United States, have a history of monopoly control laws dating back to the last half of the nineteenth century. By contrast, control of monopolies was not introduced in the United Kingdom until 1948 with the first Monopolies and Restrictive Practices Act. This act set up the Monopolies and Mergers Commission (MMC) and the Restrictive Practices Court (RPC) as the agencies of control. The 1973 Fair Trading Act created a new agency called the Office of Fair Trading. The agency is now run by the Director General of Fair Trading (DGFT), who controls the work of the MMC and the RPC. Current UK monopoly control laws have three elements:

◆ Monopoly

◆ Mergers

◆ Restrictive practices

Monopoly   Our economic model defines a monopoly as a single firm in the industry, but UK government policy defines *monopoly* as substantial market power – when a firm has 25 per cent or more of the market. Any industry that has a firm defined as a monopoly in this way can be referred by the DGFT to the MMC for investigation. The MMC produces a report on the industry and makes recommendations. The final decision rests with the secretary of state for trade and industry. For example, the 1989 MMC report on the brewing industry found evidence of a monopoly in the supply of beer. The monopoly power was created by extensive vertical integration. Most brewers owned or controlled their own pubs, and could restrict the beers that pubs could sell. The MMC recommended that the number of pubs that a brewer could own should be limited. These recommendations were implemented by government in a revised form, resulting in a major restructuring of the industry.

Mergers **Mergers** are one of the main methods by which firms grow. They occur when two firms combine by mutual agreement, but we also use the term merger when one firm mounts an unwelcome takeover for another. The reason why mergers and takeovers arise are examined in Chapter 16, pp. 404–405. Mergers can result in the formation of a dominant firm with monopoly power. The DGFT can refer any proposed merger to the MMC if it is likely to create a firm with 25 per cent of the market or more, or with assets in excess of £30 million. The MMC investigates the merger and makes a report, recommending acceptance or rejection of the proposed merger. The final decision rests with the secretary of state.

Restrictive Practices **Restrictive practices** are formal agreements between firms to set prices, to swap information or to act as a cartel. Restrictive practices are assumed to reduce competition and are illegal, unless the firms involved can prove that the practice is in the public interest. All agreements must be registered with the Office of Fair Trading and are judged by the Restrictive Practices Court. Until 1965, retail price maintenance – the practice of producers determining the minimum price a retailer can set – was widespread. It is now virtually eliminated. In 1995, retail price maintenance on books was challenged, and there is strong pressure from supermarket retailers and discount chemists to eliminate the last remaining agreement on pharmaceutical goods.

To understand why the government intervenes in markets for goods and services, and to work out the effects of its interventions, we need to identify the gains and losses that government actions can create. These gains and losses are the consumer surplus and producer surplus associated with different output levels and prices. Let's refresh our understanding of these concepts.

Surpluses and Their Distribution

Consumer surplus is the gain from trade accruing to consumers. It is calculated as the maximum price that consumers are willing to pay minus the price actually paid for each unit bought, summed over all the units bought (see Chapter 7, pp. 164–165). *Producer surplus* is the gain from trade accruing to producers. It is calculated as price minus marginal cost (opportunity cost) for each unit produced, summed over all the units produced (see Chapter 12, p. 300). **Total surplus** is the sum of consumer surplus and producer surplus.

Figure 19.1 shows these surpluses. In Fig. 19.1(a), there is perfect competition. The market demand curve is D and the market supply curve is S. The price is P_C and the quantity is Q_C. Because the demand curve shows the maximum price that consumers are willing to pay for each unit bought, consumer surplus is the amount shown by the green triangle. Because the supply curve shows marginal cost, producer surplus is the amount shown by the blue triangle. Total surplus is the amount shown by the combined green and blue triangles.

In Fig. 19.1(b), the industry is a (single-price) monopoly. What in a perfectly competitive industry is the supply curve is the marginal cost curve for a monopoly. The firm's marginal revenue curve is MR. To maximize profit, the firm restricts output to Q_M, the quantity at which marginal revenue equals marginal cost. It sells the quantity Q_M at the price P_M. Consumer surplus is shown by the smaller green triangle and producer surplus is shown by the blue area. Compared with perfect competition, consumer surplus is smaller and producer surplus is larger. Some of the consumer surplus becomes a producer surplus but some of it disappears. Also, some of the producer surplus is lost. The lost consumer surplus and producer surplus is *deadweight loss*, which is shown by the grey triangle in Fig. 19.1(b) (see Chapter 12, pp. 300–301).

Total surplus is maximized when deadweight loss is zero. When output is restricted to increase the price and increase producer surplus, total surplus falls. Thus there is a tension between the special interest of producers and the public interest. This tension is the key to understanding the economic theory of regulation. Let's examine this theory.

FIGURE 19.1

FIGURE 19.1

Consumer and Producer Surplus

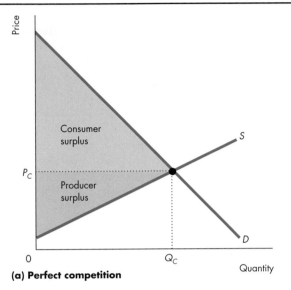

(a) Perfect competition

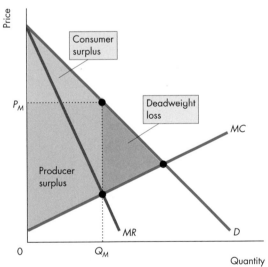

(b) Monopoly

With perfect competition (part a), the market demand curve (*D*) and market supply curve (*S*) intersect to determine the price P_C and quantity Q_C. Consumer surplus is shown by the green triangle and producer surplus is shown by the blue triangle. Total surplus is the sum of these two triangles. With monopoly (part b), the firm restricts output to Q_M, the level at which marginal revenue (*MR*) equals marginal cost (*MC*), and sells that quantity for a price of P_M. In this case consumer surplus (the green triangle) decreases, producer surplus (the blue area) increases and a deadweight loss, which is shown by the grey triangle, arises. Total surplus is maximized under perfect competition.

Economic Theory of Regulation

The economic theory of regulation is part of the broader theory of public choice that is explained in Chapter 18. We're going to re-examine the main features of public choice theory but with an emphasis on the regulatory aspects of government behaviour. We'll examine the demand for government actions, the supply of those actions and the political equilibrium – the balancing of demands and supplies.

Demand for Regulation

The *demand for regulation* is expressed through political activity – voting, lobbying and making campaign contributions. But engaging in political activity is costly and people demand political action only if the benefit that they individually receive from such action exceeds their individual costs in obtaining the action. The four main factors that affect the demand for regulation are:

1. Consumer surplus per buyer
2. Number of buyers
3. Producer surplus per firm
4. Number of firms

The larger the consumer surplus per buyer resulting from regulation, the greater is the demand for regulation by buyers. Also, as the number of buyers increases, so does the demand for regulation. But numbers alone do not necessarily translate into an effective political force. The larger the number of buyers, the greater is the cost of organizing them, so the demand for regulation does not increase proportionately with the number of buyers.

The larger the producer surplus per firm arising from a particular regulation, the larger is the demand for that regulation by firms. Also, as the number of firms that might benefit from some regulation increases, so does the demand for that regulation. But again, as in the case of consumers, large numbers do not necessarily mean an effective political force. The larger the number of firms, the greater is the cost of organizing them.

For a given surplus, consumer or producer, the smaller the number of households or firms which share that surplus, the larger is the demand for the regulation that creates it.

Supply of Regulation

Regulation is supplied by politicians and bureaucrats. Politicians choose policies that appeal to a majority of voters, thereby enabling themselves to achieve and maintain office. Bureaucrats support policies that maximize their budgets (see Chapter 18, pp. 447–448). Given these objectives of politicians and bureaucrats, the *supply of regulation* depends on the following factors:

1. Consumer surplus per buyer
2. Producer surplus per firm
3. The number of persons affected

The larger the consumer surplus per buyer or producer surplus per firm generated, and the larger the number of persons affected by a regulation, the greater is the tendency for politicians to supply that regulation. If regulation benefits a large number of people significantly enough for it to be noticed and if the recipients know who is the source of the benefits, that regulation appeals to politicians and it is supplied. If regulation benefits a *small* number of people by a large amount per person, that regulation also appeals to politicians provided its costs are spread widely and are not easily identified. If regulation affects markets that benefit a large number of people but by a small amount per person, and if such benefits do not attract notice, that regulation does not appeal to politicians and is not supplied.

Political Equilibrium

In equilibrium, the regulation that exists is such that no interest group feels it is worthwhile to use additional resources to press for changes, and no group of politicians feels it is worthwhile to offer different regulations. Being in a *political equilibrium* is not the same thing as everyone being in agreement. Interest groups will devote resources to trying to change regulations that are already in place; others will devote resources to maintaining the existing regulations. But no one will feel it is worthwhile to *increase* the resources they are devoting to such activities. Also, political parties might not agree with each other. Some support the existing regulations and others propose different regulations. In equilibrium, no one wants to change the proposals that they are making.

What will a political equilibrium look like? The answer depends on whether the regulation serves the public interest or the interest of the producer. Let's look at these two possibilities.

Public Interest Theory   The **public interest theory** is that regulations are supplied to satisfy the demand of consumers and producers to maximize total surplus – that is, to attain allocative efficiency. Public interest theory implies that the political process relentlessly seeks out deadweight loss and introduces regulations that eliminate it. For example, where monopoly practices exist, the political process will introduce price regulations to ensure that outputs increase and prices fall to their competitive levels.

Capture Theory   The **capture theory** is that the regulations are supplied to satisfy the demand of producers to maximize producer surplus – that is, to maximize economic profit. The key idea of capture theory is that the cost of regulation is high and only those regulations that increase the surplus of small, easily identified groups and that have low organization costs are supplied by the political process. Such regulations are supplied even if they impose costs on others, provided these costs are spread thinly and widely enough so that they do not decrease votes.

The predictions of the capture theory are less clear cut than the predictions of the public interest theory. According to the capture theory, regulations benefit cohesive interest groups by large and visible amounts and impose small costs on everyone else. But these costs are so small, in per person terms, that no one feels it is worthwhile to incur the cost of organizing an interest group to avoid them. To make these predictions concrete enough to be useful, the capture theory needs a model of the costs of political organization.

Whichever theory of regulation is correct, according to public choice theory, the political system delivers amounts and types of regulations that best further the electoral success of politicians. Because producer-oriented and consumer-oriented regulation are in conflict with each other, the political process can't satisfy both groups in any particular industry. Only one group can win. This makes the regulatory actions of government a bit like a unique good – for example, a painting by Rembrandt. There is only one original and it will be sold to just one buyer. Normally, a unique commodity is sold through an auction; the highest bidder takes the prize. Equilibrium in the regulatory process can be thought of in much the same way: the suppliers of regulation will satisfy the demands of the higher bidder. If the producer demand offers a bigger return to the politicians, either directly through votes or indirectly through political contributions, then the producers' interests will be served. If the consumer demand translates into a larger number of votes, then the consumers' interests will be served by regulation.

R E V I E W

◆ The demand for regulation is expressed by both consumers and producers who spend scarce resources voting, lobbying and campaigning for regulations that best further their own interests.

◆ Regulation is supplied by politicians and bureaucrats. Politicians choose actions that appeal to a majority of voters, and bureaucrats choose actions that maximize their budgets.

◆ The regulation that exists is the political equilibrium that balances the opposing demand and supply forces. The political equilibrium either achieves efficiency – the public interest theory – or maximizes producer surplus – the capture theory.

We have now completed our study of the theory of regulation in the marketplace. Let's turn our attention to the regulations that exist in our economy today. Which of these regulations are in the public interest and which are in the interests of producers?

Regulation and Deregulation

The past 20 years have seen dramatic changes in the way in which European economies are regulated by government. We're going to examine some of these changes. To begin we'll look at what is regulated and also at the scope of regulation. Then we'll turn to the regulatory process itself and examine how regulators control prices and other aspects of market behaviour. Finally, we'll tackle the more difficult and controversial questions. Why do we regulate some things but not others? Who benefits from this regulation – consumers or producers?

The Scope of Regulation

What exactly do regulatory agencies do? How do they regulate industries and firms? Table 19.1 shows the hierarchy of regulatory agencies that operate in the United Kingdom. At the top are institutions created by agreement among countries. These institutions regulate firms indirectly by restricting government protection of domestic industry. The World Trade Organization (WTO) was set up in 1995 to replace the GATT, the General Agreement on Tariffs and Trade. The agency's aim is to avoid an outbreak of tariff wars among countries and to promote unilateral reductions in tariffs. Agreements are made during occasional negotiation rounds, the last of which was the Uruguay Round in 1993. The WTO now monitors and enforces the agreements made between the 124 participating governments. Below this are the 23 Directorates General of the European Commission. The European Commission is responsible for ensuring its member states comply with EU level regulation of industry, based on the Treaty of Rome and the Treaty of European Union. Its directives control many aspects of business activity directly and indirectly. For example, its directives determine standards of production and marketing, the pricing of agricultural products, employment practices, health and safety, pollution, monopoly power, restrictive practices and mergers.

Firms are also subject to general and specific regulation at the national level. Table 19.1 shows that some agencies are responsible for general regulation across all industries – the Environment Agency, the Health and Safety Executive and the Monopolies and Mergers Commission are all examples. Other agencies have responsibility for specific regulation of particular industries – the Civil Aviation Authority, the Bank of England and the Securities and Investments Board are all examples of these. The agencies set up to regulate the newly privatized industries – OFFER, OFWAT, OFGAS, OFTEL and OFRAIL – are also industry-specific regulators.

Many firms are also subject to voluntary regulation by professional and industrial organizations. Voluntary self-regulation usually involves setting up a code of practice to which firms registered with the professional or industrial organizations must adhere.

TABLE 19.1

The Regulation Hierarchy

LEVEL	AGENCY	ACTIVITY	METHOD
Global	World Trade Organization	Monitors and enforces rules on tariff agreements	International agreements
European Union	European Commission	Monitors and enforces rules on member states	Directives
National Government	Departments	Monitor and control public provision in the NHS, education, and so on	Circulars
◆ General	MMC	Investigates monopoly and recommends action	Investigative reports
	Health and Safety Executive	Investigates breaches of health and safety law	Inspectorate
	Environment Agency	Monitors and enforces environmental law	Inspectorate
	Securities and Investments Board	Regulates financial investment firms and other financial agencies	Code of practice and licence
	Bank of England	Regulates banks and building societies and enforces monetary policy	Licence
	Civil Aviation Authority	Monitors and regulates airlines, airports and air-traffic control	Route and price control, code of practice
◆ Specific	OFFER Office of Electricity Regulation	Monitors and regulates electricity companies	Price cap formula
	OFWAT Office of Water Services	Monitors and regulates water companies	Price cap formula
	OFGAS Office of Gas	Monitors and regulates British Gas and new suppliers	Price cap formula and licence
	OFTEL Office of Telecommunications	Monitors and regulates British Telecom and new suppliers	Price cap formula and licence
	OFRAIL Office of Rail Transport	Monitors and regulates Railtrack and travel companies	Price cap formula
Local government	Departments	Control and monitor planning, education, taxis, traders, and so on	Licences and bye-laws
Industry	Professional organizations	Control and monitor participating industries	Code of practice and membership

Examples are the British Medical Association, the Press Association and the British Association of Pharmaceutical Industries. In some cases the professional organization is required by law to set up a code of practice and to enforce that code, although the law does not dictate what should be in the code of practice. Local government, which has responsibility for issuing planning regulations and the licensing of taxis and local traders, is the final regulatory tier.

The Regulatory Process

Although regulatory agencies vary in size and scope and in the detailed aspects of economic life that they control, there are certain features common to all agencies.

First, the bureaucrats, who are the key decision makers in the main regulatory agencies, are appointed by central and local governments. In addition, all agencies have a permanent bureaucracy made up of experts in the industry being regulated, who are often recruited from the regulated firms. Agencies are allocated financial resources by government to cover the costs of their operations.

Second, each agency adopts a set of practices or operating rules for controlling prices and other aspects of economic or professional performance. We will concentrate on the main agencies and on industry-specific economic regulation. These rules and practices are based on well-defined physical and financial accounting procedures that are quite easy to administer and to monitor.

In a regulated industry, individual firms are usually free to determine the technology that they will use in production. The exceptions are those industries whose production technology is regulated by the Environment Agency. Regulation usually involves limiting the power of firms to determine one or more of the following: the price of output, the quantities sold, the quality of the product, or the markets served. The regulatory agency grants certification to a company to serve a particular market with a particular line of products, and it determines the level and structure of prices that will be charged. In some cases, the agency also determines the scale and quality of output permitted.

To analyse the way in which industry-specific regulation works, it is convenient to distinguish between the regulation of natural monopoly and the regulation of cartels. Let's begin with natural monopoly.

Natural Monopoly

Natural monopoly was defined in Chapter 12 (p. 287) as an industry in which one firm can supply the entire market at a lower price than can two or more firms. As a consequence, a natural monopoly experiences economies of scale, no matter how high an output rate it achieves. Examples of natural monopolies include telephone and cable companies, local electricity and water companies, and rail services. It is much more expensive to have two or more competing sets of wires, pipes and railway lines serving every area than it is to have a single set. (What is a natural monopoly changes over time as technology changes. With the introduction of fibre optic cables, both telephone companies and cable television companies can compete with each other in both markets, so what was once a natural monopoly is becoming a more competitive industry.)

Let's consider the example of cable TV, which is shown in Fig. 19.2. The demand curve for cable TV is *D*. The cable TV company's marginal cost curve is *MC*. That marginal cost curve is (assumed to be) horizontal at £10 per household per month – that is, the cost of providing each additional household with a month of cable programming is £10. The cable company has a heavy investment in satellite receiving dishes, cables and control equipment and so has high fixed costs. These fixed costs are part of the company's average total cost curve, shown as *ATC*. The average total cost curve slopes downward because as the number of households served increases, the fixed cost is spread over a larger

FIGURE 19.2

Natural Monopoly: Marginal Cost Pricing

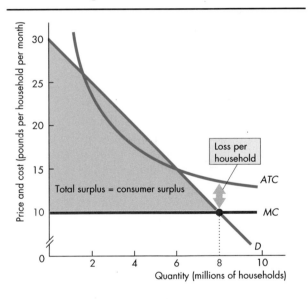

A natural monopoly is an industry in which average total cost is falling even when the entire market demand is satisfied. A cable TV operator faces the demand curve *D*. The firm's marginal cost is constant at £10 per household per month, as shown by the curve *MC*. Fixed costs are large and the average total cost curve, which includes average fixed cost, is shown as *ATC*. A marginal cost pricing rule that maximizes total surplus sets the price at £10 a month, with 8 million households being served. It also maximizes consumer surplus, shown as the green area. The firm incurs a loss on each household, indicated by the red arrow. To remain in business, the cable operator must either price discriminate or receive a subsidy.

number of households. (If you need to refresh your memory on how the average total cost curve is calculated, take a quick look back at Chapter 10, pp. 233–234.)

Regulation in the Public Interest   How will cable TV be regulated according to the public interest theory? In the public interest theory, regulation maximizes total surplus, which occurs if marginal cost equals price. As you can see in Fig. 19.2, that outcome occurs if the price is regulated at £10 per household per month and if 8 million households are served. Such a regulation is called a marginal cost pricing rule. A **marginal cost pricing rule** sets price equal to marginal cost. It maximizes total surplus and consumer surplus in the regulated industry.

A natural monopoly that is regulated to set price equal to marginal cost incurs an economic loss. Because its average total cost curve is falling, marginal cost is below average total cost. Because price equals marginal cost, price is below average total cost. Average total cost minus price is the loss per unit produced. It's pretty obvious that a cable TV operator that is required to use a marginal cost pricing rule will not stay in business for long. How can a company cover its costs and, at the same time, obey a marginal cost pricing rule?

One possibility is price discrimination. Some natural monopolies can fairly easily price discriminate using a two-part tariff that gives consumers a bill for connection and a bill for units used. For example, a gas supply company can charge consumers a monthly fee for being connected to the gas supply and then charge a price equal to marginal cost for each unit of gas supplied. A cable TV operator can price discriminate by charging a one-time connection fee that covers its fixed cost and then charging a monthly fee equal to marginal cost.

But a natural monopoly cannot always price discriminate. It is difficult to operate a two-part tariff on a rail network. When a natural monopoly cannot price discriminate, it can cover its total cost and follow a marginal cost pricing rule only if it receives a subsidy from the government. In this case, the government raises the revenue for the subsidy by taxing some other activity. But as we saw in Chapter 18, taxes themselves generate deadweight loss. Thus the deadweight loss resulting from additional taxes must be offset against the allocative efficiency gained by forcing the natural

monopoly to adopt a marginal cost pricing rule.

It is possible that deadweight loss will be minimized by permitting the natural monopoly to charge a higher price than marginal cost rather than by taxing some other sector of the economy in order to subsidize the natural monopoly. This pricing arrangement is called an average cost pricing rule. An **average cost pricing rule** sets price equal to average total cost. Figure 19.3 shows the average cost pricing solution. The cable TV operator charges £15 a month and serves 6 million households. A deadweight loss arises, which is shown by the grey triangle in the figure.

Capturing the Regulator   What does the capture theory predict about the regulation of this industry? According to the capture theory, regulation serves the interests of the producer. The interests of the producer are best satisfied by

FIGURE 19.3

Natural Monopoly: Average Cost Pricing

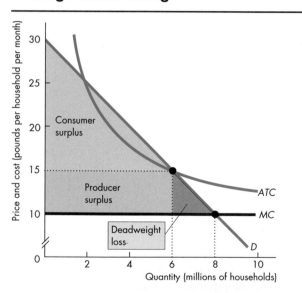

Average cost pricing sets price equal to average total cost. The cable TV operator charges £15 a month and serves 6 million households. In this situation the firm breaks even – average total cost equals price. Deadweight loss, shown by the grey triangle, is generated. Consumer surplus is reduced to the green area.

maximizing profit. To work out the price that achieves this goal, we need to look at the relationship between marginal revenue and marginal cost. A monopoly maximizes profit by producing the output at which marginal revenue equals marginal cost. The monopoly's marginal revenue curve in Fig. 19.4 is the curve *MR*. Marginal revenue equals marginal cost when output is 4 million households and the price is £20 a month. Thus a regulation that best serves the interest of the producer will set the price at this level.

But how can a producer go about obtaining regulation that results in this monopoly profit-maximizing outcome? To answer this question, we need to look at the way agencies determine a regulated price. A key method used is called rate of return regulation.

FIGURE 19.4

Natural Monopoly: Profit Maximization

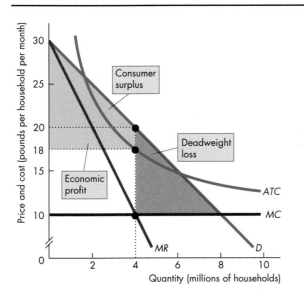

The cable TV operator would like to maximize profit. To do so, marginal revenue (*MR*) is made equal to marginal cost. At a price of £20 a month, 4 million households buy cable services. Consumer surplus is reduced to the green triangle. The deadweight loss increases to the grey triangle. The monopoly makes the profit shown by the blue rectangle. If the producer can capture the regulator, the outcome will be the situation shown here.

Rate of Return Regulation **Rate of return regulation** determines a regulated price by setting the price at a level that enables the regulated firm to earn a specified target percentage return on its capital. The target rate of return is determined with reference to what is normal in competitive industries. This rate of return is part of the opportunity cost of the natural monopolist and is included in the firm's average total cost. By examining the firm's total cost, including the normal rate of return on capital, the regulator attempts to determine the price at which average total cost is covered. Thus rate of return regulation is equivalent to average cost pricing.

In the example that we have just been examining – in Fig. 19.3 – average cost pricing results at a regulated price of £15 a month with 6 million households being served. Thus rate of return regulation, based on a correct assessment of the producer's average total cost curve, results in a price and quantity that favour the consumer and do not enable the producer to maximize monopoly profit. The special interest group will have failed to capture the regulator and the outcome will be closer to that predicted by the public interest theory of regulation.

But there is a feature of many real-world situations that the above analysis does not take into account – the ability of the monopoly firm to mislead the regulator about its true costs.

Inflating Costs The managers of a regulated firm might be able to inflate the firm's costs by spending part of its revenue on inputs that are not strictly required for the production of the good. By this device, the firm's apparent cost curves exceed the true cost curves. This is sometimes called X-inefficiency. On-the-job luxury in the form of sumptuous office suites, expensive company cars, free football match tickets (disguised as public relations expenses), lavish international travel and entertainment are all ways in which managers can inflate costs.

If the managers of the cable firm inflate costs and persuade the regulator that the firm's true cost curve is that shown as *ATC (inflated)* in Fig. 19.5, then the regulator, applying the normal rate of return principle, will regulate the price at £20 a month. In this example, the price and quantity will be the same as in an unregulated monopoly. It might be impossible for firms to inflate their costs by as much as that shown in the figure. But to the extent that costs can be inflated, the apparent average total cost curve lies somewhere between the true *ATC* curve and *ATC (inflated)*. The greater the ability of the firm to pad its costs in this way, the closer its profit (measured in economic terms) approaches the maximum possible. The shareholders of this firm don't receive this economic profit because it gets used up in football match tickets, luxury offices and the other actions taken by the firm's managers to inflate the firm's costs.

Incentive Regulation Schemes   Partly for the reasons we've just examined, rate of return regulation is increasingly being replaced by incentive regulation schemes. An **incentive regulation scheme** is a type of regulation that gives a firm an incentive to operate efficiently and keep costs under control. These new schemes take two main forms:

FIGURE 19.5

Natural Monopoly: Inflating Costs

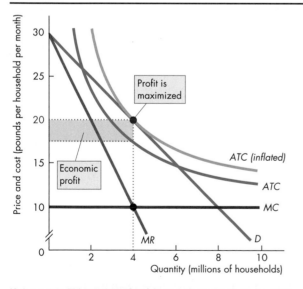

If the cable TV operator is able to inflate its costs to *ATC* (inflated) and persuade the regulator that these are genuine minimum costs of production, rate of return regulation results in a price of £20 a month – the profit-maximizing price. To the extent that the producer can inflate costs above average total cost, the price rises, output falls and deadweight loss increases. The profit is captured by the managers, not the shareholders (owners) of the firm.

price caps and earnings sharing plans. Under a price cap regulation, the regulators set the maximum price that may be charged and hold that price cap for a number of years. If profits are considered too high, the price cap will be lowered. Under earnings sharing regulation, if profits rise above a certain level, they must be shared with the firm's customers.

The newly privatized industries in the United Kingdom are all subject to a form of price cap regulation. You can read about price cap regulation in the gas industry in *Reading Between the Lines* on pp. 488–489, and we'll look at this in more detail later in this chapter.

Public Interest or Capture?

It is not clear whether actual regulation produces prices and quantities that more closely correspond with the predictions of capture theory or public interest theory. One thing is clear, however. Price regulation does not require natural monopolies to use the marginal cost pricing rule. If it did, most natural monopolies would make losses and receive hefty government subsidies to enable them to remain in business. But there are even exceptions to this conclusion. For example, British Telecommunications does not appear to use marginal cost pricing for telephone calls. It covers its total cost by charging a flat fee each month for being connected to its telephone system but then permitting each call to be made at its marginal cost.

A test of whether natural monopoly regulation is in the public interest or the interest of the producer is to examine the rates of return earned by regulated natural monopolies. If these rates of return are significantly higher than those in the rest of the economy, then, to some degree, the regulator may have been captured by the producer. If the rates of return in the regulated monopoly industries are similar to those in the rest of the economy, then we cannot tell, for sure, whether the regulator has been captured or not for we cannot know the extent to which costs have been inflated by the managers of the regulated firms.

It is difficult to assess regulatory capture in the United Kingdom because all the regulated natural monopolies were under public ownership in the 1970s and 1980s. Some of them have been privatized recently and there is insufficient evidence to make a meaningful comparison. Table 19.2 compares the rates of return on assets before and after privatization. Two of the monopolies are natural monopolies and were subject to regulation after privatization. Rates of return had improved in all the monopolies by 1990. The improvement was small in the case of the regulated natural monopoly, gas, and the improvement was cut back substantially by 1992 in the case of the non-regulated monopoly, steel. There is no evidence to suggest that rates of return are substantially higher for regulated natural monopolies and so the evidence on capture is inconclusive.

A final test of whether regulation of natural monopoly is in the public interest or the interest of producers is to study the changes in consumer surplus and producer surplus following deregulation. Microeconomists have examined this issue in the United States. In the case of rail deregulation, which occurred during the 1980s, both consumers and producers gained, and by large amounts. The gains from deregulation of telecommunications and cable television were smaller and accrued only to the consumer. These findings suggest that rail regulation hurt everyone, while regulation of telecommunications and cable television hurt only the consumer.

We've now examined the regulation of natural monopoly. Let's next turn to regulation in oligopolistic industries – to the regulation of cartels.

TABLE 19.2

Rates of Return in Monopolies

	Before privatization	After privatization	
	1979	1990	1992
		(percentage)	
Regulated natural monopolies			
British Gas	5	6	7
British Telecommunications	14	24	21
Other monopolies			
British Steel	3	18	1
British Airways	14	24	12

Source: D. Parker, 'Privatization and Business Restructuring: Change and Continuity in the Privatized Industries', *The Review of Policy Issues*, 1994, 1 (2).

Cartel Regulation

A *cartel* is a collusive agreement among a number of firms designed to restrict output and achieve a higher profit for the cartel's members. Cartels are illegal in the United Kingdom, the European Union and most other countries. But international cartels can sometimes operate legally, such as the international cartel of oil producers known as OPEC (the Organization of Petroleum Exporting Countries).

Illegal cartels can arise in oligopolistic industries. An oligopoly is a market structure in which a small number of firms compete with each other. We studied oligopoly (and duopoly – two firms competing for a market) in Chapter 13. There we saw that if firms manage to collude and behave like a monopoly, they can set the same price and sell the same total quantity as a monopoly firm would. But we also discovered that in such a situation, each firm will be tempted to 'cheat', increasing its own output and profit at the expense of the other firms. The result of such 'cheating' on the collusive agreement is the unravelling of the monopoly equilibrium and the emergence of a competitive outcome with zero economic profit for producers. Such an outcome benefits consumers at the expense of producers.

How is oligopoly regulated? Does regulation prevent monopoly practices or does it encourage those practices?

According to the public interest theory, oligopoly is regulated to ensure a competitive outcome. Consider, for example, the market for road haulage of carrots from East Anglia to Yorkshire, illustrated in Fig. 19.6. The demand curve for trips is *D*. The industry marginal cost curve – and the competitive supply curve – is *MC*. Public interest regulation will regulate the price of a trip at £20 and there will be 300 trips a week.

How would this industry be regulated according to the capture theory? Regulation that is in the producer interest will maximize profit. To find the outcome in this case, we need to determine the price and quantity when marginal cost equals marginal revenue. The marginal revenue curve is *MR*. So marginal cost equals marginal revenue at 200 trips a week. The price of a trip is £30.

One way of achieving this outcome is to place an output limit on each firm in the industry. If there are 10 haulage companies, an output limit of 20 trips per company ensures that the total number of trips in a week is 200. Penalties can be imposed to ensure

FIGURE 19.6

Collusive Oligopoly

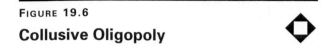

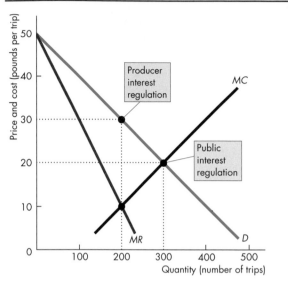

Ten road haulage firms transport carrots from East Anglia to Yorkshire. The demand curve is *D* and the industry marginal cost curve is *MC*. Under competition, the *MC* curve is the industry supply curve. If the industry is competitive, the price of a trip will be £20 and 300 trips will be made each week. Producers will demand regulation that restricts entry and limits output to 200 trips a week. This regulation raises the price to £30 a trip and results in each producer making maximum profit – as if it were a monopoly. Industry marginal revenue is equal to industry marginal cost.

that no single producer exceeds its output limit.

All the firms in the industry would support this type of regulation because it helps to prevent cheating and to maintain a monopoly outcome. Each firm knows that without effectively enforced production quotas every firm has an incentive to increase output. (For each firm, price exceeds marginal cost so a greater output brings a larger profit.) So each firm wants a method of preventing output from rising above the industry profit-maximizing level and the quotas enforced by regulation achieve this end. With this type of cartel regulation, the regulator enables a cartel to operate legally and in its own best interest.

What does cartel regulation do in practice? Although there is disagreement about the matter, the consensus view is that regulation tends to favour the producer. Regulating taxis (by local authorities) and airlines (by the Civil Aviation Authority) are specific examples in which profits of producers increased as a result of regulation.

Making Predictions

Most industries have a few producers and many consumers. In these cases, public choice theory predicts that regulation will protect producer interests because a small number of people stand to gain a large amount and so they will be fairly easy to organize as a cohesive lobby. Under such circumstances, politicians will be rewarded with political contributions rather than votes. But there are situations in which the consumer interest is sufficiently strong and well-organized and thus able to prevail. There are also cases in which the balance switches from producer to consumer, as seen in the deregulation process that began in the late 1970s.

Deregulation raises some hard questions for economists seeking to understand and make predictions about regulation. Why were the bus and financial sectors deregulated? If producers gained from regulation and if the producer lobby was strong enough to achieve regulation, what happened in the 1980s to change the equilibrium to one in which the consumer interest prevailed? We do not have a complete answer to this question at the present time. But regulation had become so costly to consumers, and the potential benefits to them from deregulation so great, that the cost of organizing the consumer voice became a price worth paying.

One factor that increased the cost of regulation borne by consumers and brought deregulation in the airline and bus sectors was the large increase in energy prices in the 1970s. These price hikes made route regulation extremely costly and changed the balance in favour of consumers in the political equilibrium. Technological change was the main factor at work not only in the finance sector but also in the airline sector. Computerized accounts, automatic tellers and telephone services all made smaller producers able to offer low-cost services, forcing deregulation. Let's look at the EU airline example.

The European Union has begun to deregulate scheduled air services within and among its member states. Until recently, most governments allowed only two airlines on any one route, and regulated fares and traffic in such a way that airlines could not compete. These restrictions have been lifted to encourage competition. Since 1997, airlines from one European country can launch domestic services in another. Ryanair and EasyJet are already operating dramatic cut-price services. How can they cut prices so much? These airlines can use direct telephone sales technology, pick the cheapest airports to run from, cut red tape and can adopt a 'no frills' service approach. Of course customers get what they pay for, as you can see in the cartoon.

If the political equilibrium has swung towards the consumer, it should lead to more consumer-oriented regulation in the future. Deregulation creates more competition, as we have seen, but it could erode consumer rights. We can expect the current emphasis on deregulation to switch regulation from serving the interests of producers to serving the interests of consumers. So deregulation does not mean less regulation overall.

© Nick Baker, *Financial Times,* 18 December 1995.

REVIEW

◆ Regulation of a natural monopoly in the public interest sets price equal to marginal cost or, to avoid a tax-financed subsidy, sets price equal to average total cost.

◆ In practice, natural monopolies face either rate of return regulation or incentive regulation schemes.

◆ With rate of return regulation, firms have an incentive to inflate costs and move as closely as possible to the profit-maximizing output. Incentive regulation – price caps and earnings sharing – encourage cost cutting.

◆ Cartel regulation that establishes output levels for each firm can help perpetuate a cartel and work against the public interest.

Let's now leave specific industry regulation and turn to the other main methods of intervention in markets – monopoly and competition policy and public ownership.

Monopoly and Competition Policy

Monopoly and competition policy is an alternative way in which government can influence the marketplace. This is a form of general regulation, where government can control the actions of any industry. As in the case of specific regulation, monopoly and competition policy can operate in the public interest, maximizing total surplus, or in the private interest, maximizing the surpluses of particular interest groups such as producers. Firms operating in the United Kingdom are subject to two levels of monopoly and competition policy – the national and the EU level policy. Let's look at how these work and how they differ.

There was no monopoly or merger control in the United Kingdom until after World War II. Monopoly and merger control laws aim to avoid the creation of monopoly structures but also regulate monopoly practices. Competition law is more general and covers all non-competitive practices by firms – for example, mergers and the creation of cartels in oligopoly market structures. So monopoly and merger control laws can be seen as one part of general competition policy.

The historical development of UK competition policy is shown in Table 19.3. The initial Monopolies and Restrictive Practices Act created an agency called the Monopolies and Restrictive Practices Commission (MRPC). Its role was to investigate the activities of reported monopolies and any restrictive practices to assess whether they acted against the public interest. The act defined a monopoly as a firm having a market share greater than 30 per cent – this was reduced to 25 per cent in the Fair Trading Act of 1973. The 1973 act also allowed the investigation of an industry where one firm has a 25 per cent share of a local market rather than a national market. As a result, monopoly investigations are focused on oligopoly industries and their abuse of monopoly power, rather than on pure monopolies and single firms. The traditional emphasis of UK policy is on the behaviour of oligopolies rather than the structure of industries.

The 1956 act removed the control of restrictive practices from the MRPC, creating the Monopolies Commission. This legislation was the direct result of the early work of the MRPC. Its reports found widespread evidence of restrictive practice agreements between firms, which tended to operate against the public interest. The Monopolies Commission became the Monopolies and Mergers Commission (MMC) as a result of the 1965 act. With its new powers, it could now investigate any merger likely to create a monopoly or lead to abuse of monopoly power which would be against the public interest. The Office of Fair Trading (OFT) was set up in the 1973 act, and its Director General (DGFT) now recommends monopolies and mergers to the government for investigation. Since the 1980 Competition Act, the DGFT has been able to recommend investigation of a single firm rather than the whole industry, including public corporations.

Until 1973, there was no statement of what was meant by the criterion of the 'public interest'. This makes the operation of the law vague and open to interpretation. As MMC recommendations are accepted or rejected by the secretary of state for trade and industry, the interpretation of public interest is a political matter. Public interest could mean the interest of consumers, the interest of producers, or even the interest of bureaucrats. Some attempt was made to clarify the meaning of 'public interest' in the 1973 Fair Trading Act, which stated it was any practice that maintains and promotes effective competition – or total surplus. The act suggested consumer surplus should be given a higher weighting than producer surplus. It also shifted the emphasis of UK policy from monopoly control to promoting competition.

So let's take a look at some more recent examples of monopoly and merger investigations.

TABLE 19.3

The Main UK Monopoly and Competition Laws

Name of law	Year	Changes introduced
Monopolies and Restrictive (Inquiry and Control) Act	1948	Set up Monopolies and Restrictive Practices Commission (MRPC). Defined monopoly as 30 per cent of national market
Restrictive Trade Practices Act	1956	Removed restrictive practices from MRPC. Set up Monopolies Commission (MC)
Monopolies and Mergers Act	1965	Set up Monopolies and Mergers Commission (MMC). Added merger investigation to MMC
Fair Trading Act	1973	Redefined national and local monopoly. Set up Office of Fair Trading (OFT) and duties of Director General (DGFT). Competition defined as the 'public interest'
Competition Act	1980	Allows referral of individual firms and small-scale MMC reports. Public corporations included

UK Monopoly Investigations

Despite the emphasis on promoting competition rather than controlling monopoly, the MMC started to promote structural remedies to monopoly in the late 1980s and early 1990s. This was a result of the move towards deregulation. If an oligopoly industry could be broken up into smaller parts to operate without regulation, this was better than regulating the oligopoly. You have already heard about the investigation into UK brewers in 1989 and the recommendation that they should sell off a large proportion of their pubs. The government accepted a weaker version of the proposals. In 1993, the MMC investigated the monopoly supply of gas. British Gas controlled gas supply, pipelines and storage units. The MMC found that British Gas could use its control of the pipelines and storage to reduce competition from new entrants into gas supply. Its recommendation that British Gas should sell its gas supply business was not accepted.

The problem with deregulation is that it can result in an increase in concentration and monopoly power. This was the problem investigated by the MMC in 1995 when it looked at the supply of bus services in the north of England. The enquiry was started after allegations of predatory pricing by Busways Travel Services Ltd, a subsidiary of Stagecoach Holdings plc. Predatory pricing involves starting a bus war by undercutting prices. The MMC found evidence of monopoly power as four bus companies, including Busways, supplied more than 90 per cent of local bus services, two with more than 25 per cent each. After a failed bid to buy the local authority bus company, Busways recruited the majority of the local authority's drivers, and started operating free bus services on local authority routes. The successful bidder pulled out and the local authority bus company went into liquidation, removing a potential competitor. The MMC decided that predatory pricing had reduced competition against the public interest, and recommended new regulation to improve market entry and reduce predatory pricing.

UK Merger Investigations

All mergers must be notified to the OFT. These cases are then considered by the DGFT for evidence of potential monopoly creation. A potential monopoly may exist if the merged firms control 25 per cent or more of their market, or their combined assets are worth more than a specific amount. The asset value criterion was raised in 1994 from £30 million to £70 million. The merger investigations of the OFT are shown in Table 19.4. In 1994, the OFT considered 381 merger cases and investigated 231 of these – a total asset value of £160,000 million. The DGFT eventually referred 8 cases to the MMC for a full investigation. Despite the fact that the threshold for investigation had been raised, there was a 23 per cent increase in the number of cases considered by the OFT.

Mergers investigated by the MMC are of three types:

1. Horizontal
2. Vertical
3. Conglomerate

Horizontal mergers are mergers between firms operating in the same industry, producing the same types of products. They can reduce the number of competitors in the industry and create monopoly power in the new combined firm. *Vertical mergers* are mergers between suppliers and customers. A vertical merger results in forward integration when a manufacturer merges with a retailer, and backward integration when a manufacturer merges with a raw materials supplier. These mergers limit access by other manufacturers to suppliers and retailers, creating monopoly power. *Conglomerate mergers* are mergers between firms that operate in different markets with unrelated products. Conglomerate mergers are likely to reduce competition only if there is some similarity between the products produced.

In deciding whether a merger is against the public interest, the MMC must balance the benefits of merger against any total surplus loss from a reduction in competition. Merger can lead to an

TABLE 19.4

Merger Investigations by the OFT

	Considered	Investigated	Referred to MMC
1993	309	197	3
1994	381	231	8

improvement in efficiency if it results in a reduction in costs through economies of scale. A merger will be in the public interest if the value of the reduction in costs is greater than the value of the loss of consumer surplus. Conglomerate and vertical mergers have less effect on competition than horizontal mergers, and are more likely to be in the public interest. This explains why most of the mergers recommended to the MMC are of the horizontal type. It also explains why most are accepted with minor recommendations about the activities of the combined firm after the merger.

A recent example of vertical mergers illustrates the investigation process. In 1995, two mergers were announced between electricity generators and electricity suppliers – PowerGen and Midland Electricity, and National Power and Southern Electricity. PowerGen had 24 per cent of the electricity generating market and National Power had 33 per cent. Midland Electricity and Southern Electricity were both electricity supply companies with a local monopoly. So these mergers are examples of vertical integration, which would reduce the number of suppliers. While the MMC found that the mergers would operate against the public interest, the impact was not considered strong enough to stop them going ahead. Let's see why.

Since privatization, new independent producers have entered the market and reduced the share of the two big generators from 73 per cent to 57 per cent. The MMC noted that both supply companies were minority shareholders in some of these new independent producers. The mergers would make the two big producers privy to new information on the operation of the independent production market, increasing their influence. This would reduce competition in the electricity market, raising prices to consumers, and would be against the public interest. The MMC recognized that there would be benefits from cost reductions, and suggested that the merger would not be against the public interest if the two regional electricity companies were to sell their shareholdings in the independent producers within 18 months of the mergers going ahead.

We have looked at UK monopoly and merger control and shown that it works by comparing the costs and benefits of increased market share on a case-by-case basis. The meaning of public interest operated by the MMC has changed but its impact is politically determined. Some economists believe that this process is too vague and costly and that

we should change to a rules-based system similar to that operated in the United States. Clear rules defining monopoly and acceptable mergers operated by a court would remove a great deal of uncertainty for firms and cut the cost of operating the policy. Other economists argue that a flexible system is needed to ensure that beneficial mergers can go ahead, and that competitive oligopolies are not destroyed. The European Union operates a compromise system – more flexible than the UK system but not subject to political control. Let's see if it is a better system.

EU Monopolies and Mergers Investigations

National competition policy controls the actions of firms within national borders, and EU policy controls the impact of monopolies and mergers on trade among member states. EU policy is also designed to promote free competition, but it defines monopoly power in a different way. Under European law, abuse of power by a firm in a dominant position is illegal if it affects trade among member states by creating unfair trading conditions. The important aspect triggering investigation is the abuse of power, not the existence of a dominant firm as it is in the United Kingdom. Abuse includes imposing unfair price and purchase conditions, limiting production, applying different conditions in different countries and imposing restrictive contracts. The European Commission is the investigating agency. Unlike its UK counterpart, it can act on its recommendations and has wide-ranging powers to enforce its decisions with fines for offending firms. For example, the Commission fined British Sugar 3 million ecu in 1988. It found that the company's vertically integrated structure – producing and packaging refined sugar – allowed it to abuse its dominant position by slashing the price of packaged sugar to drive out competitors.

EU merger control was not an explicit policy until 1990. The EU Merger Control Regulation of 1990 allowed the Commission to investigate mergers which have a 'European Dimension'. This is defined as a total worldwide turnover value of 5 billion ecu or more, and where two firms have a turnover value within the European Union of at least 250 million ecu. The Commission accepts a merger providing any strengthening of the dominant position does not lead to an effective reduction in competition. By 1993, only one merger had been blocked, and 95 per cent were accepted without any conditions.

So is EU competition policy more efficient than the UK approach? It depends on whether you think the administrative decision of the Commission is more accountable than the political decision of the UK secretary of state. The commissioners are bureaucrats but also have their national allegiance. It also depends on whether you think an investigation triggered by abuse of power leads to better decision making than an investigation triggered by changes in industrial structure. The debate can only be settled by empirical evidence. In the meantime, the United Kingdom is considering making its monopoly control policy more like the EU policy, and has introduced a system of negotiation between the OFT and firms to cut the costs of MMC investigation. We'll find similar problems in the last element of monopoly regulation – restrictive practices.

UK Restrictive Practices Investigations

In monopoly and merger investigations, the MMC must prove that firms are acting against the public interest. The opposite is true for restrictive practices. A *restrictive practice* is defined in the 1973 Fair Trading Act and covers agreements between firms on prices, terms and conditions of sale, and market share. All restrictive practices in the United Kingdom are deemed illegal unless the parties can prove to the Restrictive Practices Court that they are in the public interest. There are eight clearly defined arguments for proving this. These arguments are called gateways and include proving beneficial effects on trade, on unemployment and on consumer interests. The firms must prove that the agreement passes at least one gateway and that, on balance, the benefits of the agreement outweigh the costs.

In 1994, 581 new agreements were registered with the OFT, bringing the total number of registered agreements to 12,000. The OFT started 80 new investigations and issued 36 notices against agreements arising from nine of its investigations in 1994. Most investigations are resolved through voluntary negotiation with firms and less than 100 cases end up in the Restrictive Practices Court. This does not necessarily indicate success. The process of investigation is slow and the fines imposed are small in relation to the turnover of the

firms. Also, it is virtually impossible to uncover secret agreements. Nevertheless, an increasing number of firms are abandoning agreements because of the costs involved in proving their cases.

Retail price maintenance – where manufacturers dictate the minimum selling price to retailers – only became a restrictive practice in 1964. Firms then had to prove that retail price maintenance was in the public interest by passing one of five new gateways. These gateways included beneficial effects on health, prices, quality, competition in retailing and services associated with the sale of the goods. By 1990, the only two remaining agreements were in books and pharmaceutical products. Publishers argued that price maintenance was needed to stop small booksellers going out of business, and the pharmaceuticals industry argued that price maintenance was needed to keep small chemists in business and preserve the specialist pharmacy advice service that they offer. These have both been challenged by large-scale retailers in recent years.

In 1988, the Department of Trade and Industry agreed to review the restrictive practices system. Some economists have suggested that the EU system would be better. Let's look at how it works.

EU Restrictive Practices Investigations

The EU law and UK law are similar in their purpose. EU law prohibits any agreement that affects trade among member states and any agreement designed to reduce competition. Firms can register their agreements but they do not have to. Agreements are exempted if they improve production and distribution or technical progress and do not reduce competition. Exemptions can be granted by the Commission as a block, for example to an industry, or for individual firms. The main difference is that EU law is concerned with the *effect* of the agreement and not its *form*, which is the basis for requiring agreements to be registered in the United Kingdom. This reduces the cost of investigation and increases the chances of anti-competitive agreements being identified. Also, the Commission has much greater powers of enforcement than the UK Restrictive Practices Court – imposing fines of up to 10 per cent of a firm's turnover.

EU law has been effective in identifying and removing agreements on price fixing, market sharing and the use of exclusive dealerships. It has also identified secret agreements and potential collusive cartel agreements and initiated investigations. In 1996, the Commission began an investigation into an alleged secret cartel in the £600 million district heating market – a form of communal heating. You can read about the alleged secret cartel activities in *Reading Between the Lines* in Chapter 12, pp. 304–305. Following this success, the Department of Trade and Industry recommended adopting the EU approach, so that the OFT could investigate potential cartels and award block exemptions to cut administration costs.

Public or Special Interest?

Our discussion shows that monopoly control law has evolved to protect and pursue the public interest and to restrain the profit-seeking and anti-competitive actions of producers. Although the interests of the producer can influence the way in which the law is interpreted and applied, the overall thrust of it appears to have been directed towards achieving allocative efficiency and serving the public interest.

There is a key difference between EU law and UK law in the way it is administered. UK monopoly control and regulation are administered by a bureaucracy and the final decisions are political. EU law is administered by a bureaucracy but interpreted and enforced by the legal process – the courts. Economists are now beginning to extend theories of public choice to include an economic analysis of the law and the way the courts interpret the law. It is interesting to speculate whether the courts are more sensitive to the public interest than politicians in interpreting monopoly control law and regulation.

We have now looked at all the aspects of EU and UK monopoly control law. There is one other form of control that has been widely used in the past – public ownership or nationalization. Let's look at this now.

Public Ownership and Privatization

After World War II, most European countries took a wide range of industries and firms into public ownership. However, many European governments are now in the process of privatizing firms and industries in public ownership. **Privatization**, in this context, means the sale of assets in public ownership to the private sector. To explain this shift, we'll compare the benefits and costs of regulation through public ownership with the benefits and costs of regulating privatized industries. The UK is an interesting example because it is extreme. The progress of the UK privatization programme of nationalized industries since 1979 is shown in Table 19.5. Before this, we need to understand what public ownership means.

Public Ownership

The main form of **public ownership** is nationalization – the compulsory purchase of major industries by government to satisfy a political belief that public ownership is better. The gas, electricity generation, transport, iron, steel and coal industries came into public ownership through nationalization. Governments also bought some firms through direct dealings on the stock market because of their importance to the economy. Examples include British Petroleum, Britoil and British Airways. Other 'lame duck' firms – those struggling to retain their markets under intense international competition – were bought for their national image and employment potential. Examples of these are Rolls-Royce and British Leyland (now Rover).

UK governments followed a continuous programme of nationalization and purchase after World War II. Some industries were denationalized for short periods, but soon returned to public ownership. The range of firms in public ownership in 1979 included the main utilities, transport, key industries and many firms from relatively competitive industries. Among these were Jaguar Cars, Sealink Ferries, Cable and Wireless, Britoil and Unipart. So why were so many firms brought into public ownership?

Reasons for Public Ownership

There are three main reasons why firms and whole industries have been brought into public ownership. They are:

1. Social
2. Political
3. Economic

Social reasons arise from the use of public ownership to generate an equitable distribution of goods

TABLE 19.5

UK Privatizations of Nationalized Industries 1979–1996

NATIONALIZED INDUSTRIES

Full privatization	Partial privatization
British Aerospace	Electricity:
British Airports Authority	England and Wales Area Boards
British Airways	PowerGen and National Power
British Coal	South of Scotland Electricity Board
British Gas	North of Scotland Hydro-Electric Board
British National Oil Corporation	National Grid Company
British Rail	Nuclear Electric and Scottish Nuclear (due 1996)
British Shipbuilders (Warships)	Water and Sewerage:
British Steel	England and Wales water boards
British Telecommunications	
National Bus Company	
National Freight Consortium	

Source: S. Bailey (1995), *Public Sector Economics: Theory, Policy and Practice*, London, Macmillan, adapted from Table 13.1.

and services. For example, suppose there is no gas or electricity on a remote Scottish island. The one family living on the island decides it is time to enjoy the benefits of modern utility services. It asks for a quote. The private gas and telecommunications firms quote on the basis of the marginal cost of laying pipe connections out to the Scottish islands. This price is much higher than any one family could afford – leaving them without basic utility services. A public industry can cross-subsidize the provision of these services by spreading the cost among other customers. It can also ensure uniform quality of service by charging a flat-rate price. But equity could be achieved equally by a government subsidy – to the firm or the customer. Public ownership will be preferred if the transactions costs of achieving equity are lower under public ownership than under regulation or subsidies to private firms and individuals. Governments try to achieve this by making equity a major objective of the firm under public ownership.

Political reasons stem from the belief that public ownership is better than private ownership in major industries. The post-war UK Labour government believed that private ownership of capital led to the exploitation of labour. Public ownership of the means of production, distribution and exchange could control the exploitation of labour in major industries – wages and conditions could be fairly negotiated. This political belief no longer has prominence in the United Kingdom, but it was the major reason for post-war nationalization.

Economic reasons include generating economic benefits for the whole economy and generating benefits for the firm or industry concerned. Benefits for the whole economy arise from controlling unemployment and wage demands through public ownership, and through saving flagging industries and their potential export markets. If private capital markets fail to provide the capital needed for investment in flagging industries, whole industries can be lost, with disastrous impacts on local economies. This was part of the reason for public ownership of shipbuilding and steel, together with car manufacturing. Public ownership means that the return on the government's investment does not leak back to shareholders, but goes back to the government. Wage control can be effective through public ownership only if a large proportion of employees are employed by the government. This is no longer the case in the United Kingdom.

Economic benefits at the firm or industry level include the control of monopoly power, the promotion of economies of scale, the provision of public goods and the control of externalities. We looked at the control of monopoly and oligopoly earlier in this chapter. Most UK nationalized industries were subject to rate of return control and were expected to use a form of long-run marginal cost pricing. Economies of scale could be promoted through investment and the creation of natural monopolies. Public goods, such as defence, would not be provided by the private sector and the fear of extreme externalities, such as nuclear power disasters, could be reduced if safety standards could be raised at lower cost under public ownership. But if most of these benefits could be realized at a lower cost by regulating private firms, the argument for privatization is stronger.

Between 1979 and 1996, 12 nationalized industries were fully privatized and 2 were partially privatized. By 1996, the Post Office was the only remaining industry in public ownership and its future in the public sector was uncertain. In addition to the nationalized industries, 17 competitive firms were also privatized during this period. So why has the UK government followed such an intensive privatization programme? Let's look at the reasons for privatization.

Reasons for Privatization

The reasons for privatization are similar to those for public ownership. How can this be? Economists who support privatization would argue that the economic and social benefits of public ownership can be achieved in the private sector with appropriate regulation – but at lower cost to the taxpayer. Only the political reasons differ. Political reasons include reducing government expenditure, deregulating industry and widening share ownership.

Why might privatization achieve the same benefits as public ownership but at a lower cost? Firms like Unipart, Britoil and Cable and Wireless, which were in public ownership in 1979, could easily have operated as private firms without additional regulation. After privatization, these firms were released from government regulation and exposed to the competitive forces of the market. This reduced the total level and cost of government regulation. Other privatized firms were examples of natural monopolies or large-scale oligopolies which had to be

regulated after privatization. Privatizing these firms did not reduce the total cost of regulation, but exposed their management to shareholder pressure for dividends. This should lead to reductions in costs and more efficient production. Why?

Privatized firms will be more efficient if they have less inflated costs, as shown in Fig. 19.5. When the MMC investigated the nationalized industries in the 1980s, it found evidence of poor management and high costs. There are three reasons to expect lower costs – less X-inefficiency – in the private sector. They are:

1. Exposure to competition and merger
2. Exposure to shareholder preferences
3. More efficient regulation of monopoly power

When firms like Jaguar and Rover were privatized, they entered a competitive international market. Managers had to look for ways to deflate costs to raise shareholders returns in the private sector. Competitive pressure will be much lower when privatization creates a near monopoly as in the case of British Gas and British Telecommunications. Merger threats are also limited because of the sheer size and value of these firms. Competition can only be achieved by separating out the service part of the business from the ownership of physical networks. For example, the sale of gas and electricity, telecommunications and travel services are retail activities and can be highly competitive. It is only the network of pipes, lines and road or track that is a natural monopoly. Careful regulation to remove entry barriers in retail and control the price of access to the network encourages new entrants and competition, forcing managers to reduce average costs.

Our model of regulatory capture suggested that private monopolies will have inflated costs under rate of return regulation. The new regulatory bodies, such as OFTEL and OFFER, have adopted price cap regulation using the RPI minus X formula to improve efficiency. RPI is the retail price index and the X-factor is a percentage reduction to improve X-efficiency. The formula sets the price cap in real terms and forces real prices in the industry to fall over time, forcing managers to improve efficiency to maintain profits. It is applied only to a basket of the industry's prices. So if retail prices are rising at 6 per cent and the X-factor set by OFFER is 2 per cent, the maximum increase in overall electricity service prices is 4 per cent. The formula cuts the cost of regulation in other ways. It avoids the problem of estimating average costs, gaining access to detailed accounting information, setting individual prices or tariffs, or directly controlling profits.

You can see the impact of privatization on a sample of nine nationalized firms in Fig. 19.7. Labour productivity has been increasing steadily in the economy as a whole, but it was falling in the nationalized firms during the 1970s. Labour productivity in the sample of privatized firms increased more rapidly than in the economy as a whole in the 1980s. This was because of increased capital investment and substantial shedding of labour. Performance-related pay was also introduced into privatized firms in the 1980s with dramatic effects on top executive pay. Between 1979 and 1988 the pay of top executives in the private sector increased by 85 per cent on average. By comparison, the pay of top executives still under public ownership increased by 111 per cent, but the pay of top executives in privatized firms increased by 247 per cent[1]. Some of the increase in pay to top executives in nationalized industries during the period may have been part of an incentive to prepare for privatization.

The benefits of privatization have been questioned by some economists. If increased efficiency arises from improved competition rather than shareholder preferences, there will be little improvement in privatized monopolies[2]. Government wealth, and therefore social welfare, may be lower after privatization if firms are sold at a discount price. Cost cutting will lead to a fall in quality and service provision, reducing consumer surplus. If privatization merely shifts surplus from consumers and employees to shareholders and managers, it will not have achieved its objectives. So has privatization gained the benefits of public ownership at a lower cost? The jury is still out – empirical studies of performance in the privatized industries are inconclusive[3].

◆ ◆ ◆ ◆ In this chapter, we've seen how the government intervenes in markets to affect prices, quantities, the gains from trade and the division of

[1] J. Haskel and S. Szymanski, 'Privatization and the Labour Market: Facts, Theory and Evidence'. In *Privatization and Economic Performance*, M. Bishop, J. Kay, and C. Mayer (eds.), Oxford, Oxford University Press, 1995.

[2] J. Vickers and G. Yarrow, *Privatization: An Economic Analysis*, London, MIT Press, 1988.

[3] M. Bishop, J. Kay and C. Mayer (eds.), *Privatization and Economic Performance*, Oxford, Oxford University Press, 1995.

FIGURE 19.7

Productivity in the Privatized Industries

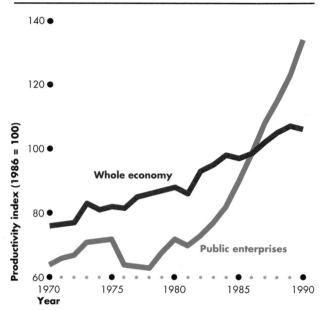

Labour productivity in the economy as a whole increased steadily between 1970 and 1988. By comparison, changes in labour productivity in the sample of 9 privatized firms declined in the 1970s and then increased much more rapidly in the 1980s. It appears that privatization after 1979 improved labour productivity, probably as a result of substantial cuts in the size of the work-force in privatized firms together with increased investment in technology.

Source: M. Bishop and D. Thompson (1994), 'Privatization in the UK: Internal Organization and Productive Efficiency.' In *Privatization and Economic Performance*, M. Bishop, J. Kay and C. Mayer (eds.), Oxford, OUP 1994 reproduced by permission of Oxford University Press.

these gains between consumers and producers when there is monopoly or oligopoly. We've seen that there is a conflict between the pursuit of the public interest – achieving allocative efficiency – and the pursuit of the special interests of producers – maximizing producer surplus or economic profit. The political and legal arenas are the places in which these conflicts are resolved. We've reviewed the two theories – public interest and capture – concerning the type and scope of government intervention. We've explained the shift from public ownership to privatization by comparing the benefits and costs of regulation through public ownership and regulation after privatization.

Regulation and Competition in Gas Supply

The Essence of the Story

THE TIMES, 6 DECEMBER 1995

Falling price sends UK to bottom of gas price league

Philip Bassett

Gas prices in Britain are now the cheapest of the leading economies, a new international study showed yesterday, though it gave warning that the gas market is in 'chaos'. ...The study also suggested there will be more casualties among independent gas companies as suppliers battle for market share.

In its latest annual survey of gas prices in leading countries, National Utility Services... said 'dramatically falling' gas prices in Britain had pushed the United Kingdom to the very bottom of the gas price league table, with the cheapest gas prices of all the countries studied....

Looking at industrial users, the survey said gas prices in Britain fell 41 per cent in the year to September to 57p per kilowatt hour, the lowest of the 13 countries studied. ...Italy again headed the gas price league table, at £2.08 pkwh, followed by Sweden, France and Germany....

In the UK, the ... 'unprecedented upheaval' in the gas industry resulting from the introduction of competition had forced prices down, as well as other factors including new gas fields coming on stream, delays in commissioning new gas-fired power stations and mild weather....

The study said that ... further restructuring in British Gas could not be ruled out, since the opening of the gas market was now questioning BG's profitability and leading Ofgas, the industry's regulator, to struggle with 'how to keep British Gas in business'.

This marked a 'complete reversal of roles' for Ofgas, after it had endeavoured to curtail BG and promote competition in the gas market. In placing Ofgas in such an 'awkward position', the survey said that Ofgas 'now must respond to British Gas's needs, acting on behalf of Goliath rather than David'.

■ Gas prices in the UK are now the cheapest in 13 leading economies. Italy tops the league at over 200 pence per kilowatt hour (pkwh) and the United Kingdom hits the bottom at 57 pence pkwh.

■ Competition in the new supply market has been fierce following the privatization of British Gas, and industrial gas prices fell 41 per cent in 1995.

■ Some other factors have also reduced prices, including mild weather and new gas fields coming on stream.

■ But falling prices have brought the profitability of British Gas into question and OFGAS, the industry regulator, has switched its concern from promoting competition to keeping British Gas in business.

Economic Analysis

■ When British Gas (BG) was privatized it was still acting as a monopoly supplier.

■ OFGAS, the industry regulator, uses a price cap incentive scheme (RPI − X) to limit BG's ability to set a monopoly price or inflate costs, as well as licensing new gas suppliers.

■ In Fig. 1, after privatization, BG faces the demand curve for industrial sales, D_0, marginal cost is MC and marginal revenue is MR. OFGAS holds price to P_r pence pkwh, below the profit maximizing price, P_M, restricting economic profits to the blue shaded area.

■ Figure 2 shows the industrial market for gas in 1995. At the beginning of the year, demand is D_0, the supply is S_0, price is 100 pence pkwh and quantity traded is Q_1.

■ More new entrants shift the supply curve rightward to S_1, and the price falls to 60 pence pkwh. A mild winter shifts the demand curve leftward to D_1, and price falls to 57 pence pkwh at quantity level Q_3.

■ The overall effect on BG is shown in Fig. 3. BG's demand curve, D_1, becomes more elastic and price moves towards the unregulated price and profit maximizing levels.

■ BG has already shed 25,000 jobs and more restructuring will be needed to avoid further losses at these low prices, as BG's costs are still higher than those of its competitors.

■ OFGAS may have to act in BG's interests during this transition to avoid further losses, relaxing price caps rather than promoting further competition.

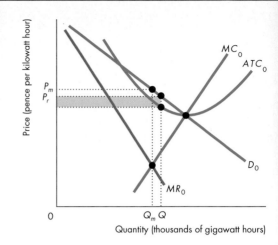

Figure 1

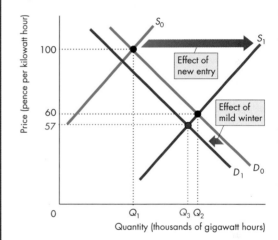

Figure 2

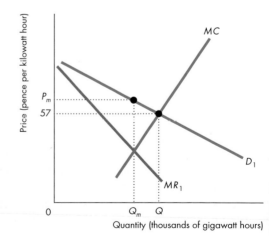

Figure 3

SUMMARY

Market Intervention

The government intervenes to regulate monopolistic and oligopolistic markets in two ways: regulation and monopoly control law. Both of these methods are widely used in the United Kingdom and European Union.

Government action can influence consumer surplus, producer surplus and total surplus. Consumer surplus is the difference between what consumers are willing to pay for a given consumption level and what they actually pay. Producer surplus is the difference between a producer's revenue from its sales and the opportunity cost of production. Total surplus is the sum of consumer surplus and producer surplus. Total surplus is maximized under competition. Under monopoly, producer surplus is increased and consumer surplus decreased, and a deadweight loss is created. (pp. 467–469)

Economic Theory of Regulation

Consumers and producers express their demand for the regulation that influences their surpluses by voting, lobbying and making campaign contributions. The larger the surplus that can be generated by a particular regulation and the smaller the number of people adversely affected, the larger is the demand for the regulation. A smaller number of people is easier to organize into an effective political lobby. Regulation is supplied by politicians who pursue their own best interest. The larger the surplus per person generated and the larger the number of persons affected by it, the larger is the supply of regulation. In equilibrium, the regulation that exists is such that no interest group feels it is worthwhile to employ additional scarce resources to press for further changes. But the political equilibrium depends on whose interests are served by regulation. The public interest theory predicts that total surplus will be maximized; the capture theory predicts that producer surplus will be maximized. (pp.469–471)

Regulation and Deregulation

Firms are regulated at all levels, from the decisions of the European Union, to national government regulation, local authority regulation and voluntary regulation through industrial and professional organizations. Regulation is conducted by regulatory agencies controlled by politically appointed bureaucrats and staffed by a permanent bureaucracy of experts. Regulated firms are required to comply with rules about price, product quality and output levels. Two types of industries are regulated: natural monopolies and cartels. In both cases, regulation has enabled firms in the regulated industries to achieve profit levels equal to or greater than those attained, on the average, in the rest of the economy.

Although the number of regulatory agencies continues to grow with the creation of special agencies to control privatized monopolies, there has been a tendency to deregulate many areas of the economy. Deregulation has focused on those industries where regulation has reduced the degree of competition. Public interest theory tells us that deregulation has occurred because the balance of power has shifted to consumers who demand lower prices, but they are also likely to demand more regulation serving their interests. (pp.471–479)

Monopoly and Competition Policy

Monopoly control law provides an alternative way in which the government can control monopoly and monopolistic practices. The law defines monopoly in terms of market power and is also used to control oligopolies and mergers. While the focus of UK legislation is on establishing the *form* of monopoly and restrictive practice, the focus of EU law is on impact of monopoly power and the *effect* of restrictive practices. The overall thrust of monopoly control law is directed towards serving the public interest, but it may favour producers because it is administered by bureaucrats and politicians. (pp.479–484)

Public Ownership and Privatization

European countries have a long history of public ownership of firms, but many of these firms have now been privatized – sold to private investors. There are three reasons for public ownership –

social, political and economic. The social objectives are to create equity, the political objectives are to avoid exploitation, and the economic objectives are to generate economy-wide benefits and benefits within each industry or firm. The same social and economic reasons hold for privatization, but the political objectives differ. Privatization will achieve the same economic and social outcomes if the costs of regulation are lower in the private sector than in the public sector. Regulatory costs fall where privatization of monopolies exposes firms to competition for service provision, shareholder preferences for profits and an alternative regulatory framework adopting a price cap formula. (pp.484–487).

KEY ELEMENTS

Key Terms

Average cost pricing rule, 474
Capture theory, 470
Deregulation, 467
Incentive regulation scheme, 476
Marginal cost pricing rule, 474
Mergers, 468
Monopoly control law, 467
Privatization, 484
Public interest theory, 470
Public ownership, 484
Rate of return regulation, 475
Regulation, 467
Restrictive practices, 468
Total surplus, 468

◆ Key Figures and Tables

Figure 19.2	Natural Monopoly: Marginal Cost Pricing, 473
Figure 19.3	Natural Monopoly: Average Cost Pricing, 474
Figure 19.4	Natural Monopoly: Profit Maximization, 475
Figure 19.6	Collusive Oligopoly, 478
Table 19.1	The Regulation Hierarchy, 472
Table 19.3	The Main UK Monopoly and Competition Laws, 480

REVIEW QUESTIONS

1 What are the two main ways in which the government can intervene in the marketplace?

2 What is consumer surplus? How is it calculated and how is it represented in a diagram?

3 What is producer surplus? How is it calculated and how is it represented in a diagram?

4 What is total surplus? How is it calculated and how is it represented in a diagram?

5 Why do consumers demand regulation? In what kinds of industries would their demands for regulation be greatest?

6 Why do producers demand regulation? In what kinds of industries would their demands for regulation be greatest?

7 Explain the public interest and capture theories of the supply of regulation. What does each theory imply about the behaviour of politicians?

8 How is oligopoly regulated in the United Kingdom? In whose interest is it regulated?

9 What are the main monopoly control laws in force in the United Kingdom today?

PROBLEMS

1 Cascade Springs plc is an unregulated natural monopoly that bottles water from a natural spring high in the Scottish highlands. The total fixed cost incurred by Cascade Springs is £160,000 and its marginal cost is 10 pence a bottle. The demand for bottled water from Cascade Springs is as follows:

Price (pence per bottle)	Quantity demanded (thousands of bottles per year)
100	0
90	200
80	400
70	600
60	800
50	1,000
40	1,200
30	1,400
20	1,600
10	1,800
0	2,000

a What is the price of a bottle of water?
b How many bottles does Cascade Springs sell?
c Does Cascade Springs maximize total surplus or producer surplus?

2 The government regulates Cascade Springs in Problem 1 by imposing a marginal cost pricing rule.

a What is the price of a bottle of water?
b How many bottles does Cascade Springs sell?
c What is Cascade Springs' producer surplus?
d What is consumer surplus?
e Is the regulation in the public interest or in the private interest?

3 The government regulates Cascade Springs in Problem 1 by imposing an average cost pricing rule.

a What is the price of a bottle of water?
b How many bottles does Cascade Springs sell?
c What is Cascade Springs' producer surplus?
d What is consumer surplus?

e Is the regulation in the public interest or in the private interest?

4 The value of the capital invested in Cascade Springs in Problem 1 is £2 million. The government introduces a rate of return regulation requiring the firm to sell its water for a price that gives it a rate of return of 5 per cent on its capital.

a What is the price of a bottle of water?
b How many bottles does Cascade Springs sell?
c What is Cascade Springs' producer surplus?
d What is consumer surplus?
e Is the regulation in the public interest or in the private interest?

5 Faced with the rate of return regulation of Problem 4, Cascade Springs pads its costs by paying a special bonus to its owner that it counts as a cost.

a Counting the bonus as part of the producer surplus, what is the size of the bonus that maximizes producer surplus and that makes the measured rate of return equal to 5 per cent as required by the regulation?
b How many bottles does Cascade Springs sell?
c What is Cascade Springs' producer surplus?
d What is consumer surplus?
e Is the regulation in the public interest or in the private interest?

6 Read the story about the UK gas industry in *Reading Between the Lines* on pp. 488–489 and then answer the following questions:

a What was the initial impact on prices and profits of the price cap regulation imposed on British Gas privatization?
b What factors other than regulation have helped to make gas prices in the United Kingdom lower than in any other leading economy?
c Why might the industry regulator, OFGAS have to promote the industry interests over public interest while prices are so low?

CHAPTER

20

EXTERNALITIES, THE ENVIRONMENT AND KNOWLEDGE

After studying this chapter you will be able to:

- ◆ Describe the nature of externalities
- ◆ Explain how property rights can sometimes be used to overcome externalities
- ◆ Identify how emission charges, standards, marketable permits and taxes can be used to achieve efficiency in the face of external costs
- ◆ Explain the costs and benefits of a carbon-fuel tax, and explain why we do not have such a tax
- ◆ Explain how grants, subsidies and public provision can make the quantity of education, training and invention more efficient
- ◆ Explain how patents increase the efficiency of the process of developing new products and processes

W E HEAR A LOT ABOUT OUR ENDANGERED PLANET. WE BURN HUGE quantities of fossil fuels – coal, natural gas and oil – that cause acid rain and possibly global warming. The persistent and large-scale use of chlorofluorocarbons (CFCs) may have caused irreparable damage to the earth's ozone layer. We clear acres of rain forest every day. In doing so we destroy rare trees and plants, the habitats of thousands of species of animals, and also the most important storage place for the carbon dioxide that our cars and power stations pump out. We dump toxic waste into rivers, lakes and oceans. Everyone is put at risk by the continued damage to our environment and yet no one individual can take the necessary action to protect it. What, if anything, can government do to protect our environment? How can government action help us to take account of the damage that we cause others every time we turn on our heating or drive our cars? ◆ Almost every day, we hear about a new discovery. The advance of knowledge seems boundless. And

Greener and Smarter

more and more people are learning more and more of what is already known. The stock of knowledge – what is known and how many people know it – is increasing apparently without bound each year. But is our stock of knowledge advancing fast enough? Are we spending enough on research and development? And do we spend enough on education? Do enough people remain in school for long enough? Would we be better off if we spent more on research and education?

◆ ◆ ◆ ◆ In this chapter we study market failure problems that arise because many of our actions affect other people, for good or ill, in ways that we do not take into account when we make our own market choices. We study two important areas – the environment and the accumulation of knowledge. But first we need to look at the underlying market failure problem of externalities.

Externalities

An **externality** is a cost or benefit of a production or consumption activity that spills over to affect people other than those who decide the scale of the activity. An *external cost* is the cost of producing a good or service that is not borne by its consumers or producers but by other people. An *external benefit* is the benefit of consuming a good or service that does not accrue to its consumers or producers but to other people. Externalities occur when the consumption or production of a good or service creates another good or service that does not have a market. Let's consider some examples.

External Costs

When a chemicals factory produces packaged chemicals it also produces another good – toxic waste. If there is no market for toxic waste, the factory will decide to dump it in the cheapest possible way. If the waste is dumped in a nearby river and kills the fish, it imposes an *external cost* on the members of the fishing club located downstream. The chemicals factory does not have to take these costs into account because toxic waste has no price. Similarly, when people used leaded fuels in their cars in the 1970s, an external cost was imposed on everyone who tried to breathe the toxic air. Again, because there is no market for exhaust fumes and most of these costs were not borne by the driver, they were not taken into account when deciding how often to drive.

Two particularly dramatic external costs have received a lot of attention in recent years. One arises from the use of chlorofluorocarbons (CFCs). These chemicals are used in a wide variety of products – from coolants in refrigerators and air conditioners, to propellants in aerosols and cleaning solvents for computer circuits. Although the precise chemistry of the process is not understood, many atmospheric physicists believe that CFCs damage the atmosphere's protective ozone layer. Discoveries of depleted ozone over Antarctica in 1983 heightened fears of extended ozone depletion. The US National Academy of Sciences has estimated that a 1 per cent drop in ozone levels might cause a 2 per cent rise in the incidence of skin cancer. When you use an aerosol spray you don't think about the minute additional damage you are doing to the ozone layer. You only count the cost of replacing the aerosol.

The other external cost arises from burning fossil fuels. This adds carbon dioxide and other gases to the atmosphere, preventing infrared radiation from escaping. These gases are collectively known as 'greenhouse gases' because they maintain the earth's temperature. An increase in the concentration of these gases might be responsible for an increase in the earth's average temperature – an increase that could continue into the next century and beyond. If the greenhouse scenario is correct (which is by no means certain), parts of North America will become deserts and parts of southern India will be flooded. When you take a car trip – and burn petrol, a fossil fuel – you do not count the cost of the effects of a warmer planet. You compare your private benefit with your private motoring costs.

Not all externalities are negative – external costs. Let's look at some activities that bring external benefits.

External Benefits

When a home owner fills her garden with spring bulbs, she generates an external benefit for the neighbours and walkers who pass by. In deciding how much to spend on this lavish display, she pays more attention to the pleasure she receives herself than the pleasure she gives to others.

The biggest external benefits are in our schools, colleges and research laboratories. Well-educated people derive many benefits for themselves, such as higher incomes and the enjoyment of a wide range of artistic and cultural activities. But they also bring benefits to others through social interaction. People find more exciting partners and spouses, children get more imaginative parents, and we get to see more creative and entertaining movies and television shows. The list is almost endless. Despite all these external benefits, each one of us decides how much schooling to undertake by assessing our own costs and benefits, not those enjoyed by the wider community.

Health services also create external benefits. Widespread good health and vaccination reduce the risk that any one person will come into contact with an infectious disease – say, polio or tuberculosis. When we make individual choices about how much to spend on health and prevention, we mainly take account of the costs we bear and the benefits we get rather than the greater benefit that our actions bring to others.

Market Failure and Public Choice

The existence of external costs and external benefits is a major source of *market failure*. There is a tendency for the market economy to overproduce goods and services that have external costs and to underproduce goods and services that have external benefits. That is, externalities create inefficiency.

When market failure occurs, either we live with the inefficiency it creates or we try to achieve greater efficiency by making some *public choices* to use government policy. Governments can use several policies to achieve a more efficient allocation of resources in the face of externalities – to decrease production where there are external costs and increase it where there are external benefits – and this chapter explains these actions. Let's look first at the external costs that affect the environment.

Economics of the Environment

Popular discussions of the environment usually pay little attention to economics. They focus on physical aspects of the environment, not costs and benefits. A common assumption is that if people's actions cause *any* environmental degradation, these actions must cease. In contrast, an economic study of the environment emphasizes costs and benefits. An economist talks about the efficient amount of pollution or environmental damage. This emphasis on costs and benefits does not mean that economists, as citizens, do not share the same goals as others and do not value a healthy environment. Nor does it mean that economists have the right answers and everyone else has the wrong ones (or vice versa). Economics provides a set of tools and principles which clarify the issues. It does not provide an agreed list of solutions.

The starting point for an economic analysis of the environment is the demand for a healthy environment.

The Demand for Environmental Quality

Environmental problems are not new, nor is the desire to find solutions to environmental problems new. The demand for a clean and healthy environment has grown and is higher today than it has ever been. We express our demand for a better environment in a number of ways. We can join 'green' organizations to lobby governments for environmental regulations and policies. We can vote for political parties that reflect our views and we can buy 'green' products. Figure 20.1 gives one indicator of the growth in the demand for a better environment – the growth in the number of people who pay subscriptions to environmental organizations. Between 1981 and 1994, the demand for membership of most voluntary environmental organizations in the United Kingdom more than doubled. By 1994, there were 4.4 million members of environmental organizations.

The demand for a better environment has grown for two reasons:

1. Increased incomes
2. Increased knowledge of the sources of environmental problems.

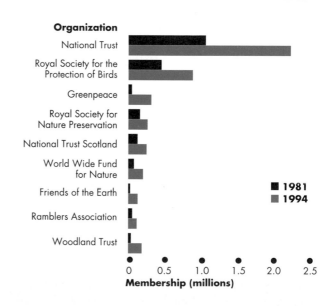

FIGURE 20.1

Membership of Environmental Groups

There were 4.4 million members of UK voluntary environmental organizations in 1994. The demand for membership of most organizations more than doubled between 1981 and 1994.

Source: Central Statistical Office, *Membership of Voluntary Environmental Organizations, Social Trends*, London, HMSO, 1996, Table 11.4.

As our incomes increase, we demand a larger range of goods and services and one of these 'goods' is a high-quality environment. We value clean air, unspoiled natural scenery and wildlife, and we are willing to pay to protect these valuable resources.

As our knowledge of the effects of our actions on the environment grows, so we are able to take measures that improve the environment. For example, now that we know how sulphur dioxide causes acid rain and how clearing rain forests destroys natural stores of carbon dioxide, we are able, in principle, to design measures that limit these problems.

Let's look at the range of environmental problems that have been identified and the actions that create these problems.

The Sources of Environment Problems

Environmental problems arise from pollution of the air, water and land and these individual sources of pollution interact through the *ecosystem*.

Air Pollution Figure 20.2(a) shows the five economic activities that create most of our air pollution. It also shows the relative contributions of each activity. More than two-thirds of air pollution comes from road transport and industrial processes. Only one-sixth arises from coal and gas-fired electric power generation.

A common belief is that air pollution is getting worse. On many fronts, as we will see later in this chapter, *global* air pollution is getting worse. But air pollution in the United Kingdom is getting less severe for some substances. Figure 20.2(b) shows projected trends in the emissions of a major pollutant – carbon dioxide. Carbon dioxide is a 'greenhouse' gas thought to create global warming and increases are mostly created by economic activity. Total emissions fell between 1970 and 1980 but increased after 1980. The projected rise to 2020 is mainly owing to increasing use of cars and rising trends in fuel consumption in the production of goods and services.

FIGURE 20.2

Air Pollution

(a) Sources of emission

Part (a) shows that road transport is the largest source of air pollution, followed by industrial production and power stations. Part (b) shows that carbon dioxide emissions – the most important gas thought to cause global warming –

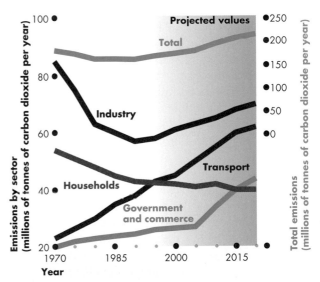

(b) UK carbon dioxide emissions

fell after 1970 but have recently begun to rise. Forecasts of future emissions suggest the most important source of increase will be from transport – particularly increased use of cars.

Source: Royal Commission on Environmental Pollution, *18th Report*, London, HMSO, 1994.

While the facts about the sources and trends in air pollution are not in doubt, there is considerable disagreement in the scientific community about the *effects* of air pollution. The least controversial problem is *acid rain,* which is caused by sulphur dioxide and nitrogen oxide emissions from coal- and oil-fired power stations. Acid rain begins with air pollution and it leads to water pollution and damages vegetation.

More controversial are airborne substances (suspended particulates) such as lead from leaded petrol. Some scientists believe that in sufficiently large concentrations, these substances (of which currently 189 have been identified) cause cancer and other life-threatening conditions.

Even more controversial is *global warming,* which some scientist believe results from the carbon dioxide emissions of road transport and power stations, methane created by cows and other livestock, nitrous oxide emissions from power stations and from fertilizers, and chlorofluorocarbons or CFCs from refrigeration equipment and (in the past) aerosols. The earth's average temperature has increased over the past 100 years, but most of the increase occurred *before* 1940. Determining what causes changes in the earth's temperature and separating out the effect of carbon dioxide and other factors is proving to be difficult.

Equally controversial is the problem of *ozone layer depletion.* There is no doubt that a hole in the ozone layer exists over Antarctica. There is also no doubt that the ozone layer protects us from cancer-causing ultraviolet rays from the sun. But how the ozone layer is influenced by our industrial activity is simply not understood at this time.

While air pollution from leaded petrol has almost been eliminated in developed economies, sulphur dioxide and the so-called greenhouse gases are a much tougher problem to tackle. The alternatives to road vehicles and power stations are costly or have environmental problems of their own. Road vehicles can be made greener in a variety of ways. One way is to use alternative fuels such as alcohol, natural gas, propane and butane, and hydrogen. Another way is to reduce exhaust emissions by fitting catalytic converters and changing the chemistry of petrol. Similarly, electric power can be generated in cleaner ways by harnessing solar power, tidal power, or geothermal power. Although technically possible, these methods are more costly than conventional carbon-fuelled generators. Another alternative is nuclear power. This method

is good for air pollution but bad for land and water pollution because there is no known safe method of disposing of spent nuclear fuel.

Water Pollution   The largest sources of water pollution are the dumping of industrial waste and treated sewage in lakes and rivers and the run-off from agricultural fertilizers. A more dramatic source is the accidental spilling of crude oil into the oceans, such as the Exxon Valdez spill in Alaska and an even larger spill in the Russian Arctic in 1994. The most frightening is the dumping of nuclear waste in the ocean.

Polluting the waterways and oceans has two main alternatives. One is the chemical processing of waste to render it inert or biodegradable. The other, in wide use for nuclear waste, is to use land sites for storage in secure containers.

Land Pollution   Land pollution arises from dumping toxic waste products. Ordinary household rubbish does not pose a pollution problem unless toxic elements in the rubbish seep into the water supply. This possibility increases as less suitable landfill sites are used. It is estimated that 80 per cent of existing landfills will be full by 2010. Some countries such as Japan and the Netherlands have run out of landfills already. The alternatives to landfill are recycling and incineration. Recycling is an apparently attractive alternative, but it requires an investment in new technologies to be effective. Incineration is a high-cost alternative to landfill and it produces air pollution.

We've seen that the demand for a quality environment has grown and we've described the range of environmental problems. Let's now look at the ways these problems can be handled. We'll begin by looking at property rights and how they relate to environmental externalities.

Property Rights and Environmental Externalities

Externalities arise when there are no markets for a good or service because of an *absence* of property rights. **Property rights** are social arrangements that govern the ownership, use and disposal of factors of production and goods and services. In modern societies, a property right is a legally established title that is enforceable in the courts.

You can see that property rights are absent when externalities arise by thinking about the examples we've already reviewed. No one owns the air, the rivers and the oceans. So it is no one's private business to ensure that these resources are used in an efficient way. In fact, there is an incentive to use them more than if there were property rights.

Figure 20.3 shows how an environmental externality arises in the absence of property rights using our earlier example of a chemicals factory which dumps toxic waste upstream from a fishing club. The *MB* curve in part (a) is the factory's marginal benefit curve. It tells us how much an additional tonne of waste dumped into the river is worth to the factory. The marginal value to the firm of dumping waste in the river falls as the quantity increases. If the factory has the property rights, the *MB* curve would also be the firm's demand curve for the use of the river, which is a factor of production. The demand for a factor of production slopes downward because of the law of diminishing returns (see Chapter 14, pp. 349–355). As there are no external benefits from dumping waste, the *MB* curve is also the marginal social benefit, *MSB*.

The *MSC* curve in part (a) of Fig. 20.3 is the marginal social cost of one additional tonne of waste being dumped in the river. It rises as the quantity of waste being dumped increases. The *MSC* curve measures the marginal cost to the fishing club of reduced fish stocks and fish quality as the firm dumps an additional tonne of waste in the river. If the fishing club has the property rights, the *MSC* curve would also be the fishing club's supply curve of river use to the firm. The supply curve slopes upward because the greater the quantity of waste, the smaller is the quantity of fish and the more the club's members are willing to pay for a marginal increase in fish stock and quality.

The factory is upstream from the fishing club and the factory must decide how to dispose of its waste. If no one owns the stream, the marginal cost of waste disposal to the factory is zero. The factory maximizes total benefit – the area under *MB* – by dumping 8 tonnes of waste a week as shown in part (a) of Fig. 20.3. The *MSC* curve, shows that the fishing club bears a cost of £200 a tonne when 8 tonnes of waste a week are dumped. So the factory has an incentive to dump 8 tonnes of waste a week because it can ignore the cost borne by the members of the fishing club. Dumping 8 tonnes of waste a week is inefficient and social welfare is not maximized. Let's see why.

The efficient level of dumping waste is 4 tonnes a week, where *MSB* equals *MSC*. This amount generates the maximum level of total social welfare – £400

FIGURE 20.3

Externalities and the Coase Theorem

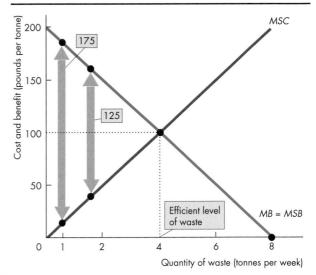

(a) Marginal cost and marginal benefit

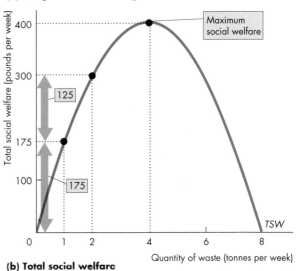

(b) Total social welfare

The *MB* curve in part (a) is the factory's marginal benefit curve which equals marginal social benefit, *MSB*. The *MSC* curve measures the marginal social cost to the fishing club of one additional tonne of waste being dumped in the river. If no one owns the river, the factory maximizes *MB* by dumping 8 tonnes a week. This is inefficient. The efficient level of dumping shown in part (b) is 4 tonnes a week – where *MSB* equals *MSC* and *TSW* is maximized. Using the Coase theorem from part (a), if the polluter owns the river, the victim will pay £400 a week (£100 a tonne x 4 tonnes a week) to the polluter for the assurance that pollution will not exceed 4 tonnes a week. If the victim owns the river, the polluter will pay £400 for pollution rights to dump 4 tonnes a week.

a week – as shown in part (b) of Fig. 20.3. Total social welfare is the difference between total social benefit – the area under the *MSB* curve – and total social cost – the area under the *MSC* curve. Each additional unit of waste dumped adds more to total social benefit than total social cost up to 4 tonnes of waste a week. The first tonne dumped generates £175 of total social welfare. The second tonne dumped adds £125 pounds raising total social welfare to £300 (£175 + £125). After the fourth tonne, each additional tonne of waste dumped adds more to total social cost than to total social benefit, so total social welfare falls. If property rights to the river are not clearly defined, the market will lead to an inefficient amount of dumping of waste – at 8 tonnes a week – and total social welfare will fall to zero.

Sometimes it is possible to correct an externality by establishing a market – creating property rights where they did not exist before. For example, suppose that the property right in the river was assigned by law to the chemicals factory. Because the river is now the property of the factory, the fishing club must pay the factory for the right to fish in the river. But the price that the club is willing to pay depends on the number and quality of fish, which in turn depends on how much waste the factory dumps in the river. The greater the amount of pollution, the smaller is the amount the fishing club is willing to pay for the right to fish. Similarly, the smaller the amount of pollution, the greater is the amount the fishing club is willing to pay for the right to fish. The chemicals factory is now confronted with the cost of its pollution decision. It might still decide to pollute, but if it does it faces the opportunity cost of its actions – forgone revenue from the fishing club.

Suppose that the fishing club, not the chemicals factory, owns the river. In this case, the factory must pay a fee to the fishing club for the right to dump its waste. The more waste it dumps (equivalently, the more fish it kills), the more it must pay. Again, the factory faces an opportunity cost for the pollution it creates – the fee paid to the fishing club.

The Coase Theorem

So does it matter how property rights are assigned? At first thought, the assignment seems crucial, but in 1960, Ronald Coase had a remarkable insight, now known as the Coase theorem. The **Coase theorem** states that if property rights exist and transactions costs are low, private transactions are efficient. In other words, with property rights and low transactions costs, there are no externalities. All the costs and benefits are taken into account by the transacting parties. So it doesn't matter how the property rights are assigned.

You can see the Coase theorem at work by looking again at part (a) of Fig. 20.3. At the efficient level of waste – 4 tonnes a week – the fishing club bears a cost of £100 for the last tonne dumped in the river, and the factory gets a benefit of £100 a tonne dumped. If waste disposal is restricted below 4 tonnes a week, an increase in waste disposal benefits the factory more than it costs the club. The factory will bribe the club to put up with more waste disposal and both the club and the factory can gain. If waste disposal exceeds 4 tonnes a week, an increase in waste disposal costs the club more than it benefits the factory. The club will now bribe the factory to cut its waste disposal and again, both the club and the factory can gain. Only when the level of waste disposal is 4 tonnes a week – the efficient level – can neither party do any better.

The outcome is the same regardless of who owns the river. If the factory owns it, the club pays £400 for fishing rights and for an agreement that waste disposal will not exceed 4 tonnes a week. If the club owns the river, the factory pays £400 for the right to dump 4 tonnes of waste a week.

Assigning property rights works in this example because the transactions costs are low. The factory and the fishing club can easily sit down and negotiate the deal that produces the efficient outcome. When property rights are assigned in this way, external factors become *internalized*. Property rights create markets that work like Adam Smith's 'invisible hand' to achieve an efficient outcome – marginal cost equals marginal benefit – with everyone pursuing their own self-interest.

But in many situations transactions costs are high and property rights cannot be enforced. Imagine, for example, the transactions costs of 8 million people who live in Sweden trying to negotiate an agreement with the 5,000 factories in the United Kingdom that emit sulphur dioxide and cause acid rain! In a case such as this, governments resort to alternative methods of coping with externalities. They use a range of policies including:

- Emission charges
- Emission standards
- Marketable permits
- Taxes

Economics in History on pp. 512–513 reviews some examples of the use of these methods and how ideas about how to cope with externalities have changed. In the United Kingdom, the government has established an agency, the Environment Agency (EA), to coordinate and administer the country's environment policies. Let's look at the tools the EA could use and see how they work.

Emission Charges

Emission charges are a method of using the market to achieve efficiency, even in the face of externalities. The government (or the regulatory agency established by the government) sets the emission charges, which are, in effect, a price per unit of pollution. The more pollution a firm creates, the more it pays in emission charges. This method of dealing with environmental externalities is common throughout Europe. For example, in France, Germany and the Netherlands water polluters pay a waste disposal charge.

To work out the emission charge that achieves efficiency, the regulator must determine the marginal social cost and marginal social benefit of pollution. **Marginal social cost** is the marginal cost incurred by the producer of a good – marginal private cost – *plus* the marginal cost imposed on others – the external cost. **Marginal social benefit** is the marginal benefit received by the consumer of a good – marginal private benefit – *plus* the marginal benefit to others – the external benefit. To achieve efficiency, the price per unit of pollution must be set to make the marginal social cost of the pollution equal to its marginal social benefit.

Figure 20.4 illustrates an efficient emissions charge for sulphur dioxide pollution. The marginal benefit of pollution is *MB* and accrues to the polluters alone. It is also the marginal social benefit of pollution, *MSB*, as there is no external benefit. The marginal social cost of pollution is *MSC* and is entirely an external cost, falling on other firms and people who live in the affected country. The efficient level of sulphur dioxide emissions is 10 million tonnes a year – where *MSB* = *MSC*. This can be achieved by setting an emission charge of £10 per tonne. Polluters carry on increasing emissions until the marginal benefit just equals the charge per tonne.

In practice, it is hard to determine the marginal benefit of pollution. The people who are best informed about the marginal benefit, the polluters, have an incentive to mislead the regulators about the

benefit. As a result, if a pollution charge is used, the most likely outcome is for the price to be set too low. For example, in Fig. 20.4, the price might be set at £7 per tonne. At this price, polluters find it worthwhile to pay for 15 million tonnes a year. At this level of pollution, the marginal social cost is £15 a tonne and the amount of pollution exceeds the efficient level.

One way of overcoming excess pollution is to impose general emission standards, which dictate the maximum safe quantity of a pollutant in any output of waste. A more sophisticated method is to issue quantitative limits that firms can buy and sell – marketable permits. Let's look at these two methods.

Emission Standards

Instead of imposing emission charges on polluters, pollution agencies might set a single emission standard. An **emission standard** is a regulation which

FIGURE 20.4

Emission Charges

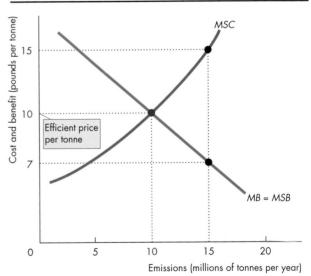

Power stations obtain marginal benefits from sulphur dioxide emissions of *MB* and everyone else bears a marginal social cost of *MSC*. The efficient level of pollution – 10 million tonnes a year in this example – is achieved by imposing an emission charge on power stations of £10 a tonne. If the emission charge is set too low, at £7 a tonne, the resulting amount of pollution is greater than the efficient amount – at 15 million tonnes a year. In this case, the marginal social cost is £15 a tonne, and it exceeds the marginal benefit of £7 a tonne.

limits the quantity of the pollutant in any volume of waste and sets penalties for breaking the regulation. Emission standards for water and air are widely used in the United Kingdom and in the European Union's environmental policy. For example, since 1994, the UK government has set car exhaust emission standards, and all cars over three years old are now tested as part of the annual MOT (Ministry of Transport) certificate. The benefit of using a uniform standard is that it is simple and cheap to apply. The problem is that standards are inefficient. Let's see why.

If firm H has a higher marginal benefit than firm L, an efficiency gain can be achieved by decreasing the standard for firm L and increasing the standard for firm H. As it is virtually impossible to determine the marginal benefits of each firm in practice, quantitative restrictions cannot be allocated to each producer in an efficient way. Uniform emission standards will always be inefficient. Despite their inefficiency, standards are widely used because it is easy for producers to comply with a uniform standard. Also, it is often difficult to value the damage caused by pollutants to establish the marginal

external cost. Policies that attempt to set a price for pollution cannot succeed unless the value of the marginal external cost is known. The efficiency of vehicle emission standards compared to road pricing is examined in *Reading Between the Lines* on pp. 510–511.

Marketable Permits

Marketable permits are a clever way of overcoming the need for the regulator to know every firm's marginal benefit schedule. Permit trading is a key element of the US Clean Air Acts but has not been implemented in Europe. Each firm can be allocated a permit to emit a certain amount of pollution. Firms may also buy and sell such permits.

Figure 20.5 shows how such a system works and can achieve efficiency. Some firms have low marginal benefits from sulphur emissions, shown as MB_L in part (a). Others have a high marginal benefit, shown as MB_H in part (b). For the economy as a whole, the marginal benefit is MB_E in part (c). The marginal social cost of sulphur emissions is MSC, also shown in part (c). The efficient level of

FIGURE 20.5

Marketable Pollution Permits

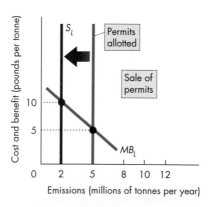

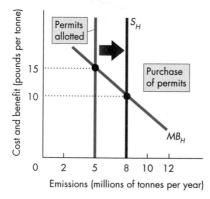

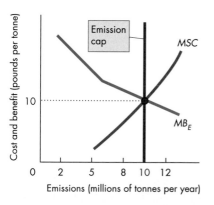

(a) Low-benefit firms

(b) High-benefit firms

(c) Economy

Some firms obtain low marginal benefits from pollution, MB_L in part (a), and some obtain high marginal benefits, MB_H in part (b). The marginal social cost is MSC in part (c). Marginal benefit for the economy is MB_E in part (c). Pollution permits are issued that limit pollution to 10 million tonnes a year (the efficient level) and each type of firm gets the same

limit, 5 million tonnes a year. Initially, low-benefit firms value their permits at £5 a tonne and high-benefit firms value their permits at £15 a tonne. High-benefit firms buy permits for 3 million tonnes of pollution from low-benefit firms for a market price of £10 a tonne.

emissions is 10 million tonnes a year, the quantity at which marginal social cost equals marginal social benefit.

Suppose the EA allocates permits for a total of 10 million tonnes of sulphur emissions a year. And suppose the permits are allocated equally to the two groups of firms – 5 million tonnes each. The firms in part (a) value their last tonne of pollution permitted at £5. The firms in part (b) value their last tonne of pollution permitted at £15 a tonne. With a market in permits, the firms in part (a) sell some of their permits to those in part (b). Both types of firms gain from the trade.

If the market in permits is competitive, the price at which permits trade is £10 per tonne. At this price, low-benefit firms (part a) sell permits for 3 million tonnes of sulphur emissions to the high-benefit firms (part b). After these transactions, the low-benefit firms (part a) have S_L permits and the high-benefit firms (part b) have S_H permits and the allocation is efficient.

Evidence from the United States suggests that permit trading can be administratively costly if there are a great many polluters. By contrast, if there are only a few polluters, these firms may buy up all available permits and refuse to trade them – leading to a barrier to entry to new firms. Also, permit trading will not lead to the efficient level of emissions in each firm unless the efficient level of total emissions is known to start with. The benefit of permit trading is that for any given level of permits allocated, trading will ensure that they are efficiently distributed between different producers.

Taxes and External Costs

Taxes can be used to provide incentives for producers or consumers to cut back on an activity that creates external costs. A tax used in this way to control pollution is called a **green tax**. The European Union plans to introduce a 'green' tax on carbon fuels in power stations and vehicles because they are a major source of pollution. To see how this type of 'green' tax works, let's look at the market for petrol shown in Fig. 20.6. The demand curve for petrol, D, is also the marginal benefit curve, MB. This curve tells us how much consumers value different amounts of petrol. The curve MC measures the marginal *private* cost of using petrol – the costs directly incurred by the producers of these services.

FIGURE 20.6

Taxes and Pollution

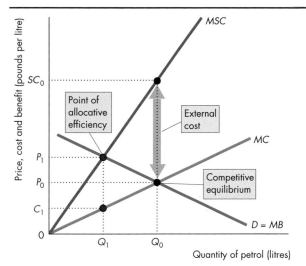

The demand curve for petrol is also the marginal benefit curve ($D = MB$). The marginal cost curve of producing petrol is MC. If the market is competitive, Q_0 litres of petrol are produced and the price is P_0 per litre. The marginal social cost of petrol is shown by the curve MSC. Because of environmental pollution, the marginal social cost of petrol, SC_0, exceeds the marginal private cost, P_0, when the quantity of petrol is Q_0. If the government imposes a tax on petrol supply equal to the external cost, producers face a marginal cost equal to the MSC curve. The price of petrol increases to P_1 per litre and the quantity decreases to Q_1 litres. Allocative efficiency is achieved.

The costs borne by drivers are not the only costs. External costs arise from the urban smog, air toxins and greenhouse gases caused by vehicle emissions. When all the external marginal costs are added to the marginal cost faced by the producer, we obtain the marginal *social* cost of petrol, shown by MSC in the figure.

If the petrol market is competitive and unregulated, drivers will balance the marginal cost of petrol, MC, against their own marginal benefit, MB, and buy Q_0 litres of petrol at a price of P_0 per litre. At this level of petrol use, the marginal social cost is SC_0. The marginal social cost minus the marginal private cost, $SC_0 - P_0$, is the marginal cost imposed on others – the marginal external cost.

Suppose the EA imposes a new 'green' tax on petrol and that it sets the tax equal to the external marginal cost. The tax makes the suppliers of petrol incur a marginal cost equal to the marginal social cost. That is, the marginal private cost plus the tax equals the marginal social cost. The market supply curve is now the same as the *MSC* curve. The price of petrol rises to P_1 a litre and at this price, the quantity bought falls to Q_1. The marginal cost of the resources used in producing Q_1 litres of petrol is C_1, and the marginal external cost is P_1 minus C_1. That marginal external cost is paid by the consumer through the tax.

The situation at the price P_1 and the quantity Q_1 is efficient. At an output rate above Q_1, marginal social cost exceeds marginal benefit, so net benefit increases by decreasing petrol production. At an output rate below Q_1, marginal benefit exceeds marginal social cost, so net benefit increases by increasing petrol production.

A Carbon-fuel Tax?   The European Union introduced the idea of a green tax on carbon emissions as part of its new sustainable environmental policy in 1992. The issue is still pressing. Today, annual carbon emissions worldwide are a staggering 6 billion tonnes. By 2050, with current policies, that annual total is predicted to be 24 billion tonnes. If the rich countries used carbon taxes to keep emissions to their 1990 level and the developing countries remove subsidies from coal and oil, total emissions in 2050 might be held at 14 billion tonnes. So why have the European Union and other rich countries worldwide failed to introduce carbon taxes?

Uncertainty About Global Warming   Part of the reason we do not have a high, broad-based, carbon-fuel tax is that the scientific evidence that carbon emissions produce global warming is not accepted by everyone. Climatologists are uncertain about how carbon emissions translate into atmospheric concentrations – about how the *flow* of emissions translates into a *stock* of pollution. The main uncertainty arises because carbon drains from the atmosphere into the oceans and vegetation at a rate that is not well understood. Climatologists are also uncertain about the connection between carbon concentration and temperature. Economists are uncertain about how a temperature increase translates into economic costs and benefits. Some economists believe the costs and benefits are almost zero, while others believe that a temperature

increase of 3°C by 2090 will reduce the total output of goods and services by 20 per cent.

Present Cost and Future Benefit   Another factor weighing against a large change in fuel use is that the costs would be borne now while the benefits, if any, would accrue many years in the future. To compare future benefits with current costs, we must use an interest rate. If the interest rate is 5 per cent a year, a pound today becomes more than £17,000 in 200 years. So at an interest rate of 5 per cent a year, it is worth spending £1 million today only if this expenditure avoids £17 billion in environmental damage in 2195.

Because large uncertain future benefits are needed to justify small current costs, a general tax on carbon fuels is not a high priority on the political agenda.

International Factors   A final factor against a large change in fuel use is the international pattern of the use of carbon fuels. At present, carbon pollution comes in even doses from the industrial (OECD)[1] countries and the developing countries. But by 2050, three-quarters of the carbon pollution will come from the developing countries (if the trends persist). One reason for the high pollution rate in some developing countries is that their governments *subsidize* the use of coal or oil. These subsidies lower producers' marginal costs and encourage the use of fuel beyond the efficient quantity – and by a large amount.

A Global Warming Dilemma

With the high output rate of greenhouse gases in the developing world, the European Union and the other industrial countries are faced with a global warming dilemma[2]. Decreasing pollution is costly

---

[1] The OECD is the Organization for Economic Cooperation and Development, an international agency based in Paris, the member nations of which include the United States, Canada, Japan and the industrial countries of Western Europe and Australasia.

[2] This dilemma is like the 'prisoners' dilemma' that is explained in Chapter 13 on pp. 322–324.

and brings benefits. But the benefits depend on all countries taking action to limit pollution. If the European Union acts alone, other countries will gain benefits, but the European Union bears the cost of limiting pollution and gets almost no benefits. So it is worthwhile taking steps to limit global pollution only if all nations act together.

The global warming dilemma faced by the European Union and the developing countries is shown in Table 20.1. The numbers are hypothetical. Each country (we'll call the developing countries a country) has two possible policies: to introduce a carbon tax or to pollute. If each country pollutes, it receives a zero net return (by assumption) shown in the top left square in the table. If each country introduces a carbon tax, it bears the cost of using more expensive fuels and gets the benefit of less pollution. Its net return is £25 billion, as shown in the bottom right square of the table. If the European Union alone introduces a carbon tax, the European Union pays £50 billion more than it benefits and the developing countries benefit by £50 billion more than they pay, as shown in the top right corner of the table. Finally, if the developing countries alone introduce a carbon tax, they lose £50 billion and the European Union gains £50 billion, as shown in the bottom left corner of the table.

Confronted with these possible payoffs, the European Union reasons as follows. If the developing countries do not introduce a carbon tax, we break even if we pollute and we lose £50 billion if we introduce a tax. Conclusion, we are better off polluting. If the developing countries introduce a tax, we gain £50 billion if we pollute and £25 billion if we introduce a tax. Again, we are better off polluting. The developing countries reach the same conclusion. So no one introduces a carbon tax and pollution continues unabated.

Treaties and International Agreements

To break the dilemma, international agreements – treaties – might be negotiated. But such treaties must have incentives for countries to comply with their agreements. Otherwise, even with a treaty, the situation remains as we've just described and illustrated in Table 20.1.

One such international agreement is the *climate convention* that came into effect on 21 March,

1994. This convention is an agreement among 60 countries to limit their output of greenhouse gases. But the convention does not have economic teeth. The poorer countries are merely asked to list their sources of greenhouse gases. The rich countries must show how, by 2000, they will return to their 1990 emission levels.

To return to the 1990 emission levels, the rich countries will need stiff increases in energy taxes, and such taxes will be costly. Energy taxes will induce a substitution towards more costly but cleaner alternative fuels. Without energy taxes, only a large technological advance in solar, wind, tidal, or nuclear power that makes these sources less costly than coal can create the incentive needed to give up carbon fuels.

TABLE 20.1

A Global Warming Dilemma

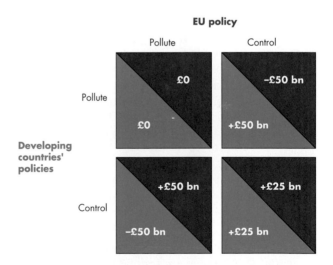

If the European Union and developing countries both pollute, their payoffs are those shown in the top left square. If neither pollutes, their payoffs are shown in the bottom right square. When one country pollutes and the other one does not, their payoffs are shown in the top right and bottom left squares. The outcome of this game is for both countries to pollute. The structure of this game is the same as that of the prisoners' dilemma.

REVIEW

◆ When externalities are present, the market allocation is not efficient.

◆ If by assigning property rights an externality can be eliminated, an efficient allocation can be achieved.

◆ With the right information, governments can use emission charges, pollution standards, taxes or permits to induce the efficient quantity of pollution, even in the face of externalities.

◆ When an externality goes beyond the scope of one country, effective international cooperation is necessary to achieve an efficient outcome.

Economics of Knowledge

Knowledge is both a consumer good and a factor of production. The demand for knowledge – the willingness to pay to acquire knowledge – depends on the marginal benefit it provides to its possessor. As a consumer good, knowledge provides utility and this is one source of its marginal benefit. As a factor of production – part of the stock of capital – knowledge increases productivity and this is another source of its marginal benefit.

Knowledge creates benefits not only for its possessor, but for others as well – external benefits. External benefits arise from education and training – passing on existing knowledge to others. When children learn basic skills at school, they are better able to communicate and interact with each other. Similarly, when people are trained at work, they make better employees for other firms. But when people make decisions about how much schooling to undertake, or when firms decide about how much training to provide, they do not value the external benefits created.

External benefits also arise from research and development activities that lead to the creation of new knowledge. Once someone has worked out how to do something, others can copy the basic idea. They do have to work to copy an idea, so they face an opportunity cost. But (usually) they do not

have to pay the person who made the discovery to use it. When Isaac Newton worked out the formulas for calculating the rate of response of one variable to another – calculus – everyone was free to use his method. When a spreadsheet program called VisiCalc was invented, others were free to copy the basic idea. Lotus Corporation developed its 1-2-3 and later Microsoft created Excel and both became highly successful, but they did not pay for the key idea first used in VisiCalc.

When people make decisions about the quantity of education to undertake, or when firms decide on the amount of research and development and training that they provide, they balance the *private* marginal costs against the private marginal benefits. They do not take into account the value of the external benefits. As a result, if we were to leave education, training and research and development to individual market choice we would get too little of these activities. To deliver them in efficient quantities, we make public choices through government policy to modify the market outcome.

Governments can use a range of policies to achieve an efficient allocation of resources in the presence of the external benefits from education and research and development. Three important policies are:

◆ Subsidies

◆ Below-cost provision

◆ Patents

Subsidies

A **subsidy** is a payment made by the government to producers that depends on the level of output. By subsidizing private activities, government can in principle encourage private decisions to be taken in the public interest. A government subsidy programme might alternatively enable private producers to capture resources for themselves. Although subsidies cannot be guaranteed to work successfully, we'll study an example in which they do achieve their desired objective.

Figure 20.7 shows how subsidizing education can increase the amount of education undertaken and achieve allocative efficiency. Suppose that the marginal cost of producing a student–year of college or university education is a constant £10,000. This marginal social cost is shown by the *MSC* curve. We'll assume that all these costs are borne by the colleges

FIGURE 20.7

Efficiency in Education

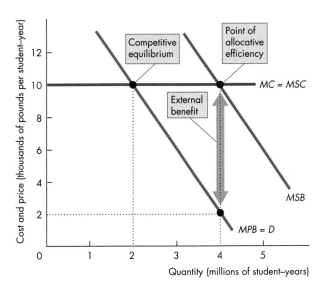

The demand curve for education measures the marginal private benefit of education (*MPB = D*). The curve *MSC* shows the marginal social cost of education – in this example, £10,000 per student–year. If college education is provided in a competitive market with no government intervention, tuition is £10,000 a year and 2 million students are enrolled in college. Education produces an external benefit and adding the external benefit to the marginal private benefit gives marginal social benefit, *MSB*. Allocative efficiency is achieved if the government provides education services on a scale such that marginal social cost equals marginal social benefit. This scale of provision is 4 million students a year, which is achieved if the government either subsidizes private colleges or provides education below cost in public colleges. In this example, people pay an annual tuition fee of £2,000 and the government pays £8,000.

and there are no external costs. The maximum price that students (or parents) are willing to pay for an additional year of study determines the marginal private benefit curve and the demand curve for education. This curve is *MPB = D*. In this example, a competitive market in private university or college education results in 2 million students being enrolled and tuition fees of £10,000 a year.

Suppose that the external benefit – the benefit derived by people other than those who receive the education – results in external benefits. The

marginal social benefit – marginal private benefit plus marginal external benefit – is the curve *MSB*. Allocative efficiency occurs when marginal social cost equals marginal social benefit. In the example in Fig. 20.7, this occurs when 4 million students are enrolled. One way of getting 4 million students enrolled is to subsidize private universities or colleges. In our example, a subsidy of £8,000 per student per year paid to the colleges does the job. With a subsidy of £8,000 and marginal cost of £10,000, colleges and universities earn an economic profit on any fee above £2,000. Competition drives the tuition fee down to £2,000 and at this price, the quantity demanded is 4 million. So a subsidy can achieve an efficient outcome.

A subsidy can also be used to increase the stock of knowledge through research and development in industry and through subsidized training. By subsidizing these activities, the government can move the allocation of resources towards a more efficient outcome. Another way to achieve an efficient amount of education and research and development is through public provision sold below cost.

Below-cost Provision

Instead of subsidizing private colleges and universities, the government can establish public sector colleges and universities that provide schooling below cost. Instead of subsidizing research and development in industry and the universities, the government can establish its own research facilities and make discoveries available to others. Let's see how this approach works by returning to the example in Fig. 20.7

By creating public sector universities with places for 4 million students, the government can supply the efficient quantity of higher education directly. To ensure that this number of places is taken up, the public universities charge a tuition fee, in this example, of £2,000 per student per year. At this price, the number of people who choose to attend college makes the marginal social benefit of education equal to its marginal cost.

In a similar way, government could set up its own research centres to develop technology and test innovations in defence and agriculture, or in health or transport. The government centres would undertake research to create new technology and sell the right to use the technology to private industry at a price below marginal cost. This would ensure that technology is widely transferred throughout industry so that the marginal social benefit of technology use is equal to its marginal cost.

We've now looked at two examples of how government action can help market participants take account of the external benefits deriving from education to achieve an outcome different from that of a private unregulated market. In reality, governments use both methods of encouraging an efficient quantity of education. They subsidize private colleges and universities and run their own institutions, selling their services at below cost. But in education, the public sector is by far the larger. In research and development, subsidies to the private sector are far larger and government provides little direct research.

Patents

Knowledge may well be the only factor of production that does not display *diminishing marginal productivity*. More knowledge (about the right things) makes people more productive. And there seems to be no tendency for the additional productivity from additional knowledge to diminish.

For example, in just 15 years, advances in knowledge about microprocessors has given us a sequence of processor chips that has made our personal computers increasingly powerful. Each advance in knowledge about how to design and manufacture a processor chip has brought apparently ever larger increments in performance and productivity. In the space of 80 years, we have moved from a simple one-seater plane to the most modern Boeing 747, which can carry 400 people halfway around the world non-stop. These examples can be repeated again and again in fields as diverse as agriculture, biogenetics, communications, engineering, entertainment, medicine and publishing.

A key reason why the stock of knowledge increases without diminishing returns is the sheer number of different techniques that can in principle be tried. Paul Romer (see *Economics in History*, pp. 512–513) explains this fact with an amazing example. Suppose, says Romer,

'that to make a finished good, 20 different parts have to be attached to a frame, one at a

time. A worker could proceed in numerical order, attaching part one first, then part two... Or the worker could proceed in some other order, starting with part 10, then adding part seven...With 20 parts, a standard (but incredible) calculation shows that there are about 10^{18} different sequences one can use for assembling the final good. This number is larger than the total number of seconds that have elapsed since the big bang created the universe, so we can be confident that in all activities, only a very small fraction of the possible sequences have ever been tried.[3]'

Think about all the processes and all the products and all the different bits and pieces that go into each, and you can see that we have only begun to scratch around the edges of what is possible.

Because knowledge is productive and creates external benefits, it is necessary to use government policy to ensure that markets face sufficient incentives to produce the efficient level of effort in invention and innovation. The main way of creating the right incentives is to provide the creators of knowledge with property rights in their discoveries – called **intellectual property rights**. The legal device for creating intellectual property rights is the patent or copyright. A **patent** or **copyright** is a government-sanctioned exclusive right granted to the inventor of a good, service, or productive process, to produce, use and sell the invention for a given number of years. A patent enables the developer of a new idea to prevent, for

---

[3] From Paul Romer 'Ideas and Things', in *The Future Surveyed*, a supplement to *The Economist*, 11 September, 1993, pp. 71–72. © 1993 The Economist Newspaper Group, Inc. The 'standard calculation' that Romer refers to is the number of ways of selecting and arranging in order 20 objects from 20 objects – also called the number of permutations of 20 objects 20 at a time. This number is *factorial* 20, or 20! = 20 ¥ 19 ¥ 18 ¥ ... ¥ 2 ¥ 1 = $10^{18.4}$.

A standard theory (challenged by observations made by the Hubble space telescope in 1994) is that a big bang started the universe 15 billion years, or $10^{17.7}$ seconds, ago. Although $10^{18.4}$ and $10^{17.7}$ look similar, $10^{18.4}$ is *five* times as large as $10^{17.7}$, so if you started trying alternative sequences at the moment of the big bang and took only one second per trial you would still have

a limited number of years, others from benefiting freely from an invention. But to obtain the protection of the law, an inventor must make knowledge of the invention public.

Although patents encourage invention and innovation, they do so at an economic cost. While a patent is in place, its holder has a monopoly – generating more market failure. To maximize profit, a monopoly (patent holder) produces the quantity at which marginal cost equals marginal revenue. The monopoly sets the price above marginal cost and equal to the highest price at which the profit-maximizing quantity can be sold. In this situation, consumers value the good more highly (are willing to pay more for one more unit of it) than its marginal cost. So the quantity of the good available is less than the efficient quantity.

But without a patent, less effort is put into developing new goods, services, or processes and the flow of new inventions is slowed. So the efficient outcome is a compromise that balances the social welfare gain of more inventions against the social welfare loss of temporary monopoly power in newly invented activities.

◆ ◆ ◆ ◆ When we started looking at government regulations and policy at the beginning of Part 4, in Chapter 18, we identified three reasons for government intervention. You might want to go back to Fig. 18.2, p. 444, to remind yourself that governments intervene to reduce the inefficiency caused by market failure, to improve equity and to stabilize the macroeconomic environment. We've now completed our study of the main problems of market failure. In Part 4, we have looked at the inefficiency arising from the provision of public goods, the impact of monopoly and oligopoly in industry and finally, in this chapter, the problems of externalities. We've also seen that regulation and policies, and even the politicians and bureaucrats who supply them, can lead to inefficiency. So efficient intervention must balance the benefits of intervention against costs. ◆ Our next task is to examine the problem of inequality in our economy and to try to identify the factors which determine the distribution of wealth and income. We will look at the ways in which government can redistribute income and provide services to reduce inequality, and the extent to which we might have to trade some efficiency to achieve greater equity.

R E V I E W

◆ Knowledge is a good and a factor of production that creates external benefits.

◆ External benefits arise from education and training – passing on existing knowledge to others; and from research and development – creating new knowledge.

◆ Government policy can achieve an efficient stock of education and training through subsidies, below-cost provision.

◆ Subsidies, below-cost provision and patents can deliver an efficient stock of knowledge.

◆ Knowledge does not seem to have diminishing returns, so government policy is needed to encourage the development of new ideas.

◆ Patents and copyrights create a temporary monopoly so the gain from more knowledge must be balanced against the loss from monopoly.

Externalities and Air Pollution

The Essence of the Story

THE FINANCIAL TIMES, 5 AUGUST 1996

Race on to clean air

Leyla Boulton & Gillian Tett

Most UK drivers – 71 per cent – see air pollution and traffic congestion as the greatest problems of road travel. But reducing traffic congestion, the single most important cause of urban air pollution, remains difficult....

'Changing driver behaviour is the nub of the matter,' says a UK official who is drafting a national strategy for eradicating health threats from air pollution by 2005....

Every year, up to 20,000 people are admitted to UK hospitals suffering from respiratory ailments.... 10,000 deaths a year are attributable to respiratory problems aggravated by summertime smog and pollution from diesel vehicles....

Efforts to tackle the twin problems of congestion and air pollution have so far concentrated on tightening standards for vehicle emissions and fuel quality....

European car emission and fuel standards – published by the European Commission in June ... would cut emissions from vehicles by between 20 per cent and 40 per cent by 2000.... The cost is ... likely to be about Ecu766m (£610m) a year for the oil sector and Ecu2.4bn a year for car manufacturers. For consumers, this means an increase in average annual petrol bills of just £1.80 in 2000, and a rise in the cost of a medium sized car by around £180....

The real challenge facing European governments is not whether industry will foot the bill, ... but whether individuals can be persuaded to use their cars less frequently.

UK motorists may complain about congestion, but they are reluctant to choose other means of transport.... 'The advantage for many of improved public transport would lie in attracting other car users off the road,' the Department of Transport concluded....

A study by Westminster University showed that 'people considered that personal, voluntary change of behaviour was a self-sacrifice which would be ineffective if not undertaken by the majority – which was thought to be unlikely without government action.'...

Many European countries are considering financial penalties to persuade drivers to leave their cars at home. There are several different schemes, but all involve charging motorists for using urban roads to reduce their use.... There could be a public backlash if government measures are seen as socially unfair.

- Most drivers believe air pollution and congestion are the main problems of road travel.

- The costs of air pollution include 20,000 hospitalizations a year and 10, 000 deaths from respiratory problems aggravated by air pollution.

- Governments aim to reduce air pollution by introducing tighter EU emissions and fuel standards. Industry costs and prices will rise as a result.

- But the main problem is changing driver behaviour. Most drivers admit they will not use public transport unless forced to by government.

- Many European countries are now considering introducing road charges to change driver behaviour.

Economic Analysis

■ Congestion causes most urban air pollution. Congestion and air pollution generate external costs on third parties – costs not taken into account by drivers.

■ By estimating the monetary value of the costs of damage – hospital costs and the loss of life – we can plot the marginal external cost curve of urban pollution, MEC_0, shown in Fig. 1. A better estimate would include the value of environmental damage as well.

■ In Fig. 1, the marginal private benefit of car travel for drivers is MPB, which equals marginal social benefit, MSB, if there are no external benefits to car travel. The marginal private cost of car travel is MPC_0 and includes travel time, fuel and car maintenance costs.

■ To maximize utility, car drivers equate MPB with MPC_0 and choose to drive Q_0 kilometres a year.

■ Tighter emission and fuel standards raise annual marginal private costs just £1.80 for petrol and £180 for a car to MPC_1, and reduce marginal external costs a little to MEC_1, resulting in a slight reduction in kilometres driven to Q_1.

■ Figure 2 shows the impact of a road pricing scheme where drivers are charged the value of MEC on each road section after tighter emission standards are introduced.

■ The charge raises driver costs to MSC at Q_1, where costs exceed benefits, and drivers cut kilometres driven to the efficient level of Q^*. Although efficient, road pricing may be unfair for drivers on low incomes.

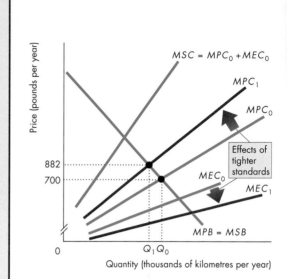

Figure 1

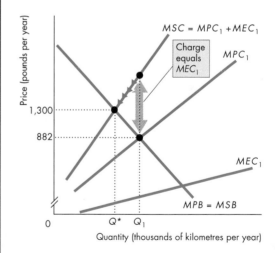

Figure 2

'The question to be decided is: is the value of the fish lost greater than the value of the product which contamination of the stream makes possible?'

Ronald H. Coase, THE PROBLEM OF SOCIAL COST

Understanding Externalities

THE ISSUES AND IDEAS

As knowledge accumulates, we are becoming more sensitive to environmental externalities. We are also developing more sensitive methods of dealing with them. But all the methods involve a public choice.

Urban smog forms when sunlight reacts with emissions from the exhausts of motor vehicles and is both unpleasant and dangerous to breathe. Because of these external costs, emission standards are set by regulation and petrol is taxed. Emission standards increase the cost of vehicles, and petrol taxes increase the cost of the marginal kilometre travelled. The higher costs decrease the quantity demanded of road transport and so decrease the amount of pollution created. Is the value of cleaner urban air worth the higher cost of transport? The public choice of voters, regulators and law-makers answered this question.

Acid rain falls from clouds laden with the output of electric utility chimneys. This external cost is being tackled with a market solution that to some extent replaces the values of law-makers and bureaucrats with those of the people who bear the costs. This solution is marketable permits, the price and allocation of which is determined by the forces of demand and supply. Private choices determine the demand for pollution permits, but a public choice determines the supply.

As cars stream onto a motorway at morning rush hour, the motorway clogs and becomes an expensive car park. Each rush hour traveller imposes external costs on all the others. Today, road users bear private congestion costs and do not face a share of the external congestion costs they create. But a market solution to this problem is now feasible. This solution would charge road users a toll that varies with time of day and degree of congestion. Confronted with the marginal social cost of his or her actions, each road user would make a choice, and the market for motorway space would be efficient. Here a public choice to use a market solution leaves the final decision about the degree of congestion to private choices.

THEN ...

The River Thames had a reputation in early Victorian times for sustaining many aspects of commercial trade, including fishing. However, as the nineteenth century progressed, the number of factories sited near the river and using it as a dumping ground for waste products increased greatly. The result was a decline in fish stocks, particularly in salmon, until the 1940s when the Thames became incapable of sustaining a viable fish stock.

... AND NOW

Today, the Thames supports a diverse fish stock including the occasional salmon just as it did many years ago. The river is no longer viewed as a conduit for rubbish, industrial waste and chemicals and the result is a burgeoning ecosystem including many nesting birds. Pollutants are recognized as having potential externalities and the Department for the Environment is enforcing much more stringent laws regarding dumping. The imposition of penalties has shown how the River Thames's externality problem has been reduced by government regulation.

THE ECONOMISTS: THE PUBLIC INTEREST AND PUBLIC CHOICES

James Buchanan

Externalities are solved by *public choices*. But for a time, economists lost sight of this fact. During the 1920s, Arthur Cecil Pigou (1877–1959), of Cambridge, United Kingdom, pioneered a branch of economics designed to guide public choices – *welfare economics*. Pigou, who attended school with Winston Churchill and relaxed by climbing in the Swiss Alps with some of the best mountaineers of the day, devised rules which, if followed, ensured that decisions about externalities were in the *public interest*. But the rules were not followed.

Not until the 1950s did economists develop public choice theory and explain the choices actually made by politicians and bureaucrats. A leader in this field is 1986 Nobel laureate James Buchanan (1919–), of George Mason University. Working in the inspiring setting of his mountainside summer cottage near Blacksburg, Virginia, Buchanan has led us to appreciate that the solutions to externalities adopted depend not on the public interest, but on private interests – on private costs and benefits.

Arthur Cecil Pigou

SUMMARY

Externalities

An externality is a cost or a benefit of a production or consumption activity that falls on a third party who cannot affect the scale of the activity. An external cost is the cost of producing a good or service that is not borne by its consumers but by other people. An external benefit is the benefit of consuming a good or service that does not accrue to its consumers but to other people. Externalities arise when there is no market for the benefit or cost produced from an activity.

The main external costs in our economies are the costs arising from activities which pollute the air, the land, our rivers and oceans. The main external benefits are the benefits of education and scientific research.

External costs and benefits are forms of market failure and lead to inefficiency because they are not taken into account by those who undertake the activities that produce them. There is a tendency for markets to overproduce goods and services that generate external costs, and to underproduce goods and services that generate external benefits. Government policy can be used to increase the efficiency of the market, raising social welfare, when external costs and benefits are created. (pp. 495–496)

Economics of the Environment

Popular discussion of the environment frames the debate in terms of right and wrong. In contrast, economists emphasize costs and benefits and a need to find a way to balance the two.

The demand for environmental policies has grown because incomes have grown and awareness of the connection between actions and the environment has increased.

Air pollution in the form of urban smog, air toxins, acid rain, global warming, and ozone layer depletion arise from road transport, power stations and industrial processes. Water pollution arises from dumping industrial waste, treated sewage and fertilizers in lakes and rivers and spilling oil and dumping waste in the oceans. Land pollution arises from dumping household and industrial waste and toxic products.

Externalities (environmental and others) arise when property rights are absent. Sometimes it is possible to overcome an externality by assigning a property right. If property rights exist and transactions costs are low, the Coase theorem states that private market transactions are efficient – there are no externalities. In this case, the same efficient outcome is achieved regardless of who has the property right, the polluter or the victim.

When property rights cannot be assigned, governments might overcome environmental externalities by using emission charges, uniform standards, marketable permits, or taxes. Standards are inefficient but widely used because it is difficult to identify the information needed to set efficient charges, permits or taxes.

Global externalities, such as greenhouse gases and substances that deplete the earth's ozone layer, can be overcome only by international action. Each country acting alone has insufficient incentive to act in the interest of the world as a whole. There is also a great deal of scientific uncertainty and disagreement about the effects of greenhouse gases and ozone depletion, and in the face of this uncertainty, international resolve to act is weak. The world is locked in a type of 'prisoners' dilemma' game in which it is in every country's self-interest to let other countries carry the costs of environmental policies. (pp. 496–506)

Economics of Knowledge

Knowledge is both a consumer good and a factor of production that creates external benefits. External benefits from education – passing on existing knowledge to others – arise because the skills and training equip people to interact and communicate more effectively. External benefits from research – creating new knowledge – arise because once someone has worked out how to do something, others can copy the basic idea.

Governments can use policies to encourage the efficient level of education, training and innovation to take place. Three devices are available to governments: subsidies, below-cost provision and patents.

Subsidies and public provision can achieve an efficient provision of education and training. Patents and copyrights create intellectual property rights and increase the incentive to innovate. As patents create a temporary monopoly, the cost must be balanced against the benefit of more inventive activity. (pp. 506–509)

KEY ELEMENTS

Key Terms

Coase theorem, 500
Copyright, 508
Emission charges, 501
Emission standard, 501
Externality, 495
Green tax, 503
Intellectual property rights, 508
Marginal social benefit, 501
Marginal social cost, 501
Marketable permits, 502
Patent, 508
Property right, 498
Subsidy, 506

Key Figures

Figure 20.3   Externalities and the Coase Theorem, 499
Figure 20.4   Emission Charges, 501
Figure 20.5   Marketable Pollution Permits, 502
Figure 20.6   Taxes and Pollution, 503
Figure 20.7   Efficiency in Education, 507

REVIEW QUESTIONS

1   What are externalities?

2   Why is an external cost a problem?

3   Why is an external benefit a problem?

4   What are the main air pollution problems and what are their sources?

5   What are the main economic activities that cause air pollution?

6   Why has the demand for a better environment increased?

7   What do property rights have to do with externalities?

8   State the Coase theorem. Under what conditions does the Coase theorem apply?

9   Explain why property rights assigned either to the polluter or to the victim of pollution give an efficient amount of pollution if transactions costs are low.

10   What is an emission charge and how does it work?

11   What are the pros and cons of a high, broad-based carbon tax and why don't we have such a tax?

12   What is a marketable pollution permit and how does it work?

13   How might a tax be used to overcome an external cost?

14   Why are emission standards inefficient and why are they widely used?

15   Is the efficient rate of pollution zero? Explain your answer.

16   What are the externalities problems posed by knowledge?

17   Why do we have free schooling?

18   What is a patent and how does it work?

PROBLEMS

1 A trout farmer and a pesticide maker are located next to each other on the side of a lake. The pesticide maker can dispose of waste by dumping it in the lake or by transporting it to a safe land storage place. The marginal cost of road haulage is a constant £100 a tonne. The trout farmer's profit depends on how much waste the pesticide maker dumps in the lake and is as follows:

Quantity of waste (tonnes per week)	Trout farmer's profit (pounds per week)
0	1,000
1	500
2	300
3	200
4	150
5	125
6	110
7	100

a What is the efficient amount of waste to be dumped in the lake?

b If the trout farmer owns the lake, how much waste will be dumped and how much will the pesticide maker pay to the farmer for each tonne dumped?

c If the pesticide maker owns the lake, how much waste will be dumped and how much will the farmer pay to the factory to rent space on the lake?

2 Using the information given in Problem 1, suppose that no one owns the lake, and that the government introduces a pollution charge.

a What is the price per tonne of waste dumped that will achieve an efficient outcome?

b Explain the connection between the answer to this Problem and the answer to Problem 1.

3 Using the information given in Problem 1, suppose that no one owns the lake, and that the government issues marketable pollution permits to both the farmer and the factory. They may each dump equal amounts of waste in the lake and the total that may be dumped is the efficient amount.

a What is the quantity that may be dumped in the lake?

b What is the market price of a permit? Who buys and who sells?

c What is the connection between the answer to this Problem and the answers to Problems 1 and 2?

4 The marginal cost of educating a student is £5,000 a year and is constant. The marginal private benefit schedule is as follows:

Quantity of education (student–years)	Marginal private benefit (pounds per student–year)
0	10,000
1,000	5,000
2,000	3,000
3,000	2,000
4,000	1,500
5,000	1,250
6,000	1,100
7,000	1,000

a With no government involvement in education and if the colleges are competitive, how many students are enrolled in college and what is the annual tuition fee?

b Suppose the external benefit from education is £4,000 per student–year and is constant. If the government provides the efficient amount of education, how many college places does it offer and what is the annual tuition fee?

5 Go back and read the article and analysis in *Reading Between the Lines* on pp. 510–511 and then answer these questions:

a What is the impact on drivers' marginal private cost of introducing tighter emission standards compared to an efficient road pricing scheme?

b What information would you need in order to be able to identify a price for road use in a road pricing scheme

c Which method of reducing congestion and its associated pollution is better and why?

CHAPTER

21

INEQUALITY, REDISTRIBUTION AND WELFARE

After studying this chapter you will be able to:

◆ Describe inequality in income and wealth

◆ Explain why wealth inequality is greater than income inequality

◆ Explain how economic inequality arises

◆ Explain the effects of taxes and cash benefits on economic incquality

◆ Explain the effects of health care as a benefit in kind on economic inequality

◆ Compare different forms of health-care provision

◆ Compare different views about fairness in the distribution of income and wealth

WALK THROUGH THE LEAFY SUBURBS OF ANY MAJOR CITY AND YOU WILL find plenty of evidence OF conspicuous consumption, clear signs that some people are very rich. Walk down some private road and you'll find 10-bedroom mansions for families of four, immaculate lawns tended by gardeners, heated swimming pools and several double garages. Outside the garages there'll be not one, not two, but three or more cars – a Porsche for fun, a 4-wheel drive Land Rover for shopping and a large, powerful BMW as a family saloon car. It's what people wish for when they play the National Lottery. Walk into the centre of the city and you'll pass people who are cold and miserable huddled in doorways. You'll see the homeless – living in cardboard boxes, unemployed and begging for change – owning nothing more than the clothes they stand in. ◆ Why are some people exceedingly rich while others are very poor and own almost nothing? Are the rich getting richer and

Riches and Rags

the poor poorer? Does the information we have about the inequality of income and wealth paint an accurate picture or a misleading one? How do taxes, social security benefits and the health service influence economic inequality? What is an equitable distribution of economic well-being?

◆ ◆ ◆ ◆ In this chapter, we study economic inequality – its extent, its sources and its potential remedies. We look at taxes and government policies that redistribute incomes, and study their effects on economic inequality. We also study the different ways in which health care can be delivered and its effects on economic efficiency and equality. Let's begin by looking at some facts about economic inequality.

Economic Inequality in the United Kingdom

We can study inequality by looking at the distribution of income or wealth. A family's income is the amount that it receives in a given period of time. A family's wealth is the value of the things it owns at a point in time. We can measure family income inequality by looking at the percentage of total income received by a given percentage of households. We measure wealth inequality by looking at the percentage of total wealth owned by a given percentage of individuals, as household figures are not recorded.

In 1994, the average income in the United Kingdom was £369 a week. But there was considerable inequality around that average. The poorest 20 per cent received only 3 per cent of total income.

Their incomes were just one-fifth of the average at £79 a week. The next poorest 20 per cent received just 6 per cent of total income. But the richest 20 per cent received over 50 per cent of total income, their incomes being more than twice the average at £854 a week.

The wealth distribution shows even greater inequality. Average individual wealth in 1994 was £50,000. But the range was enormous. The wealthiest 10 per cent of the population owned 48 per cent of the nation's wealth and the wealthiest 25 per cent owned a staggering 72 per cent of the nation's wealth. The poorest half of the population owned just 8 per cent of the nation's wealth.

Lorenz Curves

Income and wealth distributions are shown in Fig. 21.1. Part (a) of the table divides households into five income groups, called *quintiles*, ranging

---

FIGURE 21.1

Lorenz Curves for Income and Wealth

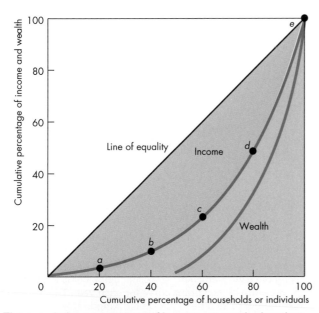

Part (a)	Households		Income	
	Percentage	Cumulative percentage	Percentage	Cumulative percentage
a Lowest 20	20	3	3
b Second 20	40	6	9
c Third 20	60	15	24
d Fourth 20	80	25	49
e Highest 20	100	51	100

Part (b)	Individuals		Wealth	
	Percentage	Cumulative percentage	Percentage	Cumulative percentage
a' Lowest 50	50	8	8
b' Next 25	75	20	28
c' Next 10	85	24	52
d' Next 5	90	12	64
e' Next 8	98	12	76
f' Highest 2	100	24	100

The cumulative percentages of income are graphed against the cumulative percentage of households. If income were distributed equally, each 20 per cent of households would have 20 per cent of the income – the line of equality. Points *a* to *e* on the Lorenz curve for income correspond to the rows in part (a) of the table. The Lorenz curve for wealth plots the cumulative percentage of wealth against the cumulative percentage of adults from part (b) of the table. The distribution of wealth is more unequal than the distribution of income.

Sources: Income: Central Statistical Office, *Economic Trends, 1995,* London, HMSO. Wealth: Inland Revenue, *Inland Revenue Statistics, 1995,* London, HMSO.

from the income of the lowest 20 per cent (row *a*) to the income of the top 20 per cent (row *e*). It shows the percentage share of total income taken by each of these income groups. For example, row *a* tells us that the lowest quintile of households received 3 per cent of total income. The table also shows the *cumulative* percentages of households and original income. Original income is income before any taxes are deducted and before any government benefits are received. For example, row *b* tells us that the lowest two quintiles (lowest 40 per cent) received 9 per cent of total income (3 per cent for the lowest quintile and 6 per cent for the next lowest). The data on cumulative income shares are illustrated by a Lorenz curve. A **Lorenz curve** graphs the cumulative percentage of income against the cumulative percentage of households.

If income was distributed equally to every household, the cumulative percentages of income received by the cumulative percentages of households would fall along the straight line labelled 'Line of equality' in Fig. 21.1. The actual distribution of income is shown by the Lorenz curve labelled 'Income'.

The Lorenz curve shows the degree of inequality. The closer the Lorenz curve is to the line of equality, the more equal is the distribution. Figure 21.1 also shows a Lorenz curve for wealth, based on the distribution in part (b) of the table. As you can see from the two Lorenz curves, the Lorenz curve for wealth is much farther away from the line of equality than the Lorenz curve for income. As the data for income are based on households and the data for wealth are based on individuals, the two Lorenz curves for the United Kingdom are not directly comparable. For example, an unemployed 21 year old may have little personal wealth but be living in a household with a high income. Despite this, the two Lorenz curves show the basic pattern found in most market economies – the distribution of wealth is much more unequal than the distribution of income.

Inequality Over Time

The Lorenz curve picture of inequality can be converted into a measure of inequality called the Gini coefficient. This measure lets us look at how inequality changes over time. The Gini coefficient is calculated by dividing the value of the area under the Lorenz curve (the blue shaded area in Fig. 21.1), by the value of the area under the line of total equality (the blue shaded area plus the green

shaded area). The closer the Gini coefficient is to 0, the closer the distribution is to total equality. The closer the Gini coefficient is to 1, the closer the distribution is to total inequality.

Changes in the distribution of income in the United Kingdom are shown in Fig. 21.2. You can see that inequality (the value of Gini coefficient) was falling between 1961 and 1968, and between 1972 and 1976. Inequality in incomes increased between 1968 and 1972, and has continued to rise since 1977 without falling.

Who are Rich and Who Are Poor?

What are the characteristics of poor and rich households? The lowest-income household in the United Kingdom today is likely to comprise a retired

---

FIGURE 21.2

UK Income Inequality: 1961–1991

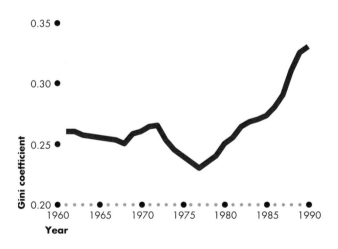

Changes in the distribution of income can be measured using the Gini coefficient. The Gini coefficient is a numerical measure of the Lorenz curve for each year. The distribution of income in the United Kingdom became more equal in two periods in the early 1960s and 1970s. Inequality in income rose in the late 1960s and has been steadily increasing since 1977.

Source: A. Goodman and S. Webb, For richer, for poorer: the changing distribution of income in the UK, 1961–1991, *Fiscal Studies,* 1994 Vol. 15 (4), 31.

woman over 75 years of age, with no qualifications, who lives alone somewhere in Wales. The highest-income household in the United Kingdom today is likely to comprise two adults aged between 30 and 50, both graduates with skilled jobs, living together with two children somewhere in the South East.

These snapshot profiles are the extremes in Fig. 21.3. The figure shows how incomes vary around the mean household income of £369 a week by different characteristics. The mean (average) income is higher than the most commonly occuring income because it is inflated by a few households with very high incomes. Figure 21.3 illustrates the importance of household size, the age, education and economic status of the householder, and the region of residence, in influencing the size of a household's income.

The households most likely to be on low incomes are usually those with just one adult. This person might be a pensioner living alone, or a single parent with children. He, or more likely she, is probably unemployed or retired, has few qualifications and is likely to be over the age of 65 years. There are also several regions with a higher concentration of low-income households. Many of these are in areas where traditional industries such as mining, ship-building, textiles and steel manufacture have declined.

Poverty

Households at the low end of the income distribution are so poor that they are considered to be living in poverty. **Poverty** is a state in which a household's income is too low for it to be able to buy the quantities of food, shelter and clothing that are deemed necessary. Poverty is a relative concept: so poverty in one country might be considered an acceptable standard of living in another. Because poverty is relative, it is necessary to decide on a *poverty line* – an imaginary benchmark which distinguishes poor people from everyone else. There are two widely used definitions of the poverty line:

1. People living on an income less than 50 per cent of average income

2. People living on an income at or below the current means-tested benefit level.

FIGURE 21.3

The Distribution of Income by Selected Household Characteristics in 1992

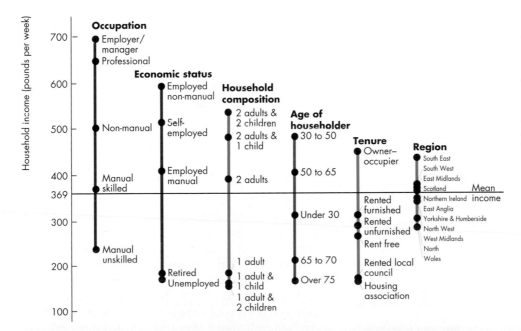

The figure shows that being a single adult household or one parent family, being unemployed or aged over 75 are common characteristics of poor households in the United Kingdom. You are also likely to be poor if you are employed as a manual worker, if you are living in unfurnished accommodation, or if you live in Wales.

Source: Central Statistical Office, *Family Spending: A Report on the 1994/95 Family Expenditure Survey, 1995*, London, HMSO.

According to government figures, 11.4 million people in the United Kingdom had an income below 50 per cent of average income in 1992 – one-fifth of the population. Using the second definition, 13.6 million people – 24 per cent of the population – had an income at or below the level of income support in 1992. There are significant differences in poverty rates among countries – even within the European Union. Figure 21.4 shows the latest comparable figures using a poverty line of 50 per cent of national average household expenditure rather than income. The UK rate is in the middle of the range. The highest rates are in those countries with low national incomes and a high dependency on the low-wage agricultural sector.

Looking back at the factors which determine low income in Fig. 21.3, we can see that within any one country, poverty results from two main factors –

limited access to high-paid employment and the extra costs associated with having children – which may vary through someone's lifetime. There is more poverty among women and racial minorities because they tend to have less well-paid jobs. Women still take a larger share of domestic responsibilities, leading to more time out of work and lower pensions when they retire.

REVIEW

◆ Income and wealth are distributed unequally, but wealth is more unequal than income.

◆ The distribution of income became more equal in two short periods in the early 1960s and 1970s but has become steadily more unequal since 1977.

◆ The main influences on a household's income are: family size, economic status, age of householder, occupation and related skill, and region of residence. Gender and race are also contributing factors.

Factor Prices, Endowments and Choices

A household's income depends on the prices of the factors of production supplied, the endowment of the factors owned by the household, and the choices the household members make. To what extent do differences in income arise from differences in factor prices and from differences in the quantities of factors that people supply?

Labour Market and Wages

Wages are the biggest single source of income. To what extent do variations in wage rates account for the unequal distribution of income? Figure 21.5 helps answer this question. It sets out the median real wage rate per hour for men for different occupational groups. It is clear that professional and managerial workers earn consistently more than skilled and unskilled workers – and these differentials are maintained over time. Professional workers

FIGURE 21.4

Poverty in the European Union

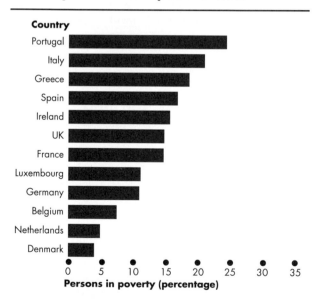

The figure shows comparable EU poverty rates for the latest available year, 1988. The poverty line is 50 percent of national average household expenditure adjusted for family size. Poverty rates were highest in Portugal, Italy, Greece, Spain and Ireland in 1988. These countries tend to have lower national income and are highly dependent on agricultural output – a low wage sector.

Source: Eurostat, *Poverty Statistics in the Late 1980s: research based on microdata*, Luxembourg, Office for Official Publications of the EC, 1994.

FIGURE 21.5

Growth in Occupational Wage Rates

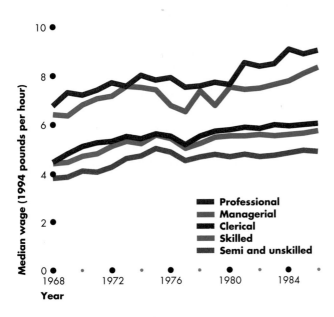

The figure shows the growth in the median real wage per hour for men in different occupational groups over time. In the late 1960s and early 1970s, the wages of lower-paid workers increased faster than those of higher-paid workers. After 1977, the wages of professional and managerial workers increased faster than the wages of lower-paid workers, making overall income inequality increase.

Source: A. Gosling, S. Machin and C. Meghir, 'What has happened to men's wages since the mid-1960s?', *Fiscal Studies*, 1994, Vol. 15 (4), p.74.

earn about twice as much as unskilled and skilled workers. Using the log scale allows us to compare the slopes of the different lines across time. The steeper the slope, the faster the rate of growth in income. In the late 1960s and early 1970s, wages were growing faster for the lowest-paid occupational groups. But by the 1980s, the wages of professional and managerial workers were growing faster than the wages of skilled and unskilled workers. One of the things that wage rate differences reflect is differences in skills or human capital, as we saw in Chapter 15. So one explanation of the faster rate of growth of wages for professional and managerial workers may be the increasing amount of training and education undertaken by these workers.

Looking back at Fig. 21.2, you can see that changes in the rate of growth of wages between occupational groups explains the overall changes in income inequality. During the period when wages of the lower-paid occupational groups were growing faster than those of the higher-paid groups, overall income inequality was falling. After 1977, the incomes of higher-paid occupational groups rose faster than those of the lower-paid groups, so overall income inequality started to rise.

Differences in wage rates are one source of income inequality. Differences in endowments of factors of production are another.

Distribution of Endowments

There is a large amount of variety in a household's endowments of abilities. Physical and mental differences (some inherited, some learned) are such an obvious feature of human life that they hardly need mentioning. These differences across individuals have a normal, or bell-shaped distribution – like the distribution of heights or weights.

The distribution of individual ability across individuals is a major source of inequality in income and wealth. But it is not the only source. If it were, the distributions of income and wealth would look like the bell-shaped curve that describes the distribution of heights. In fact, these distributions are skewed towards high incomes and look like the curve in Fig. 21.6. This figure shows income on the horizontal axis and the percentage of households receiving each income on the vertical axis. The median income is £325 per week. The most common income – called the modal income – is less than the median income and is £130. The mean income – also called the average income – is greater than the median income and is £369. A skewed distribution like the one shown in Fig. 21.6 is one in which many more people have incomes below the average than above it, a large number of people have very low incomes, and a small number of people have very high incomes. The distribution of (non-human) wealth has a similar shape to the distribution of income but is even more skewed.

The skewed shape of the distribution of income cannot be explained by the bell-shaped distribution of individual abilities. It results from the choices that people make.

FIGURE 21.6

The Distribution of Income

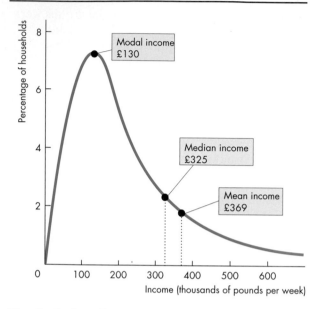

The distribution of income is unequal and is not symmetric around the mean. There are many more people below the mean than above the mean. Also, the distribution has a long thin upper tail representing a small number of people earning very large incomes.

Choices

A household's income and wealth depend partly on the choices that its members make. People choose how much of each of the factors of production they own to supply. They also choose whether to babysit or look for a job in a bank, whether to put their savings in the bank or in shares. We are going to discover that the choices people make exaggerate the differences among households. Their choices make the distribution of income more unequal than the distribution of abilities and they make the distribution of income skewed.

Wages and the Supply of Labour   Other things remaining the same, the quantity of labour that a person supplies increases as that person's wage rate increases. A person who has a low wage rate chooses to work fewer hours than a person who has a high wage rate. Compare two people, one whose wage rate is £5 an hour and another whose wage rate is £10 an hour. If each person works the same

number of hours, one has an income that is twice as much as the other. But a higher wage rate can induce a greater number of hours of work. So if the person whose wage is £10 an hour chooses to work more hours, she earns an income that exceeds twice the income of the other person.

Thus because the quantity of labour supplied increases as the wage rate increases, the distribution of income is more unequal than the distribution of hourly wages. It is also skewed. People whose wage rates are below the average tend to work fewer hours than the average, and their incomes bunch together much below the average. People whose wage rates are above the average tend to work more hours than the average, and their incomes stretch out above the average.

Saving and Bequests   Another choice that results in unequal distributions in income and wealth is the decision to save and make bequests. A *bequest* is a gift from one generation to the next. The higher a family's income, the more that family tends to save and bequeath to later generations. By making a bequest, a family can spread consumption across the generations. One common way in which people make bequests is to provide educational resources for their children and grandchildren.

Saving and bequests are not inevitably a source of increased inequality. If a family saves to redistribute an uneven income over the life cycle and enable consumption to be constant, the act of saving decreases the degree of inequality. If a lucky generation that has a high income saves a large amount and makes a bequest to a generation that is unlucky, this act of saving also decreases the degree of inequality. But there are two important features of bequests that do make inter-generational transfers of wealth a source of increased inequality:

◆   Debts cannot be bequeathed

◆   Mating is assortative

Debts Cannot be Bequeathed   Although a person may die with debts that exceed assets – with negative wealth – debts cannot be forced on to other family members. Because a zero inheritance is the smallest inheritance that anyone can receive, bequests can only add to future generations' wealth and income potential.

The vast majority of people inherit nothing or a very small amount. A few people inherit enormous fortunes. As a result, bequests make the distribution of income and wealth not only more unequal than the distribution of ability and job skills but also more persistent. A family that is poor in one generation is more likely to be poor in the next. A family that is wealthy in one generation is likely to be wealthy in the next. Even so, there is also a tendency for income and wealth to converge, across generations, to the average. One feature of human behaviour that slows down convergence and makes inequalities persist is assortative mating.

Assortative Mating *Assortative mating* is the tendency for people to marry within their own socioeconomic class – like attracts like. Although there is a good deal of folklore that 'opposites attract', perhaps such Cinderella tales appeal to us because they are so rare in reality. Marriage partners tend to have similar socioeconomic characteristics. Wealthy individuals seek wealthy partners. The consequence of assortative mating is that inherited wealth becomes more unequally distributed.

R E V I E W

◆ Income inequality arises from unequal wage rates, unequal endowments and choices.

◆ Wage rates are unequal because of differences in skills or human capital.

◆ Endowments are unequal and have a bell-shaped distribution.

◆ The distribution of income is skewed because people with higher wage rates tend to work longer hours and so make a disproportionately larger income.

◆ The distribution of wealth is skewed because people with higher incomes save more, bequeath more to the next generation and marry people with similar wealth.

We've now described the extent of inequality and examined some of the reasons it exists. Next we're going to see how government policy modifies the outcome of the market economy and changes the distributions of income and wealth.

Income Redistribution

Governments use three main types of policies to redistribute income and relieve poverty. They are:

◆ Income taxes
◆ Transfer payments
◆ Goods and services in kind

Income Taxes

The scale of redistribution of income achieved through income taxes depends on the form that the income taxes take. Income taxes may be progressive, regressive, or proportional. A **progressive income tax** is one that taxes income at a marginal rate which increases with the level of income. The term 'marginal', applied to income tax rates, refers to the fraction of the last pound earned that is paid in taxes. A **regressive income tax** is one that taxes income at a marginal rate which decreases with the level of income. A **proportional income tax** (also called a *flat-rate income tax*) is one that taxes income at a constant rate regardless of the level of income.

The income tax rates that apply in the United Kingdom are progressive. The poorest households pay no income tax as everyone is allowed to earn a certain amount before paying any tax at all. Middle-income households pay 20 per cent initially and then 24 per cent of each additional pound they earn, and richer households pay 40 per cent of each additional pound earned above the middle-income tax band.

Transfer Payments

Transfer payments redistribute income by making direct payments to people in the lower part of the income distribution. In 1995, the UK government paid out £130 billion in transfer payments. The main types of payments are:

◆ Income support payments
◆ Unemployment benefits
◆ State pensions

Income Support Payments The UK government uses two main forms of income support payments to raise household incomes and reduce poverty. Family credit helps families where at least one person is in work, but the family wage is very low. Income support helps people whose incomes are low because they are not working. These people may also be claiming other sorts of income support payments such as incapacity benefit – a benefit for those who cannot work because of a disability. In 1996, income support was £46.50 a week for a single person over 25 years old. The average amount claimed under family credit was £51.06 a week.

Unemployment Benefits   The job seekers allowance is a payment for individuals who have lost their jobs involuntarily and have no other main source of income. It is available for six months and is awarded on the condition that individuals register as unemployed and are actively seeking work. They may also be required to attend training courses and attend for interviews for suitable jobs. The allowance was £47.90 for those aged over 25 in 1997.

State Pensions   State pensions are a major component of transfer payments. All European economies operate a system whereby the current taxpayers pay for the pensions of the current elderly people. In the United Kingdom state pensions are a contributory benefit – you must have made sufficient National Insurance tax contributions to be eligible. The full basic pension was £61.15 a week in 1996 and was paid to 7 million people, 70 per cent of people of pensionable age. Many women do not get a full state pension because part-time work generates insufficient contributions.

So what is the impact of transfer payments? They certainly relieve poverty because they raise the income of the poorest people. But do they remove poverty? The answer depends on how the poverty line is defined and the value of the benefits. If we define the poverty line as 50 per cent of average UK income, then a single person needed at least £65 a week after housing costs to stay above the poverty line in 1995. The income support paid, after housing costs, was just £36.80 – not enough to remove poverty with this definition.

Benefits in Kind

A great deal of redistribution takes place in most European countries through the provision of benefits in kinds. These are the goods and services provided by the government at prices below marginal cost.

The taxpayers who consume these goods and services receive a transfer in kind from the taxpayers who do not consume them. The two most important areas in which this form of redistribution takes place are education – from nursery care through to university – and health care.

In the United Kingdom, 50 per cent of government expenditure is on benefits in kind – 24 per cent on the National Health Service (NHS), 21 per cent on education, the remainder on other services. The NHS provides almost all health care free at the point of demand. Primary and secondary education are provided free for all children in the United Kingdom. Vouchers are available to help parents pay for the cost of nursery care and, although student grants are being withdrawn, the government still subsidizes the cost of university education by paying tuition fees for most undergraduate students.

Because the NHS and free basic education ensure that everyone can gain access to good-quality health care and education, benefits in kind help to reduce inequality in health status and basic human capital. They also help to reduce inequality in income. Although rich households receive the value of the benefits in kind as well as poor households, rich households pay more in tax – reducing income inequality. Richer households often pay for these services privately, without any compensatory tax rebate.

Take-up and Targeting Benefits

Up to 30 per cent of people eligible for income support and family credit benefits do not claim them, whereas virtually everyone eligible for child benefit claims this benefit. Why are these *take-up* rates so different? Child benefit, the NHS and primary and secondary schooling are universal benefits, available to anyone without a means test or an eligibility test. As a result, there is no stigma attached to claiming these benefits and take-up is high. Other benefits are means tested on income. Only those people with very low incomes and wealth are eligible. Means testing involves filling in complex forms and generates a high level of stigma for recipients. This stops many people claiming and so take-up is poor.

If government wants to redistribute income efficiently, it needs to achieve a high level of take-up. So why are so many benefits means tested rather than universal benefits? The answer lies in the problem of *targeting* and its opportunity cost.

Universal benefits are paid to everyone, rich and poor. The high level of take-up has an opportunity cost – the waste involved in taxing the rich to pay benefits back to the rich. Means-tested benefits have low take-up but they reach only the poor – targeting is high.

Because the NHS is such an important benefit, we'll study it more fully later in this chapter. But before doing so, let's bring all the different methods of redistribution together and look at their impact on incomes.

The Impact on Income Redistribution

A household's income in the absence of government redistribution is called *original income* and a household's income after taxes and benefits is called *final income*. The tax and benefit system works as a redistributive mechanism, making final income more equally distributed than original income. Let's look at the impact on income distribution of the UK tax and benefit system.

Figure 21.7 shows the impact of taxes and benefits for the five quintile income groups, from bottom fifth (the poorest) to top fifth (the richest). You can see that the value of cash benefits received by the poorest group is much higher than the value of cash benefits received by the richest group. On average, the poorest fifth received £4,500 of cash benefits each year, while the richest fifth received only £1,000. The richest group receives a small amount of benefit because some are universally available. The impact on income of benefits in kind – the NHS and education – is more evenly distributed across all income groups, but the poorest groups still receive more in total. Benefits in kind are strongly progressive as they are worth over 70 per cent of post-tax income to the poorest fifth, but just 7 per cent for the richest fifth.

Direct taxes also have a strong effect on the distribution of income. Figure 21.7 shows that the richest fifth pay £10,000 in direct taxes on income each year and the poorest fifth pay just £800 each year. Indirect taxes on expenditure have a less dramatic redistributive effect because the poorest groups spend proportionately more of their total income on goods. Overall, the net impact on income distribution as shown in Fig. 21.7 is to redistribute income from the top 40 per cent to the bottom 40 per cent, with no net gain to the middle 20 per cent.

FIGURE 21.7

The Effect of Taxes and Benefits on the Distribution of Income

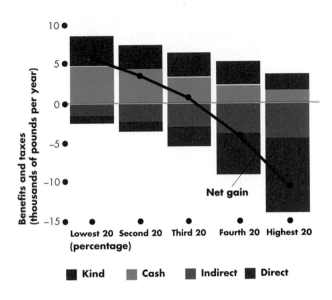

The impact of taxes and benefits overall is to redistribute income from the richest (top) 40 per cent to the poorest (bottom) 40 per cent. The poorest groups receive more income as cash benefits and benefits in kind than the richest groups and the poorest groups pay less tax than the richest groups. Cash benefits and direct taxes on income have the strongest redistributive effects on income.

Source: Central Statistical Office, *Social Trends, 1996*, London, HMSO, Fig.5.13.

The Leaky Bucket

An economist, Arthur Okun, once described the process of redistributing income as like trying to transfer water from one barrel to another with a leaky bucket[1]. Some of the water – income – is always lost in the process as it spills through the holes in the bucket. The more we try to improve social welfare by increasing equity, the more we will lose social welfare by reducing efficiency. There is a trade-off between equity and efficiency.

---

[1] The idea comes from a book by Arthur Okun, *Equality and Efficiency: The Big Tradeoff*, Washington DC, Brookings Institution, 1975.

So why does the redistribution bucket leak? Any redistribution policy requires the use of skilled labour and other scarce resources. The bigger the redistributive policy, the greater is the opportunity cost of running it. Redistributive policies also involve taxing richer people to pay benefits to poorer people. This reduces the income of richer people so they work and save less, resulting in less output and consumption for everybody – rich and poor.

Another form of leakage is the deadweight loss of a tax. A lower wage (as a result of increasing income tax) reduces the opportunity cost of leisure and leads to a substitution towards leisure – a reduction in work hours. (You can review this argument by looking back to Fig. 8.12 in Chapter 8, p.189). The substitution effect leads to an inefficient choice and a reduction in welfare.

A final source of inefficiency in most benefit systems is the benefit trap. This has been the main reason for reforming the benefits system in Australia, the United Kingdom and the United States. Let's look at benefit traps in more detail.

The Benefit Trap   The benefit system has been criticized for creating disincentives to work by catching people in the *benefit trap*. Benefit traps arise when people who are receiving benefits do not think it is worthwhile taking up employment or working longer hours. If people lose £1 of benefit for every extra £1 that they earn – a *withdrawal rate* of 100 per cent – they will be no better off. They are facing a marginal tax rate of 100 per cent, much higher than all other taxpayers! This problem is unavoidable if benefits are withdrawn as people earn additional income.

There are two main types of benefit traps – the unemployment trap and the poverty trap. In the unemployment trap, people make decisions based on the replacement ratio – the ratio of the expected wage to the benefits received. If the expected wage is only marginally higher than the level of unemployment benefit, the rational choice for most people is to remain unemployed. In the poverty trap, people are already in low-paid work but still receiving benefit. They may want to work longer hours to earn an extra £10, but they will pay tax on the extra £10 and lose up to £10 of benefit. As a result, they are facing a marginal tax rate in excess of 100 per cent! The rational choice is not to work more hours.

Reform Proposals

There are two broad ways in which the problem of the benefit traps can be tackled. They are:

◆ Piecemeal reforms

◆ Radical reform

Piecemeal Reforms   For practical reasons, most reforms that actually get implemented are piecemeal. They are a response to the most pressing problems of the day. The process of reform in the United Kingdom began in 1988 when the Social Security Act of 1986 was implemented. At the time, some people faced marginal tax rates of up to 120 per cent in the poverty trap. Although the number of people facing such extreme marginal tax rates was not high – about 100,000 – the idea that anyone could earn an extra pound and actually be worse off as a result was unacceptable.

The UK reforms removed the worst aspect of the benefit trap by introducing a simple mechanism. Benefit changes for people who are already receiving benefit, but work extra hours, are now calculated on their income after tax, rather than income before tax. This has eliminated marginal tax rates in excess of 100 per cent. But many more people now face extremely high marginal tax rates of between 60 and 90 per cent.

Radical Reform   A more radical reform proposal is a negative income tax. A **negative income tax** gives every household a *guaranteed annual income* and decreases the household's benefit at a specified *withdrawal rate* as the household's original income increases. For example, suppose the guaranteed annual income is £10,000 and the withdrawal rate and the income tax rate are set at 25 per cent. A household with no earnings receives the £10,000 guaranteed income. A household with earnings of £8,000 loses 25 per cent of that amount – £2,000 – and receives a total income of £16,000 (£8,000 earnings plus £10,000 guaranteed income minus £2,000 benefit loss). A household earning £40,000 receives an income of £40,000 (£40,000 earnings plus £10,000 guaranteed income minus £10,000 benefit loss). Such a household is at the break-even income level. Households with earnings exceeding £40,000 pay more in taxes than they receive in benefits.

A negative income tax is illustrated and compared with our current arrangements in Fig. 21.8.

FIGURE 21.8

Comparing the Current Benefit System and a Negative Income Tax

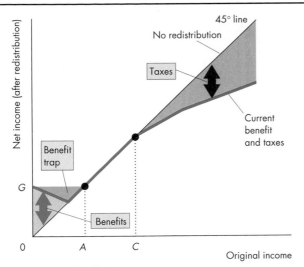

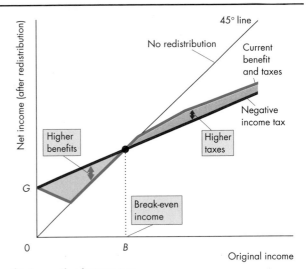

(a) Current redistribution arrangements

(b) A negative income tax

Part (a) shows the current redistribution arrangements – the blue line. Benefits of *G* are paid to those with no income. As incomes increase from zero to *A*, benefits are withdrawn, *lowering* income after redistribution below *G* and creating a welfare trap – the grey triangle. As incomes increase from *A* to *C*, there is no redistribution. As incomes increase above *C*, income taxes are paid at successively higher rates.

In part (b), a negative income tax gives a guaranteed annual income of *G* and decreases benefits at the same rate as the tax rate on incomes. The red line shows how market incomes translate into income after redistribution. Households with market incomes below *B*, the break-even income, receive net benefits. Those with market incomes above *B* pay net taxes.

In both parts of the figure, the horizontal axis measures *original income* – that is, income *before* taxes are paid and benefits received – and the vertical axis measures net income *after* taxes are paid and benefits received. The 45° line shows the hypothetical case of 'no redistribution'.

Part (a) shows the current redistribution arrangements – the blue line. Benefits of *G* are paid to those with no income. As original incomes increase from zero to *A*, benefits are withdrawn, *lowering* net income below *G*. This arrangement creates a *benefit trap* shown as the grey triangle. Over the income range *A* to *C*, each additional pound of original income increases net income by a pound. At incomes greater than *C*, income taxes are paid at successively higher rates, and net income is smaller than original income.

Part (b) shows the negative income tax. The guaranteed annual income is *G* and the break-even income is *B*. Households with original incomes

below *B* receive a net benefit (blue area) and those with incomes above *B* pay taxes (red area). You can see why such a scheme is called a negative income tax. Every household receives a guaranteed minimum income and every household pays a tax on its earnings – losing benefits is like paying a tax – but households with incomes below the break-even income receive more than they pay and so, in total, pay a negative amount of tax.

A negative income tax removes the benefit trap (the grey triangle) and gives greater encouragement to low-income households to seek additional employment, even at a low wage. It also overcomes many of the other problems arising from existing benefit systems.

So why don't we have a negative income tax scheme? The main reason is cost. Assume the guaranteed annual income that puts a household comprising two adults and two children on the official *poverty* line is £6,000. With a withdrawal rate equal to 20 per cent – a rate similar to the income tax rate for most households – the break-even income is £31,000. This income is much higher than the average income and the taxes on households with incomes above this level would increase substantially (as shown in Fig. 21.8b).

It has been suggested that a small level of guaranteed annual income supported by the existing system of means-tested benefit could improve both equity and the efficiency of the existing system. A computerized negative income tax system would contain details of everyone's income on a database – rich and poor. The system could be used to identify who should be receiving means-tested benefits and these could be sent out automatically, avoiding the stigma of claiming. The guaranteed income received would be negligible, but take-up and targeting of existing benefits would be radically improved.

R E V I E W

◆ Government redistributes income in the United Kingdom by using transfer payments, income taxes and benefit payments – and benefits in kind goods and services provided below cost.

◆ The overall impact of the tax and benefit system is progressive, redistributing income from the richest 40 per cent to the poorest 40 per cent.

◆ Increasing equity implies a reduction in efficiency as benefit traps create disincentives to work.

◆ Welfare reform aims to reduce the problems of benefit traps.

Health and the cost of health care are major sources of inequality. We are now going to study the economics of health care, public provision of health care to reduce inequality and how market mechanisms can be used to improve the efficiency of public health services.

Health-care Provision

Health-care provision is one of the most widely used methods of improving redistribution in European economies – but at a cost. Rising health-care costs and increasing government expenditure have led many economists to consider the alternative – a private market in health care. But would we be better off with private health-care systems modelled on the United States? Is a national health service the best method of producing health care? We'll try to answer these questions by comparing the benefits of different systems in terms of equity and efficiency. Before that we need to look at the different systems and the problem of rising health-care costs.

Health-care Systems

There are three basic types of health-care systems:

1. Mainly private finance and private supply
2. Mainly government finance and private supply
3. Mainly government finance and government supply

The private finance and supply system is one where people buy and sell health-care in health-care markets, like in the United States. Many European countries like Belgium, France, Germany, Italy and the Netherlands have a system of private suppliers, financed by government expenditure rather than private individuals. Finally, countries like the United Kingdom, Greece and Portugal have national health services, while Scandinavian countries have local government health services. These are all mainly government financed and supplied. All of these systems have some mix of private and government provision.

So which of these systems is better? Which system will maximize social welfare? The answer lies in our model of market failure and efficiency and in the preferences of voters for equity. The best system is the most efficient system which also maximizes voters' preferences for equity. We can start by comparing systems in terms of the cost of producing health care.

Health-care Costs

Health-care costs have increased more rapidly than consumer prices on the average in most developed countries as shown in Fig. 21.9. The percentage growth in health-care costs relative to other prices is highest in the United States, Ireland and Canada. There appears to be a cost crisis in health care in these countries, and there is evidence of rising real costs in many other

FIGURE 21.9

Health-care Costs

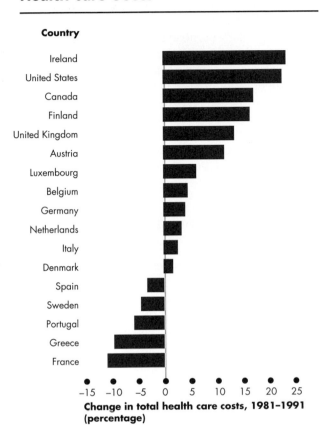

Health care costs have increased relative to consumer prices in most developed countries. The percentage growth in health care costs between 1981 and 1991 is highest in the United States, Ireland and Canada, and positive in many other European countries.

Source: T. Besley and M. Gouveia, 'Alternative systems of health care provision', Economic Policy, October 1994, 19.

European countries. Why has this happened? First, health care is labour-intensive with limited scope for labour-saving technological change. Health-care labour costs generally increase at a faster rate than do prices. Because there is limited scope for labour-saving changes higher labour costs lead to higher prices for final health-care services.

Second, the main effect of any technological change in health care is to improve the quality of the service. For example, the application of computer technology and advances in drugs have broadened the range of conditions that can be treated. Costs rise steadily as we constantly improve quality and use new technologies to treat previously untreatable conditions.

Figure 21.10 shows the market for health care. Initially, the demand curve is D_0, the supply curve is S_0, the quantity is Q_0 and the price is P_0. Increasing incomes and advances in medical technology increase the demand for health-care services and the demand curve shifts rightward to D_1. Technological advances also increase supply, but by a smaller amount than the increase in demand because some factors have worked to decrease supply. One of these factors is the increasing wage rates of health-care workers and another is the

FIGURE 21.10

The Market for Health Care

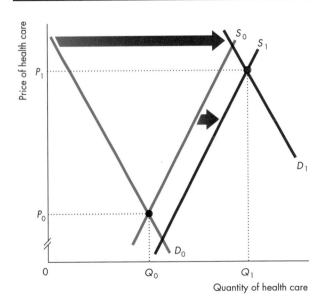

Quantity of health care

Initially (say in 1980), demand was D_0, supply was S_0, the quantity was Q_0, and the price was P_0. Increasing incomes and technological advances that expand the range of conditions that can be treated increase demand and shift the demand curve rightward to D_1. Advancing technology also increases supply but increasing wages and more costly equipment and drugs counteract this increase in supply. The result is that the supply curve rightward to S_1. The quantity increases by a small amount to Q_1 and the price increases steeply to P_1.

increasing cost of health-care technologies. The net effect of the positive and negative influences on supply over time is a rightward shift in the supply curve to S_1. The quantity of health care increases to Q_1– a relatively small increase – and the price rises to P_1– a relatively large increase.

The forces at work that produce the changes shown in Fig. 21.10 do not appear to be temporary, and appear to work in all health-care systems. So do we have any reason to believe that introducing more competition and private provision can improve health-care efficiency in Europe. Or will introducing more government finance improve efficiency in North America? Let's look at our model of market failure to see if there are any reasons to prefer one system over the other in terms of efficiency.

Private Health Care and Insurance

Everyone demands health care at some point in their life, but the people with the largest demands are the elderly, the very young and the chronically sick. The costs for most people are high and the frequency of use is low. Uncertainty about your future income makes planning health-care expenditure difficult, so in a purely private market system most people choose to finance their health care by insurance. But insurance markets can fail as we saw in Chapter 17. Let's look at the problem of health care insurance.

Health-care insurance, like all types of insurance, faces two problems: *moral hazard* and *adverse selection*[2] . Moral hazard is the tendency for people who are covered by insurance to use more health services or to be less careful about avoiding health risks than they otherwise would. Adverse selection is the tendency for people who know they have a greater chance than the average of falling ill to be the ones more likely to buy health insurance.

Insurance companies set their premium levels sufficiently high to cover claims arising from people who have been adversely selected and who face moral hazard. But to attract profitable business from low-risk customers, insurance companies give preference to healthy and employed people.

Insurance markets work well if the probabilities of getting a certain type of illness can be estimated by insurance companies, and if the probabilities are independent of other people getting the disease. Some diseases are so rare that probabilities cannot be estimated. The probability of my getting flu (an infectious disease) is clearly linked to the probability of your getting flu if we live or work together. Also, there is no profit in insuring people against a disease they already have – perhaps one they were born with. So many people will not be able to buy health-care insurance even if they want it in a private system. Many of the economic benefits of health care will be lost. To avoid this problem, governments can provide health insurance.

Private Health Care and Government Insurance

Many countries have a mixed system of compulsory social insurance (taxation) to pay for privately provided health care. This removes the market failure problem in insurance. But private provision may still be inefficient. Economies of scale in local hospital services may lead to monopoly supply where the quantity of health care is cut back below the efficient level and price is raised above marginal cost. Although government can determine the price it pays private suppliers, the private sector will only provide health care if the return is at least as good as that available in other industries. Some high-cost health care – heart transplants and specialized brain scanners – may never be provided.

Introducing a third party – government – to pay for costs generates another type of inefficiency shown in Fig. 21.11. For simplicity, we'll assume there are no benefits from health care, so the marginal social benefit, MSB, equals demand, D. Marginal social cost is shown by the line MSC. The efficient quantity of health care is at Q_e where $MSC = MSB$. If doctors are paid a fee for their private service, neither doctor nor patient has to bear the cost directly. The marginal private cost (MPC) will appear to be zero and they provide and consume the maximum quantity of health care at Q_m. Doctors maximize their income and patients maximize their total benefit. The result of third party payment is inefficiency – overconsumption and high cost.

Third party problems can be removed through the introduction of a national health service, where government finances and supplies health care.

---

[2] These problems and other aspects of insurance are explained more fully in Chapter 17, pp 425–428.

FIGURE 21.11

Third Party Payments Inefficiency

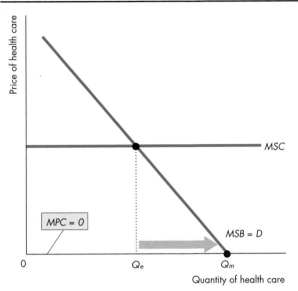

The efficient quantity of health-care provision is where *MSB* = *MSC* at Q_e. In a health-care system where government pays private sector doctors a fee for service, there is a third party payments problem. The marginal private cost to doctors and patients is zero. Doctors have an incentive to maximize income and total patient benefit at Q_m. This leads to over consumption of Q_m– Q_e, and inefficiency.

National Health Services

A national health service avoids the problems of third party payments, economies of scale and insurance markets. But other forms of inefficiency tend to arise. One major criticism of a national health service is that it is a monopoly. Monopoly provision on a national scale can result in bureaucratic inefficiency and high cost as we saw in Chapter 18. The National Health Service (NHS) in the United Kingdom is one of the world's largest organizations, employing more than 1 million people. Rising costs led real expenditure on the NHS to increase by more than 38 per cent between 1983 and 1993, from £30 billion to £42 billion at 1993 prices.

Another problem arises in the allocation of resources among different forms of health care. If there are no prices, there is no information on cost. The forces of demand and supply are not working and there are no incentives to allocate

resources efficiently among different types of care. Decisions about the allocation of resources between prevention and treatment, between care for the chronically sick and emergency treatment, and between hospitals and general practitioners, are made by NHS managers from politically determined budgets. As most voters do not have access to this information, voting behaviour is unlikely to reflect preferences for different political allocations.

Some economists also believe that monopoly restricts patient choice. While patients are free to choose a private alternative, only 14 per cent of households in the United Kingdom had private insurance in 1994. Private insurance does not cover chronic illness or maternity care, and deals mainly with non-life-threatening illnesses. So there is little alternative choice in many areas of health care.

We have looked at the different forms of health-care provision and seen that they all generate inefficiency and all face rising costs. Let's look at the policies that have been used to contain costs and reduce inefficiency in health care.

Reforming Private Systems

The pressure for reform is greatest in those countries that operate mainly private systems. In the United States, government pays the health-care costs of people on low incomes through the Medicaid and Medicare programmes. Although it is a private system, half of all health-care expenditure is paid for by government. Removing the effects of inflation, US government expenditure on health has increased more than fourfold since 1970, while the cost of private health care has less than doubled. One reason for this might be the third party payment problem generated by the government support element.

A recent attempt by the Clinton administration to expand the role of government in health-care provision failed in 1993. It included capping insurance premiums, creating universal cover and raising more funds through taxation. These changes would have made the system more like those in Canada and Europe but its critics say it would do no more than swap one form of inefficiency for another. For example, capping insurance premiums creates shortages which lead to quantity rationing. This form of rationing – waiting lists – is common in most European systems.

Reforming Mixed Systems and the NHS

Third party payment problems are also a source of inefficiency in mixed systems of government finance with private supply. Some countries such as Germany and the Netherlands have introduced a per head fee, replacing a fee for service system. A per head fee removes any incentive to maximize earnings through increasing treatment. Introducing co-payments – making patients pay part of the cost at the point of demand – makes patients more aware of costs and reduces the incentive to maximize total benefits. Co-payments have been introduced in Germany and in the NHS for dental care and prescriptions. Other European countries have implemented stringent regulation of prices and quantities and imposed annual health-care spending budgets to contain costs.

The problem of bureaucratic inefficiency in national health services can be tackled through privatization and the introduction of internal markets. An internal market is a system that generates prices within government-provided services by creating separate and independent groups of purchasers and providers. Each group is given a budget – providers set prices and market their services and purchasers look for the best buys. In the United Kingdom, after the NHS reforms of 1990, the District Health Authorities, budget-holding general practitioners, insurance companies, employers and individuals became purchasers. The District Health Authority hospitals, the new Trust status hospitals, some general practioners and private providers became the providers.

In an internal market, competition among purchasers, among providers, and between purchasers and providers should reduce costs and increase producer efficiency. It cannot improve allocative efficiency as the proportion spent on health care is determined by poltical choice at any point in time. Producer efficiency will increase if the monopoly of the NHS can be broken without raising other costs. The problem with the internal market is that it may generate more inefficiency than it removes. Let's see why.

To compete, the new purchasers and providers in the NHS must have good information. They must put prices on all goods and services and create contracts among themselves. This is time consuming and expensive. If these transactions costs are high

in the new internal market it will be less efficient than the old monopoly NHS. Uncertainty about future demand for health care is also likely to increase the transactions costs of contracting in an internal market. Finally, many health professionals use their professional organizations to negotiate for wages. The old NHS was a monopsonist – a monopoly buyer of labour – whose power balanced the power of professional organizations in setting wages. The internal market has changed the NHS into a monopoly buyer of services without the power to control labour costs – the vast majority of its expenditure.

The Impact of Reforms

Figure 21.12 shows the change in government expenditure on health as a percentage of all health expenditure between 1980 and 1991. It is clear that health-care reforms in most countries have reduced the share of health-care spending paid for by government. In particular, the biggest cuts have been made by those countries with national health services – the United Kingdom, Greece and Portugal. However, total spending on health care (government and private) is rising as a proportion of total expenditure in most countries as predicted in Fig. 21.10. So private finance and supply is becoming more common in countries with national health services and mixed systems. Health-care systems are slowly becoming more similar, but there is no reason to believe that the systems are converging on the most efficient model.

So which system is better? Is the NHS doomed? It depends upon voter preferences for equity. A national health service is a benefit in kind and has an important redistributive effect as we saw in Fig. 21.7. Comparative studies have shown that national health services are highly progressive – redistributing incomes from richer households to poorer households[3]. Private supply systems that are financed by governments are slightly regressive – redistributing incomes from poorer households to richer households. Private systems, like the one operated in the United States, are highly regressive.

---

[3] The study is by E. Van Doorslaer and A. Wagstaff, 'Equity in the Delivery of Health Care: Some International Comparisons', *Journal of Health Economics*, 1992.

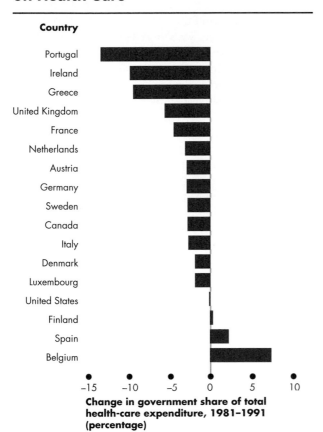

FIGURE 21.12

Changing Government Expenditure on Health Care

Country

Change in government share of total health-care expenditure, 1981–1991 (percentage)

Over the period 1981–1991, governments have succeeded in reducing the proportion of government expenditure in total health-care expenditure in most countries. Government expenditure on health care as a percentage of total health-care expenditure has increased in only three countries. Some of the largest reductions are in those countries with national health services.

Source: T. Besley and M. Gouveia, Alternative systems of health care provision, *Economic Policy*, October, 1994, 19.

Our median voter model suggests that the NHS is better – maximizes social welfare – if the median voter has a preference for the redistributive impact of the NHS. The British Social Attitudes survey shows that 91 per cent of those who have no private insurance and 85 per cent of those who have private insurance still want more government expenditure on the NHS. The vast majority prefer to trade off a more certain gain in equity for an uncertain level of efficiency in other systems.

It is clear that private systems are least able to control rising costs driven by technology change, while systems with rigid budget controls like the NHS are better able to contain these costs. This may also make the relative efficiency of the NHS appear more certain to the median voter in the longer run. The relative efficiency of European and North American healthcare are compared in *Reading Between the Lines* on pp. 538–539.

R E V I E W

◆ There are three types of health-care systems: mostly private supply and finance, mostly private supply and government finance, and mostly government supply and finance.

◆ Health-care costs are high and rising in all systems.

◆ Health-care costs increase more quickly than average prices because health care is a labour-intensive personal service and it experiences continuous improvements in product quality.

◆ All health-care systems suffer from some form of inefficiency. Private insurance (like all types of insurance) faces moral hazard and adverse selection problems. Mixed systems face a third party payment problem and national health services face monopoly problems.

◆ Health-care reforms have tried to reduce inefficiency in all systems and systems are more similar as a result.

◆ Key differences still exist in terms of equity. National health services are the most equitable – progressive, mixed systems are slightly regressive and private systems are highly regressive in their impact.

We've studied economic inequality and redistribution but we have not asked one crucial question. Is it fair that some people are so incredibly rich and others so abjectly poor? In the final section of this chapter, we examine the ways in which economists and philosophers have tried to wrestle with this question.

Ideas about Fairness

Everyone has views about fairness. Our views are diverse and are a source of political and philosophical debate. Throughout the ages, moral philosophers have tried to find a theory of distributive justice. A *theory of distributive justice* is a set of principles against which we can test whether a particular distribution of economic well-being is fair. The two broad classes of theories of distributive justice are end-state theories and process theories.

An *end-state theory* of distributive justice focuses on the justice or fairness of the *outcomes* or *ends* of economic activity. A *process theory* of distributive justice focuses on the fairness of the *mechanisms* or *means* whereby the ends are achieved. For example, the belief that everyone should have exactly the same income and wealth is an end-state theory. The belief that everyone should have the same *opportunity* to earn and accumulate wealth is a process theory. Equality of income and wealth requires an equality of outcomes or ends. That is, when the process is over, everyone has to have the same income and wealth. Requiring that people have equal opportunity does not imply that they will have equal income and wealth because people will use their opportunities in different ways. Depending on how they use their opportunities and on a variety of chance events (good and bad luck), unequal income and wealth will emerge.

End-state Theories

The two end-state theories of distributive justice are the utilitarian and maximin theories. Each theory assumes that we can make comparisons about utility among individuals by treating everyone as deriving the same marginal utility at a given level of income (or wealth).

The *utilitarian* theory is that the outcome must make the sum of the utilities of all the individuals in a society as large as possible. If Rob gets less utility than does Ian from the last pound spent, then fairness requires that a pound be taken from Rob and given to Ian. The reduction in Rob's utility is less than the gain in Ian's utility, so society is better-off – total social welfare is maximized. Redistribution should take place until the marginal utility of the last pound spent by each individual is the same.

The *maximin* theory is that the outcome must result in the maximum possible utility (income) for the person with the minimum utility (income). In the maximin view, if the poorest person can be made better off by taking income from any other person, justice requires that such redistribution take place. The fairest distribution – on the maximin criterion – might be one of complete equality but not necessarily so. The reason why complete equality might not be the fairest is that redistribution creates disincentives. So too much equality might result in lower average income and a lower income for the least well-off person.

The two end-state theories of justice differ in what they regard as the desirable end-state or outcome: for the utilitarian, it is the average income or sum of the incomes of all the individuals that counts; for maximin, it is the income of the least well-off individual or individuals that counts.

How Much Inequality is Consistent with End-state Theories? It used to be thought that an end-state theory of justice implied that complete equality in the distribution of income was the best outcome. This conclusion was reached by reasoning along the following lines. First, people are much alike in their capacity for enjoyment. (In the technical language of economics, they have the same marginal utility of income schedule.) Second, marginal utility declines with income. Therefore by taking a pound from a rich person and giving it to a poorer person, the marginal utility lost by the rich person is less than the marginal utility gained by the poorer person. Thus taking from rich people and giving to poor people increases total utility. Maximum utility occurs when each individual has the same marginal utility, a point that is reached only when incomes – after redistribution – are equal. When incomes have been equalized, total utility of the society has been maximized and 'fair shares' have been achieved.

The Big Trade-off

Although it used to be thought that justice implied complete equality it is now recognized that there exists what has been called a 'big trade-off' between fairness and economic efficiency[4].

---

[4] The term is from the title of A. Okun's book, *Equality and Efficiency: The Big Trade-off*, Washington DC, Brookings Institution, 1975.

The big trade-off is based on the following idea. Greater equality can be achieved only by taxing productive activities. Taxing people's income from their work and saving lowers the after-tax income they receive. This lower income makes them work and save less. Less work and less saving result in smaller output and less consumption not only for rich people but also for poor people. According to this line of reasoning, the correct amount of redistribution to undertake depends on the balance between greater equality and lower average consumption.

Also redistribution uses resources – it has an opportunity cost. Tax-collecting agencies as well as all the tax accountants, auditors and lawyers together with the welfare-administering agencies, use skilled labour and computers to do their work. A pound collected from a rich person does not translate into a pound received by a poor person. The bigger the scale of redistribution, the greater is the opportunity cost of administering it. Taking account of the disincentive effects of redistribution and the resource costs of administering redistribution produces the 'big trade-off'. A more equally shared pie is a smaller pie.

The Process View of Justice

The process view is that justice depends on the mechanisms through which the distribution of income and wealth arises[5]. A system based on private property rights, where private property can be acquired and transferred only through voluntary exchange, is just – or fair. The argument can be illustrated with the following story.

Start out with a distribution of income that you regard as the best possible. Then suppose that your favourite rock singer enters into a contract with a recording company. The deal is that she will get £1 on every CD sold. In a given year, she sells 3 million CDs and her total income is £3,000,000. This income is much larger than the average and much larger than she had under the original 'ideal' distribution.

The original distribution was fair. But then you and 2,999,999 other fans contributed £1 each to the income of this successful singer. Nozick believes that the rock singer is entitled to the income and that there is nothing illegitimate about you and your friends buying CDs and attending concerts. The key question is: is the new distribution unfair?

The philosophical debate continues and will perhaps never be settled. But this state of affairs is no deterrent to the political marketplace. While moral philosophers continue their disagreement about fairness, voters, politicians and bureaucrats interact in the political marketplace to create and implement laws that change the distribution of income in a political equilibrium.

◆ ◆ ◆ ◆ We've examined economic inequality in the United Kingdom, and we've seen that there is a large amount of inequality across households and individuals. Some of that inequality arises from comparing households at different stages in the life cycle. But even taking a lifetime view, inequality remains. Some of that inequality arises from differences in wage rates. Economic choices accentuate these differences. We've seen that government policy can redistribute income to alleviate the worst aspects of poverty. ◆ We've now completed our study of *microeconomics*. We've learned how all economic problems arise from scarcity, that scarcity forces us to make choices and that choice imposes cost – opportunity cost. Prices (*relative prices*) are opportunity costs and are determined by the interactions of buyers and sellers in markets. People choose what goods to buy and what factors of production to sell to maximize utility. Firms choose what goods to sell and what factors to buy to maximize profit. People and firms interact in markets, but the resulting equilibrium is inefficient because of market failure and often unfair because of the resulting distribution of incomes and wealth. Government policy can raise social welfare by modifying the market outcome to provide public goods, redistribute income and wealth, curb monopoly and cope with externalities, limited knowledge and uncertainty.

---

[5] The modern approach to process theory was set up by a Harvard philosopher, Robert Nozick, in his book '*Anarchy, State and Utopia*', New York, Basic Books, 1974.

Health-Care Spending

The Essence of the Story

THE INDEPENDENT, 16 JUNE 1996

Welcome to Britain's bargain basement

Nicholas Timmins

In international terms, the NHS is either a bargain basement buy, or chronically underfunded....

In 1993, according to Organisation for Economic Co-operation and Development figures, the UK spent 7.1 per cent of its gross national product – or national income – on health care. The average for the 25 OECD members was 8.3 per cent....

Of the UK total, only 17 per cent is spent privately against an average 30 per cent in the rest of the OECD. Only Norway, Sweden, Finland and Denmark spend such a small proportion privately....

In 1985, NHS spending as a share of gross domestic product was significantly below the average for public health spending. Now it is fractionally above – thanks mainly to the ... NHS ... reforms....

Comparisons of GDP spending can, however, mislead.... Comparisons need to allow for different costs of living ... using purchasing power parities.... On that basis the UK ... rates 17th out of 25, ... and the Nordic countries spend a little more. France and Germany ... spend at least half as much again, ... and the US almost three times as much.

Higher spending may produce better facilities. But there is little evidence, above minimal levels, that it produces better health care, let alone better health.

The US spends twice as much of its national income on health and six times more in terms of purchasing parities than anyone else, yet millions of Americans are not covered and the country has one of the worst infant mortality rates in the OECD. Greek men, for example, can expect to live two years longer than their American counterparts.

With every operation and most medical treatments carrying a risk, and with the value of much treatment unproven, too much health care may be as dangerous as too little.

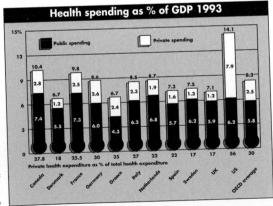

Health spending as % of GDP 1993

Public spending | Private spending

Private health expenditure as % of total health expenditure

Country	Public	Private	Total	% private
Canada	7.4	2.8	10.4	27.8
Denmark	5.5	1.2	6.7	18
France	7.3	2.5	9.8	25.5
Germany	6.0	2.6	8.6	30
Greece	4.3	2.4	6.7	35
Italy	6.2	2.3	8.5	27
Netherlands	6.8	1.9	8.7	22
Spain	5.7	1.6	7.3	22
Sweden	6.2	1.3	7.5	17
UK	5.9	1.2	7.1	17
US	6.2	7.9	14.1	56
OECD average	5.8	2.5	8.3	30

■ In 1993 the United Kingdom spent 7.1 per cent of its national output on health care, well below the average of 8.3 per cent for the 25 OECD countries and the US level of 14.1 per cent, which may indicate chronic underfunding.

■ In the United Kingdom, as in Norway, Sweden, Finland and Denmark, private health-care spending accounts for less than 17 per cent of total health-care spending, and the United Kingdom now spends more on public provision than the OECD average.

■ A higher level of total health-care expenditure does not mean that people are in better health. It may simply indicate a higher cost of living and a higher proportion of people using private care, with more extensive use of high-cost treatments.

■ A high level of health-care spending may also result in higher levels of mortality and more limited access to health care.

Economic Analysis

■ The figure in the article shows total health-care expenditure is well above average in the United States, Canada and France and well below average in Denmark, Greece, the United Kingdom, Spain and Sweden.

■ We can think of health-care expenditure as just one input into the output that we all want — good health status. Other inputs might include genetic factors, exposure to disease, and lifestyle, such as exercise and smoking.

■ Figure 1 shows a production function for health status, P, which shows how output of health status (measured by indicators such as mortality) changes with expenditure on health care, all other factors remaining the same.

■ If the production functions for health are similar in North America and Europe, the higher level of average health-care expenditure in North America leads to a higher level of health outcome M_2, than in Europe, M_1.

■ Figure 2 shows a situation where health-care expenditure is more efficient, on the average, in Europe than in North America. The production function for Europe, P_E, is higher at every level of expenditure than for North America, P_A.

■ Europe achieves a higher level of health-care outcomes for a lower level of expenditure, at M_2, than North America, at M_1, perhaps because Europeans are genetically healthier, have a healthier lifestyle, and have less exposure to disease.

■ But the extent and type of private provision may also be a factor. Efficiency gains from private health care in North America may be outweighed by efficiency losses associated with greater inequality in access to health care in a private system — an example of the 'leaky bucket' discussed on p. 527 of this chapter.

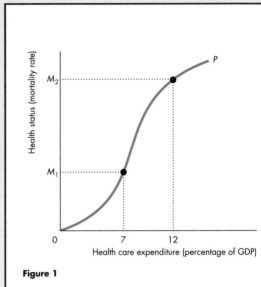

Figure 1

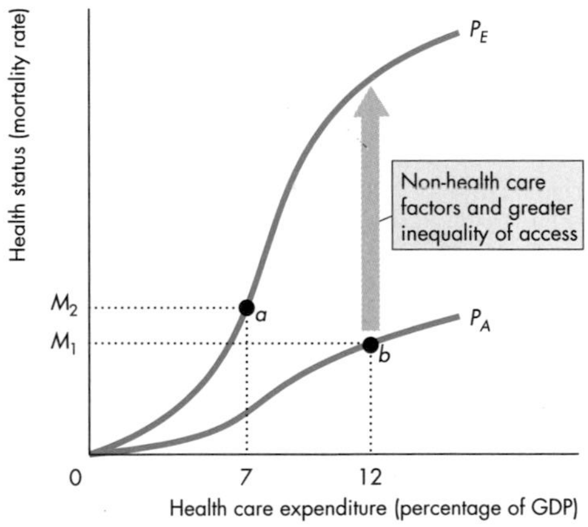

Figure 2

SUMMARY

Economic Inequality in the United Kingdom

The richest 1 per cent of the population own almost one-third of the total wealth in the United Kingdom. Income is distributed less unevenly than wealth. Income inequality was reduced in the early 1960s and 1970s but increased in all other periods. The poorest people in the United Kingdom are likely to be single retired women over the age of 75, with no qualifications, living in Wales. The richest are university-educated couples, aged between 30 and 50, who live in the South East. (pp. 519–522)

Factor Prices, Endowments and Choices

Differences in income and wealth arise partly from differences in individual endowments and partly from differences in factor prices. Wage rates vary considerably, depending on skill and other factors. But these differences, on their own, are not enough to account for differences in the distribution of income and wealth. These differences are exaggerated by the economic choices that people make.

People who face a high hourly wage rate generally choose to work longer than those who face a low wage rate. As a result, the distribution of income becomes more unequal than the distribution of wage rates. Also, saving and bequests affect wealth across the generations. Bequests accentuate inequality because of assortative mating. (pp. 522–525)

Income Redistribution

Governments redistribute income through transfer payments such as income taxes, cash benefits and benefits in kind. Cash benefits (social security) include family credit, income support, job seekers allowance, pensions and disability payments. Benefits in kind are the provision of health care through the NHS, free schooling and subsidized housing.

Redistribution suffers from the 'leaky bucket' problem, which means there is a trade-off between equity and efficiency. The trade-off arises because the process of redistribution uses resources and weakens incentives to work and save.

Means-tested cash benefits create benefit traps that discourage work, keeping people in poverty. Benefit system reforms try to lessen the severity of the benefit traps. A more radical reform known as negative income tax would strengthen the incentives but increase the tax burden. A minimal negative income tax system could increase the efficiency of the means-tested system. (pp. 525–530)

Health-care Provision

There are three types of health-care systems: private supply and finance, private supply and government finance, and government supply and government finance. The main problems for all health-care systems are high and rising costs and inefficient production.

All health-care systems suffer from some form of inefficiency. Private insurance (like all types of insurance) faces moral hazard and adverse selection problems. Mixed systems face a third party payment problem and national health services face monopoly problems. Health-care reforms have reduced inefficiency, making the different systems increasingly similar. The main differences are in terms of equity. National health services are the most progressive, shifting income from rich people to poor people. Government finance with private supply systems are slightly regressive, and private systems are very regressive. Voters in the United Kingdom appear to prefer the redistributive impact of the NHS over the efficiency of other systems. (pp. 530–535)

Ideas About Fairness

People disagree on what constitutes a fair distribution of income. Moral philosophers have tried to resolve the issue by finding principles on which we can all agree, but agreement still has not been reached. Two broad groups of theories have been developed: end-state theories and process theories. End-state theories of fairness assert that it is the outcome that matters. Process theories assert that it is equality of opportunity that matters. (pp. 536–537)

KEY ELEMENTS

Key Terms

Lorenz curve, 520
Negative income tax, 528
Poverty, 521
Progressive income tax, 525
Proportional income tax, 525
Regressive income tax, 525

Key Figures

Figure 21.1 Lorenz Curves for Income and Wealth, 519

Figure 21.3 The Distribution of Income by Selected Household Characteristics in 1992, 521

Figure 21.8 Comparing the Current Benefit System and a Negative Income Tax, 529

REVIEW QUESTIONS

1 Which of the following describe the distributions of personal income and wealth in the United Kingdom today?

   a The distributions of income and wealth are best represented by normal or bell-shaped curves.

   b More than 50 per cent of the population is wealthier than the average.

   c More than 50 per cent of the population is poorer than the average.

2 What is a Lorenz curve? How does a Lorenz curve illustrate inequality? Explain how the Lorenz curves for the distributions of income and wealth in the United Kingdom differ from each other.

3 Which is more unequally distributed, income or wealth? In answering this question, pay careful attention both to the way in which income and wealth are measured by official statistics and to the fundamental concepts of income and wealth.

4 How has income inequality changed over the past 30 years? What factors have contributed to changes in inequality of income over time?

5 What is a gini-coefficient?

6 How has the gini-coefficient changed over time and what does this indicate?

7 Why do we need a poverty line and how can it be measured?

8 What is wrong with the way in which the official statistics measure the distribution of wealth?

9 Explain why the work/leisure choices made by individuals can result in a distribution of income that is more unequal than the distribution of ability. If ability is distributed normally (bell-shaped), will the resulting distribution of income also be bell-shaped?

10 What is meant by a benefit trap?

11 Explain what is meant by transfer payments and benefits in kind.

12 Explain the difference between take-up and targetting of benefits.

13 Explain the difference between a poverty trap and an unemployment trap.

14 What is a negative income tax, and why don't we have one?

15 What are the three main types of health-care systems?

16 How do different health-care systems compare in terms of efficiency and equity?

17 What factors will determine whether the NHS is retained or whether a different form of health-care system is introduced in the United Kingdom?

18 What is the difference between an end-state theory of equity and a process theory of equity?

19 Explain the utilitarian theory of distributive justice.

20 Explain the maximin theory of distributive justice.

21 What is meant by the big trade-off?

PROBLEMS

1 Imagine an economy in which there are five people who are identical in all respects. They each live for 70 years. For the first 14 of those years, they earn no income. For the next 35 years, they work and earn £30,000 a year from their work. For their remaining years, they are retired and have no income from labour. To make the arithmetic easy, let's suppose that the interest rate in this economy is zero; the individuals consume all their income during their lifetime and at a constant annual rate. What are the distributions of income and wealth in this economy if the individuals have the following ages:

a All are 45?
b 25, 35, 45, 55, 65?

Is case (a) one of greater inequality than case (b)?

2 You are given the following information about income and wealth shares:

	Income shares (per cent)	Wealth shares (per cent)
Lowest 20%	5	0
Second 20%	11	1
Third 20%	17	3
Fourth 20%	24	11
Highest 20%	43	85

Draw the Lorenz curves for income and wealth for this economy. Explain which of the two variables – income or wealth – is more unequally distributed.

3 An economy consists of 10 people, each of whom has the following labour supply schedule:

Wage rate (pounds per hour)				
1	2	3	4	5
Hours worked per day				
0	1	2	3	4

The people differ in ability and earn different wage rates. The distribution of wage rates is as follows:

Wage rate (pounds per hour)				
1	2	3	4	5
Number of people				
1	2	4	2	1

a Calculate the average wage rate.
b Calculate the ratio of the highest to the lowest wage rate.
c Calculate the average daily income.
d Calculate the ratio of the highest to the lowest daily income.
e Sketch the distribution of hourly wage rates.
f Sketch the distribution of daily incomes.
g What important lesson is illustrated by this problem?

4 Read the article about health-care spending in *Reading Between the Lines* on pp. 538–539 and then answer the following questions:

a Describe the differences in health-care expenditure in different countries.
b What factors explain the differences in health-care expenditure between countries?
c What is a production function for health status and how does it relate to health-care expenditure?
d What factors determine the shape of the health status production function?
e Why might European health-care systems be more efficient than North American health-care systems, even though they spend less on health-care as a percentage of GDP?

Part 5
PRELIMINARIES AND LONG-TERM FUNDAMENTALS

TALKING WITH NICK CRAFTS

Nick Crafts is currently the Professor of Economic History at the London School of Economics, a position he has held since 1995. He is also Fellow of the British Academy. After his time as Fellow and CUF Lecturer of economics at University College, Oxford, he spent a short time as Professor of Economics at the University of Leeds. In 1988 he became Professor of Economic History and Chairman of the Department of Economics at the University of Warwick. He is the author and co-editor of many publications, including *Economic Growth in Europe Since 1945*, *The British Economy Since 1945*, *Can De-Industrialization Seriously Damage Your Wealth?* and his forthcoming publication: *Relative Economic Decline in Britain, 1870–1995: A Quantitative Perspective*. He has many research interests, especially in comparative experience of economic growth and long-run economic perspectives, and was recently described by Peter Jay (TLS, 20/9/96) as 'probably now the leading expert on British economic growth since 1945'.

What made you take up the study of economic history?

I started reading economics at Cambridge in the 1960s, and I became interested in growth and development. I remember good economic historians at Cambridge, all of whom seemed to have interesting things to say on this subject. So I came into economic history through an interest in economic development.

You have been a student of long-term economic growth in the United Kingdom and Europe. Tell me about your work.

I began by thinking about how well we measured economic growth. A focal point for a lot of my early work was the Industrial Revolution. In studying this subject you are working with imperfect data and a controversial episode. When you start thinking seriously about measurement, index number problems loom quite large. This is because as the structure of the economy changes quickly, relative prices adjust fast. As I delved into the index number problem, I came to the conclusion that previous attempts to measure growth during the Industrial Revolution had got it seriously wrong, and in particular that British growth was much less rapid than had previously been believed. Although the Industrial Revolution was a period of dramatic change, the performance of the British economy was, in some ways, modest. That is, it was modest from a contemporary perspective, but it was of course impressive compared with what had gone before. Britain was certainly not a 'Japan' during the Industrial Revolution. The implication was that Britain had grown well by the standards of the time without accumulating any of the things that would be important for rapid growth in the twentieth century. One particular twist, which is still unresolved, is how, if at all, Britain's early start, impeded subsequent growth. In conclusion, the acceleration of growth during the Industrial Revolution was remarkable relative to the seventeenth century, but not relative to the twentieth.

What about Europe? Your studies have also encompassed other countries, have they not?

Absolutely! It seems to me that there is a lot to be gained from international comparisons in growth economics. Looking at international growth performance, you can see how idiosyncratic the United Kingdom's development was in the nineteenth and early twentieth centuries. For example, it was epitomized by the extremely small share of agriculture in GDP and in employment. We are talking about 10 per cent of the work-force in agriculture in the United Kingdom in 1900 – a level that the

major continental economies reach round about 1965–70. This is a striking feature.

During the Industrial Revolution Britain pushed an enormous number of people into industry. This, rather than the productivity they achieved, was really impressive. This in turn relates to a particular story of comparative advantage during the Industrial Revolution. The most tradeable item at the time was textiles. Britain became a leader in international textiles, a lead which it preserved for a long time. It allowed a reasonably free trade regime, the implications of which were rapid expansion of exportable manufactures and a fairly rapid contraction in agriculture. This is an interesting comparative advantage story to quote because it then looks at some of the issues that people such as Paul Krugman have been featuring heavily in the last five or six years.

Your study of UK economic growth has covered the Thatcher decade of the 1980s which some people refer to as the Thatcher Economic Miracle. Have your studies found any evidence for this?

I think it is a natural progression to look at the recent past, and if you do this, then there is an advantage from also knowing the distant past. The answer to your question is not straightforward and there are several ways of tackling it. One is

simply to look at the raw data of growth. Since 1979 the United Kingdom's growth is less impressive than it was in the 'Golden Age' of the 1950s and 1960s when UK growth was at an all-time high. But relatively speaking, the United Kingdom has done much better compared with its peer group in Europe. One way of thinking about this is to say that the other European economies have slowed down much more than the United Kingdom has since the 'Golden Age', so that the United Kingdom on the raw data looks like an average performer in the 1980s. You wouldn't say that was a miracle. The rates of growth we are talking about are moderate. The United Kingdom is probably achieving total factor productivity growth of about 2 per cent a year, depending on how you try and measure it. Income per person is probably growing at a fairly similar rate. It's a change in relative performance rather than an absolute increase.

In answering your question I would argue that had the policies of the 1970s continued for much longer, growth performance would have been worse than actually turned out to be the case in the 1980s. In particular, a number of things we were doing in the post-war period made us worse than our European peer group at catching up with the United States, which is where the fast growth was in the 1950s and 1960s. We imported technology but got much less

'I personally think that technical progress is crucial to sustaining long-term growth'

productivity improvement out of it. One of the reasons is that productivity outcomes at firm level are the result of the bargaining process, and I suspect that British industrial relations were less satisfactory than was generally the case in the rest of Europe. This inhibited our catch-up and led to some of these productivity failures. We were not getting anything like full value out of technological change. The example that everyone thinks of is the nationalized industries. For instance, in British Railways the person who was the fireman with the steam locomotive became the assistant driver with the diesel locomotive. It isn't exactly the worst example but I think it embodies quite a lot of what was happening. Technology did change but the productivity growth from it was less impressive than it might have been. In the 1980s one big change was the conduct of British industrial relations, which resulted in a shift of bargaining power during the Thatcher years. Some of this was because of trade union reform, but a lot was the result of nasty economic shocks: tight monetary policy, North Sea oil and rapidly rising unemployment in many manufacturing sectors during 1979–81.

This brings me to the third aspect of your question, which is whether or not the effect of the 1980s change in policy increased the long-run growth rate. I think this is much harder to be sure of

because the jury is still out. We need to see the evidence in a decade or two. On the plus side, there were some palpable changes in institutions, which if you take a modern endogenous growth-type story could conceivably have growth rate effects in the future. We certainly started to tackle some of the United Kingdom's weaknesses in the area of human capital, which again may have a long gestation period. I suspect reforms in taxation were positive and conceivably might have an investment implication. So there are some things which might in theory be good and could have a positive result. On the negative side, it might be argued that some of the growth in the 1980s was a once and for all adjustment of levels. You can't rule that out. What has been achieved is controversial, and there is no measurement of it at present. It could be said that some things weren't tackled which may be important. For example, the attempt to reform the capital market is something you might want to look at. I am thinking of institutional relationships and the issue of under-investment. Under-investment is probably a better phrase than the commonly used 'short termism'. The question is whether a world in which there is high exposure to hostile takeover and outside investors tend to rule the roost is better than, say, a German-style alternative. I don't know, but those who worry about this kind of problem would say that

there were other reforms which could have been more productive and which weren't undertaken. The way to look at the 1980s is against a background of relative economic decline and missed opportunities.

In your examination of the 1970s and 1980s you refer to 'X' inefficiency. What has X inefficiency to do with growth?

X inefficiency means obtaining less output per unit of input than you would expect to if you were on the production function and being as efficient as technology would permit you to be. It would be reflected in a lower level of measured total factor productivity. Why might this happen? For a variety of reasons which essentially imply that firms will not minimize cost. It could be to do with managerial discretion in the context of managers who can't be effectively monitored by shareholders. It might be, and this is more important in the post-war United Kingdom, to do with the relationship between firms and their workers in imperfectly competitive situations where there is some rent to be bargained over. The bargaining between firms and their workers includes such things as effort levels and who shares the benefits. This could quite easily show up in what conventionally would be thought of as over-manning. When things in the environment that affect the bargain change, so too might the bargain. So, for example, the introduction of more competition will change the observed effort level. A big shock in unemployment changes the workers' position. This, too, will be reflected in a change in bargaining. The sort of bargain that you see will also depend on how many unions you have to deal with. During the 1980s, firms faced an increase in international competition. The macroeconomic shocks of the period delivered a severe blow to workers' bargaining power. These things were reflected in a change in productivity.

Can you tell us about endogenous growth theory?

An endogenous growth theory argues that productivity growth is determined within the economic system rather than coming as manna from heaven or as exogenous technical innovation. Productivity growth comes from investment. The notion of investment that we appeal to in modern growth theory tends to be a broad one. It is both physical capital and human capital. The most important version of this growth theory concerns the acquisition and utilization of knowledge. This is something which has to be invested in. Strictly, to have endogenous

growth means if you increase investment you will have a permanent increase in the growth rate because such investment does not run into diminishing returns. So what endogenous growth theory tries to deny is the diminishing returns to capital formation, which has a transitory rather than a permanent effect on the growth rate, and that in the long run the rate of growth is independent of the rate of saving or investment. If there are constant returns to the relevant concept of accumulation then you can in principle get a permanent increase in the growth rate from an increase in investment.

If these models are right, then paying attention to investment has much more impact on long-term living standards. This delivers different agendas to different people. For right-wing economists or politicians it might mean that low marginal direct tax rates are needed to get a high investment rate. For left-wing economists or politicians the argument might be that constant returns arise because there are big externalities to investment. So the right agenda is to devise the appropriate package of subsidies to prevent under-investment. In European economic history, Barry Eichengreen, for example, would use this sort of model to argue that the contracts between capital and labour made after World War II had the effect of producing more investment in return for wage

moderation. I don't believe in growth models which achieve increases in the long-run growth rate through greater routine investment, that is, more and more investment in the same sort of physical capital or the same sort of human capital. I believe the evidence is in favour of diminishing returns, but if you take a broader notion of capital it might take an economy longer to converge to the steady state. Another branch of endogenous growth is associated with the work of Paul Romer in the 1990s. There we are looking for a notion of endogenizing innovation in the form of the development of new varieties of capital goods. It may be that the fruits of the innovative activity are then embodied in capital. The important thing would be that growth comes from the new sorts of capital, not simply more and more accumulation.

What advice would you give a student starting out in economics?

To pursue a balanced course of study. Having taught for so many years at Warwick, it is important to say that students need a sound mathematical background. It's important to be well trained in econometrics. It is also important to have knowledge of the economic past and in particular a strong sense of historiography.

CHAPTER

22

A
FIRST
LOOK
AT
MACROECONOMICS

After studying this chapter you will be able to:

◆ Describe the origins of macro-economics and the problems it deals with

◆ Describe the long-term trends and short-term fluctuations in economic growth, unemployment, inflation and the balance of international payments

◆ Explain why economic growth, unemployment, inflation and the balance of international payments are important

◆ Identify the macroeconomic policy challenges and describe the tools available for meeting them

D URING THE PAST 100 YEARS, THE QUANTITY OF GOODS AND SERVICES PRODUCED IN the United Kingdom has increased by 550 per cent. In 1994, production expanded more quickly than the average and although the United Kingdom was emerging from a long recession, this rapid growth raised fears that the economy was overheating. How does an economy overheat? Why was rapid economic growth feared? Isn't more output always a good thing? ◆ One reason overheating was feared was the rapid growth in production. It was thought that output growth was faster than the economy's capacity to sustain that growth. Another reason was the decrease in unemployment to 2.4 million. But how can the economy be overheating when so many people are unemployed? Why can't *everyone* who wants a job find one? ◆ Prices have increased slowly in recent years. But with rapid production growth and falling unemployment, it was feared that inflation might break out again. That's what overheating means – an economy growing so quickly that inflation increases. What exactly is inflation, and why does it matter? ◆ A consequence of an overheated economy is that it sucks in goods and services from abroad on a large scale and brings a larger balance of international payments deficit. Why does it matter if we have a

Overheating?

balance of payments deficit? ◆ To prevent the economy from overheating and to prevent the opposite condition, an economic slowdown, the government may take policy actions. These policy actions will be influenced by the advice it receives from economists in government and the Bank of England. But what kinds of actions does the government take? How do those actions influence production, jobs, inflation and the ability of people to compete in the global marketplace?

◆ ◆ ◆ ◆ These questions are the subject matter of macroeconomics – the branch of economics that seeks to understand economic growth, unemployment, inflation and the balance of international payments and to design policies to improve macroeconomic performance. The macroeconomic events through which we are now living are tumultuous and exciting. With what you learn in these chapters, you will be able to understand these events, the policy challenges they bring and the political debate they stir. ◆ Let's begin by looking at the origins of macroeconomics and the key issues it deals with.

Origins and Issues of Macroeconomics

Economists began to study long-term economic growth, inflation and international payments as long ago as the 1750s, and this work was the beginning of macroeconomics. But modern macroeconomics emerged much later, as a response to the **Great Depression**, a decade (1929–39) of high unemployment and stagnant production throughout the world economy. In the United Kingdom, the Great Depression came on top of an existing situation of slump and mass unemployment. In the worst year, 1931, total production fell by over 5 per cent and in the following year unemployment reached a record 15 per cent of the work-force. These were years of human misery on a scale that is hard to imagine today. A deep pessimism about the ability of the market economy to work properly was created. Many people believed that the experience of mass unemployment demonstrated that the economic system of private ownership and free markets was a failure. The perceived failure was so extreme that it raised the deeply disturbing question of whether liberal–democratic political institutions could survive.

The economic dogma of the period had no solutions. The major alternative economic system of central planning and the political system of socialism that went with it seemed increasingly attractive to many people. It was in this climate of economic depression and political and intellectual turmoil that macroeconomics emerged. Its origin was the publication in 1936 of John Maynard Keynes' *The General Theory of Employment, Interest, and Money* (see *Economics in History* on pp. 572–573).

Short-term versus Long-term Goals

Keynes' theory was that depression and high unemployment result from insufficient private spending and that to cure these problems, the government must increase its spending. Keynes' focus was primarily the *short term*. He wanted to cure an immediate and serious problem almost regardless of what the *long-term* consequences of the cure might be. 'In the long run,' said Keynes, 'we're all dead.'

But Keynes believed that after his cure for depression had restored the economy to a normal condition, the long-term problems of inflation and economic growth would become the central ones.

He even suspected that his cure for depression, increased government spending, might trigger inflation and also might lower the long-term growth rate of production. With a lower long-term growth rate, fewer jobs would be created. If this outcome did occur, a policy aimed at lowering unemployment might end up increasing it.

By the late 1960s and through the 1970s, these long-term concerns became a reality. Inflation increased, economic growth slowed down, and in some countries unemployment became persistently high. The causes of these developments are complex. But they point to an inescapable conclusion: the long-term issues of inflation, slow growth and persistent unemployment and the short-term issues of depression and economic fluctuations intertwine, and are most usefully studied together. So although macroeconomics was reborn during the Great Depression, it has today returned to its older tradition. Nowadays, it is a subject that tries to understand the long-term issues of economic growth and inflation as well as short-term economic fluctuations and the unemployment these fluctuations bring.

The Road Ahead

There is no unique way to study macroeconomics. Because its rebirth was a product of economic depression, it was common for many years to pay most attention to short-term output fluctuations and unemployment. But long-term issues were never completely forgotten. During the late 1960s and 1970s, when a serious inflation emerged, this topic returned to prominence. Rising inflation in this period was coupled with a slowing down in long-term growth and rising unemployment. A new word had come into being to describe this phenomenon – **stagflation**. Economists redirected their energy towards tackling this problem. In the 1990s, when information technologies have shrunk the globe, the international dimension of macroeconomics has become more prominent. The result of all these events is that modern macroeconomics is a broad subject that pays attention to all the issues we've just reviewed: long-term economic growth, unemployment, inflation and international economic activity.

Over the past 40 years, economists have developed a clearer understanding of the forces that determine macroeconomic performance and they have devised policies that, while imperfect, stand some chance of preventing the extremes of depression and inflation. Your main goal is to become familiar with the theories of macroeconomics and the policies they make possible. To set you on your path towards this goal, we're going to take a first look at the macroeconomic issues of economic growth, unemployment, inflation and the balance of international payments and learn why they are problems that merit our attention.

REVIEW

◆ Macroeconomics was born out of the experience of mass unemployment following the Great Depression.

◆ Macroeconomics studies the long-term trends and short-term fluctuations in economic growth, unemployment, inflation and the balance of international payments.

◆ One goal of macroeconomics is to devise policies to improve macroeconomic performance.

Economic Growth

It is highly likely that your parents are richer than your grandparents were when they were young. But are you going to be richer than your parents? And are your children going to be richer than you? The answers depend on the rate of economic growth.

Economic growth is the expansion of the economy's capacity to produce goods and services. It is an expansion of the economy's production possibilities and can be pictured as an outward shift of the production possibility frontier (*PPF*) (see Chapter 3, pp. 52–55).

We measure economic growth by the increase in real gross domestic product. **Real gross domestic product** (also called **real GDP**) is the value of *aggregate* or *total* production – the output of all the country's farms, factories, shops and offices – measured in the prices of a single year. At the present time, real GDP in the United Kingdom is measured in prices that prevailed in 1990 (1990 prices). We use the prices of a single year so that we can eliminate the influence of *inflation* – the

increase in prices – and determine how much production has grown from one year to another. (The concept of real GDP is explained more fully in Chapter 23 on pp. 576–586.)

Real GDP is not a perfect measure of total production. For example, it does not include the things we produce for ourselves such as do-it-yourself jobs (DIY) in the home or other housework. Nor does it include things people produce but hide to avoid taxes – known as the underground economy. But despite its shortcomings real GDP is the broadest measure of total production available. What does it tell us about economic growth in the United Kingdom and other countries in Europe?

Economic Growth in the United Kingdom

Figure 22.1 shows real GDP in the United Kingdom since 1960 and it highlights two features of economic growth:

◆ The growth of potential GDP

◆ Fluctuations of real GDP around potential GDP

The Growth of Potential GDP **Potential GDP** is the real GDP the economy would produce if all its resources – labour, capital, land and entrepreneurial ability – were fully employed. The rate of long-term economic growth is measured by the steepness of the potential GDP line.

If you look closely at Fig. 22.1, you can see that there are three trends in potential GDP. The potential GDP line is steeper in the 1960s than in the 1970s and steeper again in the 1980s. During the 1960s, potential GDP grew at an average annual rate of 2.9 per cent a year. Growth slowed during the 1970s as a result of a **productivity growth slowdown** – a slowdown in the growth rate of output per person. Growth in potential GDP in the 1970s was at an average of only 2.0 per cent. Faster growth in potential GDP returned during the 1980s and 1990s. Growth in potential GDP in the 1980s was 2.2 per cent.

Why did the productivity growth slowdown occur? Was the United Kingdom alone in experiencing such an event? Why was the poor productivity performance reversed in the 1980s? What are the consequences of both events?

The two 'why' questions are not easy ones to answer fully. Many factors were at work in the 1970s,

FIGURE 22.1

Economic Growth in the United Kingdom: 1960–1994

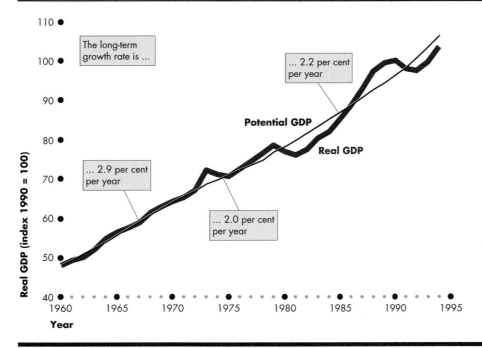

The long-term economic growth rate, measured by the growth of potential GDP, was 2.9 per cent a year during the 1960s but slowed to 2.0 per cent a year during the 1970s and 2.2 in the 1980s. Real GDP fluctuates around potential GDP.

Sources: Central Statistical Office, *Economic Trends Annual Supplement*, 1996; Lombard Street Research Ltd; estimates of potential GDP are obtained by applying a Hodrick–Prescott Filter.

but two were critical: oil price shocks and rapid inflation. The oil price shocks of 1973–74 triggered the development of new energy-saving technologies and a high level of investment in energy efficient equipment. But these innovations and investments did not increase labour productivity. The rapid inflation of the 1970s brought increased uncertainty and made it hard for people to make wise long-term investment decisions. This brief explanation of the productivity slowdown is expanded on in Chapter 26 on pp. 663–664. The improvement in productivity growth in the 1980s and 1990s in the United Kingdom may have also been owing to the supply side policies of the Conservative government under the then prime minister, Margaret Thatcher, and the return of low inflation.

Was the United Kingdom alone in experiencing a productivity growth slowdown? No. We'll see some other examples later in this chapter when we look at long-term growth around the world. But it was alone in experiencing a productivity growth revival in the 1980s. The consequence is that we have much smaller incomes today than we would

have had if productivity growth had not slowed. For opposite reasons we have larger incomes as a result of the improvement in the 1980s. These issues will be expanded on later on in this chapter.

Let's look at the second feature of economic growth, namely the fluctuations around trend.

Fluctuations Around Trend   Real GDP fluctuates around potential GDP in a business cycle. A **business cycle** is the periodic but irregular up and down movement in economic activity. It is measured by fluctuations in real GDP around potential GDP. When real GDP is less than potential GDP, some resources are underused. For example, some labour is unemployed and capital is underutilized. When real GDP is greater than potential GDP, some resources are being overused. For example, many people are working longer hours than they are willing to put up with in the long run and capital is being worked so intensively that there is no time to keep it in prime working order.

Business cycles are not regular, predictable, or repeating cycles like the phases of the moon. Their timing changes unpredictably. But cycles do have some things in common. Every business cycle has two turning points:

1. Peak
2. Trough

and two phases:

1. Recession
2. Expansion

Figure 22.2 shows these features of the most recent business cycle A *peak* is the upper turning point of a business cycle where an expansion ends and a recession begins. A peak occurred in the second quarter of 1990. A *trough* is the lower turning point of a business cycle where a recession ends and a recovery begins. A trough occurred in the first quarter of 1992.

A **recession** is a period during which real GDP decreases – the growth rate of real GDP is negative – for at least two successive quarters. In Fig. 22.2, a recession began in the second quarter of 1990 and ended in the first quarter of 1992.

An **expansion** is a period during which real GDP increases. It begins at a trough and ends at a peak. In Fig. 22.2, an expansion ended at the 1990 peak and another expansion began at the 1992 trough.

The Recent Recession in Historical Perspective
The recession of 1990–92 that is shown in Fig. 22.2 seemed pretty severe while we were passing through it, but compared with earlier recessions it was relatively mild. You can see how mild it was by looking at Fig. 22.3, which shows a longer history of economic growth. The most precipitous decline in real GDP occurred immediately after World War I. A large fall in real GDP also occurred in 1931 and immediately following World War II. In more recent times, milder decreases in real GDP occurred during the mid-1970s – the time of oil price hikes by OPEC – and during the early 1980s and early 1990s.

While each of these economic downturns was considered to be severe at the time, you can see that the downturn that occurred in the interwar period was more severe than anything that followed it. This

---

FIGURE 22.2

The Most Recent UK Business Cycle

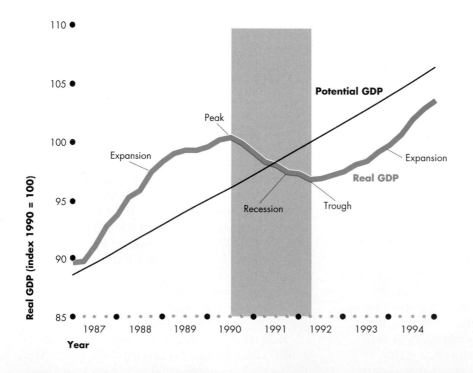

A business cycle has two turning points: a peak and a trough. In the most recent business cycle, the peak occurred in the second quarter of 1990 and the trough occurred in the first quarter of 1992. A business cycle has two phases: recession and expansion. The most recent recession ran from the peak in 1990 to the trough in 1992 as indicated by the pink area on the figure. The expansion ran from the trough in 1992 to end-1994.

FIGURE 22.3

Long-term Economic Growth in the United Kingdom

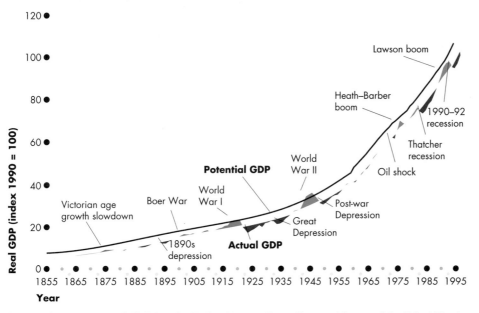

The thin black line shows potential GDP. Along this line, real GDP grew at an average rate of 1.9 per cent a year between 1856 and 1994. The blue areas show when real GDP was above potential GDP and the red areas show when it was below potential GDP. During some periods, such as World War II, real GDP expanded quickly. During other periods, such as the Great Depression and more recently in 1974–75, 1980–81, and 1990–92, real GDP declined.

Sources: GDP 1855–1947: C. H. Feinstein, *National Income Expenditure and Output of the United Kingdom, 1855–1965*, 1972, Cambridge, Cambridge University Press; GDP 1948–1994 Central Statistical Office, *Economic Trends Annual Supplement*, 1996; Potential GDP Lombard Street Research Ltd.

---

episode was so extreme that we don't call it a recession. We call it a depression. The term *depression* is used to describe a severe contraction of production that brings extreme and prolonged hardship.

The fact that the last truly great depression occurred before governments started taking policy actions to stabilize the economy (and before the birth of macroeconomics) has led to speculation that perhaps macroeconomics has made a contribution to economic stability. We'll examine this speculation on a number of occasions in this book.

We've seen that real GDP has increased over the long term. We've seen that long-term growth slowed during the 1970s and picked up in the 1980s. We've seen that recessions have interrupted the broad upward sweep of real GDP. Is the UK experience typical? Do other countries share this experience? Let's see if they do.

Economic Growth Around the World

A country might have a rapid growth rate of real GDP, but it might also have a rapid population growth rate. To compare growth rates over time

and across countries, we use the growth rate of real GDP *per person* measured in a common currency, in this case US dollars. **Real GDP per person** is real GDP divided by the population.

Figure 22.4 shows the growth of real GDP per person between 1960 and 1990 for some of the major OECD economies: the United States, Japan, Germany and the United Kingdom. In these countries, three features of the paths of real GDP per person stand out:

♦ Similar productivity growth slowdowns

♦ Similar business cycles

♦ Different long-term trends in potential GDP

Similar Productivity Growth Slowdowns

The countries shown in Fig. 22.4 have similar productivity growth slowdowns. Between 1960 and 1973 UK real GDP growth per person was 2.7 per cent a year, but it slowed to 2.0 per cent in the 1970s and 1980s. In the United States, growth of real GDP per person was 2.9 per cent a year during the 1960s, but it slowed to 1.5 per cent a year during the 1970s and 1980s. In Germany, the growth of real GDP per

FIGURE 22.4

Economic Growth in Four Major OECD Economies

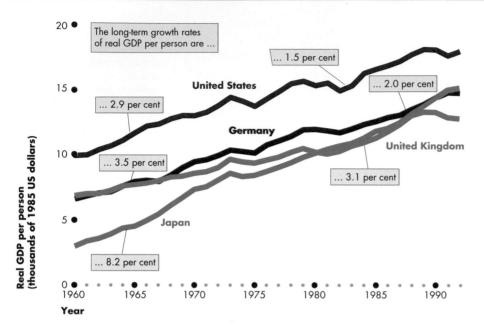

The long-term growth rates of real GDP per person are ...

... 1.5 per cent

United States

... 2.9 per cent

... 2.0 per cent

Germany

... 3.5 per cent

United Kingdom

... 3.1 per cent

Japan

... 8.2 per cent

Real GDP per person (thousands of 1985 US dollars)

Year

Economic growth in the four large economies, the United States, Germany, Japan and the United Kingdom has followed a similar pattern. The growth rate in all three countries slowed during the 1970s and 1980s and each country has similar business cycles. But Japan has grown fastest and Germany too has grown faster than the United States.

Source: Robert Summers and Alan Heston, New computer diskette (Mark 5.5), 15 June 1993, distributed by the National Bureau of Economic Research to update The Penn World Table (Mark 5): An Expanded Set of International Comparisons, 1950–1988, *Quarterly Journal of Economics*, May 1991, pp. 327–368. The data uses comparable international prices converted to 1985 US dollars.

person slowed from 3.5 per cent a year in the 1960s to 2.0 per cent a year during the 1970s and 1980s. In Japan, the slowdown was more spectacular, from 8.2 per cent a year during the 1960s to 3.1 per cent a year during the 1970s and 1980s.

The slowdown experienced by the major OECD countries was also experienced by almost every country. The exceptions were the major oil producers. The recovery in growth performance in the mid-1980s occurred in the United Kingdom, the United States and Japan.

Similar Business Cycles   The major economies have experienced similar business cycles. Each economy had an expansion running from the early or mid-1960s to 1973, a recession from 1973 to 1975, an expansion to 1979, another recession in the early 1980s, and a long expansion through the rest of the 1980s.

Like the common productivity growth slow-down, this common business cycle is shared by most economies around the world.

Different Long-term Trends in Potential GDP
Perhaps the most striking feature of Fig. 22.4 is the variation in the long-term growth rates of the big economies. In 1960, real GDP per person was $6,800 in the United Kingdom, $9,800 in the United States, $6,600 in Germany and $3,000 in Japan[1]. So, in round numbers, in 1960, the United Kingdom produced over twice as much per person as Japan and a little more than Germany. The United States produced three times as much per person as Japan and nearly half as much more than the United Kingdom.

But during the 1960s, Japan's output streaked upward like a rocket. When UK long-term growth in real GDP per person was 2.3 per cent a year, in the United States it was 2.9 per cent, while Germany achieved a rate of 3.5 per cent a year, and real GDP in Japan grew at an astonishing 8.2 per cent a year. These differences in the long-term growth trend sur-

---

[1] These dollars are based on prices in 1985 and have been calculated to make the most valid possible international comparison (see the note on Fig. 22.4).

vived the productivity growth slowdown. After the slowdown, when Japan's growth rate more than halved, its growth of real GDP per person still exceeded the US rate before the slowdown.

Because it has achieved such a high growth rate, Japan has narrowed the gap between its own production level and that of the other major economies.

Differences in growth rates like those shown in Fig. 22.4 can also be seen in the broader regions of the world. Figure 22.5 shows some average yearly growth rates of real GDP per person between 1973 and 1990. Among the industrial countries (shown by the red bars) Japan has grown the fastest and the countries of Oceania (Australia and New Zealand) have grown the slowest. The growth rate of Western Europe has been at the middle end of the range experienced by these countries. The developing countries and the countries in transition to a market economy have experienced a wide range of growth rates. The most rapid growth has occurred in Asia, where the average growth rate has been close to 5 per cent a year – two and a half times the Western European growth rate. The slowest growth has been experienced by the developing countries in Africa and Latin America. With the exception of these regions, growth rates in the developing countries have exceeded that of Western Europe.

Benefits and Costs of Economic Growth

We've studied some facts about economic growth. But why is economic growth important? What are the benefits of economic growth? Does it matter if the long-term growth rate slows down as it did during the 1970s?

The main benefit of long-term economic growth is expanded consumption possibilities, including greater welfare and support for poor people, higher pensions for retired people and better benefits for disadvantaged people. Other benefits include more expenditure on education and health, better roads, and more and better housing. We can even have cleaner rivers and cleaner air by devoting more resources to these environmental problems.

When the long-term growth rate slows, the resources that would have been used for these benefits are lost and the loss can be large. However, it must be understood that the proportion of a country's resources devoted to welfare issues and the long-term rate of growth are interrelated. It is certainly the case that the lower the long-term rate of growth the

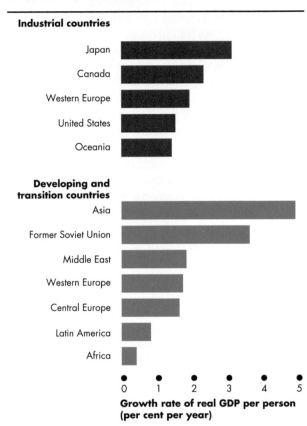

FIGURE 22.5

Long–term Growth Rates Around the World: 1973–1990

Industrial countries

Developing and transition countries

Growth rate of real GDP per person (per cent per year)

After the productivity growth slowdown of the 1970s, the growth rate of real GDP per person has been lower in the United States than in some other industrial countries. The developing countries of Asia have had the most rapid growth rates and those of Latin America and Africa have had the slowest growth.

Source: Robert Summers and Alan Heston, New computer diskette (Mark 5.5), 15 June, 1993, distributed by the National Bureau of Economic Research to update The Penn World Table (Mark 5): An Expanded Set of International Comparisons, 1950–1988, *Quarterly Journal of Economics*, May 1991, pp. 327–368. The data use comparable international relative prices converted to 1985 US dollars.

fewer resources are available for welfare. But it is also true that if more resources are spent on welfare there are fewer available for the productive sectors that generate growth. Finding the balance between resources available for current consumption such as welfare spending and resources devoted to future consumption through growth is one of the big issues of macroeconomics.

While economic growth brings enormous benefits, it also has costs. The main cost of economic growth is the current consumption forgone. To sustain a high growth rate over a large number of years, resources must be devoted to advancing technology and accumulating capital rather than to producing goods and services for current consumption.

A second possible cost of faster long-term economic growth is more rapid depletion of exhaustible natural resources such as oil and natural gas. A third possible cost is environmental degradation such as increased pollution of the air, rivers and oceans. But none of these problems are inevitable. The technological advances that bring economic growth often help us to economize on natural resources and to achieve a cleaner environment. For example, more efficient internal combustion engines have decreased the amount of petrol a car uses and cut lead and carbon emissions.

A fourth possible cost of faster long-term economic growth is more frequent changes in what we produce, the job we do and the place we live. Faster long-term growth means that the number of new businesses starting up increases and possibly existing businesses fail at a faster pace. With the birth and death of businesses, jobs are created and destroyed. Faster long-term growth increases the pace of job creation and job destruction. In a fast-growing economy, people must be ready to accept changes in the jobs they do and the places in which they live and to bear the costs of these changes.

The choices that people make, both private choices and public choices made through government institutions, to balance the benefits and costs of economic growth, determine the actual pace of economic growth. We'll study these choices and their consequences in Chapters 25 and 26.

REVIEW

◆ Economic growth is the expansion of production possibilities. The long-term trend in economic growth is measured by the growth rate of potential GDP.

◆ Long-term growth in Europe, the United States, Japan and other countries slowed during the 1970s, but was restored to some extent in the 1980s in the United Kingdom, the United States and Japan.

◆ Real GDP growth fluctuates in a business cycle. An expansion to a peak is followed by a recession, trough, recovery, and finally a new expansion.

◆ The main benefit of economic growth is expanded consumption possibilities. The main costs are less current consumption, possibly resource depletion and environmental pollution, and rapid changes in jobs and locations.

We've seen that real GDP grows and that it also fluctuates over the business cycle. Business cycles bring fluctuations in jobs and unemployment. Let's now examine this core macroeconomic problem.

Jobs and Unemployment

What kind of labour market will you enter when you graduate? Your decision to take a university course may have been prompted by your assessment of the chances of securing a good job after taking a degree. Whether there will be plenty of good jobs to choose from, or whether you will be forced to take a low-paying job that doesn't use your education will depend, in part, on the total number of jobs available and on the unemployment rate.

Jobs

Between 1979 and 1994 3.6 million jobs were created in the European Union. This number may appear to be impressive but let's put it in an international perspective. In the United States – a comparably sized economy – nearly 27 million jobs were created over the same period. Since the middle of 1979, the number of jobs created in the United Kingdom equalled the number destroyed, so that there have been no additional jobs created. But these figures disguise the considerable changes that have been going on in the jobs market. There has been a general switch from manufacturing jobs to services, from male to female workers and from full-time to part-time. Of course new jobs are created every month, but there are many that are also destroyed. The pace of job creation and destruction fluctuates over the business cycle. More jobs are destroyed than created during a recession, so the number of jobs decreases. But more jobs are created than destroyed during a recovery and expansion, so the number of jobs increases. For example, 1.7 million jobs were lost between 1979 and 1983. In the long recovery to 1989 3.2 million jobs were created and in the recession of 1990–1992 the number of jobs fell by nearly 1.9 million. But the prospects for university graduates are a little better. At the end of 1994, when the overall unemployment rate for the United Kingdom was 9 per cent, the unemployment rate of graduates was 7 per cent six months after graduation. At the same time starting salaries were £13,600, which was close to average earnings for the economy as a whole.

Unemployment

An internationally recognized definition of unemployment is that a person is defined as being **unemployed** if he or she does not have a job but is available for work, willing to work and has made some effort to find work within the previous four weeks[2]. The sum of the people who are unemployed and the people who are employed is called the **work-force**. The **unemployment rate** is the percentage of the people in the work-force who are

---

[1] In the United Kingdom the definition of unemployment is someone who is in receipt of the jobseekers allowance (Chapter 24).

unemployed. (The concepts of the work-force and unemployment are explained more fully in Chapter 24 on pp. 602–604.)

The unemployment rate is not a perfect measure of the underutilization of labour for two main reasons. First, it excludes discouraged workers. A **discouraged worker** is a person who does not have a job, is available for work and willing to work, but who has given up the effort to find work. Many people switch between the unemployment and discouraged worker categories in both directions every month. Second, the unemployment rate measures unemployed persons rather than unemployed labour hours. It excludes those people who have a part-time job but who want a full-time job.

Despite these two limitations, the unemployment rate is the best available measure of underused labour resources. Let's look at some facts about unemployment.

Unemployment in the United Kingdom

Figure 22.6 shows the unemployment rate in the United Kingdom from 1855 to 1994. Two features stand out. First, we have had high unemployment in

---

FIGURE 22.6

Unemployment in the United Kingdom: 1855–1994

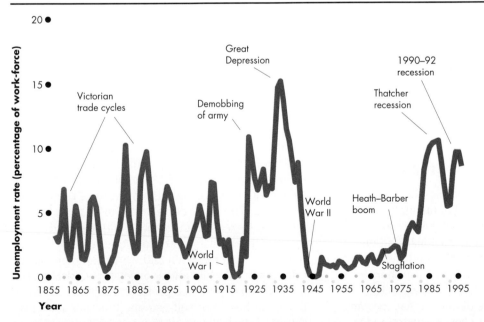

Unemployment is a persistent feature of economic life, but its rate varies. At its worst – during the Great Depression – nearly 16 per cent of the work-force was unemployed. Even in recent recessions, the unemployment rate climbed to 11 per cent. Between 1945 and the late 1960s unemployment remained stable. From the mid 1970s, there has been a general tendency for the unemployment rate to increase.

Sources: C.H.Feinstein, *National Income Expenditure and Output of the United Kingdom, 1855–1965*, 1972, Cambridge, Cambridge University Press; Cental Statistical Office, *Economic Trends Annual Supplement*, 1996.

the past, indeed unemployment in the depressed interwar years reached peaks of between 11.3 and 15.6 per cent. In the period after World War II the average unemployment rate remained low until the late 1970s.

Second, although in recent years we have not experienced anything as devastating as the mass unemployment of the interwar years, we have seen some high unemployment rates during recessions. The figure highlights two recent experiences – the 1980–81 recession and the 1990–1992 recession.

How does UK unemployment compare with unemployment in other countries?

Unemployment Around the World

Figure 22.7 shows the unemployment rate in the United States, the European Union, Japan and the United Kingdom. Over the period shown in this figure, US unemployment averaged 6.7 per cent, much higher than Japanese unemployment, which averaged 2.2 per cent, but lower than unemployment in the European Union, which averaged 7.1 per cent, and in the United Kingdom, which averaged 7.3 per cent.

The figure shows that unemployment fluctuates over the business cycle. It increases during a recession and decreases during an expansion. The cycle in the United States is out of phase with the United Kingdom and Europe. Also, European and UK unemployment was on a rising trend through the 1970s and most of the 1980s. In contrast with the other countries, Japanese unemployment has been remarkably stable.

We've looked at some facts about unemployment in the United Kingdom and in other countries. Let's now look at some of the consequences of unemployment that make it the serious problem that it is.

Why Unemployment is a Problem

Unemployment is a serious economic, social and personal problem. A prolonged spell of unemployment can permanently damage a person's job prospects. For example, Patricia finishes law school at a time when the unemployment rate is high and she just can't find a job in a law office. Desperately short of income, she becomes a telephone sales operator. After a year in this work, she discovers that she can't compete with the new crop of law graduates and is stuck with selling over the telephone.

FIGURE 22.7

Unemployment in the Industrial Economies

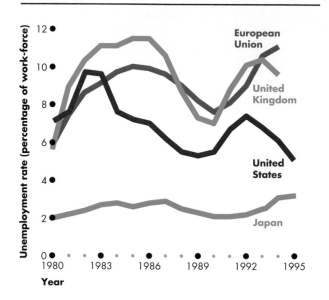

The unemployment rate in the European Union has in general been higher than that in the United States. The UK unemployment rate has increased faster than the EU average but also fallen faster. EU unemployment has a cycle that is out of phase with the United States. Japanese unemployment barely changes.

Source: *European Economy,* November, European Union, (Brussels), November, 1995.

Many social problems become more severe in times of high unemployment. Among them are an increase in crime, alcoholism, depression, suicide and domestic violence. It is sometimes argued that the main reason for the correlation between crime and unemployment is that some people, when they cannot earn an income from legal work, turn to illegal activities. As a result, the amount of theft increases. The other correlations arise from low incomes, increased uncertainty and fear, and increased personal frustration. These factors put family life under a strain and lead to an increase in crimes such as child and spouse abuse. Also, many people who experience prolonged periods of unemployment lose their self-esteem. It is probably this aspect of unemployment that makes it so highly charged with political and social significance.

◆ The total number of jobs in the United Kingdom today is about the same as in 1979.

◆ The unemployment rate fluctuates but unemployment never disappears.

◆ Prolonged unemployment can permanently damage a person's job prospects and a high unemployment rate brings increased social problems.

Let's now turn to the third major issue for macroeconomics: inflation.

Inflation

Inflation is a process of rising prices. We measure the *inflation rate* as the percentage change in the *average* level of prices or **price level**. A common measure of the price level is the *Retail Prices Index* (RPI). The RPI tells us how the average price of all the goods and services bought by a typical household changes from month to month. (The RPI is explained in Chapter 23, pp. 586–587). Every month the television news and the newspapers report the rate of inflation. How is this calculated?

So that you can see in a concrete way how the inflation rate is measured, let's do a calculation. In December 1993, the RPI was 141.9, and in December 1994, it was 146.0, so the inflation rate during 1994 was

$$\text{Inflation} = \frac{146.0 - 141.9}{141.9} \times 100$$
$$= 2.9\%$$

Inflation in the United Kingdom

Figure 22.8 shows the UK inflation rate from 1960 to 1994. You can see from this figure that during the early 1960s the inflation rate was between 2 and 3 per cent a year. Inflation began to increase in the late 1960s, but the largest increases occurred in

FIGURE 22.8

Inflation in the United Kingdom: 1960–1994

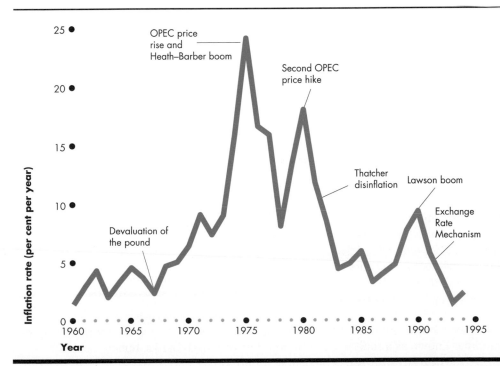

Inflation has been a persistent feature of economic life in the United Kingdom. The inflation rate was low in the first half of the 1960s, but it increased during the second half with the rise in world inflation. It increased further with the OPEC oil price hikes but declined during the Thatcher years of the 1980s as a result of policy actions. The inflation rate rose at the end of the 1980s and has fallen during the 1990s.

Source: Central Statistical Office, *Economic Trends Annual Supplement*, 1996.

1975 and 1980. These were years in which the actions of OPEC resulted in exceptionally large increases in the price of oil, but domestic policies also contributed to the inflation process. Inflation was brought under control in the early 1980s when the then prime minister, Margaret Thatcher, made inflation control her top priority. On the government's instructions, the Bank of England pushed interest rates up in an effort to reduce demand.

The inflation rate rises and falls over the years, but it rarely becomes negative. If the inflation rate is negative, the price *level* is falling. Since the 1930s, the price level has generally risen – the inflation rate has been positive. Thus even when the inflation rate is low, as it was in 1961 and 1986, the price level is rising.

Inflation Around the World

Figure 22.9 shows inflation in the major industrial countries since 1961. You can see in part (a) that the UK inflation rate has been similar to that of other industrial countries. You can also see that all the industrial countries shared the burst of double-digit inflation during the 1970s and the fall in inflation during the 1980s. You can see in part (b) that the average inflation rate of industrial countries has been low compared with that of the developing countries. Among the developing countries, the most extreme inflation has occurred in Latin America where, in 1990, the inflation rate hit almost 600 per cent. This means that a commodity which costs £10 at the start of the year costs £60 by the end of the year. A period of inflation brings changes in two other key variables:

1. Interest rates
2. The foreign exchange rate

Inflation and Interest Rates

An **interest rate** is the amount received by a lender and paid by a borrower expressed as a percentage of the amount of the loan. For example, suppose you borrow £1,000 for one year and at the end of the year, you repay the £1,000 plus £50 of interest. In this case, you have paid an *interest rate* of 5 per cent a year.

There are many interest rates in our economy. On a deposit account (sometimes known as a time deposit) at a bank, you receive the *deposit interest rate*. On a loan to buy a car, you pay the *loan*

FIGURE 22.9

Inflation Around the World

(a) The United Kingdom and other industrial countries

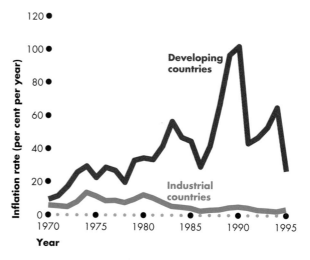

(b) Industrial countries and developing countries

Inflation in the UK is similar to that in the other industrial countries. Its peaks have typically been above that of the EU average and higher than in the United States. Compared with the developing countries, inflation in the industrial countries is low.

Source: International Monetary Fund, *International Financial Statistics Yearbook*, 1994, Washington, DC.

interest rate, which includes a margin on the bank's operating *base rate*. On the money the government borrows from banks, businesses and people for up to one year, it pays the *treasury bill rate*. On the loans that banks make to each other, they pay and receive the *interbank rate*, sometimes referred to as LIBOR (London interbank offered rate). And on the loans that banks make to big businesses, the banks earn a margin over the *LIBOR rate*.

Although there are many interest rates, they all move up and down together. Usually, the higher the inflation rate, the higher are interest rates. You can see this relationship between inflation and interest rates in Fig. 22.10. This figure shows the UK Treasury bill rate alongside the inflation rate. As inflation increased during the 1960s and early 1970s, interest rates also increased, but not as quickly as inflation. The result, between 1974 and 1977, was that most interest rates were lower than the inflation rate. But interest rates continued to rise into the early 1980s and when inflation decreased through the 1980s, interest rates also came down, but much more slowly than inflation. The gap between interest rates and the inflation rate widened.

The Real Interest Rate   When inflation is present, money is losing value. The *value of money* is the quantity of goods and services that can be bought with a given amount of money. When an economy experiences inflation, the value of money falls – you cannot buy as many goods with £100 this year as you could last year. The rate at which the value of money falls is equal to the inflation rate. When the inflation rate is high, as it was in 1980, money loses its value at a rapid pace. When the inflation rate is low, as it was in 1994, the value of money falls slowly.

When money is losing value, people who have funds to lend are willing to do so only if they receive an interest rate that they expect will compensate them for the fact that they will be repaid with money that buys less than the money they lend. And people who borrow are willing to pay such an interest rate. The interest rate calculated in terms of money is called the **nominal interest rate**. But when the value of money is falling, money itself is not a good measuring rod of value. So instead of calculating interest in terms of money, we calculate it in terms of the goods and services that the money will buy. The result is the **real interest rate,** which is the nominal interest rate minus the inflation rate.

Let's calculate a real interest rate. Suppose you borrow £1,000 for one year at a nominal interest rate of 5 per cent a year. Suppose the inflation rate

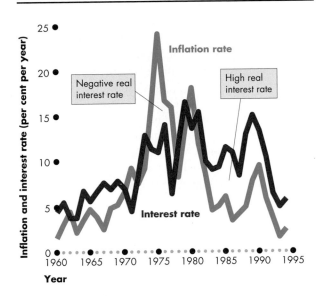

FIGURE 22.10

Interest Rates and Inflation: 1960–1994

Interest rates and inflation generally fluctuate together. During the 1960s, both increased together, but inflation increased faster than interest rates and real interest rates fell. During the 1980s, when inflation decreased, interest rates did not fall as quickly and real interest rates increased. Real interest rates remained high until the 1990s.

Source: Central Statistical Office, *Economic Trends Annual Supplement*, 1996.

is 2 per cent a year. At the end of the year, you pay £1,050 to repay the loan and pay the interest. But with 2 per cent inflation, this £1,050 buys what £1,030 would have bought at the beginning of the year. So the real interest paid is £30 and the real interest rate is only 3 per cent a year – 5 per cent minus 2 per cent.

You can see the real interest rate in Fig. 22.10. It is the vertical distance between the (nominal) interest rate and the inflation rate. During the 1960s, the real interest rate was positive but decreasing. It became negative between 1974 and 1976 and then positive again and quite high during the mid-1980s.

Fluctuations in the nominal interest rate occur because of fluctuations in the inflation rate and the real interest rate. You will learn what determines real interest rates in Chapter 25 and what determines inflation and nominal interest rates in Chapter 32.

Inflation and the Foreign Exchange Rate

All countries experience inflation. But inflation *rates* vary from one country to another. When inflation rates across countries differ over a prolonged period of time, the result is a change in the foreign exchange value of money. A *foreign exchange rate* is the rate at which one country's money (or currency) exchanges for another country's money. For example, in January 1995, £1 exchanged for US$1.58. But in January 1970, you could have got $2.40 for £1. The pound sterling has fallen in value against the US dollar. Part of the reason for this fall in the value of the pound in terms of the dollar was the fact that UK inflation has been higher than US inflation.

Why is Inflation a Problem?

Inflation is a problem because it makes the economy behave like a giant casino in which some people gain and some lose and no one can accurately predict where the gains and losses will fall. Gains and losses occur because of unpredictable changes in the value of money. Money is used as a measuring rod of value in the transactions that we undertake. Borrowers and lenders, workers and employers all make contracts in terms of money. If the value of money varies unpredictably over time, then the amounts *really* paid and received – the quantity of goods that the money will buy – also fluctuate unpredictably. Measuring value with a measuring rod whose units vary is a bit like trying to measure a piece of cloth with an elastic ruler. The size of the cloth depends on how tightly the ruler is stretched.

In a rapid inflation, resources are diverted from productive activities to forecasting inflation. It becomes more profitable to forecast the inflation rate correctly than to invent a new product. Doctors, lawyers, accountants, farmers – just about everyone – can make themselves better off, not by practising the profession for which they have been trained but by becoming amateur economists and inflation forecasters. From a social perspective, this diversion of talent resulting from inflation is like throwing our scarce resources on to the rubbish heap. This waste of resources is a cost of inflation.

The most serious type of inflation is called *hyperinflation* – an inflation rate that exceeds 50 per cent a month. Such high inflation rates are rare, but they occurred in Germany, Poland and Hungary during the 1920s and Hungary and China during the 1940s. At the height of these hyperinflations, workers were paid twice a day because money lost its value so quickly. As soon as they were paid, people rushed off to spend their wages before they lost too much value. Prices were so high that a shopping trolley of money was needed to buy just a handful of groceries. People who lingered too long in the coffee shop found that the price of their cup of coffee had increased between the time they placed their order and when the bill was presented. Children played with bundles of bank notes, which was cheaper than buying toys.

Hyperinflation is not just a historical curiosity. In 1994, the African country of Zaire had a hyperinflation that peaked at a *monthly* inflation rate of 76 per cent. Also during 1994, Brazil almost reached the hyperinflation stratosphere with a monthly inflation rate of 40 per cent. A cup of coffee that cost 15 cruzeiros in 1980 would have cost 22 *billion* cruzeiros in 1994. With numbers this big, Brazil twice changed the name of its currency and twice lopped off three zeros to keep the magnitudes of monetary values manageable. Bank deposits in Brazil earned 30 per cent a month interest – just about enough to keep up with inflation. With a cashpoint machine on every street corner, people get cash at the moment they need it. When they take a taxi, they stop at a cashpoint machine at the end of the trip and get just enough cash for the fare. Hyperinflation and near-hyperinflation like that in Brazil bring economic chaos and severely disrupt normal economic life.

REVIEW

◆ Inflation is a process of rising prices and a falling value of money.

◆ Fluctuations in the inflation rate bring fluctuations in interest rates.

◆ When inflation in the United Kingdom exceeds inflation in another country, the value of the pound in terms of the money of the other country falls.

◆ Inflation is a serious problem because it brings unpredictable gains and losses to borrowers and lenders, workers and employers, and because it diverts resources from producing goods and services to predicting inflation.

We've now looked at economic growth and the business cycle, unemployment and inflation. There's a fourth macroeconomic issue that generates a lot of excitement: the balance of international payments.

What happens when a country buys more from other countries than it sells to them? Does it face the problem that you and I would face if we spent more than we earned? Does it run out of money? Let's look at these questions.

International Payments

When we import goods and services from the rest of the world, we make payments to foreigners. When we export goods and services to the rest of the world, we receive payments from foreigners. We keep track of the values of our imports and exports in our international current account.

The Current Account

The **current account** records the receipts from exports (the sale of goods and services to other countries), the payments for imports (the purchase of goods and services from other countries), the receipts of interest income from other countries, the payments of interest to other countries, and gifts and other transfers (such as international aid payments).

If our exports plus interest receipts from other countries exceed our imports plus interest payments to other countries plus gifts and other transfers, we have a current account surplus. If our imports plus interest payments to other countries plus gifts and other transfers exceed our exports plus interest received from other countries, we have a current account deficit.

The Current Account in the United Kingdom

Figure 22.11 shows the history of the UK current account since 1960. It shows that the United Kingdom has always had a problem with the balance of trade. The current account was in deficit in several years in the 1960s. It built up a surplus between 1969 and 1972 and slipped into deficit at the time of the OPEC oil crisis. Large surpluses occurred in the first half of the 1980s and deficits in the second half.

The current account balance fluctuates with the business cycle. In a recession, imports fall and the deficit decreases (or the surplus increases). During an expansion, imports rise and the current account deficit increases. For example, a large deficit emerged during the period of the major expansion of

FIGURE 22.11

The UK Current Account Balance: 1960–1994

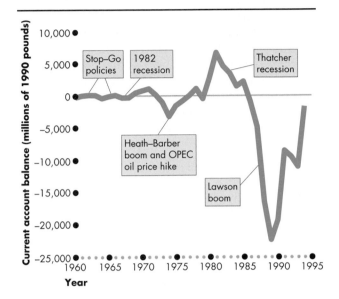

The current account records our exports and imports of goods and services. During the 1960s, our current account was generally in balance. In the mid-1970s, a deficit emerged following the expansionary policies of the Conservative Heath government. The early 1980s saw a sizeable surplus following the deflationary policies of Mrs Thatcher. During the expansion of the late 1980s, a large deficit emerged, but it has fallen since the recession of 1990–92.

Source: Central Statistical Office, *Economic Trends Annual Supplement*, 1996.

demand engineered by the Conservative Heath administration between 1973 and 1974. During the early 1980s, a huge surplus was generated following the deflationary policies of the Conservative Thatcher administration. But after 1986, a persistent current account deficit emerged with the economic boom of the late 1980s. At times the deficit has been large. In 1989, for example, it exceeded £22.4 billion. How can we have a persistent current account deficit? The answer is because we have a capital account surplus.

The Capital Account

The **capital account** records the receipts from foreign investments in the United Kingdom and UK investments in the rest of the world. When we have a current account deficit, we borrow from foreigners or we sell some UK assets to foreigners to pay for it. When we have a current account surplus, we loan our surplus to the rest of the world or we buy foreign assets.

So a current account surplus is always matched by a capital account deficit, and a current account deficit is always matched by a capital account surplus. We do not, as a nation, run out of cash to pay our bills. But is borrowing from the rest of the world a problem? It might be, but it is not inevitably a problem.

Just as an individual can borrow to consume, so also can a country. Borrowing to consume is usually not a good idea. It builds up a debt that grows as interest is added to the debt, and at some point the debt plus the interest must be paid off. But an individual or a country can also borrow to invest in assets that earn interest. Borrowing to invest in assets that earn interest is potentially profitable. It creates an income stream that can pay off a debt and the interest on the debt. So long as the interest rate earned on the investment exceeds that on the debt, the deficit and the debt do not pose a problem.

In Chapters 25, 28, and 36 you will learn more about the balance of international payments, why we have had a current account deficit for 10 years, why the current account balance fluctuates with the business cycle, and whether we have been borrowing to consume or to invest.

R E V I E W

◆ The current account records the receipts from exports and the payments for imports.

◆ When imports exceed exports, we have a current account deficit.

◆ We have had a persistent current account deficit since 1986.

◆ The current account balance is cyclical. It increases during an expansion and decreases during a recession.

◆ A current account deficit is matched by a capital account surplus.

Let's close this chapter by looking at the macroeconomic policy challenges.

Macroeconomic Policy Challenges and Tools

From the time of Adam Smith's *Wealth of Nations* until the establishment of macroeconomics in 1936, the general view was that the proper role of government in economic life was to provide the legal framework in which people could freely pursue their own best interests. The macroeconomics of Keynes, published in the *General Theory of Employment, Interest, and Money* in 1936, challenged this view and argued that government could (and should) take policy actions aimed at achieving and maintaining full employment.

The policy goal of full employment became the declared objective of the government following the publication of the White Paper on Employment Policy in 1944.

Policy Challenges

Today, the widely agreed challenges for macroeconomic policy are to:

1. Boost long-term growth
2. Stabilize the business cycle
3. Lower unemployment
4. Tame inflation
5. Prevent a large current account deficit
6. Reduce the government deficit

By boosting long-term growth, we can try to avoid the problems that have arisen over the past 20 years from the productivity growth slowdown of the mid-1970s. You've seen in this chapter how much that slowdown has cost us. By stabilizing the business cycle, we can try to smooth out the fluctuations in unemployment and in income growth. By lowering the unemployment rate, we can try to avoid some of the social problems that unemployment creates, and by taming inflation, we can encourage people to focus on the activities at which they have a comparative advantage and not get diverted to becoming amateur inflation forecasters. By avoiding a large current account deficit, we avoid having to borrow large amounts from the rest of the world. Finally by reducing the government budget deficit, the real interest rate could fall, which would aid the process of boosting long-term growth.

But how can we do all these things? What are the tools available to pursue the macroeconomic policy challenges?

Policy Tools

Macroeconomic policy tools are divided into two broad categories:

◆ Fiscal policy

◆ Monetary policy

Fiscal Policy   **Fiscal policy** is the government's attempt to influence the economy by setting and changing taxes, government spending, and the government's deficit and debt. This range of policy actions is under the control of the Chancellor of the Exchequer and the Treasury. Fiscal policy can be used to try to change the total amount of spending or to change incentives so that investment and productivity increase. When the economy is in a recession, the government might cut taxes or increase its spending in an attempt to lower the unemployment rate. Conversely, when the economy is expanding and real GDP is above potential, the government might increase taxes or cut its spending in an attempt to prevent the economy from overheating.

Through most of the 1970s and 1980s, the government has spent more than it has raised in taxes. When government spending exceeds tax revenues, the government has a **budget deficit**. This deficit is referred to as the General Government Financial Deficit. A more popularly known concept is the **Public Sector Borrowing Requirement** (PSBR). The PSBR is the government budget deficit plus the interest payments the government pays to those who have lent to the government. In the second half of the 1980s, the government ran a budget surplus. There was a surplus even after the government paid interest to those who had lent to the government. This surplus was referred to as the **Public Sector Debt Repayment** (PSDR). But since 1991 the government has run a PSBR that reached a record height of £42.5 billion in 1993. The government has stated as a long-term objective the desirability of eliminating the budget deficit. Also the Maastricht Treaty imposes certain constraints on the fiscal deficits of member countries in the European Union as conditions of economic convergence prior to full European Monetary Union (EMU). The constraints include a budget deficit target of 3 per cent of GDP. While the UK government is a signatory to the treaty it has an opt-out clause that can stop it from joining EMU, but it has

not categorically rejected the option to join. In either case the existence of a budget deficit target has limited the scope for using fiscal policy to stabilize the business cycle.

Monetary Policy   **Monetary policy** consists of changes in interest rates and in the amount of money in the economy. This range of policy actions is under the control of the Treasury but ultimately carried out by the Bank of England. When the economy is in recession, the government might lower interest rates and inject money into the economy in an attempt to lower the unemployment rate. And when the economy is expanding quickly, it might increase interest rates in an attempt to prevent the economy from overheating.

By mid-1994, the governor of the Bank of England, Eddie George, became concerned that the economy was overheating and heading towards a period of rising inflation (see *Reading Between the Lines* on pp. 566–567). Monetary policy was used to push interest rates up so as to discourage borrowing and spending, to curb the growth of production and to forestall a rise in inflation.

R E V I E W

◆ The macroeconomic policy challenges are to boost long-term growth, stabilize the business cycle, lower unemployment, tame inflation and prevent a large current account deficit.

◆ To meet these challenges, the government uses fiscal policy tools – taxes and government spending.

◆ Since 1979, the government has made the reduction of the government sector and the reduction of the government deficit a new policy challenge.

◆ The Bank of England uses monetary policy tools – interest rates and money supply.

◆ ◆ ◆ ◆ In your study of macroeconomics, you will find out what is currently known about the causes of long-term economic growth, business cycles, unemployment, inflation and the international balance of payments, and about the policy choices and challenges that the government faces. The next step in your pursuit of these goals is to learn more about macroeconomic measurement – about how we measure real GDP and the price level.

The Developed Economies in 1995

The Essence of the Story

THE FINANCIALTIMES, 14 JUNE 1996

'Feel bad' factor grips western world

Gillian Tett

BIS shows subtle change of tone by cautioning against both inflation and deflation

The western world is gripped by a lack of confidence and a "feel bad" factor that is unprecedented in recent economic history, the Bank for International Settlements said in its annual report yesterday.

While growth in the US remained steady and the recovery in Japan was gathering pace, consumption had been dampened by job insecurity and the need to trim fiscal deficits, it warned.

Central bankers now need to consider the risks of falling prices as well as inflation in settling their monetary policy, it said. 'Price stability has been reached or nearly reached in a large number of countries.

'The forces bearing on the price level... are now more balanced than they have been for some decades.'...

In recent years the BIS, ...has emphasised the need to combat inflation at all costs, and limited its analysis of labour market problems.

But with central banks having been accused in some countries of curbing growth in their zeal to control inflation, the BIS emphasised that monetary policy could be both expansionary and restrictive – and called on policy makers to 'resist both inflation and deflation'.

This subtle change in tone may fuel market speculation that central banks might be slower to raise interest rates again in the next economic cycle. However, the BIS denied that it was encouraging lax monetary policy, while Mr Wim Duisenberg, BIS president, warned that the 'continuing buoyancy of the US economy' might pose an inflation risk in the future.

Nevertheless, it admitted that some new deflationary factors were emerging in the world – namely increased global competition, wage flexibility and continuing attempts to cut fiscal deficits.

With these factors partly to blame for the 'feel bad' problem, the BIS acknowledged that central bankers could do little themselves to boost sentiment. In the longer term, however, it argued that consumer confidence should rebound.

Although the timing of the upturn in Europe was still uncertain, growth elsewhere in the world was healthy and the world markets were unlikely to trigger any recessionary jolts....

- The major western economies grew steadily during 1995, but a lack of confidence in the prospects for the future have raised the possibility of new types of risk.

- Growth in the United States and Germany was steady but declining during 1995. Growth in Japan gathered pace in the same period.

- The US economy is above potential output whereas the German and Japanese economies are below potential output.

- While growth has continued in all three economies, consumption has been weak because of job insecurity and the need to reduce fiscal deficits.

- The economic authorities need to consider the dangers of falling prices as well as inflation when setting monetary policies.

Economic Analysis

■ The recovery in the world economy was not consistent during 1995. Growth of GDP output declined in the United States and Germany but recovered in Japan.

■ At the same time, GDP output was below potential GDP in Germany and Japan but above potential GDP in the United States. Consumer spending has remained weak because of uncertainty about future job prospects.

■ Figures 1–3 show GDP growth and the difference between actual GDP and potential GDP for the three major economies in the western world. A positive output gap means that actual GDP is above potential GDP and a negative output gap means that actual GDP is below potential GDP. Potential GDP is not known exactly in any of the three countries. Any figure is only one possible estimate.

■ The inconsistency in the output gaps of the three major economies means that the western world is finely balanced between inflation and falling prices. While the continued strength of the US economy might pose an inflation risk in the future, the weakness of the German and Japanese economies suggests the reverse.

■ Price stability has been reached in the major western economies and there are as many forces bearing down on the price level as there are pushing the price level up.

■ Increased global competition, wage flexibility and attempts by governments to cut their expenditure has contributed to a world 'feel bad' factor.

■ In the United States, a positive output gap poses the danger that the economy could overheat and inflation could pick up. The negative output gap in Japan and Germany poses the danger of falling prices.

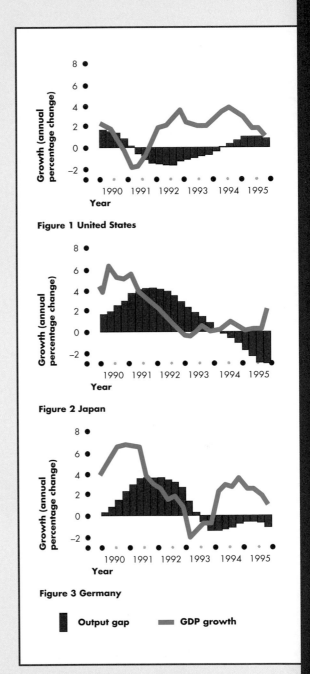

Figure 1 United States

Figure 2 Japan

Figure 3 Germany

■ Output gap ▬ GDP growth

SUMMARY

Origins and Issues of Macroeconomics

Macroeconomics emerged during the mid-eighteenth century but it was reborn during the Great Depression of the 1930s. Macroeconomics studies both the long-term trends and short-term fluctuations in economic growth, unemployment, inflation and the balance of international payments. Its main purpose is to devise policies that might boost long-term economic growth, prevent the extremes of depression and inflation, and avoid large international payments deficits. (pp. 549–550)

Economic Growth

Economic growth is the expansion of the economy's capacity to produce goods and services, measured by the increase in real GDP. The long-term trend growth rate is measured by the rate of increase of potential GDP. The long-term growth rate slowed during the 1970s. Real GDP fluctuates around potential GDP in a business cycle. Other macroeconomic variables such as unemployment also fluctuate over a business cycle. Every business cycle has an expansion, peak, recession, trough, recovery and new expansion.

To compare countries, we use the growth rate of real GDP per person – real GDP divided by the population. When we compare countries, we find similar productivity growth slowdowns and similar business cycles but different long-term trends in potential GDP.

The main benefit of long-term economic growth is expanded consumption possibilities, and the main costs are reduced current consumption, resource depletion, environmental pollution, and the need to face rapid and often costly changes in job type and location. (pp. 550–556)

Jobs and Unemployment

The United Kingdom is not a large job-creating economy. The rate at which jobs are created and destroyed varies with the business cycle. Just over 500,000 jobs a year are created in the expansion phase of a business cycle. But just under 500,000 jobs a year are lost in the contraction phase. During the 1990s there have been on average 2.5 million people unemployed.

An internationally accepted definition of unemployment is that it is a state in which people do not have jobs but are willing to work, are available for work and have looked for work during the previous four weeks. In the United Kingdom, unemployment is measured by the number of people in receipt of the job seekers allowance. The work-force is the number of people employed plus the number unemployed. The unemployment rate is the percentage of the work-force who are unemployed. The unemployment rate excludes discouraged workers and people with a part-time job who want a full-time job.

The UK unemployment rate fluctuates over the business cycle. It rises during a recession and falls during an expansion. The UK unemployment rate is lower than the average for the European Union but higher than in Japan or the United States.

Unemployment is a serious economic, social and personal problem. It can permanently damage a person's job prospects. It can also bring increased crime, alcoholism, depression, suicide and domestic violence. (pp. 556–559)

Inflation

Inflation is a process of rising prices. The inflation rate is measured by the percentage change in a price index such as the RPI. Inflation is a persistent feature of economic life in the United Kingdom and the other major economies, but the inflation rate fluctuates. During the 1960s and 1970s, inflation was on an upward trend. Since 1980, it has generally been on a downward trend. Inflation in the United Kingdom is similar to that in other developed countries. But inflation in the developed countries has been mild compared with that of the developing countries.

Changes in the inflation rate lead to changes in interest rates and in the foreign exchange rate. Inflation is a problem because it lowers the value of money at an unpredictable rate and makes money less useful as a measuring rod of value. A rapid inflation diverts resources from productive activities to forecasting inflation. (pp. 559–562)

International Payments

Our receipts from exports (the sale of goods and services to foreigners), payments for imports (the purchase of goods and services from foreigners), international interest receipts and payments, and gifts and other transfers (such as foreign aid payments) are recorded in the current account. The United Kingdom has always had a problem with the current account. It had a current account deficit in the late 1960s and most of the 1970s. The United Kingdom had a current account surplus in the early 1980s, but has had a deficit since the late 1980s. The current account balance is cyclical and fluctuates with the business cycle – the current account deficit decreases in a recession and increases in an expansion.

A current account deficit is financed by borrowing from abroad or by selling UK assets to foreigners. International borrowing and lending and asset sales and purchases are recorded in the capital account. (pp. 563–564)

Macroeconomic Policy Challenges and Tools

The challenges for macroeconomic policy are to boost long-term growth, stabilize the business cycle, lower unemployment, tame inflation and prevent a large current account deficit. The tools available for meeting these challenges are fiscal policy and monetary policy. (pp. 564–565)

K E Y   E L E M E N T S

Key Terms

Budget deficit, 565
Business cycle, 551
Capital account, 563
Current account, 563
Discouraged worker, 557
Economic growth, 550
Expansion, 552
Fiscal policy, 565
Great Depression, 549
Inflation, 559
Interest rate, 560
Monetary policy, 565
Nominal interest rate, 561
Potential GDP, 550
Price level, 559
Productivity growth slowdown, 550
Public Sector Borrowing Requirement (PSBR), 565
Public Sector Debt Repayment (PSDR), 565
Real GDP per person, 553
Real gross domestic product (real GDP), 550
Real interest rate, 561
Recession, 552
Stagflation, 549
Unemployed, 557
Unemployment rate, 557
Work-force, 557

◆ Key Figures

Figure 22.1   Economic Growth in the United Kingdom: 1960–1994, 551
Figure 22.2   The Most Recent UK Business Cycle, 552
Figure 22.3   Long-term Economic Growth in the United Kingdom, 553
Figure 22.6   Unemployment in the United Kingdom: 1855–1994, 557
Figure 22.8   Inflation in the United Kingdom: 1960–1994, 559
Figure 22.11   The UK Current Account Balance: 1960–1994, 563

REVIEW QUESTIONS

1 Distinguish between real GDP and potential GDP.

2 Is real GDP an ideal measure of total production? Explain why or why not.

3 What is economic growth?

4 How is the long-term economic growth rate measured?

5 What are the benefits of long-term economic growth?

6 What are the costs of long-term economic growth?

7 What is a business cycle? Describe its phases.

8 In what phase of the business cycle was the UK economy during 1973, 1981, 1988 and 1994?

9 What is unemployment? How is it measured in the United Kingdom? Do you think it is an accurate measure?

10 What does the unemployment rate tell us about the amount of joblessness? Explain your answer.

11 What are the main costs of unemployment?

12 What is inflation?

13 What are some of the costs of inflation?

14 Explain the connection between inflation and interest rates and define the real interest rate.

15 Explain the connection between inflation and the exchange rate.

16 What are the main challenges and tools of macroeconomic policy?

PROBLEMS

1 The figure shows real GDP per person in Barbados and Mexico during the 1980s.

   a In which years was economic growth in Barbados positive?

   b In which years was economic growth in Barbados negative?

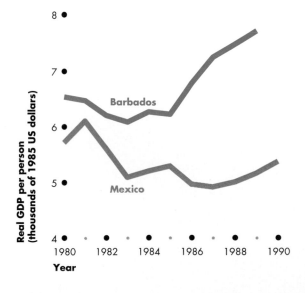

   c In which year was economic growth in Barbados fastest?

   d In which years was economic growth in Mexico positive?

   e In which years was economic growth in Mexico negative?

   f What is the most striking difference between real GDP per person in these two countries?

   g In which country is the average person becoming richer?

2 The figure shows real GDP in Germany from the first quarter of 1991 to the second quarter of 1994.

   Use the figure to answer the following questions:

   a How many recessions did Germany experience during this period?

   b In which quarters, if any, did Germany experience a recovery?

   c In which quarters, if any, did Germany experience a business cycle peak?

   d In which quarters, if any, did Germany experience a business cycle trough?

   e In which quarters, if any, did Germany experience an expansion?

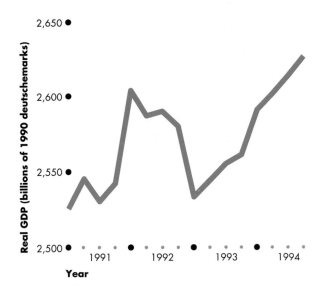

Year

3   Obtain data on quarterly real GDP for the United Kingdom since the fourth quarter of 1994 and update Fig. 22.2. You will find the data in recent issues of *Economic Trends*, which is published monthly by the Central Statistical Office. (Find out if your college library has a subscription to Datastream, which gives you access to the latest data online.) Using what you have discovered, answer the following questions:

  a   Is the UK economy now in a recession or a recovery?
  b   If the economy is still in a recovery, how long has it lasted?
  c   During 1995, was the growth rate speeding up or slowing down?

  d   Compare the recession of 1980–81 with the recession that began in 1990. Which recession was the longest, and during which recovery did real GDP grow most quickly?

4   Obtain data on unemployment in your region. This can be obtained from *Regional Trends*, *Annual Abstract of Statistics* or selected issues of *Economic Trends*. Compare the behaviour of unemployment in your region with that in the United Kingdom as a whole. Why do you think your region might have a higher or a lower unemployment rate than the national average?

5   Obtain data on inflation in the United Kingdom, the United States, Japan and Germany since 1980. You will find these data in *International Financial Statistics* or the *European Economy* in your college library. Draw a graph of the data and answer the following questions. Which country has had:

  a   The highest inflation rate?
  b   The lowest inflation rate?
  c   The fastest rising inflation rate?
  d   The fastest falling inflation rate?

6   Study *Reading Between the Lines* on pp. 566–567 and then answer the following questions:

  a   In what phase of the business cycle were the US, Japanese and German economies in 1995?
  b   What has been the growth performance of these three economies in 1995?
  c   What dangers are posed by the position of each economy in the phase of their respective business cycles?

> '*The ideas of economists and political philosophers, both when they are right and when they are wrong, are more powerful than is commonly understood. Indeed the world is ruled by little else.*'

John Maynard Keynes (1883–1946), THE GENERAL THEORY OF EMPLOYMENT, INTEREST AND MONEY, CHAPTER 24, 'CONCLUDING NOTES' (1936).

The Keynesian Revolution

THE ISSUES AND IDEAS

During the Industrial Revolution in England and on the European continent, new inventions destroyed jobs. Waves of new prosperity for the majority were accompanied by unemployment for a significant minority. In this climate, there was controversy as to whether the economy could expand indefinitely or whether it would reach a limit beyond which there would not be sufficient demand to buy the goods and services that could be produced.

Jean-Baptiste Say argued that in the long run, there can be no problem about supply outstripping demand. The production of goods and services, he claimed, creates incomes that are sufficient to buy those goods and services – supply creates its own demand. The idea that supply creates its own demand came to be known as *Say's Law.*

As the economies of the world became industrialized, they fluctuated in a business cycle – alternating recessions and expansions. But Say seemed to be correct. On average, supply appeared to create its own demand.

But as the Great Depression of the 1930s became more severe and more prolonged, Say's Law looked less and less relevant. John Maynard Keynes revolutionized macroeconomic thinking by turning Say's Law on its head, arguing that real GDP does not depend on what can be produced – on supply. Instead, real GDP depends on what people are willing to buy – on demand, or as Keynes put it, on *effective demand*. It is possible, argued Keynes, for people to refuse to spend all of their incomes. If businesses also fail to spend new capital, demand might be less than supply. In this case, resources might go unemployed and remain unemployed indefinitely.

THE SPINNING JENNY.

THEN ...

In 1776, James Hargreaves, an English weaver and carpenter, developed a simple hand-operated machine called the spinning jenny (pictured here). Using this machine, a person could spin 80 threads at once. Thousands of hand-wheel spinners, operators of machines that could spin only one thread at once, lost their jobs. They protested and tried to protect their jobs by wrecking spinning jennies. In the long run, the displaced hand-wheel spinners found work, often in factories that manufactured the machines that had destroyed their previous jobs. Since the earliest days of the Industrial Revolution to the present day, people have lost their jobs as new technologies have automated what human effort had previously been needed to accomplish.

... AND NOW

Advances in computer technology have made it possible for us to dial our own telephone calls to any part of the world and get connected in a flash. A task that was once performed by telephone operators, who made connections along copper wires, is now performed faster and more reliably by computers, which make connections along fibre optic cables. Just as the Industrial Revolution transformed the textiles industry, so today's Information Revolution is transforming the telecommunications industry. In the process, the mix of jobs is changing. There are fewer jobs for telephone operators but more for telephone systems designers, builders, managers and marketers. In the long run, as people spend the incomes they earn in their new and changing jobs, supply creates its own demand just as Say predicted. But does supply create its own demand in the short run, when displaced workers are unemployed?

THE ECONOMISTS: JEAN-BAPTISTE SAY AND JOHN MAYNARD KEYNES

John Maynard Keynes

Jean-Baptiste Say

Say and Keynes would have had a lot to disagree about. Jean-Baptiste Say, born in Lyon, France, in 1767 (he was 9 years old when Adam Smith's *Wealth of Nations* was published), suffered the wrath of Napoleon for expressing the view that the government should not intervene in the economy. As a result, for several years he was forced to work as a journalist and then as a cotton manufacturer before resuming his career as an economics professor. In the early nineteenth century, Say was the most famous economist in both Europe and the United States. His book *Traité d' économie politique* (*A Treatise on Political Economy*), published in 1803, became a best-selling university economics textbook on both sides of the Atlantic.

John Maynard Keynes, born in the United Kingdom in 1883, was one of the truly great minds of the twentieth century. He wrote on probability as well as economics, represented the UK government at the Versailles peace conference following World War I, was a master speculator in international financial markets (an activity that he conducted from bed every morning), and played a prominent role in establishing the International Monetary Fund and a new global financial system after World War II. He was a prominent member of the Bloomsbury Group, an astonishing circle of artists and writers that included E.M. Forster, Bertrand Russell and Virginia Woolf. Keynes was a controversial and quick-witted figure. A critic once complained that Keynes was constantly shifting his position, to which Keynes retorted: 'When I discover I am wrong, I change my mind. What do you do?'

CHAPTER
23

MEASURING GDP,
INFLATION
AND
ECONOMIC
GROWTH

**After studying this chapter
you will be able to:**

◆ Distinguish between the stocks of
capital and wealth and the flows of
production, income, investment and
saving

◆ Describe the circular flow of income
and expenditure, and explain why
aggregate income, expenditure and
product are equal

◆ Explain how GDP is measured

◆ Explain how the Retail Prices Index
(RPI) and the GDP deflator are
measured

◆ Explain the shortcomings of changes
in the RPI and the GDP deflator as
measures of inflation

◆ Explain how real GDP is measured

◆ Explain the shortcomings of real
GDP growth as a measure of
improvements in economic well-
being

WHEN MERCEDES-BENZ CONTEMPLATES OPENING A CAR PLANT IN THE United States, it pays close attention to long-term forecasts of US real GDP. When British Telecommunications plans to expand its fibre optics network, it uses forecasts of long-term growth in the UK economy. The outcome of many business decisions turns on the quality of forecasts of global and national macroeconomic conditions. ◆ Key inputs for making economic forecasts are the latest estimates of the gross domestic product, or GDP. The GDP data are a barometer of our country's economy. Economists pore over the latest numbers looking at past trends and seeking patterns that might give a glimpse of the future. How do economic statisticians add up all the economic activity of the country to arrive at the number called GDP? What exactly *is* GDP? ◆ Most of the time, our economy grows and sometimes it shrinks. But to reveal the rate of growth (or shrinkage), we must remove the effects of inflation on GDP and assess how *real* GDP is changing. How do we remove the inflation component of GDP to reveal real GDP? ◆ From economists to housewives, all types of people pay close attention to another economic barometer, the Retail Prices Index, or RPI. The Office for National Statistics publishes new figures each month, and analysts in newspapers and on TV quickly leap to conclusions about the causes of recent changes in prices and the prospects for future changes. How does the government determine the RPI? How well does it measure a consumer's living costs and the inflation rate? ◆ Some countries are rich while others are poor and only now are in the process of developing their industries and reaching their productive potential. How do we compare incomes in one country with incomes in another? How can we make international comparisons of GDP?

◆ ◆ ◆ ◆ In this chapter you are going to find out how economic statisticians measure real GDP and the price level. You are also going to learn how they use these measures to assess the economic growth rate and the inflation rate and to compare macroeconomic performance across countries.

Economic Barometers

Gross Domestic Product

Gross domestic product (GDP) is the value of *aggregate* or *total* production of goods and services in a country during a given time period – usually a year. The GDP of the United Kingdom, which measures the value of aggregate production in the United Kingdom during a year, was £688.9 billion in 1994. How was this number calculated, what does it mean and why do we care about it?

You are going to discover the answers to all these questions in this chapter. But first, how is GDP calculated? Two fundamental concepts form the foundation on which GDP measurements are made:

◆ The distinction between stocks and flows

◆ The equality of income, expenditure and the value of production

Stocks and Flows

To keep track of our personal economic transactions and the economic transactions of a country, we distinguish between stocks and flows. A **stock** is a quantity that exists at a point in time. The water in a bath is a stock. So is the number of CDs that you own and the amount of money in your savings deposit. A **flow** is a quantity per unit of time. The water that is running from an open tap into a bath is a flow. So is the number of CDs that you buy in a month and the amount of income that you earn in a month. GDP is another flow. It is the value of production in a country *in a given time period*.

Capital and Investment The key macroeconomic stock is **capital**, the plant, equipment, buildings and stocks of raw materials and semi-finished goods that are used to produce other goods and services. The amount of capital in the economy is a crucial factor that influences GDP. Two macroeconomic *flows* change the *stock* of capital: investment and depreciation. **Investment** is the purchase of new plant, equipment and buildings and the additions to stocks. Investment *increases* the stock of capital. **Depreciation** is the decrease in the stock of capital that results from wear and tear and the passage of time. Another name for depreciation is capital consumption. The total amount spent on adding to

the stock of capital and on replacing depreciated capital is called **gross investment.** The amount spent on adding to the stock of capital is called **net investment.** Net investment equals gross investment minus depreciation.

Figure 23.1 illustrates these concepts. On 1 January, 1995, the Best Jeans Denim factory had 3 sewing machines and this quantity was its initial capital. During 1995, Best Jeans scrapped an older machine. This quantity is its depreciation. After depreciation, Best Jeans' stock of capital was down to 2 machines. But also during 1995, Best Jeans bought 2 new machines. This amount is its gross investment. By 31 December, 1995, Best Jeans had 4 sewing machines so its capital had increased by 1 machine. This amount is Best Jeans' net investment. Best Jeans' net investment equals its gross investment (the purchase of 2 new machines) minus its depreciation (1 machine scrapped).

FIGURE 23.1

Capital and Investment

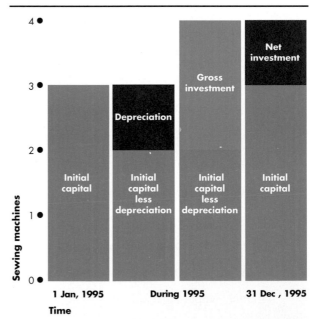

The Best Jeans denim factory's capital stock at the end of 1995 equals its capital stock at the beginning of the year plus its net investment. Net investment is equal to gross investment less depreciation. Best Jeans' gross investment is the 2 new sewing machines bought during the year, and its depreciation is the 1 sewing machine that it scrapped during the year.

The example of Best Jeans Denim factory can be applied to the economy as a whole. The nation's capital stock decreases because capital depreciates and increases because of gross investment. The change in the nation's capital stock from one year to the next equals its net investment.

Wealth and Saving Another macroeconomic stock is **wealth**, which is the value of all the things that people own. What people *own,* a stock, is related to what they *earn,* a flow. People *earn* an *income,* which is the amount they receive during a given time period from supplying the services of factors of production. Income can be either consumed or saved. **Consumption expenditure** is the amount spent on consumption goods and services. **Saving** is the amount of income left over after meeting consumption expenditures. Saving adds to wealth, and dissaving (negative saving) decreases wealth.

For example, at the end of the academic year, you have a £500 overdraft on your bank account and computer equipment worth £1,000. That's all you own. Your wealth is £500. Suppose that you take a summer job and earn an income of £3,000. You are extremely careful and spend only £500. When college starts again you have paid off your overdraft and you have £2,000 in your savings account. Your wealth is now £3,000. Your wealth has increased by £2,500 which equals your saving of £2,500. And your saving of £2,500 equals your income during the summer of £3,000 minus your consumption expenditure of £500.

National wealth and national saving work just like this personal example. The wealth of a nation at the start of a year equals its wealth at the start of the previous year plus its saving during the year. And its saving equals its income minus its consumption.

We'll make the idea of the nation's income and consumption more precise a bit later in this chapter. Before doing so, let's see what the stocks and flows that we've just learned about imply for the recurring theme of macroeconomics: short-term fluctuations and long-term trends in production.

The Short Term Meets the Long Term You saw in Chapter 22 that potential GDP grows steadily, year after year. You also saw that real GDP grows and fluctuates around potential GDP. Both the long-term growth in potential GDP *and* the short-term

fluctuations in real GDP are influenced by the stocks and flows that you've just studied. One of the reasons that potential GDP grows is that the capital stock grows. And one of the reasons that real GDP fluctuates is that investment fluctuates. So capital and investment as well as wealth and saving are part of the key to understanding the growth and fluctuations of GDP.

The flows of investment and saving together with the flows of income and consumption expenditure interact in a circular flow of income and expenditure. In this circular flow, income equals expenditure, which also equals the value of production. This amazing equality is the foundation on which a nation's economic accounts are built and from which its GDP is measured.

The Equality of Income, Expenditure and the Value of Production

To see why, for the economy as a whole, income equals expenditure and also equals the value of production, we study the circular flow of income and expenditure. Figure 23.2 illustrates the circular flow. In the figure, the economy consists of four sectors: households, firms, governments and the rest of the world (the purple diamonds). It has three aggregate markets: factor markets, goods (and services) markets and financial markets. Focus first on households and firms.

Households and Firms Households sell and firms buy the services of labour, capital, land and entrepreneurship in factor markets. For these factor services, firms pay income to households – wages for labour services, interest for the use of capital, rent for the use of land and profits for entrepreneurship. Firms' retained earnings – profits that are not distributed to households – are also part of the household sector's income. (You can think of retained earnings as being income that households save and lend back to firms.) The *total income* received by all households in payment for the services of factors of production is *aggregate income*. Figure 23.2 shows aggregate income by the blue dots labelled Y.

Firms sell and households buy consumer goods and services – such as cola, cinema tickets and pizzas, microwave ovens and dry cleaning services – in the markets for goods (and services). The aggregate payment that households make for these goods

FIGURE 23.2

The Circular Flow of Income and Expenditure

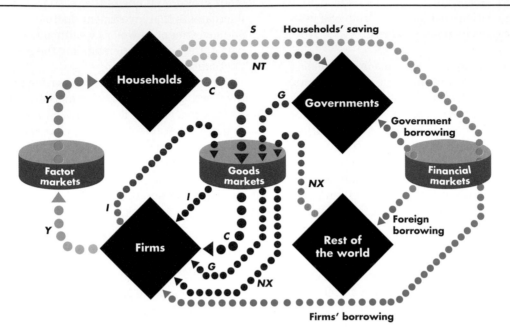

In the circular flow of income and expenditure, households receive incomes (*Y*) from firms (blue flow) and make consumption expenditures (*C*); firms make investment expenditures (*I*); governments purchase goods and services (*G*); the rest of the world purchases net exports (*NX*) – (red flows). Aggregate income (blue flow) equals aggregate expenditure (red flows).

Households' saving (*S*) and net taxes (*NT*) leak from the circular flow. Firms borrow to finance their investment expenditures and governments and the rest of the world borrow to finance their deficits or lend their surpluses – (green flows).

and services is *consumption expenditure*. Figure 23.2 shows consumption expenditure by the red dots labelled *C*.

Firms buy and sell new capital equipment in the goods market. For example, IBM sells 1,000 PCs to Vauxhall or BAC sells an aircraft to British Airways. Some of what firms produce might not be sold at all and is added to stock. For example, if Ford (UK) produces 1,000 cars and sells 950 of them, the other 50 cars remain unsold and Ford's stock of cars increases by 50. When a firm adds unsold output to stock, we can think of the firm as buying goods from itself. The purchase of new plant, equipment and buildings and the additions to stocks are *investment*. To finance investment, firms borrow from households in financial markets. Figure 23.2 shows investment by the red dots labelled *I*. Notice that in the figure investment flows from firms through the goods markets

and back to firms. Some firms produce capital goods and other firms buy them (and firms 'buy' stocks from themselves).

Households place their saving and firms do their borrowing in the financial markets. Figure 23.2 shows these flows by the green dots labelled 'Households' saving' or *S* and 'Firms' borrowing'. These flows are neither income nor expenditure. Income is a payment for the services of a factor of production and expenditure is a payment for goods or services.

Governments Governments buy goods and services from firms. In Fig. 23.2, these **government purchases** are shown as the red flow *G*. Governments pay for their purchases with taxes. Figure 23.2 shows taxes as net taxes by the green dots *NT*. **Net taxes** are taxes paid to governments minus transfer payments received from governments. *Transfer payments* are cash transfers from governments to households and firms such as social security benefits, unemployment compensationand subsidies[1].

When government purchases (G) exceed net taxes (NT), the government sector has a budget deficit, which it finances by borrowing in financial markets. This borrowing is shown by the green dots labelled 'Government borrowing'.

Rest of World Sector   The rest of the world exports goods and services to firms and imports goods and services from firms. The value of exports minus the value of imports is called **net exports.** Figure 23.2 shows net exports by the red flow NX.

If the value of exports exceeds the value of imports, net exports are positive and flow from the rest of the world to firms. But if the value of exports is less than the value of imports, net exports are negative and flow from firms to the rest of the world.

When net exports are positive, the rest of the world either borrows from the domestic economy or sells domestic assets that it has bought previously. These transactions take place in financial markets and they are shown by the green flow labelled 'Foreign borrowing'. When net exports are negative, the domestic economy either borrows from the rest of the world or sells foreign assets that it has previously acquired. Again, these transactions take place in financial markets. To illustrate this case in the figure, we would reverse the directions of the flows of net exports and foreign borrowing.

To help you keep track of the different types of flows that make up the circular flow of income and expenditure, they are colour-coded. In Fig. 23.2, red flows are expenditures on goods and services, blue flows are incomes, and green flows are financial transfers. So the expenditure flows (red flows) are consumption expenditure, investment, government purchases and net exports. The income flow (blue flow) is aggregate income. The financial transfers (green flows) are saving, net taxes, government borrowing, foreign borrowing and firms' borrowing.

Gross Domestic Product   Gross domestic product is the value of *aggregate* production in a country during a year. Production can be valued in two ways:

1. By what buyers pay for it
2. By what it costs producers to make it

From the viewpoint of buyers, goods are worth the prices paid for them. From the viewpoint of producers, goods are worth what it costs to make them. It will be a real nuisance if these two values are different because we will then have two different measures of GDP. But if these two values are always equal, we'll have a unique concept of GDP regardless of which one we use.

Fortunately, the two concepts of value do give the same answer. Let's see why.

Expenditure Equals Income   The total amount that buyers pay for the goods and services produced is *aggregate expenditure*. Let's focus on aggregate expenditure in Fig. 23.2. The expenditures on goods and services are shown by the red flows. Firms' revenues from the sale of goods and services equal consumption expenditure (C) plus investment by firms (I) plus government purchases of goods and services including investment (G) plus net exports (NX). The sum of these four flows is equal to aggregate expenditure on goods and services.

The total amount it costs producers to make goods and services is equal to the incomes paid for factor services. This amount is shown by the blue flow in Fig. 23.2.

The sum of the red flows equals the blue flow. The reason is that everything a firm receives from the sale of its output is paid out as incomes to the owners of the factors of production that it employs. That is,

$$Y = C + I + G + NX$$

or aggregate income (Y) equals aggregate expenditure $(C + I + G + NX)$.

The buyers of aggregate production pay an amount equal to aggregate expenditure, and the sellers of aggregate production pay an amount equal to aggregate income. But because aggregate expenditure equals aggregate income, these two methods

---

[1] The diagram does not show firms paying any (net) taxes. In reality, firms pay taxes and receive subsidies. You can think of net taxes paid by firms as being paid on behalf of the households that own the firms. For example, a tax on a firm's profit means that the households owning the firm receive less income. It is as if the households receive all the profit and then pay the tax on the profit. This way of looking at taxes makes Fig. 23.2 simpler but does not change any conclusions.

of valuing aggregate production give the same answer. So aggregate production, that is GDP, equals aggregate expenditure or aggregate income.

The circular flow of income and expenditure is the foundation for measuring GDP. But it is also the foundation for understanding how the flows that we've just studied finance investment and translate into a growing capital stock.

How Investment is Financed

Investment is financed by national saving and by borrowing from the rest of the world. **National saving** equals household saving plus government saving. Borrowing from the rest of the world equals imports minus exports (or the negative of net exports). Let's see how these sources of funds combine to finance investment.

National Saving   Look at the flows into and out of households in Fig. 23.2. Aggregate income (Y) flows in and consumption expenditure (C), saving (S) and net taxes (NT) flow out. Everything received by households is either spent on consumption goods and services, saved, or paid in net taxes so,

$$Y = C + S + NT$$

and household saving is

$$S = (Y - NT) - C$$

Aggregate income minus net taxes ($Y - NT$) is called *disposable income*, so household saving equals disposable income minus consumption expenditure.

Government saving equals net taxes minus government purchases, ($NT - G$), which is the government budget surplus. If net taxes exceed government purchases, that is if ($NT - G$) is positive, the government has a budget surplus and this surplus is added to household saving as an additional source of finance for investment. But if net taxes are less than government purchases, that is if ($NT - G$) is negative, the government has a budget deficit. In this case, part of household saving is used to finance the government deficit.

National saving equals household saving plus government saving:

$$\text{National saving} = S + (NT - G)$$

But because household saving equals disposable income minus consumption expenditure,

$$\text{National saving} = Y - NT - C + (NT - G)$$

You can see that net taxes cancel in the above equation. Households pay them and governments receive them, so when we add household saving and government saving together, they wash out and we are left with

$$\text{National saving} = Y - C - G$$

National saving equals aggregate income (GDP) minus consumption expenditure minus government purchases.

Borrowing From the Rest of the World   If foreigners spend more on UK goods and services than we spend on theirs, they must borrow from us to pay the difference. That is, if the value of exports (EX) exceeds the value of imports (IM), we must lend to the rest of the world an amount equal to $EX - IM$. In this situation, part of our national saving flows to the rest of the world and is not available to finance investment.

Conversely, if we spend more on foreign goods and services than the rest of the world spends on ours, we must borrow from the rest of the world to pay the difference. That is, if the value of imports (IM) exceeds the value of exports (EX), we must borrow from the rest of the world an amount equal to $IM - EX$. In this case, part of the rest of the world's saving flows into the United Kingdom and becomes available to finance investment.

Investment Financing   The total funds available to finance investment equals national saving, $S + (NT - G)$, plus borrowing from the rest of the world, ($IM - EX$). This amount equals investment. That is,

$$I = S + (NT - G) + (IM - EX)$$

That is, investment (I) equals household saving (S) plus government saving ($NT - G$) plus borrowing from the rest of the world ($IM - EX$).

In 1994, private investment in the United Kingdom was £86 billion. Saving was £116.3 billion. The government sector had a deficit of £37.1 billion, so government saving was –£37.1 billion. As a result, national saving was £79.2 billion. Net borrowing from the rest of the world, imports minus exports, was £6.8 billion. Adding this amount to national saving equals £86 billion, the level of investment.

Injections and Leakages   You can think of the circular flow of income and expenditure as a system of tubes with liquid flowing through them. The flow of factor incomes equals the flow of expenditures. But some liquid leaks from the circular flow. The *leakages* from the circular flow are saving, net taxes and imports. For the flows not to run dry, there must also be some injections into the circular flow. The *injections* are investment, government purchases of goods and services, and exports. You are going to see that injections always equal leakages.

Start with the investment financing equation that you've just seen:

$$I = S + (NT - G) + (IM - EX)$$

Add government purchases (G) and exports (EX) to both sides of this equation and you get:

$$I + G + EX = S + NT + IM$$

The left side is injections into the circular flow of income and expenditure and the right side is leakages from the circular flow. So

$$\text{Injections} = \text{Leakages.}$$

REVIEW

◆ Production, income, expenditure, investment and saving are flows – quantities per unit of time. Capital and wealth are stocks – quantities at a point in time. The flow of investment adds to the stock of capital and the flow of saving adds to the stock of wealth.

◆ Aggregate expenditure, the sum of consumption expenditure, investment, government purchases and net exports, equals aggregate income.

◆ Investment is financed by national saving plus borrowing from the rest of the world.

◆ Investment, government purchases and exports are *injections* into the circular flow of income, and expenditure and saving, net taxes and imports are *leakages* from the circular flow. Injections equal leakages.

Let's now see how economic statisticians at the Central Statistical Office (CSO) use the circular flow of income and expenditure to measure GDP.

Measuring UK GDP

To measure GDP, the CSO uses three approaches:

◆ Expenditure approach
◆ Factor incomes approach
◆ Output approach

The Expenditure Approach

The *expenditure approach* measures GDP by collecting data on consumption expenditure (C), investment (I), government purchases of goods and services (G) and net exports (NX). Table 23.1 illustrates this approach. The numbers refer to 1994 and are in billions of pounds. The name of the item used in the *United Kingdom National Accounts* tables (published by the Office for National Statistics since April 1996; previously published by the CSO) appears in the first column, and the symbol we have used in our GDP equations appears in

---

TABLE 23.1

GDP: The Expenditure Approach

Item	Symbol	Amount in 1994 (millions of pounds)	Percentage of GDP
Personal consumption expenditures	C	428,084	64.0
Gross private domestic investment + stockbuilding	I	86,060	12.9
Government purchases of goods and services	G	161,526	24.1
Net exports	NX	−6,804	−1.0
Gross domestic product	Y	668,866	100.0

The expenditure approach measures GDP by adding together personal consumption expenditures (*C*), gross private domestic investment plus stockbuilding (*I*), government purchases of goods and services (*G*), and net exports (*N X*). In 1994, GDP measured by the expenditure approach was £668,866 million. Sixty four per cent of aggregate expenditure is on personal consumption goods and services.

Source: Central Statistical Office, *Economic Trends Annual Supplement* 1996, Table 1.3.

the next column. To measure GDP using the expenditure approach, we add together personal consumption expenditures (C), gross private domestic investment (I), government purchases of goods and services (G), and net exports of goods and services (NX).

Personal consumption expenditures are the expenditures by households on goods and services produced in the United Kingdom. They include goods such as beer, CDs, books and magazines as well as services such as insurance, banking and legal advice. They do not include the purchase of new residential houses, which is counted as part of investment.

Gross private domestic investment is expenditure on capital equipment and buildings by firms and expenditure on new residential houses by households. It also includes the change in firms' stocks.

Government purchases of goods and services are the purchases of goods and services by all levels of government – from Westminster to the local town hall. This item of expenditure includes the cost of providing national defence, law and order, street lighting, refuse collection, and so on. It does not include *transfer payments*. As we have seen, such payments do not represent a purchase of goods and services but rather a transfer of funds from government to households.

Net exports of goods and services are the value of exports minus the value of imports. When Rover sells a car to a buyer in the United States, the value of that car is part of UK exports. When your local Volvo dealer stocks up on 850s, its expenditure is part of UK imports.

Table 23.1 shows the relative importance of the four items of aggregate expenditure. The largest component is personal consumption expenditure and the smallest is net exports (negative in 1994).

Expenditures Not in GDP   Aggregate expenditure, which equals GDP, does not include all the things that people and businesses buy. To distinguish total expenditure on GDP from other items of spending, we call the expenditure included in GDP *final expenditure*. Items that are not part of final expenditure and not part of GDP include the purchase of:

1. Intermediate goods and services
2. Second-hand goods
3. Financial securities

Intermediate goods and services are the goods and services that firms buy from each other and use as inputs in the goods and services that they eventually sell to final users. An example of an intermediate good is a computer chip that Dell buys from Intel. A Dell computer is a final good, but an Intel chip is an intermediate good. To count the expenditure on intermediate goods and services as well as the expenditure on the final good involves counting the same thing twice – known as *double counting*.

Some goods are sometimes intermediate goods and sometimes final goods. For example, the ice cream that you buy on a hot summer day is a final good, but the ice cream that a restaurant buys and uses to make a dessert is an intermediate good. Whether a good is intermediate or final depends on what it is used for, and not on what it is.

Expenditure on *second-hand* goods is not part of GDP because these goods were counted as part of GDP in the period in which they were produced and in which they were new goods. For example, a 1988 car was part of GDP in 1988. If the car is sold in the second-hand car market in 1995, the amount paid for the car is not part of GDP in 1995.

Firms often sell *financial securities* such as bonds and stocks to finance purchases of newly produced capital goods. The expenditure on newly produced capital goods is part of GDP, but the expenditure on financial securities is not. GDP includes the amount spent on new capital, not the amount spent on pieces of paper.

Let's look at the second way of measuring GDP.

The Factor Incomes Approach

The *factor incomes approach* measures GDP by adding together all the incomes paid by firms to households for the services of the factors of production they hire – wages for labour, interest for capital, rent for land and profits paid for entrepreneurship. Let's see how the factor incomes approach works.

The *National Income, Product and Expenditure Accounts* divide factor incomes into four categories:

1. Income from employment
2. Rent
3. Gross trading profits and surplus
4. Income from self-employment

Income from employment is the total payments by firms for labour services. This item includes the net wages and salaries (called take-home pay) that workers receive each week or month plus taxes withheld on earnings plus fringe benefits such as social security and pension fund contributions.

Rent is the payment for the use of land and other rented inputs. It includes payments for rented housing and imputed rent for owner-occupied housing. (Imputed rent is an estimate of what homeowners would pay to rent the housing they own and use themselves. By including this item in the national income accounts, we measure the total value of housing services, whether they are owned or rented.)

Gross trading profits and surplus are the total profits made by corporations and the surpluses generated by publicly owned enterprises. Some of these profits are paid to households in the form of dividends, and some are retained by corporations as undistributed profits. The surpluses from public enterprises are either retained by the enterprises or paid to the government as part of its general revenue.

Income from self-employment is a mixture of the elements that we have just reviewed. The proprietor of an owner-operated business supplies labour, capital and perhaps land and buildings to the business. It is difficult to split up the income earned by an owner–operator into its component parts – compensation for labour, payment for the use of capital, rent payments for the use of land or buildings and profit – so the national income accounts lump all these separate incomes into a single category.

The sum of these four components of factor incomes is called *net domestic income at factor cost*. It is not GDP. Two further adjustments are needed to get to GDP, one from factor cost to market price and another from *net* to *gross*.

Factor Cost to Market Price   When we add up all the final expenditures on goods and services, we arrive at a total called gross domestic product at *market price.* These expenditures are valued at the market prices that people pay for the various goods and services. Another way of valuing goods and services is at factor cos*t. Factor cost* is the value of a good or service measured by adding together the costs of all the factors of production used to produce it. If the only economic transactions were between households and firms – if there were no

government taxes or subsidies – the market price and factor cost values would be the same. But the presence of indirect taxes and subsidies makes these two methods of valuation differ.

An *indirect tax* is a tax paid by consumers when they buy goods and services. (In contrast, a *direct tax* is a tax on income.) Value added tax (VAT) and purchase taxes on alcohol, petrol and tobacco are indirect taxes. Because of indirect taxes, consumers pay more for some goods and services than producers receive. The market price is greater than the factor cost. For example, at a VAT rate of 17.5 per cent the purchase of a CD at a cost of £10.99 means you will have paid £9.35 as the cost price and £1.64 VAT.

A *subsidy* is a payment by the government to a producer. Payments made to your local Training and Enterprise Council (TEC) are to subsidize training courses. Because of subsidies, consumers pay less for some goods and services than producers receive. The market price is less than the factor cost.

To use the factor incomes approach to measure GDP, we must add indirect taxes to total factor incomes and subtract subsidies. Making this adjustment gets us one step closer to GDP, but it does not quite get us there. We must make one further adjustment.

Net Domestic Product to Gross Domestic Product   If we total all the factor incomes and then add indirect taxes and subtract subsidies, we arrive at *net* domestic product at market prices. What do the words *gross* and *net* mean?

The word *gross* means *before* subtracting *depreciation* – the decrease in the value of the capital stock that results from wear and tear and the passage of time. Similarly, the word *net* means *after* subtracting depreciation.

A component of aggregate expenditure is *gross investment* – the purchase of new capital and the replacement of depreciated capital. So when we total all the expenditures, we arrive at a number that includes that amount of depreciation, a gross measure.

A component of aggregate factor incomes is the *net profit* of businesses – profit *after* subtracting the depreciation of capital. So when we total all the factor incomes, we arrive at a number that excludes depreciation, a net measure.

To reconcile the factor incomes and expenditure approaches, we must add depreciation (which is also called capital consumption) to net domestic product.

Table 23.2 summarizes these calculations and shows how the factor incomes approach leads to the same estimate of GDP as the expenditure approach. The table also shows the relative magnitudes of the various factor incomes. As you can see, wages and salaries (compensation of employees) make up by far the largest factor income.

The Output Approach

The third method used to measure GDP is the output method. This method measures the contribution that an industry makes to GDP. But to measure the value of production of an individual industry, we must be careful to count only the value added by that industry. **Value added** is the value of a firm's production minus the value of the *intermediate goods* bought from other firms. Equivalently, it is the sum of the incomes (including profits) paid to the factors of production used by the firm to produce its output. Let's illustrate value added by looking at the production of a loaf of bread.

Figure 23.3 takes you through the brief life of a loaf of bread. It starts with the farmer, who grows the wheat. To do so, the farmer hires labour, capital

FIGURE 23.3

Value Added and Final Expenditure

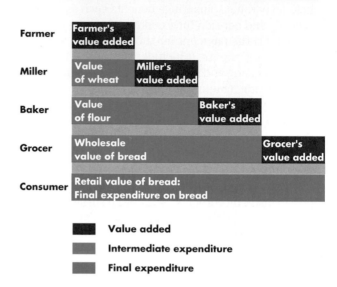

- ■ Value added
- ■ Intermediate expenditure
- ■ Final expenditure

A consumer's expenditure on a loaf of bread is equal to the sum of the value added at each stage in its production. Intermediate expenditure, for example the amount paid for the purchase of flour by the baker from the miller, equals the value added by the farmer and the miller. If intermediate expenditure is included in the total, then parts of value added are counted twice.

TABLE 23.2

GDP: The Factor Incomes Approach

Item	Amount in 1994 (millions of pounds)	Percentage of GDP
Compensation of employees	362,758	54.2
Rental income	56,793	8.5
Profits and surplus	96,204	14.4
Income from self-employment	63,655	9.5
Indirect taxes *less* Subsidies	89,726	13.4
Capital consumption (depreciation) *less* stock appreciation	−270	0.0
Gross domestic product	668,866	100.0

The sum of all factor incomes equals net domestic income. GDP equals net domestic income plus capital consumption (depreciation). In 1994, GDP measured by the factor incomes approach was £668,866 million. The compensation of employees – labour income – was by far the largest part of total factor incomes.

Source: Central Statistical Office, *National Income and Expenditure*, 1995.

equipment and land. Wages are paid to farm workers and interest and rent are paid. The farmer also earns a profit. The entire value of the wheat produced is the farmer's value added. The miller buys wheat from the farmer and turns it into flour. To do so, the miller hires labour and capital equipment. Wages are paid to mill workers, interest is paid on the capital and the miller earns a profit. The miller has now added value to the wheat bought from the farmer. The baker buys flour from the miller. The price of the flour includes the value added by the farmer and by the miller. The baker adds more value by turning the flour into bread. Wages are paid to bakery workers, interest is paid on the capital used by the baker and the baker earns a profit. The grocer buys the bread from the baker. The price paid by the grocer includes the value added by the farmer, the miller and the baker. At this stage the value of the loaf is its *wholesale* value. The grocer adds further value by making the loaf available in a convenient place at a convenient time. The consumer buys the bread for a price – its *retail price* – that includes the value added by the farmer, the miller, the baker and the grocer.

Final Goods and Intermediate Goods

To value output, we count only *value added* because the sum of the value added at each stage of production equals expenditure on the *final good*. By using value added, we avoid double counting. In the above example, the only thing that has been produced and consumed is a loaf of bread – shown by the green bar in Fig. 23.3. The value added at each stage is shown by the red bars, and the sum of the red bars equals the green bar. The transactions

involving intermediate goods, shown by the blue bars, are not part of value added and are not counted as part of the value of output or of GDP.

Figure 23.4 shows the contribution of each sector to total output in the United Kingdom. The share of each sector is given by the value added contribution of each sector. The sum of the value of each sector gives GDP at factor cost.

Aggregate Expenditure, Income and GDP

You've seen that aggregate expenditure equals aggregate income. And you've seen that the CSO uses both aggregate expenditure and aggregate income to measure GDP. Why does it use two approaches when they are supposed to be the

---

FIGURE 23.4

Aggregate Expenditure, Output and Income

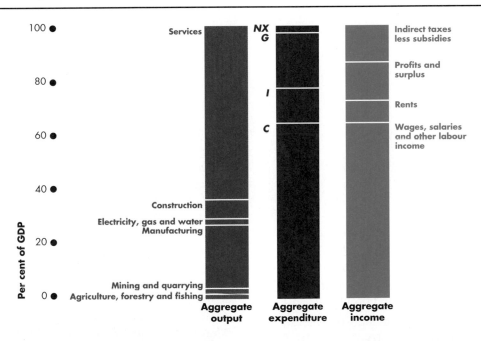

The orange bar illustrates the components of aggregate output and their relative magnitudes. It shows the share of each industrial sector's contribution to GDP. The total GDP is the value added by all activities that produce goods and services. The smallest components are agriculture, forestry and fishing, mining and quarrying, and electricity, gas and water. The largest contribution is from services.

The red bar illustrates the components of aggregate expenditure as well as their relative magnitudes. Net

exports, the smallest component, can be either a positive or negative value.

The green bar illustrates the components of aggregate income and their relative magnitudes. The smallest component is rents and the largest is wages, salaries and other labour income.

The figure illustrates the equality between aggregate expenditure, aggregate output and aggregate income.

Source: Central Statistical Office, *National Income Accounts*, 1995, *Blue Book*.

same? The answer is that although the two concepts of the value of aggregate production are identical, the actual measurements, which are based on samples of information, give slightly different answers. The expenditure approach uses data from *Family Expenditure Survey*, house building, business investment, the accounts of central and local government, HM Customs and Excise records and many other sources. The factor incomes approach uses data supplied by the Inland Revenue. None of these sources gives a complete coverage of all the items that make up aggregate expenditure and aggregate factor incomes. So by using the two approaches, the CSO can check one aggregate against the other. The discrepancy (known as the *Initial Residual Difference* – IRD) has at times been large and has been used as an indicator of the underground economy. The discrepancy is used to adjust both approaches to make them equal.

Figure 23.4 shows this equality between the approaches to measuring GDP and gives a snapshot summary of the expenditure, income and product concepts. It also shows the relative magnitudes of the components of aggregate expenditure and aggregate income.

R E V I E W

◆ The expenditure approach to measuring GDP sums consumption expenditure, investment, government purchases and net exports.

◆ The factor incomes approach to measuring GDP sums wages, interest, rent and profits.

◆ To value the production of an industry, we use the value added of that industry.

So far, in our study of GDP and its measurement, we've been concerned with the nominal (or money) value of GDP and its components. But GDP can change either because prices change or because there is a change in the volume of goods and services produced – a change in real GDP. Let's now see how we measure the price level and distinguish between the nominal value and the real value of GDP.

The Price Level and Inflation

The *price level* is the average level of prices measured by a *price index*. To construct a price index, we take a basket of goods and services and calculate its value in the current period and its value in a base period. The price index is the value of the basket in the current period expressed as a percentage of the value of the same basket in the base period.

Two main price indexes are used to measure the price level in the United Kingdom today. They are the:

◆ Retail Prices Index
◆ GDP deflator

Retail Prices Index

The **Retail Prices Index (RPI)** measures the average level of prices of the goods and services that a typical UK household consumes. The RPI is published every month by the CSO. To construct the RPI, the CSO first selects a base period. Currently, it is 13 January, 1987. Then it surveys consumer spending patterns to determine the typical or average 'basket' of goods and services that people buy in the base period. Around 500 different goods and services feature in the RPI.

Every month, the CSO sends a team of observers to more than 180 geographical locations in the United Kingdom and takes some 150,000 price quotations to record the prices for the 500 items. When all the data are in, the RPI is calculated by valuing the basket of goods and services at the current month's prices. That value is expressed as a percentage of the value of the same basket in the base period.

To see more precisely how the RPI is calculated, let's work through a simplified example. Table 23.3 summarizes the calculations. Let's suppose that there are only three goods in the typical consumer's basket: apples, haircuts and bus rides. The table shows the quantities bought and the prices prevailing in the base period. It also shows total expenditure in the base period. The typical consumer buys 200 bus rides at 30 pence each and so spends £60 on bus rides. Expenditure on apples and haircuts is worked out in the same way. Total expenditure is the sum of expenditures on the three goods, which is £98.

TABLE 23.3

The Retail Price Index: A Simplified Calculation

Base period basket	Base period		Current period	
	Price	Expenditure	Price	Expenditure
5 kilograms of apples	£0.40/kilogram	£2.00	£0.24/kilogram	£1.20
6 haircuts	£6.00 each	£36.00	£6.10 each	£36.60
200 bus rides	£0.30 each	£60.00	£0.35 each	£70.00
Total expenditure		£98.00		£107.80
RPI	$\frac{£98.00}{£98.00} \times 100 = 100$		$\frac{£107.80}{£98.00} \times 100 = 110$	

A fixed basket of goods – 5 kilograms of apples, 6 haircuts and 200 bus rides – is valued in the base period at £98. Prices change, and that same basket is valued at £107.80 in the current period. The RPI is equal to the current-period value of the basket divided by the base-period value of the basket multiplied by 100. In the base period the RPI is 100, and in the current period the RPI is 110.

To calculate the price index for the current period, we need only to discover the prices of the goods in the current period. We do not need to know the quantities bought. Let's suppose that the prices are those set out in Table 23.3 under 'Current period'. We can now calculate the current period's value of the (base-period) basket of goods by using the current period's prices. For example, the current price of apples is down to 24p a kilogram, so the current period's value of the base-period quantity (5 kilograms) is £1.20. The base-period quantities of haircuts and bus rides are valued at this period's prices in a similar way. The total value of the base-period basket in the current period is £107.80.

We can now calculate the RPI – the ratio of this period's value of the basket to the base period's value, multiplied by 100. In this example the RPI for the current period is 109. The RPI for the base period is, by definition, 100.

In recent times, the government has expressed a preference for a new price index that eliminates the mortgage interest component of typical household expenditure on the basket of goods. The main reason is that by including mortgage interest, the RPI will show a rise in prices when the government raises interest rates to try and control inflation. The new price index is known as the RPIX. The government argues that RPIX is a better indicator of underlying inflation. While there is some truth in what the government says, it is also true that mortgage interest payment is a valid expenditure by households.

GDP Deflator

The **GDP deflator** measures the average level of prices of all the goods and services that are included in GDP. Currently, the base period for the GDP deflator is 1990.

We are going to learn how to calculate the GDP deflator by studying an imaginary economy that has just three final goods: a consumption good that households buy (apples), a capital good that firms buy (computers) and a good that the government buys (red tape). Net exports are zero in this example. Table 23.4 summarizes the calculations of the GDP deflator in this economy.

To calculate the GDP deflator, we use the formula

$$\text{GDP deflator} = \frac{\text{Nominal GDP}}{\text{Real GDP}} \times 100$$

To calculate nominal GDP, we use the expenditure approach. The table shows the quantities of the final goods and their prices. To calculate nominal GDP, we work out the expenditure on each good and then total the three expenditures. Consumption expenditure (apples) is £2,226, investment (computers) is £5,250 and government purchases (red tape) are £530, so nominal GDP is £8,006.

TABLE 23.4

Nominal GDP, Real GDP and the GDP Deflator: Simplified Calculations

Current year output	Base-period values		Current-period values	
	Price	Expenditure	Price	Expenditure
4,240 kilograms of apples	50p/ kilogram	£2,120	52.5p/kilogram	£2,226
5 computers	£1,000 each	£5,000	£1,050 each	£5,250
1,060 metres of red tape	50p/metre	£530	50p/metre	£530
	Real GDP	**£7,650**	**Nominal GDP**	**£8,006**

$$\text{GDP deflator} = \frac{£8,606}{£7,650} \times 100 = 104.7$$

An imaginary economy produces only apples, computers and red tape. In the current period, nominal GDP is £8,006. If the current-period quantities are valued at the base-period prices, we obtain a measure of real GDP, which is £7,650.

The GDP deflator in the current period – which is calculated by dividing nominal GDP by real GDP in that period and multiplying by 100 – is 104.7.

Now let's calculate real GDP, a measure of the physical volume of output. To do so, we value the current-period quantities at the base-period prices. Because the base year is 1990, we refer to the units in which real GDP is measured as '1990 prices'. The table shows the prices for the base period. Real expenditure on apples for the current period is 4,240 kilograms valued at 50 pence a kilogram, which is £2,120. If we perform the same types of calculations for computers and red tape and add up the real expenditures, we arrive at a real GDP of £7,650.

Let's put the numbers we've found into the formula for the GDP deflator. Nominal GDP is £8,006 and real GDP is £7,650, so the GDP deflator is

$$\text{GDP deflator} = \frac{£8,606}{£7,650} \times 100 = 104.7$$

Notice that when the current period is also the base period, nominal GDP equals real GDP and the GDP deflator is 100.

You can think of nominal GDP as a balloon that is being blown up by growing production and rising prices. Figure 23.5 illustrates this idea. In part (a), real GDP is measured by the height of the red area and nominal GDP by the height of the red area plus the green area. In part (b), the GDP deflator lets the inflation air out of the nominal GDP balloon – the contribution of rising prices – so that we can see what has happened to *real* GDP. The red balloon for 1990 shows real GDP in that year. The green balloon shows *nominal* GDP in 1994. The red balloon for 1994 shows real GDP for that year. To see real GDP in 1994, we *deflate* nominal GDP using the GDP deflator.

What the Inflation Numbers Mean

A major purpose of the RPI and the GDP deflator is to measure inflation, and the measures are put to practical use. For example, the RPI is used to determine cost of living adjustments to state pensions, unemployment benefits, family income supplements, other social security payments and upward adjustment of tax allowances – the income ranges over which different income tax rates apply. How good a measure of inflation does the RPI or the GDP deflator give? Does a 2.7 per cent increase in the RPI mean that the cost of living has increased by 2.7 per cent? And does a 3 per cent increase in the GDP deflator mean that the prices of the goods and services that make up real GDP have increased by 3 per cent? Let's find out.

Measuring the inflation rate accurately is of crucial importance. It tells us how the value of money is changing, and it affects our assessment of changes in real GDP. A 1 per cent upward bias in the estimated inflation rate translates into a 1 per cent downward bias in the estimated growth rate of real GDP and real wage rates. And a 1 per cent a year bias sustained over 10 years throws the estimate of real GDP and real wages off by more than 10 per cent.

FIGURE 23.5

The GDP Balloon

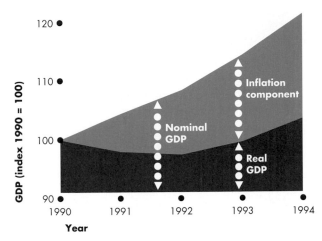

(a) Nominal GDP and real GDP

(b) Deflating nominal GDP

Part of the rise in GDP comes from inflation and part from increased production – an increase in real GDP (part a). The

GDP deflator lets some air out of the GDP balloon (part b) so that we can see the extent to which production has grown.

Source: Central Statistical Office, *Economic Trends Annual Supplement*, 1996.

Despite the importance of getting the numbers right, the RPI and the GDP deflator give different views of the inflation rate, and neither index is a perfect measure. Figure 23.6 shows the difference in the two measures. The average inflation rate over the period shown is 7.4 per cent a year for the RPI and 7.5 per cent a year for the GDP deflator and as you can see at times they give different messages about inflation.

Worse, *both* measures of inflation probably overstate the inflation rate. The main sources of bias are:

◆ New goods bias
◆ Quality change bias
◆ Substitution bias

New Goods Bias   New goods keep replacing old goods. For example, CDs have replaced LP records and PCs have replaced typewriters. If you want to compare the price level in 1995 with that in 1975, you somehow have to compare the price of a CD and a computer today with that of an LP and typewriter in 1975. Because CDs and PCs are more

expensive today than LPs and typewriters, the arrival of these new goods puts an upward bias into the estimate of the price level.

Quality Change Bias   Most goods undergo constant quality improvement. Cars, computers, CD players and even textbooks get better year after year. Improvements in quality often mean increases in price. But such price increases are not inflation. For example, suppose that a 1995 car is 5 per cent better and costs 5 per cent more than a 1994 car. Adjusted for the quality change, the price of the car has been constant. But in calculating the RPI, the price of the car will be counted as having increased by 5 per cent.

Estimates have been made of the importance of quality change bias, especially for obvious changes such as those in cars and computers. Allowing for quality improvements changes the inflation picture by between 1 and 2 percentage points a year, on the average, according to some economists. That is, correctly measured, the inflation rate might be as much as 2 percentage points a year less than the published numbers.

FIGURE 23.6

Measures of Inflation

The RPI and the GDP deflator have similar averages – RPI 7.4 per cent a year and GDP deflator 7.5 per cent a year – over the period shown here. The government has put forward the RPIX as a more appropriate measure of the underlying inflation rate. The RPIX is the RPI *excluding* mortgage interest. The main reason the government prefers the RPIX is because if the rate of interest is raised to choke off a build-up in inflationary pressure, the resulting rise in mortgage interest rates raises the general RPI but not the RPIX. In general, the RPI fluctuates more than the GDP deflator but both measures probably overstate the inflation rate.

Source: Central Statistical Office, *Economic Trends Annual Supplement*, 1996.

Substitution Bias A change in the RPI measures the percentage change in the price of a *fixed* basket of goods and services. But changes in relative prices lead consumers to seek less costly items. For example, by shopping more frequently at discount stores and less frequently at convenience stores, consumers can cut the prices they pay. By using discount fares on airlines, they can cut the cost of travel. This kind of substitution of cheaper items for more costly items is not picked up by the RPI. Because consumers make such substitutions, a price index based on a fixed basket overstates the effects of a given price change on the inflation rate.

To reduce the bias problems, the CSO (and previously the Department of Employment) revises the basket used for calculating the RPI about every five

years based on the spending patterns of households within a specified income group. Yet despite periodic updating, the RPI is of limited value for making comparisons of the cost of living over long periods of time and even has shortcomings as a measure of year-to-year inflation rates.

REVIEW

◆ The Retail Prices Index measures the average prices of a fixed basket of consumption items bought by a typical urban household.

◆ The GDP deflator measures the average prices of the items that make up GDP.

◆ The RPI and GDP deflator overstate the inflation rate by an estimated 1 per cent and 2 per cent a year.

You now know how inflation is calculated and what the inflation numbers mean. You also know that by letting the inflationary air out of the GDP balloon, we can reveal real GDP. But what does real GDP really mean? Let's find out.

What Real GDP Means

Estimates of real GDP and the real GDP growth rate are used for many purposes. But the three main uses are to:

◆ Make international comparisons of GDP

◆ Assess changes in economic welfare over time

◆ Determine the current phase of the business cycle

International Comparisons of GDP

To make international comparisons, the GDP of one country must be converted into the same currency units as the other. For example, in 1990, the GDP of China was 1,769 billion yuan. In that year, US$1 was worth 4.78 yuan. If we convert the GDP of China into US dollars using this exchange rate, we get a value of $370 billion. The population of China in 1990 was 1,139 million, so according to these estimates, GDP per person in China in 1990 was $325.

In comparison, US GDP in 1990 was $5,546 billion and the population of the United States was 250 million, so GDP per person in the United States in 1990 was $22,200, some 68 times larger than GDP per person in China.

This comparison of China and the United States makes China look extremely poor. And this is the impression given by the official statistics published by the International Monetary Fund (IMF) and the World Bank. But data on China's GDP in the Penn World Table (PWT) compiled by Robert Summers and Alan Heston, economists at the University of Pennsylvania, tell a remarkably different story. The difference arises from the prices used. The official statistics use Chinese prices converted to US dollars at the market exchange rate. But these prices are misleading. Some goods that are expensive in the United States cost little in China. By converting these items into US dollars, they get a small weight in China's GDP. If, instead, all the goods and services are valued at the prices prevailing in the United States, then a true comparison can be made. Such a comparison uses prices called *purchasing power parity prices.*

The result of this correction to the prices at which China's production is valued changes the picture by an incredible amount. Instead of real GDP per person in 1990 being $325, it was perhaps as much as $2,000 – more than 6 times the official estimate. Figure 23.7 shows this amazing difference.

The World Bank and the IMF tell us that China is a poor developing country. The PWT data tell us that China has become a middle income country. The PWT data also tell us that China's GDP exceeds Germany's, and that China's economy is the third largest in the world after those in the United States and Japan.

Despite large differences in estimates of the *level* of China's GDP, there is much less doubt about its growth rate. The economy of China is expanding at an extraordinary rate and it is for this reason that most businesses are paying a great deal of attention to the prospects of expanding their activities in China and the other Asian economies.

The alternative measures of China's GDP are to some degree unreliable and the truth is not known. But even if it were, there would still be problems in comparing the United States and China. These problems also affect comparisons in a single country over time. They arise because real GDP is an imperfect measure of economic welfare.

FIGURE 23.7

Two Views of GDP in China

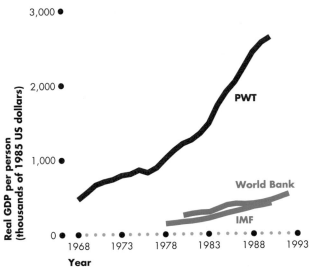

According to the official statistics of the International Monetary Fund and the World Bank, China is a poor developing country. But according to an alternative view based on purchasing power prices, China has a GDP more than 6 times the official view and has the world's third largest total production.

Sources: IMF, *International Financial Statistics Yearbook*, 1994, Washington, DC; World Bank, *World Development Report*, 1994, Washington, DC; Robert Summers and Alan Heston, New computer diskette (Mark 5.5), 15 June 1993, distributed by the National Bureau of Economic Research to update The Penn World Table (Mark 5): An Expanded Set of International Comparisons, 1950–1988, *Quarterly Journal Of Economics*, May 1991, 327–368; and author's calculations.

Economic Welfare

Economic welfare is a comprehensive measure of the general state of well-being. Improvements in economic welfare depend on the growth of real GDP. But they also depend on many other factors not measured by GDP. Some of these factors are:

◆ Quality improvements

◆ Household production

◆ The underground economy

◆ Health and life expectancy

◆ Leisure time

◆ The environment

◆ Political freedom and social justice

Quality Improvements   The price indices that we use to measure inflation give a downward biased estimate of the growth rate of real GDP. When car prices rise because cars have improved (becoming safer, faster, more fuel efficient, more comfortable), the RPI and the GDP deflator count the price increase as inflation. So what is really an increase in production is counted as an increase in price rather than an increase in real GDP. It is deflated away by the wrongly measured higher price level.

Household Production   An enormous amount of production takes place every day in our homes. Changing a light bulb, cutting the grass, washing the car, growing vegetables and teaching a child to catch a ball are all examples of productive activities that do not involve market transactions and are not counted as part of GDP.

Household production has become much more capital intensive over the years. As a result, less labour is used in household production than in earlier periods. For example, a microwave meal that takes just a few minutes to prepare uses a great deal of capital and almost no labour. Because we use less labour and more capital in household production, it is not easy to work out whether this type of production has increased or decreased over time. But it is likely that market production counted in GDP has increasingly replaced household production. Two trends point in this direction. One is the trend in female employment, which has increased from 46 per cent of the female population of working age in 1960 to 65 per cent in 1994. The other trend is the marketization of traditionally home-produced goods and services. For example, more and more households now buy takeaways, eat in fast food restaurants and use nursery services. This trend means that increasing proportions of food preparation and child care that used to be part of household production are now measured as part of GDP.

The Underground Economy   The *underground economy* is the part of the economy purposely hidden from view by the people operating in it to avoid taxes and regulations or because the goods and services they are producing are illegal. Because underground economic activity is unreported, it is omitted from GDP.

The underground economy is easy to describe, even if it is hard to measure. It includes the production and distribution of drugs, production that uses illegal labour that is paid less than the minimum wage, and jobs done for cash to avoid paying income taxes. This last category might be quite large and includes tips earned by taxi drivers, hairdressers, and hotel and restaurant workers. Estimates of the scale of the underground economy range between 3.5 and 14.5 per cent of GDP (£23 billion to £97 billion) in the United Kingdom and much more in some countries.

Provided the underground economy is a reasonably stable proportion of the total economy, its omission from GDP does not pose a problem. The growth rate of real GDP still gives a useful estimate of the long-term growth rate and of business cycle fluctuations. But sometimes production shifts from the underground to the rest of the economy and sometimes it shifts the other way. The underground economy expands relative to the rest of the economy if taxes become especially high or if regulations become especially restricting. And the underground economy shrinks relative to the rest of the economy if the burden of taxes and regulations are eased. During the 1980s, when tax rates were cut, there was an increase in tax revenues. Some of this may have been owing to the existing work-force, particularly high-paid labour, working harder, taking greater risks and being more productive, but some of it could have been owing to a switch from what was previously underground activity to recorded activity. So some part (but probably a small part) of the expansion of real GDP during the 1980s represented a shift from the underground economy rather than an increase in production.

Health and Life Expectancy   Good health and a long life – the hopes of everyone – do not show up in real GDP, at least not directly. A higher real GDP does enable us to spend more on medical research, health care, healthy food and exercise equipment. And as real GDP has increased, our life expectancy has lengthened – from 70 years at the end of World War II to approaching 80 years today. Infant deaths and death in childbirth, two fearful scourges of the nineteenth century, have almost been eliminated.

But we face new health and life expectancy problems every year. AIDS, drug abuse, suicide and murder are taking young lives at a rate that causes serious concern. And in recent years, the number of households, mostly single parent families, which are living below the official poverty level has increased.

When we take these negative influences into account, we see that real GDP growth overstates the improvements in economic welfare.

Leisure Time   Leisure time is an economic good that adds to our economic welfare. Other things remaining the same, the more leisure we have, the better off we are. Our time spent working is valued as part of GDP, but our leisure time is not. Yet from the point of view of economic welfare, that leisure time must be at least as valuable to us as the wage that we earn for the last hour worked. If it was not, we would work instead of taking the leisure. Over the years, leisure time has steadily increased. The working week has become shorter, and the number and length of holidays have increased.

These improvements in economic well-being are not reflected in GDP.

The Environment   The environment is directly affected by economic activity. The burning of hydrocarbon fuels is the most visible activity that damages our environment. But it is not the only example. The depletion of exhaustible resources, the mass clearing of forests, and the pollution of lakes and rivers are other major environmental consequences of industrial production.

Resources used to protect the environment are valued as part of GDP. For example, the value of catalytic converters that help to protect the atmosphere from carbon emissions are part of GDP. But if we did not use such pieces of equipment and instead polluted the atmosphere, we would not count the deteriorating air that we were breathing as a negative part of GDP.

An industrial society possibly produces more atmospheric pollution than an agricultural society does. But it is not always the case that such pollution increases as we become wealthier. One of the things that wealthy people value is a clean environment, and they devote resources to protecting it. Compare the pollution that was discovered in the former East Germany and the former Soviet Union in the late 1980s with pollution in the western developed countries. East Germany, a relatively poor country, polluted its rivers, lakes and atmosphere in a way that would have been unimaginable in wealthy West Germany.

Political Freedom and Social Justice   Most people value political freedoms such as those pro-

vided by the western democracies. They also value social justice or fairness – equality of opportunity and of access to social security safety nets that protect people from the extremes of misfortune.

A country might have a large real GDP per person, but have limited political freedom and equity. For example, a small elite might enjoy political liberty and extreme wealth while the vast majority are effectively enslaved and live in abject poverty. Such an economy would generally be regarded as having less economic welfare than one that had the same amount of real GDP but in which political freedom were enjoyed by everyone. Today, China has rapid real GDP growth but limited political freedoms, while Russia has a decreasing real GDP and an emerging democratic political system. Economists have no easy way to determine which of these countries is better off.

The Bottom Line   What is the bottom line? Do we get the wrong message about changes (or differences) in economic welfare by looking at changes (or differences) in real GDP? The influences omitted from real GDP are probably important and could be large. Developing countries have a larger underground economy and a larger amount of household production than do developed countries. So as an economy develops and grows, part of the apparent growth might reflect a switch from underground to recorded production and from home production to market production. This measurement error overstates the rate of economic growth and the improvement in economic welfare.

Other influences on living standards include the amount of leisure time available, the quality of the environment, the security of jobs and homes, the safety of city streets, and so on. It is possible to construct broader measures that combine the many influences that contribute to human happiness. Real GDP will be one element in these broader measures, but it will by no means be the whole of them.

Phase of the Business Cycle

Did the UK government need to raise interest rates and slow down the economy during 1994? On the basis of the information available the Bank of England decided that it did indeed need to take such action. But don't the measures of inflation used to calculate real GDP overstate the inflation rate? They do, but not in a cyclical way. They are

Diagnosing the Economy

The Essence of the Story

THE FINANCIAL TIMES, 6 AUGUST 1996

German economy returns to growth

Peter Norman

Germany returned to growth in the second quarter, but rising unemployment last month and a sober report on the economy from the Organisation for Economic Cooperation and Development gave little hope of an easing of the country's job crisis.

On a seasonally-adjusted basis, gross domestic product jumped by a slightly better than expected 1.5 per cent from the first quarter, when the economy declined 0.5 per cent, the federal statistics office said yesterday....

Mr Günter Rexrodt, the economics minister, hailed the news as evidence that Germany had overcome a 'dip in growth', but the federal labour office announced that...on an adjusted basis, the August jobless total of 3.9m was 9,950 below that of July but 323,500 higher than in August last year. The national rate held steady at 10.2 per cent of the working population last month, with a continuing sharp divergence between former Communist eastern Germany with 15 per cent, and the west, with 9 per cent.

In its annual report on the German economy, the OECD said yesterday that the expected rate of growth 'would be too weak to make any inroads into the high level of unemployment.' Although the organisation forecast GDP increases of 0.5 per cent this year and 2.4 per cent in 1997, it warned that employment in Germany would fall by about 1 per cent this year and that the jobless rate would not stabilise before next year....

Germany's return to growth between the first and second quarters owed much to an unprecedented 11.5 per cent jump in construction activity, which more than made up for a 9.5 per cent drop during the severe weather of the first quarter.

The statistics office pointed to a 2.5 per cent increase in export demand and a 3.6 per cent jump in public sector consumption as important factors behind the year-on-year growth of 1.2 per cent.

■ Real GDP growth in Germany increased by 1.5 per cent in the second quarter of 1996 after a fall of 0.5 per cent in the first quarter. GDP was 1.2 per cent higher than in the second quarter of 1995.

■ Unemployment in August was 9,950 below that of July but 323,500 higher than in August 1995. The level of unemployment was 3.9 million.

■ The unemployment rate was 10.2 per cent of the working population. In former communist East Germany the unemployment rate was 15 per cent and in former West Germany it was 9 per cent.

■ Output in the construction sector jumped 11.5 per cent in the second quarter after a 9.5 per cent fall in the first quarter.

■ Exports increased by 2.5 per cent and consumption by the public sector increased by 3.6 per cent in the second quarter.

Economic Analysis

■ The German economy returned to growth in the second quarter of 1996 after a fall in output in the first quarter. But the return to growth did not signal an improvement in unemployment.

■ The OECD produces an annual report and forecast on each of the member countries. The governments of the member countries tend to treat the forecasts and reports of the OECD seriously, even when they do not agree with their own.

■ Figure 1 shows the rate of growth of GDP a year from the first quarter of 1992 to the second quarter of 1996. The figure shows that the German economy slowed down during 1992 and went into a deep recession in 1993. The economy recovered in 1994 but slowed down again in 1995.

■ You can see that the recovery in 1994 was not sustained and unemployment, shown in Fig. 2, fell during 1994, then rose and dipped in 1995 and again in 1996. Notice that the rise in unemployment in June 1996 was from a higher point than in June 1995. Each time unemployment rises when the economy turns down, it does not fall back to its original level when the economy picks up.

■ Figure 3 shows the output gap, which is the percentage difference between real GDP and potential GDP. Although the German economy improved during 1994 and 1995, it was still below potential GDP. Unless real GDP rises at a faster rate than potential GDP, unemployment will stay high or continue to rise.

■ The improvement in GDP growth in the second quarter was due to a sharp increase in construction output (Fig. 4). Construction spending accounts for 10 per cent of German GDP. When the construction sector picks up GDP growth improves, and when the construction sector declines, GDP growth falls. A surge in demand from former East Germany has fuelled a construction sector boom, but now the boom has come to an end.

■ The fall in unemployment during 1996 is also related to the recovery in the construction sector. However, because real GDP is below potential GDP, unemployment will decline only if growth is greater than potential GDP growth.

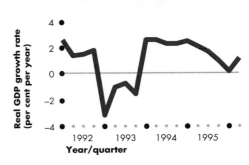

Figure 1 Real GDP growth

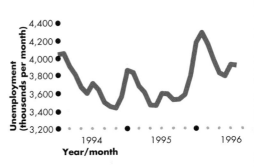

Figure 2 Unemployment

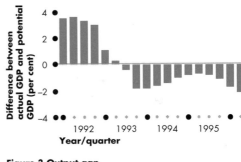

Figure 3 Output gap

Figure 4 Construction output

Reading Between the Lines

out by a similar amount every year. So while the possible mismeasurement of inflation may lead to wrong estimates of long-term real GDP growth, it probably does not cause a wrong assessment of the phase of the business cycle.

On the whole, the fluctuations in economic activity measured by real GDP probably tell a reasonably accurate story about the phase of the business cycle the economy is in. When real GDP grows the economy is in a business cycle expansion phase and when real GDP shrinks (for two quarters) the economy is in a recession. Also, real GDP fluctuations are correlated with other indicators of the business cycle. For example, in a recession, jobs disappear and unemployment increases, inflation (eventually) subsides and imports decrease. Similarly, in an expansion, more jobs become available and unemployment falls, inflation (eventually) increases, and imports increase. By studying *Reading Between the Lines* on pp. 594–595, you can see how real GDP in Germany during 1994 showed the economy to be in a strong business cycle expansion phase. But the growth in real GDP was not maintained and began to slow in 1995. Unemployment in Germany fell during 1994 and rose during 1995 as growth slowed down. Real GDP has to grow faster than potential GDP for a business cycle expansion phase to be sustained over any period of time. It is often difficult to know what stage of the business cycle the economy is in until after the event.

But real GDP fluctuations probably exaggerate or overstate the fluctuations in total production and economic welfare. The reason is that when business activity slows down in a recession, household production increases and so does leisure time. When business activity speeds up in an expansion phase, household production and leisure time decrease. Because household production and leisure time

increase in a recession and decrease in an expansion, they are countercyclical. As a result, real GDP fluctuations tend to overstate the fluctuations in total production and in economic welfare. But the directions of change of real GDP, total production, and economic welfare are probably the same.

R E V I E W

◆ Real GDP is not an accurate measure of economic welfare because it undervalues quality improvements, omits some production and ignores indicators of economic welfare such as health and life expectancy, leisure time, the environment and political freedom.

◆ Real GDP probably understates the long-term growth rate and overstates business cycle fluctuations.

◆ ◆ ◆ ◆ In Chapter 22 we studied the macroeconomic performance of the United Kingdom in recent years – the growth and fluctuations in real GDP, unemployment, inflation and the balance of international payments. We've now studied the methods used to measure some of these indicators of macroeconomic performance. We've seen how real GDP and the price level are measured, and we've seen what these measures mean. ◆ In Chapter 24 we will learn about the labour market and the measurement of employment and unemployment. The chapters that follow build on this knowledge of the measurement and meaning of the indicators of macroeconomic performance and explain the choices and the interactions that determine the performance of the economy.

SUMMARY

Gross Domestic Product

Gross domestic product (GDP) is the value of aggregate production in a country in a given time period (usually a year). The concept of GDP is based on the distinction between stocks and flows and the circular flow of expenditure and income.

Capital is the key macroeconomic stock and investment is the flow that increases the stock of capital. Wealth is also a stock, and saving – income minus consumption expenditure – increases the stock of wealth.

The circular flow of income and expenditure arises from the expenditures of households, firms, governments and the rest of the world, and the payment of factor incomes by firms. Aggregate expenditure on goods and services equals aggregate income. The value of aggregate production – GDP – is equal to aggregate expenditure or aggregate income.

Injections into the circular flow – investment, government purchases and exports – equal the leakages from the circular flow – saving, net taxes and imports. Investment is financed by national saving plus borrowing from the rest of the world. (pp. 576–581)

Measuring UK GDP

Because aggregate expenditure, aggregate income and the value of aggregate production are equal, national income accountants can measure GDP by using one of two approaches: the expenditure approach or the factor incomes approach.

The expenditure approach adds together consumption expenditure, investment, government purchases of goods and services and net exports to arrive at an estimate of GDP. This approach includes only expenditure on new final goods and services. It does not include expenditure on intermediate goods and services, second-hand goods and financial services.

The factor incomes approach adds together the incomes paid to the factors of production – labour, capital, land and profit paid to entrepreneurs. To use the factor incomes approach, it is necessary to add capital consumption (depreciation) to arrive at GDP.

To value the output of a firm or sector in the economy, we measure value added. The use of value added avoids double counting. (pp. 581–586)

The Price Level and Inflation

The two main indices that measure the price level are the Retail Prices Index and the GDP deflator. The RPI measures the average price level of goods and services typically consumed by UK households. It is measured as the ratio of the value of the typical (base-period) basket at current-period prices to its value at base-period prices, multiplied by 100. The GDP deflator measures the average price level of all the goods and services that make up GDP. It is measured as the ratio of GDP to real GDP, multiplied by 100. Real GDP is the current year's production valued at base-period prices.

Inflation is measured by the rate of change of the RPI or the GDP deflator. The RPI and the GDP deflator give an upward-biased measure of inflation because some goods disappear and new goods become available, the quality of goods and services changes over time, and as relative prices change consumers substitute less expensive items for more expensive items. (pp. 586–590)

What Real GDP Means

Real GDP is not a perfect measure of either aggregate economic activity or economic welfare. It excludes quality improvements, household production, underground production, environmental damage and the contribution to economic welfare of health and life expectancy, leisure time, and political freedom and equity. (pp. 590–596)

KEY ELEMENTS

Key Terms

Capital, 576
Consumption expenditure, 577
Depreciation, 576
Flow, 576
GDP deflator, 587
Government purchases, 578
Gross domestic product, (GDP), 576
Gross investment, 576
Intermediate goods and services, 582
Investment, 576
National saving, 580
Net exports, 579
Net investment, 576
Net taxes, 578
Retail Prices Index (RPI), 586

Saving, 577
Stock, 576
Value added, 584
Wealth, 577

◆ Key Figures and Tables

Figure 23.1   Capital and Investment, 576
Figure 23.2   The Circular Flow of Income and
              Expenditure, 578
Figure 23.3   Value Added and Final Expenditure,
              584
Table 23.1   GDP: The Expenditure Approach, 581
Table 23.2   GDP: The Factor Incomes Approach,
              584

REVIEW QUESTIONS

1 List the components of aggregate expenditure.

2 What are the components of aggregate income?

3 Why does aggregate income equal aggregate expenditure?

4 Why does the value of output (or GDP) equal aggregate income?

5 Distinguish between government purchases of goods and services and transfer payments.

6 What are injections into the circular flow of income and expenditure ? What are leakages?

7 Explain why injections into the circular flow of income and expenditure equal leakages from it.

8 How does the CSO measure GDP?

9 Explain the expenditure approach to measuring GDP.

10 Explain the factor incomes approach to measuring GDP.

11 What is the distinction between expenditure on final goods and expenditure on intermediate goods?

12 What is value added? How is it calculated?

13 What are the two main price indices used to measure the price level?

14 How is the Retail Prices Index (RPI) calculated? Why does the government prefer to use the RPIX as a measure of inflation?

15 How is the basket of goods and services used in constructing the RPI chosen? Is it the same basket in 1995 as it was in 1955? If not, how is it different?

16 Is the RPI a good measure to use to compare the cost of living today with that in the 1980s? If not, why not?

17 How is the GDP deflator calculated?

18 Is real GDP a good measure of economic welfare? If not, why not?

PROBLEMS

1 The following transactions took place in Euroland last year:

Item	Billions of euros
Wages paid to labour	800,000
Consumption expenditure	600,000
Taxes	250,000
Government transfer payments	50,000
Firms' profits	200,000
Investment	250,000
Government purchases	200,000
Exports	300,000
Saving	300,000
Imports	250,000

  a Calculate Euroland's GDP.
  b Did you use the expenditure approach or the factor incomes approach to make this calculation?
  c What extra information do you need in order to calculate net domestic product?

2 Anne, the owner of The Cheesecake factory in Liverpool, spends in a week £100 on eggs, £50 on flour, £45 on milk, £10 on gas and electricity, and £60 on wages to produce 200 cakes. She sells her cakes for £1.50 each. Calculate the value added per cake at The Cheesecake factory.

3 A typical family living on Rocky Island consumes only apple juice, bananas and cloth. Prices in the base year were £4 a litre for apple juice, £3 a kilogram for bananas and £5 a metre for cloth. In the base year, the typical family spent £40 on apple juice, £45 on bananas and £25 on cloth. In the current year, apple juice costs £3 a litre, bananas cost £4 a kilogram and cloth costs £7 a metre. Calculate the Retail Prices Index on Rocky Island in the current year and the inflation rate between the base year and the current year.

4 An economy has the following real GDP and nominal GDP in 1993, 1994 and 1995. The currency units are denoted in EuroMarks (EM):

Year	Real GDP	Nominal GDP
1999	EM1,000 billion	EM1,000 billion
2000	EM1,050 billion	EM1,200 billion
2001	EM1,200 billion	EM1,500 billion

  a What was the GDP deflator in 1999?
  b What was the GDP deflator in 2000?
  c What is the inflation rate as measured by the GDP deflator between 2000 and 2001?
  d What is the percentage increase in the price level between 1999 and 2000 as measured by the GDP deflator?

5 Study *Reading Between the Lines* on pp. 594–595 and then answer the following questions:

  a What phase of the business cycle is the German economy in 1996?
  b If the rate of growth of potential GDP is 2.5 per cent a year, what is the likely outcome for unemployment if growth in 1996 is 1.5 per cent?
  c Study Figures 3 and 4. Roughly calculate the average level of unemployment in the second quarter of 1995. What is the negative output gap in 1995, second quarter?
  d If the rate of growth of potential GDP is 2.5 per cent a year, make a rough calculation as to what the rate of growth should be in the remainder of 1996 and in 1997 for unemployment to fall to the same position as in the second quarter of 1995.

CHAPTER 24

EMPLOYMENT, UNEMPLOYMENT AND WAGES

After studying this chapter you will be able to:

◆ Define the unemployment rate, the work-force participation rate, the economic activity rate and aggregate hours

◆ Describe the trends and fluctuations in the indicators of labour market performance

◆ Describe the sources of unemployment, its duration and the groups most affected by it

◆ Explain the different types of unemployment

◆ Define the natural rate of unemployment and full employment

◆ Explain how employment and wage rates are determined by demand and supply in the labour market

E ACH MONTH, WE CHART THE COURSE OF THE UNEMPLOYMENT RATE AS A MEASURE OF the economic health of the nation with the intensity of a doctor tracking a patient's temperature. How do we measure the unemployment rate? What does it tell us? Is it a reliable vital sign for the economy? ◆ December 1992 was a month in which unemployment peaked at almost 3 million. How can this large number of people be unemployed? How do people become unemployed? Do most of them get the sack or do most simply quit their jobs to look for better ones? How long do spells of unemployment last for most people? A week or two or several months? And how does the length of unemployment spells vary over the business cycle? ◆ You may know that unemployment affects young people much more severely than older people. It affects ethnic minorities much more severely than whites. Why isn't unem- ployment 'shared' more equitably by all age and racial groups? ◆ Another feature of the labour market that we regularly monitor is the number of people working. This number fluctuates as the unemployment rate fluctu- ates. At the start of 1995, 25.5 million people in the United Kingdom had a job. But this is

Vital Signs

no more than what existed in 1979. What does this information tell us about the health of the economy? ◆ In mid-1994, the working-age population of the United Kingdom was estimated to be 39.6 million. In mid-1981 it was 37.2 million. This is an average increase of 180,000 a year. Does the number of jobs grow quickly enough to keep pace with the increase in population? ◆ Yet other signs of economic health are the hours people work and the wages they receive. Are work hours growing as quickly as the number of people with jobs? Or are most of the new jobs part time? Also, are most new jobs high-wage or low-wage jobs?

◆ ◆ ◆ ◆ These are the questions we study in this chapter. You will discover that while there are things about the UK labour market that are not healthy there are other aspects that give grounds for optimism. The economy has been creating good jobs that pay good wages and benefits. But you'll also see that the economy has destroyed many jobs. While some people have seen their wages rise, others have seen no change and a few have seen their wages fall. So there have been big changes in the distribution of jobs and big changes in spread between the highest and the lowest wages. We begin by looking at the key labour market indicators and the way they are measured.

Employment and Wages

Real GDP, which measures the economy's total production of goods and services, depends on the quantities of labour and capital employed, on entrepreneurship and on the state of technology, which influences the productivity of the factors of production. We'll study what determines the quantity of capital employed in Chapters 25 and 26 and what influences technology and productivity in Chapter 26. In this chapter we study the forces that determine the quantity of labour employed, and we take an initial look at the productivity of labour. We begin by learning how the state of the labour market is observed and measured.

Population Survey

The Office for National Statistics (ONS), formerly known as the Central Statistical Office (CSO), periodically publishes two complementary measures of employment in the United Kingdom. One is based on the Labour Force Survey[1] (LFS), which is a survey of households in the United Kingdom, and the other on information from employers obtained from the Work-force in Employment (WiE) survey. The LFS conforms to internationally recognized norms set out by the International Labour Organization and includes demographic information such as age, qualifications and ethnic origin. Because LFS surveys are conducted in all EU and OECD countries they are also useful for international comparison. The WiE survey provides detailed information on employment by industry and is the estimate that is used to calculate the total work-force in the national accounts.

Unemployment figures are also obtained in two different ways: from the LFS and from the claimant count. To be counted as *unemployed* in the LFS, people must be available for work within the two weeks following their interview and must be in one of three categories:

1. Without work, but having made specific efforts to find a job within the previous four weeks
2. Waiting to be called back to a job from which they have been laid off
3. Waiting to start a new job within 30 days

---

[1] Until winter 1994/95,the Work-force Survey covered only Great Britain. It has now been extended to include Northern Ireland.

The claimant count measures unemployment as the number of people who are eligible and claim unemployment-related benefits (jobseekers allowance). This measure differs from the LFS and is sensitive to changes in the regulations for benefit entitlement. For example, a married woman who wishes to return to work after a period of absence from the labour market is not counted as being unemployed according to the claimant count but is counted in the LFS. Similarly, young people under the age of 18 are excluded from the claimant count but are included in the LFS.

The LFS defines the **working-age population** as the total number of people aged between 15 years and retirement who are not in jail, hospital, or some other form of institutional care. The working-age population is divided into two groups: those in the work-force and those not in the work-force. The work-force is also divided into two groups: the employed and the unemployed. So the **work-force** is the sum of the employed and the unemployed.

To be counted as employed in the LFS, a person must have either a full-time job or a part-time job. This includes students who do part-time work while at college. People in the working-age population who are neither employed nor unemployed are classified as not in the work-force.

The CSO estimates the official size of the work-force by combining the figures from the WiE survey with the claimant count. The LFS is used to estimate the working-age population and economic activity rates. But the total numbers that come out of the two methods are remarkably similar. Figure 24.1 compares the population categories obtained by the WiE and the claimant count with that of the LFS. The LFS estimates total employment including part-time workers in the first quarter of 1995 as 25.4 million, which is 446,000 more than that obtained by the WiE method. The LFS also estimates that unemployment is 122,000 larger than that measured by the claimant count.

Three Labour Market Indicators

We can use the WiE survey to calculate three indicators of the state of the labour market which are shown in Fig 24.2. They are:

◆ The unemployment rate
◆ The participation rate
◆ The employment-to-population ratio

FIGURE 24.1

Two Measures of the Work-force

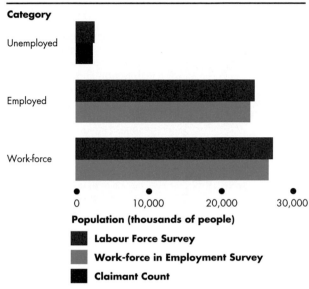

Category

The number of people employed plus the number unemployed make up the work-force. The CSO publishes two measures of employment, one based on information from employers and another based on the Labour Force Survey. Similarly, estimates of the unemployed are obtained from two sources: the Labour Force Survey and the count of those in receipt of unemployment benefit.

Source: Department of Employment, *Labour Market Trends*, November 1995.

The Unemployment Rate   The amount of unemployment is an indicator of the extent to which people who want jobs can't find them. The **unemployment rate** is the percentage of the people in the work-force who are unemployed. That is,

$$\text{Unemployment rate} = \frac{\text{Number of people unemployed}}{\text{Work-force}} \times 100$$

and

$$\text{Work-force} = \frac{\text{Number of}}{\text{people employed}} + \frac{\text{Number of}}{\text{people unemployed}}$$

In June 1995, the number of people employed in the United Kingdom according to official estimates was 25,729,000 and the number unemployed was 2,314,000. By using the above equations, you can verify that the work-force was 28,043,000, and the unemployment rate was 8.3 per cent.

The unemployment rate in Fig 24.2 (graphed in orange and plotted on the right scale) shows how labour market conditions have changed. The average unemployment rate in the 1960s and 1970s was 2.5 per cent, but the average rate in the 1980s and 1990s is 9%. Unemployment reached its most recent peak in 1993 following the recession of 1990–92, and a trough in 1990.

The Participation Rate   The number of people who join the work-force is an indicator of the willingness of the people of working age to take jobs. The **participation rate** is the percentage of the working-age population who are members of the work-force. That is,

$$\text{Participation rate} = \frac{\text{Work-force}}{\text{Working-age population}} \times 100$$

In mid-1994, the work-force was 28,108,000 and the working-age population was 37,713,000. By using the above equation, you can calculate the work-force participation rate. It was 74.5 per cent.

In Fig 24.2, the participation rate (graphed in red and plotted on the left scale) tells us about the growth of the work-force relative to the population. It has increased a little rising from 73 per cent in 1960 to 74.5 per cent in 1994. It peaked in 1989. It has also had some mild fluctuations, resulting from unsuccessful job seekers becoming discouraged workers. **Discouraged workers** are people who during a recession temporarily leave the work-force and who during a recovery and expansion re-enter the work-force and become more active job seekers. The movements of discouraged workers out of and back into the work-force change the participation rate. Fluctuations in the work-force participation rate give an estimate of the number of discouraged workers.

The Employment-to-population Ratio   The number of people of working age who have jobs is an indicator of the availability of jobs and the degree of match between people's skills and jobs. The **employment-to-population ratio** is the percentage of the people of working age who have jobs. That is,

$$\text{Employment-to-population ratio} = \frac{\text{Number of people employed}}{\text{Working-age population}} \times 100$$

In mid-1994, employment in the United Kingdom was 25,689,000 and the working-age population was 37,713,000. By using the above equation, you can calculate the employment-to-population ratio. It was 68.1 per cent.

FIGURE 24.2

Employment, Unemployment and the Work-force: 1960–1994

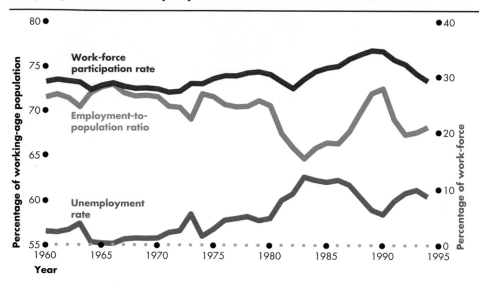

The state of the labour market is indicated by the participation rate, the employment-to-population ratio and the unemployment rate. The participation rate has not increased much since 1960. The employment-to-population ratio has decreased slightly and fluctuates with the business cycle, but it has fluctuated more in the 1980s and 1990s.

Sources: Central Statistical Office, *Annual Abstract of Statistics*, 1995; Department of Employment, *Department of Employment Gazette*, various; Department of Employment, *Employment Gazette Historical Supplement*, October 1994.

The employment-to-population ratio in Fig 24.2 (graphed in blue and plotted against the left scale) tells us about the growth in the number of people employed relative to the population. This ratio has decreased slightly from 71 per cent during the 1960s to 68 per cent in the 1990s. The fact that the employment-to-population ratio has decreased means that the economy has created jobs at a slower rate than the working-age population has grown. This labour market indicator also fluctuates, and its fluctuations coincide with but are opposite to those in the unemployment rate. The employment-to-population ratio falls during a recession and increases during a recovery and expansion.

Why has the participation rate stayed the same and the employment-to-population ratio decreased? The main reason is an increase in the unemployment rate. Between 1960 and 1994, the rate of unemployment increased from 2.5 per cent to 8.5 per cent, reaching a peak of 12 per cent in 1983. In other words, the total number of jobs has not kept up with the increase in the working-age population. But this statement has to be qualified. Figure 24.3 shows that the female work-force participation rate has increased from 48 per cent in 1960 to 65 per cent in 1994. Other things are also changing. Shorter working hours, higher productivity and an

increased emphasis on white-collar jobs have expanded the job opportunities and wages available to women. At the same time, technological advances have increased productivity in the home and freed women from some of their more traditional jobs outside the job market.

Figure 24.3 also shows another remarkable fact about the UK work-force: the participation rate and the employment-to-population ratio for men have *decreased*. Between 1960 and 1994, the male work-force participation rate decreased from 99 per cent to 84 per cent. It has decreased because increasing numbers of men are in higher education, some are retiring earlier and some are specializing in the household jobs that previously were done almost exclusively by women.

Aggregate Hours

The three labour market indicators that we've just examined are useful signs of the health of the economy and directly measure what matters to most people: jobs. But they don't tell us the quantity of labour used to produce GDP, and we can't use them to calculate the productivity of labour. The productivity of labour is significant because it influences the wages people earn.

FIGURE 24.3

The Changing Face of the Labour Market

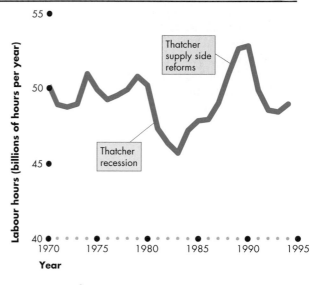

The male participation rate and the employment-to-population ratio have decreased. This is because increasing numbers of men are in higher education, some are retiring earlier and some are specializing in the household jobs that were previously done by women. The female participation rate has been rising and many new jobs are part time employing female labour.

Source: Department of Employment, *Employment Gazette Historical Supplement*, October 1994.

The reason the number of people employed does not measure the quantity of labour employed is that jobs are not all the same. Some jobs are part time and involve just a few hours of work a week. Others are full time, and some of these involve regular overtime work. For example, one shop might hire six students who each work for three hours a day. Another might hire two full-time workers who each work nine hours a day. The number of people employed in these two shops is eight, but six of the eight do the same total amount of work as the other two. To determine the total amount of labour used to produce GDP, we measure labour in hours rather than in jobs. **Aggregate hours** is the total number of hours worked by all the people employed, both full time and part time, during a year.

Figure 24.4(a) shows aggregate hours in the economy from 1970 to 1994. They fluctuate around a flat trend. Between 1970 and 1994, the number of people employed in the UK economy increased by less than 2 per cent. However, during that same

---

FIGURE 24.4

Aggregate Hours: 1970–1994

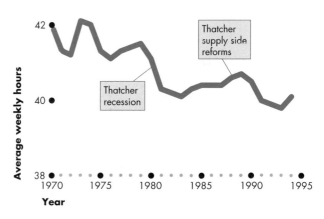

(a) Aggregate hours

(b) Average weekly hours per person

Aggregate hours (part a) measure the total labour used to produce real GDP more accurately than does the number of people employed because an increasing proportion of jobs are part time. Between 1970 and 1994, aggregate hours fluctuated around a flat trend. Fluctuations in aggregate hours coincide with business cycle fluctuations. Aggregate hours have stayed the same while the number of jobs has increased because the average workweek has shortened (part b).

Sources: Labour Force Survey; Quantime Ltd; and the author's calculations.

period, aggregate hours fell by 3 per cent. Why the difference? Because average weekly hours per worker have fallen over the same period.

Figure 24.4(b) shows average weekly hours per worker. From around 42 hours a week in 1970, average hours per worker decreased to about 40 hours a week in 1994. This shortening of the average workweek has arisen partly because of a decrease in the average hours worked by full-time workers but mainly because the number of part-time jobs has increased faster than the number of full-time jobs.

Fluctuations in aggregate hours and average hours per worker line up with the business cycle. Figure 24.4 highlights the past three recessions during which aggregate hours decreased and average hours per worker decreased more quickly than the trend. While both measures show a fall that corresponds with the downturn of the economy in a recession, aggregate hours fall by more because people lose their jobs.

Wage Rates

The **real wage rate** is the quantity of goods and services that an hour's work can buy. It is equal to the money wage rate (pounds per hour) divided by the price level. If we use the GDP deflator as the price level, the real wage rate is expressed in 1990 pounds because the GDP deflator is 100 in 1990. The real wage rate is a significant economic variable because it measures the reward for labour.

What has happened to the real wage rate in the United Kingdom? Figure 24.5 answers this question. It shows three measures of the average hourly real wage rate in the UK economy between 1970 and 1994.

The first measure of the real wage rate is the New Earnings Survey calculation of the average hourly earnings of adult manual workers measured in 1990 pounds. This measure of the hourly wage rate reached a peak of £4.05 in 1976. It fell to £3.91 in 1977 but accelerated in the second half of the 1980s and slowed down in the 1990s.

The second measure of the hourly real wage rate is based on the national income accounts. It is calculated by dividing total wages and salaries by aggregate hours. This measure of the hourly wage rate is broader than the first and includes the incomes of all types of labour, whether their rate of pay is calculated by the hour or not. It includes man-

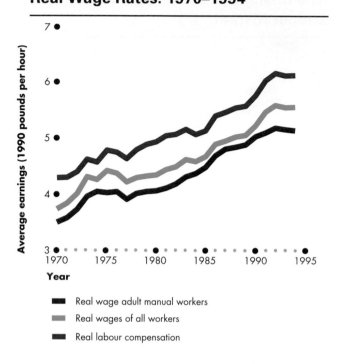

FIGURE 24.5

Real Wage Rates: 1970–1994

The average hourly real wage rate of manual workers kept pace with the other two measures based on national income accounts. It accelerated in the late 1980s but slowed in the 1990s. All three measures of average hourly real wage rates reflect the productivity growth slowdown of the 1970s.

Sources: New Earnings Survey; Liverpool Macroeconomics Research Group; and the author's calculations.

agers and supervisors and all types of workers. This measure shows a sustained upward trend during the 1970s and 1980s and acceleration in 1989–92.

An increasing proportion of labour cost now takes the form of employer's add-on costs, such as employer's National Insurance contributions, and graduated pension contributions. To take this trend into account, Fig. 24.5 shows a third measure of the hourly real wage rate, which equals *real labour compensation* – wages, salaries, and supplements – divided by aggregate hours. This measure is the most comprehensive one available, and it shows that the average hourly wage rate has increased. All three measures show that there was a common slowdown coinciding with the productivity slowdown of the 1970s.

◆ The work-force participation rate and the employment-to-population ratio have an upward trend and fluctuate with the business cycle.

◆ The female work-force participation rate has increased but the male work-force participation rate has decreased.

◆ Aggregate hours have fluctuated with total employment but have not grown as quickly because the average working week has shortened.

◆ Average hourly earnings have grown, but their growth rate slowed with the productivity growth slowdown of the 1970s.

We've seen that employment grows and that employment and unemployment fluctuate with the business cycle. Let's now focus more sharply on unemployment.

Unemployment and Full Employment

How do people become unemployed, how long do they remain unemployed and who is at greatest risk of becoming unemployed? Let's answer these questions by looking at the anatomy of unemployment.

The Anatomy of Unemployment

People become unemployed if they:

1. Lose their jobs

2. Leave their jobs

3. Enter or re-enter the work-force

People end a spell of unemployment if they:

1. Are hired or recalled

2. Withdraw from the work-force

People who are laid off, either permanently or temporarily, from their jobs are called **job losers**. Some job losers become unemployed but some immediately withdraw from the work-force. People who voluntarily quit their jobs are called **job leavers**. Like job losers, some job leavers become unemployed and search for a better job, while others withdraw from the work-force temporarily or perma-

nently retire from work. People who enter or re-enter the work-force are called **entrants** and **re-entrants**. Entrants are mainly people who have just left school. Some entrants get a job straight away and are never unemployed, but many spend time searching for their first job and during this period they are unemployed. Re-entrants are people who have previously withdrawn from the work-force. Most of these people are formerly discouraged workers or women returning to the labour market after an extended absence while raising a family. But an increasing number of unemployed people have been in this state for a period longer than a year. They are referred to as the **long-term unemployed**. Figure 24.6 shows these labour market categories.

FIGURE 24.6

Labour Market Flows

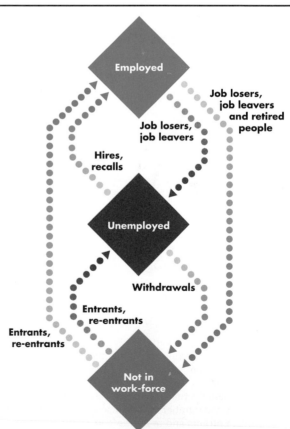

Unemployment results from employed people losing or leaving their jobs (job losers and job leavers) and from people entering the work-force (entrants and re-entrants). Unemployment ends because people get hired or recalled or because they withdraw from the work-force.

Let's see how much unemployment arises from the three different ways in which people can become unemployed.

The Sources of Unemployment   Figure 24.7 shows unemployment by reason for becoming unemployed. Job losers are the biggest source of unemployment. These are the people that make up the redundancy statistics we hear so regularly on the television news and read in the newspapers. Their number fluctuates a great deal. In the recession of 1992, nearly 34 per cent of the unemployment was due to job losses. In contrast, in the business cycle peak year of 1990, fewer than 22 per cent of the unemployed were job losers.

Entrants are also a significant component of the unemployed. Although they do not figure in the official claimant count of unemployed, they are picked up in the LFS as school leavers. On any given day in 1994, nearly one-fifth of those unemployed were entrants to the labour market.

Job leavers are the smallest and most stable source of unemployment. On any given day, fewer than 175,000 people are unemployed because they are job leavers. The number of job leavers is remarkably constant.

The Duration of Unemployment   Some people are unemployed for a week or two, and others are unemployed for periods of a year or more. Figure 24.8 examines the duration of unemployment at the peak and the trough of the business cycle. We can see that in the peak a higher proportion of the unemployed were jobless for under 13 weeks than in the trough, and a lower proportion of the unemployed were jobless for more than 13 weeks than in

FIGURE 24.7

Unemployment by Reasons

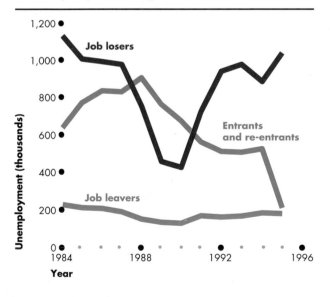

Everyone who is unemployed is a job loser, a job leaver, or an entrant/re-entrant into the work-force. Most of the unemployment that exists results from job loss. The number of job losers fluctuates more closely with the business cycle than do the numbers of job losers and entrants and re-entrants. Entrants and re-entrants are the second most commonly unemployed people. Their number fluctuates with the business cycle because of discouraged workers. Job leavers are the least common unemployed people.

Sources: Labour Force Survey; Quantime Ltd; and the author's calculations.

FIGURE 24.8

Unemployment by Duration

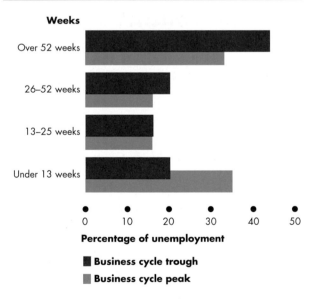

At a business cycle peak when unemployment is at its lowest level, 35 per cent of unemployment lasts for under 13 weeks, 16 per cent lasts for 13–25 weeks, 16 per cent lasts for 26–52 weeks and 33 per cent lasts for one year or more. At a business cycle trough when unemployment is at its highest level, only 20 per cent of unemployment lasts for under 13 weeks, 16 per cent lasts for 13–25 weeks, 20 per cent lasts for 26–52 weeks and 44 per cent lasts for one year or more.

Sources: Labour Force Survey; Quantime Ltd.

the trough. But the most noticeable feature is the proportion of people who have been unemployed for over one year. This is the definition of long-term unemployment, which is a pressing social problem both in the United Kingdom and in the rest of the European Union. In the peak of 1989, 33 per cent of the jobless population were classified as long-term unemployed; in the trough of 1992 that proportion increased to 44 per cent. While most people who are unemployed find work within a year, the proportion of the long-term unemployed has remained stubbornly in the range 35–45 per cent over the business cycle.

The Demographics of Unemployment   Figure 24.9(a) and (b) shows unemployment for different demographic groups. The figure shows that the high unemployment rates occur among young workers, especially young men, and also ethnic minority groups, especially among blacks. In the summer of 1994, the unemployment rate of all ethnic minorities was about 20 per cent; for blacks as a whole it was about 25 per cent compared with whites for whom it was about 9 per cent. Figure 24.9(b) shows that the gap between white and non-white unemployment increases in the trough and decreases in the peak. Teenagers also have a higher than average unemployment rate. In summer 1994, the unemployment rate of all 16–19 year olds was 22 per cent, while that of teenage men was 25 per cent.

Why are teenage unemployment rates so high? There are three reasons. First, young people are still in the process of discovering what they are good at and trying different lines of work. So they leave their jobs more frequently than older workers. Second, firms sometimes hire teenagers on a short-term trial basis. So the rate of job loss is higher for teenagers than for other people. Third, most teenagers are not in the work-force but are at school. This means that the percentage of the teenage population unemployed is much lower than the teenage unemployment rate. For example, in summer 1994, 396,000 teenagers were unemployed and 1,372,000 were employed, and the teenage unemployment rate (all races) was 22.4 per cent. But 1,209,000 teenagers were at school or on government-sponsored training schemes. The ratio of teenage unemployment to the teenage population is 15.3 per cent. That is, 22 per cent of the teenage work-force or 15 per cent of the teenage population is unemployed.

FIGURE 24.9

Unemployment by Demographic Group

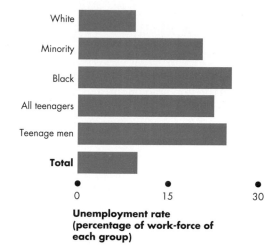

(a) Demographic groups

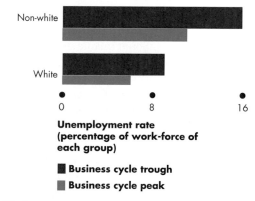

Unemployment rate (percentage of work-force of each group)

■ Business cycle trough
■ Business cycle peak

(b) Ethnic groups

Teenagers experience unemployment rates nearly two-and-a-half times higher than the average, and unemployment among blacks is over two-and-a-half times the average. Even at a business cycle trough when unemployment is at its highest rate, the ratio of non-white to white unemployment is 1.7.

Sources: Labour Force Survey; Quantime Ltd.

Why are ethnic minorities' unemployment rates higher than white unemployment rates? One reason is that many ethnic minority workers are low-skilled. In the downturn of the business cycle more low-skilled than high-skilled jobs are lost. Another possible reason is that ethnic minorities face unequal opportunities in the labour market.

Types of Unemployment

Unemployment is classified into three types that are based on its causes. They are:

◆ Frictional
◆ Structural
◆ Cyclical

Frictional Unemployment   **Frictional unemployment** is the unemployment that arises from normal labour turnover. Frictional unemployment is not usually regarded as a problem, but it is a permanent, long-term phenomenon.

Normal labour turnover arises for two reasons. First, people are constantly entering the work-force – young people leave school, mothers return to the work-force and previously discouraged workers try once more to find jobs. At the same time, other people retire and create job vacancies for the new entrants and re-entrants to fill. This constant churning of the individuals in the work-force is the first reason for normal labour turnover.

The second reason is the constant churning of individual businesses. Some businesses fail, close down and lay off their workers. Other new businesses start up and hire workers. The people who lose their jobs in this process are frictionally unemployed and are trying to match their skills to jobs that are opening up.

The unending flow of people into and out of the work-force and of job creation and job destruction creates the need for people to search for jobs and for businesses to search for workers. Always there are businesses with unfilled jobs and people seeking jobs. Look in your local newspaper and you will see that there are always some jobs being advertised. Businesses don't usually hire the first person who applies for a job, and unemployed people don't usually take the first job that comes their way. Instead, both firms and workers spend time searching out what they believe will be the best match available. By this process of search, people can match their own skills and interests with the available jobs and find a satisfying job and income. While these unemployed people are searching, they are frictionally unemployed.

The amount of frictional unemployment depends on the rate at which people enter and re-enter the work-force and on the rate at which jobs are created and destroyed. During the 1960s, the amount of frictional unemployment increased as a consequence of the post-war baby boom that began during the 1940s. By the 1960s, the baby boom created a bulge in the number of school leavers. As these people entered the work-force, the amount of frictional unemployment increased.

The amount of frictional unemployment is also influenced by the level of unemployment benefit. The greater the number of people covered by unemployment benefit (jobseekers allowance) and the more generous the benefit, the longer is the average time taken in job search and the greater is the amount of frictional unemployment. The LFS indicates that 92 per cent of the unemployed are covered by unemployment benefit. Studies of unemployment in the European Union indicate that a strong statistical correlation exists between the length of time people are able to receive unemployment benefit and the duration of unemployment.

Structural Unemployment   **Structural unemployment** is the unemployment that arises when changes in technology or international competition destroy jobs that use different skills or are located in different regions from the new jobs that are created. Structural unemployment usually lasts longer than frictional unemployment because it is often necessary to retrain and possibly relocate to find a job. For example, on the day the shipyards in the Upper Clyde announced the loss of 600 jobs, a computer chip company in Gwent announced the creation of 750 new jobs. The unemployed former shipyard workers remain unemployed for several months until they move home, retrain and get one of the new jobs being created in other parts of the country.

Structural unemployment is painful, especially for older workers for whom the best available option might be to retire early, but with a lower income than they had expected. For example, a shipyard worker from Humberside who is made redundant may reluctantly accept to remain unemployed rather than retrain, accept a lower wage for another type of job, or move south where new jobs are being created. Such a person has opted to join the ranks of the long-term unemployed. The decision to accept long-term unemployment is governed by the options available to and the constraints on the structurally unemployed person. A person with different circumstances may make an entirely different decision. A younger person with family commitments may retrain, or take a job as a taxi driver in the short term until a better opportunity turns up, or relocate to take advantage of job opportunities elsewhere. One of the many factors that influence a person's decision is the level of unemployment benefit. The higher the level of benefit, the less incentive there is to accept the alternatives to long-term unemployment.

At certain times structural unemployment can become a serious long-term problem. It began to increase in the 1970s during the period of stagflation, when an increasingly competitive international environment brought a decline in the number of jobs in traditional industries.

Cyclical Unemployment   **Cyclical unemployment** is the fluctuating unemployment that coincides with the business cycle. It is a repeating short-term problem. The amount of cyclical unemployment increases during a recession and decreases during a recovery and expansion. A worker in a car components factory who is laid off because the economy is in a recession and who gets rehired some months later when the recovery begins has experienced cyclical unemployment.

Figure 24.10 illustrates cyclical unemployment in the United Kingdom between 1980 and 1994. Part (a) shows the fluctuations of real GDP around potential GDP. Part (b) shows fluctuations in the unemployment rate around a line labelled 'Natural rate of unemployment'. The **natural rate of unemployment** is the unemployment rate when there is no cyclical unemployment or, equivalently, when all the unemployment is frictional and structural. The divergence of the unemployment rate from the natural rate is cyclical unemployment.

In Fig. 24.10, the unemployment rate fluctuates around the natural rate of unemployment (part b) just as real GDP fluctuates around potential GDP (part a). When the unemployment rate equals the natural rate of unemployment, real GDP equals potential GDP. When the unemployment rate is less than the natural rate of unemployment, real GDP is greater than potential GDP. And when the unemployment rate is greater than the natural rate of unemployment, real GDP is less than potential GDP. However, it is not always the case that when GDP equals potential GDP, unemployment equals the natural rate. While it is true to argue that when unemployment is at its natural rate GDP is at its potential, the reverse is not always the case. This is because, while production of goods and services can be increased by

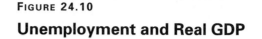

FIGURE 24.10

Unemployment and Real GDP

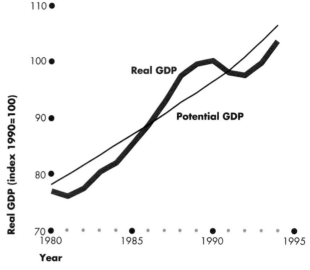

(a) Real GDP

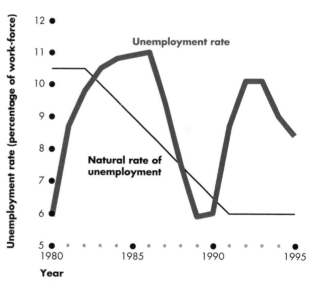

(b) Unemployment rate

As real GDP fluctuates around potential GDP (part a), the unemployment rate fluctuates around the natural rate of unemployment (part b). In the deep recession of 1982, unemployment reached almost 10 per cent. In the milder recession of 1992–1993, the unemployment rate peaked at 10 per cent. The labour market reforms of the 1980s helped to reduce the natural rate of unemployment. We don't know how far the natural rate of unemployment has fallen.

Sources: Department of Employment, *Labour Market Trends*; Lombard Street Research Ltd; and author's estimates.

working the existing employed work-force more intensively through increased overtime, the process of hiring labour takes time. Hence adjustments to the unemployment rate can lag behind the movements in GDP.

Full Employment

There is always *some* unemployment – someone looking for a job or laid off and waiting to be recalled. So what do we mean by full employment? **Full employment** occurs when the unemployment rate equals the natural rate of unemployment. There can be quite a lot of unemployment at full employment, and the term 'full employment' is an example of a technical economic term that does not correspond with everyday ideas. The term 'natural rate of unemployment' is another example of a technical economic term that does not correspond with everyday language. For most people, there is nothing *natural* about unemployment – especially for the unemployed. These terms remind us that frictions and structural changes are unavoidable features of the economy and that they create unemployment.

In Fig. 24.10(b), the natural rate of unemployment is 10.5 per cent during the early 1980s and it falls to 8 per cent during the late 1980s and further to 6 per cent in the 1990s. This view of the natural rate of unemployment in the United Kingdom is an estimate that some, but not all, economists would accept.

There is not much controversy about the existence of a natural rate of unemployment. Nor is there much controversy that it fluctuates. The natural rate of unemployment arises from the existence of frictional and structural unemployment, and it fluctuates because the frictions and the amount of structural change fluctuate. But there is controversy about the magnitude of the natural rate of unemployment and the extent to which it fluctuates. Some economists believe that the natural rate of unemployment fluctuates frequently, and that at times of rapid demographic and technological change, its rate can be high. Others argue that restrictive practices by trade unions and increases in real unemployment benefits will increase the natural rate, and that the labour market reforms associated with the decade of Mrs Thatcher's economic policies led to a reduction in the natural rate to an even lower figure than that shown in Fig. 24.10(b).

REVIEW

◆ The people who become unemployed are job losers, job leavers and work-force entrants or re-entrants.

◆ Between 40 and 50 per cent of the unemployed are the long-term unemployed.

◆ Unemployment can be frictional (normal labour market turnover), structural (a long-lasting decline in a region or industry), or cyclical (in line with the business cycle).

◆ When all the unemployment is frictional and structural (when there is no cyclical unemployment), the unemployment rate is equal to the natural rate of unemployment.

◆ When the unemployment rate is equal to the natural rate of unemployment, there is full employment.

We've described the trends and fluctuations in employment, wage rates and unemployment. And we've described the labour market flows that bring changes in employment and unemployment. We've also described the anatomy of unemployment and classified it as frictional, structural and cyclical. It is now time to explain the trends and fluctuations. We begin by explaining the trends in employment and wage rates.

Explaining Employment and Wage Rates

We can understand the amount of employment and the wage rate by using the model of demand and supply and applying it to the labour market.

Demand and Supply in the Labour Market

Figure 24.11 illustrates the labour market in 1994. The *x*-axis measures the quantity of labour employed as *aggregate hours* – billions of hours per year. The *y*-axis measures the real wage rate. The figure has three curves, a labour demand curve, a labour supply curve and a work-force

FIGURE 24.11

The Labour Market

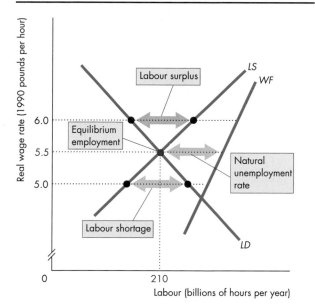

The labour demand curve, *LD,* shows the aggregate hours of labour that firms plan to hire at each real wage rate. The labour supply curve, *LS,* shows the aggregate hours that households plan to work at each wage rate. In equilibrium, the real wage rate is £5.50 an hour in 1990 prices. The *WF* curve shows the potential hours available if everyone of working age who wants to work at a particular wage rate is employed. The gap between the *LS* curve and the *WF* curve defines the natural rate of unemployment. The slope of the *WF* curve is steeper than the *LS* curve because as the real wage rises the gap between the *LS* and *WF* curves narrows.

curve. In the labour market, firms demand labour and households supply labour.

The **labour demand curve** shows the quantity of labour that firms plan to hire at each possible real wage rate. The lower the real wage rate, the greater is the quantity of labour that firms plan to hire. That is, the labour demand curve slopes downward. The reason the quantity of labour demanded depends on the *real* wage rate is that firms care only about the amount they pay for labour relative to the amount they get for their output. If money wages and prices change in the same proportion, the quantity of labour that firms plan to hire is unaffected.

The **labour supply curve** shows the quantity of available labour that households plan to supply at

each possible real wage rate. The higher the real wage rate, the greater is the quantity of labour that households plan to supply. That is, the labour supply curve slopes upward. The reason the quantity of labour supplied depends on the *real* wage rate is that households care only about the amount they are paid for their labour relative to the price they must pay for the things they buy. If money wages and prices change in the same proportion, the quantity of labour that households plan to supply is unaffected. An increase in restrictive practices by trade unions will reduce the number of hours worked and will result in a leftward shift of the labour supply curve.

The **work-force curve** shows the potential quantity of labour available for employment at a particular real wage rate. The potential quantity of labour is made up of the actual supply of available labour and labour hours expended in job search and in long-term structural unemployment. The gap between the labour supply curve and the work-force curve is the natural rate of unemployment. The work-force curve is steeper than the labour supply curve because as real wages rise, the amount of labour hours expended in job search declines and even those who are in long-term structural unemployment will be willing to take on any kind of work.

The reason the quantity of labour demanded increases as the real wage rate decreases – the labour demand curve slopes downward – is that firms strive to maximize profit. If the wage rate at which they can hire labour falls relative to the price they can get for their output, they have an incentive to expand production and hire more labour. And the reason the quantity of labour supplied increases as the real wage rate increases – the labour supply curve slopes upward – is that households strive to use their scarce time in the most efficient way. If the wage rate they are offered rises relative to the prices they must pay for goods and services, they have a stronger incentive to work.

Labour demand and labour supply interact to determine the equilibrium level of employment, unemployment and the real wage rate. In Fig. 24.11, at an average real wage rate below £5.50 an hour based on 1990 prices, there is a labour shortage. People find jobs easily, but businesses are short of labour. But this situation doesn't last for ever. Because there is a shortage of labour, the real wage rate rises towards the equilibrium wage rate of £5.50 an hour.

At wage rates above £5.50 an hour, there is a labour surplus. People have a hard time finding jobs and businesses can easily hire all the labour they want. Unemployment will be a mixture of the labour surplus created by the excess supply of labour and the natural rate shown by the gap between the labour supply curve and the work-force curve. In this situation, the real wage rate falls towards the equilibrium wage rate. In equilibrium the actual unemployment rate coincides with the natural rate.

The Trends in Employment and Wage Rates

We can use the model of labour demand and labour supply to understand the long-term trends in aggregate hours and real wage rates. We saw in Fig. 24.4 that aggregate hours in 1979 were much the same as in 1970. We saw in Fig. 24.5 that the real wage rate increased. The average real wage rate for the entire economy, including the value of pay supplements, increased from £4.30 an hour in 1970 to about £5 an hour in 1979. We also saw in Fig. 24.2 that the unemployment rate increased from 2.6 per cent in 1970 to 3.6 per cent in 1979.

Figure 24.12 shows how these changes came about. In 1970, the labour demand curve was LD_{70} and the labour supply curve was LS_{70}. The equilibrium real wage rate was £4.30 an hour, and 50 billion hours of labour were employed.

Throughout the period since World War II, labour has become more and more productive. The reason is that capital per worker has increased and technology has advanced. We'll explore the reasons for this increased labour productivity in Chapter 26. But regardless of the reasons, the effect of an increase in labour productivity is an increase in the demand for labour. If an hour of labour can produce more output, firms are willing to pay a higher wage rate to hire that hour of labour. This would be shown by a rightward shift in the labour demand curve, resulting in a rise in the real wage and an increase in the quantity of labour employed. However, during the 1970s there was a productivity slowdown associated with the oil price shock and the outward shift was moderate. This increase in demand is shown by a rightward shift in the labour demand curve from LD_{70} to LD_{79}.

At the same time the population grew and so did the working-age population. With a larger working-age population, the supply of labour available for work increased. This increase is shown by the

FIGURE 24.12

Explaining the Trends in Employment and Real Wage Rates

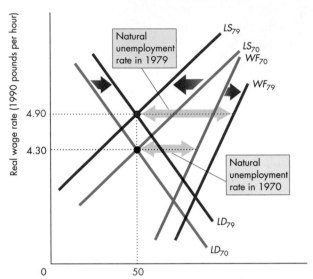

In 1970, the labour demand curve was LD_{70} and the labour supply curve was LS_{70}. The equilibrium real wage rate was £4.30 an hour in 1990 prices, and 50 billion hours of labour were employed. Over the years, labour became more and more productive. The demand curve shifted rightward to LD_{79}. At the same time, an increase in the working-age population increased the potential supply of labour, and the work-force curve shifted rightward to WF_{79}. An increase in union militancy and restrictive practices led to a leftward shift of the LS curve to LS_{79}. As a result the quantity of labour employed remained the same, the average real wage rose and unemployment increased.

rightward shift in the work-force curve from WF_{70} to WF_{79}. Normally, we would expect the supply of labour to shift in the same direction; however, during the 1970s there was an increase in trade union militancy aimed at increasing the cost of labour. This resulted in a leftward shift of the labour supply curve from LS_{70} to LS_{79}.

Thus the quantity of labour employed remained the same, the average real wage rate increased, and unemployment increased. But also the natural rate of unemployment increased.

During the 1980s, particularly the second half, trade union reform and other supply side policies of Mrs Thatcher's government resulted in the labour

FIGURE 24.13

Explaining Labour Market Trends in the 1980s

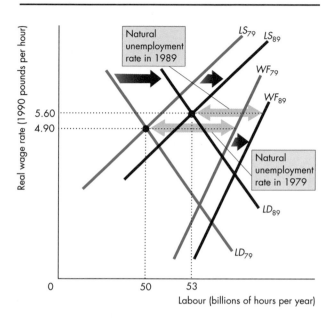

An increase in the population of working age brings an increase in the entry rate into the work-force and an increase in unemployment. This is shown by a rightward shift in the *WF* curve. The labour market reforms of the 1980s resulted in the *LS* curve shifting to the right more than the *WF* curve. By the end of the decade, total hours had increased by 3 billion and the natural rate of unemployment had declined.

supply curve shifting rightward. These policies were aimed at making the labour market more flexible. This is shown in Fig. 24.13 as a rightward shift in the *LS* curve. The working-age population increased by 1.5 million in the 10 years to 1989. This is shown as a rightward shift in the *WF* curve. It is generally accepted that the supply side policies of Mrs Thatcher's government were successful in making the labour market more competitive. This means that the labour supply curve shifted to the right more than the WF curve, narrowing the gap between the two and reducing the natural rate of unemployment.

The labour market reforms resulted in the balance of power in the workplace shifting away from trade unions and towards management. This resulted in labour being used more efficiently and worker productivity improving. The increase in

worker productivity led to a rightward shift in labour demand, resulting in higher real wages, higher aggregate hours and lower unemployment.

R E V I E W

◆ The labour demand curve shows the quantity of labour that firms plan to hire at each real wage rate. The labour demand curve slopes downward because a fall in the real wage rate gives firms a stronger incentive to increase production and hire more labour.

◆ The labour supply curve shows the quantity of labour that households plan to supply at each real wage rate. The labour supply curve slopes upward because a rise in the real wage rate gives households a stronger incentive to work.

◆ Labour demand and labour supply interact to determine the level of employment and the equilibrium real wage rate.

◆ The work-force curve shows the potential supply of labour at a particular real wage, but separates the supply of labour to the labour market by making allowance for the natural rate of unemployment.

We've now studied the main trends in employment and wage rates, and we have seen how the demand and supply model can help us to understand these trends. Our next task is to explain unemployment.

Explaining Unemployment

We've described *how* people become unemployed – they are job losers, job leavers, or work-force entrants and re-entrants. And we have classified unemployment – it can be frictional, structural and cyclical. But this description and classification do not *explain* unemployment. Why is there always some unemployment and why does its rate fluctuate? Unemployment is always present for three reasons:

◆ Job search

◆ Job rationing

◆ Sticky wages

Unemployment and Minimum Wages

The Essence of the Story

THE SUNDAY TIMES, 14 JANUARY 1996

Job market faces new shackles

David Smith

If one accepts that one of Margaret Thatcher's most important achievements, nurtured by John Major, was the creation of a flexible and responsive labour market, the risk is that Labour, with its commitment to the European social chapter and a national minimum wage, will turn back the clock, to the detriment of the economy.

For this, more than usually, is a time when Britain does not want to emulate the European market. Last week it was announced that unemployment in the united Germany had jumped to 3.79m – 8.7% of the workforce in the former west Germany and 14.9% in the old east Germany.

The total will break through 4m before the winter is through. ...In France the picture is no better. Unemployment is 11.5% and officially predicted to top 12%....

Some economists believe that the unemployment effects of a minimum wage will either be negligible, or could be positive if they increase productivity by making employers use labour more efficiently. Some argue for setting a high minimum wage (the broad area of argument runs between £3.50 and £4.30 an hour) on the grounds that once set, it may be fixed for years.

I do not believe a minimum wage creates jobs. ...A £4-an-hour minimum wage is worth £160 a week – the impact on Britain's wage bill, and on employment, could be bigger than even pessimists assume. One argument in favour of a minimum wage, that it will prevent employers abusing workers in a receipt of top-up social-security benefits (a minimum would prevent firms from cutting pay and leaving the government to pick up the tab), is not decisive. Such abuses are better tackled directly....

■ Reform of the trade union movement during the 1980s created a flexible labour market in the United Kingdom.

■ The adoption of a minimum wage and the European Social Chapter might reverse the gains produced by a flexible labour market to the detriment of the economy.

■ Unemployment in the United Kingdom is lower than in Germany or France. However, it is argued by its supporters that a minimum wage may not have an adverse effect on employment.

■ There are conflicting arguments regarding the economic implications of a minimum wage. David Smith of the *Sunday Times* argues that a minimum wage could reduce the number of jobs.

Economic Analysis

■ The economic reforms of the 1980s have made the UK labour market flexible and responsive to changing economic circumstances. The flexibility of the labour market explains why UK unemployment is lower than German or French unemployment.

■ Figure 1 shows that the reform of the trade union movement in the 1980s shifted the supply of labour rightward from LS_0 to LS_1 and reduced the equilibrium level of unemployment.

■ The argument in favour of minimum wages is that if firms are forced to pay a minimum wage they will have to use labour more efficiently and improve productivity. It is argued that the improved productivity will result in negligible effects on unemployment. This argument is illustrated in Fig. 2. The minimum wage is W^*, which is above the equilibrium defined by the intersection of labour demand, LD_0, and labour supply, LS_0. Improved productivity will increase the demand for labour, causing the labour demand curve to shift rightward to LD_1. The resulting effect would raise, lower, or keep unemployment the same as before according to the extent of the increase in labour demand.

■ The counter-argument is that the distribution of earnings is skewed towards low pay. A £4 an hour minimum wage is worth £160 a week. About a quarter of workers earn less than £4 an hour.

■ A minimum wage of £4 would raise wages throughout the economy as different groups seek higher wages to restore eroded differentials. This will reduce the supply of labour in Fig. 3 from LS_0 to LS_1, and increase unemployment.

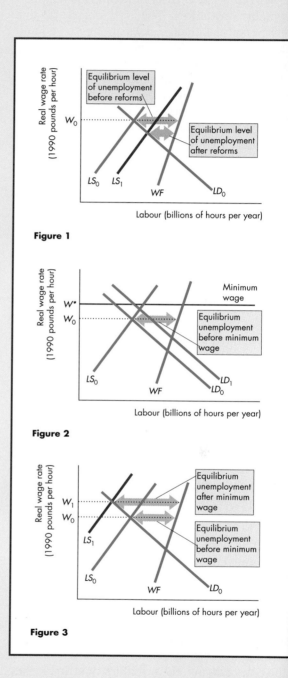

Figure 1

Figure 2

Figure 3

Job Search

Job search is the activity of people looking for acceptable vacant jobs. The labour market is in a constant state of change. Jobs are destroyed and created as businesses fail and new businesses start up and as new technologies and new markets evolve. In the process, people lose jobs. Other people enter or re-enter the labour market. Yet other people leave their jobs to look for better ones and others retire. This constant churning in the labour market means that there are always some people looking for jobs – the unemployed. Job search even takes place when the quantity of labour demanded equals the quantity supplied. In this situation, some people have not yet found a job and some jobs have not yet been filled.

Job search explains frictional, structural and cyclical unemployment. All three types of unemployment occur because job losers, job leavers, and work-force entrants and re-entrants don't know about all the jobs available to them so they must take time to *search* for an acceptable one. This search takes time, and the average amount of time varies. When there is a small amount of structural change and when the economy is close to a business cycle peak, search times are low and the unemployment rate is low. But when structural change is rapid and when the economy is in a recession, search times increase and the unemployment rate increases.

Although job search is cyclical, it also changes more slowly and brings changes in the natural rate of unemployment. The main sources of these slower changes are:

◆ Demographic change
◆ Unemployment benefit
◆ Technological change
◆ Hysteresis

Demographic Change An increase in the proportion of the working-age population brings an increase in the entry rate into the work-force and an increase in the unemployment rate. This is described by a rightward shift in the *WF* curve in Figs. 24.12 and 24.13. A bulge in the birth rate occurred in the late 1940s and early 1950s, following World War II. This bulge increased the proportion of new entrants into the work-force during the 1970s and brought an increase in the unemployment rate.

Unemployment Benefit The length of time that an unemployed person spends searching for a job depends, in part, on the opportunity cost of job search. With no income during a period of unemployment, an unemployed person faces a high opportunity cost of job search. In this situation, search is likely to be short and an unattractive job is likely to be accepted as a better alternative to continuing a costly search process. With generous unemployment benefits, the opportunity cost of job search is low. In this situation, search is likely to be prolonged. An unemployed worker will hold out for the ideal job.

The opportunity cost of job search has fallen over the years as unemployment benefits have increased. In 1966, unemployment benefit included a flat-rate component and an earnings-related component. As a result of these changes, the natural rate of unemployment was on an upward trend during the 1970s. In 1982, earnings-related benefit was abolished in the United Kingdom and during the 1990s the conditions for the receipt of benefit were tightened. During the 1980s estimates of the natural rate decreased.

Technological Change Labour market flows and unemployment are influenced by the pace and direction of technological change. Sometimes technological change brings a *structural slump*, in which some industries die and regions suffer and other industries are born and regions flourish. When these events occur, labour turnover is high – the flows between employment and unemployment and the pool of unemployed people increases. The decline of traditional heavy industries such as shipbuilding, steel and coal and the rapid expansion of industries in the electronics and car components sectors are examples of the effects of technological change and sources of the increase in unemployment during the 1970s and early 1980s. While these changes were taking place, the natural rate of unemployment increased.

Hysteresis The unemployment rate fluctuates around the natural rate of unemployment. But it is possible that the natural rate itself depends on the path of the actual unemployment rate. So where the unemployment rate ends up depends on where it has been. Such a process is called **hysteresis**.

If hysteresis is present, then an increase in the unemployment rate brings an increase in the natural rate. A possible source of hysteresis is that the human capital of unemployed workers depreciates, and people who experience long bouts of unemployment usually find it difficult to get new jobs as good as the ones they have lost. An increase in the number of long-term unemployed workers means an increase in the amount of human capital lost and possibly a permanent increase in the natural rate of unemployment. The hysteresis theory is controversial and has not yet been thoroughly tested, but it is also consistent with the view that the long-term unemployed are willing to remain on state benefits indefinitely.

Job search unemployment is present even when the quantity of labour demanded equals the quantity supplied. The other possible explanations of unemployment are based on the view that the quantity of labour demanded does not always equal the quantity supplied.

Job Rationing

Job rationing is the practice of paying employed people a wage that creates an excess supply of labour and a shortage of jobs. Three reasons why jobs might be rationed are:

◆ Efficiency wages

◆ Insider interest

◆ The minimum wage

Efficiency wages   A firm can increase its labour productivity by paying wages above the competitive wage rate. The higher wage attracts a higher quality of labour, encourages greater work effort, and cuts down on the firm's labour turnover rate and recruiting costs. But the higher wage also adds to the firm's costs. So a firm offers a wage rate that balances productivity gains and additional costs. The wage rate that maximizes profit is called the **efficiency wage**.

The efficiency wage will be higher than the competitive equilibrium wage. If it was lower than the competitive wage, competition for labour would bid the wage up. With an efficiency wage above the competitive wage, some labour is unemployed and employed workers have an incentive to perform well to avoid being fired.

The payment of efficiency wages is another reason the natural rate of unemployment is not zero.

Insider Interest   Why don't firms cut their wage costs by offering jobs to unemployed workers for a lower wage rate than that paid to existing workers? One explanation, called **insider–outsider theory**, is that to be productive, new workers – outsiders – must receive on-the-job training from existing workers – insiders. If insiders provide such training to outsiders who are paid a lower wage, the insiders' bargaining position is weakened. So insiders will not train outsiders unless outsiders receive the same rate of pay as insiders.

When bargaining for a pay deal, unions represent only the interests of insiders so the wage agreed exceeds the competitive wage and there are always outsiders unable to find work. Thus the pursuit of rational self-interest by insiders is another reason the natural rate of unemployment is positive. The weakening of trade union power through legislation may have reduced the insiders' bargaining position.

The Minimum Wage   A minimum wage is legislated by the government at a level higher than the one the market would determine – see *Reading Between the Lines* on pp.616–617. As a result, the quantity of labour supplied exceeds the quantity demanded and jobs are rationed. Currently there is no minimum wage in the United Kingdom but it does exist in many other EU countries that have signed up for the 'Social Chapter'. The Social Chapter of the Treaty on European Union gives the EU Commission and the European Court powers in three areas: minimum wages, union powers and workers' rights.

Job rationing is a possible reason for the high natural rate of unemployment. It is a source of persistent and possibly high frictional unemployment. The distinction between unemployment that arises from job search and that which arises from job rationing can be illustrated by musical chairs. If there are equal numbers of chairs (jobs) and players (people who want jobs), when the music stops, everyone finds a chair. If there are more players than chairs, when the music stops, some players can't find a chair. The chairs are rationed.

Job rationing is a source of long-term frictional unemployment. The final explanation of unemployment is one reason why unemployment is cyclical.

Sticky Wages

Wages don't change as often as prices do. So if the demand for labour decreases, the real wage rate begins to move towards its new equilibrium, but it takes some time to get there. During this process of gradual wage adjustment, there is a surplus of labour and unemployment is temporarily high.

Figure 24.14 illustrates this type of unemployment. Initially, the demand for labour is LD_0 and the supply of labour is LS. The equilibrium level of employment is L_0 billion hours and the real wage rate is W_0 an hour. The demand for labour then decreases and the demand curve shifts leftward to LD_1. But the real wage rate is temporarily sticky at W_0 an hour. At this real wage rate and in the new conditions, firms are willing to hire only L_1 billion hours of labour. So there is a surplus of $L_0 - L_1$ billion hours and extra unemployment is created.

Eventually, as prices and wages change, the real wage rate falls to its equilibrium level. In this example, when the real wage rate has fallen to W_1 an hour, the quantity of labour demanded equals the quantity supplied and the surplus of labour vanishes. The only unemployment that remains is the natural rate of unemployment consistent with the new equilibrium.

FIGURE 24.14

Sticky Wages and Unemployment

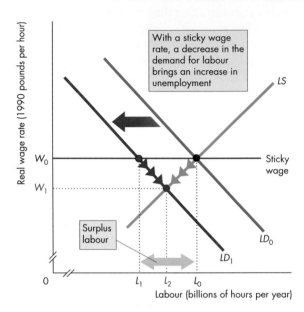

When the demand for labour is LD_0 and the supply of labour is LS, employment is L_0 billion hours and the real wage rate is W_0 an hour. The demand for labour decreases and the demand curve shifts leftward to LD_1 but the real wage rate is sticky at W_0 an hour. Employment decreases and there is a surplus of $L_0 - L_1$ billion hours. Eventually, the real wage rate falls to W_1 an hour and the quantity of labour employed increases to L_2 billion hours.

REVIEW

◆ Unemployment is always present because of job search.

◆ The natural rate of unemployment depends on the age distribution of the population, unemployment benefit and technological change.

◆ Some unemployment also results from job rationing and sticky wages.

◆ ◆ ◆ ◆ In the chapters that follow you will return to some of the themes set out here. Chapter 25 continues to look at the long-term fundamentals. It explains how consumption, investment and saving decisions are made, and it sets the scene for your study of economic growth in Chapter 26 and short-term fluctuations in Chapters 27 and 28.

SUMMARY

Employment and Wages

The population is divided into four labour market categories: employed, unemployed, not in the work-force, and young and institutionalized people. The work-force is the sum of the employed and the unemployed. The working-age population is the sum of the work-force and the people not in the work-force. And the population is the sum of the working-age population and young and institutionalized people. These population categories are used to calculate the unemployment rate, the work-force participation rate and the employment-to-population ratio.

The participation rate has been roughly constant and the employment-to-population ratio has fallen slightly. They both fluctuate with the business cycle. The female participation rate has increased but the male participation rate has decreased.

Aggregate hours, the total number of hours worked by all the people employed during a year, has remained roughly constant, but it also fluctuates in line with the business cycle. While aggregate hours have remained roughly the same in the past 25 years, average hours per worker have decreased.

The average hourly real wage rate of adult manual workers has kept pace with other measures of real wages. It increased slightly ahead of the average in the second half of the 1980s but slowed down in the 1990s. Broader measures of average hourly real wage rates were slightly ahead of the average in the second half of the 1980s but slowed down in the 1990s. A broader measure of the real wage shows the same picture, but the growth rate slows during the 1970s with the productivity growth slowdown. (pp. 602–607)

Unemployment and Full Employment

The unemployment rate rises because people lose their jobs (*job losers*), leave their jobs (*job leavers*) and enter (or re-enter) the work-force (*entrants or re-entrants*), and it falls because people get hired or recalled or withdraw from the work-force. Entrants are the largest source of unemployment. Job losers are the second largest source of unemployment, and their number also

fluctuates the most. Job leavers are the smallest source of unemployment, and their number does not fluctuate much.

The duration of unemployment fluctuates over the business cycle. When the unemployment rate is at its lowest level, almost 35 per cent of unemployment lasts for under 13 weeks, but when the unemployment rate is at its highest level, about 20 per cent of unemployment lasts for under 13 weeks.

The highest unemployment rates occur among young workers and especially among non-whites. The phase of the business cycle makes little difference to the demographic patterns in unemployment, but the gap between white and non-white unemployment increases in the trough and decreases in the peak.

Unemployment can be *frictional* (arising from normal labour market turnover), *structural* (arising when there is a long-lasting decline in the number of jobs available in a region or industry) and *cyclical* (arising from the business cycle).

When all the unemployment is frictional and structural, unemployment is at its natural rate, and there is *full employment*. There can be a substantial amount of unemployment at full employment, and the natural rate of unemployment fluctuates because of fluctuations in frictional and structural unemployment. (pp. 607–612)

Explaining Employment and Wage Rates

Employment and wage rates can be understood by using the demand and supply model and applying it to the labour market.

The *labour demand curve,* which shows the quantity of labour that firms plan to hire at each possible real wage rate, slopes downward. The quantity of labour demanded increases if the *real* wage rate falls because the cost of labour falls relative to the price firms get for their output.

The *labour supply curve,* which shows the quantity of labour that households plan to supply at each possible real wage rate, slopes upward. The quantity of labour supplied increases if the *real* wage rate increases because households face a stronger incentive to work. Labour demand and labour supply interact to determine the level of employment and the real wage rate.

The *work-force curve* shows the potential amount of labour available for employment at a particular real wage rate. The gap between the labour supply curve and the work-force curve defines the *natural rate of unemployment.* As real wages rise the natural rate of unemployment declines, since more people find it easier to match their work preferences to job availability.

Real wage rates and employment have increased over the years because both labour demand and labour supply have increased, but labour demand has increased by more than labour supply. Labour demand has increased because labour has become more productive, and labour supply has increased because the working-age population has grown and because restrictive practices have declined. (pp. 612–615)

Explaining Unemployment

Unemployment arises from *job search, job rationing* and *sticky wages*. The amount of job search unemployment fluctuates with the business cycle, but it also changes for other reasons, which bring changes in the natural rate of unemployment. These other reasons are: demographic change, changes to unemployment benefit entitlement and technological change. Job search might be subject to a hysteresis effect. A high unemployment rate brings an increase in the natural rate of unemployment because the human capital of long-term unemployed workers depreciates and they find it hard to get new jobs.

Job rationing, which can arise from efficiency wages, insider interest and the minimum wage, can be the source of long-term frictional unemployment. Sticky wages – the gradual adjustment of wage rates – can bring cyclical unemployment. (pp. 615–620)

KEY ELEMENTS

Key Terms

Aggregate hours, 605
Cyclical unemployment, 611
Discouraged workers, 603
Efficiency wage, 617
Employment-to-population ratio, 603
Entrants, 607
Frictional unemployment, 610
Full employment, 612
Hysteresis, 618
Insider–outsider theory, 617
Job leavers, 607
Job losers, 607
Job rationing, 617
Job search, 618
Labour demand curve, 613
Labour supply curve, 613
Long-term unemployed, 607
Natural rate of unemployment, 611

Participation rate, 603
Real wage rate, 606
Re-entrants, 607
Structural unemployment, 610
Unemployment rate, 603
Work-force, 602
Work-force curve, 613
Working-age population, 602

Key Figures

Figure 24.6   Labour Market Flows, 607
Figure 24.10 Unemployment and Real GDP, 611
Figure 24.11 The Labour Market, 613
Figure 24.12 Explaining the Trends in
               Employment and Real Wage Rates,
               614
Figure 24.14 Sticky Wages and Unemployment,
               620

REVIEW QUESTIONS

1 How is unemployment measured in the United Kingdom?

2 Define the unemployment rate, the participation rate and the employment-to-population ratio.

3 Define aggregate hours. Why might aggregate hours be a more accurate measure of the total labour input than the number of people employed?

4 Name three measures of average hourly earnings and describe how each one changed between 1970 and 1994.

5 How do people become unemployed? What is the most common way and which is the one that fluctuates most?

6 How does the duration of unemployment vary over the business cycle?

7 Which groups of the population experience the highest unemployment rates?

8 Distinguish between frictional, structural and cyclical unemployment.

9 What is the natural rate of unemployment and what is full employment?

10 What is the relationship between the unemployment rate and real GDP over the business cycle?

11 Explain how demand and supply in the labour market determine the level of employment and the real wage rate.

12 What are the main changes in demand and supply in the labour market that have brought employment growth?

13 What are the main changes in demand and supply in the labour market that have brought a slowdown in the rate of increase in real wage rates?

14 What are the three main explanations of unemployment?

PROBLEMS

1 The Labour Force Survey measured the following numbers in winter 1995: work-force 28 million, employment 25.7 million, working-age population 44.5 million. Calculate the

　a Unemployment rate
　b Participation rate
　c Employment-to-population ratio

2 During 1995, the working-age population increased by 133,000, employment increased by 309,000, and the work-force increased by 176,000. What happened to the level of unemployment and what do you believe happened to the number of discouraged workers?

3 In January 1996, the official claimant count unemployment rate was 7.9 per cent. In January 1995, the unemployment rate was 8.6 per cent. What do you predict happened in 1995 to the numbers of

　a Job losers?
　b Job leavers?
　c Work-force entrants and re-entrants?

4 The labour market in an economy is described by the figure. Initially, demand is LD_0 but then it decreases to LD_1.

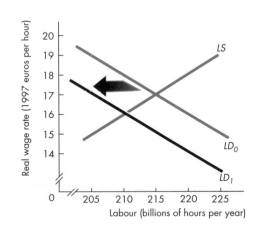

　a What are the initial levels of employment hours and real wage rate?

b When the demand for labour decreases, what are the new levels of employment hours and real wage rate if wages are completely flexible?

c When the demand for labour decreases and if the real wage rate is sticky and does not change:

1 What is the level of employment hours?

2 What is the quantity of employment hours supplied?

3 What is the number of hours that are unemployed?

4 During the time that the real wage rate is stuck above its equilibrium level, is the unemployment rate greater than, less than, or equal to the natural rate of unemployment?

5 You are told the following facts about the economy of Big Time: All the people work in either fishing, Big Time's traditional economic activity, or video game production, Big Time's new found bonanza industry. The working-age population is growing by 1 million people a year and the number of jobs is growing by 1.2 million a year. But jobs in fishing are disappearing at a rate of 2 million a year and jobs are being created in video game production at a rate of 3.2 million a year. What do you predict is happening to wage rates, employment, and unemployment in Big Time both in total and in its two industries? Draw two labour market figures, one for the fishing industry and one for the video games industry, and show how the demand and supply curves are shifting and how wage rates and employment levels are changing.

6 You have been given the following data on GDP and unemployment for the economy of Mainland. The data for real GDP and potential GDP is presented as an index and are measured in the same units.

Year	Real GDP (index)	Potential GDP (index)	Unemployment (per cent of the workforce)
1986	103.0	100.0	5.0
1987	105.1	103.0	5.7
1988	106.1	106.1	6.0
1989	107.2	109.3	6.6
1990	109.3	112.6	7.0
1991	112.6	116.0	7.0
1992	116.5	119.5	6.8
1993	121.2	123.1	6.5
1994	125.4	126.8	6.4
1995	129.8	130.6	6.2
1996	134.5	134.5	6.0
1997	138.8	138.5	5.9

a Plot real GDP and potential GDP on a graph against year as in Fig. 24.10

b Plot the rate of unemployment against year and compare it with your graph of real and potential GDP. What do you notice about the two graphs?

c What is approximate rate of growth of potential GDP?

d What is your estimate of the natural rate of unemployment?

e By approximately how much does the rate of unemployment rise or fall if the growth of real GDP differs from the growth of potential GDP?

f What would happen to the natural rate of unemployment if potential GDP grew by only 1 per cent in 1987 but then continued to grow at the long-term rate of growth shown by the data?

7 Study *Reading Between the Lines* on pp. 616–617 and then answer the following questions:

a What is the traditional argument against a minimum wage?

b What is the argument in support of a minimum wage?

c Use Fig. 24.11 to illustrate both arguments.

d Do you think a minimum wage will increase or decrease unemployment?

CHAPTER
25

INVESTMENT,
CAPITAL
AND
INTEREST

After studying this chapter you will be able to:

◆ Describe the growth and fluctuations of investment and the capital stock

◆ Compare investment in the United Kingdom with that in other countries

◆ Describe the fluctuations in the real interest rate

◆ Explain how business investment decisions are made

◆ Explain how household saving and consumption decisions are made

◆ Explain how investment, saving and consumption interact to determine the real interest rate

◆ Explain how net exports are determined and explain the role they play in influencing investment

W HEN THE WORLD CUP FINAL WAS PLAYED IN LOS ANGELES IN 1994, more than 1 billion soccer fans (one-fifth of the world's population) watched the game live. This media event was made possible by an enormous investment in a global video network. An even larger investment in a vast network of computers, telecommunications equipment and databases enables a teenager in the United Kingdom to click the mouse button and surf the Internet or send an e-mail message to a 'pen-friend' in Australia. How do businesses make the investment decisions that create the amazing tools that are building a global village? ◆ Each one of us decides how much current income to save and how much to spend on consumption goods and services. Some of us spend everything we earn and can't wait for the next payday to come around. Others of us save large amounts of income. How do people make their saving and consumption decisions? ◆ Investment, saving and consumption decisions combine to determine interest rates and the

Building the Global Village

long-term growth of potential GDP. How do investment, saving and consumption decisions influence the interest rate you pay on your credit card balance and the interest rate you'll pay when you take out a mortgage to buy a home? How do they influence the size of your pension when you retire?

◆ ◆ ◆ ◆ In this chapter, we study the decisions that determine the amount of capital in the economy and the return – the interest rate – that capital earns. The chapter parallels Chapter 24, which studies the decisions that determine the amount of labour in the economy and the return – the wage rate – that labour earns. When you have completed your study of these two topics, you will be able to combine them and learn about the forces that make potential GDP expand, which are explained in Chapter 26. We begin by looking at some facts about investment, capital and interest rates in the United Kingdom and around the world.

Capital and Interest

The total quantity of plant, equipment, buildings and stocks is the economy's **capital stock**. The purchase of new capital, called **gross investment,** increases the capital stock, and the wearing out and scrapping of existing capital, called **depreciation**, decreases the capital stock. The capital stock increases by the amount of **net investment** – gross investment minus depreciation. (See Chapter 23, pp. 576–577.)

Figure 25.1 shows investment and capital in the United Kingdom from 1970 to 1994. In part (a), you can see that gross investment has grown and fluctuated. In the recession years (1975, 1981–82 and 1991–92), gross investment decreased, and in the recovery and expansion years, it grew quickly. Part of gross investment replaces worn-out capital. The green line 'Replacement investment' in Fig. 25.1(a) shows this amount. This component of investment has grown steadily but it has not fluctuated much.

Figure 25.1(a) also shows net investment, the addition to the capital stock. Net investment has fluctuated like gross investment. In the recession year of 1981, net investment fell to about £14.4 billion. In the business cycle peak year of 1989, it was close to £52 billion.

Figure 25.1(b) shows how the capital stock has changed over the years. It grew every year and increased from around £1,389 billion in 1970 to £2,646 billion in 1994. The growth of the capital stock slowed during the recessions, but the growth rate has been steady over the long term.

The reason the capital stock has grown every year is that net investment has been positive. The reason the fluctuations in the growth rate of the capital stock are small is that net investment is a small part of the capital stock. When net investment falls to a low during a recession, the capital stock grows at about 1.8 per cent a year. When net investment rises to a high during an expansion, the capital stock grows at about 3.5 per cent a year. On the average, the capital stock has grown at a rate of 2.6 per cent a year.

Figure 25.1 shows total investment, which includes the private and public sectors and the capital stock. Private sector investment is business investment plus investment in new homes and dwellings. Public investment is part of government

FIGURE 25.1

Investment and the Capital Stock: 1970–1994

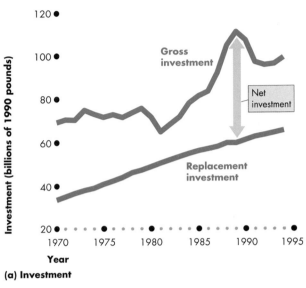

(a) Investment

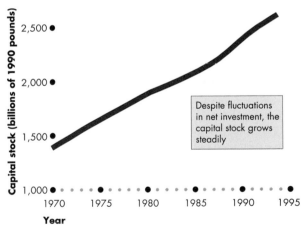

(b) Capital stock

Gross investment grows over the long term and fluctuates over the business cycle. Replacement investment grows over the long term and does not fluctuate. Net investment fluctuates between around £14 billion and £50 billion a year, but because it is a small percentage of the capital stock, the capital stock grows steadily.

Source: Central Statistical Office, *United Kingdom National Accounts: The Blue Book*, 1995, London, HMSO; and Datastream International

purchases. The part of government purchases that is public investment creates *social infrastructure capital*. The most basic element in the social infrastructure is the body of laws and the legal institutions that enforce them; without them our economy could not have developed. Motorways, bridges, schools and universities are other examples of social infrastructure capital that enhance productivity growth.

Investment Around the World

How does the amount of investment in the United Kingdom compare with that in other parts of the world? Figure 25.2 answers this question. So that we can make comparisons, we'll measure investment as the percentage of GDP devoted to it.

Figure 25.2 shows that investment in the United Kingdom has fluctuated between about 15 per cent and 22 per cent of GDP. This investment rate is lower than that in the other groups of countries shown in the figure – the industrial countries and the developing countries. The industrial countries are Canada, Japan, Australia, New Zealand and 18 other rich countries in Western Europe. The developing countries comprise the rest of the world. Investment in the industrial countries has fluctuated between about 21 per cent and 26 per cent of GDP and has been on a downward trend. Investment in the developing countries has fluctuated between about 17 per cent and 28 per cent of GDP. Investment in these countries has followed two distinct trends: an upward trend from 1970 to 1981, and a downward trend during the 1980s. Since 1975, the investment rate in the developing countries has exceeded that in the industrial countries.

Within the developing economies, those in Asia (such as South Korea, Taiwan and Malaysia) have the highest investment rates and those in Africa and Central and South America have the lowest investment rates. But most of these countries have higher investment rates than the United Kingdom.

Interest Rates

We've seen that the capital stock has grown steadily over time. But what about the return on capital? Has the return to capital grown also? Let's find out.

The return on capital is the real interest rate. The **real interest rate** is equal to the interest

FIGURE 25.2

Investment in the United Kingdom and World: 1970–1994

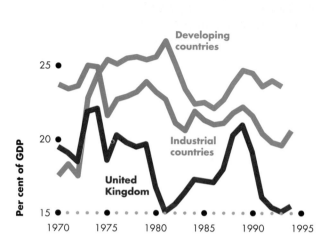

Government purchases include public investment. Total investment is business investment plus investment in new houses plus government investment. Investment in the United Kingdom is a smaller percentage of GDP than it is in many other countries. Since 1975, the developing countries have invested a larger percentage of GDP than the industrial countries.

Source: International Monetary Fund, *International Financial Statistics, Yearbook*, 1994, Washington, DC.

rate on a loan minus the inflation rate – the rate at which prices are rising. For example, if the interest rate is 10 per cent a year and the inflation rate is 4 per cent a year, then the *real* interest rate is 6 per cent a year.

Think about the following example. You borrow £1,000 to help finance a year at college. You plan to repay this loan after one year with the income from next summer's job. At the end of the year you pay out £1,100 – the £1,000 borrowed plus £100 interest. Because prices are rising by 4 per cent a year, £1,040 is needed to buy the same goods and services that £1,000 bought a year earlier. So the people who lent you £1,000 need to receive £1,040 just to replace the purchasing power that they lent. So only £60 of the interest is an addition to their purchasing power. This £60 is the *real* interest income and the real interest rate is 6 per cent a year – £60 as a percentage of the £1,000 loan.

Viewed from your perspective, the amount of summer work that earns £1,000 this year will earn £1,040 next year. So when you borrow £1,000 this year, you know that you will get £40 from the higher wages (from inflation) and will only *really* pay £60 in interest, so the real interest rate you face is 6 per cent a year.

In the world economy, there are thousands of different interest rates. But real interest rates around the world move together. One real interest rate that fluctuates with many others is the real interest rate at which blue-chip (highly creditworthy) companies borrow in the world capital markets. In 1995, this real interest rate was about 5 per cent a year. The real interest rate at which house buyers and small businesses could borrow was higher, and the rate at which the government could borrow was lower. But all real interest rates tend to move up and down together.

In 1988, the real interest rate was at a peak level. In that year, big companies could borrow at an interest rate of 15 per cent a year and the inflation rate was only about 5 per cent a year, so the real interest rate was approximately 10 per cent a year. In contrast, in 1975, the real interest rate was *negative*. Big companies could borrow at about 13 per cent a year and the inflation rate was about 24 per cent a year, so the real interest rate was about −11 per cent a year.

Figure 25.3 shows the real interest rate facing big UK companies from 1970 to 1994. Three periods are striking:

1. The 1970s – usually low and negative
2. The 1980s – the real interest rate rose sharply reaching a peak of 10 per cent
3. The 1990s – steady between 5 per cent and 6 per cent.

The 1970s were years of stagflation that resulted from huge oil price hikes and trade union militancy. The 1980s began with a deep recession, but then saw a near decade of expansion. The 1990s also began with a recession but expansion has not been consistent. We'll learn in this chapter how these events influenced the real interest rate.

FIGURE 25.3

The Real Interest Rate

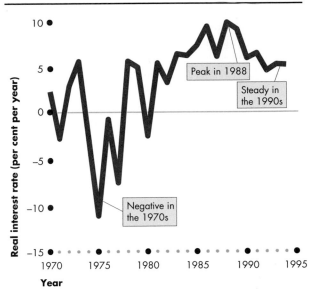

The real interest rate (here, the rate at which creditworthy UK companies can borrow) was low during the 1970s and sometimes negative. It increased strongly between 1980 and 1985 and then it decreased during 1989. It was relatively steady at between 5 per cent and 6 per cent a year during the 1990s.

Source: Central Statistical Office, *Financial Statistics*, 1995; and the author's calculations.

R E V I E W

◆ Net investment (gross investment minus depreciation) increases the capital stock.

◆ Net investment fluctuates but it never becomes negative, so the capital stock grows every year. Fluctuations in the growth rate of the capital stock are small because net investment is a small fraction of the capital stock.

◆ Government purchases include investment in social infrastructure capital.

◆ The UK investment rate (the percentage of GDP invested) is lower than the rate in many other countries, especially the developing countries.

◆ The return on capital is the real interest rate.

We've described investment. Let's now study the business investment decisions that determine its magnitude.

Investment Decisions

How does Ford (Europe) decide how much to spend on a new car assembly plant? What determines British Telecommunication's outlays on fibre optic communications systems? The main influences on business investment decisions are:

♦ The expected profit rate
♦ The real interest rate

The Expected Profit Rate

Other things remaining the same, the greater the expected profit rate from new capital, the greater is the amount of investment.

Imagine that Ford (Europe) is trying to decide whether to build a new £100 million car assembly line that will produce cars for one year and then be scrapped. Ford expects a net revenue of £120 million from operating the plant. Net revenue is equal to total revenue from sales minus the cost of labour and materials. The firm's expected profit from this assembly line is £20 million, which equals £120 million (net revenue) minus £100 million (cost of the plant). The expected *profit rate* is 20 per cent a year (£20 million ÷ £100 million).

Of the many influences on the expected profit rate, the two that stand out are:

1. The state of the business cycle
2. Advances in technology

During a business cycle expansion, the expected profit rate increases, and during a recession, it decreases. The business cycle influences the expected profit rate because sales and the utilization rate of capital fluctuate over the business cycle. In an expansion, an increase in sales and in the capacity utilization rate bring a higher profit rate. In a recession, a decrease in sales and in the capacity utilization rate bring a lower profit rate.

As technologies advance, profit expectations change. When a new technology first becomes available, firms expect to be on a learning curve and so expect a modest profit rate from switching to the new technology. But as firms gain experience with a new technology, they expect a higher profit rate.

The profit rate calculation does not include the firm's *opportunity cost* of the funds used to buy

capital as a cost. For example, the calculation of Ford's profit rate that we've just done ignores the opportunity cost of the funds used to buy the assembly line. To decide whether to invest in a new assembly line, Ford compares the expected profit rate with the opportunity cost of the funds to be used. This opportunity cost is the real interest rate that the firm faces.

The Real Interest Rate

Other things remaining the same, the lower the real interest rate, the greater is the amount of investment. The real interest rate is the opportunity cost of the funds used to finance investment. These funds might be borrowed or might be the financial resources of the firm's owners (the firm's retained earnings). But regardless of the source of the funds, the real interest rate is the opportunity cost. The real interest paid on borrowed funds is an obvious cost. The real interest rate is the cost of using retained earnings because these funds could be lent to another firm. The real interest income forgone is the opportunity cost of using retained earnings to finance an investment project.

In the Ford example, the expected profit rate is 20 per cent a year. So it is profitable for Ford (Europe) to invest as long as the real interest rate is less than 20 per cent a year. That is, at real interest rates below 20 per cent a year, Ford (Europe) will build this assembly line, and at real interest rates in excess of 20 per cent a year, it will not. Other projects will be profitable at higher real interest rates and others will become unprofitable at lower real interest rates. Consequently, the higher the real interest rate, the smaller is the number of projects that are worth undertaking and the smaller is the amount of investment.

Investment Demand

Investment demand is the relationship between the level of investment and the real interest rate, holding all other influences on investment constant. The *investment demand schedule* lists the quantities of planned investment at each real interest rate, holding all other influences on investment constant, and the *investment demand curve* graphs this relationship.

Figure 25.4(a) shows an investment demand curve. Each point (*a* to *c*) corresponds to a row in the table. If the real interest rate is 6 per cent a year, planned investment is £100 billion. A change in the real interest rate causes a movement along the investment demand curve. If the real interest rate rises to 8 per cent a year and planned investment decreases to £80 billion, there is a movement up the

investment demand curve. If the real interest rate falls to 4 per cent a year and planned investment increases to £120 billion, there is a movement down the investment demand curve.

The investment demand schedule and the position of the investment demand curve depend on

---

FIGURE 25.4

Investment Demand

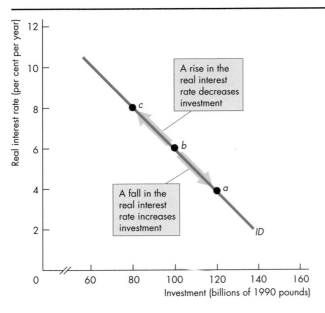

(a) The effect of a change in the real interest rate

	Real interest rate (per cent per year)	Investment (billions of 1990 pounds)		
		Profit rate expectations		
		Low	Average	High
a	4	96	120	144
b	6	76	100	124
c	8	56	80	104

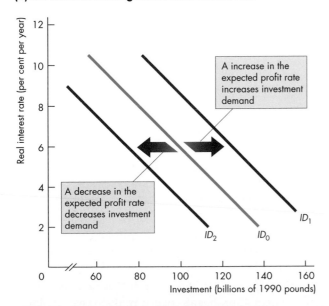

(b) The effect of a change in the expected profit rate

The table shows three investment schedules for low, average and high profit expectations. Row *b* states that when the real interest rate is 6 per cent a year, private investment is £76 billion with low profit expectations, £100 billion with average profit expectations, and £124 billion with high profit expectations. Part (a) shows the investment demand curve when firms expect the profit rate to be average. As the real interest rate rises from 6 per cent to 8 per cent, planned investment decreases – there is a movement up the investment demand curve from *b* to *c*. As the real interest rate falls from 6 per cent to 4 per cent, planned investment increases – there is a movement down the investment demand curve from *b* to *a*.

Part (b) shows how investment demand changes when the expected profit rate changes. When firms expect the profit rate to be average, the investment demand curve is *ID₀* – the same curve as in part (a). When firms expect the profit rate to be high, planned investment increases at each real interest rate and the investment demand curve shifts rightward to *ID₁*. When firms expect the profit rate to be low, investment decreases at each real interest rate and the investment demand curve shifts leftward to *ID₂*.

the expected profit rate. Figure 25.4(b) illustrates the investment demand curve for three different states of expectations. When firms expect an average profit rate, investment demand is ID_0, the same as in part (a). But when the expected profit rate increases, investment demand increases and the investment demand curve shifts rightward to ID_1. When the expected profit rate decreases, investment demand decreases and the investment demand curve shifts leftward to ID_2. Fluctuations in the expected profit rate are the main source of fluctuations in investment demand.

We've studied the *theory* of investment demand. Let's now see how that theory helps us to understand the changes in investment in the United Kingdom.

Private Investment Demand in the United Kingdom

The theory of investment demand predicts that fluctuations in private sector investment result from fluctuations in the real interest rate and in future profit expectations. Figure 25.5 shows the relative importance of these two factors. The dots in the figure show the gross private investment and the real interest rate in the United Kingdom each year from 1981 to 1994. The figure also shows three investment demand curves – ID_{81}, ID_{88}, and ID_{94}.

In the early 1980s, the investment demand curve was ID_{81}. The expected profit rate increased during the recovery of 1982 to the boom in 1988 and investment demand increased. This increase is shown by the rightward shift in the investment demand curve to ID_{88}. In 1990, 1991 and 1994, the expected profit rate decreased as the economy went into recession. Investment demand decreased and the investment demand curve shifted leftward to ID_{94}.

You can see in Fig. 25.5 that investment fluctuates for two reasons: the real interest rate changes, which brings movements along an investment demand curve, and expectations about the profit rate change, which shift the investment demand curve. You can also see that changes in the expected profit rate (shifts of the investment demand curve) create larger fluctuations in investment than changes in the real interest rate (movements along the investment demand curve).

FIGURE 25.5

Investment Demand in the United Kingdom

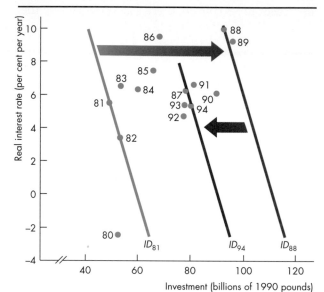

The dots show the levels of gross investment and the real interest rate in the United Kingdom for each year from 1980 to 1994. When the expected profit rate was low in the recession of the early 1980s, the investment demand curve was ID_{81}. As the expected profit rate increased during the 1980s, the investment demand curve shifted rightward. By 1988 it had shifted to ID_{88}. When the expected profit rate decreased during the recession of the 1990s, the investment demand curve shifted leftward to ID_{94}.

Source: Central Statistical Office, *National Income and Expenditure (Blue Book)*, 1995; and the author's assumptions.

R E V I E W

◆ Investment depends on the expected profit rate and the real interest rate.

◆ Other things remaining the same, if the real interest rate falls, investment increases and there is a movement along the investment demand curve.

◆ When the expected profit rate increases, the investment demand curve shifts rightward; when the expected profit rate decreases, it shifts leftward.

◆ Changes in both the real interest rate and the expected profit rate play a role in creating fluctuations in investment in the United Kingdom.

Next, we study the decisions that create the funds that finance investment: saving and consumption decisions.

Saving and Consumption Decisions

A country's investment is financed by domestic saving and by borrowing from the rest of the world. Domestic saving, which is the sum of private saving and government saving, is determined by decisions of households and by the government's fiscal policy. Here, we'll focus on the major source of finance for investment: the saving decisions of households.

Households receive a *disposable income* (earned income – wages, dividends, interest and profit – plus transfers from the government minus taxes), and they must decide how to allocate that income between saving and consumption expenditure. *Consumption expenditure* is the value of the consumption goods and services bought by households in a given time period and *saving* is defined as disposable income minus consumption expenditure. So the saving and consumption decision is a single decision. It is a decision about how to allocate disposable income between the two actions. Of the many factors that influence household saving and consumption expenditure decisions, the more important ones are:

◆ Real interest rate

◆ Disposable income

◆ Purchasing power of net assets

◆ Expected future income

Real Interest Rate

Other things remaining the same, the lower the real interest rate, the greater is the amount of consumption expenditure and the smaller is the amount of saving. The real interest rate is the opportunity cost of consumption. This opportunity cost arises regardless of whether a person is a borrower or a lender. For a borrower, increasing consumption this year means paying more interest next year. For a lender, increasing consumption this year means receiving less interest next year.

The effect of the real interest rate on consumption expenditure is an example of the principle of substitution. If the opportunity cost of an action increases, people substitute other actions in its place. In this case, if the opportunity cost of current consumption increases, people cut current consumption and substitute future consumption in its place.

For example, if the real interest rate on your student loan was 12 per cent, you would probably cut your consumption expenditure (buy cheaper food, find cheaper accommodation) and borrow a smaller amount. Similarly, with a 12 per cent real interest rate, lenders try to cut back on current consumption in order to increase their lending and profit from the high real interest rate. But if the real interest rate on your student loan was 1 per cent a year, you might increase your consumption and borrow a larger amount.

Disposable Income

The higher a household's disposable income, other things remaining the same, the greater is its consumption expenditure and the greater is its saving.

For example, a student works during the summer and earns a disposable income of £2,000. She spends the entire £2,000 on consumption during the year. When she graduates as an economist, her disposable income jumps to £12,000 a year. She now spends £10,000 on consumption and saves £2,000. The increase in disposable income of £10,000 has brought an increase in consumption of £8,000 and an increase in saving of £2,000.

Purchasing Power of Net Assets

A household's assets are what it *owns* and its liabilities are what it *owes*. A household's *net assets* are its assets minus its liabilities. The purchasing power of a household's net assets, the *real* value of its net assets, are the goods and services that its net assets can buy. The higher the purchasing power of a household's net assets, other things remaining the same, the greater is its consumption expenditure. That is, if two households have the same disposable income in the current year, the household with the larger net assets will spend a larger portion of current disposable income on consumption goods and services.

Look, for example, at the households of Cindy and Stuart. Both Cindy and Stuart are department store executives and each earns a disposable income of £15,000 a year. Cindy has £10,000 in the bank and no debts. Stuart has no money in the bank and owes £5,000 on his car loan. Cindy spends most of her £15,000 each year, but Stuart tries to keep his consumption at £14,000 so he can pay off his car loan. (Paying off a loan is not consumption expenditure. When Stuart bought his car, that was consumption expenditure. When he pays off his loan, he is saving.)

The purchasing power of net assets is influenced by the price level. The higher the price level, other things remaining the same, the smaller is the purchasing power of net assets and the smaller is the amount of consumption expenditure. For example, if the price level rises by 10 per cent, everything else remaining the same, a household with £50,000 in a savings deposit experiences a £5,000 decrease in its purchasing power. This household will probably cut its consumption and increase its saving. (A rise in the price level decreases the real value of debts, which works in the opposite direction to the effect on the real value of assets. As the purchasing power that must be given up to repay a household's debts decreases, consumption might increase. But most households have assets that exceed their debts, so an increase in the price level brings a decrease in consumption expenditure.)

Expected Future Income

The higher a household's expected future income, other things remaining the same, the greater is its consumption expenditure. That is, if two households have the same disposable income in the current year, the household with the larger expected future income will spend a larger portion of current disposable income on consumption goods and services.

Look at Cindy and Stuart again. (Recall that they are both department store executives and each earns a disposable income of £15,000 a year.) Cindy has just been promoted and will receive a £3,000 pay rise next year. Stuart has just been told that his contract will not be renewed at the end of the year. On receiving this news, Cindy buys a new car – increases her consumption expenditure – and Stuart cancels his summer holiday plans – decreases his consumption expenditure.

Although consumption and saving are influenced by several factors, we focus on two of them:

the real interest rate and disposable income. The real interest rate, which is the opportunity cost of consumption, determines the long-run allocation of disposable income between consumption and saving. Disposable income is the key short-run influence on consumption and saving. In the rest of this chapter, our focus is the long run, and in Chapters 27 and 28 we look at the short run.

Consumption Demand and Saving Supply

If the real interest rate rises, other things remaining the same, consumption expenditure decreases and saving increases. The table in Fig. 25.6 shows an example of these relationships. It lists the levels of consumption expenditure and saving that occur at three levels of the real interest rate. The relationship between consumption expenditure and the real interest rate, other things remaining the same, is called **consumption demand**, and the relationship between saving and the real interest rate, other things remaining the same, is called **saving supply**.

Consumption Demand Figure 25.6(a) shows a consumption demand curve. The x-axis measures consumption expenditure and the y-axis measures the real interest rate. Along the consumption demand curve, the points labelled a to c correspond to the rows having the same letters in the table. For example, point b indicates the real interest rate of 6 per cent a year and consumption expenditure of £350 billion. If the real interest rate rises from 6 per cent a year to 8 per cent a year, consumption expenditure decreases from £350 million to £340 billion and there is a movement along the consumption demand curve from b to c. If the real interest rate falls from 6 per cent a year to 4 per cent a year, consumption expenditure increases from £350 billion to £360 billion and there is a movement along the consumption demand curve from b to a.

Saving Supply Figure 25.6(b) shows a saving supply curve. The x-axis measures saving and the y-axis measures the real interest rate. Again, the points marked a to c correspond to the rows of the table. For example, point b indicates that when the real interest rate is 6 per cent a year, saving is £30 billion. If the real interest rate rises from 6 per cent a year to 8 per cent a year, saving increases from

FIGURE 25.6

Consumption Demand Curve and Saving Supply Curve

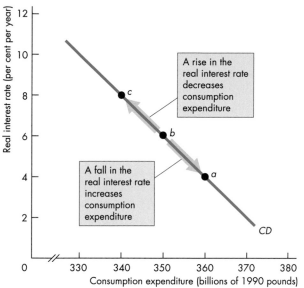

(a) Consumption demand

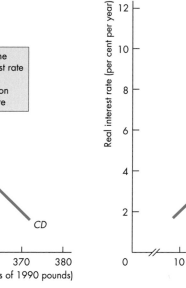

(b) Saving supply

Real interest rate (per cent per year)	Consumption expenditure	Saving	Disposable income
	(billions of 1990 pounds)		
a	4	360	20	380
b	6	350	30	380
c	8	340	40	380

The table shows consumption expenditure and saving at various levels of the real interest rate and for a disposable income of £380 billion, all other influences on consumption and saving remaining the same. Part (a) of the figure shows the relationship between consumption expenditure and the real interest rate (the consumption demand curve, *CD*). Part (b) shows the relationship between saving and the real interest rate (the saving supply curve, *SS*). Points *a* to *c* on the consumption demand curve and saving supply curve correspond to the rows in the table. At each real interest rate, consumption expenditure plus saving equals disposable income. An increase in the real interest rate decreases consumption expenditure and increases saving. The total remains unchanged.

£30 billion to £40 billion and there is a movement along the saving supply curve from *b* to *c*. If the real interest rate falls from 6 per cent a year to 4 per cent a year, saving decreases from £30 billion to £20 billion and there is a movement along the saving supply curve from *b* to *a*.

Along the consumption demand curve and saving supply curve, all the other influences on consumption and saving are constant. One of these influences, and one of the strongest influences, is disposable income. Because disposable income is constant, consumption plus saving equals the constant level of disposable income. In

the table in Fig. 25.6, disposable income is a constant £380 billion. Because households can only consume or save their disposable income, consumption demand plus saving supply always equals disposable income.

Disposable Income, Consumption Expenditure and Saving

You've seen how a change in the real interest rate brings changes in consumption expenditure and saving. And you've seen how these changes bring movements along the consumption demand curve and saving supply curve.

Changes in other influences on consumption expenditure and saving *change consumption demand* and also *change saving supply*. That is, these changes alter the quantity of consumption expenditure and saving at each interest rate. They are illustrated as shifts in the consumption demand curve and the saving supply curve. The most important of these other factors that change consumption demand and saving supply is disposable income.

When disposable income increases, both consumption expenditure and saving increase. The extent to which each increases is determined by the marginal propensity to consume and the marginal propensity to save. The **marginal propensity to consume** (*MPC*) is the fraction of a *change* in disposable income that is consumed. It is calculated as the *change* in consumption

expenditure (ΔC) divided by the *change* in disposable income (ΔYD) that brought it about. That is:

$$MPC = \frac{\Delta C}{\Delta YD}$$

In Fig. 25.7, when disposable income increases from £380 billion to £400 billion, consumption expenditure increases from £350 billion to £366 billion. The change in disposable income is £20 billion and the change in consumption expenditure is £16 billion. The *MPC* is £16 billion divided by £20 billion, which equals 0.8.

The **marginal propensity to save** (*MPS*) is the fraction of a *change* in disposable income that is saved. It is calculated as the *change* in saving (ΔS) divided by the *change* in disposable income (ΔYD) that brought it about. That is:

FIGURE 25.7

An Increase in Disposable Income

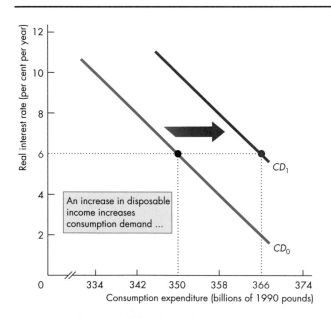

(a) Increase in consumption demand

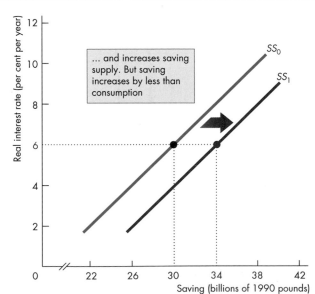

(b) Increase in saving supply

An increase in disposable income increases both consumption demand and saving supply. The marginal propensity to consume, *MPC*, determines the increase in consumption demand and the marginal propensity to save, *MPS*, determines the increase in saving supply,

other things remaining the same. Here, the *MPC* is 0.8 and the *MPS* is 0.2. An increase in disposable income of £20 billion brings an increase in consumption demand of £16 billion and an increase in saving supply of £4 billion.

$$MPS = \frac{\Delta S}{\Delta YD}$$

Again, when disposable income increases from £380 billion to £400 billion, saving increases from £30 billion to £34 billion. The change in disposable income is £20 billion and the change in saving is £4 billion. The *MPS* is £4 billion divided by £20 billion, which equals 0.2.

Because an increase in disposable income increases both consumption expenditure and saving, it shifts both the consumption demand curve and the saving supply curve rightward. Figure 25.7 shows these shifts. But also, as in this example, because the marginal propensity to consume is generally greater than the marginal propensity to save, an increase in disposable income increases consumption expenditure by more than it increases saving.

Other Influences on Consumption Expenditure and Saving

The other influences on consumption expenditure and saving – the purchasing power of net assets and expected future income – change consumption expenditure and saving in opposite directions, other things remaining the same. That is, any change that increases consumption expenditure, with disposable income constant, decreases saving. For example, an increase in the purchasing power of net assets increases consumption expenditure and decreases saving. The effect of such a change is shown by a rightward shift of the consumption demand curve and a leftward shift of the saving supply curve. Figure 25.8 illustrates these shifts.

We've studied the *theory* of consumption demand and saving supply and identified the key

---

FIGURE 25.8

FIGURE 25.8

Other Influences on Consumption Demand and Saving Supply

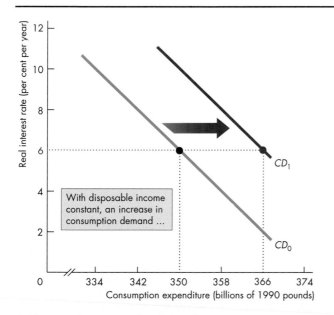

(a) Increase in consumption demand

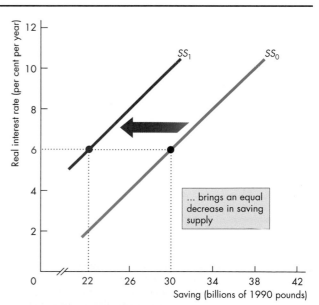

(b) Decrease in saving supply

With a given level of disposable income, an increase in the purchasing power of net assets or an increase in expected future income increases consumption demand and decreases saving supply. The consumption demand curve shifts rightward from CD_0 to CD_1 (part a) and the saving

supply curve shifts leftward from SS_0 to SS_1 in part (b). The rightward shift of the *CD* curve equals the leftward shift of the *SS* curve because consumption expenditure plus saving equal a constant disposable income.

influences on these decisions. Let's now see how that theory helps us to understand the changes in consumption expenditure and saving in the United Kingdom.

Consumption Demand and Saving Supply in the United Kingdom

Figure 25.9(a) shows the UK consumption demand curve. Each point identified by a blue dot represents consumption expenditure and the real

interest rate for a particular year. (The dots are for the years 1970–1994). In 1970, the consumption demand curve was CD_{70}. This curve indicates that when the real interest rate rises, everything else remaining the same, consumption expenditure decreases. But a large change in the real interest rate brings a small change in consumption expenditure.

Over time, the consumption demand curve has shifted rightward, mainly because disposable income has increased. During the 1970s, disposable income increased by £67.7 billion and

---

FIGURE 25.9

Consumption Demand and Saving Supply in the United Kingdom

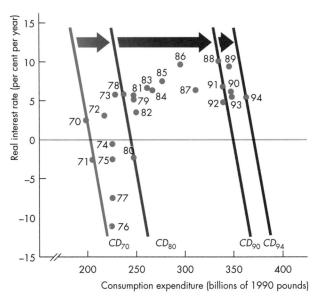

(a) Consumption demand

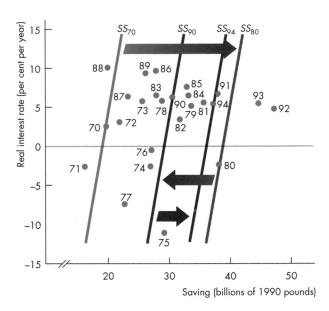

(b) Saving supply

Part (a) shows the consumption demand curve in the United Kingdom. Each dot represents consumption expenditure and the real interest rate for a particular year from 1970 to 1994. The blue curve CD_{70} is an estimate of the consumption demand curve for 1970. A large change in the real interest rate brings a small change in consumption expenditure. As disposable income increased, consumption demand increased and the consumption demand curve shifted rightward to CD_{80}, CD_{90}, and CD_{94}. Consumption demand

increased by more during the 1980s than during the 1970s.

Part (b) shows the saving supply curve. Each dot represents saving and the real interest rate for a particular year from 1970 to 1994. The blue curve SS_{70} is an estimate of the saving supply curve for 1970. As disposable income increased, saving supply increased, and the saving supply curve shifted rightward to SS_{80}. Saving supply fell during the 1980s and 1990 because of other influences and rose again during the 1990s to 1994.

Source: Central Statistical Office, *Economic Trends Annual Supplement*, 1995; and the author's assumptions.

consumption expenditure increased by £49.4 billion. The consumption demand curve shifted rightward to CD_{80}. During the 1980s, real disposable income increased by £92.9 billion and consumption expenditure increased by £100.3 billion. So the consumption demand curve shifted rightward by a larger amount than in the 1970s and in excess of the increase in real disposable income to become CD_{90}. This is because the purchasing power of households' net assets increased in the 1980s. Deregulation of the financial sector in the 1980s enabled people who had their savings tied up in the value of their homes to borrow money against the value of their homes. This is known as **equity withdrawal.** The existence of equity withdrawal meant that households could spend more than the increase in their disposable income. As disposable income increased during the 1990s, the consumption demand curve shifted farther rightward to CD_{94} in 1994.

Figure 25.9(b) shows the UK saving supply curve. Here, each point identified by a dot represents saving and the real interest rate for a particular year. In 1970, the saving supply curve was SS_{70}. The curve indicates that when the real interest rate rises, saving increases. But as in the case of consumption, a large change in the real interest rate brings a small change in saving.

Over time, the saving supply curve has shifted rightward and for the same reason that the consumption demand has shifted rightward – because disposable income has increased. But saving supply has not increased by as much as consumption demand. During the 1970s, when disposable income increased by £67.7 billion, saving increased by £18.4 billion and the saving supply curve shifted rightward to SS_{80}. During the 1980s, when real disposable income increased by £92.9 billion, saving *decreased* by £74.3 billion as people began to spend out of their assets. So the saving supply curve shifted leftward. Disposable income increased during the 1990s but saving supply increased, mainly because households began paying back some of the debts they ran up during the 1980s, and the saving supply curve shifted rightward to SS_{94}.

The reason why saving supply has at some times increased much less than consumption demand and even decreased at other times, is that influences other than the interest rate and disposable income have tended to increase consumption

expenditure and decrease saving. During the 1980s, these influences were the purchasing power of net assets and expected future incomes. A booming stock market, rising house prices and increasing personal wealth meant that people were willing to consume more and save less. Expectations of continued rapid economic expansion, which increased expected future incomes, reinforced the effect of increasing personal wealth. The result was an increase in consumption expenditure that was in excess of the increase in disposable income.

REVIEW

◆ Consumption expenditure and saving decisions are influenced by the real interest rate, disposable income, the purchasing power of net assets and expectations of future income.

◆ The consumption demand curve is the relationship between consumption expenditure and the real interest rate, other things remaining the same. The consumption demand curve slopes downward.

◆ The saving supply curve is the relationship between saving and the real interest rate, other things remaining the same. The saving supply curve slopes upward.

◆ Between 1970 and 1994, the consumption demand curve in the United Kingdom shifted rightward as disposable income and net assets increased. The saving supply curve shifted rightward during the 1970s and between 1990 and 1994 but during the 1980s other influences on saving offset the influence of increased disposable income and saving fell.

We've now studied the decisions that determine investment, consumption expenditure and saving, and seen that both sets of decisions depend on the real interest rate. *Reading Between the Lines* on pp.648–649 takes a closer look at the relationship between consumption and saving. But how is the real interest rate determined? How is a given amount of production allocated between investment and consumption?

Long-run Equilibrium in the Global Economy

We are now going to see how investment decisions together with consumption and saving decisions determine the real interest rate. To do so, we study the economy of the entire world. Why? Why don't we determine the real interest rate the way we determine the real wage rate by studying the national economy?

The reason is that there is a single world capital market. In contrast, each country has a national labour market. Immigration laws and nationality laws limit the free movement of labour in search of the highest available wage rate. So the supply of labour and the demand for labour in a national economy determine the national real wage rate. But the market in which the real interest rate is determined knows no such restrictions. Capital is free to roam the world and seek the highest possible real rate of return, unless there are legal restrictions that hinder the movement of capital. During the 1970s, various forms of capital controls existed in the United Kingdom and in the rest of Europe. During the 1980s, these controls were gradually dismantled, allowing capital to move freely. As a result the saving of one country is not necessarily used to finance the investment of that country.

Real interest rates are not identical in every country because some countries are riskier than others and have higher real interest rates. But rates move up and down together. If a higher return is available in one country where the risk is equal to that in others, capital rushes into that country. The increase in the supply of capital lowers the interest rate and brings it into line with the countries of equal risk. If the return available in one country is lower than that in other countries of equal risk, capital leaves that country. The decrease in the supply of capital raises the real interest rate and brings it into line with countries of equal risk. The world average real interest rate and changes in the real interest rate in each country are determined by global saving and global investment. So the real interest rate is in the long run determined by global saving and global investment.

Determining the Real Interest Rate: $S = I$

Figure 25.10 shows how the real interest rate is determined. The *ID* curve is the world investment demand curve. The *SS* curve is the world saving supply curve. The higher the real interest rate, the

---

FIGURE 25.10

The Saving Equals Investment Approach

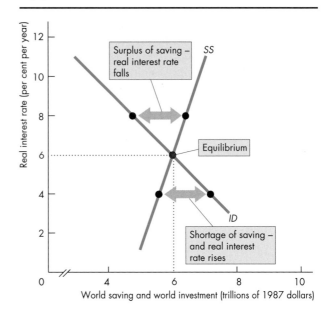

	Real interest rate (per cent per year)	Investment	Savings
		(trillions of 1987 dollars)	
a	4	7.2	5.6
b	6	6.0	6.0
c	8	4.8	6.4

The table sets out a world investment demand schedule and saving supply schedule and the figure shows the world investment demand curve, *ID*, and saving supply curve, *SS*. If the real interest rate is 4 per cent a year, investment exceeds saving. There is a shortage of saving and the real interest rate rises. If the real interest rate is 8 per cent a year, investment is less than saving. There is a surplus of saving and the real interest rate falls. When the real interest rate is 6 per cent a year, investment equals saving and the real interest rate is at its equilibrium level.

greater is the amount of saving and the smaller is the amount of investment. In the figure, when the real interest rate exceeds 6 per cent a year, saving exceeds investment. If saving exceeds investment, borrowers have an easy time finding the loans they want, but lenders are unable to lend all the funds they have available. In this situation, the real interest rate falls. As it falls, planned investment increases and planned saving decreases. The interest rate continues to fall so long as saving exceeds investment.

When the interest rate is less than 6 per cent a year, saving is less than investment. If there is a shortage of saving, borrowers can't find the loans they want, but lenders are able to lend all the funds they have available. In this situation, the real interest rate rises. As it rises, there is a decrease in planned investment and an increase in planned saving. The interest rate continues to rise as long as there is a shortage of saving.

Regardless of whether there is a surplus or a shortage of saving, the real interest rate changes and is pulled towards an equilibrium level. In Fig. 25.10, this equilibrium is 6 per cent a year. At this interest rate there is neither a surplus nor a shortage of saving. Investors can get the funds they demand and savers can lend all the funds they have available. The plans of savers and investors are consistent with each other.

Let's use this model of global saving and investment to explain changes in the real interest rate in the world economy.

Explaining Changes in the Real Interest Rate

In 1995, the real interest rate was unusually high. For the biggest and safest companies in the world, it was about 6 per cent a year. During 1985–88, the real interest rate was even higher. It averaged over 8 per cent. In contrast, 20 years earlier in 1975, the real interest rate was *negative*. Figure 25.11 explains why these changes in the real interest rate occurred. Each point identified by a blue dot represents world investment and world saving and the real interest rate for a particular year. Part (a) focuses on a short period from 1973 to 1975. In 1973, the saving supply curve was SS_{73} and the investment demand curve was ID_{73}. The real interest rate was 4 per cent, and the amount of saving

and investment in the world economy was $3.2 trillion in 1987 prices.

In 1973, the price of a barrel of oil was $2.70. By 1975, this price was $10.70. Oil producers and exporters experienced a huge increase in income and their saving increased. The world saving supply curve shifted rightward to SS_{75}. Oil users and importers faced steep cost increases and a collapse of profits. With a low expected profit rate, investment demand decreased and the world investment demand curve shifted leftward to ID_{75}. So in 1975, world saving supply was high, world investment demand was low and the real interest rate fell to −1 per cent a year.

Figure 25.11(b) takes up the story at this point. Gradually, investment demand recovered and, except for severe recession in 1981–82, increased each year. By 1984, the investment demand curve had shifted rightward to ID_{84}. During these same years, saving supply increased slowly. In fact, in 1984, the saving supply curve was the same as it had been in 1977. The reasons for this slow saving growth are complex. But one factor at work was the productivity growth slowdown of the 1970s. At first, the productivity growth slowdown was seen as temporary, so people still expected their future income to grow. With expected future income growth, consumption expenditure increased and saving decreased. The combination of a large increase in investment demand and a small increase in saving supply increased the real interest rate to 8.5 per cent in 1984, and world investment and world saving increased to $4.2 trillion.

The rest of the 1980s saw a more rapid growth in the supply of saving relative to the increase in investment demand. A possible reason is that by then, the productivity growth slowdown was perceived to be persisting and people expected the income growth rate to fall. As a result, consumption was cut and saving increased. By 1989, the investment demand curve had shifted rightward to ID_{89} and the saving supply curve had shifted to SS_{89}. As a result of these changes, the real interest rate fell to 5 per cent.

You've now seen how saving and investment in the world economy determine the world real interest rate. There is another way of viewing the equilibrium interest rate. Not only does it bring saving and investment plans into balance. At the same time, it ensures that the demand for world GDP

FIGURE 25.11

Explaining Changes in the Real Interest Rate

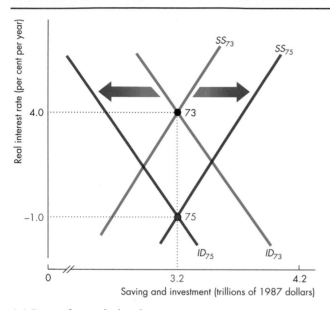

(a) Onset of growth slowdown

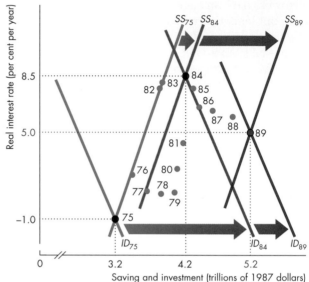

(b) 1975–1989

In 1973 (part a), world saving supply was SS_{73} and world investment demand was ID_{73}. The real interest rate was 4 per cent a year. A large increase in the world price of oil increased world saving supply and decreased world investment demand. By 1975, world saving supply was SS_{75} and world investment demand was ID_{75}, and the real interest rate was negative. By 1984 (part b), a strong economic expansion was under way and investment demand

had increased to ID_{84}, but saving supply had not increased by much and was at SS_{84}. The real interest rate increased and reached a peak of 8.5 per cent in 1984. During the rest of the 1980s, saving supply increased by more than investment demand, and by 1989, the saving supply curve was at SS_{89} and the investment demand curve was at ID_{89}. The real interest rate had fallen to 5 per cent a year.

Sources: Robert Summers and Alan Heston, New computer diskette (Mark 5.5), 15 June 1993, distributed by the National Bureau of Economic Research to update The Penn World Table (Mark 5): An Expanded Set of International Comparisons, 1950–1988, *Quarterly Journal of Economics*, May 1991, 327–368; International Monetary Fund, *International Financial Statistics Yearbook*, 1994, Washington DC; *Economic Report of the President*, 1995; and the author's assumptions and calculations.

equals the supply of world GDP. This alternative view of the equilibrium real interest rate is interesting because it helps us to see more clearly how decisions in national economies are coordinated. Let's explore this alternative view of the equilibrium real interest rate by studying the demand for world GDP and the way it is influenced by the real interest rate.

The Demand for Real GDP

The consumption demand curve tells us how consumption demand changes as the real interest rate changes, other things remaining the same, and the investment demand curve tells us how investment changes as the real interest rate changes, other things remaining the same. Figure 25.12 shows

these two demand curves for the world economy.

In part (a), world consumption expenditure is shown on the *x*-axis and the real interest rate on the *y*-axis. At point *b*, world consumption expenditure is $16 trillion in 1987 prices at a real interest rate of 6 per cent a year. Along this consumption demand curve, as the real interest rate rises, world consumption expenditure decreases. This consumption demand curve is related to the saving supply curve that you've already used in Fig. 25.10. At each real interest rate, consumption demand plus saving supply equals disposable income. In this example, disposable income is $22 trillion. At a real interest rate of 6 per cent a year, world consumption expenditure is $16 trillion and world saving is $6 trillion.

Figure 25.12(b) shows the world investment

demand curve. At point *b*, world investment is $6 trillion at an interest rate of 6 per cent a year. Along this investment demand curve, as the real interest rate rises, world investment decreases.

Total demand for world GDP equals consumption demand plus investment demand plus government demand. Figure 25.12(c) generates the demand curve for world GDP. First, it adds consumption demand and investment demand together to create the *C* + *I* line. For example, when the real interest rate is 6 per cent a year, *C* + *I* is $22 trillion ($16 trillion of consumption expenditure and $6 trillion of investment). The rest of the *C* + *I* line is constructed in a similar way.

Second, Fig. 25.12(c) adds government purchases to the *C* + *I* line. We examine the influences on government purchases when we study fiscal policy in Chapter 29. Here, we will assume that whatever the factors that determine government purchases, they do not depend on the real interest rate. For this example, we assume that world government purchases are a constant $5 trillion. Adding this amount to the *C* + *I* line at each real interest rate gives the *C* + *I* + *G* line. This line tells us the quantity of real GDP demanded in the world economy as the real interest rate changes, all other influences on consumption expenditure, investment, and government purchases remaining the same.

FIGURE 25.12

Demand for Real GDP

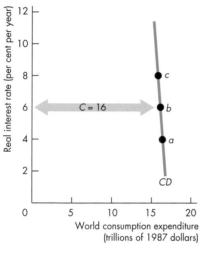
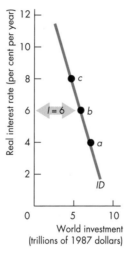
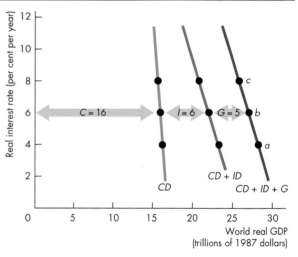

(a) Consumption demand   **(b) Investment demand**   **(c) Demand for real GDP**

	Real interest rate	Consumption expenditure (*C*)	Investment (*I*)	(*C* + *I*)	Government purchases (*G*)	(*C* + *I* + *G*)
	(per cent per year)			(trillions of 1987 dollars)		
a	4	16.4	7.2	23.6	5.0	28.6
b	6	16.0	6.0	22.0	5.0	27.0
c	8	15.6	4.8	20.4	5.0	25.6

The table shows global consumption, investment, government purchases and total expenditure (*C* + *I* + *G*) at each of three real interest rates. By adding global consumption demand (part a) and global investment demand (part b),

we get the *C* + *I* line (part c). By adding global government purchases to this amount, we get the *C* + *I* + *G* line, which shows how the demand for global real GDP changes as the real interest rate changes.

Determining the Real Interest Rate: $C + I + G = Y_{POT}$

The equilibrium real interest rate, which ensures that world saving equals world investment, also ensures that the demand for world real GDP equals the supply of world real GDP. You've just learned how to construct the $C + I + G$ line, which tells us the quantity of real GDP demanded in the global economy at each real interest rate. What determines the quantity of real GDP supplied in the global economy?

On the average, ignoring the ebb and flow of the business cycle, the quantity of real GDP supplied is potential GDP – Y_{POT}. That is, when there is full employment, the quantity of real GDP equals potential GDP.

Figure 25.13 shows the $C + I + G$ line. It also shows a vertical line labelled Y_{POT}, which is potential GDP for the global economy. Here, potential GDP is a constant $27 trillion regardless of the

real interest rate. Given the $C + I + G$ line and the Y_{POT} line, we can determine the real interest rate.

The equilibrium real interest rate is 6 per cent a year. At this real interest rate, the quantity of real GDP demanded equals potential GDP. The supply of saving also equals investment demand. If the real interest rate were 8 per cent a year, the quantity of real GDP demanded would be less than potential GDP and the supply of saving would exceed investment. The interest rate would fall. If the real interest rate were 4 per cent a year, the quantity of real GDP demanded would exceed potential GDP and the supply of saving would be less than investment demand. The interest rate would rise.

This alternative way of viewing the equilibrium interest rate is most interesting when we use it to study an individual country and the forces that determine its net exports. This is our next task.

FIGURE 25.13

The Real Interest Rate

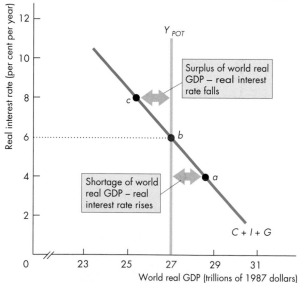

When the world economy is producing on its long-term trend, world real GDP equals potential GDP, which is shown by the Y_{POT} line. If the quantity of world real GDP demanded exceeds potential GDP, there is an excess demand for world real GDP and the real interest rate rises. If the quantity of world real GDP demanded is less than potential GDP, there is an excess supply of world real GDP and the real interest rate falls.

R E V I E W

◆ At the equilibrium real interest rate, the world saving supply equals world investment demand and the demand for world GDP equals world potential GDP.

◆ The world oil price explosion of 1973–74 increased oil exporters' incomes and increased saving supply. It also squeezed profit rates and decreased investment demand. The real interest rate fell to a low point.

◆ The 1980s expansion increased investment demand, but saving supply grew by less and the real interest rate rose.

◆ During the late 1980s, investment demand increased less than saving supply and the real interest rate fell.

We've now studied the decisions that determine investment, consumption expenditure and saving, and we've seen how the real interest rate is determined. The real interest rate is determined by saving and investment in a global market. Our final task in this chapter is to return to the national economy and see how national investment, consumption and saving decisions influence a country's net exports and its net lending to or borrowing from the rest of the world.

Net Exports and Equilibrium in the National Economy

I n the national economy, real GDP equals consumption expenditure plus investment plus government purchases plus *net exports*. Each country determines its consumption expenditure, investment and government purchases. We've seen that these consumption expenditure and investment decisions depend on the real interest rate. But we've also seen that the real interest rate is determined partly by *world* saving and *world* investment. So what do *national* investment, consumption and saving decisions determine?

The answer has three parts. First, each country contributes to world saving and investment and so helps to influence the world real interest rate. The larger the country, the greater is that influence. So, for example, the investment, consumption and saving decisions of the European Union, the United States and Japan have a significant impact on the world economy and influence the world real interest rate. Other countries individually have a less significant influence.

Second, for all countries, regardless of their size, their investment, consumption and saving decisions, along with the world real interest rate, determine their net exports and their net lending to or borrowing from the rest of the world. For an individual country, net exports equals real GDP *minus* the total of consumption expenditure, investment and government purchases. In the long run, when real GDP is equal to potential GDP, net exports equal potential GDP minus the total of consumption expenditure, investment and government purchases.

Third, in the short run, national macroeconomic policies can alter real interest rates temporarily to stimulate or constrain domestic demand. However, in the long run governments must borrow at the world real rate of interest.

Figure 25.14 illustrates the determination of UK net exports in the long run. Potential GDP is £525 billion, as shown by the vertical line, Y_{POT}. The downward-sloping line is the $C + I + G$ line for the United Kingdom. It tells us the quantity of GDP demanded in the United Kingdom and it is derived just like the world $C + I + G$ line in Fig. 25.12. The world real interest rate is 6 per cent a year. At this real interest rate, the quantity of $C + I + G$ demanded in the United Kingdom is below potential

FIGURE 25.14

Net Exports and Equilibrium in the UK Economy

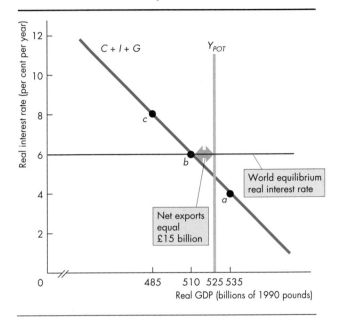

	Consumption expenditure + Investment + Government purchases ($C + I + G$)	Net exports (NX)	Potential GDP
Real interest rate (per cent per year)			
	(billions of 1990 pounds)		
a	4	535	−10	525
b	6	510	15	525
c	8	485	40	525

For three levels of the real interest rate, the table shows the levels of consumption expenditure plus investment plus government purchases ($C + I + G$), net exports (NX) and potential GDP. When the UK economy is producing on its long-term trend, real GDP equals potential GDP, which is shown by the Y_{POT} line at £525 billion. World equilibrium determines the real interest rate (6 per cent a year). If the quantity of real GDP demanded exceeds potential GDP, (point *c*), net exports are negative. If the quantity of real GDP demanded is less than potential GDP, (points *a* and *b*), net exports are positive.

GDP. Net exports in the long run are positive (current net exports are negative because the short-run aggregate supply is less than aggregate demand). The amount of net exports is shown by the arrow in the figure.

Net Exports and the Exchange Rate

What makes UK net exports adjust in the long run to fill the gap between potential GDP and $C + I + G$? The answer is the exchange rate. Let's see why the exchange rate adjusts.

A country's export and import decisions depend on prices in that country compared with prices in the rest of the world. If you can buy an item from a Japanese producer at a lower price than you can buy it from a UK producer, the item will be imported by the United Kingdom and exported by Japan. The higher the prices of UK-produced goods and services relative to the prices of similar foreign-produced goods and services, the larger is the quantity of UK imports, other things remaining the same. For example, if the prices of Japanese-produced cars fall and the prices of UK-produced cars remain constant, UK car imports from Japan increase.

Similarly, if people in Japan can buy an item from a UK producer at a lower price than they can buy it from a Japanese producer, that item will be exported by the UK and imported by Japan. The lower the price of UK-produced goods and services relative to the prices of similar goods and services produced in other countries, the greater is the quantity of UK exports, other things remaining the same. For example, if the prices of UK-produced cars fall while the prices of Japanese-produced cars remain constant, UK car exports to Japan increase.

The price comparisons we've just considered actually depend on three sets of prices:

1. Prices in the United Kingdom
2. Prices in Japan
3. The exchange rate between the pound sterling and the Japanese yen

Suppose the price of a UK-produced car is £20,000. A similar car produced in Japan might cost ¥2,000,000. To compare the price in the United Kingdom with the price in Japan, we need to convert the prices into common currency units. To make this conversion, we use the exchange rate between the pound sterling and the Japanese yen. If the exchange rate is £1 = ¥100, then a Japanese-produced car that costs ¥2,000,000 equivalently costs £20,000. Similarly, the UK-produced car that costs £20,000 equivalently costs ¥2,000,000. If these two cars are similar, it is likely that they will be neither exported nor imported by either country.

But suppose the exchange rate is £1 = ¥90. In this case, the Japanese-produced car that costs ¥2,000,000 now costs £22,222 and the UK-produced car that costs £20,000 now costs ¥1,800,000. If these two cars are similar, it is likely that Japan will begin to import the UK-produced car.

On the other hand, suppose the exchange rate is £1 = ¥120. In this case, the Japanese-produced car that costs ¥2,000,000 now costs £16,667 and the UK-produced car that costs £20,000 now costs ¥2,400,000. At these prices, it is likely that the United Kingdom will begin to import the Japanese-produced car.

The Real Exchange Rate The three sets of prices that enable us to make international price comparisons can be summarized in a single *opportunity cost*. If the price of a UK-produced car is £20,000 and the price of a similar Japanese-produced car is ¥2,000,000, and the exchange rate between the pound sterling and the Japanese yen is £1 = ¥100, then 1 Japanese-made car costs 1 UK-produced car and the real exchange rate is 1. If the prices remain the same but the exchange rate changes to £1 = ¥90, then 1 Japanese-produced car costs 1.11 UK-produced cars. If the prices remain the same but the exchange rate changes to £1 = ¥120, then 1 Japanese-produced car costs 0.83 UK-produced cars.

To compare the prices of all goods and services, we use the concept of the real exchange rate. The **real exchange rate** is an index number that tells us the opportunity cost of foreign-produced goods and services in terms of UK-produced goods and services. Other things remaining the same, the lower the real exchange rate (the real value of the pound sterling in terms of other currencies), the greater is the demand by foreigners for UK-produced goods and services (for UK exports), and the smaller is the demand in the United Kingdom for foreign-produced goods and services (for UK imports). But exports minus imports are net exports so other things remaining the same, the lower the real exchange rate, the greater is the value of UK net exports.

You can turn the last proposition around. The greater is the value of UK net exports, the lower the real exchange rate (the lower is the real value of the pound sterling in terms of other currencies).

We can now connect the real exchange rate with the expenditure decisions. If consumption expenditure plus investment plus government purchases increase relative to potential GDP, then net exports decrease (and possibly become negative). In this case, the real exchange rate rises and net exports fall.

FIGURE 25.15

The Adjustment of Net Exports

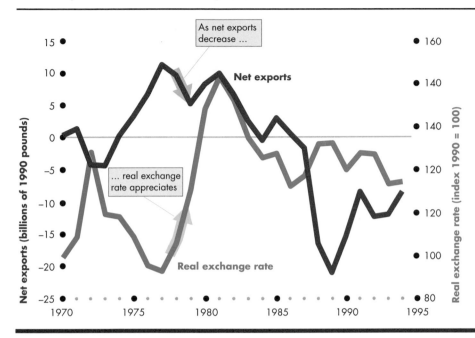

The real exchange rate adjusts to ensure that import and export decisions are compatible with consumption, investment and government purchases decisions. A decrease in the real exchange rate increases net exports and an increase in the real exchange rate decreases net exports, other things remaining the same. In the United Kingdom, the real exchange rate increased from 1973 to 1977 and net exports decreased.

Source: Central Statistical Office, *Economic Trends Annual Supplement*, 1995; International Monetary Fund, *International Financial Statistics Yearbook* 1995, and *Liverpool Macroeconomic Research Group*.

Does the real exchange rate actually change in the way we've just described? It does so only to a degree. Figure 25.15 shows the relationship between net exports and the real exchange rate for the United Kingdom. Net exports are shown as the red line graphed against the left scale. The real exchange rate is shown in blue and graphed against the right scale. You can see that when the real exchange rate rises (the real value of the pound rises), net exports fall. This was particularly true of the late 1970s. During the 1980s, other factors were important. The domestic demand in the United Kingdom was greater than potential output and thus net exports fell even when the real exchange rate declined. However, net exports improved during 1986–89 and worsened in the early 1990s, while the real exchange rate rose during the period when the pound sterling was in the *Exchange Rate Mechanism* of the *European Monetary System* (see Chapter 36, pp.971–974).

R E V I E W

◆ Other things remaining the same, net exports adjust to fill the gap between potential GDP and $C + I + G$.

◆ The real exchange rate adjusts to make decisions about exports and imports compatible with decisions about consumption expenditure, saving and investment.

◆ When consumption expenditure plus investment plus government purchases rises relative to potential GDP, the real exchange rate rises and net exports fall.

◆ ◆ ◆ ◆ In this chapter, we've studied the factors that influence investment decisions, and consumption and saving decisions. We've also studied the way these decisions interact in global markets to determine the real interest rate. Finally, we've studied the way the real interest rate determines consumption, investment and net exports in a national economy such as the United Kingdom. ◆ We've now laid the foundation on which you can study both long-term economic growth and short-term fluctuations. In Chapter 26, you will learn how investment, consumption and saving decisions influence the long-term growth of potential GDP, and in Chapters 27 and 28, you will learn how these decisions influence our economy in the short run and create fluctuations around the long-term growth trend.

Real Interest Rates and Consumer Spending

The Essence of the Story

THE TIMES, 1 DECEMBER 1996

Consumer demand robust

Janet Bush, Economics Correspondent

The consumer sectors of the economy continue their robust growth, with demand for mortgage finance and other types of credit remaining strong in August.

The latest figures further convinced the City that another cut in base rates should be ruled out....

Consumer credit jumped by £997 million, higher than economists had expected. Together with July's increase in credit of £1.05 billion – the second biggest on record – this confirmed that, if anything, consumer spending is accelerating. Compared with a year ago, consumer credit is now up by 15.5 per cent, the highest year-on-year gain since the first quarter of 1990.

Net mortgage loans rose by £1.7 billion in August after a £1.6 billion jump in July.

Taking mortgages and other credit together, total personal borrowing rose by £2.7 billion and 0.6 per cent in the month. Michael Saunders, UK economist at Salmon Brothers, said that this is the biggest rise since 1991 and fits in with a picture of big gains in retail sales and house prices in August.

Separate figures published yesterday showed that M0 narrow money supply rose by 0.2 per cent in September, the lowest month-on-month gain since May. M0's annual rate fell to 7.0 per cent, from 7.4 per cent.

Although this drop was exaggerated by a sharp fall in bankers' operational deposits, which are notoriously volatile, the latest figures suggest that retail spending may have cooled off a little in September.

- Consumer spending in the United Kingdom accelerated during the second half of 1996.

- The sectors that showed a strong growth in demand in August 1996 were mortgage finance and consumer credit.

- Consumer credit grew at an annual rate of 15.5 per cent a year in August 1996. Net mortgage loans rose by £1.7 billion in August.

- Retail sales and house prices grew during this period.

- However, another indicator suggests that spending may have actually weakened in September. The annual rate of growth of the money supply measured by the amount of currency in circulation fell from 7.4 per cent in August to 7 per cent in September.

Economic Analysis

■ Weak demand at the beginning of 1996 prompted the Chancellor of the Exchequer to instruct the Bank of England to cut its base rate to 5.75 per cent in January. Interest rates had been falling during 1995. Figure 1 shows that real interest rates for preferred bank customers during 1995–96 have fallen considerably.

■ Consumption and savings plans depend on the real rate of interest, not the nominal rate of interest.

■ Figure 1 also shows the annual rate of growth of consumer credit issued by banks and lending institutions. The decline in real interest rates has lowered the cost of obtaining credit and the demand for consumer credit has increased.

■ Consumer spending has recovered as a result of the reduction in real interest rates. Figure 2 shows the year-on-year rate of growth in the volume of retail sales. This is a measure of the rate of growth of real household spending.

■ There is still a lot of uncertainty in the economy. Although real interest rates have fallen, they remain historically high and may not have fallen sufficiently to stimulate a strong consumer-led recovery.

■ Another indicator of spending is the rate of growth of currency. More spending in the shops means that more notes and coins are circulating in the economy.

■ The narrow measure of the money supply known as M0 is largely currency in circulation. This was increasing during 1996 as seen in Figure 3, but as the news article says the rate of growth in September was 7 per cent, compared with 7.4 per cent in August.

■ The unsteady growth in the amount of currency may yet signal a weak rather than a robust increase in consumer demand.

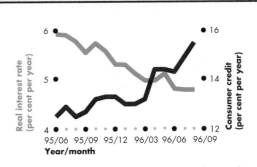

Figure 1 Real interest rate and consumer credit growth

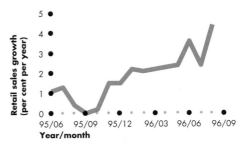

Figure 2 Retail sales growth

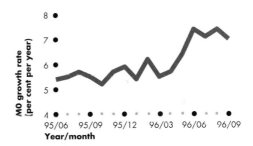

Figure 3 Rate of growth of currency in circulation

SUMMARY

Capital and Interest

The capital stock increases by the amount of net investment which fluctuates between £14 billion and £50 billion a year. Because net investment is always positive the capital stock grows steadily.

Investment is business investment plus investment in new houses. Some government purchases are investment in *social infrastructure capital.*

The return on capital is the real interest rate – the interest rate on a loan minus the inflation rate. Real interest rates around the world move together. (pp. 627–629)

Investment Decisions

Gross private investment is determined by two main factors: the real interest rate and expected profit rate.

The higher the expected profit rate on new capital, the greater is the amount of investment, other things remaining the same. The two main influences on the expected profit rate are the phase of the business cycle and advances in technology.

To decide whether to undertake an investment, a firm compares the expected profit rate with the opportunity cost of funds. This opportunity cost is the real interest rate. The lower the real interest rate, the greater is the amount of investment undertaken, other things remaining the same.

Investment demand is the relationship between the level of planned investment and the real interest rate, holding all other influences on investment constant. When firms expect a high profit rate, investment demand increases and the investment demand curve shifts rightward, and when firms expect a low profit rate, investment demand decreases and the investment demand curve shifts leftward. (pp. 630–632)

Saving and Consumption Decisions

A household's consumption expenditure depends on its disposable income, the purchasing power of its net assets and its expected of future income.

The higher a household's disposable income, the purchasing power of its net assets and expected future income, the greater is its permanent income and, other things remaning the same, the greater is its consumption expenditure.

The relationship between consumption expenditure and disposable income is called the consumption demand curve, and the relationship between saving and disposable income is called the saving supply curve. As disposable income increases, other things remaining the same, both consumption expenditure and saving increase. (pp. 633–639)

Long-run Equilibrium in the Global Economy

Because capital is free to move internationally to seek the highest possible real rate of return, the real interest rate is determined in a global market. The equilibrium real interest rate makes global consumption expenditure plus global investment plus global government purchases equal to global potential GDP. Equivalently, the equilibrium real interest rate makes global saving equal to global investment. (pp. 640–644)

Net Exports and Equilibrium in the National Economy

In the national economy, foreign borrowing (the negative of net exports) fills the gap between domestic resources and investment. That is, net exports adjust to fill the gap between potential GDP and $C + I + G$, or, equivalently, they adjust to fill the gap between investment and national saving.

Changes in the real exchange rate occur to make decisions about exports and imports compatible with decisions about investment, consumption and saving. When investment exceeds national saving by a large amount, net exports become increasingly negative and the real exchange rate rises to make UK-produced goods expensive relative to foreign-produced goods. (pp. 645–647)

KEY ELEMENTS

Key Terms

Capital stock, 627
Consumption demand, 634
Depreciation, 627
Equity withdrawal, 639
Gross investment, 627
Investment demand, 630
Marginal propensity to consume, 636
Marginal propensity to save, 636
Net investment, 627
Real exchange rate, 646
Real interest rate, 628
Saving supply, 634

◆ Key Figures

Figure 25.4   Investment Demand, 631
Figure 25.6   Consumption Demand Curve and
               Saving Supply Curve, 635
Figure 25.7   An Increase in Disposable Income,
               636
Figure 25.8   Other Influences on Consumption
               Demand and Saving Supply, 637
Figure 25.10   The Saving Equals Investment
               Approach, 640
Figure 25.13   The Real Interest Rate, 644
Figure 25.14   Net Exports and Equilibrium in the
               UK Economy, 645

REVIEW QUESTIONS

1 Which component of gross investment fluctuates the most, net investment or replacement investment?

2 Why does the capital stock grow smoothly when net investment fluctuates?

3 Describe how the real interest rate has changed since 1975.

4 Explain how investment is financed.

5 What determines investment?

6 Why does a fall in the real interest rate increase investment?

7 List the main influences on consumption expenditure.

8 What is the consumption demand curve?

9 What is the saving supply curve?

10 What is the relationship between the saving supply curve and the consumption demand curve?

11 How do consumption demand and saving supply change when disposable income changes?

12 What are the marginal propensity to consume and the marginal propensity to save? Why are they less than 1 and why do they sum to 1?

13 What happens to the consumption demand curve and the saving supply curve when expected future incomes or the purchasing power of assets increases?

14 Explain how the real interest rate is determined.

15 Describe the two approaches to determining the real interest rate and explain why they are equivalent.

16 How are net exports determined?

PROBLEMS

1 A cellular telephone assembly plant can be built for £10 million and it will have a life of one year. The firm will have to hire labour at a cost of £3 million and buy parts and fuel at a cost of a further £3 million. If the firm builds the plant, it will be able to produce cellular telephones that will sell for £17 million. Does it pay the firm to invest in this new production line at the following real interest rates:

  a 5 per cent a year?
  b 10 per cent a year?
  c 15 per cent a year?

2 Suppose the phone producer in Problem 1 expects its total revenue to increase to £17.5 million with unchanged costs. What, in this situation, is the highest real interest rate at which it will undertake the investment? How does the firm's investment demand curve change as a result of the firm's expected profit rate increasing?

3 You are given the following information about a household:

Household Consumption and Saving in 1994

Real interest rate (per cent per year)	Consumption expenditure	Saving	Disposable income
	(thousands of pounds a year)		
a 4	80	20	100
b 6	75	25	100
c 8	60	40	100

Household Consumption and Saving in 1995

Real interest rate (per cent per year)	Consumption expenditure	Saving	Disposable income
	(thousands of pounds a year)		
a 4	88.0	22.0	110
b 6	82.5	27.5	110
c 8	66.0	44.0	110

  a Draw a graph of the household's consumption demand curve and saving supply curve for 1994 and 1995.
  b Calculate the household's marginal propensity to consume.
  c Calculate its marginal propensity to save.

4 The year is 3050 and the economy of Alpha Centura, still isolated from all other planets, has the following consumption demand and investment demand schedules:

Real interest rate (per cent per year)	Investment	Consumption expenditure
	(trillions of 3050 zips)	
a 4	7	28
b 5	6	24
c 6	5	20
d 7	4	16
e 8	3	12

The Alpha Centurans have a balanced government budget rule that works and government purchases are 10 trillion 3050 zips. Potential GDP on Alpha Centura is 30 trillion 3050 zips.

  a What is the equilibrium real interest rate?
  b What is the equilibrium level of investment?
  c What is the equilibrium level of consumption expenditure?
  d Find the level of saving on Alpha Centura at each interest rate shown in the table.

5 Alpha Centura and Earth discover each other and begin to pursue intergalactic economic activity. The real interest rate on Earth is 6 per cent a year. On Alpha Centura, it is the number you have calculated for Problem 4.

  a Which planet borrows from the other?
  b Do consumption and saving on Alpha Centura increase or decrease?
  c Do consumption and saving on Earth increase or decrease?

6 Study *Reading Between the Lines* on pp. 648–649 and then answer the following questions:

  a What was the reason for the cut in interest rates at the beginning of 1996?
  b What happened to the real interest rate in 1995 and 1996?
  c What has happened to the demand curve for consumer credit in 1995 and 1996?
  d Describe the relationship between the real interest rate and consumption expenditure in 1995 and 1996.

CHAPTER
26

After studying this chapter you will be able to:

- ◆ Describe the long-term growth trends in the United Kingdom and other countries and regions
- ◆ Explain the main factors that influence the long-term growth rate of real GDP
- ◆ Explain the productivity growth slowdown during the 1970s and recovery in the 1980s
- ◆ Explain the rapid economic growth rates being achieved in East Asia
- ◆ Explain the theories of economic growth
- ◆ Describe the policies that might be used to speed up economic growth

Almost every year, we become more productive. Our economy expands and our incomes grow. In the United Kingdom, real GDP per person doubled between 1960 and 1995. If you stay in a university residence, the chances are that it was built during the 1960s and equipped with two electric plug-points, one for a desk lamp and one for a bedside lamp. Today, with the help of a multi-plug (or two), your room bulges with a television and VCR, CD player, electric kettle and computer – the list goes on – which were not contemplated in the 1960s when the residence was built. What has brought about this growth in productivity and incomes? ◆ Although our economy expands, its growth is uneven. In some periods, such as the 1960s, growth is rapid. In other periods, such as the 1970s and early 1980s, growth slows down. What makes our long-term growth rate vary? What can be done to prevent growth from slowing down? And what can be done to speed up economic growth? ◆ We can see even greater extremes of economic growth if we look at modern Asia. On the banks of the Li River in southern China, Songman Yang breeds cormorants, amazing birds that he trains to fish and to deliver their catch to a basket on his simple bamboo raft. Songman's work, the capital equipment and tech-

Economic Miracles

nology he uses, and the income he earns are similar to those of his ancestors going back some 2,000 years. Yet all around Songman, in China's bustling towns and cities, people are participating in an economic miracle. They are creating businesses, investing in new technologies, developing both local and global markets, and experiencing income growth of more than 6 per cent a year. Similar rapid economic growth is taking place in other economies in Asia such as Hong Kong, South Korea, Singapore and Taiwan. In all these countries, real GDP has doubled *three times* – an eightfold increase – between 1960 and 1995. Why have incomes in these Asian economies grown so rapidly? What makes an economic miracle?

◆ ◆ ◆ ◆ In this chapter we study long-term economic growth. We begin by looking more closely at the facts about long-term economic growth in the United Kingdom and other parts of the world. We then discover what makes real GDP grow, why some countries grow faster than others and why the long-term growth rate sometimes slows down. We'll also look at ways of achieving faster economic growth.

Long-term Growth Trends

The long-term growth trends that we study in this chapter are the trends in *potential GDP*. But potential GDP growth has two components, population growth and growth in potential GDP per person. It is the growth of potential GDP per person that brings rising living standards. And it is changes in the growth of potential GDP per person that are the main causes for concern about economic growth. Let's look at the growth of real GDP per person.

Growth in the UK Economy

Figure 26.1 shows real GDP per person in the United Kingdom for the 140 years from 1855 to 1995. The average growth rate over this entire period is 1.3 per cent a year. But the long-term growth rate has varied. For example, the long-term growth rate slowed during the 1970s to 1.8 per cent a year, down from 2.4 per cent a year during the 1960s. But growth picked up again in the 1980s to 2 per cent a year. This productivity growth slowdown and pickup was described in Chapter 22 (pp. 550–556).

You can see the present productivity growth slowdown in a longer perspective in Fig. 26.1, and you can see that it is not unique. The interwar period and the early years of the 1900s had even slower growth than we have today.

In the middle of the graph are two extraordinary events: the two recessions of the interwar period and World War II in the 1940s. The recession in the interwar period and the bulge during the war obscure changes in the long-term growth trend that might have occurred within these years. But between 1919 and 1953, averaging out the depression and the war, the long-term growth rate was 1.2 per cent a year.

A major goal of this chapter is to explain why our economy grows and why the long-term growth rate varies. A related goal is to explain variations in the economic growth rate across countries. Let's look at some facts about these variations.

FIGURE 26.1

A Hundred and Forty Years of Economic Growth in the United Kingdom

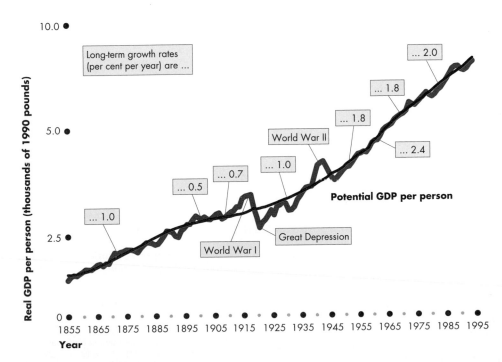

During the 140 years from 1855 to 1995, long-run real GDP per person in the United Kingdom grew by 1.3 per cent a year, on the average. The growth rate was above average during the 1950s, 1960s and 1980s, and it was below average in the 1900s, the interwar period and 1973–1979.

Source: Charles Feinstein, *National Income Expenditure and Output of the United Kingdom 1855–1965*, Cambridge, Cambridge University Press, 1972; Central Statistical Office, *Economic Trends Annual Supplement*, 1995; Datastream International.

Real GDP Growth in the World Economy

Figure 26.2 shows real GDP growth in the largest economies in the world since 1960. The data shown in this figure are from the Penn World Tables and are measured in a common currency (1985 US dollars). Part (a) looks at the richest countries. The United States has the highest real GDP per person and Canada has the second highest. But Canada has grown faster than the United States and so has been catching up.

Until 1984, the third richest countries were France, Germany, Italy and the United Kingdom. They are shown in the figure as Europe Big 4. But in 1984, the fastest growing rich country, Japan, caught up with Europe Big 4. All the countries shown in Fig. 26.2(a) are catching up with the United States.

Japan has caught up most, Canada has got closest and Europe Big 4 has caught up least.

Not all countries are growing faster than and catching up with the United States. Figure 26.2(b) looks at some of these. The economies of Africa and Central and South America were stagnating, not growing, during the 1980s. As a result, the gap between them and the United States widened. The former communist countries of Central Europe grew during the 1970s and 1980s, but at a rate roughly equal to that of the United States. So the gap remained constant. (After 1990, real GDP per person shrank in some of these countries as they went through a process of traumatic political change.)

Taking both parts of Fig. 26.2 together, we can see that the catch-up in real GDP per person that is visible in part (a) is not a global phenomenon. Some rich countries are catching up with the United States but

FIGURE 26.2

Economic Growth Around the World: Catch-up or Not?

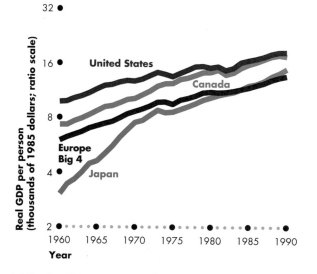

(a) Catch-up?

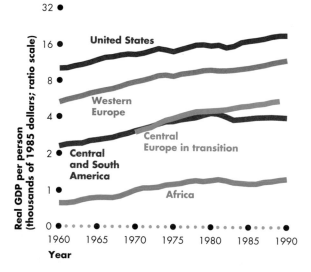

(b) No catch-up?

Real GDP per person has grown throughout the world economy. Among the rich industrial countries (part a), real GDP growth has ben faster in low-income countries and income levels have converged. The most spectacular growth was in Japan during the 1960s. But Canada and the big four West European countries (the United Kingdom, France, Germany and Italy) have got closer to the United States income level.

Among a wider range of countries (part b), there is less sign of convergence. The gaps between the income levels

of the United States, West European countries, Central and Eastern Europe, Central and South America, and Africa have remained remarkably constant.

Sources: Robert Summers and Alan Heston, New computer diskette (Mark 5.5), June 15 1993, distributed by the National Bureau of Economic Research to update 'The Penn World Table (Mark 5): An Expanded Set of International Comparisons, 1950-1988', *Quarterly Journal of Economics*, May 1991, 327-368.

the gaps between the United States and many poor countries are not closing.

There is another group of countries that in 1960 had low levels of real GDP per person and that are catching up with the United States and the other Western economies in a dramatic way. These are the economies of Hong Kong, South Korea, Singapore and Taiwan. Figure 26.3 shows how these economies are catching up with the United States. The figure also shows Asia's giant economy, China. It too is catching up, but from a long way behind. In 1960 China's real GDP per person was 8 per cent that of the United Kingdom and 6 per cent that of the United States, but by 1992 it was 12 per cent that of the United Kingdom and 8 per cent that of the United States.

FIGURE 26.3

Catch-up in Asia

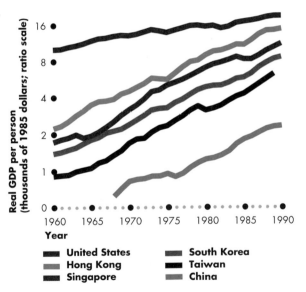

The clearest examples of catch-up have occurred in five economies in Asia. Starting out in 1960 with incomes as little as one-tenth of that in the United States, four Asian economies (Hong Kong, South Korea, Singapore and Taiwan) have substantially narrowed the gap on the United States. And from being a very poor developing country in 1960, China has caught up with the income level that Hong Kong had in 1960 and is growing at a rate that is enabling it to continue catching up with the United States.

Source: Robert Summers and Alan Heston, New computer diskette (Mark 5.5), June 15 1993, distributed by the National Bureau of Economic Research to update The Penn World Table (Mark 5): An Expanded Set of International Comparisons, 1950-1988, *Quarterly Journal of Economics*, May 1991, 327-368.

◆ Over the 140 years between 1855 and 1995, long-run real GDP per person in the United Kingdom grew at an average rate of 1.3 per cent a year. Slow growth occurred during the early 1900s and the interwar period, and rapid growth occurred in the 1960s and more recently in the 1980s.

◆ Some countries are catching up with the developed economies, but the gaps between the rich and many poor countries are not closing.

◆ The economies that are catching up with the Western developed economies are Hong Kong, South Korea, Singapore, Taiwan and China.

We've described some facts about economic growth in the developed economies and around the world. Our next task is to study the causes of economic growth. Economic growth is a complex process and its causes are difficult to discover. We'll study the causes of economic growth in three stages. First, we'll describe the sources of growth. Second, we'll study 'growth accounting', which is an attempt to measure the quantitative importance of the sources of growth. Third, we'll study the theories of economic growth that explain how the sources of growth interact to determine the growth rate.

The Sources of Economic Growth

Most human societies have lived for centuries and even thousands of years, with no economic growth. The key reason is that they have lacked some fundamental social institutions and arrangements that are essential preconditions for economic growth. Let's see what these preconditions are.

Preconditions for Economic Growth

The most basic precondition for economic growth is an appropriate *incentive* system. Three institutions are crucial to the creation of incentives. They are:

1. Markets
2. Property rights
3. Monetary exchange

You studied these institutions in Chapter 3 (pp. 59–60), so here we'll give you just a brief reminder of what you've already learned. Markets enable buyers and sellers to get information and to do business with each other, and market prices send signals to buyers and sellers that create *incentives* to increase or decrease the quantities demanded and supplied. Markets enable people to specialize and trade and to save and invest. But to work well, markets need property rights and monetary exchange.

Property rights are the social arrangements that govern the ownership, use and disposal of factors of production and goods and services. They include the right to physical property (land, buildings and capital equipment), to financial property (claims by one person against another) and to intellectual property (such as inventions). Clearly established and enforced property rights give people an assurance that the income they earn and their savings will not be confiscated by a capricious government. Monetary exchange facilitates transactions of all kinds, including the orderly transfer of private property from one person to another. Property rights and monetary exchange create incentives for people to specialize and trade, to save and invest, and to discover new technologies.

There is no unique political system that is necessary to deliver the preconditions for economic growth. Liberal democracy, founded on the fundamental principle of the rule of law, is the system that does the best job. It provides a solid base on which property rights can be established and enforced. But authoritarian political systems have sometimes provided an environment in which economic growth has occurred.

Early human societies, based on hunting and gathering, did not experience economic growth because they lacked the preconditions we've just described. Economic growth began when societies evolved these institutions. The presence of an incentive system and the institutions that create it do not guarantee that economic growth will occur. They permit it but do not make it inevitable.

The simplest way in which growth happens when the appropriate incentive system exists is that people begin to specialize in the activities at which they have a comparative advantage and trade with each other. You saw in Chapter 3 how everyone can gain from such activity. By specializing and trading, everyone can acquire goods and services at the lowest possible cost. Equivalently, everyone can obtain a greater volume of goods and services from their labour.

As an economy moves from one with little specialization to one that is highly specialized, it grows. Real GDP per person increases and the standard of living rises. But once the economy is highly specialized, this source of economic growth runs its course.

For growth to continue, people must face incentives that encourage them to pursue three activities that generate ongoing economic growth. These activities are:

◆ Saving and investment in new capital

◆ Investment in human capital

◆ Discovery of new technologies

These three sources of growth, which interact with each other, are the primary sources of the extraordinary growth in productivity during the past 200 years. Let's look at each in turn.

Saving and Investment in New Capital

Saving and investment in new capital increase the amount of capital per worker and increase human productivity. Human productivity took the most dramatic upturn when the amount of capital per worker increased during the Industrial Revolution. Production processes that use hand tools can create beautiful objects, but production methods that use large amounts of capital per worker, such as car plant assembly lines, are much more productive. The accumulation of capital on farms, in textiles factories, in iron foundries and steel mills, in coal mines, on building sites, in chemical plants, in car plants, in banks and insurance companies, and in retail stores, have added incredibly to the productivity of our economy. From your knowledge of life 100 years ago try to imagine how productive you would be in such circumstances compared with your productivity today.

Growth in Human Capital

Human capital is fundamental to the growth process. The basic human skills of reading, writing and mathematics as well as knowledge of physical forces and chemical and biological processes are the foundation of all technological change.

But much human capital, which is extremely productive, is much more humble. It takes the form of millions of individuals learning and repetitively doing simple production tasks and becoming remarkably more productive in the task. One carefully studied example illustrates this kind of human capital. Between 1941 and 1944 (during World War II), US shipyards produced some 2,500 units of a cargo ship, called the Liberty Ship, to a standardized design. In 1941, it took 1.2 million person hours to build a ship. By 1942, it took 600,000, and by 1943, it took only 500,000. Thousands of workers and managers learned from experience and accumulated human capital that more than doubled their productivity in two years.

Discovery of New Technologies

People are many times more productive today than they were 100 years ago, not because we have more steam engines per person and more horse-drawn carriages per person, but because we have engines and transport equipment that use technologies unknown 100 years ago, which are more productive than those old technologies were. Technological change makes an enormous contribution to our increased productivity. It arises from formal research and development programmes and from informal trial and error, and it involves discovering ways of getting more out of our resources.

To reap the benefits of technological change, capital must increase. Some of the most powerful and far-reaching fundamental technologies are embodied in human capital – for example, language, writing and mathematics. But most technologies are embodied in physical capital. For example, to reap the benefits of the internal combustion engine, millions of horse-drawn carriages and horses had to be replaced by cars; and, more recently, to reap the benefits of computerized word processing, millions of typewriters had to be replaced by PCs.

R E V I E W

◆ Economic growth cannot occur without institutional capital that creates incentives to specialize and exchange, save and invest, and develop new technologies.

◆ The most significant sources of economic growth are saving and investment in new capital, the growth of human capital and the discovery of new technologies. These sources interact: human capital creates new technologies, which are embodied in both human and physical capital.

We've described the sources of economic growth. Let's now see how we can begin to quantify their contributions by studying growth accounting.

Growth Accounting

Real GDP grows because the quantities of labour and capital grow and because technology advances. The purpose of **growth accounting** is to calculate how much real GDP growth has resulted from growth of labour and capital and how much is attributable to technological change.

The first task of growth accounting is to define productivity. **Productivity** is real GDP per hour of work. It is calculated by dividing real GDP by aggregate labour hours. (Chapter 23, pp. 581–586, explains how real GDP is measured and Chapter 24, pp. 605–606, explains how aggregate hours are measured.) We are interested in productivity because it determines how much income an hour of labour can earn. Figure 26.4 shows productivity for the period 1960–95. In the 1960s productivity growth was 4.2 per cent a year. Productivity growth was only 0.8 per cent per year in the period 1973–79. It speeded up again in the 1980s to 2 per cent and again to 2.4 per cent in the 1990s.

The second (and main) task of growth accounting is to explain the fluctuations in productivity. Why did productivity growth slow down during the 1970s and then speed up again in the 1980s? Growth accounting answers these questions by dividing the growth in productivity into two components and then measuring the contribution of each. The components are:

1. Growth in capital per hour of work
2. Technological change

The technological-change component contains everything that is not included in capital per hour. In particular, it includes human capital. But as you've seen, human capital and technological change are intimately interrelated, so calling this catch-all component 'technological change' is not misleading.

The analytical engine of growth accounting is a relationship called the productivity function. Let's learn about this relationship and see how it is used.

The Productivity Function

The **productivity function** is the relationship that shows how real GDP per hour of work changes as the amount of capital per hour of work changes with no change in technology. Figure 26.5 illustrates the productivity function. Capital per hour of work is measured on the x-axis and real GDP per hour of

FIGURE 26.4

Real GDP per Hour of Work

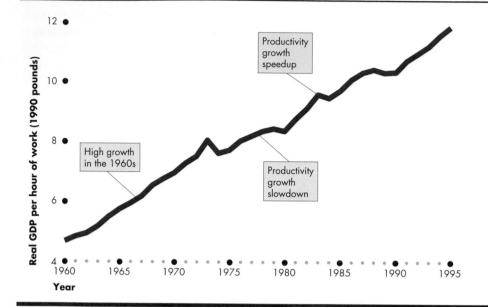

Real GDP divided by aggregate hours equals real GDP per hour of work, which is a broad measure of productivity. During the 1960s, the productivity growth rate was high. It slowed during the 1970s and speeded up again during the 1980s.

Sources: Central Statistical Office, *Economic Trends Annual Supplement*, 1995; Labour Force Survey; R.C.O. Matthews, C.H. Feinstein and J.C. Odling-Smee, *British Economic Growth 1856–1953*, 1982, Oxford, Clarendon Press.

work is measured on the y-axis. The figure shows two productivity functions as the curves labelled PF_0 and PF_1.

An increase in the amount of capital per hour of work results in an increase in real GDP per hour of work, which is shown by a movement along a productivity function. For example, on the curve labelled PF_0, when capital per hour of work is £20, real GDP per hour of work is £5. As capital per hour of work increases to £40, real GDP per hour of work increases to £7.

Technological change increases the amount of GDP per hour of work that can be produced by a given amount of capital per hour of work. It is shown by an upward shift of the productivity function. For example, if capital per hour of work is £20 and a technological change increases real GDP per hour of work from £5 to £7, the productivity function shifts upward from PF_0 to PF_1 in Fig. 26.5. Similarly, if capital per hour of work is £40, the same technological change increases real GDP per hour of work from £7 to £10 and shifts the productivity function upward from PF_0 to PF_1.

To calculate the contributions of capital growth and technological change to productivity growth, we need to know the shape and slope of the productivity function. The shape of the productivity function reflects a fundamental economic law – the law of

diminishing returns. The **law of diminishing returns** states that as the quantity of one input increases with the quantities of all other inputs remaining the same, output increases but by ever smaller increments. For example, in a factory that has a given amount of capital, as more labour is hired, production increases. But each additional hour of work produces less additional output than the previous hour produced. Two typists working with one computer type fewer than twice as many pages per day as one typist working with one computer.

Applied to capital, the law of diminishing returns states that if a given number of hours of work use more capital (with the same technology), the additional output that results from the additional capital gets smaller as the amount of capital increases. One typist working with two computers types fewer than twice as many pages per day as one typist working with one computer. More generally, one hour of work working with £40 of capital produces less than twice the output of one hour of work working with £20 hours of capital. But how much less? The answer is given by the 'one-third rule'.

The One-third Rule On the average, across all types of work, a 1 per cent increase in capital per hour of work, with no change in technology, brings a *one-third of 1 per cent* increase in output per

FIGURE 26.5

How Productivity Grows

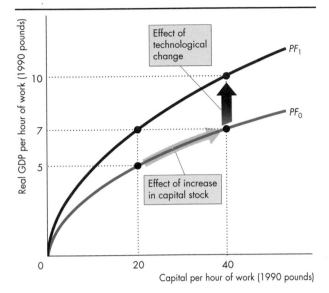

Productivity can be measured by real GDP per hour of work. Productivity can grow for two reasons: (1) capital per hour of work increases, and (2) technological advances occur. The productivity function, *PF*, shows the effects of an increase in capital per hour of work on productivity. Here, when capital per hour of work increases from £20 to £40, real GDP per hour of work increases from £5 to £7 along the productivity curve PF_0. Technological advance shifts the productivity curve upward. Here, an advance in technology shifts the productivity curve from PF_0 to PF_1. With this technological advance, real GDP per hour of work increases from £7 to £10 when there is £40 of capital per hour of work.

hour of work. In the aggregate a 1 per cent increase in capital per hour of work, with no change in technology, brings a *one-third of 1 per cent* increase in real GDP per hour of work.

This one-third rule, which was first discovered by Robert Solow of the Massachusetts Institute of Technology (MIT), can be used to calculate the contributions of an increase in capital per hour of work and technological change to the growth of real GDP. Let's do such a calculation. Suppose that capital per hour of work grows by 3 per cent a year and real GDP grows by 2.5 per cent a year. The one-third rule tells us that capital growth has contributed one-third of 3 per cent, which is 1 per cent. The rest of the 2.5 per cent growth of real GDP comes from technological change. That is, technological change has contributed 1.5 per cent, which is the 2.5 per

cent growth of real GDP minus the estimated 1 per cent contribution of capital growth.

Why The One-third Rule   Why is the one-third rule used to separate contributions of capital growth and technological change to productivity growth? How do we know that one-third is the correct proportion? The answer is that we don't know for sure, but there is one strong piece of evidence pointing to one-third being the correct proportion. This evidence is the share of real GDP received by capital and labour.

A fundamental principle of economics is that factors of production receive incomes in proportion to their contributions to production. On the average, capital receives one-third of real GDP and labour receives two-thirds. (In 1995, for example, UK GDP was £604 billion and capital income was £233 billion[1], nearly one-third of GDP.) If the factors of production are rewarded in proportion to their contributions, then a 1 per cent increase in capital brings a one-third of 1 per cent increase in real GDP. The one-third rule is based on historical experience. It is an average and not a hard and precise fixed number.

Accounting for the Productivity Growth Slowdown and Speedup

We can use the productivity function and the one-third rule to study the reasons for the slowdown and subsequent speedup of productivity growth in the United Kingdom. Figure 26.6 shows you what has been happening[2].

The story begins in 1950, which is shown in Fig. 26.6(a). Between 1950 and 1973 capital per hour grew at about 2.2 per cent a year and GDP per hour increased at about 2.8 per cent a year. This occurred at a time when the total number of hours worked fell at the rate of 0.5 per cent a year. During this period, rapid technological change increased productivity and shifted the productivity function upward from PF_0 to PF_1. With no increase in capital per hour of work, real GDP per hour of work would

---

[1] In current accounting practices, £233 is an overestimate as it includes the income from self-employment, which cannot easily be separated into labour and capital income.

[2] A continuous series for data for total hours worked is not available for the United Kingdom before 1970. We therefore turn to various studies of growth accounting that have used approximations to calculate output per hour.

FIGURE 26.6

Growth Accounting and the Productivity Growth Slowdown

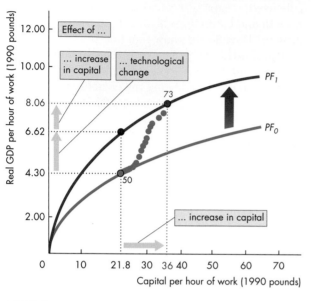

(a) 1950 to 1973

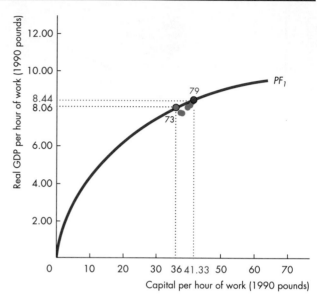

(b) 1973 to 1979

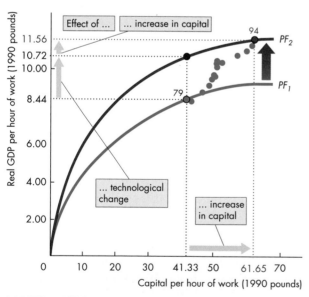

(c) 1979 to 1994

Between 1950 and 1973, which was a period of rapid growth in potential GDP, capital per hour of work increased from £21.80 to £36, and technological progress shifted the productivity function upward from PF_0 to PF_1. Between 1973 and 1979, when potential GDP grew slowly, capital per hour of work increased from £36 to £41.33 but the productivity function did not shift. The technological change that occurred was absorbed by the negative effects of oil price shocks, change in the composition of output and X-inefficiency. Between 1979 and 1994, capital per hour of work increased from £41.33 to £61.65, and technological progress shifted the productivity function upward from PF_1 to PF_2. Although the growth in potential GDP was not as rapid as in the 1960s, the productivity growth rate did increase.

Sources: Figures derived from R.C.O Matthews, C.H. Feinstein and J.C. Odling-Smee, *British Economic Growth 1856–1953*, 1982, Oxford, Clarendon Press; and A. Maddison, *Dynamic Forces in Capitalist Development*, 1991, Oxford, Oxford University Press; Central Statistical Office, *Economic Trends Annual Supplement,* 1995; Datastream International; and the author's calculations.

have increased from £4.30 to £6.62. But capital per hour of work increased from £21.80 to £36. This increase in capital per hour of work increased real GDP per hour of work further to £8.06.

You can see how the one-third rule works here. GDP per hour in the period 1950–73 increased in total by about 87.4 per cent (£4.30 to £8.06). The increase in capital per hour of work over this period was about 65.1 per cent (£21.80 to £36). The increase in real GDP per hour of work produced by this was 21.8 per cent (£6.62 to £8.06) or roughly one-third of the increase in capital per hour of work. The remaining increase in real GDP, 65.6 per cent, is attributed to the advance in technology. This is roughly 2.2 per cent per year.

The story continues between 1973 and 1979 in Fig. 26.6(b), when capital per hour of work increased from £36 in 1973 to £41.33 in 1979. This is an increase of 14.8 per cent. Real GDP per hour of work increased by 38 pence to £8.44, from £8.06 in 1973, which is a 4.7 per cent increase. This increase is slightly less than one-third of 14.8 per cent, so technological change made no contribution to real GDP growth during this period.

The reason for the productivity growth slow-down has now been isolated. It was not the result of slower growth in capital per hour of work. Rather it occurred because the contribution of technological change to real GDP growth dried up. Technological change itself did not stop. On the contrary, there was a lot of it. But the technological change that occurred did not increase productivity. Instead, it offset negative shocks to productivity. We'll look at these negative factors below.

The most recent episode in the story is shown in Fig. 26.6(c). It begins in 1979, when capital per hour of work was £41.33 and real GDP per hour of work was £8.44. Technological change shifted the productivity function upward from PF_1 to PF_2 and investment in new capital increased capital per hour of work from £41.33 in 1979 to £61.65 in 1994, a 49.2 per cent increase in total. Real GDP per hour of work increased from £8.44 to £11.56, a 37 per cent increase. Using the one-third rule, the 49.2 per cent increase in capital per hour of work increased real GDP per hour of work by 16.4 per cent (16.4 is one-third of 49.2). Technological change contributed the remaining 20.6 per cent (37 per cent minus 16.4 per cent) – roughly 1.2 per cent per year. Thus technological change resumed its contribution to productivity growth but at a slower pace than during the 1960s.

Accounting for the Productivity Slowdown: A Summary

We can bring the elements we've been studying together and describe the productivity slowdown in terms of these elements. Figure 26.7 summarizes them. Aggregate hours fell between 1950 and 1973 at a rate of 0.5 per cent a year. They then rose at a rate of 0.6 per cent per year during 1973–79 and fell by 0.2 per cent per year during 1979–94. Growth in capital per hour (remember the one-third rule, p. 663) was over 0.7 per cent a year in the 1950–73 period, 0.7 per cent in the 1973–79 period and 0.9 per cent in the 1979–94 period. The major source of variation in productivity is the rate of technological change. Technological improvements contributed the most to growth in the 1950–73 period. There was no contribution to growth from technological progress in the 1970s, but the 1980s saw a resumption of the contribution to growth from technological developments.

Technological Change During the Productivity Growth Slowdown

We've seen that during the productivity growth slowdown of the 1970s, the contribution of technological change dried up. But why? Three factors have been identified as being responsible. They are:

◆ Energy price shocks
◆ Changes in the composition of output
◆ X-inefficiency

Energy Price Shocks   The price of oil quadrupled during 1973–74 and quickly on the tail of this increase, the prices of coal and natural gas – substitutes for oil – also increased dramatically. Energy prices increased sharply again in 1979–80.

The immediate effect of higher energy prices was an increase in the rate at which fuel-intensive cars, aircraft and heating systems were scrapped. But this effect shows up in Fig. 26.6(b) as a leftward movement along the productivity function as capital per hour of work decreased. A longer drawn out effect was the development of new energy-saving technologies. Research and development efforts concentrated on developing new types of automobile and aircraft engines, heating furnaces and industrial processes that used fuel more sparingly than their predecessors. As a result, despite a huge amount of technological change and investment in new technologies, productivity did not increase. The new

FIGURE 26.7

Real GDP Growth

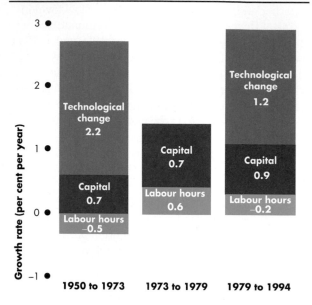

Real GDP grows because aggregate hours grow, capital per hour grows and technology advances. The growth in aggregate hours contributed about –0.5 to the average annual growth of output of 2.4 per cent per year from 1950 to 1973. Capital contributed about 0.7 per cent a year, but the main contribution was from technological change which added 2.2 per cent a year. In the period of the slow-down, 1973–1979, aggregate hours contributed 0.6 per cent and capital added 0.7 per cent. Technological change made no contribution. The pattern of the 1950s and 1960s was resumed in the 1980s. The contribution of technological change to real GDP growth has fluctuated much more than the contribution of capital per hour.

Sources: Central Statistical Office, *Economic Trends Annual Supplement*, 1995; Labour Force Survey; and the author's calculations.

technologies produced a given amount of real GDP with a much smaller amount of fuel, but not with a smaller amount of capital per hour of work. So the productivity function did not shift upward.

Changes in the Composition of Output   During the 1950s and 1960s, a lot of our growth came from a movement of resources out of the farm sector into the small business sector. Farm productivity grows less quickly than small business productivity, so as resources move, average productivity grows quickly. During the 1970s and 1980s, the main movement

of resources was out of manufacturing into services. Productivity growth in services is less than in manufacturing, so average productivity growth slowed. In the growth accounting exercise, this type of change shows up as a slowdown in aggregate productivity growth.

X-inefficiency   During the 1970s, trade union membership as a proportion of the employed labour force increased from 45 per cent to 59 per cent. The growth in union membership brought with it an increase in restrictive practices, overmanning and an increase in strikes. The period of the 1970s is characterized as one of X-inefficiency that contributed to the increasing productivity gap between the United Kingdom and other developed economies.

REVIEW

◆ Growth accounting separates out the contributions to economic growth of the growth of aggregate hours, of capital per hour and of technological change.

◆ The key to growth accounting is the one-third rule – the rule that a 1 per cent increase in capital per hour of work brings a one-third of 1 per cent increase in real GDP per hour of work.

◆ Growth accounting isolates the reason for the productivity growth slowdown. Technological change made no contribution to GDP growth between 1973 and 1979.

Growth Theory

We've seen that real GDP grows when aggregate hours of work grow, when the quantity of capital per hour of work grows and when improvements in technology (including additions to human capital) bring increases in productivity. But what is the *cause* of economic growth and what is the *effect*? How do the influences on economic growth interact with each other to make some economies grow quickly and others slowly? And what are the deeper forces that make a country's long-term growth rate sometimes speed up and sometimes slow down?

The causes of economic growth are hard to unravel because so many factors interact with each other. Population growth might create pressures on land use which result in advances in plant biology which increase crop yields, and advances in architecture and building technology which increase building heights. Here, population growth causes technological change, which in turn causes saving and investment, which in turn brings economic growth. Alternatively, a surplus of saving might lower interest rates and bring an increase in the pace of investment in human capital and physical capital which speed up the growth rate. Here, saving and investment have caused economic growth. A lucky break might bring an unlooked-for and unexpected technological advance which increases the productivity of labour and capital and causes a burst of saving and investment and rapid economic growth. Each of these possible sources of growth can operate.

But there are more complex interactions to consider. Rapid economic growth might set in motion a sequence of events which eventually bring that growth to an end. For example, other things remaining the same, growth in the work-force brings a diminishing marginal product of labour and, again other things remaining the same, growth in the capital stock brings a diminishing marginal product of capital. How does the diminishing marginal product of a factor of production influence that growth rate?

Let's look at the progress economists have made in finding the answers to these questions. There are three main theories of economic growth. They are:

◆ Classical growth theory
◆ Neoclassical growth theory
◆ New growth theory

Classical Growth Theory

Classical growth theory is a theory of economic growth based on the view that population growth is determined by the level of income per person. This theory was suggested by Adam Smith, Thomas Robert Malthus and David Ricardo, the leading economists of the late eighteenth century and early nineteenth century (see *Economics in History*, pp. 676–677).

To understand classical growth theory let's transport ourselves back to the world of 1710. Many of the 5.3 million people who live in England at this time work on farms or on their own land and perform their tasks using simple tools and animal power. They earn about 1 shilling and 4 pence for

working a 10-hour day.[3] Then advances in farming technology bring new types of ploughs and seeds that increase farm productivity. As farm productivity increases, farm production rises and some farm workers move from the land to the cities, where they get work producing and selling the expanding range of farm equipment. Incomes rise and the people seem to be prospering. But will the prosperity last? Classical growth theory says it will not.

Figure 26.8 illustrates classical growth theory and explains why it reaches a pessimistic conclusion. Before growth begins, the economy is in the situation shown in part (a). The labour demand curve is LD_0 and the labour supply curve is LS_0. There is equilibrium in the labour market: the quantity of labour demanded equals the quantity supplied at a real wage rate of 1 shilling a day and 5 million people are employed. (We will use constant 1710 prices in this example to keep it in its historical context.)

Advances in technology – in both agriculture and industry – lead to investment in new capital and labour becomes more productive. More and more businesses start up and try to hire the now more productive labour. So the demand for labour increases and the labour demand curve shifts rightward to LD_1. With this greater demand for labour, the real wage rate rises from 1 shilling a day to 2 shillings a day and this higher wage rate causes an increase in the quantity of labour supplied (a movement along the labour supply curve). In the new situation, 5.5 million people are employed.

At this stage, economic growth has occurred and everyone has benefited from it. Real GDP has increased and real wages have also increased. But the classical economists believed that this new situation could not last and would be disturbed because it would induce an increase in the population.

Classical Theory of Population Growth The classical theory of population growth is based on the idea of a subsistence real wage rate. The **subsistence real wage rate** is the minimum real wage rate needed to maintain life. By its definition, if the actual real wage rate is less than the subsistence real wage rate, some people cannot survive

---

[3] B.R. Mitchell, *British Historical Studies*, 1988, Cambridge, Cambridge University Press, p.153.

FIGURE 26.8

FIGURE 26.8

Classical Growth Theory

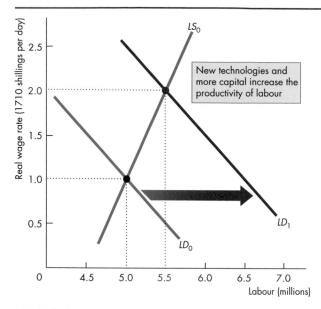

(a) Initial effect

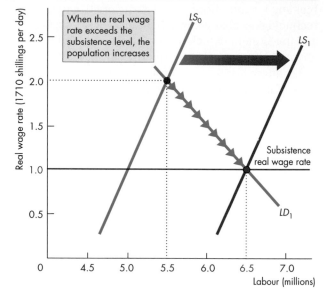

(b) Long-term effect

In classical growth theory, economic growth is temporary and the real wage rate keeps returning to the subsistence level. Initially, in part (a), the demand for labour is LD_0 and the supply of labour is LS_0. There are 5 million people employed and they earn 1 shilling a day. An advance in technology and an increase in capital increases the productivity of labour and the demand for labour increases to LD_1. The real wage rate rises to 2 shillings and the quantity of labour supplied increases to 5.5 million.

The real wage rate is now above the subsistence real wage, which in this example is 1 shilling a day. The population begins to increase. With an increase in population, the supply of labour increases and the labour supply curve shifts rightward to LS_1. As it does so, the real wage rate falls and the quantity of labour employed increases. The population stops growing when the real wage rate is back at the subsistence level.

and the population decreases. But in the classical theory, whenever the real wage rate exceeds the subsistence real wage rate, the population grows. This assumption, combined with the diminishing marginal product of labour, has a dismal implication – one that resulted in economics being called the *dismal science*. This implication is that no matter how much investment and technological change occurs, real wage rates are always pushed towards the subsistence level.

Figure 26.8(b) shows this process. Here, the subsistence real wage rate is (by assumption) 1 shilling a day. The actual real wage rate, at the intersection of LS_0 and LD_1, is 2 shillings a day. Because the actual real wage rate exceeds the subsistence real wage rate, the population grows and the labour supply increases. The labour supply

curve shifts rightward to LS_1. As it does so, the real wage rate falls and the quantity of labour increases. Eventually, in the absence of further technological change, the economy comes to rest at the subsistence real wage rate of 1 shilling a day and 6.5 million people are employed.

The economy has grown, real GDP is higher and a larger population is earning the subsistence wage rate. But the benefits of economic growth have gone to the suppliers of capital and the entrepreneurs who have put the new technology to work.

The Modern Theory of Population Growth

When the classical economists were developing their ideas about population growth, a population explosion was under way. In the United Kingdom and other West European countries, advances in medicine and hygiene had lowered the death rate but the birth rate remained high. For several decades, population growth was extremely rapid. But eventually the birth rate fell and while the population continued to increase, its rate of increase was moderate.

The population growth rate is influenced by economic factors. For example, the birth rate has fallen as women's wage rates have increased and job opportunities have expanded. Also the death rate has fallen as greater investment has been made in advances in medicine. But despite the influence of economic factors, to a good approximation, the rate of population growth is independent of the rate of economic growth. To the extent that there is a connection, as incomes increase, the population growth rate eventually decreases. This inverse relation between real income growth the and the population growth rate is contrary to the assumption of the classical economists and it invalidates their conclusions.

Neoclassical Growth Theory

Neoclassical growth theory is a theory of economic growth that explains how saving, investment and economic growth respond to population growth and technological change. This theory was suggested during the 1950s by Robert Solow of MIT. In the neoclassical theory, the population growth rate influences the rate of economic growth. But economic growth does not influence population growth. Similarly, in neoclassical growth theory the rate of technological change influences the rate of economic growth, but economic growth does not influence the pace of technological change. Rather, technological change is determined by chance. When we are lucky, we have rapid technological change, and when bad luck strikes, the pace of technological advance slows down. But there is nothing we can do to influence its pace. When variables are determined outside a theory, they are called *exogenous* variables. Thus in the neoclassical growth theory population growth and technological change are exogenous.

At the heart of the neoclassical growth theory is the stock of capital and the *productivity function* – the relationship between capital per unit of labour and output per unit of labour. For simplicity, the theory assumes that people work a fixed number of hours and that everyone works. So it measures labour as the population. The faster the capital stock per person grows, the faster real GDP and income per person grow. But what determines the growth rate of the capital stock per person? The answer is the demand for and supply of capital per person.

The Demand for and Supply of Capital per Person Figure 26.9 illustrates the neoclassical growth theory by showing how the demand for and supply of capital determine the capital stock and its growth rate. In this figure, we measure the capital stock per person on the x-axis and the real interest rate on the y-axis. The demand for capital and the supply of capital are determined by investment and saving decisions, which are described in Chapter 25 (see pp. 630–639). Briefly, the lower the real interest rate, the larger is the number of capital projects that are profitable and the greater is the demand for capital. On the other hand, in the short run, the lower the interest rate, the less strong is the incentive to save, rather than consume, and the smaller is the supply of capital.

In Fig. 26.9, the demand for capital is shown by the downward-sloping KD_0 curve in part (a). Along this curve, as the real interest rate falls, other things remaining the same, the quantity of capital demanded increases. The supply of capital is shown by the upward-sloping KS_0 curve. Along this curve, as the real interest rate falls, other things remaining the same, the quantity of capital supplied decreases.

The real interest rate adjusts to achieve an equilibrium in which the quantity of capital demanded equals the quantity supplied. In Fig. 26.9, the economy is in equilibrium at a real interest rate of 4 per cent a year and with a capital stock of £40,000 per person, shown in part (a). In the absence of technological change, capital per person converges to its equilibrium level. As a result, real GDP per person converges to a constant level and there is no economic growth.

But with technological change, real GDP per person grows. Figure 26.9 illustrates this growth process. A technological advance increases the productivity of capital and the demand for capital increases. The capital demand curve shifts rightward to KD_1. The greater demand for capital raises the real interest rate to 6 per cent a year and the higher real interest rate causes an increase in saving. The quantity of capital supplied increases to £50,000 per person.

The economy has experienced a period of economic growth. Because the capital stock per person has increased, output per person has increased. Also, labour has become more productive and the demand for labour has increased, bringing an increase in real wages and employment. But economic growth continues beyond the point shown in Fig. 26.9(a). To understand why, we need to look at the neoclassical theory of saving.

FIGURE 26.9

Neoclassical Growth Theory

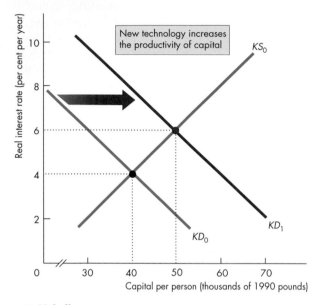

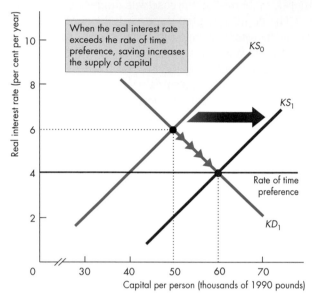

(a) Initial effect

(b) Long-term effect

In neoclassical growth theory, economic growth results from technological change. In the absence of technological change, real GDP per person converges to a constant level. Initially, in part (a), the demand for capital is KD_0 and the supply of capital is KS_0. The capital stock is £40,000 per person and the real interest rate is 4 per cent a year. An advance in technology increases the productivity of capital and the demand for capital increases to KD_1. The real interest rate rises to 6 per cent a year and the quantity of capital

supplied increases to £50,000.

The real interest rate is now above the rate of time preference, which in this example is 4 per cent a year (part b). Saving is positive and the supply of capital increases. The capital supply curve shifts rightward to KS_1. As it does so, the real interest rate falls and the quantity of capital per person increases. The quantity of capital per person stops growing when the real interest rate is back at the rate of time preference.

Neoclassical Theory of Saving The neoclassical theory of saving is based on the idea called a constant rate of time preference. The **rate of time preference** is the target real interest rate that savers want to achieve. If the real interest rate exceeds the rate of time preference, saving is positive and the supply of capital increases. If the real interest rate is less than the rate of time preference, saving is negative and the supply of capital decreases. If the real interest rate equals the rate of time preference, people are happy with the amount of wealth they have accumulated and saving is zero.

Figure 26.9(b) illustrates the consequences of a constant rate of time preference. Here, the rate of time preference is 4 per cent a year. So when the real interest rate rises to 6 per cent a year, saving is positive and the supply of capital increases. The capital

supply curve shifts rightward towards KS_1. As the supply of capital increases, the real interest rate falls and the quantity of capital demanded increases. Eventually, the economy reaches the point at which the real interest rate has fallen to equal the rate of time preference. At this point, saving is zero and the supply of capital is constant.

Throughout the process just described, real GDP per person has been increasing. The capital stock per person and real wage rates have also been increasing. The economy has experienced long-term growth.

Ongoing advances in technology are constantly increasing the demand for capital and raising the real interest rate above the rate of time preference. The process we've just examined repeats indefinitely to create an ongoing process of long-term economic growth.

Problems with Neoclassical Growth Theory

Neoclassical growth theory tells us how capital accumulation and saving interact to determine the economy's growth rate. But the growth rate itself depends on the *exogenous* rate of technological change. We need to go one step further and determine the rate of technological change.

Because all economies have access to the same technologies, and because capital is free to roam the world seeking the highest available rate of return, neoclassical growth theory predicts that growth rates and income levels per person will converge. While there is some sign of convergence among the rich countries (shown in Fig. 26.2a), convergence does not appear to be present for all countries (as we saw in Fig. 26.2b).

New growth theory attempts to overcome these two shortcomings of neoclassical growth theory.

New Growth Theory

New growth theory is a theory of economic growth based on the idea that technological change results from the choices that people make. (New growth theory is sometimes called *endogenous growth theory* and sometimes also called *neo-Schumpeterian growth theory* – see *Economics in History*, pp. 676–677). New growth theory starts with four facts about market economies:

◆ Discoveries result from choices and actions

◆ Discoveries bring profits

◆ Discoveries can be used by many people at the same time

◆ Physical activities can be replicated

Discoveries and Choices   When someone discovers a new product or technique, they think of themselves as being lucky. They are right. But the pace at which new discoveries are made – at which technology advances – is not determined by chance. It depends on how many people are looking for a new way of doing something and how intensively they are looking.

Discoveries and Monopoly Profits   The spur to seeking new and better ways of producing is profit. The forces of competition are constantly squeezing profits, so to make a profit greater than the average, a person must constantly seek out either lower-cost methods of production or new and better products for which people are willing to pay a higher price.

Eventually, the new discovery is copied and profits disappear. But in the meantime, monopoly profit can be enjoyed, and when it disappears, another new innovation can be found.

Discoveries Used by All   Once a profitable new discovery has been made, it is difficult to prevent others from copying it. But also, unlike inputs such as labour and capital, it can be used by everyone who knows about it without reducing its availability to others. This means that as the benefits of a new discovery are dispersed through the economy, resources are made available free to those who reap the benefit but didn't pay the price of making the discovery. But there is more.

Replicating Activities   Replicas can be made of many (perhaps most) production activities. For example, there might be two, three or 53 identical firms making fibre optic cable using an identical assembly line and production technique. This means that the economy as a whole does not experience diminishing returns. (Each firm experiences diminishing returns but the economy does not).

These features of the economy can be summarized in the neat idea that knowledge – the stock of productive ideas that has been accumulated as a result of research and development efforts – is a special kind of capital that can be used by all and whose marginal product does not diminish. The implication of this simple and appealing idea is shown in Fig. 26.10, which illustrates new growth theory. In this figure, we measure the knowledge capital stock on the x-axis and the real interest rate on the y-axis.

The supply of knowledge capital is shown by the upward-sloping S_0 curve. Along this curve, as the real interest rate rises, other things remaining the same, the quantity of saving and of resources devoted to accumulating knowledge capital increases.

Because the marginal product of knowledge capital does not diminish, the demand for knowledge capital does not slope downward like the demand curve for other types of capital. If knowledge capital yields a higher return than the rate of time preference, the quantity of knowledge capital demanded is unlimited. And if knowledge capital yields a lower return than the rate of time preference, then the demand for knowledge capital is zero.

Initially, before growth begins, the marginal product of knowledge capital is 2 per cent a year, shown by the horizontal line R_0 in Fig. 26.10(a). At this rate of return, and given the supply of knowledge capital curve, the economy is in equilibrium at a real interest rate of 2 per cent a year and has no knowledge capital. The economy is stuck at point a.

The invention of such basic tools as language and writing (the two most basic pieces of knowledge capital), and later the development of the scientific method and the establishment of communities of scientists, inventors and research institutions. The rate of return line shifted upward to R_1. The initial effect of this increase in the return on knowledge capital was to increase the real interest rate to 6 per cent a year and to cause an increase in the quantity of knowledge capital supplied (to £100 billion in the figure). The economy moved to point b.

The economy has experienced a period of economic growth. Because the stock of knowledge capital has increased, real GDP has increased. But

economic growth continues and it continues indefinitely. The reason is that the real interest rate now exceeds the rate of time preference. So saving is positive and the supply of capital (which includes knowledge capital) increases.

Figure 26.10(b) illustrates the process. The rate of time preference is 4 per cent a year and the rate of return on knowledge capital is 6 per cent a year. With positive saving, the supply curve shifts rightward and continues to do so indefinitely. The speed with which the saving supply curve shifts rightward depends on the extent to which the real interest rate exceeds the rate of time preference. The higher the marginal productivity of knowledge capital, the higher is the real interest rate and the faster the saving curve shifts rightward, so the faster the economy grows.

FIGURE 26.10

New Growth Theory

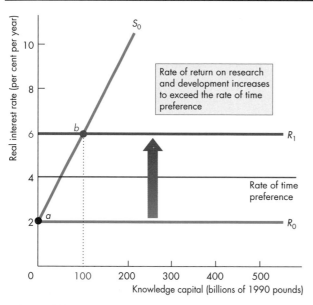

(a) Growth begins

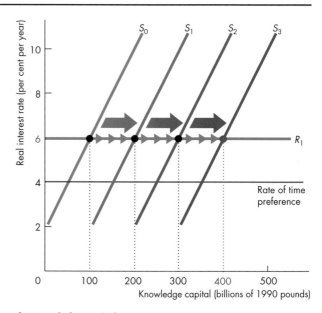

(b) Knowledge capital grows

In new growth theory, economic growth results from *endogenous* technological change. The returns to knowledge capital do not diminish and growth proceeds indefinitely. Initially, in part (a), the rate of return on knowledge capital is R_0 and the supply of knowledge capital is S_0. The stock of knowledge capital is zero. The development of the scientific method and the creation of research and development organizations increases the rate of return on knowledge capital to R_1. The real interest rate rises to 6 per cent a year and the quantity of knowledge capital supplied

increases to £100 billion.

The real interest rate is now above the rate of time preference, which in this example is 4 per cent a year. Saving is positive and the supply of knowledge capital increases. The knowledge capital supply curve shifts rightward successively to S_1, S_2, S_3, and so on. As it does so, the economy grows but the real interest rate does not fall because there are no diminishing returns to knowledge capital. Growth continues as long as the rate of return on knowledge capital exceeds the rate of time preference.

Unlike the neoclassical theory, with its diminishing marginal productivity of capital, which eventually lowers the real interest rate to the rate of time preference, there is no such mechanism at work in the new growth theory. Real GDP per person increases and does so indefinitely as long as people can undertake research and development that yields a higher return than the rate of time preference.

New growth theory sees the economy as a kind of perpetual motion mechanism. Economic growth is driven by our insatiable wants that lead us to pursue profit and innovate. The result of this process is new and better products. But new and better products result in firms going out of business and new firms starting up. In this process, jobs are destroyed and created. The outcome is more consumption, new and better jobs, and more leisure. All this adds up to a higher standard of living. But our insatiable wants are still there: profits, innovation, new products and higher living standards.

The economy's growth rate depends on people's ability to innovate, the rate of return to innovation and the rate of time preference, which influences the rate of saving. *Reading Between the Lines* on pp. 674–675 further explores the connection between saving and economic growth in the world economy.

REVIEW

- ◆ Economic growth arises from improvements in human capital, increases in the capital stock and improvements in technology.
- ◆ The classical growth theory is that there is no long-term growth in the real wage rate because when the real wage rate exceeds its subsistence level, the population expands and the real wage rate falls to the subsistence level.
- ◆ The neoclassical growth theory is that growth results from technological advances that are themselves determined by chance.
- ◆ The new growth theory is that scarcity leads people to devote resources to innovation in the pursuit of monopoly profit. The pace of innovation depends on the resources devoted to it. Profitable new discoveries are copied and replicated so their benefits spread without diminishing returns.

Achieving Faster Growth

To achieve faster economic growth, we must either increase the growth rate of capital per hour of work or increase the pace of technological advance. Let's begin to examine the policies that might speed up economic growth by looking at the miracle economies of Asia. How have they managed to grow so quickly?

The Miracle Economies

The full story of the miracle economies of the 1980s and 1990s has not yet been told. But the parts of the story that look relevant are:

1. High saving rate
2. High rate of investment in human capital
3. Learning-by-doing in high-technology industries

Singapore, Hong Kong and China save a much larger fraction of income than we save in the United Kingdom. A high saving rate enables a country to accumulate both physical capital and human capital at a rapid rate and thereby keep close to the frontier of new technologies. The miracle economies have also concentrated on giving their work-forces experience with the latest technologies. Singapore has been the most aggressive in this respect. It has virtually replaced its entire capital stock and transformed its work-force every few years and now has one of the most adaptable and highly skilled work-forces in the world.

Policies for Faster Growth

The suggestions that come from growth theory to increase the economic growth rate all centre on speeding up the pace of technological change and capital accumulation. The main suggestions are:

- ◆ Stimulate saving
- ◆ Subsidize research and development
- ◆ Target high-technology industries
- ◆ Encourage international trade

Stimulate Saving There is a direct link between economic growth and saving, so stimulating saving can also stimulate economic growth. It is not an accident that China, Hong Kong, Japan, South Korea, Singapore and Taiwan have the highest growth rates.

They also have the highest saving rates. It is also no accident that the countries of Africa have the lowest growth rates. For they have the lowest saving rates. The saving rates in the United Kingdom and the other rich countries are modest.

The most obvious way in which saving could be increased is by providing tax incentives. Some incentives already exist, but more radical measures are possible. For example, instead of taxing incomes (which means taxing both consumption and saving), we could tax only consumption. Such a tax would encourage additional saving and probably increase the economy's growth rate.

Subsidize Research and Development

Because the fruits of research and development efforts can be used by all, there is a tendency to allocate too few resources to these activities. It is true that inventions can be patented, but it is virtually impossible to prevent a near copy that does not violate a patent. For example, VisiCalc invented the spreadsheet, but it did not take long for Lotus Corporation to develop a similar product, the famous 1-2-3, and for Microsoft Corporation to bring out a Lotus 1-2-3 lookalike, Excel. Intel developed the microprocessor that powers IBM and compatible PCs. Again, clones were soon developed that broke Intel's monopoly. Because inventions can be copied, the inventor's profit is limited and the resources that are worth devoting to making an invention or innovation are also limited.

This situation is one in which government subsidies might help. By using public funds to finance research and development that bring social benefits, it might be possible to encourage an efficient level of research. But the solution is not foolproof. The main problem is that some mechanism must be designed for allocating the public funds. The universities and research councils are the main channels through which public funds in the United Kingdom are used to finance research. But it might be more productive to give public funds to private firms. But which firms?

Target High-technology Industries

One answer to the question 'which firms?' is to direct the publicly funded research effort towards high-technology firms and industries. The argument is that by encouraging such industries, a country can become the first to exploit a new technology and can earn monopoly profits for a period while others are busy catching up. But to exploit fully the potential of a new technology, it must be marketed worldwide. Hence the fourth element in the growth programme.

Encourage International Trade

Economists have generally favoured free international trade. Since the time of Adam Smith, they have appreciated the connection between trade and growth. But endogenous growth theory points to an advantage of international trade that had not previously been appreciated – *dynamic comparative advantage.* Dynamic comparative advantage is the ability to produce a good at a lower opportunity cost than that of any other supplier and results from being first in the field and getting the first crack at accumulating specialized human capital to exploit a new technology. Eventually, all countries can produce all goods at the same opportunity cost (to a reasonable approximation), but the first in a field can dominate that field for some time. However, there are many fields. So free international trade enables the first-comers in the many fields to engage in mutually advantageous international trade.

As a technology ages and is copied, so the dynamic comparative advantage disappears and a new field must be found. This is the story of Singapore over the past three decades as it has moved from textiles in the 1950s, through successively more complex electronic information technology products in the 1960s, 1970s and 1980s, to the most advanced biotechnology products in the 1990s.

◆ ◆ ◆ ◆ In this chapter, we've looked at long-term growth rates in the United Kingdom and around the world. We've studied the sources of economic growth, learned how we can measure the contributions of hours, capital and technological change, and we've studied the theories of economic growth. Finally, we've seen some policy actions that might speed up growth rates. ◆ Economic growth is the single most decisive factor in influencing a country's living standard, but it is not the only one. Another is the extent to which the country fully employs its scarce resources, especially its labour. In recent years, unemployment has become a severe problem for many countries. In Part 6, we study the fluctuations of real GDP and employment and unemployment around their long-term trends.

SUMMARY

Long-term Growth Trends

Over the 140 years between 1855 and 1995, real GDP per person in the United Kingdom grew at an average rate of 1.3 per cent a year. The early 1900s, the inter-war years, and 1973-1979 were the periods of slowest growth and the 1950s, 1960s and 1980s were periods of rapid growth.

Catch-up in real GDP per person occurs some-times but it is not a global phenomenon. The United States is still the richest country. Some rich countries are catching up with the United States, but the gaps between the United States and many poor countries are not closing. Canada, France, Germany, Italy, the United Kingdom and Japan have grown faster than the United States and have been catching up. The gap between the United States and Africa and Central and South America has widened, and the gap has remained constant with the former communist countries of Central and Eastern Europe. Hong Kong, South Korea, Singapore, Taiwan and China are catch-ing up the fastest. (pp.655–657)

The Sources of Economic Growth

Economic growth occurs when an *incentive* system, which is created by markets, property rights and monetary exchange, encourages saving and invest-ment in new capital, the growth of human capital and the discovery of new technologies.

Saving and investment in new capital, human capital accumulation and technological advances interact to increase production and raise living stan-dards and they are the main sources of economic growth. (pp. 657–659)

Growth Accounting

Growth accounting divides the sources of economic growth between the growth of aggregate hours and productivity growth, and it divides productivity growth between growth in capital per hour and tech-nological change (which includes all other influences on growth.)

The analytical engine of growth accounting is the productivity function, which is the relationship between real GDP per hour of work and capital per hour of work, holding technology constant. A change in capital per hour of work brings a movement along a productivity function, and technological change shifts the productivity function.

The contributions of capital growth and techno-logical change to productivity growth are estimated by using the *one-third rule* – a 1 per cent increase in capital per hour of work brings a one-third of 1 per cent increase in real GDP per hour of work.

Growth accounting isolates the reason for the productivity growth slowdown of the 1970s. Technological change made no contribution to real GDP growth. Three factors have been suggested as producing this situation: energy price shocks, changes in the composition of output and X-ineffi-ciency caused by trade union restrictive practices. (pp. 659–664)

Growth Theory

The three main theories of economic growth are the classical theory, the neoclassical theory, and new growth theory. The classical theory is that the popu-lation grows whenever incomes rise above the *subsistence* level and declines whenever incomes fall below the subsistence level. This assumption, com-bined with the diminishing marginal product of labour, implies that incomes are always pushed towards the subsistence level. The neoclassical growth theory is that the long-term growth rate is determined by the rate of technological change, which in turn is determined by chance. New growth theory is that the growth rate depends on the costs and benefits of developing new technologies. (pp. 664–671)

Achieving Faster Growth

To achieve faster economic growth, we must increase the growth of capital per hour of work or increase the pace of technological advance.

The miracle economies grew quickly because they had a high saving rate and a high rate of invest-ment in human capital, and they took advantage of learning-by-doing in high technology industries. It might be possible to achieve faster growth by stimu-lating saving, subsidizing research and development, targeting (and possible subsidizing) high-technology industries and encouraging more international trade. (pp. 671–672)

Saving and Growth

The Essence of the Story

THE ECONOMIST, 6 MAY 1995

Rattling the piggy bank

When bond yields rose many economists got into a tizzy about the possibility that the world would start to run short of capital. This triggered an avalanche of studies, of which the latest, from the IMF, finds some evidence for such fears. It is this savings shortfall, says the Fund, that is largely to blame for high real interest rates.

By saving rather than consuming current output, countries enjoy less jam today, but because these savings are invested they can look forward to higher income and consumption tomorrow. So if the total supply of savings (whether by individuals, firms, or governments) falls, global investment and hence growth will be constrained....

Countries that save more tend to grow faster. Over the past ten years, 14 of the 20 fastest growing economies had savings rates of more than 25% of GDP. In contrast, 14 of the 20 slowest growing economies had savings rates below 15%. But which way does the causality run?

Higher saving clearly boosts growth by spurring investment. But, intriguingly, the IMF argues that there is also evidence that faster growth itself causes savings rates to rise. Many East Asian economies, for example, enjoyed rapid growth before they began saving more. South Korea was one of the world's least thrifty countries in the early 1960s; now it is one of the biggest savers. This suggests that a virtuous circle connects growth and savings, with faster growth spurring higher savings and higher savings boosting growth. The reason this matters is that it implies that most of the savings needed to finance investment of fast-growing developing countries will be self generated...

■ A study by the International Monetary Fund (IMF) says that interest rates increased during 1994 because saving decreased.

■ A low saving rate implies a low investment rate and a low growth rate of GDP.

■ Countries that save more tend to grow faster, but does a higher saving rate bring a higher growth rate or does a higher growth rate bring a higher saving rate?

■ If the IMF is correct, fast growth will produce the savings needed to sustain it.

Economic Analysis

■ For the world economy, a *closed economy,* saving (from all sources — individual, business and government) equals investment.

■ Investment increases the capital stock, which brings higher productivity.

■ Figure 1 shows how the world saving rate (and investment rate) has fluctuated since 1960. It increased during the 1960s, peaked in 1974, and fluctuated around a slightly falling trend through the 1980s and into the 1990s.

■ Figure 2 shows the saving rates of the developing and the industrial countries since 1970. The saving rate of the industrial countries has decreased, and that of the developing countries has increased.

■ The article is correct when it says that a decrease in world saving, other things remaining the same, brings an increase in the world average interest rate (see Chapter 25, pp. 641–642). But the article is not completely correct about the connection between a country's saving rate and its growth rate.

■ Figure 3 shows the relationship between the saving rate and the growth rate of more than 100 countries over the 30 years from 1960 to 1990. Some high savers are fast growers, but there are many exceptions, several of which are identified in the figure.

■ A high saving rate does not always bring fast growth (Venezuela and Gabon are counter-examples), and fast growth does not always bring a high saving rate (the Republic of Yemen, Malta, Lesotho and Reunion are counter-examples).

■ The reason why growth rates and saving rates are only loosely linked is that saving does not limit investment, and it is investment that brings growth. Capital is internationally mobile and people seek the highest available return on their savings. So capital flows into countries that offer the highest rate of return (for equal risk) and enables those countries to invest more than they can save and grow faster.

Figure 1 World saving rate

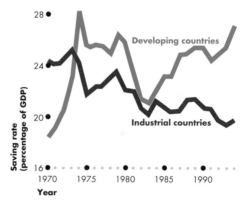

Figure 2 Saving rates

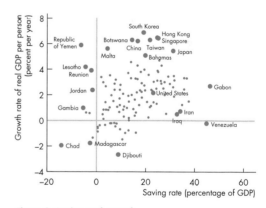

Figure 3 Saving and growth

Sources: Figures 1 and 2 from International Monetary Fund and *The Economist* feature article. Figure 3 from Robert Summers and Alan Heston, New computer diskette (Mark 5.5), 15 June 1993, distributed by the National Bureau of Economic Research to update The Penn World Table (Mark 5): An Expanded Set of International Comparisons, 1950–1988, *Quarterly Journal of Economics*, May 1991, 327–368.

'Economic progress, in capital society, means turmoil.'

Joseph Schumpeter, CAPITALISM, SOCIALISM AND DEMOCRACY

Economic Growth

THE ISSUES AND IDEAS

Technological change, capital accumulation and population growth all interact to produce economic growth. But what is cause and what is effect, and can we expect productivity and income per person to keep on growing?

The classical economists of the eighteenth and nineteenth centuries believed that technological change and capital accumulation were the engines of growth. But they also believed that no matter how successful people were in inventing more productive technologies and investing in new capital, they were destined to live at the subsistence level. These classical economists based their conclusion on a belief that productivity growth causes population growth, which in turn causes productivity to fall. They believed that whenever economic growth raises incomes above the subsistence level, the population will increase. And, they went on to reason, the increase in population brings diminishing returns that lower productivity. As a result, incomes must always fall back to subsistence level. Only when incomes are at the subsistence level is population growth held in check.

The new growth theories in the 1980s and 1990s stand the classical belief on its head. Today's theory of population growth is that rising incomes slow the population growth rate because they increase the opportunity cost of having children. Productivity and incomes grow because technology advances and the scope for further productivity growth, which is stimulated by the search for profit, is practically unlimited.

THEN ...

In 1830, a strong and experienced farm worker could harvest 3 acres of wheat in a day. The only capital employed was a scythe (to cut the wheat), which had been used since Roman times, and a cradle (to lay the stalks on), which had been invented by Flemish farmers in the 15th century. With newly developed horse-drawn ploughs, harrows and planters, farmers could plant more wheat then they could harvest. But despite big efforts, no one had been able to make a machine that could replicate the swing of a scythe. Then in 1831, 22-year-old Cyrus McCormick built a machine that worked. It scared the horse that pulled it, but it did in a matter of hours what three men could accomplish in a day. Technological change has increased productivity on farms and brought economic growth. Do the facts about productivity growth mean that the classical economists, who believed that diminishing returns would push us relentlessly back to a subsistence living standard, were wrong?

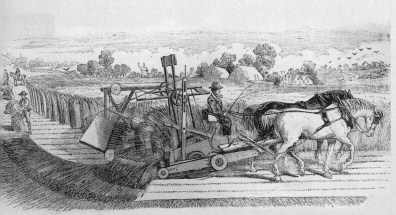

McCormick's Reaper. By Burgess & Key.

... AND NOW

Today's technologies are expanding our horizons beyond the confines of our planet and are expanding our minds. Geosynchronous satellites bring us global television, voice and data communication, and more accurate weather forecasts, which incidentally increase agricultural productivity. In the foreseeable future, we may have superconductors that revolutionize the use of electric power, virtual reality theme parks and training facilities, pollution-free hydrogen cars, wristwatch telephones and optical computers that we can talk to. Equipped with these new technologies, our ability to create yet more dazzling technologies will increase. Technological change begets technological change in an (apparently) unending process that makes us ever more productive and brings ever higher incomes.

Robert Solow

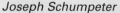

THE ECONOMISTS: JOSEPH SCHUMPETER, ROBERT SOLOW AND PAUL ROMER

Joseph Schumpeter, who was born in Austria in 1883 and became a professor of economics at Harvard in the depths of the Great Depression in 1932, was the unwitting founder of modern growth theory. Schumpeter saw the development and diffusion of new technologies by profit-seeking entrepreneurs as the source of economic progress. But he saw economic progress as a process of creative *destruction* – the creation of new profit opportunities and the destruction of currently profitable businesses. When Schumpeter died, in 1950, he had achieved his self-expressed life ambition: he was the world's greatest economist.

Robert Solow, who was born in New York City in 1924 and is now a professor of economics at MIT, was one of Schumpeter's students. He gave modern growth theory its next push forward with the *neo-classical growth model*, for which he received the Nobel Prize for Economic Science.

Joseph Schumpeter

But Paul Romer, who was born in Denver, Colorado, in 1955 and is now a professor of economics at the University of California, Berkeley, has transformed the way economists think about economic growth. Like Schumpeter, Romer believes that sustained economic growth arises from competition among firms. Firms try to increase their profits by devoting resources to creating new products and developing new ways of making existing products. One goal of Romer's research programme is to understand why China and some other East Asian countries are growing quickly, while other countries are stagnating. Romer also wants to discover ways of designing economic incentives that foster faster growth.

KEY ELEMENTS

Key Terms

Classical growth theory, 665
Growth accounting, 659
Law of diminishing returns, 660
Neoclassical growth theory, 667
New growth theory, 669
Productivity, 659
Productivity function, 659
Rate of time preference, 668
Subsistence real wage rate, 665

Key Figures

Figure 26.1   A Hundred and Forty Years of
              Economic Growth in the United
              Kingdom, 655
Figure 26.5   How Productivity Grows, 661
Figure 26.6   Growth Accounting and the
              Productivity Growth Slowdown, 662
Figure 26.8   Classical Growth Theory, 666
Figure 26.9   Neoclassical Growth Theory, 668
Figure 26.10 New Growth Theory, 670

REVIEW QUESTIONS

1 What was the average growth rate of real GDP per person in the United Kingdom between 1855 and 1995?

2 Which countries have grown fastest since 1960 and which have grown slowest?

3 Have levels of real GDP per person across countries caught up with each other?

4 What are the three necessary preconditions for economic growth to occur?

5 What three activities can create ongoing economic growth?

6 Explain how economic growth can occur even in the absence of investment and new technologies.

7 What is growth accounting?

8 What is the main concept used in growth accounting?

9 How are the effects of capital accumulation and technological change separated by growth accounting techniques?

10 What is the one-third rule and how is it used?

11 Explain the main sources of the productivity slowdown in the United Kingdom during the 1970s.

12 Why did technological advances stop increasing productivity during the 1970s?

13 What are the main theories of economic growth?

14 What are the key assumptions of classical growth theory?

15 What are the key assumptions of neoclassical growth theory?

16 What are the key assumptions of new growth theory?

17 Contrast the neoclassical growth theory and the new growth theory.

18 Describe the main reasons why the miracle economies of Asia have been so successful.

19 What are the main policy actions that governments might take to increase the growth rate?

1 The following information has been discovered about the economy of Europa. The economy's productivity function is:

Capital per hour of work (1997 euros per hour)	Real GDP per hour of work (1997 euros per hour)
10	3.80
20	5.40
30	6.80
40	8.00
50	9.00
60	9.80
70	10.40
80	10.80

Does this economy conform to the one-third rule? If so, explain why. If not, explain why not and also explain what rule, if any, it does conform to.

2 The figure illustrates the productivity function of Macaroonia in 1995 and 1997. In 1995, capital per hour of work was E10 and in 1997 it was E25.

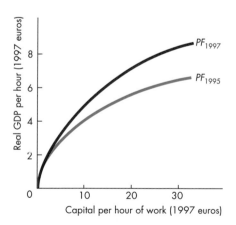

a Does Macaroonia experience diminishing returns? Explain your answer.

b Use growth accounting to find the contribution of the change in capital between 1995 and 1997 to the growth of productivity in Macaroonia.

c Use growth accounting to find the contribution of technological change between 1995 and 1997 to the growth of productivity in Macaroonia.

3 The figure illustrates the labour market in Desperado, a country that performs exactly as predicted by the classical growth theory.

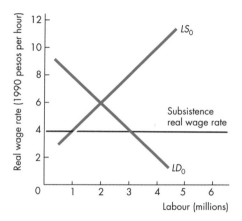

a What is the real wage rate and level of employment in Desperado?

b Is the population of Desperado growing, constant, or shrinking?

c With no further change in technology and labour productivity, what is the eventual level of employment in Desperado?

4 The following information has been discovered about the economy of Morovia. The subsistence real wage rate is 9 florins an hour. Whenever the real wage rate rises above this level the population grows, and when the real wage rate falls below this level the population falls. With its current population, the demand and supply schedules for labour in Morovia are as follows:

Real wage rate (1997 florins per hour)	Quantity of labour demanded (billions of hours per year)	Quantity of labour supplied (billions of hours per year)
3	8	4
5	7	5
7	6	6
9	5	7
11	4	8
13	3	9
15	2	10
17	1	11

Initially, the work-force of Morovia is constant and the real wage is at the subsistence level. Then a technological advance increases the amount that firms are willing to pay for labour by 2 florins at each level of employment.

a What is the initial level of employment and real wage rate in Morovia?

b What happens to the real wage rate immediately following the technological advance?

c What happens to the population growth rate following the technological advance?

d What is the new population when Morovia returns to a long-run equilibrium?

5 The figure illustrates the economy of Technologia, a country that behaves according to the predictions of the neoclassical growth model.

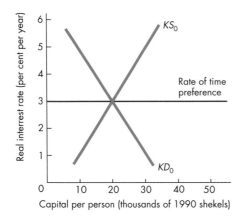

Capital per person (thousands of 1990 shekels)

a What is the real interest rate in Technologia?

b What is the real amount of capital per person in Technologia?
A technological advance increases the demand for capital by 10,000 shekels per person.

c What is the immediate effect of this change on the real interest rate and the amount of capital per person in Technologia?

d With no further technological change, what is the eventual real interest rate and amount of capital per person in Technologia?

6 Solovia is an economy that behaves according to the neoclassical growth model. The rate of time preference is 3 per cent a year. A technological advance increases the demand for capital and raises the interest rate to 5 per cent a year. Describe what happens in Solovia.

7 An increase in the rate of technological change to 6 per cent a year occurs in Solovia. What is the new steady-state growth rate?

8 The figure illustrates the economy of New Labouria, a country that behaves according to the predictions of new growth theory. Initially, the rate of return on capital is 2 per cent a year.

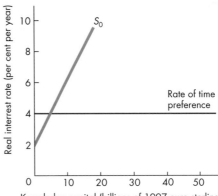

Knowledge capital (billions of 1997 euro sterling)

It then rises to 6 per cent a year.

a What initially is the real interest rate and quantity of knowledge capital in New Labouria?

b What is the immediate effect of the increase in the rate of return on knowledge capital to 6 per cent a year on the real interest rate and the quantity of knowledge capital?

c If the rate of return on knowledge capital remains at 6 per cent a year, what happens in New Labouria to the real interest rate, the quantity of knowledge capital, and real income per person?

9 Set out your policy recommendations for speeding up the growth rate of the UK. economy.

10 After studying *Reading Between the Lines* on pp. 674–675, answer the following questions:

a For the world economy, why does an increase in the saving rate bring faster real GDP growth?

b For an individual country, why does its saving not limit its investment?

c Which countries have had the highest saving rates and the highest growth rates?

d Which of the three economic growth theories – classical, neoclassical, and new – do you think best explains the facts about saving and growth rates in this news article?

Part 6
MACROECONOMIC
FLUCTUATIONS AND POLICIES

TALKING WITH
PATRICK MINFORD

Professor Patrick Minford has been Edward Gonner Professor of Applied Economics, University of Liverpool, since 1976, and a visiting Professor at the University of Cardiff Business School since 1993. He was a member of the Monopolies and Mergers Commission from 1990–1996 and one of H.M. Treasury's Panel of Forecasters ('Six Wise Men') for four years from its inception in January 1993. He is the author of many books on exchange rates, unemployment, housing and macroeconomics, and articles on trade, monetary economics, UK and international economy. In 1979 he started the Liverpool Research Group in Macroeconomics with the aim of developing new methods of macroeconomic forecasting and policy analysis. He also has a regular City column in the *Daily Telegraph*.

You have made your name as a student of New Classical Economics. Can you explain what New Classical economics is?

The key element of New Classical Economics is the idea that people have rational expectations. This implies that people form inflation expectations as a function of expected nominal variables. The old-fashioned models show inflation as being automatically generated by the business cycle. New Classical Economics says that expected inflation is determined by an expected excess of money supply growth over growth of the economy. Inflation is connected to the business cycle only by surprises. So when actual inflation is higher than expected inflation there is a surprise upturn, and when it is lower than expected inflation there is a surprise downturn.

How does rational expectation help you to understand economic fluctuation in the United Kingdom?

It helps me enormously. You and I worked on this sort of model of the UK economy in the 1970s and 1980s. It suggests that trend output and unemployment, depend on supply side fundamentals, just as inflation depends on monetary fundamentals. The business cycle, that is surprise fluctuations around those fundamentals, is not particularly important, although demand has its role – it can obviously be mismanaged. Demand is important in this analysis only if it is badly managed; unfortunately, there are plenty of instances of this in the UK economy. What New Classical Economics has taught me is that you have to think of the UK economy in terms of fundamentals and of demand as something you should try to manage competently so it can get out of the way of the fundamentals.

Looking back at UK economic history, the fundamentals of both the supply side and inflation were disastrous in the 1970s. As we moved into the Thatcher period it was essential to put those fundamentals right. The Thatcher policies were divided into two phases. Phase I was getting the inflation fundamentals right: cutting the growth of the money supply and cutting budget deficits. This phase revealed just how bad the supply side was. Phase 2 was to address the supply side: union laws, cutting tax rates, and so on. I think the New Classical Programme was essential in pushing policy makers to get these things right.

Do you think the well-known policy ineffectiveness result is relevant to the United Kingdom?

I don't think the ineffectiveness result is relevant to the UK economy or any other economy that I am familiar with. It is very much a special case. Having said that, however, it does highlight the fact that because policy responses are incorporated into people's expectations, they should not affect the behaviour of the economy a great deal. The exception to this is severe mismanagement. It was a surprise

to me to find that at the end of the 1980s we had gross mismanagement: first, the Lawson boom, fed largely by the decision to cap the exchange rate and shadow the ERM; second, the ERM recession of 1990–92; and third, the post-ERM period when demand was a sequence of negative monetary surprises which kept the recovery from really getting a grip. Whereas in the mid-1980s I was fairly confident that demand would not be a serious problem, in fact we had a series of bad cases of demand mismanagement.

Do you think that active monetary policy can stabilize the business cycle?

I don't think that active monetary policy is sensible because we do not have sufficient knowledge of the economy's detailed behaviour. That was Milton Friedman's argument and I think it is still true to today. We now know how to write down sensible rules for the behaviour of monetary policy. They are little more than conditions for interest rates that act as an automatic stabilizer and quite a lot of them work reasonably well. I don't feel at all doctrinaire about rules of this sort; certainly, I would not at present regard money supply rules as highly reliable. Financial deregulation has made the monetary indicators extremely difficult to use. Freeing up the financial markets has destabilized the monetary aggregates. So the rules that I pay more attention to today are interest rates which regulate behaviour. For example, a nominal GDP rule, or the John Taylor rule, which has nominal interest rates reacting to the GDP gap and the excess of inflation, over some target rate. These rules, broadly speaking, do the same job

as the monetarist rules of keeping the rate of growth of money stable.

Unfortunately, one of the absurd developments of rational expectations has been to create a hang-up about credibility. This is because people have assumed that a natural consequence of allowing a government to conduct policy according to one of these rules will be that it would try to exploit the Phillips curve in order to boost the economy at

> '*I* don't think that active monetary policy is sensible because we do not have sufficient knowledge of the economy's detailed behaviour. That was Milton Friedman's argument and I think it is still true today.'

convenient moments. I feel this is a red herring because we know, thanks to the work of Kydland and Prescott, and Barro and Gordon, that if the electorate rewards the government for such behaviour there will be severe stagflation. Equally, we know, as a result of this work, that it will be irrational for the electorate to reward governments for this behaviour. Now we have got to the stage of rethinking this subject, and people are beginning to realize that rational expectations does not apply just within the economy; it must also be allowed to apply to the electorate. Electorates must be assumed to have rational expectations and to reward politicians in a strategic way. Once this is accepted the issue of credibility disappears. If the electorate can set rules that penalize governments for trying to boost the economy before an election, then politicians will not do it. Politicians will be rewarded for conducting stabilization policies in a sensible manner.

Do you think that the rational expectations revolution has run its course?

The rational expectations assumption is the right one to use in most analyses of the macroeconomy, except when there is a complete upheaval in policy and no one knows what the policy is. In these circumstances, I think it is perfectly reasonable to appeal to some sort of learning model. But of course these models are unreliable because nobody really knows how people learn. There are occasions when the cards are thrown up in the air because of a regime change and everyone is wondering what is going on. In these circumstances, as Benjamin Friedman pointed out, something like adaptive expectations may work while people are figuring out what is going on, but there will come a point when they say Ah! we know what's going on, and then we are back to rational expectations. The learning models that have been suggested are not robust because nobody knows the point when people say Ah! we understand.

What is the next big step? Not a revolutionary one, I think, but rather the progressive application of a new paradigm. Rational expectations was a paradigm shift. It moved macroeconomics from

being a process of writing down rule-of-thumb assumptions which could not be justified rigorously into one where everything can in principle be justified rigorously by the appeal to *homo economicus*. The first-generation rational expectations models were supply and demand models with rational expectations bolted on. The problem is that the supply and demand models were still not fully based on optimizing behaviour. The interesting challenge we are now facing is whether we can develop models that can incorporate the way we write down the parameters of tastes and technology of the agents in the model. So instead of writing down supply and demand equations, we write down equations that have in them the parameters of their tastes and technology. This is obviously the challenge of the real business cycle theory. I am not keen on real business cycles. I think that money matters, but I like to think we can build models where money is included.

We are now in a second generation of modelling that stems from the new rational expectations paradigm. I think it will be successful, but it is difficult to judge the extent of its success. I am struck by the fact that we are developing the estimation technology, and although at the moment we calibrate these models (that is, we put in values that seem plausible from other work), it will

not be long before we estimate them. There is no model around at the moment that solves these problems, but I think the work we have been doing at Liverpool is advancing the practical techniques that are needed to do these things properly.

Who are the economists that have inspired you?

Oh, a lot. Certainly Milton Friedman has always been a great inspiration as both a researcher and a persuader, but there have been others that I have learned so much from. Harry Johnson was a tremendous inspiration, as were Alan Walters, who also taught me at LSE, and Michael Parkin and David Laidler at Manchester.

What advice would you give a student who is setting out to study economics?

Do not be put off by its appalling complexity. Economics is a circular subject. Everything depends on everything else and therefore it can be extremely baffling for beginners. The advice I would give is to persist and not give up on understanding it as a whole, as a logical system. I think it is fatal to learn economics as a series of disconnected propositions. The other thing is never lose your interest in the data and the real world because ultimately economics is supposed to be explaining, and helping to improve, the real world.

CHAPTER 27

AGGREGATE SUPPLY AND AGGREGATE DEMAND

After studying this chapter you will be able to:

◆ Explain the purpose of the aggregate supply–aggregate demand model

◆ Explain what determines aggregate supply and aggregate demand

◆ Define macroeconomic equilibrium

◆ Explain the effects of changes in aggregate demand and aggregate supply on economic growth inflation and business cycles

◆ Explain the recent history of economic growth inflation and business cycles in the United Kingdom

O UR ECONOMY IS A BIT LIKE AN OCEAN. LIKE THE TIDE, THE GENERAL DIRECTION OR long-term trend of the economy is predictable and is governed by fundamental forces that are reasonably well understood. And like individual waves that ebb and flow, the economy rises and falls in a sequence of cycles that seem to repeat but are never quite like anything that went before and that are hard to predict. World class surfers know how to catch a wave and get a good ride. Like champion surfers, people who study the economy sometimes learn how to catch a wave and get a good economic ride. But the economic waves are hard to read. What makes the economy ebb and flow in waves around its long-term trend? ◆ Sometimes the economic waves rise high and then crash, and sometimes they rise and roll on a high for a long period like they did during the mid-1980s. Sometimes the waves are inflationary like they were during the 1970s. And sometimes they hit a low and remain there for some time like they did during the depression years of the interwar period, and like they did during the early 1980s and early 1990s. What makes the economic waves vary so much, with real GDP growth and inflation fluctuating in unpredictable ways? ◆ The UK economy is influenced by economic and

Catching the Wave

political events in other parts of the world. For example, the economic policies of our partners in the rest of the European Union, particularly the interest rate policy of the Bundesbank have implications for economic policy at home. A medium-term concern is the rapid economic and industrial expansion in Asia, which has increased the competition we face in markets for manufactured goods. The economy is also influenced by policy actions taken by the government and the Bank of England. How do events in the rest of the world and domestic policy actions affect production and prices?

◆ ◆ ◆ ◆ To address questions like these, we need a model of macroeconomic fluctuations – of fluctuations around the long-term trends. Our main task in this chapter is to build such a model – the *aggregate supply–aggregate demand model*. Our second task is to use the aggregate supply–aggregate demand model to answer the questions we've just posed. You'll discover that the model of aggregate supply and aggregate demand enables us to understand many important economic events which have a major impact on our lives.

Aggregate Supply

The purpose of the aggregate supply–aggregate demand model is to understand and predict deviations of real GDP from potential GDP and fluctuations in the price level. The model uses an aggregate supply curve and an aggregate demand curve, each of which shows a relationship between real GDP and the price level. We begin by studying aggregate supply.

The *aggregate quantity of goods and services supplied* is the sum of the quantities of final goods and services produced by all firms in the economy, which is measured by real GDP. Aggregate supply is the relationship between the quantity of real GDP supplied and the price level (the GDP deflator), other things remaining the same. This relationship depends on the time-frame we are considering and we distinguish two time-frames for aggregate supply:

♦ Long-run aggregate supply

♦ Short-run aggregate supply

Long-run Aggregate Supply

The economy is constantly bombarded by events that move real GDP away from potential GDP and, equivalently, that move the unemployment rate away from equilibrium employment. Following such an event, forces operate to take real GDP back towards potential GDP and restore full employment. The **macroeconomic long run** is a time-frame that is sufficiently long for these forces to have done their work so that real GDP equals potential GDP and full employment prevails.

The **long-run aggregate supply curve** is the relationship between the quantity of real GDP supplied and the price level in the long run when real GDP equals potential GDP. Figure 27.1 illustrates long-run aggregate supply as the vertical line labelled *LAS*. Along the long-run aggregate supply curve, as the price level changes, real GDP remains at potential GDP, which in Fig. 27.1 is £525 billion. The long-run aggregate supply curve is always vertical and located at potential GDP.

The long-run aggregate supply curve is vertical because potential GDP is independent of the price level. The reason for this independence is that a movement along the long-run aggregate supply curve is accompanied by changes in *two* sets of prices: the prices of goods and services (the price level) and the prices of factors of production. A 10

FIGURE 27.1

Long-run Aggregate Supply

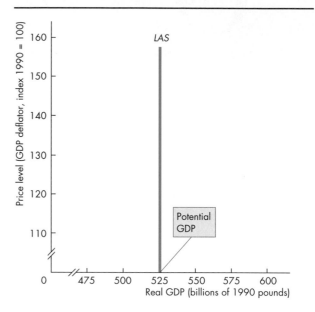

The long-run aggregate supply (*LAS*) curve shows the relationship between the quantity of real GDP supplied and the price level when real GDP equals potential GDP and there is full employment. This level of real GDP is independent of the price level so the *LAS* curve is vertical at potential GDP.

per cent increase in the prices of goods and services is matched by a 10 per cent increase in wage rates and in other factor prices. That is, the price level, wage rate and other factor prices all change by the same percentage and *relative prices* and the *real wage rate* remain constant. When the price level changes but relative prices and the real wage rate remain constant, real GDP also remains constant.

Production at a Pepsi Plant   You can see why real GDP remains constant in these circumstances by thinking about production decisions at a Pepsi bottling plant. The plant has increased its production to the point at which it is making the largest available profit. It could increase production further but to do so it would have to incur additional costs that exceed the additional revenue from higher sales, so its profit would fall. In this situation, if the price of bottled Pepsi increased and wage rates and other bottling costs did not change, the firm would have an incentive to increase its production. The higher price for Pepsi would more than cover the extra cost of hiring more labour, and profit would rise. But if the price of bottled Pepsi increases and wage rates and other bottling costs also increase by the same percentage, the firm has no incentive to change its production. The extra revenue from the higher price just equals the extra cost of hiring more labour, so profit can't be increased by increasing production. In this case, production remains constant.

What's true for Pepsi bottlers is true for the producers of all goods and services. So aggregate production – real GDP – does not change when the price level and the prices of all factors of production change by the same percentage.

Short-run Aggregate Supply

Following an event that has moved real GDP away from potential GDP (and moved the unemployment rate away from full employment), the economy enters the **macroeconomic short run**, which is a period of adjustment towards potential GDP and full employment. The short run is not a point in time but a possibly long drawn out period of adjustment.

At the start of a short run, spending, production, and sales begin to change but the price level and the money wage rate do not change. After some time, firms begin to change their prices so the price level changes. But the money wage rate and possibly some raw materials prices do not change. Money wage rates are determined by labour contracts that usually run for a year and that can run for longer. As a result, money wage rates change more slowly than prices do. The prices of some raw materials also move more slowly than other prices. For example, the price of oil is influenced by the actions of a small number of producers who keep their prices steady in some periods but change them by large amounts in others. Eventually the money wage rate and raw materials prices begin to change. But until all prices and wages have changed by the same percentage, the economy remains in a period of short-run adjustment.

The **short-run aggregate supply curve** is the relationship between the quantity of real GDP supplied and the price level in the short run when the money wage rate and all other influences on production plans remain constant. In the shortest of short runs, firms produce and sell the quantity demanded at the prices they have announced. In this situation, real GDP changes with no change in the price level. So the short-run aggregate supply curve is horizontal. But this *sticky price* situation does not last for long. If sales have increased, firms increase production and raise their prices. Similarly, if sales have

decreased, firms decrease production and cut their prices. For the economy as a whole, with the money wage rate and other factor prices remaining the same, a rise in the price level brings an increase in the quantity of real GDP supplied, and a fall in the price level brings a decrease in the quantity of real GDP supplied.

Figure 27.2 illustrates this short-run aggregate supply response as an aggregate supply schedule and as the upward-sloping curve labelled *SAS*.

FIGURE 27.2

Short-run Aggregate Supply

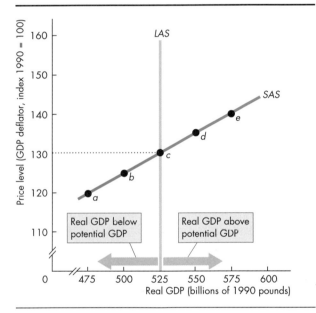

	Price Level (GDP deflator)	**Real GDP** (billions of 1990 pounds)
a	120	475
b	125	500
c	130	525
d	135	550
e	140	575

The short-run aggregate supply (*SAS*) curve shows the relationship between the quantity of real GDP supplied and the price level when the money wage rate, other factor prices and potential GDP are constant. The short-run aggregate supply curve *SAS* is based on the schedule in the table. The *SAS* curve is upward-sloping because firms' costs increase as the rate of output increases so a higher price is needed to bring forth an increase in the quantity produced.

This short-run aggregate supply curve is based on the aggregate supply schedule and each point on the aggregate supply curve corresponds to a row of the aggregate supply schedule. For example, point *a* on the short-run aggregate supply curve and row *a* of the schedule tell us that if the price level is 120, the quantity of real GDP supplied is £475 billion.

Back at the Pepsi Plant You can see why the short-run aggregate supply curve slopes upward by going back to the Pepsi bottling plant. Recall that the plant has increased its production to the point at which it is making the largest available profit. To increase production further, it must incur additional costs that exceed the additional revenue from higher sales, so its profit would fall. But if the price of bottled Pepsi rises and wage rates and other bottling costs don't change, the firm has an incentive to increase its production. The higher price for Pepsi more than covers the extra cost of hiring more labour, and its profit rises. So in this situation, the firm increases its production.

Again, what's true for Pepsi bottlers is true for the producers of all goods and services. So when the price level rises and the money wage rate and other factor prices remain constant, aggregate production and the quantity of real GDP supplied increase.

Movements Along *LAS* and *SAS*

Figure 27.3 summarizes what you've just learned about the *LAS* and *SAS* curves. A rise in the price level and an equal percentage rise in the money wage rate brings a movement along the *LAS* curve. Real GDP remains constant at potential GDP. A rise in the price level and no change in the money wage rate bring a movement along the *SAS* curve. When the price level rises and there is no change in the money wage rate, the quantity of real GDP supplied increases and the economy moves away from the long-run aggregate supply.

You've now learned about the long-run and short-run aggregate supply curves and the factors that make the long-run aggregate supply curve vertical and the short-run aggregate supply curve slope upward. But what makes aggregate supply change? Let's find out.

Changes in Aggregate Supply

You've just seen that a change in the price level, other things remaining the same, brings a movement

FIGURE 27.3

Movements Along the Aggregate Supply Curves

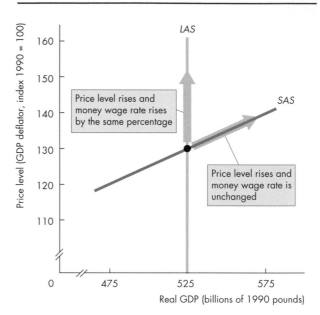

A rise in the price level with the money wage rate unchanged brings an increase in the quantity of real GDP supplied and a movement along the short-run aggregate supply curve. A rise in the price level with an equal percentage rise in the money wage rate keeps the quantity of real GDP supplied constant and brings a movement along the long-run aggregate supply curve.

along the aggregate supply curves but it does not change aggregate supply. Aggregate supply changes when any other influences on production plans change. Let's study these influences beginning with those that affect long-run aggregate supply.

Changes in Long-run Aggregate Supply Long-run aggregate supply changes when potential GDP changes and potential GDP changes for two reasons:

1. Growth of aggregate labour hours
2. Growth of productivity

Suppose there are two identical Pepsi bottling plants except that one employs 100 hours of labour and the other employs 10 hours of labour. The plant with more labour produces more bottles of Pepsi. The same is true for the economy as a whole. The larger the number of labour hours available, the greater is potential GDP, and the faster the growth rate of labour hours, the faster is the growth rate of potential GDP (other things remaining the same).

Growth in productivity means getting more output from given inputs (or the same output from fewer inputs). It is measured by the growth in real GDP per hour of labour. The growth in productivity is influenced by three main factors:

1. Growth of the capital stock
2. Growth of human capital
3. Technological change

Suppose one Pepsi plant has two production lines and the other has only one. The plant with two lines has more capital and produces more output than the other. For the economy as a whole, the larger the capital stock, the more productive is the work-force and the greater is the output that it can produce. Also, the faster the capital stock grows, the faster real GDP grows. The capital-rich UK economy produces a vastly greater real GDP per hour of labour than countries that have a small amount of capital, such as the developing countries. But the fast-growing capital stock of the Asian economies is bringing faster real GDP growth than the United Kingdom and other EU countries have achieved.

The manager of one Pepsi plant is an economics graduate with an MBA and its work-force has an average of 10 years' experience. The manager of another identical plant has no business training and its work-force has just been hired and is new to bottling. The first plant has a higher stock of human capital than the second and its output is larger. For the economy as a whole, the larger the stock of *human capital* – the skills that people have acquired at school and through on-the-job training – the greater is real GDP, and the faster the stock of human capital grows, the faster real GDP grows (other things remaining the same).

One Pepsi plant has a production line that was designed in the 1970s before the computer age. Another uses the latest robot technology. Even with a smaller work-force, the second plant produces more bottles per day than the first plant. Technological change – inventing new and better ways of doing things – enables firms to produce more from any given amount of inputs. So even with a constant work-force and constant capital stock, improvements in technology increase production and increase aggregate supply (Chapter 26, pp.659–664). Technological advances have been by far the most important source of increased production over the past two centuries. As a result of technological advances, in the UK today, one farm worker produces enough to feed 60 people in a year, and one carworker can produce 12 cars and trucks in a year.

Changes in Short-run Aggregate Supply All the factors that influence long-run aggregate supply also influence short-run aggregate supply. That is, if potential GDP increases, more real GDP is supplied in the long run but more real GDP is supplied at each price level in the short run. So if potential GDP increases, short-run aggregate supply increases.

The only influences on short-run aggregate supply that do not also change long-run aggregate supply are the money wage rate and the prices of other factors of production. Factor prices affect short-run aggregate supply through their influence on firms' costs. The higher the money wage rate and other factor prices, the higher are firms' costs and the smaller is the quantity that firms are willing to supply at each price level. Thus an increase in the money wage rate and other factor prices decreases short-run aggregate supply.

Why do factor prices affect short-run aggregate supply but not long-run aggregate supply? The answer lies in the definition of long-run aggregate supply. Along the long-run aggregate supply curve real GDP remains constant at potential GDP because when the money wage changes, the price level also changes by the same percentage. So real wages are unchanged and the labour market is back in equilibrium

Shifts in *LAS* and *SAS* Figure 27.4 illustrates changes in long-run aggregate supply and short-run aggregate supply as shifts in the aggregate supply curves. Part (a) shows the effects of a change in potential GDP. Initially, the long-run aggregate supply is LAS_0 and short-run aggregate supply is SAS_0. An increase in labour hours or an increase in productivity increases potential GDP to £575 billion. As a result, the long-run aggregate supply increases and the long-run aggregate supply curve shifts rightward to LAS_1. Short-run aggregate supply also increases and the short-run aggregate supply curve shifts rightward to SAS_1.

Figure 27.4(b) shows the effects of an increase in the money wage rate (or other factor price) on aggregate supply. Initially, the short-run aggregate

FIGURE 27.4

Changes in Aggregate Supply

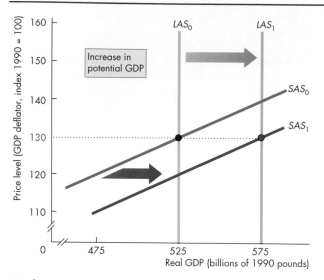

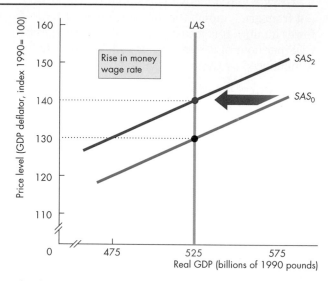

(a) Change in potential GDP shifts LAS and SAS

In part (a), an increase in potential GDP increases both long-run aggregate supply and short-run aggregate supply and shifts both aggregate supply curves rightward from LAS_0 to LAS_1 and from SAS_0 to SAS_1.

(b) Change in the money wage rate shifts SAS

In part (b), a rise in the money wage rate decreases short-run aggregate supply and shifts the short-run aggregate supply curve leftward from SAS_0 to SAS_2. A rise in the money wage rate does not change long-run aggregate supply so the LAS curve does not shift.

supply curve is SAS_0. A rise in the money wage rate *decreases* short-run aggregate supply and shifts the short-run aggregate supply curve leftward to SAS_2. Long-run aggregate supply does not change when the money wage rate changes, so the LAS curve remains at LAS.

REVIEW

◆ On the long-run aggregate supply curve, a change in the price level is accompanied by an equal percent change in the money wage rate and the quantity of real GDP supplied is constant at potential GDP.

◆ On the short-run aggregate supply curve, a rise in the price level with no change in the money wage rate brings an increase in the quantity of real GDP supplied.

◆ An increase in labour hours and an increase in productivity increase potential GDP, which

increases both long-run aggregate supply and short-run aggregate supply and shifts the LAS curve and the SAS curve rightward.

◆ An increase in the money wage rate (or other factor price) decreases short-run aggregate supply but leaves long-run aggregate supply unchanged and shifts the SAS curve leftward.

Aggregate Demand

Real GDP equals aggregate expenditure and aggregate expenditure is the sum of consumption expenditure, investment, government purchases and net exports (see Chapter 23, pp. 577–581). *Aggregate planned expenditure* is the sum of planned consumption expenditure, planned investment, planned government purchases and planned net exports and aggregate planned expenditure equals the *quantity of real GDP demanded*. **Aggregate demand** is the relationship between the quantity of real GDP demanded and the price level (the GDP deflator).

Figure 27.5 illustrates aggregate demand as an aggregate demand schedule and as the downward-sloping curve labelled *AD*. This aggregate demand curve is based on the aggregate demand schedule and each point on the aggregate demand curve corresponds to a row of the aggregate demand schedule. For example, point *c'* on the aggregate demand curve and row *c'* of the aggregate demand schedule tell us that if the price level is 130, the quantity of real GDP demanded is £525 billion.

In constructing the aggregate demand schedule and aggregate demand curve, we hold constant all the influences on the quantity of real GDP demanded other than the price level and the interest rate. As the price level changes, the interest rate also changes (for a reason that is explained below) and there is a movement along the aggregate demand curve. A change in any of the other influences on the quantity of real GDP demanded results in a new aggregate demand schedule and a shift in the aggregate demand curve.

Let's look more closely at the effects of a change in the price level on the quantity of real GDP demanded. You can see from the numbers that describe the aggregate demand schedule that the higher the price level, the smaller is the quantity of real GDP demanded. The aggregate demand curve slopes downward. But why?

Why the Aggregate Demand Curve Slopes Downward

If the price of Pepsi rises, the quantity of Pepsi demanded decreases because some people can't afford to buy as much fizzy drink (an income effect) and because some people switch to drinking Coke and other fizzy drinks (a substitution effect). The demand curve for Pepsi slopes downward because of an income effect and a substitution effect.

The aggregate demand curve slopes downward for analogous reasons. Real GDP has three main substitutes: money, future real GDP and foreign real GDP, and these substitutes give rise to three influences of the price level on the quantity of real GDP demanded:

◆ Real money balances effect

◆ Intertemporal substitution effect

◆ International substitution effect

FIGURE 27.5

Aggregate Demand

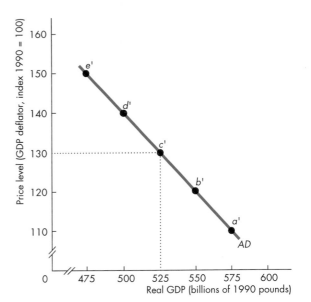

	Price level (GDP deflator)	Real GDP (billions of 1990 pounds)
a'	110	575
b'	120	550
c'	130	525
d'	140	500
e'	150	475

The aggregate demand curve (*AD*) shows the relationship between the quantity of real GDP demanded and the price level. The aggregate demand curve is based on the schedule in the table. Each point *a'* to *e'* on the curve corresponds to the row in the table identified by the same letter. Thus when the price level is 130, the quantity of real GDP demanded is £525 billion, illustrated by point *c'* in the figure.

Real Money Balances Effect **Money** in the United Kingdom is currency and bank and building society deposits – the things you use to buy goods and services and pay bills. In most other countries of the European Union, money is simply currency and bank deposits. **Real money** is the *purchasing power* of money or the quantity of goods and services that money will buy. It is measured by the quantity of money divided by the price level. The

real money balances effect is the change in the quantity of real GDP demanded that results from a change in the quantity of real money. The greater the quantity of real money – the greater the purchasing power of money – the greater is the quantity of real GDP demanded. But the quantity of real money increases if the price level falls, so a fall in the price level brings an increase in the quantity of real GDP demanded and a movement along the aggregate demand curve.

To see how the real money balances effect works, think about your own spending plans. You have £5 to spend, and coffee costs £1 a cup. Your money can buy 5 cups of coffee. But if coffee costs 50 pence a cup, your £5 can buy 10 cups. The lower the price, the more you can buy with a given quantity of money so the greater is your purchasing power. And the greater your purchasing power, the more goods you plan to buy.

The real money balances effect is analogous to the income effect on the demand for individual goods and services. But income is a flow and money is a stock, so the two effects are not identical. The other two reasons for the downward-sloping aggregate demand curve are substitution effects.

Intertemporal Substitution Effect   The **intertemporal substitution effect** is the change in the quantity of real GDP demanded resulting from a change in the *opportunity cost* of goods and services now in terms of goods and services in the future. The main influence in this opportunity cost is the *interest rate*. The higher the interest rate, the greater is the opportunity cost of buying today. By not buying today, but by saving instead, you can earn interest and increase the amount available for spending in the future. The higher the interest rate, the greater is the amount you earn on your savings and the more you can buy in the future. So the higher the interest rate, the greater is the opportunity cost of buying today.

The interest rate is influenced by the price level. The higher the price level, other things remaining the same, the higher is the interest rate. The reason is connected to the *real money balances effect* that you've just learned about. With a higher price level, people have less purchasing power, so the amount they want to lend decreases and the amount they want to borrow increases (again, other things remaining the same). A decrease in the supply of loans and an increase in the demand for loans means that interest rates rise.

So as the price level rises, other things remaining the same, the interest rate also rises and the quantity of real GDP demanded decreases.

International Substitution Effect   The **international substitution effect** is the change in the quantity of real GDP demanded resulting from a change in the *opportunity cost* of domestic goods and services in terms of foreign goods. An example of international substitution is your decision to buy a Fiat car that was made in Italy instead of a Ford Fiesta made in the United Kingdom. Another example is your decision to take a holiday in Spain instead of Cornwall.

The higher the price level in the United Kingdom, other things remaining the same, the higher are the prices of UK-produced goods and services relative to foreign-produced goods and services and the fewer UK-produced goods and services people buy. So the higher the price level, other things remaining the same, the smaller is the quantity of real GDP demanded.

For the three reasons we've just reviewed, the aggregate demand curve slopes downward. The higher the price level in the United Kingdom, the smaller is the quantity demanded of UK-produced goods and services – UK real GDP. The lower the price level in the United Kingdom, the larger is the quantity demanded of UK-produced goods and services – UK real GDP.

Changes in the Quantity of Real GDP Demanded

When the price level changes (and the interest rate changes with it), other things remaining the same, there is a change in the quantity of real GDP demanded. Such a change is illustrated as a movement along the aggregate demand curve. Figure 27.6 illustrates changes in the quantity of real GDP demanded. It also summarizes the three reasons why the aggregate demand curve slopes downward.

We've now seen how the quantity of real GDP demanded changes when the price level (and interest rate) change. How do other influences on spending plans affect aggregate demand?

Changes in Aggregate Demand

The aggregate demand schedule and aggregate demand curve describe aggregate demand at a point in time. But aggregate demand frequently changes.

FIGURE 27.6

Changes in the Quantity of Real GDP Demanded

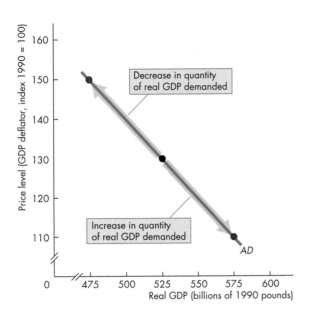

The quantity of real GDP demanded

Decreases if the price level *increases*

Increases if the price level *decreases*

because of the:

Real money balances effect

◆ An increase in the price level decreases the quantity of real money

◆ A decrease in the price level increases the quantity of real money

Intertemporal substitution effect

◆ An increase in the price level increases interest rates

◆ A decrease in the price level decreases interest rates

International substitution effect

◆ An increase in the price level increases the cost of domestic goods and services relative to foreign goods and services

◆ A decrease in the price level decreases the cost of domestic goods and services relative to foreign goods and services

As a consequence, the aggregate demand curve frequently shifts. The main influences on aggregate demand that shift the aggregate demand curve are:

◆ Expectations
◆ International factors
◆ Fiscal policy
◆ Monetary policy

Expectations

Expectations about all aspects of future economic conditions play a crucial role in determining people's decisions about spending on consumer goods and services and business decisions about spending on investment. But three expectations are especially important. They are expectations about future incomes, future inflation and future profits.

Expected Future Incomes An increase in expected future income, other things remaining the same, increases the amount that households plan to spend today on consumption goods and consumer durables and increases aggregate demand. When households expect slow future income growth, or even a decline in income, they scale back their spending plans today and aggregate demand decreases.

Expectations about future income growth were pessimistic during 1990 and this factor contributed to the decrease in spending that brought on the recession in 1991.

Expected Inflation An increase in the expected inflation rate, other things remaining the same, leads to an increase in aggregate demand. The higher the expected inflation rate, the higher is the expected price of goods and services in the future and the lower is the expected real value of money and other financial assets in the future. As a consequence, when people expect a higher inflation rate, they plan to buy more goods and services today and hold smaller quantities of money and other financial assets. As a result, aggregate demand increases.

Inflation expectations increased during the 1970s, and by 1979 people expected inflation in 1980 to rise to around 18 per cent a year. But a severe recession in 1980 reduced inflation and inflation expectations. By the mid-1980s a low future inflation rate was expected. But then, during 1987–88, as the economy expanded quickly, higher inflation became expected.

Expected Future Profits   A change in firms' expected future profit changes their demands for new capital equipment. For example, suppose that there has been a recent wave of technological change that has increased productivity. Firms might expect that large profit opportunities exist from using the latest technology. This expectation leads to an increase in demand for new plant and equipment and so to an increase in aggregate demand.

Profit expectations were pessimistic in 1991 and led to a decrease in aggregate demand. Expectations were optimistic through the mid-1980s and led to sustained increases in aggregate demand.

International Factors

There are two main international factors that influence aggregate demand. They are the foreign exchange rate and foreign income.

The Foreign Exchange Rate   A change in the UK price level, other things remaining the same, changes the prices of domestically produced goods and services *relative* to the prices of goods and services produced in other countries. Another influence on the price of UK-produced goods and services relative to those produced abroad is the *foreign exchange rate*. The foreign exchange rate is the amount of a foreign currency that you can buy with £1. For example, £1 might buy US $1.50.

The foreign exchange rate affects aggregate demand because it affects the prices that foreigners have to pay for UK-produced goods and services and the prices that we have to pay for foreign-produced goods and services. To see how, suppose that £1 is worth 1,200 South Korean won. You can buy a Samsung portable TV (made in South Korea) that costs 180,000 won for £150. What if for the same price you can buy a Ferguson TV (made in the United Kingdom) that is just as good as the Samsung ? In this case, you may be willing buy the Ferguson TV.

But which TV will you buy if the value of the pound rises to 1,250 won and everything else remains the same? Let's work out the answer. At 1,250 won per pound, you pay only £144 to buy the 180,000 won needed to buy the Samsung TV. Since the Ferguson TV costs £150, the Samsung is now cheaper and you will substitute the Samsung for the Ferguson. The demand for UK-made TVs falls as the foreign exchange value of the pound rises. So as the foreign exchange value of the pound rises, everything else remaining the same, aggregate demand decreases.

There have been huge swings in the foreign exchange value of the pound during the 1980s and 1990s, leading to large swings in aggregate demand.

Foreign Income   The income of foreigners affects the aggregate demand for UK-produced goods and services. For example, an increase in income in the United States, Japan and Germany increases the demand by American, Japanese and German consumers and producers for UK-produced consumption goods and capital goods.

The United Kingdom is an open economy, which means that it exports and imports a significant part of its GDP (approximately one-third). Thus these sources of change in aggregate demand have always been important in UK history. The long-term economic growth of the United States, Japan, Western Europe and of some of the newly industrializing countries of the Pacific Rim, such as Hong Kong and Singapore, has led to a sustained increase in demand for UK-produced goods and services. Also, fluctuations in income growth in the rest of the world have contributed to fluctuations in UK aggregate demand.

Fiscal Policy

Fiscal policy is the government's attempt to influence the economy by setting and changing taxes, government spending, and the government's deficit and debt. Fiscal policy influences aggregate demand.

Government Purchases of Goods and Services
The scale of government purchases of goods and services has a direct effect on aggregate demand. If taxes are held constant, the more hospitals, motorways, schools, and colleges the government funds, the larger are government purchases of goods and services and so the larger is aggregate demand. The most important changes in government purchases of goods and services arise from the state of international tension and conflict. In times of war government purchases increase dramatically. In this century, government purchases increased sharply during World Wars I and II and then declined. These changes in spending exerted a large influence on aggregate demand.

Taxes and Transfer Payments   A decrease in taxes increases aggregate demand. An increase in transfer payments – unemployment benefits, social security benefits and welfare payments – also increases aggregate demand. Both of these influences operate by increasing households' *disposable* income. The higher the level of disposable income, the greater is the demand for goods and services. Because lower taxes and higher transfer payments increase disposable income, they also increase aggregate demand.

This source of changes in aggregate demand has been an important one in the post-war period. During the 1980s, the Thatcher government tax cuts increased aggregate demand, and tax increases in the 1990s decreased aggregate demand.

Monetary Policy

Decisions about the money supply and interest rates are made by the Chancellor of the Exchequer in consultation with the governor of the Bank of England. These decisions influence aggregate demand. The government's and Bank of England's attempt to influence the economy by varying the money supply and interest rates is called **monetary policy**.

Money Supply The money supply is determined by the Bank of England and the banks and building societies (in a process described in Chapters 30 and 31). The greater the *quantity of money* the greater is the level of aggregate demand. An easy way to see why money affects aggregate demand is to imagine what would happen if the Bank borrowed the army's helicopters, loaded them with millions of pounds worth of new £10 notes, and sprinkled the notes like confetti across the country. We would all stop whatever we were doing and rush out to pick up our share of the newly available money. But we wouldn't just put the money we picked up in the bank. We would spend some of it, so our demand for goods and services would increase. Although this story is pretty extreme, it does illustrate that an increase in the quantity of money increases aggregate demand.

In practice, changes in the quantity of money are brought about by a change in the interest rate at which the Bank of England is willing to lend to the commercial banks (the bank rate), and so have an additional influence on aggregate demand by changing the amount of investment and the demand for consumer durables. The Bank speeds up the rate at which new money is being injected into the economy by lowering the bank rate, banks

have more funds to lend and interest rates fall. The Bank slows down the pace at which it is creating money by raising the bank rate, commercial banks have less funds to lend and interest rates rise. Thus a change in the quantity of money has a second effect on aggregate demand, operating through its effects on commercial bank interest rates.

Interest Rates If the Bank of England increases interest rates, households and firms change their borrowing, lending and spending plans. They try to borrow less, lend more and cut back their spending on durable goods – investment. The cut in spending on durable goods is a decrease in aggregate demand.

Fluctuations in the quantity of money and interest rates have been important sources of changes in aggregate demand. Rapid increases in the quantity of money through the 1970s made aggregate demand increase quickly and contributed to the inflation of those years; decreases in the growth rate of the quantity of money in 1980–83 and 1991–93 slowed aggregate demand growth and contributed to the recessions of those years.

Now that we've reviewed the factors that influence aggregate demand, let's summarize their effects on the aggregate demand curve.

Shifts of the Aggregate Demand Curve

We illustrate a change in aggregate demand as a shift in the aggregate demand curve. Figure 27.7 illustrates two changes in aggregate demand, and summarizes the factors bringing about such changes. Aggregate demand is initially AD_0, the same as in Fig. 27.5.

The aggregate demand curve shifts rightward, from AD_0 to AD_1 when expected future profit increases, the expected inflation rate increases, the foreign exchange rate falls, income in the rest of the world increases, government purchases of goods and services increase, taxes are cut, transfer payments increase, or the money supply increases and interest rates fall.

The aggregate demand curve shifts leftward, from AD_0 to AD_2, when expected future profit decreases, the expected inflation rate decreases, the foreign exchange rate rises, income in the rest of the world decreases, government purchases of goods and services decrease, taxes are increased, transfer payments decrease, or the money supply decreases and interest rates rise.

FIGURE 27.7

Changes in Aggregate Demand

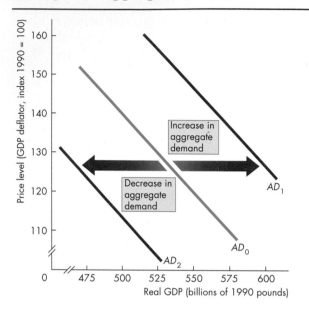

Aggregate demand

Decreases if

◆ Expected inflation
  or expected profits
  decrease

◆ The exchange rate
  increases or
  foreign income
  decreases

◆ Fiscal policy decreases
  government spending or
  increases taxes

◆ Monetary policy
  decreases the money supply
  and increases interest rates

Increases if

◆ Expected inflation
  or expected profits
  increase

◆ The exchange rate
  decreases or
  foreign income
  increases

◆ Fiscal policy increases
  government spending or
  decreases taxes

◆ Monetary policy
  increases the money supply
  and decreases interest rates

R E V I E W

◆ The aggregate demand curve shows the effect of
  a change in the price level on the quantity of real
  GDP demanded, other things remaining the same.

◆ An increase in the price level brings a decrease
  in the quantity of real GDP demanded because
  it decreases the quantity of real money balances, increases the price of goods in the
  present relative to goods in the future, and

increases the price of domestic goods relative to
foreign goods.

◆ Other influences on aggregate spending plans
  (expectations, international factors, fiscal policy
  and monetary policy) change aggregate demand
  and shift the aggregate demand curve.

Macroeconomic Equilibrium

The purpose of the aggregate supply–aggregate
demand model is to understand and predict
changes in real GDP and the price level. To achieve
this purpose, we combine aggregate supply and
aggregate demand and determine macroeconomic
equilibrium. There is a macroeconomic equilibrium
for each of the time-frames for aggregate supply: a
long-run equilibrium and a short-run equilibrium.
Long-run equilibrium is the state towards which the
economy is heading. Short-run equilibrium describes
the state of the economy at each point in time on its
path towards long-run macroeconomic equilibrium.
We'll begin our study of macroeconomic equilibrium
by looking at the short run.

Determination of Real GDP and the Price Level

The aggregate demand curve tells us the quantity
of real GDP demanded at each price level, and the
short-run aggregate supply curve tells us the
quantity of real GDP supplied at each price level.
Short-run macroeconomic equilibrium occurs
when the quantity of real GDP demanded equals the
short-run quantity of real GDP supplied at the point
of intersection of the *AD* curve and the *SAS* curve.
Figure 27.8 illustrates such an equilibrium at a
price level of 130 and real GDP of £525 billion
(point *c* and *c'*).

To see why this position is an equilibrium, let's
work out what happens if the price level is something other than 130. Suppose, for example, that
the price level is 140 and that real GDP is £575 billion (at point *e*) on the *SAS* curve. The quantity of
real GDP demanded is less than £575 billion so
firms are unable to sell all their output. Unwanted
stocks pile up and firms cut both production and
prices. Production and prices are cut until firms can
sell all their output. This situation occurs only when
real GDP is £525 billion and the price level is 130.

FIGURE 27.8

Short-run Macroeconomic Equilibrium

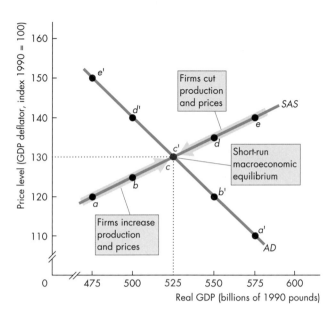

Short-run macroeconomic equilibrium occurs when real GDP demanded equals real GDP supplied at the intersection of the aggregate demand curve (*AD*) and the short-run aggregate supply curve (*SAS*). Here, such an equilibrium occurs at points *c* and *c'* where the price level is 130 and real GDP is £525 billion. If the price level was 140 and real GDP was £550 billion, point *e*, firms would not be able to sell all their output. They would decrease production and cut prices. If the price level was 120 and real GDP was £500 billion, point *b*, people would not be able to buy all the goods they demanded. Firms would increase production and raise their prices. Only when the price level is 130 and real GDP is £525 billion can firms sell all they produce and people buy all they demand. This is the short-run macroeconomic equilibrium.

Next consider what happens if the price level is 120 and real GDP is £475 billion (at point *a*) on the *SAS* curve. The quantity of real GDP demanded exceeds £475 billion so firms are not able to meet demand. Stocks are running out and customers are clamouring for goods. So firms increase production and raise their prices. Production and prices are increased until firms can meet demand. This situation occurs only when real GDP is £525 billion and the price level is 130.

Short-run Macroeconomic Equilibrium and Full Employment

Short-run macroeconomic equilibrium does not necessarily occur at full employment. At full employment, the economy is on its *long-run* aggregate supply curve. But short-run macroeconomic equilibrium occurs at the intersection of the *short-run* aggregate supply curve and the aggregate demand curve and can occur at, below, or above potential GDP. We can see this fact by considering the three possible cases shown in Fig. 27.9.

In part (a) there is a below full-employment equilibrium. A **below full-employment equilibrium** is a macroeconomic equilibrium in which potential GDP exceeds real GDP. The amount by which potential GDP exceeds real GDP is called a **recessionary gap**. This name reminds us that a gap has opened up between potential GDP and real GDP either because the economy has experienced a recession or because real GDP, while growing, has grown more slowly than the long-term growth rate.

The below full-employment equilibrium illustrated in Fig. 27.9(a) occurs where aggregate demand curve AD_0 intersects short-run aggregate supply curve SAS_0 at a real GDP of £475 billion and a price level of 130. The recessionary gap is £50 billion. The UK economy was in a situation similar to that shown in Fig. 27.9(a) in 1980–81 and again in 1991–92. In those years, unemployment was high and real GDP was less than potential GDP.

Figure 27.9(b) is an example of full-employment equilibrium. **Full-employment equilibrium** is a macroeconomic equilibrium in which real GDP equals potential GDP. In this example, the equilibrium occurs where the aggregate demand curve AD_1 intersects the short-run aggregate supply curve SAS_1 at an actual and potential GDP of £525 billion. The economy was in a situation such as that shown in Fig. 27.9(b) in 1986.

Figure 27.9(c) illustrates an above full-employment equilibrium. An **above full-employment equilibrium** is a macroeconomic equilibrium in which real GDP exceeds potential GDP. The amount by which real GDP exceeds potential GDP is called an **inflationary gap**. This name reminds us that a gap has opened up between real GDP and potential GDP which is placing inflationary pressure on the economy.

The above full-employment equilibrium illustrated in Fig. 27.9(c) occurs where the aggregate demand curve AD_2 intersects the short-run aggregate supply

FIGURE 27.9

Three Types of Macroeconomic Equilibrium

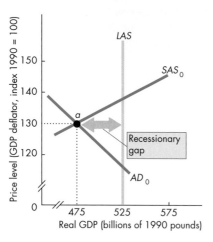

(a) Below full-employment equilibrium

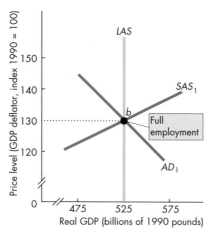

(b) Full-employment equilibrium

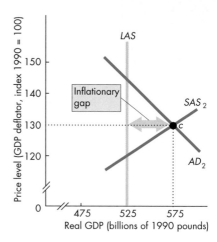

(c) Above full-employment equilibrium

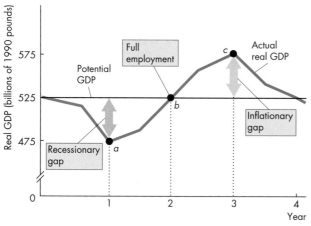

(d) Fluctuations in real GDP

Part (a) shows a below full-employment equilibrium, part (b) shows a full-employment equilibrium, part (c) shows an above full-employment equilibrium and part (d) shows how real GDP fluctuates around potential GDP in a business cycle. In year 1, there is a recessionary gap and the economy is at point *a* (in parts a and d). In year 2, there is full employment and the economy is at point *b* (in parts b and d). In year 3, there is an inflationary gap and the economy is at point *c* (in parts c and d).

curve SAS_2 at a real GDP of £575 billion and a price level of 130. There is an inflationary gap of £50 billion. The economy was in a situation similar to that depicted in part (c) in 1987–89.

The economy moves from one type of equilibrium to another as a result of fluctuations in aggregate demand and in short-run aggregate supply. These fluctuations produce fluctuations in real GDP and the price level. Figure 27.9(d) shows how real GDP fluctuates around potential GDP.

Long-term Growth and Inflation

Long-term economic growth comes about because, over time, the long-run aggregate supply curve shifts rightward. The pace at which it shifts is determined by the growth rate of potential GDP (see Chapter 26 pp.655).

Inflation comes about because, over time, the aggregate demand curve shifts rightward at a faster pace than the shift in the long-run aggregate supply curve. The pace at which it shifts is determined mainly by the growth rate of the quantity of money. At times when the quantity of money is increasing rapidly, aggregate demand is increasing quickly and the inflation rate is high. When the growth rate of the quantity of money slows down, other things remaining the same, the inflation rate eventually slows down.

But the economy does not experience steady real GDP growth and steady inflation. Instead, it fluctuates around its long-term growth path and its long-term inflation rate. When we study these fluctuations, we ignore the long-term trends. We examine how GDP and the price level are determined in a model economy that has no trends. By ignoring the trends, we can see the short-term fluctuations more clearly.

Let's now look at some of the sources of fluctuations around the long-term trends.

Fluctuations in Aggregate Demand

We're going to work out how real GDP and the price level change following an increase in aggregate demand. Let's suppose that the economy starts out at full employment and, as illustrated in Fig. 27.10(a), is producing £525 billion worth of goods and services at a price level of 130. The economy is on the aggregate demand curve AD_0, the short-run aggregate supply curve SAS_0 and the long-run aggregate supply curve LAS.

Now suppose that the world economy grows more quickly and the demand for UK-made goods increases in Japan and the United States. The increase in exports increases aggregate demand and the aggregate demand curve shifts rightward. Suppose that the aggregate demand curve shifts from AD_0 to AD_1 in Fig. 27.10(a).

Faced with an increase in demand firms increase production and raise prices. For the economy as a whole, real GDP increases and the price level rises. Real GDP rises to £550 billion and the price level rises to 135. In this short-run macroeconomic equilibrium, firms are producing the quantities they want to produce, given the price level and the money wage rate. But the economy is at an above full-employment equilibrium. Real GDP exceeds potential GDP, and there is an inflationary gap.

The increase in aggregate demand has increased the prices of all goods and services. Faced with higher prices, firms have increased their output rates. At this stage, prices of goods and services

have increased but wage rates have not changed. (Recall that as we move along a short-run aggregate supply curve, wage rates are constant.)

The economy cannot produce in excess of potential GDP for ever. Why not? What are the forces at work that bring real GDP back to potential GDP and restore full employment?

If the price level has increased and wage rates have remained constant, workers have experienced a fall in the purchasing power of their wages. Furthermore, firms have experienced an increase in revenue and no change in their costs. Firms' profits have increased. In these circumstances, workers demand higher wages, and firms, anxious to maintain their employment and output levels, meet those demands. If firms do not raise wage rates, they either lose workers or have to hire less productive ones.

As wage rates rise, the short-run aggregate supply curve begins to shift leftward. In Fig. 27.10(b), the short-run aggregate supply curve moves from SAS_0 towards SAS_1. The rise in wages and the shift in the SAS curve produce a sequence of new equilibrium positions. Along the adjustment path, real GDP falls and the price level rises and the economy moves up along its aggregate demand curve as shown by the arrow heads in the figure. Eventually, wages will have risen by so much that the SAS curve is SAS_1. At this time, the aggregate demand curve AD_1 intersects SAS_1 at a full-employment equilibrium. The price level has risen to 145, and real GDP is back where it started, at potential GDP. Unemployment is again at its natural rate.

Throughout the adjustment process, higher wage rates raise firms' costs and, with rising costs, firms offer a smaller quantity of goods and services for sale at any given price level. By the time the adjustment is over, firms are producing the same amount as they initially produced, but at higher prices and higher costs.

We've just worked out the effects of an increase in aggregate demand. A decrease in aggregate demand has similar but opposite effects to those that we've just studied. That is, a decrease in aggregate demand decreases real GDP to less than potential GDP and unemployment increases above its natural rate. A recessionary gap emerges. Firms cut prices. The lower price level increases the purchasing power of wages, and increases firms' costs relative to their output prices because wages remain unchanged. Eventually, the slack economy leads to falling wage rates and the short-run aggregate supply curve

FIGURE 27.10

An Increase in Aggregate Demand

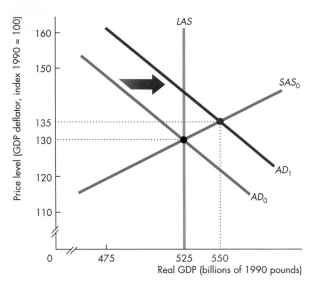

(a) Short-run effect

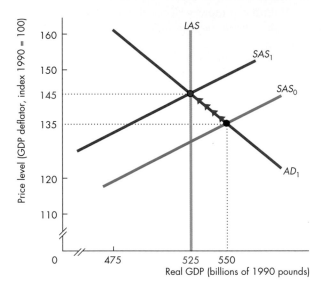

(b) Long-run effect

An increase in aggregate demand shifts the aggregate demand curve from AD_0 to AD_1. Initially (part a), with sticky prices, real GDP increases from £525 billion to £550 billion along the SAS curve. Firms start to raise their prices and cut back production (part b) and the SAS curve shifts upward. In the short-run equilibrium, real GDP is £550 billion and the price level rises to 135. In this situation, there

is an inflationary gap. The money wage rate rises and the short-run aggregate supply curve shifts leftward from SAS_0 to SAS_1 in part (b). As it shifts, it intersects the aggregate demand curve AD_1 at higher price levels and lower real GDP levels. Eventually, the price level rises to 145 and real GDP falls back to £525 billion – potential GDP and full employment.

shifts rightward. Real GDP gradually returns to potential GDP and full employment is restored. But the adjustment process will take a long time to complete because firms and workers will resist decreasing prices and wages.

You've seen how a change in aggregate demand changes real GDP and the price level. Let's now work out how real GDP and the price level change when aggregate supply changes.

Fluctuations in Aggregate Supply

Fluctuations in short-run aggregate supply can bring fluctuations in real GDP around potential GDP. We'll study a decrease in aggregate supply. Suppose that initially, real GDP equals potential GDP. Then there is a large but temporary rise in the

money price of raw materials. (Similar to an increase in the price of oil as in 1973–74 and again in 1979–80 when OPEC used its market muscle). What happens to real GDP and the price level?

Figure 27.11 shows the effects of this rise in the price of raw materials. The aggregate demand curve is AD_0, the short-run aggregate supply curve is SAS_0 and the long-run aggregate supply curve is LAS_0. Equilibrium real GDP is $525 billion, which equals potential GDP, and the price level is 130. Then the price of oil rises. Faced with a higher price of raw materials, firms' costs rise and they decrease production. Short-run aggregate supply decreases, and the short-run aggregate supply curve shifts leftward to SAS_1.

As a result of this decrease in short-run aggregate supply, the economy moves to a new

FIGURE 27.11

A Decrease in Aggregate Supply

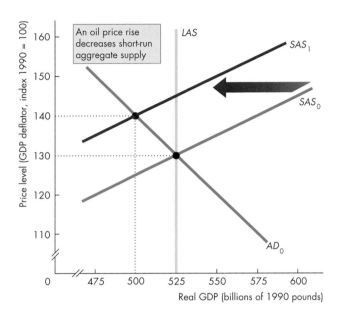

An increase in the price of oil decreases short-run aggregate supply and shifts the short-run aggregate supply curve leftward from SAS_0 to SAS_1. Real GDP falls from £525 billion to £500 billion and the price level increases from 130 to 140. The economy experiences both recession and inflation – stagflation.

keep on raising the price of oil and keep the relative price of oil high, potential GDP will fall and the economy will get stuck with a permanently lower level of real GDP.

◆ Short-run macroeconomic equilibrium explains how real GDP and the price level change over time.

◆ There are three types of short-run macroeconomic equilibrium: (1) below full-employment equilibrium (a situation in which potential GDP exceeds real GDP and there is a recessionary gap); (2) full-employment equilibrium (a situation in which real GDP equals potential GDP); (3) above full-employment equilibrium (a situation in which real GDP exceeds potential GDP and there is an inflationary gap).

◆ The price level fluctuates and real GDP fluctuates around potential GDP because of fluctuations in aggregate demand and short-run aggregate supply.

We've now seen how changes in aggregate supply and aggregate demand influence real GDP and the price level. Let's put our new knowledge to work and see how it helps us understand macroeconomic performance.

equilibrium where SAS_1 intersects the aggregate demand curve AD_0. The price level rises to 140, and real GDP decreases to £500 billion. Because real GDP falls, the economy experiences recession. Because the price level increases, the economy experiences inflation. Such a combination of recession and inflation – called *stagflation* – actually occurred in the mid-1970s.

Where the economy goes from this short-run equilibrium depends on whether aggregate demand changes. If aggregate demand does not change, the price of oil might eventually fall. Also, with real GDP below potential GDP and unemployment above the natural rate, the money wage rate might fall. But these adjustments are likely to take a long time. It is more likely that aggregate demand will eventually increase, in which case real GDP will increase and the price level will rise. As the price level increases, the relative price of oil falls. But if the oil producers

Long-term Growth, Inflation, and Cycles in the UK Economy

The economy is continually changing. If you imagine the economy as a video, then an aggregate supply–aggregate demand figure such as Fig. 27.11 is a freeze-frame. We're going to run the video – an instant replay – but keep our finger on the freeze-frame button, looking at some important parts of the previous action. Let's run the video from 1960.

Figure 27.12 shows the state of the economy in 1960 at the point of intersection of its aggregate demand curve AD_{60} and short-run aggregate supply curve SAS_{60}. Real GDP was £230 billion and the GDP deflator was 10 (less than one-tenth of its 1994 level).

FIGURE 27.12

Aggregate Supply and Aggregate Demand: 1960–1994

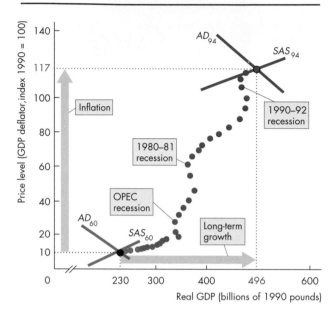

Each point indicates the value of the GDP deflator and real GDP in a given year. In 1960, these variables were determined by the intersection of the aggregate demand curve AD_{60} and the short-run aggregate supply curve SAS_{60}. Each point is generated by the gradual shifting of the AD and SAS curves. By 1994, the curves were AD_{94} and SAS_{94}. Real GDP grew and the price level increased. But growth and inflation did not proceed smoothly. Real GDP grew quickly and inflation was moderate in the 1960s; real GDP growth sagged in 1974–75 and again, more strongly, in 1980–81. The 1974–75 slowdown was caused by an unusually sharp increase in oil prices. The 1980–81 recession was caused by a sharp slowdown in the growth of aggregate demand, which resulted mainly from Mrs Thatcher's tough monetary policy. Inflation was rapid during the 1970s but slowed after the 1980–81 recession. The period from 1982 to 1989 was one of strong, persistent recovery. A recession began in 1990 and a small recovery took place in 1994.

By 1994, the economy had reached the point marked by the intersection of aggregate demand curve AD_{94} and short-run aggregate supply curve SAS_{94}. Real GDP was £496 billion and the GDP deflator was 117.

There are three important features of the economy's path traced by the points:

◆ Long-term growth

◆ Inflation

◆ Cycles

Long-term Growth Over the years, real GDP grows – shown in Fig. 27.12 by the rightward movement of the points. The more rapid the growth rate of real GDP, the larger is the horizontal distance between successive dots in the figure. The force generating long-term growth is an increase in long-run aggregate supply. And long-run aggregate supply increases because of work-force growth, the accumulation of capital – both physical plant and equipment and human capital – the discovery of new resources and technological change.

Inflation The price level rises over the years – shown in Fig. 27.12 by the upward movement of the points. The more rapid the inflation rate, the larger is the vertical distance between successive dots in the figure. The main force generating the persistent increase in the price level is a tendency for aggregate demand to increase at a faster pace than the increase in long-run aggregate supply. All of the factors that increase aggregate demand and shift the aggregate demand curve influence the pace of inflation. But one factor – the growth of the quantity of money – is the most important source of *persistent* increases in aggregate demand and persistent inflation.

Cycles Over the years, the economy grows and shrinks in cycles – shown in Fig. 27.12 by the wave-like pattern made by the points, with recessions highlighted in red. The cycles arise because both the expansion of short-run aggregate supply and the growth of aggregate demand do not proceed at a fixed, steady pace. Although the economy has cycles, recessions do not usually follow quickly on the heels of their predecessors; 'double-dip' recessions like the one in the cartoon are rare.

The Evolving Economy: 1960–1994

During the 1960s, real GDP growth was rapid and inflation was low. This was a period of rapid increases in aggregate supply and of moderate increases in aggregate demand.

The mid-1970s were years of rapid inflation and recession – of stagflation. The major sources of these developments were a series of massive oil price increases and domestic supply side factors that produced X-inefficiency in production that shifted the short-run aggregate supply curve leftward, and rapid increases in the quantity of money that shifted the aggregate demand curve rightward. Recession occurred because the aggregate supply

"it appears to be levelling out, cause for optimism perhaps!"

Drawing by Brian Tyrer.

curve shifted leftward at a faster pace than the aggregate demand shifted rightward.

The rest of the 1970s saw high inflation – the price level increased quickly – and only moderate growth in real GDP. This inflation was the product of the government through the Bank of England increasing the money supply (known as monetary accommodation) in response to increasing union militancy. What started off as the result of the oil price shock was continued by the unions in the United Kingdom, with wages being demanded in excess of productivity. The government had the choice of whether to accommodate the wage claims by expanding aggregate demand or to let the rise in wages take its toll on the labour market. Rising wages also responded to rising prices (and expectations of rising prices) which in turn resulted from an expansionary monetary policy. Up until the late 1970s the government chose accommodation. In 1979 there was a change in government and a change in policy.

In June 1979 the new government of Mrs Thatcher introduced a policy to keep aggregate demand growth in check. In Fig. 27.12, you can see the effects of Mrs Thatcher's actions in 1980–81. In this period, most people expected high inflation to persist, and wages grew at a rate consistent with

those expectations. The short-run aggregate supply curve shifted leftward. Aggregate demand increased only a little, but not fast enough to make inflation as high as most people expected. As a consequence, during 1980–81 the leftward shift of the short-run aggregate supply curve was so strong relative to the growth of aggregate demand that the economy went into a deep recession.

Improved capital accumulation and steady technological advance played only a small part in the recovery in growth performance in the United Kingdom during 1982–90. The main factor in the recovery in long-term growth was the supply side policies of Mrs Thatcher. A combination of industrial relations legislation, which weakened the power of trade unions and altered work practices, lower direct taxes and greater competition through deregulation of markets (and privatization) resulted in a sustained rightward shift of the long-run aggregate supply curve. Wage growth was moderate and the short-run aggregate supply curve also shifted rightward. Aggregate demand growth kept pace with the growth of aggregate supply. Sustained-but-steady growth in aggregate supply and aggregate demand kept real GDP growing and inflation steady up until 1986–87. The economy moved from a recession with real GDP less than potential GDP in 1980–81 to above full-employment in 1987–90. Inflation began to rise during this period and it was in this condition when a decrease in aggregate demand led to the 1990–92 recession. The economy again embarked on a path of expansion during 1994 but faltered in 1995. A pick up in the economy in 1996 created a policy dilemma for the government, which is explained in *Reading Between the Lines* on pp. 704–705.

◆ ◆ ◆ ◆ The aggregate supply–aggregate demand model can be used to understand long-term growth, inflation and business cycles. The model is a useful one because it enables us to keep our eye on the big picture – on the broad trends and cycles in inflation and real GDP. But the model lacks detail. It does not tell us as much as we need to know about the components of aggregate demand – consumption, investment, government purchases of goods and services, and exports and imports. It doesn't tell us what determines interest rates or wage rates or even, directly, what determines employment and unemployment. In the following chapters, we're going to start to fill in that detail.

Aggregate Supply and Aggregate Demand in Action

The Essence of the Story

THE SUNDAY TIMES, 28 JULY 1996

Hotting up but this is not 1988 all over again

David Smith

The spectre of 1988 casts a long shadow over British economic policy. When consumer spending rises, and the housing market lifts itself off the floor, many people become twitchy. When this is combined with rapid money-supply growth and stock-market turbulence, those same people nod knowingly and say: 'Here we go again.'

Last week's news that non-food retail sales in the April-June quarter grew at their fastest rate since September 1988 – up 2.4% on the previous three months – got the twitchers agitated....

The big question then, is straightforward. Is this 1988, or something like it, all over again? Let us have a look at the evidence.

The most obvious echoes of that earlier period are the strength of consumer spending, low interest rates (in 1988 they dropped to 7.5%) and Tim Congdon tolling the warning bell of runaway money-supply growth.

Perky though consumer spending is, however, it is a mere shadow of the late 1980s. In 1988, consumer spending rose 7.5%. Over the 1985-89 period its growth averaged more than 5%. By comparison, the Treasury predicts 3.25% growth this year, picking up to 4.25% next. Combining the rise in consumer demand this year and next thus gives a similar growth rate to that achieved in the single year of 1988....

Then, growth was associated with rising prices and retailers' margins. This time, stores gain their volume by holding down prices. In some sectors, such as clothing and electrical goods, this summer's prices are below last year's. The price-resistant consumer, who emerged in the 1990-92 recession and who was reinforced in his or her behaviour during the subsequent tax-raising period, is still with us.

But what about interest rates? Last week Nationwide building society grabbed a few headlines and struck a blow for mutuality by cutting its mortgage rate a quarter of a point to 6.49%, the lowest since the mid-1960s. ...And, whereas 7.5% was achieved only briefly in 1988, rates in the current cycle have been 6.75% or below since January 1993.

The difference in real interest rates, of course, is less marked. In May 1988 inflation was 4.2%, compared with a 2.1% headline rate now. One could argue, in fact, that real interest rates are higher now than they were then.

The thing about the low rates then was that they were dangerously, and mistakenly, low. Surely, even low rates now must be dangerous? I think not.

One of the key factors in the late 1980s boom, which reached its zenith in 1988, was that consumers were experimenting with the new freedoms that were the product of financial liberalisation....

But we are still in the backwash of the liberalisation. People may not have cut their debt burden much in recent years, but they have been reluctant to add to it. And, despite a modest upturn in consumer credit and mortgage lending, this remains the prevailing consideration....

So this is not 1988 all over again.

■ The first half of 1996 saw a rise in consumer spending and rapid growth in consumer credit. The housing market was reviving and share prices were rising sharply.

■ The question the article poses is whether the signs of 1996 represent a repeat of the recent history of an overheating economy in 1988.

■ 1988 was the beginning of a strong consumer boom. An abundance of credit following the deregulation of the banking system enabled households to increase their debt. Expenditure grew in April–June 1996 at the fastest rate since September 1988.

■ Interest rates fell to a low of 7.5 per cent in 1988 and house prices rose rapidly, as did inflation.

■ A comparison of the two periods suggests that 1996 is not like 1988. The economy has changed fundamentally since then.

Economic Analysis

■ The article considers the similarities and differences between 1996 and 1988. From Fig. 1 we can see that inflation was slightly higher in 1988 than in 1996.

■ The article points out that inflation in May 1988 was 4.2 per cent compared with 2.1 per cent in mid-1996. Real mortgage interest rates were 3.3 per cent in 1988 and 4.39 per cent in 1996.

■ House prices rose rapidly, peaking at an annual rate of 35 per cent between 1988 and 1989, but although house prices began to rise in 1996, it is not like 1988.

■ The important difference is the phase of the business cycle. Figure 2 shows real GDP and potential GDP. In 1988, the economy was overheating with real GDP above potential GDP. In 1996, real GDP was still below potential GDP.

■ Figure 3 shows the situation in 1988. In 1988, aggregate demand had increased in excess of potential GDP. This is shown at the intersection of AD_{88} and SAS_{88}. With the inflationary gap indicated in Fig. 3, the inflation rate would rise further.

■ Figure 4 shows the situation in 1996. An increase in aggregate demand shifted the AD curve to AD_{95}, but the increase in potential GDP is seen as a shift from LAS_{91} to LAS_{95}. The recessionary gap will cause the money wage rate to fall or rise very slowly and therefore the inflationary pressures are likely to be moderate. This is the point that is made about 'labour market flexibility'. The recessionary gap will help to keep wage costs down.

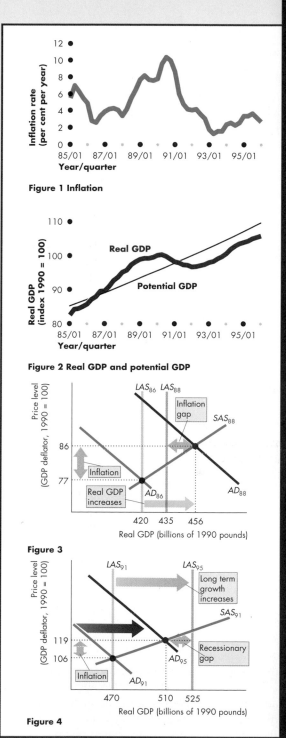

Figure 1 Inflation

Figure 2 Real GDP and potential GDP

Figure 3

Figure 4

SUMMARY

Aggregate Supply

There are two macroeconomic time-frames: the long run and the short run. In the long run, real GDP equals potential GDP and there is full employment. In the short run, real GDP deviates from potential GDP.

Long-run aggregate supply is the relationship between the quantity of real GDP supplied and the price level when real GDP equals potential GDP and there is full employment. The long-run aggregate supply curve is vertical – long-run aggregate supply is independent of the price level – at potential GDP. Long-run aggregate supply changes only when potential GDP changes.

Short-run aggregate supply is the relationship between the quantity of real GDP supplied and the price level when wage rates and other factor prices are constant. The short-run aggregate supply curve is upward-sloping – with factor prices and all other influences on supply held constant, the higher the price level, the larger is the output that firms plan to supply. Short-run aggregate supply changes when factor prices change and when potential GDP changes. (pp.686–690)

Aggregate Demand

Aggregate demand is the relationship between the quantity of real GDP demanded and the price level holding all other influences constant. Other things held constant, the higher the price level, the smaller is the quantity of real GDP demanded – the aggregate demand curve slopes downward. The aggregate demand curve slopes downward for three reasons: money and goods are substitutes (*real money balances effect*); goods today and goods in the future are substitutes (*intertemporal substitution effect*); domestic goods and foreign goods are substitutes (*international substitution effect*).

The main factors that change aggregate demand – and shift the aggregate demand curve – are expectations (especially expectations about future inflation and profits), international factors (economic conditions in the rest of the world and the foreign exchange rate), fiscal policy (government purchases of goods and services and taxes) and monetary policy (the money supply and interest rates). (pp.690–696)

Macroeconomic Equilibrium

In a long-run macroeconomic equilibrium, real GDP equals potential GDP and aggregate demand determines the price level. In a sticky-price equilibrium, the price level is stuck at its current level and aggregate demand determines real GDP. In a short-run macroeconomic equilibrium, real GDP and the price level are determined simultaneously by the interaction of aggregate demand and short-run aggregate supply. Short-run macroeconomic equilibrium tells us how real GDP and the price level evolve.

Short-run macroeconomic equilibrium does not always occur at potential GDP and full employment – that is, at a point on the long-run aggregate supply curve. Below full-employment equilibrium occurs when equilibrium real GDP is less than potential GDP. There is a recessionary gap and unemployment exceeds its natural rate. When equilibrium real GDP exceeds potential GDP, there is an inflationary gap and unemployment is less than its natural rate.

Long-term growth of real GDP occurs because the *LAS* curve shifts rightward as potential GDP increases. Inflation occurs because growth in the quantity of money makes the *AD* curve shift rightward more quickly than the *LAS* curve shifts.

Fluctuations in aggregate demand and short-run aggregate supply bring fluctuations in the price level and deviations of real GDP from potential GDP. An increase in aggregate demand shifts the aggregate demand curve rightward and initially increases real GDP and the price level to a short-run macroeconomic equilibrium. When real GDP exceeds potential GDP, the money wage rate rises and short-run aggregate supply decreases. The *SAS* curve shifts leftward. The leftward shift of the short-run aggregate supply curve results in a yet higher price level and lower real GDP. Eventually, real GDP returns to equal potential GDP.

An increase in factor prices decreases short-run aggregate supply and shifts the short-run aggregate supply curve leftward. Real GDP decreases and the price level rises – stagflation. (pp.696–701)

Long-term Growth, Inflation and Cycles in the UK Economy

Long-term growth is the growth of potential GDP. Inflation persists in the economy because of steady increases in aggregate demand brought about by increases in the quantity of money. The economy experiences cycles because the short-run aggregate supply and aggregate demand curves shift at an uneven pace.

Large oil price hikes in 1973 and 1974 signalled the beginning of stagflation. Union militancy coupled with government accommodation using expansionary monetary policy intensified the infla-

tionary situation. Restraint in aggregate demand growth in 1980 and 1981 resulted in a severe recession in those years. This recession resulted in lower real GDP and a lower inflation rate. Moderate increases in wage rates and steady technological advance and capital accumulation resulted in a sustained expansion from 1982 to 1989. A slowdown in aggregate demand growth brought recession in 1991. (pp. 701–703)

K E Y   E L E M E N T S

Key Terms

Above full-employment equilibrium, 697
Aggregate demand, 690
Below full-employment equilibrium, 697
Fiscal policy, 694
Full-employment equilibrium, 697
Inflationary gap, 697
International substitution effect, 692
Intertemporal substitution effect, 692
Long-run aggregate supply curve, 686
Macroeconomic long run, 686
Macroeconomic short-run, 687
Monetary policy, 695
Money, 691
Real money, 691
Real money balances effect, 692
Recessionary gap, 697
Short-run aggregate supply curve, 687
Short-run macroeconomic equilibrium, 696

◆ Key Figures

Figure 27.2   Short-run Aggregate Supply, 687
Figure 27.3   Movements Along the Aggregate Supply Curves, 688
Figure 27.4   Changes in Aggregate Supply, 690
Figure 27.5   Aggregate Demand, 691
Figure 27.6   Changes in the Quantity of Real GDP Demanded, 693
Figure 27.7   Changes in Aggregate Demand, 696
Figure 27.8   Short-run Macroeconomic Equilibrium, 697
Figure 27.9   Three Types of Macroeconomic Equilibrium, 698
Figure 27.10 An Increase in Aggregate Demand, 700
Figure 27.11 A Decrease in Aggregate Supply, 701

R E V I E W   Q U E S T I O N S

1 Name and distinguish between two macroeconomic time-frames.

2 What is long-run aggregate supply?

3 What is short-run aggregate supply?

4 Distinguish between short-run aggregate supply and long-run aggregate supply.

5 Consider the following events:

   a Potential GDP increases

   b The money wage rate rises

   c The price level rises

   d The money wage rate and the price level rise by the same percentages

Say which of these events, if any, change: (1) long-run aggregate supply but not short-run aggregate supply; (2) short-run aggregate supply but not long-run aggregate supply; (3) both short-run aggregate supply and long-run aggregate supply; and which, if any, bring a movement along (4) the long-run aggregate supply curve, (5) the short-run aggregate supply curve; and (6) both the short-run and the long-run aggregate supply curves.

6 What is aggregate demand?

7 What is the difference between aggregate demand, the quantity of real GDP demanded and aggregate planned expenditure?

8 List the main factors that affect aggregate demand. Separate them into those that increase aggregate demand and those that decrease it.

9 Which of the following do not affect aggregate demand:

a Quantity of money?
b Interest rates?
c Technological change?
d Human capital?

10 Define short-run macroeconomic equilibrium.

11 Distinguish between a below full-employment equilibrium and full-employment equilibrium.

12 Work out the initial, the short-run and the long-run effects of an increase in the quantity of money on the price level and real GDP.

13 Work out the short-run effect of an increase in the price of oil on the price level and real GDP.

14 What are the main factors generating growth of real GDP in the UK economy?

15 What are the main factors generating persistent inflation in the UK economy?

PROBLEMS

1 The following events occur that influence the economy of Yahooland:

♦ A deep recession hits the world economy
♦ Oil prices rise sharply
♦ Firms expect a downturn in the economy in the future

Yahooland is an oil importer.

a Explain the separate effects of each of these events on real GDP and the price level in Yahooland, starting from a position of long-run equilibrium.

b Explain the combined effects of these events on real GDP and the price level in Yahooland, starting from a position of long-run equilibrium.

c Explain what the government of Yahooland can do to overcome the problems faced by the economy.

2 The following events occur that influence the economy of Lilliput:

♦ A strong expansion of the world economy
♦ The government of Lilliput raise taxes
♦ Businesses expect profits to fall in the near future

a Explain the separate effects of each of these events on real GDP and the price level in Lilliput, starting from a position of long-run equilibrium.

b Explain the combined effects of these events on real GDP and the price level in Lilliput,

starting from a position of long-run equilibrium.

c Explain what the government of Lilliput can do to overcome the problems faced by the economy.

3 The economy of Mainland has the following aggregate demand and supply schedules:

Price level	Real GDP demanded	Real GDP supplied in the short run
	(billions of 1990 euros)	
90	450	350
100	400	400
110	350	450
120	300	500
130	250	550
140	200	600

a Plot the aggregate demand curve and short-run aggregate supply curve in a figure.

b What is real GDP and the price level in Mainland in a short-run macroeconomic equilibrium?

c Mainland's potential GDP is E500 billion. Plot the long-run aggregate supply curve in the same figure in which you answered part (a).

d Is Mainland at, above, or below its natural rate of unemployment?

4 In Problem 3, aggregate demand is increased by E10 billion. What is the change in real GDP and the price level in the short run?

5 In Problem 3, aggregate supply decreases by E10 billion. What is the new short-run macroeconomic equilibrium?

6 You are the chief economic adviser at HM Treasury and you are trying to work out where the economy is likely to go next year. You have the following forecasts for the *AD*, *SAS*, and *LAS* curves:

Price level	Real GDP demanded	Short-run real GDP supplied	Long-run aggregate supply
	(billions of 1990 pounds)		
115	650	350	520
120	600	450	520
125	550	550	520
130	500	650	520

This year, real GDP is £500 billion and the price level is 120.

The prime minister wants answers to the following questions:

a What is your forecast of next year's real GDP?

b What is your forecast of next year's price level?

c What is your forecast of the inflation rate?

d Will unemployment be above or below its natural rate?

e Will there be a recessionary gap or an inflationary gap? By how much?

7 The following figure shows the aggregate supply and aggregate demand curves in an economy. Initially, short-run aggregate supply is SAS_0 and aggregate demand is AD_0. Then some events change aggregate demand and the aggregate demand curve shifts rightward to AD_1. Later,

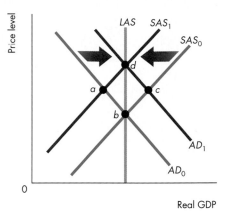

some further events change aggregate supply and the short-run aggregate supply curve shifts leftward to SAS_1.

8 Carefully draw some figures similar to those in this chapter and use the information in Problem 3 to explain:

a What has to be done to aggregate demand to achieve full employment.

b What the inflation rate is if aggregate demand is manipulated to achieve full employment.

9 After you have studied *Reading Between the Lines* on pp. 704–705, answer the following questions.

a What were the common features of the economy in 1988 and 1996?

b What were the differences in the economy in 1988 and 1996?

c Draw a figure to illustrate the economy in 1988.

d Draw a figure to illustrate the economy on 1996.

CHAPTER 28

EXPENDITURE MULTIPLIERS

After studying this chapter you will be able to:

◆ Explain how expenditure plans are determined when the price level is sticky

◆ Explain how real GDP is determined when the price level is sticky

◆ Explain the expenditure multiplier

◆ Explain how imports and taxes influence the multiplier

◆ Explain how recessions and recoveries begin

◆ Explain the relationship between aggregate expenditure and aggregate demand

◆ Explain how the multiplier gets smaller as the price level changes

A T THE BATHS OF CARACALLA IN ROME, LUCIANO PAVAROTTI BEGINS HIS passionate rendition of 'Nessun Dorma' in the bel canto style he is famous for. Moving to a louder passage, the volume of his voice increases and, with the aid of electronic amplification, booms across the open-air concert stadium. ◆ Brian Tyrer, an Everton supporter, is driving some of his friends in his BMW to Goodison Park to see Everton play Manchester. Some of the roads around Liverpool are badly potholed. The car's wheels are bouncing and vibrating, but Brian and his friends are completely undisturbed, thanks to the car's efficient shock absorbers. ◆ Investment and exports fluctuate like the volume of Pavarotti's voice and the uneven surface of a Liverpool road. How does the economy react to those fluctuations? Does it react like Brian's BMW, absorbing the shocks and providing a smooth ride for the economy's passengers? Or does it behave like Pavarotti's amplifier, blowing up the fluctuations and spreading them out to affect the many millions of participants in an economic opera concert? And is the economic machine built to a design

Economic Amplifier or Shock Absorber?

that we simply have to put up with, or does it change over time? Also, can the government modify the design of the economy and change its amplifying and shock-absorbing powers in a way that gives us all a smoother ride?

◆ ◆ ◆ ◆ You will explore these questions in this chapter. You will learn how a recession or a recovery begins when a change in investment or exports triggers a larger change in *aggregate* expenditure and real GDP – like the amplifier. You will also learn how, over the years, imports and income taxes have lowered the power of the amplifier. Finally, you will discover that in contrast to the initial amplification effect, the economy's imperfect shock absorbers, which are price and wage changes, pull real GDP back towards the long-term growth path of potential GDP.

Sticky Prices and Expenditure Plans

Most firms are like your local supermarket. They set their prices, advertise their products and services, and sell the quantities their customers are willing to buy. If they persistently sell a greater quantity than they plan to and are constantly running out of stocks, they eventually raise their prices. And if they persistently sell a smaller quantity than they plan to and have stocks piling up, they eventually cut their prices. But in the very short term their prices are sticky. They hold the prices they have set, and the quantities they sell depend on demand, not supply.

The Aggregate Implications of Sticky Prices

Sticky prices have two immediate implications for the economy as a whole:

1. Because each firm's price is sticky, the *price level* is sticky.

2. Because demand determines the quantities that each firm sells, *aggregate demand* determines the aggregate quantity of goods and services sold, which equals real GDP.

So to understand the fluctuations in real GDP when the price level is sticky, we must understand aggregate demand fluctuations. The aggregate expenditure model explains fluctuations in aggregate demand by identifying the forces that determine expenditure plans.

Expenditure Plans

The components of aggregate expenditure are:

1. Consumption expenditure
2. Investment
3. Government purchases of goods and services
4. Net exports (exports *minus* imports)

These four components of aggregate expenditure sum to real GDP (see Chapter 23, pp. 577–581).

Aggregate planned expenditure is equal to *planned* consumption expenditure plus *planned* investment plus *planned* government purchases plus *planned* exports minus *planned* imports. Chapter 26 describes the influences on these expenditure plans and explains how in the long run, when real GDP equals potential GDP, expenditure plans determine the real interest rate. Chapter 27 combines aggregate demand, which is based on aggregate expenditure plans, with aggregate supply and explains how in the short run, real GDP deviates from potential GDP. Here, we look at expenditure plans on a much shorter-term horizon.

In the very short term, *planned* investment, *planned* government purchases and *planned* exports are fixed. But *planned* consumption expenditure and *planned* imports are not fixed. They depend on the level of real GDP itself.

A Two-way Relationship Between Aggregate Expenditure and GDP   Because real GDP influences consumption expenditure and imports, and because consumption expenditure and imports are components of aggregate expenditure, there is a two-way relationship between aggregate expenditure and GDP. Other things remaining the same:

1. An increase in real GDP increases aggregate planned expenditure, and

2. An increase in aggregate expenditure increases real GDP.

You are going to learn how this two-way relationship between aggregate expenditure and real GDP determines real GDP when the price level is sticky. The starting point is to consider the first piece of the two-way relationship – the influence of real GDP on planned consumption expenditure and saving.

Consumption Function and Saving Function

Consumption and saving are influenced by several factors and the more important ones are:

◆ Real interest rate
◆ Disposable income
◆ Purchasing power of assets minus debts
◆ Expected future income

The ways that consumption and saving are influenced by these factors are explained in Chapter 25 (see pp. 633–634). In the short time-frame we are considering, the real interest rate, the purchasing power of assets minus debts and expected future income are fixed. But disposable income is not fixed. It equals real GDP plus transfer payments minus taxes. So it depends on real GDP, which in turn depends on aggregate expenditure.

Consumption and Saving Plans The table in Fig. 28.1 shows an example of the relationship among planned consumption expenditure, planned saving and disposable income. It lists the consumption expenditure and the saving that people plan to undertake at each level of disposable income.

Notice that at each level of disposable income, consumption expenditure plus saving always equals disposable income. The reason is that households can only consume or save their disposable income. So planned consumption plus planned saving always equals disposable income.

The relationship between consumption expenditure and disposable income, other things remaining the same, is called the **consumption function**. The relationship between saving and disposable

---

FIGURE 28.1

Consumption Function and Saving Function

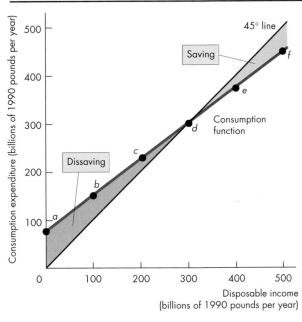

(a) Consumption function

	Disposable income	Planned consumption expenditure	Planned saving
		(billions of 1990 pounds per year)	
a	0	75	−75
b	100	150	−50
c	200	225	−25
d	300	300	0
e	400	375	25
f	500	450	50

The table shows consumption expenditure and saving plans at various levels of disposable income. Part (a) of the figure shows the relationship between consumption expenditure and disposable income (the consumption function). Part (b) shows the relationship between saving and disposable income (the saving function). Points *a* to *f* on the consumption and saving functions correspond to the rows in the table.

The 45° line in part (a) is the line along which consumption expenditure equals disposable income. Consumption expenditure plus saving equals disposable income. When the consumption function is above the 45° line, saving is negative (dissaving occurs) and the saving function is below the horizontal axis. When the consumption function is below the 45° line, saving is positive and the saving function is above the horizontal axis. At the point where the consumption function intersects the 45° line, all disposable income is consumed, saving is zero and the saving function intersects the horizontal axis.

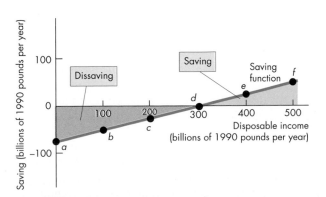

(b) Saving function

income, other things remaining the same, is called the **saving function**. Let's study the consumption and saving functions, beginning with the consumption function.

Consumption Function   Figure 28.1(a) shows a consumption function. The y-axis measures consumption expenditure and the x-axis measures disposable income. Along the consumption function, the points labelled a to f correspond to the rows of the table. For example, point e shows that when disposable income is $375 billion, consumption expenditure is $375 billion. Along the consumption function, as disposable income increases, consumption expenditure also increases.

At point a on the consumption function, consumption expenditure is $75 billion even though disposable income is zero. This consumption expenditure is called *autonomous consumption*. It is the amount of consumption expenditure that would take place in the short run, even if people had no current income. Consumption expenditure in excess of this amount is called *induced consumption*. It is expenditure that is induced by an increase in disposable income.

45° Line   Figure 28.1(a) also contains a line labelled '45° line'. At each point on this line, consumption expenditure (on the y-axis) equals disposable income (on the x-axis). In the range over which the consumption function lies above the 45° line – between a and d – consumption expenditure exceeds disposable income; in the range over which the consumption function lies below the 45° line – between d and f – consumption expenditure is less than disposable income; and at the point at which the consumption function intersects the 45° line – at point d – consumption expenditure equals disposable income.

Saving Function   Figure 28.1(b) shows a saving function. The x-axis is exactly the same as that in part (a). The y-axis measures saving. Again, the points marked a to f correspond to the rows of the table. For example, point e shows that when disposable income is $400 billion, saving is $25 billion. Along the saving function, as disposable income increases, saving also increases. At disposable income levels below point d, saving is negative. Negative saving is called *dissaving*. At disposable income levels above point d, saving is positive, and at point d, saving is zero.

Notice the connection between the two parts of Fig. 28.1. When consumption expenditure exceeds disposable income in part (a), saving is negative in part (b). When disposable income exceeds consumption expenditure in part (a), saving is positive in part (b). And when consumption expenditure equals disposable income in part (a), saving is zero in part (b).

When saving is negative (when consumption expenditure exceeds disposable income), past saving is used to pay for current consumption. Such a situation cannot last forever but it can occur if disposable income falls temporarily.

Marginal Propensities to Consume and Save

The extent to which consumption expenditure changes when disposable income changes depends on the marginal propensity to consume. The **marginal propensity to consume** (MPC) is the fraction of a *change* in disposable income that is consumed. It is calculated as the *change* in consumption expenditure (ΔC) divided by the *change* in disposable income (ΔYD) that brought it about. That is:

$$MPC = \frac{\Delta C}{\Delta YD}$$

In the table in Fig. 28.1, when disposable income increases from $300 billion to $400 billion, consumption expenditure increases from $300 billion to $375 billion. The change in disposable income of $100 billion brings about a change in consumption expenditure of $75 billion. The MPC is $75 billion divided by $100 billion, which equals 0.75. In Fig. 28.1, the MPC is a constant 0.75. For example, an increase in disposable income from $200 billion to $300 billion increases consumption expenditure from $225 billion to $300 billion, so again the MPC is 0.75.

The **marginal propensity to save** (MPS) is the fraction of a *change* in disposable income that is saved. It is calculated as the *change* in saving (ΔS) divided by the *change* in disposable income (ΔYD) that brought it about. That is:

$$MPS = \frac{\Delta S}{\Delta YD}$$

Again, using the numbers in the table in Fig. 28.1, an increase in disposable income from $300 billion to $400 billion increases saving from zero to $25 billion. The change in disposable income of $100 billion brings about a change in saving of £25 billion. The *MPS* is £25 billion divided by £100 billion, which equals 0.25. In Fig. 28.1, the *MPS* is a constant 0.25. For example, an increase in disposable income from £200 billion to £300 billion increases saving from −£25 billion to zero, so again the *MPS* is 0.25.

Marginal Propensities and Slopes   You might find it helpful to visualize the marginal propensities to consume and save in a graph. They can be seen as the slopes of the consumption function and the saving function. You can see the marginal propensity to consume as the slope of the consumption function in Fig. 28.2(a). A £100 billion increase in disposable income from £300 billion to £400 billion is the base of the red triangle. The increase in consumption expenditure that results from this increase in income is £75 billion and is the height of the triangle. The slope of the consumption function is given by the formula 'slope equals rise over run' and is £75 billion divided by £100 billion, which equals 0.75 – the *MPC*.

You can see the marginal propensity to save as the slope of the saving function in Fig. 28.2(b). A £100 billion increase in disposable income from £300 billion to £400 billion (the base of the red triangle) increases saving by £25 billion (the height of the triangle). The slope of the saving function is £25 billion divided by £100 billion, which equals 0.25 – the *MPS*.

The marginal propensity to consume plus the marginal propensity to save always equals 1. These two marginal propensities add up to 1 because consumption expenditure and saving exhaust disposable income. Part of each pound increase in disposable income is consumed and the remaining part is saved. You can see that these two marginal propensities add up to 1 by using the following equation:

$$\Delta C + \Delta S = \Delta YD$$

Divide both sides of the equation by the change in disposable income to obtain

$$\frac{\Delta C}{\Delta YD} + \frac{\Delta C}{\Delta YD} = 1$$

$\Delta C / \Delta YD$, is the *marginal propensity to consume* (*MPC*) and $\Delta S / \Delta YD$ is the *marginal propensity to save* (*MPS*), so

$$MPC + MPS = 1$$

FIGURE 28.2

Marginal Propensities to Consume and Save

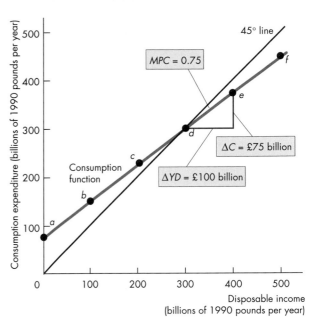

(a) Consumption function

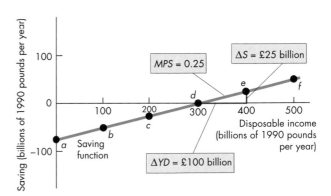

(b) Saving function

The marginal propensity to consume, *MPC*, is equal to the change in consumption expenditure divided by the change in disposable income, other things remaining the same. It is measured by the slope of the consumption function. In part (a), the *MPC* is 0.75. The marginal propensity to save, *MPS*, is equal to the change in saving divided by the change in disposable income, other things remaining the same. It is measured by the slope of the saving function. In part (b), the *MPS* is 0.25.

Other Influences on Consumption Expenditure and Saving

You've seen that a change in disposable income leads to changes in consumption expenditure and saving. A change in disposable income brings movements along the consumption function and saving function. A change in other influences on consumption expenditure and saving shifts both the consumption function and the saving function. These other factors include the real interest rate, expected future income and the purchasing power of net assets (see Chapter 25, pp. 633–634).

When the real interest rate falls or when the purchasing power of net assets (assets minus debts) or expected future income increases, consumption expenditure increases and saving decreases. Figure 28.3 shows the effects of these changes on the consumption function and the saving function. The consumption function shifts upward from CF_0 to CF_1, and the saving function shifts downward from SF_0 to SF_1. Such shifts commonly occur during the expansion phase of the business cycle because, at such times, expected future income increases.

When the real interest rate rises or when the purchasing power of net assets or expected future income decreases, consumption decreases and saving increases. Figure 28.3 also shows the effects of these changes on the consumption function and the saving function. The consumption function shifts downward from CF_0 to CF_2, and the saving function shifts upward from SF_0 to SF_2. Such shifts often occur when a recession begins because at such a time, expected future income decreases.

We've studied the theory of the consumption function. Let's now see how that theory applies to the economy.

The Consumption Function

Figure 28.4(a) shows the consumption function in the United Kingdom. Each point identified by a blue dot represents consumption expenditure and disposable income for a particular year. (The dots are for the years 1970–94). The orange line shows the average relationship between consumption expenditure and disposable income and is an estimate of the consumption function. The slope of this line is 0.9, which means that a £100 billion increase in disposable income brings a £90 billion increase in consumption expenditure. That is, on the average, over the period

FIGURE 28.3

Shifts in the Consumption and Saving Functions

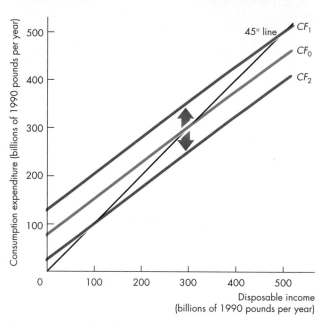

(a) Consumption function

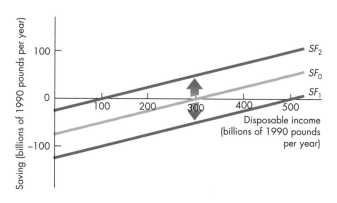

(b) Saving function

A fall in the real interest rate, an increase in the purchasing power of net assets, or an increase in expected future income increases consumption expenditure, shifts the consumption function upward from CF_0 to CF_1 and shifts the saving function downward from SF_0 to SF_1. Similarly, a rise in the real interest rate, a decrease in the purchasing power of net assets, or a decrease in expected future income shifts the consumption function downward from CF_0 to CF_2 and shifts the saving function upward from SF_0 to SF_2.

FIGURE 28.4

The UK Consumption Function

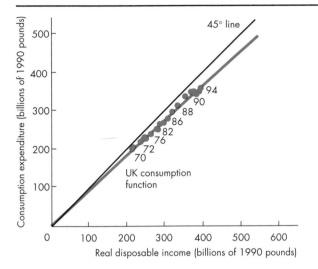

(a) Consumption as a function of disposable income

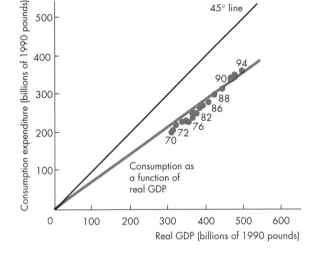

(b) Consumption as a function of real GDP

Part (a) shows the UK consumption function. Each blue dot represents consumption expenditure and disposable income for a particular year. The orange line is an estimate of the UK consumption function. Its slope is the marginal propensity to consume, which is 0.9. The table shows the connection between consumption as a function of disposable income and consumption as a function of real GDP. Disposable income equals real GDP minus net taxes. The net tax rate is 20 per cent, so disposable income (YD) is 80 per cent of real GDP. With a marginal propensity to consume of 0.9, consumption expenditure is 0.9 × YD or 0.9 × 0.8 × real GDP, which is 0.72 × real GDP. Part (b) shows consumption expenditure as a function of real GDP. The slope of this function is 0.72.

Real GDP (Y)	Disposable income (YD = 0.9Y)	Consumption expenditure (C = 0.9YD = 0.72Y)
	(billions of 1990 pounds per year)	
100	80	72
200	160	144
300	240	216
400	320	288

1970–94, the marginal propensity to consume in the United Kingdom was about 0.9. Also, on the average, autonomous consumption is zero. That is, if disposable income were zero, consumption expenditure would also be zero.

The relationship between consumption expenditure and disposable income in any given year does not fall exactly on the orange line. The reason is that the position of the consumption function in each year depends on other factors – such as the real interest rate, expected future income and the purchasing power of net assets – which influence consumption expenditure and shift the consumption function.

Consumption as a Function of Real GDP

Because our goal is to determine real GDP when the price level is sticky, our next step is to link consumption expenditure with real GDP. Figure 28.4(b) shows this link for the United Kingdom. The blue dots illustrate the actual values of the two variables in each year, again for the period 1970–94. The orange line shows the average relationship between consumption expenditure and real GDP.

Consumption expenditure is a function of real GDP because disposable income depends on real

GDP. Disposable income is real GDP minus net direct taxes. *Net direct taxes* are equal to taxes paid to the government minus transfer payments (such as unemployment benefits or income supplements) received from the government.

Net direct taxes increase as real GDP increases. Almost all the direct taxes that we pay – personal taxes, corporate taxes and national insurance contributions – increase as our incomes increase. Transfer payments, such as welfare benefits, decrease as our incomes increase. In 1995, net taxes were about 21 per cent of real GDP. With net taxes equal to 21 per cent of real GDP, disposable income is 79 per cent of real GDP.

The table in Fig. 28.4 sets out the relationship between real GDP, disposable income and consumption expenditure. For example, when real GDP is £400 billion, disposable income is 80 per cent of that amount, which is £320 billion. And if the marginal propensity to consume is 0.9, as in Fig. 28.4(a), then consumption expenditure is 0.9 of £320 billion, which is £288 billion.

When consumption expenditure is plotted against real GDP, the slope of the curve tells us the amount by which consumption expenditure changes as real GDP changes. In Fig. 28.4, the slope is 0.72. When real GDP increases by £100 billion, consumption expenditure increases by £72 billion. This slope is equal to the marginal propensity to consume (0.9) multiplied by 1 minus the net tax rate ($1 - 0.2 = 0.80$).

Two components of aggregate planned expenditure are influenced by real GDP: consumption expenditure and imports. We've seen that consumption expenditure increases as real GDP increases. Let's now study the relationship between imports and real GDP.

Import Function

Imports to the United Kingdom are determined by three main factors:

1. Real GDP
2. Prices of foreign-produced goods and services relative to the prices of similar UK-produced goods and services
3. Foreign exchange rates

Other things remaining the same, the greater the United Kingdom real GDP, the larger is the quantity of United Kingdom imports. For example, the growth in United Kingdom real GDP between 1986 and 1989 resulted in a large increase in imports. Real GDP grew by a total of nearly 13 per cent between 1986 and 1989 (an annual average of 4.1 per cent). Meanwhile exports less imports went from a surplus of £792 million (1990 prices) in 1986 to a deficit of £20779 million in 1989.

Again, other things remaining the same, the lower the prices of foreign-produced goods and services relative to the prices of similar UK-produced goods and services, the larger is the quantity of United Kingdom imports. To compare prices of foreign-produced and UK-produced goods and services, we use foreign exchange rates. A **foreign exchange rate** is the value of one national money in terms of another, for example, the value of the pound in terms of the US dollar or the Deutschemark. The higher the value of the pound against the dollar or Deutschemark, the more dollars or Deutschemarks will one pound buy and the cheaper are US or German-produced goods and services. That is, the higher the value of the pound against other currencies, the larger are imports into the United Kingdom.

In 1989, strong real GDP growth in the United Kingdom produced an increase in imports. But the increase was more than it otherwise would have been because at the same time the value of the pound against other currencies rose. The stronger pound made foreign-produced goods and services less expensive and so increased, to some degree, the growth of imports.

The response of imports to changes in prices and foreign exchange rates occurs slowly and is spread out over a long period. But real GDP influences imports quickly.

The relationship between imports and real GDP is called the **import function**. Figure 28.5(a) shows an import function. The x-axis measures real GDP, and the y-axis measures imports. The points labelled a to e in the figure correspond to the rows of the table. For example, point d indicates a real GDP of £400 billion and imports of £120 billion.

An increase in real GDP brings an increase in imports, and the magnitude of the increase in imports is determined by the marginal propensity to import. The **marginal propensity to import** is the fraction of an increase in real GDP that is spent on imports. It is calculated as the change in

FIGURE 28.5

The Import Function

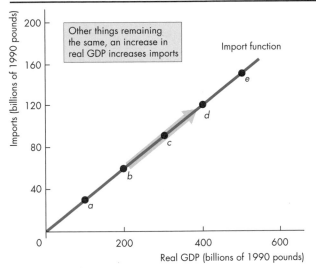

(a) An import function

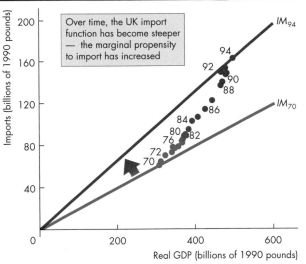

(b) The UK import function

	Real GDP	Imports
	(billions of 1990 pounds per year)	
a	100	30
b	200	60
c	300	90
d	400	120
e	500	150

Part (a) shows an import function, the relationship between imports and real GDP with all other influences on imports remaining constant. Here, the marginal propensity to import is 0.30. Part (b) shows the relationship between imports and real GDP in the United Kingdom. In 1970, the import function was IM_{70} and the marginal propensity to import was 0.2. By 1994, the marginal propensity to import had increased to 0.33 and the import function was IM_{94}.

imports divided by the change in real GDP that brought it about, other things remaining the same. Along the import function in Fig. 28.5(a), the marginal propensity to import is a constant 0.3. That is, when real GDP increases by £100 billion, imports increase by £30 billion.

Figure 28.5(b) shows the UK import function. In 1970, the UK import function was IM_{70}. Along this import function, the marginal propensity to import is 0.2. A £100 billion increase in UK real GDP increased imports by £20 billion. Over the years, influences other than real GDP increased the marginal propensity to import and the UK import function has gradually become steeper. By 1994, it was IM_{94}. Along this import function, the marginal propensity to import is 0.33, an increase of more than half the value in 1970.

REVIEW

◆ With a sticky price level, *aggregate demand* determines real GDP.

◆ Two components of aggregate planned expenditure – consumption expenditure and imports – are influenced by real GDP.

◆ The influence of real GDP on consumption expenditure is determined by the marginal propensity to consume, and the influence of real GDP on imports is determined by the marginal propensity to import.

We've studied the influence of real GDP on consumption expenditure and imports. Next we will see how these components of aggregate expenditure interact with investment, government purchases and exports to determine aggregate expenditure and real GDP.

Real GDP with a Sticky Price Level

We are now going to discover how aggregate expenditure plans interact to determine real GDP when the price level is sticky. The first step in this process is to look at the relationship between aggregate planned expenditure and real GDP.

The relationship between aggregate planned expenditure and real GDP can be described by either an aggregate expenditure schedule or an aggregate expenditure curve. The *aggregate*

expenditure schedule lists aggregate planned expenditure generated at each level of real GDP. The *aggregate expenditure curve* is a graph of the aggregate expenditure schedule.

Aggregate Expenditure Schedule

The table in Fig. 28.6 sets out an aggregate expenditure schedule together with the components of aggregate planned expenditure. To calculate aggregate planned expenditure at a given real GDP, we add the various components together. The first column of the table shows real GDP and the second column shows the consumption expenditure generated by

FIGURE 28.6

Aggregate Expenditure

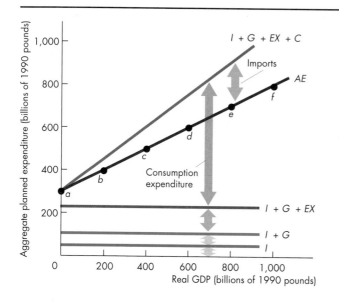

The relationship between aggregate planned expenditure and real GDP is shown by an aggregate expenditure schedule and illustrated by an aggregate expenditure curve. Aggregate planned expenditure is the sum of planned consumption expenditure, investment, government purchases of goods and services, and net exports. For example, in row *b* of the table, when real GDP is £200 billion, planned consumption expenditure is £225 billion, planned investment is £50 billion, planned government purchases of goods and services are £55 billion, planned exports are £120 billion, and planned imports are £50 billion. Thus when real GDP is £200 billion, aggregate planned expenditure is £400 billion (£225 + £50 + £55 + £120 − £50). The schedule shows that aggregate planned expenditure increases as real GDP increases. This relationship is graphed as the aggregate expenditure curve *AE*, the line *af*. The components of aggregate expenditure that increase with real GDP are consumption expenditure and imports. The other components – investment, government purchases and exports – do not vary with real GDP.

	Real GDP (*Y*)	Consumption expenditure (*C*)	Investment (*I*)	Government purchases (*G*)	Exports (*EX*)	Imports (*IM*)	Aggregate expenditure (*AE* = *C* + *I* + *G* + *NX*)
				(billions of 1990 pounds)			
a	0	75	50	55	120	0	300
b	200	225	50	55	120	50	400
c	400	375	50	55	120	100	500
d	600	525	50	55	120	150	600
e	800	675	50	55	120	200	700
f	1,000	825	50	55	120	250	800

each level of real GDP. When real GDP is £200 billion, consumption expenditure is £225 billion. A £200 billion increase in real GDP generates an £150 billion increase in consumption expenditure.

The next two columns show investment and government purchases of goods and services. Investment depends on the real interest rate and the expected rate of profit (see Chapter 25, p. 630). At a given point in time these factors generate a level of investment that is independent of real GDP. Suppose this amount of investment is £50 billion. Government purchases of goods and services are also independent of real GDP and their value is £55 billion.

The next two columns show exports and imports. Exports are influenced by events in the rest of the world, prices of foreign-produced goods and services relative to the prices of similar goods and services produced at home, and foreign exchange rates. But they are not directly affected by real GDP in the United Kingdom. In the table, exports appear as a constant £120 billion. In contrast, imports increase as real GDP increases. A £200 billion increase in real GDP generates a £50 billion increase in imports.

The final column of the table shows aggregate planned expenditure. This amount is the sum of planned consumption expenditure, investment, government purchases of goods and services, and exports minus imports.

Aggregate Expenditure Curve

Figure 28.6 plots an aggregate expenditure curve. Real GDP is shown on the x-axis and aggregate planned expenditure on the y-axis. The aggregate expenditure curve is the red line *AE*. Points *a* to *f* on this curve correspond to the rows of the table. The *AE* curve is a graph of aggregate planned expenditure (the last column) plotted against real GDP (the first column).

Figure 28.6 also shows the components of aggregate expenditure. The constant components – investment (*I*), government purchases of goods and services (*G*), and exports (*EX*) – are shown by the horizontal lines in the figure. Consumption expenditure (*C*) is the vertical gap between the lines labelled $I + G + EX + C$ and $I + G + EX$.

To construct the *AE* curve, subtract imports (*IM*) from the $I + G + EX + C$ line. Aggregate expenditure is expenditure on UK-produced goods and services. But the components of aggregate expenditure, *C*, *I* and *G*, include expenditure on

imported goods and services. For example, a student's purchase of a new motorbike is part of consumption expenditure, but if that motorbike is a Honda made in Japan, expenditure on it must be subtracted from consumption expenditure to find out how much is spent on goods and services produced in the United Kingdom – on UK real GDP. Money paid to Honda for car imports from Japan does not add to aggregate expenditure in the United Kingdom.

Figure 28.6 shows that aggregate planned expenditure increases as real GDP increases. But as real GDP increases only some of the components of aggregate planned expenditure increase. These components are consumption expenditure and imports. The sum of the components of aggregate expenditure that vary with real GDP is called **induced expenditure**. The sum of the components of aggregate expenditure that are not influenced by real GDP is called **autonomous expenditure**. The components of autonomous expenditure are investment, government purchases, exports and the part of consumption expenditure that does not vary with real GDP. That is, autonomous expenditure is equal to the level of aggregate planned expenditure when real GDP is zero. In Fig. 28.6, autonomous expenditure is £300 billion. As real GDP increases from zero to £200 billion, aggregate expenditure increases from £300 billion to £400 billion. Induced expenditure is £100 billion – £400 billion minus £300 billion.

The aggregate expenditure curve summarizes the relationship between aggregate planned expenditure and real GDP. But what determines the point on the aggregate expenditure curve at which the economy operates? What determines real GDP?

Actual Expenditure, Planned Expenditure and Real GDP

Actual aggregate expenditure is always equal to real GDP, as we saw in Chapter 23, pp. 585–586. But aggregate *planned* expenditure is not necessarily equal to actual aggregate expenditure and, therefore, is not necessarily equal to real GDP. How can actual expenditure and planned expenditure differ from each other? Why don't expenditure plans get implemented? The main reason is that firms might end up with more stocks than planned or with less stocks than planned. People carry out their consumption expenditure plans, the government implements its planned purchases of goods and services, and net exports are as planned. Firms carry out their plans to purchase new buildings, plant and equipment. One component of investment, however, is the increase in firms' stocks of goods. When aggregate planned expenditure differs from real GDP, firms end up with more or less stocks than they had planned. If aggregate planned expenditure is less than real GDP, stocks increase, and if aggregate planned expenditure exceeds real GDP, stocks decrease.

Equilibrium Expenditure

Equilibrium expenditure is the level of aggregate expenditure that occurs when aggregate *planned* expenditure equals real GDP. It is a level of aggregate expenditure and real GDP at which everyone's spending plans are fulfilled. When the price level is sticky, equilibrium expenditure determines real GDP. When aggregate planned expenditure and actual aggregate expenditure are unequal, a process of convergence towards equilibrium expenditure occurs. And throughout this convergence process real GDP adjusts. Let's examine equilibrium expenditure and the process that brings it about.

Figure 28.7(a) illustrates equilibrium expenditure. The table sets out aggregate planned expenditure at various levels of real GDP. These values are plotted as points *a* to *f* along the *AE* curve. The 45° line shows all the points at which aggregate planned expenditure equals actual aggregate expenditure (and equals real GDP). Thus where the aggregate expenditure curve intersects the 45° line, point *d*, aggregate planned expenditure equals actual aggregate expenditure. Point *d* illustrates equilibrium expenditure and determines real GDP. At this point, real GDP is £600 billion.

Convergence to Equilibrium

What are the forces that move aggregate expenditure towards its equilibrium level? To answer this question, we must look at a situation in which aggregate expenditure is away from its equilibrium level. Suppose that in Fig. 28.7, real GDP is £200 billion. With real GDP at £200 billion, aggregate expenditure is also £200 billion. But aggregate *planned* expenditure is £400 billion (point *b* in Fig. 28.7a). Aggregate planned expenditure exceeds *actual* expenditure. When people spend £400 billion, and firms produce goods and services worth £200 billion, firms' stocks fall by £200 billion (point *b* in Fig. 28.7b). Because the change in stocks is part of investment, *actual* investment is

£200 billion less than *planned* investment.

Real GDP doesn't remain at £200 billion for long. Firms have stock targets based on their sales. When the ratio of stocks to sales falls below target, firms increase production to restore stocks to the target level. To increase stocks, firms hire additional labour and increase production. Suppose that they increase production in the next period by £200 billion. Real GDP increases by £200 billion to £400 billion. But again, aggregate planned expenditure exceeds real GDP. When real GDP is £400 billion, aggregate planned expenditure is £500 billion (point *c* in Fig. 28.7a). Again, stocks decrease but this time by less than before. With real GDP of £400 billion and aggregate planned expenditure of £500 billion, stocks decrease by £100 billion (point *c* in Fig. 28.7b). Again, firms hire additional labour and production increases; real GDP increases yet further.

The process that we have just described – planned expenditure exceeds real GDP, stocks decrease and production increases to restore the level of stocks – ends when real GDP has reached £600 billion. At this real GDP, there is an equilibrium. There are no unplanned stock changes and firms do not change their production.

You can do a similar experiment to the one we've just done, but starting with a level of real GDP greater than equilibrium expenditure. In this case, planned expenditure is less than actual expenditure, stocks pile up and firms cut production. As before, real GDP keeps on changing (decreasing this time) until it reaches its equilibrium level of £600 billion.

REVIEW

◆ Equilibrium expenditure occurs when aggregate planned expenditure equals real GDP.

◆ Equilibrium expenditure results from an adjustment in real GDP.

◆ If real GDP and aggregate expenditure are less than their equilibrium levels, an unplanned fall in stocks leads firms to increase production and real GDP increases.

◆ If real GDP and aggregate expenditure are greater than their equilibrium levels, an unplanned rise in stocks leads firms to decrease production and real GDP decreases.

FIGURE 28.7

Equilibrium Expenditure

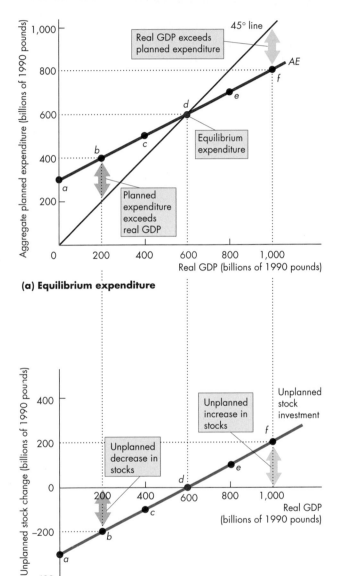

(a) Equilibrium expenditure

(b) Unplanned stock changes

Real GDP (Y)	Aggregate planned expenditure (AE)	Unplanned stock change (Y – AE)
	(billions of 1990 pounds)	
a	0	300	-300
b	200	400	-200
c	400	500	-100
d	600	600	0
e	800	700	100
f	1,000	800	200

The table shows expenditure plans at different levels of real GDP. When real GDP is £600 billion, aggregate planned expenditure equals real GDP. Part (a) of the figure illustrates equilibrium expenditure, which occurs when aggregate planned expenditure equals real GDP at the intersection of the 45° line and the AE curve. Part (b) of the figure shows the forces that bring about equilibrium expenditure. When aggregate planned expenditure exceeds real GDP stocks decrease – for example, point b in both parts of the figure. Firms increase production and real GDP increases. When aggregate planned expenditure is less than real GDP stocks increase – for example, point d in both parts of the figure. Firms decrease production and real GDP decreases. When aggregate planned expenditure equals real GDP there are no unplanned stock changes and real GDP remains constant at equilibrium expenditure.

We've learned that when the price level is sticky, real GDP is determined by equilibrium expenditure. And we have seen how unplanned changes in stocks and the production response they generate bring a convergence towards equilibrium. We're now going to study *changes* in equilibrium. And we are going to discover an economic amplifier called the multiplier.

The Multiplier

Investment and exports – two components of autonomous expenditure – can change for many reasons. A fall in the real interest rate might induce firms to increase their planned investment. A major wave of innovation, such as occurred with the spread of IT in the 1980s, might increase expected future profits and lead firms to increase their planned investment. Stiff competition in the car industry from Japanese or South Korean imports might force Ford, Vauxhall and Rover to increase their investment in robotic assembly lines. An economic boom in developing countries might lead to a large increase in their expenditure on UK-produced goods and services – on UK exports. These are all examples of increases in autonomous expenditure.

When autonomous expenditure increases, aggregate expenditure increases, and so too does equilibrium expenditure. The increase in equilibrium expenditure and real GDP is larger than the change in autonomous expenditure. The **multiplier** is the amount by which a change in autonomous expenditure is magnified or multiplied to determine the change in equilibrium expenditure and real GDP.

It is easiest to get the basic idea of the multiplier if we work with an example economy in which there are no income taxes and no imports. So we'll first assume that these factors are absent. Then, when you understand the basic idea, we'll bring these factors back into play and see what difference they make to the multiplier.

The Basic Idea of the Multiplier

Suppose that investment increases. The additional expenditure by businesses means that aggregate expenditure and real GDP increases. Disposable income also increases, and with no income taxes, real GDP and disposable income increase by the same amount. The increase in disposable income brings an increase in consumption expenditure. And the increased consumption expenditure adds even more to aggregate expenditure. Real GDP and disposable income increase further, and so does consumption expenditure. The initial increase in investment brings an even bigger increase in aggregate expenditure because it induces an increase in consumption expenditure. The magnitude of the

increase in aggregate expenditure that results from an increase in autonomous expenditure is determined by the *multiplier*.

The table in Fig. 28.8 sets out aggregate planned expenditure. Initially, when real GDP is £500 billion, aggregate planned expenditure is £525 billion. For each £100 billion increase in real GDP, aggregate planned expenditure increases by £75 billion. This aggregate expenditure schedule is

FIGURE 28.8

The Multiplier

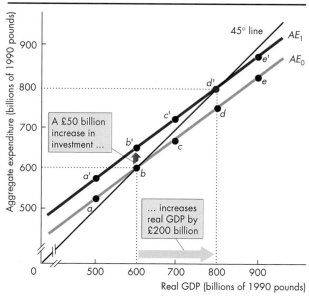

Real GDP (Y)	Aggregate planned expenditure Original (AE₀)		Aggregate planned expenditure New (AE₁)	
		(billions of 1990 pounds)		
500	a	525	a'	575
600	b	600	b'	650
700	c	675	c'	725
800	d	750	d'	800
900	e	825	e'	875

A £50 billion increase in autonomous expenditure shifts the *AE* curve upward by £50 billion from *AE₀* to *AE₁*. Equilibrium expenditure increases by £200 billion from £600 billion to £800 billion. The increase in equilibrium expenditure is 4 times the increase in autonomous expenditure, so the multiplier is 4.

shown in the figure as the aggregate expenditure curve AE_0. Initially, equilibrium expenditure is £600 billion. You can see this equilibrium in row b of the table, and in the figure where the curve AE_0 intersects the 45° line at the point marked b.

Now suppose that autonomous expenditure increases by £50 billion. What happens to equilibrium expenditure? You can see the answer in Fig. 28.8. When this increase in autonomous expenditure is added to the original aggregate planned expenditure, aggregate planned expenditure increases by £50 billion at each level of real GDP. The new aggregate expenditure curve is AE_1. The new equilibrium expenditure, highlighted in the table (row d'), occurs where AE_1 intersects the 45° line and is £800 billion (point d'). At this point, aggregate planned expenditure equals real GDP.

The Multiplier Effect

In Fig. 28.8, the increase in autonomous expenditure of £50 billion increases equilibrium expenditure by £200 billion. That is, the change in autonomous expenditure leads to an amplified change in equilibrium expenditure. This amplified change is the *multiplier effect* – equilibrium expenditure increases by *more than* the increase in autonomous expenditure.

Initially, when autonomous expenditure increases, aggregate planned expenditure exceeds real GDP. As a result, stocks decrease. Firms respond by increasing production so as to restore their stocks to the target level. As production increases, so does real GDP. With a higher level of real GDP, *induced expenditure* increases. Thus equilibrium expenditure increases by the sum of the initial increase in autonomous expenditure and the increase in induced expenditure. In this example, induced expenditure increases by £150 billion, so equilibrium expenditure increases by £200 billion.

Although we have just analysed the effects of an *increase* in autonomous expenditure, the same analysis applies to a decrease in autonomous expenditure. If initially the aggregate expenditure curve is AE_1, equilibrium expenditure and real GDP are £800 billion. A decrease in autonomous expenditure of £50 billion shifts the aggregate expenditure curve downward by £50 billion to AE_0. Equilibrium expenditure decreases from £800 billion to £600 billion. The decrease in equilibrium expenditure (£200 billion) is larger than the decrease in autonomous expenditure that brought it about.

Why is the Multiplier Greater than 1?

We've seen that equilibrium expenditure increases by more than the increase in autonomous expenditure. This makes the multiplier greater than 1. How come? Why does equilibrium expenditure increase by more than the increase in autonomous expenditure?

The multiplier is greater than 1 because of induced expenditure – an increase in autonomous expenditure *induces* further increases in expenditure. If British Telecommunications spends £10 million on a new video communications system, aggregate expenditure and real GDP immediately increase by £10 million. But that is not the end of the story. Electrical engineers and construction workers now have more income, and they spend part of the extra income on cars, microwaves, holidays and a host of other goods and services. Real GDP now rises by the initial £10 million plus the extra consumption expenditure induced by the £10 million increase in income. The producers of cars, microwaves, holidays and other goods now have increased incomes, and they, in turn, spend part of the increase in their incomes on consumption goods and services. Additional income induces additional expenditure, which creates additional income.

We have seen that a change in autonomous expenditure has a multiplier effect on real GDP. But how big is the multiplier effect?

The Size of the Multiplier

Suppose that the economy is in a recession. Profit prospects start to look better and firms are making plans for large increases in investment. The world economy is also heading towards recovery, and exports are increasing. The question on everyone's lips is: how strong will the recovery be? This is a hard question to answer. But an important ingredient in the answer is working out the size of the multiplier.

The *multiplier* is the amount by which a change in autonomous expenditure is multiplied to determine the change in equilibrium expenditure that it generates. To calculate the multiplier, we divide the change in equilibrium expenditure by the change in autonomous expenditure. Let's calculate the multiplier for the example in Fig. 28.8. Initially, equilibrium expenditure is £600 billion. Then autonomous expenditure increases by £50 billion, and equilibrium expenditure increases by £200 billion to £800 billion.

The multiplier is

$$\text{Multiplier} = \frac{\Delta \text{ equilibrium expenditure}}{\Delta \text{ autonomous expenditure}}$$

$$= \frac{£200 \text{ billion}}{£50 \text{ billion}}$$

$$= 4$$

Figure 28.9 illustrates the multiplier process. In round 1, autonomous expenditure increases by £50 billion. At this time, induced expenditure does not change, so aggregate expenditure and real GDP increase by £50 billion. In round 2, the larger real GDP induces more consumption expenditure. Induced expenditure increases by 0.75 times the increase in real GDP, so the increase in real GDP of £50 billion induces a further increase in expenditure of £37.5 billion. This change in induced expenditure, when added to the initial change in autonomous expenditure, increases aggregate expenditure and real GDP by £87.5 billion. The round 2 increase in real GDP induces a round 3 increase in expenditure. The process repeats through successive rounds. Each increase in real GDP is 0.75 times the previous increase. The cumulative increase in real GDP gradually approaches £200 billion.

The Multiplier and the Marginal Propensities to Consume and Save

What determines the magnitude of the multiplier? The answer is the marginal propensity to consume. The larger the marginal propensity to consume, the larger is the multiplier. To see why, let's do a calculation.

Aggregate expenditure and real GDP (Y), change because consumption expenditure, (C), changes and investment, (I), changes. The change in GDP equals the change in consumption expenditure plus the change in investment. That is

$$\Delta Y = \Delta C + \Delta I$$

But the change in consumption expenditure is determined by the change in real GDP and the *MPC*. It is

$$\Delta C = MPC \times \Delta Y$$

Now combine these two facts to give:

$$\Delta Y = MPC \times \Delta Y + \Delta I$$

Now, solve for the change in Y as

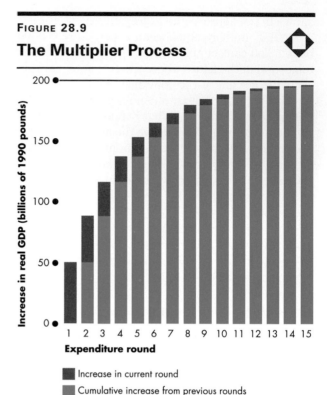

FIGURE 28.9

The Multiplier Process

Autonomous expenditure increases in round 1 by £50 billion. As a result, real GDP increases by the same amount. With a marginal propensity to consume of 0.75, each additional pound of real GDP induces an additional 0.75 of a pound of aggregate expenditure. The round 1 increase in real GDP induces an increase in consumption expenditure of £37.5 billion in round 2. At the end of round 2, real GDP has increased by £87.5 billion. The extra £37.5 billion of real GDP in round 2 induces a further increase in consumption expenditure of £28.1 billion in round 3. Real GDP increases yet further to £115.6 billion. This process continues with real GDP increasing by ever smaller amounts. When the process comes to an end, real GDP has increased by a total of £200 billion.

$$(1 - MPC) \times \Delta Y = \Delta I$$

and rearranging,

$$\Delta Y = \frac{\Delta I}{(1 - MPC)}$$

The multiplier that we want to calculate is

$$\text{Multiplier} = \frac{\Delta Y}{\Delta I}$$

so divide both sides of the previous equation by the change in I to give

$$\text{Multiplier} = \frac{\Delta Y}{\Delta I} = \frac{1}{(1 - MPC)}$$

Using the numbers for Fig. 28.8, the *MPC* is 0.75 so the multiplier is

$$\text{Multiplier} = \frac{1}{(1 - 0.75)} = \frac{1}{0.25} = 4$$

There is another formula for the multiplier. Because the marginal propensity to consume (*MPC*) plus the marginal propensity to save (*MPS*) adds up to 1, the term (1 − *MPC*) equals *MPS*. Therefore, another formula for the multiplier is:

$$\text{Multiplier} = \frac{1}{MPS}$$

Again using the numbers in Fig. 28.8,

$$\text{Multiplier} = \frac{1}{0.25} = 4$$

Because the marginal propensity to save (*MPS*) is a fraction – a number lying between 0 and 1 – the multiplier is greater than 1.

So far, we've ignored imports and income taxes. Let's now see how these two factors influence the multiplier.

Imports and Income Taxes

The multiplier is determined, in general, not only by the marginal propensity to consume but also by the marginal propensity to import and by the marginal tax rate. Imports make the multiplier smaller than it otherwise would be. To see why, think about what happens following an increase in investment. An increase in investment increases real GDP, which in turn increases consumption expenditure. But part of investment and part of the consumption expenditure are expenditure on imported goods and services, not UK-produced goods and services. It is the expenditure on only UK-produced goods and services that increases real GDP in the United Kingdom.

Income taxes also make the multiplier smaller than it otherwise would be. Again, think about what happens following an increase in investment. An increase in investment increases real GDP. Because income taxes increase with income, the increase in real GDP increases income taxes. And the increase in income taxes decreases disposable income. Consumption expenditure depends on disposable income, so the greater the increase in income taxes, the smaller is the increase in consumption expenditure, other things remaining the same. It is only the

increase in *disposable* income that induces an increase in consumption expenditure.

The marginal propensity to import and the marginal tax rate together with the marginal propensity to consume determine the slope of the *AE* curve and the multiplier. The multiplier is equal to 1 divided by 1 minus the slope of the *AE* curve. Figure 28.10 compares two situations. In Fig. 28.10(a), there are no imports and no taxes. The marginal propensity to consume, which also equals the slope of the *AE* curve, is 0.75 and the multiplier is 4. In Fig. 28.10(b), imports and income taxes decrease the slope of the *AE* curve to 0.5. In this case, the multiplier is 2.

Over time, the value of the multiplier changes as tax rates change and as the marginal propensity to consume and the marginal propensity to import change. These ongoing changes make the multiplier hard to predict. But they do not change the fundamental fact that an initial change in autonomous expenditure leads to a magnified change in aggregate expenditure and real GDP.

Now that we've studied the multiplier and the factors that influence its magnitude, let's use what we've learned to gain some insights into the most critical points in the life of an economy: business cycle turning points.

Business Cycle Turning Points

At a business cycle trough, the economy moves from recession into recovery and at a peak, it moves from recovery, into recession. Economists understand these turning points like seismologists understand earthquakes. They know quite a lot about the forces that produce them and the mechanisms at work when they occur, but they can't predict them. The forces that bring business cycle turning points are the swings in autonomous expenditure – in investment and exports. The mechanism that gives momentum to the new direction the economy is taking is the multiplier process that we've just studied. Let's use what we've now learned to examine these turning points.

A Recovery Begins   A recovery is triggered by an increase in autonomous expenditure that increases aggregate planned expenditure. At the moment the economy turns the corner into recovery, aggregate planned expenditure exceeds real GDP. In this situation, firms see their stocks taking

FIGURE 28.10

The Multiplier and the Slope of the *AE* Curve

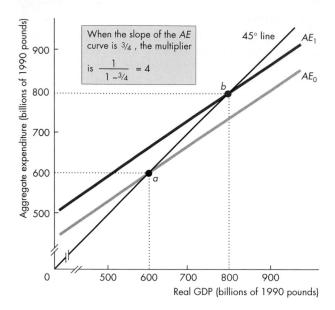

(a) Multiplier is 4

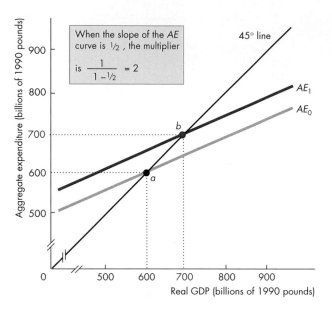

(a) Multiplier is 2

Imports and income taxes make the *AE* curve less steep and reduce the value of the multiplier. In part (a), with no imports and income taxes the slope of the *AE* curve is 0.75 (the marginal propensity to consume) and the multiplier

is 4 . But with imports and income taxes, the slope of the *AE* curve is less than the marginal propensity to consume. In part (b), the slope of the *AE* curve is 0.5. In this case, the multiplier is 2.

---

an unplanned dive. The recovery now begins. To meet their stock targets, firms increase production and real GDP begins to increase. This initial increase in real GDP brings higher incomes that stimulate consumption expenditure. The multiplier process kicks in and the recovery picks up speed. The expansion ends when real GDP has increased to equal aggregate planned expenditure and there are no unplanned stock changes.

A Recession Begins The process we've just described works in reverse at a business cycle peak. A recession is triggered by a decrease in autonomous expenditure that decreases aggregate planned expenditure. At the moment the economy turns the corner into recession, real GDP exceeds aggregate planned expenditure. In this situation, firms see unplanned stocks piling up. The recession now begins. To lower their stocks, firms cut production and real GDP begins to decrease. This

initial decrease in real GDP brings lower incomes that cut consumption expenditure. The multiplier process reinforces the initial cut in autonomous expenditure and the recession takes hold. The recession ends when real GDP has fallen to equal aggregate planned expenditure and there are no unplanned stock changes. *Reading Between the Lines* on pp. 734–735 examines the French multiplier in action.

The Next UK Recession? During 1995, stocks increased rapidly in the United Kingdom. Were these stock changes planned or unplanned? If they were planned, they would *not* trigger a change in production. But if they were unplanned, firms would cut production and real GDP growth could fall in 1996. However, a reduction in the rate of growth of GDP is not a reduction in the level of GDP. The next recession will not occur in the foreseeable future.

◆ A change in autonomous expenditure changes real GDP by an amount determined by the multiplier.

◆ The greater the marginal propensity to consume, the smaller is the marginal propensity to import, and the smaller the marginal tax rate, the larger is the multiplier.

◆ Fluctuations in autonomous expenditure brings business cycle turning points.

We've seen that the economy does not operate like the shock absorbers on Brian Tyrer's car. The economy's potholes and bumps are changes in autonomous expenditure – mainly brought about by changes in investment and exports. And while the price level is sticky, these economic potholes and bumps are not smoothed out. Instead they are amplified. But we've only considered the adjustments in spending that occur in the very short term when the price level is sticky. What happens when the price level changes? And what happens in the long run? Let's answer these questions.

The Multiplier, Real GDP and the Price Level

When firms are having trouble keeping up with sales and their stocks fall below target, they increase production, but at some point they raise their prices. Similarly, when firms find unwanted stocks piling up, they decrease production, but eventually they cut their prices. So far, we've studied the macroeconomic consequences of firms changing their production levels when their sales change, but we've not looked at the effects of price changes. When individual firms change their prices, the economy's price level changes.

To study the simultaneous determination of real GDP and the price level, we use the *aggregate demand–aggregate supply model*, which is explained in Chapter 27. There is a connection between the aggregate demand–aggregate supply model and the equilibrium expenditure model that we've used in this chapter. The key to the relationship between these two models is the distinction between the aggregate *expenditure* curve and the aggregate *demand* curve.

Aggregate Expenditure and Aggregate Demand

The aggregate expenditure curve is the relationship between the aggregate planned expenditure and real GDP, all other influences on aggregate planned expenditure remaining the same. The aggregate demand curve is the relationship between the aggregate quantity of goods and services demanded and the price level, all other influences on aggregate demand remaining the same. Let's explore the links between these two relationships.

Aggregate Expenditure and the Price Level

At a given price level, there is a given level of aggregate planned expenditure. But if the price level changes, so does aggregate planned expenditure. Why? There are three main reasons[1]. They are:

1. Real money balances effect
2. Intertemporal substitution effect
3. International substitution effect

Real money is the purchasing power of money, which is measured by the quantity of money divided by the price level. A rise in the price level, other things remaining the same, decreases the quantity of real money and a smaller quantity of real money decreases aggregate planned expenditure – the *real money balances effect*. A rise in the price level, other things remaining the same, makes current goods and services more costly relative to future goods and services, and results in a delay in purchases – the *intertemporal substitution effect*. A rise in the price level, other things remaining the same, makes UK-produced goods more expensive relative to foreign-produced goods and services, and increases imports and decreases exports – the *international substitution effect*.

When the price level rises, each of these effects reduces aggregate planned expenditure at each level of real GDP. As a result, when the price level rises, the aggregate expenditure curve shifts downward. A fall in the price level has the opposite effect. When the price level falls, the aggregate expenditure curve shifts upward.

---

[1] These reasons are explained more fully in Chapter 27, pp. 691–693.

Figure 28.11(a) illustrates these effects. When the price level is 130, the aggregate expenditure curve is AE_0, which intersects the 45° line at point b. Equilibrium expenditure and real GDP are £600 billion. If the price level increases to 170, the aggregate expenditure curve shifts downward to AE_1, which intersects the 45° line at point a. Equilibrium expenditure and real GDP are £400 billion. If the price level decreases to 90, the aggregate expenditure curve shifts upward to AE_2, which intersects the 45° line at point c. Equilibrium expenditure and real GDP are £800 billion.

We've just seen that when the price level changes, other things remaining the same, the aggregate expenditure curve shifts and equilibrium expenditure changes. And when the price level changes, other things remaining the same, there is a movement along the aggregate demand curve. Figure 28.11(b) illustrates these movements. At a price level of 130, the aggregate quantity of goods and services demanded is £600 billion – point b on the aggregate demand curve AD. If the price level increases to 170, the aggregate quantity of goods and services demanded decreases to £400 billion. There is a movement along the aggregate demand curve to point a. If the price level decreases to 90, the aggregate quantity of goods and services demanded increases to £800 billion. There is a movement along the aggregate demand curve to point c.

Each point on the aggregate demand curve corresponds to a point of equilibrium expenditure. The equilibrium expenditure points a, b and c in Fig. 28.11(a) correspond to points a, b and c on the aggregate demand curve in Fig. 28.11(b).

When the price level changes, other things remaining the same, the aggregate expenditure curve shifts and there is a movement along the aggregate demand curve. When any other influence on aggregate planned expenditure changes, both the aggregate expenditure curve and the aggregate demand curve shift. For example, an increase in investment or in exports increases both aggregate planned expenditure and aggregate demand and shifts both the AE curve and the AD curve. Figure 28.12 illustrates the effect of such an increase.

Initially, the aggregate expenditure curve is AE_0 in part (a) and the aggregate demand curve is AD_0 in part (b). The price level is 130, real GDP is £600 billion, and the economy is at point a in both parts of the figure. Now suppose that investment increases by £100 billion. At a constant price level of 130, the aggregate expenditure curve shifts upward to AE_1.

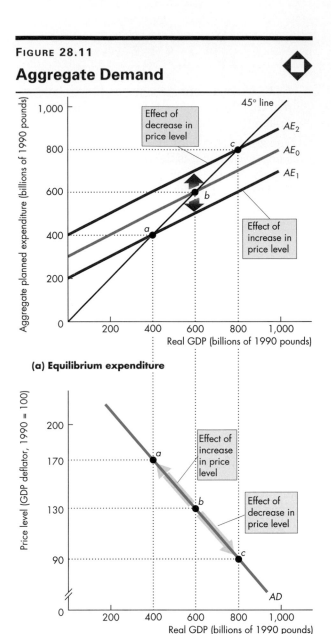

FIGURE 28.11

Aggregate Demand

(a) Equilibrium expenditure

(b) Aggregate demand

The position of the AE curve depends on the price level. When the price level is 130, the AE curve is AE_0. Equilibrium expenditure is at point b, and real GDP demanded is £600 billion. When the price level rises to 170, the AE curve shifts downward to AE_1, and equilibrium expenditure is at point a. Real GDP demanded is £400 billion. When the price level falls to 90, the AE curve shifts upward to AE_2, and equilibrium expenditure is at point c. Real GDP demanded is £800 billion.

Part (b) shows the AD curve. A change in the price level shifts the AE curve but results in a *movement along* the AD curve. Points a, b and c on the AD curve correspond to the equilibrium expenditure points a, b and c in part (a).

This curve intersects the 45° line at an equilibrium expenditure of £800 billion (point *b*). This equilibrium expenditure of £800 billion is the aggregate quantity of goods and services demanded at a price level of 130, as shown by point *b* in part (b). Point *b* lics on a ncw aggregate demand curve. The aggregate demand curve has shifted rightward to AD_1.

But how do we know by how much the *AD* curve shifts? The answer is determined by the multiplier. The larger the multiplier, the larger is the shift in the aggregate demand curve that results from a given change in autonomous expenditure. In this example, the multiplier is 2. A £100 billion increase in investment produces a £200 billion increase in the aggregate quantity of goods and services demanded at each price level. That is, a £100 billion increase in autonomous expenditure shifts the aggregate demand curve rightward by £200 billion.

A decrease in autonomous expenditure shifts the aggregate expenditure curve downward and shifts the aggregate demand curve leftward. You can see these effects by reversing the change that we've just studied. Suppose that the economy is initially at point *b* on the aggregate expenditure curve AE_1 and the aggregate demand curve AD_1. A decrease in autonomous expenditure shifts the aggregate planned expenditure curve downward to AE_0. The aggregate quantity of goods and services demanded falls from £800 billion to £600 billion and the aggregate demand curve shifts leftward to AD_0.

We can summarize what we have just discovered in the following way. An increase in autonomous expenditure arising from some source other than a change in the price level shifts the *AE* curve upward and the *AD* curve rightward. The magnitude of the shift of the *AD* curve is determined by the change in autonomous expenditure and the multiplier.

Equilibrium GDP and the Price Level

In Chapter 27, we learned that aggregate demand and short-run aggregate supply determine equilibrium real GDP and the price level. We've now put aggregate demand under a more powerful microscope and discovered that a change in investment (or in any component of autonomous expenditure) changes aggregate demand and shifts the aggregate demand curve. The magnitude of the shift depends on the multiplier. But whether a change in autonomous expenditure results ultimately in a change in real GDP, or a change in the price level, or some combination of the two depends on aggregate supply. There are two time-frames to consider:

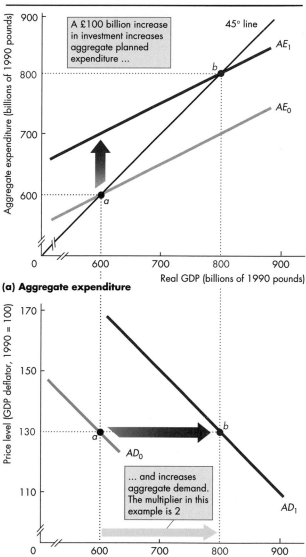

FIGURE 28.12

A Change in Aggregate Demand

(a) Aggregate expenditure

(b) Aggregate demand

The price level is 130. When the aggregate expenditure curve is AE_0 (part a), the aggregate demand curve is AD_0 (part b). An increase in autonomous expenditure shifts the aggregate expenditure curve upward to AE_1. The new equilibrium occurs where AE_1 intersects the 45° line at a real GDP of £800 billion. Because the quantity of real GDP demanded at a price level of 130 increases to £800 billion, the aggregate demand curve shifts rightward to AD_1. The magnitude of the rightward shift of the aggregate demand curve is determined by the change in autonomous expenditure and the size of the multiplier.

1. The short run

2. The long run

First, we'll see what happens in the short run. Then we'll look at the long run.

An Increase in Aggregate Demand in the Short Run

Figure 28.13 describes the economy. In part (a), the aggregate expenditure curve is AE_0, and equilibrium expenditure and real GDP are £600 billion – point a. In part (b), aggregate demand is AD_0 and the short-run aggregate supply curve is SAS. (Look at Chapter 27 if you need to refresh your understanding of this curve.) Equilibrium is at point a, where the aggregate demand and short-run aggregate supply curves intersect. The price level is 130 and real GDP is £600 billion.

Now suppose that investment increases by £100 billion. With the price level sticky at 130, the aggregate expenditure curve shifts upward to AE_1. Equilibrium expenditure increases to £800 billion – point b in part (a). In part (b), the aggregate demand curve shifts rightward by £200 billion, from AD_0 to AD_1. How far the aggregate demand curve shifts is determined by the multiplier when the price level is sticky. But with this new aggregate demand curve, the price level does not remain fixed. The price level rises and as it does so, the aggregate expenditure curve shifts downward. The short-run equilibrium occurs when the aggregate expenditure curve has shifted downward to AE_2 and the new aggregate demand curve, AD_1, intersects the short-run aggregate supply curve. Real GDP is £760 billion and the price level is 136 (at point c).

Taking price level effects into account, the increase in investment still has a multiplier effect on real GDP, but the effect is smaller than it would be if the price level was sticky forever. The steeper the slope of the short-run aggregate supply curve, the larger is the increase in the price level and the smaller is the multiplier effect on real GDP.

An Increase in Aggregate Demand in the Long Run

In the long run, the economy is at full-employment equilibrium and on its long-run aggregate supply curve. When the economy is at full employment, an increase in aggregate demand has the same short-run effect as we've just worked out, but its long-run effect is different.

Figure 28.14 illustrates the long-run effect. Potential GDP is £600 billion so long-run aggregate supply is LAS. When investment increases by £100

FIGURE 28.13

The Multiplier in the Short Run

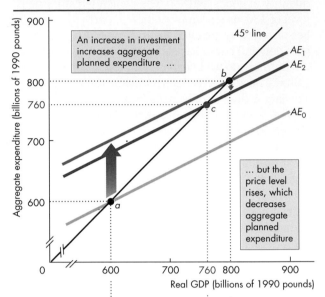

(a) Aggregate expenditure

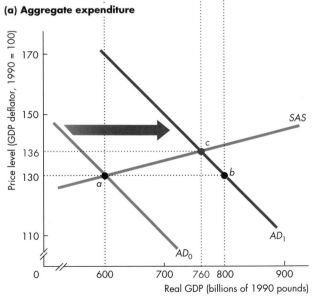

(b) Aggregate demand

An increase in investment shifts the AE curve upward from AE_0 to AE_1 (part a). As a result, the AD curve shifts from AD_0 to AD_1 (part b). The distance ab is determined by the multiplier when the price level is sticky. At the price level 130, there is excess demand. The price level rises, and the higher price level shifts the AE curve downward to AE_2. The economy moves to point c in both parts. With flexible prices, the multiplier is smaller than when prices are sticky. The steeper the SAS curve, the larger is the increase in the price level, the smaller is the increase in real GDP, and the smaller is the multiplier.

FIGURE 28.14

The Multiplier in the Long Run

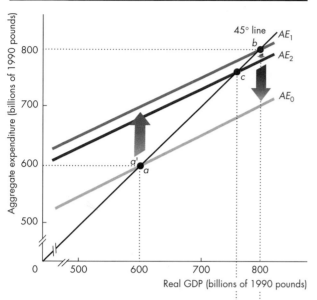

(a) Aggregate expenditure

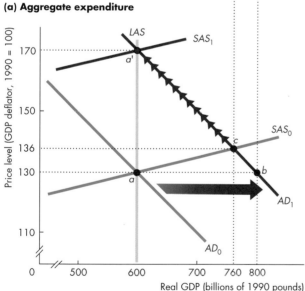

(b) Aggregate demand

Starting from point *a*, an increase in investment shifts the *AE* curve to AE_1 and shifts the *AD* curve to AD_1. In the short run, the economy moves to point *c*. In the long run, the money wage rate rises, the *SAS* curve shifts to SAS_1, the *AE* curve shifts back to AE_0, the price level rises and real GDP falls. The economy moves to point *a'* and the long-run multiplier is zero.

billion, the aggregate expenditure curve shifts upward to AE_1 and the aggregate demand curve shifts rightward to AD_1. The price level rises to a short-run equilibrium with real GDP at £760 billion and the price level at 136. But this situation is an above full-employment equilibrium. The work-force is more than fully employed, and there are shortages of labour. The money wage rate begins to rise. The higher money wage rate increases costs, and short-run aggregate supply decreases. The *SAS* curve begins to shift leftward. As a result, the price level increases further. As the price level rises, aggregate planned expenditure decreases and the *AE* curve shifts downwards toward AE_0. Eventually, when the money wage rate and the price level have increased by the same percentage, real GDP is again at its full-employment level. The multiplier in the long run is zero.

REVIEW

◆ A change in the price level shifts the *AE* curve and brings a movement along the *AD* curve.

◆ A change in autonomous expenditure not caused by a change in the price level shifts both the *AE* curve and the *AD* curve, and the multiplier determines the magnitude of the shift in the *AD* curve.

◆ The increase in real GDP that results from an increase in autonomous expenditure is smaller than the increase in aggregate demand.

◆ An increase in aggregate demand at full employment leaves real GDP unchanged but increases the price level. The long-run multiplier is zero.

◆ ◆ ◆ ◆ We've now seen how real GDP deviates from its long-term growth path when aggregate demand fluctuates, and we've studied the multiplier effect that amplifies the disturbances to aggregate demand. ◆ In the next three chapters we're going to see how macroeconomic policy can be used to smooth economic fluctuations. In Chapter 29, we study fiscal policy and discover what the government can do (and can't do) with taxes and its own spending to smooth economic fluctuations and stimulate production, and in Chapters 30 and 31, we study money and the actions the government and the Bank of England can take to smooth fluctuations and to keep inflation in check.

The French Multiplier in Action

The Essence of the Story

BUSINESS WEEK, 15 APRIL 1996

The economy lacks *joie de vivre*

James C. Cooper and Kathleen Madigan

France   For months, private forecasters knew the French government's projection of 2.8% economic growth for 1996 was optimistic. On March 25, the forecast was slashed to 1.3%. Still, Finance Minister Jean Arthuis maintains that the government will meet this year's target of 288 billion francs ($57 billion) and that the overall public-sector shortfall will dip to 4% of gross domestic product in 1996, and to the Maastricht criterion of 3% in 1997. Don't count on it.

The problem: a weak economy. France has averted a recession, thanks to a lift from government spending and tax incentives that buoyed growth during last year's sharp second-half slowdown. But weak private-sector demand has left businesses with excess inventories that will have to be run down at the expense of gains in output and jobs. In March, businesses were more upbeat about the future, but readings on recent orders, output, and pricing stayed soft.

Consumer demand appears to have rebounded in the first quarter, but that's a temporary bounce from December's strike-depressed levels. Going forward, higher taxes, including a February hike to cut the social security deficit, will depress buying power, and a weak job market will limit income growth. The jobless rate held at 11.8% in February and is expected to top 12% this year, making it unlikely that households will dip into their savings by as much as Arthuis' budget projections require. And the franc's recent strength and German-led weakness in Europe will restrain exports.

Government demand is set to decline. On top of other restrictive budget measures, the recent freeze in spending credit intends to save 20 billion francs. Still, the combination of a spending overshoot, due to rising unemployment compensation, and a revenue shortfall, due to the weak economy, is shaping up to be larger than that planned saving. The social security deficit is expected to miss its target as well.

With 2% inflation and a strong franc, the Bank of France has room to trim interest rates. But attempts to squeeze the deficit more will put the economy – and the government of Prime Minister Alain Juppé – at risk.

■ Official predictions of French GDP growth for 1996 have proved to be too optimistic. In March 1996, the forecast was cut from 2.8 per cent to 1.3 per cent.

■ The budget deficit is expected to be 4 per cent of GDP in 1996 and 3 per cent in 1997.

■ Domestic demand has weakened but a recession was averted by an expansion in government spending.

■ A build-up of stocks will be run down during 1996 and demand is expected to decline further. Unemployment is expected to rise in the future but taxes will rise to pay for some of the deficit on the social security budget. Government spending is expected to decline in an attempt to meet the target of a budget deficit of 3 per cent of GDP by 1997.

Economic Analysis

■ A prediction of GDP growth of 2.8 per cent in 1996 by the French government was too optimistic because of a fall in private sector demand. Figure 1 shows that French economic growth slowed down sharply in 1995. It picked up in the first quarter of 1996 but fell back in the second quarter.

■ The downturn in private sector demand has led to a build-up in stocks which signals a cut in orders and production.

■ A recession was avoided because government spending increased to offset the decline in private spending. Figure 2 shows that a fall in private sector demand shifts the *AE* curve downward from AE_0 to AE_1, but a rise in government spending shifts AE1 to AE2. However, the rise in government spending was insufficient to close the recessionary gap indicated by the difference between real GDP and potential GDP.

■ Figure 3 shows real GDP and potential GDP with a projection made by the OECD for the second half of 1996 and for 1997. The projection shows that although demand rises, potential GDP also rises so that the recessionary gap is not closed.

■ A rise in taxes in 1996 and cuts in government spending in 1997 to meet the target of a deficit of 3 per cent of GDP will reduce demand in 1997. Aggregate demand will grow at a moderate rate in 1997.

■ The article suggests that the fall in demand will reduce tax revenues and make it harder for the government to meet its fiscal target. Interest rates could be lowered to stimulate private demand but further cuts in government spending will worsen the recessionary gap.

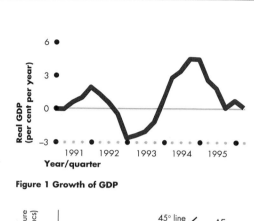

Figure 1 Growth of GDP

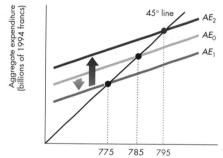

Figure 2

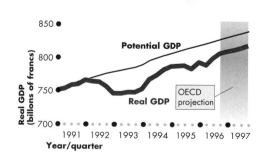

Figure 3 Real GDP and potential GDP

SUMMARY

Sticky Prices and Expenditure Plans

When the *price level* is sticky, *aggregate* expenditure determines real GDP. There is a two-way relationship between aggregate expenditure and real GDP. An increase in real GDP brings an increase in aggregate *planned* expenditure and an increase in aggregate expenditure brings an increase in real GDP.

Planned consumption expenditure is described by the consumption function – the relationship between consumption expenditure and disposable income. *Planned* saving is described by the saving function – the relationship between saving and disposable income. The influence of disposable income on consumption expenditure is determined by the marginal propensity to consume (*MPC*), which is equal to the slope of the consumption function. Similarly, the influence of disposable income on saving is determined by the marginal propensity to save (*MPS*), which is equal to the slope of the saving function.

The influence of real GDP on imports is described by the import function. An increase in real GDP brings an increase in imports, and the magnitude of the increase in imports is determined by the marginal propensity to import. (pp. 712–719)

Real GDP with a Sticky Price Level

The aggregate expenditure curve shows the relationship between aggregate *planned* expenditure and real GDP. *Actual* aggregate expenditure is always equal to real GDP. But aggregate *planned* expenditure is not necessarily equal to actual aggregate expenditure and real GDP. Equilibrium expenditure occurs when aggregate planned expenditure equals real GDP. When aggregate planned expenditure and real GDP are unequal, a process of convergence towards equilibrium expenditure occurs. When real GDP is below its equilibrium level, an unplanned fall in stocks stimulates an increase in production and an increase in real GDP. When real GDP is above its equilibrium level, an unplanned rise in stocks brings a decrease in production and decrease a in real GDP. (pp. 720–723)

The Multiplier

The multiplier is the magnified effect of a change in autonomous expenditure on real GDP. An increase in investment (or any other component of autonomous expenditure) increases real GDP and disposable income, which in turn increases consumption expenditure and adds more to real GDP than the initial increase in investment.

The multiplier is equal to 1 divided by the marginal propensity to save. The larger the marginal propensity to consume, the smaller the marginal propensity to save, the larger is the multiplier. The multiplier is also influenced by the marginal propensity to import and by the marginal income tax rate. For a given marginal propensity to consume, the larger the marginal propensity to import and the higher the marginal tax rate, the smaller is the multiplier. (pp. 724–729)

The Multiplier, Real GDP and the Price Level

The aggregate demand curve is the relationship between the quantity of real GDP demanded and the price level, other things remaining the same. The aggregate expenditure curve is the relationship between aggregate planned expenditure and real GDP, other things remaining the same. At a given price level, there is a given aggregate expenditure curve. A change in the price level changes aggregate planned expenditure and shifts the aggregate expenditure curve. A change in the price level also creates a movement along the aggregate demand curve. Thus a movement along the aggregate demand curve is associated with a shift in the aggregate expenditure curve.

A change in autonomous expenditure not caused by a change in the price level shifts the aggregate expenditure curve and also shifts the aggregate demand curve. The size of the shift in the aggregate demand curve depends on the size of the multiplier and the change in autonomous expenditure.

Because real GDP and the price level are determined by both aggregate demand and aggregate supply, the short-run multiplier is smaller than when the price level is sticky (pp. 729–733)

K E Y   E L E M E N T S

Key Terms

Aggregate planned expenditure, 712
Autonomous expenditure, 721
Consumption function, 713
Equilibrium expenditure, 722
Foreign exchange rate, 718
Import function, 718
Induced expenditure, 721
Marginal propensity to consume, 714
Marginal propensity to import, 718
Marginal propensity to save, 714
Multiplier, 724
Saving function, 714

◆ Key Figures

Figure 28.1   Consumption Function and Saving
              Function, 713
Figure 28.2   Marginal Propensities to Consume
              and Save, 715
Figure 28.6   Aggregate Expenditure, 720
Figure 28.7   Equilibrium Expenditure, 723
Figure 28.8   The Multiplier, 724
Figure 28.9   The Multiplier Process, 726
Figure 28.11 Aggregate Demand, 730
Figure 28.12 A Change in Aggregate Demand, 731
Figure 28.13 The Multiplier in the Short Run, 732
Figure 28.14 The Multiplier in the Long Run, 733

R E V I E W   Q U E S T I O N S

1 What are the main implications of sticky prices for the economy as a whole?

2 Explain the two-way relationship between real GDP and aggregate expenditure.

3 What is the main influence on consumption expenditure and saving in the short term?

4 What are the consumption function and the saving function?

5 What is the relationship between the consumption function and the saving function?

6 What is the marginal propensity to consume? Why is it less than 1?

7 Explain the relationship between the marginal propensity to consume and the marginal propensity to save.

8 What is the relationship between the marginal propensity to consume and the slope of the consumption function?

9 What is the relationship between consumption expenditure and GDP and why does the relationship arise?

10 What is the import function and the marginal propensity to import?

11 What is the aggregate expenditure schedule and aggregate expenditure curve?

12 Distinguish between induced expenditure and autonomous expenditure.

13 How is equilibrium expenditure determined?

14 Explain how a recovery gets going when aggregate planned expenditure exceeds real GDP.

15 Explain why an increase in autonomous expenditure shifts the aggregate expenditure curve upward.

16 What is the multiplier?

17 Explain the multiplier process.

18 Why is the multiplier greater than 1? What determines the size of the multiplier?

19 Explain the influence of the marginal propensity to consume, imports and taxes on the size of the multiplier.

20 Describe the relationship between the aggregate expenditure curve and the aggregate demand curve.

21 Explain why the aggregate expenditure curve shifts downward when the price level increases.

22 What happens to the aggregate expenditure curve and the aggregate demand curve when the price level changes and everything else is constant?

23 Explain why an increase in autonomous expenditure increases aggregate demand.

24 Explain why the multiplier is larger in the very short run when the price level is sticky than it is when the price level changes.

25 Explain why the multiplier is zero in the long run.

PROBLEMS

1 You are given the following information about the economy of Eurasthania:

Disposable income (millions of euros per year)	Consumption expenditure (millions of euros per year)
0	5
10	10
20	15
30	20
40	25

a Calculate Eurasthania's marginal propensity to consume.

b Calculate Eurasthania's saving at each level of disposable income.

c Calculate Eurasthania's marginal propensity to save.

d Draw a graph to illustrate the consumption function. Calculate its slope.

e Over what range of disposable income does Eurasthania dissave?

2 You are given the following information about the economy of Happy Isle. When disposable income is zero, consumption expenditure is £80 billion. The marginal propensity to consume is 0.75. Investment is £400 billion; government purchases of goods and services are £600 billion; taxes are a constant £500 billion and do not vary as income varies.

a Calculate autonomous expenditure.

b What is the consumption function?

c What is the saving function?

d Calculate the marginal propensity to consume.

e Calculate the marginal propensity to save.

f What is the equation that describes the aggregate expenditure curve?

g Calculate equilibrium expenditure.

3 You are given the following information about the economy of Zeeland. Autonomous consumption expenditure is £100 billion and the marginal propensity to consume is 0.9. Investment is £460 billion, government purchases of goods and services are £400 billion, taxes are a constant £400 billion – they do not vary with income. Exports are £350 billion and imports are 10 per cent of GDP.

a What is the consumption function?

b What is the equation that describes the aggregate expenditure curve.

c Calculate equilibrium expenditure.

d Calculate the slope of the aggregate expenditure curve in Zeeland.

e If investment falls to £360 billion, what is the change in equilibrium expenditure and what is the size of the multiplier?

4 Suppose that the economy of Zeeland is as described in Problem 3. The price level in Zeeland is 100 and real GDP equals potential GDP.

a If investment increases by £100 billion, what happens to the quantity of real GDP demanded?

b In the short run, does equilibrium real GDP increase by more than, less than, or the same amount as the increase in the quantity of real GDP demanded?

c In the long run, does equilibrium real GDP increase by more than, less than, or the same amount as the increase in the quantity of real GDP demanded?

d In the short run, does the price level in Zeeland rise, fall, or remain unchanged?

e In the long run, does the price level in Zeeland rise, fall, or remain unchanged?

5 Study *Reading Between the Lines* on pp. 734–735 and then answer the following questions.

a Why was the French GDP growth in 1996 weaker than expected?

b How was a recession averted?

c Draw a figure to illustrate the position of the French economy in 1996.

d Draw a figure to illustrate the expected position of the French economy in 1997 as viewed from 1996.

APPENDIX

TO

CHAPTER

28

IMPORTS, TAXES
AND THE
MULITPLIER

To work out the effects of imports and taxes on the multiplier, begin with the aggregate expenditure equation. Real GDP, Y, equals consumption expenditure, C, plus investment, I, plus government purchases, G, plus exports, EX, minus imports, IM. That is:

$$Y = C + I + G + EX - IM$$

Investment plus government purchases plus exports are *autonomous expenditure,* which we'll call A. So, more simply,

$$Y = C + A - IM$$

The changes in real GDP and the component of aggregate expenditure are:

$$\Delta Y = \Delta C + \Delta A - \Delta IM$$

The change in consumption expenditure is equal to the marginal propensity to consume, MPC, multiplied by the change in disposable income, YD. That is:

$$\Delta C = MPC \times \Delta YD$$

The change in disposable income, YD, equals the change in real GDP minus the change in taxes, T. That is:

$$\Delta YD = \Delta Y - \Delta T$$

The change in taxes equals the change in real GDP multiplied by the marginal tax rate, MTR. That is:

$$\Delta T = MTR \times \Delta Y$$

Combining these last three relationships gives:

$$\Delta C = MPC \times (\Delta Y - MTR \times \Delta Y)$$

Or:

$$\Delta C = MPC \times (1 - MTR) \times \Delta Y$$

The change in imports equals the marginal propensity to import, *MPI*, multiplied by real GDP. That is:

$$\Delta IM = MPI \times \Delta Y$$

Using the last two equations with the fact that

$$\Delta Y = \Delta C + \Delta A - \Delta IM$$

gives:

$$\Delta Y = MPC \times (1 - MTR) \times \Delta Y + \Delta A - MPI \times \Delta Y$$

which means that:

$$(1 - MPC(1 - MTR) + MPI) \times \Delta Y = \Delta A$$

So the multiplier is:

$$\frac{\Delta Y}{\Delta A} = \frac{1}{(1 - MPC(1 - MTR) + MPI)}$$

CHAPTER

29

THE GOVERNMENT BUDGET AND FISCAL POLICY

After studying this chapter you will be able to:

◆ Describe the budget statement

◆ Describe the recent history of government expenditures, tax revenues, and the budget deficit in the UK

◆ Distinguish between automatic and discretionary fiscal policy

◆ Define and explain the fiscal policy multipliers

◆ Explain the effects of fiscal policy in both the short run and the long run

◆ Distinguish between and explain the demand side and the supply side effects of fiscal policy

I N 1994, THE GOVERNMENT PLANNED TO SPEND £301.8 BILLION BETWEEN 1995 AND 1996. What are the effects of government spending on the economy? Does it create jobs? Or does it destroy them? Does a pound spent by the government on goods and services have the same effect as a pound spent by someone else? ◆ Although the government planned to *spend* 42 pence of every pound earned, it did not plan to tax us by that amount. Its plans were for tax and social security revenues of £278.7 billion or 38 pence of every pound earned. What are the effects of taxes on the economy? Do taxes harm employment and economic growth? ◆ The plan to have tax revenues fall short of expenditures is not uncommon in developed economies. The last time the United Kingdom had a budget surplus was in 1990, but usually the government has planned to spend more than it expected to receive. ◆ The United Kingdom is not alone in Europe in this respect. All the governments of the countries in the European Union, except for Luxembourg, ended up spending more than they received in revenues during the 1990s. ◆ Government debt as a percentage of GDP rose from 35.3 per cent in 1990 to 51.5 per cent in 1995. Does it matter if the government doesn't balance its books? What are the effects of an ongoing government deficit

Balancing Acts at Westminster

and accumulating debt? Do they slow down economic growth? Do they impose a burden on future generations – on you and your children? Many of the countries of Europe have different levels of government deficits and government debt as a proportion of GDP. Some of the conditions for joining a European Monetary Union before the millennium are for countries to converge to a government budget deficit of 3 per cent of GDP and a level of debt of 60 per cent of GDP. For some countries this will mean reducing government expenditure and possibly imposing higher taxes. What will be the likely effects of such a policy on the individual countries and in Europe generally?

◆ ◆ ◆ ◆ These are the questions that you will explore in this chapter. We'll begin by describing the budget and the components that contribute to it. We'll also look at the development of the budget in the United Kingdom and other EU countries. We'll then use the multiplier analysis of Chapter 28 and the aggregate supply–aggregate demand model of Chapter 27 to study the effects of the budget on the economy.

The Government Budget

The *Financial Statement and Budget Report by Her Majesty's Treasury* is an annual statement of the expenditures and tax revenues of the government put to Parliament by the Chancellor of the Exchequer. The main purposes of the Financial Statement, sometimes referred to as the Budget Statement, are:

1. To state the items of expenditure of the government and to lay out the plans to finance its activities

2. To stabilize the economy

The first purpose of the budget – and its original purpose – is to ensure that funds are available to finance the business of the government. Until the view that government spending can play a part in generating aggregate demand became generally accepted, the budget had no other purpose. The second purpose is to pursue the government's fiscal policy. **Fiscal policy** is the use of the budget to achieve macroeconomic objectives such as full employment, sustained long-term economic growth and price level stability. The November 1995 Financial Statement begins: 'This budget continues the work of recent years to promote sustainable economic growth with low inflation.'[1] It is this second purpose that we focus on in this chapter.

Highlights of the 1995 Budget

Table 29.1 shows the main items in the **government budget**. The numbers are projected amounts for the fiscal years April 1995 to end-March 1996 – fiscal 1995 – and April 1996 to end- March 1997 – fiscal 1996. Notice first the three main parts of the table: *expenditures* are the government's outlays, *total receipts* are the government's receipts and the *deficit* (referred to as the General Government Borrowing Requirement or GGBR) is the amount by which the government's expenditures exceed its tax revenues. The next item is the public corporations' market and overseas borrowing. This represents the net borrowing of the industries that come under state control. In the United Kingdom this item is small and is expected to decline as more and more

---

[1] *Financial Statement and Budget Report 1996–97*, No 30, London, HMSO, November 1995.

TABLE 29.1

The Public Finances in 1995–1996 and 1996–1997

Item	1995/96	1996/97
	(billions of pounds)	
Expenditure	**302.1**	**308.3**
Expenditure on goods and services	149.6	152.4
Transfer payments	127.0	129.0
Debt interest	25.5	26.9
Total receipts	**271.9**	**284.8**
Value added taxes and other indirect taxes	77.2	84.1
Income taxes	68.9	70.2
Social security contributions	44.4	46.9
Other receipts and royalties	43.1	42.3
Corporate taxes and rates	38.3	41.3
GGBR	**30.2**	**23.5**
Public corporations	**−1.2**	**−1.1**
PSBR	**29.0**	**22.4**

Source: HM Treasury, *Financial Statement and Budget Report 1996–97*, No 30, London, HMSO, November 1995.

public enterprises are privatized. The final item is the Public Sector Borrowing Requirement (PSBR) which refers to the deficit for the public sector as a whole.

Expenditures Expenditures are classified in three categories:

1. Expenditure on goods and services
2. Transfer payments
3. Debt interest

The largest item of spending, is government expenditure. *Expenditure on goods and services* are expenditures on final goods and services, and in 1995/96 they were expected to total £149.6 billion. These expenditures include those on defence, the National Health Service, computers for schools, construction of new roads and motorways, and urban regeneration. This component of the budget is government purchases of goods and services that appears in the circular flow of expenditure and income and in the national income and product accounts (see Chapter 23, pp. 577–581).

Transfer payments are payments to individuals, businesses, other levels of government and the rest of the world. In 1995/96, this item was expected to be £127 billion. It includes social security benefits, health care, unemployment benefits, welfare supplements, grants to local authorities and aid to developing countries.

Debt interest is the interest on the government debt minus interest received by the government on its own investments. In 1995/96 this item was expected to be £25.5 billion – about 15 per cent of total current and capital spending.

Total current receipts   Total current receipts were projected to be £271.9 billion in fiscal 1995. These revenues come from five sources:

1. Taxes on income

2. Social security contributions

3. Value added taxes (VAT) and other taxes on expenditure

4. Corporate taxes and business rates

5. Other receipts and royalties

The largest source of revenue is *taxes on expenditure*. These are the taxes paid by consumers on goods that carry VAT (currently 17.5 per cent), and special duties and taxes on gambling, alcoholic drinks, petrol and luxury items. The total from taxes on expenditure is projected to be £77.2 billion. The second largest source is taxes on *income*, which in 1995 were expected to be £68.9 billion. These are the taxes paid by individuals on their incomes. Third in size are *social security contributions*. These are taxes paid by workers and employers to fund the welfare and health programmes. Fourth is *other*

receipts and royalties. These are small items including oil royalties, stamp duties, car taxes, miscellaneous rents, dividends from abroad and profits from nationalized industries. The final item is *corporate taxes and rates*. This is the taxes expected from the profits of businesses and the rates businesses pay for government services.

Deficit   The government's budget balance is equal to its tax revenues minus its expenditures. That is,

Budget balance = Tax revenues − Expenditures

If tax revenues exceed expenditures, the government has a **budget surplus**. If expenditures exceed tax revenues, the government has a **budget deficit**. If tax revenues equal expenditures, the government has a **balanced budget**. In 1995/96, with projected expenditures of £302.1 billion and tax revenues of £271.9 billion, the government projected a budget deficit of £30.2 billion. After allowing for a small repayment from public corporations the projected PSBR was £29 billion.

Big numbers like these are hard to visualize and hard to compare over time. To get a better sense of the magnitude of taxes, spending and the deficit we often express them as percentages of GDP. Expressing them in this way let us see how large government is relative to the size of the economy, and it also helps us to study *changes* in the scale of government over time.

How typical is the budget of 1995? Let's look at its recent history.

FIGURE 29.1

The UK Government Budget Deficit

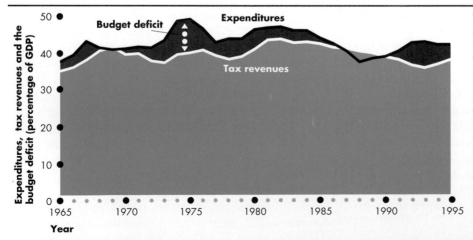

The figure records the UK government's expenditures, tax revenues, and budget deficit from 1965/66 to 1995/96. In the late 1960s, the deficit was small, but during the 1970s it became large and persisted through to the 1980s. A budget surplus occurred in the late 1980s, but the budget deficit increased again in the 1990s. The increase in the 1990s came about through a combination of a decrease in tax revenues from tax cuts in the 1980s and an increase in expenditures.

Source: HM Treasury, *Financial Statement and Budget Report 1996–97*, No 30, London, HMSO, November 1995.

The Budget in Historical Perspective

Figure 29.1 shows the government's tax revenues, expenditures and budget deficit since 1965/66. Throughout most of this period there was a budget deficit. The deficit rises in recessions and falls in recoveries. The deficit rose to a peak following the recession of the 1970s. Government receipts were actually higher than expenditures in the fiscal years 1987–89. But the deficit increased again during the 1990s.

Why did the government deficit grow so sharply in the 1990s? The immediate answer is that expenditures increased and tax revenues decreased. But which components of expenditures increased and which sources of tax revenues decreased? Let's look at tax revenues and expenditures in a bit more detail.

Tax Revenues Figure 29.2(a) shows the components of tax revenues received by the government as a percentage of GDP, between 1988 and 1995. Central government receipts increased as a percentage of GDP to 1991 and then declined in the following three years. The reason for this is that the recession reduced the amount of tax receipts obtained from direct taxes. Firms' profits declined, reducing the take from corporate taxes, and the

---

FIGURE 29.2

UK Government Tax Revenues and Expenditures

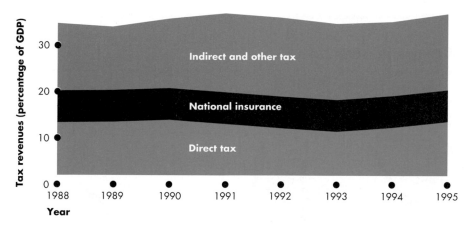

(a) Tax revenues

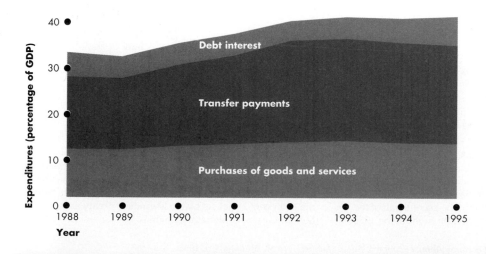

Part (a) shows the three components of government tax revenues: direct income taxes (including corporate income taxes), indirect taxes (including VAT) and national insurance contributions. Revenues from direct income taxes declined in 1993 but rose in 1995. The other two components of tax revenues remained steady.

Part (b) shows three components of government expenditures: purchases of goods and services, debt interest and transfer payments. Purchases of goods and services has remained largely constant in the past eight years. Transfer payments have risen in the 1990s recession. Debt interest has remained steady.

Source: HM Treasury, *Financial Statement and Budget Report 1996–97*, No 30, London, HMSO, November 1995.

increase in unemployment reduced the amount of tax gained from personal taxes.

Expenditures   Figure 29.2(b) shows the components of central government expenditures as percentages of GDP, between 1988 and 1995. Total expenditures increased as a proportion of GDP during the first half of the 1990s. The main reason for this is that transfer payments increased substantially while purchases of goods and services increased only slightly. Transfer payments increased because the unemployment and early retirements caused by the recession have led to a higher level of benefit and welfare payments.

Part of government expenditure is the payment of interest on the existing level of debt held by individuals. A high level of debt means that more interest payments have to be made. The United Kingdom does not have a high level of debt in relation to its GDP in comparison with many other countries in the

European Union. However, high debt interest payments can make it difficult for a country to control its deficit. To understand why, we need to see the connection between the deficit and government debt.

Deficit and Debt   **Government debt** is the total amount of borrowing by the government. It is the sum of past deficits minus the sum of past surpluses. If the government has a deficit, its debt increases, and if it has a surplus, its debt decreases. Once a persistent deficit emerges, the deficit begins to feed on itself. The deficit leads to increased borrowing; increased borrowing leads to larger interest payments; and larger interest payments lead to a larger deficit. This is one of the reasons high-debt countries like Italy and Belgium find it difficult to reduce their debt.

Figure 29.3(a) shows the history of government debt in Italy and Belgium since 1970. In the case of Italy, the level of debt as a proportion of GDP

FIGURE 29.3

The Government Debt of Italy and Belgium

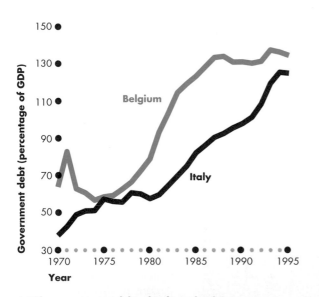

(a) The government debt of Italy and Belgium

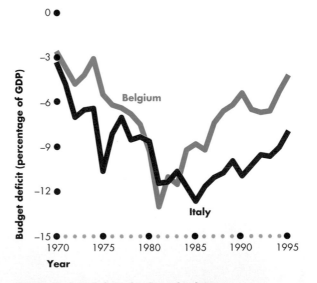

(b) The budget deficit of Italy and Belgium

In part (a) you can see the government debt (the accumulation of past budget deficits less past budget surpluses) of Italy and Belgium. Both countries had debt in excess of 120 per cent of GDP in 1995. While Belgium has made some attempt to control the growth of its debt during the second half of the 1980s, Italy has allowed its debt to grow throughout the 1980s

and into the 1990s. In part (b) you can see the budget deficits of both countries. The peak in the deficit occured in the recession of the early 1980s. Since the 1980s, both countries have been struggling to get their respective budget deficits below the 3 per cent target set by the Maastricht Treaty as a condition for European Monetary Union.

Source: European Union, *European Economy Annual Economic Report for 1995*, No 59, Brussels, EU, 1995.

doubled in the decade of the 1980s. With Belgium, the level of debt increased sharply in the recession years of the early 1980s but has declined only moderately at the end of the decade. Figure 29.3(b) shows the budget deficits of each country as a percentage of GDP. A negative value in the chart indicates that revenues are less than expenditures. The peak in the deficit occurred in the recession of the early 1980s, but Belgium has had greater success in controlling its deficit than Italy in subsequent years.

Debt and Capital   When individuals and businesses incur debts, they usually do so to buy capital – assets that yield a return. In fact, the main point of debt is to enable people to buy assets that will earn a return that exceeds the interest paid on the debt. The government is similar to individuals and businesses in this regard. Much government expenditure is on public assets that yield a return. Roads, bridges, schools and universities, public libraries and the stock of national defence capital all yield a social rate of return that probably far exceeds the

interest rate the government pays on its debt.

Total government debt in the United Kingdom was around £340 billion in 1994, whereas the capital stock of the general government – that is, central government, local governments and public enterprises – was £405 billion, including £85 billion of the assets of public enterprises. Therefore the UK public finances are not in bad shape. But how do the deficit and debt compare with deficits and debts in the rest of the European Union?

The Budget Deficit and Debt Levels in a European Perspective

Do other countries in Europe have large budget deficits or do they have budget surpluses? Are their levels of debt comparable with that of the United Kingdom? Figure 29.4 answers these questions. Figure 29.4(a) shows the government budget deficits of all countries in the European Union as a percentage of GDP. Figure 29.4(b) shows the levels of debt as a percentage of GDP. All the members of

FIGURE 29.4

Government Deficits and Debt in the European Union

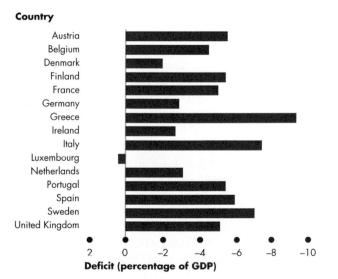

(a) Government deficits in European Union

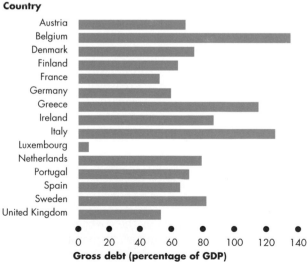

(a) General government gross debt

Part (a) shows that almost all countries in the European Union have budget deficits. The largest ones are Greece, Italy and Sweden, and the smallest are Denmark, Germany, Ireland and Luxembourg, which has a budget surplus. Part (b) shows that many countries in the European Union have

large levels of debt in relation to GDP. These include Belgium, Greece and Italy. Countries with low relative levels of debt include Luxembourg, Germany, France and the United Kingdom.

Source: European Union, *European Economy Annual Report for 1995*, No 59, Brussels, EU, 1995.

© Peter Brooks, *The Times*, 26th July 1996

the European Union except Luxembourg, have budget deficits. Some countries have levels of debt in excess of 100 per cent of GDP. The Treaty of Maastricht 1992 set out certain conditions that countries must achieve prior to European Monetary Union (EMU). Two of these conditions relate to fiscal policy and levels of government debt. Countries that aim to join EMU must reduce their budget deficits to a maximum of 3 per cent of GDP and their debt levels to 60 per cent of GDP. Only Luxembourg satisfies both conditions at this time. Member countries of the European Union face severe pressures to reduce their budget deficits and debt levels before the deadline for EMU in 1999. These reductions can only be brought about by cuts in government spending or increases in taxes. What will be the likely effects of such cuts in spending? This question will be examined in the next section.

REVIEW

◆ Fiscal policy is created by the government and ratified by Parliament and is a key tool designed to influence employment and economic activity.

◆ Each year, the budget is proposed by the Chancellor of the Exchequer and usually enacted in April.

◆ For many years, the government has run a budget deficit – expenditures have exceeded tax revenues – but the United Kingdom is not unusual. Virtually all EU countries run budget deficits.

We have now described the government budget – as the cartoon suggests, the budget is not an easy thing for a government to control. Your next task is to study the effects of fiscal policy on the economy. We'll begin by learning about its effects on expenditure plans when the price level is sticky. You will see that fiscal policy has multiplier effects like the expenditure multipliers that are explained in Chapter 28. Then we'll study the influences of fiscal policy on both aggregate demand and aggregate supply and look at its short-run and long-run effects on real GDP and the price level.

Fiscal Policy Multipliers

Fiscal policy actions can be either automatic or discretionary. **Automatic fiscal policy** is a change in fiscal policy that is triggered by the state of the economy. For example, an increase in unemployment triggers an *automatic* increase in payments to unemployed workers. A fall in incomes triggers an *automatic* decrease in tax receipts. That is, fiscal policy adjusts automatically. **Discretionary fiscal policy** is a policy action that is initiated by the Chancellor of the Exchequer. It requires a change in tax laws or in some spending programme. For example, a decrease in the standard rate of income tax or an increase in defence spending are discretionary fiscal policy actions. That is, discretionary fiscal policy is a deliberate policy action.

We begin by studying the effects of *discretionary* changes in government spending and taxes. To focus on the essentials, we'll initially study a model economy that is simpler than the one in which we live. In our model economy, there is no international trade and the taxes are all lump sum. **Lump-sum taxes** are taxes that do not vary with real GDP. They are fixed by the government and they change only when the government changes them. Lump-sum taxes are rare in reality and they are generally considered to be unfair because rich people and poor people pay the same amount of tax. (It is said that the former prime minister, Margaret Thatcher, lost her job because of the unpopularity of a lump-sum tax called the 'poll-tax', which was a fixed tax per person to pay for local government services.) We use lump-sum taxes in our model economy only because they make the principles we are studying easier to understand. Once we've grasped the principles, we'll explore our real economy with its international trade and income taxes – taxes that *do* vary with real GDP.

Like our real economy, the model economy we study is constantly bombarded by shocks. Exports fluctuate because incomes fluctuate in the rest of the world. Business investment fluctuates because of swings in profit expectations and interest rates. These fluctuations set up multiplier effects that begin a recession or a recovery. If a recession takes hold, unemployment increases and incomes fall. If a recovery becomes too strong, inflationary pressures build up. To minimize the effects of these swings in spending, the government might change either its purchases of goods and services or net taxes (taxes minus transfer payments, see Chapter 23, pp. 578–579). By changing either of these items, the government can influence aggregate expenditure and real GDP. But it also changes its budget deficit or surplus. An alternative fiscal policy action is to change purchases and taxes together so budget balance does not change. We are going to study the initial effects of these discretionary fiscal policy actions in the very short run when the price level is sticky. Each of these actions creates a multiplier effect on real GDP. These multipliers are:

◆ The government purchases multiplier
◆ The lump-sum tax multiplier
◆ The balanced budget multiplier

The Government Purchases Multiplier

The **government purchases multiplier** is the amount by which a change in government purchases of goods and services is multiplied to determine the change in equilibrium expenditure that it generates.

Government purchases are a component of aggregate expenditure. So when government purchases change, aggregate expenditure changes and so does real GDP. The change in real GDP induces a change in consumption expenditure which brings an additional change in aggregate expenditure. A multiplier process ensues. This multiplier process is like the one described in Chapter 28, pp. 724–727. Let's look at an example.

Peace Dividend Multiplier   After the fall of the Berlin Wall and the ending of the cold war, the NATO countries looked forward to a reduction in expenditure on defence and a scaling back of arms spending. In the United Kingdom, this has led to a rationaliza-

tion of military installations and restructuring of operations. Part of the restructuring has been the downgrading of the Rosyth naval base in Scotland, and the removal of its main operations to Portsmouth in the south of England. The downgrading of the Rosyth naval base will hit hard a region that is already blighted by high unemployment. The reduction in military expenditure will have severe effects on the region's GDP and employment in the short term. Because military personnel and workers on the base spend most of their incomes locally, consumption expenditure in the region depends on defence spending in the area. Retail shops and hotels depend on the spending power of people whose incomes are associated or linked with the base. In the long term the Rosyth area will learn to develop other types of industries but in the short term there will be negative multiplier effects for the region.

The Size of the Multiplier   Table 29.2 illustrates the government purchases multiplier with a numerical example. The first column lists various possible levels of real GDP. Our task is to find equilibrium expenditure and the change in real GDP when government purchases change. The second column shows taxes. They are fixed at £50 billion, regardless of the level of real GDP. (This is an assumption that keeps your attention on the key idea and makes the calculations easier to do.) The third column calculates disposable income. Because taxes are lump sum, disposable income equals real GDP minus the £50 billion of taxes. For example, in row *b*, real GDP is £600 billion and disposable income is £550 billion. The next column shows consumption expenditure. In this example, the *marginal propensity to consume* is 0.75 or 3/4. That is, a £1 increase in disposable income brings a 75 pence increase in consumption expenditure. Check this fact by calculating the increase in consumption expenditure when disposable income increases by £100 billion from row *b* to row *c*. Consumption expenditure increases by £75 billion. The next column shows investment, which is a constant of £100 billion. And the next column shows the initial level of government purchases, which is £50 billion. Aggregate planned expenditure is the sum of consumption expenditure, investment and government purchases.

Equilibrium expenditure and real GDP occur when aggregate planned expenditure equals real GDP. In this example, equilibrium expenditure is £600 billion (highlighted in row *b* of the table.)

The final two columns of the table show what

TABLE 29.2

The Government Purchases Multiplier

	Real GDP (Y)	Taxes (T)	Disposable income (Y − T)	Consumption expenditure (C)	Investment (I)	Initial government purchases (G)	Initial aggregate planned expenditure (AE = C + I + G)	New government purchases (G')	New aggregate planned expenditure (AE' = C + I + G')
					(billions of pounds)				
a	500	50	450	375	100	50	525	100	575
b	600	50	550	450	100	50	600	100	650
c	700	50	650	525	100	50	675	100	725
d	800	50	750	600	100	50	750	100	800
e	900	50	850	675	100	50	825	100	875

---

happens when government purchases increase by £50 billion to £100 billion. Aggregate planned expenditure increases by £50 billion at each level of real GDP. For example, at the initial real GDP of £600 billion, aggregate planned expenditure increases to £650 billion. Because aggregate planned expenditure exceeds real GDP, stocks decrease and firms increase production to restore their stocks. Output, incomes and expenditure continue to increase. The increased incomes bring a further increase in aggregate planned expenditure. But aggregate planned expenditure increases by less than income, and eventually a new equilibrium is reached. In this example, the new equilibrium expenditure is at a real GDP of £800 billion.

A £50 billion increase in government purchases has increased equilibrium expenditure and real GDP by £200 billion. Therefore the government purchases multiplier is 4. The size of the multiplier depends on the marginal propensity to consume, which in this example, is 3/4. The following formula shows the connection between the government purchases multiplier and the marginal propensity to consume (MPC).

$$\text{Government purchases multiplier} = \frac{1}{(1 - MPC)}$$

Let's check this formula by using the numbers in the above example. The marginal propensity to consume is 3/4, so the government purchases multiplier is 4.

Figure 29.5 illustrates the government purchases multiplier. Initially, aggregate planned expenditure is shown by the curve labelled AE_0. The points on this curve, labelled a to e, correspond with the rows of

FIGURE 29.5

The Government Purchases Multiplier

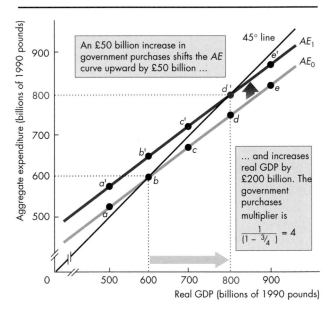

Initially, the aggregate expenditure curve is AE_0 and real GDP is £600 billion (at point b). An increase in government purchases of £50 billion increases aggregate planned expenditure at each level of real GDP by £50 billion. The aggregate planned expenditure curve shifts upward from AE_0 to AE_1 – a parallel shift. At the initial real GDP of £600 billion, aggregate planned expenditure is now £650 billion. Because aggregate planned expenditure is greater than real GDP, real GDP increases. The new equilibrium is reached when real GDP is £800 billion – the point at which the AE_1 curve intersects the 45° line (at d'). In this example, the government purchases multiplier is 4.

Table 29.2. This aggregate expenditure curve intersects the 45° line at the equilibrium level of real GDP, which is £600 billion.

When government purchases increase by £50 billion, the aggregate expenditure curve shifts upward by that amount to AE_1. With this new aggregate expenditure curve, equilibrium real GDP increases to £800 billion. The increase in real GDP is 4 times the increase in government purchases. The government purchases multiplier is 4.

You've seen that in the very short term, when the price level is sticky, an increase in government purchases increases real GDP. But to produce more output, more people must be employed, so in the short term an increase in government purchases can create jobs.

Changing its purchases of goods and services is one way in which the government can try to stimulate the economy. A second way in which the government might act to increase real GDP in the very short run is by decreasing lump-sum taxes. Let's see how this action works.

The Lump-sum Tax Multiplier

The **lump-sum tax multiplier** is the amount by which a change in lump-sum taxes is multiplied to determine the change in equilibrium expenditure that it generates. An *increase* in taxes leads to a *decrease* in disposable income and a decrease in aggregate expenditure. The amount by which aggregate expenditure initially decreases is determined by the marginal propensity to consume. In our example, the marginal propensity to consume is 3/4, so a £1 tax cut increases disposable income by £1 and increases aggregate expenditure initially by 75 pence.

This initial change in aggregate expenditure has a multiplier just like the government purchases multiplier. We've seen that the government purchases multiplier is $1/(1 - MPC)$. Because a tax *increase* leads to a *decrease* in expenditure, the lump-sum tax multiplier is *negative*. And because a change in lump-sum taxes changes aggregate expenditure initially by only the MPC multiplied by the tax change, the lump-sum tax multiplier is equal to :

$$\text{Lump-sum tax multiplier} = \frac{-MPC}{(1 - MPC)}$$

In our example, the marginal propensity to consume is 3/4, so the lump-sum multiplier is:

$$\text{Lump-sum tax multiplier} = \frac{-3/4}{(1 - 3/4)} = -3$$

Figure 29.6 illustrates the lump-sum tax multiplier. Initially, the aggregate expenditure curve is AE_0 and equilibrium expenditure is £800 billion. Taxes increase by £100 billion and disposable income falls by that amount. With a marginal propensity to consume of 3/4, aggregate expenditure decreases initially by £75 billion and the aggregate expenditure curve shifts downward by that amount to AE_1. Equilibrium expenditure and real GDP fall by £300 billion to £500 billion. The lump-sum tax multiplier is –3.

FIGURE 29.6

The Lump-sum Tax Multiplier

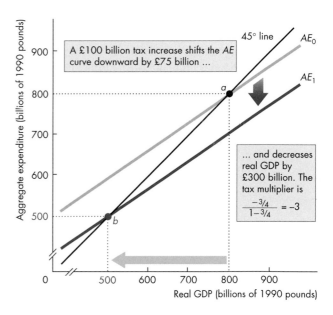

Initially, the aggregate expenditure curve is AE_0, and equilibrium expenditure is £800 billion. The marginal propensity to consume is 0.75. Lump-sum taxes increase by £100 billion, so disposable income falls by £100 billion. The decrease in aggregate expenditure is found by multiplying this change in disposable income by the marginal propensity to consume and is £100 billion × 0.75 = £75 billion. The aggregate expenditure curve shifts *downward* by this amount to AE_1. Equilibrium expenditure falls by £300 billion, and the lump-sum tax multiplier is –3.

Lump-sum Transfers The lump-sum tax multiplier also tells us the effects of a change in lump-sum transfer payments. Transfer payments are like negative taxes, so an increase in transfer payments works like a decrease in taxes. Because the tax multiplier is negative, a decrease in taxes increases expenditure. An increase in transfer payments also increases expenditure. So the lump-sum transfer payments multiplier is positive. It is:

$$\text{Lump-sum transfer payments multiplier} = \frac{MPC}{(1 - MPC)}$$

The Balanced Budget Multiplier

A balanced budget fiscal policy action is one that changes *both* government purchases and taxes by the same amount so that the government's budget deficit or surplus remains *unchanged*. The **balanced budget multiplier** is the amount by which a simultaneous and equal change in government purchases and taxes is multiplied to determine the change in equilibrium expenditure. What is the multiplier effect of this fiscal policy action?

To find out, we must combine the government purchases multiplier and the lump-sum tax multiplier. These two multipliers are:

$$\text{Government purchases multiplier} = \frac{1}{(1 - MPC)}$$

$$\text{Lump-sum tax multiplier} = \frac{-MPC}{(1 - MPC)}$$

Adding these two multipliers gives the balanced budget multiplier, which is:

$$\text{Balanced budget multiplier} = \frac{1 - MPC}{1 - MPC}$$
$$= 1$$

The balanced budget is smaller than the other multipliers but it is not zero. This fact is interesting because it means that in principle, fiscal policy can be used to increase aggregate planned expenditure if a recession is expected without increasing the government deficit. It also means that in the long run, as government grows, even if the growth of taxes keeps pace with the growth of expenditures, government adds to aggregate demand and squeezes out some private consumption expenditure or private investment, or both.

Induced Taxes and Welfare Spending

In the examples we've studied so far, taxes are lump-sum taxes. But in reality, net taxes (taxes minus transfer payments) vary with the state of the economy.

On the tax revenues side of the budget, the government passes tax laws that define the tax *rates* to be paid, not the tax *pounds* to be paid. As a consequence, tax *revenues* depend on real GDP. We call those taxes that vary as real GDP varies **induced taxes**. If the economy is in an expansion phase of the business cycle, induced taxes increase because real GDP increases. If the economy is in a recession phase of the business cycle, induced taxes decrease because real GDP decreases.

On the government expenditures side of the budget, the government pays out various benefits, principally to unemployed workers in the form of job seekers allowance. But it also subsidizes training programmes and start-up schemes, which result in transfer payments that depend on the economic state of individual citizens and businesses. For example, when the economy is in a recession, unemployment is high and government transfer payments increase. When the economy is in a boom, transfer payments decline.

The existence of induced taxes and benefits decreases the government purchases and lump-sum tax multipliers because they loosen the link between real GDP and disposable income and so dampen the effect of a change in real GDP on consumption expenditure. When real GDP increases, induced taxes increase and benefits decrease. So disposable income does not increase by as much as the increase in real GDP. As a result, consumption expenditure does not increase by as much as it otherwise would have done and the multiplier effect is reduced.

The extent to which induced taxes and benefits decrease the multiplier depends on the *marginal tax rate*. The marginal tax rate is the proportion of an additional pound of real GDP that flows to the government in net taxes (taxes minus transfer payments). The higher the marginal tax rate, the larger is the proportion of an additional pound of real GDP that is paid to the government and the smaller is the induced change in consumption expenditure. The smaller the change in consumption expenditure induced by a change in real GDP, the smaller is the multiplier effect of a change in government purchases or lump-sum taxes.

International Trade and Fiscal Policy Multipliers

Not all expenditure on final goods and services in the United Kingdom is on domestically produced goods and services. Some of it is on imports – foreign-produced goods and services. The extent to which an additional pound of real GDP is spent on imports is determined by the *marginal propensity to import*. Expenditure on imports does not generate UK real GDP and does not lead to an increase in UK consumption expenditure. The larger the marginal propensity to import, the smaller is the increase in consumption expenditure induced by an increase in real GDP and the smaller are the government purchases and lump-sum tax multipliers. (Imports affect the fiscal policy multipliers in exactly the same way that they influence the investment multiplier, as explained in Chapter 28, see pp. 726–727).

In today's increasingly global economy in which the marginal propensity to import is much greater than it was 20 years ago, the fiscal policy multipliers are smaller than they used to be.

So far, we've studied *discretionary* fiscal policy. Let's look at automatic stabilizers.

Automatic Stabilizers

Automatic stabilizers are mechanisms that operate without the need for explicit action by the government. Their very name is borrowed from engineering and conjures up images of shock absorbers, thermostats and sophisticated devices that keep aircraft and ships steady in turbulent air and seas. Automatic fiscal stabilizers arise from the fact that income taxes and transfer payments fluctuate with real GDP. If real GDP begins to fall, tax revenues also fall and transfer payments rise. These changes in taxes and transfers affect the economy. Let's study the budget deficit over the business cycle.

Fiscal Policy over the Business Cycle   Figure 29.7 shows the business cycle and fluctuations in the budget deficit since 1980. Part (a) shows the fluctuations of real GDP around potential GDP. Part (b) shows the government budget deficit (the PSBR). Both parts highlight the most recent recession by shading this period. By comparing the two parts of the figure, you can see the relationship between the business cycle and the budget deficit. As a rule, when the economy is in the expansion phase of a business cycle, the budget deficit declines.

FIGURE 29.7

The Business Cycle and the Budget Deficit

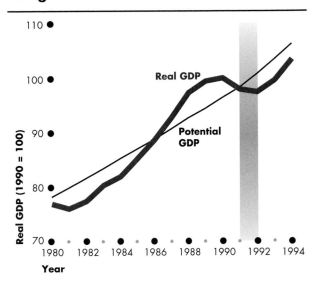

(a) Growth and recessions

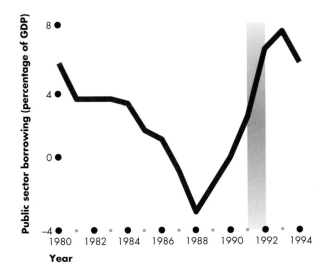

(b) The UK public sector borrowing requirement

As real GDP fluctuates around potential GDP (part a), the budget deficit fluctuates (part b). During a recession (shaded areas), tax revenues decrease, transfer payments increase and the budget deficit increases. The deficit also increases *before* a recession as the growth rate of real GDP slows and *after* a recession before the growth rate of real GDP speeds up. When the growth rate of real GDP is high during a recovery, tax revenues increase, transfer payments decrease and the deficit decreases.

Sources: Central Statistical Office; and Lombard Street Research Ltd.

(In the figure, a declining deficit means a deficit that is getting closer to zero.) As the expansion slows before the recession begins, the budget deficit increases. It continues to increase during the recession and for a further period after the recession is over. Then, when the expansion is well under way, the budget deficit declines again.

The budget deficit fluctuates with the business cycle because both tax revenues and expenditures fluctuate with real GDP. As real GDP increases during an expansion, tax revenues increase and transfer payments decrease, so the budget deficit automatically decreases. As real GDP decreases during a recession, tax revenues decrease and transfer payments increase, so the budget deficit automatically increases.

As investment or exports fluctuate, real GDP fluctuates. And as real GDP fluctuates, tax revenues fluctuate and so the budget deficit fluctuates. For example, when a large increase in investment causes the economy to boom, real GDP increases by a multiple of the increase in investment. But the multiplier effect of the increase in investment is reduced by the automatic increase in tax revenues and decrease in the budget deficit (or increase in a budget surplus). The higher tax revenues act as an automatic stabilizer. They decrease disposable income and induce a decrease in consumption expenditure. This decrease in consumption expenditure dampens the effects of the initial increase in investment on aggregate expenditure and moderates the increase in equilibrium expenditure and real GDP. The expansion slows.

Conversely, when a large decrease in investment is pushing the economy into recession, tax revenues decrease and the budget deficit increases (or the budget surplus decreases). Again, tax revenues – this time lower revenues – act as an automatic stabilizer. They limit the fall in disposable income and moderate the extent of the decline in aggregate expenditure and real GDP. The recession slows.

Because the budget deficit increases when the economy is in a recession and decreases when the economy is in an expansion, economists have developed a modified deficit concept called the cyclically adjusted deficit. The **cyclically adjusted deficit** is the budget deficit that would occur if the economy were at full employment.

The Cyclically Adjusted Deficit The cyclically adjusted deficit is a measure for judging whether the budget deficit is cyclical or structural. A **cyclical deficit** is a budget deficit that is present only

because real GDP is less than potential GDP and taxes are temporarily low and transfer payments are temporarily high. A **structural deficit** is a budget that is in deficit even though real GDP equals potential GDP. With a structural deficit, expenditures are too high relative to tax revenues over the entire business cycle.

Figure 29.8 illustrates the concepts of cyclical and structural deficits. The blue curve shows expenditures. When real GDP is less than potential GDP, transfer payments are temporarily high. As real GDP increases, transfer payments fall and expenditures decrease. The green curve shows tax revenues. Because most taxes increase with income,

---

FIGURE 29.8

Cyclical and Structural Deficits

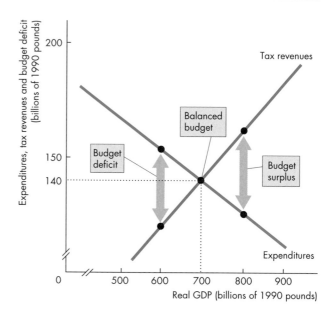

Government expenditures (blue line) decrease as real GDP increases because transfer payments decrease. Tax revenues (green line) increase as real GDP increases because most taxes are linked to income and expenditures. If real GDP is £700 billion, the government has a *balanced budget*. If real GDP is less than £700 billion, expenditures exceed tax revenues and the government has a budget deficit. If real GDP exceeds £700 billion, expenditures are less than tax revenues and the government has a budget surplus. If potential GDP is £700 billion, there is not a structural deficit – the budget deficits and surpluses are cyclical. But if potential GDP is less than £700 billion, there is a structural deficit.

tax revenues increase as real GDP increases. In this example, if real GDP is £700 billion, the government has a *balanced budget*. Expenditures and tax revenues each equal £140 billion. If real GDP is £600 billion, expenditures exceed tax revenues and there is a budget deficit. And if real GDP is £800 billion, expenditures are less than tax revenues and there is a budget surplus.

To determine whether there is a structural deficit, we need to know potential GDP. If, in Fig. 29.8, potential GDP is £700 billion, the budget has a structural deficit of zero. As the real GDP fluctuates, the budget fluctuates around zero. If, in Fig. 29.8, potential GDP is £600 billion, there is a structural deficit, and if potential GDP is £800 billion, there is a structural surplus.

The OECD calculates that the United Kingdom has a structural budget deficit of 3.6 per cent of potential GDP. But the United Kingdom is not alone. The OECD calculate that virtually all the countries in the European Union have structural budget deficits. Figure 29.9 shows a selection of countries' structural budget deficits. Sweden, Italy and Greece have larger structural budget deficits than the United Kingdom, but Germany, Denmark and Belgium have smaller structural budget deficits.

<table>
<tr><td colspan="2">

FIGURE 29.9

Structural Budget Deficits in the European Union

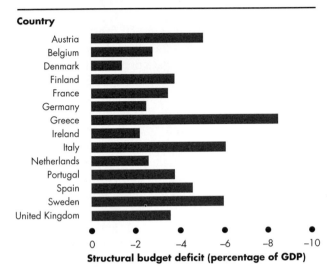

The OECD calculates that most of the countries in the European Union will have had a structural budget deficit in 1995. The United Kingdom is projected to have a structural budget deficit of 3.6 per cent of potential GDP. Sweden, Italy and Greece are expected to have higher structural budget deficits, while Germany, Ireland, Denmark, Belgium and the Netherlands are expected to have lower structural budget deficits.

Source: *OECD Economic Outlook*, December 1995. Reproduced by permission of the OECD.
</td></tr>
</table>

REVIEW

◆ In the very short run when the price level is sticky, a change in government purchases or lump-sum taxes has a multiplier effect on real GDP.

◆ The multiplier effect of a change in government purchases is greater than that of a change in lump-sum taxes because a pound of taxes initially changes aggregate expenditure by less than a pound.

◆ The presence of income taxes and international trade reduces the fiscal policy multipliers.

◆ Income taxes and unemployment benefits work as automatic stabilizers to dampen the business cycle.

We have now seen the immediate effects of fiscal policy when the price level is sticky. The next task is to see how, with the passage of more time and with some price level adjustments, these multiplier effects are modified.

Fiscal Policy in the Short Run and the Long Run

We've seen how real GDP responds to changes in fiscal policy when the price level is sticky and all the adjustments that take place are in spending, income and production. In the short run, the price level also adjusts and in the long run, both the price level and the wage rate adjust. You are now going to see how these further adjustments change the outcome of fiscal policies.

Fiscal Policy and Aggregate Demand

You learned about the relationship between aggregate demand, aggregate expenditure, and equilibrium expenditure in Chapter 28. You are now going to use what you learned there to work out what happens to aggregate demand, the price level, real GDP and jobs when fiscal policy changes. We'll start by looking at the effects of a change in fiscal policy on aggregate demand.

Fiscal Policy and Aggregate Demand   Figure 29.10 shows the effects of an increase in government purchases on aggregate demand. Initially, the aggregate expenditure curve is AE_0 in part (a), and the aggregate demand curve is AD_0 in part (b). The price level is 130, real GDP is £600 billion, and the economy is at point a in both parts of the figure. Now suppose that government purchases increase by £50 billion. At a constant price level of 130, the aggregate expenditure curve shifts upward to AE_1. This curve intersects the 45° line at an equilibrium expenditure of £800 billion at point b. This amount is the aggregate quantity of goods and services demanded at a price level of 130, as shown by point b in part (b). Point b lies on a new aggregate demand curve. The aggregate demand curve has shifted rightward to AD_1.

The distance by which the aggregate demand curve shifts rightward is determined by the government purchases multiplier. The larger the multiplier, the larger is the shift in the aggregate demand curve resulting from a given change in government purchases. In this example, a £50 billion increase in government purchases produces a £200 billion increase in the aggregate quantity of goods and services demanded at each price level. The multiplier is 4. So the £50 billion increase in government purchases shifts the aggregate demand curve rightward by £200 billion.

Figure 29.10 shows the effects of an increase in government purchases. But a similar effect occurs for *any* expansionary fiscal policy. An **expansionary fiscal policy** is an increase in government expenditures or a decrease in tax revenues.

Figure 29.10 can also be used to illustrate the effects of a contractionary fiscal policy. A **contractionary fiscal policy** is a decrease in government expenditures or an increase in tax revenues. In this case, start at point b in each part of the figure and decrease government expenditure. Aggregate demand decreases from AD_1 to AD_0.

Equilibrium GDP and the Price Level in the Short Run   We've seen how an increase in government purchases increases aggregate demand. Let's now see how it changes real GDP and the

---

FIGURE 29.10

Changes in Government Purchases and Aggregate Demand

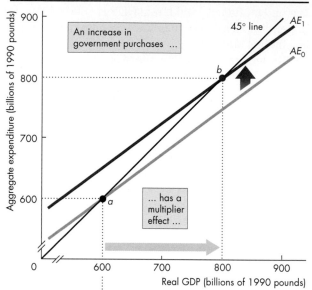

(a) Aggregate expenditure

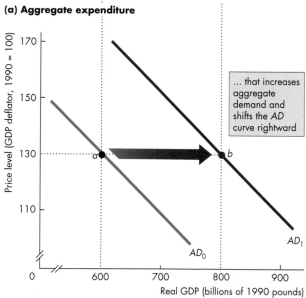

(b) Aggregate demand

The price level is 130. When the aggregate expenditure curve is AE_0 (part a), the aggregate demand curve is AD_0 (part b). An increase in government purchases shifts the aggregate expenditure curve upward to AE_1. The new equilibrium occurs where AE_1 intersects the 45° line at a real GDP of £800 billion. Because the quantity of real GDP demanded at a price level of 130 increases to £800 billion, the aggregate demand curve shifts rightward to AD_1. The magnitude of the rightward shift of the aggregate demand curve is determined by the change in government purchases and the size of the multiplier.

price level. Figure 29.11 describes the economy. Aggregate demand is AD_0 and the short-run aggregate supply curve is *SAS*. (Check back to Chapter 27 if you need to refresh your understanding of the *SAS* curve.) Equilibrium is at point *a*, where the aggregate demand and short-run aggregate supply curves intersect. The price level is 130, and real GDP is £600 billion.

An increase in government purchases of £50 billion shifts the aggregate demand curve rightward from AD_0 to AD_1. While the price level is sticky at 130, the economy moves towards point *b* and real GDP increases towards £800 billion. But during the adjustment process, the price level does not remain constant. It gradually rises and the economy moves along the short-run aggregate supply curve to the point of intersection of the short-run aggregate supply curve and the new aggregate demand curve – point *c*. The price level rises to 146 and real GDP increases to £760 billion.

When we take the price level effect into account, the increase in government purchases still has a multiplier effect on real GDP, but the effect is

smaller than it would be if the price level remained constant. Also, the steeper the slope of the short-run aggregate supply curve, the larger is the increase in the price level, and the smaller is the increase in real GDP, the smaller is the government purchases multiplier. But the multiplier is not zero.

Because the fiscal policy multipliers are not zero, fiscal policy can in principle be used to increase real GDP and decrease the unemployment rate in a recession. It can also be used if the economy is overheating to decrease real GDP and help to keep inflation in check. In practice, the use of fiscal policy is limited by two factors.

First, the parliamentary process is slow, which means that it is difficult to take fiscal policy actions in a timely way. By the time the action is taken, the economy might need an entirely different fiscal medicine.

Second, it is not always easy to tell whether real GDP is below (or above) trend because aggregate demand has changed and moved real GDP away from potential GDP, or whether potential GDP itself has fluctuated.

FIGURE 29.11

Fiscal Policy, Real GDP and the Price Level

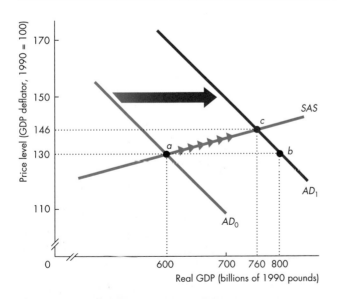

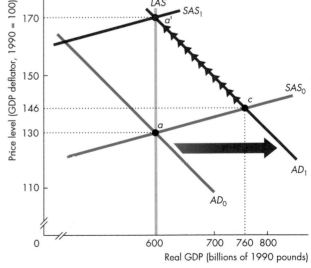

An increase in government purchases shifts the *AD* curve from AD_0 to AD_1. With a sticky price level, real GDP would have increased from £600 billion to £800 billion – to point *b*. But in the short run, the price level is not sticky and the economy moves along the *SAS* curve to point *c*. The price level increases to 146, and real GDP increases to £760 billion. The steeper the *SAS* curve, the larger is the increase in the price level and the smaller is the increase in real GDP.

Fiscal Expansion at Potential GDP

In the long run, real GDP equals potential GDP – the economy is at full-employment equilibrium. When real GDP equals potential GDP, an increase in aggregate demand has the same short-run effect as we've just worked out, but its long-run effect is different.

Figure 29.11(b) shows the effect of an expansionary fiscal policy when real GDP equals potential GDP. In this example, potential GDP is £600 billion. The government might be concerned that the unemployment rate is too high, even though real GDP is equal to potential GDP. Such a situation can arise if the natural rate of unemployment is high (see Chapter 24, pp. 610—611). To lower the unemployment rate, the government increases its purchases. Aggregate demand increases and the aggregate demand curve shifts rightward from AD_0 to AD_1. The short-run equilibrium, point c, is an above full-employment equilibrium. The work-force is more than fully employed, and there are shortages of labour. Wage rates begin to increase. Higher wage rates increase costs, and short-run aggregate supply decreases. The SAS curve begins to shift leftward from SAS_0 to SAS_1. The economy moves up along the aggregate demand curve AD_1 toward point a'.

Eventually, when all adjustments to wage rates and the price level have been made, the price level is 170 and real GDP is again at potential GDP of £600 billion. The multiplier in the long run is zero. There has been a temporary decrease in the unemployment rate during the process you've just looked at but not a permanent decrease.

Fiscal Policy and Aggregate Supply

So far we've considered only the demand side effects of fiscal policy. But fiscal policy also has supply side effects. On the expenditures side, the government buys capital goods, which increases the quantity of real GDP supplied. On the tax revenues side, taxes on labour income act as a disincentive to work and decrease the quantity of labour employed and the quantity of real GDP supplied. With fewer people employed, the jobless rate is higher.

Similarly, taxes on interest income weaken the incentive to save and invest and so decrease the quantity of capital and decrease the quantity of real GDP supplied. This effect is an ongoing one that affects not only the current level of real GDP but also the trend growth rate of potential GDP. The influences of fiscal policy on the quantity of real GDP supplied mean that to assess the impact of an expansionary fiscal policy, especially a tax cut, we must take into account changes in both aggregate demand and aggregate supply.

Figure 29.12 shows the supply side effects of an expansionary fiscal policy such as a tax cut. Part (a) shows the effects that are most likely to occur. An expansionary fiscal policy has a large effect on aggregate demand and a small effect on aggregate supply. The aggregate demand curve shifts rightward by a larger amount than the rightward shift in the short-run aggregate supply curve. The outcome is a rise in the price level and an increase in real GDP.

During the 1980s, a school of thought known as the *supply-siders* became prominent in the United States. Although their ideas did not catch on as well in the United Kingdom, they did have their supporters and some of these were close to the then prime minister, Margaret Thatcher. Supply-siders believed that tax cuts would strengthen incentives and have a large effect on aggregate supply. Figure 29.12(b) shows the effects that supply-siders believe might occur. An expansionary fiscal policy still has a large effect on aggregate demand but it has a similarly large effect on aggregate supply. The aggregate demand curve and the short-run aggregate supply curve shift rightward by similar amounts. In this particular case, the price level remains constant and real GDP increases. A slightly larger increase in aggregate supply would have brought a fall in the price level, a possibility that some supply-siders believe could occur.

The general point that everyone agrees with is that an expansionary fiscal policy that strengthens incentives increases real GDP by more and is less inflationary than one that does not change or that weakens incentives. *Reading Between the Lines* on pp. 762–763 looks at the supply side effects of German fiscal policy.

We've studied the long-run effects of fiscal policy but we've not studied the long-run effects of the budget deficit. What are those effects?

A Burden on Future Generations?

It is a common and popular view that the budget deficit places a burden on future generations. The idea behind this view is that the current generation is enjoying the benefits of government expenditures but it is not paying for all those benefits. The budget deficit is financed by selling bonds and it is

FIGURE 29.12

Supply Side Effects of Fiscal Policy

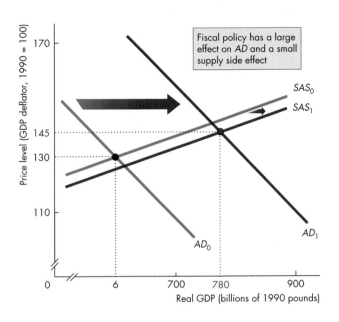

(a) The traditional view

An expansionary fiscal policy such as a tax cut increases aggregate demand and shifts the AD curve rightward from AD_0 to AD_1 (both parts). Such a policy change also has a supply side effect. If the supply side effect is small, the SAS curve shifts rightward from SAS_0 to SAS_1 in part (a). In this case, the demand side effect dominates the supply side effect, real GDP increases and the price level rises.

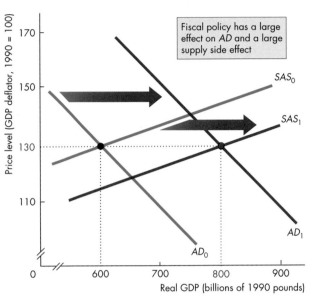

(b) The supply side view

If the supply side effect of a tax cut is large, the SAS curve shifts rightward from SAS_0 to SAS_1 in part (b). In this case, the supply side effect is as large as the demand side effect. Real GDP increases and the price level remains constant. But if the supply side effect was larger than the demand side effect, the price level would actually fall.

future generations that will pay either in the form of ongoing interest payments or in repayment of the debt now being incurred.

But wait. Doesn't the interest paid each year get financed with tax revenues collected each year? So how can the deficit be a burden to *future* generations? It might be a burden to those members of future generations who pay taxes, but it must be a benefit to those who receive the interest payments. In the aggregate, the burden and the benefit cancel out.

Although in the aggregate the interest paid equals the tax revenues collected, there might still be undesirable redistribution effects. For example, one feature of our present budget deficit is that

some government debt is being bought not by British investors but by foreign investors. So part of the future burden of the current deficit is that future British taxpayers will have to pay sufficient tax revenues so that the interest can be paid to foreign holders of UK government debt. In this case, the burden on future British taxpayers will exceed the interest received by British holders of UK government debt.

There's another way in which today's budget deficit can make people poorer tomorrow. By slowing investment today, the rate of growth of real GDP will slow and the stock of productive capital equipment available for future generations will be smaller. This phenomenon is called crowding out.

Crowding out

Crowding out is the tendency for an increase in government purchases of goods and services to bring a decrease in investment. Full crowding out is when an increase in government purchases results in an equivalent decrease in investment. If crowding out does occur, there will be a larger stock of government debt and a smaller stock of capital in the future.

Full crowding out does *not* occur if:

◆ Real GDP is less than potential GDP.

◆ The budget deficit arises from the government's purchases of capital on which the return equals (or exceeds) that on privately purchased capital.

Full crowding out *does* occur if:

◆ Real GDP equals or exceeds potential GDP.

◆ The government purchases consumption goods and services or capital on which the return is less than that on privately purchased capital.

Real GDP and Potential GDP   If real GDP equals (or exceeds) potential GDP, an increase in government purchases of goods and services (and an increase in the budget deficit) must result in a decrease in the purchases of other goods and services. But if real GDP is below potential GDP, it is possible that an increase in government purchases (and an increase in the budget deficit) could result in an increase in real GDP (and a decrease in the unemployment rate). In such a case, the budget deficit does not fully crowd out other expenditure.

Productive Government Purchases   Much of what the government purchases is productive capital. Extending the M25 motorway and building bridges, airports, schools and universities are some obvious examples. But there are some not-so-obvious examples of productive government purchases that have an investment element. Expenditures on teachers' and nurses' wages are investments in productive human capital. Defence expenditure protects both our physical and our human capital resources and is also productive capital expenditure. To the extent that the deficit results from our acquisition of such assets, it does not crowd out productive capital. On the contrary, it contributes to it.

But it is possible for government purchases to crowd out the accumulation of private capital. Let's see how.

How Crowding Out Occurs   Crowding out occurs if the government's deficit increases the real interest rate and decreases investment. Figure 29.13 shows how this outcome arises. Part (a) shows the demand and supply curves for loans. Initially, the demand for loans is D_0 and the supply of loans is S_0. The real interest rate is 3 per cent a year and the quantity of loans made is £100 billion a year. Part (b) shows investment. The investment demand curve *ID* shows how investment depends on the opportunity cost of funds, the real interest rate. At a real interest rate of 3 per cent, investment is £80 billion. Now suppose that the government begins to run a deficit, and to finance the deficit it borrows. The government's demand for loans is added to the original demand and the demand curve in part (a) shifts rightward to D_1. There is no change in the supply of loans so the real interest rate rises to 4 per cent. At this interest rate, investment decreases to £50 billion in part (b). Because investment has decreased, the capital stock is lower than it would have been. The government deficit has crowded out investment and government debt has crowded out productive capital.

Ricardian Equivalence

Some economists do not believe that budget deficits crowd out investment. On the contrary, they argue, debt financing and paying for government spending with tax revenues are equivalent. The level of purchases of goods and services matters. Government purchases can crowd out investment and increase the real interest rate. But the way in which government purchases are financed is irrelevant.

The first economist to advance this idea (known as *Ricardian equivalence*) was a great British economist, David Ricardo. Ricardo's idea has been given a forceful restatement by Robert Barro of Harvard University. Barro argues as follows. If the government decreases its tax revenues and increases its deficit, people are smart enough to recognize that the government must increase taxes in the future to pay the increased interest charges on the debt being issued today and, eventually, to repay the debt. In recognition of having to pay higher taxes in the

FIGURE 29.13

The Deficit, Borrowing and Crowding Out

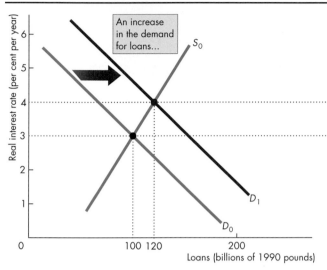

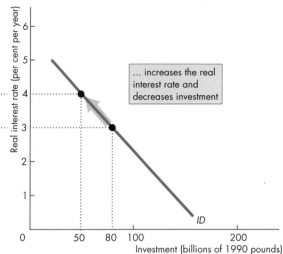

(a) The market for loans

(b) Investment

Part (a) shows the market for loans. The demand for loans is D_0, and the supply of loans is S_0. The equilibrium quantity of loans is £100 billion and the real interest rate is 3 per cent a year. In part (b), the investment demand curve is ID and at an interest rate of 3 per cent, investment is £80 billion. The government runs a deficit, which it finances by borrowing. The

government's increased demand for loans increases the market demand and shifts the demand curve rightward to D_1. The real interest rate rises to 4 per cent and in part (b), investment decreases to £50 billion. The deficit has crowded out investment in productive capital.

future, people will cut their consumption now and save more. They'll increase their saving so that when the higher taxes are finally levied, they will have accumulated sufficient wealth to meet those tax liabilities without a further cut in consumption. The increased saving matches the decreased taxes and national saving is unchanged.

Whether Ricardian equivalence is relevant to the economy or not is controversial and unsettled. Most economists believe that Ricardian equivalence has no practical relevance. Deficits have the potential to redistribute resources across generations and if Ricardian equivalence really works, people's consumption and saving choices must prevent any such redistribution. But for such an outcome to occur, people must be as concerned about the consumption of future generations as they are about their own consumption. Most economists believe that while people do care about future generations, they don't care enough to make Ricardian equivalence relevant.

But Ricardian equivalence has many defenders and the empirical evidence against it is not decisive.

REVIEW

◆ In the short run, changes in government purchases and taxes change the price level, and the multiplier effect on real GDP is smaller than when the price level is sticky.

◆ In the long run, fiscal policy actions influence wage rates, the price level, interest rates, and the level and growth rate of aggregate supply.

◆ The long-run effects of a budget deficit are possibly slower economic growth and less capital and lower incomes in the future, but whether these consequences do arise is controversial.

◆ ◆ ◆ ◆ You have now completed your study of the effects of fiscal policy. You've seen how fiscal policy influences the way real GDP fluctuates around its trend and how it influences the long-term growth rate of real GDP. Your next task is to study the other main arm of macroeconomic policy, monetary policy. We begin in the next chapter by describing the monetary system of a modern economy.

Fiscal Policy in Germany

The Essence of the Story

THE FINANCIAL TIMES, 9 JULY 1996

Bonn plans 2.5% cuts in spending to meet Emu limit

Peter Norman

The German federal government plans to cut spending in 1997 for the third year in succession as part of its intensifying efforts to bring the country's public sector deficit below the limit set by the Maastricht treaty.

The draft budget, to be presented tomorrow to the cabinet by Mr Theo Waigel, the finance minister, envisages a 2.5 per cent drop in federal spending to DM440.2bn ($289.6bn) next year from a planned DM451.3bn this year and a decline in Bonn's net borrowing requirement to DM56.5bn from DM59.9bn.

Mr Waigel will tell his colleagues that the federal government will fulfil the promise made in April to cut existing spending plans by DM25bn next year as part of its programme of spending reductions, supply side reforms and welfare restructuring to boost growth and jobs.

Bonn is aiming to bring Germany's overall deficit down to 2.5 per cent of gross domestic product next year and so below the 3 per cent Maastricht ceiling. But success will depend crucially on whether the federal states or Länder can produce a total of DM25bn of budget cuts through their individual efforts after failing last week to agree a joint austerity programme....

Details of the 1997 draft federal budget were circulating unofficially in Bonn yesterday. Cuts are envisaged in 18 of 26 individual spending plans next year, with the ministries of economics, transport, defence and agriculture accounting for DM4bn of the DM7bn of cuts negotiated in recent weeks.

The transport budget is set for a particularly sharp fall this year.

Defence...will see its budget cut to DM46.5bn next year from DM48.2bn. The budget of Mr Günter Rexrodt, the economics minister...will decline by 8.4 per cent to DM17bn from a planned DM18.6bn.

The labour and social affairs ministry remains the biggest federal spender by far next year, although its budget is set to decline to DM122.1bn from a planned DM124.6bn in 1996.

- ■ The Maastricht Treaty has imposed a condition that the budget deficit of countries that intend to make a European Monetary Union (EMU) should be no more than 3 per cent of GDP by 1997.

- ■ The German federal government plans to cut its spending by 2.5 per cent in 1997. It aims to bring the government budget deficit to 2.5 per cent of GDP.

- ■ Success will depend on whether the federal states can produce total budget cuts of DM25 billion.

- ■ Welfare spending by the ministry of labour and social affairs remains the largest component of the federal budget.

- ■ This will be the third year of budget cuts and the latest budget target for 1997 was announced in April 1996.

Economic Analysis

■ What are the likely effects of the proposed cuts in government expenditure and the deficit if they do actually occur? Any effects will depend on whether the cuts are considered to be permanent or temporary.

■ Figure 1 shows the possible effect of the federal government plan to cut expenditure. The economy is initially at point a. Figure 2 shows that the economy was in a recessionary gap in 1995. If the cuts are temporary or if they are not believed, aggregate demand in Fig. 1 will decrease from AD_0 to AD_1 and output and inflation will fall.

■ Because the cuts were announced in advance and budget cuts had been carried out effectively in the previous year, it is possible that the cut in federal spending will be seen as permanent. Aggregate demand will decrease from AD_0 to AD_1 in Fig. 3.

■ If the planned cut in federal spending is viewed as permanent, the cut in expenditure could lower long-term interest rates and boost private investment and increase aggregate supply.

■ In Fig. 3, potential GDP increases to DM2,780 billion the long-run aggregate supply curve shifts from LAS_0 shifts to LAS_1, and the short-run aggregate supply curve shifts to SAS_1. The real GDP growth rate increases and the inflation rate slows.

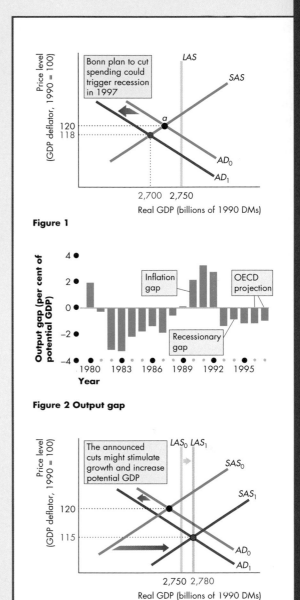

Figure 1

Figure 2 Output gap

Figure 3

SUMMARY

The Government Budget

The government budget finances the activities of the government and is used to achieve full employment, sustained long-term economic growth and price level stability. The budget is proposed by the Chancellor, presented to Parliament, debated in the House of Commons and signed into law by the Queen.

Tax revenues come from personal income taxes, social security contributions, corporate income taxes, indirect taxes and rents. Government expenditures include transfer payments, purchases of goods and services, and debt interest. The budget balance is equal to tax revenues minus expenditures.

The United Kingdom government has had a budget deficit for most of the post-war period. During the late 1980s the government had surpluses. These surpluses were referred to as Public Sector Debt Repayments. Almost all the countries in the European Union have budget deficits nowadays and the UK budget deficit is *smaller* than that of most countries.

The general government sector of the United Kingdom includes the central government, local governments and public enterprises. (pp 743–748)

Fiscal Policy Multipliers

Fiscal policy actions are either automatic and triggered by the state of the economy, or discretionary and initiated by the Treasury and approved by Parliament. The government purchases multiplier equals $1/(1 − MPC)$. The lump-sum tax multiplier equals $−MPC/(1 − MPC)$. The balanced budget multiplier equals 1.

Income taxes and benefits make each of the multipliers smaller than they otherwise would be. They also bring fluctuations in tax revenues and transfer payments over the business cycle and help the shock-absorbing capacities of the economy. (pp 748–755)

Fiscal Policy in the Short Run and the Long Run

An expansionary fiscal policy (an increase in government purchases or a decrease in taxes) increases aggregate demand and shifts the aggregate demand curve rightward. It increases real GDP and raises the price level. A contractionary fiscal policy (a decrease in government purchases or an increase in taxes) decreases aggregate demand and shifts the aggregate demand curve leftward. It decreases real GDP and lowers the price level. In the short run, the fiscal policy multipliers are smaller than when the price level is sticky.

In the long run, when real GDP equals potential GDP, an expansionary fiscal policy increases the price level but leaves real GDP unchanged. The fiscal policy multipliers are zero.

Fiscal policy has supply side effects because the government buys capital goods that increase aggregate supply and taxes weaken the incentives to work, save and invest. These supply side influences mean that an expansionary fiscal policy increases real GDP and if the supply side effect is stronger than the demand side effect, an expansionary fiscal policy might lower the price level.

A deficit can place a long-run burden on future generations if it results in increased international debt or a smaller capital stock caused by crowding out. First, it might result in increased international debt. In this case, part of the increased income of future generations will be paid to foreigners instead of being used for consumption or investment. Second, it might result in a smaller future stock of productive capital, which means that future production will be lower than it otherwise could have been. This outcome results from 'crowding out', which is the tendency for public expenditure to displace private expenditure. The controversial Ricardian equivalence view is that a deficit is equivalent to a tax. Government expenditure crowds out private expenditure but the way the expenditure is financed is irrelevant. (pp. 755–761)

KEY ELEMENTS

Key Terms

Automatic fiscal policy, 748
Balanced budget, 744
Balanced budget multiplier, 752
Budget deficit or PSBR, 744
Budget surplus or PSDR, 744
Contractionary fiscal policy, 756
Crowding out, 760
Cyclically adjusted deficit, 754
Cyclical deficit, 754
Discretionary fiscal policy, 748
Expansionary fiscal policy, 756
Fiscal policy, 743
Government budget, 743
Government debt, 746
Government purchases multiplier, 749
Induced taxes, 752
Lump-sum taxes, 748
Lump-sum tax multiplier, 751
Structural deficit, 754

◆ Key Figures

Figure 29.1 The UK Government Budget Deficit, 744
Figure 29.4 Government Deficits and Debt in the European Union, 747
Figure 29.5 The Government Purchases Multiplier, 750
Figure 29.6 The Lump-sum Tax Multiplier, 751
Figure 29.7 The Business Cycle and the Budget Deficit, 753
Figure 29.8 Cyclical and Structural Deficits, 754
Figure 29.10 Changes in Government Purchases and Aggregate Demand, 756
Figure 29.11 Fiscal Policy, Real GDP and the Price Level, 757
Figure 29.12 Supply Side Effects of Fiscal Policy, 759
Figure 29.13 The Deficit, Borrowing and Crowding Out, 761

REVIEW QUESTIONS

1 Describe the main purposes of the government budget.

2 Describe the features of the 1995 UK government budget.

3 List the main sources of tax revenues and the main components of expenditures in the UK.

4 Compare the UK government budget deficit with deficits in other EU countries.

5 Compare the UK debt–income ratio with those of other EU countries.

6 Distinguish between automatic and discretionary fiscal policy.

7 Explain why an increase in government purchases has a multiplier effect on real GDP when the price level is sticky.

8 Explain why the lump-sum tax multiplier is smaller than the government purchases multiplier.

9 Explain why there is an increase in real GDP when both taxes and expenditures increase by the same amount.

10 Explain how induced taxes and benefits influence the fiscal policy multipliers.

11 Explain how international trade influences the fiscal policy multipliers.

12 Explain how the deficit fluctuates over the business cycle and define the structural deficit.

13 Explain how the multiplier effect is modified in the short run when the price level begins to change.

14 Explain what happens following an increase in government purchases if real GDP equals potential GDP.

15 Explain why the deficit can be a burden on future generations.

PROBLEMS

1 You are given the following information about the economy of Euroland. Autonomous consumption expenditure is 10 billion euros and the marginal propensity to consume is 0.9. Investment is 50 billion euros, government purchases of goods and services are 40 billion euros, lump-sum taxes are 40 billion euros. Euroland has no exports and no imports.

   a The government cuts its purchases of goods and services to 30 billion euros. What is the change in equilibrium expenditure?

   b What is the value of the government purchases multiplier?

   c The government continues to purchase 40 billion euros worth of goods and services and cuts lump-sum taxes to 30 billion euros. What is the change in equilibrium expenditure?

   d What is the value of the tax multiplier?

   e The government simultaneously cuts both its purchases of goods and services and taxes to 30 billion euros. What is the change in equilibrium expenditure?

   f What is the value of the balanced budget multiplier?

2 Euroland becomes outward looking and starts to export. Its exports are 50 billion euros. It also begins to import and its imports are 10 per cent of GDP. Everything else is the same as in Problem 1.

   a The government cuts its purchases of goods and services to 30 billion euros. What is the change in equilibrium expenditure?

   b What is the value of the government purchases multiplier?

   c Is the new government purchases multiplier in Euroland greater or smaller than it was in Problem 1? Why?

   d The government continues to purchase 40 billion euros worth of goods and services and cuts lump-sum taxes to 30 billion euros. What is the change in equilibrium expenditure?

   e What is the value of the tax multiplier?

   f The government simultaneously cuts both its purchases of goods and services and taxes to 30 billion euros. What is the change in equilibrium expenditure?

   g What is the value of the balanced budget multiplier? Compare the balanced budget multiplier in this case with the one in Problem 1.

3 An economy has no foreign trade and has only lump-sum taxes. Its lump-sum tax multiplier is four-fifths the magnitude of its government purchases multiplier. What is the marginal propensity to consume in this economy?

4 Suppose that the price level in the economy of Euroland as described in Problem 1 is 100. The economy is also at full employment.

   a If the government of Euroland increases its purchases of goods and services by 10 billion euros, what happens to the quantity of real GDP demanded?

   b In the short run, does equilibrium real GDP increase by more than, less than, or the same amount as the increase in the quantity of real GDP demanded?

   c In the long run, does equilibrium real GDP increase by more than, less than, or the same amount as the increase in the quantity of real GDP demanded?

   d In the short run, does the price level in Euroland rise, fall, or remain unchanged?

   e In the long run, does the price level in Euroland rise, fall, or remain unchanged?

5 Study *Reading Between the Lines* on pp. 762–763, and then answer the following questions.

   a Analyse the potential outcome on the German economy of a cut in government spending.

   b What are the implications for the budget deficit and the 'crowding out' debate?

   c How does your answer change if supply side factors are significant?

CHAPTER
30

MONEY

After studying this chapter you will be able to:

◆ Define money and describe its functions

◆ Explain the economic functions of banks and other financial institutions

◆ Describe the financial innovations of the 1980s

◆ Explain how banks create money

◆ Explain why the quantity of money is an important economic magnitude

◆ Explain the quantity theory of money

MONEY, LIKE FIRE AND THE WHEEL, HAS BEEN AROUND FOR A VERY LONG TIME. An incredible array of items have served as money. Cowrie shells were used in the Pacific Islands, wampum (beads made from shells) were used by North American Indians, whales' teeth were used by Fijians and tobacco was used by early American colonists. In ancient Greece, cattle served as money, indeed the word 'pecuniary' is derived from *pecunia*, the Latin for money, which in turn is derived from *pecus*, meaning cattle. Today, when we want to buy something, we use coins or notes, write a cheque, or present a credit card. Tomorrow, we'll use a 'smart card' that keeps track of spending and that our pocket computer can read. Are all these things money? ◆ When we deposit some coins or notes into a bank or building society, is that still money? What happens when the bank or building society lends the money in our deposit to someone else? How can we get our money back if it's been lent out? Does lending by banks and building societies create money – out of thin air? ◆ In the 1970s, there were two types of accounts with banks. There were demand deposits that did not pay interest, and there were time deposits, or deposit accounts as they are known in the United Kingdom, that did pay interest. Today, there's a

Money Makes the World Go Around

wide variety of accounts that provide the convenience of a cheque facility and the income of a savings deposit. Why were these new kinds of bank deposits introduced? ◆ During the 1970s and periods of the 1980s, the quantity of money in existence in the United Kingdom increased very quickly, but in the 1990s it increased at a much slower pace. In Russia and in some Latin American countries the quantity of money has increased at an extremely rapid pace. In Switzerland and Germany, the quantity of money has increased at a slower pace. Does the rate of increase in the quantity of money matter? What are the effects of an increasing quantity of money on our economy?

◆ ◆ ◆ ◆ In this chapter we'll study that useful invention: money. We'll look at its functions, its different forms, and the way it is defined and measured in the United Kingdom today. We'll also study banks and other financial institutions and explain how they create money. Finally, we'll examine the effects of money growth on the economy.

What Is Money?

What do cowrie shells, wampum, whales' teeth, tobacco, cattle and pennies have in common? Why are they all examples of money? To answer these questions we need a definition of money. **Money** is any commodity or token that is generally acceptable as the means of payment. A **means of payment** is a method of settling a debt. When a payment has been made there is no remaining obligation between the parties to a transaction. So what cowrie shells, wampum, whales' teeth, cattle and pennies have in common is that they have served (or still do serve) as the means of payment. But money has three other functions. They are:

◆ Medium of exchange

◆ Unit of account

◆ Store of value

Medium of Exchange

A *medium of exchange* is an object that is generally accepted in exchange for goods and services. Money acts as such a medium. Without money, it would be necessary to exchange goods and services directly for other goods and services – an exchange called **barter.** For example, if you want to buy a hamburger, you offer the paperback novel you've just finished reading in exchange for it. Barter requires a *double coincidence of wants*, a situation that occurs when Erika wants to buy what Kazia wants to sell, and Kazia wants to buy what Erika wants to sell. To get your hamburger, you must find someone who's selling hamburgers and who wants your paperback novel. Money guarantees that there is a double coincidence of wants because people with something to sell will always accept money in exchange for it. Money acts as a lubricant that smoothes the mechanism of exchange.

Unit of Account

A *unit of account* is an agreed measure for stating the prices of goods and services. To get the most out of your budget you have to figure out, among other things, whether seeing one more film is worth the price you have to pay, not in pounds and pence, but in terms of the number of ice creams, beers and cups of tea that you have to give up. It's easy to do such calculations when all these goods have prices in terms of pounds and pence (see Table 30.1). If a cinema ticket costs £4 and a pint of beer in the Students' Union costs £1, you know straight away that seeing one more film costs you 4 pints of beer. If a cup of tea costs 50 pence, one more cinema ticket costs 8 cups of tea. You need only one calculation to figure out the opportunity cost of any pair of goods and services.

But imagine how troublesome it would be if your local cinema posted its price as 4 pints of beer; and if the Students' Union announced that the price of a pint of beer was 2 ice-cream cones; and if the corner shop posted the price of an ice-cream cone as 1 cup of tea; and if the cafe priced a cup of tea as 5 rolls of mints! Now how much running around and calculating do you have to do to work out how much that film is going to cost you in terms of the beer, ice cream, tea, or mints that you must give up to see it? You get the answer for beer straight away from the sign posted at the cinema, but for all the other goods you're going to

---

TABLE 30.1

The Unit of Account Function of Money Simplifies Price Comparisons

Good	Price in money units	Price in units of another good
Cinema ticket	£4.00 each	4 pints of beer
Beer	£1.00 per pint	2 ice-cream cones
Ice cream	£0.50 per cone	1 cup of tea
Tea	£0.50 per cup	5 rolls of mints
Mints	£0.10 per roll	1 local phone call

Money as a unit of account. 1 cinema ticket costs £4 and 1 cup of tea costs 50 pence, so a film costs 8 cups of tea (£4.00/0.5 = 24).

No unit of account. You go to a cinema and learn that the price of a film is 4 pints of beer. You go to a cafe and learn that a cup of tea cost 5 rolls of mints. But how many rolls of mints does seeing a film cost you? To answer that question, you go to the Students' Union bar and find that a pint of beer costs 2 ice-cream cones. Now you head for the ice-cream shop, where an ice cream costs one cup of tea. Now you get out your pocket calculator: 1 film costs 4 pints of beer, or 8 ice-cream cones, or 8 cups of tea, or 40 rolls of mints!

have to visit many different stores to establish the price of each commodity in terms of another and then calculate prices in units that are relevant for your own decision. Cover up the column labelled 'price in money units' in Table 30.1 and see how hard it is to figure out the number of local telephone calls it costs to see one film. How much simpler it is for everyone to express their prices in terms of pounds and pence.

Store of Value

Any commodity or token that can be held and exchanged later for goods and services is called a *store of value*. Money acts as a store of value. If it did not, it would not be acceptable in exchange for goods and services. The more stable the value of a commodity or token, the better it can act as a store of value, and the more useful it is as money. There are no stores of value that are completely safe. The value of a physical object, such as a house, a car, or a work of art, fluctuates over time. The value of commodities and tokens used as money also fluctuate and, when there is inflation, they persistently fall in value.

Money must satisfy all three functions discussed above. Therefore money must be a medium of exchange, a unit of account and a store of value. But the most important function is the medium of exchange. Something can be a store of value, like a national savings account you can obtain at the post office, but it cannot be used to buy something. When Erika wants to buy something from Kazia she may go to the local post office and withdraw £25 from her saving account. The £25 will then be used in the process of exchange to buy goods that Kazia wants to sell. The process takes us from store of value to medium of exchange and then to goods. Similarly, a unit of account alone is not money unless it is first a medium of exchange. An example of a unit of account that is not money is the European Currency Unit or ECU. An ECU is defined as the basket of currencies of all the members of the European Union. It is the unit of account the European Union uses to disburse funds throughout the Union. If the value of one currency in the basket alters in relation to another, the value of the ECU in terms of either of the currencies will also alter. The value of the ECU in terms of the pound sterling in mid-1996 was £0.796.

The objects used as money have evolved over many centuries and we can identify four main forms of money:

◆ Commodity money
◆ Convertible paper money
◆ Fiat money
◆ Deposit money

Commodity Money

A physical commodity that is valued in its own right and also used as a means of payment is **commodity money**. An amazing array of items have served as commodity money at different times and places, seven of which were described at the beginning of this chapter. But the most common commodity monies have been coins made from metals such as gold, silver and copper. The first known coins were made in Lydia, a Greek city-state, at the beginning of the seventh century BC.

There are two problems with commodity money. First, there is a constant temptation to cheat on the value of the money. Two methods of cheating have been commonly used – clipping and debasement. *Clipping* is reducing the size of coins by an imperceptible amount, thereby lowering their metallic content. *Debasement* is the creation of a coin that has a lower silver or gold content (the balance being made up of some cheaper metal).

The temptation to lower the value of commodity money led to a phenomenon known as Gresham's Law, after the sixteenth-century British financial expert, Sir Thomas Gresham. **Gresham's Law** is the tendency for bad (debased) money to drive good (not debased) money out of circulation. To see why Gresham's Law works, suppose you are paid with two coins, one debased and the other not. Each coin has the same value if you use it to buy goods. But the good coin is more valuable as a commodity than it is as money. You will not, therefore, use the good coin as money. You will always pay with a debased coin (if you have one). In this way, bad money drives good money out of circulation.

The second problem with commodity money is its opportunity cost. Gold and silver used as money could be used to make jewellery or ornaments instead. This opportunity cost creates incentives to find alternatives to the commodity itself for use in the exchange process. One such alternative is a paper claim to commodity money.

Convertible Paper Money

When a paper claim to a commodity circulates as a means of payment, that claim is called **convertible paper money**. The first known example of paper money occurred in China during the Ming dynasty (1368–99 AD). This form of money was also used extensively throughout Europe in the Middle Ages.

The inventiveness of goldsmiths and their clients led to the widespread use of convertible paper money. Because gold was valuable, goldsmiths had well-guarded safes in which to keep their own gold. They also rented space to artisans and others who wanted to put their gold in safe-keeping and issued a receipt entitling them to reclaim their 'deposits' on demand. (These receipts were similar to the cloakroom ticket that you get at a theatre or museum.) Because the gold receipts entitled the holder of the receipt to reclaim gold, they were 'as good as gold' and circulated as money. When Isabella of Spain bought some land from Henry IV, she simply gave him a gold receipt for the appropriate value. The paper money is *backed* by the gold held by a goldsmith and is *convertible* into commodity money – gold.

Fractional Backing – the Origin of Banking

Once a convertible paper money system is operating and people are using paper claims to gold rather than gold itself as the means of payment, goldsmiths notice that their vaults are storing a lot of gold that is never withdrawn. This gives them a brilliant idea. Why not lend people gold receipts? The goldsmith can charge interest on the loan and the loan is created just by writing on a piece of paper. As long as the number of such receipts created is not too large in relation to the stock of gold in the goldsmith's safe, the goldsmith is in no danger of not being able to honour his promise to convert receipts into gold on demand. The gold in the goldsmith's safe is a *fraction* of the gold receipts in circulation. By this device, *fractionally backed* convertible paper money was invented.

Except for a brief period after World War I, between 1821 and 1931, the United Kingdom was on a **gold standard**. The gold standard was a monetary system with fractionally backed convertible paper in which the pound sterling could be converted into gold at a guaranteed value on demand. The gold value of the pound was fixed by the market price of gold in terms of silver and the silver content of the

shilling. The old units of account had 20 shillings to the pound, which gave the convertible value of the pound to gold as the value of the silver content of 20 shillings. Until the 1880s the United Kingdom was the only country in the world that maintained a gold standard. Being on the gold standard meant that it was easy to calculate the value of one currency, such as the pound, in terms of another, such as the US dollar. The amount of gold one pound sterling could be exchanged for was just over 486 per cent of the amount of gold one US dollar could buy, and so the value of the pound was fixed at $4.86 until 1931.

Even with fractionally backed paper money, valuable commodities that could be used for other productive activities are tied up in the exchange process. There remains an incentive to find a yet more efficient way of facilitating exchange and of freeing up the commodities used to back the paper money. This alternative is fiat money.

Fiat Money

The term *fiat* means 'let it be done' or 'by order of the authority.' **Fiat money** is an intrinsically worthless (or almost worthless) commodity that serves the functions of money. Some of the earliest fiat monies were the continental currency issued during the American War of Independence and the 'greenbacks' issued during the American Civil War, which circulated until 1879. These early experiments with fiat money ended in rapid inflation because the amount of money created was allowed to increase quickly, causing the money to lose value. Provided the quantity of fiat money is not allowed to grow too rapidly, it has a reasonably steady value in terms of the goods and services that it buys.

The notes and coins that we use in the United Kingdom today – collectively known as **currency** – are examples of fiat money. They are money because the government, through the Bank of England, declares them to be so. The Bank of England, which is the UK central bank, has a virtual monopoly in issuing notes in the UK. In Scotland, various banks issue similar notes but they are fully backed by Bank of England notes. Because of the creation of fiat money, people are willing to accept a piece of paper with a special watermark, printed in special ink and worth not more than a few pence as a commodity, in exchange for £20 worth of goods and services. The small metal coin that we call 10 pence is worth almost nothing as a piece of metal, but it pays for a local phone call and many other small commodities. The replacement of commodity money by fiat money enables the commodities themselves to be used productively.

Deposit Money

In the modern world, there is a fourth type of money – deposit money. **Deposit money** consists of deposits at banks and building societies. This type of money is an accounting entry in an electronic database in the banks' and building societies' computers. It is money because it is used to settle debts. In fact, it is the main means of settling debts in modern societies. The owner of a deposit transfers ownership to another person simply by writing a cheque – an instruction to a bank – that tells the bank to change its database, debiting the account of one depositor and crediting the account of another.

We'll have more to say about deposit money shortly. But before doing so, let's look at the different forms of money and their relative magnitudes in the United Kingdom today.

Money in the United Kingdom Today

In most countries, money consists of *currency* and *deposits* at banks and other financial institutions. There are different types of deposits and, as a result, different measures of money. The two official measures of money are known as **M0** and **M4**. M0 consists of currency held by the public plus currency reserves held by banks and building societies, and banks deposits held at the Bank of England. This measure of money is referred to as *narrow money*. M4 includes currency held by the public and their holdings of bank and building society deposits, but does *not* include currency held by banks and building societies. Deposits are classified as sight deposits and time deposits. A sight deposit is a chequeable deposit. A person holding such a deposit will issue cheques from their sight deposit account. In the United Kingdom a sight deposit is more familiarly known as a *current account*. A time deposit is a deposit that has a fixed term to maturity. Although this is not usually a chequeable deposit, technological advances in the banking industry have made it easy to switch funds from time deposits to sight deposits. The cost of switching funds is the bank charge and the penalty of lost interest. Because of the ease with which time deposits can be switched into sight

deposits, they are included in the definition of money. A time deposit is more familiarly known in the United Kingdom as a *deposit account*. Another familiarly used term for M4 is *broad money*.

The many definitions of money used by the authorities during the 1980s have been superseded by the definitions for M0 and M4 shown in Table 30.2. Other definitions of money that have been in use include non-interest bearing M1, M1, M2, M3 and £M3. Each definition includes various types of bank and building society deposits. For example, M1 includes only bank sight deposits and £M3 includes sterling time deposits. Figure 30.1 gives a schematic description of money.

Are M0 and M4 Really Money? Money is the means of payment. So the test of whether an asset is money is whether it serves as a means of payment. Currency passes the test. M0 consists of currency held by people and businesses and currency held by banks and building societies. The currency held by the banks and building societies is part of their reserves and is referred to as *till money*. These reserves are held to meet the withdrawals of cash by bank and building society customers. The currency held by people and businesses is for spending. This represents the largest component of M0 – 80 per cent. Thus M0 is largely money, but a significant amount of M0 is not technically money. What about deposits? Chequeing deposits are money because they can be transferred

---

TABLE 30.2

Two Measures of Money

M0

◆ Currency held outside banks

◆ Currency held by banks and building societies

◆ Bankers' deposits at the Bank of England

M4

◆ Currency held outside banks

◆ Sight deposits at banks

◆ Time deposits at banks

◆ Building society share accounts and other deposits at building societies

◆ Certificates of Deposits at banks and building societies

FIGURE 30.1

Schematic Representation of Money Supply

Notes & coin in circulation with the public	+	Notes & coin held by the banks and building societies
+		+
Private sector non-interest bearing sterling sight bank deposits		Bankers' balance with the Bank of England
=		=
Non-interest bearing M1		**M0**
+		+
Private sector interest bearing sterling sight bank deposits	+	Private sector interest retail sterling deposits with banks and building societies and national savings bank ordinary accounts
=		=
M1		**M2**
+		
Private sector sterling time deposits	+	Private sector foreign currency bank deposits
=		
£M3		=
+		**M3**
Private sector holdings of building society shares and deposits and sterling certificates of deposits		
–		
Building society holdings of bank deposits and bank certificate of deposits, notes and coin		
=		
M4		

There are many definitions of money in he United Kingdom. The narrowest definition is M0 and the broadest is M4. In between there is non-interest bearing M1, M1, M2, £M3 and M3.

from one person to another by writing a cheque. Such a transfer of ownership is equivalent to handing over currency. Both banks and building societies issue chequeable deposits.

But what about time deposits? A few time deposits are just as much a means of payment as a sight deposit. You can use the cash dispenser (automated teller machine – ATM) to transfer funds directly from such accounts to pay for your purchase. But most time deposits are not direct means of payments. They are *liquid assets*. **Liquidity** is the property of being instantly convertible into a means of payment with little loss in value. Most time deposits have this property, but there are some deposits that do not. These are large deposits known as *Certificates of Deposits* or CDs. CDs have maturities from three months to up to two years. They are not bank and building society deposits in the normal sense as they have to be held for the period of the maturity, but they can be sold in the financial markets quickly and easily. Because most time deposits are quickly and easily converted into currency or chequeing deposits, they are operationally similar to sight deposits but technically they are not money.

You can see in Fig. 30.2 that currency is a small part of our money. It accounts for only 3 per cent of M4, while bank deposits account for 62 per cent and building society deposits represent 35 per cent. Chequeing deposits at banks and building societies total more than 66 per cent.

Deposits are Money but Cheques are Not In defining money, we included, along with currency, deposits at banks and other financial institutions. But we did not count the cheques that people write as money. Why are deposits money and cheques not?

To see why deposits are money but cheques are not, think about what happens when Colleen buys some roller blades for £100 from Rocky's Rollers. When Colleen goes to Rocky's shop she has £250 in her deposit account at the Co-op Bank. Rocky has £1,000 in his deposit account – at the same bank, as it happens. The total deposits of these two people is £1,250. On June 11, Colleen writes a cheque for £100. Rocky takes the cheque to Co-op Bank straight away and deposits it. Rocky's bank balance rises from £1,000 to £1,100. But when the bank credits Rocky's account with £100, it also debits Colleen's account £100, so that her balance falls from £250 to £150. The total deposits of Colleen and Rocky are

---

FIGURE 30.2

Two Official Measures of Money

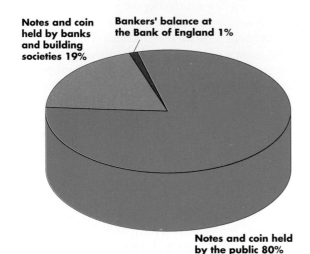

Notes and coin held by banks and building societies 19%

Bankers' balance at the Bank of England 1%

Notes and coin held by the public 80%

(a) M0 £24 billion in March 1996

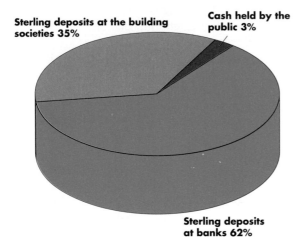

Sterling deposits at the building societies 35%

Cash held by the public 3%

Sterling deposits at banks 62%

(b) M4 £640 billion in March 1996

The M0 measure of money consists of currency held by the public, currency held by the banks and banks' own deposits at the Bank of England. Currency held by the public is a means of payment and makes up 80 per cent of M0. Currency held by the banks and deposits at the Bank of England are part of bank reserves and are not really used for transactions. Therefore not all of M0 is technically money. M4 consists of currency held by the public plus sight deposits at banks, time deposits at banks, building society share accounts and other building society deposits, and Certificates of Deposits issued by banks and building societies.

Source: *Bank of England Quarterly Bulletin*, November 1995.

---

still the same as before, £1,250. Rocky now has £100 more and Colleen £100 less than before. These transactions are summarized in Table 30.3.

This transaction has transferred money from Colleen to Rocky. The cheque itself was never money. There wasn't an extra £100 worth of money while the cheque was in circulation. The cheque was an instruction to the bank to transfer money from Colleen to Rocky.

In the example, Colleen and Rocky use the same bank. The same story, but with additional steps, describes what happens if Colleen and Rocky use different banks. Rocky's bank credits the cheque to Rocky's account and then takes the cheque to a cheque-clearing centre. Colleen's bank pays Rocky's bank £100 and then debits Colleen's account £100. This process can take a few days, but the principles are the same as when two people use the same bank.

Credit Cards are Not Money   So cheques are not money. But what about credit cards? Isn't having a credit card in your wallet and presenting the card to pay for your roller blades the same thing as using money? Why aren't credit cards somehow valued and counted as part of the quantity of money?

When you pay by cheque you are usually asked to guarantee the cheque with a *cheque guarantee card*. It would never occur to you to think of your

---

TABLE 30.3

Paying by Cheque

Colleen's Chequeing Deposit Account

Date	Item	Debit	Credit	Balance
June 1	Opening balance			£250.00 CR *
June 11	Rocky's Rollers	£100.00		£150.00 CR

Rocky's Rollers Chequeing Deposit Account

Date	Item	Debit	Credit	Balance
June 1	Opening balance			£1,000.00 CR
June 11	Colleen buys roller blades		£100.00	£1,100.00 CR

*CR means 'credit': the bank owes the depositor.

cheque guarantee card as money. It's just an ID card. But it is an ID card that enables you to guarantee your cheque up to a certain value. A credit card is also an ID card but one that lets you take a loan at the instant you buy something. When you sign a credit card sales slip, you are saying: 'I agree to pay for these goods when the credit card company bills me.' Once you get your statement from the credit card company, you must make the minimum payment due (or clear your balance). To make that payment you need money – you need to have currency or a chequeing deposit to pay the credit card company. So although you use a credit card when you buy something, the credit card is not the *means of payment* and it is not money.

REVIEW

◆ Money is the means of payment and has three functions: medium of exchange, unit of account and store of value.

◆ A commodity can serve as money, but modern societies use fiat money and deposit money.

◆ The main component of money in the UK today is deposits at banks and building societies.

◆ Neither cheques nor credit cards are money.

We've seen that the main component of money in the United Kingdom is deposits at banks and building societies. Let's take a closer look at these institutions.

Financial Intermediaries

We are going to study the banking and financial system by first describing the variety of financial intermediaries that operate in the United Kingdom today. Then we'll examine the operations of banks and of other financial intermediaries. After describing the main features of financial intermediaries, we'll examine their economic functions, describing what they produce and how they make a profit.

A **financial intermediary** is a firm that takes deposits from households and firms and makes loans to other households and firms. There are two types of financial intermediaries whose deposits are components of the nation's money:

◆ Banks

◆ Building societies

Let's begin by looking at the banks.

Banks

A **bank** is a private firm, licensed by the Bank of England under the Banking Act of 1987 to take deposits and make loans and operate in the United Kingdom. There are over 400 commercial banks in the United Kingdom today. These banks can be categorized into two main groups: retail banks and wholesale banks. The distinction between retail banks and wholesale banks is based on the size of deposit. In general, the minimum deposit accepted by a wholesale bank is £250,000 while retail banks accept deposits as small as £1. Retail banks operate extensive branch networks, while wholesale banks have few branches and operate mainly in London. Wholesale banks form a varied group, comprising UK merchant banks, other UK banks such as finance houses that specialize in lending to businesses, leasing companies that specialize in financing the leasing of equipment to businesses, other small regional banks and overseas banks.

To understand the operations of commercial banks, it is useful to study their balance sheets. The *balance sheet* of a bank (or of any other business) is a list of assets, liabilities and net worth. *Assets* are what the bank owns, *liabilities* are what the bank owes and *net worth*, which is equal to assets minus liabilities, is the value of the bank to its shareholders – its owners. A bank's balance sheet can be described by the equation

Liabilities + Net worth = Assets

Among a bank's liabilities are the deposits that are part of the nation's money. Your deposit at the bank is a liability to your bank (and an asset to you) because the bank must repay your deposit (and sometimes the interest on it too) whenever you decide to take your money out of the bank.

Profit and Prudence: A Balancing Act   The aim of a bank is to maximize its net worth – its value to its stockholders. To achieve this objective, a bank lends the money deposited with it at interest rates higher than the rates it pays for deposits. But a bank must perform a delicate balancing act. Lending is risky, and the more it ties up its deposits in high-risk, high-interest rate loans, the bigger is its chance of not being able to repay its depositors. And if depositors perceive a high risk of not being repaid, they withdraw their funds and create a crisis for the bank. So a bank must be prudent in the way it uses its deposits, balancing security for the depositors against profit for its shareholders.

Reserves and Loans   To achieve security for its depositors, a bank divides its funds into two parts: reserves and loans. **Reserves** are cash in a bank's vault plus its deposits at the Bank of England. The cash in a bank's vaults is a reserve to meet the demands that its customers place on it – it keeps that ATM replenished every time you and your friends need to use it for a midnight pizza. A commercial bank's deposit at the Bank of England is similar to your deposit at your own bank. Commercial banks use these deposits in the same way that you use your bank account. A commercial bank deposits cash into or draws cash out of its account at the Bank of England and writes cheques on that account to settle debts with other banks.

If a bank kept all its assets as cash in its vault or as deposits at the Bank of England, it wouldn't make any profit. In fact it keeps only a small fraction of its funds in reserves and lends the rest. A bank makes three different types of loans, or equivalently, holds three different types of assets. They are:

1. Liquid assets
2. Investment securities
3. Loans

A bank's *liquid assets* are government Treasury bills and commercial bills. These assets can be sold and instantly converted into cash with virtually no risk of loss. Because liquid assets are virtually risk free, they have a low interest rate.

A bank's *investment securities* are longer-term government bonds and other bonds. These assets can be sold quickly and converted into cash but at prices that fluctuate. Because their prices fluctuate, these assets are riskier than liquid assets but they also have a higher interest rate.

A bank's *loans* are lines of credit extended to companies to finance the purchase of capital equipment and stocks, and to households – personal loans – to finance consumer durable goods, such as cars or boats. The outstanding balances on credit card accounts are also bank loans. Loans are the riskiest assets of a bank because they cannot be converted into cash until they are due to be repaid. And some borrowers default and never repay. Because they are the riskiest of a bank's assets, they are also carry the highest interest rate.

Table 30.4 describes the balance sheet of all the commercial banks in the United Kingdom. The sterling assets of the banks include the notes and coin held in their vaults and the bankers' balances at the Bank of England. These are part of the banks' reserves. The bankers' balances at the Bank of England are a bit like your own deposit at a bank. Just as you sign cheques to pay your debts or expenditures, banks will meet their obligations to other banks by drawing on their balances at the Bank of England. The banks also hold some liquid assets and these are loans to financial intermediaries, government bills and other securities. These liquid assets earn a rate of interest, but banks make the most of their money by giving loans and overdrafts to people and businesses. These items come under the heading of *advances*. The banks also make money by lending in other currencies to businesses, other banks and governments. These are other currency assets. The banks that have a lot of other currency assets are the wholesale banks. On the other side of the balance sheet is the liabilities of the banks. The first item is notes issued. These are bank notes issued by the Scottish banks – the Royal Bank of Scotland, Bank of Scotland and Clydesdale Bank – just like the sterling notes issued by the Bank of England. The remainder of sterling liabilities are sight and time deposits, which form part of the money supply. The wholesale banks also take large deposits in other currencies which represent the majority of other currency liabilities.

We have seen that commercial bank deposits are one component of the nation's money. But building societies also take deposits that form part of the nation's money.

Building Societies

A **building society** is a financial intermediary that traditionally obtained its funds from savings deposits (sometimes called share accounts) and that made long-term mortgage loans to home buyers. The first building societies were founded in the late eighteenth century as *mutuals*. A mutual is an organization that belongs to its members. In the case of a building society, its mutual status

TABLE 30.4

The Balance Sheet of All Banks in the United Kingdom, March 1995

Assets (billions of pounds)		Liabilities (billions of pounds)	
Sterling assets		**Sterling liabilities**	
Notes and coin	3.7	Notes issued	2.1
Balances with the Bank of England	1.5	Sight deposits	217.0
Market loans	171.4	Time deposits	317.9
Bills	20.9	CDs	66.3
Advances	403.4	Other liabilities	87.8
Other assets	90.6		
Total sterling assets	**691.5**	**Total sterling liabilities**	**691.1**
Other currency assets		**Other curency liabilities**	
Loans to financial intermediaries	750.0	Sight and time deposits	826.2
Bills	11.0	CDs	67.1
Other investments	148.4	Other liabilities	45.3
Miscellaneous assets	28.8		
Total other currency assets	**938.2**	**Total other currency liabilities**	**938.6**
Total assets	**1,630.**	**Total liabilities**	**1,630.**

Source: *Bank of England Quarterly Bulletin*, November 1995, Table 3.

means that by law it belongs to its depositors and borrowers. Up until the 1980s the societies had concentrated on their traditional function of lending to home buyers. However, the societies had begun to compete with the banks in the late 1970s by offering depositors accounts that gave them instant access to their money but paid a rate of interest for a minimum amount left in the account. The Building Societies Act of 1986 allowed for the progressive deregulation of the societies enabling them to offer financial products that brought them directly into competition with the banks. The act also enabled building societies to give up their mutual status and become banks. One of the United Kingdom's most well known building societies, the Abbey National, took this route in 1989, and the merged Halifax/Leeds building society plan to do the same in 1997.

The structure and balance sheets of building societies are similar to those of banks. Like banks, they have developed a branch network, and they have liabilities that are deposits and CDs. Like bank deposits, building society deposits are chequeable

and are accepted in shops in exchange for goods. Building societies also offer similar services to banks, such as credit cards, personal lending and foreign currency.

The assets of building societies include cash reserves, but unlike the banks they do not have to hold deposits at the Bank of England. However, they do hold deposits and CDs at commercial banks. They also hold liquid assets such as CDs of other building societies and Treasury bills. Like banks, they also hold government bonds, but unlike banks most of building society lending is for house purchase. These assets have a much longer maturity than the normal lending of the commercial banks. Mortgage loans are typically for 25 years and are viewed as very safe assets. This is because the house technically belongs to the building society until the mortgage loan is paid off. The building society has the right to sell the house to recover the debt if a home buyer defaults. Table 30.5 shows the balance sheet of all building societies. As you can see, one of the differences between building societies and banks is that the liquid assets of building societies include bank deposits. In calculating the nation's money supply, the deposits of the building societies at the banks are subtracted from the total figures.

The Economic Functions of Financial Intermediaries

All financial intermediaries make a profit from the spread between the interest rate they pay on deposits and the interest rate at which they lend. Why can financial intermediaries borrow at a low interest rate and lend at a higher one? What services do they perform that makes their depositors willing to put up with a low interest rate and their borrowers willing to pay a higher one?

Financial intermediaries provide four main services that people are willing to pay for:

◆ Creating liquidity

◆ Minimizing the cost of obtaining funds

◆ Minimizing the cost of monitoring borrowers

◆ Pooling risk

Creating Liquidity Financial intermediaries create liquidity. *Liquid* assets are those that are easily and with certainty convertible into money. Some of the liabilities of financial intermediaries are themselves money; others are highly liquid assets that are easily converted into money.

Financial intermediaries create liquidity by borrowing short and lending long. Borrowing short means taking deposits but standing ready to repay them at short notice (and on even no notice in the case of chequeing deposits). Lending long means making loan commitments for a prearranged, and often quite long, period of time. For example, when a person makes a deposit with a building society, that deposit can be withdrawn at any time. But the building society makes a lending commitment for perhaps up to 25 years to a home buyer.

Minimizing the Cost of Obtaining Funds
Finding someone from whom to borrow can be a costly business. Imagine how troublesome it would be if there were no financial intermediaries. A firm that was looking for £1 million to buy a new production plant would probably have to hunt around for several dozen people from whom to borrow in order to acquire enough funds for its capital project. Financial intermediaries lower such costs. A firm needing £1 million can go to a single financial intermediary to obtain those funds. The financial intermediary has to borrow from a large number of people, but it's not doing that just for this one firm and the £1 million it wants to borrow. The financial intermediary can establish an organization capable of raising funds from a large number of depositors and can spread the cost of this activity over a large number of borrowers.

TABLE 30.5

The Balance Sheet of All Building Societies in the United Kingdom, March 1996

Assets (billions of pounds)		Liabilities (billions of pounds)	
Notes and coin	0.4	Shares and deposits	214.1
Bank deposits and CDs	30.9	CDs	8.4
Bank bills	0.2	Wholesale liabilities	46.5
Building society deposits and CDs	2.3	Other liabilities and reserves	30.6
Government stocks	8.2		
Mortgage and other loans	244.0		
Other assets	13.6		
Total assets	**299.6**	**Total liabilities**	**299.6**

Source: *Bank of England Quarterly Bulletin*, March 1996, Table 5.2.

Borrowing a very large amount may be too much for one financial intermediary. This is because a single financial intermediary may not be willing to take the risk of exposing itself to one large borrower. In such cases a number of financial intermediaries are brought together and each intermediary will lend a proportion of the total loan. This is called a 'syndicated loan' and is typical of the way a large loan, such as the loan to build the Channel Tunnel, is raised in the international financial market.

Minimizing the Cost of Monitoring Borrowers

Lending money is a risky business. There's always a danger that the borrower may not repay. Most of the money lent gets used by firms to invest in projects that they hope will return a profit. But sometimes these hopes are not fulfilled. Checking up on the activities of a borrower and ensuring that the best possible decisions are being made for making a profit and avoiding a loss is a costly and specialized activity. Imagine how costly it would be if each and every household that lent money to a firm had to incur the costs of monitoring that firm directly. By depositing funds with a financial intermediary, households avoid those costs. The financial intermediary performs the monitoring activity by using specialized resources that have a much lower cost than what each household would incur if it had to undertake the activity individually.

Pooling Risk   As we noted above, lending money is risky. There is always a chance of not being repaid – of default. The risk of default can be reduced by lending to a large number of different individuals. In such a situation, if one person defaults on a loan it is a nuisance but not a disaster. In contrast, if only one person borrows and that person defaults on the loan, the entire loan is a write-off. Financial intermediaries enable people to pool risk in an efficient way. Thousands of people lend money to any one financial intermediary and, in turn, the financial intermediary re-lends the money to hundreds, and perhaps thousands, of individual firms. If any one firm defaults on its loan, that default is spread across all the depositors with the intermediary and no individual depositor is left exposed to a high degree of risk.

Lending a large amount of money to one person or one firm is also a risky business. If that person or firm defaults on the loan, the write-off of the loan will endanger the viability of the financial intermediary.

R E V I E W

◆ Most of the nation's money is made up of deposits in financial intermediaries – commercial banks and building societies.

◆ The main economic functions of financial intermediaries are to create liquidity, to minimize the cost of obtaining funds and of monitoring borrowers, and to pool risk.

Financial Regulation, Deregulation and Innovation

Financial intermediaries are highly regulated institutions. But regulation is not static, and in the 1980s some important changes in their regulation as well as deregulation took place. Also, the institutions are not static. In their pursuit of profit, they constantly seek lower-cost ways of obtaining funds, monitoring borrowers, pooling risk and creating liquidity. They are also inventive in seeking ways to avoid the costs imposed on them by financial regulation. Let's take a look at regulation, deregulation and innovation in the financial sector in recent years.

Financial Regulation

Financial intermediaries face two types of regulation:

◆ Deposit insurance
◆ Balance sheet rules

Deposit Insurance   The deposits of financial intermediaries are insured by the Bank of England deposit protection scheme. The scheme is financed by a flat rate contribution by banks in proportion to their deposits. The scheme covers 90 per cent of the first £20,000 per depositor. Therefore small depositors are basically covered for up to 90 per cent of the value of their deposits but large depositors have cover only up to £20,000.

The existence of deposit insurance provides protection for depositors in the event that a financial intermediary fails. But it also limits the incentive for the owner of a financial intermediary to make safe investments and loans. Some economists believe that deposit insurance can create a banking system that is prone to take excessive risks with depositors' money. This is the problem of *moral hazard*. Because depositors are sure that their deposits are insured, they do not keep an eye on what banks are doing with their money. Banks in turn, knowing that depositors are not worried about their funds, will aim to maximize profits by lending to high-risk businesses. It has been argued that this is precisely what happened with Savings & Loans associations (S&Ls) in the United States in the 1980s. Savers, knowing that their deposits were being used to make high-risk loans, did not remove their deposits from S&Ls because they knew they had the security of deposit insurance. The S&L owners making high-risk loans knew they were making a one-way bet. If their loans paid off, they made a high rate of return. If they failed and could not meet their obligations to the depositors, the insurance fund would step in. Bad loans were good business!

Because of this type of problem, all financial intermediaries face regulation of their balance sheets.

Balance Sheet Rules The most important balance sheet regulations are:

1. Capital requirements
2. Reserve requirements

Capital requirements are the minimum amount of an owner's own financial resources that must be put into an intermediary. This amount must be sufficiently large to discourage owners from making loans that are too risky. Capital requirements are also referred to as capital adequacy and depend on the types of assets of a bank. An international agreement on the capital requirements of all banks operating in the major industrial economies came into effect in 1993. Known as the Basle Agreement of 1986, it recommended a common system of requirements for all banks based on the types of assets they held.

Reserve requirements are rules setting out the minimum percentages of deposits that must be held in currency or other safe, liquid assets. These minimum percentages vary across the different types of intermediaries and deposits. The Bank of England does not specify the percentage of liquid assets that any specific bank holds but ensures through supervision that banks maintain an appropriate mix of liquid assets. However, banks in other EU countries have reserve requirements.

Deregulation in the 1980s

The 1980s was a period of deregulation of the banking and financial system in the United Kingdom. In 1979 exchange controls were abolished. The abolition of these controls meant that banks could borrow and lend overseas unhindered. The most important deregulatory measure in 1980 was the abolition of the *corset*. The corset was a system of regulation that controlled the amount of deposits the banks were allowed to take. With the removal of this and other controls, banks were free to compete with building societies in the market for housing finance. A further deregulatory measure was the removal in 1983 of the arrangement whereby the building societies fixed the interest rate on mortgages. This measure injected further competition into the mortgage market, because now any individual building society could set its interest rate according to the pressures of the market and not wait for all the remaining building societies to change their interest rates together. In 1986 the Building Societies Act allowed the societies to offer similar services to those of banks.

Financial Innovation

The development of new financial products – of new ways of borrowing and lending – is called **financial innovation**. The aim of financial innovation is to lower the cost of borrowing or increase the return from lending or, more simply, to increase the profit from financial intermediation. There are three main influences on financial innovation. They are:

◆ Economic environment
◆ Technology
◆ Regulation

The pace of financial innovation was remarkable in the 1980s, and all three of these forces played a role.

Economic Environment Some of the innovations that occurred in the 1970s and 1980s were a response to high inflation and high interest rates. An important example is the development of variable interest rate loans for businesses. Traditionally, companies had borrowed long-term funds at fixed interest rates. Rising interest rates brought rising borrowing costs for banks, which led them to develop variable rate lending. Another important innovation in the 1970s was the payment of interest on sight deposits. This had the effect of making the holding of bank deposits as opposed to a savings account more attractive. In the 1980s, depositors who maintained a certain minimum amount in their sight deposit accounts had all bank charges waived, making such accounts even more attractive.

Technology   Other financial innovations resulted from technological change, most notably that associated with the decreased cost of computing and long-distance communication. The use of ATMs and direct debit cards such as Switch cards, which allow stores to debit your bank or building society account directly, is an example of the advance of financial innovation caused by improved technology. The growth in the use of credit cards and the development of international financial markets – for example, the increased importance of Eurodollar[1] – are consequences of technological change.

Regulation   A good deal of financial innovation takes place to avoid regulation. For example, when the corset was in operation in the 1970s, banks were not allowed to expand their deposits beyond a certain point. Other financial intermediaries sprang up with different types of deposits to grab the business that banks had to turn away.

Deregulation, Innovation and Money

Deregulation and financial innovation that have led to the development of new types of deposit accounts have brought important changes in the composition of the nation's money. In the 1960s, M1 consisted of only currency and chequeing sight deposits at commercial banks. In the 1980s, other new types of chequeing deposits expanded while traditional chequeing sight deposits declined. Similar changes took place in the composition of money. Bank time deposits expanded and building

society share accounts began to offer the same services as bank accounts. The result of these changes was that the definition of the money supply altered and a new measure – M4 – was born.

R EVIEW

◆ Financial intermediaries are required to insure their deposits, and their lending is regulated.

◆ The 1980s saw a wave of financial deregulation that blurred the distinction between commercial banks and building societies.

◆ Financial intermediaries constantly seek new ways of making a profit and react to the changing economic environment, new technologies and regulations.

◆ Deregulation and innovation in the 1980s brought new types of deposits that changed the composition of the nation's money.

Because financial intermediaries are able to create liquidity and to create assets that are a means of payment – money – they occupy a unique place in our economy and exert an important influence on the quantity of money in existence. Let's see how money is created.

How Banks Create Money

Banks create money[2]. But this doesn't mean that they have smoke-filled back rooms in which counterfeiters are busily working. Remember, most money is deposits, not currency. What banks create is deposits and they do so by making loans. But the amount of deposits they can create is limited by their reserves.

Reserves: Actual and Required

We've seen that banks don't have £100 in notes for every £100 that people have deposited with them.

---

[1] Eurodollars are US dollar bank accounts held in other countries, mainly in Europe. They were 'invented' during the 1960s when the former Soviet Union wanted the security and convenience of holding funds in US dollars but was unwilling to place deposits in US banks.

[2] In this section, we'll use the term *banks* to refer to all the depository institutions whose deposits are part of the money supply: commercial banks and building societies.

In fact, a typical bank today has about 60 pence in currency and another 26 pence on deposit at the Bank of England, a total reserve of less than £1, for every £100 deposited in it. But there is no need for panic. Banks have learned, from experience, that these reserve levels are adequate for ordinary business needs.

The fraction of a bank's total deposits that are held in reserves is called the **reserve ratio**. The value of the reserve ratio is influenced by the actions of a bank's depositors. If a depositor withdraws currency from a bank, the reserve ratio decreases. If a depositor puts currency into a bank, the reserve ratio increases.

The **required reserve ratio** is the ratio of reserves to deposits that banks are required, by regulation, to hold. A bank's *required reserves* are equal to its deposits multiplied by the required reserve ratio. A bank's **desired reserve ratio** is the ratio of reserves to deposits that banks consider as prudent to hold in order to meet withdrawals and to carry on their business. A bank's desired reserves are equal to its deposits multiplied by the desired reserve ratio. Actual reserves minus *required* or *desired reserves* are **excess reserves**. Whenever banks have excess reserves, they are able to create money.

To see how banks create money we are going to look at two model banking systems. In the first model there is only one bank. In the second model there are many banks.

Creating Deposits by Making Loans in a One-bank Economy

In the model banking system that we'll study, there is only one bank and its required reserve ratio is 25 per cent. That is, for each £1 deposited, the bank keeps 25 pence in reserves and lends the rest. The balance sheet of One-and-Only Bank is shown in Fig. 30.3(a). Its deposits are £400 million and its reserves are 25 per cent of this amount – £100 million. Its loans are equal to deposits minus reserves and are £300 million.

The story begins with Silas Marner, who has decided that it is too dangerous to keep on hiding his fortune under his mattress. Silas has been holding his fortune in currency and has a nest egg of £1 million. He decides to put his £1 million on deposit at the One-and-Only Bank. On the day that Silas makes his deposit, the One-and-Only Bank's balance sheet changes and the new situation is shown

FIGURE 30.3

Creating Money at the One-and-Only Bank

(a) Balance sheet on January 1

Assets (millions of pounds)		Liabilities (millions of pounds)	
Reserves	£100	Deposits	£400
Loans	£300		
Total	£400	Total	£400

(b) Balance sheet on January 2

Assets (millions of pounds)		Liabilities (millions of pounds)	
Reserves	£101	Deposits	£401
Loans	£300		
Total	£401	Total	£401

(c) Balance sheet on January 3

Assets (millions of pounds)		Liabilities (millions of pounds)	
Reserves	£101	Deposits	£404
Loans	£303		
Total	£404	Total	£404

In part (a), the One-and-Only Bank has deposits of £400 million, loans of £300 million and reserves of £100 million. The bank's desired reserve ratio is 25 per cent. When the bank receives a deposit of £1 million (part b), it has excess reserves. It lends £3 million and creates a further £3 million of deposits. Deposits increase by £3 million and loans increase by £3 million (in part c).

in Fig. 30.3(b). The bank now has £101 million in reserves and £401 million in deposits. It still has loans of £300 million.

The bank now has *excess reserves*. With reserves of £101 million, the bank would like to have deposits of £404 million and loans of £303 million. And being the One-and-Only Bank, the manager knows the reserves will remain at £101 million. That is, she knows that when she makes a loan, the amount lent remains on deposit at the One-and-Only Bank. She knows, for example, that all the suppliers of Sky's-the-Limit Construction, her biggest borrower, are also depositors of One-and-Only. So she knows that if she makes the loan that Sky's-the-Limit has just requested, the deposit she lends will never leave One-and-Only. When Sky's-the-Limit uses part of its new loan to pay £100,000 to I-Dig-It Building Company for some excavations, the One-and-Only Bank simply moves the funds from Sky's-the-Limit's chequeing account to I-Dig-It's chequeing account.

So the manager of One-and-Only calls Sky's-the-Limit's accountant and offers to lend the maximum that she can. How much does she lend? She lends £3 million. By lending £3 million, One-and-Only's balance sheet changes to the one shown in Fig. 30.3(c). Loans increase by £3 million to £303 million. The loan shows up in Sky's-the-Limit's deposit initially and total deposits increase to £404 million – £400 million plus Silas Marner's deposit of £1 million plus the newly created deposit of £3 million. The bank now has no excess reserves and has reached the limit of its ability to create money.

The Deposit Multiplier

The **deposit multiplier** is the amount by which an increase in bank reserves is multiplied to calculate the increase in bank deposits. That is:

$$\text{Deposit multiplier} = \frac{\text{Change in deposits}}{\text{Change in reserves}}$$

In the example we've just worked through, the deposit multiplier is 4. The £1 million increase in reserves created a £4 million increase in deposits. The deposit multiplier is linked to the required reserve ratio by the following equation:

$$\text{Deposit multiplier} = \frac{1}{\text{Desired revenue ratio}}$$

In the example, the desired reserve ratio is 25 per cent, or 0.25. That is:

$$\text{Deposit multiplier} = 1/0.25$$
$$= 4$$

Creating Deposits by Making Loans with Many Banks

If you told the student loans officer at your own bank that she creates money, she wouldn't believe you. Bankers see themselves as lending the money they receive from others, not creating money. But

in fact, even though each bank only lends what it receives, the banking *system* creates money. To see how, let's look at another example.

Figure 30.4 is going to keep track of what is happening in the process of money creation by a banking system in which each bank has a required reserve ratio of 25 per cent. The process begins when Alan decides to decrease his currency holding and put £100,000 on deposit. Now Alan's bank has £100,000 of new deposits and £100,000 of additional reserves. With a required reserve ratio of 25 per cent, the bank keeps £25,000 on reserve and lends £75,000 to Amy. Amy writes a cheque for £75,000 to buy a photocopy-shop franchise from Barbara. At this point, Alan's Bank has a new deposit of £100,000, new loans of £75,000 and new reserves of £25,000. You can see this situation in Fig. 30.4 as the first row of the 'running tally'.

For Alan's bank, that is the end of the story. But it's not the end of the story for the entire banking system. Barbara deposits her cheque for £75,000 in another bank, which has an increase in deposits and reserves of £75,000. This bank puts 25 per cent of its increase in deposits, £18,750 into reserve and lends £56,250 to Bob. And Bob writes a cheque to Carl to pay off a business loan. The current state of play is seen in Fig. 30.4. Now, bank reserves have increased by £43,750 (£25,000 plus £18,750), loans have increased by £131,250 (£75,000 plus £56,250) and deposits have increased by £175,000 (£100,000 plus £75,000).

When Carl takes his cheque to his bank, its deposits and reserves increase by £56,250, £14,060 of which it keeps in reserve and £42,190 of which it lends. This process continues until there are no excess reserves in the banking system. But the process takes a lot of further steps. One additional step is shown in Fig. 30.4. The figure also shows the final tallies – reserves increase by £100,000, loans increase by £300,000 and deposits increase by £400,000.

The sequence in Fig. 30.4 is the first four stages of the entire process. To figure out the entire process, look closely at the numbers in the figure. At each stage, the loan is 75 per cent (0.75) of the previous loan and the deposit is 0.75 of the previous deposit. Call that proportion L ($L = 0.75$). The complete sequence is

$$1 + L + L^2 + L^3 + \dots$$

Remember, L is a fraction, so at each stage in this sequence the amount of new loans gets smaller.

FIGURE 30.4

The Multiple Creation of Bank Deposits

The sequence	The running tally			When a bank receives deposits, it keeps 25 per cent in reserves and lends 75 per cent.

The sequence

Deposit
£100,000

Reserve £25,000 — Loan £75,000

Deposit £75,000

Reserve £18,750 — Loan £56,250

Deposit £56,250

Reserve £14,063 — Loan £42,187

Deposit £42,187

Reserve £10,547 — Loan £31,640

and so on ...

The running tally

Reserves	Loans	Deposits
£25,000	£75,000	£100,000
£43,750	£131,250	£175,000
£57,813	£173,437	£231,250
£68,360	£205,077	£273,437
•	•	•
•	•	•
▼	▼	▼
£100,000	£300,000	£400,000

When a bank receives deposits, it keeps 25 per cent in reserves and lends 75 per cent. The amount lent becomes a new deposit at another bank. The next bank in the sequence keeps 25 per cent and lends 75 per cent ,and the process continues until the banking system has created enough deposits to eliminate its excess reserves. The running tally tells us the amount of deposits and loans created at each stage. At the end of the process, an additional £100,000 of reserves creates an additional £400,000 of deposits.

The total number of loans made at the end of the process is the above sum which is[3]

$$\frac{1}{(1-L)}$$

---

[3] Both here and in the expenditure multiplier process in Chapter 28, the sequence of values is called a convergent geometric series. To find the sum of such a series, begin by calling the sum S. Then write out the sum as,

$$S = 1 + L + L^2 + L^3 + ...$$

Multiply by L to give,

$$LS = L + L^2 + L^3 + ...$$

and then subtract the second equation from the first to give.

$$S(1 - L) = 1$$

or

$$S = 1 \div (1 - L)$$

Using the numbers from the example, the total increase in deposits is:

$£100,000 + 75,000 + 56,250 + 42,190 + ...$

$= £100,000 \times (1 + 0.75 + 0.5625 + 0.4219 + ...)$

$= £100,000 \times (1 + 0.75 + 0.75^2 + 0.75^3 + ...)$

$= £100,000 \times (1 \div (1 - 0.75))$

$= £100,000 \times (1 \div 0.25)$

$= £100,000 \times 4$

$= £400,000$

By using the same method, you can check that the totals for reserves and loans are the ones shown in Fig. 30.4.

So even though each bank only lends the money it receives, the banking system as a whole does create money by making loans. And the amount created is the same in a multibank system as in a one-bank system.

The Deposit Multiplier in the United Kingdom

The deposit multiplier in the United Kingdom works in the same way as the deposit multiplier we've just worked out for a hypothetical economy. But the actual deposit multiplier differs from the one we've just calculated for two reasons. First, there is no required reserve ratio for UK banks, and retail banks, wholesale banks and building societies have different desired reserves of highly liquid assets, which include government Treasury bills and short-term loans. The desired ratio will be smaller than what we have used here. Second, not all the loans made by banks return to them in the form of reserves. Some of the loans remain outside the banks and are held as currency. The smaller required reserve ratio makes the UK multiplier larger than the above example. But the other two factors make the UK multiplier smaller.

R E V I E W

◆ Banks create deposits by making loans, and the amount they can lend is determined by their reserves and their desired reserve ratio.

◆ Each time a bank makes a loan, both deposits and desired reserves increase.

◆ When deposits are at a level that makes desired reserves equal to actual reserves, the banks have reached the limit of their ability to create money.

◆ A change in reserves brings about a multiple change in deposits and the deposit multiplier equals 1 divided by the desired reserve ratio.

We've now seen what money is and how banks create it. The amount of money created by the banks has a powerful influence on the economy. Our next task is to examine that influence.

Money, Real GDP and the Price Level

You now know that in a modern economy such as that of the United Kingdom today, most of the money is bank deposits. You've seen that banks actually create money by making loans. Does the quantity of money created by the banking and financial system matter? What effect does money have? Does it matter whether the quantity of money increases quickly or slowly? In particular, how does the quantity of money influence real GDP, the price level and the inflation rate?

We're going to answer these questions first by using the aggregate supply–aggregate demand model, which explains how money affects real GDP and the price level in the short run. Then we're going to study a theory called the quantity theory of money, which explains how money growth influences inflation in the long run. We'll also look at some historical and international evidence on the relationship between money growth and inflation.

The Short-run Effects of a Change in the Quantity of Money

Figure 30.5 illustrates the *AS–AD* model that explains how real GDP and the price level are determined in the short run. (For a full explanation of the *AS–AD* model, see Chapter 27, pp. 686–696) We are going to use this model to study the short-run effect of a change in the quantity of money on real GDP and the price level. Potential GDP is £600 billion and the long-run aggregate supply curve is *LAS*. The short-run aggregate supply curve is *SAS*. Initially, the aggregate demand curve is AD_0. Equilibrium real GDP is £550 billion and the price level is 125 at the intersection of the *AD* curve and the *SAS* curve.

Suppose there is now an increase in the quantity of money. This increase results from the process of money creation we've just studied. With more money in their bank accounts, people plan to increase their consumption expenditure and businesses plan to increase their investment. Aggregate demand increases and the aggregate demand curve shifts rightward to AD_1. A new equilibrium emerges at the intersection point of AD_1 and *SAS*. Real GDP expands to £600 billion and

FIGURE 30.5

Short-run Effects of a Change in the Quantity of Money

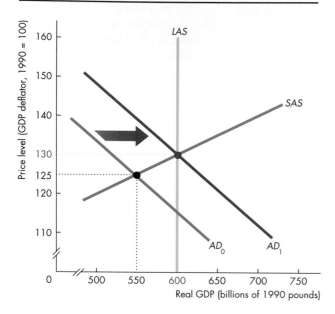

Real GDP is less than potential GDP. An increase in the quantity of money increases aggregate demand and shifts the aggregate demand curve rightward from AD_0 to AD_1. The price level rises to 130 and real GDP expands to £600 billion. The increase in the quantity of money moves real GDP to potential GDP.

the price level rises to 130. Real GDP now equals potential GDP and there is full employment. This increase in the quantity of money has increased both real GDP and the price level.

Now imagine the reverse situation. Real GDP is initially £600 billion and the price level is 130 at the intersection point of AD_1 and SAS. The quantity of money *decreases*. With *less* money in their bank accounts, people and businesses plan to decrease their expenditures. Aggregate demand decreases and the aggregate demand curve shifts leftward to AD_0. A recession occurs as real GDP shrinks to £550 billion and the price level falls to 125.

These influences of the quantity of money on real GDP and the price level are *short-run* effects. In the long run, a change in the quantity of money, perhaps surprisingly, has no effect on real GDP. All its effects are on the price level. Let's see why this outcome occurs.

The Long-run Effects of a Change in the Quantity of Money

Figure 30.6 explains how real GDP and the price level are determined in both the short run and the long run. Again, potential GDP is £600 billion and the long-run aggregate supply curve is *LAS*. The short-run aggregate supply curve is SAS_1. Initially, the aggregate demand curve is AD_1. Equilibrium real GDP is £600 billion and the price level is 130. So real GDP equals potential GDP and there is full employment.

Now suppose the quantity of money increases. Aggregate demand increases and the aggregate demand curve shifts rightward to AD_2. The new short-run equilibrium is at the intersection point of

FIGURE 30.6

Long-run Effects of Change in Quantity of Money

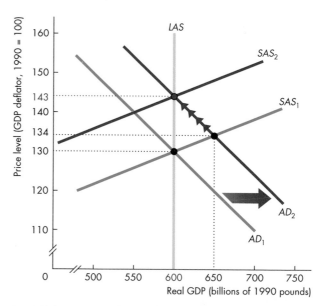

Real GDP equals potential GDP. An increase in the quantity of money shifts the aggregate demand curve from AD_1 to AD_2. The price level rises to 134 and real GDP increases to £650 billion. Real GDP exceeds potential GDP and the money wage rate rises. Short-run aggregate supply decreases and the *SAS* curve shifts leftward from SAS_1 to SAS_2. Real GDP returns to potential GDP and the price level rises to 143. In the long run, the increase in the quantity of money increases the price level and has no effect on real GDP.

AD_2 and SAS_1. The price level rises to 134, and real GDP expands to £650 billion. This short-run adjustment has put real GDP above potential GDP and decreased unemployment below the natural rate. A shortage of labour raises the money wage rate. As the money wage rate rises, short-run aggregate supply decreases and the SAS curve shifts leftward towards SAS_2. As short-run aggregate supply decreases, the price level rises to 143 and real GDP decreases back to potential GDP at £600 billion.

Thus from one full-employment equilibrium to another, an increase in the quantity of money increases the price level and has no effect on real GDP. This relationship between the quantity of money and the price level at full employment is made more precise by the quantity theory of money, which tells us about the quantitative link between money growth and inflation.

The Quantity Theory of Money

The **quantity theory of money** is the proposition that in the long run, an increase in the quantity of money brings an equal percentage increase in the price level. The original basis of the quantity theory of money is a concept known as the velocity of circulation and an equation called the equation of exchange.

The **velocity of circulation** is the average number of times a unit of money is used annually to buy the goods and services that make up GDP. GDP is equal to the price level (P) multiplied by real GDP (Y). That is:

$$GDP = PY$$

Call the quantity of money M. The velocity of circulation, V, is determined by the equation:

$$V = PY/M$$

For example, if GDP is £600 billion and the quantity of money is £300 billion, the velocity of circulation is 2. On the average, each unit of money circulates twice in its use to purchase the final goods and services that make up GDP. That is, each unit of money is used twice in a year to buy GDP.

Figure 30.7 shows the history of the velocity of circulation of M0 and M4, the two main official

---

FIGURE 30.7

The Velocity of Circulation in the United Kingdom: 1963–1995

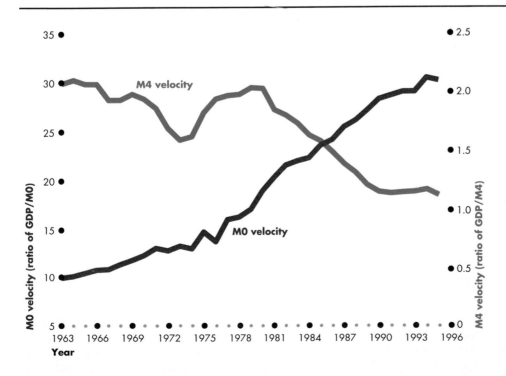

The velocity of circulation of M0 has increased over the years because financial innovation has developed cash substitutes. The velocity of circulation of M4 has declined steadily because the cash substitutes that have resulted from financial innovation are new types of deposits that are part of M4.

Sources: *Bank of England Statistical Abstract*, 1995 Bank of England CD ROM Database V3.0, and Central Statistical Office, *Economic Trends Annual Supplement*, 1996.

definitions of money. You can see that the velocity of circulation of M0 increased between 1963 and 1995. In contrast, the velocity of circulation of M4 has been falling steadily. The reason the velocity of M0 has increased is that deregulation and financial innovation have created new types of deposits and payments technologies that are substitutes for M0. More and more people are having their salaries and wages paid directly into bank accounts and now use cheques and direct debit cards. Direct debit cards enable shops to electronically debit sums of money from your bank account. They are substitutes for cheques.

Banks also have developed better methods of cash management and need to keep fewer stocks in their vaults. Except in the 'hidden' economy where cash is the main medium of exchange, today more people use cheques and cards than use cash. As a result, the quantity of M0 per pound of GDP has decreased and, equivalently, the velocity of circulation of M0 has increased. The reason why the velocity of M4 has increased is that there has been an increase in different types of deposits, and higher interest rates on those deposits have attracted funds that were normally held as savings. So the ratio of M4 to GDP and the velocity of circulation of M4 have increased.

The **equation of exchange** states that the quantity of money (M) multiplied by the velocity of circulation (V) equals GDP, or:

$$MV = PY$$

Given the definition of the velocity of circulation, this equation is always true – it is true by definition. With M equal to £300 billion and V equal to 2, MV is equal to £600 billion, the value of GDP.

The equation of exchange becomes the quantity theory of money by making two assumptions:

1. The velocity of circulation is not influenced by the quantity of money.
2. Potential real GDP is not influenced by the quantity of money.

If these two assumptions are true, the equation of exchange tells us that in the long run, a given percentage change in the quantity of money brings about an equal percentage change in the price level. You can see why by solving the equation of exchange for the price level. Dividing both sides of the equation by real GDP (Y) gives:

$$P = (V/Y)M$$

In the long run, real GDP, Y, equals potential GDP, so if potential GDP and velocity are not influenced by the quantity of money, the relationship between the change in the price level (ΔP) and the change in the quantity of money (ΔM) is:

$$\Delta P = (V/Y)\,\Delta M$$

Divide this equation by the previous one ($P = (V/Y)M$) to give:

$$\Delta P/P = \Delta M/M$$

($\Delta P/P$) is the percentage increase in the price level and ($\Delta M/M$) is the percentage increase in the quantity of money. So this equation is the quantity theory of money. In the long run, the percentage increase in the price level equals the percentage increase in the quantity of money.

The Quantity Theory and the *AS–AD* Model

The quantity theory of money can be interpreted in terms of the *AS–AD* model. The aggregate demand curve is a relationship between the quantity of real GDP demanded (Y) and the price level (P), other things remaining constant. We can obtain such a relationship from the equation of exchange,

$$MV = PY.$$

Dividing both sides of this equation by real GDP (Y) gives

$$P = MV/Y$$

This equation may be interpreted as describing an aggregate demand curve. In Chapter 27 (pp. 690–693) you saw that the aggregate demand curve slopes downward – as the price level increases the quantity of real GDP demanded decreases. The above equation also shows such a relationship between the price level and the quantity of real GDP demanded. For a given quantity of money (M) and a given velocity of circulation (V), the higher the price level (P), the smaller is the quantity of real GDP demanded (Y).

In general, when the quantity of money changes, the velocity of circulation might also change. But the quantity theory asserts that velocity is not influenced by the quantity of money. If this assumption is correct, an increase in the quantity of money increases aggregate demand and shifts the aggregate demand curve upward by the same amount as the percentage change in the quantity of money.

The quantity theory of money also asserts that real GDP, which in the long run equals potential GDP, is not influenced by the quantity of money. This assertion is true in the *AS–AD* model. Figure 30.6 shows the quantity theory result in the *AS–AD* model. Initially the economy is at full employment on the long-run aggregate supply curve *LAS* and at the intersection of the aggregate demand curve AD_1 and the short-run aggregate supply curve SAS_1. A 10 per cent increase in the quantity of money shifts the aggregate demand curve from AD_1 to AD_2. This shift, measured by the vertical distance between the two demand curves, is 10 percent. In the long run, wages rise (also by 10 per cent) and shift the *SAS* curve leftward to SAS_2. A new full-employment (long-run) equilibrium occurs at the intersection of AD_2 and SAS_2. Real GDP remains at potential GDP of £600 billion and the price level rises to 143. The new price level is 10 per cent higher than the initial

one (143 − 130 = 13, which is 10 per cent of 130).

So the *AS–AD* model predicts the same outcome as the quantity theory of money. The *AS–AD* model also predicts a less precise relationship between the quantity of money and the price level in the short run than in the long run. For example, Fig. 30.5 shows that starting out with unemployment, an increase in the quantity of money increases real GDP. In this case, a 10 per cent increase in the money supply increases the price level from 125 to 130 – a 4 per cent increase. That is, the price level changes by a smaller percentage than the percentage change in the quantity of money.

How good a theory is the quantity theory of money? (*Economics in History* on pp. 794–795 looks at the development of this theory.) Let's answer this question by looking at the relationship between money and the price level, both historically and internationally.

FIGURE 30.8

Money Growth and Inflation in the United Kingdom: 1964–1995

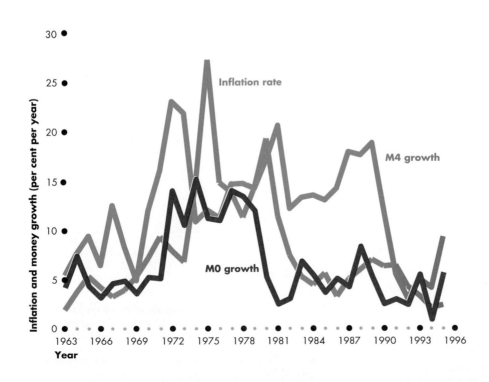

Year-to-year fluctuations in money growth and inflation are loosely correlated. The growth of M4 and inflation appeared to have a strong correlation in the 1960s and 1970s but that correlation has weakened in the 1980s. The growth of M0 and inflation have a stronger correlation in the 1980s.

Sources: *Bank of England Statistical Abstract*, 1995, Bank of England CD ROM Database V3.0, and Central Statistical Office, *Economic Trends Annual Supplement*, 1996.

Historical Evidence on the Quantity Theory of Money

The percentage increase in the price level is the inflation rate, and the percentage increase in the quantity of money is the money supply growth rate. So the quantity theory predictions can be cast in terms of money growth and inflation. The quantity theory predicts that at a given level of potential GDP and in the long run, the inflation rate will equal the money growth rate. But over time, potential GDP expands. Taking this expansion into account, the quantity theory predicts that in the long run, the inflation rate will equal the money growth rate minus the growth rate of potential GDP.

We can test the quantity theory of money by looking at the historical relationship between money growth and inflation in the United Kingdom. Figure 30.8 shows this relationship for the years between 1963 and 1995. The inflation rate is the percentage change in the GDP deflator and the two alternative money growth rates are based on M0 and M4. The chart shows year-to-year changes in money and the price level. These changes show the relationship between money growth and inflation. If the quantity theory is a reasonable guide to reality, there should be a strong correlation between inflation and money growth.

The data are broadly consistent with the quantity theory. The money growth rate and the inflation rate are correlated but the relationship is not precise. In the 1960s and 1970s, M4 growth preceded changes in inflation and M0 appeared to follow. In the 1980s, the relationship between M4 growth and inflation appears to have broken down, but a closer relationship can be observed between M0 growth and inflation. The reason why the correlation between M4 and inflation in the 1980s was weaker is because of the deregulation and financial innovation during that period.

International Evidence on the Quantity Theory of Money

Another way to test the quantity theory of money is to look at the cross-country relationship between money growth and inflation. Figure 30.9 shows this relationship for 60 countries during the 1980s. By looking at a decade average, we again are smoothing out the short-run effects of money growth and focusing on the long-run effects. There is in these

FIGURE 30.9

Money Growth and Inflation in the World Economy

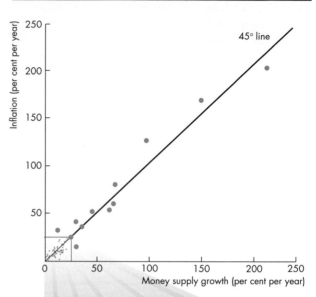

(a) All countries

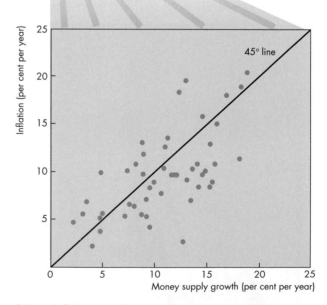

(b) Low-inflation countries

Inflation and money growth in 60 countries (in part a) and low-inflation countries (in part b) show that money growth is one influence, though not the only influence, on inflation.

Source: Federal Reserve Bank of St Louis, *Review*, May/June 1988, p. 15.

data an unmistakable tendency for high money growth to be associated with high inflation. Some further evidence from the experience of Brazil during the 1980s can be seen in *Reading Between the Lines* on pp. 792–793.

Correlation, Causation and Other Influences

Both the historical evidence for the United Kingdom and the international data tell us that in the long run, money growth and inflation are correlated. But the correlation between money growth and inflation does not tell us that money growth causes inflation. Money growth might cause inflation; inflation might cause money growth; or some third variable might simultaneously cause inflation and money growth.

According to the quantity theory and according to the *AS–AD* model, causation runs from money growth to inflation. But neither theory denies the possibility that at different times and places, causation might run in the other direction, or that some third factor might be the root cause of both rapid money growth and inflation. One possible third factor is a large and persistent government budget deficit that gets financed by newly created money.

But some occasions give us an opportunity to test our assumptions about causation. One of these is World War II and the years immediately following it. Rapid money growth during the war years accompanied by price controls almost certainly caused inflation to rise in the immediate post-war period. The inflationary consequences of the money growth were delayed by the controls but not removed. It is inconceivable that this was an example of reverse causation – of post-war inflation causing war-time money growth. Another is the early 1970s. Rapid money growth that began during the early 1970s almost certainly caused the high and persistent inflation of the mid-1970s.

The combination of historical and international correlations between money growth and inflation, and independent evidence about the direction of causation, leads to the conclusion that the quantity

theory is correct in the long run. It explains the long-term fundamental source of inflation. But the quantity theory is not correct in the short run. To understand the short-term fluctuations in inflation, the joint effects of a change in the quantity of money on real GDP, the velocity of circulation and the price level must be explained. The *AS–AD* model provides this explanation. It also points to the possibility of other factors that influence both aggregate supply and aggregate demand influencing the inflation rate independently of the money growth rate.

REVIEW

- The quantity of money influences the price level and real GDP.
- In the short run, an increase in the quantity of money increases aggregate demand and increases both the price level and real GDP.
- In the long run, when real GDP equals potential GDP, an increase in the quantity of money brings an equal percentage increase in the price level (the quantity theory of money).
- The long–run historical and international evidence on the relationship between money growth and inflation supports the quantity theory.

◆ ◆ ◆ ◆ In the next chapter, we're going to study the role of the central bank and monetary policy. We'll see how the central bank's actions can change the quantity of money. We'll also learn how the central bank is able to influence interest rates, which in turn influence aggregate demand. It is through its effects on the quantity of money and interest rates and their wider ramifications that the central bank is able to help steer the course of the economy. Then, in Chapter 32, we'll return to the problem of inflation and explore more deeply its causes, its consequences and ways of keeping it under control.

Unstable Money

The Essence of the Story

THE NEW YORK TIMES, 25 JULY 1993

In Brazil, wild ways to counter inflation

James Brooke

Rio de Janeiro, July 20 – At a fashion industry fair, a clothing manufacturer and boutique owner haggled recently over payment for blouses to be delivered in October. Mistrusting Government-manipulated dollar exchange rates and inflation indexes, buyer and seller finally agreed on a neutral pricing unit: bars of margarine.

Pricing blouses according to the margarine standard is but one of many ways Brazilians have developed to survive, and sometimes thrive, amid high inflation.

Since 1980, Brazil has had 4 currencies, 5 wage-and-price freezes, 9 economic stabilisation programs, 11 inflation indexes, 12 finance ministers, and an accumulated inflation rate of 146 billion percent. Without the currency changes, a cup of coffee that sold in 1980 for 15 cruzeiros would sell today for 22 billion cruzeiros.

The cardinal rule is to keep no cash, or to spend it as quickly as possible.

'My currency is the electronic cash card,' Carlos Decotelli, an economist for the Brazilian Institute for Capital markets, said recently. 'I left my house this morning without any cruzeiros in my pocket. I told the taxi driver to stop at a money machine. They are on every corner now.'

Others use checks to pay for taxis, pizzas, and even newspapers. Most bank accounts bear interest daily. The 30 percent monthly rates, which sound fabulous elsewhere, merely keep account holders abreast of inflation....

Another inflation dodge is to use credit cards. By timing a purchase carefully, a shopper can get a free 30-day float, by which time the real cost of his purchase will have dropped by 30 percent....

■ Since 1980 Brazil has had an accumulated inflation rate of 146 billion per cent.

■ To cope with the unstable value of money, some people use bars of margarine as a unit of account.

■ To avoid losses, people hold as little cash as possible and use electronic cash cards and cheques as much as possible.

■ Bank deposits pay interest at a rate of 30 per cent a month, which just keeps up with inflation.

■ By timing credit card purchases, it is possible to get a 30-day loan that is paid off with money that is worth 30 per cent less than when the goods were bought.

Economic Analysis

■ The last time the inflation rate in Brazil dipped below 100 per cent a year was 1982. During the 1980s, Brazil's inflation increased, and by 1989 it exceeded 1,000 per cent a year. The rate peaked in July 1994, when it briefly hit 5,600 per cent a year.

■ Figure 1 shows the record of Brazil's inflation. It also shows the money growth rate in Brazil over the same period.

■ When inflation is as high and variable as it has been in Brazil, money ceases to work well as a medium of exchange, a unit of account, or a store of value.

■ You can see in the news article that people use ingenious ways of getting around these problems, but not without incurring costs.

■ Brazil's experience is so extreme that it enables us to test the quantity theory of money in a much sharper way than we can on the more limited inflation experience of the United Kingdom.

■ The quantity theory predicts that there will

be a correlation between money growth and inflation, and Fig. 1 shows such a correlation in Brazil. But look closely at the graph.

■ In 1990, when the inflation rate leapt to 3,000 per cent a year, the money growth rate also increased, but only to around 2,000 per cent a year.

■ Why did inflation jump by so much more than money growth? The answer is that the velocity of circulation increased.

■ To account for experiences like those in Brazil, a more sophisticated version of the quantity theory is used that recognizes that when the inflation rate increases, the velocity of circulation sometimes also increases.

■ The reason for this response to high inflation is that people try to hold as little money as possible — as described in the news article — to avoid incurring losses from holding an asset whose value is falling rapidly.

■ In 1990 the inflation rate outstripped the interest rate on depo-

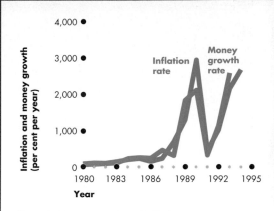

Figure 1 Money growth and inflation

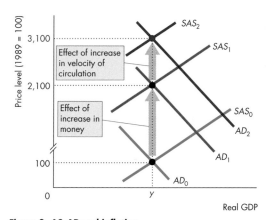

Figure 2 AS–AD and inflation

sits. As a result, an increase in the money stock and an increase in velocity both increased aggregate demand.

■ Figure 2 illustrates these *two* effects in 1990. In 1989 the aggregate demand curve was AD_0, and the short-run aggregate supply curve was SAS_0. The increase in money increased aggregate demand to AD_1, and the anticipation of inflation increased wages and decreased

aggregate supply to SAS_1. On its own, this factor would have taken the inflation rate to around 2,000 per cent.

■ The increase in velocity increased aggregate demand further to AD_2, and the anticipation of this additional inflation increased wages and decreased aggregate supply to SAS_2. This additional factor took the inflation rate up to 3,000 per cent.

'Inflation is always and everywhere a monetary phenomenon.'

Milton Friedman, THE COUNTER-REVOLUTION IN MONETARY THEORY

Money and Inflation

THE ISSUES AND IDEAS

The combination of history and economics has taught us a lot about the causes of inflation. Severe inflation – hyperinflation – arises from a breakdown of the normal fiscal policy processes at times of war or political upheaval. Tax revenues fall short of government spending, and the gap between them is filled by printing money. As inflation increases, the quantity of money that is needed to make payments increases, and there can even be a *shortage* of money. So the rate of money growth is increased yet further, and prices rise yet faster. Eventually, the monetary system collapses. Such was the experience of Germany in the 1920s and Brazil in the 1990s.

In earlier times, when commodities were used as money, inflation resulted from the discovery of new sources of money. The most recent occurrence of this type of inflation was in the nineteenth century when gold, then used as money, was discovered in Australia, the Klondike and South Africa.

In modern times, inflation has resulted from increases in the money supply that has accommodated increases in costs. The most dramatic of such inflations occurred during the 1970s when oil price increases were accommodated by central banks around the world.

To avoid inflation, money supply growth must be held in check. But at times of severe cost pressure, central banks feel a strong tug in the direction of avoiding recession and accommodating the cost–push.

Yet some countries have avoided inflation more effectively than others. A key source of success is central bank independence. In low-inflation countries, such as Germany and Japan, the central bank decides how much money to create and at what level to set interest rates and does not take instructions from the government. In high-inflation countries, such as the United Kingdom in the 1970s and Italy, the central bank takes direct orders from the government about interest rates and money supply growth. This connection between central bank independence and inflation has been noticed by the architects of a new monetary system for the European Union who are modelling the European Central Bank on Germany's Bundesbank.

THEN ...

When inflation is especially rapid, as it was in Germany in 1923, money becomes almost worthless. In Germany at that time, bank notes were more valuable as kindling than as money, and the sight of people burning Reichmarks was a common one. To avoid having to hold money for too long, wages were paid and spent twice a day. Banks took deposits and made loans, but at interest rates that compensated depositors and the bank for the falling value of money – rates that could exceed 100 per cent a day. The price of a dinner might double during the course of an evening, making lingering over coffee an expensive pastime.

... AND NOW

In 1994, Brazil had a computer-age hyperinflation, an inflation rate that was close to 50 per cent a month. Banks installed ATMs on almost every street corner and refilled them several times an hour. Brazilians tried to avoid holding currency. As soon as they were paid, they went shopping and bought enough food to get them through to the next payday. Some shoppers filled as many as six trolleys on a single monthly trip to the supermarket. Also, instead of using currency, Brazilians used credit cards whenever possible. But they paid their card balances off quickly because the interest rate on unpaid balances was 50 per cent a month. Only at such a high interest rate was it worthwhile for banks to lend to cardholders, because banks themselves were paying interest rates of 40 per cent a month to induce customers to keep their money in the bank.

David Hume

THE ECONOMISTS: DAVID HUME AND MILTON FRIEDMAN

Born in Edinburgh, Scotland, in 1711 and a close friend of Adam Smith, David Hume was a philosopher, historian and economist of extraordinary breadth. His first book, by his own description, 'fell dead-born from the press'. But his essays – on topics ranging from love and marriage and the immortality of the soul to money, interest and the balance of payments – were widely read and earned him a considerable fortune. Hume gave the first clear account of the way in which an increase in the quantity of money causes an increase in prices. He even anticipated the discovery, some 220 years later, of the Phillips curve and the Keynesian theory of aggregate demand.

Milton Friedman

Milton Friedman, now a Senior Fellow at the Hoover Institution at Stanford University, was from 1946 to 1983 one of the leading members of the 'Chicago School', an approach to economics developed at the University of Chicago and based on the views that free markets allocate resources efficiently and that stable and low money supply growth delivers macroeconomic stability. Friedman was awarded the Nobel Prize for Economic Science for his work on money and other macroeconomic problems.

By reasoning from basic economic principles, Friedman predicted that persistent demand stimulation would *not* increase output but *would* cause inflation. When output growth slowed and inflation broke out in the 1970s, Friedman seemed like a prophet and, for a time, his policy prescription, known as 'monetarism,' was embraced around the world.

SUMMARY

What is Money?

Money is the means of payment and it has three functions. It is a medium of exchange, a unit of account and a store of value. The earliest forms of money were commodities. In the modern world, we use a fiat money system. The biggest component of money is deposit money.

The two main measures of money in the United Kingdom today are M0 and M4. M0 consists of currency held by the public, the banks, the building societies and banks' deposits at the Bank of England. M4 is currency held by the public and all bank and building society sight and time deposits. Currency held by the public is the means of payment and constitutes the largest part of M0. M4 includes sight deposits, which are chequeable, and time deposits, which are not. However, time deposits are easily converted into sight deposits and are highly liquid. Chequeing deposits are money but cheques and credit cards are not money. (pp. 769–775)

Financial Intermediaries

The main financial intermediaries whose liabilities are money are commercial banks and building societies. These institutions take in deposits, hold cash and liquid assets as reserves to ensure that they can meet their depositors' demands for currency, and use the rest of their financial resources either to buy securities or to make loans. Financial intermediaries make a profit by borrowing at a lower interest rate than that at which they lend. All financial intermediaries provide four main economic services. They create liquidity, minimize the cost of obtaining funds, minimize the cost of monitoring borrowers and pool risks. (pp. 775–779)

Financial Regulation, Deregulation and Innovation

Financial intermediaries are regulated to protect depositors. Small depositors have their deposits insured by the Bank of England and owners of intermediaries are required to put a certain minimum amount of their own financial resources into the financial intermediary. Minimum cash and liquid

assets reserves are not required of UK banks, but most EU Central Banks have reserve requirements for banks operating in their countries.

In the 1980s, banks began to make mortgage loans and building societies began to offer bank services. Deregulation in the 1980s removed restrictions on bank and building society activities.

The continual search for profitable financial opportunities leads to financial innovation – to the creation of new financial products such as new types of deposits and loans. Interest-bearing instant access accounts are an example of some of the new financial products of the 1980s. Deregulation and financial innovation have brought important changes in the composition of the nation's money. (pp. 779–781)

How Banks Create Money

Banks create money by making loans. When a loan is made to one person and the amount lent is spent, much of it ends up as someone else's deposit. The total quantity of deposits that can be supported by a given amount of reserves (the deposit multiplier) is equal to 1 divided by the desired reserve ratio. (pp. 781–785)

Money, Real GDP and the Price Level

The quantity of money affects aggregate demand. An increase in the quantity of money increases aggregate demand and, in the short run, increases both the price level and real GDP. Over the long run, real GDP grows and fluctuates around its full-employment level, and increases in the quantity of money bring increases in the price level. The quantity theory of money predicts that an increase in the quantity of money increases the price level by the same percentage as the quantity of money increased and leaves real GDP unchanged. Both historical and international evidence suggest that the quantity theory of money is correct only in a broad average sense. The quantity of money exerts an influence not only on the price level but also on real GDP. There are other influences on the price level. Further, the correlation between money growth and inflation does not tell us the direction of causation. (pp. 785–791)

KEY ELEMENTS

Key Terms

Bank, 775
Barter, 769
Building society, 776
Commodity money, 770
Convertible paper money, 771
Currency, 771
Deposit money, 772
Deposit multiplier, 783
Desired reserve ratio, 782
Equation of exchange, 788
Excess reserves, 782
Fiat money, 771
Financial innovation, 781
Financial intermediary, 775
Gold standard, 771
Gresham's Law, 770
Liquidity, 773
M0, 772
M4, 772

Means of payment, 769
Money, 769
Quantity theory of money, 787
Required reserve ratio, 783
Reserve ratio, 782
Reserves, 776
Velocity of circulation, 787

◆ Key Figures and Table

Figure 30.1 Schematic Representation of Money Supply, 773
Figure 30.2 Two Official Measures of Money, 774
Figure 30.3 Creating Money at the One-and-Only Bank, 782
Figure 30.4 The Multiple Creation of Bank Deposits, 784
Figure 30.5 Short-run Effects of a Change in the Quantity of Money, 786
Table 30.2 Two Measures of Money, 772

REVIEW QUESTIONS

1 What is money? What are its functions?

2 What are the different forms of money?

3 What are the two main measures of money in the United Kingdom today?

4 Are cheques and credit cards money? Explain your answer.

5 What is a financial intermediary?

6 What are the main items in the balance sheet of a commercial bank?

7 What are the economic functions of financial intermediaries?

8 How do banks make a profit and how do they create money?

9 Describe the main types of financial regulation that financial intermediaries face.

10 Describe the deregulation of financial intermediaries that took place in the 1980s.

11 What is financial innovation? Explain the financial innovation that took place in the 1980s.

12 Define the deposit multiplier. Explain why it equals 1 divided by the desired reserve ratio.

13 What does the aggregate supply–aggregate demand model predict about the effects of a change in the quantity of money on the price level and real GDP when the economy is initially:

a In a recession?
b At full employment?

14 What is the equation of exchange and the velocity of circulation? What assumptions are necessary to make the equation of exchange the quantity theory of money?

15 What is the evidence on the quantity theory of money?

PROBLEMS

1 Money includes which of the following items?

   a Bank of England notes in the commercial bank's vaults

   b Your Visa card

   c The coins inside public phones

   d Bank of England notes in your wallet

   e The cheque you have just written to pay for your rent

   f The student loan you took last August to pay for your hall of residence fees

2 Which of the following items are fiat money? Which are private debt money?

   a Chequeing deposits at National Westminster Bank

   b IBM shares held by individuals

   c Gold bars held by banks

   d The £5 commemorative crown for the Queen's Jubilee

   e A government Treasury bill

   f A building society share account

3 Sara withdraws £1,000 from her share account at the Burnley Building Society, keeps £50 in cash and deposits the balance in her chequeing deposit at the Midland Bank. What is the immediate change in M0 and M4?

4 The commercial banks in the kingdom of Ruritania have the following assets and liabilities:

Total reserves	250 million euros
Loans	1,000 million euros
Deposits	2,000 million euros
Total assets	2,500 million euros

   a Construct the commercial banks' balance sheet. If you are missing any assets call them 'other assets', if you are missing any liabilities call them 'other liabilities'.

   b Calculate the commercial banks' reserve ratio.

   c If the reserve ratio in (b) is equal to the commercial banks' desired reserve ratio, calculate the deposit multiplier.

5 An immigrant arrives in Transylvania with 1,200 euros. The 1,200 euros is put into a bank deposit. All the banks in Transylvania have a required reserve ratio of 10 per cent.

   a What is the initial increase in the quantity of money of Transylvania?

   b What is the initial increase in the quantity of bank deposits when the immigrant arrives?

   c How much does the immigrant's bank lend out?

   d Use a format similar to that in Fig. 30.2 to set out the transactions that take place and calculate the amount lent and the amount of deposits created, assuming that all the funds lent are returned to the banking system in the form of deposits.

   e By how much has the quantity of money increased after the bank has made 20 loans?

   f What is the total increase in the quantity of money, in bank loans and in bank deposits?

6 Quantecon is a country in which the quantity theory of money operates. The country has a constant population, capital stock and technology. In year 1, real GDP was £400 million, the price level was 200 and the velocity of circulation of money was 20. In year 2, the quantity of money was 20 per cent higher than in year 1.

   a What was the quantity of money in Quantecon in year 1?

   b What was the quantity of money in Quantecon in year 2?

   c What was the price level in Quantecon in year 2?

   d What was the level of real GDP in Quantecon in year 2?

   e What was the velocity of circulation in Quantecon in year 2?

7 Study *Reading Between the Lines* on pp. 792–793 and then answer the following questions:

   a How has Brazil coped with the problem of finding a stable unit of account?

   b What has happened to the velocity of circulation of money in Brazil?

   c How do people protect themselves from a falling value of money in Brazil?

   d Why has Brazil's inflation rate been higher than its money supply growth rate in some years? Does this fact contradict the quantity theory of money?

CHAPTER
31

THE
CENTRAL BANK
AND
MONETARY
POLICY

After studying this chapter you will be able to:

◆ Describe the role of the Bank of England

◆ Describe the tools used by the Bank of England to conduct its monetary policy

◆ Explain what an open market operation is and how it works

◆ Explain how an open market operation changes the money supply

◆ Explain how a central bank controls the money supply

◆ Explain what determines the demand for money

◆ Explain how the Bank of England influences interest rates

◆ Explain how interest rates influence the economy

D URING THE 1980s MANY YOUNG ECONOMISTS WORKING IN FINANCIAL INSTITUTIONS in the City of London used a great deal of ingenuity in trying to predict the monthly money supply figures ahead of their publication. Why did they do this? The reason is that by predicting the money supply figures ahead of the Bank of England they were hoping to predict the movement of interest rates and the reaction of the financial markets so that they could take speculative positions on behalf of their institutions. ◆ During 1994, interest rates were lowered to 5$1/4$ per cent and many economic analysts working in the City of London warned of an overheating economy. Indeed, the economy grew at nearly 4 per cent. Between the end of 1994 and the middle of 1995, interest rates went up in three steps to 6$3/4$ per cent. The rate of growth of the economy slowed in 1995. From the end of 1995 to June 1996 interest rates fell in four consecutive $1/4$ percentage points. ◆ Why do interest rates move up and down in this yo-yo fashion? What determines interest rates? Is there some reason

Inside the Old Lady

for their up-and-down behaviour or is it purely random? You suspect that there is some reason. You may read in the newspapers that the Bank of England supports an interest rate rise because output growth is too high. Then, some months later, you may read that the Bank of England supports an interest rate cut because inflation is expected to remain low. How does the Bank of England change interest rates? How do interest rates influence the economy? And how do interest rates keep inflation in check?

◆ ◆ ◆ ◆ In this chapter you will learn about the Bank of England and monetary policy. You will learn how the Bank of England and other central banks influence interest rates and how interest rates influence the economy. You'll discover that interest rates depend, in part, on the amount of money in existence. You will also discover how the Bank of England influences the quantity of money to influence interest rates as it attempts to smooth the business cycle and keep inflation in check.

The Bank of England

The **Bank of England**, affectionately known as the 'Old Lady of Threadneedle Street' and referred to as the Bank, is the central bank of the United Kingdom. A **central bank** is a bankers' bank and a public authority charged with regulating and controlling a nation's monetary and financial institutions and markets. As the bankers' bank, the Bank provides banking services to the commercial banks. But a central bank is not a citizens' bank. That is, the Bank does not provide general banking services for businesses and individual citizens.

The Bank conducts the nation's **monetary policy**, which means that it adjusts the quantity of money in circulation. The Bank's goals in its conduct of monetary policy are to moderate the business cycle, manage and sometimes defend the exchange rate, and keep inflation within a specified target range. Complete success in the pursuit of these goals is impossible, and the Bank's more modest goal is to improve the performance of the economy and to get closer to the goals than a 'hands off' approach would achieve. Whether the Bank succeeds in improving economic performance is a matter on which there is a variety of opinion.

Our aim in this chapter is to learn about the tools available to the Bank in its conduct of monetary policy and the effects of the Bank's actions on the economy. Our starting point is to examine the origins and describe the structure of the Bank.

The Origins and Functions of the Bank of England

The Bank was formally recognized as the central bank of the United Kingdom in the 1946 Bank of England Act. It had been established in 1694 by an act of Parliament following a loan of £1.2 million by a syndicate of wealthy individuals to the government of King William and Queen Mary. The creation of the Bank formalized the process whereby the syndicate lent to the government in return for the right to issue bank notes. Between 1688 and 1815, the United Kingdom was involved in seven wars and several small conflicts which needed funding. The growing dependence on the Bank for raising funds in times of crisis created the role of the government's bank. The functions of the Bank of England

as a central bank have developed over the three centuries since its creation. Today these functions can be summarized as:

◆ Banker to the government
◆ Bankers' bank
◆ Lender of last resort
◆ Regulator of banks
◆ Manager of monetary policy

Let us briefly examine each of these functions.

Banker to the Government The banker to the government means that the government's own deposits – called public deposits – are held at the Bank of England. These are the accounts of the revenue raising agencies such as the Inland Revenue and HM Customs and Excise, and the spending departments such as the Ministry of Defence. A business that needs to pay tax will pay a cheque to the Inland Revenue, which will eventually be deposited at the Bank of England. If the Ministry of Defence has to pay for a new fighting ship, it will issue a cheque based on its account at the Bank. Acting as the government's bank also means that the Bank handles the government's borrowing needs. There are two ways in which the government can borrow: directly from the Bank of England in the form of a loan or by selling bonds. Direct lending amounts to the same thing as printing money. The alternative is to manage the government's borrowing by selling government bonds to the public. The function of selling government debt gives the Bank a pivotal role in the conduct of monetary policy.

Banker's Bank The commercial banks keep a certain amount of money as deposits at the Bank of England. This is a convenient means by which banks can settle debts they have with each other by simply transferring funds between accounts at the Bank. The Bank is also the sole effective issuer of bank notes. If the general public increase their demand for notes, this will result in a decrease in the amount of notes kept by the banks. The banks will replenish their stock of notes by cashing their deposits at the Bank of England. The Bank of England in turn will issue bank notes as it has an effective monopoly. Even though the Scottish banks issue their own bank notes they must be backed fully by Bank of England notes.

Lender of Last Resort The Bank of England acts as the lender of last resort to the banking system. It operates on two levels. On a day-to-day basis, when the banks run short of cash, it is the Bank of England that restores the cash levels of the banks. Unlike in other countries, the banks borrow not directly from the Bank of England but through the *discount houses*. Discount houses exist by borrowing very short-term money from banks – called *money at call* – and buying Treasury bills, commercial bills and local authority bills. The discount houses also have a special relationship with the Bank of England, so that if the commercial banks are short of cash and they call in their short-term loans to the discount houses, the discount houses can obtain the cash to pay the banks from the Bank of England. Figure 31.1 describes the pivotal role of the discount houses in the UK financial system. The rate of interest at which the Bank is prepared to lend to the discount houses will have implications for short-term interest rates and the general level of interest rates. The Bank of England also acts as lender of last resort to any individual bank or group of banks that are experiencing liquidity problems. The aim of the Bank is to ensure the smooth working of the financial system.

Regulator of Banks As the Bank ultimately guarantees the stability of the banking and financial system, it also faces the problem of moral hazard (see Chapter 30, p. 779). Some economists argue that banks may be tempted to act imprudently if they think that the central bank is always there to provide liquidity in a crisis. To guard against this possibility, the Bank also undertakes the prudential regulation of commercial banks. Regulation is based on the supervision of individual banks by the Bank of England. At one level, it deals with the entry and establishment of a bank. The Bank must be convinced that a new commercial bank is a fit and proper organization to conduct the business of banking, and any breach of the set criteria will result in loss of authorization to act as a bank. At the second level, the Bank monitors the liquidity and capital adequacy of the commercial bank. We examined such regulations in Chapter 30.

Manager of Monetary Policy The Bank of England is the agent of government monetary policy. The main channel by which the Bank pursues the monetary policy of the government is through

FIGURE 31.1

The Discount Houses and the Financial System

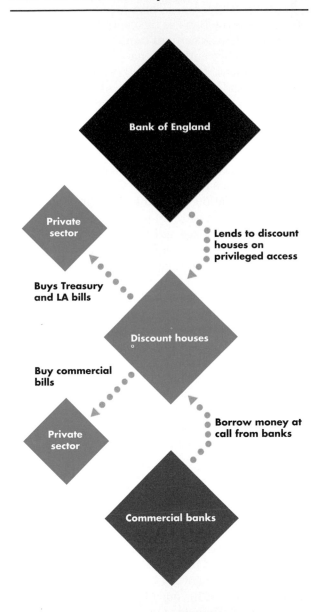

The discount houses play a pivotal role in the UK financial system. They take very short-term loans from the commercial banks, known as money at call. These loans are part of the banking system's liquid reserves and can be recalled at any time. When the discount houses are short of funds they have privileged access to lender of last resort loans from the Bank of England. They use their funds to buy Treasury bills, commercial bills and local authority bills.

the setting of the rate of interest at which it deals with the discount houses. For 270 years to 1972, the rate of interest at which the Bank lent to the discount houses was announced and known as the *bank rate*. After 13 October, 1972, the rate at which the Bank acted as lender of last resort was referred to as the *minimum lending rate* or MLR. The MLR ceased to be continuously posted after 20 August, 1981. After this date the discount houses had to apply to the Bank to find out the rate at which it would make last resort loans. Following the abandonment of the continuous posting of the MLR, the base rates of the major banks became the indicator of the broad level of interest rates. The banks' base rates are in turn influenced by the rate at which the discount houses can obtain funds from the Bank of England. The Bank influences the commercial banks' base rate by signalling to the discount houses that it will be willing to lend at a specific rate.

The Bank's Financial Structure

For accounting purposes, the Bank of England is separated into two departments: the Issue department and the Banking department. The Issue department is treated as part of the government, whereas the Banking department is a public corporation. The separation is largely historical and is not particularly important from an analytical viewpoint. The Issue department is the bank note issuing arm of the Bank of England and the Banking department takes deposits from the commercial banks. Also, the Issue department has as its liabilities the notes in circulation including the notes held by the Banking department. Table 31.1 shows the consolidated balance sheet of the Bank of England. It is arrived at by adding the assets and liabilities of the two departments and subtracting the assets of the one department that are liabilities of the other.

The largest liability of the Bank of England is notes in circulation. The reason these are entered as a liability is because when Bank of England notes were in principle convertible into coin or gold, the note represented a liability which could be redeemed on demand. Up until 1931, it was possible in principle to redeem Bank of England notes for gold. Since 1931, the note issue has been backed by securities, most of which are government securities as seen on the asset side of the balance sheet. Bank notes are non-convertible, which

---

TABLE 31.1

Balance sheet of the Bank of England, 27 June, 1996

Assets (billions of pounds)		Liabilities (billions of pounds)	
Government securities	17.2	Notes in circulation	19.8
Other securities	4.3	Public deposits	0.8
Advances and other accounts	1.4	Bankers' deposits	1.9
Premises, equipment and other	2.9	Reserves and other accounts	3.3
Total	**25.8**	**Total**	**25.8**

Source: *Bank of England Quarterly Bulletin*, May 1996.

---

means that they cannot be converted into anything. But the tradition of being able to convert Bank of England notes remains even though the reality is different. If you look at a £10 note it says on it *I promise to pay the bearer on demand the sum of Ten pounds.* This only means that the Bank of England is willing to accept one £10 note for another. While notes are the liability of the Bank of England, coin is issued by the Royal Mint and is therefore not a liability.

The other important liability of the Bank of England is the commercial banks' deposits it holds. These are the deposits that the commercial banks keep at the Bank of England to act as a means of clearing interbank debt. At the end of the working day, if the National Westminster Bank has a deficit with Barclays Bank, funds can be transferred from the National Westminster account to the Barclays account held at the Bank of England. The banks' deposits at the Bank of England include a mandatory 0.35 per cent of the eligible deposits at commercial banks. Eligible deposits are defined as sterling deposits of up to two years' maturity.

Public deposits are the deposits of individual government departments. The final item on the liability side of the balance sheet are accounts held by foreign central banks such as the German Bundesbank or the US Federal Reserve.

The asset side of the balance sheet shows that the Bank of England holds government securities, such as Treasury bills and government bonds and lending to the government. Other securities that are held by the Issue department include commercial bills issued by businesses.

The two largest items on the liabilities side of the Bank's balance sheet make up most of the monetary base. The **monetary base** is also known as M0. In theory, a central bank can control the supply of the monetary base, and through it control the total money supply and interest rates. However, traditionally the Bank of England has not attempted to control the supply of M0. As we shall see the main instrument of control is the rate of interest.

The Bank's Policy Tools

We have seen that the Bank of England has many responsibilities, but we'll examine its most important one – regulating the amount of money floating around in the United Kingdom. How does a central bank control the money supply? It uses three main policy tools to achieve its objectives:

◆ Required reserve ratios

◆ Discount rate

◆ Open market operations

Required Reserve Ratios   As a rule central banks require that commercial banks have minimum reserve requirements in the form of cash or liquidity holdings as a percentage of deposits. This minimum percentage is known as a *required reserve ratio*. The practice of minimum required reserve ratios varies from central bank to central bank. Most central banks determine a required reserve ratio for each type of deposit. Table 31.2 shows the ratios in force in selected countries. They vary from near zero to 12 per cent in Greece and 15 per cent in Italy.

By increasing required reserve ratios, the central bank can create a shortage of reserves for the banking system and decrease bank lending. A decrease in lending decreases the money supply by a process similar to that described in Chapter 30. We'll look at this process later in this chapter (see pp. 812–818).

Although changes in required reserve ratios can be used to influence the money supply, a central bank rarely uses this policy tool. That is, the central bank does not often *change* required reserve ratios as an active tool to *change* the money supply. In the United Kingdom, the last time the Bank of England used this method was in the mid-1970s.

TABLE 31.2

Reserve Requirements in Selected Countries

Country	Demand deposits	Time deposits
	(percentage of deposits)	
France	1.0	0.5
Germany	6.6–12.1	2.0
Greece	12.0	12.0
Ireland	3.0	3.0
Italy	15.0	15.0
Netherlands	1.1	1.1
Portugal	2.0	2.0
Spain	2.0	2.0
Japan	0.1–1.3	0.05–1.2
Switzerland	2.5	2.5
United States	3–10	0.0

Sources: R. M. Levich, 'The Euromarkets after 1993', J. Dermine (ed), *European Banking in the 1990s*, 1993, Oxford; Blackwell, and private correspondence European Monetary Institute, Frankfurt.

The current requirement for United Kingdom banks is to keep 0.35 per cent of their eligible deposits with the Bank of England. The banks keep a little extra at the Bank of England to cover interbank transactions. These extra deposits are called *operational deposits*.

Discount Rate   The **discount rate** is the interest rate at which the central bank stands ready to lend reserves to commercial banks. In the United Kingdom this is done by altering the cost of lender of last resort facilities to the discount houses. A rise in the discount rate makes it more costly for banks to borrow reserves from the central bank and encourages them to cut their lending, which reduces the money supply. A fall in the discount rate makes it less costly for banks to borrow reserves from the central bank and stimulates bank lending, which increases the money supply. In the United Kingdom, a rise in the lender of last resort interest rate to discount houses means that if the commercial banks recall any of their loans to the discount houses – remember that these are the highly liquid assets of the commercial banks – the discount houses will have to borrow the extra funds from the Bank of England at these new rates. To avoid lending at lower rates than those imposed by the Bank of England, the discount houses will raise their lending rates, which will cause borrowers to borrow less from them and more from the commercial banks. But if the discount houses do not lend as much as they did before the rise in the interest rate, they will not borrow as much from the commercial banks. Since the commercial banks need to lend to the discount houses as part of their liquid assets, they will find that they do not have enough reserves to maintain a prudent balance between their need to lend and make money and their need to meet withdrawals of deposits by depositors. To guard against this possibility, the commercial banks will reduce their lending by raising their own lending rates. In reality, as soon as the Bank of England signals that the interest rate to the discount houses is to rise, the commercial banks respond immediately by raising their base rates.

Open Market Operations

An **open market operation** is the purchase or sale of government securities – Treasury bills and bonds – by the Bank of England in the open market. The term 'open market' refers to commercial banks and the general public but not the government. Thus when the Bank of England conducts an open market operation, it does a transaction with a bank or some other business but it does not transact with the government.

Open market operations influence the money supply. We'll study the details of this influence in the next section. Briefly, when the Bank sells government securities it receives payment with bank deposits and bank reserves, which creates tighter monetary and credit conditions. With lower reserves, the banks cut their lending, and the money supply decreases. When the Bank buys government securities, it pays for them with bank deposits and bank reserves, which creates looser monetary and credit conditions. With extra reserves, the banks increase their lending, and the money supply increases.

Accountability and Control of the Central Bank

In some countries central banks decide monetary policy and in other countries the central bank is virtually an arm of government policy. In the United Kingdom, the government sets monetary policy in consultation with the Bank of England.

But the government is in charge of monetary policy. In the past the Chancellor of the Exchequer might consult the governor of the Bank but still announce a change in policy against the advice of the Bank. Because the Bank is an agent of the government, the governor can do little more than carry out the policy. Nowadays, the governor of the Bank of England has a monthly meeting with the Chancellor of the Exchequer to review the monetary conditions of the economy. It is only after one of these meetings that the Treasury announces a change in monetary policy. The minutes of the monthly meeting are published so that everyone can see the level of agreement and cooperation between the two agencies. The purpose of publishing the minutes is to introduce a sense of openness to the deliberations. If there is a difference between the Chancellor of the Exchequer and the governor of the Bank of England, the Bank will still carry out the policy dictated by the Treasury, but the prospect of a public disagreement may constrain the Chancellor and the Treasury from certain types of policies.

Central banks all over the world face some kind of political pressure at some time. The political constraints will depend on the legal relationship between the government and the central bank, and the history and traditions that have governed this relationship. The relationship can range from total dependence to one of total independence.

Dependence versus Independence for the Central Bank

A dependent central bank acts entirely as the agent of the government and carries out monetary policy dictated by it. Most central banks are subservient to the authority of the government. The argument for dependence is that monetary policy is a political issue and therefore central banks must follow the dictates of their political masters. While the Bank of England is subservient in the sense of having to follow the policy dictated by the Chancellor of the Exchequer, it does not mean that the Bank has no power. No government will be willing to run the risk of the governor resigning because of a strong disagreement with the Chancellor. Therefore the notion of dependence is one of degree. A low degree of dependence means a high degree of independence and vice versa.

However, economists have argued that higher inflation is usually associated with countries that have central banks with low degrees of independence. The reason for this is that governments are inclined to conduct relaxed monetary policies at election times. The evidence appears to confirm that countries with central banks that have high degrees of independence are associated with lower inflation than the average, while countries with central banks that have low degrees of independence are associated with higher inflation than the average. Countries that have relatively independent central banks are the United States, Germany, Switzerland and New Zealand. Countries that have relatively dependent central banks are the United Kingdom, France, Spain and Sweden. The notion that low inflation is the outcome of monetary policy followed by an independent central bank is not entirely convincing. Japan, for instance, has a dependent central bank but a history of relatively low inflation.

If the European Union adopts a single currency, the new European Central Bank will be an independent central bank modelled on the existing Bundesbank.

R E V I E W

◆ The Bank of England is the central bank of the United Kingdom.

◆ A central bank conducts a nation's monetary policy and supervises the financial system.

◆ A central bank's policy tools are the required reserve ratio, the discount rate and open market operations.

◆ Monetary policy in the United Kingdom is determined by the Chancellor of the Exchequer in consultation with the governor of the Bank of England.

◆ To change the quantity of money, the Bank of England changes the rate of interest or conducts open market operations.

◆ Evidence supports the argument that an independent central bank follows a low inflation monetary policy

Next, we're going to study how the Bank of England influences the quantity of money.

Controlling the Money Supply

The Bank constantly monitors and adjusts the quantity of money in the economy. To change the quantity of money, the Bank conducts an open market operation. When the Bank *buys* securities in an open market operation, the monetary base *increases*, banks *increase* their lending and the quantity of money *increases*. When the Bank *sells* securities in an open market operation, the monetary base *decreases*, banks *decrease* their lending and the quantity of money *decreases*.

Let's study these changes in the quantity of money, beginning with the effects of open market operations on the monetary base.

How an Open Market Operation Works

When the Bank of England conducts an open market operation, the reserves of the banking system, a component of the monetary base, change. To see why this outcome occurs, we'll trace the effects of an open market operation both when the Bank *buys* securities and when it *sells* securities.

The Bank Buys Securities   Suppose the Bank buys £100 million of government securities in the open market. There are two cases to consider: when the Bank buys from a commercial bank and when it buys from the public (a person or business that is not a commercial bank). The outcome is essentially the same in either case, but you need to be convinced of this fact so we'll study the two cases, starting with the simplest case in which the Bank buys from a commercial bank.

Buys from Commercial Bank   When the Bank buys £100 million of securities from Barclays de Zoete Wedd (BZW), the investment banking arm of Barclays Bank plc, two things happen:

1. BZW has £100 million fewer securities and the Bank of England has £100 million more securities.
2. The Bank of England pays for the securities by crediting BZW's deposit account at the Bank of England by £100 million.

Figure 31.2(a) shows the effects of these actions on the balance sheets of the Bank of England and BZW. Ownership of the securities

FIGURE 31.2

The Bank Buys Securities in the Open Market

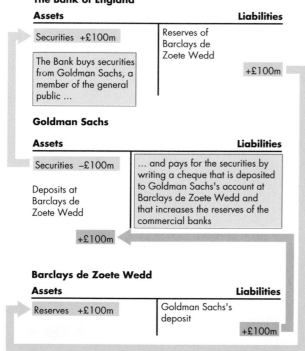

(a) The Bank buys securities from a commercial bank

The Bank of England

Assets	Liabilities
Securities +£100m	Reserves of Barclays de Zoete Wedd
The Bank buys securities from a commercial bank ...	+£100m
	... and pays for the securities by increasing the reserves of the commercial bank

Barclays de Zoete Wedd

Assets	Liabilities
Securities –£100m	
Reserves +£100m	

(b) The Bank buys securities from the public

The Bank of England

Assets	Liabilities
Securities +£100m	Reserves of Barclays de Zoete Wedd
The Bank buys securities from Goldman Sachs, a member of the general public ...	+£100m

Goldman Sachs

Assets	Liabilities
Securities –£100m	... and pays for the securities by writing a cheque that is deposited to Goldman Sachs's account at Barclays de Zoete Wedd and that increases the reserves of the commercial banks
Deposits at Barclays de Zoete Wedd	
+£100m	

Barclays de Zoete Wedd

Assets	Liabilities
Reserves +£100m	Goldman Sachs's deposit
	+£100m

When the Bank buys securities in the open market, bank reserves increase. If the Bank buys from a commercial bank (part a), bank reserves increase when the Bank pays the bank for the securities. If the Bank buys from the public (part b), bank deposits and bank reserves increase when the seller of the securities deposits the Bank's cheque and the commercial bank collects payment from the Bank.

passes from BZW to the Bank of England, so BZW's assets decrease by £100 million and the Bank of England's assets increase by £100 million – shown by the blue arrow running from BZW to the Bank of England. The Bank of England pays for the securities by crediting BZW's deposit account – its reserves – at the Bank by £100 million – shown by the green arrow running from the Bank to BZW. This action increases the monetary base and increases the reserves of the banking system.

The Bank of England's assets increase by £100 million and its liabilities also increase by £100 million. BZW's total assets remain constant but their composition changes. Its deposits at the Bank increase by £100 million and its holdings of government securities decrease by £100 million. So the bank has additional reserves, which it can use to make loans.

We've just seen that when the Bank buys government securities from a bank, the bank's reserves increase. But what happens if the Bank buys government securities from the public – say from Goldman Sachs International, a financial services company?

Buys from Public   When the Bank of England buys £100 million of securities from Goldman Sachs, three things happen:

1. Goldman Sachs has £100 million fewer securities and the Bank has £100 million more securities.

2. The Bank pays for the securities with a cheque for £100 million drawn on itself, which Goldman Sachs deposits in its account at BZW.

3. BZW collects payment of this cheque from the Bank of England, and £100 million is deposited in BZW's deposit account at the Bank of England.

Figure 31.2(b) shows the effects of these actions on the balance sheets of the Bank, Goldman Sachs and BZW. Ownership of the securities passes from Goldman Sachs to the Bank, so Goldman Sachs's assets decrease by £100 million and the Bank's assets increase by £100 million – shown by the blue arrow running from Goldman Sachs to the Bank. The Bank pays for the securities with a cheque payable to Goldman Sachs. This payment increases Goldman Sachs's deposit at BZW by £100 million and it also increases BZW's reserves by £100 million – shown by the green arrow running from the Bank to BZW and the red arrow running from BZW to Goldman Sachs. Just as when the Bank of England buys from a bank, this action increases the monetary base and increases the reserves of the banking system.

Again, the Bank's assets increase by £100 million and its liabilities also increase by £100 million. Goldman Sachs has the same total assets as before, but their composition has changed. It now has more money and fewer securities. BZW's total assets increase and so do its liabilities. Its deposits at the Bank of England – its reserves – increase by £100 million and its deposit liability to Goldman Sachs increases by £100 million. Because its reserves have increased by the same amount as its deposits, the bank has excess reserves, which it can use to make loans.

We've now studied what happens when the Bank of England buys government securities from either a bank or the public. Let's reinforce what we've learned by examining the reverse case, in which the Bank *sells* securities.

The Bank Sells Securities Suppose the Bank sells £100 million of government securities in the open market. Again, there are two cases to consider: when the Bank sells to a commercial bank and when it sells to the public.

Sells to Commercial Bank When the Bank sells £100 million of securities to BZW, two things happen:

1. BZW has £100 million more securities and the Bank of England has £100 million fewer securities.
2. BZW pays for the securities by using the Barclays Bank deposit account at the Bank of England.

Figure 31.3(a) shows the effects of these actions on the balance sheets of the Bank and BZW. Ownership of the securities passes from the Bank of England to BZW, so that BZW's assets increase by £100 million and the Bank of England's assets decrease by £100 million – shown by the blue arrow running from the Bank to BZW. BZW pays for the securities by using its deposit account – its reserves – at the Bank of England. These reserves fall by £100 million shown by the green arrow running from BZW to the Bank of England. This action decreases the monetary base and decreases the reserves of the banking system.

FIGURE 31.3

The Bank Sells Securities in the Open Market

(a) The Bank sells securities to a commercial bank

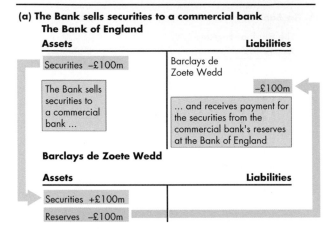

The Bank of England

Assets	Liabilities
Securities −£100m	Barclays de Zoete Wedd
The Bank sells securities to a commercial bank ...	−£100m
	... and receives payment for the securities from the commercial bank's reserves at the Bank of England

Barclays de Zoete Wedd

Assets	Liabilities
Securities +£100m	
Reserves −£100m	

(b) The Bank sells securities to the public

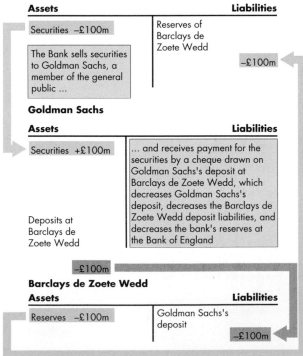

The Bank of England

Assets	Liabilities
Securities −£100m	Reserves of Barclays de Zoete Wedd
The Bank sells securities to Goldman Sachs, a member of the general public ...	−£100m

Goldman Sachs

Assets	Liabilities
Securities +£100m	... and receives payment for the securities by a cheque drawn on Goldman Sachs's deposit at Barclays de Zoete Wedd, which decreases Goldman Sachs's deposit, decreases the Barclays de Zoete Wedd deposit liabilities, and decreases the bank's reserves at the Bank of England
Deposits at Barclays de Zoete Wedd	
−£100m	

Barclays de Zoete Wedd

Assets	Liabilities
Reserves −£100m	Goldman Sachs's deposit
	−£100m

When the Bank sells securities in the open market, bank reserves decrease. If the Bank sells to a commercial bank (part a), bank reserves decrease when the bank pays the Bank for the securities. If the Bank sells to the public (part b), bank deposits and bank reserves decrease when the buyer of the securities draws a cheque payable to the Bank and the commercial bank pays the cheque using its reserves at the Bank.

The Bank of England's assets decrease by £100 million and its liabilities also decrease by £100 million. BZW's total assets remain constant but their composition changes. Its deposits at the Bank of England decrease by £100 million and its holdings of government securities increase by £100 million. So BZW has fewer reserves.

Sells to Public   When the Bank of England sells £100 million of securities to Goldman Sachs, three things happen:

1. Goldman Sachs has £100 million more securities and the Bank has £100 million fewer securities.

2. Goldman Sachs pays for the securities with a cheque for £100 million drawn on its account at BZW.

3. BZW pays this cheque from Barclays Bank's reserves at the Bank of England.

Figure 31.3(b) shows the effects of these actions on the balance sheets of the Bank of England, Goldman Sachs and BZW. Ownership of the securities passes from the Bank to Goldman Sachs, so Goldman Sachs's assets increase by £100 million and the Bank's assets decrease by £100 million – shown by the blue arrow running from the Bank to Goldman Sachs. Goldman Sachs pays for the securities with a cheque drawn on its account at BZW. This payment decreases Goldman Sachs's deposit at BZW by £100 million and it also decreases BZW's reserves by £100 million – shown by the red arrow running from Goldman Sachs to Barclays/BZW and the green arrow running from Barclays/BZW to the Bank of England. Just as when the Bank of England sells to a bank, this action decreases the monetary base and decreases the reserves of the banking system.

Again, the Bank of England's assets decrease by £100 million and its liabilities also decrease by £100 million. Goldman Sachs has the same total assets as before, but their composition has changed. It now has less money and more securities. BZW's total assets decrease and so do its liabilities. BZW's deposits at the Bank of England – its reserves – decrease by £100 million and its deposit liability to Goldman Sachs decreases by £100 million. Because its reserves have decreased by the same amount as its deposits, the bank has a shortage of reserves, and it must decrease its loans.

The effects of an open market operation on the balance sheets of the Bank of England and the banks that we've just described are not the end of the story – they are just the beginning. With an increase in their reserves, the banks are able to make more loans, which increases the quantity of money. With a decrease in reserves, the banks must cut their loans, which decreases the quantity of money.

We learned how loans create deposits in Chapter 30. Here, we build on that basic idea but instead of studying the link between bank reserves and deposits, we examine the related broader link between the quantity of money and the monetary base.

Monetary Base and Bank Reserves

We've defined the *monetary base* – M0 – as the sum of notes and coins, and bankers' deposits at the Bank. The monetary base is held either by banks as *reserves* or outside the banks as currency in circulation. When the monetary base increases, both bank reserves and currency in circulation increase. Only the increase in bank reserves can be used by banks to make loans and create additional money. An increase in currency held outside the banks is called a **currency drain**. A currency drain reduces the amount of additional money that can be created from a given increase in the monetary base.

The **money multiplier** is the amount by which a change in the monetary base is multiplied to determine the resulting change in the quantity of money. It is related to but differs from the deposit multiplier that we studied in Chapter 30. The *deposit multiplier* is the amount by which a change in bank reserves is multiplied to determine the change in bank deposits.

Let's now look at the money multiplier.

The Multiplier Effect of an Open Market Operation

Let's work out the multiplier effect of an open market operation in which the Bank buys securities from the banks. In this case, although the open market operation increases the banks' reserves, it has no immediate effect on the quantity of money. The banks are holding more reserves and fewer securities and they have excess reserves. When the banks have excess reserves, the sequence of events shown in Fig. 31.4 takes place. These events are:

◆ Banks lend excess reserves.

◆ Deposits are created equal in value to the new loans.

◆ The new deposits are used to make payments.

◆ Households and firms receive payments from the borrowers.

◆ Part of the receipts are held as currency – a *currency drain*.

◆ Part of the receipts remain as deposits in banks.

◆ Desired reserves increase (by a fraction – the desired reserve ratio – of the increase in deposits).

◆ Excess reserves decrease, but remain positive.

◆ Banks lend the excess reserves and the process repeats itself.

The sequence repeats in a series of rounds, but each round begins with a smaller quantity of excess reserves than did the previous one. The process continues until excess reserves have finally been eliminated.

Figure 31.5 illustrates these rounds and keeps track of the magnitudes of the increases in reserves, loans, deposits, currency and money that result from an open market operation of £100,000. In this figure, the *currency drain* is 33.33 per cent and the *desired reserve ratio* is 10 per cent.

The Bank buys £100,000 of securities from the banks. The banks' reserves increase by this amount but deposits do not change. The banks have excess reserves of £100,000, and they lend those reserves. When the banks lend £100,000 of excess reserves, £66,667 remains in the banks as deposits and £33,333 drains off and is held outside the banks as currency. The quantity of money has now increased

FIGURE 31.4

A Round in the Multiplier Process Following an Open Market Operation

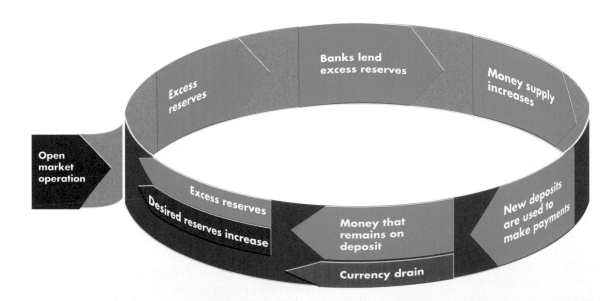

An open market purchase of government securities increases bank reserves and creates excess reserves. Banks lend the excess reserves and new loans are used to make payments. Households and firms receiving payments keep some of the receipts in the form of currency – a currency drain – and place the rest on deposit in banks. The increase in bank deposits increases banks' reserves, but also increases banks' desired reserves. Desired reserves increase by less than actual reserves, so the banks still have some excess reserves, although less than before. The process repeats until excess reserves have been eliminated. There are two components to the increase in the quantity of money: the currency drain and the increase in deposits.

FIGURE 31.5

The Multiplier Effect of an Open Market Operation

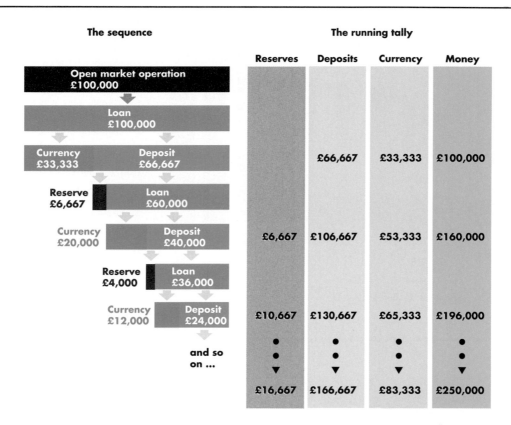

When the Bank provides the banks with £100,000 of additional reserves in an open market operation, the banks lend those reserves. Of the amount lent, £33,333 (33.33 per cent) leaves the banks in a currency drain and £66,667 remains on deposit. With additional deposits, desired reserves increase by £6,667 (10 per cent required reserves ratio) and the banks lend £60,000. Of this amount, £20,000 leaves the banks in a

currency drain and £40,000 remains on deposit. The process keeps repeating until the banks have created enough deposits to eliminate their excess reserves. The running tally tells us the amounts of reserves, deposits, currency drain and money created at each stage. At the end of the process, an additional £100,000 of reserves creates an additional £250,000 of money.

by $100,000 – the increase in deposits plus the increase in currency holdings.

The increased bank deposits of $66,667 generate an increase in desired reserves of 10 per cent of that amount, which is $6,667. Actual reserves have increased by the same amount as the increase in deposits – $66,667. So the banks now have excess reserves of $60,000. At this stage we have gone around the circle shown in Fig. 31.4 once. The process we've just described repeats but begins with excess reserves of $60,000. Fig. 31.5 shows the next two rounds. At the end of the process, the quantity of money has increased by $250,000.

Figure 31.6 illustrates the accumulated increase in the quantity of money and in its components: bank deposits and currency. When the open market operation takes place (labelled OMO in the figure), there is no initial change in either the quantity of money or its components. Then, after the first round of bank lending, the quantity of money increases by $100,000 – the size of the open market operation. In successive rounds, the quantity of money and its components continue to increase but by successively smaller amounts until, after 10 rounds, the quantities of currency and deposits and their sum, the quantity of money, have almost reached the values to which they are ultimately heading.

FIGURE 31.6

The Cumulative Effects of an Open Market Operation

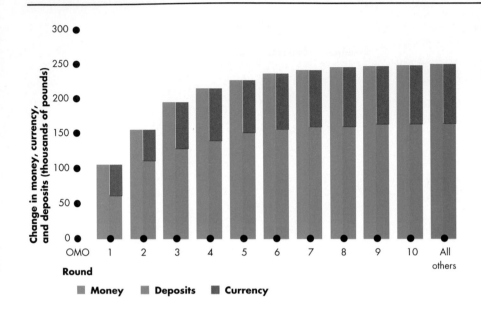

An open market operation (OMO) in which the Bank buys £100,000 government securities from the commercial banks has no immediate effect on the money supply but creates excess reserves in the banking system. When loans are made with these reserves, bank deposits and currency holdings increase. Each time new loans are made, part of the loan drains out from the banks and is held as currency, and part of the loan stays in the banking system in the form of additional deposits and additional reserves. The commercial banks continue to increase their lending until excess reserves have been eliminated. The magnitude of the ultimate increase in the money supply is determined by the money multiplier.

REVIEW

◆ When the central bank buys securities in the open market, the monetary base and bank reserves increase and an expansion of bank lending increases the quantity of money.

◆ When the central bank sells securities in the open market, the monetary base and bank reserves decrease and the resulting contraction of bank lending decreases the quantity of money.

United Kingdom Money Supply

Let us briefly review the factors that contribute to changes in the money supply from what we have learned so far. We know that increased bank lending raises the money supply. The sale of government bonds, an open market operation, decreases the money supply. An increase in monetary base decreases the money supply through the money multiplier. We also know that in principle the money supply can be increased by reducing the reserve ratio, although this method of monetary control is rarely used by central banks. Let us bring all these factors together to set out a complete statement of the determinants of the change in the money supply. The ingredients for this statement will need the balance sheets of the commercial banks and building societies, the financing requirement of government fiscal policy and the two official definitions of the money supply.

The Banks' and Building Societies' Balance Sheets From our examination of the balance sheets of the banks and building societies in Tables 30.4 and 30.5, we can think of the consolidated balance sheet as the assets that are made up of loans (advances) to the private sector and cash reserves including bankers' deposits at the Bank of England. We are ignoring all the other types of assets such as Treasury bills, commercial bills and other securities. Let's call the level of loans issued A and cash reserves R. The largest liabilities of the banks and building societies are their deposits. These are the sight deposits and time deposits of the commercial banks, the share accounts of the building societies and certificates of deposits. Again we will ignore the other smaller assets and call the total level of deposits D. Then we can write the balance sheet statement *assets = liabilities* as

$$A + R = D$$

The Financing of Fiscal Policy

In Chapter 29 we examined the role of fiscal policy in the macro-economy. The government deficit, which is government sector spending less revenues, is referred to as the *Public Sector Borrowing Requirement* (PSBR). It is called the PSBR because the deficit has to be financed by borrowing. The three ways the government finances its deficit are: borrowing from the public by selling bonds, borrowing from abroad by selling bonds to foreigners and borrowing from the Bank of England, issuing base money. The sale of bonds to the public is the addition to the existing stock of bonds (B) and is denoted as ΔB - the *change in bonds*. The sale of bonds to foreigners is the addition to the existing stock of bonds held by people outside the United Kingdom (F) and is denoted as ΔF – the *change in the stock of bonds held by foreigners*. The issue of base money is the addition to the existing stock of base money (M0) and is denoted as ΔM0 – the *change in* M0. Therefore the PSBR can be stated as follows. The government deficit can be financed by selling bonds to the public, selling bonds to foreigners or issuing base money or any combination of all three.

$$PSBR = \Delta M0 + \Delta B + \Delta F$$

The Definition of Money

We examined the definition of the two measures of money in the United Kingdom in Chapter 30. We can state M0 as being made up of currency in circulation with the public, and cash reserves of the banks and building societies including bankers' deposits at the Bank of England (R). Let us denote the amount of currency in circulation as C. The definition of M4 is currency in circulation with the public plus all bank and building society deposits and share accounts including certificates of deposits. These two definitions can be stated as:

$$M0 = C + R$$
$$M4 = C + D$$

The Change in the Money Supply

We can use the above four equations to arrive at a statement about the factors that determine the money supply in the United Kingdom. We can begin by eliminating currency from the two equations for M0 and M4. This is done by equating $C = $ M0 $- R$ and $C = $ M4 $- D$. This gives us an expression for M4 as: M4 $= $ M0 $-R + D$. We can now eliminate D from this expression by using the equation describing the bank and building society balance sheet. Now the equation becomes: M4 $= $ M0 $- R + A + R$. Notice that reserves get cancelled out and we arrive at a shorter expression: M4 $= $ M0 $+ A$. Before we proceed any further, we note that the expression for M4 can be also be stated in terms of changes. That is, the change in M4 is the change in M0 and the change in bank and building society loans and advances A:

$$\Delta M4 = \Delta M0 + \Delta A$$

We can now eliminate ΔM0 from this expression by using the statement describing the financing of the government deficit - the PSBR. From the expression for the PSBR we have: ΔM0 $= $ PSBR $- \Delta B - \Delta F$. Substituting this into the expression for ΔM4 above we arrive at our final statement:

$$\Delta M4 = PSBR - \Delta B - \Delta F + \Delta A$$

The expression for the *change in* M4 describes what is known as the M4 *counterparts*. This expression states that the money supply increases as a result of the government deficit – the PSBR and increases in bank and building society lending. The money supply decreases if the government, through the Bank of England, increases its sales of government bonds and increases if it decreases its sales of government bonds – an open market operation. The money supply will increase if the government reduces its borrowing from foreigners, and the money supply will decrease if it increases its borrowing from abroad. Table 31.3 shows how the counterparts to M4 have evolved in recent years[1]. The columns in Table 31.3 correspond to each of the counterparts of M4. You can see that in recent years the government deficit has been contributing to the

---

[1] In reality the external component of the counterparts will include the currency transactions of the Bank of England in carrying out policies to defend the value of the pound, and the foreign currency transactions of the commercial banks.

TABLE 31.3

M4 Counterparts

Year	PSBR	Purchases of public sector debt by UK private sector $-\Delta B$	External and foreign currency counterparts $-\Delta F$	Sterling lending to the UK private sector ΔA	Net non-deposit sterling liabilities	Change in money stock $\Delta M4$
1991	7,661	−5,543	−2,525	36,762	−8,621	27,682
1992	28,664	−20,092	−3,721	25,757	−12,314	18,115
1993	42,503	−30,195	3,478	22,636	−14,766	23,843
1994	37,888	−22,938	−6,626	31,129	−14,862	24,595
1995	35,486	−24,233	−5,014	58,038	−8,008	56,265

Source: Office for National Statistics, *Financial Statistics, May 1996,* No 409, HMSO, London. Numbers do not add up to ∆M4 because of rounding.

increase in the money supply, but that this increase has been largely offset by borrowing from the UK public – that is, the non-bank private sector. The penultimate column is the change in non-deposit lia-bilities, which is the increase in banks' share capital. The shareholders capital is also a liability of the bank, but it is a non-deposit liability. The major contributor to the increase in the money supply has been the increase in bank and building society lending.

REVIEW

◆ The change in the total supply of money in the United Kingdom is influenced by the financing of the government budget deficit (the PSBR), by open market operations (the sale or pur-chase of government bonds), and the increase in bank and building society lending.

◆ The M4 counterparts describe the different influences on the change in the money supply. Bank lending has the largest influence. The sec-ond largest influence is the PSBR.

The central bank's objective in conducting open market operations, or taking other actions that influence the quantity of money in circulation are not simply to affect the money supply for its own sake. An important objective is to influence the course of the economy – especially the level of out-put, employment and prices – by influencing aggregate demand. But the central bank's influence

on aggregate demand is indirect. Its immediate objective is to move interest rates up or down. To work out the effects of the central bank's actions on interest rates, we need to work out how and why interest rates change when the quantity of money changes. We'll discover the answer to these ques-tions by first studying the demand for money

The Demand for Money

The amount of money we *receive* each week in payment for our labour is income – a flow. The amount of money that we hold in our wallets or in a sight deposit account at our local bank is an inventory – a stock. There is no limit to how much income – or flow – we would like to receive each week. But there is a limit to how big a stock of money each of us would like to hold, on the average.

The Influences on Money Holding

The quantity of money that people choose to hold depends on four main factors. They are:

◆ The price level
◆ The interest rate
◆ Real GDP
◆ Financial innovation

Let's look at each of them.

The Price Level The quantity of money mea-sured in current pounds is called the quantity of *nominal money*. The quantity of nominal money demanded is proportional to the price level, other things remaining the same. That is, if the price level (GDP deflator) increases by 10 per cent, people will want to hold 10 per cent more nominal money than before, other things remaining the same. What matters is not the number of pounds that you hold but their buying power. If you hold £20 to buy your weekly groceries and beer at the Students' Union, you will increase your money holding to £22 pounds if the prices of groceries and beer – and your student grant – increase by 10 per cent.

The quantity of money measured in constant pounds (for example, in 1990 pounds) is called *real money*. Real money is equal to nominal money divided by the price level. The quantity of real money demanded is independent of the price level. In the above example, you held £20, on the average, at the original price level. When the price level increased by 10 per cent, you increased your average cash holding by 10 per cent, keeping your *real* cash holding constant. Your £22 pounds at the new price level is the same quantity of *real money* as your £20 pounds at the original price level.

The Interest Rate   A fundamental principle of economics is that as the opportunity cost of something increases, people try to find substitutes for it. Money is no exception. The higher the opportunity cost of holding money, other things remaining the same, the lower is the quantity of real money demanded. But what is the opportunity cost of holding money? It is the interest rate. But which interest rate? Bank and building society deposits of a certain type earn interest. So money, if held as a time deposit, earns interest. Do we mean the interest rate on bank and building society deposits? Surely a rise in the bank and building society deposit rate makes money more attractive and a rise in this rate will increase the demand for money not lower it. The interest rate we mean is the interest paid on a financial asset that is a close substitute for money. To see why, recall that the opportunity cost of any activity is the value of the best alternative forgone. The alternative to holding money is holding an interest-earning financial asset such as a savings bond or Treasury bill. By holding money instead, you forgo the additional interest that you otherwise would have received. This forgone additional interest is the opportunity cost of holding money.

Money loses value because of inflation. Why isn't the inflation rate part of the cost of holding money? It is – other things remaining the same, the higher the expected inflation rate, the higher are interest rates and the higher, therefore, is the opportunity cost of holding money.

Real GDP   The quantity of money that households and firms plan to hold depends on the amount they are spending, and the quantity of money demanded in the economy as a whole depends on aggregate expenditure – real GDP.

Again, suppose that you hold an average of £20 to finance your weekly purchases of goods. Now imagine that the prices of these goods and of all other goods remain constant but that your income increases. As a consequence, you now spend more and you also keep a larger amount of money on hand to finance your higher volume of expenditure.

Financial Innovation   Financial innovations have altered the quantity of money held by people. Specifically these are the introduction of:

1. Interest-bearing sight deposits
2. Automatic transfers between sight and time deposits
3. Automatic teller machines
4. Credit cards
5. Bank debit cards

These innovations have occurred because of the development of low-cost computing power. Without computers, it would be too costly to calculate the interest owing on balances at any moment in time, to switch funds from one account to another automatically, to get cash at midnight any time from a 'hole-in-the-wall' ATM, to shuffle sales slips and keep credit card records, and to use your Switch card to pay for your groceries. These innovations have decreased the quantity of cash held. But they have increased the demand for bank and building society deposits. Since more types of bank and building society deposits pay a rate of interest, people have switched from savings accounts to bank accounts.

The Demand for Money Curve

The *demand for money* is the relationship between the quantity of real money demanded and the interest rate, holding constant all other influences on the amount of money that people wish to hold. Figure 31.7 shows a demand for money curve, *MD*. When the interest rate rises, everything else remaining the same, the opportunity cost of holding money rises and the quantity of money demanded decreases – there is a movement along the demand for money curve. Similarly, when the interest rate falls, the opportunity cost of holding money falls and the quantity of money demanded increases – there is a downward movement along the demand for money curve.

Shifts in the Demand Curve for Real Money

Figure 31.8 shows the effects of factors that change the demand for money. A decrease in real GDP decreases the demand for money and shifts the demand curve leftward from MD_0 to MD_1. An increase in real GDP has the opposite effect. It

increases the demand for money and shifts the demand curve rightward from MD_0 to MD_2. The influence of financial innovation on the demand for money curve is more complicated. It might increase the demand for some types of deposits and decrease the demand for others – and decrease the demand for currency. We'll look at its effects by studying the demand for money in the United Kingdom.

The Demand for Money in the United Kingdom

Figure 31.9 shows the relationship between the interest rate and the quantity of real money demanded in the United Kingdom since 1963. Each dot shows the interest rate and the amount of real money held in a given year.

FIGURE 31.7

The Demand for Money

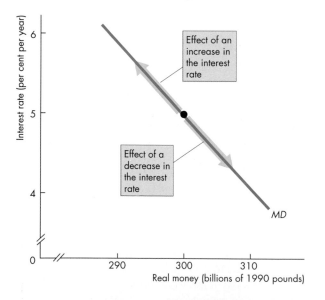

The demand for money curve, *MD*, shows that the lower the interest rate, the larger is the quantity of money that people plan to hold. The demand curve for money slopes downward because the interest rate is the opportunity cost of holding money. The higher the interest rate, the larger is the interest forgone on holding another asset. A change in the interest rate leads to a movement along the demand curve.

FIGURE 31.8

Changes in the Demand for Money

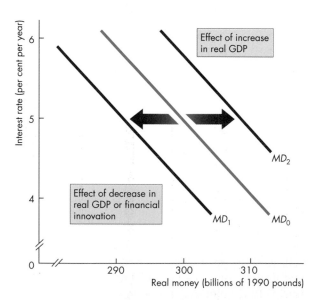

A decrease in real GDP decreases the demand for money and shifts the demand curve leftward from MD_0 to MD_1. An increase in real GDP increases the demand for money and shifts the demand curve rightward from MD_0 to MD_2. Financial innovation generally decreases the demand for money.

FIGURE 31.9

The Demand for Money in United Kingdom

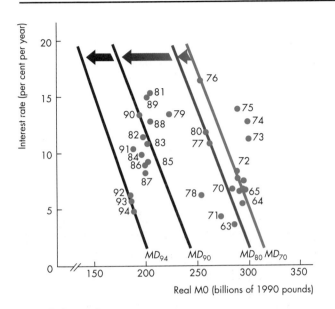

(a) M0 demand

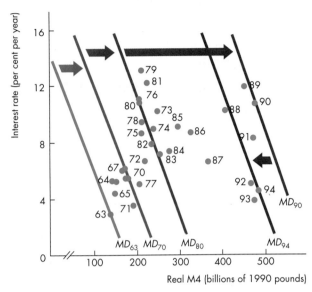

(b) M4 demand

Part (a) shows the demand for M0 – the quantity of real M0 graphed against the interest rate (the three-month Treasury bill rate). There is a negative relationship between the quantity of real M0 demanded and the interest rate, but the demand for M0 has persistently decreased and its demand curve has shifted leftward. Part (b) shows the demand for real M4 – the quantity of M4 graphed against the interest

rate. During the 1960s–1980s, the demand for M4 increased – its demand curve shifted rightward – because financial innovation developed new types of deposits that are part of M4. But in the 1990s, the demand for M4 decreased – its demand curve shifted leftward as incomes fell and better substitutes for M4 developed.

Source: *Bank of England Statistical Abstract*, 1996.

Even though real GDP has increased and this would cause the demand for M0 (part a) to increase and the demand curve to shift rightward, the evidence is that the demand for M0 has persistently decreased and the demand curve has shifted leftward. But there is a potential negative relationship between the interest rate and the quantity of M0 demanded. Because M0 is mostly currency held by the public and used almost entirely for expenditure, we would not expect a strong negative relationship.

The demand for M4 (part b) is more complicated. During the 1960s and 1970s, the demand for M4 increased and the demand curve shifted rightward. During the 1980s – a period of strong financial innovation and deregulation – the demand for M4 increased and the demand curve

shifted further to the right. During the recession of the 1990s, the demand for M4 fell and the demand curve shifted leftward.

Why did these changes in the demand for M0 and M4 occur? The answer is financial innovation. The evolution of new financial products has lead to a steady decrease in the demand for currency – M0. Some of the factors that led to a decrease in the demand for currency have led to an increase in the demand for deposits. So as the demand for M0 decreased, the demand for M4 increased. In addition, the abolition of certain types of controls on the commercial banks' ability to take deposits meant that more and more businesses and financial institutions began to deposit their money with banks, causing the demand for M4 to shift rightward.

◆ The demand for money curve shows the relationship between the quantity of real money demanded and the interest rate with all other influences on money holding unchanged.

◆ An increase in the interest rate brings a decrease in the quantity of money demanded and a movement along the demand curve for real money.

◆ Other influences on the quantity of real money demanded are real GDP and financial innovation.

◆ An increase in real GDP increases the demand for money and shifts the demand curve rightward.

◆ Financial innovations have decreased the demand for M0 and increased the demand for M4.

We now know what determines the demand for money. And we've seen that a key factor is the interest rate – the opportunity cost of holding money. But what determines the interest rate? Let's find out.

Interest Rate Determination

$\underset{\text{}}{\text{A}}$n interest rate is the percentage yield on a financial security such as a *bond* or a *share*. There is a relationship between the interest rate and the price of a financial asset. Let's spend a moment studying that relationship before analysing the forces that determine interest rates.

Interest Rates and Asset Prices

A bond is a promise to make a sequence of future payments. There are many different possible sequences but the most simple one, for our purposes, is the case of a bond called a perpetuity. A *perpetuity* is a bond that promises to pay a certain fixed amount of money each year forever. The issuer of such a bond will never buy the bond back (redeem it); the bond will remain outstanding forever, and will earn a fixed pound payment each year. The fixed pound payment is called the *coupon*. Because the coupon is a fixed pound amount, the

TABLE 31.4

The Interest Rate and the Price of a Bond

FORMULA FOR INTEREST RATE:

r = interest rate, *c* = coupon, *p* = price of bond

$$r = \frac{c}{p} 100$$

EXAMPLES

	Price of bond	Coupon	Interest rate (per cent per year)
a	50	10	20
b	100	10	10
c	200	10	5

interest rate on the bond varies as the price of the bond varies. Table 31.4 illustrates this fact.

First, the table shows the formula for calculating the interest rate on a bond. The interest rate (r) is the coupon (c) divided by the price of the bond (p) all multiplied by 100 to convert it into a percentage. The table goes on to show some numerical examples for a bond whose coupon is £10 a year. If the bond costs £100 (row *b* of Table 31.4), the interest rate is 10 per cent per year. That is, the holder of £100 worth of bonds receives £10 a year.

Rows *a* and *c* of Table 31.4 show two other cases. In row *a*, the price of the bond is £50. With the coupon at £10, this price produces an interest rate of 20 per cent – £10 returned on a £50 bond holding is an interest rate of 20 per cent. In row *c*, the bond costs £200 and the interest rate is 5 per cent – which gives £10 return on a £200 bond holding.

There is an inverse relationship between the price of a bond and the interest rate earned on the bond. As a bond price rises, the bond's interest rate declines. Understanding this relationship will make it easier for you to understand the process whereby the interest rate is determined. Let's now turn to studying how interest rates are determined.

Money Market Equilibrium

The interest rate is determined at each point in time by equilibrium in the markets for financial assets. The quantity of money supplied is determined by the actions of the banking system and the Bank of England. On any given day, the supply of broad money is a fixed quantity. The *real* quantity of money supplied is equal to the nominal quantity supplied divided by the price level. At a given moment in time, there is a particular price level and so the quantity of real money supplied is also a fixed amount. The supply curve of real money is shown in Fig. 31.10 as the vertical line labelled *MS*. The quantity of real money supplied is £300 billion.

The demand for real money depends on the level of real GDP and on the interest rate. When the quantity of money supplied equals the quantity of money demanded, the money market is in equilibrium. Figure 31.10 illustrates equilibrium in the

money market. Equilibrium is achieved by changes in the interest rate. If the interest rate is too high, people demand a smaller quantity of money than the quantity supplied. They are holding too much money. In this situation, they try to get rid of money by buying bonds. As they do so, the price of bonds rises and the interest rate falls. Conversely, if the interest rate is too low, people demand a larger quantity of money than the quantity supplied. They are holding too little money. In this situation, they try to get more money by selling bonds. As they do so, the price of bonds falls and the interest rate rises. Only when the interest rate is at the level at which people are holding the quantity of money supplied do they willingly hold the money and take no actions to change the interest rate.

Changing the Interest Rate

Suppose that the economy is overheating and the central bank fears that inflation is about to rise. It decides to take action to decrease aggregate demand and spending. To do so, it wants to raise interest rates and discourage borrowing and expenditure on goods and services. What does the central bank do?

The central bank sells securities in the open market. As it does so, it mops up bank reserves and induces the banks to cut their lending. The banks make a smaller quantity of new loans each day until the stock of loans outstanding has fallen to a level consistent with the new lower level of reserves. The money supply decreases.

Suppose that the central bank undertakes open market operations on a sufficiently large scale to decrease the money supply from £300 billion to £290 billion. As a consequence, the supply curve of real money shifts leftward, as shown in Fig. 31.11, from MS_0 to MS_1.

The demand for money is shown by *MD*. This curve tells us the quantity of money that households and firms plan to hold at each interest rate. With an interest rate of 5 per cent, and with £290 billion of money in the economy, firms and households are now holding less money than they wish to hold. They attempt to increase their money holding by selling financial assets. As they do so, the prices of bonds and stocks fall and the interest rate rises. When the interest rate has increased to 6 per cent, people are willing to hold the smaller £290 billion stock of money that the Bank and the banks have created.

FIGURE 31.10

Money Market Equilibrium

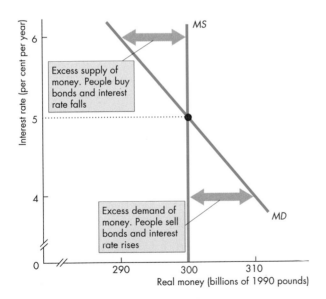

Money market equilibrium occurs when the interest rate has adjusted to make the quantity of money demanded equal to the quantity supplied. Here, equilibrium occurs at an interest rate of 5 per cent. At interest rates above 5 per cent, the quantity of money demanded is less than the quantity supplied, so people sell bonds and the interest rate falls. At interest rates below 5 per cent, the quantity of real money demanded exceeds the quantity supplied, so people buy bonds and the interest rate rises. Only at 5 per cent is the quantity of real money in existence willingly held.

Conversely, suppose that the economy is slowing and the central bank fears recession. It decides to take action to stimulate spending and increases the money supply. In this case, the Bank buys securities. As it does so, it increases bank reserves and induces the banks to increase their lending. The banks make new loans until the stock of loans outstanding has increased to a level consistent with the new higher level of reserves. Suppose that the Bank undertakes an open market sale of securities on a scale big enough to increase the real money supply to £310 billion. Now the supply of money curve shifts rightward, as shown in Fig. 31.11, from MS_0 to MS_2. With more money available, people attempt to get rid of money by buying interest-earning assets. As they do so, asset prices rise and interest rates fall. Equilibrium occurs when the interest rate has fallen to 4 per cent, at which point the new higher money stock of £310 billion is willingly held.

The Bank of England and Control of the Money Supply

This description of how the central bank controls the money supply through open market operations is a simplification of how the Bank of England actually operates in the money market. If the Bank sells government securities through an open market purchase, the commercial banks will find that they are short of reserves and their first action is to recall the overnight loans – money at call – with the discount houses. The discount houses in turn will exercise their access to the Bank of England by taking a lender of last resort loan. The Bank will then post a higher rate of interest at which it will be prepared to lend. This will force discount houses to raise the interest rates on their lending and commercial banks will do the same, as described on pp. 810–811. The higher rate of interest will lead to a cut in bank lending and the money supply will decline, and for a given price level, the real money supply declines.

FIGURE 31.11

Interest Rate Changes

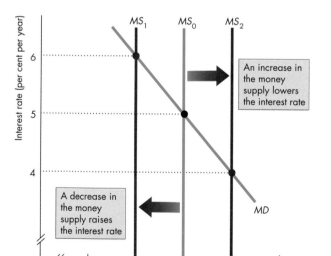

An open market sale of securities shifts the money supply curve leftward to MS_1 and the interest rate rises to 6 per cent. An open market purchase3 of securities shifts the money supply curve rightward to MS_2 and the interest rate falls to 4 per cent.

REVIEW

◆ Interest rates are determined by equilibrium in asset markets.

◆ Short-term interest rates are determined by the demand for and supply of money. When the quantity of money demanded equals the quantity supplied, the interest rate is at its equilibrium level.

◆ To increase the interest rate, the Bank sells securities and decreases the money supply. (To decrease the interest rate, the Bank buys securities and increases the money supply.)

You've now seen how the interest rate is determined and how the actions of the Bank of England can influence the interest rate. We are now going to look at the Bank in action and see how its monetary policy actions influence the course of the economy.

Monetary Policy

You have now learned a great deal about the Bank of England, the monetary policy actions it can take and the effects of those actions on short-term interest rates. But you are possibly thinking: all this sounds nice in theory, but does it really happen? Does the Bank actually do the things we've learned about in this chapter? Indeed, it does happen, and sometimes with dramatic effect. To see the Bank in action, we'll do two things. First, we'll look at the fluctuations in short-term interest rates in the United Kingdom since 1979 and see how the Bank has influenced those fluctuations. Second, we'll focus on two episodes in the life of the Bank, one from the turbulent years of the early 1980s and the other in recent years since the United Kingdom left the Exchange Rate Mechanism of the European Monetary System.

The Bank of England in Action

You've seen that the immediate effect of the Bank's actions is a change in the short-term interest rate. But does the short-term interest rate rise and fall in response to changes in the quantity of money, like the theory we've just studied predicts? Mostly, but not quite always, it does. Figure 31.12 illustrates this connection. It shows the Treasury bill rate at the end of the year and a measure of the quantity of money. This measure of money is M4 expressed as a percentage of GDP. The reason for looking at M4 is that it is a measure of money on which the Bank has placed great emphasis, and it has stated a monitoring range for its growth. The reason for expressing M4 as a percentage of GDP is that we can see both the supply side and demand side effects on interest rates in a single measure. Interest rates rise if the quantity of money decreases. Interest rates also rise if the demand for money increases. But the demand for money

---

FIGURE 31.12

Money and Interest Rates

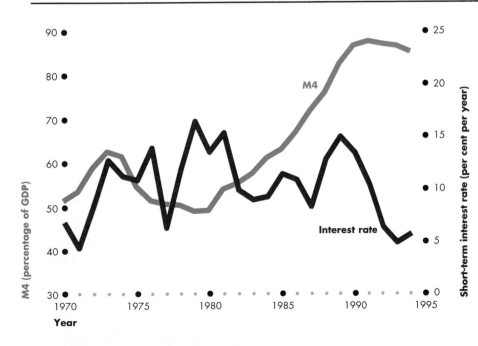

When the ratio of M4 to GDP (measured on the left scale) rises, either the supply of money increases or the demand for money decreases. The result, before 1985, is that a fall in the short-term rate of interest (measured on the right scale) is matched by a rise in M4 relative to GDP. Similarly, when the ratio of M4 to GDP falls, either the supply of money decreases or the demand for money increases and (again before 1985) this is associated with the short-term rate rising. After 1985, the relationship between M4 and interest rates broke down because of deregulation and financial innovation.

Sources: *Bank of England Statistical Abstract*, 1995, and *Economic Trends Annual Supplement*, 1996.

increases if GDP increases. So the ratio of M4 to GDP rises either if the supply of money increases (M4 increases) or if the demand for money decreases (GDP decreases).

You can see by studying Fig. 31.12 that between 1973 and 1980, the rise in the interest rate is matched by a decrease in the ratio of M4 to GDP. Lower interest rates between 1982 and 1987 were matched by an increase in the ratio of M4 to GDP. An increase in the supply of money relative to the demand for money brought a fall in the interest rate in the 1980s. And a decrease in the supply of money relative to the demand for money brought a rise in the interest rate between 1979 and 1981.

You can also see in Fig. 31.12 that after 1987, the relationship between money and interest rates broke down. When the interest rate rose in 1989, the M4 to GDP ratio did not fall but its rate of increase began to decrease. The reason the demand for M4 continued to rise is that as interest rates rose so did the interest rate on time deposits, and people continued to demand M4 deposits. It was only when the differential between the time deposit rate and the rate of interest on government securities widened that the increase in M4 relative to GDP began to decline.

You've now seen that we can explain short-term interest rate fluctuations as arising from fluctuations in the supply of money relative to the demand for money. But this relationship doesn't tell us whether actions by the Bank or fluctuations in GDP brought the fluctuations in the M4 to GDP ratio. Do the Bank's own actions move interest rates around? Let's answer this question by looking at two episodes in the life of the Bank.

The Bank in Action 1979-1982 Figure 31.13(a) shows the course of the Bank of England lending rate to the discount houses – the retail banks' base rate, the rate at which the commercial banks lend to each other – the interbank rate and the three–month Treasury bill rate between January 1979 and December 1992. Notice how closely the three interest rates move together. The Bank of England lending rate to the discount houses moves intermittently because it is a rate that is administered by the Bank. The interbank rate and the Treasury bill rate are market rates, which means that they are determined in the financial asset markets. We have chosen this period to examine the Bank in action as this was when the U K government under Margaret Thatcher pursued a strong counter-inflationary monetary policy. Mrs Thatcher was elected in June 1979 and

immediately embarked on a policy aiming to reduce inflation. In June 1979 the Bank's lending rate was raised to 14 per cent in an attempt to bring the money supply under control. In November the interest rate was raised sharply to 17 per cent. The rate of growth of the money supply did not decline immediately; indeed, it increased in the short-term partly because of financial innovation and deregulation of the banking system (see p. 821). But slowly the rate of growth of money began to decline and inflation fell. As these events occurred, the Bank lending rate was reduced. You can see that at times the market rates of interest preceded the movement in the Bank's rate and at other times they followed. The reason for this is that at times the markets were anticipating the Bank of England's action, and at other times they either did not anticipate it or they were waiting to see if the Bank would stick to or reverse its action.

The Bank in Action 1992–1996 Being the agent of the government of the day, the policies of the government constrain the actions of the Bank. One of the additional constraints the Bank faced was to sustain the value of the pound within the Exchange Rate Mechanism (ERM) of the European Monetary System. In 1990 the United Kingdom joined the ERM. This caused the Bank to raise the rate of interest and to keep it high to help maintain the value of the pound in the ERM (see Chapter 36, pp. 971–974). The policy of a high rate of interest was brought in to curb inflation, which had begun to rise sharply in the late 1980s. The ERM was expected to underpin the counter-inflation policy. The policy was effective in reducing aggregate demand and inflation, but the reduction in aggregate demand also resulted in a rise in unemployment and a fall in output. The pound was viewed by many people, including speculators, as being overvalued and in need of a devaluation. The pressure for a devaluation grew and on 17 September 1992 the pound left the ERM, was devalued and interest rates were allowed to fall to stimulate aggregate demand.

You can see from Fig. 31.13(b) that the Bank was successful in reducing interest rates and raising them when it thought that the economy was recovering too quickly in 1994. Again, the markets try to guess the position of the Bank and the Treasury bill rate may actually lead the Bank's action. During 1996, short-term market rates of interest fell before the base lending rate of the Bank of England. In April 1996, the interbank rate was 5.88 per cent

FIGURE 31.13

Short-term Interest Rates

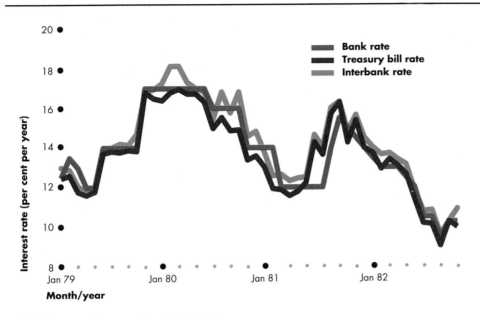

Legend:
- Bank rate
- Treasury bill rate
- Interbank rate

(a) Short-term interest rates, 1979–1982

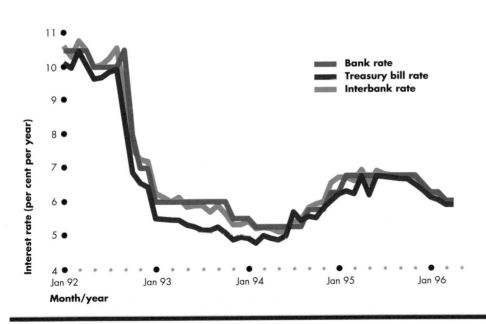

Legend:
- Bank rate
- Treasury bill rate
- Interbank rate

Part (a) shows the movement of the Bank of England base rate – referred to in the chart as the Bank rate – at which it lends to discount houses, with the rate of interest at which banks lend to each other – the interbank rate – and the Treasury bill rate between 1979 and 1982.

Part (b) shows the same rates of interest between 1992 and 1996. Notice how the rates of interest move together. The Bank directly determines the base rate at which the Bank lends to the discount houses, but all short-term interest rates move up and down together so the Bank influences all short-term rates such as the three-month Treasury bill rate (the rate at which the government borrows in the short term) and the interbank rate (the rate at which banks lend to each other).

Source: *Economic Trends Annual Supplement*, 1996, Table 5.8.

and the Treasury bill rate was 5.97 per cent, while the Bank of England base lending rate to the discount houses was 6 per cent. In June 1996, the Bank cut the base rate to 5.75 per cent. *Reading Between the Lines* on pp. 828–829 looks closer at recent monetary policy.

Profiting by Predicting the Bank of England

The Bank of England influences interest rates by its open market operations and as lender of last resort to loans to discount houses. By increasing the money supply, the Bank can lower interest rates; by lowering the money supply, the Bank can increase interest rates. Sometimes such actions are taken to offset other influences and keep interest rates steady. At other times the Bank moves interest rates up or down. The higher the interest rate, the lower is the price of a bond; the lower the interest rate, the higher is the price of a bond. Thus predicting interest rates is the same as predicting bond prices. Predicting that interest rates are going to fall is the same as predicting that bond prices are going to rise – a good time to buy bonds. Predicting that interest rates are going to rise is the same as predicting that bond prices are going to fall – a good time to sell bonds.

Because the Bank is the major player whose actions influence interest rates and bond prices, predicting what the Bank will do is profitable and a good deal of effort goes into this activity. But people who anticipate that the Bank is about to ease monetary policy and increase the money supply buy bonds straight away, pushing their prices upward and pushing interest rates downward, *before* the Bank acts. Similarly, people who anticipate that the Bank is about to tighten monetary policy and decrease the money supply sell bonds straight away, pushing their prices downward and pushing interest rates upward, before the Bank acts. In other words, bond prices and interest rates change as soon as the Bank's actions are foreseen. By the time the Bank actually takes its actions, if those actions are correctly foreseen, they have no effect. The effects occur in anticipation of the Bank's actions. Only changes in the money supply that are not foreseen change the interest rate at the time that those changes occur.

The Ripple Effects of Monetary Policy

You've now seen that the Bank's actions do indeed change interest rates and seek to influence the course of the economy. These monetary policy measures work by changing aggregate demand. When the Bank slows money growth and pushes interest rates up, it decreases aggregate demand, which slows both real GDP growth and inflation. When the Bank speeds up money growth and lowers interest rates, it increases aggregate demand, which speeds up real GDP growth and inflation. The mechanism through which aggregate demand changes involves several channels. Higher interest rates bring a decrease in consumption expenditure and investment. Higher

interest rates bring an appreciation in the exchange rate that makes UK exports more expensive and imports less costly. So net exports decrease. Tighter bank credit brings fewer loans, which reinforce the effects of higher interest rates on consumption expenditure and investment. What we have just described is sometimes refered to as the transmission mechanism of monetary policy.

Schematically, the effects of the Bank's actions ripple through the economy in the following way:

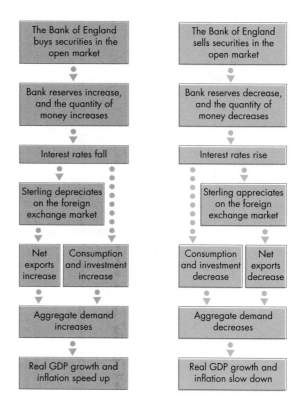

Interest Rates and the Business Cycle

You've seen the connection between the Bank's actions and interest rates in Figs. 31.12 and 31.13. What about the ripple effects that we've just described? Do they really occur? Do changes in interest rates ultimately influence the real GDP growth rate? Yes they do. You can see these effects in Fig. 31.14. The blue line shows the short-term interest rate minus the long-term interest rate. The short-term interest rate is influenced by the Bank in the way that you've studied earlier in this chapter. The long-term interest rate is determined by saving and investment plans (see Chapter 25, pp. 640–641) and by long-term inflation expectations (see Chapter 32, pp. 855–858). The red line in Fig. 31.14 is the real

---

FIGURE 31.14

Interest Rates and Real GDP Growth

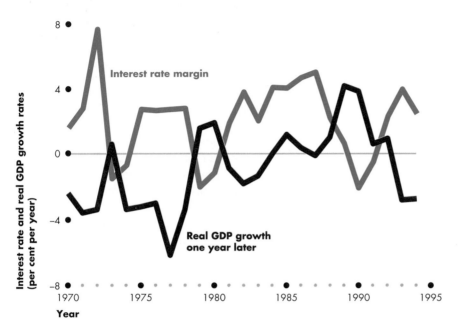

When the Bank increases short-term interest rates, the short-term rate rises above the long-term rate and later real GDP growth slows down. Similarly, when the Bank decreases short-term interest rates, the short-term rate falls below the long-term rate and later real GDP growth speeds up.

Source: Economic Trends Annual Supplement, 1996.

GDP growth rate *one year later*. You can see that when short-term interest rates rise or long-term interest rates fall the real GDP growth rate slows down in the following year. Long-term interest rates fluctuate less than short term rates, so when short-term rates rise above long-term rates, it is because the Bank has pushed short-term rates upward. And when short-term rates fall below long-term rates, it is because the Bank has pushed short-0term rates downward. So when the Bank stimulates aggregate demand the GDP growth rate speeds up, and when the Bank lowers aggregate demand, the real GDP growth rate slows down. The inflation rate also increases and decreases in sympathy with these fluctuations in real GDP growth.

REVIEW

◆ The Bank directly controls the interest rate at which lender of last resort loans are made to discount houses and ultimately the banking system.

◆ Most of the time fluctuations in short-term interest rates mirror fluctuations in the ratio of M4 to GDP.

◆ When the money supply change is unanticipated, interest rates change at the same time as the change in the money supply. When a money supply change is anticipated, interest rates change ahead of the change in the money supply.

◆ When the Bank lowers (raises) interest rates, aggregate demand increases (decreases) and real GDP growth and inflation speed up (slow down).

◆ ◆ ◆ ◆ In this chapter, we've studied the determination of interest rates and discovered how the Bank can influence interest rates by open market operations that change the quantity of money. We've also seen how interest rates influence expenditure plans, which in turn influence aggregate demand. In the next chapter, we're going to explore the influence of money and other factors on inflation.

SUMMARY

The Bank of England

The Bank of England is the central bank of the United Kingdom. Known as 'the Bank', it influences the economy by setting the base lending rate at which it is willing to lend to the discount houses and ultimately to the banking system– and by open market operations. (pp. 801–806)

Controlling the Money Supply

By buying government securities in the market (an open market purchase), the Bank is able to increase the reserves available to banks. As a result, there is an expansion of bank lending and the quantity of money increases. By selling government securities, the Bank is able to decrease the reserves of banks and other financial institutions, thereby curtailing loans and decreasing the quantity of money. (pp. 806–812)

United Kingdom Money Supply

The process of the money supply in the United Kingdom is best understood by themethod of counterparts. The M4 counterpart describes the different influences on the money supply. The change in the money supply is influenced by the government budget deficit, by the sale or purchase of goverement bonds, and by the increase in bank and building society lending. (pp. 812–814)

The Demand for Money

The quantity of money demanded is the amount of money that people plan to hold on the average. The quantity of nominal money demanded is proportional to the price level, and the quantity of real money demanded depends on the interest rate and real GDP. A higher interest rate induces a smaller quantity of real money demanded – a movement along the demand curve for real money. A higher level of real GDP induces a larger demand for real money – a shift in the demand curve for real money. Technological changes in the financial sector also change the demand for money and shift the demand curve for real money. (pp. 814–818)

Interest Rate Determination

There is an inverse relationship between the interest rate and the price of a financial asset. The higher the interest rate, the lower is the price of a financial asset. Money market equilibrium achieves an interest rate and asset price that make the quantity of real money demanded equal to the quantity supplied.

Changes in interest rates achieve equilibrium in the markets for money and financial assets. There is an inverse relationship between the interest rate and the price of a financial asset. The higher the interest rate, the lower is the price of a financial asset. Money market equilibrium achieves an interest rate and asset price that make the quantity of real money available willingly held. If the quantity of real money is increased by the actions of the Bank, the interest rate falls and the prices of financial assets rise. (pp. 818–821)

Monetary Policy

The Bank directly controls the rate at which it lends to the discount houses, but all short-term rates fluctuate together and the Bank influences all short-term interest rates. The fluctuations in short-term interest rates are usually mirrored by fluctuations in the ratio of M4 to GDP. This ratio increases when the supply of money (M4) increases and when the demand for money (determined by GDP) decreases. Before the 1980s, rises and falls in the interest rate were matched by decreases or increases in the ratio of M4 to GDP. After 1980, the relationship between M4 and interest rates broke down because of financial innovation and deregulation of the banking market.

People attempt to profit by predicting the actions of the Bank. To the extent that they can predict the Bank, interest rates and the prices of financial assets move in anticipation of the Bank's actions rather than in response to them. As a consequence, interest rates change when the Bank changes the money supply only if the Bank catches people by surprise. Anticipated changes in the money supply produce interest rate changes by themselves.

When the Bank lowers interest rates, it increases aggregate demand, which speeds real GDP growth and inflation. And when the Bank raises interest rates, it decreases aggregate demand, which slows real GDP growth and inflation. (pp. 821–825)

KEY ELEMENTS

Key Terms

Bank of England, 801
Central bank, 801
Currency drain, 809
Discount rate, 804
Monetary base, 804
Monetary policy, 801
Money multiplier, 809
Open market operation, 805

Key Figures

Figure 31.1   The Discount House and the Financial System, 802
Figure 31.5   The Multiplier Effect of an Open Market Operation, 811
Figure 31.6   The Cumulative Effects of an Open Market Operation, 812
Figure 31.7   The Demand for Money, 816
Figure 31.8   Changes in the Demand for Money, 816
Figure 31.10 Money Market Equilibrium, 819
Figure 31.11 Interest Rate Changes, 820
Figure 31.12 Money and Interest Rates, 821
Figure 31.14 Interest Rates and Real GDP Growth, 825

REVIEW QUESTIONS

1 What are the main functions of the Bank of England?

2 What are the three policy tools of the Bank? Which of these is the Bank's most frequently used tool?

3 If the central bank of a country wants to decrease the quantity of money, does it buy or sell government securities in the open market?

4 Describe the events that take place when banks have excess reserves.

5 What is the money multiplier?

6 Distinguish between nominal money and real money.

7 What do we mean by the M4 counterpart?

8 What determines the demand for money?

9 What determines the demand for real money?

10 What is the opportunity cost of holding money?

11 What happens to the interest rate on a bond if the price of the bond increases?

12 How does equilibrium come about in the money market?

13 What happens to the interest rate if the money supply increases?

14 Explain why it pays people to try to predict the Bank's actions.

15 Explain the ripple effects of the Bank's actions when it increases the interest rate.

Monetary Policy in the United Kingdom

The Essence of the Story

THE ECONOMIST, 8 JUNE 1996

Ken's short cut

British interest rates were reduced from 6% to 5.75% on June 6th, causing as much surprise as it is possible for so tiny a cut to do. The decision came the day after the monthly monetary meeting between Kenneth Clarke, the chancellor, and Eddie George, the governor of the Bank of England. 'It is hard to think of a City of London economist who anticipated a rate cut this month,' says Geoffrey Dicks, an economist at NatWest Markets, a stockbroker.

It is more likely that Mr Clarke made the cut against the advice of Mr George. Last month the Bank made it clear that it regarded this year's previous rate cuts as 'insurance' against a short-term decline in the economy, and that if there were no detoriation it would soon become more concerned about the risk of too rapid growth rather than too slow. Economic data published since suggest that although manufacturing output remains sluggish, consumption is growing fast and will produce strong growth over the next couple of years. Conclusion: there is no need for this month's extra 'insurance' against a slow-down.

Mr Clarke probably pointed to sterling's sharp rise since early May, which has hurt exporters, and to the Treasury's panel of independent economic advisers' controversial claim, published just before the cut, that GDP might grow faster, by over 3% annually for five years, without risking higher inflation. He has said repeatedly that he would raise interest rates again should that be in the best interests of the economy. Putting up rates before a general election goes against all conventional political wisdom. By cutting this week, Mr Clarke has increased the likelihood that he will have to do it, probably soon.

■ The Bank of England base interest rate has been falling in a staggered fashion during 1995 and 1996. On June 6, 1996, the Bank of England interest rate was reduced from 6 per cent to 5.75 per cent.

■ The cut came as a surprise to the markets. Most economists felt that the Chancellor of the Exchequer would heed the advice of the governor of the Bank of England, Eddie George, who has argued that the economy is improving and does not need a further reduction in interest rates.

■ Although manufacturing output growth has remained weak, household consumption has grown rapidly.

■ The Chancellor would raise interest rates if the need arose, but putting up interest rates in an election year goes against conventional political wisdom.

Economic Analysis

■ Between 1993 and 1996, the Chancellor of the Exchequer, Kenneth Clarke, has had interest rates rising and falling. In 1994 interest rates came down to a low of less than 5.5 per cent, but the Chancellor showed that he was prepared to raise the Bank of England base rate when the economy looked like overheating.

■ Interest rates reached a high of 6.75 per cent in early 1995 and have since been falling steadily in 0.25 percentage point stages. The economy slowed down during 1995 but showed signs of revival in 1996.

■ However, the signals of recovery in 1996 were mixed. The Bank of England pointed to the increase in bank and building society credit and the increase in the money supply.

■ Figure 1 shows how the demand and supply of commercial bank reserves interact with the Bank of England base rate. An increase in the supply of base money from RS_0 to RS_1 lowers the rate of interest.

■ Figure 2 shows the path of the base rate of the Bank of England and commercial banks with the rate of growth of base money. As the rate of interest has fallen the rate of growth of base money has increased. The figure also shows the rate of growth of M4.

■ Faced with lower interest rates, firms and individuals gradually increase their borrowing and spending. The increase in spending will be spread over a period of time, which could be as long as 18 months or two years.

■ The increase in spending raises aggregate demand which raises the prospect of higher inflation. The response of the price level to an increase in aggregate demand will depend on the size of the recessionary gap.

■ The Chancellor's advisers believe that GDP could grow annually at over 3 per cent for five years without stoking up inflation. The governor of the Bank of England and his advisers think that the rate of growth of money will eventually fuel higher inflation.

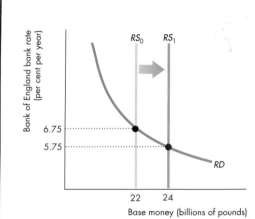

Figure 1

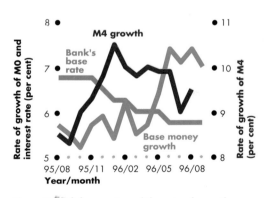

Figure 2 Bank base rate and the rate of growth of money

PROBLEMS

1 You are given the following information about the economy of Nocoin. The banks have deposits of £300 billion. Their reserves are £15 billion, two-thirds of which is in deposits with the central bank. There are £30 billion notes outside the banks. There are no coins in Nocoin!

 a Calculate the monetary base.
 b Calculate the currency drain.
 c Calculate the money supply.
 d Calculate the money multiplier.

2 Suppose that the Bank of Nocoin, the central bank, undertakes an open market purchase of securities of £500,000 What happens to the money supply? Explain why the change in the money supply is not equal to the change in the monetary base.

3 You are given the following information about the economy of Miniland. For each £1 increase in real GDP, the demand for real money increases by 25 pence, other things remaining the same. Also, if the interest rate increases by 1 percentage point (for example, from 4 per cent to 5 per cent), the quantity of real money demanded falls by £50. If real GDP is £1,000 and the price level is 1:

 a At what interest rate is no money held?
 b How much real money is held at an interest rate of 10 per cent?
 c Draw a graph of the demand for real money.

4 Given the demand for real money in Miniland, if the price level is 1, real GDP is £1,000 and the real money supply is £150, what is the equilibrium in the money market?

5 Suppose that the Bank of Miniland, the central bank, wants to lower the interest rate by 1 percentage point. By how much would it have to change the real money supply to achieve this objective?

6 You are given the following information about the economy of Miniland. For each £1 increase in real GDP, the demand for real money increases by 25 pence, other things remaining the same. Also, if the interest rate increases by 1 percentage point (for example, from 4 per cent to 5 per cent), the quantity of real money demanded falls by £50. Suppose that the Bank of Miniland, the central bank, wants to lower the interest rate by 1 percentage point. By how much would it have to change the real money supply to achieve that objective?

7 Study *Reading Between the Lines* on pp. 828–829 and then answer the following questions:

 a Why did the Chancellor reduce the Bank base rate in June 1996?
 b What were the arguments the Bank made against such a cut?
 c What are the likely effects of the interest rate cut on the economy?

CHAPTER

3 2

INFLATION

After studying this chapter you will be able to:

◆ Distinguish between inflation and a one-time rise in the price level

◆ Explain the different ways in which inflation can be generated

◆ Describe how people try to forecast inflation

◆ Explain the short-run and long-run relationships between inflation and unemployment

◆ Explain the short-run and long-run relationships between inflation and interest rates

◆ Describe the political origins of inflation

A T THE END OF THE THIRD CENTURY AD, DURING THE DYING DAYS OF THE Roman empire, Emperor Diocletian struggled to contain a rampant inflation. Prices increased at a rate of more than 300 per cent a year. At the end of the twentieth century, during the years of transition from a central planning system to a market economy, President Boris Yeltsin struggled to contain an even more severe inflation in Russia. At its peak, in the winter of 1993–94, prices increased in Russia at a rate of close to 1,000 per cent a year. But the most rapid inflations in today's world are in Latin America and Africa. For example, in 1994, Brazil's inflation hit 40 per cent *per month* and the tiny African country of Zaire had in inflation rate of 75 per cent *per month*. What causes rapid inflation? ◆ In comparison with the cases just described, the United Kingdom has had remarkable price stability. Nevertheless, during the 1970s, the UK price level trebled – a decade inflation of more than 200 per cent. Today, along with the other rich industrial countries, the United Kingdom has a low inflation rate of about 2.5 per cent a year. Why do some countries have a low inflation rate? And why did a more serious inflation break out in the United Kingdom during the 1970s? ◆ Most of life's big economic decisions

From Rome to Russia

– whether to buy or rent a house, whether to save more for retirement, whether to buy stocks or keep more money in the bank – turn on what is going to happen to inflation. Will inflation increase so our savings buy less? Will inflation decrease so our debts are harder to repay? To make good decisions, we need good forecasts of inflation, not just for next year but for many years into the future. How do people try to forecast inflation? And how do expectations of inflation influence the economy? ◆ As the inflation rate rises and falls, the unemployment rate and interest rates also fluctuate. What are the links between inflation and the economy that make unemployment and interest rates fluctuate when inflation fluctuates?

◆ ◆ ◆ ◆ In this chapter you will learn about the forces that generate inflation, the effects of inflation and the way that people try to forecast inflation. You will pull together several of the threads you have been following through your study of macroeconomics. In particular, you will use the *AS–AD* model of Chapter 27 and the analysis of the money market of Chapter 31 and put them to work in understanding the process of inflation. But first, let's recall what inflation is and how its rate is measured.

Inflation and the Price Level

Inflation is a process in which the *price level is rising* and *money is losing value.* Two features of this definition of inflation must be emphasized. First, inflation is a *monetary* phenomenon. It is the price *level* and therefore the *value of money* that is changing, not the price of some particular commodity. For example, if the price of oil rises but prices of computers fall so that the price level (an average of prices) is constant, there is no inflation. Second, inflation is an ongoing *process*, not a one-shot affair. Figure 32.1 illustrates the distinction between an ongoing process of rising prices and a one-time rise in the price level. In part (a), the price level rises continuously. In part (b), the price level rises at the beginning of 1993, a one-time rise, but is constant in the other years. The economy in part (a) is experiencing inflation but the economy in part (b) is not. It has had a one-time rise in its price level.

To measure the inflation *rate,* we calculate the annual percentage change in the price level. Call this year's price level P_1 and last year's price level

P_0. Then,

$$\text{Inflation rate} = \frac{P_1 - P_2}{P_0} \times 100$$

For example, if this year's price level is 126 and last year's price level was 120, the inflation rate is 5 per cent per year. That is,

$$\text{Inflation rate} = \frac{126 - 120}{P_{120}} \times 100$$

$$= 5 \text{ per cent per year.}$$

This equation shows the connection between the *inflation rate* and the *price level*. For a given price level last year, the higher the price level in the current year, the higher is the inflation rate. If the price level is *rising*, the inflation rate is *positive*. If the price level rises at a *faster* rate, the inflation rate *increases*. Also, the higher the price level, the lower is the value of money and the higher the inflation rate.

Inflation can occur from an increase in aggregate demand, or a decrease in aggregate supply, or both. To study the forces that generate inflation, we distinguish two types of impulses that can get an

---

FIGURE 32.1

Inflation versus a One-time Rise in the Price Level

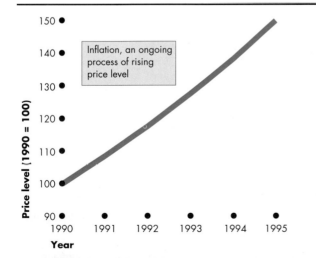

(a) Inflation

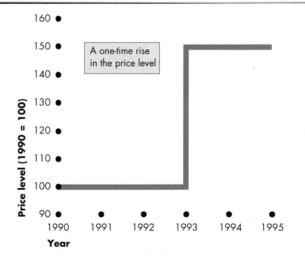

(b) One-time rise in price level

An economy experiences inflation when the price level rises persistently, as shown in part (a). An economy experiences a one-time rise in the price level if some

disturbance increases the price level but does not set off an ongoing process of a rising price level, as shown in part (b).

inflation started. These impulses are called:

◆ Demand pull

◆ Cost push

We'll first study a demand-pull inflation.

Demand-pull Inflation

An inflation that results from an initial increase in aggregate demand is called **demand-pull inflation.** Such an inflation may arise from any individual factor that increases aggregate demand such as an:

◆ Increase in the money supply

◆ Increase in government purchases

◆ Increase in the price level or real GDP in the rest of the world

When aggregate demand increases, the aggregate demand curve shifts rightward. Let's trace the effects of such an increase.

Inflation Effect of an Increase in Aggregate Demand

Suppose that last year the price level was 130 and real GDP was £600 billion. Long-run real GDP was also £600 billion. This situation is shown in Fig. 32.2(a). The aggregate demand curve is AD_0, the short-run aggregate supply curve is SAS_0, and the long-run aggregate supply curve is LAS.

In the current year, aggregate demand increases to AD_1. Such a situation arises if, for example, the government increases its purchases of goods and services or the Bank of England (the Bank) loosens its grip on the money supply. The economy moves to the point where the aggregate demand curve AD_1 intersects the short-run aggregate supply curve SAS_0. The price level rises to 135, and real GDP increases above potential GDP to £650 billion. The economy experiences 3.8 per cent inflation (a price level of 135 compared with 130 in the previous year) and a rapid expansion of real GDP. Unemployment falls below the natural rate. The next step in the unfolding story is a rise in wages.

FIGURE 32.2

A Demand-pull Rise in the Price Level

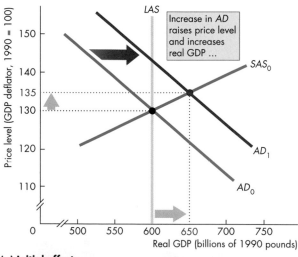

(a) Initial effect

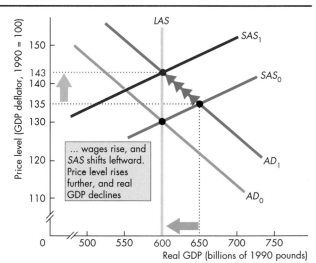

(b) Wages adjust

In part (a), the aggregate demand curve is AD_0, the short-run aggregate supply curve is SAS_0 and the long-run aggregate supply curve is LAS. The price level is 130 and real GDP is £600 billion, its long-run level. Aggregate demand increases to AD_1 (because the Bank increases the money supply or the government increases its purchases of goods and services). The new equilibrium occurs where

AD_1 intersects SAS_0. The economy experiences inflation (the price level rises to 135) and real GDP increases to £650 billion. In part (b), starting from above full employment, wages begin to rise and the short-run aggregate supply curve shifts leftward towards SAS_1. The price level rises further, and real GDP returns to its long-run level.

Wage Response

Real GDP cannot remain above potential GDP for ever. With unemployment below its natural rate, there is a shortage of labour. Wages begin to increase, and the short-run aggregate supply curve starts to shift leftward. Prices rise further, and real GDP begins to fall. With no further change in aggregate demand – the aggregate demand curve remains at AD_1 – this process comes to an end when the short-run aggregate demand curve has moved to SAS_1 in Fig. 32.2(b). At this time, the price level has increased to 143 and real GDP has returned to potential GDP of £600 billion, the level from which it started.

A Demand-pull Inflation Process

The process we've just studied eventually comes to an end when, for a given increase in aggregate demand, wages have adjusted enough to restore the real wage rate to its full-employment level. We've studied a one-time rise in the price level like that described in Fig. 32.1(b). For inflation to proceed, aggregate demand must persistently increase.

The only way in which aggregate demand can persistently increase is if the quantity of money persistently increases. The quantity of money persistently increases (usually) only when the government has a large budget deficit to finance. Suppose the government has a large budget deficit that it finances by creating more and more money each year. In this situation, aggregate demand increases year after year. The aggregate demand curve keeps shifting rightward and puts continual upward pressure on the price level. The economy now experiences demand-pull inflation.

Figure 32.3 illustrates the process of demand-pull inflation. The starting point is the same as that shown in Fig. 32.2. The aggregate demand curve is AD_0, the short-run aggregate supply curve is SAS_0, and the long-run aggregate supply curve is LAS. Real GDP is £600 billion and the price level is 130. Aggregate demand increases, shifting the aggregate demand curve to AD_1. Real GDP increases to £650 billion, and the price level rises to 135. The economy is at an above full-employment equilibrium. There is a shortage of labour and the wage rate rises, shifting the short-run aggregate supply curve to SAS_1. The price level rises to 143, and real GDP returns to its long-run level.

FIGURE 32.3

A Demand-pull Inflation Spiral

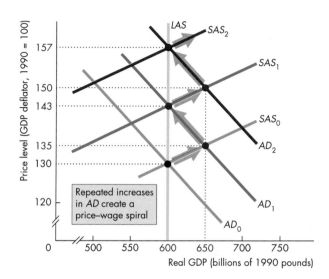

Each time the money supply increases, aggregate demand increases and the aggregate demand curve shifts rightward from AD_0 to AD_1 to AD_2, and so on. Each time real GDP goes above potential GDP and unemployment goes below the natural rate, the money wage rate rises and the short-run aggregate supply curve shifts leftward from SAS_0 to SAS_1 to SAS_2, and so on. As aggregate demand continues to increase, the price level rises from 130 through 135, 143, 150 to 157, and so on. There is a perpetual demand-pull inflation. Real GDP fluctuates between £600 billion and £650 billion.

But the money supply increases again and aggregate demand continues to increase. The aggregate demand curve shifts rightward to AD_2. The price level rises further to 150 and real GDP again exceeds potential GDP at £650 billion. Yet again, the wage rate rises and decreases short-run aggregate supply. The SAS curve shifts to SAS_2 and the price level rises further to 157. As the money supply continues to grow, aggregate demand increases and the price level rises in an ongoing demand-pull inflation process.

The process you have just studied generates inflation – an ongoing process of a rising price level like that shown in Fig. 32.1(a).

Demand-pull Inflation in Kalamazoo You may better understand the inflation process that we've just described by considering what is going on in an individual part of the economy, such as a Kalamazoo lemonade bottling plant. Initially, when aggregate demand increases, the demand for lemonade increases and the price of lemonade rises. Faced with a higher price, the lemonade plant works overtime and increases production. Conditions are good for workers in Kalamazoo, and the lemonade factory finds it hard to hang on to its best people. To do so it has to offer higher wages. As wages increase, so do the costs of the lemonade factory.

What happens next depends on what happens to aggregate demand. If aggregate demand remains constant (as in Fig. 32.2b), the firm's costs are increasing, but the price of lemonade is not increasing as quickly as its costs. Production is scaled back. Eventually, wages and costs increase by the same percentage as the price of lemonade. In real terms, the lemonade factory is in the same situation as initially – before the increase in aggregate demand. The bottling plant produces the same amount of lemonade and employs the same amount of labour as before the increase in demand.

But if aggregate demand continues to increase, so does the demand for lemonade, and the price of lemonade rises at the same rate as wages. The lemonade factory continues to operate above full employment, and there is a persistent shortage of labour. Prices and wages chase each other upward in an unending spiral.

Demand-pull Inflation in the United Kingdom
A demand-pull inflation like the one you've just studied occurred in the United Kingdom during the 1970s. In 1972–73 the government expanded the economy to reduce the level of unemployment that had been growing steadily since the late 1960s. As a consequence, the aggregate demand curve shifted rightward, the price level increased quickly and real GDP moved above its long-run or full-employment level. The money wage rate then started to rise more quickly and the short-run aggregate supply curve shifted leftward. The Bank responded with a further increase in the money supply growth rate and a demand-pull inflation spiral unfolded.

◆ Demand-pull inflation begins when an increase in aggregate demand increases real GDP and increases the price level.

◆ At above full employment, the wage rate rises, short-run aggregate supply decreases, real GDP decreases and the price level rises further.

◆ If aggregate demand keeps increasing, wages chase prices in an unending price–wage inflation spiral.

Next, let's see how shocks to aggregate supply can create a cost-push inflation.

Cost-push Inflation

An inflation that results from an initial increase in costs is called **cost-push inflation**. The two main sources of increases in costs are:

1. An increase in money wage rates
2. An increase in the money prices of raw materials

At a given price level, the higher the cost of production, the smaller is the amount that firms are willing to produce. So if money wage rates rise or if the prices of raw materials (for example oil) rise, firms decrease their supply of goods and services. Aggregate supply decreases and the short-run aggregate supply curve shifts leftward[1]. Let's trace the effects of such a decrease in short-run aggregate supply on the price level and real GDP.

Initial Effect of a Decrease in Aggregate Supply

Suppose that last year the price level was 130 and real GDP was $600 billion. Long-run real GDP was also $600 billion. This situation is shown in Fig. 32.4. The aggregate demand curve was AD_0, the short-run aggregate supply curve was SAS_0 and the long-run

---

[1] Some cost-push forces, such as an increase in the price of oil accompanied by a decrease in the availability of oil, can also decrease long-run aggregate supply. We'll ignore such effects here and examine cost-push factors that change only short-run aggregate supply.

FIGURE 32.4

A Cost-push Rise in the Price Level

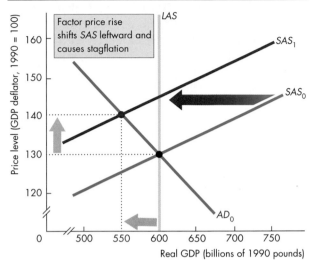

Initially, the aggregate demand curve is AD_0, the short-run aggregate supply curve is SAS_0 and the long-run aggregate supply curve is LAS. A decrease in aggregate supply (for example, resulting from an increase in the world price of oil) shifts the short-run aggregate supply curve to SAS_1. The economy moves to the point where the short-run aggregate supply curve SAS_1 intersects the aggregate demand curve AD_0. The price level rises to 140, and real GDP decreases to £550 billion. The economy experiences inflation and a contraction of real GDP – *stagflation*.

FIGURE 32.5

Aggregate Demand Response to Cost Push

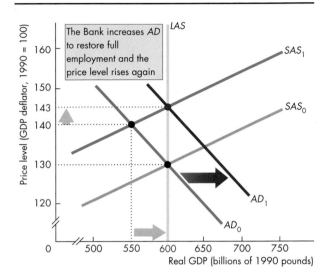

Following a cost-push increase in the price level, real GDP is below potential GDP and unemployment is above the natural rate. If the Bank responds by increasing aggregate demand to restore full employment, the aggregate demand curve shifts rightward to AD_1. The economy returns to full employment, but at the expense of higher inflation. The price level rises to 143.

aggregate supply curve was LAS. In the current year, a sharp increase in world oil prices decreases short-run aggregate supply. The short-run aggregate supply curve shifts leftward to SAS_1. The price level rises to 140, and real GDP decreases to £550 billion. The combination of a rise in the price level and a fall in real GDP is called **stagflation.**

The events we've just studied have created a one-shot change in the price level, like that in Fig. 32.1(b). A supply shock on its own cannot cause inflation. To convert a supply shock into a process of inflation, something more must happen. And it often does as you will now see.

Aggregate Demand Response

When real GDP falls the unemployment rate rises above the natural rate. In such a situation, there is usually an outcry of concern and a call for action to restore full employment. Suppose the Bank

increases the money supply. Aggregate demand increases. In Fig. 32.5, the aggregate demand curve shifts rightward to AD_1. The increase in aggregate demand has restored full employment. But the price level rises to 143, a 10 per cent rise over the original price level.

A Cost-push Inflation Process

Suppose now that the oil producers, who see the prices of everything that they buy with the dollars they receive increase by 10 per cent, decide to increase the price of oil again. Figure 32.6 continues the story. The short-run aggregate supply curve now shifts to SAS_2, and another bout of stagflation ensues. The price level rises further to 154, and real GDP falls to £550 billion. Unemployment increases above its natural rate. If the Bank responds yet again with an increase in the money supply, aggregate demand increases and the aggregate demand curve shifts to AD_2. The price level rises even

FIGURE 32.6

A Cost-push Inflation Spiral

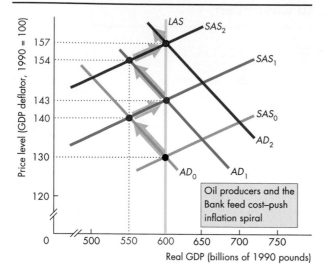

When a cost increase (for example, an increase in the world oil price) decreases short-run aggregate supply from SAS_0 to SAS_1, the price level rises to 140 and real GDP decreases to £550 billion. The Bank responds with an increase in the money supply that shifts the aggregate demand curve from AD_0 to AD_1. The price level rises again to 143 and real GDP returns to £600 billion. A further cost increase occurs, which shifts the short-run aggregate supply curve again, this time to SAS_2. Stagflation is repeated and the price level now rises to 154. The Bank responds again and the cost-push inflation spiral continues.

higher – to 157 – and full employment is again restored. A cost-push inflation spiral results. But if the Bank does not respond, the economy remains below full employment.

You can see that the Bank has a dilemma. If it increases the money supply to restore full employment, it invites another oil price hike that will cause yet a further increase in the money supply. Inflation will rage along at a rate decided by the oil exporting countries. If the Bank keeps the lid on money supply growth, the economy operates with a high level of unemployment.

Cost-push Inflation in Kalamazoo   What is going on in the Kalamazoo lemonade bottling plant when the economy is experiencing cost-push inflation? When the oil price increases, so do the costs of bottling lemonade. These higher costs decrease

the supply of lemonade, increasing its price and decreasing the quantity produced. The lemonade plant lays off some workers. This situation will persist until either the Bank increases aggregate demand or the price of oil falls. If the Bank increases aggregate demand, as it did in the mid-1970s, the demand for lemonade increases and so does its price. The higher price of lemonade brings higher profits and the bottling plant increases its production. The lemonade factory re-hires the laid-off workers.

Cost-push Inflation in the United Kingdom   A cost-push inflation like the one you've just studied occurred in the United Kingdom during the 1970s. It began in 1974 when OPEC raised the price of oil four fold. The higher oil price decreased aggregate supply, which caused the price level to rise more quickly and real GDP to shrink. The Bank then faced a dilemma. Would it increase the quantity of money and accommodate the cost-push forces, or would it keep aggregate demand growth in check by limiting money growth? Money wages began to grow as fast as prices as the unions fought to maintain real wages. The Bank repeatedly allowed the money supply to grow fast and inflation proceeded rapidly.

R E V I E W

◆ Cost-push inflation starts with an increase in the money wage rate or in the money price of a raw material that decreases aggregate supply.

◆ Real GDP decreases and the price level rises – stagflation occurs.

◆ If the Bank increases aggregate demand to restore full employment, a freewheeling cost-push inflation ensues.

Anticipating Inflation

Regardless of whether inflation is demand-pull or cost-push, the failure to *anticipate* it correctly results in unintended consequences. These unintended consequences impose costs on firms and workers. Let's examine these costs.

Unanticipated Inflation in the Labour Market

Unanticipated inflation has two main consequences for the operation of the labour market. They are:

◆ Redistribution of income

◆ Departure from full employment.

Redistribution of Income Unanticipated inflation redistributes income between employers and workers. Sometimes employers gain at the expense of workers and sometimes they lose. If an unexpected increase in aggregate demand increases the inflation rate, then wages will not have been set high enough. Profits will be higher than expected and wages will buy fewer goods than expected. In this case, employers gain at the expense of workers. But if aggregate demand is expected to increase rapidly and it fails to do so, workers gain at the expense of employers. Anticipating a high inflation rate, wages are set too high and profits are squeezed. Redistributions between employers and workers create an incentive for both firms and workers to try to forecast inflation correctly.

Departures from Full Employment Redistribution brings gains to some and losses to others. But departures from full employment impose costs on everyone. To see why, let's return to the lemonade bottling plant in Kalamazoo. If the bottling plant and its workers do not anticipate inflation, but inflation occurs, the money wage rate does not rise to keep up with inflation. The real wage rate falls and the firm tries to hire more labour and increase production. But because the real wage rate has fallen, the firm has difficulty in attracting the labour it wants to employ. It pays overtime rates to its existing work-force and because it runs its plant at a faster pace, it incurs higher plant maintenance and parts replacement costs. Also, because the real wage rate has fallen, workers begin to quit the bottling plant to find jobs that pay a real wage rate closer to that prevailing before the outbreak of inflation. This labour turnover imposes additional costs on the firm. So even though its production increases, the firm incurs additional costs and its profit does not increase. The workers incur additional costs of job search and those who remain at the bottling plant end up feeling cheated. They've worked overtime to produce the extra output and, when they come to spend their wages, they discover that prices have increased, so their wages buy a smaller quantity of goods and services than expected.

If the bottling plant and its workers anticipate a high inflation rate that does not occur, they increase the money wage rate by too much and the real wage rate rises. At the higher real wage rate, the firm lays off some workers and the unemployment rate increases. Those workers who keep their jobs gain, but those who become unemployed lose. The bottling plant also loses because its output and profits fall.

So unanticipated inflation imposes costs regardless of whether the inflation turns out to be higher or lower than anticipated. The presence of these costs gives everyone an incentive to forecast inflation correctly. Let's see how people go about this task.

How People Forecast Inflation

People devote considerable resources to forecasting inflation. Some people specialize in economic forecasting and make a living from it. Other people buy the services of these specialists. The specialist forecasters are economists who work for public and private macroeconomic forecasting agencies and for banks, insurance companies, trade unions and large corporations. The returns these specialists make depend on the quality of their forecasts, so they have a strong incentive to forecast as accurately as possible. The most accurate forecast possible is one that is correct on the average and that has the minimum possible range of error.

Specialist forecasters use statistical models of the economy that are based on (but more detailed than) the aggregate supply–aggregate demand model that you are studying in this book. In the United Kingdom, there are publicly available forecasts of the economy produced by a range of institutions such as the National Institute of Economic and Social Research, the London Business School, Liverpool University Macroeconomic Group and Oxford Economic Forecasting. Short-term forecasts are produced by HM Treasury, but City of London financial institutions also produce forecasts of the economy for their clients and there are several private forecasting agencies such as Lombard Street Research and the St James Group.

Predicting People's Forecasts

Economics tries to predict the choices that people make. Because people's choices depend on their forecasts, we must predict these forecasts in order to predict their choices. How can we predict people's forecasts?

We assume that people are rational in their use of information. In particular, we assume they use all the relevant information available to them. If some information is available that can lead to a better forecast, it will be used. We call a forecast based on all the available relevant information a **rational expectation**. A rational expectation has two features:

1. It is correct on the average.
2. The range of the forecast error is as small as possible.

A forecast that is correct *on the average* is not always correct. Suppose you forecast the outcome of tossing a coin 10 times. You predict there will be 5 heads and 5 tails. On the average (repeating the experiment of coin tossing many times) you are correct. But often you will get 6 heads and 4 tails.

The assumption that people use all the relevant information when they make forecasts does not tell us what information they actually use. So we make one further assumption. They use the *information that economic theory predicts is relevant.* For example, to predict people's expectations of the price of orange juice, we use the economic model of demand and supply, together with all the available information about the positions of the demand and supply curves for orange juice. To make a prediction about people's expectations of the price level and inflation, we use the economic model of aggregate demand and aggregate supply.

Let's see how we can use the model of aggregate demand and aggregate supply to work out the rational expectation of the price level.

Rational Expectation of the Price Level

We use the aggregate supply–aggregate demand model to forecast the price level in much the same way that a meteorologist uses a model of the atmosphere to forecast the weather. But there is a difference between the meteorologist's model of the atmosphere and the economist's model of the economy. In the meteorologist's model, tomorrow's

weather does not depend on people's forecasts of it. In the economist's model, next year's price level *does* depend on people's forecasts of it, because individuals' and firms' behaviour will be influenced by such forecasts. To work out the rational expectation of the price level, we must take account of this dependence of the actual price level on the forecasted price level.

We're going to work out the rational expectation of the price level, using Fig. 32.7 to guide our analysis. The aggregate supply–aggregate demand model predicts that the price level is at the point of intersection of the aggregate demand and short-run aggregate supply curves. To forecast the price level, therefore, we have to forecast the positions of these curves.

Let's begin with aggregate demand. To forecast the position of the aggregate demand curve we must forecast all the variables that influence aggregate demand. Suppose that we have done this and come up with a forecast of aggregate demand given by the curve *EAD*, the *expected* aggregate demand curve.

Our next task is to forecast the position of the short-run aggregate supply curve, but here we have a problem. We know that the position of the short-run aggregate supply curve is determined by two things:

1. Price level falls
2. The money wage rate

The short-run aggregate supply curve intersects the long-run aggregate supply curve at the full-employment price level. So we need a forecast of the position of the long-run aggregate supply curve. To make such a forecast we must forecast all the factors that determine potential GDP. Suppose that we have made the best forecast we can of long-run real GDP and that we expect potential GDP to be $600 billion. The *expected* long-run aggregate supply curve is *ELAS* in Fig. 32.7.

The final ingredient we need is a forecast of the wage rate. Armed with this information, we have a forecast of the point on the *ELAS* curve at which the short-run aggregate supply intersects it. There are two cases to deal with:

◆ The short run
◆ The long run

Rational Expectations in the Short Run   In the short run, the money wage rate is set, so forecasting it is easy. The forecast is the current actual

FIGURE 32.7

Rational Expectation of the Price Level

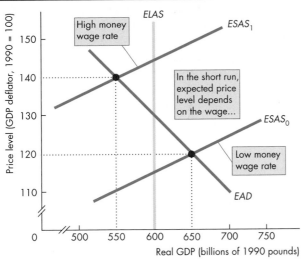

(a) The short run

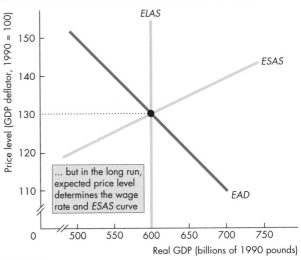

(b) The long run

The rational expectation of the price level is the best available forecast. That forecast is constructed by using the *AS–AD* model and forecasting the variables on which *SAS, LAS* and *AD* depend. These forecasts are the expected short-run aggregate supply curve, *ESAS*, the expected long-run aggregate supply curve, *ELAS*, and the expected aggregate demand curve, *EAD*. In the short run, part (a), wages are fixed and the rational expectation of the price level occurs at the point of intersection of the *ESAS* and *EAD* curves. With a low money wage rate, the expected

short-run aggregate supply curve is $ESAS_0$ and the rational expectation of the price level is 120. With a high money wage rate, the expected short-run aggregate supply curve is $ESAS_1$ and the rational expectation of the price level is 140. In the long run, part (b), wages are flexible and the rational expectation of the price level occurs at the point of intersection of *ELAS* and *EAD*. The money wage rate is expected to adjust to place the expected short-run aggregate supply curve, *ESAS*, through the point of intersection of *ELAS* and *EAD*.

wage rate. Given this fixed wage rate and the expected long-run aggregate supply curve, *ELAS*, there is an expected short-run aggregate supply curve. In Fig. 32.7(a), if the money wage rate is low then the expected short-run aggregate supply curve is $ESAS_0$.

The rational expectation of the price level is the point of intersection of *EAD* and $ESAS_0$, a price level of 120. The rational expectation of inflation is calculated as the percentage amount by which the forecasted future price level exceeds the current price level. For example, if the current price level is 110, and next year's forecasted price level is 120, the expected inflation rate over the year is 9 per cent.

There is also a rational expectation of real GDP. Given the wage rate and the expected short-run aggregate supply curve $ESAS_0$, the rational expectation is that real GDP will be £650 billion and unemployment will be less the natural rate.

Figure 32.7(a) shows another case – one in which the money wage rate is high. With this higher money wage rate, the expected short-run aggregate supply curve is $ESAS_1$. Here the rational expectation of the price level is determined at the point of intersection of *EAD* and $ESAS_1$, an expected price level of 140. With a current price level of 110, the expected inflation rate over the year is 27 per cent. The economy is expected to have an equilibrium real GDP of £550 billion and to have unemployment exceeding the natural rate.

Rational Expectations in the Long Run   In the long run, the expected price level is determined by expected aggregate demand, *EAD*, and expected long-run aggregate supply, *ELAS*. That is, in the long run, wages are flexible and adjust to achieve full employment. As a result, the short-run aggregate supply curve passes through the intersection of the

AD and *LAS* curves. Thus in the long run, the expected short-run aggregate supply curve, *ESAS*, passes through the intersection of the *EAD* and *ELAS* curves.

Figure 32.7(b) illustrates the long-run rational expectation of the price level. The forecasted price level is 130, determined at the intersection of the *EAD* and *ESAS* curves. Here we forecast the position of the short-run aggregate supply curve and the price level at the same time, and the two forecasts are consistent with each other.

You've now seen how we can predict the forecasts of inflation that people make when those forecasts are rational expectations. Suppose people make accurate forecasts of inflation. Do the forecasts of inflation influence the inflation process itself? To answer this question, we must study an anticipated inflation.

Anticipated Inflation

In the demand-pull and cost-push inflations that we studied earlier in this chapter, money wages are sticky. When aggregate demand increases, either to set off a demand-pull inflation or to accommodate a cost-push inflation, the money wage does not change immediately. But if people correctly anticipate increases in aggregate demand, they will adjust money wage rates so as to keep up with anticipated inflation.

In this case, inflation proceeds with real GDP equal to potential GDP and unemployment equal to the natural rate. Figure 32.8 explains why. Suppose that last year the price level was 130 and real GDP was $600 billion, which is also potential GDP. The aggregate demand curve was AD_0, the aggregate supply curve was SAS_0 and the long-run aggregate supply curve was *LAS*. Because real GDP equals potential GDP, the actual price level equals the expected price level.

Suppose that potential GDP does not change and is not expected to change, so the actual and expected long-run aggregate supply curve does not change. Also suppose that aggregate demand is expected to increase and that the expected aggregate demand curve for this year is AD_1. We can now calculate the rational expectation of the price level for this year. It is a price level of 143, the level at which the new expected aggregate demand curve intersects the expected long-run aggregate supply curve. The expected inflation rate is 10 per cent, the percentage change in the price level from 130 to 143.

Anticipating this inflation, money wage rates rise and the short-run aggregate supply curve shifts leftward. In particular, given that expected inflation is 10 per cent, the short-run aggregate supply curve for next year (SAS_1) passes through the long-run aggregate supply curve (*LAS*) at the expected price level.

If aggregate demand turns out to be the same as expected, the actual aggregate demand curve is AD_1. The intersection point of AD_1 and SAS_1 determines the actual price level – where the price level is 143. Between last year and this year, the price level increased from 130 to 143 and the economy experienced an inflation rate of 10 per cent, the same as the inflation rate that was anticipated.

What caused the inflation? The immediate answer is that because people expected inflation, they increased wages and increased prices. But the expectation was correct. Aggregate demand was expected to increase and it did increase. Because aggregate demand was *expected* to increase from AD_0 to AD_1, the short-run aggregate supply curve shifted upward from SAS_0 to SAS_1. Because aggregate demand actually did increase by the amount that was expected, the actual aggregate demand curve shifted from AD_0 to AD_1. The combination of the anticipated and actual shifts of the aggregate demand curve rightward produced an increase in the price level that was anticipated.

Only if aggregate demand growth is correctly forecasted does the economy follow the course described in Fig. 32.8. If the expected growth rate of aggregate demand is different from its actual growth rate, the expected aggregate demand curve shifts by an amount different from the actual aggregate demand curve. The inflation rate departs from its expected level and, to some extent, there is unanticipated inflation.

Unanticipated Inflation

Demand-pull inflation can be interpreted as unanticipated inflation. Some inflation is expected and the money wage rate is set to reflect that expectation. The *SAS* curve intersects the *LAS* curve at the expected price level. Aggregate demand then increases, but by more than expected. The *AD* curve intersects the *SAS* curve at a level of real GDP that exceeds potential GDP. The money wage rate adjusts, aggregate demand increases again and the demand-pull spiral unwinds. So demand-pull

FIGURE 32.8

Anticipated Inflation

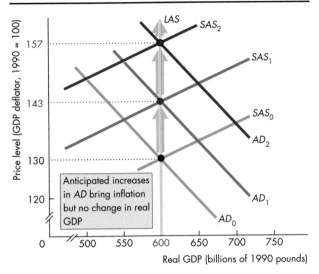

The actual and expected long-run aggregate supply curve (*LAS*) is at a real GDP of £600 billion. Last year, aggregate demand was *AD*$_0$ and the short-run aggregate supply curve was *SAS*$_0$. The actual price level was the same as the expected price level – 130. This year, aggregate demand is expected to rise to *AD*$_1$. The rational expectation of the price level changes from 130 to 143. As a result, the short-run aggregate supply curve shifts up to *SAS*$_1$. If aggregate demand actually increases as expected, the actual aggregate demand curve *AD*$_1$ is the same as the expected aggregate demand curve. Equilibrium occurs at a real GDP of £600 billion and an actual price level of 143. The inflation is correctly anticipated. Next year the process continues with aggregate demand increasing as expected to *AD*$_2$ and wages rising to shift the short-run aggregate supply curve to *SAS*$_2$. Again, real GDP remains at £600 billion and the price level rises, as anticipated, to 157.

inflation can be interpreted as being an unanticipated inflation in which aggregate demand increases by *more* than was expected.

Cost-push inflation can also be interpreted as unanticipated inflation. Expectations are formed about the increase in aggregate demand. Based on this expectation, the money wage rate rises and the *SAS* curve shifts leftward. Aggregate demand then increases, but by *less* than expected. The *AD* curve intersects the *SAS* curve at a level of real GDP below potential GDP. Aggregate demand increases to restore full employment. But if the increase in aggregate demand is less than expected wages again rise

and short-run aggregate supply again decreases and a cost-push spiral unwinds. So cost-push inflation can be interpreted as being an unanticipated inflation in which aggregate demand increases by *less* than was expected.

We've seen that only when inflation is unanticipated does real GDP depart from potential GDP. When inflation is anticipated, real GDP remains at potential GDP. Does this mean that an anticipated inflation has no costs?

The Costs of Anticipated Inflation

An anticipated inflation at a moderate rate – 2 or 3 per cent a year – probably has a small cost. But an anticipated inflation at a rapid rate is extremely costly. The costs can be summarized under four broad headings:

◆ 'Shoeleather costs'

◆ Efficiency costs

◆ Decrease in potential GDP

◆ Economic growth costs

'Shoeleather Costs'   The so-called 'shoeleather costs' of inflation are costs that arise from an increase in the velocity of circulation of money and an increase in the amount of running around that people do to try to avoid incurring losses from the falling value of money.

When money loses value at a rapid anticipated rate, it does not function well as a medium of exchange and people try to avoid holding money. They spend their incomes as soon as they receive them, and firms pay out incomes – wages and dividends – as soon as they receive revenue from their sales. The velocity of circulation increases. During the 1920s, when inflation in Germany reached *hyperinflation* levels (rates in excess of 50 per cent a month), wages were paid and spent twice in a single day!

The 'shoeleather costs' have been estimated to be between 1 per cent and 2 per cent of GDP for a 10 per cent inflation. For a rapid inflation they are much more.

Efficiency Costs   At high anticipated inflation rates, people seek alternatives to money as a means of payment and use tokens and commodities or even barter, all of which are less efficient than money as means of payment. For example, during the 1980s when inflation in Israel reached 1,000 per cent a year, the US dollar started to replace the increasingly worthless shekel. As a result, people had to keep track of the exchange rate between the shekel and the dollar hour by hour and engage in many additional and costly transactions in the foreign exchange market.

A Decrease in Potential GDP Because anticipated inflation increases transactions costs, it diverts resources from producing goods and services and it decreases potential GDP. In terms of the aggregate supply–aggregate demand model, a rapid anticipated inflation decreases potential GDP and shifts the *LAS* curve leftward. The faster the anticipated inflation rate, the further leftward the *LAS* curve shifts. By how much does potential GDP fall?

Economic Growth Costs The most serious cost of an anticipated inflation is a fall in the long-term growth rate of GDP. This cost has three sources. The first comes from the way inflation interacts with the tax system. Anticipated inflation swells the money returns on investments, but it does not change the real returns. However, money returns are taxed, so effective tax rates rise. With lower after-tax returns, businesses have less incentive to invest in new capital. A decrease in investment cuts the rate of real GDP growth. This effect becomes serious at even modest inflation rates. Let's consider an example.

Suppose the real interest rate is 4 per cent a year and the tax rate is 50 per cent. With no inflation, the nominal interest is also 4 per cent a year and 50 per cent of this rate is taxable. The real *after-tax* interest rate is 2 per cent a year (50 per cent of 4 per cent). Now suppose the inflation rate is 4 per cent a year so that the nominal rate is 8 per cent a year. The *after-tax* nominal rate is 4 per cent (50 per cent of 8 per cent). Now subtract the 4 per cent inflation rate from this amount and you see that the *after-tax real interest* rate is zero! The true tax rate on interest income is 100 per cent. If the inflation rate was greater than 4 per cent in this example, the true tax rate would exceed 100 per cent and the after-tax real interest rate would be negative.

With a low or possibly even negative after-tax real interest rate, the incentive to save is weakened and the saving rate falls. With a fall in saving, the pace of capital accumulation slows and so does the long-term growth rate of real GDP.

The second economic growth cost arises because instead of concentrating on the activities at which they have a comparative advantage, people find it more profitable to search for ways of avoiding the losses that inflation inflicts. As a result, inventive talent that might otherwise work on productive innovations works on finding ways of profiting from or avoiding losses from the inflation.

The third source of a fall in the economic growth rate arises because when the inflation rate is high, there is increased uncertainty about the long-term inflation rate. Will inflation remain high for a long time or will price stability be restored? This increased uncertainty makes long-term planning difficult and gives people a shorter-term focus. Investment falls and so the growth rate slows.

Efficiency costs and economic growth costs are estimated to be much higher than the shoeleather and other costs and range between 5 per cent and 7 per cent of GDP for a 10 per cent inflation. The productivity growth slowdown of the 1970s can partly be attributed to the inflation outburst at that time.

There are many examples of rapid anticipated inflations around the world, especially in Argentina, Bolivia and Brazil, in Russia and other East European countries, and in some of the African countries where the costs of anticipated inflation are much greater than the modest numbers given here.

REVIEW

◆ Wrong inflation forecasts are costly. To minimize forecasting errors, people use all the available information and make a rational expectation.

◆ Anticipated changes in aggregate demand and aggregate supply result in anticipated inflation.

◆ A rapid anticipated inflation diverts resources from producing goods and services and decreases potential GDP.

Inflation and Unemployment: The Phillips Curve

W e've seen that a speedup in aggregate demand growth that is not fully anticipated increases both inflation and real GDP growth. It also decreases unemployment. Similarly, a slow-down in the growth rate of aggregate demand that is not fully anticipated slows down both inflation and real GDP growth. It also increases unemployment. We've seen that a fully anticipated change in the growth rate of aggregate demand changes the inflation rate and has no effect on real GDP or unemployment. Finally, we've seen that a decrease in aggregate supply increases inflation and decreases real GDP growth. In this case, unemployment increases.

The aggregate supply–aggregate demand model that we have used to obtain these results gives predictions about the level of real GDP and the price level. Given these predictions, we can work out how unemployment and inflation have changed. But the aggregate supply–aggregate demand model does not place inflation and unemployment at the centre of the stage.

An alternative way of studying inflation and unemployment focuses directly on their joint movements and uses a relationship called the Phillips curve. The Phillips curve approach uses the same basic ideas as the *AS–AD* model, but it views the economy in an alternative way. The Phillips curve is so named because it was popularized by a New Zealand economist, A. W. Phillips, when he was working at the London School of Economics in the 1950s. A **Phillips curve** is a curve showing the relationship between inflation and unemployment. There are two time-frames for Phillips curves:

- ◆ The short-run Phillips curve
- ◆ The long-run Phillips curve

The Short-run Phillips Curve

The **short-run Phillips curve** is a curve showing the relationship between inflation and unemployment, holding constant:

1. The expected inflation rate
2. The natural unemployment rate

Figure 32.9 shows a short-run Phillips curve, *SRPC*. Suppose that the expected inflation rate is 10 per cent a year and the natural unemployment rate is 6 per cent, point *a* in the figure. A short-run Phillips curve passes through this point. If inflation rises above its expected rate, the unemployment rate falls below its natural rate. This joint movement in the inflation rate and the unemployment rate is illustrated as a movement up the short-run Phillips curve from point *a* to point *b* in the figure. Similarly, if inflation falls below its expected rate, unemployment rises above the natural rate. In this case, there is movement down the short-run Phillips curve from point *a* to point *c*.

This negative relationship between inflation and unemployment along the short-run Phillips curve is explained by the aggregate supply–aggregate

---

FIGURE 32.9

A Short-run Phillips Curve

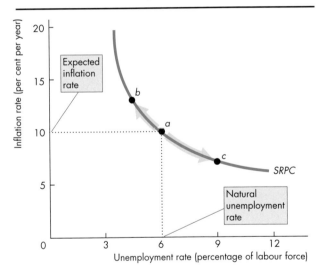

The short-run Phillips curve *SRPC* shows the relationship between inflation and unemployment at a given expected inflation rate and given natural unemployment rate. With an expected inflation rate of 10 per cent a year and a natural unemployment rate of 6 per cent, the short-run Phillips curve passes through point *a*. An unanticipated increase in aggregate demand lowers unemployment and increases inflation – a movement up the short-run Phillips curve. An unanticipated decrease in aggregate demand increases unemployment and lowers inflation – a movement down the short-run Phillips curve.

demand model. Figure 32.10 explains the connection between the two approaches. Suppose that, initially, inflation is anticipated to be 10 per cent a year and unemployment is at its natural rate.

In Fig. 32.10 the aggregate demand curve is AD_0, the short-run aggregate supply curve is SAS_0, and the long-run aggregate supply curve is LAS. Real GDP is £600 billion and the price level is 100. Money growth increases aggregate demand and the aggregate demand curve shifts rightward to AD_1, and anticipating this increase in aggregate demand, the money wage rate rises, which shifts the short-run aggregate supply curve to SAS_1. The price level rises from 100 to 110 and the inflation rate is an antici-

pated 10 per cent a year. We can describe the economy as being at point a in Fig. 32.10. It is also at point a on the short-run Phillips curve in Fig. 32.9.

Now suppose that instead of increasing as expected to AD_1, aggregate demand increases to AD_2. The price level now rises to 113, a 13 per cent inflation rate and real GDP rises above potential GDP. We can now describe the economy as being at point b in Fig. 32.10 or at point b on the short-run Phillips curve in Fig. 32.9.

Finally, suppose that instead of increasing as expected to AD_1, aggregate demand remains constant at AD_0. The price level now rises to 107, a 7 per cent inflation rate, and real GDP falls below potential GDP. We can now describe the economy as being at point c in Fig. 32.10 or at point c on the short-run Phillips curve in Fig. 32.9.

FIGURE 32.10

AS–AD and the Short-run Phillips Curve

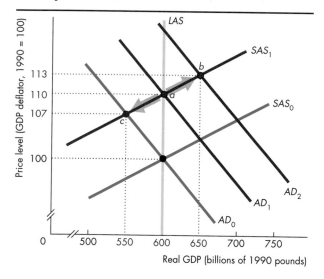

If aggregate demand is expected to increase and shift the aggregate demand curve from AD_0 to AD_1, then the money wage rate rises by an amount that shifts the short-run aggregate supply curve from SAS_0 to SAS_1. The price level rises to 110, a 10 per cent rise, and the economy is at point a in this figure and at point a on the short-run Phillips curve in Fig. 32.9. If with the same expectations, aggregate demand increases and shifts the aggregate demand curve from AD_0 to AD_2, the price level rises to 113, a 13 per cent rise, and the economy is at point b in this figure and at point b on the short-run Phillips curve in Fig. 32.9. If with the same expectations, aggregate demand does not change, the price level rises to 107, a 7 per cent rise, and the economy is at point c in this figure and at point c on the short-run Phillips curve in Fig. 32.9.

The Long-run Phillips Curve

The **long-run Phillips curve** is a curve that shows the relationship between inflation and unemployment, when the actual inflation rate equals the expected inflation rate. The long-run Phillips curve is vertical at the natural unemployment rate. It is shown in Fig. 32.11 as the vertical line $LRPC$. The long-run Phillips curve tells us that any anticipated inflation rate is possible at the natural unemployment rate. This proposition is the same as the one you discovered in the AS–AD model. When inflation is anticipated, real GDP remains at potential GDP. Real GDP being at potential GDP is equivalent to unemployment being at the natural rate.

If the expected inflation rate is 10 per cent a year, the short-run Phillips curve is $SRPC_0$. If the expected inflation rate falls to 7 per cent a year, the short-run Phillips curve shifts downward to $SRPC_1$. The distance by which the short-run Phillips curve shifts downward when the expected inflation rate falls is equal to the change in the expected inflation rate.

To see why the short-run Phillips curve shifts when the expected inflation rate changes let's do an experiment. The economy is at full employment and a fully anticipated inflation is raging at 10 per cent a year. The Bank now begins a permanent attack on inflation by slowing money supply growth and cutting the deficit. Aggregate demand growth slows down and the inflation rate falls to 7 per cent a year. At first, this decrease in inflation is unanticipated, so wages continue to rise at their original rate, shifting the short-run aggregate supply curve

FIGURE 32.11

FIGURE 32.11

Short-run and Long-run Phillips Curves

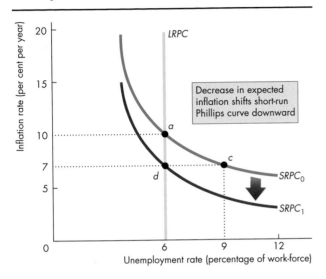

The long-run Phillips curve is *LRPC*, a vertical line at the natural unemployment rate. A fall in inflation expectations shifts the short-run Phillips curve downward by the amount of the fall in the expected inflation rate. In this figure, when the expected inflation rate falls from 10 per cent a year to 7 per cent a year, the short-run Phillips curve shifts downward from $SRPC_0$ to $SRPC_1$. The new short-run Phillips curve intersects the long-run Phillips curve at the new expected inflation rate – point *d*. With the original expected inflation rate (of 10 per cent), an inflation rate of 7 per cent a year would occur at an unemployment rate of 9 per cent, at point *c*.

leftward at the same pace as before. Real GDP falls and unemployment increases. In Fig. 32.11, the economy moves from point *a* to point *c* on the short-run Phillips curve $SRPC_0$.

If the actual inflation rate remains steady at 7 per cent a year, eventually this rate will come to be expected. As this happens, wage growth slows down and the short-run aggregate supply curve shifts leftward less quickly. Eventually it shifts leftward at the same pace at which the aggregate demand curve is shifting rightward. The actual inflation rate equals the expected inflation rate and full employment is restored. Unemployment is back at its natural rate. In Fig. 32.11, the short-run Phillips curve has shifted from $SRPC_0$ to $SRPC_1$ and the economy is at point *d*.

Changes in the Natural Unemployment Rate

The natural unemployment rate changes for many reasons that are explained in Chapter 24 (pp. 610–612). A change in the natural unemployment rate shifts both the short-run and the long-run Phillips curves. Such shifts are illustrated in Fig. 32.12. If the natural unemployment rate increases from 6 per cent to 9 per cent, the long-run Phillips curve shifts from $LRPC_0$ to $LRPC_1$, and if expected inflation is constant at 10 per cent a year, the short-run Phillips curve shifts from $SRPC_0$ to $SRPC_1$. Because the expected inflation rate is constant, the short-run Phillips curve $SRPC_1$ intersects the long-run curve $LRPC_1$ (point *e*) at the same inflation rate at which the short-run Phillips curve $SRPC_0$ intersects the long-run curve $LRPC_0$ (point *a*).

FIGURE 32.12

A Change in the Natural Unemployment Rate

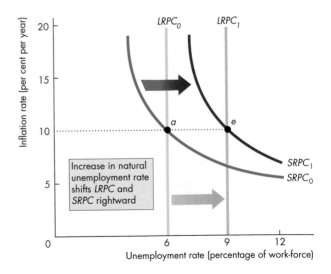

A change in the natural unemployment rate shifts both the short-run and long-run Phillips curves. Here the natural unemployment rate increases from 6 per cent to 9 per cent, and the two Phillips curves shift rightward to $SRPC_1$ and $LRPC_1$. The new long-run Phillips curve intersects the new short-run Phillips curve at the expected inflation rate – point *e*.

The Phillips Curve in the United Kingdom

Figure 32.13 shows the relationship between inflation and unemployment in the United Kingdom. Begin by looking at part (a), a scatter diagram of inflation and unemployment since 1960. Each dot in the figure represents the combination of inflation and unemployment for a particular year. As you can see, there does not appear to be any clear relationship between inflation and unemployment. We certainly cannot see a Phillips curve similar to that shown in Fig. 32.9.

But we can interpret the data in terms of a shifting short-run Phillips curve. Figure 32.13(b) provides such an interpretation. Four short-run Phillips curves appear in the figure. The short-run

Phillips curve of the 1960s is $SRPC_0$. At that time, the expected inflation rate was 2 per cent a year and the natural unemployment rate was also 2 per cent.

The short-run Phillips curve of the 1970s is $SRPC_1$. The second period has a natural unemployment rate higher than that of the 1960s, and an expected inflation rate that is much higher. The short-run Phillips curve of the late 1970s and early 1980s is $SRPC_2$. This Phillips curve is the result of a series of supply shocks that raised the natural rate. The short-run Phillips curve of the late 1980s and 1990s is $SRPC_3$. This period marks the many supply side policies followed by the government of the former prime minister, Mrs Thatcher. These supply side policies, which made the labour market more flexible, had profound effects on the natural unemployment rate, which decreased possibly to 6 per cent but some economists think it could even be lower.

FIGURE 32.13

Phillips Curves in the United Kingdom

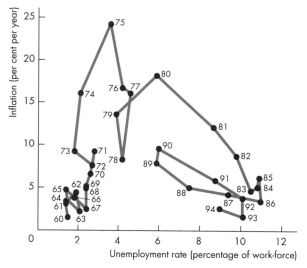

(a) Time sequence

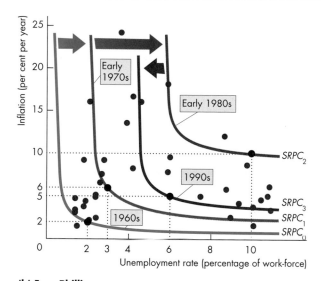

(b) Four Phillips curves

In part (a) each dot represents the combination of inflation and unemployment for a particular year in the United Kingdom. There is no clear relationship between the two variables. Part (b) interprets the data in terms of a shifting short-run Phillips curve. The short-run Phillips curve of the 1960s when the expected inflation rate was 2 per cent a year, and the natural unemployment rate was also 2 per cent is $SRPC_0$. The short-run Phillips curve of the early 1970s is $SRPC_1$. This period has a natural unemployment rate of 3 per cent, but a higher expected

inflation rate. The oil price shock increased both the natural unemployment rate and the expected inflation rate in the early 1970s. By the early 1980s, the effect of the oil shock and domestic supply factors had increased the natural rate of unemployment to over 10 per cent. The short-run Phillips curve is $SRPC_2$. The monetary policy and supply side reforms of the Thatcher government during the 1980s caused the natural rate of unemployment to decline to 6 per cent and the expected rate of inflation to fall to 5 per cent in the 1990s, as shown by $SRPC_3$.

<table>
<tr><td>

REVIEW

◆ An unanticipated change in the inflation rate changes the unemployment rate in the opposite direction and results in a movement along the short-run Phillips curve.

◆ A change in the expected inflation rate shifts the short-run Phillips curve (upward for an increase in inflation and downward for a decrease in inflation) by an amount equal to the change in the expected inflation rate.

◆ A change in the natural unemployment rate shifts both the short-run and the long-run Phillips curves (rightward for an increase in the natural rate and leftward for a decrease).

◆ The relationship between inflation and unemployment in the United Kingdom can be interpreted in terms of a shifting short-run Phillips curve.

</td></tr>
</table>

So far, we've studied the effects of inflation on real GDP, real wages, employment and unemployment. But inflation lowers the value of money and changes the real value of the amounts borrowed and repaid. As a result, interest rates are influenced by inflation. Let's see how.

Interest Rates and Inflation

In the mid-1990s, companies could borrow at interest rates of less than 7 per cent a year. But in the early 1980s, borrowing interest rates were around 14 per cent a year. Why do interest rates fluctuate so much and why were they so high in the early 1980s? Part of the answer is explained in Chapter 25, where the forces that determine the real interest rate are explained. (The **real interest rate** is the *nominal* interest rate minus the inflation rate.) Fluctuations in the real interest rate are caused by fluctuations in saving supply and investment demand. But another part of the answer – a major part – is that the inflation rate was low during the 1960s and high during the early 1980s. With changes in the inflation rate, nominal interest rates change to make borrowers pay and to compensate lenders for the fall in the value of money. Let's see how inflation affects borrowers and lenders.

The Effects of Inflation on Borrowers and Lenders

The *nominal* interest rate is the price paid by a borrower to compensate a lender only for the amount loaned. The *real* interest rate is the price paid by a borrower to compensate a lender for the amount loaned and for the fall in the value of money that results from inflation. The forces of demand and supply determine an equilibrium real interest rate that does not depend on the inflation rate. These same forces also determine an equilibrium nominal interest rate that *does* depend on the inflation rate and that equals the equilibrium *real* interest rate plus the expected inflation rate.

To see why these outcomes occur, imagine there is no inflation and that the nominal interest rate is 4 per cent a year. The real interest rate is also 4 per cent a year. The amount that businesses and people want to borrow equals the amount that businesses and people want to lend at this real interest rate. British Petroleum (BP) is willing to pay an interest rate of 4 per cent a year to get the funds it needs to pay for its global investment in new oil exploration sites. Sue, and thousands of people like her, are willing to lend BP the amount it needs for its exploration work if they can get a *real* return of 4 per cent a year. (Sue wants to buy a new car and she plans a consumption and saving strategy to achieve this objective.)

Now suppose inflation breaks out at a steady 6 per cent a year. All prices and values, including oil exploration profits and car prices, rise by 6 per cent a year. If BP was willing to pay a 4 per cent interest rate when there was no inflation, it is now willing to pay 10 per cent interest. The reason is that its profits are rising by 6 per cent a year, owing to the 6 per cent inflation, so it is *really* paying only 4 per cent. Similarly, if Sue was willing to lend at a 4 per cent interest rate when there was no inflation, she is now willing to lend only if she gets 10 per cent interest. The price of the car Sue is planning to buy is rising by 6 per cent a year, owing to the 6 per cent inflation, so she is *really* getting only a 4 per cent interest rate.

Because borrowers are willing to pay the higher rate and lenders are willing to lend only if they receive the higher rate, when inflation is anticipated the *nominal interest rate* increases by an amount equal to the expected inflation rate. The *real interest rate* remains constant. (The real interest rate might change because the supply of saving or investment demand has changed for some other reason. But a change in the expected inflation rate alone does not change the real interest rate.)

We've seen why the behaviour of borrowers and lenders makes the nominal interest rate change when the expected inflation rate changes. Let's look at the mechanism in the money market that brings this change about. We'll first see what happens when the inflation rate changes but the change is *not* anticipated. Then we'll see what happens as the inflation comes to be expected.

Interest Rates and Unanticipated Inflation

We'll work out the effects of inflation on interest rates by using Fig. 32.14. This figure is similar to Fig. 31.12 (p. 821) which explains the effects of the Bank's actions on interest rates. Initially, the economy is at full employment and there is no inflation and none is expected. The *real* quantity of money is £500 billion and the money supply curve is MS_0. The demand for money curve is MD and the interest rate is 4 per cent a year. This interest rate is both the *nominal* interest rate and the *real* interest rate. To see why, recall that

$$\text{Real interest} \atop \text{rate} = {\text{Nominal interest} \atop \text{rate}} - {\text{Inflation} \atop \text{rate}}$$

Because the inflation rate is zero, the real and nominal interest rates are the same.

To get an inflation going, the Bank must increase the quantity of money. Suppose the Bank increases the quantity of money to £530 billion – a 6 per cent increase – so that the money supply curve shifts rightward to MS_1. The nominal interest rate falls to 3 per cent a year.

With a lower interest rate, aggregate planned expenditure increases and the aggregate demand curve shifts rightward. Both real GDP and the price level rise. The higher real GDP increases the demand for money. (To prevent the figure from becoming too crowded, this shift is not shown in Fig. 32.14.) The higher price level decreases the quantity of *real* money and the money supply curve shifts leftward. Both of these influences increase the interest rate.

With real GDP above its long-run level, wages begin to rise. As they do so, the short-run aggregate supply curve shifts leftward. The price level rises

Money Growth, Inflation and the Interest Rate

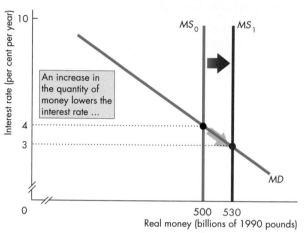

(a) Unanticipated increase in money

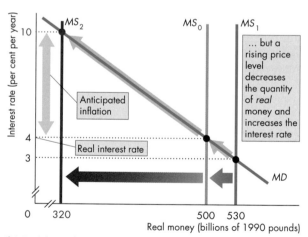

(b) Anticipated money growth

Initially, there is no inflation and none is expected. The demand for money curve is MD, the supply of money curve is MS_0 and the interest rate (*nominal* and *real*) is 4 per cent a year. The Bank increases the quantity of money and the money supply curve shifts rightward to MS_1. In part (a), the nominal interest rate falls to 3 per cent a year.

In part (b), as the price level rises, the quantity of real money decreases and the interest rate returns to its original level. If the Bank continues to increase the quantity of money and if people anticipate the resulting inflation, the price level continues to rise and the quantity of real money falls until the interest rate increases above its original level by an amount equal to the anticipated inflation rate.

yet higher and real GDP decreases as the economy heads back towards full employment. When full employment is again restored, real GDP is back at its original level and the price level has increased by the same percentage as the money supply. Fig. 32.14(b) shows the effects of these events in the money market as the money supply curve shifts leftward from MS_1 back to MS_0. The quantity of real money is back at its original level of £500 billion and the interest rate is back at 4 per cent.

Interest Rates and Anticipated Inflation

Suppose the Bank increases the quantity of money just once and then holds the quantity steady. In this case, the price level remains constant at its higher level, inflation returns to zero and the interest rate returns to its initial level – 4 per cent in the example we've just studied. But suppose the Bank continues to increase the quantity of money by 6 per cent a year and that people come to anticipate a resulting 6 per cent a year inflation. (To keep things simple, we are ignoring growing potential GDP.) In these circumstances, people are not willing to hold bonds at an interest rate of 4 per cent a year. Why not? Because the *real* interest rate has fallen.

Because people don't want to hold as many bonds, they sell bonds and increase their demand for goods and services. As they do so, the price of bonds falls and the interest rate increases. At the same time, aggregate demand increases faster and the inflation rate speeds up to a rate that for a period exceeds the rate at which the quantity of money is increasing. The quantity of *real* money decreases further as the interest rate increases.

Only when interest rates have increased by enough to compensate bond holders for the anticipated falling value of money is a long-run equilibrium restored. Such an equilibrium is shown in Fig. 32.14(b). When the real money supply has decreased to MS_2 and the interest rate has increased to 10 per cent, the *real* interest rate has returned to its original level of 4 per cent a year. This is the long-run equilibrium.

We've seen that an unanticipated inflation leads to a decrease in the real interest rate and that an anticipated inflation leads to an increase in the nominal interest rate and no change in the real interest rate. Therefore, the higher the anticipated inflation rate, the higher is the nominal interest rate. To the extent that inflation is in fact anticipated, interest rates and the inflation rate will move up and down together. Let's see if they do.

Inflation and Interest Rates in the United Kingdom

The relationship between inflation and nominal interest rates in the United Kingdom is illustrated in Fig. 32.15. The interest rate measured on the vertical axis is that paid by large corporations on short-term (3-month) loans. Each point on the graph represents a year in recent UK macroeconomic history between 1960 and 1994. The blue line shows the relationship between the nominal interest rate and the inflation rate if the real interest rate is constant at 3 per cent a year, its actual average value in this period. As you can see, there is a clear relationship between the inflation rate and

FIGURE 32.15

Inflation and the Interest Rate

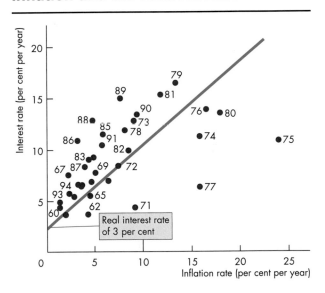

Other things remaining the same, the higher the expected inflation rate, the higher is the nominal interest rate. A graph showing the relationship between interest rates and the actual inflation rate reveals that the influence of inflation on interest rates is a powerful one. Here, the interest rate is that paid by banks on 3-month loans between each other. Each point represents a year in UK macroeconomic history between 1960 and 1994.

Source: Central Statistical Office, *Economic Trends Annual Supplement*, 1995.

the interest rate, but it is not exact. As we have just seen, it is only *anticipated* inflation that influences interest rates. Thus only to the extent that a higher inflation rate is anticipated, does it result in higher interest rates.

During the 1960s, both actual and expected inflation were moderate and so were nominal interest rates. In the early 1970s, inflation began to increase, but it was not expected to increase much and certainly not to persist. As a result, nominal interest rates did not rise much at that time. By the mid-1970s, there was a burst of unexpectedly high inflation. Interest rates increased somewhat but not by nearly as much as the inflation rate. During the late 1970s and early 1980s, inflation of between 15 and 20 per cent a year came to be expected as an ongoing and highly persistent phenomenon. As a result, nominal interest rates increased to around 12–14 per cent a year. Then in 1982, the inflation rate fell – at first unexpectedly. Interest rates began to fall but not nearly as quickly as the inflation rate. Short-term interest rates fell more quickly than long-term interest rates because, at that time, it was expected that inflation would be lower in the short term but not so low in the longer term.

The relationship between inflation and interest rates is even more dramatically illustrated by international experience. For example, in recent years Chile has experienced an inflation rate of around 30 per cent with nominal interest rates of about 40 per cent. Brazil has experienced inflation rates and nominal interest rates of 30 per cent a *month*. At the other extreme, such countries as Japan and Belgium have low inflation and low nominal interest rates.

R E V I E W

◆ The nominal interest rate is the rate actually paid and received in the marketplace.

◆ The real interest rate is the rate really paid and received when the effects of inflation are taken into account.

◆ The real interest rate is equal to the nominal interest rate minus the inflation rate.

◆ There is a strong correlation between the inflation rate and the nominal interest rate – other things remaining the same, an anticipated increase in the inflation rate brings an equal increase in the nominal interest rate.

The Politics of Inflation

We noted at the beginning of this chapter that inflation has plagued nations over many centuries, from the Roman empire to modern Russia. (There are examples of inflation from even earlier times going back to the earliest civilizations.) What are the deeper sources of inflation that are common to all these vastly different societies? The answer lies in the political situation. There are two main political sources of inflation. They are:

◆ Inflation tax
◆ Credibility and reputation

Inflation Tax

Inflation is not a tax in the usual sense. Governments don't pass inflation tax laws like income tax and sales tax laws. But inflation works just like a tax. One way in which a government can finance its expenditure is by selling bonds to the central bank. If the government sells bonds to the central bank, those bonds are paid for with new money – with an increase in the monetary base. When the government finances its expenditure in this way, the quantity of money increases. So the government gets revenues from inflation just as if it had increased taxes. And the holders of money pay this tax to the government. They do so because the real value of their money holdings decreases at a rate equal to the inflation rate.

Inflation is not used as a major source of tax revenue in the United Kingdom or in any developed economy. But in some countries it is. The closing years of the Roman empire and the transition years to a market economy in Russia and Eastern Europe are examples. In the case of the Roman empire, the empire had grown beyond its capacity to administer the collection of taxes on a scale sufficient to cover the expenditures of the government. In the case of Russia, the traditional source of government revenue was from state-owned enterprises. In the transition to a market economy, government revenue from these enterprises dried up but expenditure commitments did not decline in line with this loss of revenue. In both cases, the inflation was used to finance expenditures.

As a general rule, the inflation tax is used when conventional revenue sources are insufficient to cover expenditures and the larger the revenue shortfall, the larger is the inflation tax and the inflation rate.

Credibility and Reputation

One objective of fiscal and monetary policy is to stabilize aggregate demand and keep the economy close to full employment. If demand increases too quickly, the economy overheats and inflation increases. If demand increases too slowly, recession occurs and inflation declines.

One of the problems with conducting a low inflation policy is that people who need to forecast inflation and interest rates may have a different expectation of inflation from the central bank. The government, through the central bank, may conduct a policy that decreases the rate of growth of money and reduces inflation. Short-term rates of interest may decline because inflation in the short term may be lower, but long-term rates may not decline because people expect long-term inflation to remain high. This can occur if people anticipate that the policy of low monetary growth now will be reversed at some point in the future. While current inflation may be low, bond holders may anticipate higher inflation in the future and decide to sell some bonds, thus reducing the price of bonds and raising the long-term rate of interest. Why would people have such an expectation? The reason is that they do not believe that the central bank, and through it the government, will stick to its plans of keeping inflation low. They may believe that once people adjust their expectations of inflation and anticipate low inflation, the government may be tempted to increase the money supply growth and increase aggregate demand by more than expected. In other words, people do not think that the policy has *credibility*. One reason people do not trust the government is that it may not have a *reputation* for trustworthiness. Too often have governments said one thing and done another.

A policy is credible if the cost of conducting it is perceived by the people as less than an alternative policy. There is always an incentive for a government that has promised low inflation to expand the economy by increasing the growth rate of money and to temporarily reduce unemployment – particularly before an election year. The benefits of lower unemployment will be reaped immediately, but the costs of higher inflation and unemployment will be felt in the future. A government may avoid the temptation to expand demand after reducing inflation only if it values its reputation.

Some economists argue that independence for the central bank improves the credibility of a programme; others suggest that credibility is obtained by joining an exchange rate agreement such as the European Monetary System (see Chapter 36). A good reputation for consistent macroeconomic policy can only be earned over a period of time. The German central bank, the Bundesbank, has a good reputation for low inflation. *Reading Between the Lines* on pp. 854–855 examines the credibility of recent UK inflation policy.

R E V I E W

◆ Inflation is a source of government revenue – inflation is a tax – and when conventional revenue sources are inadequate, then an inflation tax is used.

◆ Inflation makes it harder for governments to establish an anti-inflation reputation.

◆ A low inflation policy is credible only if the costs of having such a policy are lower than any other, or if governments have a reputation for low inflation and trustworthiness.

◆ ◆ ◆ ◆ You have now completed your study of inflation. This material, together with that on economic growth (Chapter 27), gives a good overview of the long-term problems that confront a modern economy. Our next task (in the following chapter) is to focus more sharply on the problems of the business cycle and unemployment. Then, with a good understanding of both the long-term trends and the business cycle fluctuations, we'll study in Chapter 34 the policy challenges that make it difficult to achieve rapid growth and avoid excessive unemployment and inflation.

Inflation: Keeping the Enemy at Bay

The Essence of the Story

THE FINANCIAL TIMES, 3 SEPTEMBER 1996

Inflation tea leaves reveal a mixed picture

Graham Bowley

The longer-term looks less rosy, despite a current rate of 2.2%

Mr Kenneth Clarke, the chancellor, and Mr Eddie George, governor of the Bank of England, meet again tomorrow in the latest round of their fight against public enemy number one – inflation.

As the two men inspect the latest inflationary tea leaves, they will be reassured that the prospects look good – although Mr George, whose job it is to be the hawk on inflation, may point to some worrying signs such as yesterday's jump in money supply growth.

One of the bright aspects of the current economic upturn is how subdued inflation has been. After the inflationary binges of the 1970s and 1980s, this time, the optimists say, it may all be very different.

But although inflation is running at an annual rate of just 2.2 per cent and looks set to fall further for several months at least, the longer-term prospect is less rosy.

The men's monthly meetings reflect a now widely held consensus that keeping inflation low is the primary target of economic policy. But there are people who believe that slightly higher inflation may be more desirable. For example, home-owners stuck with negative equity pray for it because it boosts house prices.

The pressures these people exert may tempt the government to take chances with higher inflation in order to engineer faster output growth, lower unemployment and more votes.

'In the short-term, inflation's clearly going to head downwards but already there are signs that it will rise again in a year or so,' said David Hillier, UK economist at BZW.

Perhaps the main argument against high inflation is that, since it tends to be more variable than low inflation, it is more disruptive to economic decision making.

'If it were high but certain, then people could take account of it in their expectations and the economic contracts they set,' explained Mr Ray Barrell, at the National Institute of Economic and Social Research.

'But if it becomes more unpredictable as it rises, the more uncertain people become, risk premia grow, people invest less and output is ultimately lower.'...

But there are also good arguments why relatively high inflation might be beneficial. Farmers have also lobbied for higher inflation since it boosts land prices. Debtors – individuals, companies or even governments – can be excused for preferring faster price rises since inflation for them reduces the value of their nominal loans....

For the next few months at least, inflation looks set to remain low.

Mr David Owen, UK economist at Kleinwort Benson, emphasised the subdued conditions in the labour market. 'The key driver of inflation in the UK, as in most developed economies, is unit labour costs, which are subdued.'

The inflationary signs are also benign away from the labour market. Manufacturers' input costs have declined as commodity prices have fallen. Partly as a result of this, producers' output price inflation has been the lowest for nearly 30 years. Yesterday's purchasing managers' survey again showed prices in industry falling although at a slightly slower rate than before.

But now some suspect such subdued conditions may only be temporary.

The economy is beginning to pick up speed, driven primarily by a rebound in consumer spending. Already, rising demand is beginning to affect retail prices. While goods retail price inflation has fallen steadily since the beginning of the year, inflation in services – which account for much consumer spending – has accelerated markedly. If retailers use the consumer rebound to raise margins further, the chancellor may find his inflation target seriously threatened.

The Bank of England itself has warned that the government is now more likely than not to miss its target of 2.5 per cent inflation in two years' time. Public enemy number one may be cowed but it is not ready to succumb yet.

- The Chancellor of the Exchequer and the governor of the Bank of England have a monthly meeting to review the state of the economy and the prospects for inflation.

- The governor is the most cautious about inflationary prospects. At the next meeting he will point to the sharp rise in monetary growth. But inflation has remained low compared with the 1980s and 1970s.

- The main aim of economic policy is to keep inflation under the government's own target of 2.5 per cent.

- High inflation is associated with high variable inflation and the variability of inflation adds a 'risk premium' to interest rates which reduces investment.

Economic Analysis

■ The rate of growth of the money supply is the ultimate determinant of the rate of inflation. The news article reports that the governor of the Bank of England, Eddie George, worries that the high rate of growth of the money supply in Fig. 1 will lead to a breach of the government inflation target of 2.5 per cent.

■ The Chancellor has to balance meeting the inflation target with political pressure to expand the economy in time for the 1997 election.

■ The sharp rise in the rate of growth of money in 1995 was largely the result of takeover activity, in particular the Glaxo takeover of Wellcome. This inflated the money supply figures and may not have any inflationary implications.

■ Other takeovers and mergers occurred in 1995, but the high rate of growth of money continued into 1996.

■ Rising demand and the high rate of growth of the money supply have made financial markets nervous that inflation may increase in the future. A rise in expected future inflation will lead to rise in long-term interest rates. Figure 2 shows the 20-year interest rate and the rate of inflation measured by the GDP deflator. The figure shows that long-term bond rates fell at the end of 1995 but rose during 1996.

■ There is a direct measure of the real rate of interest in the United Kingdom. This is the yield on inflation-indexed UK government bonds called index-linked gilts. The long-term rate of interest less the yield on index-linked bonds is a measure of the expected rate of inflation.

■ Figure 3 shows the actual rate of inflation given by the Retail Price Index and the expected rate of inflation for January 1995 to October 1996. The expected rate of inflation is above the actual rate of inflation. But while actual inflation fell sharply and reached a low in 1996, expected inflation fell at a less rapid rate indicating the continued scepticism of the market that inflation is down for good.

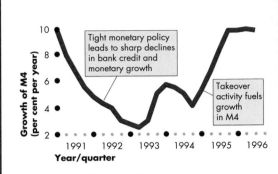

Figure 1 Rate of growth of money supply M4

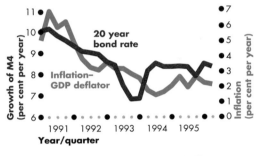

Figure 2 Long-term rate of interest and inflation

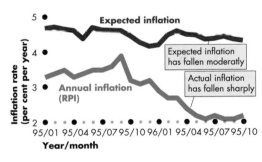

Figure 3 Inflation and expected inflation

SUMMARY

Inflation and the Price Level

Inflation is a process of persistently rising prices and falling value of money. The price level rises when the inflation rate is positive and falls when the inflation rate is negative. The price level rises *faster* when the inflation rate *increases* and *slower* when the inflation rate *decreases*. (pp. 833–834)

Demand-pull Inflation

Demand-pull inflation arises from increasing aggregate demand. Its origin can be any of the factors that shift the aggregate demand curve rightward. The main factor that increases aggregate demand is an increase in the money supply. When the aggregate demand curve shifts rightward, other things remaining the same, both real GDP and the price level increase and unemployment falls. With a shortage of labour, wages begin to increase and the short-run aggregate supply curve shifts leftward, raising the price level still more and decreasing real GDP. If aggregate demand continues to increase, the aggregate demand curve keeps shifting rightward and the price level keeps on rising. Wages respond, aggregate demand increases again and a price–wage inflation spiral ensues. (pp. 834–836)

Cost-push Inflation

Cost-push inflation can result from any factor that decreases aggregate supply, but the main factors are increasing wage rates and increasing prices of key raw materials. These sources of a decreasing aggregate supply bring increasing costs that shift the short-run aggregate supply curve leftward. Firms decrease the quantity of labour employed and cut production. Real GDP declines and the price level rises. Action by the Bank of England (an increase in the money supply) to restore full employment increases aggregate demand and shifts the aggregate demand curve rightward, resulting in a yet higher price level and higher real GDP. If the original source of cost-push inflation repeats, costs rise again and the short-run aggregate supply curve shifts leftward again. If the Bank responds again with a further increase in aggregate

demand, the price level rises even higher. Inflation proceeds at a rate determined by the cost-push forces. (pp. 836–838)

Anticipating Inflation

Decisions made by firms and households are based on forecasts of inflation. But the actual levels of real GDP, real wages and employment depend on actual inflation. Errors in forecasting inflation are costly and people have an incentive to anticipate inflation as accurately as possible.

Forecasters use data and statistical models to generate expectations and economists predict people's forecasts by using the rational expectations hypothesis. The rational expectations hypothesis is that inflation forecasts are made by using the aggregate supply–aggregate demand model together with all the available information on the positions of the aggregate demand and aggregate supply curves.

When changes in aggregate demand are correctly anticipated, inflation is anticipated, and, if its rate is moderate, it does not affect real GDP, real wages, or employment. But a rapid anticipated inflation decreases potential GDP. (pp. 838–844)

Inflation and Unemployment: The Phillips Curve

Phillips curves describe the relationships between inflation and unemployment. The short-run Phillips curve shows the relationship between inflation and unemployment, holding constant the expected inflation rate and the natural unemployment rate. The long-run Phillips curve shows the relationship between inflation and unemployment when the actual inflation rate equals the expected inflation rate. The short-run Phillips curve slopes downward – the higher the inflation rate, other things remaining the same, the lower is the unemployment rate. The long-run Phillips curve is vertical at the natural unemployment rate – the natural rate hypothesis.

Changes in aggregate demand, with a constant expected inflation rate and natural unemployment rate, bring movements along the short-run Phillips curve. Changes in expected inflation shift the short-run Phillips curve. Changes in the natural unemployment rate shift both the short-run and the long-run Phillips curves.

There is no clear relationship between inflation and unemployment in the UK, but the joint movements in these variables can be interpreted in terms of a shifting short-run Phillips curve. (pp. 845–849)

Interest Rates and Inflation

Expectations of inflation affect nominal interest rates. The higher the expected inflation rate, the higher is the nominal interest rate. As the anticipated inflation rate rises, borrowers willingly pay a higher interest rate and lenders successfully demand a higher interest rate. Saving and investment and borrowing, lending and asset-holding plans are made consistent with each other by adjustments in the real interest rate – the nominal interest rate minus the expected inflation rate. (pp. 849–852)

The Politics of Inflation

The government can print or create new base money, so inflation is another source of revenue – it is a tax – and its rate increases when the government has financial needs that exceed the income taxes and other taxes it is able to collect. This source of revenue explains the extremely high inflation rates that sometimes occur and that today are present in many developing countries. Inflation breeds mistrust of the intentions of the government. People do not trust a government with a low reputation when it conducts policy with the aim of reducing inflation. (pp. 852–853)

KEY ELEMENTS

Key Terms

Cost-push inflation, 836
Demand-pull inflation, 834
Inflation, 833
Long-run Phillips curve, 846
Phillips curve, 845
Rational expectation, 840
Real interest rate, 849
Short-run Phillips curve, 845
Stagflation, 837

◆ Key Figures

Figure 32.2   A Demand-pull Rise in the Price Level, 834
Figure 32.3   A Demand-pull Inflation Spiral, 835
Figure 32.4   A Cost-push Rise in the Price Level, 837
Figure 32.6   A Cost-push Inflation Spiral, 838
Figure 32.7   Rational Expectation of the Price Level, 841
Figure 32.8   Anticipated Inflation, 843
Figure 32.9   A Short-run Phillips Curve, 845
Figure 32.11   Short-run and Long-run Phillips Curves, 847
Figure 32.12   A Change in the Natural Unemployment Rate, 847
Figure 32.14   Money Growth, Inflation and the Interest Rate, 850

REVIEW QUESTIONS

1 Distinguish between a one-time change in the price level and inflation.

2 Distinguish between the price level and the inflation rate.

3 Distinguish between demand-pull inflation and cost-push inflation.

4 Explain how a demand-pull inflation spiral occurs.

5 Explain how a cost-push inflation spiral occurs.

6 Why are wrong inflation expectations costly? Suggest some of the losses that an individual would suffer in labour markets as well as in asset markets.

7 Explain why wrong expectations do more than redistribute income.

8 What is a rational expectation? Explain the two features of a rational expectation.

9 Explain the rational expectations hypothesis.

10 What is the rational expectation of the price level in:

a The short run?
b The long run?

11 Explain how anticipated inflation arises.

12 What does the short-run Phillips curve show?

13 What does the long-run Phillips curve show?

14 What have been the main shifts in the UK short-run Phillips curve during the 1960s, 1970s, 1980s and 1990s?

15 What is the connection between expected inflation and nominal interest rates?

PROBLEMS

1 Work out the effects on the price level of the following unexpected events:

a An increase in the money supply
b An increase in government purchases of goods and services
c An increase in income taxes
d An increase in investment demand
e An increase in the wage rate
f An increase in labour productivity

2 Work out the effects on the price level of the same events listed in Problem 1 when they are correctly anticipated.

3 An economy's potential GDP is £400 billion, and it has the following expected aggregate demand and short-run aggregate supply curves:

Price level (GDP deflator)	Expected GDP demanded	Expected GDP supplied
	(billions of 1990 pounds)	
80	500	100
100	400	300
120	300	500
140	200	700

a What is the expected price level?
b What is expected real GDP?
c Are wages expected to be fixed?

4 In the economy of Problem 3, the expected price level rises to 120.

a What is the new *SAS* curve if wages are fixed?
b What is the new *SAS* curve if wages are flexible?
c In parts (a) and (b) is real GDP expected to be above or below full employment?

5 In year t, the expected aggregate demand schedule for $t + 1$ is as follows:

Price level (GDP deflator)	Expected real GDP demanded (billions of 1990 pounds)
120	400
121	390
122	380
123	370
124	360

In year t, the long-run real GDP is £380 billion and the real GDP expected for $t + 1$ is £390 billion. Calculate the period t rational expectation of the price level for period $t + 1$ if wages are:

a Fixed until $t + 1$
b Going to be renegotiated before period $t + 1$.

6 The economy in Problem 3 has the following short-run aggregate supply schedule:

Price level (GDP deflator)	Real GDP supplied (billions of 1990 pounds)
120	320
121	350
122	380
123	410
124	440

a Under what conditions is this short-run aggregate supply schedule consistent with your answer to Problem 3?

b Calculate the actual and expected inflation rate if the aggregate demand curve is expected to shift upward by 10 per cent and if it actually does shift upward by that amount.

7 An economy has a natural unemployment rate of 4 per cent when its expected inflation is 6 per cent. Its inflation and unemployment history is as follows:

Inflation rate (per cent per year)	Unemployment rate (per cent)
10	2
8	3
6	4
4	5
2	6

a Draw a diagram of this economy's short-run and long-run Phillips curves.

b If the actual inflation rate rises from 6 per cent a year to 8 per cent a year, what is the change in the unemployment rate? Explain why it occurs.

c If the natural unemployment rate rises to 5 per cent, what is the change in the unemployment rate? Explain why it occurs.

d Go back to part (a). If the expected inflation rate falls to 4 per cent a year, what is the change in the unemployment rate? Explain why it occurs.

8 Study *Reading Between the Lines* on pp. 854–855 and then answer the following questions.

a Why is the governor of the Bank of England worried for the prospects for inflation in the future?

b What is the stated objective of the government? What other objectives might it have?

c What was the reason for the rise in the money supply in 1995?

d What has happened to expectations of long-term inflation as inflation has fallen?

e Why do you think the markets are sceptical that inflation is down for good?

CHAPTER 33

THE BUSINESS CYCLE

After studying this chapter you will be able to:

- ◆ Distinguish between business cycle impulses and propagation mechanisms
- ◆ Distingush among the several theories of the business cycle
- ◆ Explain the main traditional theories of the business cycle
- ◆ Explain real business cycle theory
- ◆ Describe the origins and mechanisms at work during a recent recession and expansion
- ◆ Describe the origins and mechanisms at work during the Great Depression

T HE PERIOD BETWEEN THE TWO WORLD WARS WAS A TIME OF MIXED FORTUNES FOR many of the people in the United Kingdom who survived the horrors of World War I (1914–18). The end of the war saw a severe recession; returning soldiers were de-mobbed and the economy was thrown back into peacetime production. After a shaky start, the economic machine was slowly getting back to work. Then, almost without warning, in October 1929, came the Wall Street crash. Share prices in the United States fell by 30 per cent and a wave of deflation was sent around the whole world. By 1933, real GDP in the United States had fallen by 30 per cent and unemployment had increased to 25 per cent of the work-force. This major down-turn in the world's largest economy had severe effects on the economies of Europe. In Germany unemployment rose to 5.6 million or 30 per cent of the work-force in 1932 and in the United Kingdom it reached nearly 16 per cent. In 1931 the United Kingdom left the gold standard and joined the rest of the world in the Great Depression. ◆ By the standard of the inter-war years, recent recessions have been mild. But recessions have not gone away. Our economy has experienced five recessions since World War II ended in 1945. In 1974, real GDP decreased by 1.5 per cent; in 1980, it decreased by 2 per cent; in 1981 it decreased

Must What Goes Up Always Come Down?

again in a back-to-back recession by 1.2 per cent, and most recently, in 1991–92, it decreased by 2.6 per cent over the two years. Between these recessions, expansions took real GDP to new heights. Since the 1990s recession, real GDP has recovered. In 1994, GDP grew by nearly 4 per cent, and at the end of the year it stood some 6.3 per cent higher than at the bottom of the recession and 3.5 per cent higher than its peak before the 1990s recession. What causes a repeating sequence of recessions and expansions in our economy? Must what goes up always come down? Will we have another recession before 2000?

◆ ◆ ◆ ◆ In this chapter we are going to explore these questions. You will see how all the strands of macroeconomics that you've been following come together and weave a complete picture of the forces and mechanisms that generate economic growth and fluctuations in production, employment and unemployment, and inflation. You will draw on your study of the labour market, consumption, saving and investment, economic growth, aggregate supply and aggregate demand, expenditure multipliers and the money market. ◆ We'll begin by summarizing the key business cycle facts that we want to understand and then distinguish between the impulses and the propagation mechanisms that can create the business cycle.

861

Patterns, Impulses and Propagation Mechanisms

The business cycle is an irregular and non-repeating up-and-down movement of business activity that takes place around a generally rising trend and that shows great diversity. Figure 33.1 shows some of this diversity by comparing business cycles since the turn of the century. You can see that there are basically nine business cycle turning points we can identify since 1990. On the average, recessions have lasted about two years and real GDP has fallen from peak to trough by nearly 10 per cent. Expansions have, on the average, lasted for just over six years and real GDP has risen from trough to peak at an average of nearly 10 per cent. But these averages mask huge variations from one cycle to another. Each cycle has a different story to tell. The onset of World War I near the beginning of the century led to a boom followed by a sharp slump at the end of the war. The interwar period witnessed two cycles with a severe recession occurring in the 1930s, earning it the title of the 'Hungry Thirties'. The

next big expansion occurred during World War II. But there have been five cycles since World War II with major expansions occurring during the 1960s and 1980s.

You can see by examining Fig. 33.1 that although the average of peak to trough decline and trough to peak boom is almost the same, most of the downturns are not as severe as the upturns. This is because the post-World War I recession was so severe that it pulled the average down. If we exclude the years up to 1918, the average trough to peak is 10.4 per cent and the average peak to trough is 8.8 per cent. Another interesting observation is the *amplitude* – the slump–boom–slump movement of the business cycle. You can see that the slump–boom–slump cycle was greater before World War II than after. Also the *frequency* of the cycle was greater before World War II than after. The 1960s heralded a long expansion period which looks unusual compared with other expansion phases of the cycle. There is no correlation between the length of an expansion and the length of the preceding recession.

With this enormous diversity of experience, there is no simple explanation of the business cycle. Also there is no (currently available) way of

FIGURE 33.1

Some Business Cycle Patterns

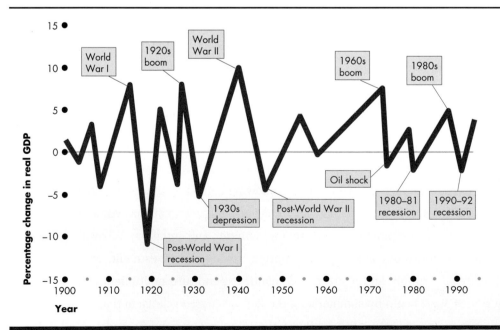

There have been nine business cycle turning points since the turn of the century. Recessions have lasted on average two years. Real GDP has fallen from peak to trough by nearly 9 per cent. Expansions have, on the average, lasted for about six years and real GDP has risen from trough to peak at an average of 10 per cent.

forecasting when the next turning point will come. But there is a body of theory about the business cycle that helps us to understand its causes. A good place to begin studying this theory is to distinguish the possible ways in which cycles can be created.

Impulses and Propagation Mechanisms

The business cycle can occur either because the economy is hit by a succession of impulses that alternate between the up-and-down directions or because the economy has a built-in cycle mechanism that causes it to move up and down regardless of how it is hit. Some analogies might help you to see the distinction between cycle impulses and cycle mechanisms. In a tennis match, the ball cycles from one side of the court to the other and back again in a way that is determined entirely by the impulses that hit the ball. The tide is a cycle that is determined purely by a mechanism and has no impulses. The rotation of the earth and the gravitational pull of the moon interact to bring the ebb and flow of the tide with no outside forces intervening. A child's rocking horse is an example of a cycle mechanism that needs an external force to create the cycle. If the horse is pushed, it rocks to-and-fro in a cycle. The cycle will eventually die out unless the horse is pushed again, and each time the horse is pushed the cycle temporarily becomes more severe.

The economy seems to be a bit like all three of these examples. It can be hit like a tennis ball by shocks that send it in one direction or another; it can cycle indefinitely like the ebb and flow of the tide; and it can cycle like a rocking horse in swings that get milder until another shock sets off a new burst of bigger swings. But no one is sure which of these analogies is correct because there is no fully developed theory that explains all business cycles equally well. While none of the analogies we use is perfect, they all contain some insights into the business cycle. Different theories of the cycle emphasize different outside forces (different tennis racquets) and different cycle mechanisms (rocking horse designs).

Although there are several different theories of the business cycle, they all agree about one aspect of the cycle: the central role played by investment and the accumulation of capital.

The Crucial Role of Investment and Capital

Whatever the shocks are that hit the economy, they hit one crucial variable: investment. Recessions begin when investment in new capital slows down and they turn into expansions when investment speeds up. Investment and capital also create a cycle propagation mechanism. They interact like the spinning earth and the sun to create an ongoing cycle.

If in an expansion investment proceeds at a rapid rate, the capital stock grows quickly. Capital per hour of labour grows and labour becomes more productive. But the *law of diminishing returns* begins to operate and this brings a fall in the rate of return on capital as the gain in productivity from the additional units of capital declines. With a lower rate of return, the incentive to invest weakens and investment eventually falls. When it falls by a large amount, recession begins. If in a recession investment proceeds at a modest rate, the capital stock grows slowly and diminishing returns work in reverse.

The *AS–AD* Model

Investment and capital are just part of the business cycle mechanism. To study the broader business mechanism, we need a broader framework. That framework is the *AS–AD* model. All the theories of the business cycle can be described in terms of the *AS–AD* model of Chapter 27. Theories differ in what they identify as the impulse and the propagation mechanism. But all theories can be thought of as making assumptions about the factors that make either aggregate supply or aggregate demand fluctuate and assumptions about their interaction with each other to create a business cycle. Business cycle impulses can hit either the supply side or the demand side of the economy or both. But there are no pure supply side theories. We can classify all theories of the business cycle as:

◆ Aggregate demand theories, or
◆ Real business cycle theory

We'll study the aggregate demand theories first. Then we'll study real business cycle theory, a more recent approach which isolates a shock that has both aggregate supply and aggregate demand effects.

Aggregate Demand Theories of the Business Cycle

Three types of aggregate demand theories of the business cycle have been proposed. They are:

◆ Keynesian theory
◆ Monetarist theory
◆ Rational expectations theory

Keynesian Theory of the Cycle

The **Keynesian theory of the business cycle** regards volatile expectations as the main source of economic fluctuations. This theory is distilled from Keynes' *General Theory of Employment, Interest and Money*. We'll explore the Keynesian theory by looking at its main impulse and the mechanism that converts this impulse into a real GDP cycle.

Keynesian Impulse The *impulse* in the Keynesian theory of the business cycle is expected future sales and profits. A change in expected future sales and profits changes the demand for new capital and changes the level of investment.

Keynes had an interesting and sophisticated view about *how* expectations of sales and profits are determined. He reasoned that these expectations would be volatile because most of the events that shape the future are unknown and impossible to forecast. So, he reasoned, news or even rumours about future tax rate changes, interest rate changes, advances in technology, global economic and political events, or any of thousands of other relevant factors that influence sales and profits, change expectations in ways that can't be quantified but that have large effects.

To emphasize the volatility and diversity of sources of changes in expected sales and profits, one of Keynes' followers, Joan Robinson, described these expectations as *animal spirits*. In using this term, Keynesians are not saying that expectations are irrational. Rather, they mean that because future sales and profits are impossible to forecast, it is rational to take a view about them based on rumours, guesses, intuition and instinct. Further, it might be rational to *change* one's view of the future, perhaps radically, in the light of scraps of new information.

Keynesian Cycle Mechanism In the Keynesian theory, once a change in animal spirits has changed investment, a cycle mechanism begins to operate that has two key elements. First, the initial change in investment has a multiplier effect. The change in investment changes *aggregate* expenditure, real GDP and disposable income. The change in disposable income changes consumption expenditure and aggregate demand changes by a multiple of the initial change in investment. (This mechanism is described in detail in Chapter 28, pp. 724–727.) The aggregate demand curve shifts rightward in an expansion and leftward in a recession.

The second element of the Keynesian cycle mechanism is the aggregate supply response to a change in aggregate demand. The short-run aggregate supply curve is horizontal (or nearly so). With a horizontal *SAS* curve, swings in aggregate demand translate into swings in real GDP with no changes in the price level. But the short-run aggregate supply curve depends on the money wage rate. If the money wage rate is fixed (sticky), the *SAS* curve does not move. And if the money wage rate changes, the *SAS* curve shifts. In the Keynesian theory, the response of the money wage rate to changes in aggregate demand depends on whether aggregate demand decreases or increases.

When aggregate demand decreases and unemployment rises, the money wage rate does not change. It is rigid in the down direction. With a decrease in aggregate demand and no change in the money wage rate, the economy gets stuck in an unemployment equilibrium. There are no natural forces operating to restore full employment. The economy remains in that situation until animal spirits are lifted and investment increases again.

When aggregate demand increases and unemployment falls below the natural rate, the money wage rate rises quickly. It is completely flexible in the up direction. Above full employment, the horizontal *SAS* curve plays no role and only the vertical *LAS* curve is relevant. With an increase in aggregate demand and an accompanying rise in the money wage rate, the price level rises quickly to eliminate the shortages and bring the economy back to full employment. The economy remains in that situation until animal spirits fall and investment and aggregate demand decrease.

Figures 33.2 and 33.3 illustrate the Keynesian theory of the business cycle by using the aggregate demand–aggregate supply model. In Fig. 33.2, the

FIGURE 33.2

A Keynesian Recession

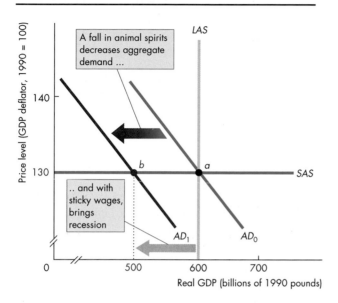

The economy is operating at point *a* at the intersection of the aggregate demand curve, AD_0, the short run aggregate supply curve, SAS_0, and the long-run aggregate supply curve, *LAS*. A Keynesian recession begins when a fall in animal spirits causes investment demand to decrease. Aggregate demand decreases and the *AD* curve shifts leftward to AD_1. With sticky money wages and sticky price level, real GDP falls to £500 billion and the economy moves to point *b*.

FIGURE 33.3

A Keynesian Expansion

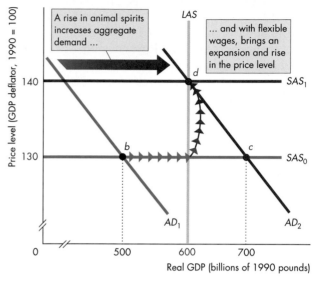

Starting at point *b*, a Keynesian expansion begins when a rise in animal spirits causes investment demand to increase. Aggregate demand increases and the *AD* curve shifts rightward to AD_2. With sticky money wages, real GDP increases to £600 billion. But the economy does not go all the way to point *c*. When full employment is reached, the money wage rate rises and the *SAS* curve shifts toward SAS_1. The price level rises as the economy heads towards point *d*.

economy is initially at full employment (point *a*) on the long-run aggregate supply curve, *LAS*, the aggregate demand curve, AD_0, and the short-run aggregate supply curve, SAS_0. A fall in animal spirits decreases investment, and aggregate demand decreases. The aggregate demand curve shifts leftward to AD_1. Real GDP falls to £500 billion and the economy moves to point *b*. Unemployment has increased and there is a surplus of labour, but the money wage rate does not fall and the economy remains at point *b* until some force moves it away.

That force is shown in Fig. 33.3. Here, starting out at point *b*, a rise in animal spirits increases aggregate demand and shifts the *AD* curve to AD_2. The multiplier process comes in to play and real GDP begins to increase. An expansion is under way. As long as real GDP remains below potential GDP

(£600 billion in this example), the money wage rate and the price level remain constant. But real GDP never gets to point *c*, the point of intersection of SAS_0 and AD_2. The reason is that once real GDP exceeds potential GDP and unemployment falls below the natural rate, the money wage rate begins to rise and the *SAS* curve starts to shift upward towards SAS_1. As the money wage rate rises, the price level also rises and real GDP growth slows down. The economy follows a path like the one shown by the arrows connecting point *b*, the initial equilibrium, with point *d*, the final equilibrium.

The Keynesian business cycle is mainly like a tennis match. It is caused by outside forces – animal spirits – that change direction and set off a process that ends at an equilibrium that must be hit again by the outside forces to disturb it.

Monetarist Theory

The **monetarist theory of the business cycle** regards fluctuations in the money stock as the main source of economic fluctuations. This theory is distilled from the writings of Milton Friedman and several other economists. We'll explore the monetarist theory as we did the Keynesian theory, by looking first at its main impulse and second at the mechanism that creates a cycle in real GDP.

Monetarist Impulse The *impulse* in the monetarist theory of the business cycle is the *growth rate of the quantity of money*. A speedup in money growth brings expansion, and a slowdown in money growth brings recession. The source of the change in the growth rate of quantity of money is the monetary policy actions of the Bank of England.

Monetarist Cycle Mechanism In the monetarist theory, once the Bank of England has changed the money growth rate, a cycle mechanism begins to operate which, like the Keynesian mechanism, first affects aggregate demand. When the money growth rate increases, the quantity of real money in the economy increases. Interest rates fall and real money balances increase. The foreign exchange rate also falls – the pound loses value on the foreign exchange market. These initial financial market effects begin to spill over into other markets. Investment demand and exports increase, and consumers spend more on durable goods. These initial changes in expenditure have a multiplier effect, just as investment has in the Keynesian theory. Through these mechanisms, a speedup in money growth shifts the aggregate demand curve rightward and brings an expansion. Similarly, a slowdown in money growth shifts the aggregate demand curve leftward and brings a recession.

The second element of the monetarist cycle mechanism is the response of aggregate supply to a change in aggregate demand. The short-run aggregate supply curve is upward-sloping. With an upward-sloping *SAS* curve, swings in aggregate demand translate into swings in both real GDP and the price level. But monetarists think that real GDP deviations from full employment are temporary in both directions.

In monetarist theory, the money wage rate is only *temporarily sticky*. When aggregate demand decreases and unemployment rises, the money wage rate eventually begins to fall. As the money wage rate falls, so does the price level and after a period of adjustment, full employment is restored. When aggregate demand increases and unemployment falls below the natural rate, the money wage rate begins to rise. As the money wage rate rises so does the price level, and after a period of adjustment, real GDP returns to potential GDP and the unemployment rate returns to the natural rate.

Figure 33.4 illustrates the monetarist theory. In part (a), the economy is initially at full employment (point a) on the long-run aggregate supply curve, LAS, the aggregate demand curve, AD_0, and the short-run aggregate supply curve, SAS_0. A slowdown in the money growth rate decreases aggregate demand and the aggregate demand curve shifts leftward to AD_1. Real GDP falls to £550 billion and the economy moves to point b. Unemployment increases, and there is a surplus of labour. The money wage rate begins to fall. As the money wage rate falls, the short-run aggregate supply curve shifts from SAS_0 to SAS_1. The price level falls and real GDP begins to expand as the economy moves to point c, its new full-employment equilibrium, and GDP is back at its full-employment level or potential GDP level (£600 billion in this example).

Figure 33.4(b) shows the effects of the opposite initial money shock – a speedup in money growth. Here, starting out at point c, a rise in the money growth rate increases aggregate demand and shifts the AD curve to AD_2. Both real GDP and the price level rise as the economy moves to point d, the point of intersection of SAS_1 and AD_2. With real GDP above potential GDP and unemployment below the natural rate, the money wage rate begins to rise and the SAS curve starts to shift leftward towards SAS_2. As the money wage rate rises, the price level also rises and real GDP decreases. The economy moves from point d to point e, its new full-employment equilibrium.

The monetarist business cycle is like a rocking horse. It needs an outside force to get it going but once going, it rocks to-and-fro (but just once). It doesn't matter how the economy is hit. If it is hit with a money growth slowdown, the economy cycles with a recession followed by recovery. If it is hit by a money growth speedup, the economy cycles with a recovery followed by recession.

Rational Expectations Theories

A **rational expectation** is a forecast that is based on all the available relevant information.

FIGURE 33.4

A Monetarist Business Cycle

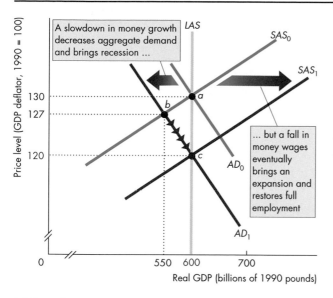

(a) Recession

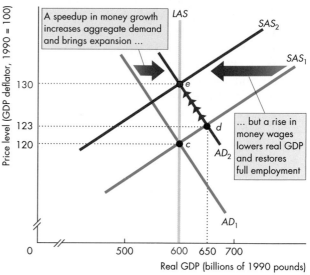

(b) Expansion

A monetarist recession begins when a slowdown in money growth decreases aggregate demand. The *AD* curve shifts leftward from AD_0 to AD_1 (part a). With sticky money wages, real GDP decreases to £550 billion and the price level falls to 127 as the economy moves from point *a* to point *b*. With a surplus of labour, the money wage rate falls and the *SAS* curve shifts rightward to SAS_1. The price level falls further, and real GDP returns to potential GDP at point *c*.

Starting at point *c* (part b), a monetarist expansion begins when an increase in money growth increases aggregate demand and shifts the *AD* curve rightward to AD_2. With sticky money wages, real GDP rises to £650 billion, the price level rises to 123, and the economy moves to point *d*. With a shortage of labour, the money wage rate rises and the *SAS* curve shifts towards SAS_2. The price level rises and real GDP decreases to potential GDP as the economy heads towards point *e*.

Rational expectations theories of the business cycle are theories based on the view that money wages are determined by a rational expectation of the price level. Two distinctly different rational expectations theories of the cycle have been proposed. A **new classical theory of the business cycle** regards *unanticipated* fluctuations in aggregate demand as the main source of economic fluctuations. This theory is based on the work of Robert E. Lucas Jr (see *Economics in History* on pp. 888–889) and has been applied to the United Kingdom by several other economists, including Patrick Minford (see *Talking with Patrick Minford* on pp. 681–683). A different **new Keynesian theory of the business cycle** regards *both anticipated and unanticipated* fluctuations in aggregate demand as sources of economic fluctuations. We'll explore these theories as we did the Keynesian and monetarist theories, by looking first at the main impulse and second at the cycle mechanism.

Rational Expectations Impulse The *impulse* that distinguishes the rational expectations theories from the other aggregate demand theories of the business cycle is the *unanticipated change in aggregate demand.* A larger than anticipated increase in aggregate demand brings an expansion and a smaller than anticipated increase in aggregate demand brings a recession. Any factor that influences aggregate demand – for example, fiscal policy, monetary policy, or developments in the world economy that influence exports – whose change is not anticipated, can bring a change in real GDP.

Rational Expectations Cycle Mechanisms

To describe the rational expectations cycle mechanisms, we'll deal first with the new classical version. When aggregate demand decreases, if the money wage rate doesn't change, real GDP and the price level both decrease. The fall in the price level increases the *real* wage rate, and employment decreases and unemployment rises. In the new classical theory, the events you've just reviewed occur only if the decrease in aggregate demand is not anticipated. If the decrease in aggregate demand *is* anticipated, both firms and workers will agree to a lower money wage rate. By doing so, they can prevent the real wage from rising and avoid a rise in the unemployment rate.

Similarly, if firms and workers anticipate an increase in aggregate demand, they expect the price level to rise and will agree to a higher money wage rate. By doing so, they can prevent the real wage from falling and avoid a fall in the unemployment rate below the natural rate.

Only fluctuations in aggregate demand that are unanticipated and not taken into account in wage contracts bring changes in real GDP. *Anticipated* changes in aggregate demand change the price level, but they leave real GDP and unemployment unchanged and do not create a business cycle.

New Keynesian economists, like new classical economists, think that money wages are influenced by rational expectations of the price level. But new Keynesians emphasize the long-term nature of most wage contracts. They say that *today's* money wages are influenced by *yesterday's* rational expectations. These expectations, which were formed in the past, are based on old information that might now be known to be incorrect. After they have made a long-term wage agreement, both firms and workers might anticipate a change in aggregate demand, which they expect will change the price level. But because they are locked into their agreement, they are unable to change money wages. So money wages are sticky in the new Keynesian theory and with sticky money wages, even an *anticipated* change in aggregate demand changes real GDP.

New classical economists say that long-term contracts are renegotiated when conditions change to make them outdated. So they do not regard long-term contracts as an obstacle to money wage flexibility, provided both parties to an agreement recognize the changed conditions. If both firms and workers expect the price level to change, they will change the agreed money wage rate to reflect that shared expectation. In this situation, anticipated changes in aggregate demand change the money wage rate and the price level and leave real GDP unchanged.

The distinctive feature of both versions of the rational expectations theory of the business cycle is the role of unanticipated changes in aggregate demand, and Fig. 33.5 illustrates its effect on real GDP and the price level. Potential GDP is $600 billion and the long-run aggregate supply curve is *LAS*. Aggregate demand is expected to be *EAD*. Given potential GDP and *EAD*, the money wage rate is set at the level that is expected to bring full employment. At this money wage rate, the short-run aggregate supply curve is *SAS*. Imagine that, initially, aggregate demand equals expected aggregate demand, so there is full employment. Real GDP is $600 billion and the price level is 130. Then, unexpectedly, aggregate demand turns out to be less than expected and the aggregate demand curve shifts leftward to AD_0 (in Fig. 33.5a). Many different aggregate demand shocks, such as a slowdown in the money growth rate or a collapse of exports, could have caused this shock. A recession begins. Real GDP falls to $550 billion and the price level falls to 127. The economy moves to point *b*. Unemployment increases and there is surplus of labour. But aggregate demand is expected to be at *EAD* so the money wage rate doesn't change and the short-run aggregate supply curve remains at *SAS*.

The recession ends when aggregate demand increases again to its expected level. A larger shock that takes aggregate demand to a level that exceeds *EAD* brings an expansion. In Fig. 33.5(b), the aggregate demand curve shifts rightward to AD_1. Such an increase in aggregate demand might be caused by a speedup in the money growth rate or an export boom. Real GDP now increases to $650 billion and the price level rises to 133. The economy moves to point *c*. Unemployment is now below the natural rate. But aggregate demand is expected to be at *EAD* so the money wage rate doesn't change and the short-run aggregate supply curve remains at *SAS*.

Fluctuations in aggregate demand between AD_0 and AD_1 around expected aggregate demand *EAD* bring fluctuations in real GDP and the price level between points *b* and *c*.

FIGURE 33.5

A Rational Expectations Business Cycle

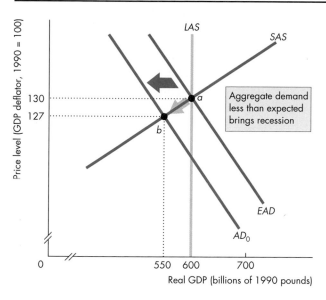

(a) Recession

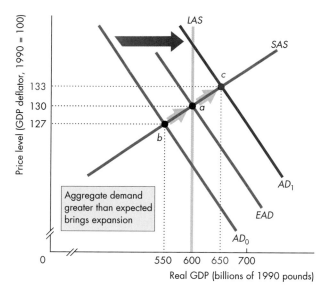

(b) Expansion

The economy is expected to be at point *a* at the intersection of the *expected* aggregate demand curve, *EAD*, the short-run aggregate supply curve, *SAS*, and the long-run aggregate supply curve, *LAS*. A rational expectations recession begins when an unanticipated decrease in aggregate demand shifts the *AD* curve leftward to AD_0. With money wage rates based on the expectation that aggregate demand will be *EAD*, real GDP decreases to £550 billion and the price level falls to 127 as the economy moves to point *b*. As long as aggregate demand is *expected* to be

EAD there is no change in the money wage rate.

A rational expectations expansion begins when an unanticipated increase in aggregate demand shifts the *AD* curve rightward from AD_0 to AD_1. With money wage rates based on the expectation that aggregate demand will be *EAD*, real GDP increases to £650 billion and the price level rises to 133 as the economy moves to point *c*. Again, as long as aggregate demand is *expected* to be *EAD*, there is no change in the money wage rate.

The two versions of the rational expectations theory differ in their predictions about the effects of a change in expected aggregate demand. The new classical theory predicts that as soon as expected aggregate demand changes, the money wage rate also changes so the *SAS* curve shifts. The new Keynesian theory predicts that the money wage rate changes gradually when new contracts are made so that the *SAS* curve moves slowly. This difference between the two theories is crucial for policy. According to the new classical theory, anticipated policy actions change only the price level and have no effect on real GDP and unemployment. The reason is that when policy is expected to change, the money wage rate changes so the *SAS* curve shifts and offsets the effects of the policy action on

real GDP. In contrast, in the new Keynesian theory, because money wages change only when new contracts are made, even anticipated policy actions change real GDP and can be used in an attempt to stabilize the cycle.

Like the monetarist business cycle, these rational expectations cycles are similar to rocking horses. They need an outside force to get going, but once going the economy rocks around its full-employment point. The new classical horse rocks faster and comes to rest more quickly than the new Keynesian horse.

AD–AS General Theory

All the theories of the business cycle that we've considered can be viewed as particular cases of a more general *AD–AS* theory. In this more general theory, the impulses of both the Keynesian and monetarist theories can change aggregate demand. A multiplier effect makes aggregate demand change by more than any initial change in one of the components of expenditure. The money wage rate can be viewed as responding to changes in the rational expectation of the future price level. Even if the money wage is flexible, it will change only to the extent that price level expectations change. As a result, the money wage will adjust gradually.

Although in all three types of business cycle theories that we've considered the cycle is caused by fluctuations in aggregate demand, the possibility that an occasional aggregate supply shock might occur is not ruled out. A recession could occur because aggregate supply falls. For example, a widespread drought that cuts agricultural production could cause a recession in an economy that has a large agricultural sector. But these demand theories of the cycle regard supply shocks as rare rather than normal events. Aggregate demand fluctuations are the normal ongoing sources of fluctuations.

R E V I E W

◆ Keynesian theory says the business cycle is caused by volatile expectations about future sales and profits (animal spirits), a multiplier effect and sticky money wages.

◆ Monetarist theory says the business cycle is caused by the Bank of England speeding up and slowing down the growth rate of money, which changes spending plans.

◆ New classical and new Keynesian theories (rational expectations theories) say the business cycle is caused by unanticipated fluctuations in aggregate demand. In the new classical theory, the money wage rate responds to price level expectations, and in the new Keynesian theory, the money wage rate is set by long-term contracts.

A new theory of the business cycle challenges the mainstream and traditional demand theories that you've just studied. It is called the real business cycle theory. Let's take a look at this new theory.

Real Business Cycle Theory

The newest theory of the business cycle, known as **real business cycle theory** (or RBC theory), regards random fluctuations in productivity as the main source of economic fluctuations. These productivity fluctuations are assumed to result mainly from fluctuations in the pace of technological change, but they might also have other sources such as international disturbances, climate fluctuations, or natural disasters. The origins of real business cycle theory can be traced to the rational expectations revolution set off by Robert E. Lucas Jr, but the first demonstration of the power of this theory was given by Edward Prescott and Finn Kydland, and by John Long and Charles Plosser. Today, real business cycle theory is part of a broad research agenda called *dynamic general equilibrium*, and hundreds of young macroeconomists do research on this topic.

Like our study of the demand theories, we'll explore the RBC theory by looking first at its impulse and second at the mechanism that converts that impulse into a cycle in real GDP.

The RBC Impulse

The *impulse* in the RBC theory is the *growth rate of productivity that results from technological change*. RBC theorists think this impulse is generated mainly by the process of research and development that leads to the creation and use of new technologies. Sometimes technological progress is rapid and productivity grows quickly; and at other times, progress is slow and productivity grows moderately. Occasionally, technological change is so far-reaching that it makes a large amount of existing capital, especially human capital, obsolete. It also, initially, destroys jobs and shuts down businesses. These initial effects of far-reaching technological change *decrease* productivity and can create recession. Other supply shocks, such as the world oil embargo of the mid-1970s, can temporarily decrease productivity.

To isolate the RBC theory impulse – the growth rate of productivity that results from technological change – economists use the tool of growth accounting, which is explained in Chapter 26, pp. 659–664.

Figure 33.6 shows the RBC impulse for the United Kingdom from 1971 to 1995. This figure also shows that fluctuations in productivity growth are correlated with GDP fluctuations.

The RBC Mechanism

The mechanism that creates the business cycle according to the RBC theory is more complex and intricate than the demand theory mechanisms. Two immediate effects follow from a change in productivity that get an expansion or a contraction going:

1. Investment demand changes
2. Demand for labour changes

We'll study these effects and their consequences during a recession. In an expansion, they work in the opposite direction to what is described here.

A wave of technological change makes some existing capital obsolete and temporarily lowers productivity. Firms expect the future profit rate to fall and see their labour productivity falling. With lower profit expectations, they cut back their purchases of

new capital, and with lower labour productivity they plan to lay off some workers. So the initial effect of a decrease in productivity is a decrease in investment demand and a decrease in the demand for labour.

Figure 33.7 illustrates these two initial effects of a decrease in productivity. Part (a) shows investment demand, *ID*, and saving supply, *SS*. Initially, investment demand is ID_0, and the equilibrium level of investment and saving is £100 billion at a real interest rate of 6 per cent a year. A decrease in productivity lowers the expected profit rate and decreases investment demand. The *ID* curve shifts leftward to ID_1. The real interest rate falls to 4 per cent a year, and investment and saving decrease to £70 billion.

Part (b) shows the demand for labour, *LD*, and the supply of labour, *LS*. Initially, the demand for labour is LD_0, and the equilibrium level of employment is 45 billion hours a year at a real wage rate of £5.50 an hour. The decrease in productivity decreases the demand for labour and the *LD* curve shifts leftward to LD_1.

FIGURE 33.6

The Real Business Cycle Impulse

The real business cycle is caused by changes in technology that bring fluctuations in productivity. The fluctuations in productivity shown here are calculated by using growth accounting (the one-third rule) to remove the contribution of capital accumulation to productivity growth. Productivity fluctuations are correlated with real GDP fluctuations. Economists are not sure what the productivity variable actually measures or what causes it to fluctuate.

Sources: *National Income and Expenditure* 1996, Datastream; and the authors' calculations.

FIGURE 33.7

Factor Markets in a Real Business Cycle

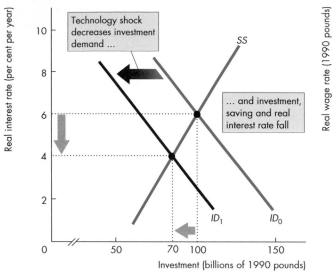

(a) Investment, saving, and interest rate

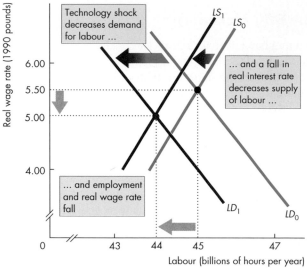

(b) Labour and wage rate

Saving supply is *SS* (part a) and, initially, investment demand is ID_0. The real interest rate is 6 per cent a year and saving and investment are £100 billion. In the labour market (part b), the demand for labour is LD_0 and the supply of labour is LS_0. The real wage rate is £5.50 an hour and employment is 45 billion hours. A technological change decreases productivity, and both investment demand and the demand for labour decrease. The two demand curves

shift leftward to ID_1 and LD_1. In part (a), the real interest rate falls to 4 per cent a year, and investment and saving fall. In part (b), the fall in the real interest rate decreases the supply of labour (the when-to-work decision) and the supply curve shifts leftward to LS_1. Employment decreases to 44 billion hours and the real wage rate falls to £5 an hour. A recession is under way.

Before we can determine the new level of employment and the real wage rate, we need to take a ripple effect into account – the key ripple effect in RBC theory.

The Key Decision: When to Work? According to the RBC theory, people decide *when* to work by doing a cost–benefit calculation. They compare the return from working in the current period with the *expected* return from working in a later period. You make such a comparison every day at college Suppose your goal in this course is to get a first. To achieve this goal, you work pretty hard most of the time. But during the few days before the mid-term and final exams, you work especially hard. Why? Because you think the return from studying close to the exam is greater than the return from studying when the exam is a long time away. So during the

term you hang around the Students' Union bar, go to parties, play squash and enjoy other leisure pursuits, but at exam time you work every evening and weekend.

Real business cycle theory says that workers behave like you. They work fewer hours, and sometimes zero hours, when the real wage rate is temporarily low and they work more hours when the real wage rate is temporarily high. But to compare properly the current wage rate with the expected future wage rate, workers must use the real interest rate. If the real interest rate is 6 per cent a year, a real wage rate of £1 an hour earned this week will become £1.06 a year from now. If the real wage rate is expected to be £1.05 an hour next year, today's wage of £1 looks good. By working longer hours now and shorter hours a year from now, a person can get a 1 per cent higher real wage.

But suppose the real interest rate is 4 per cent a year. In this case, £1 earned now is worth £1.04 next year. Working fewer hours now and more next year is the way to get a 1 per cent higher real wage.

So the when-to-work decision depends on the real interest rate. The lower the real interest rate, other things remaining the same, the smaller is the supply of labour. Many economists think this *intertemporal substitution effect* to be of negligible size. RBC theorists say the effect is large, and it is the key element in the RBC mechanism.

You've seen in Fig. 33.7(a) that the decrease in investment demand lowers the real interest rate. This fall in the real interest rate lowers the return to current work and decreases the supply of labour. In Fig. 33.7(b), the labour supply curve shifts leftward to LS_1. The effect of a productivity shock on demand is larger than the effect of the fall in the real interest rate on the supply of labour. That is, the LD curve shifts farther leftward than does the LS curve. As a result, the real wage rate falls to £5 an hour and employment falls to 44 billion hours. A recession has begun and is intensifying.

Real GDP and the Price Level   The next part of the RBC story traces the consequences of the changes you've just seen for real GDP and the price level. With a decrease in employment, aggregate supply decreases; and with a decrease in investment demand, aggregate demand decreases. Figure 33.8 illustrates these effects, using the *AD–AS* framework. Initially, the aggregate demand curve is AD_0 and the long-run aggregate supply curve is LAS_0. The price level is 130 and real GDP is £600 billion. There is no short-run aggregate supply curve in this figure because in the RBC theory, the *SAS* curve has no meaning. The labour market moves relentlessly toward its equilibrium, and the money wage rate adjusts freely (either upward or downward) to ensure that the real wage rate keeps the quantity of labour demanded equal to the quantity supplied. In the RBC theory, unemployment is always at the natural rate, and the natural rate fluctuates over the business cycle because the amount of job search fluctuates.

The decrease in employment lowers total production, and aggregate supply decreases. The *LAS* curve shifts leftward to LAS_1. The decrease in investment demand decreases aggregate demand, and the *AD* curve shifts leftward to AD_1. The price

FIGURE 33.8

AD–AS in a Real Business Cycle

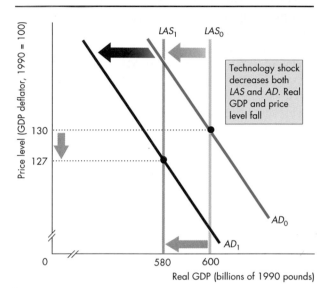

Initially, the aggregate demand curve is AD_0 and the long-run aggregate supply curve is LAS_0. Real GDP is £600 billion (which equals potential GDP) and the price level is 130. There is no *SAS* curve in the real business cycle theory because the money wage rate is flexible. The technological change described in Fig. 33.6 decreases potential GDP and the *LAS* curve shifts leftward to LAS_1. The decrease in investment demand decreases aggregate demand, and the *AD* curve shifts leftward to AD_1. Real GDP decreases to £580 billion and the price level falls to 127. The economy goes into recession.

level falls to 127, and real GDP decreases to £580 billion. The economy has gone through a recession.

What Happened to Money?   The name *real business cycle theory* is no accident. It reflects the central prediction of the theory: that the business cycle is caused by real things and not by nominal or monetary things. If the quantity of money changes, aggregate demand changes. But with no real change – with no change in the use of the factors of production and no change in potential GDP – the change in money changes only the price level. In real business cycle theory, this outcome occurs because the aggregate supply curve is the *LAS* curve, which pins real GDP down at potential GDP, so that when the *AD* curve changes only the price level changes.

Cycles and Growth   The shock that drives the business cycle of the RBC theory is the same as the force that generates economic growth: technological change. On the average, as technology advances, productivity grows. But it grows at an uneven pace. You saw this fact when you studied growth accounting in Chapter 26. There, we focused on slow-changing trends in productivity growth. Real business cycle theory uses the same idea but says there are frequent shocks to productivity that are mostly positive but that are occasionally negative.

Criticisms of RBC Theory

RBC theory is contentious, and when economists discuss it they often generate more heat than light. Its detractors claim that its basic assumptions are just too incredible. Money wages *are* sticky, they claim, so to assume otherwise is at odds with a clear fact. Intertemporal substitution is too weak, they say, to account for large fluctuations in labour supply and employment with small changes in the real wage rate.

But what really kills the RBC story, say most economists, is an implausible impulse. Technology shocks are not capable of creating the swings in productivity that growth accounting reveals. These shocks are caused by something, they concede, but they are as likely to be caused by *changes in aggregate demand* as by technology. If they are caused by demand fluctuations, then the traditional demand theories are needed to explain these shocks. Fluctuations in productivity do not cause the cycle but are caused by it!

Building on this theme, the critics point out that the so-called productivity fluctuations that growth accounting measures are correlated with changes in the growth rate of money and other indicators of changes in aggregate demand.

Defence of RBC Theory

The defenders of RBC theory claim that the theory works. It explains the macroeconomic facts about the business cycle and is consistent with the facts about economic growth. In effect, a single theory explains *both growth and cycles*. The growth accounting exercise that explains slowly changing trends also explains the more frequent business cycle swings. Its defenders also claim that RBC theory is consistent with a wide range of *microeconomic* evidence about labour supply decisions, labour demand and investment demand decisions, and information on the distribution of income between labour and capital.

RBC theorists acknowledge that money and the business cycle are correlated. That is, rapid money growth and expansion go together, and slow money growth and recession go together. But, they argue, causation does not run from money to real GDP as the traditional aggregate demand theories state. Instead, they view causation as running from real GDP to money – so-called reverse causation. In a recession, the initial fall in investment demand that lowers the interest rate decreases the demand for bank loans and lowers the profitability of banking. So banks increase their reserves and decrease their loans. The quantity of bank deposits and hence the quantity of money decreases. This reverse causation is responsible for the correlation between money growth and real GDP according to real business cycle theory.

Its defenders also argue that the RBC view is significant because it at least raises the possibility that the business cycle is efficient. The business cycle does not signal an economy that is misbehaving; it is business as usual. If this view is correct, it means that policy to smooth the cycle is misguided. Smoothing the troughs can be done only by taking out the peaks. But peaks are bursts of investment to take advantage of new technologies in a timely way. So smoothing the business cycle means delaying the benefits of new technologies.

R E V I E W

◆ The real business cycle (RBC) theory says that economic fluctuations are caused by technological change that makes productivity growth fluctuate.

◆ A fall in productivity decreases both investment demand and the demand for labour and lowers the real interest rate. The lower real interest rate decreases the supply of labour and employment and the real wage rate falls.

◆ A fall in productivity decreases both long-run aggregate supply and aggregate demand and decreases both real GDP and the price level.

You've now reviewed the main theories of the business cycle. Your next task is to examine some actual business cycles. In pursuing this task, we will focus on the recession phase of the cycle. We'll do this mainly because it is the recessions that cause most trouble. We begin by looking at the 1990–92 recession.

The 1990–1992 Recession

I n the theories of the business cycle that you've studied, recessions can be triggered by a variety of forces, some on the aggregate demand side and some on the aggregate supply side. Let's identify the shocks that triggered the most recent recession in the United Kingdom – the 1990–92 recession.

The Origins of the 1990–1992 Recession

Two forces were at work in United Kingdom during 1990 that appear to have contributed to the recession and subsequent sluggish growth and false dawns in 1993 – see the cartoon. They were:

◆ Monetary policy
◆ A slowdown in economic expansion in the world economy

Monetary Policy   Three factors made monetary policy deflationary during 1990. First, the United Kingdom joined the Exchange Rate Mechanism (ERM)[1] of the European Monetary System (EMS). Second, the Bank of England slowed the growth rate of the money supply. Third, German reunification put upward pressure on interest rates which, through the ERM, were transmitted quickly to the United Kingdom.

Inflation had reached a peak of 10 per cent by the time the United Kingdom was taken into the ERM in October 1990. Keen to restore its anti-inflation credentials, the government decided that the best way to achieve price stability was through the discipline of the ERM. The ERM is a pegged

The promised green shoots of recovery showed no signs of sprouting.

Drawing by Austin. *The Guardian.*

exchange rate system with a central rate and a wide or narrow band of fluctuations with other currencies in the system. The central rate was set at DM2.95 to the £1 with a band of ±6 per cent around its central rate.

Although inflation had peaked and was on the way down by the time the United Kingdom had entered the ERM, inflation was still above that of the EU average. With the exchange rate fixed around a band of ±6 per cent this meant that UK goods became increasingly uncompetitive in European markets. The high real interest rates that were needed to take the economy into the ERM and the loss of competitiveness had a strong negative influence on aggregate demand. The economy went into recession. Currency speculators anticipated that the UK economy could not carry on at the existing central rate of DM2.95 and expected a devaluation, causing a continuous downward pressure on the pound.

Bank of England Response   To convince currency speculators that the government did not intend to devalue, the Bank of England kept interest rates

---

[1] For a detailed explanation of the ERM, see Chapter 36.

higher than in the rest of Europe. However, the more the Bank resisted currency speculators by keeping interest rates high, the wider was the belief that the economy could not continue in recession with high real interest rates and that a devaluation must occur[2]. This is like a game of 'chicken' between two cars, except that it is between the Bank and speculators. Like a game of chicken, someone has to give way and be the chicken. In September 1992 the government of the United Kingdom became the chicken and left the ERM.

The extent to which the Bank slowed the economy can be seen from the slowdown in the growth rate of the money supply between 1990 and 1992 shown in Fig. 33.9. The growth rate of the broad definition of money, M4, slowed from 19 per cent in the first quarter of 1990 to 3 per cent in the fourth quarter of 1992.

German Reunification In November 1989 the Berlin Wall came down, and in October 1990 East Germany was reunited with West Germany. The cost of the reunification was enormous. Fiscal transfers to the eastern states pushed the government budget into deficit. From being a net lender in the world capital market, the new Germany began its life as a net borrower. The German central bank, the Bundesbank, raised interest rates to forestall the inflationary implications of the unification. As the Deutschemark was the anchor currency for the ERM, the rise in German interest rates meant that the rest of the members of the ERM had to raise their interest rates if they were to remain within the specified bands of their respective central rates. Figure 33.10 shows the influence German interest rates had on the interest rates of the United Kingdom and France. Because France remained committed to the ERM, the Bank of France raised and lowered its short-term rate of interest in line with the German short-term interest rate. The initial aim of the Bank of England was to try and stay within the bands of the ERM by keeping interest rates high. After September 1992, the short-term rate of interest in the United Kingdom was allowed to fall below that of Germany.

---

[2] This process is known as the 'Walters critique' after Professor Sir Alan Walters, who suggested that the ERM would create such destabilizing forces.

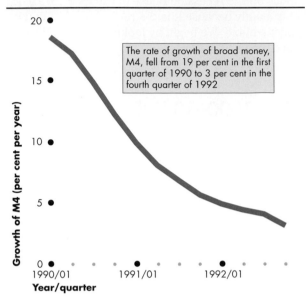

FIGURE 33.9

Money Supply Growth: 1990–1992

The rate of growth of broad money, M4, fell from 19 per cent in the first quarter of 1990 to 3 per cent in the fourth quarter of 1992

The entry of the United Kingdom into the ERM meant that the Bank of England had to pursue a tight monetary policy. The money supply growth rate began to slow during 1989. It slowed even further during 1990.

Source: *Bank of England Statistical Abstract*, 1995.

A Slowdown in Economic Expansion in the World Economy After its longest ever period of peacetime expansion, US real GDP growth began to slow in 1989 and 1990 and the United States went into recession in mid-1990. The slowdown of the US economy brought slower growth in demand for the rest of the world's exports and resulted in lower export volumes and a decline in world economic activity.

Let's see how the events we've just described influenced the UK economy in 1990.

Aggregate Demand and Aggregate Supply in the 1990–1992 Recession

The UK economy was at its peak in the second quarter of 1990. Figure 33.11 describes the effects of the various events that triggered the recession of 1990–92. The aggregate demand curve was AD_{90} and the short-run aggregate supply curve was SAS_{90}. Real GDP was £479 billion and the price level was 100.

FIGURE 33.10

European Interest Rates, 1989–1993

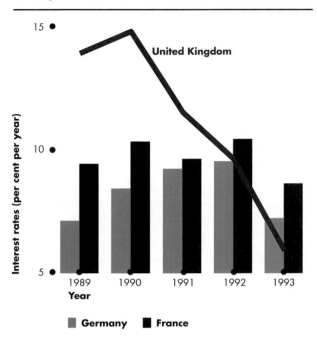

The French interest rate moved up and down with the German interest rate during this period. The UK interest rate moved up with German interest rate when the United Kingdom joined the ERM. It slipped down in 1991 as German interest rates rose. The narrowing gap between UK and German interest rates raised speculation of a withdrawal from the ERM. In September 1992, the United Kingdom left the ERM following a concerted speculative attack on the currency. UK interest rates were able to fall below German interest rates in 1993.

Source: European Union, *Annual Economic Report for the European Economy 1995* , No 59, ECSC–EC, EAEC, Brussels, 1995.

FIGURE 33.11

The 1990–1992 recession

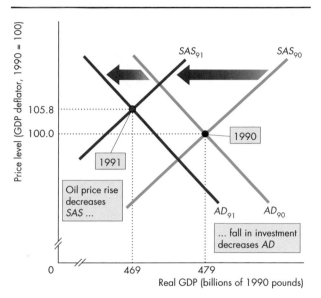

At the end of 1990, the economy was on its aggregate demand curve, AD_{90} and its short-run aggregate supply curve, SAS_{90}, with real GDP at £479 billion and a GDP deflator of 100. The combination of a decrease in both aggregate supply and aggregate demand put the economy into recession. Real GDP decreased to £469 billion and the price level increased to 105.8.

The 1990–92 recession was caused by a decrease in both aggregate demand and aggregate supply. Aggregate demand decreased, initially, because of the high real interest rate, the overvalued exchange rate and the slowdown in the growth rate of the quantity of money. These factors were soon reinforced by the slowdown in the world economy that brought a decline in the growth of exports. The combination of these factors triggered a massive decline in investment. The resulting decrease in aggregate demand is shown by the shift of the aggregate demand curve leftward to AD_{91}. Aggregate supply decreased because money wages continued to increase throughout 1990 at a rate similar rate to that

in 1989. This decrease in aggregate supply is shown in Fig. 33.11 as the shift in the short-run aggregate supply curve leftward to SAS_{91}. (The figure does not show the long-run aggregate supply curve.)

The combined effect of the decreases in aggregate supply and aggregate demand was a decrease in real GDP to £469 billion – a 2.1 per cent decrease – and an increase in the price level to 105.8 – a 5.8 per cent increase.

You've seen how aggregate demand and aggregate supply changed during the 1990–92 recession. What happened in the labour market during this recession?

The Labour Market in the 1990s

The unemployment rate increased persistently from the beginning of 1990 to the end of 1993. Figure 33.12 shows two other facts about the labour market during this period – facts about employment and the real wage rate. As employment decreased

FIGURE 33.12

The Labour Market in the 1990s

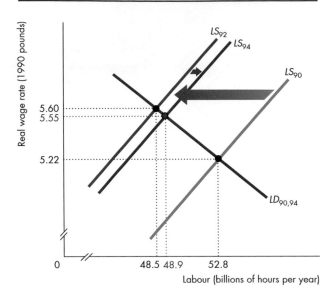

In 1990, the demand for labour was LD_{90} and the supply of labour was LS_{90}. If the quantity of labour supplied equalled the quantity of labour demanded, the real wage was £5.22 an hour and employment was 52.8 billion of hours. Money wages continued to rise because people did not anticipate the fall in inflation in 1991 and 1992, and LS shifted leftward to LS_{92}. Real wages increased to £5.60 and employment fell to 48.5 billion hours. In 1993 and 1994 money wages grew less than inflation, LS shifted rightward to LS_{94}, and real wages fell to £5.55 an hour and employment increased to 48.9 billion hours. The shifts in the LD curve were small relative to the shifts in the LS curve during this episode and are not shown here.

through 1990, 1991 and 1992, the real wage rate increased. Later, during the recovery in mid-1993, employment increased and the real wage rate decreased. These movements in employment and the real wage rate suggest that the forces of supply and demand do not operate smoothly in the labour market. Money wages continued to rise because people did not anticipate the slowdown in inflation. When inflation did slow down, the real wage rate increased and the quantity of labour demanded decreased. The loss of employment meant that when inflation fell money wages fell faster. The recovery in mid-1993 also led to a rise in labour demand in 1994.

◆ The 1990–92 recession was triggered by the government's decision to take the United Kingdom into the ERM at an overvalued exchange rate. The situation was aggravated by two further factors: first, the costs of German reunification raised interest rates within the ERM, and second, the world economy slowed down.

◆ Money wages continued to rise and the fall in inflation increased the real wage rate and lowered employment and real GDP.

You've now seen what caused the 1990–92 recession. Let's look next at the greatest of recessions – the Great Depression.

The Great Depression

The late 1920s were years of economic revival in some parts of the UK economy. While the traditional industries like coal and shipbuilding stagnated, others like motor manufacturing were booming. New firms were created, and the capital stock of the nation expanded. At the beginning of 1929, UK real GDP nearly equalled potential GDP. But as that eventful year unfolded, increasing signs of economic weakness began to appear. The most dramatic events occurred in October when the US stock market collapsed, losing more than one-third of its value in two weeks. The four years that followed were years of monstrous economic depression all over the world.

Figure 33.13 shows the dimensions of the Great Depression. On the eve of the Great Depression in 1929, the economy was on aggregate demand curve AD_{29} and short-run aggregate supply curve SAS_{29}. Real GDP was £123 billion (1990 pounds) and the GDP deflator was 3.4 (1990 = 100).

In 1931, there was a widespread expectation that the price level would fall, and the money wage rate fell. With a lower money wage rate, the short-run aggregate supply curve shifted from SAS_{29} to SAS_{31}. But increased pessimism and lower trade decreased investment, and the demand for consumer durables and aggregate demand decreased to AD_{31}. In 1931, real GDP decreased by 7 per cent from its 1929 position,

FIGURE 33.13

The Great Depression

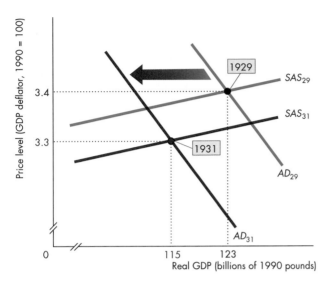

In 1929, real GDP was £123 billion and the GDP deflator was 3.4 – at the intersection of AD_{29} and SAS_{29}. Increased pessimism from a fall in world trade resulted in a drop in investment, resulting in a decrease in aggregate demand to AD_{31}. To some degree, this decrease was reflected in the labour market and wages fell, so the short-run aggregate supply curve shifted to SAS_{31}. Real GDP and the price level fell. By 1931, real GDP had fallen to £115 billion (93 per cent of its 1929 level) and the GDP deflator had fallen to 3.3 (97 per cent of its 1929 level).

and the price level fell by 3 per cent to 3.3.

Although the Great Depression brought enormous hardship, the distribution of that hardship was uneven. At its worst point, 16 per cent of the work–force had no jobs at all. Although there was unemployment benefit and other forms of poor relief, there was a considerable level of poverty for those on the dole. But the wallets of those who kept their jobs barely noticed the Great Depression. It is true that wages fell. But at the same time, the price level fell by more, so real wages actually rose. Thus those who had jobs were paid a wage rate that had an increasing buying power during the Great Depression.

You can begin to appreciate the magnitude of the Great Depression if you compare it with the 1990–92 recession. In 1991, real GDP fell by 2.1 per cent. In comparison, in 1931, it fell by 5.3 per cent.

Why the Great Depression Happened

The late 1920s were years of economic recovery in the world economy, but they were also years of increasing uncertainty. The main source of increased uncertainty was international. The world economy was going through tumultuous times. The patterns of world trade were changing as the United Kingdom began its period of relative economic decline and new economic powers such as Japan began to emerge. International currency fluctuations and the introduction of restrictive trade policies by many countries (see Chapter 35) further increased the uncertainty faced by firms. There was also domestic uncertainty arising from the restrictive monetary and fiscal policy followed by the government to ensure that the pound remained on the gold standard. Because prices in the United States fell, prices in the United Kingdom had to fall to maintain an exchange rate of $4.86 per pound sterling, and remain on the gold standard. This meant that the recovery in the United Kingdom was good but not booming like in the United States.

This environment of uncertainty was fuelled by the slowdown in the world economy following the stock market crash of 1929. It was this slowdown in the world economy which led to a drop in exports, which led to a fall in income, consumer spending and investment, which led to the initial leftward shift of the aggregate demand curve from AD_{29} to AD_{31} in Fig. 33.13.

Output fell for two years after 1929, but what stopped the Great Depression in the United Kingdom developing into the disaster that hit the United States was the fact that the United Kingdom left the gold standard. Leaving the gold standard meant that the pound was no longer convertible into gold, and interest rates that were kept high to make the pound attractive relative to the price of gold in US dollars could now be lower. Indeed, interest rates fell dramatically in the 1930s. Money was cheap, and lower interest rates fuelled a consumer revival and a house-building boom.

What really distinguishes the Great Depression was not what happened in the United Kingdom but what happened to the world's largest economy – the United States. Between 1929 and 1933 in the United States real GDP fell by nearly 30 per cent. But economists, even to this day, have not reached an agreement on how to explain those events. One view, argued by Peter Temin[3], is that spending continued

---

[3] Peter Temin, *Did Monetary Forces Cause the Great Depression?* 1976 (New York, W. W. Norton).

to fall for a wide variety of reasons – including a continuation of increasing pessimism and uncertainty. According to Temin's view, the continued contraction resulted from a collapse of expenditure that was independent of the decrease in the quantity of money. The investment demand curve shifted leftward. Milton Friedman and Anna J. Schwartz have argued that the continuation of the contraction was almost exclusively the result of the subsequent worsening of financial and monetary conditions[4]. According to Friedman and Schwartz, it was a severe cut in the money supply that lowered aggregate demand, prolonging the contraction and deepening the depression.

Although there is disagreement about the causes of the contraction phase of the Great Depression in the United States, the disagreement is not about the elements at work but the degree of importance attached to each. Everyone agrees that increased pessimism and uncertainty lowered investment demand, and everyone agrees that there was a massive contraction of the real money supply. Temin and his supporters assign primary importance to the fall in autonomous expenditure and secondary importance to the fall in the money supply. Friedman and Schwartz and their supporters assign primary responsibility to the money supply and regard the other factors as being of limited importance.

Let's look at the contraction of aggregate demand a bit more closely. Between 1930 and 1933, the nominal money supply in the United States decreased by 20 per cent. This decrease in the money supply was not directly induced by the Federal Reserve's actions. The *monetary base* (currency in circulation and bank reserves) hardly fell at all. But the bank deposits component of the money supply suffered an enormous collapse. It did so primarily because a large number of banks failed. Before the Great Depression, fuelled by increasing share prices and booming business conditions, bank loans expanded. But after the stock market crash and the downturn, many borrowers found themselves in hard economic times. They could not pay the interest on their loans, and they could not meet

the agreed repayment schedules. Banks had deposits that exceeded the realistic value of the loans that they had made. When depositors withdrew funds from the banks, the banks lost reserves and many of them simply couldn't meet their depositors' demands to be repaid.

Bank failures feed on themselves and create additional failures. Seeing banks fail, people become anxious to protect themselves and so take their money out of the banks. This happened in the United States in 1930. The quantity of notes and coins in circulation increased and the volume of bank deposits declined. But the very action of people who took money out of the bank to protect their wealth accentuated the process of banking failure. Banks were increasingly short of cash and unable to meet their obligations.

Monetary contraction also occurred in the United Kingdom, although on a less serious scale than in the United States. The broad money supply fell in 1931 by 1 per cent and did not decline in any other year, in contrast to the whopping 20 per cent in the United States. Also, the United Kingdom had no serious problems with bank failure in contrast to the United States. This was because lower interest rates meant that money was cheap and also banks always had access to the Bank of England. Another reason was the development of branch banking in the United Kingdom, which meant that if a particular sector that was concentrated in a geographical region was to collapse, the commercial bank would not go down with it. The main bank office in London could shore up any loss-making branches in a region.

What role did the stock market crash of 1929 play in producing the Great Depression in the United States? It certainly created an atmosphere of fear and panic, and probably contributed to the overall air of uncertainty that dampened investment spending. It also reduced the wealth of shareholders, encouraging them to cut their consumption spending. But the direct effect of the stock market crash on consumption, although a contributory factor to the Great Depression, was not the major source of the drop in aggregate demand. It was the collapse in investment arising from increased uncertainty that brought the 1930 decline in aggregate demand.

The stock market crash was, however, a predictor of severe recession. It reflected the expectations of shareholders concerning future profit prospects.

---

[4] This explanation was developed by Milton Friedman and Anna J. Schwartz in *A Monetary History of the United States 1867-1960,* 1963 (Princeton, Princeton University Press), Chapter. 7.

As those expectations became pessimistic, people sold their shares. There were more sellers than buyers and the prices of shares were bid lower and lower. That is, the behaviour of the stock market was a consequence of expectations about future profitability and those expectations were lowered as a result of increased uncertainty.

Can It Happen Again?

Since, even today, we have an incomplete understanding of the causes of the Great Depression, we are not able to predict such an event or to be sure that it cannot occur again. The stock market crash of 1987 did not translate into a world slowdown or a contraction anything like that of 1929. But there are some significant differences between the economy of the 1990s and that of the 1930s that make a severe depression much less likely today than it was 60 years ago. The most significant features of the economy that make severe depression less likely today are:

◆ Bank deposit protection
◆ The Bank of England's role as lender of last resort
◆ Taxes and government spending
◆ Multi-income families

Let's examine these in turn.

Bank Deposit Protection   The Bank of England deposit protection scheme covers 90 per cent of the first £20,000 per depositor of the banks that come under the scheme. So small depositors are virtually fully covered. With some form of deposit insurance, depositors have little to lose if a bank fails and so have no incentive to cause a panic by withdrawing their deposits, and thereby precipitating a bank crisis.

Although bank failure was not a severe problem in the United Kingdom during the Great Depression, it clearly was an important factor in intensifying the depression in the United States. And the severity of the US recession certainly had an impact on the United Kingdom and the rest of the world. World trade fell dramatically in 1930–33 with the fall in aggregate demand in the United States.

Lender of Last Resort   The Bank of England is the lender of last resort in the UK economy. If a

single bank is short of reserves, it can borrow reserves from other banks. If the entire banking system is short of reserves, banks can borrow from the Bank of England. By making reserves available (at a suitable interest rate), the Bank of England is able to make the quantity of reserves in the banking system respond flexibly to the demand for those reserves. Bank failure can be prevented, or at least contained, to cases where bad management practices are the source of the problem. Widespread failures of the type that occurred in the Great Depression can be prevented.

Taxes and Government Spending   The government sector was a much smaller part of the economy in 1929 than it has become today. On the eve of that earlier recession, government purchases of goods and services were less than 25 per cent of GDP. Today, government purchases exceed 40 per cent of GDP. Government transfer payments were about 6 per cent of GDP in 1929. Today, they are 18 per cent of GDP.

A higher level of government purchases of goods and services means that when recession hits, a large component of aggregate demand does not decline. But government transfer payments are the most sensitive economic stabilizer. When the economy goes into recession and depression, more people qualify for unemployment insurance and social assistance. As a consequence, although disposable income decreases, the extent of the decrease is moderated by the existence of such programmes. Consumption expenditure, in turn, does not decline by as much as it would in the absence of such government programmes. The limited decline in consumption spending further limits the overall decrease in aggregate expenditure, thereby limiting the magnitude of an economic downturn.

Multi-income Families   At the time of the Great Depression, families with more than one wage earner were much less common than they are today. The work-force participation rate in 1929 was around 45 per cent. Today, it is 75 per cent. Thus even if the unemployment rate increased to around 20 per cent today, 60 per cent of the adult population would actually have jobs. During the Great Depression, only 40 per cent of the adult population had work. Multi-income families have greater security than single-income families. The chance of both (or all) income earners in a family losing their

The Recession Watch is On

The Essence of the Story

THE FINANCIAL TIMES, 31 MARCH 1996

Sunny forecasts fail to dispel gloom

Wolfgang Münchau, Judy Dempsey and Michael Lindermann

Germans do not like the economic outlook – no matter what anyone says

The sharp downturn in the German economy has proved a problem to most of the country's forecasters – they did not predict it, then they denied it was happening and now they are saying it may be over soon.

But while they have been consistently optimistic, companies and consumers have been consistently pessimistic. Their current mood suggests that the economic picture is bound to get worse as sector after sector reports deteriorating returns.

Profit growth, where it exists at all, originates mostly from a squeeze on suppliers and from staff cuts, the companies say, and this in turn adds to spending restraint.

The level of car purchases – generally considered to be one of the best indicators of the state of the German soul – suddenly dropped off in the middle of last year....

Mr Rainer Guttmann, a consultant at Autohaus Müller ...said 'In many ways, the situation now is worse than in the last recession, unlike then, people have more money, there is a lot of inherited money swirling around. But people are afraid of losing their jobs, so they keep driving their old cars a little while longer....

He said many Germans, once punctilious about paying on time, were frequently resorting to delays, putting small suppliers at risk.

Similar pessimism prevails in the rest of the retail sector, apart from aggressive discount department stores.

Mr George Hardy, who owns three interior design shops in one of Berlin's fashionable districts, shrugs his shoulders when he thinks about the future. 'I've seen times when people hold back for a few weeks in terms of ordering or buying furniture. But over the past year I have seen a change. People are simply not spending.'

Mr Hardy expects no improvement in the coming months: 'The taxes are too high. Consumer spending is flat. I see no signs of a let up.'

Mr Steffen Kern from Germany's association of retailers (HDE) said: 'The problem is that the growing fear of unemployment will damp down any expectations of an improvement in the retail sector over the coming months.'

HDE expects zero growth in the retail sector this year – and that follows three years of negative growth. Economists believe consumer spending will not grow by more than 2 per cent this year. This bodes ill for the industry, which accounts for about 27 per cent of the total gross domestic product and employs 3.2 million people....

The other reason is that real incomes fell in 1994 and 1995, as higher taxes and social security contributions outstripped pay rises. This year, the government cut some taxes, giving Germans at least an extra DM10bn (£4.5bn) to spend, according to conservative estimates, but few see this feeding through into significantly higher consumption.

The chief executive of a medium-sized electronics company was blunt about the prospects for higher consumer spending. 'It's all window dressing. There may be less taxes to pay but other costs – health insurance, national insurance contributions, the fees for public services – have all gone up. There can't be any higher consumer spending.'

Other industrialists point out that German industry is working below full capacity anyway, so there is no incentive, and not much money, to make further capital investments.

The bigger companies may be slightly more optimistic but point out that whatever growth rates there may be will be insufficient.

Mr Gerhard Cromme, who heads the Krupp Hoesch steel and engineering group, said 'investments in plant will rise by perhaps 3 or 4 per cent this year, but what we really need is 6 or 8 per cent'. He and others say there was a 'psychological collapse' last autumn when German companies first felt the impact of the stronger D-Mark on their order books.

The debate about Germany's competitiveness, its high labour costs and tough regulatory environment, has added to the prevailing uncertainty. Some companies have now moved production abroad, especially to countries like Poland or the Czech Republic.

■ The sharp downturn in the German economy in 1995 was not expected by most of the country's economic forecasters. The optimism of the economists was not matched by consumers and firms.

■ Consumer spending was weak because people were cautious about making medium-term expenditure commitments owing to rising unemployment.

■ The retail sector expected zero growth in spending in 1996 while economic forecasters expected consumer spending to grow by 2 per cent.

■ Consumer spending was also weakened by higher taxes. Taxes were reduced in 1996, but other costs had increased.

■ Investment was expected to remain low because of a 'psychological collapse' in late 1995 with the impact of a strong Deutschemark on export orders.

Economic Analysis

■ Because a recession can be triggered by many factors and economists do not fully understand the business cycle mechanism, it is always difficult to forecast when a recession begins.

■ In looking for signs of recession, economists use their own preferred theory of the business cycle.

■ The theory used in the news article – a consumer sentiment theory – is not a standard theory in economics but has a resemblance to the Keynesian 'animal spirits' view. One commentator representing the steel and engineering sectors referred to a 'psychological collapse' in 1995.

■ If consumers become anxious about jobs, they cut spending. Lower spending leads to job losses, which validates the anxiety. Investment falls and recession begins.

■ Figure 1 shows how the components of aggregate expenditure changed during 1993–96. You can see from Fig. 1 that all the components show a dip in their respective growth rates in the second quarter of 1995, which

means than none of them were good leading indicators of a change in direction of the economy. Investment is usually a leading indicator and you can see that the fall in investment at the end of 1995 had a strong effect on growth.

■ Figure 2 shows that unemployment is not an early indicator of recession. Unemployment is often referred to as a lagging indicator. Unemployment tends to react after the direction of growth has altered.

■ Two things have made a recession in late 1996 possible in Germany. Cuts in government spending to meet the Maastricht Treaty conditions for European Monetary Union in 1999 have deflated demand. Low inflation from historically tight monetary policy has led to a strong Deutschemark, which has led to a fall in export growth.

■ Economic forecasters have remained optimistic about the German economy because the lowering of interest rates was expected to stimulate demand in 1996–97. Table 1 shows the forecast made by the OECD in December 1995.

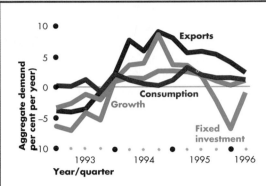

Figure 1 Components of aggregate demand

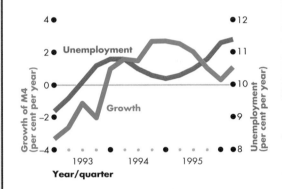

Figure 2 GDP growth and unemployment

Table 1

Germany: forecast of growth rates (1991 prices)			
	1995	1996	1997
Private consumption	1.8	2.4	2.2
Government consumption	2.1	2.0	1.6
Gross fixed investment	2.2	3.6	5.1
Exports	3.8	6.5	6.9
GDP	2.1	2.4	2.7

Source: OECD, *Economic Outlook*, 58, Paris, December 1995.

jobs simultaneously is much lower than the chance of a single earner losing work. With greater family income security, family consumption is likely to be less sensitive to fluctuations in family income that are seen as temporary. Thus when aggregate income falls, it does not induce an equivalent cut in consumption. For example, during the 1980–81 recession real GDP fell but personal consumption expenditure did not.

For the four reasons we have just reviewed, it appears the economy has better shock-absorbing characteristics today than it had in the 1920s and 1930s. Even if there is a collapse of confidence leading to a decrease in investment, the recession mechanism that is now in place will not translate that initial shock into the large and prolonged decrease in real GDP and increase in unemployment that occurred more than 60 years ago.

Because the economy is now more immune to severe recession than it was in the 1930s, even a stock market crash of the magnitude that occurred in 1987 had barely noticeable effects on spending. A crash of a similar magnitude in 1929 resulted in the collapse of investment and consumer durable purchases in the United Kingdom. In the period following the 1987 stock market crash, investment and spending on durable goods continued to grow.

None of this is to say that there might not be a deep recession or even a Great Depression in the last half of the 1990s (or beyond). But it would take a very severe shock to trigger one.

R E V I E W

◆ The Great Depression was brought on by the collapse in demand in the world's largest economy – the United States. The fall in demand in the United States led to a sharp downturn in world trade.

◆ What stopped the Great Depression in the United Kingdom developing into the scale of the collapse in the United States was that, in September 1931, the United Kingdom left the gold standard.

◆ ◆ ◆ ◆ We have now completed our study of the business cycle. Economic analysts use theories of the business cycle to forecast recessions and booms. You can see an example of this in *Reading Between the Lines* on pp. 882–883. We have also completed our study of the science of macroeconomics and learned about the influences on long-term economic growth and inflation as well as the business cycle. We have discovered that these issues pose huge policy challenges. How can we speed up the rate of economic growth while at the same time keeping inflation low and avoiding big swings of the business cycle? Our task in the next chapter is to study these macroeconomic policy challenges.

S U M M A R Y

Patterns, Impulses and Propagation Mechanisms

Since the turn of the century, there have been nine business cycle turning points. Recessions have on the average lasted about two years, while expansions have lasted on the average about six years. The economy can be hit (like a tennis ball), cycle indefinitely (like the turning of day into night) and cycle in swings that get milder until another shock hits (like a rocking horse). (pp. 862–863)

Aggregate Demand Theories of the Business Cycle

Aggregate demand theories of the cycle are based on the aggregate supply–aggregate demand model. Keynesian theory is based on volatile expectations about future sales and profits. Monetarist theory regards fluctuations in the money stock as the main source of economic fluctuations. Rational expectations theories identify unanticipated fluctuations in aggregate demand as the main source of economic fluctuations. (pp. 864–870)

Real Business Cycle Theory

In real business cycle (RBC) theory, economic fluctuations are caused by fluctuations in the influence of technological change on productivity growth. A temporary slowdown in the pace of technological change decreases investment demand and both the demand for labour and the supply of labour.

The name *real* business cycle theory reflects the central prediction of the theory: that the business cycle is caused by real things and not by money. (pp. 870–875)

The 1990–1992 Recession

Three forces contributed to the weak performance of the UK economy in the early 1990s: the ERM, the reunification of Germany and a slowdown in economic expansion in the world economy. (pp. 875–878)

The Great Depression

The Great Depression in the United States that began in 1929 lasted longer and was more severe than any before it or since. The Great Depression started with increased uncertainty and pessimism that brought a fall in investment and spending on consumer durables. Increased uncertainty and pessimism also brought on the stock market crash. The crash added to the pessimistic outlook and further spending cuts occurred. In the United States, the financial system nearly collapsed. Banks failed and the money supply decreased, resulting in a continued decrease in aggregate demand. The United Kingdom financial system held up better, but the chaos in the United States influenced economic activity throughout the world. Expectations of falling prices led to falling wages, but the decrease in aggregate demand continued to exceed expectations and real GDP continued to decrease.

A repeat of such a depression is much less likely today. The Bank of England's willingness to act as lender of last resort and the introduction of the deposit protection scheme both reduce the risk of bank failure and financial collapse. Higher taxes and government spending have given the economy greater resistance against depression, and an increased work-force participation rate provides a greater measure of security, especially for families with more than one wage earner. For these reasons, an initial change in either aggregate demand or aggregate supply is much less likely to translate into an accumulative depression than it did in the early 1930s. (pp. 878–884)

KEY ELEMENTS

Key Terms

Keynesian theory of the business cycle, 864
Monetarist theory of the business cycle, 866
New classical theory of the business cycle, 867
New Keynesian theory of the business cycle, 867
Rational expectation, 866
Real business cycle (RBC) theory, 870

Key Figures

Figure 33.2   A Keynesian Recession, 865
Figure 33.3   A Keynesian Expansion, 865
Figure 33.4   A Monetarist Business Cycle, 867
Figure 33.5   A Rational Expectations Business Cycle, 869
Figure 33.7   Factor Markets in a Real Business Cycle, 872
Figure 33.8   *AD–AS* in a Real Business Cycle, 873
Figure 33.11 The 1990–1992 recession, 877
Figure 33.13 The Great Depression, 879

REVIEW QUESTIONS

1 Distinguish between a cycle impulse and a cycle mechanism and identify the impulse and mechanism in three analogies given in this chapter.

2 What is the Keynesian theory of the business cycle? Carefully distinguish its impulse and its mechanism.

3 What is the monetarist theory of the business cycle? Carefully distinguish its impulse and its mechanism.

4 What are the rational expectations theories of the business cycle? Carefully distinguish their impulses and their mechanisms.

5 What is the key difference between the new classical theory and new Keynesian theory of the business cycle?

6 What is the impulse that causes economic fluctuations according to real business cycle theory?

7 What happens to investment demand and the demand for labour if a technological change brings a large increase in productivity?

8 How is the labour supply decision influenced by the real interest rate?

9 Why is there no *SAS* curve in real business cycle theory?

10 List the main arguments against and in favour of real business cycle theory.

11 What triggered the 1990–92 recession?

12 When did the Great Depression occur? Why did it affect the United States more than the United Kingdom?

13 Describe the changes in employment and real wages in the 1990–92 recession. What is the sticky wage theory of these changes? What is the flexible wage theory of these changes?

14 What were the main causes of the onset of the Great Depression in the United States in 1929?

15 What four features of today's economy make it less likely now than in 1929 that a Great Depression will occur? Why do they make it less likely?

PROBLEMS

1 Here is a news report about the past year in Gloomland:

'Business confidence is low. Firms have cut back on investment and laid off tens of thousands of workers. Productivity has collapsed. Real GDP has decreased and the price level, the real wage rate, the real interest rate and the money supply have all fallen.'

Try to explain these events by using the alternative theories of the business cycle. Are the facts as reported inconsistent with any of the theories? Use diagrams to illustrate your reasoning.

2 Here is a news report about the past year in Coolland:

'Business confidence is high. Business investment is booming. Jobs are easy to find

and firms have a hard time hiring. Productivity is growing rapidly. Real GDP has increased and the price level is stable.'

Try to explain these events by using the alternative theories of the business cycle. Are the facts as reported inconsistent with any of the theories? Use diagrams to illustrate your reasoning.

3 Use carefully drawn figures to illustrate the evolution of the economy during the recession of 1980–81 and the expansion through the rest of the 1980s according to:

a Keynesian theory
b Monetarist theory
c Rational expectations theories
d Real business cycle theory

4 The table illustrates the economy of Virtual-reality. When the economy is in a long-run equilibrium, it is at row *b*. When a recession occurs in Virtualreality, the economy moves away from this position to another identified by rows *a*, *c* and *d* in the three separate markets.

Labour market			AS–AD		Investment	
	Real Wage	Employment	Price level	Real GDP	Real interest rate	Investment
a	5	100	150	5	5	1
b	4	200	100	10	4	2
c	4	100	100	5	4	1
d	3	100	50	5	3	1

  a If the Keynesian theory is the correct explanation for the recession, to which positions does the economy move?

  b If the monetarist theory is the correct explanation for the recession, to which positions does the economy move?

  c If the new classical rational expectations theory is the correct explanation for the recession, to which positions does the economy move?

  d If the new Keynesian rational expectations theory is the correct explanation for the recession, to which positions does the economy move?

  e If real business cycle theory is the correct explanation for the recession, to which positions does the economy move?

5 Suppose that when the recession occurs in Virtualreality shown in the table accompanying Problem 4, the economy moves to *a* in the labour market, *d* in *AS–AD* and *d* in investment. Which, if any, theory of the business cycle could explain this outcome?

6 Suppose that when the recession occurs in Virtualreality shown in the table accompanying Problem 4, the economy moves to row *d* in these markets. Which, if any, theory of the business cycle could explain this outcome?

7 Suppose that when the recession occurs in Virtualreality shown in the table accompanying Problem 4, the economy moves to *a* in the labour market, *a* in *AS–AD* and *d* in investment. Which, if any, theory of the business cycle could explain this outcome?

8 Suppose that when the recession occurs in Virtualreality shown in the table accompanying Problem 4, the economy moves to *c* in the labour market, *a* in *AS–AD* and *d* in investment. Which, if any, theory of the business cycle could explain this outcome?

9 Suppose that when the recession occurs in Virtualreality shown in the table accompanying Problem 4, the economy moves to *a* in the labour market, *d* in *AS–AD* and *a* in investment. Which, if any, theory of the business cycle could explain this outcome?

10 During the 1990–92 recession, real wages increased from £5.22 an hour in 1990 to £5.59 in 1992 and employment decreased from 46.3 billion hours in 1990 to 42.6 billion hours in 1992. How can these changes be explained by the sticky and flexible wage theories?

11 Study *Reading Between the Lines* on pp. 882–883 and then answer the following questions:

  a What were the factors that contributed to the recessionary expectations of consumers and firms?

  b Explain the theory of consumer spending used to forecast the impending recession in Germany.

  c What were the main developments in the German economy in 1995 that made a near-future recession look possible?

  c Why are economic forecasters optimistic about the German economy in the near future?

'We don't want to manage the US economy. And we don't think anybody else should take the job either.'

Robert E. Lucas Jr, PERSONAL INTERVIEW

Business Cycles

THE ISSUES AND IDEAS

Economic activity has fluctuated between boom and bust for as long as we've kept records. The range of fluctuations became especially pronounced during the nineteenth and early twentieth centuries.

Understanding the sources of economic fluctuations has turned out to be difficult. One reason is that there are no simple patterns. Every new episode of the business cycle is different from its predecessor in some way. Some cycles are long and some short, some are mild and some severe, some begin in Europe and some in other parts of the world. We never know with any certainty when the next turning point (down or up) is coming or what will cause it. A second reason is that the apparent waste of resources during a recession or depression seems to contradict the very foundation of economics: resources are limited and people have unlimited wants – there is scarcity. A satisfactory theory of the business cycle must explain why scarce resources don't *always* get fully employed.

One theory is that recessions result from insufficient aggregate demand. The solution is to increase government spending, cut taxes and cut interest rates. But demand stimulation must not be overdone. Countries that stimulate aggregate demand too much, such as Brazil, find their economic growth rates sagging, unemployment rising and inflation accelerating.

Today's new theory, real business cycle theory, predicts that fluctuations in aggregate demand have no effect on output and employment and change only the price level and inflation rate. But this theory ignores the *real* effects of financial collapse of the type that occurred in the 1930s. If banks fail on a large scale and people lose their wealth, other firms also begin to fail and jobs are destroyed. Unemployed people cut their spending, and output falls yet further. Demand stimulation may not be called for, but action to ensure that sound banks survive certainly is.

While economists are trying to understand the sources of the business cycle, the government and the Bank of England are doing the best they can to moderate it. In the years since World War II, there appears to have been some success. Although the business cycle has not disappeared, it has become much less severe.

THEN ...

What happens to the economy when people lose confidence in banks? They withdraw their funds. These withdrawals feed on themselves, creating a snowball of withdrawals and, eventually, panic. Short of funds with which to repay depositors, banks call in loans, and previously sound businesses are faced with financial distress. They close down and lay off workers. Recession deepens and turns into depression. Bank failures and the resulting decline in the nation's supply of money and credit were a significant factor in deepening and prolonging the Great Depression. But they taught us the importance of stable financial institutions and gave rise to the establishment of a bank deposit protection scheme to prevent such financial collapse.

... AND NOW

How can it be that a building designed as a shop has no better use than to be boarded up and left empty? Not enough aggregate demand, say the Keynesians. Not so, say the real business cycle theorists. Technological change has reduced the building's current productivity as a shop to zero. But its expected future productivity is sufficiently high that it is not efficient to refit the building for some other purpose.

All unemployment, whether of buildings or people, can be explained in a similar way. For example, how can it be that during a recession a person trained as a shop assistant is without work? Not enough aggregate demand is one answer. Another is that the current productivity of shop assistants is low, but their expected future productivity is sufficiently high that it does not pay an unemployed assistant to retrain for a job that is currently available.

THE ECONOMIST: ROBERT E. LUCAS JR

Robert E. Lucas Jr

Many economists, past and present, have advanced our understanding of business cycles. But one contemporary economist stands out. He is Robert E. Lucas Jr of the University of Chicago, who was the 1995 recipient of the Nobel Prize for Economic Science. In 1970, then a 32-year-old professor at Carnegie Mellon University, Lucas challenged the Keynesian theories of economic fluctuations and launched a macroeconomic revolution that was based on two principles: people and businesses make rational decisions based on rational expectations; and markets reconcile individual decisions by balancing supply and demand, even in a recession. Like all scientific revolutions, the one touched off by Lucas was controversial. Twenty years later, the concept of rational expectations (whether right or wrong) is accepted by most economists. But the idea that in a recession when unemployment is high supply equals demand, remains controversial. Along with his teacher Milton Friedman, Lucas believes that governments cannot smooth out business cycles and that their attempts to do so are misguided and sometimes do more harm than good.

CHAPTER 34

MACROECONOMIC POLICY CHALLENGES

After studying this chapter you will be able to:

◆ Describe the goals of macroeconomic policy

◆ Describe the main features of recent fiscal and monetary policy in the United Kingdom and the European Union

◆ Explain how fiscal policy and monetary policy influence long-term economic growth

◆ Distinguish between and evaluate fixed-rule and feedback-rule policies to stabilize the business cycle

◆ Explain how fiscal policy influences the natural unemployment rate

◆ Evaluate fixed-rule and feedback-rule policies to contain inflation and explain why lowering inflation usually brings recession

B Y ALL ACCOUNTS THE UK ECONOMY HAD AN OUTSTANDING YEAR IN 1994. REAL GDP expanded by 3.9 per cent, unemployment fell to 9.6 per cent and inflation remained low with only a 2.4 per cent rise in the consumer price index. The United Kingdom was not alone in achieving a strong macro-economic performance in 1994. Within the European Union above 4 per cent real GDP growth in 1994 was recorded by Denmark, Ireland, Luxembourg and Finland. Real GDP in Canada expanded by more than 4 per cent, and in the developing countries of Asia by 8 per cent. But not all countries and regions shared in this solid growth. The EU average for real GDP growth in 1994 was 2.8 per cent. Greece's real GDP grew by only 1.5 per cent and Portugal's by 1.1 per cent. Japan's real GDP expanded by a lacklustre 0.9 per cent and in Russia, real GDP shrank for the fourth successive year to less than two-thirds of its 1990 level. ◆ There were clouds, even in the United Kingdom's eco-nomic sky. Interest rates increased through the year and the government budget deficit remained high at 6.8 per cent of GDP. Also, no one believed that UK real GDP growth of 4 per cent a year could be maintained. Looking at the longer-term trend, potential GDP growth was little more than 2 per cent a year

What Can Policy Do?

and as real GDP growth overtook potential GDP growth, the fear of renewed inflation was awakened, to be followed, most likely, by another recession. ◆ The wide variety of macroeconomic performance raises questions about macroeconomic policy. How do fis-cal and monetary policy influence the economy? What can policy do to improve macroeconomic performance? Can the government use its fiscal policy to speed up long-term growth, keep inflation in check and maintain a low unemployment rate? Can the central bank use its monetary policy to achieve any of these ends? Are some policy goals better achieved by fiscal policy and some by monetary policy? And what specific policy actions do the best job? Are some ways of conducting policy better than others?

◆ ◆ ◆ ◆ In this chapter we're going to study the challenges of using policy to influ-ence the economy and achieve the highest sustainable long-term growth rate and low unemployment while avoiding high inflation. At the end of the chapter, you will have a clearer and deeper understanding of the macroeconomic policy problems facing the United Kingdom and other EU countries today and of the debates that surround us concerning those problems.

Policy Goals

The goals of macroeconomic policy are to:

◆ Achieve the highest sustainable rate of long-term real GDP growth

◆ Smooth out avoidable business cycle fluctuations

◆ Maintain low unemployment

◆ Maintain low inflation

Long-term Real GDP Growth

We examined growth briefly in Chapter 22 (Fig. 22.3). Rapid sustained real GDP growth can make a profound contribution to economic well-being. With a growth rate of 2 per cent a year, it takes more than 30 years for production to double. With a growth rate of 5 per cent a year, production doubles in just 15 years. The limits to *sustainable* growth are determined by the availability of natural resources, by environmental considerations, and by the willingness of people to save and invest in new capital and new technologies rather than consume everything they produce.

How fast can the economy grow over the long term? Between 1987 and 1994, through one complete business cycle, potential GDP grew at a rate of 2.3 per cent a year. Because the UK population grows at about 0.5 per cent a year, a real GDP growth rate of 2.3 per cent a year translates into a growth rate of real GDP per person of 1.8 per cent a year, which means that output per person doubles every 39 years. So increasing the long-term growth rate is of critical importance.

The Business Cycle

Potential GDP probably does not grow at a constant rate. Fluctuations in the pace of technological advance and in the pace of investment in new capital bring fluctuations in potential GDP. So some fluctuations in real GDP represent fluctuations in potential GDP. But when real GDP grows less quickly than potential GDP, output is lost, and when real GDP grows more quickly than potential GDP, bottlenecks arise that create inefficiencies and inflationary pressures. Keeping real GDP growth steady and equal to long-run aggregate supply growth avoids these problems.

It is not known how smooth real GDP can be made. Real business cycle theory regards all the fluctuations in real GDP as arising from fluctuations in potential GDP. The aggregate demand theories of the business cycle regard most of the fluctuations in real GDP as being avoidable deviations from potential GDP.

Unemployment

When real GDP growth slows, unemployment increases and rises above the natural rate of unemployment. The higher the unemployment rate, the longer is the time taken by unemployed people to find jobs. Productive labour is wasted and there is a slowdown in the accumulation of human capital. If high unemployment persists, serious psychological and social problems arise for the unemployed workers and their families.

When real GDP growth speeds up, unemployment decreases and falls below the natural rate of unemployment. The lower the unemployment rate, the harder it becomes for expanding industries to get the labour they need to keep growing. If extremely low unemployment persists, serious bottlenecks and production dislocations occur, sucking in imports and creating inflationary pressure.

Keeping unemployment at the natural rate avoids both of these problems. But just what is the natural rate of unemployment? Assessments vary. The actual average unemployment rate over the most recent business cycle – 1987 to 1994 – was 8.3 per cent. Most economists would put the natural rate at below 8 per cent and possibly about 6 per cent. A few economists believe the natural rate is much lower than this, perhaps as low as 3 per cent. At the other extreme, real business cycle theorists believe the natural rate fluctuates and equals the actual unemployment rate.

If the natural unemployment rate becomes high, then a goal of policy is to lower the natural rate itself. This goal is independent of smoothing the business cycle.

Inflation

When inflation fluctuates unpredictably, money becomes less useful as a measuring rod for conducting transactions. Borrowers and lenders and employers and workers must take on extra risks. Keeping the inflation rate steady and predictable avoids these problems.

Keeping inflation steady also helps keep the value of the pound abroad steady. Other things remaining the same, if the inflation rate goes up by 1 per centage point, the pound loses 1 per cent of its value against the currencies of other countries. Large and unpredictable fluctuations in the foreign exchange rate – the value of the pound against other currencies – make international trade and international borrowing and lending less profitable and limit the gains from international specialization and exchange. Keeping inflation low and predictable helps avoid such fluctuations in the exchange rate and enables international transactions to be undertaken at minimum risk and on the desired scale (see also the Exchange Rate Mechanism in Chapter 36).

What is the most desirable inflation rate? Some economists say that the *rate* of inflation doesn't matter much as long as the rate is *predictable*. So, say these economists, any predictable inflation rate will serve well as a target for policy. But most economists believe that price stability, which they translate at an inflation rate of between 0 and 3 per cent, is desirable. The reason zero is not the target is that some price increases are due to quality improvements – a measurement bias in the price index – so a positive average *measured* inflation rate is equivalent to price stability. It has been suggested that a good definition of price stability is a situation in which no one considers inflation to be a factor in the decisions they make.

The Two Core Policy Indicators: Unemployment and Inflation

Although macroeconomic policy pursues the four goals we've just considered, the goals are not independent. Three of these goals – increasing real GDP growth, smoothing the business cycle and maintaining low unemployment – are interlinked. But two of these goals lie at the core of policy analysis in Europe. They are unemployment and inflation. The level of unemployment tells us about the state of the business cycle. The goal of reducing the number of long-term unemployed people – a particularly pressing problem in the European Union – is linked to the goal of high and sustainable long-term growth. If unemployment falls below the natural rate, then growth may be too rapid. If unemployment rises above the natural rate, then growth may be too slow. So monitoring unemployment at its natural rate is

equivalent to avoiding business fluctuations and keeping real GDP growing steadily at its maximum sustainable rate.

Policy performance, judged by the two core policy targets – inflation and unemployment – is shown in Fig. 34.1. Here the blue dot is the coordinate of inflation and unemployment for each of the European Union countries in 1995. The arrows point to the movement in both inflation and unemployment since the previous year, 1994. You can see that the movement in inflation and unemployment in most countries has been towards the origin on the

FIGURE 34.1

Macroeconomic Performance: EU Inflation and Unemployment, 1995

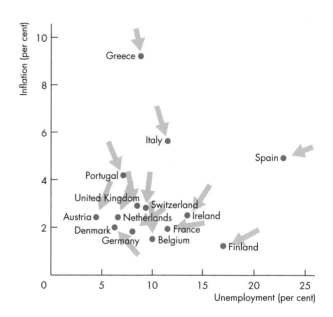

Unemployment and inflation are important objectives of the EU states. Most countries were successful in reducing inflation and unemployment between 1994 and 1995. The countries that reduced inflation but not unemployment were Greece and Belgium. Italy and Portugal reduced inflation but at the cost of increasing unemployment. The United Kingdom reduced unemployment but inflation increased slightly.

Source: *The European Monetary Institute Annual Report*, April 1995.

graph. This means that between 1994 and 1995, most countries have been successful in meeting the goal of reducing inflation and unemployment. Spain, Sweden, Finland, France, Germany, the Netherlands, Austria and Ireland have been successful in reducing both inflation and unemployment. Portugal and Italy have been successful in reducing inflation but only at the cost of raising unemployment. Belgium and Greece have reduced inflation without incurring any change in unemployment. Only Denmark and the United Kingdom have reduced unemployment but show a small rise in inflation. Most economists believe that after the recession of 1990–92, the majority of countries in the European Union have unemployment rates above the natural rate. The stated objectives of the European Commission are to raise the sustainable rate of growth of GDP in the European Union to 3 per cent a year to aid the process of unemployment reduction, and to carry out microeconomic reforms to reduce the natural rate of unemployment. The stated aim of the European Commission is to halve the present rate of unemployment in the European Union by 2000[1].

R E V I E W

◆ The goals of macroeconomic policy are: the highest sustainable rate of long-term real GDP growth, small business fluctuations, low unemployment, and low inflation.

◆ Keeping unemployment at the natural rate is equivalent to avoiding business fluctuations and keeping real GDP growing steadily at its highest sustainable rate.

We've examined the policy goals. Let's now look at the policy tools and the way they have been used.

---

[1] European Commission, *Growth, Competitiveness, Employment: The Challenges and Ways Forward into the 21st Century*, White Paper, 1994.

Policy Tools and Performance

The tools used to try to achieve macroeconomic performance objectives are fiscal policy and monetary policy. **Fiscal policy**, which is described in Chapter 29 (pp. 743–748), is the use of the government budget to achieve macroeconomic objectives. The detailed fiscal policy tools are tax rates and government purchases of goods and services. These tools work by influencing aggregate supply and aggregate demand in the ways explained in Chapter 29. **Monetary policy**, which is described in Chapter 31, is the adjustment of the quantity of money in circulation and interest rates by the central bank (the Bank of England) to achieve macroeconomic objectives. How have the tools actually been used in the United Kingdom and other parts of the European Union? Let's answer this question by summarizing the main directions of fiscal and monetary policy in recent years.

Recent Fiscal Policy in the European Union

Figure 34.2 gives a broad summary of fiscal policy since 1993 for the countries of the European Union. It shows general government spending as a percentage of GDP in part (a) and the general government deficit as a percentage of GDP in part (b). The recession of the early 1990s has made it difficult for the member states to tighten fiscal policy. *Automatic fiscal policy* led to a loosening of the government budget. The recession has raised the amount governments spend on unemployment benefits and reduced the revenues obtained from taxation. Even so, except for Greece, discretionary fiscal policy was tight. Most governments reduced government spending as a proportion of GDP between 1993 and 1995. The movement of the budget deficit also supported a general fiscal tightening. Except for Austria and Ireland, most of the EU governments reduced the government budget deficit as a proportion of GDP in 1995 compared with 1993. Luxembourg was the only country that had a fiscal loosening, with its budget surplus in 1993 being reduced in 1995. Economists of the Keynesian school argue that the general fiscal tightening in Europe has made it difficult to reduce the additional unemployment caused by the recession of 1990–92.

FIGURE 34.2

The Fiscal Policy Record

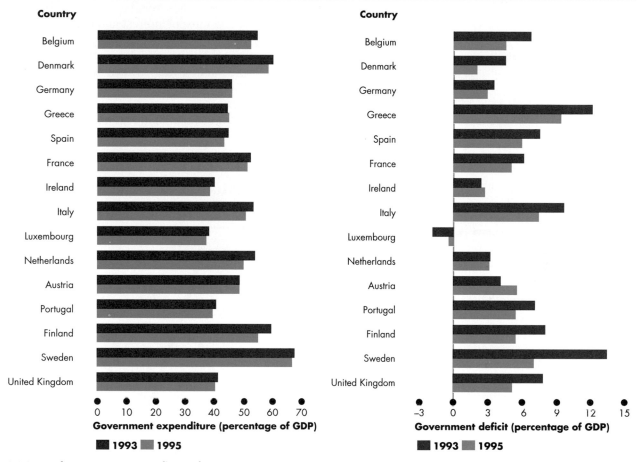

(a) General government expenditure of EU member states, 1993–1995

(b) General government budget deficit of EU member states, 1993–1995

Fiscal policy is summarized here by the performance of general government spending (part a) and the deficit (part b) between 1993 and 1995 for the EU member states. The general trend was for a tightening in fiscal policy. Most countries reduced government expenditure as a proportion of GDP and the budget deficit between 1993 and 1995. Greece raised its government expenditure but the budget deficit was reduced considerably. Ireland and Austria increased their government budget deficit.

Source: *European Commission Report on Convergence*, 1996.

The role of fiscal policy has been compromised to some extent by the need to meet the Maastricht Treaty criteria for European Monetary Union (EMU). The target of a budget deficit of 3 per cent of GDP has hindered governments from using fiscal policy to stabilize the economy according to Keynesian theory.

Let's now look at monetary policy.

Recent Monetary Policy in the United Kingdom and the European Union

Monetary policy in the European Union in recent years has been geared towards fulfilling stage 2 of EMU – namely coordination of monetary policy among member states' central banks with the aim of ensuring price stability. Table 34.1 shows the

TABLE 34.1

Monetary Policy Targets and Guidelines of Selected EU Member States

Country	Reference variable	1994		1995	
		Target	Actual	Target	Actual
Germany	M3	4–6	5.7	4–6	2.1
Greece	M3	8–11	8.8	7–9	10.4
Spain	Liquid assets	3–7	8.2	<8	9.2
France	M3	5	0.8	5	3.7
Italy	M2	5–7	2.8	5	2.1
United Kingdom	M4	3–9	5.6	3–9	5.5

Source: *European Monetary Institute Annual Report 1995*, April 1996.

monetary policy targets and guidelines for selected countries. The policies have been to raise short-term interest rates to abate inflationary pressures, and to lower them when inflationary pressure has subsided.

The table shows the target ranges for the rate of growth of money of selected member states of the European Union (in the case of Spain it is specified as liquid assets held by the public). Countries that do not state a specific monetary target use monetary policy to stabilize the exchange rate against the Deutschemark. The task of monetary policy has been to keep a lid on inflationary pressure, but there has been an equal amount of political pressure to use monetary policy to ease the burden of the recession by lowering interest rates and allowing the money supply to increase beyond the targets specified by the central banks. In 1994, fears that inflationary pressure may have built up because growth of real GDP in some countries in the European Union was greater than potential GDP growth led to a tightening of monetary policy during 1994 and early 1995. Spain, Italy, Finland, Sweden and the United Kingdom tightened monetary policy by raising short-term interest rates. In the remaining countries – Belgium, Luxembourg, Denmark, Germany, France, Ireland, the Netherlands, Austria, Greece and Portugal – monetary policy was eased during 1995 as inflation declined. Even in countries where monetary policy had been tightened interest rates were reduced during 1996 to ease monetary policy.

The monetary policy of member states is strongly influenced by that of the German central bank, the

Bundesbank. The Bundesbank cut its interest rate during 1995 in response to the weak growth in the money supply relative to its targets. Part of the low growth in German money supply was caused by people removing their funds from bank deposits that were paying low rates of interest and putting them into longer-term financial assets that paid higher rates of interest. The financial innovations that helped to expand monetary growth in the United States and Europe in the 1980s, including Germany, was now working in reverse. As a result of financial innovation a lower rate of interest makes the

FIGURE 34.3

The Monetary Policy Record: UK Monetary Policy, 1987–1995

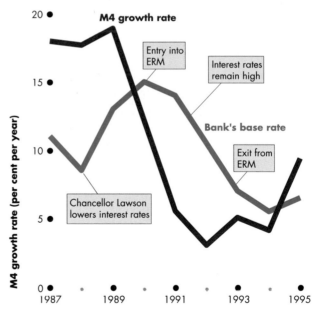

The monetary policy record is summarized here by the growth rate of M4 and the retail banks' base rate, which is closely linked to the Bank of England lender of last resort loan rate to the discount houses. The rate of interest is the rate that existed at the beginning of the year and the rate of growth of money was based on the end of year level of M4. The bank rate was raised in 1989 after a high growth rate of money in 1987 and 1988. In 1990 the United Kingdom entered the ERM. The rate of growth of money declined sharply. In 1992 the United Kingdom left the ERM and the rate of growth of money began to rise. The bank rate was lowered further until 1995 when the rate of growth of money began to rise.

Sources: Central Statistical Office, *Economic Trends Annual Supplement*, 1996; and *Bank of England Statistical Abstract*, 1995.

demand for money rise by less than in its' absence because bank deposits are less attractive relative to long-term financial assets.

The United Kingdom has been able to follow a monetary policy in recent years that is less influenced by the Bundesbank than most other countries in the European Union because it is no longer is part of the Exchange Rate Mechanism (ERM). Figure 34.3 shows how monetary policy has been used in the United Kingdom since 1987. The red line shows the rate of growth of money between 1987 and 1995 at the end of the year. The blue line shows the retail banks' base rate of interest, which is closely linked to the rate of interest at which the Bank of England lends to the discount houses. The rate of interest is taken at the beginning of the year. The figure shows that monetary policy was loose during the last few years of the 1980s. The Bank lowered interest rates in 1988 and monetary growth rose further in the following year. This was a period of rapidly rising inflation. In autumn 1990 the government took the United Kingdom into the ERM and monetary policy was guided by the Bundesbank. Interest rates remained high during the recession of 1990–92 and the rate of growth of money fell dramatically, as did inflation. It was only after the United Kingdom left the ERM in 1992 that interest rates were allowed to fall, and the rate of growth of money picked up in 1995.

REVIEW

◆ The macroeconomic policy tools are fiscal policy and monetary policy.

◆ Automatic fiscal policy was expansionary during the 1990–92 recession but discretionary fiscal policy was contractionary in most EU countries in recent years, including the United Kingdom.

◆ Monetary policy in EU countries was tightened during 1994 but was loosened in 1995.

◆ Monetary policy in the United Kingdom was tight during the recession years of 1990–92 but loosened after it left the ERM in 1992.

You've now studied the goals of policy and seen the broad trends in fiscal and monetary policy in recent years for the United Kingdom and the European Union. Let's now study the ways in which policy might be better used to achieve its goals. We'll begin by looking at long-term growth policy.

Long-term Growth Policy

The sources of the long-term growth of potential GDP, which are explained in Chapter 27 (p. 689), are the accumulation of physical and human capital and the advance of technology. Chapter 27 briefly examines the range of policies that might achieve faster growth. Here, we probe more deeply into the problem of boosting the long-term growth rate – without tears, as shown in the cartoon.

The factors that determine long-term growth result from millions of individual decisions; the role of government in influencing growth is limited. The European Commission believes that any role that government can play should be coordinated with other members of the European Union. Policy can influence the private decisions on which long-term growth depends in three areas. Such policies would increase:

◆ National saving

◆ Investment in human capital

◆ Investment in new technologies

'I hear they're laying off at the paper hankie factory'

National Saving Policies

National saving within the EU countries equals private saving plus government saving. Figure 34.4 shows the scale of national saving within the European Union since 1960 and its private and government components. The government component is obtained by subtracting private saving from government saving. From 1960 to 1975, national saving fluctuated around an average of 25 per cent of GDP. There then began a steady slide that saw national saving fall to 21 per cent in 1975 and fluctuate between 21 and 19 per cent of GDP between 1982 and 1992. Private saving has remained remarkably stable over a long period. It actually increased a little as a percentage of GDP between 1960 and 1979, when it peaked at 22 per cent of GDP, but over the whole period it has remained between 20 and 22 per

cent of EU GDP. Government saving became increasingly negative during the 1980s.

EU investment, one of the engines of growth, is not limited by saving by the European Union. The reason is that foreign saving can be harnessed to finance EU investment. But the European Union is a mature economy with the demographic problem of an ageing population. It needs to have sufficient saving to lend to the developing world and the emerging economies to meet the consumption needs of its population. Boosting the EU saving rate can help to bring faster real GDP growth for two reasons. First, the European Union represents a significant proportion of the world economy, so an increase in EU saving would increase world saving and bring lower real interest rates around the world. With lower real interest rates, investment would be boosted everywhere. The EU economy and the world economy could grow faster. Second, with more domestic saving, there might be an increase in investment in domestic high-risk, high-return new technologies that could boost long-term EU growth.

How can national saving be increased? The two points of attack are:

◆ Increasing government saving

◆ Increasing private saving

Increasing Government Saving Government saving was negative during most of the 1980s, and has been −1 to −1.4 per cent of GDP during the 1990s. The decline in the national savings of the EU economy is due to the increase in the public sector deficit in many European countries. Increasing government saving means eliminating the public sector deficit of the EU countries. They are one and the same action. But achieving a substantial cut in the deficit will be difficult and will only be achieved by cuts in such sensitive areas as welfare spending.

Increasing Private Saving Private saving in the European Union as a whole has remained remarkably stable over the three decades since 1960. The only way that government actions can boost private saving is by increasing the after-tax rate of return on saving.

The most effective way of stimulating private saving is to cut taxes on interest income. But such a tax cut would be costly and could only be financed either by a further decrease in government expenditures or by increases in taxes on labour incomes or in value added tax (VAT). This would be difficult politically and cannot be carried out at the EU level on existing

---

FIGURE 34.4

National Saving Rates in the European Union: 1960–1992

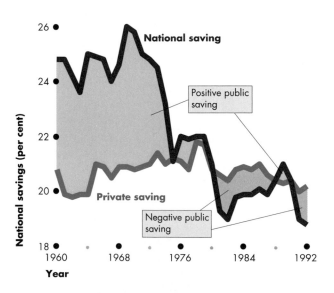

The EU gross saving rate peaked in 1970 at 25.8 per cent of EU GDP. Gross saving has fallen since that year and government saving has been the highest contributor to the fall. Private savings have remained remarkably constant since 1960, ranging between 19 and 22 per cent.

Source: European Commission, *Growth, Competitiveness and Employment*, White Paper, 1994

political arrangements. So governments are limited to making minor changes to the taxation of interest income, which will have negligible effects on the saving rate.

Private Saving and Inflation   Inflation erodes the value of saving, and uncertainty about future inflation is bad for saving. One further policy, therefore, that increases the saving rate is a monetary policy that preserves stable prices and minimizes uncertainty about the future value of money. Chapter 32 (pp. 842–844) spells out the broader connection between inflation and real GDP and explains why low inflation may bring greater output and faster growth.

Human Capital Policies

The accumulation of human capital plays a crucial role in economic growth and two areas are relevant: schooling and on-the-job experience. Economic research shows that schooling and training pay. That is, on the average, the greater the number of years a person remains at school or in training, the higher are that person's earnings. Schooling and higher education training in Europe are fairly good by international standards. The UK government has made it a policy issue to increase the number of university places to allow one-third of all school leavers to enter higher education.

If education and on-the-job training yield higher earnings, why does the government or the European Commission need a policy towards investment in human capital? Why can't people simply be left to get on with making their own decisions about how much human capital to acquire? The answer is that the *social* returns to human capital possibly exceed the *private* returns. The extra productivity that comes from the interactions of well-educated and experienced people exceeds what each individual can achieve alone. So left to ourselves we would probably accumulate too little human capital.

Economic research has also shown that on-the-job training pays. This type of training can be formal, such as a school at work, or informal, such as learning-by-doing. The scope for government involvement in these areas is limited, but it can set an example as an employer and it can encourage best-practice training programmes for workers.

Investment in New Technologies

As Chapter 26 explains, investment in new technologies is special for two reasons. First, it appears not to run into the problem of diminishing returns that plague all other factors of production. Second, the benefits of new technologies spill over to influence all parts of the economy, not just the firms undertaking the investment. For these reasons, a particularly promising way of boosting growth is to stimulate investment in the research and development efforts that create new technologies.

Governments can fund and provide tax incentives for research and development activities. Through the various research councils, the universities and research institutes, the governments of the European Union already fund a large amount of basic research. However, the European Commission points out that in 1991 total public, private, civil and military spending on research and technological development (RTD) was 104 billion ecu, compared with 124 billion ecu in the United States and 77 billion ecu in Japan. This was respectively equivalent to 2 per cent of EU GDP, 2.8 per cent of US GDP and 3 per cent of Japanese GDP. However, the figures for EU-wide expenditure on RTD hide wide variations. Germany spends 2.6 per cent of GDP on RTD, whereas Greece and Portugal spend only 0.7 per cent of their respective GDP. The Commission also points out that investment in research by businesses is weak in the European Union. Only 52 per cent of all research is funded by the EU business community compared with 78 per cent in Japan.

R E V I E W

♦ Long-term growth policies focus on increasing saving and increasing investment in human capital and new technologies.

♦ To increase the national saving rate of the EU economies, government saving and the after-tax return on private saving must be increased and inflation must be kept in check.

♦ Human capital investment might be increased with improved education and on-the-job training programmes.

♦ Investment in new technologies can be encouraged by tax incentives.

We've seen how government might use its fiscal and monetary policies to influence long-term growth. How can it influence the business cycle and unemployment? Let's now address this question.

Business Cycle and Unemployment Policies

Many different fiscal and monetary policies can be pursued to stabilize the business cycle and prevent swings in real GDP growth and the inflation rate. But all these polices fall into three broad categories:

◆ Fixed-rule policies
◆ Feedback-rule policies
◆ Discretionary policies

Fixed-rule Policies

A **fixed-rule policy** specifies an action to be pursued independently of the state of the economy. An everyday example of a fixed rule is a stop sign. It says 'stop regardless of the state of the road ahead – even if no other vehicle is trying to use the road.' Several fixed-rule policies have been proposed for the economy. One, proposed by Milton Friedman, is to keep the quantity of money growing at a constant rate year in and year out, regardless of the state of the economy, to make the *average* inflation rate zero. Another fixed-rule policy is to balance the government budget. Fixed rules are rarely followed in practice, but they have some merits in principle; later in this chapter we'll study the way they would work if they were pursued. However, as Table 34.1 shows, several countries in the European Union have targets or monitoring ranges for the money supply. Countries outside the European Union that also publish monetary targets or monitoring ranges include the United States, Japan and Switzerland.

Feedback-rule Policies

A **feedback-rule policy** specifies how policy actions respond to changes in the state of the economy. A give way sign is an everyday feedback rule. It says 'stop if another vehicle is attempting to use the road ahead but otherwise, proceed'. A macroeconomic feedback-rule policy is one that changes the money supply, or interest rates, or even tax rates, in response to the state of the economy. Some feedback rules guide the actions of policy-makers. For example, the Chancellor of the Exchequer and the governor of the Bank of England used a feedback rule when they kept pushing interest rates ever higher during 1994 and 1995 in response to strong

real GDP growth. Other feedback-rule policies are automatic. For example, the automatic rise in taxes during an expansion and the automatic fall in taxes during a recession are feedback-rule policies.

Discretionary Policies

A **discretionary policy** responds to the state of the economy in a possibly unique way that uses all the information available, including perceived lessons from past 'mistakes'. An everyday discretionary policy occurs at an unmarked junction. Each driver uses discretion in deciding whether to stop and how slowly to approach the junction. Most macroeconomic policy actions have an element of discretion because every situation is to some degree unique. For example, between 1994 and 1995, the Bank of England increased interest rates three times but by half per centage points in each case. It might have delayed increasing rates until it was more sure that higher rates were needed and then increased them in a larger increment. The governor, Eddie George, and the Chancellor, Kenneth Clarke, used discretion based on lessons they had learned from earlier expansions. But despite the fact that all policy actions have an element of discretion, they can be regarded as modifications to a basic feedback-rule policy. Discretionary policy is sophisticated feedback policy, where the rules gradually evolve to reflect new knowledge about the way the economy works.

We'll study the effects of business cycle policy by comparing the performance of real GDP and the price level with a fixed rule and a feedback rule. Because the business cycle can result from demand shocks or supply shocks, we need to consider these two cases. We'll begin by studying demand shocks.

Stabilizing Aggregate Demand Shocks

We'll study an economy that starts out at full employment and has no inflation. Fig. 34.5 illustrates this situation. The economy is on aggregate demand curve AD_0 and short-run aggregate supply curve *SAS*. These curves intersect at a point on the long-run aggregate supply curve, *LAS*. The GDP deflator is 130 and real GDP is $600 billion. Now suppose that there is an unexpected and temporary fall in aggregate demand. Let's see what happens.

Perhaps investment falls because of a wave of pessimism about the future, or perhaps exports fall because of a recession in the rest of the world.

FIGURE 34.5

A Decrease in Aggregate Demand

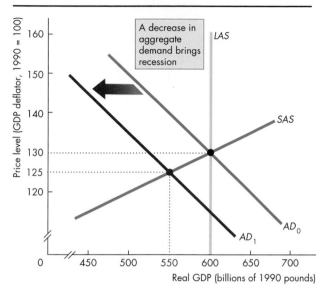

The economy starts out at full employment on aggregate demand curve AD_0 and short-run aggregate supply curve *SAS*, with the two curves intersecting on the long-run aggregate supply curve *LAS*. Real GDP is £600 billion and the GDP deflator is 130. A fall in aggregate demand (owing to pessimism about future profits, for example) unexpectedly shifts the aggregate demand curve to AD_1. Real GDP falls to £550 billion, and the GDP deflator falls to 125. The economy is in a recession.

Regardless of the origin of the fall in aggregate demand, the aggregate demand curve shifts leftward, to AD_1 in the figure. The aggregate demand curve AD_1 intersects the short-run aggregate supply curve *SAS* at a GDP deflator of 125 and a real GDP of £550 billion. The economy is in a depressed state. Real GDP is below its long-run level and unemployment is above its natural rate.

Assume that the fall in aggregate demand from AD_0 to AD_1 is temporary. As confidence in the future improves, firms' investment picks up, or as economic recovery proceeds in the rest of the world, exports gradually rise. As a result, the aggregate demand curve gradually returns to AD_0, but it takes some time to do so.

We are going to work out how the economy responds under two alternative monetary policies during the period in which aggregate demand gradually increases to its original level: a fixed rule and a feedback rule.

Fixed Rule: Monetarism   The fixed rule that we'll study here is one in which the level of government purchases of goods and services, taxes and the deficit remain constant and the money supply remains constant. Neither fiscal policy nor monetary policy responds to the depressed economy. This is the rule advocated by *monetarists*.

The response of the economy under this fixed-rule policy is shown in Fig. 34.6(a). When aggregate demand falls to AD_1, no policy measures are taken to bring the economy back to full employment. But the fall in aggregate demand is only *temporary*. As aggregate demand returns to its original level, the aggregate demand curve shifts rightward gradually back to AD_0. As it does so, real GDP and the GDP deflator gradually increase. The GDP deflator gradually returns to 130 and real GDP to its long-run level of £600 billion, as shown in Fig. 34.6(a). Throughout this process, the economy experiences more rapid growth than usual but beginning from a state of excess capacity. Unemployment remains high until the aggregate demand curve has returned to AD_0.

Figure 34.6(b) illustrates the response of the economy under a fixed rule when the decrease in aggregate demand to AD_1 is *permanent*. Gradually, with unemployment above the natural rate, the money wage rate falls and the short-run aggregate supply curve shifts rightward to SAS_1. As it does so, real GDP gradually increases and the GDP deflator falls. Real GDP gradually returns to potential GDP of £600 billion and the GDP deflator falls to 115, as shown in Fig. 34.6(b). Again, throughout the adjustment, real GDP is less than potential GDP and unemployment exceeds the natural rate.

Let's contrast this adjustment with what occurs under a feedback-rule policy.

Feedback Rule: Keynesian Activism   The feedback rule that we'll study is one in which government purchases of goods and services increase, taxes decrease, the deficit increases and the money supply increases when real GDP falls below its long-run level. In other words, both fiscal and monetary policy become expansionary when real GDP falls below long-run real GDP. When real GDP rises above its long-run level, both policies operate in reverse, becoming contractionary. This rule is advocated by *Keynesian activists*.

The response of the economy under this feedback rule policy is shown in Fig. 34.6(c). When aggregate demand falls to AD_1, the expansionary fiscal and monetary policy increases aggregate demand,

FIGURE 34.6

Two Stabilization Policies: Aggregate Demand Shock

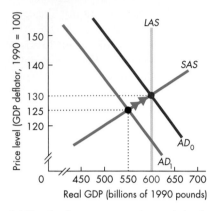

(a) Fixed rule: temporary demand shock

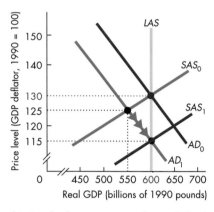

(b) Fixed rule: permanent demand shock

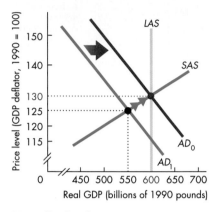

(c) Feedback rule

The economy is in a depressed state with a GDP deflator of 125 and real GDP of £550 billion. The short-run aggregate supply curve is *SAS*. If the depressed state of the economy is temporary, fixed-rule stabilization policy (part a) leaves aggregate demand initially at AD_1, so the GDP deflator remains at 125 and real GDP at £550 billion. As other influences on aggregate demand gradually increase, the aggregate demand curve shifts back to AD_0. As it does, real GDP gradually rises back to £600 billion and the GDP deflator increases to 130. When the decrease in demand is permanent, the money wage rate falls and the short-run

aggregate supply curve shifts rightward to SAS_1, shown in part (b). Part (c) shows a feedback-rule stabilization policy. Expansionary fiscal and monetary policy increase aggregate demand and shift the aggregate demand curve from AD_1 to AD_0. Real GDP returns to £600 billion and the GDP deflator returns to 130. Fiscal and monetary policy becomes contractionary as the other influences on aggregate demand increase its level. As a result, the aggregate demand curve is kept steady at AD_0, real GDP remains at £600 billion and the deflator remains at 130.

which shifts the aggregate demand curve immediately to AD_0. As other influences begin to increase aggregate demand, fiscal and monetary policy become contractionary and hold the aggregate demand curve steady at AD_0. Real GDP is held steady at £600 billion and the GDP deflator remains at 130.

The Two Rules Compared Under a fixed-rule policy, the economy goes into a recession and stays there for as long as it takes for aggregate demand to increase again under its own steam. Only gradually does the recession come to an end and the aggregate demand curve return to its original position.

Under a feedback-rule policy, the economy is pulled out of its recession by the policy action. Once back at its long-run level, real GDP is held there by a gradual, policy-induced decrease in aggregate demand that exactly offsets the increase in aggregate demand coming from private spending decisions.

The price level and real GDP fall and rise by exactly the same amounts under the two policies, but real GDP stays below capacity GDP for longer with a fixed rule than it does with a feedback rule.

So Feedback Rules are Better? Isn't it obvious that a feedback rule is better than a fixed rule? Can't the government and the Bank use feedback rules to keep the economy close to full employment with a stable price level? Of course, unforecasted events – such as a collapse in business confidence – will hit the economy from time to time. But by responding with a change in tax rates, spending, interest rates and money supply, can't the government and the Bank minimize the damage from such a shock? It appears to be so from our analysis.

Despite the apparent superiority of a feedback rule, many economists remain convinced that a fixed rule stabilizes aggregate demand more effectively than a feedback rule. These economists argue that fixed rules are better than feedback rules because:

◆ Full-employment real GDP is not known.

◆ Policy lags are longer than the forecast horizon.

◆ Feedback-rule policies are less predictable than fixed-rule policies.

Let's look at these arguments.

Knowledge of Full-employment Real GDP   To decide whether a feedback policy needs to stimulate aggregate demand or retard it, it is necessary to determine whether real GDP is currently above or below its full-employment level. But full-employment real GDP is not known with certainty. It depends on a large number of factors, one of which is the level of employment when unemployment is at its natural rate. But there is uncertainty and disagreement about how the labour market works, so we can only estimate the natural rate of unemployment. As a result, there is uncertainty about the *direction* in which a feedback policy should be pushing the level of aggregate demand.

Policy Lags and the Forecast Horizon   The effects of policy actions taken today are spread out over the following two years or even more. But no one is able to forecast that far ahead. The forecast horizon of the policy-makers is less than one year. Furthermore, it is not possible to predict the precise timing and magnitude of the effects of policy itself. Thus feedback policies that react to today's economy may be inappropriate for the state of the economy at that uncertain future date when the policy's effects are felt.

For example, suppose that today the economy is in a recession. The government through the Bank reacts with an increase in the money supply growth rate. When the Bank puts on the monetary accelerator, the first reaction is a fall in interest rates. Some time later, lower interest rates produce an increase in investment and the purchases of consumer durable goods. Some time still later, this rise in expenditure increases income which in turn induces higher consumption expenditure. Later yet, the higher expenditure increases the demand for labour and eventually wages and prices rise. The sectors in which the spending increases occur vary and so does the impact on employment. It can take from nine months to two years for an initial action by the government to cause a change in real GDP, employment and the inflation rate.

By the time the government's actions are having their maximum effect, the economy has moved on to a new situation. Perhaps a world economic slowdown has added a new negative effect on aggregate demand that is offsetting the government's expansionary actions. Or perhaps a boost in business confidence has increased aggregate demand yet further, adding to the government's own expansionary policy. Whatever the situation, the government can only take the appropriate actions today if it can forecast those future shocks to aggregate demand.

Thus to smooth the fluctuations in aggregate demand, the government needs to take actions today, based on a forecast of what will be happening over a period stretching two or more years into the future. It is no use taking actions a year from today to influence the situation that then prevails. It will be too late.

If the government, through the Treasury economics team, is good at economic forecasting and bases its policy actions on its forecasts, then the government can deliver the type of aggregate demand-smoothing performance that we assumed in the model economy we studied earlier in this chapter. But if the government takes policy actions that are based on today's economy rather than on the forecasted economy a year into the future, then those actions will often be inappropriate ones.

When unemployment is high and the government puts its foot on the accelerator, it speeds the economy back to full employment. But the government cannot see far enough ahead to know when to ease off the accelerator and gently tap the brake, holding the economy at its full-employment point. Usually it keeps its foot on the accelerator for too long and, after the government has taken its foot off the accelerator pedal, the economy races through the full-employment point and starts to experience shortages and inflationary pressures. Eventually, when inflation increases and unemployment falls below its natural rate, the government steps on the brake, pushing the economy back below full employment.

The government's own reaction to the current state of the economy has become one of the major sources of fluctuations in aggregate demand and the major factor that people have to forecast in order to make their own economic choices.

During 1994 and 1995, the UK government and the Bank of England tried hard to avoid the problems just described. The government increased interest rates early in the expansion and by small increments. In late 1995 and 1996, after real GDP growth slowed down but before any serious signs of recession were on the horizon, it began to cut interest rates. It is too early to tell whether the government now knows enough to avoid some of the mistakes of the past.

The problems for fiscal policy feedback rules are similar to those for monetary policy, but they are more severe because of the lags in the implementation of fiscal policy. The government can take actions fairly quickly. But before a fiscal policy action can be taken, the entire legislative process must be completed. Thus even before a fiscal policy action is implemented, the economy may have moved on to a new situation that calls for a different feedback from the one that is in the legislative pipeline.

Predictability of Policies   To make decisions about long-term contracts for employment (wage contracts) and for borrowing and lending, people have to anticipate the future course of prices – the future inflation rate. To forecast the inflation rate, it is necessary to forecast aggregate demand. And to forecast aggregate demand, it is necessary to forecast the policy actions of the government and the Bank.

If the government and the Bank stick to rock-steady, fixed rules for tax rates, spending programmes, and money supply growth, then policy itself cannot be a contributor to unexpected fluctuations in aggregate demand.

In contrast, when a feedback rule is being pursued there is more scope for the policy actions to be unpredictable. The main reason is that feedback rules are not written down for all to see. Rather, they have to be inferred from the behaviour of the government and the Bank.

Thus with a feedback policy it is necessary to predict the variables to which the government and Bank react and the extent to which they react. Consequently, a feedback rule for fiscal and monetary policy can create more unpredictable fluctuations in aggregate demand than a fixed rule.

Economists disagree about whether these bigger fluctuations offset the potential stabilizing influence of the predictable changes the government and the Bank make. No agreed measurements have been made to settle this dispute. Nevertheless, the unpredictability of the government in its pursuit of feedback policies is an important fact of economic life, and the government does not always go out of its way to make its reactions clear. However, in recent years the open monthly meeting between the Chancellor of the Exchequer and the governor of the Bank of England have gone some way towards lifting the curtain of mystery that used to

surround the deliberations of the two institutions.

To the extent that the government's and the Bank's actions are discretionary and unpredictable, they lead to unpredictable fluctuations in aggregate demand. These fluctuations, in turn, produce fluctuations in real GDP, employment and unemployment.

It is difficult for the government to pursue a predictable feedback stabilization policy. Such policies are formulated in terms of spending programmes and tax laws announced at the time of the Budget. Because these programmes and tax laws are the outcome of a political process of negotiation between the Treasury and the spending departments of government, there can be no effective way in which a predictable feedback fiscal policy can be adhered to.

We reviewed three reasons why feedback policies may not be more effective than fixed rules in controlling aggregate demand. But there is a fourth reason why fixed rules are preferred by some economists: not all shocks to the economy are on the demand side. Advocates of feedback rules believe that most fluctuations do come from aggregate demand. Advocates of fixed rules believe that aggregate supply fluctuations are the dominant ones. Let's now see how aggregate supply fluctuations affect the economy under a fixed rule and a feedback rule. We will also see why those economists who believe that aggregate supply fluctuations are the dominant ones also favour a fixed rather than a feedback rule.

Stabilizing Aggregate Supply Shocks

Real business cycle (RBC) theorists believe that fluctuations in real GDP (and in employment and unemployment) are caused not by fluctuations in aggregate demand but by fluctuations in productivity growth. According to RBC theory, there is no useful distinction between long-run aggregate supply and short-run aggregate supply. Because wages are flexible, the labour market is always in equilibrium and unemployment is always at its natural rate. The vertical long-run aggregate supply curve is also the short-run aggregate supply curve. Fluctuations occur because of shifts in the long-run aggregate supply curve. Normally, the long-run aggregate supply curve shifts to the right – the economy expands. But the pace at which the long-run aggregate supply curve shifts to the right varies. Also, on occasion, the long-run aggregate supply curve shifts leftward, bringing a decrease in aggregate supply and a fall in real GDP.

Economic policy that influences the aggregate demand curve has no effect on real GDP. But it does affect the price level. If a feedback policy is used to increase aggregate demand every time real GDP falls, and if the RBC theory is correct, the feedback policy will make price level fluctuations more severe than they otherwise would be. To see why, consider Fig. 34.7.

Imagine that the economy starts out on aggregate demand curve AD_0 and long-run aggregate supply curve LAS_0 at a GDP deflator of 130 and with real GDP equal to £600 billion. Now suppose that the long-run aggregate supply curve shifts to LAS_1. An actual decrease in long-run aggregate supply can occur as a result of a severe drought or other natural catastrophe, or perhaps as the result of a disruption of international trade such as the OPEC embargo of the 1970s.

Fixed Rule   With a fixed rule, the fall in the long-run aggregate supply has no effect on the Bank or the government and no effect on aggregate demand. The aggregate demand curve remains AD_0. Real GDP falls to £550 billion and the GDP deflator increases to 140.

Feedback Rule   Now suppose that the Bank and the government use feedback rules. In particular, suppose that when real GDP falls, the Bank increases the money supply and Parliament approves a tax cut to increase aggregate demand. In this example, the money supply increase and the tax cut shift the aggregate demand curve to AD_1. The policy goal is to bring real GDP back to £600 billion. But the long-run aggregate supply curve has shifted so long-run real GDP has decreased to £550 billion. The increase in aggregate demand cannot cause an increase in output if the economy does not have the capacity to produce that output. So real GDP stays at £550 billion but the price level rises still further – the GDP deflator goes to 150. You can see that in this case the attempt to stabilize real GDP using a feedback policy has no effect on real GDP, but it generates a substantial price level increase.

We've now seen some of the shortcomings of using feedback rules for stabilization policy. Some economists believe that these shortcomings are serious and would like to see simple fixed rules. A popular view among some economists is to have an exchange rate rule, as in the ERM. Others, regarding the potential advantages of feedback rules as greater than their costs, advocate the continued use of such policies but with an important modification that we'll now look at.

FIGURE 34.7

Responding to a Productivity Growth Slowdown

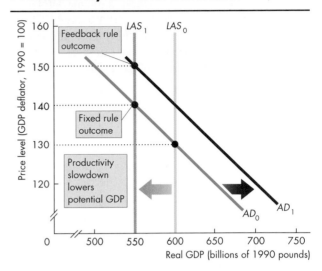

A productivity slowdown shifts the long-run aggregate supply curve from LAS_0 to LAS_1. Real GDP falls to £550 billion and the GDP deflator rises to 140. With a fixed rule, there is no change in the money supply, taxes or government spending, aggregate demand stays at AD_0, and that is the end of the matter. With a feedback rule, the Bank increases the money supply and/or the government cuts taxes or increases spending, intending to increase real GDP. Aggregate demand moves to AD_1, but the long-run result is an increase in the price level – the GDP deflator rises to 150 – with no change in real GDP.

Nominal GDP Targeting   Attempting to keep the growth rate of nominal GDP steady is called **nominal GDP targeting**. This policy target was first proposed by a leading Keynesian activist economist, James Tobin of Yale University. It is a policy that recognizes the strengths of a fixed rule but that regards the monetarist fixed rule as inappropriate. Instead, nominal GDP targeting uses feedback rules for fiscal and monetary policy to hit a fixed nominal GDP growth target.

Nominal GDP growth equals the real GDP growth rate plus the inflation rate. When nominal GDP grows quickly, it is usually because the inflation rate is high. When nominal GDP grows slowly, it is usually because real GDP growth is negative – the economy is in recession. Thus if nominal GDP growth is held steady, excessive inflation and deep recession might be avoided.

Nominal GDP targeting uses feedback rules. Expansionary fiscal and/or monetary actions increase aggregate demand when nominal GDP is below target and contractionary fiscal and/or monetary actions decrease aggregate demand when nominal GDP is above target. The main problem with nominal GDP targeting is that there are long and variable time lags between the identification of a need to change aggregate demand and the effects of the policy actions taken.

Natural Rate Policies   All the business cycle stabilization policies we've considered have been directed at smoothing the cycle and keeping unemployment close to the natural rate. It is also possible to pursue policies directed towards lowering the natural rate of unemployment. But there are no simple costless ways of lowering the natural rate of unemployment.

The main policy tools that influence the natural rate of unemployment are supply side factors dealing with tax rates, employers' additional costs of hiring labour, unemployment benefits, union regulation and minimum wages. But to use these tools the government faces tough trade-offs. To lower the natural rate of unemployment, the government could lower the tax rate on income or employers' social security contributions, or lower unemployment benefits or even shorten the period for which benefits are paid. These policy actions might create hardships and have costs that exceed the cost of a high natural rate of unemployment.

Some economists have argued that the supply side policies during the 10 years of Mrs Thatcher's government had the effect of reducing the natural rate of unemployment. Taxes on income were reduced, trade union activity was regulated, employers' social security contributions were reduced and the eligibility for unemployment benefits was reduced. The outcome of all these policies has been to make the labour market more flexible and labour less costly to employ.

R E V I E W

◆ Fixed-rule policies keep fiscal and monetary policy steady and independent of the state of the economy.

◆ Feedback policies cut taxes, increase spending and speed up money supply growth when the

economy is in recession and reverse these measures when the economy is overheating.

◆ Feedback rules apparently do a better job but we are not sure this is the case. Their successful use requires a good knowledge of the current state of the economy, an ability to forecast as far ahead as the policy actions have effects, and clarity about the feedback rules being used.

We've studied growth policy and business cycle and unemployment policy. Let's now study inflation policy.

Inflation Policy

There are two inflation policy problems. In times of price level stability, the problem is to prevent inflation from breaking out. In times of inflation, the problem is to reduce its rate and restore price stability. Avoiding demand inflation is just the opposite of avoiding demand driven recession. So keeping aggregate demand steady is an anti-inflation policy as well as an anti-recession policy. But avoiding cost-push inflation raises some special issues that we need to consider. So we will look at two issues for inflation policy:

◆ Avoiding cost-push inflation
◆ Slowing inflation

Avoiding Cost-push Inflation

Cost-push inflation is inflation that has its origins in cost increases. In 1973–74, the world oil price exploded. Cost shocks such as these become inflationary if they are accommodated by an increase in the quantity of money. Such an increase in the quantity of money can occur if a monetary policy feedback rule is used. A fixed-rule policy for the money stock makes cost-push inflation impossible. Let's see why.

Figure 34.8 shows the economy at full employment. Aggregate demand is AD_0, short-run aggregate supply is SAS_0 and long-run aggregate supply is LAS. Real GDP is £600 billion and the GDP deflator is 130. Now suppose that OPEC tries to gain a temporary advantage by increasing the price of oil. The short-run aggregate supply curve shifts leftward from SAS_0 to SAS_1.

Monetarist Fixed Rule   Figure 34.8(a) shows what happens if a fixed rule for monetary policy is

FIGURE 34.8

Responding to an OPEC Oil Price Increase

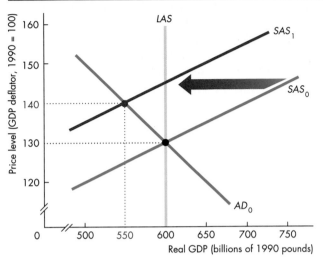

(a) Fixed rule

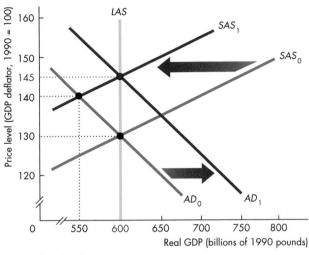

(b) Feedback rule

The economy starts out on AD_0 and SAS_0, with a GDP deflator of 130 and real GDP of £600 billion. OPEC forces up the price of oil and the short-run aggregate supply curve shifts to SAS_1. Real GDP decreases to £550 billion and the GDP deflator increases to 140. With a fixed money supply rule (part a), the Bank makes no change to aggregate demand. The economy stays depressed until the price

of oil falls again, and the economy returns to its original position. With a feedback rule (part b), the Bank injects additional money and aggregate demand increases to AD_1. Real GDP returns to £600 billion (full employment) but the GDP deflator increases to 150. The economy is set for another round of cost-push inflation.

followed and the government follows a fixed rule for fiscal policy. Suppose that the fixed rule is for zero money growth and no change in taxes or government purchases of goods and services. With these fixed rules, the government pays no attention to the fact that there has been an increase in the price of oil. No policy actions are taken. The short-run aggregate supply curve has shifted to SAS_1 but the aggregate demand curve remains at AD_0. The GDP deflator rises to 140, and real GDP falls to £550 billion. The economy has experienced *stagflation*. Unless the price of oil falls, the economy will remain depressed. But eventually, the low level of real GDP and low sales will probably bring a fall in the price of oil. When this happens, the short-run aggregate supply curve will shift back to SAS_0. The GDP deflator will fall to 130 and real GDP will increase to £600 billion.

Keynesian Feedback Rule Figure 34.8(b) shows what happens if the Bank and the government operate a feedback rule. The starting point is the same as

before – the economy is on SAS_0 and AD_0 with a GDP deflator of 130 and real GDP of £600 billion. OPEC raises the price of oil and the short-run aggregate supply curve shifts to SAS_1. Real GDP falls to £550 billion and the price level rises to 140.

A monetary feedback rule is followed. That rule is to increase the quantity of money when real GDP is below potential GDP. With potential GDP perceived to be £600 billion and with actual real GDP at £550 billion, the Bank pumps money into the economy. Aggregate demand increases and the aggregate demand curve shifts rightward to AD_1. The price level rises to 145 and real GDP returns to £600 billion. The economy moves back to full employment but at a higher price level.

What if the government and Bank reacted in a different way? Let's run through the example again. OPEC engineers a new rise in the price of oil which decreases aggregate supply, and the short-run aggregate supply curve shifts leftward once more. The Bank, realizing this danger, does *not* respond to the OPEC price increase. Instead, it holds firm and even slows down the growth of aggregate demand to dampen further the inflationary consequences of OPEC's actions.

Incentives to Push Up Costs   You can see that there are no checks on the incentives to push up costs if the government accommodates price rises. If some groups see a temporary gain from pushing up the price at which they are selling their resources, and if the Bank always accommodates to prevent unemployment and slack business conditions from emerging, then cost-push elements will have a free rein. But when the Bank pursues a fixed-rule policy, the incentive to attempt to steal a temporary advantage from a price increase is severely weakened. The cost of higher unemployment and lower output is a consequence that each group will have to face and recognize.

Thus a fixed rule is capable of delivering a steady inflation rate (and even zero inflation), while a feedback rule, in the face of cost-push pressures, leaves the inflation rate free to rise and fall at the whim of whichever group believes a temporary advantage to be available from pushing up its price.

Slowing Inflation

So far, we've concentrated on *avoiding* inflation. But often the problem is not to avoid inflation but to tame it. How can inflation, once it has set in, be cured? We'll look at two cases:

◆   A surprise inflation reduction
◆   A credible, announced inflation reduction

A Surprise Inflation Reduction   We'll use two equivalent approaches to study the problem of lowering inflation: the aggregate supply–aggregate demand model and the Phillips curve. The *AS–AD* model tells us about real GDP and the price level, while the Phillips curve, which is explained in Chapter 32 (pp. 845–849), lets us keep track of inflation and unemployment.

Figure 34.9 illustrates the economy at full employment with inflation raging at 10 per cent a year. In part (a), the economy is on aggregate demand curve AD_0 and short-run aggregate supply curve SAS_0. Real GDP is £600 billion and, at a moment in time, the GDP deflator is 130. With real GDP equal to potential GDP on the *LAS* curve, there is full employment. Equivalently, in part (b), the economy is on its long-run Phillips curve, *LRPC*, and short-run Phillips curve, $SRPC_0$. The inflation rate of 10 per cent a year

is anticipated so unemployment is at its natural rate.

Next year, aggregate demand is *expected* to increase and the aggregate demand curve in Fig. 34.9(a) is expected to shift rightward to AD_1. Expecting this increase in aggregate demand, wages increase to shift the short-run aggregate supply curve to SAS_1. If expectations are fulfilled, the GDP deflator rises to 143 – a 10 per cent inflation – and real GDP remains at its long-run level. In part (b), the economy remains at its original position – unemployment is at the natural rate and the inflation rate is 10 per cent a year.

Suppose, when no one is expecting the action, the Bank tries to slow inflation. It increases interest rates and slows money growth. Aggregate demand growth slows and the aggregate demand curve (in part a) shifts to AD_2. With no change in the expected inflation rate, wages rise by the same amount as before and the short-run aggregate supply curve shifts leftward to SAS_1. Real GDP decreases to £550 billion and the GDP deflator rises to 140.4 – an inflation rate of 8 per cent a year. In Fig. 34.9(b), there is a movement along the short-run Phillips curve $SRPC_0$ as unemployment rises to 9 per cent and inflation falls to 8 per cent a year. The policy has succeeded in slowing inflation, but at the cost of recession. Real GDP is below potential GDP and unemployment is above its natural rate.

A Credible Announced Inflation Reduction
Suppose that instead of simply slowing down the growth of aggregate demand, the government announces its intention ahead of its action in a credible and convincing way, so that its announcement is believed. The lower level of aggregate demand is expected so wages increase at a pace consistent with the lower level of aggregate demand. The short-run aggregate supply curve (in Fig. 34.9a) shifts leftward but only to SAS_2. Aggregate demand increases by the amount expected and the aggregate demand curve shifts to AD_2. The GDP deflator rises to 136.5 – an inflation rate of 5 per cent a year – and real GDP remains at its full-employment level.

In Fig. 34.9(b), the lower expected inflation rate shifts the short-run Phillips curve downward to $SRPC_1$, and inflation falls to 5 per cent a year while unemployment remains at its natural rate.

Inflation Reduction in Practice

When the UK government under Mrs Thatcher in fact slowed down inflation in 1980, we all paid a high

FIGURE 34.9

Lowering Inflation

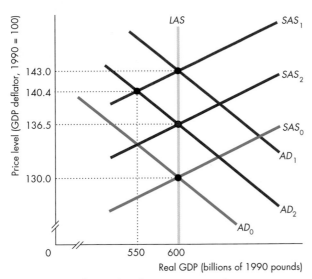

(a) Aggregate demand and aggregate supply

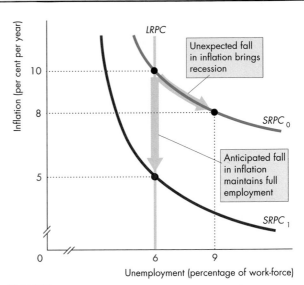

(b) Phillips curves

Initially, aggregate demand is AD_0 and short-run aggregate supply is SAS_0. Real GDP is £600 billion (its full-employment level on the long-run aggregate supply curve *LAS*). Inflation is proceeding at 10 per cent a year. If it continues to do so, the aggregate demand curve shifts to AD_1 and the short-run aggregate supply curve shifts to SAS_1. The GDP deflator rises to 143. This same situation is shown in part (b) with the economy on the short-run Phillips curve $SRPC_0$.

With an unexpected slowdown in aggregate demand growth, the aggregate demand curve (part a) shifts to AD_2,

real GDP falls to £550 billion and inflation slows to 8 per cent (a GDP deflator of 140.4). In part (b), unemployment rises to 9 per cent as the economy slides down $SRPC_0$.

If a credible, announced slowdown in aggregate demand growth occurs, the short-run aggregate supply curve (part a) shifts to SAS_2, the short-run Phillips curve (part b) shifts to $SRPC_1$, inflation slows to 5 per cent, real GDP remains at £600 billion and unemployment remains at its natural rate of 6 per cent.

---

price. The government's monetary policy action was unpredicted. As a result, it occurred in the face of wages that had been set at too high a level to be consistent with the growth of aggregate demand that the government subsequently allowed. The consequence was recession – a decrease in real GDP and a rise in unemployment. Couldn't the government have lowered inflation without causing recession by telling people far enough ahead of time that it did indeed plan to slow down the growth rate of aggregate demand?

The answer appears to be no. The main reason is that people form their expectation of the government's action (as they form expectations about anyone's actions) on the basis of actual behaviour, not on the basis of stated intentions. How many times have you told yourself that it is your firm intention to reduce weight, or to keep within a bud-

get and put a few pounds away for a rainy day, only to discover that, despite your best intentions, your old habits win out in the end?

Forming expectations about the government's behaviour is no different except, of course, it is more complex than forecasting your own behaviour. To form expectations of the government's actions, people look at its past *actions*, not its stated intentions. On the basis of such observations they try to work out what the government's policy is, to forecast its future actions, and to forecast the effects of those actions on aggregate demand and inflation. When Mrs Thatcher came to power in June 1979, the forecast for her policy was to do the same as all previous governments had done – that is, to say one thing and do another. In other words, Mrs Thatcher's government had no reputation for an anti-inflation policy. Its credibility was low.

Stabilization Policy
Dilemma

The Essence of the Story

THE FINANCIAL TIMES, 12 JUNE 1996

Economists ponder shorter dole queues and stable pay deals

Graham Bowley

Deregulation in the job market may have cut 'natural' unemployment but experts differ on the extent of the fall

Something remarkable is happening in Britain's labour market. Since January, unemployment has fallen below levels associated in the past with rising wage inflation – yet pay settlements have hardly moved.

Some economists believe that this is evidence of a decline in the so-called 'natural rate' of unemployment – when wage inflation is stable because the effect of workers' fear of job loss is offset by companies' willingness to concede pay increases. They believe unemployment can now fall further than it did after the last recession before labour shortages trigger an upward spiral of wage inflation.

The natural rate – estimated in the 1980s to have been about 8 per cent of the workforce or even as high as 10 per cent – is now much lower.

'There is some suggestion that the natural rate has probably fallen some way, 7 per cent, maybe 6 per cent, but exactly what it is is uncertain,' said Mr Charles Bean, at the London School of Economics....

'The natural rate peaked in the mid-1980s at around 9.5 per cent and has since fallen to 8.25 per cent... We doubt whether there is much scope for the unemployment rate to fall much further without triggering labour shortages and additional wage pressure,' said Mr David Walton, an economist at Goldman Sachs.

The credit for the improvement in the natural rate – be it large or small – is given to the labour market reforms of the past 15 years. These, the optimists contest, have delivered a more flexible labour market which avoids bottlenecks as demand for labour picks up.

The reforms have...one overarching theme... the government's reduced willingness to protect labour.

Changes to the benefits regime have increased incentives for people to move from the dole queue back into work.

These include the tightening of requirements to receive benefits and the shortening of the period of time for which benefits are payable.

The weakening of trade unions and the deregulation of work and pay contracts have shifted power in the workplace to the employer. Union power has declined through legislation and falling union membership – reflecting the general shift in economic activity away from highly unionised manufacturing and public sectors towards services and the private sector, which tend to be less unionised....

Mr Patrick Minford, Liverpool University, thinks the natural rate has declined to between 2 per cent and 3 per cent....

Mr Ray Barrell at the National Institute of Economic and Social Research, thinks the natural rate could fall as low as 4 per cent over the next 10 years – as long as the UK does not encounter another recession which makes many people unemployed, undoing all the work of getting the long-term jobless back to work.

But perhaps the most immediate test for how far the natural rate has fallen will come this year. So far the economic recovery has been concentrated away from the south-east – the region seen as the culprit for rising inflation during the 1980s boom.

But if, as the chancellor predicts, this year the UK is set to experience rapid consumer-led growth, attention will switch to the south-east's mainly service-sector economy.

'The final test of whether the labour market has changed is if we can go into a consumer-led, south-east region led recovery and still pay hardly moves,' said Mr Robert Barrie, an economist at BZW.

■ The natural rate of unemployment in the 1980s was estimated to be between 8 and 10 per cent of the work-force.

■ The natural rate may have fallen to possibly 6 or 7 per cent in the 1990s.

■ The reason for the fall in the natural rate is the labour market reforms of the past 15 years which have created a more flexible labour market. The specific factors have been the tightening of the rules for eligibility for unemployment benefit, and the shift in the balance of power towards employers and away from trade unions.

■ Patrick Minford believes that the natural rate of unemployment has declined to between 2 and 3 per cent of the work-force. Ray Barrell believes that the natural rate could fall as low as 4 per cent in the next 10 years as long as there is no recession in this period.

Economic Analysis

■ The size of the natural rate of unemployment is a determining factor in stabilization policy. If unemployment is below the natural rate, inflation rises. If unemployment is above the natural rate, inflation falls.

■ The government face a constant stabilization policy dilemma: whether to tighten or loosen their grip on monetary policy by raising or lowering interest rates, according to whether the rate of unemployment is above or below the natural rate.

■ In 1994, the economy expanded rapidly. But while unemployment fell, inflation also fell.

■ The governor of the Bank of England believed that the unemployment rate in mid-1996 was perilously close to the natural rate and that monetary policy would have to be tightened by raising interest rates.

■ The Chancellor believed that unemployment was still above the natural rate and that monetary pol-icy could remain loose and interest rates could remain low.

■ Figure 1 shows that if the unemployment rate is below the natural rate the rate of inflation will rise. But during the late 1980s and 1990s the natural rate decreased. In Fig. 1 the $LRPC_0$ and $SRPC_0$ curves shift leftward.

■ Figure 2 shows that in the 1980s the natural rate of unemployment increased to 11 per cent. Figure 3 shows that the natural rate has fallen to 6.5 per cent in the 1990s. By studying the shifting relationship between the change in the inflation rate and the unemployment rate, the government and the Bank of England try to estimate the natural rate and decide whether to tighten or loosen monetary policy.

■ Figure 3 shows that there is little evidence in the data for the belief that the natural rate has fallen to 3 per cent. However, the diversity of opinion between economists suggests that no one knows the correct natural rate.

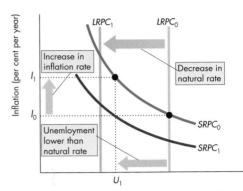

Figure 1

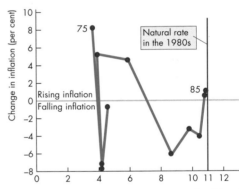

Figure 2 The late 1970s and early 1980s

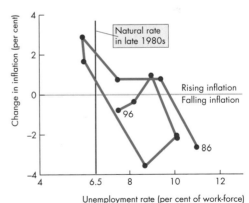

Figure 3 The late 1980s and the 1990s

Over a period of time, Mrs Thatcher won credibility for her anti-inflation policies by earning a reputation for being tough with monetary policy. In recent years, several EU governments have adopted explicit inflation targets as a means of enhancing their credibility. They work like the feedback rules we've just reviewed. If the central bank and the government think that real GDP is growing faster than potential GDP, they will expect inflation to rise from its current position. The central bank will reduce the money supply and raise the rate of interest to slow the growth of the economy and forestall a potential rise in inflation. If the central bank and the government think that real GDP is growing more slowly than potential GDP, they expect inflation to fall from its current position so the central bank will increase the money supply and lower the rate of interest.

New Zealand was the first country to experiment with the use of published inflation targets and it has developed an impressive record of success in meeting the targets. Table 34.2 shows that other countries have followed this route as a means of developing an anti-inflation reputation.

A radical suggestion for strengthening the Bank of England's reputation as the guardian of price stability is to make the Bank independent of government and to charge it with the single responsibility of achieving and maintaining price level stability. Some central banks are more independent than others. The German and Swiss central banks are the best examples. Another example is the New Zealand central bank. All these central banks have the responsibility of stabilizing prices but not real GDP, and of doing so without interference from the government.

If a durable arrangement could be devised for making the Bank of England take a longer term-view concentrating only on inflation, it is possible that inflation could be kept low at a low cost.

REVIEW

◆ A fixed rule gives more effective protection against a cost-push inflation than a feedback rule.

◆ When inflation is tamed, a recession usually results because people form policy expectations based on past policy actions.

◆ An independent central bank pursuing only price stability could possibly achieve price stability with greater credibility and at lower cost in terms of unemployment and lost production.

◆ ◆ ◆ ◆ You've examined the main issues of macroeconomic policy. You've looked at the goals of policy and the fiscal and monetary policies pursued. You've examined policies for achieving faster long-term real GDP growth and you've seen how fixed and feedback rules operate to stabilize the business cycle and contain inflation. You've also seen why lowering inflation is usually accompanied by recession and higher unemployment. *Reading Between the Lines* on pp. 910–911 examines the relationship between inflation and unemployment. ◆ You have now completed your study of macroeconomics and of the problems and challenges of improving macroeconomic performance. In this study, your main focus has been the UK and EU economies. Occasionally, we have taken into account linkages between the United Kingdom and the rest of the world. ◆ In Chapter 37, we turn our attention to the problems of the economies of the developing world and of former communist countries and see how they are moving towards industrial market economies like our own.

TABLE 34.2

Published Inflation Objectives of Selected Countries

Country	Target (per cent)	Period	Set by
UK	1 – 4	1 – 2.5 by 1997	Government
Canada	1 – 3	Until 1998	Central bank and government
France	< 2	As from 1995	Central bank
Italy	2	By 1996	Government
Spain	< 3	By late 1997	Central bank
Sweden	2 ± 1	As from 1995	Central bank
Finland	2	As from 1995	Central bank
Australia	2 – 3	Medium term	Central bank
New Zealand	0 – 2	As from 1993	Central bank and government

Source: *Bank for International Settlements Annual Report,* 1996.

SUMMARY

Policy Goals

The goals of macroeconomic policy are to achieve the highest sustainable rate of long-term real GDP growth, smooth out avoidable business fluctuations, maintain low unemployment and low inflation, and prevent a large international current account deficit.

These five goals boil down to two: unemployment and inflation. Keeping unemployment at its natural rate is equivalent to keeping real GDP growing steadily at its maximum sustainable rate and it is equivalent to avoiding business fluctuations. (pp. 892–894)

Policy Tools and Performance

The macroeconomic policy tools are fiscal policy and monetary policy. Fiscal and monetary policy within the EU is dictated by the targets set by the Maastricht Treaty. The budget deficit is to be kept below 3 per cent of GDP and monetary policy is to be coordinated by the central banks of the other EU member states. (pp. 894–897)

Long-term Growth Policy

The sources of the long-term growth of potential GDP are the accumulation of physical and human capital and the advance of technology. Policies to increase the long-term growth rate focus on increasing saving and investment in human capital and new technologies.

The EU national saving rate has been on a generally falling path since 1970. To increase the saving rate, government saving, which was negative in much of the 1980s, must be increased and incentives for private saving must be strengthened. The incentive to save depends on the after-tax rate of return. A radical policy is to eliminate taxes on interest income, but such measures are regarded as inequitable. Saving can be increased by keeping inflation under control.

Human capital investment might be increased with improved education and by improving on-the-job training programmes. Investment in new technologies can be encouraged by tax incentives and EU sponsored research programmes. (pp.897–899)

Business Cycle and Unemployment Policy

In the face of an aggregate demand shock, a fixed-rule policy takes no action to counter the shock. It permits aggregate demand to fluctuate as a result of all the independent forces that influence it. Consequently, there are fluctuations in real GDP and the price level. A feedback-rule policy adjusts taxes, government purchases, or the money supply to offset the effects of other influences on aggregate demand. An ideal feedback rule keeps the economy at full employment, with stable prices.

Some economists argue that feedback rules make the economy less stable because they require greater knowledge of the state of the economy than we have, they operate with time lags that extend beyond the forecast horizon, and they introduce unpredictability about policy reactions.

In the face of a productivity growth slowdown, a fixed rule results in lower output (and higher unemployment) and a higher price level. A feedback rule that increases the money supply or cuts taxes to stimulate aggregate demand results in an even higher price level and higher inflation. Output (and unemployment) follows the same course as with a fixed rule.

By using feedback policies aimed at keeping nominal GDP growth steady – nominal GDP targeting – it is possible that the extremes of inflation and recession might be avoided. (pp. 900–906)

Inflation Policy

A fixed rule minimizes the threat of cost-push inflation. A feedback rule validates cost-push inflation and leaves the price level and inflation rate free to move to wherever they are pushed.

Inflation can be tamed, and at little or no cost in terms of lost output or excessive unemployment, by slowing the growth of aggregate demand in a credible and predictable way. But usually, when inflation is slowed down, a recession occurs. Published inflation targets aid the process of building up a good inflation reputation. (pp. 906–912)

KEY ELEMENTS

Key Terms

Discretionary policy, 900
Feedback-rule policy, 900
Fiscal policy, 894
Fixed-rule policy, 900
Monetary policy, 894
Nominal GDP targeting, 905,

◆ Key Figures

Figure 34.1   Macroeconomic Performance: EU
              Inflation and Unemployment, 1995,
              893
Figure 34.2   The Fiscal Policy Record, 895
Figure 34.3   The Monetary Policy Record: UK
              Monetary Policy 1987–1995, 896
Figure 34.6   Two Stabilization Policies: Aggregate
              Demand Shock, 902
Figure 34.7   Responding to a Productivity Growth
              Slowdown, 905
Figure 34.8   Responding to an OPEC Oil Price
              Increase, 907
Figure 34.9   Lowering Inflation, 909

REVIEW QUESTIONS

1 What are the goals of macroeconomic policy?

2 Describe the main features of recent fiscal policy in EU countries.

3 Describe the main features of recent monetary policy in the United Kingdom since 1988.

4 Explain the main ways in which policy can try to speed up long-term real GDP growth.

5 Explain the distinction between a fixed-rule policy and a feedback-rule policy.

6 Analyse the effects of a temporary decrease in aggregate demand if a fixed money supply rule is employed.

7 Analyse the behaviour of real GDP and the price level in the face of a permanent decrease in aggregate demand under:

a A fixed monetary rule.
b A feedback monetary rule.

8 Explain the main problems in using fiscal policy for stabilizing the economy.

9 Why do economists disagree with each other on the appropriateness of fixed and feedback rules?

10 Analyse the effects of a rise in the price of oil on real GDP and the price level if the central bank employs:

a A fixed monetary rule.
b A feedback monetary rule.

11 Explain nominal GDP targeting and why it reduces real GDP fluctuations and inflation.

12 Explain why the government's credibility affects the cost of lowering inflation.

PROBLEMS

1 A productivity growth slowdown has occurred. Explain its possible origins and describe a policy package that is designed to speed up growth again.

2 The economy is experiencing 10 per cent inflation and 7 per cent unemployment. Set out policies for the central bank and parliament to pursue that will lower both inflation and unemployment. Explain how and why your proposed policies will work.

3 The economy shown in the figure is initially on aggregate demand curve AD_0 and short-run aggregate supply curve SAS_0. Then aggregate demand decreases and the aggregate demand curve shifts leftward to AD_1.

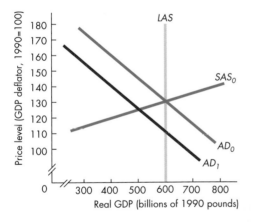

a What is the initial equilibrium real GDP and price level?

b If the decrease in aggregate demand is temporary and the government follows a fixed rule fiscal policy, what happens to real GDP and the price level? Trace the immediate effects and the adjustment as aggregate demand returns to its original level.

c If the decrease in aggregate demand is temporary and the government follows a feedback-rule policy, what happens to real GDP and the price level? Trace the immediate effects and the adjustment as aggregate demand returns to its original level.

d If the decrease in aggregate demand is temporary and the government follows a fixed-rule fiscal policy, what happens to real GDP and the price level?

4 The economy is booming and inflation is beginning to rise, but it is widely agreed that a massive recession is just around the corner. Weigh the advantages and disadvantages of the government pursuing a fixed- and a feedback-rule fiscal policy.

5 The economy is in a recession and inflation is falling. It is widely agreed that a strong recovery is just around the corner. Weigh the advantages and disadvantages of the central bank pursuing a fixed- and a feedback-rule monetary policy.

6 You have been hired as the chief economic adviser by the Chancellor to draw up an economic plan that will maximize the chance of the government being re-elected.

a What are the macroeconomic stabilization policy elements in that plan?

b What do you have to make the economy do in an election year?

c What policy actions would help the government achieve its objectives?

(In dealing with this problem, be careful to take into account the effects of your proposed policy on expectations and the effects of those expectations on actual economic performance.)

7 Study *Reading Between the Lines* on pp. 910–911 and then answer the following questions.

a Why do economists believe that the natural rate of unemployment has declined in the United Kingdom?

b Use the theory of the Phillips curve to explain the inflation implications of stabilization policy if the natural rate varied according to the estimates in the newspaper article.

b What, according to the article, would be a test of how far the natural rate of unemployment has fallen and why?

TALKING WITH
PAUL DE GRAUWE

Paul De Grauwe has a BA in economics from the Katholieke Universiteit Leuven and a PhD in Economics from the John Hopkins University in Baltimore, USA. Whilst completing his PhD he worked at the IMF as an economist. His first academic post, in 1974, was in the very university he obtained his first degree, where in 1982 he became Professor of Economics. He has held many visiting posts throughout Europe and America, which include the College of Europe, University of Pennsylvania and University of Paris. He has held research fellow posts at CEPS and CEPR and in 1991 he became a member of the Belgian Parliament. His main research interests are international monetary relations, monetary integration, open economy macroeconomics, and theory and empirical analysis of the foreign exchange markets. His publications include: *International Money, Post-war Trends and Theories* and *The Economics of Monetary Integration*.

The Maastricht Treaty has a series of convergence criteria that countries have to satisfy if European Monetary Union (EMU) is to be achieved. Do you agree that this is the best strategy for EMU?

No, I disagree. I do not think that the Maastricht Treaty approach is the correct one. In fact it is probably the most difficult way to organize a monetary union. I think historical evidence shows that monetary unions can be organized without any of these convergence criteria being imposed as prior conditions. The latest example was East and West Germany, where a monetary union was created without any convergence criteria being imposed on East Germany. If they had been there would be no German monetary union today. My interpretation of these convergence criteria is that they are there to solve a German problem, which is that Germany does not want a monetary union with high-inflation countries. It is afraid that by associating itself with such countries it will lose part of its reputation for having a strong currency. It therefore uses the convergence criteria as road blocks, making it difficult for high-inflation countries to enter into the monetary union. This has the effect of keeping the monetary union small so that Germany's dominant position in European monetary affairs can be more or less maintained.

Do you think there will be a two-speed Europe? What do you think are the dangers of that?

Yes, this Maastricht Treaty may lead to a two-speed monetary unification process and I see quite a lot of dangers. One is that the countries which are left out will have great difficulty in converging with the core group of countries so that they may be left out for some time. They will not move smoothly and quickly into the monetary union because of their poor reputation, and the fact that they are 'outside' will not improve things. Being left outside means their reputation will worsen, thereby making it more difficult to reduce interest rates and to stabilize the exchange rate. The result will be that Europe will face a division between North and South, creating economic

> *'A monetary union certainly has costs especially of a monetary union of countries that have very different economic structures.'*

problems. This will make integration more difficult and will also create political problems.

Why do you suggest that countries with high debt/income ratios have a poor reputation? Hasn't Belgium got a high debt/income ratio but not a poor reputation?

The reputation of Belgium is not as good as you say. During the 1990s it has faced several speculative crises. In general I would say that those countries with high debt have difficulty in maintaining low inflation and stable macroeconomic policies. By being left out, things will not become easier for them because they will always face the risk of devaluation. This risk leads to higher interest rates on government bonds, making the process of debt reduction more painful.

What are the costs of joining the EMU too early – are they worth the benefits?

This is a fundamental question. The question that should be asked first is: what are the costs and benefits of monetary union? A monetary union certainly has costs, especially a monetary union of countries that have very different economic structures. One of the dangers of a union of countries that differ too much is that it could place a lot of pressure on the European Central Bank (ECB). Suppose, for example, some countries face a boom and others a recession. The former may then pressure the ECB to follow tight monetary policies, whereas the latter may urge for more monetary stimulus. Such a situation, if it occurred frequently, would lead to erratic ECB monetary policies.

To avoid this problem, countries participating in EMU should have a similar economic structure so that they face similar economic disturbances. Against these costs, however, we must set the benefits and these are also significant: lower transactions costs, less exchange rate uncertainty. Unfortunately, there is no consensus among economists on how large these costs and benefits are.

How do you say that EMU should be organized? What are the proper conditions for it?

I think that the right approach should be to tell each country to do its own cost benefit analysis. If a country feels it is beneficial to be part of the EMU, then it should be allowed to join. Of course the rules that will be used in the monetary union should be announced beforehand, and accepted by prospective members. In this connection, the rules that the ECB would be politically independent and that it should pursue price stability are extremely important. Individual EU countries, which believe it to be in their national interest to join should not be prevented from doing so.

I think that the rules that will govern the monetary union must be made clear from the start. Countries with low inflation must have guarantees that monetary union will be inflation free. These guarantees can be ensured if the ECB has the right incentives to keep inflation low. One way to do this, for example, is to make the Board of the ECB accountable for keeping inflation low. If it fails to do so, it should be fired. Such rules reduce the risk for low-inflation countries of previously high-inflation countries joining and jeopardizing price stability in the union, thereby affecting the cost benefit relation of the low-inflation countries.

How do you think the European Central Bank should be organized?

I think we can learn something from the German model of central

banking, which has been extremely successful. The key ingredients of the German model are, first, that the primary objective of the central bank should be price stability, and second, that in order to achieve this objective the central bank should be politically independent. These have made the German model successful in maintaining monetary stability in Germany. I think they should be the guiding principles of the ECB. They are already enshrined in the Maastricht Treaty, so we have it there on paper at least. Some people say that the ECB will be more German than the Bundesbank. The wording in the treaty seems to be even stronger than the wording in German law. Of course there is always the risk that things may turn out to be different from the blueprint. This is what the Germans are still afraid of. They fear that certain countries, after joining the ECB, may introduce far too much inflation, despite the statutes.

Do you think that EMU will be one of the big questions for Europe?

Yes, and it will become a major issue as we come closer to the date. One of the reasons for this is that as we approach the date, the turbulence in the foreign exchange markets will increase. This is because some basic issues have yet to be solved. For example, the membership issue is to be solved in early 1998, and the EMU should start on 1 January, 1999, so this will lead to great uncertainty in the foreign exchange markets about who will be in, and who will be out. Speculators will take positions based on information which will be sometimes favourable and sometimes unfavourable. This will lead to great volatility in the foreign exchange markets. The question is whether we will be able to contain all this; and whether it will lead to a dynamic which makes it impossible to maintain the fixity of the exchange rate (another condition of the Maastricht Treaty to start EMU). This could be a self-defeating process which would lead some countries, in particular Germany, to conclude that the time is not ripe. The whole process may well collapse.

In your assessment what are the prospects for EMU?

The prospects have improved recently, but there is still likelihood that we will not be able to master the turbulence that will occur in the foreign exchange markets. There is another issue that leads to the same conclusion. In many countries these days hostility towards EMU has increased. In Germany it was present from the beginning. In other countries, such as France, there has been a change in the attitude of the population, who are now against monetary union. The reason is that we have linked two good ideas. One is monetary union and the other is fiscal prudence and reducing government debt. These things should not be linked. By doing so, a situation is created in which hostility towards budget cuts spills over to monetary union. People increasingly ask why should we have EMU if it means hardship? This leads to an erosion of the social consensus in favour of monetary union.

What are the dangers if EMU does not occur by 1999?

There will be the turbulence in the foreign exchange markets that I have mentioned. This may take us to the position we were in during the 1970s. One may say: so what! Maybe it is not that bad, many countries have survived this kind of regime. It would certainly be a setback to the integration process in Europe.

What advice would you give a person studying economics for the first time?

To be a good economist it is not sufficient to be good at maths. Students also need to study the social sciences and history. They should be willing to study 'hard' and 'soft' sciences.

CHAPTER 35

TRADING
WITH
THE
WORLD

After studying this chapter you will be able to:

◆ Describe the trends and patterns in international trade

◆ Explain comparative advantage and why all countries can gain from international trade

◆ Explain how economies of scale and diversity of taste lead to gains from international trade

◆ Explain why trade restrictions reduce the volume of imports and exports and reduce our consumption possibilities

◆ Explain the arguments used to justify trade restrictions and show how they are flawed

◆ Explain why we have trade restrictions

S INCE ANCIENT TIMES, PEOPLE HAVE STRIVEN TO EXPAND THEIR TRADING AS FAR AS technology allowed. Marco Polo opened up the silk route between Europe and China in the thirteenth century. Today, container ships laden with cars and machines and Boeing 747s stuffed with farm-fresh foods ply sea and air routes, carrying billions of pounds worth of goods. Why do people go to such great lengths to trade with those in other countries? ◆ Low-wage Mexico has entered into a free trade agreement with high-wage Canada and the United States – the North American Free Trade Agreement or NAFTA. Within the European Union it has been estimated by the US Bureau of Labor Statistics that a German manufacturing worker is paid twice that of an equivalent British one, but a worker in Hong Kong costs one-third of his or her British equivalent. How can any country compete with another that pays its workers a fraction of European wages? Are there any industries in which Europe has an advantage? The Uruguay Round of the GATT produced the most recent international

Silk Routes and Containers

treaty of trade liberalization. The process of trade liberalization around the world has been going on since the end of World War II, bringing about a gradual reduction of tariffs. What are the effects of tariffs on international trade? Why don't we have completely unrestricted international trade?

◆ ◆ ◆ ◆ In this chapter we're going to learn about international trade. We'll discover how *all* nations can gain by specializing in producing the goods and services in which they have a comparative advantage and trading with other countries. We'll discover that all countries can compete, no matter how high their wages. We'll also explain why, despite the fact that international trade brings benefits to all, countries restrict trade.

Patterns and Trends in International Trade

The goods and services that we buy from people in other countries are called **imports.** The goods and services that we sell to people in other countries are called **exports.** What are the most important things that we import and export? Most people would probably guess that a relatively rich country such as the United Kingdom imports raw materials and exports manufactured goods. While that is one feature of UK international trade, it is not its most important feature. The vast bulk of our merchandise exports *and* imports are manufactured goods. We sell foreigners Land Rovers, aircraft, machines and scientific equipment, and we buy televisions, video recorders, blue jeans and T-shirts from them. Also, we are a major exporter of primary materials, particularly North Sea oil, and we export chemical goods. We import and export a huge volume of services. Let's look at the international trade of the United Kingdom in a recent year.

UK International Trade

Table 35.1 classifies UK international trade in five major categories – agricultural products, primary materials and fuels, manufactured goods, chemicals and services. The second column gives the value of UK exports and the third column the value of UK imports. The fourth column tells us the balance of trade in the various categories. The **balance of trade** is the value of exports minus the value of imports. If the balance is positive, then the value of exports exceeds the value of imports and the United Kingdom is a **net exporter**. But if the balance is negative, the value of imports exceeds the value of exports and the United Kingdom is a **net importer**.

Trade in Goods   About 55 per cent of UK international trade is trade in goods and 45 per cent is trade in services. Of the categories of goods traded, by far the most important is manufactured goods. The total value of exports of manufactured goods is less than the total value of imports – the United Kingdom is a net importer of manufactured goods. The United Kingdom is also a net importer of primary materials and fuels and of agricultural products. It

TABLE 35.1

UK Exports and Imports in 1994

Category	Exports	Imports (billions of pounds)	Balance
Agricultural products	6.3	12.4	−6.1
Primary materials and fuels (excluding agricultural)	11.5	12.2	−0.7
Manufactured goods	98.0	106.1	−8.1
Chemicals	18.8	14.6	4.2
Total visible trade	134.6	145.3	−10.7
Services	123.0	114.1	8.9
Total balance	**257.6**	**259.4**	**−1.8**

Source: Central Statistical Office, *Annual Abstract of Statistics,* 1996.

is a net exporter of chemical goods and services. Figure 35.1 highlights some of the major items of UK imports and exports of goods. The largest items of both imports and exports are machinery and transport equipment (including motor vehicles). Our imports of machinery and transport equipment (shown by the red bars) are greater than the value of exports of these items (shown by the blue bars).

Trade in Services   Nearly half of UK international trade is not of goods but of services. You may be wondering how a country can 'export' and 'import' services. Let's look at some examples.

Suppose that you decided to take a holiday in Spain, travelling there from Manchester on Iberian Airways. What you buy from Iberian Airways is not a good but a transport service. Although the concept may sound odd at first, in economic terms you are importing that service from Spain. The money you spend in Spain on hotel bills, restaurant meals and other things is also classified as the import of services. Similarly, the holiday taken by a Spanish student in the United Kingdom counts as an export of services to Spain.

When we import TV sets from South Korea, the owner of the ship that carries these TV sets might be Greek and the company that insures the cargo might be with Lloyds in London. The payment that we make for the transport to the Greek company is a payment for the import of services, and the payment the Greek shipowner makes to the London

FIGURE 35.1

UK Exports and Imports: 1994

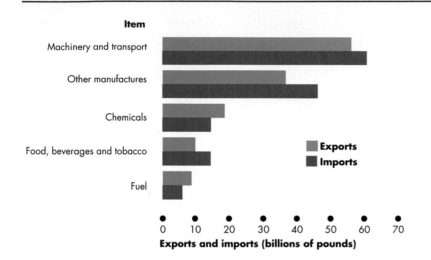

We export large quantities of capital goods such as machinery and transport equipment. We also export large quantities of manufactured goods and cars. But we import even larger quantities of some of these items. We also export and import fuel.

Source: Central Statistical Office, *Annual Abstract of Statistics*, 1996.

insurance company is a payment for the export of a service. Similarly, when an UK shipping company transports Scotch whisky to Tokyo, the transport cost is an export of a service to Japan.

The importance of the various components of trade in services is set out in Table 35.2. As you can see, investment income is the largest items – accounting for more than 60 per cent of exports and more than 55 per cent of imports. The export

of investment income is interest, profits and dividends remitted to UK businesses and citizens from holding foreign shares, bonds and stocks. The import of investment income is the remission of interest, profits and dividends on UK stocks, shares and bonds held by foreigners. We also do a large amount of international trade in financial services and insurance.

Geographical Patterns

The United Kingdom has trading links with almost every part of the world. Figure 35.2 shows the scale of these links in 1994. Our trade with the rest of the European Union is the largest. Within Europe, the largest market for our exports is Germany. In 1994 the United Kingdom exported more to Germany than to the United States – traditionally the United Kingdom's largest market. North America, which includes the United States, Canada and Mexico, takes a significant share of UK trade at 14 per cent of exports and 13 per cent of imports. Our imports from the newly industrialized countries of Asia are 6.5 per cent of total imports. However, our largest international trade deficit was almost exclusively with the rest of the European Union. The next largest deficit was with the other OECD countries, not including the United States and Canada.

TABLE 35.2

UK Trade in Services in 1993

	Exports	Imports	Balance
		(billions of pounds)	
Travel and transport	19.7	25.1	−5.4
General government	5.2	15.0	−9.8
Investment income	76.7	63.6	13.1
Financial services and insurance	19.3	8.0	11.3
Transfers	2.1	2.4	−0.3
Total invisible balance	**123.0**	**114.1**	**8.9**

Source: Central Statistical Office, *Annual Abstract of Statistics*, 1996.

FIGURE 35.2

The Geographical Pattern of UK International Trade: 1994

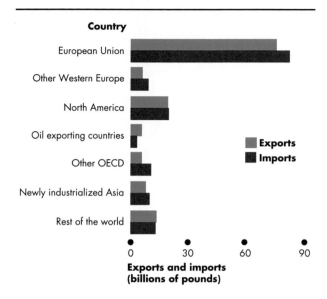

In 1994, our largest trading partner was the rest of the European Union. Within the Union our largest trading partner was Germany. Traditionally our largest trading partner was the United States, but in recent years our trade with Germany has overtaken our trade with the United States.

Source: Central Statistical Office, *Annual Abstract of Statistics*, 1996.

Trends in Trade

International trade has always been an important part of our economic life. In 1960, we exported 14 per cent of GDP and imported 15 per cent of GDP. Since then these percentages have steadily increased and today they are nearly double their 1960 levels.

On the export side, all the major commodity categories have shared in the increased volume of international trade. Mechanical and electrical machinery and semi-manufactured goods have remained the largest components of exports and have roughly maintained their share in total exports. The one major change has been the export of fuel, which has increased from 4 per cent of exports in 1963 to 7 per cent in 1994.

But there have been dramatic changes in the composition of imports. Food and raw materials

imports have declined steadily, from a total of 55 per cent in 1963 to 14 per cent in 1994. Imports of fuel have decreased as North Sea oil came on stream in the 1970s. Imports of machinery of all kinds and semi-manufactured goods have increased dramatically, from 33 per cent of imports in 1963 to 80 per cent in 1994.

Figure 35.3 shows the United Kingdom's overall *balance of trade* (of goods and services) since 1960. As you can see, there was a small deficit (a negative balance) during the 1960s. The balance then went into a surplus in the mid-1970s. But since the mid-1980s, there has been a downward trend in the balance of UK international trade.

Balance of Trade and International Borrowing

When people buy more than they sell, they have to finance the difference by borrowing. When they sell

FIGURE 35.3

The UK Balance of Trade: 1960–1995

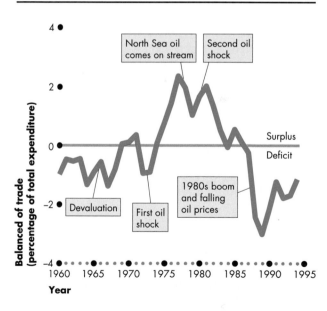

The balance of trade was a small negative (a deficit) between 1960 and 1968. From 1975 to 1986 the balance was positive (a surplus) largely because of the export of North Sea oil. In the remaining 1980s and the 1990s the balance of trade became strongly negative (a deficit).

Source: Central Statistical Office, *Annual Abstract of Statistics*, 1996.

more than they buy, they can use the surplus to make loans to others. This simple principle that governs the income and expenditure and borrowing and lending of individuals and firms is also a feature of our balance of trade. If we import more than we export, we have to finance the difference by borrowing from foreigners. When we export more than we import, we make loans to foreigners to enable them to buy goods in excess of the value of the goods they have sold to us.

This chapter does *not* cover the factors that determine the balance of trade and the scale of international borrowing and lending that finance that balance. It is concerned with understanding the volume, pattern and directions of international trade rather than its balance. So that we can keep our focus on these topics, we'll build a model in which there is no international borrowing and lending – just international trade in goods and services. Because there is no international borrowing or lending, the trade balance must be zero. We'll find that we are able to understand what determines the volume, pattern and directions of international trade and also establish its benefits and the costs of trade restrictions within this framework. This model can be expanded to include international borrowing and lending, but this extension does not change the conclusions that we'll reach here about the factors that determine the volume, pattern, directions and benefits of international trade.

Let's now begin to study these factors.

Opportunity Cost and Comparative Advantage

Let's apply the lessons that we learned in Chapter 3 about the gains from trade to the trade between countries. We'll begin by recalling how we can use the production possibility frontier to measure opportunity cost.

Opportunity Cost in Farmland

Farmland (a fictitious country) can produce grain and cars at any point inside or along the production possibility frontier shown in Fig. 35.4. (We're holding constant the output of all the other goods that Farmland produces.) The Farmers (the people of

FIGURE 35.4

Opportunity Cost in Farmland

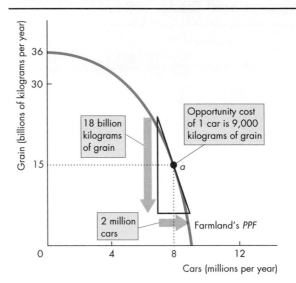

Farmland produces and consumes 15 billion kilograms of grain and 8 million cars a year. That is, it produces and consumes at point *a* on its production possibility frontier. Opportunity cost is equal to the magnitude of the slope of the production possibility frontier. The red triangle tells us that at point *a*, 18 billion kilograms of grain must be forgone to get 2 million cars. That is, at point *a*, 2 million cars cost 18 billion kilograms of grain. Equivalently, 1 car costs 9,000 kilograms of grain or 9,000 kilograms of grain cost 1 car.

Farmland) are consuming all the grain and cars that they produce and they are operating at point *a* in the figure. That is, Farmland is producing and consuming 15 billion kilograms of grain and 8 million cars each year. What is the opportunity cost of a car in Farmland?

We can answer this question by calculating the slope of the production possibility frontier (*PPF*) at point *a* . The magnitude of the slope of the *PPF* measures the opportunity cost of one good in terms of the other. To measure the slope of the frontier at point *a*, place a straight line tangential to the frontier at point *a* and calculate the slope of that straight line. Recall that the formula for the slope of a line is the change in the value of the variable measured on the *y*-axis divided by the change in the value of the variable measured on the *x*-axis as we move along the line. Here, the variable measured on the *y*-axis is billions of kilograms of grain and the variable measured on the x-axis is millions of cars. So the slope is the change in the number of kilograms of grain divided by the change in the number of cars. As you can see from the red triangle at point a in the figure, if the number of cars produced increases by 2 million, grain production decreases by 18 billion kilograms. Therefore the magnitude of the slope is 18 billion divided by 2 million, which equals 9,000. To get one more car, the people of Farmland must give up 9,000 kilograms of grain. Thus the opportunity cost of 1 car is 9,000 kilograms of grain. Equivalently, 9,000 kilograms of grain cost 1 car. For the people of Farmland, these opportunity costs are the prices they face. The price of a car is 9,000 kilograms of grain and the price of 9,000 kilograms of grain is 1 car.

Opportunity Cost in Mobilia

Now consider the production possibility frontier in Mobilia (another fictitious country and the only other country in our model world). Figure 35.5 illustrates its *PPF*. Like the Farmers, the Movers (the people in Mobilia) consume all the grain and cars that they produce. Mobilia consumes 18 billion kilograms of grain a year and 4 million cars, at point a'.

At point a', the magnitude of the slope of Mobilia's *PPF* is 6 billion kilograms of grain divided by 6 million cars, which equals 1,000 kilograms of grain per car. To get one more car, the people of Mobilia must give up 1,000 kilograms of grain. Thus the opportunity cost of 1 car is 1,000 kilograms of grain, or, equivalently, the opportunity cost of 1,000 kilograms of grain is 1 car. These are the prices faced in Mobilia.

Comparative Advantage

Cars are cheaper in Mobilia than in Farmland. One car costs 9,000 kilograms of grain in Farmland but only 1,000 kilograms of grain in Mobilia. But grain is cheaper in Farmland than in Mobilia – 9,000 kilograms of grain costs only 1 car in Farmland while that same amount of grain costs 9 cars in Mobilia.

Mobilia has a comparative advantage in car production. Farmland has a comparative advantage in grain production. A country has a **comparative advantage** in producing a good if it can produce that good at a lower opportunity cost than any other country. Let's see how opportunity cost differences and comparative advantage generate gains from international trade.

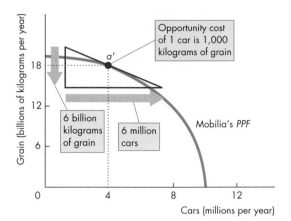

FIGURE 35.5

Opportunity Cost in Mobilia

Mobilia produces and consumes 18 billion kilograms of grain and 4 million cars a year. That is, it produces and consumes at point a' on its production possibility frontier. Opportunity cost is equal to the magnitude of the slope of the production possibility frontier. The red triangle tells us that at point a', 6 billion kilograms of grain must be forgone to get 6 million cars. That is, at point a', 6 million cars cost 6 billion kilograms of grain. Equivalently, 1 car costs 1,000 kilograms of grain or 1,000 kilograms of grain cost 1 car.

Gains from Trade

If Mobilia bought grain for what it costs Farmland to produce it, then Mobilia could buy 9,000 kilograms of grain for 1 car. That is much lower than the cost of growing grain in Mobilia, for there it costs 9 cars to produce 9,000 kilograms of grain. If the Movers can buy grain at the low Farmland price, they will reap some gains.

If the Farmers can buy cars for what it costs Mobilia to produce them, they will be able to obtain a car for 1,000 kilograms of grain. Because it costs 9,000 kilograms of grain to produce a car in Farmland, the Farmers would gain from such an opportunity.

In this situation, it makes sense for Movers to buy their grain from Farmers and for Farmers to buy their cars from Movers. Let's see how such profitable international trade comes about.

Reaping the Gains from Trade

We've seen that the Farmers would like to buy their cars from the Movers and that the Movers would like to buy their grain from the Farmers. Let's see how the two groups do business with each other, concentrating attention on the international market for cars.

Figure 35.6 illustrates such a market. The quantity of cars *traded internationally* is measured on the x-axis. On the y-axis we measure the price of a car. This price is expressed as the number of kilograms of grain that a car costs – the opportunity cost of a car. If no international trade takes place, the price of a car in Farmland is 9,000 kilograms of

FIGURE 35.6

International Trade in Cars

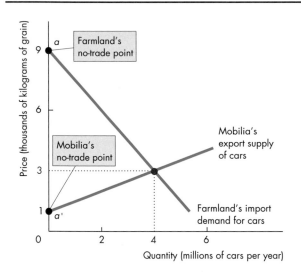

As the price of a car decreases, the quantity of imports demanded by Farmland increases – Farmland's import demand curve for cars is downward-sloping. As the price of a car increases, the quantity of cars supplied by Mobilia for export increases – Mobilia's export supply curve of cars is upward-sloping. Without international trade, the price of a car is 9,000 kilograms of grain in Farmland (point *a*) and 1,000 kilograms of grain in Mobilia (point *a'*). With free international trade, the price of a car is determined where the export supply curve intersects the import demand curve – a price of 3,000 kilograms of grain. At that price, 4 million cars a year are imported by Farmland and exported by Mobilia. The value of grain exported by Farmland and imported by Mobilia is 12 billion kilograms a year, the quantity required to pay for the cars imported.

grain, indicated by point *a* in the figure. Again, if no trade takes place, the price of a car in Mobilia is 1,000 kilograms of grain, indicated by point *a'* in the figure. The no-trade points *a* and *a'* in Fig. 35.6 correspond to the points identified by those same letters in Figs. 35.4 and 35.5. The lower the price of a car (in terms of grain), the greater is the quantity of cars that the Farmers are willing to import from the Movers. This fact is illustrated in the downward-sloping curve, which shows Farmland's import demand for cars.

The Movers respond in the opposite direction. The higher the price of cars (in terms of kilograms of grain), the greater is the quantity of cars that Movers are willing to export to Farmers. This fact is reflected in Mobilia's export supply of cars – the upward-sloping line in Fig. 35.6.

The international market in cars determines the equilibrium price and quantity traded. This equilibrium occurs where the import demand curve intersects the export supply curve. In this case, the equilibrium price of a car is 3,000 kilograms of grain. Four million cars a year are exported by Mobilia and imported by Farmland. Notice that the price at which cars are traded is lower than the initial price in Farmland but higher than the initial price in Mobilia.

Balanced Trade

The number of cars exported by Mobilia – 4 million a year – is exactly equal to the number of cars imported by Farmland. How does Farmland pay for its cars? By exporting grain. How much grain does Farmland export? You can find the answer by noticing that for 1 car Farmland has to pay 3,000 kilograms of grain. Hence for 4 million cars it has to pay 12 billion kilograms of grain. Thus Farmland's exports of grain are 12 billion kilograms a year. Mobilia imports this same quantity of grain.

Mobilia is exchanging 4 million cars for 12 billion kilograms of grain each year and Farmland is doing the opposite, exchanging 12 billion kilograms of grain for 4 million cars. Trade is balanced between these two countries. The value received from exports equals the value paid out for imports.

Changes in Production and Consumption

We've seen that international trade makes it possible for Farmers to buy cars at a lower price than they can produce them for themselves. Equivalently, Farmers can sell their grain for a higher price. International trade also enables Movers to sell their cars for a higher price. Equivalently, Movers can buy grain for a lower price. Thus everybody gains. How is it possible for *everyone* to gain? What are the changes in production and consumption that accompany these gains?

An economy that does not trade with other economies has identical production and consumption possibilities. Without trade, the economy can only consume what it produces. But with international trade an economy can consume different quantities of goods from those that it produces. The production possibility frontier describes the limit of what a country can produce, but it does not describe the limits to what it can consume. Figure 35.7 will help you to see

the distinction between production possibilities and consumption possibilities when a country trades with other countries.

First, notice that the figure has two parts, part (a) for Farmland and part (b) for Mobilia. The production possibility frontiers that you saw in Figs. 35.4 and 35.5 are reproduced here. The slopes of the two black lines in the figure represent the opportunity costs in the two countries when there is no international trade. Farmland produces and consumes at point *a* and Mobilia produces and consumes at *a'*. Cars cost 9,000 kilograms of grain in Farmland and 1,000 kilograms of grain in Mobilia.

Consumption Possibilities The red line in each part of Fig. 35.7 shows the country's consumption possibilities with international trade. These two red

Expanding Consumption Possibilities

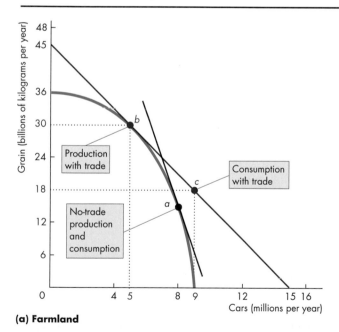

(a) Farmland

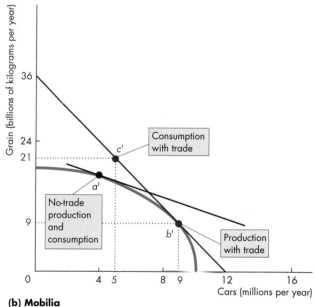

(b) Mobilia

With no international trade, the Farmers produce and consume at point *a* and the opportunity cost of a car is 9,000 kilograms of grain (the slope of the black line in part a). Also, with no international trade, the Movers produce and consume at point *a'* and the opportunity cost of 1,000 kilograms of grain is 1 car (the slope of the black line in part b).

Goods can be exchanged internationally at a price of 3,000 kilograms of grain for 1 car along the red line in each part of the figure. In part (a), Farmland decreases its production of cars and increases its production of grain,

moving from *a* to *b*. It exports grain and imports cars, and it consumes at point *c*. The Farmers have more of both cars and grain than they would if they produced all their own consumption goods – at point *a*. In part (b), Mobilia increases car production and decreases grain production, moving from *a'* to *b'*. Mobilia exports cars and imports grain, and it consumes at point *c'*. The Movers have more of both cars and grain than they would if they produced all their own consumption goods – at point *a'*.

lines have the same slope and the magnitude of that slope is the opportunity cost of a car in terms of grain on the world market – 3,000 kilograms per car. The *slope* of the consumption possibilities line is common to both countries because its magnitude equals the *world* price. But the position of a country's consumption possibilities line depends on the country's production possibilities. A country cannot produce outside its production possibility curve so its consumption possibility curve touches its production possibility curve. Thus Farmland could choose to consume at point *b* with no international trade or, with international trade, at any point on its red consumption possibilities line.

Free Trade Equilibrium With international trade, the producers of cars in Mobilia can get a higher price for their output. As a result, they increase the quantity of car production. At the same time, grain producers in Mobilia are getting a lower price for their grain and so they reduce production. Producers in Mobilia adjust their output by moving along their production possibility frontier until the opportunity cost in Mobilia equals the world price (the opportunity cost in the world market). This situation arises when Mobilia is producing at point *b'* in Fig. 35.7(b).

But the Movers do not consume at point *b'*. That is, they do not increase their consumption of cars and decrease their consumption of grain. Instead, they sell some of their car production to Farmland in exchange for some of Farmland's grain. They trade internationally. But to see how that works out, we first need to check in with Farmland to see what's happening there.

In Farmland, producers of cars now get a lower price and producers of grain get a higher price. As a consequence, producers in Farmland decrease car production and increase grain production. They adjust their outputs by moving along the production possibility frontier until the opportunity cost of a car in terms of grain equals the world price (the opportunity cost on the world market). They move to point *b* in part (a). But the Farmers do not consume at point *b*. Instead, they exchange some of their additional grain production for the now cheaper cars from Mobilia.

The figure shows us the quantities consumed in the two countries. We saw in Fig. 35.6 that

Mobilia exports 4 million cars a year and Farmland imports those cars. We also saw that Farmland exports 12 billion kilograms of grain a year and Mobilia imports that grain. Thus Farmland's consumption of grain is 12 billion kilograms a year less than it produces and its consumption of cars is 4 million a year more than it produces. Farmland consumes at point *c* in Fig. 35.7(a).

Similarly, we know that Mobilia consumes 12 billion kilograms of grain more than it produces and 4 million cars fewer than it produces. Thus Mobilia consumes at *c'* in Fig. 35.7(b).

Calculating the Gains from Trade You can now literally see the gains from trade in Fig. 35.7. Without trade, Farmers produce and consume at *a* (part a) – a point on Farmland's production possibility frontier. With international trade, Farmers consume at point *c* in part (a) – a point *outside* the production possibility frontier. At point *c*, Farmers are consuming 3 billion kilograms of grain a year and 1 million cars a year more than before. These increases in consumption of both cars and grain, beyond the limits of the production possibility frontier, are the gains from international trade.

Movers also gain. Without trade, they consume at point *a'* in part (b) – a point on Mobilia's production possibility frontier. With international trade, they consume at point *c'* – a point outside the production possibility frontier. With international trade, Mobilia consumes 3 billion kilograms of grain a year and 1 million cars a year more than without trade. These are the gains from international trade for Mobilia.

Gains for All

In popular discussions about international trade, we hear about the need for a 'level playing field' and other measures to protect people from foreign competition. International trade seems like a type of contest in which there are winners and losers. But the trade between the Farmers and the Movers that you've just studied does not create winners and losers. Everyone wins.

Sellers add the net demand of foreigners to their domestic demand, and so their market expands. Buyers are faced with domestic supply plus net foreign supply and so have a larger total supply available to them. As you know, prices rise when there is an increase in demand and they fall when there is an increase in supply. So the increased demand (from foreigners) for exports increases their price and the increased supply (from foreigners) of imports decreases their price. Gains in one country do not bring losses in another. Everyone, in this example, gains from international trade.

Absolute Advantage

Suppose that in Mobilia, fewer workers are needed to produce any given output of either grain or cars than in Farmland – productivity is higher in Mobilia than in Farmland. In this situation, Mobilia has an absolute advantage over Farmland. A country has an **absolute advantage** if has greater productivity than another country in the production of all goods. With an absolute advantage, can't Mobilia outsell Farmland in the markets for both cars and grain? Why, if Mobilia has greater productivity than Farmland, does it pay Mobilia to buy *anything* from Farmland?

The answer is that the cost of production in terms of the factors of production employed is irrelevant for determining the gains from trade. It does not matter how many resources are required to produce 1,000 kilograms of grain or a car. What matters is how many cars must be given up to produce an additional kilogram of grain or how much grain must be given up to produce an additional car. That is, what matters is the opportunity cost of one good in terms of the other good. (For a further explanation of why absolute advantage does not influence the gains from trade, see Chapter 3, pp. 56–58.)

Mobilia might have an absolute advantage in the production of all goods, but it cannot have a comparative advantage in the production of all goods. The statement that the opportunity cost of a car in Mobilia is lower than in Farmland is identical to the statement that the opportunity cost of grain is higher in Mobilia than in Farmland. Thus *whenever opportunity costs diverge, everyone has a comparative advantage in something.* All countries can potentially gain from international trade.

The story of the discovery of the logic of the gains from international trade is presented in *Economics in History* on pp. 948–949.

◆ When countries have divergent opportunity costs, they can gain from international trade.

◆ Each country can buy some goods and services from another country at a lower opportunity cost than it can produce them for itself.

◆ Gains arise when each country increases its production of those goods and services in which it has a comparative advantage (goods and services that it can produce at an opportunity cost that is lower than that of other countries) and exchanges some of its production for that of other countries.

◆ All countries gain from international trade. Everyone has a comparative advantage in something.

Gains from Trade in Reality

The gains from trade that we have just studied between Farmland and Mobilia in grain and cars occur in a model economy – in a world economy that we have imagined. But these same phenomena occur every day in the real global economy.

Comparative Advantage in the Global Economy

We buy cars made in Japan and Europe and we sell chemicals, pharmaceuticals and financial services to those countries in return. We buy shirts and fashion goods from the people of Sri Lanka and sell them machinery in return. We buy TV sets and video recorders from South Korea and Taiwan and sell them financial and other services as well as manufactured goods in return. We make some kinds of machines, and Europeans and Japanese make other kinds, and we exchange one type of manufactured good for another.

These are all examples of international trade generated by comparative advantage, just like the international trade between Farmland and Mobilia in our model economy. All international trade arises from comparative advantage, even when it is trade in similar goods such as tools and machines. At first, it seems puzzling that countries exchange manufactured goods. Why doesn't each developed country produce all the manufactured goods its citizens want to buy? Let's look a bit more closely at this question.

Trade in Similar Goods

Why does it make sense for the United Kingdom to produce cars for export and at the same time to import large quantities of them from Japan, Germany, Italy and Sweden? Wouldn't it make more sense to produce all the cars that we buy here in the United Kingdom? After all, we have access to the best technology available for producing cars. Car workers in the United Kingdom are surely as productive as their fellow workers in Germany and Japan. Capital equipment, production lines, robots and so on used in the manufacture of cars are as available to UK car producers as they are to any others. This line of reasoning leaves a puzzle concerning the sources of international exchange of similar commodities produced by similar people using similar equipment. Why does it happen? Why does the United Kingdom have a comparative advantage in some types of cars and Japan and Europe in others?

Diversity of Taste   The first part of the answer to the puzzle is that people have a tremendous diversity of taste. Let's stick with the example of cars. Some people prefer sports cars, some prefer estates, some prefer hatchbacks and some prefer the urban jeep look. In addition to size and type of car, there are many other ways in which cars vary. Some have low fuel consumption, some have high performance, some are spacious and comfortable, some have a large boot, some have four-wheel drive, some have front-wheel drive, some have manual gears, some have automatic gears, some are durable, some are flashy, some have a radiator grill that looks like a Greek temple, others look like a wedge. People's preferences across these many variables differ.

The tremendous diversity in tastes for cars means that people would be dissatisfied if they were forced to consume from a limited range of standardized cars. People value variety and are willing to pay for it in the marketplace.

Economies of Scale   The second part of the answer to the puzzle is economies of scale. *Economies of scale* are the tendency, present in

many production processes, for the average cost of production to be lower, the larger is the scale of production. In such situations, larger and larger production runs lead to ever lower average production costs. Many manufactured goods, including cars, experience economies of scale. For example, if a car producer makes only a few hundred (or perhaps a few thousand) cars of a particular type and design, the producer must use production techniques that are much more labour-intensive and much less automated than those employed to make hundreds of thousands of cars in a particular model. With low production runs and labour-intensive production techniques, costs are high. With very large production runs and automated assembly lines, production costs are much lower. But to obtain lower costs, the automated assembly lines have to produce a large number of cars.

It is the combination of diversity of taste and economies of scale that produces comparative advantages and generates such a large amount of international trade in similar commodities. Diversity of taste and the willingness to pay for variety does not guarantee that variety will be available. It could simply be too expensive to provide a highly diversified range of different types of cars, for example. If every car bought in the United Kingdom today was made in the United Kingdom – no cars were imported – and if the present range of diversity and variety was available, production runs would be remarkably short. Car producers would not be able to reap economies of scale. Although the current variety of cars could be made available, it would be at a high price, and perhaps at a price that no one would be willing to pay.

But with international trade, each manufacturer of cars has the whole world market to serve. Each producer can specialize in a limited range of products and then sell its output to the world market. This arrangement enables large production runs on the most popular cars and feasible production runs even on the most customized cars demanded by only a handful of people in each country.

The situation in the market for cars is also present in many other industries, especially those producing specialized equipment and parts. For example, the United Kingdom exports machines but imports machine tools, and it exports mainframe computers but imports PCs. Thus international exchange of similar but slightly differentiated manufactured products is a highly profitable activity.

This type of trade can be understood with exactly the same model of international trade that we studied earlier. Although we normally think of cars as a single commodity, we have to think of sports cars and saloons and so on as different goods. Different countries, by specializing in a few of these 'goods', are able to enjoy economies of scale and, therefore, a comparative advantage in their production.

You can see that comparative advantage and international trade bring gains regardless of the goods being traded. When the rich countries of the European Union, Japan and the United States import raw materials from the developing countries and from Australia and Canada, the rich importing countries gain and so do the exporting countries. When we buy cheap TV sets, video recorders, shirts and other goods from low-wage countries, both we and the exporters gain from the exchange. It's true that if we increase our imports of cars and produce fewer cars ourselves, jobs in our car industry disappear. But jobs in other industries, in which we have a comparative advantage and supply goods to other countries, expand. After the adjustment is completed, people whose jobs have been lost find employment in the expanding industries. They buy goods produced in other countries at even lower prices than those at which they were available before. The gains from international trade are not necessarily gains for some at the expense of losses for others.

But changes in comparative advantage that lead to changes in international trade patterns can take a long time to adjust to. For example, the increase in car imports and the corresponding relative decline in domestic car production have not brought increased wealth for displaced car workers. Good new jobs take time to find and often people go through a period of prolonged search, putting up with inferior jobs and lower wages than they had before. Thus only in the long run does everyone potentially gain from international specialization and exchange. Short-run adjustment costs that can be large and relatively prolonged are borne by the people who have lost their comparative advantage. Some of the people who lose their jobs may be too old for it to be worth their while making the move to another region of the country or another industry, and so they never share in the gains.

Partly because of the costs of adjustment to changing international trade patterns, but partly also for other reasons, governments intervene in international trade, restricting its volume. Let's examine what happens when governments restrict international trade. We'll contrast restricted trade with free trade. We'll see that free trade brings the greatest possible benefits. We'll also see why, in spite of the benefits of free trade, governments sometimes restrict trade.

Trade Restrictions

Governments restrict international trade in order to protect domestic industries from foreign competition. The restriction of international trade is called **protectionism.** There are two main protectionist methods employed by governments:

◆ Tariffs
◆ Non-tariff barriers

A **tariff** is a tax that is imposed by the importing country when an imported good crosses its international boundary. A **non-tariff barrier** is any action other than a tariff that restricts international trade. Examples of non-tariff barriers are quantitative restrictions and licensing regulations which limit imports. We'll consider non-tariff barriers in more detail below. First, let's look at tariffs.

The History of Tariffs

UK tariffs today are modest compared with their historical levels. Total customs duties on imports as a percentage of imports was about 1 per cent in 1995. In the United States, the average tariff rate is only 4 per cent. It was not always like this. In the 1930s many countries including the United Kingdom and the United States hid behind tariff barriers, but these barriers were slowly dismantled after World War II.

The reduction in tariffs since World War II followed the establishment of the General Agreement on Tariffs and Trade (GATT). The **General Agreement on Tariffs and Trade** is an international agreement designed to limit government intervention to restrict international trade. It was negotiated immediately following World War II and was signed in October 1947. Its goal is to liberalize trading activity and to provide an organization to administer more liberal trading arrangements. The GATT has a small bureaucracy located in Geneva, Switzerland.

Since the formation of the GATT, several rounds of negotiations have taken place that have resulted in general tariff reductions One of these, the Kennedy Round that began in the early 1960s, resulted in large tariff cuts starting in 1967. Another, the Tokyo Round, resulted in further tariff cuts in 1979.

The most recent, the Uruguay Round, which started in 1986 and was completed in 1994, was the most ambitious and comprehensive of the rounds. It was an agreement among 115 countries to lower tariffs and to prevent protection through subsidies or favourable treatment from government purchases. The agreement has been described as the biggest tax cut in the history of the world and the gains from greater specialization and exchange are predicted to boost world output by 1 per cent a year.

The most significant parts of the Uruguay Round agreement are the phasing-out of many agricultural subsidies, the strengthening of intellectual property rights (copyrights and patents) and the creation of a new World Trade Organization (WTO). Membership of the WTO imposes greater obligations on countries to observe the GATT rules and makes subsidies much harder to use as an alternative to tariffs and other forms of protection.

In addition to the agreements under the GATT and the WTO, the United Kingdom is a party to the North American Free Trade Agreement (NAFTA), which became effective on January 1, 1994. Under this agreement, barriers to international trade between the United States, Canada and Mexico will be virtually eliminated after a 15-year phasing-in period (10 years for Canada–United States trade under an earlier Canada–United Kingdom Free Trade Agreement that became effective on January 1, 1989).

In other parts of the world, trade barriers have virtually been eliminated. The *Single European Market* (SEM) in the European Union has created the largest unified tariff-free market in the world. The SEM programme has simplified border formalities for the movement of trade; capital and labour have complete freedom of movement within the European Union, other forms of protection such as non-tariff barriers are to be eliminated; and public procurement is to be made open to all EU firms. In the longer term, the SEM programme provides for all indirect taxes within the European Union to be harmonized so that no individual country can tax a good differently from another country in the Union. In 1994, discussions among the Asia-Pacific Economic group (APEC) led to an agreement in principle to work towards a free-trade area that embraces China, all the economies of East Asia and the South Pacific, and the United Kingdom and Canada. These countries include the fastest growing economies and hold the promise of heralding a global free-trade area.

The effort to achieve freer trade underlines the fact that trade in some goods is still subject to extremely high tariffs. In the European Union, buyers of agricultural products face prices that are on average 40 per cent above world prices as part of the *Common Agricultural Policy* (CAP). The CAP is a price support programme for farmers in the European Union and acts as a tariff on non-EU agricultural products. For example, when you buy 250 grams of New Zealand butter at 90 pence, you pay approximately 25 pence more than you would if there were no protective tariffs. The meat, cheese and sugar that you consume cost significantly more because of protection than they would with free international trade. Figure 35.8 shows the average protective tariff the CAP imposes on world agricultural goods. The implied tariff varies because the world price of agricultural goods varies from year to year. Tariffs are also faced by US consumers. The highest are those on textiles and footwear. A tariff of more than 10 per cent (on the average) is imposed on almost all US imports of textiles and footwear.

The temptation for governments to impose tariffs is a strong one. They do of course provide revenue to the government, but this is not particularly large compared with other sources. Their most important attribute is that they enable the government to satisfy special interest groups in import-competing industries. But, as we'll see, free international trade brings enormous benefits that are reduced when tariffs are imposed. Let's see how.

How Tariffs Work

To analyse how tariffs work, let's return to the example of trade between Farmland and Mobilia. Figure 35.9 shows the international market for cars in which these two countries are the only traders. The volume of trade and the price of a car are determined at the point of intersection of Mobilia's export supply curve of cars and Farmland's import demand curve for cars.

FIGURE 35.8

OECD Estimates of Average Implied Tariffs on EU Agricultural Products, 1979–1993

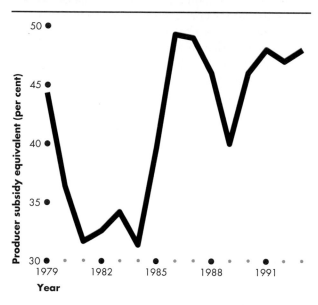

Year

The OECD estimates the average percentage subsidy paid to EU farmers that would give them the same additional income as the actual CAP intervention price, which artificially holds agricultural prices above world prices. The graph is an estimate of the percentage by which EU prices are raised above world prices.

Sources: OECD, *Agricultural Policies, Markets and Trade: Monitoring and Outlook,* 1988 and 1994, quoted in P. Minford, *Britain and Europe: The Balance Sheet,* 1996, Bradford, MCB University Press.

FIGURE 35.9

The Effects of a Tariff

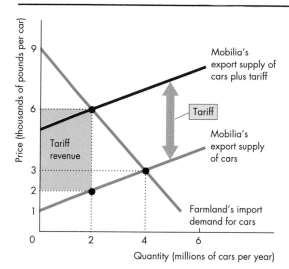

Quantity (millions of cars per year)

Farmland imposes a tariff on car imports from Mobilia. The tariff increases the price that Farmers have to pay for cars. It shifts the supply curve of cars in Farmland upward. The distance between the original supply curve and the new one is the amount of the tariff, £4,000 per car. The price of cars in Farmland increases and the quantity of cars imported decreases. The government of Farmland collects a tariff revenue of £4,000 per car – total of £8 billion on the 2 million cars imported. Farmland's exports of grain decrease because Mobilia now has a lower income from its exports of cars.

In Fig. 35.9, these two countries are trading cars and grain in exactly the same way that we analysed before in Fig. 35.6. Mobilia exports cars and Farmland exports grain. The volume of car imports into Farmland is 4 million a year and the world market price of a car is 3,000 kilograms of grain. To make the example more concrete and real, Fig. 35.9 expresses prices in pounds rather than in units of grain and is based on a money price of grain of £1 a kilogram. With grain costing £1 a kilogram, the money price of a car is £3,000.

Now suppose that the government of Farmland, perhaps under pressure from car producers, decides to impose a tariff on imported cars. In particular, suppose that a tariff of £4,000 per car is imposed. (This is a huge tariff, but the car producers of Farmland are pretty fed up with competition from Mobilia.) What happens?

The first part of the answer is obtained by studying the effects on the supply of cars in Farmland. Cars are no longer going to be available at the Mobilia export supply price. The tariff of £4,000 must be added to that price – the amount paid to the government of Farmland on each car imported. As a consequence, the supply curve in Farmland shifts upward by the amount of the tariff as shown in Fig. 35.9. The new supply curve becomes that labelled 'Mobilia's export supply of cars plus tariff.' The vertical distance between Mobilia's export supply curve and the new supply curve is the tariff imposed by the government of Farmland – £4,000 a car.

The next part of the answer is found by determining the new equilibrium. Imposing a tariff has no effect on the demand for cars in Farmland and so has no effect on Farmland's import demand for cars. Thus Farmland's import demand curve is unchanged. The new equilibrium occurs where the new supply curve intersects Farmland's import demand curve for cars. That equilibrium is at a price of £6,000 a car and with 2 million cars a year being imported. Imports fall from 4 million to 2 million cars a year. At the higher price of £6,000 a car, domestic car producers increase their production. Domestic grain production decreases as resources are moved into the expanding car industry.

The total expenditure on imported cars by the Farmers is £6,000 a car multiplied by the 2 million cars imported (£12 billion). But not all of that money goes to the Movers. They receive £2,000 a car or £4 billion for the 2 million cars. The difference – £4,000 a car or a total of £8 billion for the 2 million cars – is collected by the government of Farmland as tariff revenue.

Obviously, the government of Farmland is happy with this situation. It is now collecting £8 billion that it didn't have before. But what about the Farmers? How do they view the new situation? The demand curve tells us the maximum price that a buyer is willing to pay for one more unit of a good. As you can see from Farmland's import demand curve for cars, if one more car could be imported, someone would be willing to pay almost £6,000 for it. Mobilia's export supply curve of cars tells us the minimum price at which additional cars are available. As you can see, one additional car would be supplied by Mobilia for a price only slightly more than £2,000. Thus because someone is willing to pay almost £6,000 for a car and someone else is willing to supply one for little more than £2,000, there is obviously a gain to be had from trading an extra car. In fact, there are gains to be had – willingness to pay exceeds the minimum supply price – all the way up to 4 million cars a year. Only when 4 million cars are being traded is the maximum price that a Farmer is willing to pay equal to the minimum price that is acceptable to a Mover. Thus restricting international trade reduces the gains from international trade.

It is easy to see that the tariff has lowered the total amount Farmland pays for imports. With free trade, Farmland was paying £3,000 a car and buying 4 million cars a year from Mobilia. Thus the total amount paid to Mobilia for imports was £12 billion a year. With a tariff, Farmland's imports have been cut to 2 million cars a year and the price paid to Mobilia has also been cut to only £2,000 a car. Thus the total amount paid to Mobilia for imports has been cut to £4 billion a year. Doesn't this fact mean that Farmland is now importing less than it is exporting and has a balance of trade surplus?

To answer that question, we need to figure out what's happening in Mobilia. We've just seen that the price that Mobilia receives for cars has fallen from £3,000 to £2,000 a car. Thus the price of cars in Mobilia has fallen. But the price of grain remains at £1 a kilogram. So the relative price of cars has fallen and the relative price of grain has increased. With free trade, the Movers could buy 3,000 kilograms of grain for 1 car. Now they can buy only 2,000 kilograms for 1 car. With a higher relative price of grain, the quantity demanded by the Movers decreases. As a result, Mobilia imports less grain. But because Mobilia imports less grain, Farmland exports less grain. In fact, Farmland's grain industry suffers from two sources. First, there is a decrease in the quantity of grain sold to Mobilia. Second, there is increased competition for inputs from the now expanded car industry. Thus the tariff leads to a contraction in the scale of the grain industry in Farmland.

It seems paradoxical at first that a country imposing a tariff on cars would hurt its own export industry, lowering its exports of grain. It may help to think of it this way: Movers buy grain with the money they make from exporting cars to Farmland. If they export fewer cars, they cannot afford to buy as much grain. In fact, in the absence of any international borrowing and lending, Mobilia has to cut its imports of grain by exactly the same amount as the loss in revenue from its export of cars. Grain imports into Mobilia will be cut back to a value of £4 billion, the amount that can be paid for by the new lower revenue from Mobilia's car exports. Thus trade is still balanced in this post-tariff situation. Although the tariff has cut imports, it has also cut exports, and the cut in the value of exports is exactly equal to the cut in the value of imports. The tariff, therefore, has no effect on the balance of trade – it reduces the volume of trade.

The result that we have just derived is perhaps one of the most misunderstood aspects of international economics. On countless occasions, politicians and others have called for tariffs in order to remove a balance of trade deficit or have argued that lowering tariffs would produce a balance of trade deficit. They reach this conclusion by failing to work out all the implications of a tariff. Because a tariff raises the price of imports and cuts imports, the easy conclusion is that the tariff reduces the balance of trade deficit. But the tariff also changes the *volume* of exports as well. The equilibrium effects of a tariff are to reduce the volume of trade in both directions and the value of imports and exports by the same amount. The balance of trade itself is left unaffected.

Learning the Hard Way

Although the analysis that we have just worked through leads to the clear conclusion that tariffs cut both imports and exports and make both countries worse off, we have not found that conclusion easy to accept. Time and again in the history of world trade governments have imposed high tariff barriers on international trade. Whenever tariff barriers are increased, trade collapses. The most vivid historical example of this interaction of tariffs and trade occurred during the Great Depression years of the early 1930s when the United States imposed tariffs known as the Smoot-Hawley tariffs. The tariff changes that other countries introduced in retaliation had a strong negative effect on world trade. In the United Kingdom, the Import Duties Act 1932 raised tariffs to 33 per cent on selected goods.

Let's now turn our attention to the other range of protectionist weapons – non-tariff barriers.

Non-tariff Barriers

There are two important forms of non-tariff barriers:

1. Quotas
2. Voluntary export restraints

A **quota** is a quantitative restriction on the import of a particular good. It specifies the maximum amount of the good that may be imported in a given period of time. A **voluntary export restraint** is an agreement between two governments in which the government of the exporting country agrees to restrain the volume of its own exports. Voluntary export restraints are often called VERs.

Non-tariff barriers have become important features of international trading arrangements in the period since World War II, and there is general agreement that non-tariff barriers are now a more severe impediment to international trade than tariffs.

Quotas are especially important in the textile industries, where there exists an international agreement called the Multi-Fibre Arrangement, which establishes quotas on a wide range of textile products. Agriculture is also subject to extensive quotas. Voluntary export restraints are particularly important in regulating the international trade in cars between Japan and the United States.

It is difficult to quantify the effects of non-tariff barriers in a way that makes them easy to compare with tariffs, but some studies have attempted to do just that. Such studies attempt to assess the tariff rate that would restrict trade by the same amount as the non-tariff barriers do. With such calculations, non-tariff barriers and tariffs can be added together to assess the total amount of protection. For example, it has been estimated that when non-tariff barriers are added to tariffs in the United States, the overall amount of protection increases more than threefold – from an average of 5–6 per cent to about an 18 per cent tariff. Even so, the United States is one of the least protectionist countries in the world. Total protection in the European Union is higher, and it is higher still in other developed countries and Japan. The less developed countries and some of the newly industrializing countries have the highest protection rates of all.

How Quotas and VERs Work

To understand how non-tariff barriers affect international trade, let's return to the example of trade between Farmland and Mobilia. Suppose that Farmland imposes a quota on car imports. Specifically, suppose that the quota restricts imports to not more than 2 million cars a year. What are the effects of this action?

The answer is found in Fig. 35.10. The quota is shown by the vertical red line at 2 million cars a year. Because it is illegal to import more than that number of cars, car importers buy only that quantity from Mobilia producers. They pay £2,000 a car to the Mobilia producers. But what do they sell their cars for? The answer is £6,000 each. Because the import supply of cars is restricted to 2 million cars a year, people with cars for sale will be able to get £6,000 each for them. The quantity of cars imported equals the quantity determined by the quota.

Importing cars is now obviously a profitable business. An importer gets £6,000 for an item that costs

FIGURE 35.10

The Effects of a Quota

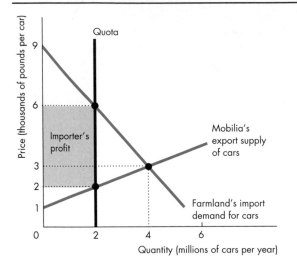

Farmland imposes a quota of 2 million cars a year on car imports from Mobilia. That quantity appears as the vertical line labelled 'Quota'. Because the quantity of cars supplied by Mobilia is restricted to 2 million, the price at which those cars will be traded increases to £6,000. Importing cars is profitable because Mobilia is willing to supply cars at £2,000 each. There is competition for import quotas – rent seeking.

only £2,000. Thus there is severe competition among car importers for the available quotas. The pursuit of the profits from quotas is called 'rent seeking.'

The value of imports – the amount paid to Mobilia – declines to £4 billion, exactly the same as in the case of the tariff. Thus with lower incomes from car exports and with a higher relative price of grain, Movers cut their imports of grain in exactly the same way as they did under a tariff.

The key difference between a quota and a tariff lies in who gets the profit represented by the difference between the import supply price and the domestic selling price. In the case of a tariff, that difference goes to the government of the importing country. In the case of a quota, that difference goes to the person who has the right to import under the import-quota regulations.

A voluntary export restraint is like a quota arrangement where quotas are allocated to each exporting country. The effects of voluntary export

restraints are similar to those of quotas but differ from them in that the gap between the domestic price and the export price is captured not by domestic importers but by the foreign exporter. The government of the exporting country has to establish procedures for allocating the restricted volume of exports among its producers.

'Invisible' Non-tariff Barriers

In addition to quotas and VERs, there are thousands of non-tariff barriers that are virtually impossible to detect – that are almost invisible. They arise from domestic laws that are not (necessarily) aimed at restricting foreign competition but they have that effect. For example, for a long time German purity laws on brewing meant that beer brewed in other countries of Europe that did not meet the specifications as set out by the ancient laws could not be sold as beer in Germany. This apparently harmless law effectively restricts competition from foreign beer-makers. In 1990 German citizens were allowed access to foreign beer.

R E V I E W

◆ When a country opens itself up to international trade and trades freely at world market prices, it expands its consumption possibilities.

◆ When trade is restricted, some of the gains from trade are lost.

◆ A country might be better off with restricted trade than with no trade but not as well off as it could be if it engaged in free trade.

◆ A tariff reduces the volume of imports, but it also reduces the volume of exports.

◆ Under both free trade and restricted trade (and without international borrowing and lending), the value of imports equals the value of exports. With restricted trade, both the total value of exports and the total value of imports are lower than under free trade, but trade is still balanced.

We've now learned about the gains from international trade and we've studied the effects of different ways in which trade can be restricted. Let's now look at the arguments about restricting international trade.

The Case Against Protection

For as long as countries and international trade have existed, people have debated whether a country is better off with free international trade or with protection from foreign competition. The debate continues, but for most economists a verdict has been delivered and it is the one you have just explored. Free trade is the arrangement most conducive to prosperity, and protection creates more problems than it solves. We've seen the most powerful case for free trade in the example of how Farmland and Mobilia both benefit from their comparative advantage. But there is a broader range of issues in the free-trade versus protection debate. Let's review these issues.

Three goals might be pursued by restricting trade and imposing tariffs or quotas. They are:

◆ Achieving national security

◆ Stimulating the growth of new industries

◆ Encouraging competition and restraining monopoly

Let's see how protection might be used to try to achieve these goals.

National Security

The national security argument for protection is that a country is better off if it protects its strategic industries – industries that produce defence equipment and armaments, and the industries on which the defence industries rely for their raw materials such as coal and steel and other intermediate inputs. This argument for protection runs into three overwhelming counter-arguments.

First, it is an argument for the protection of *every* industry. In a time of war, there is no industry that does not contribute to national defence. Agriculture, iron ore, coal mining, oil and natural gas extraction, the manufacture of steel and other metals, vehicles, aircraft, ships, machinery of all kinds and services such as banking and insurance are all vital to a nation's defence. To protect every industry would require a tariff or quota on the import of all goods and services that can be traded.

Second, the cost of lower output must be weighed against the benefit of greater national security. There is no clear and objective way of making this cost–benefit calculation. In practice, it is made in the political arena and once a national security argument is given respectability, it is exploited by anyone who can lay remote claim to it being relevant. Makers of paper clips and nail scissors will lobby as vigorously as weapons designers and shipbuilders.

Third, even if the case is made for maintaining or increasing the output of a strategic industry, there is always a more efficient way of doing so than by protecting the industry from international competition. A direct subsidy to the firms in a strategic industry, financed out of taxes on all sectors of the economy, would keep the industry operating at the scale judged appropriate. The presence of unfettered international competition would prevent the prices faced by consumers from rising.

New Industries

The second argument that is used to justify protection is the **infant-industry argument** – the proposition that protection is necessary to enable an infant industry to grow into a mature industry that can compete in world markets. The argument is based on the idea of *dynamic comparative advantage* which can arise from *learning-by-doing* (see Chapter 3).

There is no doubt that learning-by-doing is a powerful engine of productivity growth and that comparative advantage evolves and changes because of on-the-job experience. But these facts do not justify protection.

First, the infant industry argument is valid only if the benefits of learning-by-doing not only accrue to the owners and workers of the firms in the infant industry but also spill over to other industries and parts of the economy. For example, there are huge productivity gains from learning-by-doing in the manufacture of aircraft. But almost all of these gains benefit the shareholders and workers of BAe, Westland and other aircraft producers. Because the people making the decisions, bearing the risk and doing the work are the ones who benefit, they take the dynamic gains into account when they decide on the scale of their activities. In this case, almost no benefits spill over to other parts of the economy, so there is no need for government assistance to achieve an efficient outcome.

Secondly, even if the case is made for protecting an infant industry, it is more efficient to do so by a direct subsidy to the firms in the infant industry, with the subsidy financed out of taxes. Such a subsidy would keep the industry operating at the scale judged appropriate, and free international trade would keep the prices faced by consumers at their world market levels.

Restraining Monopoly

The third argument used to justify protection is the dumping argument. **Dumping** occurs when a foreign firm sells its exports at a lower price than its cost of production. Dumping might be used by a firm that wants to gain a global monopoly. In this case, the firm sells at a price below its cost in order to drive domestic firms out of business. When the domestic firms have gone, the foreign firm takes advantage of its monopoly position and charges a higher price for its product. Dumping is usually regarded as a justification for temporary – countervailing – tariffs.

But there are powerful reasons to resist the dumping argument for protection. First, it is virtually impossible to detect dumping because it is hard to determine a firm's costs. As a result, the test for dumping is whether a firm's export price is below its domestic price. But this test is a weak one because it can be rational for a firm to charge a low price in markets in which the quantity demanded is highly sensitive to price and a higher price in markets in which demand is less price-sensitive.

Second, there are virtually no goods that are natural global monopolies. So even if all the domestic firms did get driven out of business in some industry, it would always be possible to find several and usually many alternative foreign sources of supply and to buy at prices determined in competitive markets.

Third, if a good or service was a truly global natural monopoly, the best way of dealing with it would be by regulation, just as in the case of domestic monopolies. Such regulation would require international cooperation.

The three arguments for protection we've just examined have an element of credibility. The counter-arguments are in general stronger so these arguments do not make the case for protection. But they are not the only arguments that you might encounter. The many other arguments commonly heard are quite simply wrong. They are fatally flawed. The most common of them are:

◆ Protection saves jobs
◆ Because foreign labour is cheap, we need a tariff to compete
◆ Protection brings diversity and stability

◆ Protection penalizes lax environmental standards
◆ Protection prevents rich countries from exploiting developing countries

Protection Saves Jobs

The argument is that when we buy shoes from Brazil or shirts from Taiwan, workers in Lancashire lose their jobs. With no earnings and poor prospects, these workers become a drain on the welfare state and they spend less, causing a ripple effect of further job losses. The proposed solution to this problem is to ban imports of cheap foreign goods and protect jobs at home. The proposal is flawed for the following reasons.

First, free trade does cost some jobs, but it also creates other jobs. It brings about a global rationalization of labour and allocates labour resources to their highest-value activities. Because of international trade in textiles, tens of thousands of workers in the United Kingdom have lost jobs because textile mills and other factories have closed. But tens of thousands of workers in other countries have got jobs because textile mills have opened there. And tens of thousands of workers in the United Kingdom have got better-paying jobs than textile workers because other industries have expanded and created more jobs than have been destroyed.

Second, imports create jobs. They create jobs for retailers which sell imported goods and for firms which service these goods. They also create jobs by creating incomes in the rest of the world, some of which are spent on UK-made goods and services.

Although protection does not save jobs, it changes the mix of jobs. But it does so at inordinate cost. For example, in the United States jobs in the textile industry are protected by quotas imposed under an international agreement called the Multi-Fibre Arrangement. It has been estimated by the US International Trade Commission (ITC) that because of quotas 72,000 jobs exist in textiles that would otherwise disappear, and that annual clothing expenditure in the United States is $15.9 billion or $700 per family higher than it would be with free trade. Equivalently, the ITC estimates that each textile job saved costs $221,000 a year.

Because Foreign Labour is Cheap, We Need a Tariff to Compete

Sir James Goldsmith, multimillionaire and Euro MP, has argued that if Europe does not build protective tariffs against cheap imports from the newly industrializing economies of East Asia, there will be a loss of jobs that will threaten the way of life in Europe. The loss of jobs will occur as firms relocate in the Far East to take advantage of cheap labour. Let's see what's wrong with this view.

The labour cost of a unit of output equals the wage rate divided by labour productivity. For example, if a UK production assembly worker earns $30 an hour and produces 10 units of output an hour, the average labour cost of a unit of output is $3. (We will use dollars to measure the outputs of workers from different countries.) If a Chinese production assembly worker earns $3 an hour and produces 1 unit of output an hour, the average labour cost of a unit of output is $3. Other things remaining the same, the higher a worker's productivity, the higher is the worker's wage rate. High-wage workers have high productivity. Low-wage workers have low productivity.

Although high-wage UK workers are more productive, on the average, than low-wage Chinese workers, there are differences across industries. UK labour is relatively more productive at some activities than others. For example, the productivity of UK workers in producing chemical products, luxury cars and high-quality engineering is relatively higher than in the production of metals and some standardized machine parts. The activities in which UK workers are relatively more productive than their Chinese counterparts are those in which the United Kingdom has a *comparative advantage*. By engaging in free trade, increasing our production and exports of the goods at which we have a comparative advantage and decreasing our production and imports of the goods at which our trading partners have a comparative advantage, we can make ourselves and the citizens of other countries better off.

Protection Brings Diversity and Stability

A diversified investment portfolio is less risky than one that has all its eggs in one basket. The same is true for an economy's production. A diversified economy fluctuates less than an economy that produces only one or two goods.

But big, rich, diversified economies like the United States, Japan and the European Union do not have this type of stability problem. Even a country like Saudi Arabia, which produces almost only one good (oil), can benefit from specializing in

the activity at which it has a comparative advantage and then investing in a wide range of other countries to bring greater stability to its income and consumption.

Protection Penalizes Lax Environmental Standards

A new argument for protection that was used extensively in the Uruguay Round of the GATT negotiations is that many poorer countries, such as Mexico, do not have the same environment policies we have and, because they are willing to pollute and we are not, we cannot compete with them without tariffs. So if they want free trade with the richer and 'greener' countries, they must clean up their environments to our standards.

The environment argument for trade restrictions is weak. First, it is not true that all poorer countries have significantly lower environmental protection standards than the United Kingdom has. Many poor countries, and the former communist countries of Eastern Europe, do have a bad record on the environment. But some countries, one of which is Mexico, have strict laws and they enforce them. Second, a poor country cannot afford to be as concerned about its environment as a rich country can. The best hope for a better environment in Mexico and in other developing countries is rapid income growth through free trade. As their incomes grow, developing countries such as Mexico will have the *means* to match their desires to improve their environment.

Protection Prevents Rich Countries From Exploiting Developing Countries

Another new argument for protection is that international trade must be restricted to prevent the people of the rich industrial world from exploiting the poorer people of the developing countries, forcing them to work for slave wages.

Wage rates in some developing countries are, indeed, very low. But by trading with developing countries, we increase the demand for the goods that these countries produce, and, more significantly, we increase the demand for their labour. When the demand for labour in developing countries increases, the wage rate also increases. So, far from exploiting people in developing countries, trade improves their opportunities and increases their incomes.

We have reviewed the arguments commonly heard in favour of protection and the counter-arguments against them. There is one counter-argument to protection that is general and quite overwhelming. Protection invites retaliation and can trigger a trade war. The best example of a trade war occurred during the Great Depression of the 1930s when the Smoot-Hawley Tariff was introduced in the United States. Country after country retaliated with its own tariff and in a short time, world trade had almost disappeared. The costs to all countries were large and led to a renewed international resolve to avoid such self-defeating moves in future. They also led to the creation of the GATT and are the impetus behind NAFTA, APEC and the European Union.

Why is International Trade Restricted?

Why, despite all the arguments against protection, is trade restricted? The key reason is that consumption possibilities increase *on the average* but not everyone shares in the gain and some people even lose. Free trade brings benefits to some and costs to others, with total benefits exceeding total costs. The uneven distribution of costs and benefits is the principal impediment to achieving more liberal international trade.

Returning to our example of international trade in cars and grain between Farmland and Mobilia, the benefits from free trade accrue to all the producers of grain and those producers of cars who would not have to bear the costs of adjusting to a smaller car industry. These costs are transition costs, not permanent costs. The costs of moving to free trade are borne by those car producers and their employees who have to become grain producers. The number of people who gain will, in general, be enormous compared with the number who lose. The gain per person will, therefore, be rather small. The loss per person to those who bear the loss will be large. Because the loss that falls on those who bear it is large, it will pay those people to incur considerable expense in order to lobby against free trade. On the other hand, it will not pay those who gain to organize to achieve free trade. The gain from trade for any one individual is too small for that individual to spend much time or money on a political organization to achieve free trade. The loss from free trade will be seen as being so great by those bearing that loss that they *will* find it profitable to join a political organization to prevent free trade. Each group is optimizing – weighing benefits against costs and choosing the best action for themselves. The anti-free trade group will, therefore, undertake a larger quantity of political lobbying than the pro-free trade group.

Compensating Losers

If, in total, the gains from free international trade exceed the losses, why don't those who gain compensate those who lose so that everyone is in favour of free trade? To some degree, such compensation does take place.

The losers from freer or marginal improvements in international trade are compensated indirectly through the normal unemployment benefit payments. But only limited attempts are made to compensate those who lose from total free international trade. The main reason full compensation is not attempted is that the costs of identifying all the losers and estimating the value of their losses would be enormous. Also, it would never be clear whether or not a person who has fallen on hard times is suffering because of free trade or for other reasons, perhaps reasons largely under the control of the individual. Furthermore, some people who look like losers at one point in time may, in fact, end up gaining. The young coal worker in the Rhondda who loses his job and becomes a computer assembly worker in Newport resents the loss of work and the need to move. But a year or two later, looking back on events, he counts himself fortunate. He's made a move that has increased his income and given him greater job security.

It is because we do not, in general, compensate the losers from free international trade that protectionism is such a popular and permanent feature of our national economic and political life.

Political Outcome

The political outcome that emerges from this activity is one in which a modest amount of restriction on international trade occurs and is maintained.

Politicians react to constituencies pressing for protection and find it necessary, in order to get re-elected, to support legislative programmes that protect those constituencies. The producers of protected goods are far more vocal and much more sensitive swing-voters than the consumers of such goods. The political outcome, therefore, often leans in the direction of maintaining protection.

REVIEW

◆ Trade restrictions aimed at national security goals, stimulating the growth of new industries and restraining foreign monopoly have little support.

◆ Trade restrictions to save jobs, compensate for low foreign wages, make the economy more diversified and compensate for costly environmental policies are misguided.

◆ The main arguments against trade restrictions are that subsidies and anti-monopoly policies can achieve domestic goals more efficiently than protection and that protection can trigger a trade war in which all countries lose.

◆ ◆ ◆ ◆ You've now seen how free international trade enables all countries to gain from increased specialisation and exchange. By producing goods at which we have a comparative advantage and exchanging some of our own production for that of others, we expand our consumption possibilities. Placing impediments on that exchange when it crosses national borders restricts the extent to which we can gain from specialization and exchange. *Reading Between the Lines* on pp. 942–943 examines how trade restrictions have hampered economic development. By opening our country up to free international trade, the market for the things that we sell expands and the relative price rises. The market for the things that we buy also expands and the relative price falls. All countries gain from free international trade. As a consequence of price adjustments, and in the absence of international borrowing and lending, the value of imports adjusts to equal the value of exports. ◆ In the next chapter, we're going to study the ways in which international trade is financed, and also learn why international borrowing and lending that permit unbalanced international trade arise. We'll discover the forces that determine the balance of payments and the value of the pound in terms of foreign currency.

Protection versus Free Trade

The Essence of the Story

THE FINANCIAL TIMES, 9 OCTOBER 1996

Protectionism no defence for Africa

Michael Holman

Study says region pays heavy price for import barriers

Projectionist policies imposed by African governments have been costing sub-Saharan Africa as much as $11bn a year, equivalent to the total aid in the region from developed countries in 1991, according to a World Bank research paper.

The study argues that the decline in sub-Saharan Africa's share of global exports from 3.1 per cent in 1955 to 1.2 per cent in 1990 was the result of 'inappropriate domestic policies that reduced the region's ability to compete internationally'.

Import barriers in Africa are far higher, according to the report, than in other developing countries and regions with faster export growth. These barriers hamper exports and economic development by adding to the cost of essential imports, such as agricultural inputs and machinery....

Africa's market share for its 30 main exports declined from 20.8 per cent to 9.7 per cent between 1962–64 and 1991–93, 'which implies annual trade losses for the region of just under $11bn'.

Official development assistance to sub-Saharan Africa from members of the Organisation for the Economic Co-operation and Development in 1991 totalled $10.9bn.

Not only has Africa experienced a declining market share for its main exports, says the report, they are of declining relative importance in world trade. The region is now highly dependent on relatively few export products....

According to the report, 'the share of African exports subject to non-tariff barriers is far lower than that of other developing countries which launched successful sustained export-oriented industrialisation drives'.

In addition, tariff preferences extended under the European Union's Lomé Convention or under OECD members' Generalised System of Preferences, provide Africa with more favourable terms of market access than for many other exporters of similar products.

Trade barriers in Africa 'are far more restrictive' than in any other developing country groups, according to the Bank study. 'Sub-Saharan Africa's tariffs average 26.8 per cent, which is more than three times higher than those of the fast growing exporters, and are more than four times the OECD average (6.1 per cent).'

The report adds that OECD countries reduced their tariffs by almost 40 per cent in the recent Uruguay Round (to about 3.9 per cent), and many of the fast growing exporters also made important concessions on trade barriers. 'In contrast, Africa's trade barriers were virtually unchanged by the Round. As a result, the current spread between Africa's tariffs (as well as tariffs plus other import charges combined) and those in the other countries have widened.'

The divergence in the use of non-tariff protection is even sharper, says the study.

'Over one third of all African imports encounter some form of these restrictions (over 40 per cent in the case of low-income African countries) which is almost nine times higher than the corresponding average (3.9 per cent) for the fast growing exporters and 13 times greater than the high income non-OECD countries'....

'If Africa is to reverse its unfavourable export trends,' the authors conclude, 'the region must adopt appropriate trade and structural adjustment policies in order to enhance its international competitiveness, and to permit African exporters to capitalise on opportunities in foreign markets.'

■ Protectionist policies have been costing sub-Saharan Africa as much as $11 billion a year, according to a World Bank study.

■ The study argues that the decline in the sub-Saharan share of global exports from 3.1 per cent in 1955 to 1.2 per cent in 1990 was a result of weak competitiveness caused by import barriers that hamper exports and economic development.

■ Sub-Saharan Africa has received preferential tariff treatment from the developing economies. The share of exports subject to non-tariff barriers is lower than that of other developing countries.

■ Tariffs in sub-Saharan Africa average 26.8 per cent, which is three times higher than the emerging markets in the Far East and Mexico. Over one-third of African imports encounter non-tariff barriers.

Economic Analysis

■ The study argues that trade barriers in sub-Saharan Africa have hampered the ability of these countries to be competitive and retarded the economic development of the region by imposing heavy costs on imports.

■ The trade barriers are both tariff and non-tariff barriers. Figure 1 shows how tariff barriers work. Consumption of imports by African firms and consumers declines and domestic production increases. Figure 2 shows how non-tariff barriers work. By restricting imports, African distribution companies extract rents from African consumers.

■ The higher prices paid by African firms and consumers for imported products have further effects on export performance. The trade barriers raise the price of important inputs to export production such as agricultural machinery. The higher costs of export production raise the price of exports, and reduce the amount of exports. Because of the relative dependence on a few export commodities, a reduction in export sales will have severe effects on the region's export earnings and its economic development.

■ Figure 3 shows the barriers to competitiveness in sub-Saharan Africa compared with the fast-growing exporting economies of the Far East and Mexico. The barriers to trade have weakened export capability.

■ To reverse the worsening trend in trade and to improve economic development in Africa, the report calls for a change in trade policy.

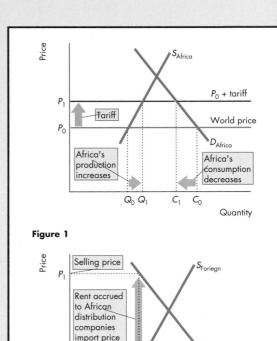

Figure 1

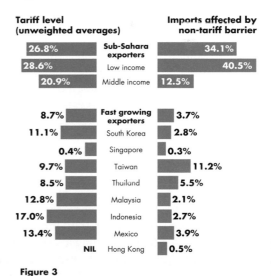

Figure 2

Figure 3

Tariff level (unweighted averages)		Imports affected by non-tariff barrier
26.8%	**Sub-Sahara exporters**	34.1%
28.6%	Low income	40.5%
20.9%	Middle income	12.5%
8.7%	**Fast growing exporters**	3.7%
11.1%	South Korea	2.8%
0.4%	Singapore	0.3%
9.7%	Taiwan	11.2%
8.5%	Thailand	5.5%
12.8%	Malaysia	2.1%
17.0%	Indonesia	2.7%
13.4%	Mexico	3.9%
NIL	Hong Kong	0.5%

SUMMARY

Patterns and Trends in International Trade

Large flows of trade take place between rich and poor countries. Resource-rich countries exchange natural resources for manufactured goods, and resource-poor countries import resources in exchange for their own manufactured goods. However, by far the biggest volume of trade is in manufactured goods exchanged among the rich industrialized countries. Finished manufactured goods constitute the largest group of export items by the United Kingdom. Trade in services has grown in recent years. Total trade has also grown over the years. The UK balance of trade moved from a small deficit in the 1960s to a surplus in the mid-1980s and then followed a downward trend from the mid-1980s through to the 1990s. Throughout the late 1980s and 1990s, the balance of trade has been negative – imports have exceeded exports. (pp. 921–924)

Opportunity Cost and Comparative Advantage

When opportunity costs differ among countries, the country with the lowest opportunity cost of producing a good is said to have a comparative advantage in that good. Comparative advantage is the source of the gains from international trade. A country can have an absolute advantage, but not a comparative advantage, in the production of all goods. Every country has a comparative advantage in something. (pp. 924–925)

Gains from Trade

Countries can gain from trade if their opportunity costs differ. Through trade, each country can obtain goods at a lower opportunity cost than it could if it produced all goods at home. Trading allows consumption to exceed production. By specializing in producing the good in which it has a comparative advantage and then trading some of that good for imports, a country can consume at points outside its production possibility frontier. Each country can consume at such a point.

In the absence of international borrowing and lending, trade is balanced as prices adjust to reflect the international supply and demand for goods. The world price balances the production and consumption plans of the trading parties. At the equilibrium price, trade is balanced. For imported goods, consumption equals domestic production plus imports. For exported goods, consumption equals domestic production minus exports. (pp. 925–929)

Gains from Trade in Reality

Comparative advantage explains the enormous volume and diversity of international trade that takes place in the world. But much trade takes the form of exchanging similar goods for each other – one type of car for another. Such trade arises because of economies of scale in the face of diversified tastes. By specializing in producing a few goods, having long production runs and then trading those goods internationally, consumers in all countries can enjoy greater diversity of products at lower prices. (pp. 929–931)

Trade Restrictions

A country can restrict international trade by imposing tariffs or non-tariff barriers – quotas and voluntary export restraints. All trade restrictions raise the domestic price of imported goods, lower the volume of imports and reduce the total value of imports. They also reduce the total value of exports by the same amount as the reduction in the value of imports.

All trade restrictions increase the domestic price of an imported good above the world price. In the case of a tariff, the government collects a tariff revenue. But the government collects no revenue from a quota. Instead, importers who have a licence to import the good increase their economic profit. A voluntary export restraint resembles a quota except that it increases the price received by the exporter. (pp. 931–936)

The Case Against Protection

Three arguments for trade restrictions – the national security argument, the infant industry argument and the dumping argument – are weak. *Every* industry contributes to national defence, and a direct subsidy to a firm in a strategic industry is more efficient than a tariff. In an infant industry, the benefits of learning-by-doing accrue to the owners and workers of the firms so they take these benefits into account and do not need protection. It is unlikely that a foreign firm will sell below cost to gain a global monopoly because there are virtually no goods that are global natural monopolies.

Other arguments for protection – that it saves jobs, is necessary because foreign labour is cheap, makes the economy diversified and stable, and is needed to offset the costs of environmental policies that poorer countries do not incur – are fatally flawed. Protection does not save jobs and its attempt to do so is costly; it is possible to com-

pete against cheap foreign labour because expensive domestic labour is more productive; protection is not needed to bring diversity and stability to the economy; and free trade is the best way to promote income growth and higher environmental standards in developing countries. A general argument against protection is that it can trigger a trade war in which all countries lose.

Trade is often restricted because, although it increases consumption possibilities *on the average*, a small number of losers bear a large loss per person and a large number of gainers enjoy a small gain per person. Those who lose from free trade undertake a larger quantity of political lobbying than those who gain from it. (pp. 937–941)

KEY ELEMENTS

Key Terms

Absolute advantage, 929
Balance of trade, 921
Comparative advantage, 925
Dumping, 938
Exports, 921
General Agreement on Tariffs and Trade, 931
Imports, 921
Infant-industry argument, 937
Net exporter, 921
Net importer, 921
Non-tariff barrier, 931
Protectionism, 931

Quota, 935
Tariff, 931
Voluntary export restraint, 935

Key Figures

Figure 35.4   Opportunity Cost in Farmland, 924
Figure 35.5   Opportunity Cost in Mobilia, 925
Figure 35.6   International Trade in Cars, 926
Figure 35.7   Expanding Consumption Possibilities, 927
Figure 35.9   The Effects of a Tariff, 933
Figure 35.10 The Effects of a Quota, 936

REVIEW QUESTIONS

1 What are the main exports and imports of the United Kingdom?
2 How does the United Kingdom trade services internationally?
3 Which items of international trade have been growing the most quickly in recent years?
4 What is comparative advantage? Why does it lead to gains from international trade?
5 Explain why international trade brings gains to all countries.

6 Distinguish between comparative advantage and absolute advantage.
7 Explain why all countries have a comparative advantage in something.
8 Explain why we import and export such large quantities of certain similar goods – such as cars, for example.
9 What are the main ways in which we restrict international trade?
10 What are the effects of a tariff?

11 What are the effects of a quota?

12 What are the effects of a voluntary export restraint?

13 Describe the main trends in tariffs and non-tariff barriers.

14 Why do countries restrict international trade?

PROBLEMS

1 Figures 35.4 and 35.5 illustrate Farmland's and Mobilia's production possibilities.

  a Calculate the opportunity cost of cars in Farmland at the point on the production possibility frontier at which 4 million cars are produced.

  b Calculate the opportunity cost of a car in Mobilia when it produces 8 million cars.

  c With no trade, Farmland produces 4 million cars and Mobilia produces 8 million cars. Which country has a comparative advantage in the production of cars?

  d If there is no trade between Farmland and Mobilia, how much grain is consumed and how many cars are bought in each country?

2 Suppose that the two countries in Problem 1 trade freely.

  a Which country exports grain?

  b What adjustments will be made to the amount of each good produced by each country?

  c What adjustment will be made to the amount of each good consumed by each country?

  d What can you say about the price of a car under free trade?

3 Compare the total production of each good produced in Problems 1 and 2.

4 Compare the situation in Problems 1 and 2 with that analysed in this chapter. Why does Mobilia export cars in the chapter but import them in Problem 2?

5 The following figure depicts the international market for soybeans.

  a What is the world price of soybeans if there is free trade between these countries?

  b If the country that imports soybeans imposes a tariff of £2 per kilogram, what is the world price of soybeans and what quantity of soybeans is traded internationally? What is the price of soybeans in the importing country? Calculate the tariff revenue.

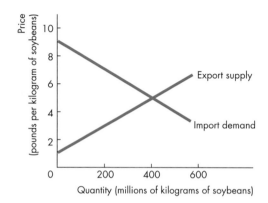

6 If the importing country in Problem 5(a) imposes a quota of 300 million kilograms, what is the price of soybeans in the importing country? What is the revenue from the quota and who gets this revenue?

7 If the exporting country in Problem 5(a) imposes a VER of 300 million kilograms of soybeans, what is the world price of soybeans? What is the revenue of soybean growers in the exporting country? Which country gains from the VER?

8 Suppose that the exporting country in Problem 5(a) subsidizes production by paying its farmers £1 a kilogram for soybeans harvested.

  a What is the price of soybeans in the importing country?

  b What action might soybean growers in the importing country take? Why?

9 Suppose that the exporting country in Problem 5 subsidizes production by paying its farmers £1 a tonne for soybeans harvested.

  a What is the price of soybeans in the importing country?

  b What action might soybean growers in the importing country take? Why?

10 Countries Atlantis and Magic Kingdom produce only food and ballon rides and have the following production possibility frontiers:

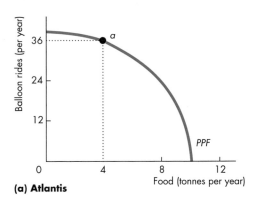

(a) Atlantis

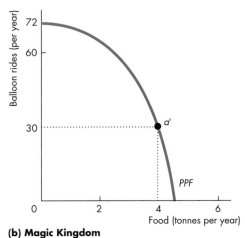

(b) Magic Kingdom

a If Atlantis produces at point a, what is its opportunity cost of a balloon ride?

b What are the consumption possibilities of Atlantis?

c If Magic Kingdom produces at point a, what is its opportunity cost of a balloon ride?

d What are the consumption possibilities of Magic Kingdom?

e Which country has a comparative advantage in producing food?

11 Study *Reading Between the Lines* on pp. 942–943 and then answer the following questions.

a What have been the effects of protectionist policies on sub-Saharan Africa's trade and development since 1955?

b What proportion of imports by sub-Saharan Africa is affected by non-tariff barriers compared with 'fast-growing exporters'?

c What is the average tariff barrier in sub-Saharan Africa compared with the 'fast-growing exporters'?

d Explain how tariff barriers have influenced trade and reduced development in sub-Saharan Africa.

e How have non-tariff barriers affected trade and development in sub-Saharan Africa?

f How far have protectionist measures worsened competitiveness and export performance in sub-Saharan Africa?

'Free trade, one of the greatest blessings which a government can confer on a people, is in almost every country unpopular.'

Lord Macaulay (1800–1859), ESSAY ON MITFORD'S HISTORY OF GREECE

Understanding the Gains from International Trade

THE ISSUES AND IDEAS

Until the mid-eighteenth century, it was generally believed that the purpose of international trade was to keep exports above imports and pile up gold. If gold was accumulated, it was believed, the nation would prosper; and if gold was lost through an international deficit, the nation would be drained of money and be impoverished. These beliefs are called *mercantilism,* and the *mercantilists* were pamphleteers who advocated with missionary fervour the pursuit of an international surplus. If exports did not exceed imports, the mercantilists wanted imports restricted.

In the 1740s, David Hume explained that as the quantity of money (gold) changes, so does the price level, and the nation's real wealth is unaffected. In the 1770s, Adam Smith argued that import restrictions would reduce the gains from specialization and make a nation poorer; and 30 years later David Ricardo proved the law of comparative advantage and demonstrated the superiority of free trade. Mercantilism was intellectually bankrupt but remained politically powerful.

Gradually, through the nineteenth century, the mercantilists' influence waned, and North America and Western Europe prospered in an environment of increasingly free international trade. But despite remarkable advances in economic understanding, mercantilism never quite died. It had a brief and devastating revival in the 1920s and 1930s, when tariff hikes brought about the collapse of international trade and accentuated the Great Depression. It subsided again after World War II with the establishment of the General Agreement on Tariffs and Trade (GATT).

But mercantilism lingers on. The often expressed view that the European Union should restrict Japanese imports is a modern manifestation of mercantilism. It would be interesting to have David Hume, Adam Smith and David Ricardo commenting on these views. But we know what they would say – the same things that they said to the eighteenth-century mercantilists. And they would still be right today.

THEN ...

In the eighteenth century, when mercantilists and economists were debating the pros and cons of free international exchange, the available transport technology severely limited the gains from international trade. Sailing ships with tiny cargo holds took close to a month to cross the Atlantic Ocean. But the potential gains were large and so was the incentive to cut shipping costs. By the 1850s, the clipper ship had been developed, cutting the journey from Liverpool to Boston to only 12¼ days. Half a century later, 10,000-ton steamships were sailing between the United Kingdom and the United States in just four days. As sailing times and costs declined, the gains from international trade increased and the volume of trade expanded.

... AND NOW

The container ship has revolutionized international trade and contributed to its continued expansion. Today, most goods cross the oceans in 'containers' – metal boxes – packed into and piled on top of ships like this one. Container technology has cut the cost of ocean shipping by economizing on handling and by making cargoes harder to steal, lowering insurance costs. It is unlikely that there would be much international trade in goods such as television sets and VCRs without this technology. High-value and perishable cargoes such as flowers and fresh food, as well as urgently needed items, travel by air. Every day, dozens of cargo-laden 747s fly between all major European cities and destinations across the Atlantic and Pacific Oceans.

THE ECONOMISTS: FROM SMITH AND RICARDO TO THE GATT

David Ricardo

David Ricardo (1772–1823) was a highly successful 27-year-old stockbroker when he stumbled on a copy of Adam Smith's *Wealth of Nations* on a weekend visit to the country. He was immediately hooked and went on to become the most celebrated economist of his age and one of the all-time great economists. One of his many contributions was to develop the principle of comparative advantage, the foundation on which the modern theory of international trade is built. The example he used to illustrate this principle was the trade between the United Kingdom and Portugal in cloth and wine.

The General Agreement on Tariffs and Trade (GATT) was established as a reaction against the devastation wrought by beggar-my-neighbour tariffs imposed during the 1930s. But it is also a triumph for the logic first worked out by Smith and Ricardo.

CHAPTER 36

THE BALANCE OF PAYMENTS AND THE EXCHANGE RATE

After studying this chapter you will be able to:

- ◆ Explain how international trade is financed
- ◆ Describe a country's balance of payments accounts
- ◆ Explain what determines the amount of international borrowing and lending
- ◆ Explain how the foreign exchange value of the pound is determined
- ◆ Explain the workings of the Exchange Rate Mechanism of the European Monetary System
- ◆ Appreciate the implications of European Monetary Union

IN 1986, THE UNITED KINGDOM OWNED £721.2 BILLION IN ASSETS ABROAD AND FOREIGNERS owned £622.9 billion of assets in the United Kingdom. Foreign assets exceeded foreigners' assets in the United Kingdom so that net foreign assets – the difference between what people in the United Kingdom hold of foreign assets and what foreigners hold of UK assets – was £98.3 billion. In 1990 the balance had tipped the other way around. Net foreign assets was –£3.8 billion. What caused this sudden turnaround? Part of the reason is that the United Kingdom is a good place to invest and foreign companies have been roaming around buying up UK firms or setting up companies. Think of BMW's acquisition of a controlling share of Rover, Nestlés purchase of Rowntree, or the Hongkong & Shanghai Bank's purchase of Midland Bank. Why have foreigners been buying more businesses in the United Kingdom than British people have been buying abroad? ◆ In 1971, one pound sterling was enough to buy 8.5 Deutschemarks, and 2.44 US dollars. In mid-1996, that same pound bought only DM2.3 and $1.55. But the slide in the value of the pound from DM8.5 to DM2.3 or from $2.44 to $1.55 was not a smooth one. At some times, the pound rose in value against all currencies, as it did, for example, in 1980. But at other times, the pound's slide was precipitous, as in September 1992 when the pound left the Exchange Rate Mechanism (ERM). What makes the pound fluctuate in value against other currencies? Why have the fluctuations been particularly extreme, as in the 1980s and in 1992? Is there anything we can do to stabilize the value of the pound? Can the ERM help us to stabilize the pound?

A Mounting Debt and a Sinking Pound

◆ ◆ ◆ ◆ International economics has always been an important issue for an economy such as the United Kingdom. In this chapter we're going to study the questions that we've just raised. We're going to discover why the United Kingdom has become such an attractive target for foreign investors; why the value of the pound fluctuates against the values of other currencies; and why interest rates vary from country to country.

Financing International Trade

When Currys, an electrical goods retail chain, imports Sony CD players, it does not pay for them with pounds – it uses Japanese yen. When Harrods imports Armani suits, it pays for them with Italian lire. And when a Japanese retail company buys a consignment of Scotch malt whisky, it uses pounds sterling. Whenever we buy things from another country, we use the currency of that country in order to make the transaction. It doesn't make any difference what the item being traded is; it might be a consumer good or a capital good, a building, or even a firm.

We're going to study the markets in which money – in different types of currencies – is bought and sold. But first we're going to look at the scale of international trading and borrowing and lending and at the way in which we keep our records of these transactions. Such records are called the balance of payments accounts.

Balance of Payments Accounts

A country's **balance of payments accounts** record its international trading and its borrowing and lending. There are three balance of payments accounts:

1 Current account
2 Capital account
3 Balance for official financing

The **current account** records the receipts from the sale of goods and services to foreigners, the payments for goods and services bought from foreigners, and gifts and other transfers (such as foreign aid payments) received from and paid to foreigners. By far the largest items in the current account are the receipts from the sale of goods and services to foreigners (the value of exports) and the payments made for goods and services bought from foreigners (the value of imports). Net transfers – gifts to foreigners minus gifts from foreigners – are relatively small items. The **capital account** records all the international borrowing and lending transactions. The capital account balance records the difference between the amount that a country lends to and borrows from the rest of the world. The **balance for official financing** shows the net

increase or decrease in a country's holdings of foreign currency reserves.

Table 36.1 shows the UK balance of payments accounts in 1994. Items in the current account and capital account that provide foreign currency to the United Kingdom have a plus sign and items that cost the United Kingdom foreign currency have a minus sign. The table shows that in 1994, UK imports exceeded UK exports and the current account had a deficit of £1.7 billion. How do we pay for imports that exceed the value of our exports? That is, how do we pay for our current account deficit? We pay by borrowing from abroad. The capital account tells us by how much. We borrowed £35.8 billion but made loans of £38.4 billion. Thus our identified net foreign lending was £2.6 billion.

In theory our net borrowing or lending from abroad minus our current account deficit represents the balance for official financing, which is the balance that is financed from official UK reserves. Official UK reserves are the government's holdings of foreign currency. In 1994, those reserves increased by £1 billion, but this did not close the gap between the current account deficit and the capital account balance. The remainder is made up by a statistical discrepancy known as the balancing

---

TABLE 36.1

UK Balance of Payments Accounts in 1994

Current account	(billions of pounds)
Import of goods and services	−180.7
Export of goods and services	+173.9
Net investment income	+10.5
Net transfers	−5.4
Current account balance	<u>−1.7</u>
Capital account	
Foreign investment in the UK	+35.8
UK investment abroad	<u>−38.4</u>
Capital account balance	<u>−2.6</u>
Balance for official financing	
Decrease (+) in official UK reserves	−1.0
Balancing item	<u>5.3</u>

Source: Central Statistical Office, *Economic Trends Annual Supplement*, 1996.

item. This discrepancy represents a combination of capital and current account transactions such as unidentified borrowing from abroad, illegal international trade – for example, the import of illegal drugs – and transactions not reported in order to evade tariffs or taxes.

The numbers in Table 36.1 give a snapshot of the balance of payments accounts in 1994. Figure 36.1 puts that snapshot into perspective by showing the balance of payments between 1975 and 1994. Because the economy grows and the price level rises, changes in the sterling value of the balance of payments do not convey much information. To remove the influences of growth and inflation, Fig. 36.1 shows the balance of payments as a percentage of nominal GDP.

As you can see, the current account balance is almost a mirror image of the capital account balance. The balance for official financing (change in reserves) is small compared with the balances on these other two accounts. A large current account deficit (and capital account surplus) emerged during the late 1980s, but was declining after 1990.

You will perhaps obtain a better understanding of the balance of payments accounts and the way in which they are linked together if you consider the income and expenditure, borrowing and lending, and bank account of an individual.

Individual Analogy An individual's current account records the income from supplying the services of factors of production and the expenditure

FIGURE 36.1

The Balance of Payments: 1975–1994

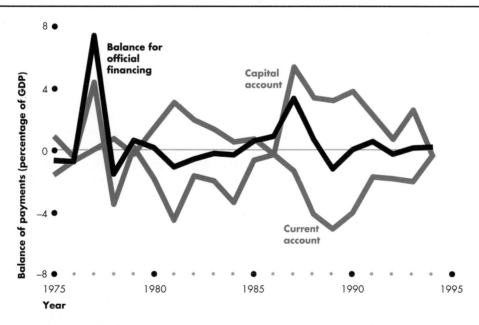

The balance of payments fluctuated during the 1970s, but during the early 1980s, a large current account surplus arose. The increase in the price of oil in 1979 helped to produce a current account surplus. The capital account balance mirrors the current account balance. When the current account balance is positive, the capital account balance is negative – we lend to the rest of the world – and when the current account balance is negative, the capital account balance is positive – we borrow from the rest of the world. Fluctuations in the balance for official financing account are usually small compared with fluctuations in the current account balance and the capital account balance. A special case was the large inflow of reserves in 1977 which was the result of IMF-initiated policies in December 1976.

Source: Central Statistical Office, *Economic Trends Annual Supplement*, 1996.

on goods and services. Consider, for example, Joanne. She earned an income in 1995 of £25,000. Joanne has £10,000 worth of investments that earned her an income of £1,000. Joanne's current account shows an income of £26,000. Joanne spent £18,000 buying goods and services for consumption. She also bought a new house, which cost her £60,000. So Joanne's total expenditure was £78,000. The difference between her expenditure and income is £52,000 (£78,000 minus £26,000). This amount is Joanne's current account deficit.

To pay for expenditure of £52,000 in excess of her income, Joanne has either to use the money that she has in the bank or to take out a loan. In fact Joanne took a mortgage of £50,000 to help buy her house. This mortgage was the only borrowing that Joanne did, so her capital account surplus was £50,000. With a current account deficit of £52,000 and a capital account surplus of £50,000, Joanne is still £2,000 short. She got that £2,000 from her own bank account. Her cash holdings decreased by £2,000.

Joanne's income from her work and investments is analogous to a country's income from its exports. Her purchases of goods and services, including her purchase of a house, are analogous to a country's imports. Joanne's mortgage – borrowing from someone else – is analogous to a country's foreign borrowing. The change in her own bank account is analogous to the change in the country's official reserves.

Borrowers and Lenders, Debtors and Creditors

A country that is borrowing more from the rest of the world than it is lending to it is called a **net borrower.** Similarly, a **net lender** is a country that is lending more to the rest of the world than it is borrowing from it. A net borrower might be going deeper into debt or might simply be reducing its net assets held in the rest of the world. The total stock of foreign investment determines whether a country is a debtor or a creditor. A **debtor nation** is a country that during its entire history has borrowed more from the rest of the world than it has lent to it. It has a stock of outstanding debt to the rest of the world that exceeds the stock of its own claims on the rest of the world. The United Kingdom briefly became a debtor nation in 1990 and 1991. A **creditor nation** is a country that has invested more in the rest of the world than other

countries have invested in it. The largest creditor nation today is Japan.

At the heart of the distinction between a net borrower/net lender and a debtor/creditor nation is the distinction between flows and stocks, which you have encountered many times in your study of macroeconomics. Borrowing and lending are flows – amounts borrowed or lent per unit of time. Debts are stocks – amounts owed at a point in time. The flow of borrowing and lending changes the stock of debt. But the outstanding stock of debt depends mainly on past flows of borrowing and lending, not on the current period's flows. The current period's flows determine the *change* in the stock of debt outstanding.

During the 1960s and the 1970s, the United Kingdom would periodically swing from surplus to deficit on its current account. When it was in current account surplus it had a deficit on its capital account. On the whole the United Kingdom was a net lender to the rest of the world. It was not until the late 1980s that it became a significant net borrower. Between 1987 and 1993, borrowing continued each year. In 1994 it became a net lender again.

Most countries are net borrowers. But a small number of countries, which includes oil-rich Saudi Arabia and Venezuela, and Japan, are huge net lenders.

The United Kingdom today is a small net lender, and it is back to being a creditor nation. That is, its total stock of lending from the rest of the world exceeds its borrowing to the rest of the world. There are many countries that are debtor nations. The United States is one. But the largest debtor nations are the capital-hungry developing countries. The international debt of these countries grew from less than a third to more than a half of their gross domestic product during the 1980s and created what was called the 'Third World debt crisis'.

Does it matter if a country is a net borrower rather than a net lender? The answer to this question depends mainly on what the net borrower is doing with the borrowed money. If borrowing is financing investment that in turn is generating economic growth and higher income, borrowing is not a problem. If the borrowed money is being used to finance consumption, then higher interest payments are being incurred and, as a consequence, consumption will eventually have to be reduced. In this case, the more the borrowing and the longer it goes on, the greater is the reduction in consumption that will eventually be necessary. We'll see below whether the United Kingdom has been borrowing for investment or for consumption.

Current Account Balance

What determines the current account balance and the scale of a country's net foreign borrowing or lending?

To answer this question, we need to recall and use some of the things that we learned about the national income accounts. Table 36.2 will refresh your memory and summarize the necessary calculations for you. Part (a) lists the national income variables that are needed, with their symbols. Their values in the United Kingdom in 1994 are also shown.

Part (b) presents two key national income equations. First, Equation (1) reminds us that GDP, Y, equals aggregate expenditure, which is the sum of consumption expenditure, C, investment, I, government purchases of goods and services, G, and net exports (exports, EX, minus imports, IM). Equation (2) reminds us that aggregate income is used in three different ways. It can be consumed, saved, or paid to the government in the form of taxes (net of transfer payments). Equation (1) tells us how our expenditure generates our income. Equation (2) tells us how we dispose of that income.

Part (c) of the table takes you into some new territory. It examines surpluses and deficits. We'll look at three surpluses/deficits – those of the current account, the government's budget and the private sector. To get at these surpluses and deficits, first subtract Equation (2) from Equation (1) in Table 36.2. The result is Equation (3). By rearranging Equation (3), we obtain a relationship for the current account – exports minus imports – that appears as Equation (4) in the table.[1]

The current account, in Equation (4), is made up of two components. The first is taxes minus government spending and the second is saving minus investment. These items are the surpluses/deficits of the government and private sectors. Taxes (net of transfer payments) minus government purchases of goods and services is the budget surplus or

---

TABLE 36.2

The Current Account Balance, Net Foreign Borrowing and the Financing of Investment

	Symbols and equations	UK in 1994 (billions of pounds)
(a) VARIABLES		
Gross domestic product (GDP)	Y	668.8
Consumption expenditure	C	428.1
Investment	I	86.0
Government purchases of goods and services	G	161.5
Exports of goods and services	EX	173.9
Imports of goods and services	IM	180.7
Saving	S	116.3
Taxes, net of transfer payments	T	124.4
(b) DOMESTIC INCOME AND EXPENDITURE		
Aggregate expenditure	(1) $Y = C + I + G + EX - IM$	
Uses of income	(2) $Y = C + S + T$	
Subtracting (1) from (2)	(3) $0 = I - S + G - T + EX - IM$	
(c) SURPLUSES AND DEFICITS		
Current account	(4) $EX - IM = (T - G) + (S - I)$ $= 173.9 - 180.7 = -6.8$	
Government budget	(5) $T - G = 124.4 - 161.5 = -37.1$	
Private sector	(6) $S - I = 116.3 - 86.0 = 30.3$	
(d) FINANCING INVESTMENT		
Investment is financed by the sum of:		
private saving,	$S = 116.3$	
net government saving and	$T - G = -37.1$	
net foreign saving	$IM - EX = 6.8$	
That is:	(7) $I = S + (T - G) + (IM - EX) = 86.0$	

Source: Central Statistical Office, *Economic Trends Annual Supplement*, 1996.

---

deficit. If that number is positive, the government's budget is a surplus and if the number is negative, it is a deficit. The **private sector surplus or deficit** is the difference between saving and investment. If saving exceeds investment, the private sector has a surplus to lend to other sectors. If investment exceeds saving, the private sector has a deficit that has to be financed by borrowing from other sectors. As you can see from our calculations, the current

---

[1] *Net exports*, minus imports, in the national income accounts, are approximately equal to the current account balance. There are some small differences in the definitions used in the national income accounts and the balance of payments accounts but, for most purposes, you can regard net exports and the current account balance as being equal.

account deficit is equal to the sum of the other two deficits – the government's budget deficit and the private sector surplus. In the UK in 1994, the private sector had a surplus of £30.3 billion and the government sector had a deficit of £37.1 billion. The government sector deficit minus the private sector surplus equalled the current account deficit of £6.8 billion.

Part (d) of Table 36.2 shows you how investment is financed. To increase investment, either private saving, the government surplus, or the current account deficit, must increase.

The calculations that we've just performed are really nothing more than bookkeeping. We've manipulated the national income accounts and discovered that the current account deficit is just the sum of the deficits of the government and private sectors. But these calculations do reveal a fundamental fact: our international balance of payments can change only if either our government budget balance changes or our private sector financial balance changes.

We've seen that our international deficit is equal to the sum of the government deficit and the private

sector surplus. Is the private sector surplus equal to the government's budget deficit so that the current account deficit is zero? Does an increase in the government budget deficit bring an increase in the current account deficit?

You can see the answer to this question by looking at Fig. 36.2. In this figure, the general government sector budget balance is plotted alongside the current account balance and the private sector balance. To remove the effects of growth and inflation, all three balances are measured as percentages of nominal GDP. Over the whole period (1972–94), the private sector balance tends to mirror the government deficit. Between 1975 and 1982, the private sector surplus was roughly a stable proportion of GDP. The current account was in deficit between 1973 and 1975 but was roughly in balance for the rest of the 1970s. The private sector surplus began to decline in the mid-1980s and the declining government sector deficit meant that the current account was in surplus. In the late 1980s the private sector was in deficit while the government sector was in surplus. During the 1990s the private sector surplus increased during the recession. Also the

FIGURE 36.2

Sector Balances

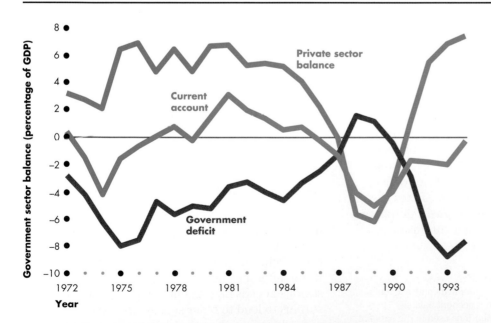

The private sector balance tends to mirror the government deficit. The private sector surplus as a proportion of GDP was stable between 1975 and 1982. It began to decline in the mid-1980s. In the late 1980s the private sector was in deficit while the government sector was in surplus. During the 1990s the private sector surplus increased as consumption fell and savings rose during the recession, but the government sector was in deficit while the current account was also in deficit. The twin deficits of the government and external sectors also occurred in the 1970s.

Source: Central Statistical Office, *Economic Trends Annual Supplement*, 1996.

government deficit was matched by a current account deficit. Notice that at the end of the 1980s the government sector was in surplus while the current account was in deficit. When the paths of the government deficit and the current account deficit diverge, their divergence is accommodated by changes in the private sector surplus.

To understand the history of the three balances shown in Fig. 36.2, we need to consider two extreme possible relationships between them:

◆ The Ricardian case
◆ The twin deficits case

The Ricardian Case

Changes in taxes or government spending, which change the budget deficit, can also influence private sector saving and investment and so change the private sector surplus/deficit. The Ricardian case is a special one in which a change in the government deficit induces an equal offsetting change in the private sector surplus and leaves the current account balance unchanged. The name Ricardian is used because this case arises from the *Ricardian equivalence*, which is explained in Chapter 29, p. 760.

Suppose the government cuts taxes and increases its deficit. The Ricardian equivalence proposition is that people will recognize that the lower taxes and higher deficit mean that taxes will *increase* later either to pay interest on the deficit for ever or eventually to repay the debt and eliminate the deficit. The *present value* of the future tax liability is equal to the current tax cut. So no one is really any better off with the tax cut. Being no better off, the entire decrease in the tax bill is saved. The private surplus increases to offset exactly the increase in the government deficit and the current account balance is unchanged.

The Twin Deficits Case

The tendency for the current account deficit and the government deficit to move together as they did in the mid-1970s and 1990s created the idea that there was a mechanism that made these deficits twin deficits.

The twin deficits can arise when two conditions prevail: real GDP is at potential GDP and capital is perfectly mobile among countries. In this situation, suppose the government increases its purchases and increases the government deficit. With the

economy at full employment the increase in aggregate demand that comes from the additional government purchases increases imports and/or decreases exports and the current account deficit increases. Saving does not change because there is no change in either disposable income or the interest rate, the two factors that determine saving. Investment does not change because there is no change in the interest rate. Foreign capital flows in to finance the increased government deficit. So the private sector surplus/deficit is unchanged and the current account changes to offset the change in the government deficit.

This extreme case does not occur if the economy is at less than full employment so it cannot explain the occurrence of the twin deficits in the 1990s. If the increase in government purchases increases GDP and increases disposable income, saving increases and the private sector surplus also increases. The extreme case does not occur if capital is not completely mobile. In this case, the change in government purchases increases the interest rate, investment decreases and the private sector surplus increases. So if an increase in the government budget deficit increases real GDP and/or induces higher interest rates, it increases the private sector surplus.

The combination of these possible cases creates the variety of responses of the current account to changes in the government deficit.

Is the UK Borrowing for Consumption or Investment?

We noted above that whether international borrowing is a problem or not depends on what that borrowing is used for. Since 1987, the United Kingdom has borrowed £11 billion a year, on the average. Over these same years, the government sector has had an average deficit of £17 billion a year, on the average, and the private sector has had an average surplus (saving minus investment has been positive) of £6 billion a year. So private sector saving has been more than sufficient to pay for investment in plant and equipment. Does the fact that foreign borrowing has financed a government deficit mean that we are borrowing to consume?

Our foreign borrowing probably has been financing public consumption to some degree. But not all government purchases are consumption purchases. Over 10 per cent of government purchases are of investment goods. But there is no sure way to divide government purchases into a consumption component and an investment component. Some items, such as the expenditure on improved roads and bridges, are clearly investment. But what about expenditure on education and health care? Are these expenditures consumption or investment? A case can be made that they are investment – investment in human capital – and that they earn a rate of return at least equal to the interest rate that we pay on our foreign debt.

However, another reason for believing that foreign lending is used to finance productive investment in the United Kingdom is that foreign investors do not buy a large volume of government bonds. In fact, in 1994, less than one-fifth of the government's deficit was *directly* financed by foreigners buying government securities. Most of the foreign investment in the United Kingdom is in the private sector and is undertaken in the pursuit of the highest available profit. Foreigners diversify their lending to spread their risk. We do the same. Some of our saving is used to finance investment in firms in the United Kingdom, some is lent to the government and some is used to finance investment in other countries.

R E V I E W

◆ When we buy goods from or invest in the rest of the world, we use foreign currency; and when foreigners buy goods from or invest in the United Kingdom, they use sterling.

◆ We record international transactions in the balance of payments accounts: current account (exports and imports of goods and services); capital account (net foreign borrowing or lending); and official settlements account (change in holdings of foreign currencies).

◆ The current account deficit is equal to the sum of the government budget deficit and the private sector surplus.

◆ Changes in the government deficit can change both the private sector surplus and the current account deficit.

Sterling in the Global Market

When we buy foreign goods or invest in another country, we have to obtain some of that country's currency to make the transaction. When foreigners buy UK-produced goods or invest in the United Kingdom, they have to obtain sterling. We get foreign currency and foreigners get pounds sterling in the foreign exchange market. The **foreign exchange market** is the market in which the currency of one country is exchanged for the currency of another. The foreign exchange market is made up of thousands of people: importers and exporters, banks, and specialists in the buying and selling of foreign exchange called foreign exchange brokers. The foreign exchange market opens on Monday morning in Hong Kong. As the day advances, markets open in Singapore, Tokyo, Bahrain, Frankfurt, London, New York, Chicago and San Francisco. As the West Coast markets in the United States close, Hong Kong is only an hour away from opening for the next day of business. As Fig. 36.3 shows, the sun barely sets on the foreign exchange market. Dealers around the world are continually in contact by telephone and on any given day, billions of dollars, yen, Deutschemarks and pounds change hands.

The price at which one currency exchanges for another is called a **foreign exchange rate**. For example, in July 1996, one pound sterling bought 2.31 Deutschemarks, 168 Japanese yen and 1.55 US dollars. The exchange rate between the US dollar and the pound sterling was £0.64 per $1. Exchange rates can be expressed either way. We've just expressed the exchange rate between the pound and the Deutschemark as the number of Deutschemarks per pound. Equivalently, we could express the exchange rate in terms of pounds per Deutschemark. That exchange rate, in July 1996, was £0.43 per DM1.

The actions of the foreign exchange brokers make the foreign exchange market highly efficient. Exchange rates are almost identical no matter where in the world the transaction is taking place. If US dollars were cheap in London and expensive in Tokyo, within a flash someone would have placed a buy order in London and a sell order in Tokyo, thereby increasing demand in one place and increasing supply in another, moving the prices to equality.

FIGURE 36.3

The Global Foreign Exchange Market

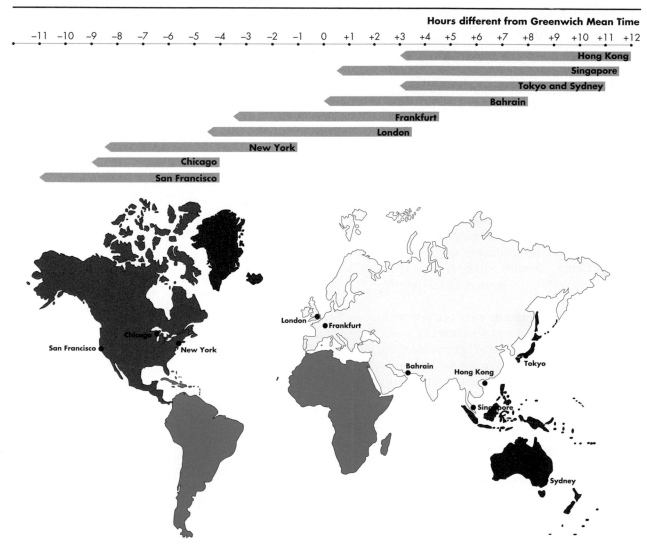

The foreign exchange market barely closes. The day begins in Hong Kong and as the globe spins, markets open up in Singapore, Tokyo, Sydney, Bahrain, Frankfurt, London, New York, Chicago and San Francisco. By the time the West Coast markets close, Hong Kong is almost ready to begin another day.

Sources: Based on a similar map in Steven Husted and Michael Melvin, *International Economics*, 1989, Harper & Row Publishers Inc.; and data from *Euromoney*, April 1979, p.14.

Foreign Exchange Systems

Foreign exchange rates are of critical importance for millions of people. They affect the costs of things as diverse as foreign holidays and imported cars. They affect the number of pounds that we get for the lamb we sell to France and the luxury cars we sell to the United States. Because of their importance, governments pay a great deal of attention to what is happening in the foreign exchange market and, more than that, take actions designed to achieve what they regard as desirable movements in exchange rates. In deciding how to act in the foreign exchange market, a government must choose among three alternative strategies that give rise to three foreign exchange systems. They are:

1. Fixed exchange rate
2.. Flexible exchange rate
3. Managed exchange rate

A **fixed exchange rate** is a system in which the value of a country's currency is pegged by the country's central bank. Under a fixed exchange rate system the Bank of England would declare the pound sterling to be worth a certain number of units of some other currency and would take actions on the foreign exchange market to try to maintain the pound's declared value. Below we'll study what those foreign exchange market actions would be.

A **flexible exchange rate** is a system in which the value of a country's currency is determined by market forces in the absence of central bank intervention. Under a flexible exchange rate, the Bank of England would take no actions on the foreign exchange market.

A **managed exchange rate** is a system in which the value of a country's currency is not fixed at some pre-announced level but is influenced by central bank intervention in the foreign exchange market. This intervention is in the form of using the official reserves to buy or sell the currency to stabilize its value.

Like many currencies the pound has experienced all three exchange rate systems at some time in its history. So before we learn how the foreign exchange market operates in these three systems, let's look at the recent history of the foreign exchange market.

Recent Exchange Rate History

At the end of World War II, the major countries of the world set up the International Monetary Fund (IMF). The **International Monetary Fund** is an international organization that monitors balance of payments and exchange rate activities. The IMF is based in Washington, DC. It came into being as a result of negotiations between the United States and the United Kingdom during World War II. In July 1944, at Bretton Woods, New Hampshire, 44 countries signed the Articles of Agreement of the IMF. At the centre of these agreements was the establishment of a worldwide system of fixed exchange rates among currencies. The anchor for this fixed exchange rate system was gold. One

ounce of gold was defined to be worth 35 US dollars. All other currencies were pegged to the US dollar at a fixed exchange rate. For example, the pound sterling was set to be worth $4.80 and the Japanese yen was set at 360 yen per dollar. The rules of the Bretton Woods system allowed for countries to alter the exchange rates subject to agreement. The pound was devalued in September 1949 and November 1967, to $2.80 and $2.40 respectively. Although the fixed exchange rate system established in 1944 served the world well during the 1950s and early 1960s, it came under increasing strain in the late 1960s and, by 1971, the order had almost collapsed. In the period since 1971, the world has operated with different countries adopting a variety of flexible and managed exchange rate arrangements as well as fixed exchange rates. Some currencies have increased in value, and others have declined. The pound sterling and the US dollar are among the currencies that have declined, while the Japanese yen is the currency that has had the most spectacular increase in value. In 1972, the pound's link with the dollar was broken and the pound began to float. At times between 1972 and 1990, the Bank of England intervened to influence the value of the pound, but there were also times when it was allowed to float freely.

Figure 36.4 shows what happened to the exchange rate between 1975 and 1996. The red line in part (a) shows the value of the pound against the German Deutschemark. The value of the pound has fallen against the Deutschemark – the pound has depreciated. **Currency depreciation** is the fall in the value of one currency in terms of another currency. For example, in 1975, the pound was worth DM5.447 and in 1996 it was worth DM2.310. So the pound has depreciated by DM3.137 or almost 58 per cent of its 1975 value.

Although the pound has depreciated in terms of the Deutschemark, it has not depreciated at the same rate against all other currencies. The green line in part (b) of Fig. 36.4 shows the value of the pound against the US dollar. During the mid-1980s the pound depreciated more against the US dollar than against other currencies.

To calculate the value of the pound sterling in terms of other currencies on the average, a trade-weighted index is calculated. The **trade-weighted index** is the value of a basket of currencies in which the weight placed on each currency is related to its importance in UK international trade. An example of the calculation of the trade-weighted

FIGURE 36.4

Exchange Rates

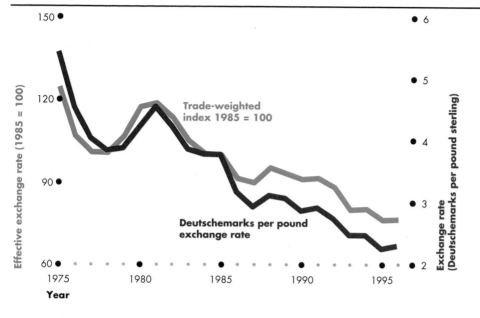

(a) Deutschemark–pound

(b) Dollar – Pound

The exchange rate is the price at which two currencies can be traded. The Deutschemark–sterling exchange rate, expressed as Deutschemarks per pound, shows that the pound has fallen in value – depreciated – against the Deutschemark. A trade-weighted index of the value of the pound sterling against all currencies shows that the pound depreciated on the average against all currencies between 1975 and 1996. It depreciated faster against the US dollar between 1980 and 1985 and appreciated against the dollar between 1985 and 1988.

Source: Office for National Statistics, *Financial Statistics*, July 1996.

---

index is set out in Table 36.3. In this example, we suppose that the United Kingdom trades with only three countries: Germany, the United States and France. Of that trade 45 per cent is with Germany, 35 per cent with the USA and 20 per cent with France. In year 1, the pound is worth DM2.5, $1.44 and Fr9. Imagine putting these three currencies into a 'basket' worth £100, where 45 per cent of the

TABLE 36.3

Trade-weighted Index Calculation

Currency	Trade weight	Exchange rate (Units of foreign currency per US dollar)		Percentage changes	
		Year 1	Year 2	Unweighted	Weighted
Deutschemark	0.45	2.50	2.35	−6.0	−2.7
US dollar	0.35	1.44	1.55	+7.6	+2.7
French franc	0.20	9.00	8.55	−5.0	−1.0
Total	1.00				−1.0

Trade-weighted index: Year 1 = 100
Year 2 = 99

value of the basket is in German Deutschemarks, 35 per cent in US dollars and 20 per cent in French francs. In year 1, the index number for the basket is 100. Suppose that in year 2, the exchange rates change in the way shown in the table. The Deutschemark appreciates to 2.35, the dollar depreciates to 1.55 and the French franc goes up in value to 8.55. What is the change in the value of the basket? The percentage changes in the value of the pound against each currency are calculated in the table. The pound goes down against the Deutschemark by 6 per cent, up against the US dollar by 7.6 per cent and down against the French franc by 5 per cent. Applying the trade weights to these percentage changes, we can calculate the weighted average change in the value of the pound. Because the weight on the French franc is 0.20 and that on the dollar is 0.35, the Deutschemark is more important than the dollar. That is, a larger fraction of the basket's value consists of Deutschemarks than of dollars. The weighted average value of the basket falls by 1 per cent. The trade-weighted index declines by 1 per cent and is 99. In this example, the pound has depreciated on the average against the other three currencies.

The calculations that we have just worked through used hypothetical numbers. How the pound has actually fluctuated against other currencies, on the average, in the period 1975–96 is shown in Fig. 36.4. As you can see, during the

1970s the value of the pound depreciated against all currencies; in 1980 it appreciated against all currencies; from 1980 to 1985 it depreciated strongly against the US dollar; and after 1985 it appreciated against the dollar but continued to depreciate against the Deutschemark.

REVIEW

◆ There are three possible foreign exchange market systems: fixed, flexible and managed.

◆ Between the end of World War II and 1971, the world economy had a fixed exchange rate system. Since 1971, it has had a mixture of flexible and managed systems.

◆ The pound has fluctuated against the dollar but has fallen against the Deutschemark and all other currencies.

Why did the pound fluctuate so much in the early 1980s? Why did it climb in value against the currencies of most countries during 1980 and then decline steadily again a few years after? To answer questions like these, we need to know what determines the foreign exchange rate. What determines the foreign currency value of the pound?

Exchange Rate Determination

The exchange rate is the price of the pound sterling in terms of other currencies. Just like any other price, the exchange rate is determined by demand and supply – the demand for pounds and the supply of pounds. But what exactly do we mean by the demand for and supply of pounds? And what is the quantity of sterling?

The quantity of sterling demanded in the foreign exchange market is the amount that people would buy on a given day at a particular exchange rate (price) if they found a willing seller. The quantity of sterling supplied in the foreign exchange market is the amount that people would sell on a given day at a particular exchange rate (price) if they found a willing buyer. What determines the quantities of sterling demanded and supplied in the foreign exchange market?

To answer this question, we need to think about the alternative to demanding and supplying pounds sterling. For a demander of sterling, the alternative is to hang on to foreign currency. For a supplier, the alternative is to hang on to sterling. The decision to buy or sell is also the decision to hold sterling or foreign currency.

To understand the forces that determine demand and supply in the foreign exchange market, we need to study people's decisions about the quantities of pounds sterling and foreign currencies to hold. Let's see what we mean by the quantity of sterling held.

The Quantity of Pounds

The **quantity of sterling assets** (which we'll call the quantity of pounds sterling) is the *net stock* of financial assets denominated in pounds sterling held outside the Bank of England and the public sector. Three things about the quantity of sterling need to be emphasized.

First, the quantity of sterling is a *stock*, not a *flow*. People make decisions about the quantity of sterling to hold (a stock) and about the quantities to buy and sell (flows) in the foreign exchange market. But it is the decision about how much sterling to hold that determines whether people plan to buy or sell sterling.

Second, the quantity of sterling is a stock *denominated in pounds sterling*. The denomination of an asset defines the units in which a debt must be repaid. It is possible to make a loan using currency of any denomination. The UK government could borrow in US dollars. If it did borrow in dollars, it would issue a bond denominated in dollars. Such a bond would be a promise to pay an agreed number of dollars at an agreed date. It would not be a sterling debt and, even though issued by the government, it would not be part of the supply of sterling. Many governments actually do issue bonds in currencies other than their own. The Canadian government, for example, issues bonds denominated in US dollars.

Third, the supply of sterling is a *net* supply – the quantity of assets *minus* the quantity of liabilities. This means that the quantity of sterling supplied does not include sterling assets created by private households, firms, financial institutions, or foreigners. The reason is that when a private debt is created, there is both an asset (for the holder) and a liability (for the issuer), so the *net* financial asset is zero. For example, if Pat loans Matt £1,000, then Pat's asset of £1,000 cancels out Matt's £1,000 liability. The quantity of sterling includes only the sterling liabilities of the government *plus* those of the Bank of England. This quantity is equal to the government debt held outside the Bank of England, plus the sterling liabilities of the Bank of England – the monetary base. In the United Kingdom, the monetary base is also known as M0. We first came across the monetary base in Chapter 30, p.769–776. The quantity of pounds sterling is:

$$\text{Quantity of pounds sterling} = \begin{array}{l} \text{Government debt held} \\ \text{outside the Bank of England} \\ + \text{Monetary base.} \end{array}$$

We've seen what sterling assets are. Let's now study the demand for and the supply of these assets and see what makes the demand and supply change.

The Demand for Sterling Assets

The law of demand applies to sterling assets just as it does to anything else that people value. The quantity of sterling demanded increases when the price of sterling in terms of foreign currency falls and decreases when the price of sterling in terms of foreign currency rises. Suppose, for example, that the pound is trading at DM2.30. If the pound rises to DM2.40, with everything else remaining the same, the quantity of sterling demanded decreases and if the pound falls to DM2.20, with everything else remaining the same, the quantity of sterling demanded increases. There are two separate reasons why the law of demand applies to sterling:

◆ Transactions effect

◆ Expected capital gains effect

Transactions Effect   A transactions cost is incurred whenever a foreign currency is converted into pounds. This transactions cost can be avoided by holding a stock of sterling. With such a stock, it is not necessary to convert foreign currency into sterling on the foreign exchange market each time a sterling payment must be made. The larger the value of sterling payments, the larger is the inventory of stock that people hold. But the value of sterling payments depends on the exchange rate. The lower the value of the pound, with everything else remaining the same, the larger is the demand for UK exports and the lower is UK demand for imports. Hence the lower the value of the pound, the larger is the value of sterling payments and the greater is the demand for sterling. Foreigners demand more pounds to buy US exports and we demand fewer units of foreign currency and more pounds as we switch from importing to buying UK-produced goods.

Expected Capital Gains Effect   Suppose you think the pound will be worth $1.50 by the end of the month. If today, it is trading at $1.55 per pound, and if your prediction about the future value of the pound is correct, you can make a quick capital gain. Suppose you buy £1,000-worth of dollars today. You get $1,550 for your £1,000. If the exchange rate at the end of the month is $1.5 per pound, as you predict it will be, you can sell your $1,550 for £1,033.33 (1,550 divided by 1.5 equals 1,033.33). (If your bank charges you £8 in fees, you've made a profit of £25.33 on these transactions.) If you are pretty confident about your prediction, you will not hold sterling during the current month. You will hold dollars instead.

If today the pound is trading not at $1.55 but at $1.45 per pound, and if your prediction about the future value of the pound – $1.50 – is correct, you will incur a capital loss if you undertake the transactions we've just looked at. If you buy £1,000-worth of dollars today, you now get only $1,450 for your £1,000. If the exchange rate at the end of the month is $1.50 per pound, as you predict

it will be, you will sell your $1,450 for £966.67 (1,450 divided by 1.5 equals 966.67). (If your bank charges you £8 in fees, you've incurred a loss of £41.33 on these transactions.) You will hang on to your pounds during the current month. You will *not* hold dollars instead.

For a given expected future value of the pound, the lower the current value of sterling, the greater is the expected capital gain from holding sterling and the greater is the quantity of sterling demanded.

Figure 36.5 shows the relationship between the foreign currency price of the pound sterling in terms of US dollars and the quantity of sterling assets demanded – the demand curve for sterling assets. When the foreign exchange rate changes, other things remaining the same, there is a movement along the demand curve.

Changes in the Demand for Sterling Assets

Any other influence on the quantity of sterling assets that people want to hold results in a shift in the demand curve. Demand either increases or decreases. These other influences are:

◆ UK GDP

◆ The expected future value of the pound

◆ The UK interest rate differential

UK GDP   You've seen that a transactions cost can be avoided by holding a stock of sterling and that the larger the value of sterling payments, the larger is the stock of sterling that people hold. A major influence on the value of sterling payments is UK GDP. An increase in UK GDP brings an increase in the value of sterling payments, which increases the demand for sterling. When the demand for sterling increases, the demand curve for sterling shifts rightward.

The Expected Future Value of Sterling   You've seen that for a given expected future value of the pound, the lower the current value of the pound, the greater is the expected capital gain from holding pounds and the greater is the quantity of sterling demanded. But what happens if the expected future value of the pound changes while the current exchange rate is unchanged?

You can answer this question by returning to the capital gain example. Suppose the pound is trading

FIGURE 36.5

The Demand for Sterling Assets

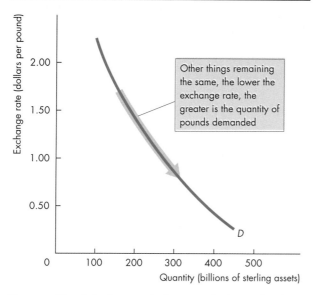

Other things remaining the same, the lower the exchange rate, the greater is the quantity of pounds demanded

The quantity of sterling assets that people demand, other things remaining the same, depends on the exchange rate. The lower the exchange rate (the smaller the amount of foreign currency per pound sterling), the larger is the quantity of sterling assets demanded. The increased quantity demanded arises from an increase in the volume of sterling trade (foreigners buy more UK goods and we buy fewer foreign goods) and an increase in the expected appreciation (or decrease in the expected depreciation) of sterling assets.

at \$1.55 and you think it is going to fall to \$1.50 by the end of the month. You are confident in your view and you buy \$1,550 with your £1,000. At the end of the month, the dollar falls to \$1.50 as you predicted it would. You now sell your \$1,550 and buy pounds. At \$1.5 per pound, you collect £1,025.33 after paying bank charges. You have made a capital gain. In this circumstance, you hold dollars rather than pounds during this month. But suppose the pound is trading at \$1.55 and you think it is going to rise to \$1.60 by the end of the month. If in this situation you do the transactions we've just considered, you will incur a capital loss. Your £1,000 still buys \$1,550 but, when you sell these dollars at the end of the month at \$1.60 per pound, you collect only £960.75 after deduction of £8 for bank charges. In this circumstance, you hold pounds rather than dollars during this month.

The lower the expected future value of the pound, other things remaining the same, the smaller is the demand for sterling (and the greater is the demand for other currencies). Similarly, the higher the expected future value of the pound, other things remaining the same, the greater is the demand for sterling (and the smaller is the demand for other currencies).

The UK Interest Rate Differential People and businesses buy financial assets to make a return that has two components: a capital gain and an interest rate. You've just seen how the expected capital gain is determined by the current exchange rate and the expected future exchange rate. Let's now look at the interest component of the return on financial assets.

People can hold sterling assets or foreign currency assets. To choose the currencies in which to hold their wealth, people look at the interest rate on sterling assets and compare it with the interest rate on a foreign currency asset. The interest rate on a sterling asset minus the interest rate on a foreign currency asset is called the **UK interest rate differential**. If the interest rate on sterling assets increases and the interest rate on a foreign currency asset remains constant, the UK interest rate differential increases. The larger the UK interest rate differential, the greater is the demand for sterling assets.

Table 36.4 summarizes the above discussion of the influences on the demand for sterling.

The Supply of Sterling Assets

Remember that the *flows* of pounds and other currencies through the foreign exchange market are determined by decisions about *stocks*. A decrease in the demand for sterling brings a flow of pounds sterling on to the foreign exchange market. But this flow of sterling on to the market is *not* what we mean when we talk about the *supply of sterling*. The supply of sterling is the quantity of sterling assets available for people to hold.

The quantity of sterling supplied is determined by the actions of the government and the Bank of England. We've seen that the quantity of sterling is equal to government debt plus the monetary base. Of these two items, the monetary base is by far the smallest. But it plays a crucial role in determining the supply of sterling. The behaviour of the monetary base depends crucially on the foreign exchange rate system.

TABLE 36.4

The Demand for Sterling Assets

THE LAW OF DEMAND

The quantity of sterling assets demanded

Increases if:	*Decreases if:*
◆The foreign exchange rate falls	◆The foreign exchange rate rises

CHANGES IN DEMAND

The demand for sterling assets

Increases if:	*Decreases if:*
◆UK GDP increases	◆UK GDP decreases
◆The expected future value pound sterling rises	◆The expected future value of the of the pound sterling falls
◆The UK interest rate differential increases	◆The UK interest rate differential decreases

---

In a fixed exchange rate system, the supply curve of sterling assets is horizontal at the chosen exchange rate. The Bank of England stands ready to supply whatever quantity of sterling assets is demanded in exchange for foreign currency assets at the fixed exchange rate. In a managed exchange rate system, the Bank of England wants to smooth fluctuations in the exchange rate, and the supply curve of sterling assets is upward-sloping. The higher the foreign exchange rate, the larger is the quantity of sterling assets supplied by the Bank of England in exchange for foreign currency assets. In a flexible exchange rate system, a fixed quantity of sterling assets is supplied, regardless of their price. As a consequence, in a flexible exchange rate system, the supply curve of sterling assets is vertical.

Changes in the Supply of Sterling Assets

There are two ways in which the quantity of sterling supplied can change:

1. The government has a budget deficit or surplus
2. The Bank of England buys or sells foreign currency assets

The government influences the quantity of sterling assets supplied through its budget. If the government has a budget deficit, it borrows by

issuing bonds, which are denominated in pounds sterling. The sale of new government bonds to finance a deficit increases the supply of sterling assets. Similarly, if the government has a budget surplus, it buys back previously issued bonds and the supply of sterling assets decreases.

The Bank of England influences the quantity of sterling supplied through its transactions in the foreign exchange market. If the Bank buys foreign currency, it increases the quantity of sterling assets supplied. If the Bank sells foreign currency, it decreases the quantity of sterling assets supplied.

An open market operation in which the Bank buys or sells government securities changes the monetary base but it does not change the quantity of sterling assets supplied. It changes the composition of sterling assets supplied. For example, if the Bank buys government bonds, the quantity of sterling denominated bonds decreases and the monetary base increases. But the increase in the monetary base equals the decrease in sterling bonds so the total quantity of sterling assets remains unchanged.

Table 36.5 summarizes the above discussion of the influences on the supply of sterling assets.

TABLE 36.5

The Supply of Sterling Assets

SUPPLY

Fixed exchange rate system

The supply curve of sterling assets is horizontal at the fixed exchange rate.

Managed exchange rate

In order to smooth fluctuations in the price of the pound sterling, the quantity of sterling assets supplied by the Bank of England increases if the foreign currency price of the pound rises and decreases if the foreign currency price of the pound falls. The supply curve of sterling assets is upward-sloping.

Flexible exchange rate

The supply curve of sterling assets is vertical.

CHANGES IN SUPPLY

The supply of sterling assets

Increases if:	*Decreases if:*
◆The UK government has a deficit	◆The UK government has a surplus
◆The Bank of England buys foreign currency	◆The Bank of England sells foreign currency

---

The Market for Sterling

Let's now bring the demand and supply sides of the market for sterling assets together and determine the exchange rate. Figure 36.6 shows how the exchange rate is determined in the three systems for fixed, flexible and managed exchange rates. The demand side of the market is the same in the three cases but the supply side differs. First, let's look at a fixed exchange rate system such as that from the end of World War II to 1971.

Fixed Exchange Rate This case is illustrated in Fig. 36.6(a). The supply curve of sterling is horizontal at the fixed exchange rate of $1.50 per pound. If the demand curve is D_0, the quantity of sterling assets is Q_0. An increase in demand to D_1 results in an increase in the quantity of sterling assets from Q_0 to Q_1 but no change in the exchange rate.

Flexible Exchange Rate Next look at Fig. 36.6(b), which shows what happens in a flexible exchange rate system. In this case, the quantity of sterling assets supplied is fixed at Q_0, so the supply curve of sterling assets is vertical. If the demand curve for sterling is D_0, the exchange rate is $1.50 per pound. If the demand for sterling increases from D_0 to D_1, the exchange rate increases to $1.60 per pound.

Managed Exchange Rate Finally, consider a managed exchange rate system, which appears in Fig. 36.6(c). Here, the supply curve is upward-sloping. When the demand curve is D_0, the exchange rate is $1.50 per pound. If demand increases to D_1, the dollar value of the pound rises but only to $1.55 per pound. Compared with the flexible exchange rate case, the same increase in demand results in a smaller increase in the exchange rate when it is

---

FIGURE 36.6

Three Exchange Rate Systems

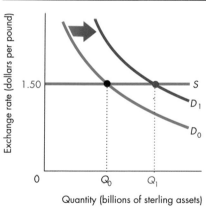

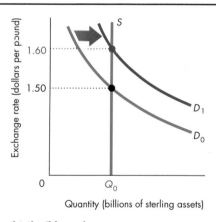

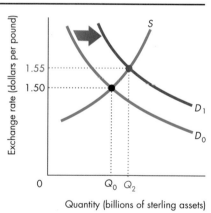

(a) Fixed exchange rate   **(b) Flexible exchange rate**   **(c) Managed exchange rate**

In a fixed exchange rate system (part a), the Bank of England stands ready to supply sterling assets or to take sterling assets off the market (supplying foreign currency in exchange) at a fixed exchange rate. The supply curve for sterling assets is horizontal. Fluctuations in demand lead to fluctuations in the quantity of sterling assets outstanding and to fluctuations in the nation's official holdings of foreign exchange. If demand increases from D_0 to D_1, the quantity of sterling assets increases from Q_0 to Q_1 and the exchange rate does not change. In a flexible exchange rate system (part b), the quantity of sterling assets is fixed so that the supply curve is vertical. An increase in the demand for sterling assets from D_0 to D_1 results only in an increase in the value of the pound – the exchange rate rises from $1.50 to $1.60. The quantity of sterling assets remains constant at Q_0. In a managed exchange rate system (part c), the Bank of England has an upward-sloping supply curve of sterling assets, so that if demand increases from D_0 to D_1, the pound sterling appreciates but the quantity of sterling assets supplied also increases – from Q_0 to Q_2. The increase in the quantity of sterling assets supplied moderates the rise in the value of the pound sterling but does not completely prevent it as in the case of fixed exchange rates.

managed. The reason for this is that the quantity supplied increases in the managed exchange rate case.

Exchange Rate System and Official Reserves

The behaviour of the balance for official financing (change in reserves) depends on the foreign exchange rate system. The official financing account of the balance of payments records the change in the country's official holdings (by the government and the Bank of England) of foreign currency. In a fixed exchange rate system (as shown in Fig. 36.6a), every time the demand for sterling assets changes, the Bank must change the quantity of sterling assets supplied to match it. When the Bank has to increase the quantity of sterling assets supplied, it does so by offering sterling assets in exchange for foreign currency assets. In this case, the official holdings of foreign exchange reserves increase. If the demand for sterling assets decreases, the Bank must decrease the quantity of sterling assets supplied. To decrease the quantity of sterling supplied, the Bank buys pounds and pays for them with its foreign exchange reserves. In this case, official foreign exchange reserves decrease. Thus with a fixed exchange rate, fluctuations in the demand for sterling assets result in fluctuations in official reserves.

In a flexible exchange rate system, there is no central bank intervention in the foreign exchange market. Regardless of what happens to the demand for sterling, no action is taken to change the quantity of sterling supplied. Therefore there are no changes in the country's official reserves. In this case, the official financing balance is zero and there is no change in official foreign currency reserves.

With a managed exchange rate, official holdings of foreign exchange are adjusted to meet fluctuations in demand but in a less extreme manner than in a fixed exchange rate system. As a consequence, fluctuations in the official financing balance are smaller in a managed floating system than in a fixed exchange rate system.

The Exchange Rate in the Long Run

We have seen how changes in the expected future exchange rate can influence the demand for sterling assets. If the exchange rate regime is floating or managed, we know that an expectation that the future exchange rate will rise results in a rightward shift of the demand for sterling assets and an appreciation of the exchange rate. So an expectation of a rise in the future exchange rate will result in a rise in the current exchange rate if the exchange rate is not fixed. But we have not said why the future exchange rate is expected to be different from the current exchange rate. However, before we discuss this we need to understand two important arguments.

First, we must recognize that the argument that the current exchange rate is influenced by the expected exchange rate in one month's time means that in turn the exchange rate in one month's time is influenced by the expectation of the exchange rate in two months' time. This argument can be extended to any future value of the exchange rate.

Second, we can appeal to rational expectations (we looked at this in Chapter 32 pp. 839–843). The expected exchange rate in one month's time will, on the average, be the actual exchange rate in one month's time. So the current exchange rate will depend partly on the expected exchange rate in one month's time. The expected future exchange rate will, on the average, be correct, and the expected future exchange rate will depend partly on the expected exchange rate further in the future. We can extend this argument to the point where the current exchange rate will depend partly on the expected exchange rate somewhere in the distant future. Another way of looking at it is that the current exchange rate is influenced by the expected exchange rate in the long-run.

Purchasing Power Parity

Purchasing power parity (PPP) is a condition that holds when the prices of goods in different countries are equalized once adjustment is made for the exchange rate. For example, suppose the price of Levi jeans in the UK is £20. Suppose the same pair of jeans costs $30 in the United States, and the exchange rate is $1.50 per pound. Then we have PPP in Levi jeans. This means that the jeans can be bought for the same price in both countries once we take into account the exchange rate (£20 = $30 divided by 1.50).

PPP is a condition that results from the application of *the law of one price* and *arbitrage* in international trade. The law of one price simply states that two identical goods must sell for the same price. How do we know that the law of one price holds? Imagine what would happen if it did not. Suppose for some reason that Doc Marten boots can be bought for £5 less in Glasgow than in London. An enterprising person could buy Doc Marten boots in Glasgow and sell them at a higher price in London. The process of buying or selling something to exploit a price differential to make a riskless profit is known as arbitrage. What would be the effect of this arbitrage process on Doc Marten boots? The retailers of Doc Martens in Glasgow will face a rundown of their stocks and will have to order more from the suppliers. The suppliers will face additional costs of diverting resources to meet the extra demand in Glasgow and will demand a higher price. In the meantime, shoe retailers in London will find that they are building up stocks as they will no longer be selling the same volume as in the past. In an attempt to move the stock they will lower the prices of Doc Martens in London. The result will be that the prices of Doc Martens in Glasgow and London will converge until it will no longer be profitable to ship the boots from one area to another. This occurs when the prices are the same. In reality small differences will exist to allow for the costs of transportation.

The same process of arbitrage can be applied to trade across countries. Let's go back to the example of the Levi jeans. Suppose Levis are selling for £30 in the United Kingdom and $30 in the United States and the exchange rate is $1.50 per pound. It will pay to import Levis into the United Kingdom from the United States and to sell them for a profit. In the long run, this process will cause prices of Levis to change in the United Kingdom and in the United States. But imagine what happens when we apply this logic to many goods, not just Levis. Identical goods in the United States will be selling at a lower price than in the United Kingdom after allowing for the exchange rate. Firms in the United Kingdom will import more US goods and pay for them in dollars. At the same time, UK exporters will export fewer goods to the United States . The demand for dollar assets will rise and the demand for sterling assets will fall. Hence the price of sterling in terms of the dollar will decline. To go back to our example of the Levi jeans, PPP in Levis will be restored when the exchange rate falls to $1 per pound (£30 = $30 divided by $1 per pound). In other words, we can state that the price of goods in the United Kingdom measured in sterling $P(£)$ is equal to the price of goods in the United States measured in dollars $P(\$)$ divided by the exchange rate (S – dollars per pound).

$$P(£) = \frac{P(\$)}{S}$$

We can rearrange this equation to arrive at an expression for the exchange rate in the long-run

$$S = \frac{P(\$)}{P(£)}$$

We now have a theory that explains what determines the exchange rate in the long run. The exchange rate will adjust so as to bring about PPP in the long run. So if the price of goods in the UK were higher than in the United States, the exchange rate with the dollar would decline in the long run. In reality there are many difficulties with the theory of PPP. There are difficulties in constructing comparable price indices between countries. The theory of PPP holds only for identical goods, but not all goods are identical – Levi jeans are an exception, not the rule. Similarly, not all goods are traded. Some goods are sold only in the United Kingdom and there is no international competition or arbitrage process that brings about a PPP in them. These goods are known as *non-traded goods*. A haircut is an often used example of a non-traded good. It is not possible to buy a cheap haircut in Spain and sell it at a profit in Sweden. Transport costs, taxes and tariffs are other factors that also reduce the convergence to PPP. However, the evidence that PPP holds on a long-run basis is strong.

Why is the Exchange Rate So Volatile? We've seen times during the 1970s, the early 1980s and even recently when the pound has moved dramatically. On some of these occasions sterling has depreciated spectacularly, but on other occasions it has appreciated strongly.

The main reason the exchange rate fluctuates so remarkably is that fluctuations in supply and demand are not always independent of each other. Sometimes a change in supply will trigger a change in demand that reinforces the effect of the change in supply. Let's see how these effects work by looking at two episodes, one in which sterling rose in value and one in which it fell.

An Appreciating Pound: 1979–81 Between 1979 and 1981, the sterling trade-weighted index appreciated by over 11 per cent. Figure 36.7(a) explains why this happened. In 1979, the demand and supply curves were those labelled D_{79} and S_{79}. The trade-weighted index was 107 – where the supply and demand curves intersect. The period between 1980 and 1981 was one of severe recession. This recession was brought about in part by the tight monetary policy pursued by the new conservative government of Mrs Thatcher. The Bank of England raised interest rates sharply in November 1979, cutting back the supply of sterling assets. The direct effect was a shift in the supply curve from S_{79}

FIGURE 36.7

Why the Exchange Rate is so Volatile

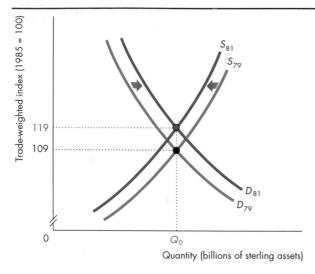

(a) 1979 to 1981

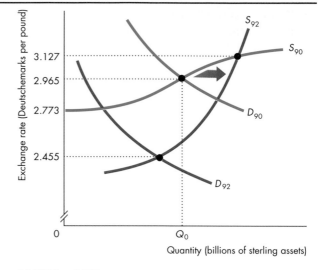

(b) 1990 to 1992

The exchange rate is volatile because shifts in the demand and supply curves for sterling assets are not independent of each other. Between 1979 and 1981 (part a), the sterling trade-weighted index appreciated from 107 to 119. The supply curve of sterling assets shifted leftward and higher interest rates and expectations of a rise in the exchange rate induced an increase in demand for sterling assets, shifting the demand curve rightward. The result was a large appreciation of the pound. The rise in the price of oil

also added to the expectation of a rise in the value of the pound sterling. Between October 1990 and October 1992 (in part b), the quantity of sterling assets increased and the supply curve of sterling shifted rightward. As the pound started to fall in value, further falls were expected so the demand for pounds sterling decreased and the demand curve shifted leftward. The result was a steep fall in the exchange rate, from DM2.965 in October 1990 to DM2.455 in October 1992.

to S_{81} – a decrease in the supply of sterling. But higher UK interest rates induced an increase in the demand for sterling assets. Furthermore, the tight monetary policy created expectations that inflation would fall in the future and that the fall in inflation would make UK inflation lower than inflation in the rest of the world. This means that people expected the UK price level to fall relative to the world price level. The implication of PPP is that the exchange rate was expected to rise in the long run. We know from our discussion of exchange rate expectations that the implication of an expected appreciation of the exchange rate in the long run is an expectation of a rise in the exchange rate in the near future, which causes the demand for sterling assets to rise even further. As a result the demand curve shifted from D_{79} to D_{81}. These two shifts reinforced each other, increasing the exchange rate to 119. But there were other factors that also contributed to the rise in the exchange rate. The oil shock of 1979

meant that UK exports of North Sea oil would result in higher dollar receipts, and a stronger current account added to the expectation of a rise in the value of sterling.

A Depreciating Pound: 1990–1992   There was a spectacular depreciation of the pound in terms of the Deutschemark from DM2.965 in October 1990 to DM2.455 in October 1992 – a fall of over 17 per cent. This fall came about in the following way. First, in October 1990, the United Kingdom was taken into the Exchange Rate Mechanism (ERM) of the European Monetary System (EMS) at a central parity of DM2.95. The ERM is a like a fixed exchange rate system but with a band around the central parity in which the value of the currency is allowed to fluctuate. The United Kingdom entered the ERM with a band of ±6 per cent around the central parity of DM2.95. The demand and supply curves were those labelled D_{90} and S_{90} in Fig. 36.7(b). The supply curve is shaped in this elongated reverse 'S' because it is meant to show the upper and lower bounds at which the Bank of England will support the currency around its central parity. The Deutschemark price of the pound – the price at which these two curves intersect – was DM2.965 per pound. In retrospect this was an unsustainable rate of exchange given the large current account deficit in 1989–90. To keep sterling at its central parity, the Bank had to raise interest rates and tighten monetary policy. The economy moved sharply into recession, raising expectations that interest rates would have to fall. The expectation of lower interest rates fuelled expectations of lower exchange rates in the future, causing the demand for sterling assets to fall and pushing the exchange rate to the bottom of the band. A large government budget deficit increased the supply of sterling assets and the supply of sterling assets curve shifted rightward from S_{90} to S_{92}. Because the expected future value of the pound fell, the demand for sterling assets decreased from D_{90} to D_{92}. The result of this combined increase in supply and decrease in demand was a dramatic fall in the value of the pound to DM2.455 on 16 September, 1992.

REVIEW

◆ The exchange rate is determined by the demand for and supply of sterling.

◆ In a fixed exchange rate system, a change in the demand for sterling is matched by a change in the quantity of sterling supplied by the Bank of England and the exchange rate does not change.

◆ In a flexible exchange rate system, fluctuations in the exchange rate can be large because changes in supply change the expected future exchange rate and induce a change in demand that reinforces the effect of the change in supply.

◆ In a managed exchange rate system, the Bank of England tries to smooth fluctuations in the exchange rate by changing the quantity of sterling supplied when the demand for sterling changes but by less than in a fixed exchange rate system.

The European Monetary System

The experience of exchange rate volatility that followed the break-up of the Bretton Woods system raised questions about whether an effective system of exchange rate management could be designed to stabilize exchange rate movements. After several unsuccessful attempts to stabilize exchange rates in the 1970s by some members of the European Union, a Franco-German initiative led to the setting up of the **European Monetary System** (EMS) in March 1979. The aim of the EMS was to create a zone of monetary stability. Low inflation and exchange rate stability were to be delivered through inter-European monetary cooperation. The key characteristics of the EMS are the **European Currency Unit** (ECU) and the **Exchange Rate Mechanism** (ERM). An amendment to the Treaty of Rome in 1987 gave a central role to the ECU and the EMS as a means of promoting economic convergence among the member states as part of the process towards a **European Monetary Union** (EMU).

European Currency Unit

The **ECU** is a constructed currency unit for the European Union. It is a weighted average of all the EMS currencies. The weights of the currencies are reviewed every five years and each time new members join the EMS, and are based on inter-European trade and individual country GDP. So the Deutschemark has the largest weight and the Portuguese escudo and Greek drachma have the lowest.

The role of the ECU was to serve as a common currency unit for the European Union. Budgets, divestments, loans and contributions to and from the European Union are denominated in ECU. It was also designed to act as a common denominator for the operation of the ERM. In particular, the ECU plays a central role as an *indicator of divergence* for the operation of intervention by member states' central banks.

Exchange Rate Mechanism

The **ERM** is a system of pegged exchange rates among participating currencies. It is a parity grid system where each currency has a set of bilateral central parities and a band in which it is allowed to float. The band defines the margin of fluctuations which in 1979 was set as either a narrow band of ±2.25 per cent or a wide band of ±6 per cent. The architects of the ERM saw its two most important features as:

1. The indicator of divergence
2. Symmetry

The indicator of divergence measures the divergence of a particular currency from its central parity. If a currency diverges significantly from its parity grid the central bank intervenes in the currency market to push the exchange rate back towards its central parity. When a currency diverges by 2.25 per cent if in the narrow band or 6 per cent if in the wide band in the same direction against all the currencies in the EMS, the arrangement of the ERM is that all the central banks of the participating currencies will intervene together. So, for example, if the French franc depreciated significantly against the Deutschemark, the rules of the ERM were that the central banks of both France and Germany should intervene jointly. The Banque de France would buy francs and sell Deutschemarks in the foreign currency market and the Bundesbank would sell Deutschemarks and buy francs. This is the meaning of symmetry. If a currency diverges significantly from its central parity, the burden of adjustment is shared by all the central banks of the participating currencies.

The ERM in Practice   The ERM was designed to be a cooperative arrangement between all the participating countries. The participating central banks were meant to coordinate their monetary and fiscal policies to keep the exchange rates stable against each other. Persistent differences in inflation rates among the participating currencies in the early 1980s led to several realignments. Between 1979 and 1983, 27 realignments occurred. Realignments were less frequent between 1984 and 1987, raising expectations that the ERM had created the exchange rate stability required as the first stage for EMU. While the theory of the ERM was a cooperative arrangement, the reality was that after 1987 the system developed into a fixed exchange rate 'leader–follower' framework reminiscent of the Bretton Woods system. The leader was Germany. The other participating countries pegged their currencies to the Deutschemark. This meant that the monetary policies of all the members of the ERM were dictated by the policy of the Bundesbank. If the Bundesbank raised interest rates, the rest of the ERM countries would be expected to do the same irrespective of the economic needs of their own economies.

In 1990, Spain, the United Kingdom and later Portugal joined the ERM with wide bands of ±6 per cent. While the United Kingdom was going through a recession, German monetary policy was tightened to offset the inflationary implications of unification. As German interest rates were raised the Bank of England was forced to keep interest rates higher than necessary, making worse the recession that was also occurring in the rest of Europe. This action fuelled expectations that the tight monetary policy of the Bank of England was unsustainable and devaluation was imminent. Expectations of a devaluation caused speculative attacks on the weaker currencies of the ERM. On 16 September, 1992 – 'Black Wednesday' – following a sustained speculative attack the United Kingdom and Italy were forced to withdraw from the ERM. According to the original rules of the ERM, all the central banks in the system were expected to intervene in the foreign currency markets to aid the weaker currencies. For the Bundesbank, this would have meant buying the weaker currencies and supplying more Deutschemark assets, and thus abandoning its tight monetary policy. The Bundesbank stuck to its monetary policy. By August 1993, after three more realignments, a broadening of the ERM bands to ±15 per cent was accepted by the participants.

European Monetary Union

The amendment to the Treaty of Rome in 1991 at Maastricht in the Netherlands laid the foundations for Economic and Monetary Union in Europe **(EMU).** A single currency is seen as the natural outcome of closer economic integration and the development of the *Single European Market*. There are good arguments in favour of a single currency. Since the purpose of a single European market is to remove all barriers to trade and to promote competition, a single currency has the advantage of ensuring that all prices in the European Union will be denominated in a common unit and the process of arbitrage will enforce the law of one price, just like our example of the Doc Marten boots in Glasgow and London. Countries will not be able to exploit a competitive advantage by artificially lowering the price of their exports through devaluation.

Other arguments are that a single currency will remove foreign exchange transactions costs – the costs associated with exchanging pounds for francs at a bank or travel agent, such as commission charges or the margin between buy and sell exchange rates we see posted in banks and currency exchanges. The removal of these costs will benefit the consumer, who will know that a Europound in the United Kingdom will buy the same as a Euromark in Germany. A single currency will also remove foreign exchange risk associated with exports and imports. For example, Alpine Gardens, an Austrian garden company, has ordered a consignment of garden gnomes to be supplied by a UK company, Britannia Gnomes Ltd, in three months' time. The contract and the price are set today, but payment will take place in three months' time. Alpine Gardens has to pay £50,000 in three months' time. To protect itself against an adverse change in the exchange rate, it pays a small premium to insure against an exchange rate change.[2] It is argued that the reduction in exchange rate risk could improve trade between EU countries. The total benefit of the removal of transactions costs associated with currency exchange has been estimated as 0.4 per cent of EU GDP.[3]

While the arguments in favour of a single currency are largely microeconomic, the arguments against are largely macroeconomic. The main cost of EMU is the loss of an independent monetary policy. In the EMU, monetary policy is to be carried out by an independent *European Central Bank* (ECB). But how important is the loss of an independent monetary policy? It depends on the frequency of shocks that hit the United Kingdom but that do not hit other EU countries. For example, if the United Kingdom were in recession but

the other countries in the European Union were not, it would not be possible for interest rates to be lowered or the exchange rate to be devalued in the United Kingdom to stimulate the economy. So how could the economy recover? There is the option of fiscal policy, but we saw in Chapter 29 (p. 760) that this may not always be effective. The Delors Report[4] states that an EMU will consist of not only a common market with free mobility of capital and labour, but also a common competition policy and a common regional policy. A common regional policy implies that fiscal transfers can be made to the United Kingdom from the other countries of the European Union. However, before fiscal transfers can be made from some countries in the European Union to others, there has to be a political consensus on the part of the donor countries and the receiver countries, which in turn can only occur if there is a political union. This is the greatest objection to EMU from some points of view. A single currency implies a political union. A loss of monetary sovereignty implies a loss of political sovereignty.

The timetable for EMU is that the single currency is to be set up in 1999. The decision as to which countries will be in, which countries will be out and which countries will have an opt-out is to be made in 1997. The qualification for membership is set out in the Treaty of Maastricht as a set of convergence conditions that would-be member states have to satisfy. These are:

1. They must be members of the ERM for at least two years before the final date for the single currency.

2. Inflation should be no more than 1.5 per cent above the three lowest inflation countries in the European Union.

3. The government budget deficit should be no more than 3 per cent of GDP.

4. Government debt should be no more than 60 per cent of GDP.

How likely is EMU to occur in the timetable envisaged by the Maastricht Treaty? It depends on how strictly the conditions of convergence will be enforced. The current 15 per cent band for the

---

[2] Alpine Gardens buys sterling in the forward market, paying a commission to the foreign currency operator which ensures the delivery of £50,000 in three months' time at an exchange rate specified today irrespective of what the exchange rate will be in three months' time.

[3] Commission of the European Communities, 'One Market, One Money: An Evaluation of the Potential Benefits and Costs of Forming an Economic and Monetary Union', 1990, *European Economy,* 44, Brussels.

[4] Committee for the Study of Economic and Monetary Union, 'Report on Economic and Monetary Union in the European Community', 1989, Luxembourg.

FIGURE 36.8

EMU and Fiscal Convergence

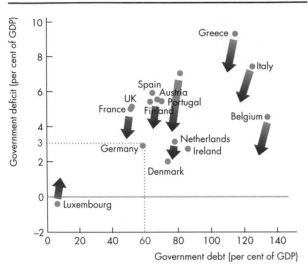

The box shows the combination of budget and debt ratios allowed by the Treaty of Maastricht if a country is to qualify for EMU. Only Luxembourg and Germany currently satisfy the fiscal convergence criteria. The arrows show the likely positions of the countries in the European Union by 1997. Although some countries will have made considerable progress towards the conditions most countries will be outside the box in 1997, the date when it will be decided which countries will qualify for EMU.

Source: 'Report on Convergence in the European Union in 1995', *European Economy*, Supplement A, No 1, January 1996.

ERM is broad and could be viewed as being no different from a managed exchange rate system. Under the existing rules, being a member of the ERM bestows no particular benefits or costs. Figure 36.8 shows the combination of the budget deficit and debt as a percentage of GDP for each of the member countries in the European Union in 1995. The arrows show the most likely position of countries in 1997 – the date when it is decided which countries can qualify. Only Germany and

Luxembourg are expected to satisfy the strict fiscal criteria by 1997. France and the United Kingdom will satisfy the debt condition but not the deficit condition, while Belgium will satisfy the deficit condition but not the debt condition. Italy, one of the original signatories of the Treaty of Rome, will still not have satisfied either condition. Postponement of the date for EMU is the most generous prediction.

R E V I E W

◆ The ERM is a system of pegged exchange rates where each participating currency has a central parity and a specified margin in which it is allowed to fluctuate against other participating currencies.

◆ In theory, the ERM is a cooperative system where each participating Central Bank helps the others to keep their currencies within specified bands. In practice, the monetary policy of each participating country is governed by the Bundesbank – the German Central Bank.

◆ The Treaty of Maastricht specifies a number of inflation and fiscal conditions that have to be met in 1997 for countries to join EMU.

◆ ◆ ◆ ◆ You've now discovered what determines a country's current account balance and the value of its currency. You have seen how the ERM works and you've examined the implications of EMU. *Reading Between the Lines* on pp. 976–977 examines the inter-relationship between expectations of EMU and the value of the pound in the foreign exchange market. In Chapter 37, we're going to look at some further global economic issues by examining the problems faced by newly emerging market economies in Asia and Central Europe.

SUMMARY

Financing International Trade

International trade, borrowing and lending are financed using foreign currency. A country's international transactions are recorded in its balance of payments accounts. The current account records receipts and expenditures connected with the sale and purchase of goods and services, as well as net transfers to and from the rest of the world; the capital account records international borrowing and lending transactions; the balance for official financing shows the increase or decrease in the country's foreign currency holdings.

The current account deficit is equal to the government budget deficit plus the private sector surplus. Changes in the government deficit change both the private sector surplus/deficit and the current account deficit. Most of the time the private sector surplus mirrors the government sector deficit, but during the early 1970s and the 1990s, the government budget and the current account were both in deficit. (pp. 952–958)

Sterling in the Global Market

Foreign currency is obtained in exchange for domestic currency in the foreign exchange market. The exchange rate can be fixed, flexible or managed. A fixed exchange rate is one that is pegged by a central bank. A flexible exchange rate is one that adjusts freely with no central bank intervention in the foreign exchange market. A managed exchange rate is one in which the central bank smoothes out fluctuations but does not peg the rate at a fixed value. (pp. 958–962)

Exchange Rate Determination

The exchange rate is determined by the demand for and supply of sterling assets. The quantity of sterling assets demanded, a stock, is greater the lower the exchange rate. A change in the exchange rate brings a movement along the demand curve for sterling. Changes in UK GDP, the expected future exchange rate and the UK interest rate differential change the demand for sterling and bring a shift in the demand curve.

The supply of sterling assets depends on the exchange rate system. In a fixed exchange rate system, the supply curve is horizontal; in a flexible exchange rate system, the supply curve is vertical; in a managed exchange rate system, the supply curve is upward-sloping. The position of the supply curve depends on the government's budget and the Bank of England's monetary policy. The larger the budget deficit or the greater the purchases of foreign currency by the Bank of England, the greater is the supply of sterling.

Fluctuations in the exchange rate occur because of fluctuations in demand and supply and sometimes these fluctuations are large. Large fluctuations arise from interlinked changes in demand and supply. A shift in the supply curve often produces an induced change in the demand curve that reinforces the effect on the exchange rate. (pp. 963–971)

The European Monetary System

The European Monetary System (EMS) was set up to create a region of monetary stability, based on low inflation and stable exchange rates. A key feature of the EMS is the ERM.

The ERM is a parity grid system, where each currency has a central parity to each other participating country's currency. A band of ±15 per cent is allowed for the currency to fluctuate around the central parity. The original rules of the ERM envisaged all the participating countries' central banks intervening in the foreign exchange market to help a currency that diverged from its central parity value to return to its parity. The reality of the ERM is that Germany has taken on the role of the leader and has set monetary policy for all the participating countries' central banks to follow. Membership of the ERM is one of the conditions for EMU. It is unlikely that the conditions set in the Treaty of Maastricht will be met by more than a few countries by the proposed start date for EMU. (pp. 971–974)

Foreign Exchange Markets in Action

The Essence of the Story

THE TIMES, 12 OCTOBER 1996

Clarke pledge propels pound to 20-month high

Janet Bush

The pound was the star performer on foreign exchanges yesterday, surging to a 20-month high against the German mark as the markets reacted with relief to the Chancellor's pledge that he will not throw away sensible economic policies to win votes.

The pound jumped to DM2.4124 from DM2.3955, its highest level since February 1995. In the past two months alone sterling has appreciated by nearly 6 per cent against the German currency. Against a basket of currencies, the pound closed at 87.8. This was its best level for 20 months and nearly 5 per cent higher than two months ago....

Kenneth Clarke's warning to the Conservative Party conference in Bournemouth on Thursday, that he would not make tax cuts unless they were sustainable, removed one element of political risk from investing in the pound. A layer of risk had already been taken out of sterling the previous week when Gordon Brown, Shadow Chancellor, promised fiscal and monetary discipline.

The apparent commitment to sensible economic policies by both main election contendors is the main reason for the latest leg of sterling's rally rather than euphoria about a successful Tory conference....

The removal of most of the obvious political risks after the conference season has added to other factors that have fuelled sterling's rise. As recently as Thursday, for example, the pound rallied after a small but disappointing rise in underlying inflation to 2.9 per cent in September, from 2.8 per cent in August. This appeared finally to rule out another cut in base rates.

Other factors helping the pound include the strength of the dollar and the developing situation in Europe. As it has appeared more likely that a single currency will go ahead but possibly on fudged economic criteria, so the preconception has grown that the euro, when established, may be a soft rather than the hard currency always envisaged.

This has undermined the mark and helped those currencies less likely to join a first wave of entrants into the euro, but which are still striving to meet the Maastricht economic convergence criteria – positive in the view of investors.

Unravelling the 'euro effect' on currencies is difficult, but as economists at Swiss Bank said yesterday: 'When it all gets confusing, you buy sterling.' However, as the European policies of the Conservative and Labour parties develop, the pound has the advantage of being backed by an economy that has shown healthy, sustained growth without inflationary pressures, while many European economies are just emerging weakly from a recession.

- ■ The value of the pound rose during September to October 1996 in reaction to the Chancellor's pledge that he will not introduce expansionist policies to win votes at the next general election.

- ■ The pound jumped to DM2.4124 in October 1996, its highest since February 1995. The value of sterling appreciated by nearly 6 per cent against the Deutschemark in September and October alone.

- ■ The commitment to sensible economic policies has reduced a source of political risk.

- ■ The rise in the pound was helped by the increased likelihood of a single European currency in 1999 based on weak economic criteria. This perception has weakened those currencies such as the Deutschemark that will join the European currency, and strengthened those currencies that will not, like the pound.

Economic Analysis

■ The value of sterling climbed from DM2.395 in September to DM2.412 in mid October 1996. Similarly, the effective exchange rate of the pound, against the currencies of the United Kingdom's main trading partners, has also edged up from 84.5 to 89.3.

■ What has caused the pound to rise so sharply? First, it should be noted that the pound has been falling for a long time. Back in 1971 the pound could be exchanged for DM9. So a small rise in the pound is nothing spectacular.

■ One of the reasons the pound has gained ground is because of the fortunes of the US dollar. The pound has had a close link with the dollar since 1993. Figure 1 shows how the dollar effective exchange rate and dollars per pound have moved in the 22 months to October 1996. The dollar has strengthened against all other currencies, but the dollar–pound relationship has remained stable for some time.

■ However, the strengthening of the pound is not entirely owing to the rise in the dollar. European governments are introducing restrictive fiscal polices in an attempt to join a European Monetary Union (EMU). The deflationary pressure in these economies has increased the likelihood that governments and central banks will reduce interest rates.

■ The United Kingdom is an attractive home for foreign investment. Figure 2 shows that the United Kingdom has relatively high short-term interest rates.

■ The markets perceive that the currencies that enter the EMU will be weakened by it because of fudged economic criteria for entry. Currencies that remain outside the EMU will be relatively attractive. Figure 3 shows that the demand for sterling assets rises and the exchange rate appreciates.

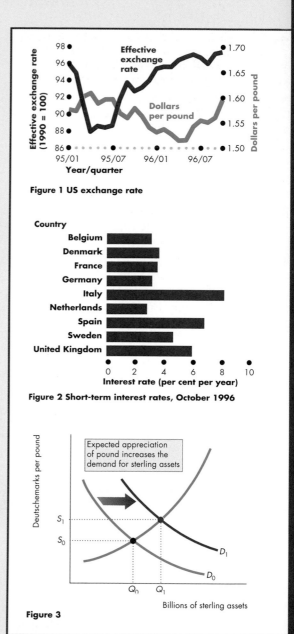

Figure 1 US exchange rate

Figure 2 Short-term interest rates, October 1996

Figure 3

K E Y   E L E M E N T S

Key Terms

Balance for official financing, 952
Balance of payments accounts, 952
Capital account, 952
Creditor nation, 954
Currency depreciation, 960
Current account, 952
Debtor nation, 954
European Currency Unit, (ECU), 971
European Monetary System, (EMS), 971
European Monetary Union, (EMU), 971
Exchange Rate Mechanism, (ERM), 971
Fixed exchange rate, 960
Flexible exchange rate, 960
Foreign exchange market, 958
Foreign exchange rate, 958
International Monetary Fund, 960
Managed exchange rate, 960
Net borrower, 954
Net lender, 954
Private sector surplus or deficit, 955
Quantity of sterling assets, 963
Trade-weighted index, 960
UK interest rate differential, 965

◆ Key Figures and Tables

Figure 36.1   The Balance of Payments, 1975–1994, 953
Figure 36.2   Sector Balances, 956
Figure 36.4   Exchange Rates, 961
Figure 36.6   Three Exchange Rate Systems, 967
Table 36.2   The Current Account Balance, Net Foreign Borrowing and the Financing of Investment, 955
Table 36.4   The Demand for Sterling Assets, 966
Table 36.5   The Supply of Sterling Assets, 966

R E V I E W   Q U E S T I O N S

1 What are the transactions recorded in a country's current account, capital account and balance for official financing account?

2 What is the relationship between the balance on the current account, the capital account, and the balance for official financing account?

3 Distinguish between a country that is a net borrower and one that is a creditor. Are net borrowers always creditors? Are creditors always net borrowers?

4 What is the connection between a country's current account balance, the government's budget deficit and the private sector surplus?

5 Why do fluctuations in the government budget balance lead to fluctuations in the current account balance?

6 Distinguish among the three exchange rate systems: fixed, flexible and managed.

7 Review the main influences on the quantity of sterling assets that people demand.

8 Review the influences on the supply of sterling assets.

9 How does the supply curve of sterling differ in the three exchange rate systems?

10 Why does the foreign exchange value of sterling fluctuate so much?

PROBLEMS

1 The citizens of Silecon, whose currency is the grain, conduct the following transactions in 1990:

Item	Billions of grains
Imports of goods and services	350
Exports of goods and services	500
Borrowing from the rest of the world	60
Lending to the rest of the world	200
Increase in official holdings of foreign currency	10

  a Set out the three balance of payments accounts for Silecon.
  b Does Silecon have a flexible exchange rate?

2 You are told the following about Ecflex, a country with a flexible exchange rate whose currency is the band:

Item	Billion bands
GDP	100
Consumption expenditure	60
Government purchases of goods and services	24
Investment	22
Exports of goods and services	20
Government budget deficit	4

Calculate the following for Ecflex:
  a Imports of goods and services
  b Current account balance
  c Capital account balance
  d Taxes (net of transfer payments)
  e Private sector deficit/surplus

3 A country's currency appreciates and its official holdings of foreign currency increase. What can you say about the following:
  a The exchange rate system being pursued by the country.
  b The country's current account.
  c The country's balance for official financing account.

4 The foreign exchange market is shown in the figure. The demand for pounds sterling decreases from D_0 to D_1.
  a Explain the influences on the market that might have caused this fall in the demand for pounds sterling.
  b Which curve is the supply of pounds sterling if

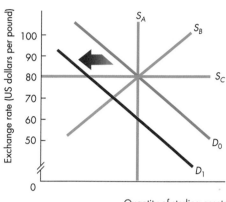

the exchange rate is fixed? Explain what happens to the exchange rate and the balance for official financing account in this case when the demand for pounds sterling decreases from D_0 to D_1.
  c Which curve is the supply of pounds sterling if the exchange rate is flexible? Explain what happens to the exchange rate and the balance for official financing account in this case when the demand for pounds sterling decreases from D_0 to D_1.
  d Which curve is the supply of pounds sterling if the exchange rate is managed? Explain what happens to the exchange rate and the balance for official financing account in this case when the demand for pounds sterling decreases from D_0 to D_1.

5 Study *Reading Between the Lines* on pp. 976–977 and then answer the following questions.
  a What events in the foreign exchange market does the news article describe?
  b How does this event influence the value of the pound?
  c What other explanations does the article give for the rise in the value of the pound?
  d Is the rise in the value of the pound remarkable in a historical context?
  e How can the Chancellor and the Bank of England influence the value of the pound?

CHAPTER
37

EMERGING
ECONOMIES

After studying this chapter you will be able to:

◆ Describe how income is distributed and is changing in the world economy of the 1990s

◆ Explain the fundamental economic problem that confronts all nations and the alternative systems that have been used to cope with it

◆ Describe the process of transition in the emerging economies of Russia and other Central European countries

THE BERLIN WALL HAS FALLEN AND GERMANY IS REUNITED. EAST GERMANY'S centrally planned economy has been replaced by a market economy. Russia, Ukraine, Poland, Hungary and the Czech and Slovak Republics have abandoned central economic planning and are making a painful transition towards a market economy. Why are these countries abandoning central planning and jumping on the market bandwagon? ◆ Dramatic change is also taking place in Asia. In 1946, as World War II ended, Hong Kong emerged from Japanese occupation as a poor outpost of the British Empire. Occupying a cluster of overcrowded rocky islands, Hong Kong today is a vibrant city of hardworking and increasingly wealthy people. A similar story can be told of Singapore. Two and a half million people crowded into an island city nation have, by their dynamism, transformed their economy, increasing their average income more than sixfold since 1960. Even in Asia's giant, China, incomes are growing at an extraordinary pace and closing the gap on those in the rich industrial countries. How have these countries managed to unshackle themselves from poverty? What do they have that other poor countries lack? Can their lessons be applied elsewhere?

Dramatic Economic Change

◆ ◆ ◆ ◆ This chapter brings you full circle and returns to the fundamental economic problem of scarcity and the various ways in which people try to cope with it. You've studied the way the economy of the United Kingdom operates. You are now going to look at the bigger picture and examine economies that are emerging from either relative economic underdevelopment or an alternative economic system, that of socialist central planning. You are going to look at the process of revolutionary change that is taking place in the world economy during the 1990s. But to set the scene, we're first going to look at a snapshot of the world economy in the mid-1990s.

A Snapshot of the World Economy

The world economy consists of more than 5 billion people, who live in 181 countries. In 1990, the most recent year for which comparable data are available for a large number of countries, world average annual income per person was $4,500. Which countries earn more than this average and which earn less? How is world income distributed around the average? And how quickly is the situation changing because of economic growth? We are going to answer these questions in this snapshot of the world economy. But to do so, and to study the anatomy of the world economy, we need a scheme for classifying countries.

Classification of Countries

Many different country classification schemes exist and none is perfect. But a commonly used scheme is one devised by the International Monetary Fund (IMF). It has three major groups of countries:

◆ Industrial countries

◆ Developing countries

◆ Countries in transition

Industrial Countries   The IMF's first group is made up of 23 countries. They are the Group of Seven, or G-7 (Canada, France, Germany, Italy, Japan, United Kingdom and United States), 14 other West European countries and Australia and New Zealand. Figure 37.1 shows these countries in blue.

Developing Countries   The IMF's second group has 130 countries, which cover the Western Hemisphere other than the United States and Canada, Asia other than Japan, the Middle East and Africa. Figure 37.1 shows these countries in red (Western Hemisphere), orange (Asia and the Middle East) and green (Africa). Four Asian countries in this group, Hong Kong, South Korea, Singapore and Taiwan, are more similar to the members of the industrial group than the other developing countries. They are sometimes called Newly Industrializing Countries or NICs and are identified separately in Fig. 37.1 in yellow.

Countries in Transition   The countries in transition are the 28 countries that have emerged from the former Soviet Union together with the countries of Central Europe that were closely allied and linked with the former Soviet Union. Figure 37.1 shows these countries in grey.

Let's now see how these three country groups differ in terms of incomes per person and income growth rates.

Incomes Per Person

Incomes per person range from $18,450 a year in the United States to $365 a year – a dollar a day – in the African country of Chad. Figure 37.1 shows some of the details of the distribution across the major countries and regions of the world. In the Western Hemisphere outside Canada and the United States, the average annual income of $3,900 contains a range from $8,500 in the Caribbean islands of Trinidad and Tobago to $1,200 in Guyana. In Western Europe, the average annual income of $12,900 contains a range from $17,700 in Switzerland to $6,500 in Portugal. In Africa, the average annual income of $1,300 contains a range from $5,700 in the Indian Ocean island of Mauritius and $3,200 in South Africa, to $365 in Chad. Incomes for the countries in transition (grey on the map) are not known with sufficient accuracy and detail for international comparisons to be made. But data for a few of these countries show their average annual incomes to be around $5,000.

Income Distribution

Figure 37.2 summarizes the world distribution in the form of a Lorenz curve. A **Lorenz curve** plots the cumulative percentage of income against the cumulative percentage of population. If income is equally distributed, the Lorenz curve is a straight diagonal line running from the origin. With an equal distribution of income, each 1 per cent of the population receives 1 per cent of the income. The degree of inequality is indicated by the extent to which the Lorenz curve departs from the line of equality. The blue Lorenz curve in Fig. 37.2 shows the degree of inequality in the world economy. The poorest 20 per cent of the world's population lives in countries that earn only 4.5 per cent of world income. The richest 20 per cent of the world's population lives in countries that earn 63 per cent of world income.

FIGURE 37.1

World Income Per Person in 1990

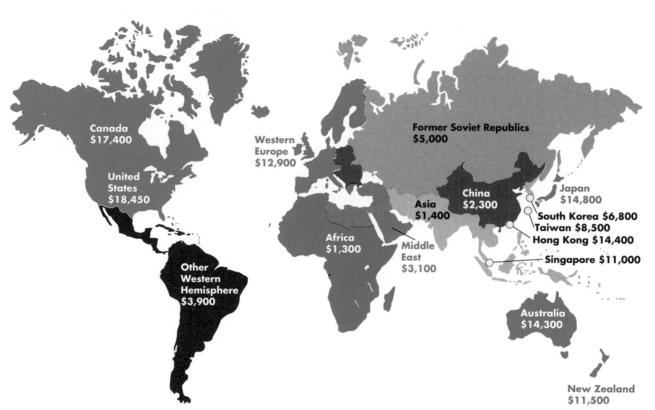

The industrial countries (blue) have the highest incomes per person, but four Asian economies (yellow) have rapidly growing incomes and are closing the gap on the industrial countries. The developing countries of Africa (green) and Asia (light orange) have the lowest incomes per person. The emerging economies are those of Central Europe (grey), the former Soviet Union (light grey), China (orange) and the fast-growing Asian countries (yellow).

Source: Robert Summers and Alan Heston, New computer diskette (Mark 5.5), 15 June 1993, distributed by the National Bureau of Economic Research to update The Penn World Table (Mark 5): An Expanded Set of International Comparisons, 1950–1988, *Quarterly Journal of Economics*, May 1991, 327–368.

Figure 37.2 also shows a Lorenz curve for the United Kingdom[1]. This curve shows the degree of inequality in the United Kingdom. It also reveals that the distribution of world income across countries is more unequal than the distribution of UK income across families. The poorest 20 per cent of UK families earn 6.7 per cent of total income – not too far from the global percentage. But the richest 20 per cent of UK families earn 43 per cent of total UK income – much less than the 63 per cent of total world income earned by the 20 per cent of the world's population living in the richest countries.

The picture of the world economy contained in Figs 37.1 and 37.2 is static. It shows the world at a point in time. But the world is changing. Many poor people live in countries in which rapid economic growth is taking place. As a result of economic growth and development, millions of people now enjoy living standards undreamed of by their parents and inconceivable to their grandparents. In the

[1] The world data are country incomes while the United Kingdom data are household incomes.

FIGURE 37.2

The World Lorenz Curve: 1990

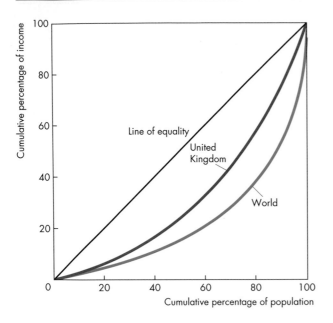

The cumulative percentage of income is plotted against the cumulative percentage of population. If income were distributed equally across countries, the Lorenz curve would be a straight diagonal line. The distribution of per head income across countries is even more unequal than the distribution of income among families in the United Kingdom.

Sources: Robert Summers and Alan Heston, New computer diskette (Mark 5.5), 15 June 1993, distributed by the National Bureau of Economic Research to update The Penn World Table (Mark 5): *An Expanded Set of International Comparisons, 1950–1988*, Quarterly Journal of Economics, May, 1991, 327–368; and HMSO, *Social Trends*, 1995, London.

countries in transition, change is taking place, and although it holds hope for the future, its present effects are putting the lives of millions of people under severe strain. Let's end our snapshot of the world economy by looking at some of the changes in incomes that have taken place in the past few years.

Economic Growth and Decline

World average income per person has grown at an average rate of 2.6 per cent a year during the 10 years 1986–1995. But the rate has fluctuated from

year to year and has varied across countries. During this 10-year period, world aggregate income growth fluctuated between a high of 4.7 per cent in 1988 and a low of 0.7 per cent in 1991. Figure 37.3(a) shows this fluctuating growth rate as the purple line. The figure also shows that the industrial countries (the green line) have grown at a slower pace than the developing countries (the orange line). The average income growth rate of the industrial countries was 2.2 per cent a year and of the developing countries 5.1 per cent a year. Within the developing countries, income per person grew at 7.5 per cent a year in Asia but at only 1.1 per cent a year in Africa. At a growth rate of 7.5 per cent a year, the *level* of income per person doubles in 10 years. At a growth rate of 1.1 per cent a year, the level of income per person increases by only a little more than 10 per cent in 10 years and takes 70 years to double.

Most countries have shared in economic growth, even if the pace has varied. But a few countries have experienced declining incomes. These are the countries in transition – the former Soviet Union and other Central European countries. Figure 37.3(b) shows the rate of change in income in these countries. Incomes have *fallen* at an average rate of 3.4 per cent a year during the years shown in the figure. In the year of peak decline, 1992, incomes fell by almost 16 per cent. To place this period of economic transition in perspective, Fig. 37.3(c) shows the growth rate in the countries in transition alongside the growth rate of income in the United States 60 years earlier during the Great Depression (the red line). During the 10 years from 1926 to 1935, incomes in the United States fell at an average annual rate of 0.5 per cent a year. Viewed in this way, it is clear that the transition taking place in Central Europe and Russia is a costly process.

Why are the countries of East Asia expanding so quickly? Why are Russia and the other countries in transition having such a painful time? Part of the answer to both of these questions lies in the economic system employed and to changes in that system. The economies of East Asia rely on a *decentralized market mechanism*. In contrast, until recently the economies in transition relied on a *centralized command mechanism* that they are dismantling and replacing with a market system. Let's look at these different economic systems and see how they differ in the way they try to cope with the economic problem.

FIGURE 37.3

World Economic Growth

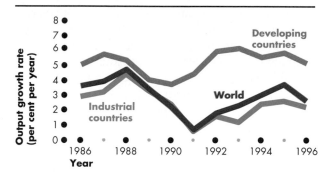

(a) Developing and industrial countries

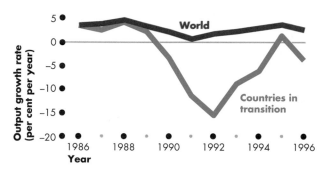

(b) Countries in transition

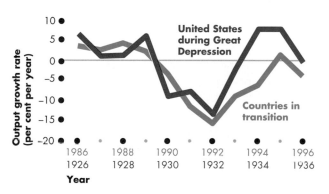

(c) Another Great Depression

The developing countries are experiencing faster economic growth than the industrial countries (part a). The countries in transition have experienced declining incomes (part b) and the scale of income decline has exceeded the decline in income in the United States during the Great Depression 60 years earlier (part c).

Source: International Monetary Fund, *World Economic Outlook*, October 1994, Washington, DC.

Alternative Economic Systems

The economic problem arises from the universal fact of scarcity – we want to consume more goods and services than the available resources make possible. Figure 37.4 illustrates the economic problem. People have preferences about what goods and services to consume and how to use the factors of production they own or control. Techniques of production – technologies – are available to transform factors of production into goods and services. The economic problem is to choose the quantities of

FIGURE 37.4

The Fundamental Economic Problem

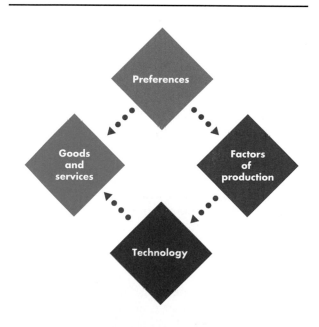

People have preferences about goods and services and the use of factors of production. Technologies are available for transforming factors of production into goods and services. People want to consume more goods and services than can be produced with the available factors of production and technology. The fundamental economic problem is to choose *what* goods and services to produce, *how* to produce them, and *who* to produce them for. Different economic systems deliver different solutions to this problem.

goods and services to produce – *what* – the ways to produce them – *how* – the timing of production – *when* – the location of production – *where* – and the distribution of goods and services to each individual – *who*.

What, how, when, and *where* goods and services are produced and *who* gets them depends on how the economy is organized. Different systems deliver different outcomes. Let's examine the different economic systems.

Economic systems vary in many ways, but two characteristics are crucial:

◆ Property rights
◆ Incentives

Property Rights

Property rights are the social arrangements that govern the ownership, use and disposal of factors of production and goods and services. Economic systems differ in the way they assign property rights to capital and land. These property rights may be granted to individuals, the state, or a mixture of the two. The private ownership of capital and land enables people to create and operate their own firms. It also enables them to buy and sell capital, land and firms freely at the going market prices. State ownership of capital and land enables bureaucrats and managers to control the use of these resources in state-owned firms, but it does not permit this control to be passed to others in a market transaction.

In practice, no economy has pure private ownership or pure and exclusive state ownership. For example, in an economy with widespread private ownership, the freedom to buy and sell firms is modified by the anti-monopoly laws. Also, national defence or the public interest might be invoked to limit private ownership and to justify public ownership. Such limitations operate to restrict the private ownership and promote public ownership of, for example, beaches and areas of natural scenic beauty.

In an economy that has predominantly state ownership, people sometimes own small plots of land and their homes. Also, in many economies, private ownership and state ownership exist side by side. In such cases, the state acts like a private firm and can buy capital, land, or even a production enterprise from its existing owner.

Incentives

Incentives are inducements to take certain actions. They can be rewards (carrots) for taking actions that bring benefits or penalties (sticks) for taking actions that impose costs. Incentives may be created by market prices, by laws and regulations, or by a mixture of the two.

An incentive system based on market prices is one in which people respond to the price signals they receive and the price signals themselves respond to people's actions. For example, suppose a severe frost in Seville wipes out the orange crop one year. The supply of orange juice falls. As a result, the price of orange juice rises. Faced with the higher price, people have an *incentive* to economize on orange juice and they decrease the quantity demanded. At the same time, the higher price of orange juice induces an increase in the demand for apple juice, a substitute for orange juice. As a result, the prices of apples and apple juice also rise. With higher prices for orange juice and apple juice, orange and apple growers in other regions and countries have an *incentive* to increase the quantity supplied.

An incentive system based on laws and regulations is one in which people are rewarded or punished in a variety of non-monetary ways to induce them to take particular actions. For example, a manager might reward a salesperson for achieving a sales goal with more rapid promotion or a bigger office. Alternatively, a salesperson might be punished for failing to achieve a sales goal by being moved to a less desirable sales district. When an entire economy is operated on administrative incentives, everyone, from the highest political authority to the lowest ranked worker, faces non-monetary rewards and punishments from their immediate superiors.

When the incentive system is based on laws and regulations, prices are determined by the law, not by the forces of demand and supply. For example, a government might want everyone to have access to low-cost bread as, was the case in France for a long time. As a result, bread might be priced at a few francs a baguette. At an artificially low price, people have an *incentive* to buy lots of bread. Poor children might even use stale loaves as footballs! This use of bread apparently did occur in the former Soviet Union.

Types of Economic Systems

Economic systems differ in how they combine property rights and incentives. Figure 37.5 illustrates the range of possibilities. There are two extreme types and many hybrid types of economic systems.

FIGURE 37.5

Alternative Economic Systems

Capital owned by

	Individuals	Mixed	State

Capitalism

Market socialism

Market prices — Hong Kong / USA / Japan

Hungary / Poland

Incentives based on Mixed — United Kingdom / Sweden

China / Former USSR / North Korea / Cuba

Laws and regulations — **Welfare state capitalism**

Socialism

Under capitalism, individuals own capital – farms, factories, plant and equipment – and incentives are created by market prices. Under socialism, the state owns capital and land and incentives are created by a planning and command system. Market socialism combines state ownership of capital with market price incentives. Welfare state capitalism combines private capital ownership with a high degree of state intervention in markets that change incentives.

The extreme types are capitalism and socialism. **Capitalism** is a system with private ownership of capital and land and incentives based on market prices. **Socialism** is a system with state ownership of capital and land and incentives based on laws and regulations.

No country uses an economic system that precisely corresponds to one of these extreme types, but the United States, Japan and Hong Kong come closest to being capitalist economies and the former Soviet Union, China before the 1980s, Cuba and North Korea come closest to being socialist economies.

The many hybrid economic systems combine private ownership with state ownership and market price incentives with laws, regulations and administered prices. **Market socialism** (also called **decentralized planning**) is an economic system that combines state ownership of capital and land with incentives based on a mixture of market and administered prices. Hungary and Poland have used market socialism. In such economies, administrators set the prices at which firms and shops buy and sell, and then leave these organizations free to choose the quantities of inputs and outputs. But the prices set by the administrators responded to the forces of demand and supply.

Another combination is welfare state capitalism. **Welfare state capitalism** combines the private ownership of capital and land with state intervention in markets that modify the price signals to which people respond. Sweden, the United Kingdom and other EU countries are examples of such economies.

Capitalism has evolved over thousands of years and is not the invention of a single philosopher. But Adam Smith was the first economist to probe the workings of capitalism and explain how the invisible hand of the price mechanism guides resources to their highest value uses. In contrast, socialism was invented. It was first imagined by Karl Marx and Frederick Engels during the nineteenth century, and then refined and put into practice in Russia during the 1930s by Joseph Stalin and in China during the 1950s by Mao Zedong.

Alternative Systems Compared

Because all economic systems are a combination of the two extreme cases – capitalism and socialism – we can study the essence of any system by studying the two extreme types. Let's see how first capitalism and then socialism cope with scarcity.

How Capitalism Copes with Scarcity

Figure 37.6 shows how capitalism copes with scarcity. Households own the factors of production and are free to use these factors and the incomes they receive from the sale of their services in any way they choose. These choices are governed by their preferences. The preferences of households are all-powerful in a capitalist economy.

Households choose the quantity of each factor of production to supply and firms choose the quantity of each factor of production to demand. Firms choose the quantity of each good or service to supply and households choose the quantity of each to demand. These choices respond to prices in factor markets and goods markets. An increase in a factor price gives households an incentive to increase the quantity supplied of that factor and gives firms an incentive to decrease the quantity demanded. An increase in the price of a good gives firms an incentive to increase the quantity supplied of that good and gives households an incentive to decrease the quantity demanded. Factor prices adjust to bring the quantities demanded of the factors into equality with the quantities supplied, and goods prices adjust to bring the quantities demanded of the goods into equality with the quantities supplied.

In Fig. 37.6, factors of production flow from households through factor markets to firms and goods flow through goods markets from firms to households. *What* is produced, *how* it is produced and *who* it is produced for is determined by the preferences of the households, the resources that they own and the technologies available to the firms.

No one *plans* a capitalist economy. Doctors perform nearly miraculous life-saving surgery by using sophisticated computer-controlled equipment. The equipment is designed by medical and electronic engineers, programmed by mathematicians, financed by insurance companies and banks, and bought and installed by hospital administrators. Each individual household and firm involved in this process allocates the resources that it controls in the way that seems best for it. Each firm tries to maximize its profit and each household tries to maximize its utility. These plans are coordinated in the markets for health-care equipment, computers, engineers, computer programmers, insurance, hospital services, nurses, doctors and hundreds of other markets for items that range from anaesthetic chemicals to paper gowns, through the 'invisible hand' of the price mechanism.

FIGURE 37.6

Capitalism's Solution to the Economic Problem

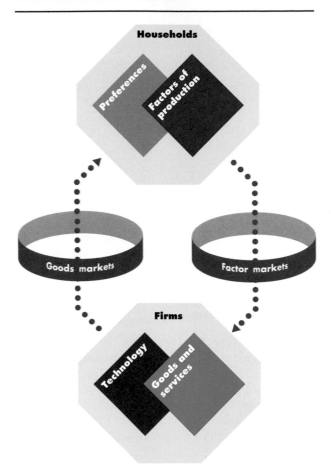

Under capitalism, the preferences of individual households dictate the choices that are made. Households own all the factors of production and sell the services of those factors in factor markets. Households decide which goods and services to consume and buy them in goods markets. Firms decide which goods and services to produce and which factors of production to employ, selling their output in goods markets and buying their inputs in factor markets. The markets find the prices that bring the quantities demanded and quantities supplied into equality for each factor of production and each good or service. Capitalism economizes on information because households and firms need to know only the prices of various goods and factors that they buy and sell.

When a surgeon performs an operation, an incredible amount of information is used. Yet no one person or firm possesses all this information. It is not centralized in one place. The capitalist economic system economizes on information. Each household or firm needs to know little about the other households and firms with which it docs business. The reason is that *prices convey most of the information it needs*. By comparing the prices of factors of production, each household chooses the quantity of each factor to supply. And by comparing the prices of goods and services, it chooses the quantity of each to buy. Similarly, by comparing the prices of factors of production, each firm chooses the quantity of each factor to use, and by comparing the prices of goods and services, it chooses the quantity of each to supply.

How Socialism Copes with Scarcity

Figure 37.7 shows how socialism copes with scarcity. In this case, the preferences of a group of administrators called *planners* carry the most weight. Those preferences dictate the activities of the production enterprises. The planners control capital and natural resources, directing them to the uses that satisfy their priorities. The planners also decide what types of jobs will be available, and the state plays a large role in the allocation of the only factor of production owned by households – labour.

The decisions of the planners are formalized in a central plan. A **central plan** is a detailed economic blueprint that sets out *what* will be produced, *how* it will be produced and *who* it will be produced for, and that establishes a set of sanctions and rewards designed to ensure that the plan is fulfilled as fully as possible.

The central plan is communicated to state-owned enterprises which use the factors of production and the available technologies to produce goods and services. These goods and services are supplied to households in accordance with the central plan. The purchases by each individual household are determined by household preferences, but the total amount available is determined by the central plan.

A centrally planned economy has prices, but they do not adjust to make the quantity demanded and supplied equal. Instead, they are set by the planners to achieve social objectives. For example, the prices of staple food products are set at low levels so that even the poorest families can afford an adequate basic diet. The effect of setting such prices at low levels is chronic shortages and long queues. In such a situation, prices do not provide the main incentives and people respond to the penalties and rewards that superiors impose on and give to their subordinates.

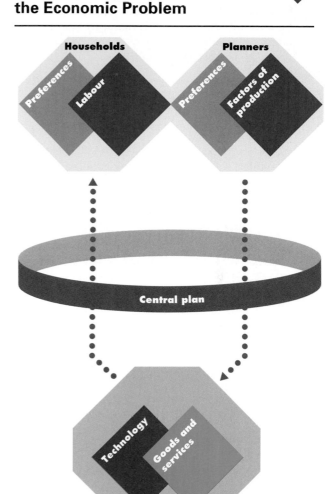

FIGURE 37.7

Socialism's Solution to the Economic Problem

Under socialism, the preferences of the planners dictate the choices that arc made. The planners control all the capital and natural resources owned by the state. Planners draw up plans and issue orders that determine how these resources will be used in the production of goods and services. Households decide which goods and services to consume and buy. State enterprises produce the goods and services and employ the factors of production required by the central plan. The output of state enterprises is shipped to other enterprises in accordance with the plan. Prices are set by the planners to achieve social objectives and bear no relation to the quantities demanded and quantities supplied. Prices set at low levels for social reasons – as in the case of basic food products – result in chronic shortages.

◆ Capitalism copes with scarcity by permitting households and firms to decide how to use the factors of production they own and coordinates these decisions through markets.

◆ Socialism copes with scarcity by central planning and state ownership – planners decide what to produce and communicate their plans to state-owned enterprises.

Now that we've examined the features of socialist and capitalist economies, let's look at some of the formerly socialist economies in transition.

Economic Transition in Russia and Central Europe

We'll begin our look at economies in transition with the republics that once made up the Soviet Union, the place where socialist central planning was developed and from which it was 'exported' to other countries in Central Europe.

History of the Soviet Union

The Soviet Union, or the Union of Soviet Socialist Republics (USSR), was founded in 1917 following the Bolshevik revolution led by Vladimir Ilyich Lenin. After more than 70 turbulent years, the Soviet Union collapsed in 1991 when it was replaced by 16 independent republics, the largest of which are Russia and Ukraine. The 16 republics are resource-rich and diverse. Their land area is almost three times that of the United States; their population is 290 million, 20 per cent larger than the United States; they have vast reserves of coal, oil, iron ore, natural gas, timber, and almost every other mineral resource. They are republics of enormous ethnic diversity with Russians making up 50 per cent of the population and many European, Asian and Arabic ethnic groups making up the other 50 per cent. A compact economic history of the Soviet Union appears in Table 37.1.

Although the Soviet Union was founded in 1917, its economic management system was not put in place until 1928. The architect of this system was Joseph Stalin. The financial, manufacturing and

TABLE 37.1

Key Periods in the Economic History of the Soviet Union

Period	Main economic events/characteristics
1917–1921 (Lenin)	◆ Bolshevik Revolution
	◆ Nationalization of banking, industry and transport
	◆ Forced requisitioning of agricultural output
1921–1924 (Lenin)	◆ New Economic Policy, 1921
	◆ Market allocation of most resources
1928–1953 (Stalin)	◆ Abolition of market
	◆ Introduction of command planning and five-year plans
	◆ Collectivization of farms
	◆ Emphasis on capital goods and economic growth
	◆ Harsh conditions
1953–1970 (Khrushchev to Brezhnev)	◆ Steady growth
	◆ Increased emphasis on consumer goods
1970–1985 (Brezhnev to Chernenko)	◆ Deteriorating productivity in agriculture and industry
	◆ Slowdown in growth
1985–1991 (Gorbachev) 1991	◆ *Perestroika* – reforms based on increased accountability
	◆ Break-up of the Soviet Union

transport sectors of the economy were placed under state ownership and control by Lenin. Stalin added farms to this list. He abolished the market and introduced a command planning mechanism, initiating a series of five-year plans that placed their major emphasis on setting and attaining goals for the production of capital goods. The production of consumer goods was given a secondary place and personal economic conditions were harsh. With emphasis on the production of capital goods, the Soviet economy grew quickly.

In the 1950s, after Stalin's death, steady economic growth continued, and the emphasis in economic planning gradually shifted away from capital goods towards consumer goods production. But there was also a heavy emphasis on both military equipment and space exploration. In the 1960s, the growth rate began to sag and by the 1970s and early 1980s, the Soviet economy was running into serious problems. Productivity was actually declining, especially in agriculture but also in industry. Growth slowed and, on some estimates, income per person began to fall. It was in these circumstances that Mikhail Gorbachev came to power with plans to restructure the Soviet economy, based on the idea of increased individual accountability and rewards based on performance.

As a unified political entity, the Soviet Union effectively disintegrated following an unsuccessful coup to topple former President Mikhail Gorbachev in August 1991. What emerged from that coup was a loose federation of independent republics. Political freedoms began to be enjoyed in the late 1980s under President Gorbachev's programmes of *perestroika* (restructuring) and *glasnost* (openness). These freedoms released nationalist and ethnic feelings that had been held in check for 50 years and created a virtual explosion of political activity. At the same time the economies of the new republics underwent tumultuous change.

We are going to look at that change. But to understand it, we need to see how the Soviet Union operated before it abandoned its central planning system.

Soviet-style Central Planning

Soviet-style central planning was a method of economic planning and control that had four key elements:

◆ Administrative hierarchy
◆ Iterative planning process
◆ Legally binding commands
◆ Taut and inflexible plans

Administrative Hierarchy   A large and complex hierarchy implemented and controlled the central economic plan that determined almost every aspect of economic activity. At the top of the hierarchy was the state's *political* authority and at the bottom were factories and farms that produced the goods and services. In between were layer upon layer of superiors and subordinates, with superiors wielding absolute and arbitrary power over their subordinates.

Iterative Planning Process   An iterative process is a repetitive series of calculations that get closer and closer to a solution. Central planning is an iterative process. A plan is proposed and adjustments are repeatedly made until all the elements of the plan are consistent with each other. But a plan is not arrived at as the result of a set of neat calculations performed on a computer. Rather, the process involves a repeated sequence of communications of proposals and reactions down and up the administrative hierarchy.

The process begins with the setting of a big picture of objectives or directives by the highest political authority. These directives are translated into targets by the planning ministry and retranslated into ever more detailed targets as they are passed down the hierarchy. Tens of millions of raw materials and intermediate goods featured in the detailed plans of the Soviet Union, which filled 70 volumes, or 12,000 pages, each year.

When the targets are specified as production plans for individual products, the factories react with their own assessments of what is feasible. Reactions as to feasibility are passed back up the hierarchy, and the central planning ministry makes the targets and reports of feasibility consistent. A good deal of bargaining takes place in this process, the superiors demanding the impossible and subordinates claiming the requests to be infeasible.

Legally Binding Commands   Once a consistent (even if not feasible) plan has been determined by the planning ministry, the plan is given the force of law in a set of binding commands from the political authority. The commands are translated into increasing detail as they pass down the chain of command and are implemented by the production units in a way that most nearly satisfies the superiors of each level.

Taut and Inflexible Plans   In the Soviet Union, the targets set by superiors for their subordinates were not feasible. The idea was that in the attempt to do the impossible, more would be achieved than if an easily attained task was set. The outcome of this planning process was a set of taut and inflexible plans. A taut plan is one that has no slack built into it. If one unit fails to meet its planned targets, all the other units that rely on the output of the first unit will fail to meet their targets also. An inflexible plan is one that has no capacity for reactions to changing circumstances.

Faced with impossible targets, factories produced a combination of products that enabled their superiors to report plan fulfillment, but the individual items produced did not meet the needs of the other parts of the economy. No factory received exactly the quantity and types of inputs needed, and the economy was unable to respond to changes in circumstances. In practice, the plan for the current year was the outcome of the previous year plus a wished-for but unattainable increment.

Living Standards in the 1980s

Figure 37.8 puts the problems of the Soviet economy in sharp focus. This figure compares the mid-1980s productivity and consumption levels of the Soviet Union with those of the United States, Western Europe (Germany, France and Italy), Japan and Portugal. As you can see, average worker productivity in the Soviet Union, measured by GDP per worker, was less than 40 per cent of real GDP per worker in the United States and lagged considerably behind the other West European countries and Japan. A similar picture is painted by comparing consumption per worker and consumption per person. The capitalist country whose level of productivity and consumption was most similar to that of the Soviet Union is Portugal.

Market Economy Reforms

By 1990, there was widespread dissatisfaction throughout the Soviet Union with the economic planning system. Incomes were falling and the old political order was under severe strain. It was in this climate that a process of transition towards a market economy began. This process had three main elements:

◆ Relaxing central plan enforcement
◆ Deregulating prices
◆ Permitting limited private ownership of firms

Relaxing Central Plan Enforcement   The transition in all three areas was one of gradual change. But the relaxation of central plan enforcement was the fastest and the most far-reaching element of the transition. The idea was that by relaxing central control over the annual plan and permitting the managers of state enterprises greater freedom to act like the managers of private firms, enterprises would be able to respond to changing

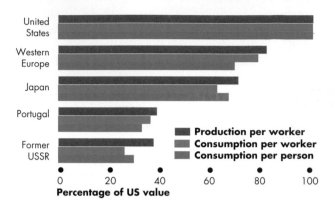

FIGURE 37.8

Productivity in the Soviet Union and Other Countries

Productivity per worker in the Soviet Union in the mid-1980s was less than 40 per cent of its level in the United States and similar to the level in Portugal. Consumption per worker and consumption per person were even lower at less than 30 per cent of the US level. The Soviet Union lagged considerably behind Western Europe and Japan in both GDP and consumption.

Source: Abram Bergson, 'The USSR Before the Fall: How Poor and Why', *Journal of Economic Perspectives*, Volume 5, Number 4, Fall, 1991, pp. 29–44.

circumstances without having to wait for orders from the central planners.

Deregulating Prices   Price deregulation was gradual and covered a limited range of products. The idea of removing price controls was to allow the price mechanism to allocate scarce resources to their highest-value uses. Shortages would disappear and be replaced by available but in some cases expensive goods and services. Higher prices would strengthen the incentive for producers to increase the quantities supplied.

Permitting Limited Private Ownership of Firms
The move towards the private ownership of firms was extremely gradual. The idea here was that enterprising individuals would be able to move quickly to seize profit opportunities by responding to price signals much more rapidly than the replaced planning system could respond to shortages and bottlenecks. But the transition process ran into problems.

Transition Problems

Three major problems confront Russia and the other republics of the former Soviet Union that complicate their transition to the capitalist market economic system. They are:

◆ Value and legal systems alien to capitalism
◆ Collapse of traditional trade flows
◆ Fiscal crisis

Value and Legal Systems   Fifty years of socialist dictatorship has left a legacy of values and memories alien to the rapid and successful establishment of a capitalist, market economy. The political leaders and people of the former Soviet Union have no personal memories of free political institutions and markets. They have been educated, both formally and informally, to believe in a political creed in which traders and speculators are not just shady characters but criminals. Unlearning these values will be a slow and perhaps painful process.

The legal system is also unsuited to the needs of a market economy in two ways. First, there are no well-established property rights and methods of protecting these rights. Second, and more important, there is no tradition for the government to behave like individuals and firms before the rule of law. In the Soviet system, the government *was* the law. Its economic plan and the arbitrary decisions made by the superiors at each level in the hierarchy were the only law that counted. Rational, self-promoting actions taken outside the plan were illegal. It will take a long time to establish a legal system based on private property rights and the rule of law.

Collapse of Traditional Trade Flows   When a centrally administered empire collapses the ensuing political reorganization can have devastating economic consequences. The most serious of these is the collapse of traditional trade flows. The Soviet Union was a highly interdependent grouping of republics organized on a wheel-hub basis with Moscow at its centre. The most heavily dependent republic, Belarus, delivered 70 per cent of its output to other republics and received a similar value of goods from the other republics. Even the least dependent republic, Kazakhstan, traded 30 per cent of its production with the other republics. The vast amount of inter-republic trade, managed by the central planners and channelled through the Moscow hub, meant that individual enterprise managers had little knowledge of where their products were finally used or of where their inputs originated.

With the collapse of the central plan, managers must search for supplies and for markets. Because they have not yet built new networks of information, shortages of raw materials and other material inputs are common and the lack of markets stunts production. This problem can be solved by the activities of specialist traders and speculators, but the emergence of intermediaries is proving to be slow because of political attitudes towards this type of activity.

Fiscal Crisis   Under its central planning system, the central government of the Soviet Union collected taxes in an arbitrary way. One source of revenue was a tax on consumer goods, the rate of which was increased to eliminate shortages. With prices now being free to adjust to eliminate shortages, this source of government revenue has dried up. Another source (the major source) of revenue was the profits of the state enterprises. Because the state owned these enterprises, it also received the profits. With the collapse of central planning and the decentralization of control and privatization of state enterprises, this source of revenue has also declined.

Money played virtually no role in the Soviet Union's system of central planning. Workers received their wages in currency and used it to purchase consumer goods and services. But for the state enterprises and the government, money was just a unit for keeping records. With the collapse of central planning, money became more important, especially for the government. And with the loss of its traditional sources of revenue but no cut in its spending, a government budget deficit emerged. The government was forced to cover this deficit by printing money, and the result was inflation. The inflation rate during the final six months of the life of the Soviet Union – the first half of 1991 – reached close to 200 per cent and it was on a rising path. By 1992 it had reached 1,300 per cent, where it remained throughout1993. But inflation fell in 1994 to 200 per cent a year and was in prospect of being lowered to less than 20 per cent a year in 1996 – see *Reading Between the Lines* on pp. 1000–1001.

Economic Transition in Central Europe

The Czech and Slovak republics, East Germany, Hungary and Poland – formerly planned economies of Central Europe – have also made transitions to market economies. Let's take a look at the transition process in these countries.

East Germany

On 3 October 1990, the 16 million people of East Germany became citizens of a new united Germany, a country with a combined population of 80 million. Even before the formal reunification of the two parts of Germany, East Germany had begun to dismantle its Soviet-style planning system and replace it with a market economy.

The former East Germany adopted the monetary system of West Germany, deregulated its prices and opened itself up to free trade with its western partner. State enterprises were permitted to fail in competition with private western firms, private firms were permitted to open up in the former East Germany and a massive sell-off of state enterprises took place.

The process of selling state enterprises began with the creation of a state corporation called Treuhandanstalt (which roughly translates as 'Trust Corporation') which took over the assets of the almost 11,000 state enterprises of East Germany. The idea was to sell off these enterprises in an orderly way over a period of a few years. In its first year of operation, Treuhandanstalt disposed of more than 4,000 firms. Most of these firms were sold to the private sector but about 900 firms were closed down or merged with other firms. By the mid-1990s, the process of privatization was far advanced.

The loss of jobs resulting from this rapid shake-out of state enterprises was large. Even by July 1990, before the two Germanies were reunited, unemployment in East Germany had reached one-third of the labour force. The unemployment rate in East Germany has remained high and will continue to be high for some years. But the safety net of the West German social security system is cushioning the blow to individual workers and their families.

East Germany has no fiscal policy crisis and no inflation problem. It has adopted the West German taxation and monetary systems and has assured financial stability. But the transition for East Germany will last for several more years, even though it will be the most rapid transition imaginable.

Czech Republic and Slovak Republic

Czechoslovakia removed its communist government in what was called the 'Velvet Revolution' in November 1989 and almost immediately embarked on a programme of economic reforms aimed at replacing its centrally planned economy with a market system.

The first step in the transition was the freeing of wages, prices and interest rates. This step was accomplished quickly but the emergence of well-functioning markets did not immediately follow. Financial markets were especially nervous and a shortage of liquidity created a financial crisis.

The second step in the transition was privatization. Czechoslovakia pursued a so-called two-track policy of 'little privatization' and 'big privatization'. 'Little privatization' is the sale or, where possible, the return to their former owners, of small businesses and shops. 'Big privatization' is the sale of shares in large industrial enterprises. One feature of this privatization process is the issue of vouchers to citizens that can be used to buy shares in former state enterprises.

Czechoslovakia's transition was slowed down by the decision of its people to divide into two parts, the Czech Republic and the Slovak Republic. Real GDP in Czechoslovakia fell by 16 per cent in 1991 and by a further 8.5 per cent in 1992. But in 1993, the two new countries turned the corner. Real GDP was roughly constant in the Czech Republic and increased by 1 per cent in the Slovak Republic. Both economies expanded in 1994.

These republics not only had a fairly rapid transition to an expanding market economy, but also avoided the worst excesses of inflation. The peak inflation rate, in 1991, was 59 per cent. By 1994, the rate of increase in consumer prices had fallen to 18 per cent in the Slovak Republic and to 9 per cent in the Czech Republic. Unemployment rates were also low in these countries – climbing to a peak of 16 per cent in the Slovak Republic and to only 4 per cent in the Czech Republic.

Hungary

Hungary has been in a long transition towards a capitalist market economy. The process began in the 1960s when central planning was replaced by decentralized planning based on a price system. It has also established a taxation system similar to that in the market economies. But the privatization of large-scale industry began only in the 1990s and proceeded slowly.

Because of its gradualism, Hungary's transition has been less disruptive than that in Russia and the other countries of the former Soviet Union. But

Hungary has felt the repercussions of the economic restructuring of the other East European countries with which it has traditionally had the strongest trade links, so it suffered some modest economic decline in its transition. Real GDP fell by 10 per cent in 1991, Hungary's worst year, and began to grow again only in 1994.

Like the Czech and Slovak Republics, Hungary has avoided rampant inflation (consumer prices have increased at a steady 20–30 per cent throughout the 1990s) and has had modest unemployment (climbing to a peak of 12 per cent).

Poland

Severe shortages, black markets and inflation were the jumping-off point for Poland's journey towards a market economy, which began in September 1989 when a non-communist government that included members of the trade union Solidarity took office. The new government has deregulated prices, and black markets have disappeared. It has also pursued a policy of extreme financial restraint, bringing the state budget and inflation under control.

Privatization has also been on a fast track in Poland. Under the a 'Mass Privatization Scheme', the shares of 400 state enterprises have been transferred through a Privatization Fund to the entire adult population. This method of privatization creates a giant insurance company that owns most of the production enterprises and that is in turn owned by private shareholders.

The economy of Poland has responded well to these measures. Real GDP fell in 1989 and 1990 by a total of 20 per cent, but by 1992 it was growing again. The growth rate increased in both 1993 and 1994. At the same time, Poland brought a severe inflation under control. It cut the rate at which consumer prices were rising from 600 per cent a year in 1993 to only 30 per cent a year in 1994. The transition brought more unemployment in Poland than it did in the other countries we've just looked at. Its rate climbed each year to 1994, by which time it had reached 17 per cent.

We've seen that economic decline accompanied the economic transition of the countries of the former Soviet Union and Central Europe. Real GDP has fallen in every country and in Russia by an extremely large amount. But the rate of output loss varies and in some cases is modest.

The economic change that is taking place in another part of the world, East Asia, is equally as profound as that in the transition economies that we've just studied. But there the process is accompanied by rapid and unprecedented expansion. Let's now turn our attention to this region. We'll begin by studying China.

China's Emerging Market Economy

China is the world's largest country. In 1994, its population exceeded 1.2 billion – almost a quarter of the world's population. Chinese civilization is ancient and has a splendid history, but the modern nation – the People's Republic of China – dates only from 1949. Table 37.2 gives a compact summary of key periods in the economic history of the People's Republic.

Modern China began when a revolutionary communist movement, led by Mao Zedong, captured control of the country and forced its previous leader, Chiang Kai-shek (Jiang Jie-shi), on to the island of Formosa – now Taiwan.

During the early years of the People's Republic, urban manufacturing industry was taken over and operated by the state and farms were collectivized. Also primary emphasis was placed on the production of capital equipment.

The Great Leap Forward

In 1958, Mao Zedong set the Chinese economy on what he called a **Great Leap Forward**, an economic plan based on small-scale, labour-intensive production. The Great Leap Forward paid little or no attention to linking individual pay to individual effort. Instead, a revolutionary commitment to the success of collective plans was relied upon. The Great Leap Forward was an economic failure. Productivity increased, but so slowly that living standards hardly changed. In the agricultural sector, massive injections of modern, high-yield seeds, improved irrigation and chemical fertilizers were insufficient to enable China to feed its population. The country became the world's largest importer of grains, edible vegetable oils and even raw cotton.

The popular explanation within China for poor performance, especially in agriculture, was that the

TABLE 37.2

Key Periods in the Economic History of the People's Republic of China

Period	Main economic events/characteristics
1949	◆ People's Republic of China established under Mao Zedong
1949–1952	◆ Economy centralized under a new communist government
	◆ Emphasis on heavy industry and 'socialist transformation'
1952–1957	◆ First five-year plan
1958–1960	◆ The Great Leap Forward: an economic reform plan based on labour-intensive production methods
	◆ Massive failure
1966	◆ Cultural Revolution: revolutionary zealots
1976	◆ Death of Mao Zedong
1978	◆ Deng Xiaoping's reforms: liberalization of agriculture and introduction of individual incentives
	◆ Growth rates accelerated
1989	◆ Democracy movement; government crackdown
1990s	◆ Continued rapid economic growth

country had reached the limits of its arable land and that its population explosion was so enormous that agriculture was being forced to use substandard areas for farming. But it is much more likely that the key problem was the adoption of inefficient techniques. A further problem was that the revolutionary and ideological motivation for the Great Leap Forward degenerated into what came to be called the Cultural Revolution. Revolutionary zealots denounced productive managers, engineers, scientists and scholars, and banished them to the life of the peasant. Schools and universities were closed and the accumulation of human capital was severely disrupted.

Deng Xiaoping's Reforms

By 1978, two years after the death of Mao Zedong, the new Chinese leader, Deng Xiaoping, proclaimed major economic reforms. Collectivized agriculture was abolished. Agricultural land was distributed among households on long-term leases. In exchange for a lease, a household agreed to pay a fixed tax

and contracted to sell part of its output to the state. But the household made its own decisions on cropping patterns, the quantity and types of fertilizers and other inputs to use, and also hired its own workers. Markets for farm produce were liberalized and farmers received higher prices for their output. Also the state increased the prices it paid to farmers, especially for cotton and other non-grain crops.

The results of Deng Xiaoping's reforms have been astounding. Annual growth rates of output of cotton and oil-bearing crops increased a staggering 14-fold. Soybean production, which had been declining at an annual rate of 1 per cent between 1957 and 1978, now started to grow at 4 per cent a year. Growth rates of yields per hectare also increased dramatically. By 1984, a country that six years earlier had been the world's largest importer of agricultural products became a food exporter!

China has gone even further and is encouraging foreign investment and joint ventures. In addition, capital markets are being created, including a stock market.

Motivated partly by political considerations, China proclaims the virtues of what it calls the 'one country, two systems' approach to economic management. One political source of this movement is the existence of two capitalist enclaves in which China has a close interest – Taiwan and Hong Kong. China claims sovereignty over Taiwan. As such, it wants to create an atmosphere in which it becomes possible for China to be 'reunified' at some future date. Hong Kong, a UK crown colony, is currently leased by the United Kingdom from China and that lease terminates in 1997. When the lease expires, Hong Kong will become part of China. Anxious not to damage the economic prosperity of Hong Kong, China proposes to continue operating Hong Kong as a capitalist economy. But capitalist 'islands' are also emerging in other cities such as Hong Kong's close neighbour Guangzhou, the capital of the most dynamic province, Guangdong, and Shanghai.

The results of this move towards capitalism in China are summarized in the country's dramatic real GDP growth statistics. Between 1978 and 1994, real GDP per person grew at an average rate of 7.5 per cent a year – a 3.2-fold increase in income per person over the 16-year period. Between 1982 and 1988, real GDP per person grew at 7.8 per cent a year, and between 1991 and 1994, it grew at 9.5 per cent a year.

No one knows how long China can keep growing at rates like these. Part of the problem of forecasting its future growth is the fact that past growth is the combined effect of becoming more efficient and expanding production possibilities. Figure 37.9 illustrates the distinction between these two sources of growth. In 1978, China's production possibility frontier was PPF_{78}. But because it was using an inefficient system of central economic planning, China was wasting resources and was producing at a point such as A, *inside* its production possibility frontier. The economic reforms of 1978 helped China's economy to become more efficient and to move closer to its *PPF*. At the same time, the reforms increased the incentives to save and invest and also increased the flow of foreign capital and enterprise into China. As a result, over the years, the country's production possibilities have expanded. By 1994, the production possibility frontier had shifted outward to PPF_{94}. Production expanded and in 1994 it was at point B and closer to its *PPF* than it had been in 1978 before the reforms. The production of consumption goods

increased almost threefold from C_{78} to C_{94} and the production of capital goods increased more than threefold from K_{78} to K_{94}.

Once China's economy becomes efficient and operates on the *PPF*, the growth rate will probably slow somewhat. Whether it will slow to the rates of Hong Kong and Singapore – a growth of income per person of around 5 per cent a year – or to the rate of the United States or average European Union country – a growth rate of around 2–2.5 per cent a year – is impossible to tell. But on its 1990s growth path, China is closing the gap with the United States and is set to become the world's largest economy before the year 2000[2].

China is not only experiencing rapid growth of real income per person but also increasing its international competitiveness. Its exports have grown during the 1980s and 1990s at a much faster rate than GDP. In 1994, China's exports were 17 per cent of GDP.

How has China achieved this dramatic success?

China's Success

China's success in achieving a high rate of economic growth has resulted from four features of its reforms[3]. They are:

◆ Massive rate of entry of new non-state firms

◆ Large increases in the productivity and profitability of state firms

◆ An efficient taxation system

◆ Gradual price deregulation

Entry of Non-state Firms   The most rapidly growing sector of the Chinese economy is industrial firms located in rural areas. In recent years, this sector has grown at an annual rate of 17.5 per cent. In 1978, it produced 22 per cent of the nation's

FIGURE 37.9

Economic Growth in China

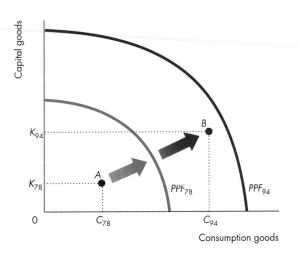

When China began its reforms in 1978, it was operating *inside* its production possibility frontier, PPF_{78}, at a point such as A, where it produced C_{78} consumption goods and K_{78} capital goods. Capital accumulation and technological change shifted the *PPF* outward to PPF_{94}. China's income growth has resulted partly from moving closer to its *PPF* and partly from a shifting *PPF*. By 1994, the economy was producing at a point such as B, where it produced C_{94} consumption goods and K_{94} capital goods.

---

[2] Because the population of China is 4.5 times that of the United States, when income per person in China exceeds 22 per cent of that in the United States, the gross domestic product of China will exceed that of the United States. In 1994, according to the most generous estimates, real income per person in China was about 17 per cent of that in the United States. If China and the United States maintain their current growth rates, real GDP in China will exceed that in the United States by about 1998.

[3] This section is based on a paper by John McMillan and Barry Naughton, 'How to Reform a Planned Economy: Lessons from China', Graduate School of International Relations and Pacific Studies, University of California, San Diego, 1991.

industrial output and by 1993, it was producing close to 50 per cent of total industrial output. By contrast, the state-owned firms – the firms organized by the state under its national plan – shrank (relatively) from producing 78 per cent of total output in 1978 to about 50 per cent in the mid-1990s.

The entry of new firms created a dramatic increase in competition both among the new firms and between the new firms and the state firms. This competition spurred both non-state and state firms into greater efficiency and productivity.

Increases in Productivity and Profitability of State Firms   China has not privatized its economy by selling state firms. Instead, privatization has come from the entry of new firms. State firms have continued to operate and the government has a strong incentive to ensure that these firms are profitable. If state firms make no profit, the government collects no taxes from them.

To achieve the greatest possible profit and tax revenue, the Chinese economic planners have changed the incentives faced by the managers of state enterprises to resemble those of the market incentives faced by non-state firms. Managers of state-owned firms are paid according to the firm's performance – similar to managers in private firms.

The Chinese system gives incentives for managers of state enterprises to be extremely enterprising and productive. As a result of this new system, the Chinese government is now able to auction off top management jobs. Potential managers bid for the right to be manager. The manager offering the best promise of performance, backed by a commitment of personal wealth, is the one who gets the job.

Efficient Taxation System   Firms (both private and state firms) are taxed but the tax system is unusual and different from that in our own economy. Firms are required to pay a fixed amount of profit to the government. Once that fixed amount of tax has been paid, the firm keeps any additional profit made. In contrast, the tax system in Western Europe requires firms to pay a fixed percentage of their profits in tax. Thus in the European Union, more profit means higher taxes, while in China, taxes are set independently of a firm's profit level. The Chinese system creates much stronger incentives than does our own system for firms to seek out and pursue profitable ventures.

Gradual Price Reform   China has not abandoned planning its prices. The socialist planning system keeps the prices of manufactured goods fairly high and keeps domestic prices higher than world prices. This pricing arrangement makes private enterprise production in China extremely profitable. In 1978, when the non-state sector was small, the profit rate in that sector was almost 40 per cent. With such a high profit rate, there was a tremendous incentive for enterprising people to find niches and engage in creative and productive activity. The forces of competition have gradually lowered prices. By 1990, rates of return had fallen to 10 per cent. The price movements were gradual. There was no big bang adjustment of prices – no abandonment of the planning mechanism and introduction of a rip-roaring free market system.

Growing Out of the Plan   As a result of the reforms adopted in the 1970s and pursued vigorously since that time, the Chinese economy has gradually become a much more market-oriented economy and is, in effect, growing out of its central plan[4]. The proportion of the economy accounted for by private enterprise and market-determined prices has gradually increased and the proportion accounted for by state enterprises and planned and regulated prices has gradually decreased.

To sustain this process, changes in fiscal policy and monetary policy have been necessary. The reform of the economy has entailed the redesigning of the tax system. In a centrally planned economy, the government's tax revenues come directly through its pricing policy. Also the government, as the controller of all financial institutions, receives all of the nation's saving. When the central planning system is replaced by the market system, the government must establish a tax collection agency similar to the Inland Revenue in the United Kingdom. Also, it must establish financial markets so that households' savings can be channelled into the growing private firms to finance their investment in new buildings, plant and equipment.

Despite the reform of its tax system, the government of China spends more than it receives in tax revenue and covers its deficit by the creation of

---

[4] Barry Naughton, *Growing Out of the Plan: Chinese Economic Reform, 1978–90*, Paper, Graduate School of International Relations and Pacific Studies, University of California, San Diego, 1992.

money. The result is inflation. But inflation in China is not out of control because the rapid growth of economic activity absorbs a great deal of the new money.

Whether China has found a way of making the transition from socialism to capitalism relatively painless is controversial. The violent suppression of the democracy movement in Tiananmen Square in the summer of 1989 suggests that China might have bought economic gains at the expense of political freedoms. But the experiment in comparative *economic* systems currently going on in China is one of the most exciting that the world has seen. Economists of all shades of political opinion will closely watch its outcome, and its lessons will be of enormous value for future generations – whatever these lessons turn out to be.

R E V I E W

◆ China embarked on a process of economic reform in 1978 that created a dynamic market economy alongside its socialist economy.

◆ Since 1978, China's rate of economic expansion has been rapid and income per person has increased more than threefold.

◆ China's success has resulted from unleashing market incentives.

Other Economic Miracles in East Asia

Four other East Asian economies that have expanded quickly are Hong Kong, Singapore, Taiwan and South Korea. Figure 37.10 shows just how rapidly these countries have grown compared with the United Kingdom. Hong Kong has overtaken the United Kingdom, and Singapore caught up with the United Kingdom in 1992. Why have these countries experienced such rapid income growth?

The first and fundamental reason is that these countries have developed economic institutions that support an entrepreneurial spirit and encourage specialization and the division of labour. The most basic of these institutions are the rule of law,

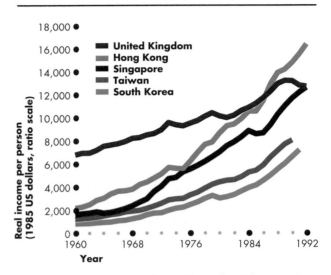

FIGURE 37.10

Economic Growth in Four Asian Economies and the United Kingdom

Economic growth in Hong Kong, Singapore, Taiwan and South Korea is more rapid than in the United Kingdom and income per person in each of these four countries is converging on that in the United Kingdom. Hong Kong has overtaken the United Kingdom and Singapore has caught up.

Source: Robert Summers and Alan Heston, New computer diskette (Mark 5.5), 15 June 1993, distributed by the National Bureau of Economic Research to update The Penn World Table (Mark 5): An Expanded Set of International Comparisons, 1950–1988, *Quarterly*

property rights and a well-functioning judicial system together with stable money. Neither domestic citizens nor foreigners have any fear about the security of their property or the stability of the currency in these countries.

The second reason for economic growth in these countries is that they have opened their borders to foreign competition and specialized in the activities at which they have a comparative advantage. As their incomes have grown and their labour forces have become more experienced, the particular goods and services in which they have specialized have changed. During the 1960s, textiles were an important part of the production and international trade of these countries. During the 1970s, electronic manufactures became more important. Today, Singapore and Hong Kong are at the forefront of the latest information technologies and Singapore is moving into bio-technologies.

Russia's Macroeconomic Performance

The Essence of the Story

THE WALL STREET JOURNAL, 28 NOVEMBER 1994

Russia's economic news: it's not all bad

Steve Leisman

MOSCOW—Russia's stormy transition to a market economy is a story of fired ministers, a plunging rouble, soaring inflation, and even violence. The cabinet has been reshuffled six times, most recently last month, and a parliament has been dissolved by military force.

Yet despite the fears about hyperinflation and an end to economic liberalisation that were expressed after each government shake-up, the reforms have shown surprisingly resilience. Indeed, the economy – albeit still precarious – has been having its best year since reforms began in 1992, when Russia broke with its socialist past by freeing prices.

After three years of decline following the collapse of the Soviet Union, Russia's potentially vast economy started growing again in October. Prices arc expected to rise a relatively modest 150% this year, compared with 840% in 1993. Outside investment has begun to filter in, with estimates that foreigners this year pumped (in) $2.5 billion to $3 billion...

President Boris Yeltsen gathered hundreds of legislative, regional and industrial leaders in the Kremlin to drum up enthusiasm for the economy and continued reforms. 'Until now, the Russian economy has remained in crisis. Now, we are close to overcoming that stage,' Mr Yeltsin said. 'In 1995, we'll start an offensive. We will complete financial stabilisation and move on to creating conditions for economic revival and growth.'...

The country still lacks coherent tax and civil codes. The government keeps promising tax reform...but it hasn't delivered...

The government's hope these days is that if it tames inflation, other reforms will fall into line. The 1995 budget proposal, now before Parliament, aims to lower inflation to between 1% and 1.5% monthly. It was 11.8% in October...

If a (budget) proposal similar to the current one passes, lending institutions such as the World Bank and International Monetary Fund are ready to inject as much as $13 billion into Russia, covering half the projected budget deficit of 7.8% of gross domestic product.... An additional $6 billion could come from the IMF to support the rouble in a plan to peg it to the dollar.

■ Russia's transition to a market economy has been accompanied by falling real GDP, a falling rouble, and high inflation.

■ But after three years of decline, Russia's economy started growing again in October 1994. Inflation in 1994 was expected to be 150 per cent a year, down from 840 per cent a year in 1993.

■ Foreign investment in 1994 was expected to be $2.5–3 billion.

■ The core of the government's plan is to lower inflation from its October 1994 rate of 11.8 per cent a month to between 1 per cent and 1.5 per cent a month.

■ Loans of $13 billion from the World Bank and International Monetary Fund (IMF) would be used to cover half the projected government budget deficit of 7.8 per cent of GDP.

Economic Analysis

■ Figure 1 shows the International Monetary Fund's (IMF) estimates of Russia's real GDP growth rate between 1991 and 1994 and its projections for 1995 and 1996.

■ Although the news article says that real GDP grew in October 1994, the IMF estimate of the growth rate for 1994 and its projected growth rate for 1995 are negative – they show a *fall* in real GDP.

■ Figure 2 shows the IMF's estimates of Russia's inflation between 1991 and 1994 and its projections for 1995 and 1996.

■ Inflation peaked at 1,350 per cent in 1992 and was more than 800 per cent in 1993. The IMF projects an inflation rate of 143 per cent for 1995.

■ The news article reports target inflation rate of 1–1.5 per cent a month which translates to a range of 13–20 per cent a year.

■ Even if Russia does not lower its inflation rate further but maintains its current rate, it will avoid *hyperinflation.*

■ Russia's problem of eliminating inflation arises from its government budget deficit. With no tax reform,

Russia has a government budget deficit of $26 billion, which is 7.8 per cent of GDP.

■ Even if the World Bank and IMF lend Russia $13 billion to finance half of its budget deficit, Russia must find the other $13 billion.

■ Without a well functioning capital market, Russia will print new money to finance the other half of its deficit.

■ It is unlikely that Russia can sell bonds to foreigners.

■ So even if the IMF and World Bank finance half of Russia's government deficit, this financing is likely to be sufficient only to lower the inflation rate to around half its present level.

■ Even if Russia could lower its inflation rate to 13–20 per cent a year, talk of pegging the rouble to the dollar is misplaced.

■ The rouble will depreciate against the dollar at a rate that reflects the gap between the Russian and US inflation rates.

■ In 1995 the US inflation rate was about 3 per cent a year, so a good deal of rouble depreciation remains likely.

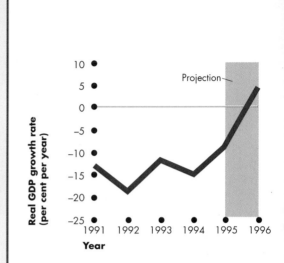

Figure 1 Real GDP growth

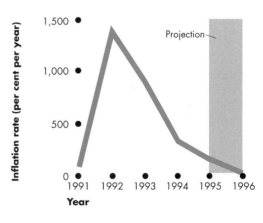

Figure 2 Inflation rate

Source: Figures 1 and Figure 2 are based on data from *World Economic Outlook,* May 1995, International Monetary Fund, Washington, DC.

The scale of international trade undertaken by some of these countries is hard to imagine. For example, Singapore's imports and exports exceed its gross domestic product by 50 per cent. (In contrast, UK imports and exports are about 30 per cent of gross domestic product.)

The third source of rapid growth in these countries is a high saving rate and well-organized stock markets, through which both domestic and international savings are channelled into firms. During the 1990s, the returns on these stock markets have been large. For example, between January 1992 and October 1994, while the New York Stock Exchange rose by less than 20 per cent, average prices on the East Asian stock markets more than doubled.

Government economic policy is the fourth source of rapid economic growth. For Hong Kong, government policy is a hands-off policy. For Singapore, at the opposite extreme, government operates a bit like the board of directors of a corporation. It seeks out strategically advantageous areas in which to expand and then takes actions to stimulate private enterprise in those areas. Government intervention in Singapore is successful, probably because it is disciplined by global competition and is not directed towards protecting vested interests.

A key role that governments have played in all the Asian miracle economies, and this is the fifth source of economic success, is to educate the population to a high standard that enables the work-force to cope effectively with new technologies and rapid change.

The lessons that are being learned from the success stories of East Asia are reverberating around the world and beginning to influence countries where success is so far more limited. But new success stories are beginning to emerge on all continents. In Africa, Botswana and the Republic of South Africa are showing signs of joining the ranks of the rapid growth economies. In South and Central America, Argentina, Brazil, Chile and Mexico are on the move. In the Middle East, Israel is growing at a rapid rate. And in Asia, India,

Indonesia, Malaysia and Thailand are performing well. While economic forecasting is much more hazardous than weather forecasting, there are definite signs that rapid and possibly sustained income growth is happening in many countries and in all regions of the world.

REVIEW

◆ Rapid growth of East Asian economies has led to Hong Kong overtaking the United Kingdom in terms of GDP per person and Singapore catching up.

◆ These countries have developed institutions that support and foster the entrepreneurial spirit.

◆ Competition, high savings and investment in education have contributed to the high growth of these countries.

◆ ◆ ◆ ◆ Rapid income growth in Asia and other parts of the world is increasing the number of people who live in rich, industrial countries. The transition to a market economy is changing Central Europe. But the world has seen change of historical proportions before. The transformation of the economies of formerly war-torn Germany and Japan into the economic powerhouses of today is one example. Throughout all this change – past, present and future – our knowledge and understanding of the economic forces that produce the change and are unleashed by it have been getting gradually better. There remains a great deal that we do not understand. But we have made some progress. The economic principles presented in this book summarize this progress and the current state of knowledge. As the world continues to change, you will need a compass to guide you into unknown terrain. The principles of economics are that compass!

SUMMARY

A Snapshot of the World Economy

More than 5 billion people live in 181 countries, 23 of which are industrial, 130 developing and 28 economies in transition. In 1990, average annual income per person was $4,500 and ranged from $18,450 in the United States to $365 in the African country of Chad. The poorest 20 per cent of the world's population live in countries that earn only 4.5 per cent of world income. The richest 20 per cent of the world's population lives in countries that earn 63 per cent of world income. World average income per person grew at an average rate of 2.6 per cent a year during the 10 years 1986–95 and fluctuated between a high of 4.7 per cent in 1988 and a low of 0.7 per cent in 1991. Income growth was slower in industrial countries (2.2 per cent per year) than in developing countries (5.1 per cent per year) and income growth was faster in Asia (7.5 per cent per year) than in Africa (1.1 per cent per year). In the countries in transition – the former Soviet Union and other Central European countries – incomes fell, and in the most extreme cases by more than they fell in the United States 60 years earlier during the Great Depression. (pp. 982–985)

Alternative Economic Systems

The economic problem is the universal fact of scarcity. Different economic systems deliver different solutions to the economic problem determining *what*, *how*, and *for whom* goods and services are produced. Alternative economic systems vary in two dimensions: ownership of capital and land and the incentives people face. Capital and land may be owned by individuals, the state, or a mixture of the two. Incentives may be created by market prices, laws and regulations, or a mixture of the two.

Economic systems differ in the ways in which they combine ownership and incentive arrangements. Capitalism is based on the private ownership of capital and land and on market price incentives. Socialism is based on state ownership of capital and land and incentives based on laws and regulations. Market socialism combines state ownership of capital and land with incentives based on a mixture of market and administered prices. Welfare state capitalism combines the private ownership of capital and land with state intervention in markets that change the price signals that people respond to. (pp. 985–990)

Economic Transition in Russia and Central Europe

The economy of the Soviet Union (1917–91) was coordinated by a central planning mechanism that involved: an administrative hierarchy, an iterative planning process, legally binding commands, and taut and inflexible plans. Money played only a minor role in the economy of the Soviet Union.

The Soviet economy grew in excess of 5 per cent per year before 1970 and more slowly during the 1970s, and began to stagnate during the 1980s. Soviet economic performance deteriorated because the economy shifted its emphasis in production from capital goods to consumption goods, and was hit by serious external shocks which its taut and inflexible planning system was incapable of coping with.

By the end of the 1980s, the Soviet Union began a process of transition towards the market economy. This process had three main elements: the relaxation of central plan enforcement, the deregulation of prices and the introduction of limited private ownership of firms. The transition was a process of gradual change but it ran into severe problems. The most important were: value and legal systems alien to capitalism, the collapse of traditional trade flows and the emergence of a large state budget deficit and inflation.

The formerly planned economies of Czechoslovakia, East Germany, Hungary and Poland are also making transitions to market economies. East Germany's transition has been the most dramatic and the most complete because its economy has been absorbed into that of West Germany. The Czech Republic and the Slovak Republic have deregulated wages, prices and interest rates and are privatizing industry by returning small businesses and shops to their former owners and by issuing their citizens with vouchers that they can use to buy shares in former state enterprises. Hungary began the process of moving towards a market economy during the 1960s when central planning was replaced by decentralized planning. Hungary has established a taxation system similar to that in the market economies. But the privatization of large-scale industry began only in the 1990s and is proceeding slowly. Poland has deregulated prices, pursued a policy of financial restraint that has brought inflation under control, and put privatization on a fast track. (pp. 990–995)

China's Emerging Market Economy

Since the foundation of the People's Republic of China, economic management has been through turbulent changes. At first, China used the Soviet system of central planning. It then introduced the Great Leap Forward, which in turn degenerated into the Cultural Revolution. China grew quickly initially with heavy reliance on state planning and capital accumulation, but growth soon slowed and,

at times, income per person actually fell. In 1978, China revolutionized its economic management, placing greater emphasis on private incentives and markets. As a consequence, productivity grew at a rapid rate and income per person increased.

China's high rate of economic growth has resulted from competition between private and state firms, productivity increases in state firms, an efficient taxation system and price deregulation. (pp. 995–999)

Other Economic Miracles in East Asia

Hong Kong, Singapore, Taiwan and South Korea – four small East Asian economies – have experienced rapid growth. This has resulted from factors such as the institution of the rule of law, property rights and the judicial system, stable money, borders that are open to foreign competition, a high saving rate and growth-oriented government economic policy. (pp. 999–1002)

KEY ELEMENTS

Key Terms

Capitalism, 987
Central plan, 989
Decentralized planning, 987
Great Leap Forward, 995
Lorenz curve, 982
Market socialism, 987
Socialism, 987
Welfare state capitalism, 987

◆ Key Figures and Tables

Figure 37.1 World Income Per Person in 1990, 983
Figure 37.2 The World Lorenz Curve: 1990, 984
Figure 37.4 The Fundamental Economic Problem, 985
Figure 37.5 Alternative Economic Systems, 987
Figure 37.6 Capitalism's Solution to the Economic Problem, 988
Figure 37.7 Socialism's Solution to the Economic Problem, 989
Figure 37.10 Economic Growth in Four Asian Economies and the United States, 999
Table 37.1 Key Periods in the Economic History of the Soviet Union, 990
Table 37.2 Key Periods in the Economic History of the People's Republic of China, 996

REVIEW QUESTIONS

1 What are the average incomes per person in the main regions and types of countries?

2 Compare the distribution of income among families in the United Kingdom with the distribution of income among countries in the world. Which distribution is more unequal?

3 What is the fundamental economic problem that any economic system must cope with?

4 What are the main economic systems? Set out the key features of each.

5 Give examples of countries that are capitalist, socialist, market socialist and welfare state capitalist. (Name some countries other than those in Fig. 37.5.)

6 How does capitalism cope with the economic problem? What determines how much of each good to produce?

7 How does socialism cope with the economic problem? What determines how much of each good to produce?

8 How does market socialism determine the price of each good and the quantity of it produced?

9 List the main economic events in the history of the Soviet Union before its collapse in 1991.

10 Describe the main elements in the Soviet Union's central planning system.

11 Why did the Soviet economy begin to fail in the 1980s?

12 What are the main features of the transition programme in the former Soviet Union?

13 What are the main problems faced by the republics of the former Soviet Union?

14 What are the problems faced by the other East European countries as they make the transition to a market economy?

15 Review the main episodes in China's economic management since 1949.

16 Compare the economic growth performance of the United States and China. What do we learn from this comparison?

17 What are the main episodes in China's economic management since 1949?

18 Explain why China has grown so quickly.

19 What are the lessons of the economic experiment that is going on in China?

20 What are the key elements in the success of the newly industrializing countries of Asia?

PROBLEMS

1 A poor country has 10 per cent of the income of a rich country. The poor country achieves a growth rate of 10 per cent per year and the rich country achieves a growth rate of 5 per cent per year. How many years will it take income in the poor country to catch up with that of the rich country?

2 A poor country has one-tenth of the GDP per person of a rich country. The poor country achieves a growth rate of 8 per cent a year but a population growth of 3 per cent a year. The rich country achieves a growth rate of 3 per cent a year but a population growth of 1/2 per cent a year. How many years will it take the poor country to catch up with the rich country's real GDP per person?

3 Three countries are identified in the figure by *A*, *B* and *C*.

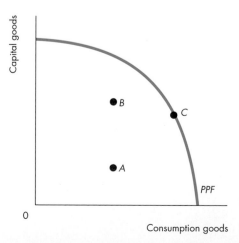

a Which country or countries are most likely to use a market mechanism and which a central planning mechanism?

b Which country is most likely to have the fastest rate of economic growth and which the slowest?

c Which country has the greatest scope for increasing incomes by becoming more efficient in the use of its resources?

d Which country most resembles China today?

e Which country most resembles Russia today?

4 Compare and contrast the methods being used in the former Soviet Union with those of China and explain why the economy of China is growing more rapidly than that of the former Soviet Union.

5 Compare and contrast the methods being used in the former Soviet Union with those of other countries in transition in Central Europe.

6 In 1960, GDP per person was $6,823 in the United Kingdom, $1,256 in Taiwan and $904 in South Korea. In 1990 the respective figures were $13,217, $8,063 and $6,673.

a Extrapolating from past trends, how long will it be before Taiwan catches up with the United Kingdom?

b How long will it be before South Korea catches up with the United Kingdom?

c What do you think has contributed to this phenomenal growth performance?

d Can the United Kingdom do anything to maintain its economic position?

7 Study *Reading Between the Lines* on pp. 1000–1001 and then answer the following questions:

a Why is Russia short of entrepreneurs?

b Why are economic profits available in some industries in Russia today?

c Why will economic profit opportunities eventually become harder to find in Russia?

d How do you think foreign investment can help Russia in its transition from a planned economy?

e How do you think foreign-owned businesses can do profitable business in Russia?

GLOSSARY

Above full-employment equilibrium   A situation in which macroeconomic equilibrium occurs at a level of real GDP above long-run real GDP.

Absolute advantage   A person has an absolute advantage in the production of two goods if by using the same quantities of inputs, that person can produce more of both goods than another person. A country has an absolute advantage if its output per unit of inputs of all goods is larger than that of another country.

Adverse selection   The tendency for people to enter into agreements in which they can use their private information to their own advantage and to the disadvantage of the less-informed party.

Aggregate demand   The relationship between the aggregate quantity of goods and services demanded (real GDP demanded) and the price level (the GDP deflator).

Aggregate hours   The total number of hours worked by all the people employed, both full-time and part-time, during a year.

Aggregate planned expenditure   The expenditure that economic agents (households, firms, governments and foreigners) plan to undertake in given circumstances.

Allocative efficiency   A situation that occurs when no resources are wasted – when no one can be made better off without someone else being made worse off. Allocative efficiency is also called Pareto efficiency.

Anti-trust law   A law that regulates and prohibits certain kinds of market behaviour, such as monopoly and monopolistic practices.

Arc elasticity of demand   The value of elasticity of demand between two points calculated by the average price method.

Automatic fiscal policy   A change in fiscal policy that is triggered by the state of the economy.

Autonomous expenditure   The sum of those components of aggregate planned expenditure that are not influenced by real GDP.

Average cost pricing rule   A rule that sets price equal to average total cost.

Average fixed cost   Total fixed cost per unit of output – total fixed cost divided by output.

Average product   The average productivity of a factor of production – total product divided by the quantity of the factor employed.

Average revenue   The revenue per unit of output sold – total revenue divided by the quantity sold. Average revenue also equals price.

Average total cost   Total cost per unit of output.

Average variable cost   Total variable cost per unit of output.

Balance for official financing   Net increase or decrease in a country's holding of foreign currency reserves.

Balance of payments accounts   A country's record of international trading, borrowing and lending.

Balance of trade   The value of exports minus the value of imports.

Balanced budget   A government budget in which tax revenues and expenditures are equal.

Balanced budget multiplier   The amount by which a simultaneous and equal change in goverment purchases and taxes is multiplied to determine the change in equilibrium expenditure.

Bank   A private firm licensed by the Bank of England under the Banking Act of 1987 to take deposits and make loans and operate in the United Kingdom.

Bank of England   The central bank of the United Kingdom.

Barriers to entry   Legal or natural impediments protecting a firm from competition from potential new entrants.

Barter   The direct exchange of one good or service for other goods and services.

Below full-employment equilibrium   A macroeconomic equilibrium in which potential GDP exceeds real GDP.

Bilateral monopoly   A situation in which there is a single seller (a monopoly) and a single buyer (a monopsony).

Black market   An illegal trading arrangement in which buyers and sellers do business at a price higher than the legally imposed price ceiling.

Bond   A legally enforceable debt obligation to pay specified amounts of money at specified future dates.

Bond market   A market in which the bonds of corporations and governments are traded.

Budget deficit   A government's budget balance that is negative – expenditures exceed tax revenues.

Budget line   The limits to a household's consumption choices.

Budget surplus   A government's budget balance that is positive – tax revenues exceed expenditures.

Building society   A financial intermediary that traditionally obtained its funds from savings deposits (sometimes called share accounts) and that made long-term mortgage loans to home buyers.

Bureaucrat   A hired official who works in a government department at the national or local level and who produces public goods and services.

Business cycle   The periodic but irregular up-and-down movement in economic activity, measured by fluctuations in real GDP and other macroeconomic variables.

Capital   The equipment, buildings, tools and manufactured goods that are used in the production of goods and services.

Capital account   A record of a country's international borrowing and lending transactions.

Capital accumulation   The growth of capital resources.

Capital stock   The stock of plant, equipment, buildings (including residential housing) and unsold finished goods.

Capitalism   An economic system with private ownership of capital and land and incentives based on market prices.

Capture theory   A theory of regulation that states that the regulations are supplied to satisfy the demand of producers to maximize producer surplus – to maximize economic profit.

Cartel   A group of firms that has entered into a collusive agreement to restrict output so as to increase prices and profits.

Central bank   A public authority charged with regulating and controlling a country's monetary policy and financial institutions and markets.

Central plan   A detailed economic blueprint that sets out *what* will be produced, *how*, *when* and *where* it will be produced, and *who* will get what is produced, and that establishes a set of sanctions and rewards designed to ensure that the plan is fulfilled as fully as possible.

Ceteris paribus   Other things being equal – all other relevant things remaining the same.

Change in demand   A change in buyers' plans that occurs when some influence on those plans other than the price of the good changes. It is illustrated by a shift of the demand curve.

Change in supply   A change in sellers' plans that occurs when some influence on those plans other than the price of the good changes. It is illustrated by a shift of the supply curve.

Change in the quantity demanded   A change in buyers' plans that occurs when the price of a good changes but all other influences on buyers' plans remain unchanged. It is illustrated by a movement along the demand curve.

Change in the quantity supplied   A change in sellers' plans that occurs when the price of a good changes but all other influences on sellers' plans remain unchanged. It is illustrated by a movement along the supply curve.

Choke price   The price at which the quantity demanded of a natural resource is zero.

Classical growth theory   A theory of economic growth based on the view that population growth is determined by the level of income per person.

Coase theorem   The proposition that if property rights exist and transactions costs are low, private transactions are efficient – equivalently, there are no externalities.

Collective bargaining   A process of negotiation between representatives of employers and unions.

Collusive agreement   An agreement between two (or more) producers to restrict output so as to increase prices and profits.

Commodity money   A physical commodity that is valued in its own right and is also used as a means of payment

Common Agricultural Policy (CAP)   The agricultural policy implemented by the European Union in member countries.

Company   A firm owned by two or more shareholders.

Comparative advantage   A person or country has a comparative advantage in an activity if that person or country can perform the activity at a lower opportunity cost than anyone else or any other country.

Competition   A situation where individuals and firms are forced into a contest for the command of scarce resources because of scarcity.

Complement   A good that is used in conjunction with another good.

Constant returns to scale   Technological conditions under which a given percentage increase in all the firm's inputs results in the firm's output increasing by the same percentage.

Consumer efficiency   A situation that occurs when consumers cannot make themselves better off by reallocating their budgets.

Consumer equilibrium   A situation in which a consumer has allocated his or her income in the way that maximizes his or her utility.

Consumer surplus The value that the consumer places on a good minus the price paid for it.

Consumption demand The relationship between consumption expenditure and the real interest rate, other things remaining the same.

Consumption expenditure The total payment made by households for consumption goods and services.

Consumption function The relationship between consumption expenditure and disposable income, other things remaining the same.

Contestable market A market structure in which there is one firm (or a small number of firms) and because of freedom of entry and exit, the firm (or firms) faces competition from potential entrants and so operates like a perfectly competitive firm.

Contractionary fiscal policy A decrease in government expenditures or an increase in tax revenues.

Convertible paper money A paper claim to a commodity (such as gold) that circulates as a means of payment.

Copyright A government-sanctioned exclusive right granted to the inventor of a good, service, or productive process to produce, use, and sell the invention for a given number of years.

Corporation A large-scale firm owned by shareholders whose liability is legally limited to the value of their initial investment.

Cost-push inflation Inflation that results from an initial increase in costs.

Creditor nation A country that has invested more in the rest of the world than other countries have invested in it.

Cross elasticity of demand The responsiveness of the demand for a good to the price of a substitute or complement, other things remaining the same. It is calculated as the percentage change in the quantity demanded of the good divided by the percentage change in the price of the substitute or complement.

Cross-section graph A graph that shows the values of an economic variable for different groups in a population at a point in time.

Crowding out The tendency for an increase in government purchases of goods and services to bring a decrease in investment.

Currency The notes and coins that we use today.

Currency depreciation The fall in the value of one currency in terms of another currency.

Currency drain An increase in currency held outside banks.

Current account A record of receipts from the sale of goods and services to foreigners, the payments for goods and services bought from foreigners, the interest income received from and paid to foreigners, and gifts and other transfers (such as foreign aid payments) received from and paid to foreigners.

Cyclical deficit A budget deficit that is present only because real GDP is less than potential GDP and taxes are temporarily low and transfer payments are temporarily high.

Cyclical unemployment The unemployment arising from the slowdown in the pace of economic expansion.

Cyclically adjusted deficit The budget deficit that would occur if the economy were at full employment.

Deadweight loss A measure of allocative inefficiency. It is equal to the loss in total surplus (consumer surplus plus producer surplus) that results from producing less than the efficient level of output.

Debtor nation A country that during its entire history has borrowed more from the rest of the world than it has lent to it.

Decentralized planning An economic system that combines state ownership of capital and land with incentives based on a mixture of market prices and laws and regulations.

Decreasing returns to scale Technological conditions under which a given percentage increase in all the firm's inputs results in the firm's output increasing by a smaller percentage.

Demand The relationship between the quantity of a good that consumers plan to buy and the price of the good, with all other influences on buyers' plans remaining the same. It is described by a demand schedule and illustrated by a demand curve.

Demand curve A curve that shows the relationship between the quantity demanded of a good and its price, all other influences on consumers' planned purchases remaining the same.

Demand-pull inflation Inflation that results from an initial increase in aggregate demand.

Deposit money Deposits at banks and other financial institutions; an accounting entry in an electronic database in the banks' and other financial institutions' computers.

Deposit multiplier The amount by which an increase in bank reserves is multiplied to calculate the increase in bank deposits.

Depreciation The decrease in the value of capital stock or the value of a durable input that results from wear and tear and the passage of time.

Deregulation The removal of regulatory rules to restrict or control economic activity in price setting, product standards, trading standards and the conditions under which firms can enter an industry.

Derived demand   Demand for an item not for its own sake but for use in the production of goods and services.

Desired reserve ratio   Ratio of reserves to deposits that banks consider as prudent to hold in order to meet withdrawals and to carry on their business.

Diminishing marginal rate of substitution   The general tendency for the marginal rate of substitution of one good for another to diminish as a consumer increases consumption of the first good.

Diminishing marginal returns   The tendency for the marginal product of a variable factor eventually to diminish as additional units of the variable factor are employed.

Diminishing marginal utility   The marginal utility that a consumer gets from a good decreases as more of the good is consumed.

Direct relationship   A relationship between two variables that move in the same direction.

Discount rate   The interest rate at which the central bank stands ready to lend reserves to commercial banks.

Discounting   The conversion of a future amount of money to its present value.

Discouraged workers   People who do not have jobs and would like to work but have stopped seeking work.

Discretionary fiscal policy   A policy action that is initiated by the Chancellor of the Exchequer.

Discretionary policy   A policy that responds to the state of the economy in a possibly unique way that uses all the information available, including perceived lessons from past 'mistakes'.

Discrimination   Occurs in the labour market when employment decisions are taken on the basis of ethnic origin or gender rather than ability.

Diseconomies of scale   Technological conditions under which long-run average cost increases as output increases.

Dominant strategy equilibrium   The outcome of a game in which there is a single best strategy (a dominant strategy) for each player, regardless of the strategy of the other players.

Dumping   The sale of a good in a foreign market for a lower price than in the domestic market or for a lower price than its cost of production.

Duopoly   A market structure in which two producers of a good or service compete.

Dynamic comparative advantage   A comparative advantage that a person or country possesses as a result of having specialized in a particular activity and then, as a result of learning-by-doing, becoming the producer with the lowest opportunity cost.

Economic depreciation   The decrease in the market price of a piece of capital over a given period.

Economic efficiency   A situation that occurs when the cost of producing a given output is as low as possible.

Economic growth   The expansion of production possibilities that results from capital accumulation and technological change.

Economic information   Data on prices, quantities and qualities of goods and services and factors of production.

Economic model   A description of some aspect of the economic world that includes only those features of the world that are needed for the purpose at hand.

Economic profit   A firm's total revenue minus its opportunity cost.

Economic rent   The income received by the owner of a factor of production in excess of the amount required to induce that owner to offer the factor for use.

Economic stability   The absence of wide fluctuations in the economic growth rate, the level of employment and average prices.

Economic theory   A generalization that summarizes what we think we understand about the economic choices that people make and the performance of industries and entire economies.

Economics   The study of the choices people make to cope with scarcity.

Economies of scale   Technological conditions under which long-run average cost decreases as output increases.

Economies of scope   Decreases in average total cost made possible by increasing the range of goods produced.

Economy   A mechanism that allocates scarce resources among competing uses.

Efficiency   A point in production where is not possible to produce more of one good without producing less of some other good.

Efficiency wage   The wage rate that maximizes profit.

Efficient market   A market in which the actual price embodies all currently available relevant information.

Elastic   Where a small percentage change in price results in a proportionately larger change in the quantity demanded

Elasticity of supply   The responsiveness of the quantity supplied of a good to a change in its price, other things remaining the same.

Emission charges   Any form of pollution control that uses the market to create incentives for producers to cut pollution emissions

Emission standards   Pollution control in the form of regulations limiting the quantity of pollution emissions.

Employment-to-population ratio   The percentage of people of working age who have jobs.

Entrants   People who enter the work-force.

Entrepreneurial ability   A special type of human resource that organizes the other three factors of production – labour, land and capital – and makes business decisions, innovates and bears business risk.

Environment capital   Includes elements of land which are lost forever when used in the production process as well as the degree of biodiversity among species and the ability of the environment to absorb waste from production.

Equal pay for equal worth   Where employees are paid the same wage for different jobs considered to be of comparable worth.

Equation of exchange   An equation that states that the quantity of money multiplied by the velocity of circulation equals GDP.

Equilibrium expenditure   The level of aggregate planned expenditure that equals real GDP.

Equilibrium price   The price at which the quantity demanded equals the quantity supplied.

Equilibrium quantity   The quantity bought and sold at the equilibrium price.

Equity   In economics, equity has two meanings: economic justice or fairness and the owner's stake in a business.

Equity withdrawal   Borrowing by owner–occupiers from the mortgage issuer against the value of their home without actually moving house.

European Currency Unit (ECU)   A composite currency unit made up of the currencies of the member countries of the European Union.

European Monetary System (EMS)   The system by which members of the European Union cooperate on monetary matters to achieve exchange rate stability.

European Monetary Union (EMU)   A currency union of all participating member countries of the European Union, where a single currency, the Euro, will replace individual country currencies.

Excess reserves   A bank's actual reserves minus its required reserves.

Exchange efficiency   A situation in which a good or service is exchanged at a price that equals both the marginal social benefit and the marginal social cost of the good or service.

Exchange Rate Mechanism (ERM)   A system of pegged exchange rates among participating currencies. It is a parity grid system where each currency has a set of bilateral central parities and a band by which it is allowed to float.

Excise tax   A tax on the sale of a good or service. The tax is paid when the good or service is bought.

Exhaustible natural resources   Natural resources that can be used only once and that cannot be replaced once they have been used.

Expansion   A business cycle phase in which there is a speedup in the pace of economic activity.

Expansionary fiscal policy   An increase in government expenditure or a decrease in tax revenues.

Expected utility   The average utility arising from all possible outcomes.

Exports   The goods and services that we sell to people in other countries.

External benefits   Benefits that accrue to members of the society other than the buyer of the good.

External costs   Costs that are borne by members of society other than the producer of the good.

External diseconomies   Factors outside the control of a firm that raise the firm's costs as the industry produces a larger output.

External economies   Factors beyond the control of a firm that lower the firm's costs as the industry produces a larger output.

Externality   A cost or a benefit arising from an economic activity that affects people other than those who decide the scale of the activity.

Factors of production   The economy's productive resources – land, labour, capital and entrepreneurial ability.

Feedback-rule policy   A rule that specifies how policy actions respond to changes in the state of the economy.

Fiat money   An intrinsically worthless (or almost worthless) commodity that serves the functions of money.

Financial capital   The supply of funds by households to firms for the purchase of capital, either directly through share ownership or indirectly through the financial and banking system.

Financial innovation   The development of new financial products – new ways of borrowing and lending.

Financial intermediary An institution that receives deposits and makes loans.

Firm An institution that hires factors of production and that organizes those factors to produce and sell goods and services.

Fiscal policy The government's attempt to influence the economy by varying its purchases of goods and services and taxes to smooth the fluctuations in aggregate expenditure; use of the government budget to achieve macroeconomic objectives such as full employment, sustained long-term economic growth and price level stability.

Five-firm concentration ratio The percentage of the value of sales accounted for by the largest five firms in one industry.

Fixed cost The cost of a fixed input; a cost that is independent of the output level.

Fixed exchange rate A system in which the value of a country's currency is pegged by the country's central bank.

Fixed-rule policy A rule that specifies an action to be pursued independently of the state of the economy.

Flexible exchange rate A system in which the value of a country's currency is determined by market forces in the absence of central bank intervention.

Flow A quantity per unit of time.

Foreign exchange market The market in which the currency of one country is exchanged for the currency of another.

Foreign exchange rate The price at which one currency exchanges for another.

Forward market A market in which a commitment is made at a price agreed here and now to exchange a specified quantity of a commodity at a particular future date.

Free rider A person who consumes a good without paying for it.

Frictional unemployment Unemployment arising from normal labour turnover – new entrants are constantly coming into the labour market, and firms are constantly laying off workers and hiring new workers.

Full employment A situation which occurs when the unemployment rate equals the natural rate of unemployment – when all unemployment is frictional and structural and there is no cyclical unemployment.

Full employment equilibrium Macroeconomic equilibrium in which real GDP equals potential GDP.

Futures market An organized market operated on a futures exchange in which large-scale contracts for the future delivery of goods can be exchanged.

Game theory A method of analysing strategic behaviour.

GDP deflator A price index that measures the average level of the prices of all goods and services that make up GDP.

General Agreement on Tariffs and Trade An international agreement that limits government intervention to restrict international trade.

Gold standard A monetary system with fractionally backed convertible paper in which a currency could be converted into gold at a guaranteed value on demand.

Government budget Finances the activities of the government.

Government debt The total amount of borrowing that the government has undertaken and the total amount that it owes to households, firms and foreigners.

Government purchases Goods and services bought by the government.

Government purchases multiplier The amount by which a change in government purchases of goods and services is multiplied to determine the change in equilibrium expenditure that it generates.

Great Depression A decade (1929–39) of high unemployment and stagnant production throughout the world economy.

Great Leap Forward An economic plan for post-revolutionary China based on small-scale, labour-intensive production.

Green tax A form of pollution control where a tax equal to the marginal external cost of pollution is charged on output.

Gresham's Law The tendency for bad (debased) money to drive good (not debased) money out of circulation.

Gross domestic product (GDP) The value of all final goods and services produced in the economy in a year.

Gross investment The amount spent on replacing depreciated capital and on net additions to the capital stock.

Growth accounting A method of calculating how much real GDP growth has resulted from growth of labour and capital and how much is attributable to technological change.

Hotelling Principle The proposition that the market for the stock of a natural resource is in equilibrium when the price of the resource is expected to rise at a rate equal to the interest rate on similarly risky assets.

Human capital The skill and knowledge of people, arising from their education and on-the-job training.

Hysteresis The idea that the natural rate of unemployment depends on the path of the actual unemployment rate; where the unemployment rate ends up depends on where it has been.

Implicit rental rate The rent that a firm pays to itself for the use of the assets that it owns.

Import function The relationship between imports and real GDP.

Imports The goods and services that we buy from people in other countries.

Incentive An inducement to take a particular action.

Incentive regulation scheme A regulation that gives a firm an incentive to operate efficiently and keep costs under control.

Income effect The change in consumption that results from a change in the consumer's income, other things remaining the same.

Income elasticity of demand The responsiveness of demand to a change in income, other things remaining the same. It is calculated as the percentage change in the quantity demanded divided by the percentage change in income.

Increasing marginal returns The tendency for the marginal product of a variable factor initially to increase as additional units of the variable factor are employed.

Increasing returns to scale Technological conditions under which a given percentage increase in all the firm's inputs results in the firm's output increasing by a larger percentage.

Indifference curve A line that shows combinations of goods among which a consumer is indifferent.

Individual demand The relationship between the quantity of a good or service demanded by a single individual and the price of a good or service.

Induced expenditure The part of aggregate planned expenditure on UK-produced goods and services that varies as real GDP varies.

Induced taxes Taxes that vary as real GDP varies.

Industrial union A group of workers who have a variety of skills and job types but who work for the same firm or industry.

Inelastic Where a small percentage change in price results in a proportionately smaller change in the quantity demanded

Infant-industry argument The proposition that protection is necessary to enable an infant industry to grow into a mature industry that can compete in world markets.

Inferior good A good for which demand decreases as income increases.

Inflation An upward movement in the average level of prices; a process in which the price level is rising and money is losing value.

Inflationary gap Actual real GDP minus potential GDP when actual real GDP exceeds potential GDP.

Information cost The cost of acquiring information on prices, quantities and qualities of goods and services and factors of production – the opportunity cost of economic information.

Insider–outsider theory A theory of job rationing that says that to be productive, new workers – outsiders – must receive on-the-job training from existing workers – insiders.

Intellectual property rights Property rights for discoveries owned by the creators of knowledge.

Interest rate The amount received by a lender and paid by a borrower expressed as a percentage of the amount of the loan.

Intermediate goods and services Goods and services that are used as inputs into the production process of another good or service.

International Monetary Fund (IMF) An international organization that monitors balance of payments and exchange rate activities.

International substitution effect The substitution of domestic goods and services for foreign goods and services or of foreign goods and services for domestic goods and services.

Intertemporal substitution effect The substitution of goods and services now for goods and services later or of goods and services later for goods and services now.

Inverse relationship A relationship between variables that move in opposite directions.

Investment The purchase of new plant, equipment and buildings and additions to stock.

Investment demand The relationship between the level of planned investment and the real interest rate, all other influences on investment remaining the same.

Job leavers People who voluntarily quit their jobs.

Job losers People who are laid off, either permanently or temporarily, from their jobs.

Job rationing The practice of paying employed people a wage that creates an excess supply of labour and a shortage of jobs, and increases the natural rate of unemployment.

Job search The activity of people looking for acceptable vacant jobs.

Keynesian theory of the business cycle   A theory that regards volatile expectations as the main source of economic fluctuations.

Labour   The time and effort that people allocate to producing goods and services.

Labour demand curve   A curve that shows the quantity of labour that firms plan to hire at each possible real wage rate.

Labour supply curve   A curve that shows the quantity of labour that households plan to supply at each possible real wage rate.

Land   All the natural resources used to produce goods and services.

Law of diminishing returns   A law stating that as the quantity of one input increases with the quantities of all other inputs remaining the same, output increases but by ever smaller increments.

Learning-by-doing   People become more productive in an activity (learn) just by repeatedly producing a particular good or service (doing).

Legal monopoly   A market structure in which there is one firm and entry is restricted by the granting of a public franchise, licence, patent or copyright, or the firm has acquired ownership of a significant portion of a key resource.

Limit pricing   The practice of charging a price below the monopoly profit-maximizing price and producing a quantity greater than that at which marginal revenue equals marginal cost so as to deter entry.

Limited information and uncertainty   A form of market failure caused when the assumption of full information and full knowledge of all future outcomes fails to hold.

Linear relationship   A relationship between two variables that is illustrated by a straight line.

Liquidity   The property of being instantly convertible into a means of payment with little loss in value.

Loan market   A market in which households and firms make and receive loans.

Long run   A period of time in which a firm can vary the quantities of all its inputs.

Long-run aggregate supply curve   The relationship between the aggregate quantity of final goods and services (GDP) supplied and the price level (GDP deflator), other things remaining the same and there is full employment.

Long-run cost   The cost of production when a firm uses the economically efficient plant size.

Long-run Phillips curve   A curve that shows the relationship between inflation and unemployment when the actual inflation rate equals the expected inflation rate.

Long-term unemployed   People who have remained unemployed for over 12 months.

Lorenz curve   A curve that plots the cumulative percentage of income against the cumulative percentage of population.

Lump-sum tax multiplier   The amount by which a change in lump-sum taxes is multiplied to determine the change in equilibrium expenditure that it generates.

Lump-sum taxes   Taxes that are fixed by the government and do not vary with real GDP.

M0   Consists of currency held by the public, the banks, the building societies and banks' deposits at the Bank of England. See also Monetary base.

M4   Currency held by the public and all bank and building society sight and time deposits.

Macroeconomic long run   A period that is sufficiently long for the prices of all the factors of production to have adjusted to any disturbance.

Macroeconomic short run   A period during which the prices of goods and services change in response to changes in demand and supply but the prices of factors of production do not change.

Macroeconomics   The study of the national economy and the global economy, the way that economic aggregates grow and fluctuate, and the effects of government actions on them.

Managed exchange rate   A system in which the value of a country's currency is not fixed at some preannounced level but is influenced by central bank intervention in the foreign exchange market.

Marginal benefit   The extra benefit received from a small increase in the consumption of a good or service. It is calculated as the increase in total benefit divided by the increase in consumption.

Marginal cost   The change in total cost that results from a unit increase in output. It is calculated as the increase in total cost divided by the increase in output.

Marginal cost pricing rule   A rule that sets the price of a good or service equal to the marginal cost of producing it.

Marginal product   The extra output produced as a result of a small increase in the variable factor. It is calculated as the increase in total product divided by the increase in the variable factor employed, when the quantities of all other factors are constant.

Marginal propensity to consume   The fraction of the last pound of disposable income that is spent on consumption goods and services.

Marginal propensity to import   The fraction of the last pound of real GDP spent on imports.

Marginal propensity to save   The fraction of the last pound of disposable income that is saved.

Marginal rate of substitution   The rate at which a person will give up one good or service in order to get more of another good or service and at the same time remain indifferent.

Marginal revenue   The extra total revenue received from selling one additional unit of the good or service. It is calculated as the change in total revenue divided by the change in quantity sold.

Marginal revenue product   The extra total revenue received from employing one more unit of a factor of production while the quantity of all other factors remains the same. It is calculated as the increase in total revenue divided by the increase in the quantity of the factor.

Marginal social benefit   The marginal benefit received by the producer of a good (marginal private benefit) plus the marginal benefit received by other members of society (external benefit).

Marginal social cost   The marginal cost incurred by the producer of a good (marginal private cost) plus the marginal cost imposed on other members of society (external cost).

Marginal utility   The change in total utility resulting from a one-unit increase in the quantity of a good consumed.

Marginal utility per pound spent   The marginal utility obtained from the last unit of a good consumed divided by the price of the good.

Market   Any arrangement that enables buyers and sellers to get information and to do business with each other.

Market activity   People undertake market activity when they buy goods and services in goods (or services) markets or sell the services of the factors of production that they own in factor markets.

Market demand   The total demand for a good or service by everyone in the population. It is illustrated by the market demand curve.

Market failure   The failure of an unregulated market to achieve an efficient allocation of resources.

Market socialism   An economic system that combines state ownership of capital and land with incentives based on a mixture of market prices and laws and regulations.

Maximize total utility   A major assumption of marginal utility theory which implies that individuals choose as if they made the marginal utility per pound spent on each good equal.

Means of payment   A method of settling a debt.

Median voter theorem   The proposition that political parties will pursue policies that appeal most to the median voter.

Merger   The combining of the assets of two firms to form a single, new firm.

Microeconomics   The study of the decisions of people and businesses, the interactions of those decisions in markets, and the effects of government regulation and taxes on the prices and quantities of goods and services.

Minimum wage   The wage below which it is illegal to employ someone under minimum wage law.

Minimum wage law   A regulation that prohibits labour services being paid at less than a specified wage rate.

Monetarist theory of the business cycle   A theory that regards fluctuations in the money stock as the main source of economic fluctuations.

Monetary base   The sum of the notes and coins in circulation and banks' deposits at the Central Bank. See also M0.

Monetary policy   The government's attempt to achieve macroecnomic objectives by adjusting the quantity of money in circulation and interest rates.

Money   Any commodity or token that is generally acceptable as a means of payment for goods and services.

Money multiplier   The amount by which a change in the monetary base is multiplied to determine the resulting change in the quantity of money.

Monopolistic competition   A market structure in which a large number of firms compete with each other by making similar but slightly different products.

Monopoly   An industry that produces a good or service for which no close substitute exists and in which there is one supplier that is protected from competition by a barrier preventing the entry of new firms.

Monopoly control law   A law that defines and regulates practices which lead to the monopoly structure and monopoly power in industry.

Monopoly power   The ability to exercise the power of a monopoly to raise price by restricting output.

Monopsony   A market structure in which there is just a single buyer.

Moral hazard   A situation in which one of the parties to an agreement has an incentive, after the agreement is made, to act in a manner that brings additional benefits to himself or herself at the expense of the other party.

Multiplier   The change in equilibrium real GDP divided by the change in autonomous expenditure.

Nash equilibrium   The outcome of a game that occurs when player A takes the best possible action given the action of player B, and player B takes the best possible action given the action of player A.

National saving Private saving plus government saving; also equals GDP minus consumption expenditure minus government purchases.

Natural monopoly A monopoly that occurs when one firm can supply the entire market at a lower price than two or more firms can.

Natural rate of unemployment The unemployment rate when the economy is at full employment.

Natural resources The non-produced factors of production, which can be exhaustible or non-exhaustible.

Negative income tax A redistribution scheme that gives every family a *guaranteed annual income* and decreases the family's benefit at a specified *benefit-loss rate* as its market income increases.

Negative relationship A relationship between variables that move in opposite directions.

Neo-classical growth theory A theory of economic growth that explains how saving, investment and economic growth respond to population growth and technological change.

Net borrower A country that is borrowing more from the rest of the world than it is lending to it.

Net exporter A country whose value of exports exceeds its value of imports – its balance of trade is positive.

Net exports The expenditure by foreigners on UK-produced goods minus the expenditure by UK residents on foreign-produced goods – exports minus imports.

Net importer A country whose value of imports exceeds its value of exports – its balance of trade is negative.

Net investment Net additions to the capital stock – gross investment minus depreciation.

Net lender A country that is lending more to the rest of the world than it is borrowing from it.

Net present value The present value of the future flow of marginal revenue product generated by capital minus the cost of the capital.

Net taxes Taxes paid to governments minus transfer payments received from governments.

New classical theory of the business cycle A rational expectations theory of the business cycle that regards unanticipated fluctuations in aggregate demand as the main source of economic fluctuations.

New growth theory A theory of economic growth based on the idea that technological change results from the choices that people make in the pursuit of ever greater profit.

New Keynesian theory of the business cycle A rational expectations theory of the business cycle that regards unanticipated fluctuations in aggregate demand as the main source of economic fluctuations.

Nominal GDP targeting An attempt to keep the growth rate of nominal GDP steady.

Nominal interest rate The interest rate actually paid and received in the marketplace.

Non-excludable A property of market failure in the form of public goods where non-payers cannot be excluded from receiving the benefits of the public good or service.

Non-exhaustible natural resources Natural resources that can be used repeatedly without depleting what is available for future use.

Non-market activity Leisure and non-market production activities, including education and training, shopping, cooking and other activities in the home.

Non-rival A property of market failure in the form of public goods where one person's consumption of the good or service does not affect the consumption possibilities of anyone else.

Non-tariff barrier An action other than a tariff that restricts international trade.

Normal good A good for which demand increases as income increases.

Normal profit The expected return for supplying entrepreneurial ability.

Oligopoly A market structure in which a small number of producers compete with each other.

Open market operation The purchase or sale of government securities by the Bank of England designed to influence the money supply.

Opportunity cost The opportunity cost of an action is the best forgone alternative.

Pareto efficiency Another term for allocative efficiency where the market could not reallocate resources through trade, production or consumption to make at least one person better off without making anybody else worse off.

Participation rate The state of the labour market is indicated by this, the employment-to-population ratio and the unemployment rate.

Patent A government-sanctioned exclusive right granted to the inventor of a good, service, or productive process to produce, use and sell the invention for a given number of years.

Payoff matrix   A table that shows the payoffs for every possible action by each player for every possible action by each other player.

Perfect competition   A market structure in which there are many firms; each firm sells an identical product; there are many buyers; there are no restrictions on entry into the industry; firms in the industry have no advantage over potential new entrants; and firms and buyers are completely informed about the price of each firm's product.

Perfectly elastic demand   Demand with an infinite price elasticity; the quantity demanded is infinitely responsive to a change in price.

Perfectly inelastic demand   Demand with a price elasticity of zero; the quantity demanded remains constant when the price changes.

Phillips curve   A curve that shows a relationship between inflation and unemployment.

Political equilibrium   A situation in which the choices of voters, politicians and bureaucrats are all compatible and in which no group can improve its position by making a different choice.

Poor definition of property rights   A form of market failure where the legal rights to property are not clearly defined

Positive relationship   A relationship between two variables that move in the same direction.

Potential GDP   A situation in which all the economy's labour, capital, land and entrepreneurial ability are fully employed.

Poverty   A state in which a family's income is too low to be able to buy the quantities of food, shelter and clothing that are deemed necessary.

Preferences   A person's likes and dislikes for goods and services which are described by the economist's measure of utility.

Present value   The amount of money that, if invested today, will grow to be as large as a given future amount when the interest that it will earn is taken into account.

Price ceiling   A regulation that makes it illegal to charge a price higher than a specified level.

Price discrimination   The practice of charging some customers a lower price than others for an identical good or of charging an individual customer a lower price per unit on a large purchase than on a small one,

even though the cost of servicing all customers is the same.

Price effect   The change in consumption that results from a change in the price of a good or service, other things remaining the same.

Price elasticity of demand   The responsiveness of the quantity demanded of a good to a change in the price of a good or service, other things remaining the same.

Price level   The average level of prices as measured by a price index.

Price taker   A firm that cannot influence the price of the good or service it produces.

Principal–agent problem   A form of market failure arising in a contractual relationship when one party, the principal, cannot fully monitor the activities of the other party, the agent.

Private information   Information that is available to one person but is too costly for anyone else to obtain.

Private sector surplus or deficit   The difference between saving and investment.

Privatization   The process of selling a public company or public sector assets to private shareholders.

Producer efficiency   A situation in which it is not possible to produce more of one good without producing less of some other good.

Producer surplus   The price a producer gets for a good or service minus the opportunity cost of producing it.

Product differentiation   Making a good or service slightly different from that of a competing firm.

Production function   The relationship that shows how the maximum output attainable varies as quantities of all inputs vary.

Production possibility frontier   The boundary between those combinations of goods and services that can be produced and those that cannot.

Productivity   The amount of output produced per unit of inputs used to produce it.

Productivity function   A relationship that shows how real GDP per hour of labour changes as the amount of capital per hour of labour changes with no change in technology.

Productivity growth slowdown   A slowdown in the growth rate of output per person.

Progressive income tax   A tax on income at a marginal rate that increases with the level of income.

Property rights   Social arrangements that govern the ownership, use and disposal of factors of production and goods and services.

Proportional income tax   A tax on income that remains at a constant rate, regardless of the level of income.

Protectionism   The restriction of international trade.

Public choice theory   A theory predicting the behaviour of the government sector of the economy as the outcome of the individual choices made by voters, politicians and bureaucrats interacting in a political marketplace.

Public good   A good or service that can be consumed simultaneously by everyone and from which no one can be excluded.

Public interest theory   A theory of regulation that states that regulations are supplied to satisfy the demand of consumers and producers to maximize total surplus – that is, to attain allocative efficiency.

Public ownership   Ownership of corporations by government rather than private shareholders.

Public Sector Borrowing Requirement (PSBR)   The budget deficit of the government and public corporations.

Public Sector Debt Repayment (PDSR)   The budget surplus of the government and public corporations.

Quantity demanded   The amount of a good or service that consumers plan to buy during a given time period at a particular price.

Quantity of sterling assets   The net stock of financial assets denominated in pounds sterling held outside the Bank of England and the government.

Quantity supplied   The amount of a good or service that producers plan to sell during a given time period at a particular price.

Quantity theory of money   The proposition that in the long run, an increase in the quantity of money brings an equal percentage increase in the price level.

Quota   A restriction on the quantity of a good that a firm is permitted to produce or that a country is permitted to import.

Rate of return regulation   A regulation that determines a regulated price by setting the price at a level that enables the regulated firm to earn a specified target percentage return on its capital.

Rate of time preference   The target real interest rate that savers want to achieve.

Rational expectation   A forecast based on all available relevant information.

Rational ignorance   The decision not to acquire information because the cost of doing so exceeds the expected benefit.

Real business cycle theory   A theory that regards random fluctuations in productivity that result from technological change as the main source of economic fluctuations.

Real exchange rate   An index number that gives the opportunity cost of foreign-produced goods and services in terms of UK-produced goods and services.

Real GDP per person   Real GDP divided by the population.

Real gross domestic product (real GDP)   The output of final goods and services valued at prices prevailing in the base period.

Real income   The quantity of a good that a consumer's income will buy. It is the consumer's income expressed in units of a good and is calculated as income divided by the price of the good.

Real interest rate   The interest rate paid by a borrower and received by a lender after taking into account the change in the value of money resulting from inflation; the nominal interest rate minus the inflation rate.

Real money   A measure of money based on the quantity of goods and services it will buy.

Real wage rate   The wage rate per hour expressed in constant pounds.

Recession   A downturn in the level of economic activity in which real GDP falls in two successive quarters.

Recessionary gap   Potential GDP minus actual real GDP when actual real GDP is less than potential GDP.

Re-entrants   People who re-enter the work-force.

Regressive income tax   A tax on income at a marginal rate that decreases with the level of income.

Regulation   Rules enforced by a government agency to restrict or control economic activity in price setting, product standards, trading standards and the conditions under which firms can enter an industry.

Relative price   The ratio of the price of one good or service to the price of another good or service. A relative price is an opportunity cost.

Rent ceiling   A regulation that makes it illegal to charge a rent higher than a specified level.

Rent seeking   The activity of searching out or creating a monopoly from which an economic profit can be made.

Required reserve ratio   The ratio of reserves to deposits that banks are required, by regulation, to hold.

Reservation price   The highest price that a buyer is willing to pay for a good.

Reservation wage   The lowest wage rate for which a person will supply labour to the market. Below that wage, the person will not supply labour.

Reserve ratio The fraction of a bank's total deposits that are held in reserves.

Reserves Cash in a bank's vault plus the bank's deposits at the Bank of England.

Restrictive practice An agreement between two firms not to compete in some respect such as price, output levels or quality.

Retail Prices Index (RPI) An index of the prices of a basket of goods purchased by a typical UK family.

Returns to scale The increase in output that results when a firm increases all its inputs by the same percentage.

Risk A situation in which more than one outcome might occur and the probability of each possible outcome can be estimated.

Saving Income minus consumption. Saving is measured in the national income accounts as disposable income (income less taxes) minus consumption expenditure.

Saving function The relationship between saving and disposable income, other things remaining the same.

Saving supply The relationship between saving and the real interest rate, other things remaining the same.

Savings bank A financial intermediary owned by its depositors that accepts deposits and makes loans, mostly for consumer mortgages.

Scarcity The universal state in which wants exceed resources.

Scatter diagram A diagram that plots the value of one economic variable against the value of another.

Search activity The time spent in looking for someone with whom to do business.

Shares Long-term assets issued by firms which can be traded in stock markets.

Short run The short run in microeconomics has two meanings. For the firm, it is the period of time in which the quantity of at least one of its inputs is fixed and the quantities of the other inputs can be varied. The fixed input is usually capital – that is, the firm has a given plant size. For the industry, the short run is the period of time in which each firm has a given plant size and the number of firms in the industry is fixed.

Short-run aggregate supply curve A curve showing the relationship between the quantity of real GDP supplied and the price level, other things remaining the same.

Short-run industry supply curve A curve that shows how the quantity supplied by the industry varies as the market price varies when the plant size of each firm and the number of firms in the industry remain the same.

Short-run macroeconomic equilibrium A situation that occurs when the quantity of real GDP demanded equals the short-run quantity of real GDP supplied at the point of intersection of the *AD* curve and the *SAS* curve.

Short-run Phillips curve A curve showing the relationship between inflation and unemployment, when the expected inflation rate and the natural rate of unemployment remain the same.

Shutdown point The price and output level at which the firm just covers its total variable cost. In the short run, the firm is indifferent between producing the profit-maximizing output and shutting down temporarily. If it produces, it makes a loss equal to its total fixed cost.

Signal An action taken outside a market that conveys information that can be used by that market.

Slope The change in the value of the variable measured on the y-axis divided by the change in the value of the variable measured on the x-axis.

Socialism An economic system with state ownership of capital and land and incentives based on laws and regulations.

Stagflation The combination of a rise in the price level and a fall in real GDP.

Stock A quantity measured at a point in time.

Stock market A market in which the shares of corporations are traded.

Strategies All the possible actions of each player in a game.

Structural deficit A budget that is in deficit even though real GDP equals potential GDP; expenditures are high relative to tax revenues over the entire business cycle.

Structural unemployment The unemployment that arises when there is a decline in the number of jobs available in a particular region or industry.

Subsidy A payment made by the government to producers that depends on the level of output.

Subsistence real wage rate The minimum real wage rate needed to maintain life.

Substitute A good that can be used in place of another good.

Substitution effect The effect of a change in price of one good or service on a consumer's consumption of goods and services when the consumer remains indifferent between the original and the new consumption bundles – that is, the consumer remains on the same indifference curve.

Sunk cost The past economic depreciation of a firm's capital (buildings, plant and equipment).

Supply The relationship between the quantity of a good that producers plan to sell and the price of the good, with all other influences on sellers' plans remaining the same. It is described by a supply schedule and illustrated by a supply curve.

Supply curve   A curve that shows the relationship between the quantity supplied and the price of a good, all other influences on producers' planned sales remaining the same.

Takeover   The purchase of the stock of one firm by another firm.

Tariff   A tax on an import by the government of the importing country.

Technological efficiency   A situation that occurs when it is not possible to increase output without increasing inputs.

Technological progress   The development of new and better ways of producing goods and services and the development of new goods.

Total cost   The sum of the costs of all the inputs a firm uses in production.

Total fixed cost   The total cost of the fixed inputs.

Total product   The total output produced by a firm in a given period of time.

Total revenue   The value of a firm's sales. It is calculated as the price of the good multiplied by the quantity sold.

Total surplus   The sum of consumer surplus and producer surplus.

Total utility   The total benefit or satisfaction that a person gets from the consumption of goods and services.

Total variable cost   The total cost of the variable inputs.

Trade-off   A constraint that entails giving up one thing to get something else.

Trade union   A group of workers organized principally for the purpose of increasing wages and improving conditions.

Trade-weighted index   The value of a basket of currencies in which the weight placed on each currency is related to its importance in UK international trade.

Transactions costs   The costs incurred in searching for someone with whom to do business, in reaching an agreement about the price and other aspects of the exchange, and in ensuring that the terms of the agreement are fulfilled.

Transfer earnings   The income that an owner of a factor of production requires to induce the owner to supply the factor.

Trend   A general direction (rising or falling) in which a variable is moving over the long term.

UK interest rate differential   The interest rate on a UK sterling asset minus the interest rate on a foreign currency asset.

Uncertainty   A situation in which more than one event might occur but it is not known which will occur.

Unemployed   A person who does not have a job but is available for work, willing to work and has made some effort to find work within the previous four weeks.

Unemployment rate   The number of people unemployed expressed as a percentage of the work-force.

Unit elastic demand   Demand with a price elasticity of 1; the percentage change in the quantity demanded equals the percentage change in price.

Utility   The benefit or satisfaction that a person gets from the consumption of a good or service.

Utility of wealth   The amount of utility that a person attaches to a given amount of wealth.

Utility maximization   The attainment of the greatest possible utility.

Value   The maximum amount that a person is willing to pay for a good.

Value added   The value of a firm's output minus the value of the intermediate goods bought from other firms.

Variable cost   A cost that varies with the output level. It is the cost of a variable input.

Velocity of circulation   The average number of times a pound is used annually to buy the goods and services that make up GDP.

Voluntary export restraint (VER)   A self-imposed restriction by an exporting country on the volume of its exports of a particular good.

Wealth   The value of all the things that people own.

Welfare state capitalism   An economic system that combines the private ownership of capital and land with state interventions in markets that modify the price signals to which people respond.

Work-force curve   This shows the potential quantity of labour available for employment at a particular real wage rate.

Work-force   The sum of employed and unemployed people.

Working-age population   The total number of people aged 16 and over who are not in jail, hospital, or some other form of institutional care.

INDEX

Notes: Page numbers for key concepts and definitions are set in bold; italic page numbers refer to figures; (n) indicates footnotes.

A

A-level examination(s) 432–433
Above full-employment equilibrium 697
Absolute advantage 56, **57**, 58, **929**
Accountability 805
Accounting depreciation 213
Actual expenditure 721–722
Administration cost(s) 460
Administrative hierarchies 991
Advance 776
Adverse selection 425
Advertising 424–425
Age *374*
Aggregate demand 690, *691*, 692–696, 699, *730*
  business cycle 863–870, 885
  change *696*, *731*
  expenditure 729, 732–733
  fiscal policy 755–757
  government purchases *756*
  increase *700*
  inflation 834, *837*
  recession 876–877
  shock *902*
  types 684, 704–705, 706
  Aggregate demand curve 695–696
Aggregate expenditure 579, 582, 585–586, *720*, 729–733
Aggregate hours 604, **605**, 606, 612
Aggregate income 577, 585–586
Aggregate planned expenditure 690, **712**
Aggregate production 550
Aggregate supply 684–690, 700, 704–705, 706
  change *690*
  decrease *701*
  fiscal policy 758–759
  recession 876–877
  shocks 904–905
Aggregate supply curve *688*
Agricultural price support system *142*
Air pollution *497*, 510–511
Alchian, Armen 219(n)
Alcoholism 558

Allocative efficiency 276, *277*, 297, *298*, 299
Alternative economic system(s) 985–986, 1003
Animal spirits 864
Anticipation of inflation 838–842, *843*, 844, 851–852, 856
Arbitration 376
Arc elasticity 101
Arc elasticity of demand 101
AS–AD model 863, 870, *873*
Asia-Pacific Economic Group (APEG) 932
Asset(s) 633–634, 775, 818
Assortive mating 525
Asymmetric information 425
Audit Commission 458
Automatic fiscal policy 748, 894
Automatic stabilizer(s) 753–755
Autonomous expenditure 721
Average cost pricing rule 474
Average cost(s) 233–234
Average fixed cost(s) 233
Average mark(s) 230, *231*, 232
Average price(s) 101
Average product(s) 230
Average quantity(ies) 101
Average revenue 260
Average total cost curve 235
Average total cost(s) 233
Average variable cost(s) 233

B

Balance for official financing 952
Balance of payments 950–952, *953*, 954–979
Balance of payments account(s) 952, 953–954
Balance sheet(s) 775, *777*
  Bank of England *803*
  rules 780
Balance of trade 921, 923–924, 926
Balanced budget multiplier 752
Balanced budget(s) 744
Bank of England 471, 565, 695, 771, **801**
  bank role 775, 776
  building society role 777
  deposit insurance 779, 782
  deposit protection 881
  ERM 897
  exchange rate determination 963, 965–966, 969

financial structure 803–804
  functions 802–803
  monetarism 866
  monetary policy 821–825
  money 828
  money supply 806–810, 820
  policy tools 804–805
  policy-making 828–829, 854–855
  recession 875–876
  unemployment 911
Bank for International Settlements (BIS) 566
Bank(s) 775
  deposit protection 881
  money creation 781–785, 796
  money supply 812–813
  multiple-deposit creation *784*
  origin 771
Barrell, Ray 910
Barrier(s) to entry 286, 313–314
Barter 60, 769
Becker, Gary 195
Below full-employment equilibrium 697
Below-cost provision 507–508
Benefit(s)
  environment 504
  external 495
  income distribution *527*
  in kind 526
  system *529*
  trap 528, 529
Bentham, Jeremy 195
Bequest(s) 524
Best affordable point *181*
Bilateral monopoly 380
Bio-technology 999
Bishop, M. 487(n)
Black economy 62–63
Black market(s) 126
Bond market(s) 395
Bond(s) 210, 813
Borrowing 396, 580, *761*, 778–779
  international 923–924
  trade 954–955, 957–958
Branson, Richard 420
Break-even point 263
Buchanan, James 513
Budget deficit(s) 565, 744
  business cycle *753*
  crowding out *761*
Budget equation 174–175
Budget line 173, 181
Budget surplus 744
Budget(s) 741–766
Building societies 776, 777, *778*
  money supply 812–813

Bureaucracy 458
Bureaucratic overprovision 452
Bureaucrat(s) 447, 448, *452*, 453,
    472–473
Business cycle(s) 551, *552*, 554,
    564, 860–887, 888–889
  budget deficit *753*
  fluctuation 592
  interest rate 824–825
  phases 593–596
  policy goals 892
  turning point 727
  unemployment 900–906, 913
Business finance 209–212
Buying plan(s) 71

C

Capacity 317
Capital 18, **576**, 577, 625–652
  business cycle 863
  cost 213–214
  demand *399*, *400*, 413
  factor prices 346
  investment *576*
  natural resource markets 393–415
  new 658
  requirement 780
  substitutes 355
  supply 358–359, 400, *401*, 402, 413
  types 17, 22, 46
Capital account(s) 563, 564, **952**
Capital accumulation 52, 53
Capital gain(s) 205, 964
Capital market equilibrium *403*
Capital market flow(s) *396*
Capital stock *627*, **627**
Capitalism 987, *988*
Capture theory 470, 471
Cartel(s) 304–305, **324**, 477–478
Catch-up *656*, *657*
Causation 29
Central bank(s) 799–830, **801**
Central planning 989, *990*, *996*
Certificate(s) of Deposit (CD) 773,
    777
Ceteris paribus **13**, 14, 22, 38, 49
Chancellor of the Exchequer 565,
    695, 743, 805
  role 828–829, 854–855
  unemployment 911
Change in demand 73, **74**
Change in demand versus change in
    the quantity demanded *75*
Change in price 82–87, 92–93
**Change in the quantity demand-
    ed 74**
**Change in the quantity supplied
    78**
Change in supply 76–77, **78**
Change in supply versus change in

the quantity supplied *79*
Cheating 326, *329*
Cheque(s) 773–774
Chiang Kai-Shek 995
Chicago School 795
Chlorofluorocarbon(s) (CFC) 495
Choice 8, 17, 22, 171–200, 522–525,
    540
  discovery 669
  under uncertainty *419*
Choke price(s) 407
Circular flow of income and expen-
    diture *578*
Civil Aviation Authority (CAA) 471,
    478
Clarke, Kenneth 828–829, 854, 900,
    976–977
Classical growth theory 665,
    666, 667
Classification of countries 982
Climate convention 505
Closed economy 17, 21
Coase, Ronald H. 256–257, 500
Coase theorem *499*, **500**, 501
Collective bargaining 376
Collusion
  cheating *327*
  monopoly profits *326*
  profit maximization 325–326
Collusive agreement(s) 324
Collusive oligopoly *478*
Command economy 20
Command mechanism(s) 20, 21, 22
Commodity money 770
**Common Agricultural Policy
    (CAP) 139**, 932
Company(ies) 203
Comparative advantage 55, 56,
    57, 924, **925**, 937
  dynamic 674
  gains from trade 929–930
  international trade 944
Comparison 30–31
Compensation 940
Competition 10, 258–283
  container line 278–279
  factor market 346–349
  gas supply 488–489
  monopoly *298*, 299–301, 307
  policy 479–484, 490
  UK laws *480*
  union *378*
Complement(s) 73, 179–180
Compliance cost(s) 460
Concentration measure(s) 312–314,
    315
Confederation of British Industries
    (CBI) 376
Congestion 510–511
Conservation 409–412
Constant returns to scale 238
Constraint(s) 227, 245, 376–378

Consumer behaviour 181–188
Consumer efficiency 276
Consumer equilibrium 157
Consumer surplus 164, 292, **299**,
    468, *469*
Consumption 633–639
  borrowing 957–958
  change 926–928
  decision-making 650
  demand 648–649
  expanding possibilities *927*
  household 180–181, 193
  individual choices 154–156
  influences *637*, 716
  possibilities *154*, 173–176, 193
Consumption demand 634, *635*,
    638
Consumption demand curve *635*
Consumption expenditure 577,
    578
Consumption function 712, **713**,
    714, 716, *717*
Contestable market(s) 312,
    318–319, 332–336
Contractionary fiscal policy 756
Convergence 722, 973, *974*
Convertible paper money 771
Cooperative equilibrium 330
Coordinate(s) 28
Coordination of decisions 19–21, 22
Copyright(s) 284, **508**, 932
Corporate structure(s) *204*
Corporate tax 744
Corporation(s) 203
Corporatist bargaining 376
Correlation 29
Cost curve 235, *236*
Cost-push inflation 836, 837–838,
    856
  avoidance 906–908
  spiral *838*
Cost-push rise in price level *837*
Cost(s) 225–55
  administration 460
  capital 213–214
  demand *325*
  environment 504
  external 495
  firm 256–257
  four ways of making 10 TV sets
      per day *217*
  glossary *235*
  health-care 530–532
  incentive 908
  inflating 475–476
  inflation 843–844
  obtaining funds 778–779
  oligopoly 324–325
  output 242–243
  plant size 237–244
  public health care 458–459
  selling 318

short-run 232–237
stocks 214
taxation 537
technology 220–221
Country types 982
Cournot, Antoine-Augustin 90–91
Crafts, Nick 543–546
Credibility 853, 909
Credit card(s) 774–775
Creditor nation(s) 954
Crime 558
Cross elasticity of demand 107
Cross-section graph(s) 28, **31**
Crowding out 760, *761*
Cultural Revolution 996
Currency 771, 772, 813, 976–977
Currency depreciation 960
Currency drain 809, 810
Current account(s) 563, 564,
952, *955*
Cycle(s) of long-term growth
701–703, 706–707
Cyclical deficit(s) *754*, **754**
Cyclical unemployment 611, 612,
622
Cyclically adjusted deficit(s)
754

D

Deadweight loss 300, **456**,
457(n), 468
Debt 524–525
Debt interest 744
Debtor nation(s) 954
Decentralized bargaining 376
Decentralized planning 987
Decision-making 17, 19–21, 22
elasticity of supply 111–12
investment 396–397, *398*,
630–633, 650
output 287–290
perfect comeptition 262
price *289*
production 266
saving 400–401, 633–639
Decreasing returns to scale 238
Deficit(s) 957
De Grauwe, Paul 916–918
Demand 73, *74*, *75*, 92, *99*
capital 396–398, *399*, *400*, 413
change 82–83, 84–86, 273
changes *348*
consumer 648–649
costs *325*
decrease *272*
factor income *348*
factor market *347*
factors 349–355, 365
income effect *183*
influences *637*

labour *351*, *354*
labour market 612–614
law 71–72, 90–91
marginal revenue *288*
money 814–815, *816*, 828
natural resources 405–406,
407–408
oligopoly 324–325
perfect competition *261*
real GDP 642, *643*
regulation 469–470
revenue 285–287
schedule 72–73
skill differentials 372
sterling assets *966*
utility 151–170
wheat price 88–89
Demand curve 72
capital 399
investment 630–632
kinked 319, *320*
labour **613**, 622
price effect *182*
Demand-pull inflation 834,
835–836, 856
spiral *835*
Demand-pull rise in price level *834*
Demography of unemployment 609
Demsetz, Harold 219(n)
Deng Xiaoping 996
Deposit insurance 779–780
Deposit interest rate(s) 560
Deposit money 772
Deposit multiplier 783
Deposit(s) 772, 782–785
Depreciation 213, 396, **576**,
583–584, **627**
hysteresis 619
Depression 558
Deregulation 467, 471–479, 490,
779–781, 796
labour market 910–911
price 992
Derived demand 349
Desired reserve ratio 782, 810
Developing countries 982
Development 939–940
Diminishing marginal product of
capital 238
Diminishing marginal productivity
508
Diminishing marginal rate of
substitution 178
Diminishing marginal returns
231
Diminishing marginal utility 155
Diminishing returns 238
Direct provision 444
Direct relationship(s) 32, *33*
Discount house(s) *802*
Discount rate(s) 804, 805
Discounting 211, 212

Discouraged worker(s) 557, **603**
Discovery 669
Discretionary fiscal policy 748
Discrimination 381, **382**, *383*
Diseconomy of scale 241
Dismal science 666
Disposable income 633, 635, *636*, 637
Distortion 32
Distribution of endowments 523
Distribution of income 445
Distributive justice theory 536–537
Diversification 428–429
Divisible goods(s) 173–174
Division of labour 66
Domestic violence 558
Dominant firm oligopoly 320, *321*
Dominant strategy equilibrium
323
Doomsday 409–412
Doorslaer, E. Van 534(n)
Double coincidence of wants 60, 769
Double counting 582
Dow, Sheila 1–4
Driving 510–511
Drugs *136*
Dumping 938
Duopoly 324, 329, *330*, 337
Dupuit, Jules 90–91
Dynamic comparative advantage
58, 674, 937

E

Earnings *374*
Economic depreciation 213
Economic efficiency 15, **216**, 227
Economic growth 15, 52, **550**,
551, **655**
comparison *54*
decline 984
emerging economies *999*
factory *53*
feel-bad factor 566–567
inflation 844
long-term 897–899, 913
macroeconomic policy 1000–1001
measurement 574–599
multiplier 734–735
national 55, 61
saving 672–673
theoretical issues 666–680
types 552, *553*, 554–556, 568,
594–595, 653–654
Economic history *990*, *996*
Economic inequality 519–522, 540
Economic information 423
Economic loss 269, 346
Economic miracle 999–1002, 1004
Economic model(s) 12, 32–35
Economic policy types 14–15, 22
Economic problem 8, *988*, *989*
Economic profit 215, **260**, 269

factor prices 346
   opportunity cost 212–216
   short run 264–265
Economic rent 299, **362**
   factor pricing 362–364, 365
   transfer earnings *363*
Economic stability 15
Economic system(s) 986–987
Economic theory 2, *13*, 22
   government 444–446, 461
   regulation 469–471, 490
Economic transition 990–995,
   993–995, 1003–1004
Economic welfare 591–593
Economics 8, 22
   environment 514
   knowledge 506–509
Economies of scale 219, **241**, *303*
   types 244, 300, 930–931
Economies of scope 219, **302**,
   303
Economy 16, *18*, 20
Ecosystem 497
Education 374–375, *507*
Effects of a change in supply *83*
Efficiency 47, 276–280, 281
   allocation of resources 444
   cost 843–844
   education *507*
   monopolistic competition 318
Efficiency wage(s) 617
Efficient market(s) 431
Ehrlich, Paul 368
Einstein, Albert 13
Elastic 101, *102*
Elasticity 97–121
   demand 354–355
   factor income *348*
   revenue 287
   straight-line demand curve *103*
   total revenue *106*
Elasticity of demand 99–100,
   101, 102–110, 113
   farm revenue 138
   glossary *110*
   taxation 131, *132*
Elasticity of supply 110, **111**, 112
Emerging economies 980–1006
Emission charge(s) 501
Emission standard(s) 501, 502
Employment 600–624
   real wage rate *614*
**Employment-to-population ratio
   603**, 604
End-state theory 536
Endowment(s) 522–525, 540
Entrant(s) 607
Entrepreneurial ability 17, **18**,
   214
Entrepreneurship 346

Entry 267–8, *269*, 312
   See also Barrier(s) to entry
Entry-deterrence game *336*
Environment 555
   air pollution 510–511
   economics 496–506, 514
   externality 512–513
   GDP 593
   group membership *496*
   protectionism 939
Environment Agency (EA) 471, 501
Environmental capital 46
Equal pay for equal worth
   387–390, **387**
Equal worth 387, *388*
Equalizing marginal utility per
   pound spent *159*
Equation of exchange 788
Equilibrium *80*, 81
   game theory 323–324
   GDP 731–733
   global economy 640–644, 650
   interest rate 403
   long-run 270
   macroeconomic 696–697, *698*,
      699–701, 706
   net export *645*, 646–647
   payoff matrix 328–329
   short-run *268*
   short-run macroeconomic *697*
   stock 407–408
Equilibrium expenditure 722,
   723
Equilibrium price 81
Equilibrium quantity 81
Equitable distribution of income 445
Equity 15, **209**
Equity withdrawal 639
Ethnic minorities 609
European Central Bank 973
European Commission 471
**European Currency Unit (ECU)
   971**
**European Monetary System
   (EMS)** 647, 875, 970, **971**,
   972–975
**European Monetary Union
   (EMU)** 565, 748, 895, **971**, 973
European Union (EU)
   Agricultural Price Support System
      142
   Common Agricultural Policy
      139–142
European Union, Treaty of 471
Excess capacity 317
Excess reserve(s) 782
Exchange efficiency 276
**Exchange Rate Mechanism
   (ERM)** 647, 875–876, 897, 970,
   971, 972

Exchange rate(s) 694, 950–979,
   961, *967*
   determination 963–971, 975
   net export 646–647
Excise tax 455, *456*
Excludable good(s) 445
**Exhaustible natural resource(s)
   405**
Exit *269*, 270, 312
Exogenous variable(s) 667
Expansion 552, 758
Expansionary fiscal policy 756
Expectation(s)
   exchange rate determination
      964–965
   income 358, 400–401, 419, 420,
      634, 693
   price 408–409, *431*
   prices 73, 77
   profit 694
   profit rate 630
   See also Rational expectation(s)
Expected utility 419
Expenditure 106–107, *581*, 583–584
   circular flow *578*
   consumption 633
   government budget 743–744, 746
   income equality 577–580
   multipliers 710–740
   saving 635–637
Experience good(s) 424
Explicit cost(s) 212
Export(s) 579, **921**
External benefit(s) 277
External cost(s) 277
External diseconomies 273
External economies 273
Externality 446, **495**, 496,
   510–511, 514
   air pollution 510–511
   Coase theorem *499*
   environmental 499–500

F

Factor cost(s) 583
Factor income
   approach 582, 583, *584*
   football 360–361
Factor market(s) 17, *347*, 365
   glossary *352*
   real business cycle *872*
Factor price(s) 522–525, 540
   incomes 346–349, 365
Factor service(s) 346
Factor substitution possibility(ies)
   111
Factor(s) of production 17, 22
   allocation 344–353
   price 76–77
Fairness 536–537

Fallacy of composition 14, 22
Fall(s) in price 159, *160*
Farm price stabilization *138*
Farm revenue 137, *138*, 139–143
Feedback-rule policy 900,
901–904, 905, 907–908
Feel-bad factor 566–567
Fiat money 771
Final expenditure 582, *584*
Final good(s) 585
Final income 527
Finance 952–958, 975
Financial capital 358, 396, 399
Financial innovation 780, 815
Financial intermediary 395, **775,**
776–779, 796
Financial market(s) 428–434, 435
Financial property 59
Financial regulation 779–781, 796
Financial security 582
Financial Statement and Budget
Report by Her Majesty's
Treasury 743
Financial system(s) *802*
Firm(s) 17, *18*, 21, 22, 46–47, **203**
cheating 326, *327*, 328, *329*
coordination 218
cost 256–257
costs *233*
demand for labour *354*
different types *209*
dominant 320, *321*
economic problem 203–209
fund-raising 209–210
labour 357
market 217–19
market constraints 227, 245
non-state 997–998
objective 227, 245
opportunity cost 48
perfect competition 262
private ownership 992
relative importance 205, *206*
short-run supply curve 266
stock market valuation 403–404
total income 577–578
First In, First Out (FIFO) 214
Fiscal crisis 993
Fiscal policy 565, 694, 743, 894,
895
government budget 741–766
real GDP *757*
supply-side effects *759*
**Five-firm concentration ratio
312**, 313
Fixed cost(s) 232
Fixed exchange rate(s) 960, 967
Fixed input 227
Fixed-rule policy 900, 901, 902,
905, 906–907

Flexible exchange rate(s) 960,
967
Flow 346, **576**
labour market *607*
stock 407–408
trade collapse 993
Fluctuation(s) 551–552, 561, 577,
592
aggregate demand 699–700
aggregate supply 700–701
Football 360–361
Forecasting
inflation 839, 840
policy lag 903–904
recession 882–883
**Foreign exchange market(s)
958**, 976–977
Foreign exchange rate 562, 694,
718, **958**
Foreign exchange system 959–960
Forestry 410–411
Forward market(s) 429, **430**
Fossil fuel(s) 495
Fractional backing 771
Franchise(s) 284
Free market(s) 66, 135
Free rider(s) 446, 448
Free trade 942–943
Frictional unemployment 610
Friedman, Milton 794–795, 866, 880,
900
Full employment 607, **612**, 621
inflation 839
real GDP 903
**Full-employment equilibrium
697**
Fund flow(s) 396
Fund-raising 209–210
Fundamental economic problem *985*
Futures market(s) 429, **430**

G

Gain(s)
insurance *422*
trade 55–56, 58, 61, 925–931, 944,
948–949
Game theory 322, 323–324, 331,
337
Gas supply 488–489
Gelderland Housing Market *125*
Gender 381–387
pay differential 384–385
**General Agreement on Tariffs
and Trade (GATT)** 471, **931,**
932, 939, 948–949
General Government Borrowing
Requirement (GGBR) 743
General insurance 421

Geography 313, 922, *923*
George, Eddie 565, 828, 900
Giffen good(s) 185–188
Gini coefficient 520
Glasnost 991
Global economy *21*, 22, 982–985
equilibrium 650
foreign exchange market *959*
long-term equilibrium 640–644
See also World trade 919–949
Global warming 498, 504–505
Gold standard 771
Goldsmith, James 938
Goods and services 46, 424–425
government expenditure 743
international trade 921–922
markets 17
net export 582
prohibited 134–137
Gorbachev, Mikhail 991
Government 6–7, 17, *18*, 21–22, 60
aggregate demand *756*
agriculture markets 139
Bank of England 801
budget 741–766
budget deficit *744*
deficit 564
growth 453
health-care expenditure *535*
insurance 532
licence 284
policy aims 443, *444*, 445–446,
461
purchases **578**, 579, 582, 694
recession 881
saving 898
size *443*
Government budget 743
Government debt 746
Government deficit *743*
**Government purchases multipli-
er 749**, *750*
Grading 432–433
Grain market(s) 88–89
Graph(s) 26–43
Great Depression 7, **549**, 572,
878–884, *879*, 885
Great Leap Forward 995, *996*
Green tax 503
Greenhouse effect 6, 412
Greenhouse gases 495, 497, 503
Gresham, Thomas 770
Gresham's Law 770
Griffiths Report 458
Gross 583
Gross domestic product (GDP)
550, **576**, *581*, *584*
balloon *589*
exchange rate determination 964
expenditure 712

measurement 574–599

Gross domestic product (GDP) deflator 587, 588

Gross investment 576, 583, **627**

Gross private domestic investment 582

Gross trading profits and surplus 583

Growth *see* Economic growth

Growth accounting 659, 660–661, *662*, 663–664, 675

Growth rate *555*

Growth theory 664–671, 675

Guaranteed annual income(s) 528

H

Hargreaves, James 572

Harvests *138*

Haskel, J. 487(n)

Health 592–593

Health and Safety Executive 471

Health-care provision 458–459, 530–535, 538–539

Heating pipe industry 304–305

Heston, Alan 591

Hey, John, 340–343

Highly contestable market(s) 313

Hotelling, Harold Jr 368–369, 406(n)

Hotelling Principle 368, **406**

Household(s) 17, *18*, 21, 22, 53–54
  choices 188–192, 193
  consumption 180–181, 193, 633–634
  income distribution *521*
  labour 356
  production 592
  total income 577–578

Housing market 124, *125*, 126–127, 143

Hubble space telescope 508(n)

Human behaviour analysis 194–195

Human capital 46, *372*, **384**, 898
  growth 658–659, 689
  wage differentials 381, 386

Hume, David 795

Hyperinflation 562, 795, 843

Hysteresis 616

I

Illegal trading 136–137

Implicit cost(s) 212

Implicit rental rate(s) 214

Import function 718, *719*

Import(s) 377, 579, 727, **921**

Impulse(s) 862–864, 866–867, *871*, 885

Incentive regulation scheme(s) 476

Incentive(s) 10, 303–306, 657–658, 984
  cost 908
  pay schemes 208

Income 6–7, 73, 982–984
  change *175*
  circular flow *578*
  elasticity 104
  employment 583
  equitable distribution 445
  expectation 634, 693
  expenditure equality 577–580
  factor pricing 362–364
  factors of production 346–349, 365
  future expectations 358
  Lorenz curve *519*
  per person 982
  redistribution 525–530, 540
  rise 161–162
  saving decision 400
  selected household characteristics *521*
  self-employment 583
  support payments 525–526
  taxes 454–455

Income effect 71–72, **183**, 184, *185*, 356
  saving 401

Income elasticity *109*

Income elasticity of demand 107, *108*

Income tax *455*, 525, 727

Increase in demand *75*

Increase in supply *79*

Increasing marginal returns 231

Increasing returns to scale 238

Indifference curve 176, 181, 186–187, 191, 193

Indirect taxation 134, 583

Individual consumption choice(s) 154–156, 168

Individual demand 153, 168

Individual demand curve *153*

Indivisible good(s) 173–174

Induced expenditure 721

Induced tax 752

Industrial countries 982

Industrial Revolution 572

Industrial union(s) 375

Industry
  markets 314
  supply curve *267*

Inefficiency 47, *533*

Inelastic 101, *102*

Inequality 517–542

Infant-industry argument 937

Inferior good(s) 73, 183(n)

Inflation 559, *560*, 831–2, **833**, 834–859
  A-level examination 432–433
  emerging economies 995
  expectations 693

long-term growth 698–699, 701–703, 706–707
  lowering *909*
  macroeconomic performance *893*
  measurement 574–599
  money 792–793, 794–795
  money growth *789*
  policy goals 892–894
  policy-making 854–855, 906–913
  price level 586–590
  saving 898
  taming 564
  types 549–551, 568

Inflationary gap 697

Inflexibility 991–992

Information 416–417, 423–428, 435
  incomplete 206–207, 446
  interest groups 452–453

Information cost 423

Information technology 999

Initial residual difference (IRD) 586

Injection 581
  Innovation 284, 303–306, 318, 779–781, 796

Input
  possibilities *250*
  price 251, 253
  substitution 248–250

Insider–outsider theory 617

Insurance 421, 423, 435
  gains *422*
  private 532

Intellectual property right(s) 59, **508**, 932

Interbank rate(s) 561

Interest 213–214, 625–652

Interest group(s) 452–453

Interest rate differential(s) 965

Interest rate(s) 346, 358, 413, **560**, 695, 704
  capital 402–405
  change *820*
  demand for money 815
  determination 818–820
  inflation 849–852, 857
  money *821*
  natural resource 407–408
  real GDP growth *825*
  saving 401

Intermediate goods and services 582, 584, 585

Internal restructuring 208

Internalization 500

International agreement(s) 505

International car trade *926*

International Monetary Fund (IMF) 591, 672, **960**, 1000–1001

International payment(s) 563–564, 569

International substitution effect 692, 730

International trade 674, 753, 919–949, 952–958, 975

Intertemporal substitution effect 692, 729, 873, 874
Inverse relationship(s) 33, *34*
Investment 396, *397*, *398*, 399, 400, **576**
  approach *640*
  borrowing 957–958
  business cycle 863
  capital *576*
  capital stock *627*
  financing 580–581, *955*
  new capital 658
  security 776
  technology 898
  types 578, 625–652
Investment demand 630, *631*
Invisible hand 280, 500
Isocost equation 251
Isocost line 250
Isocost map 251, *252*
Isoquant 249
Isoquant map 249
Iterative planning 991

J

Jevons, William S. 195
Job leaver(s) 607
Job loser(s) 607
Job rationing 617, 622
Job search 615, 619, 622
Job types 381–382
Jobs 556–559, 568
Jobseekers allowance 557(n)
Joint unlimited liability 203

K

Kay, John, 438–440, 487(n)
Keynes, John Maynard 549, 572–573, 864
Keynesian theory of business cycle 864
Keynesianism
  activists 901
  expansion *865*
  recession *865*
Kinked demand curve model 319, *320*
Knowledge 506–509, 514

L

Labour 17, 22, 46
  demand *351*, *354*
  elasticity 354–355
  factor prices 346
  glossary *375*
  intensity 354

  market 127–30, 143, 370–392
  substitutes 355
  supply 188–190, 355, 524
  union *378*
Labour demand curve 613, 621
Labour Force Survey (LFS) 602
Labour market(s) *613*
  deregulation 910–911
  flow *607*
  indicators 602–604
  minimum wage 616–617
  recession 877–878
  unanticipated inflation 839
  unemploymnet 556
  wage 522–523
Labour supply curve 613, 621
Lags 903
Land 17, 22, 46
  factor prices 346
  pollution 498
  supply 359–362
Lardner, Dionysius 90–91
Last In, First Out (LIFO) 214
Law of demand 71–72
Law of diminishing marginal rate of substitution 250
Law of diminishing returns 232, 233, *660*
Law of supply 76
Lawson, Nigel 704
Leakages 581
Leaky bucket concept 527–528
Learning-by-doing 58, 937
Least-cost technique 248–251, **252**, 253, *254*, 255
Legal barrier(s) to entry 284
Legal monopoly 286
Legislation
  binding command 991
  equal pay 387–388, 389–390
  legalizing drugs *136*
  monopoly and competition *480*
Leisure time 593
Lender of last resort 881
Lenders 954–955
Lenin, Vladimir Ilyich 990
Liabilities 775, 803
Licences 284
Life expectancy 592–593
Limit pricing 333–336, **333**
Limited information 276
Linear relationship(s) 32
Linkage(s) 21
Liquid asset(s) 776, 778
Liquidity 773
Living standards 992
Loan interest rate 560
Loan market(s) 395, 427–428
Loan(s) 776, 782–785
London interbank offered rate (LIBOR) 561
Long run 227
Long-run adjustment 124

Long-run aggregate supply 686–687
Long-run aggregate supply curve 686, 697
Long-run average cost curve *240*
Long-run cost 237, *239*, 240, 244
Long-run decision(s) 262
Long-run demand 105
Long-run equilibrium 270, *271*, 640–644, 650
Long-run fiscal policy 755–761, 764
Long-run industry supply curve 273
Long-run marginal cost(s) 253–255
Long-run marginal product(s) 253–255
Long-run multiplier *733*
Long-run Phillips curve 846, *847*
Long-run supply 111–112
Long-term contract(s) 208
Long-term economic growth *553*, 653–680
Long-term goal(s) 549
Long-term growth
  inflation 698–699, 701–703, 706–707
  policy 897–899, 913
  trends 655–657, 675
Long-term insurance 421
Long-term unemployed 607
Lorenz curve *519*, **520**, **982**, 983, *984*
Lucas, Robert E. Jr 867, 888–889
Lum-sum tax 748
Lump-sum tax multiplier 751
Lump-sum transfer(s) 752

M

M0 772, 804, 809, 813, 817, 963
M4 772, 813, 817
Maastricht Treaty 565, 748, 973, 975
McCormick, Cyrus 676
McMillan, John 997(n)
Macroeconomic long-run 686
Macroeconomic short-run 687, *697*
Macroeconomics 11, 15, 22, 547–571
  challenges 890–915
  equilibrium 696–701, 706
  market failure 445–446
  net export 645
  performance *893*
  policy-making 1000–1001
Malthus, Thomas Robert 368–369, 665
Managed exchange rate(s) 960, 967–968
Management 205–208, 428–435
Mao Zedong 995–996
Marginal analysis 158, 212, 264
Marginal benefit(s) 9, **448**

Marginal cost pricing rule *473*, **474**

Marginal cost(s) 9, **233**, 253–255, *264*
factor pricing 349

Marginal mark(s) 230, *231*, 232

Marginal product(s) 228, *229*, 253–255, 354

Marginal propensity to consume 636, **714**, *715*, 726–727

Marginal propensity to import 718

Marginal propensity to save 636, **714**, *715*, 726–727

Marginal rate of substitution 177, *178*, *249*, 250, 253

Marginal rate of substitution of labour for capital 249

Marginal revenue 260, *264*
factor pricing 349
monopoly 286
single-price monopoly *288*

Marginal revenue product 349, 382

Marginal social benefit(s) 276, **501**

Marginal social cost(s) 276, **501**

Marginal tax rate(s) 752

Marginal utility 155, *156*, 165, 168
equalizing *159*
indifference curves 191
theory 159–165, *162*
wealth 418

Marginal utility per pound spent 157

Market activity(ies) 355

Market demand 153, 168
capital 399–400
factor pricing 354

Market demand curve *153*

Market economies 20, 21
emerging 995–999, 1004
reform 992

Market equilibrium 406

Market failure 276, 409–412, 441–443, **444**, 445–464
public choice 496

Market socialism 987

Market structure(s) *314*
types 312–315, 337

Marketable permit(s) 502, 503

Market(s) 17, 19–20, 22, 59
constraints 227
container lines 278–279
coordination 218
firm 217–19
geography 313
growth 657–658
health-care *531*
industry 314

insurance 428
intervention 467–469, 490
labour 370–392, *613*
loans 427–428
natural resources 405–412, 413
price 583
prohibited good *135*
sterling 967
supply 356–357
union *378*
unskilled labour *128*
used car 426–427

Marriage 525

Marshell, Alfred 90–91

Maximin theory 536

Maximizing profit *353*

Maximizing total utility 163, 168

Maximum point 34, *35*

Mayer, C. 487(n)

Means of payment 769

Measurement of gross domestic product 574–599

Meat industry 186–187

Median voter theorem 454, 455

Medium of exchange 769

Medium-sized firm(s) 205, *206*

Membership of unions *377*

Men 381–382

Merger(s) 404, **405**, **468**, 855
investigations 481–483

Microeconomics 11, 22

Minford, Patrick 681–683, 867, 910

Minimum lending rate(s) (MLR) 803

Minimum point 34, *35*

Minimum supply price(s) 76

Minimum wage law 128, 377

Minimum wage(s) 127–30, 143, **380**, 619
unemployment *129*, 616–617

Minus sign 100

Miracle economies 671

Misleading graphs *32*

Mitchell, B.R. 665(n)

Mixed economies 20, 21, 22

Mixed system(s) 534

Momentary supply 111

Momentary supply curve 137

Monetarism 795, 901, 906–907

Monetarist theory of business cycle 866, *867*

Monetary base 804, 809

Monetary exchange 60, 657–658

Monetary policy 565, **695**, 828–829, **894**, *896*
recession 875
types 799–830

Money 8–9, 59–60, **691**, 767–798, **769**
business cycle 873
change in quantity *786*

creation *782*
demand *816*
equilibrium 818, *819*
growth *850*
inflation 792–793, 794–795, 833
official measure *772*, *774*
price *70*

Money multiplier 809

Money supply
control 806–814, 820, 828
schematic representation *773*
Monopolies and Mergers
Commission (MMC) 471, 480

Monopolistic competition 312, *317*
oligopoly 310–339

Monopoly 282–285, **286**, 287–309, 938
cartels 304–305
collusion *326*
competition *298*
control 467–468
discovery 669
franchise 284
output *289*
output-price decision *289*
policy 479–484, 490
privatization 446
revenue curve *288*
UK laws *480*

Monopoly control law(s) 467

Monopoly power 277

Monopsony 378, 379–380

Moral hazard(s) 425

Mortimer, John 55

Movement
demand curve 74–75
supply curve 78–79

Multi-divisional form (M-form) corporation(s) 203–205

Multi-Fibre Arrangement 935, 938

Multi-income families 881–882

Multiplier 724, 727, 729–731, 736
effect 725
fiscal policy 748–755, 760
growth 734–735
long-run *733*
open-market operation 809–810, *811*
process *726*
short-run *732*

Mutual 776

N

Nash equilibrium 323, 329–330

National Health Service (NHS) 458–459, 532, 534

National Income, Profit and Expenditure Account 582

National investment 645, 650
National saving(s) 580
National security 937
Nationalized industries *485*
Nation(s) 54–55
Natural monopoly 287, 474–476
  average cost pricing *474*
  marginal cost pricing *473*
  profit maximization *475*
Natural rate policy 906
**Natural rate of unemployment
  611**, 622
Natural resource(s) 405, 413
  markets 393–415
  wood 410–411
Natural unemployment rate(s) *847*
Naughton, Barry 997(n), 998(n)
Negative income tax 528, *529*
Negative interest rate(s) 629, 641
Negative relationship(s) 33, *34*
Negative slope(s) *36*
Neo-Schumpeterian growth theory
  669
Neoclassical growth theory 667,
  668, 669
Net 583
Net asset(s) 633–634
Net benefit(s) 449
Net borrower(s) 954
Net domestic income 583
Net Domestic Product (NDP)
  583–584
Net exporter(s) 921
Net export(s) 579, 582
  adjustment *647*
  equilibrium *645*, 646–647, 650
Net foreign borrowing *955*
Net importer(s) 921
Net investment 576, 627
Net lender(s) 954
Net present value *397*, **398**, 399
Net profit 583
Net tax 578
Net worth 775
**New classical theory of business
  cycle 867**
New growth theory 669, *670*
**New Keynesian theory of busi-
  ness cycle 867**
New-goods bias 589
**Nominal gross domestic product
  (GDP) targeting 905**, 906
Nominal interest rate(s) 561,
  849
Non-excludable(s) 445
**Non-exhaustible natural
  resource(s) 405**
Non-market activity(ies) 355
Non-rival(s) 445
Non-tariff barrier(s) 931, 935
Normal good(s) 73, 183[n]

Normal profit 215, **260**, 346
Normative statement(s) 11–12, 16,
  22
North American Free Trade
  Agreement (NAFTA) 932

O

Objectives of unions 376–378
Occupational wage rate growth *523*
Office of Fair Trading (OFT) 468,
  480, 483–484
Office for National Statistics (ONS)
  602
Official reserves 968
Oil refining industry 242–243
Okun, Arthur 527, 536(n)
Oligopoly 310–311, **312**, 313–339,
  477
  supermarket loyalty cards
   334–335
One-third rule 660–661
Open economies 21
Open shop(s) 375
Open-market operation(s) 805,
  806–809
  cumulative effect *812*
  multiplier effect *811*
Operational deposit(s) 804
Opportunity cost(s) 8, 22, 48,
  49–50, *51*
  commodity money 770
  economic profit 212–216
  factor prices 346
  information 423
  international trade 944
  intertemporal substitution effect
   692
  net exports 646
  price 92
  profit 260
  risk 418–420
  trade *924*, *925*
  types 52, 58, 61, 70–71
Optimal-search rule 423, *424*
Optimization 9
Organisation for Economic Co-operation and Development (OECD)
  504(n), 538, 594, *933*
Organisation of Petroleum
  Exporting Countries (OPEC) 98,
  104, *907*
Original income 527
Origin(s) 28
Output 225–247
  approach 584–586
  composition 664
  cost 242–243
  long run 269–271, 281
  monopolistic competition 316–317

monopoly *289*, 297
  price 287–290
  profit-maximizing 262–263
  short run 267–269, 281
  single-price monopoly *288*
Overprovision *452*, 453
Ownership 207–208, 214–215, 633
Ozone-layer depletion 498

P

Paradox of value 165
Pareto efficiency 276
Participation rate(s) 603
Partnership(s) 203
Patent(s) 286, **508**, 509, 932
Patterns
  business cycle 862–863, 885
  international trade 921–924, 944
Pay differentials 384–385
Payoff matrix 322
  duopoly *330*
  equilibrium 328–329
Peak(s) 552
Penn World Table (PWT) 591
Pensions 526
Perceptions 447
Perestroika 991
Perfect competition 260, *261*,
  262–267, 281
  efficiency 277–280
Perfect price discrimination 295
Perfectly elastic 102
  demand 132
  supply 133
Perfectly inelastic 101
  supply 133
Performance 894–897, 913
Personal consumption expenditure
  582
Persuasion 424–425
Phillips curve 845, 856–857
Phillips, W.A. 845
Physical capital 396, 399
Piecemeal reform of wealth redistri-
  bution 528
Pigou, Arthur 513
Planning 205–206
  central 991–992
  expenditure 712–719, 721–722,
   736
Plant size 237–244, 245–246, 270,
  271
Policy-making
  Bank of England 804–805
  growth 671–674
  macroeconomic 564–565, 569,
   890–915
  monetary 695
  stabilization 910–911

Political equilibrium 448, 470
Political freedom 593
Political marketplace 448, 461
Politician(s) 447
Politics
  inflation 852, 857
  trade 940–941
Pollution 498, 510–511
  marketable permits *502*
  taxes *503*
Population 73
  growth 399, 665–667
  survey 602
Portfolio choice 400
Positive relationship(s) *32*, **32**
Positive slope(s) *36*
Positive statement(s) 11–12, 16, 22
Possibilities 171–200
Post hoc fallacies 14, 22
Potential gross domestic product 550, 551, 655
  fiscal policy 758
  long-term trends 554–555
  real GDP 760
Poverty 6, **521**, *522*, 528–530
Precondition(s) for growth 657–659
Prediction 479
  consumer behaviour 181–188, 193
  forecasting 840
  marginal utility theory 159–163, 168
  policy-making 904
  price change 82–87, 92–93
Preference(s) 73, **154**, 171–200, 193
  indifference curves 176–180
  map *177*
  voters 453
Premium(s) 421
Present value(s) 211, 212
Price ceiling(s) 124
Price discrimination 293, 306–307
  consumer surplus 292
Price effect 181, *182*, *185*
Price elasticity of demand 100
Price level 559, 586–590
Price taker(s) 260
Price-earnings ratio 404
Price(s) 7, 70–1
  advertising 425
  average 101
  change 82–87, 104–105, *175*
  comparison *769*
  decision *289*
  demand for money 814–815
  deregulation 992
  determination 80–82, 92
  energy 663–664
  EU agricultural support system *142*
  expectations 408–409
  factor 522–525

factors of production 76–77, 346–349
fall 159, *160*
farm *138*
gas supply 488–489
grain market 88–89
increase *907*
inflation 833, 856
information 423–424
input 251, 253
long run 269–271, 281
long-run changes *274*
management strategy 88–89
money 785–791, 796
monopolistic competition 316–317
monopoly 297
multiplier 729–733, 736
opportunity cost 92
output decision 287–290
quantity demanded 99
rational expectation *431*
real GDP *757*
reform 998
related goods 73, 77
rise 160, *161*
rocket 86, *87*
roller-coaster 86, *87*
See also Sticky price(s)
short run 267–269, 281
single-price monopoly *288*
slide 86, *87*
stock *139*, 402–405, 413, 434
war 331
Pricing 344–353
Principal–agent problem 207
Principal–agent relationship(s) 276
Principle of substitution 8
Prisoners' dilemma 322, *323*, 329–330, 337, 504(n)
Private good(s) 448
Private health care 532
Private information 425, 435
Private ownership 992
Private provision 450–451
Private sector deficit(s) 955
Private sector surplus 955
Privatization 465–483, **484**, 485–492, 994–995
Privatized industries *485*
Probability 418
Process theory 536, 537
Producer efficiency 276
Producer surplus 299, 468, *469*
Product curve 231, 235, *236*
Product differentiation 312
Production 46, 201–24
  change 926–928
  decision-making 266
  fluctuations 139
  four ways of making 10 TV sets per day *216*, 217
  household 592

innovation 318
least-cost technique *252*
value 577–580
Production function 237, *248*
Production possibility frontier(s) 46, *47*, 48, *49*, 50, 61, 228
  competition 276
  economic growth 52
  trade gains 55–56
Productivity 659, *661*
  emerging economy 998
  growth *661*
Productivity function 659, 660
  neoclassical growth theory 667
Productivity growth slowdown 550, 553–554, *662*, *905*
Professional association(s) 376
Profit 260–262, *263*
  bank 775–776
  discovery 669
  emerging economy 998
  expectation 630, 694
  long run 269–271, 281
  maximization 227, *264*, 349, *353*, 424
  monopoly *326*
  oligopoly 325–326
  price discrimination 294–295
  short run *265*, 267–269, 281
  supermarket loyalty cards 334–335
Progressive income tax 525
Prohibited good(s) 134–137
  Prohibited goods market(s) *135*, 143
Propagation mechanism(s) 862–863, 885
Property right(s) 59, **277**, **498**, *987*
  types 499–500, 657–658, 986
Proportional income tax 525
Proprietorship 203
Protectionism 931, 937–941, 944–945
  trade 942–943
Prudence 775–776
Public choice 447–464, 496
Public choice theory 447, 448
Public good(s) 280, **445**, *449*, *450, 451*
  types 448, 451–454, 461
Public health care 458–459
Public interest 480, 484, 513
  capture 476–477
  regulation 474
Public interest theory 448, **470**
Public ownership 484, 485–487, 490–491
Public provision 451
Public Sector Borrowing Requirement (PSBR) 565, 743, 744, 813

Public Sector Debt Repayment (PSDR) 565, 744
Purchasing power 691
Purchasing power parity (PPP) 968–969
Purchasing power parity price 591

Q

Qualification(s) 432–433
Quality
    environmental 496–497
    improvement 592
Quality-change bias 589
Quantity
    average 101
    change 82–87, 92–93
    factor pricing 349–354
    labour 355–356
    long-run changes *274*
    money 785, *786*, 787
Quantity demanded 71
Quantity of sterling assets 963
Quantity supplied 76
Quantity theory of money 787, 788–790
Quintiles 519
Quota 935, 936, *936*

R

Race 381–387, 389
Radical reform of wealth redistribution 528–530
Rate of return regulation 475
Rate of time preference 668
Rate(s) 744
Rate(s) of growth 671–674, 675
Rate(s) of inflation 833
Rational expectation(s) 430, 434, **840**, 842–844, **866**
    business cycle 867–869, *869*
    price *431*, *841*
Rational ignorance 452
Rationing 427
Re-entrant(s) 607
Real business cycle (RBC) theory 870, 871–874, 885
Real exchange rate(s) 646
Real gross domestic product per person 553
Real gross domestic product (real GDP) 550, 590–596
    business cycle 873–874
    change 692
    change in demand *693*
    consumption 717–718
    demand 642, *643*
    demand for money 815
    fiscal policy *757*
    full employment 903

growth 656–657, 892
    interest rate *825*
    money 785–791, 796
    multiplier 729–733
    potential GDP 760
    sticky price 720–723, 736
    unemployment *611*
Real income 174, 174
Real interest rate(s) 561, 628, *629*, *640*, *644*, **849**
    change 641, *642*, *644*
    types 630, 633
Real labour compensation 606
Real money 691, 729
Real money balances effect 692, 729
Real price(s) *70*
Real property 59
Real wage rate(s) 605, *614*
Real-world income elasticities of demand *109*
Recessionary gap(s) 697
Recession(s) 552, 553, 728
    forecasting 882–883
    multiplier 734–735
    types 875–876, *877*, 878, 885
Redistribution 299, 517–542
Reform
    impact 534–535
    market economy 992
    price 998
    private system 533
    wealth redistribution 528–530
Regressive income tax 525
Regulation 465–466, 467, 468–492
    bank 802
    financial 779–781, 796
    gas supply 488–489
    hierarchy *472*
    housing market 124–126
Regulator(s) of price 80–81
Related good(s) 73, 77
Relative input price(s) 253
Relative price(s) 70, 174, 175
Rent ceiling(s) 124, 125, *126*, 127, 143
Rent seeking 301, 302, 446
Rent(s) 346, 363, 583
Replication 669–671
Reputation(s) 853
Required reserve ratio 782, 804
Research & development (R&D) 331–332, *333*, 671–674
Reservation price(s) 423
Reservation wage(s) 356
Reserve ratio 782
Reserve requirement(s) 780
Reserve(s) 776, 781–782
Residual claimant(s) 203
Restriction(s) on trade 931–936, 944
Restrictive practice(s) 468, 483–484

Retail Prices Index (RPI) 559, **586**, 587
Returns to scale 238, 239, 241–244
Revenue 260, *261*, 262, 745–746, 752
    cost and profit statement *215*
    demand 285–287
    elasticity 287
    farm 137, *138*, 139–142
Revenue curve *290*
Ricardian equivalence 760, 957
Ricardo, David 665, 760, 948–949
Ripple effect 824
Rise in price(s) 160, *161*
Risk 418, 419–420, 435
    financial markets 428–434
    insurance *422*
    neutrality *420*
Robinson, Joan 864
Rocket(s) 86, *87*
Roller-coaster(s) 86, *87*
Rome, Treaty of 471
Romer, Paul 508, 677
Royalties 744
Rules 322

S

Sales tax 130, *131*, *132*, *133*
Saving function 712, 713, *713*, **714**
Saving supply 634, *635*, *638*
Saving supply curve *635*
Saving(s) 190–191, 400–401, **577**, 633–639
    approach *640*
    bequests 524
    decision-making 650
    expenditure 635–637
    growth 672–673
    influences *637*, 716
    national policy 898–899
    new capital 658
    stimulation 671–674
Say, Jean-Baptiste 572–573
Scarcity 8, 22, 988–990
Scatter diagram(s) 28, *29*, 30
Schumpeter, Joseph 676–677
Schwartz, Anna J. 880
Search activity(ies) 126
Search good(s) 424
Second-hand good(s) 582
Second-round effect(s) 10
Sector balance(s) *956*
Securities 806, *807*, *808*
Securities and Investments Board 471
Selling cost(s) 318
Selling plan(s) 76
Service(s)
    factor 346

international trade 921–922
Sex 381–387, 389
Shareholder(s) 207
Share(s) 210, 400
Shift of demand curve 74–75
Shift of supply curve 78–79
Shipping industry 278–279
Shoeleather cost(s) 843
Short run 227
Short-run aggregate supply 686,
    688–689
**Short-run aggregate supply
    curve 687,** 697
Short-run cost curve 234–235
Short-run cost(s) 232–233, *234,*
    235–237, *239,* 240, 245
Short-run decision(s) 262
Short-run demand 105
Short-run equilibrium *268*
Short-run fiscal policy(ies) 755–761,
    764
**Short-run industry supply curve
    267,** 268
**Short-run macroeconomic equi-
    librium 696**
Short-run multiplier *732*
Short-run Phillips curve 845,
    846, 847, 848
Short-run supply 111, 112
Short-run technology constraint(s)
    228–232, 245
Short-term goal(s) 549
Shortage(s) 81
Shutdown point 266
Signal(s) 269, **426,** 427
Simon, Julian 368
Single European Market (SEM) 932
Single variable *27*
Single-price monopoly 285–290,
    288, 306
  output *292*
  price *292*
  revenue curve *290*
Size of firm(s) 205
Size of plant(s) 237–244, 245–246,
    270, *271*
Skill differentials 372, *373,* 374–375,
    389
Slide(s) 86, *87*
Slope 100
Slope of curve *37*
Slope of straight line *36*
Slowdown of growth 661–663
Small firm(s) 205, *206*
Smith, Adam 13, 66–67, 165,
    280, 500
  classical growth theory 665
  international trade 674
Social dumping 129
Social infrastructure capital 628
Social justice 593

Social security contribution(s) 744
Socialism 987, *989*
Solow, Robert 661, 667, 677
Specialization 55, *57,* 59, 61
  wage differentials 381, 386
Speculative market(s) 138–139
Speedup of growth 661–663
Stabilization policy *902,* 910–911
Stagflation 549, **837**
Stalin, Joseph 990
State pension(s) 526
Steinherr, Alfred 147–150
Sterling 958–962, 975
Sterling asset *966*
Sticky price(s)
  expenditure 712–719, 736
  real GDP 720–723
Sticky wage(s) *620,* 622
Stock market(s) 395, 403–404,
    431–434
Stock(s) 142, 214, 576, 577
  demand 406
  natural resource 407–408
  price 402–405, 413
  price change limitation *139*
  speculative markets 138–139
Store of value 770
Straight-line demand curve 102–103
Strategic behaviour 322
Strategic variable(s) 331
Strategy 322
Strike(s) 376
Structural deficit(s) 754
Structural slump(s) 618
Structural unemployment 610,
    611
Subjective probability 418
Subsidy(ies) 506, 507, 583, 674
Subsistence real wage rate 665
Substitutability 179–180
Substitute(s) 73
  closeness 103–104
  factor pricing 355
  monopoly 284
Substitution 9–10, 22
  bias 590
  elasticity 111
  taste 166–167
Substitution effect 71, 183, **184,**
    185, 356
  saving 401
Suicide 558
Summers, Robert 591
Sunk cost(s) 213
Supermarket loyalty card(s)
    334–335
Supplier(s) 77
Supply 76, 77, *78,* 79, 92, *99*
  capital 400, *401,* 402, 413
  change 83–84
  factor market *347*

factor pricing 355–362
fiscal policy *759*
gas 488–489
influences *637*
labour 188–190, 524
labour market 612–614
law 90–91
market response 124
natural resource market 405–406
regulation 470
schedule 76
skill differentials 372
sterling assets 965–966, *966*
wheat price 88–89
Supply curve 76, *77, 266*
capital 401–402
industry *267*
labour **613,** 622
skill differentials 372
Surplus 81
Sustainable economic development
    412
Szymanski, S. 487(n)

T

Take-up of benefits 526–527
Takeover(s) 404, 405, 855
Targeting of benefits 526–527
Tariff(s) 931, 932, *933,* 934–935,
    938–939
Taste(s) 166–167, 272–275, 281
Taxation 130–134, 143, 454, *455,*
    456, 457
  cost 537
  drugs *136*
  emerging economy 998
  expenditure 744
  import 727
  income 525
  income distribution *527*
  indirect 583
  orange juice *457*
  pollution *503*
  recession 881
  types 460–461, 694–695
  wine 140–141
Team production 219
Technological change 6, 53, 78,
    399–400
  aggregate supply 689
  growth 659, 660–664
  new growth theory 669–671
  unemployment 618
Technological efficiency 216, 227
Technological progress 52
Technology 77–78, 659
  advances 272–275, 281
  constraints 227, 228–232
  cost-cutting 220–221

development 676–677
innovation 781
investment 898
Teenage unemployment 609
Temin, Peter 879–880
Thatcher, Margaret 551, 906, 908–909, 912, 969
Theft 558
Third party payments inefficiency *533*
Three-variable graph *39*
Time-series graph 28, **28**, *30*
Tit-for-tat strategy 330
Tobin, James 905
Tool(s) of policy-making 894–897, 913
Total benefit(s) 448
Total cost(s) 232, *263*
Total fixed cost(s) 232
Total income 577
Total product 228
Total production 550
Total revenue *99*, **101**, *106*, **260**, *263*, 286
price discrimination 291
test 106–107
Total surplus 468
Total utility 155, *156*, 165, 168
Total variable cost(s) 232
Toxic waste 498
Trade 7, *57*, 61
economic miracle 1002
evolution 59–60, 61
finance 952–958, 975
flow collapse 993
global 919–949
international 674, 948–949
Trade union(s) 375, *378*, 389
Trade-off 47–48, 536–537
Trade-weighted index 960
Trades Union Congress (TUC) 376
Training 374–375
Transactions cost(s) 59, 60, **218**, 276
Transactions effect(s) 964
Transfer earning(s) 362
economic rent *363*
factor pricing 362–364, 365
Transfer fee(s) 360–361
Transfer payment(s) 444, 525–526, 582, 694–695
government budget 743–744
Transition problem(s) 993
Treasury 560, 565
Treaties 505
Trend(s) 30
Trigger strategies 330
Trough(s) 552
Turnover 313–314
Twin deficits 957
Two-variable graph *27*, 28

U

Unanticipated inflation 850–851
Uncertainty 205–206, **276**, **418**, *419*
government 446
types 416–417, 420–435
Underground economies 592
Undiversified risk 428–429
Unemployed 557
Unemployment *557*, *558*, **603**, *608*, *609*
benefit 526, 618
business cycle 900–906, 913
growth 594–595
inflation 845–848, 856–857
macroeconomic performance *893*
minimum wages *129*, 616–617
natural rate 910–911
policy goals 892, 893–894
real GDP *611*
reasons 615–620
role 607, 610–612, 621
sticky wages *620*
types 7, 556, 564, 568, 600–624
Unemployment rate(s) 557
Union(s) 375–381, 389
Unit elasticity 102, 287
Unitary divisional form (U-form) corporation(s) 203–204
Unit(s) of account *769*, 770
Unit(s) of measurement 100
Unrelated variable(s) *35*
Unskilled labour market(s) *128*, 372
Uruguay Round 471, 932, *939*
Used car market(s) 426–427
Utilitarianism 536
Utility 154
demand 151–170
theory 166–167
Utility maximization 157
Utility of wealth 418, *419*

V

Valuation 403–404
Value 164, 448
legal system 993
money 561, 833
Value added 584
Value added tax (VAT) 130, 744
Variable cost(s) 232, 244
Variable input(s) 227
Variable(s) *27*, 331
Velocity of circulation 787
Velvet Revolution 994
Vickers, J. 487(n)
Viner, Jacob 257
Volatility of stock price(s) 434
Volume of stock market(s) 404

Voluntary export restraint(s) (VER) 935, 936
Voluntary regulation 472
Voter(s) 447
ignorance 452–453
income tax *455*
preference 453

W

Wage(s) 600–624
differentials 381–387, 389
inflation 834
labour 355–356, 522–524
minimum 616–617
pay differential 384–385
rate 346, 614–615
skill differentials 372–374
sticky *620*, 622
unions 380–381
Wagstaff, A. 534(n)
Walters, Alan 876(n)
Walters critique 876 (n)
Warranty 426–427
Water pollution 498
Wealth 400, 517–542, **577**
sources 66–67
Weighted average(s) 419
Welfare spending 752
Welfare state capitalism 987
Willingness-and-ability-to-pay curve 72–73
Withdrawal rate(s) 528
Women 381–382
Work-force 557, **602**
Work-force curve 613
Work-force in Employment (WiE) Survey 602
Working-age population 602
World
economy 982–985
income per person *983*
Lorenz curve *984*
See also Global economy
World Bank 591, 942, 1000–1001
World Commission on Environment and Development 412
World Trade Organization (WTO) 471, 932

X

X-inefficiency 475, 486, 664

Y

Yarrow, G. 487(n)

Microeconomic Focus

Core	**Extensions and Applications**
1 What is Economics?	
	2 Making and Using Graphs
3 Production, Growth and Trade	
4 Demand and Supply	
5 Elasticity	
	6 Markets in Action
7 Utility and Demand *or*	**8** Possibilities, Preferences and Choices
	9 Organizing Production
10 Output and Costs	
11 Competition	
12 Monopoly	
	13 Monopolistic Competition and Oligopoly
14 Pricing and Allocating Factors of Production	
	15 Labour Markets
	16 Capital and Natural Resource Markets
	17 Uncertainty and Information
18 Market Failure and Public Choice	
	19 Regulation and Privatization
	20 Externalities, the Environment and Knowledge
	21 Inequality, Redistribution and Welfare
35 Trading with the World	
	37 Emerging Economies

Four Alternative Sequences for a Micro Principles Course

Microeconomic Theory	**Business Economics**	**Microeconomic Policy**	**Management Economics**
3 Production, Growth and Trade	**3** Production, Growth and Trade	**3** Production, Growth and Trade	**3** Production, Growth and Trade
4 Demand and Supply	**4** Demand and Supply	**4** Demand and Supply	**4** Demand and Supply
5 Elasticity	**5** Elasticity	**5** Elasticity	**5** Elasticity
7 Utility and Demand *or*	**9** Organizing Production	**6** Markets in Action	**9** Organizing Production
8 Possibilities, Preferences and Choices	**10** Output and Costs	**7** Utility and Demand *or*	**10** Output and Costs
10 Output and Costs	**11** Competition	**10** Output and Costs	**11** Competition
11 Competition	**12** Monopoly	**11** Competition	**12** Monopoly
12 Monopoly	**13** Monopolistic Competition and Oligopoly	**12** Monopoly	**14** Pricing and Allocating Factors of Production
13 Monopolistic Competition and Oligopoly	**14** Pricing and Allocating Factors of Production	**14** Pricing and Allocating Factors of Production	**15** Labour Markets
14 Pricing and Allocating Factors of Production	**15** Labour Markets	**15** Labour Markets	**16** Capital and Natural Resource Markets
15 Labour Markets	**16** Capital and Natural Resource Markets	**16** Capital and Natural Resource Markets	**17** Uncertainty and Information
16 Capital and Natural Resource Markets	**17** Uncertainty and Information	**18** Market Failure and Public Choice	**18** Market Failure and Public Choice
17 Uncertainty and Information	**18** Market Failure and Public Choice	**19** Regulation and Privatization	**19** Regulation and Privatization
18 Market Failure and Public Choice	**19** Regulation and Privatization	**20** Externalities, the Environment and Knowledge	**20** Externalities, the Environment and Knowledge
19 Regulation and Privatization	**20** Externalities, the Environment and Knowledge	**21** Inequality, Redistribution and Welfare	**35** Trading with the World

Macroeconomic Focus

Core	Extensions and Applications	Chapter's Prerequisites
22 A First Look at Macroeconomics		None
23 Measuring GDP, Inflation and Economic Growth		None
24 Employment, Unemployment and Wages		**4** Demand and Supply
25 Investment, Capital and Interest		**4** Demand and Supply
	26 Long-term Economic Growth	**4** Demand and Supply
27 Aggregate Supply and Aggregate Demand		**4** Demand and Supply
28 Expenditure Multipliers		**23** Measuring GDP, Inflation and Growth
29 The Government Budget and Fiscal Policy		**27** Aggregate Supply and Aggregate Demand
30 Money		None
31 The Central Bank and Monetary Policy		**30** Money
	32 Inflation	**27** Aggregate Supply and Aggregate Demand
	33 The Business Cycle	**27** Aggregate Supply and Aggregate Demand
	34 Macroeconomic Policy Challenges	**27** Aggregate Supply and Aggregate Demand
	36 The Balance of Payments and the Exchange Rate	**4** Demand and Supply
	37 Emerging Economies	

Four Alternative Sequences for a Macro Principles Course

Early Long-term Growth	Late Long-term Growth	Keynesian Perspective	Monetarist Perspective
22 A First Look at Macroeconomics	**22** A First Look at Macroeconomics	**22** A First Look at Macroeconomics	**22** A First Look at Macroeconomics
23 Measuring GDP, Inflation and Economic Growth	**23** Measuring GDP, Inflation and Economic Growth	**23** Measuring GDP, Inflation and Economic Growth	**23** Measuring GDP, Inflation and Economic Growth
24 Employment, Unemployment and Wages	**24** Employment, Unemployment and Wages (here or after Chapter 32)	**24** Employment, Unemployment and Wages	**24** Employment, Unemployment and Wages
25 Investment, Capital and Interest	**27** Aggregate Supply and Aggregate Demand	**28** Expenditure Multipliers	**27** Aggregate Supply and Aggregate Demand
26 Long-term Economic Growth	**28** Expenditure Multipliers	**27** Aggregate Supply and Aggregate Demand	**30** Money
27 Aggregate Supply and Aggregate Demand	**29** The Government Budget and Fiscal Policy	**29** The Government Budget and Fiscal Policy	**31** The Central Bank and Monetary Policy
28 Expenditure Multipliers	**30** Money	**30** Money	**32** Inflation
29 The Government Budget and Fiscal Policy	**31** The Central Bank and Monetary Policy	**31** The Central Bank and Monetary Policy	**28** Expenditure Multipliers
30 Money	**32** Inflation	**32** Inflation	**29** The Government Budget and Fiscal Policy
31 The Central Bank and Monetary Policy	**25** Investment, Capital and Interest	**25** Investment, Capital and Interest	**25** Investment, Capital and Interest
32 Inflation	**26** Long-term Economic Growth	**26** Long-term Economic Growth	**26** Long-term Economic Growth
33 The Business Cycle	**33** The Business Cycle	**33** The Business Cycle	**33** The Business Cycle
34 Macroeconomic Policy Challenges	**34** Macroeconomic Policy Challenges	**34** Macroeconomic Policy Challenges	**34** Macroeconomic Policy Challenges
36 The Balance of Payments and the Exchange Rate (optional)	**36** The Balance of Payments and the Exchange Rate (optional)	**36** The Balance of Payments and the Exchange Rate (optional)	**36** The Balance of Payments and the Exchange Rate (optional)

We want to hear your views!

Thank you for purchasing this book. We would very much like to obtain your feedback on this edition of *Economics* to assist us in the development of future publications. We want to know what you the student or lecturer are looking for. We would therefore be grateful if you could complete and return this to us at the following address:

> Lucy Everest
> Addison Wesley Longman
> Higher Education Division
> FREEPOST
> Edinburgh Gate
> Burnt Mill
> Harlow
> Essex, CM20 2JE
> UK.
> No stamp needed if posted in
> the UK, Channel Islands or Isle of Man

❀ What do you like about this book?

❀ What suggestions do you have to improve the text?

❀ What other books do you use?

❀ Which particular features and additional materials are most useful to you in your studies/teaching?

❀ Any other comments?

❀ Are you a student or lecturer?

Prize Draw

All replies received by the 31st December will be entered into our annual prize draw.

The first 5 entries will each receive Addison Wesley Longman books to the value of £25.00.

Name_____

Institution/home address_____

Department_____

Course_____

Level_____

If you would like to send us your feedback by e-mail it would be gratefully received.

Please direct all comments to the following address: b&e.feedback@awl.co.uk

Thank you for your time.